Biographical Dictionary of American Sports

BASEBALL,
REVISED AND EXPANDED EDITION
Q–Z

Edited by David L. Porter

GREENWOOD PRESS
Westport, Connecticut • London

Library of Congress Cataloging-in-Publication Data

Biographical dictionary of American sports. Baseball / edited by
   David L. Porter.—Rev. and expanded ed.
       p.   cm.
   Includes bibliographical references (p.   ) and index.
   Contents: [1] A–F — [2] G–P — [3] Q–Z.
   ISBN 0–313–29884–X (set : alk. paper). — ISBN 0–313–31174–9 (A–F
: alk. paper). — ISBN 0–313–31175–7 (G–P : alk. paper). — ISBN
0–313–31176–5 (Q–Z : alk. paper)
   1. Baseball—United States Biography Dictionaries.   2. Baseball—
United States—History.   I. Porter, David L., 1941–   .
   II. Title: Baseball.
   GV865.A1B55   2000
   796.357'092'273—dc21   99–14840
   [B]

British Library Cataloguing in Publication Data is available.

Library of Congress Catalog Card Number: 99–14840
ISBN: 0–313–29884–X (set)
         0–313–31174–9 (A–F)
         0–313–31175–7 (G–P)
         0–313–31176–5 (Q–Z)

First published in 2000

Greenwood Press, 88 Post Road West, Westport, CT 06881
An imprint of Greenwood Publishing Group, Inc.
www.greenwood.com

Printed in the United States of America

The paper used in this book complies with the
Permanent Paper Standard issued by the National
Information Standards Organization (Z39.48–1984).

10 9 8 7 6 5 4 3 2 1

Cover photographs: National Baseball Hall of Fame Library, Cooperstown, NY.

Unless otherwise credited, all photographs appearing in this volume are courtesy of the National
Baseball Hall of Fame Library, Cooperstown, NY.

Every reasonable effort has been made to trace the owners of copyright materials in this book,
but in some instances the has proven impossible. The editor and publisher will be glad to receive
information leading to more complete acknowledgments in subsequent printings of the book
and in the meantime extend their apologies for any omissions.

Contents

Illustrations

VOLUME 3

Photos for Volume 3 follow page 1509.

Preface

The *Biographical Dictionary of American Sports (BDAS)* series began because of a need for a scholarly, comprehensive biographical dictionary of notable American athletic figures. Sports encyclopedias typically had concentrated on statistical achievements of notable American athletic figures and contained comparatively little biographical background data. Sports biographies, meanwhile, usually featured just the greatest or most prominent athletic figures.

The *BDAS* series, consisting of six volumes published between 1987 and 1995, has profiled 3,383 notable American sports figures. To date, 973 entries have featured major league baseball players, managers, umpires, and/or executives. A majority appeared in a 1987 volume devoted exclusively to baseball, while the remainder were included in either the 1992 or 1995 supplemental volumes.

This three-volume book, arranged alphabetically, features 1,450 baseball entries. It contains revised and updated entries for all 973 figures included in the earlier volumes. These figures typically compiled impressive career statistical records as players, managers, coaches, umpires, and/or executives. One quarter are members of the National Baseball Hall of Fame in Cooperstown, New York. The position players often batted above .300 lifetime with at least 2,000 career hits and/or 300 career home runs. In some instances, they demonstrated remarkable fielding and/or running abilities. Starting pitchers typically compiled at least 175 major league victories with outstanding win–loss percentages and excellent earned run averages, while relief pitchers ranked among career save leaders.

An additional 477 baseball luminaries who have helped shape the development of the national pastime from the mid–nineteenth century to the present are also profiled. Roberto Alomar, Jeff Bagwell, Albert Belle, Dante Bichette, Craig Biggio, Kevin Brown, Ken Caminiti, David Cone, Andres

Galarraga, Tom Glavine, Juan Gonzalez, Ken Griffey, Jr., Randy Johnson, David Justice, Chuck Knoblauch, Barry Larkin, Kenny Lofton, Greg Maddux, Edgar Martinez, Pedro Martinez, Tino Martinez, Mike Mussina, Mike Piazza, Ivan Rodriguez, Garry Sheffield, John Smoltz, Sammy Sosa, Frank Thomas, Jr., Mo Vaughn, Larry Walker, Matt Williams, and other current stars with several years of major league experience are featured for the first time.[1] A vast majority of the new entries are former major league players, managers, umpires, and executives. New baseball entries also include 31 Negro League and 33 All-American Girls Professional Baseball League (AAGPBL) stars. The AAGPBL operated from 1943 to 1954. Jean Faut Eastman, Betty Weaver Foss, Dottie Kamenshek, Sophie Kurys, Dottie Schroeder, Joanne Weaver, Connie Wisniewski, and other AAGPBL players are profiled.

The selection of the new baseball entries proved very challenging. Before making final choices, the editor thoroughly researched several baseball encyclopedias and histories.[2] Frederick Ivor-Campbell assisted in the selection of nineteenth-century personalities, while Rick Center suggested many AAGPBL entries. Other contributors also suggested subjects worthy of inclusion. Of course, the editor assumes ultimate responsibility for any significant baseball figures inadvertently excluded from this volume.

The additional baseball entries met three general criteria. First, they either were born in or spent their childhood years in the United States. Foreigners who made exceptional impacts on the national pastime are also covered. Second, they typically compiled impressive statistical records. Major leaguers, for example, batted above .275 with at least 1,000 hits and/or 100 home runs, recorded at least 100 major league victories with fine win–loss percentages and/or earned run averages, demonstrated fine fielding and/or running abilities, or excelled as managers, coaches, umpires, or executives. Third, they made a major impact on professional baseball, earning significant awards or performing for championship teams.

Biographies usually indicate the subject's full given name at birth; date and place of birth and, when applicable, date and place of death; parental background; formal education; spouse and children, when applicable; and major personal characteristics. Entries feature the subject's baseball career through December 1999 and typically include information about his or her entrance into professional baseball; positions played; teams played for with respective leagues;[3] lifetime batting, fielding, and/or pitching records and achievements; individual records set, awards won, and All-Star and World Series appearances; and impact on baseball. Biographical and statistical data frequently proved elusive for Negro Leaguers and early major leaguers. Entries on managers usually cover their teams guided, with inclusive dates; major statistical achievements; career win–loss records with percentages; premier players piloted; and managerial philosophy, strategy, and innovations.

Biographies of club executives, league officials, umpires, sportswriters, and sportscasters describe their various positions held, notable accomplishments, and impact on baseball.

Brief bibliographies list pertinent sources for each biographical entry. Authors benefited from interviews or correspondence with biographical subjects, relatives, or acquaintances. Former major leaguers and AAGPBL players proved especially cooperative in furnishing information. The National Baseball Library in Cooperstown, New York, *The Sporting News* in St. Louis, MO, the Northern Indiana Historical Society in South Bend, IN, college, university, and public libraries, radio and television networks, newspapers, and magazines also provided invaluable assistance. When an entry cites a subject covered elsewhere in this book, an asterisk follows the person's name. Appendices list biographical entries by place of birth and players alphabetically by main position played. Other Appendices list major league managers, executives, and/or umpires, National Baseball Hall of Fame members, Negro Leaguers, and AAGPBL players.

One hundred fifty-two contributors, mostly members of the Society for American Baseball Research or North American Society for Sport History, contributed baseball entries for this revised and expanded volume. Sixty-seven people contributed new baseball entries for this volume. Most authors are university or college professors with baseball expertise. School teachers, administrators, writers, publishers, editors, journalists, librarians, businessmen, government employees, clergymen, consultants, and others also participated. Contributors are cited alphabetically with occupational affiliation following the index.

The editor deeply appreciates the enormous amount of time, energy, and effort expended by contributors in searching for biographical information. I am especially grateful to William E. Akin, Dennis S. Clark, Scott A.G.M. Crawford, John L. Evers, John R. Hillman, Frederick Ivor-Campbell, William J. Miller, Frank J. Olmsted, Frank V. Phelps, James A. Riley, Duane A. Smith, Luther W. Spoehr, Robert E. Weir, and Jerry J. Wright, each of whom wrote at least 10 new baseball entries. Akin, Evers, David Fitzsimmons, James N. Giglio, Hillman, George W. Hilton, Miller, Scot E. Mondore, Olmsted, Riley, Victor Rosenberg, William M. Simons, Edward J. Tassinari, Sarah L. Ulerick, and Weir kindly agreed to write additional entries when contributor Stan W. Carlson died in December 1996 and when other last-minute cancellations occurred. Mondore, Bill Deane, and Richard Topp supplied family information on numerous players. Biographical subjects, relatives, or acquaintances often furnished data. Richard H. Gentile and Thomas C. Eakin sent biographical material on Massachusetts and Ohio entries, respectively. William Penn University librarians again provided considerable assistance. Cynthia Harris gave adept guidance and helped in the planning and writing of this volume, while Elizabeth Meagher furnished valuable assistance in the production stage. As always, my wife, Marilyn, demonstrated considerable patience, understanding, and support throughout the project.

NOTES

1. Several other promising stars are not included because they are still in the early phases of their major league careers.

2. The principal baseball reference sources examined for major league baseball players included *The Baseball Encyclopedia*, 10th ed. (New York, 1996); John Thorn et al., eds., *Total Baseball*, 5th ed. (New York, 1997); David Nemec, *The Great Encyclopedia of 19th Century Major League Baseball* (New York, 1997); David Neft et al., eds., *The Sports Encyclopedia: Baseball* (New York, 1997); Charles F. Faber, *Baseball Ratings: The All-Time Best Players at Each Position*, 2d ed. (Jefferson, NC, 1995); *The Complete 1998 Baseball Record Book* (St. Louis, MO, 1998); *The Sporting News Official Baseball Register, 1998* (St. Louis, MO, 1998); *The Sporting News Official Baseball Guide, 1998* (St. Louis, MO, 1998); and Mike Shatzkin, ed., *The Ballplayers* (New York, 1990). James A. Riley, *The Biographical Encyclopedia for the Negro Baseball Leagues* (New York, 1994) and W. C. Madden, *The Women of the All-American Girls Professional Baseball League: A Biographical Dictionary* (Jefferson, NC, 1997) proved invaluable sources for Negro League and AAGPBL players, respectively.

3. Professional major leagues represented include the National Association (1871–1875), National League (1876–), American Association (1882–1891), Union Association (1884), Players League (1890), American League (1901–), Federal League (1914–1915), Negro National League (1920–1931, 1933–1948), Eastern Colored League (1923–1928), East-West League (1932), Negro Southern League (1932), Negro American League (1933–1950), and All-American Girls Professional Baseball League (1943–1954).

Abbreviations

The abbreviations, listed alphabetically, include associations, baseball terms, conferences, journals, leagues, organizations, and reference sources mentioned in the text and bibliographies.

AA	American Association
AAGPBL	All-American Girls Professional Baseball League
AAGPBLPA	All-American Girls Professional Baseball League Players Association
AAU	Amateur Athletic Union
ABA	American Basketball Association
ABC	American Broadcasting Company
ABCA	American Baseball Coaches Association
ABL	American Basketball League
AC	Athletic Club
ACAB	*Appleton's Cyclopaedia of American Biography*
ACBC	American College Baseball Coaches
ACC	Atlantic Coast Conference
ACFL	Atlantic Coast Football League
AFL	American Football League
AH	*American Heritage*
AHI	*American History Illustrated*
AIL	Arizona Instructional League
AL	American League
AlFL	Alabama-Florida League
AlL	Alaskan League

AlSL	Alaska Summer League
AM	*American Mercury*
AmBC	American Bowling Congress
AMeL	Arizona-Mexico League
AML	Arkansas-Missouri League
AmLit	*American Literature*
AmM	*American Magazine*
ANL	American Negro League
AOA	American Olympic Association
AP	Associated Press
ApL	Appalachian League
ArSL	Arizona State League
ArTL	Arizona-Texas League
AS	*American Scholar*
ASL	Alabama State League
AtA	Atlantic Association
AtL	Atlantic League
AtM	*Atlantic Monthly*
AV	*American Visions*
BA	*Baseball America*
BAA	Basketball Association of America
BBM	*Beckett's Baseball Monthly*
BBWAA	Baseball Writers Association of America
BC	Business College
BD	*Baseball Digest*
BDAC	*Biographical Dictionary of the American Congress*
BEaC	Big East Conference
BEC	Big Eight Conference
BeL	Bethlehem Steel League
BGL	Blue Grass League
BH	*Baseball History*
BHR	*Baseball Historical Review*
BL	Border League
BL	*Boy's Life*
BM	*Baseball Magazine*
BNC	Big Nine Conference
BoM	*Boston Magazine*

BPBP	Brotherhood of Professional Baseball Players
BPRA	Bowling Proprietory Association of America
BPY	Baseball Players of Yesterday
BQ	*Baseball Quarterly*
BR	*Boston Referee*
BRJ	*Baseball Research Journal*
BRL	Blue Ridge League
BRQ	*Baseball Research Quarterly*
BRS	Bottomley Ruffing Schalk
BRuL	Babe Ruth League
BS	*Black Sports*
BSC	Big Six Conference
BSL	Bi-State League
BStL	Big State League
BT	*Biography Today*
BTC	Big Ten Conference
BUDS	Baseball Umpire Development School
BVL	Blackstone Valley League
BW	*Baseball Weekly*
CA	Central Association
CA	*Contemporary Authors*
CAB	*Cyclopedia of American Biography*
CAD	*Coach and Athletic Director*
CaL	California League
CAL	Canadian-American League
CaPL	Canadian Provincial League
CarA	Carolina Association
CaSL	California State League
CB	*Current Biography Yearbook*
CBCA	College Baseball Coaches of America
CbL	Cumberland League
CBS	Columbia Broadcasting System
CC	Community College
CCNY	City College of New York
CCo	*Cooperstown Corner*
CCSL	Copper Country Soo League
CdL	Colorado League

CH	*Chicago History*
ChNL	Chicago National League
CIF	California Interscholastic Federation
CIL	Central Interstate League
CKAL	Central Kentucky Amateur League
CL	Central League
ClL	Colonial League
CmA	Commercial Association
CML	Connie Mack League
CnL	Canadian League
CNL	Cuban National League
CNN	Cable News Network
CntL	Continental League
CoC	Country Club
CoPL	Coastal Plain League
CPL	Central Pennsylvania League
CPrL	Canadian Provincial League
CQR	*Congressional Quarterly Researcher*
CrA	Carolina Association
CrL	Carolina League
CRL	Cocoa Rookie League
CSC	*Canadian Sports Collector*
CSL	Cotton States League
CSSL	California State Semipro League
CtL	Connecticut League
CtSL	Connecticut State League
CUL	Cuban League
CUSL	Cuban Summer League
CUWL	Cuban Winter League
CWL	California Winter League
DAB	*Dictionary of American Biography*
DaM	*Dawn Magazine*
DH	designated hitter
DIB	*Dictionary of International Biography*
DL	Dakota League
DM	*Dodgers Magazine*
DRWL	Dominican Republic Winter League

DSM	*Diamond Sports Memorabilia*
DT	*Delaware Today*
EA	Eastern Association
EaIL	Eastern Intercollegiate Athletic League
ECA	Eastern Championship Association
ECAC	Eastern Collegiate Athletic Association
ECaL	Eastern Carolina League
ECL	Eastern Colored League
EDL	Eastern Dixie League
EIL	Eastern Interstate League
EL	Eastern League
EPL	East Penn League
ERA	earned run average
ESL	Eastern Shore League
ESPN	Eastern Sports Network
ESUTS	Eastern States Umpire Training School
ETL	East Texas League
EvL	Evangeline League
EWL	East-West League
FBC	Fox Broadcasting Network
FCA	Fellowship of Christian Athletes
FECL	Florida East Coast League
FIL	Florida International League
FInL	Florida Instructional League
FL	Federal League
FlL	Florida League
FSL	Florida State League
FWL	Far West League
GAL	Georgia-Alabama League
GC	Golf Club
GCL	Gulf Coast League
GCRL	Gulf Coast Rookie League
GFL	Georgia-Florida League
GML	Green Mountain League
GQ	*Gentlemen's Quarterly*
GSL	Georgia State League
HAF	Helms Athletic Foundation

HB	*Harper's Bazaar*
HR	home run(s)
HRL	Hudson River League
IA	International Association
IAD	*Italian-American Digest*
IAL	Inter-American League
IaL	Iowa League
IBA	International Baseball Association
ID	*In Dixieland*
IdSL	Idaho State League
IIAC	Illinois Intercollegiate Athletic Conference
IIL	Illinois-Iowa League
IInL	Illinois-Indiana League
IlML	Illinois-Missouri League
IlSL	Illinois State League
IL	International League
Ind	Independent
InL	Instructional League
IOBL	Idaho-Oregon Baseball League
IOL	Iron and Oil League
IoSL	Iowa State League
IS	*Inside Sports*
ISA	Interstate Association
ISDL	Iowa and South Dakota League
ISL	Interstate League
IVL	Imperial Valley League
IvL	Ivy League
JAC	*Journal of American Culture*
JC	Junior College
JCL	Japan Central League
JEE	*Journal of Economic Education*
JeSH	*Jewish Sports History*
JPC	*Journal of Popular Culture*
JPL	Japanese Pacific League
JSH	*Journal of Sport History*
JSS	*Jewish Social Studies*
JW	*Journal of the West*

KL	Kitty League
KOML	Kansas-Oklahoma-Missouri League
KSL	Kansas State League
LCS	League Championship Series
LD	*Literary Digest*
LL	Longhorn League
LM	*Lippincott's Magazine*
LPGA	Ladies Professional Golfers Association
LSL	Lone Star League
LSU	Louisiana State University
MAC	Mid-American Conference
MAL	Middle Atlantic League
MasL	Massachusetts League
MD	*Magazine Digest*
MEL	Mexican League
MEWL	Mexican Winter League
MH	*Men's Health*
MISL	Michigan State League
MiVL	Mississippi Valley League
MkL	Mandak League
ML	Midwest League
MLPA	Major League Players Association
MLPAA	Major League Players Alumni Association
MLUA	Major League Umpires Association
MM	*Mariners Magazine*
MnL	Manila League
MOL	Michigan-Ontario League
MOVL	Mississippi-Ohio Valley League
mph	miles per hour
MSA	Massachusetts State Association
MSL	Middle States League
MtL	Montana League
MtnSL	Mountain State League
MtSL	Montana State League
MUL	Muny League
MVC	Missouri Valley Conference
MVL	Missouri Valley League

MVP	Most Valuable Player
MWL	Minnesota-Wisconsin League
NA	National Association
NaBC	National Baseball Congress
NAIA	National Association of Intercollegiate Athletics
NAL	Negro American League
NAML	National Association of Minor Leagues
NAPBL	National Association of Professional Baseball Leagues
NASSH	North American Association for Sport History
NAtL	North Atlantic League
NBA	National Basketball Association
NBBC	National Baseball Congress
NBC	National Broadcasting Company
NCAA	National Collegiate Athletic Association
NCAB	*National Cyclopedia of American Biography*
NCBWA	National Collegiate Baseball Writers Association
NCC	North Central Conference
NCL	North Carolina League
NCSL	North Carolina State League
NEA	Newspaper Enterprise Association
NEAL	Northeast Arkansas League
NECSL	Northeastern Connecticut State League
NEL	New England League
NeL	Northeastern League
NEQ	*New England Quarterly*
NeSL	Nebraska State League
NFL	National Football League
NGBL	National Girls Baseball League
NHL	National Hockey League
NIFL	Negro Independent Football League
NL	National League
NLe	*New Leader*
NNL	Negro National League
NoA	Northern Association
NoL	Northern League
NR	*New Republic*
NSD	*National Sports Daily*

NSL	Negro Southern League
NTL	North Texas League
NWL	Northwestern League
NY	*New York*
NYJ	*New York Journal*
NYNJL	New York-New Jersey League
NYPL	New York-Pennsylvania League
NYSBC	New York State Boxing Commission
NYSL	New York State League
NYT	*New York Times*
NYU	New York University
NYWT	*New York World Telegram*
OAB	*Oberlin Alumni Bulletin*
OHQ	*Ohio Historical Quarterly*
OIL	Ohio-Indiana League
OKSL	Oklahoma State League
OL	Ohio League
OPL	Ohio-Pennsylvania League
OrL	Oregon League
OSL	Ohio State League
OTBA	Old Timers Baseball Association
OTBN	*Oldtyme Baseball News*
PAPBP	Protective Association of Professional Baseball Players
PCC	Pacific Coast Conference
PCL	Pacific Coast League
PEC	Pacific Eight Conference
PIL	Pacific International League
PiL	Piedmont League
PL	Players' League
PNL	Pacific Northwest League
PoL	Pony League
POML	Pennsylvania-Ohio-Maryland League
PPAA	Pittsburgh Pirates Alumni Association
PPVL	Panhandle-Pecos Valley League
PrL	Pioneer League
PRL	Puerto Rican League
ProL	Provincial League

PRWL	Puerto Rican Winter League
PSA	Pennsylvania State Association
PSL	Pennsylvania State League
PT	*Psychology Today*
PTC	Pac-Ten Conference
PW	*People Weekly*
RAL	Rookie Appalachian League
RB	*Ragtyme Baseball*
RBI	runs batted in
RD	*Readers Digest*
RR	*Reds Report*
RRVL	Red River Valley League
RS	*Ragtyme Sports*
SA	Southern Association
SABR	Society for American Baseball Research
SAL	South Atlantic League
SBC	Sun Belt Conference
SC	Southern Conference
SCD	*Sports Collectors Digest*
SCQ	*Southern California Quarterly*
SDL	South Dakota League
SEAL	*The Scribner Encyclopedia of American Lives*
SEC	Southeastern Conference
SEL	Southeastern League
SEP	*Saturday Evening Post*
SeS	*Senior Scholastic*
SH	*Sports Heritage*
SI	*Sports Illustrated*
SIAA	Southern Intercollegiate Athletic Association
SIC	*Sports Illustrated Canada*
SIL	Southwest International League
SL	Southern League
SL	*Sport Life*
SML	Southern Michigan League
SMU	Southern Methodist University
SN	*Saturday Night*
SNEL	South New England League

SPBA	Senior Professional Baseball Association
SpL	Sophomore League
SpL	*Sporting Life*
SR	*Saturday Review*
SS	*Sports Scoop*
SSBM	*Street & Smith Baseball Magazine*
SSL	Sooner State League
ST	*Sporting Times*
STL	South Texas League
SuL	Sunset League
SW	*Sport World*
SWaL	Southwestern Washington League
SWC	Southwest Conference
SWL	Southwestern League
TAC	*The American Chronicle*
TAI	*The Annals of Iowa*
TBA	*The Berean Alumnus*
TBR	*The Baseball Review*
TCU	Texas Christian University
TD	*The Diamond*
TF	*The Fan*
3IL	Three I League
TL	Texas League
TM	*Texas Monthly*
TNP	*The National Pastime*
TNY	*The New Yorker*
TOL	Texas-Oklahoma League
TP	*This People*
TPI	Total Pitcher Index
TrM	*Trenton Magazine*
TSL	Tri-State League
TSN	*The Sporting News*
UA	Union Association
UCLA	University of California at Los Angeles
UIL	Utah-Idaho League
UL	Union League
UP	United Press

UPI	United Press International
USAT	*USA Today*
USC	University of Southern California
USL	United States League
USOC	U.S. Olympic Committee
UtA	Utah Association
VaL	Valley League
VL	Virginia League
VSL	Virginia State League
VVL	Virginia Valley League
VWL	Venezuelan Winter League
WA	Western Association
WAC	Western Athletic Conference
WC	Western Conference
WCAC	West Coast Athletic Conference
WCaL	Western Canadian League
WCL	West Carolinas League
WeIL	Western International League
WIBC	Women's International Bowling Congress
WIL	Wisconsin-Illinois League
WL	Western League
WM	*World Monitor*
WNABA	Women's National Adult Baseball Association
WPL	Western Pennsylvania League
WSC	Western State Conference
WSJ	*Wall Street Journal*
WSL	Wisconsin State League
WTL	Western Tri-State League
WTNML	West Texas-New Mexico League
WTxL	West Texas League
WWA	*Who's Who in America*
WWE	*Who's Who in the East*
WWIB	*Who's Who in Baseball*
WWM	*Who's Who in the Midwest*
WWWA	*Who Was Who in America*
YM	*Yankee Magazine*
YMCA	Young Men's Christian Association

CROSS-REFERENCE TO BIOGRAPHICAL DICTIONARY VOLUMES

*	Current Volume
FB	Football Volume
IS	Basketball and Other Indoor Sports Volume
OS	Outside Sports Volume

Q

QUINN, John Picus "Jack" (b. John Quinn Picus, July 5, 1883, Janesville, PA; d. April 17, 1946, Pottsville, PA), player, grew up in eastern Pennsylvania. Very little is known of his early life. Although his family name was Paykos (modified to Picus), he played baseball as Jack Quinn. He first pitched for semipro coal-mining teams and in 1907 entered organized baseball with Macon, GA (SAL). After his spectacular 14–0 season with Richmond, VA (VL) in 1908, he was drafted by the New York Highlanders (AL). He spent four seasons with the Highlanders, winning 18 games in 1910. After parts of two seasons with Rochester, NY (IL), he was purchased by the Boston Braves (NL) in August 1913. Quinn soon jumped to the Baltimore Terrapins in the newly upgraded FL for the 1914–1915 seasons. He won 26 games the first season, but lost 22 decisions in 1915. His performance for Vernon, CA (PCL) resulted in his purchase by the Chicago White Sox (AL) in 1918. He won five of six games, causing the New York Yankees (AL) to reclaim him. After lengthy deliberation, the National Commission awarded him to New York, with whom he spent three more seasons. He pitched in the 1921 World Series, but was traded to the Boston Red Sox (AL) that December.

Quinn, a steady but not spectacular hurler, possessed good control of his low-breaking spitball and did not allow many HR. His fame grew primarily from his remarkable longevity, although there was uncertainty about his exact age then. After Connie Mack* purchased him for the Philadelphia Athletics (AL) in 1925, the 41-year-old 6-foot, 196-pound right-hander responded with several good seasons. He pitched on the AL pennant-winning 1929 and 1930 Philadelphia Athletics teams and on October 4, 1930 became the oldest player (age 46) to participate in a World Series game. With the Brooklyn Dodgers (NL) in 1931–1932, he ranked among the leading NL relief hurlers. He hurled briefly with the Cincinnati Reds (NL) in 1933, but was released shortly after his 49th birthday on July 5. Although several players have made token appearances after age 50, Quinn was the oldest regular roster player in major league history and the oldest player to hit a HR (June 27, 1930) and win a game (August 14, 1932). In 23 seasons, he won 247 games, lost 218 decisions, and compiled a 3.29 ERA. In 756 games, he pitched 3,920.1 innings, struck out 1,329 batters, and hurled 28 shutouts.

Quinn pitched a few games for Hollywood, CA (PCL) in 1934 and the next year returned to Pennsylvania, where he managed Johnstown, PA (MAL) in 1935. He lived the rest of his life in or near Pottsville, PA. His wife, the former Jean Lambert, whom he married in November 1910, died in 1940.

BIBLIOGRAPHY: Lee Allen, "Jack Quinn Big Leaguer at 49," *TSN* (September 9, 1967); Mark Gallagher, *The Yankee Encyclopedia*, vol. 3 (Champaign, IL, 1997); Frank Graham, *The New York Yankees* (New York, 1943); Tom Hufford, "Minoso One of the Oldest," *BRJ* 6 (1977), pp. 30–36; Gene Karst and Martin J. Jones, Jr., *Who's Who in Professional Baseball* (New Rochelle, NY, 1973); Craig Carter, ed., *TSN Daguerreotypes*, 8th ed. (St. Louis, MO, 1990); John Quinn file, National Baseball Library, Cooperstown, NY; Jerome C. Romanowski, *The Mackmen* (Upper Darby, PA, 1979); Connie Mack, *My 66 Years in the Big Leagues* (Philadelphia, PA, 1950); Frederick G. Lieb, *Connie Mack* (New York, 1945).

                                                                        L. Robert Davids

QUISENBERRY, Daniel Raymond "Dan" (b. February 7, 1953, Santa Monica, CA; d. September 30, 1998, Leawood, KS), player, was the son of John Quisenberry, an automobile salesman and horse breeder, and Reberta (Meola) Quisenberry. After graduating from Costa Mesa (CA) High School in 1971, he attended Orange Coast College (1971–1973), La Verne College (1973–1975), and Fresno Pacific College (1978–1979). At La Verne, he made the NAIA All-American baseball team as a pitcher and set school records for most wins, innings pitched, and games pitched in one season. In 1984, he was named the NAIA Hall of Fame. At La Verne in 1975, Quisenberry became a sidearm hurler because the fatigue caused by his record 194 innings pitched led him to alter his pitching motion. Quisenberry's unique delivery dropped into the "submarine" position after he worked with star relief pitcher Kent Tekulve* in spring training of 1980. He became one of the finest relief pitchers in baseball.

Despite his outstanding amateur career, Quisenberry was not drafted by a professional team. The Kansas City Royals (AL) signed him as a free agent in 1975. After starting his first professional game, Quisenberry was moved to the bullpen because Waterloo, IA (ML) lacked a reliever with good control. His extraordinary control marked a four-year rise through the minor leagues at Jacksonville, FL (SL) and Omaha, NE (AA) and created much of his great success in Kansas City. He paced the AL in saves with 33 in 1980; 35 in 1982, a then major league record; 45 in 1983; 44 in 1984; and 37 in 1985 and in appearances with 75 in 1980, 69 in 1983, and 84 in 1985. In

1980 and 1982–1985, he was named AL Fireman of the Year. Due to Quisenberry's effectiveness, he rarely needed to be relieved. In 1980, 1982, 1983, and 1985, he led the AL in games finished in relief. Quisenberry was selected to the AL All-Star team from 1982 through 1984. In 1980, his heroics extended to the World Series. Quisenberry set records by appearing in and completing all six games of the Royals' losing effort against the Philadelphia Phillies. In 1985, he helped the Royals capture the Western Division title by winning eight games and saving 37 others. Quisenberry lost Game 2 of the AL Championship Series against the Toronto Blue Jays, but picked up a save in Game 6. He made four appearances in the Royals' World Series winning effort against the St. Louis Cardinals and won Game 6. After being released by the Royals in July 1988, he joined the St. Louis Cardinals (NL). His major league career ended with the San Francisco Giants (NL) in 1990. During 12 major league seasons, he appeared in 674 games with 56 wins, 46 losses, 244 saves, and a 2.76 ERA.

Quisenberry married Janie Ann Howard on September 11, 1976, had two children, and resided in Leawood, KS. A devoted family man and committed Christian, Quisenberry spent much of the off-season in religious work. He remained a popular public speaker, renowned for a delightful sense of humor. The Kansas City Royals retired his uniform number in 1998. He died after a nine-month battle with brain cancer.

BIBLIOGRAPHY: Sid Bordman, "Royals: Quisenberry Is Tekulve Disciple," *TSN*, June 28, 1980; Sid Bordman, *Expansion to Excellence* (Marcelline, MS, 1981); Alan Eskew, *A Royal Finish* (Chicago, IL, 1985); J. Friedman, "Here's an Underhanded Quiz: How Do They Spell Relief in KC? D-A-N Q-U-I-S-E-N-B-E-R-R-Y," *PW* 25 (April 7, 1986), pp. 49–50; Dan Quisenberry file, National Baseball Library, Cooperstown, NY; Bob Cairns, *Pen Men* (New York, 1993); Pat Jordan, "Oh What a Relief He Is," *Sport* 71 (November 1980), pp. 68–71; Jonathan Rand, "Dan Quisenberry: Baseball's Best Reliever Is an Underhanded Guy," *TSN* August 22, 1983, p. 2; Steve Wulf, "Special Delivery from Down Under," *SI* 59 (July 11, 1983), pp. 74–78ff.

Allen E. Hye

R

RADATZ, Richard Raymond "Dick," "The Monster" (b. April 2, 1937, Detroit, MI), player, is the son of Norman R. Radatz, an automotive engineer, and Virginia Mary (Osterman) Radatz and graduated from suburban Berkley High School, where he starred in basketball, football, and baseball. Radatz declined a $4,000 bonus from the Baltimore Orioles (AL), earning a Bachelor of Science degree in education from Michigan State University in 1959. A pitcher and teammate of Ron Perranoski,* Radatz compiled a 17–4 win–loss record, made All-BTC in 1958 and 1959, and won second team All-America honors his senior year.

Boston Red Sox (AL) scout Maurice DeLoof signed Radatz in 1959. After having modest success as a starter at Raleigh, NC (CrL) and Minneapolis, MN (AA), Radatz was converted into a relief specialist by Seattle, WA (PCL) manager Johnny Pesky* in 1961. The hard-throwing right-hander fanned 74 hitters in 71 innings and lowered his ERA from 3.50 to 2.28. The Boston Red Sox promoted him in 1962.

The 6-foot 6-inch, 250-pound Radatz replaced veteran Mike Fornieles as the Boston Red Sox bullpen mainstay his rookie year and became the dominant major league relief pitcher the next three seasons. With a deceptively easy, high sidearm delivery, an overpowering fastball, and pinpoint control, he appeared in 207 games from 1962 through 1964. Radatz won 40, lost just 21, recorded 78 saves, compiled an overall 2.17 ERA, struck out 487 batters, and surrendered only 149 walks in 414 innings. He led the AL in games pitched (62) in 1962, relief wins in 1963 (15) and 1964 (16), and saves in 1962 (24) and 1964 (29) and set the major league record for strikeouts by a relief pitcher (181) in 1964. Radatz was selected the *TSN* AL Fireman of the Year in 1962 and 1964 and made the AL All-Star team in 1963 and 1964. The lowly Boston Red Sox finished an average of 25 games out of first place during the three-year period. Radatz, one of the few crowd pleasers, appeared in 43 percent of Boston's games and contributed via wins and saves to 53 percent of the team's victories.

In 1965, Radatz changed his motion while developing a sinker ball. The velocity of his fastball diminished, making him less effective. He struck out 121 batters in 124.1 innings and recorded 22 saves, but his record slipped to 9–11 and his ERA ballooned to 3.91. In June 1966, Radatz was traded to the Cleveland Indians (AL) for pitchers Lee Stange and Don McMahon.* With the Cleveland Indians, Chicago Cubs (NL), Detroit Tigers (AL), and Montreal Expos (NL) in 1966, 1967, and 1969, Radatz continued to struggle. He won only three games and lost 11 with a 5.34 ERA, but fanned a respectable 137 in 155.1 innings. In seven major league seasons, Radatz struck out 745 batters in 693.2 innings. His 9.67 strikeouts per nine innings remains the best in baseball history, exceeding even Nolan Ryan's* 9.42.

From 1969 to 1984, Radatz worked in the industrial chemical and packaging businesses in Detroit, MI. Upon returning to the Boston area in 1984, he pursued several baseball-related ventures. He instructs coaches in the training of young ballplayers and frequently appears on radio and television. Radatz married Sharon Cooper in September 1958 and had three children. After they divorced, he married Charlene Booton in December 1987. They reside in Easton, MA. In 1997 the Boston Red Sox Hall of Fame enshrined him.

BIBLIOGRAPHY: Dick Radatz file, National Baseball Library, Cooperstown, NY; Richard Gentile, telephone interview with Dick Radatz, July 7, 1996; *The Baseball Encyclopedia*, 10th ed. (New York, 1996); Joe Jares, "Look, It's 'The Monster' of the Red Sox," *SI* 22 (April 9, 1965), pp. 101–105; Al Stump, "Dick Radatz: He's in Charge," *Sport* 34 (June 1965), pp. 64–69; Peter Golenbock, *Fenway* (New York, 1992); Donald Dewey and Nicholas Acocella, *The Biographical History of Baseball* (New York, 1995); Jack Lautier, *Fenway Voices* (Camden, ME, 1990); Howard Liss, *The Boston Red Sox* (New York, 1982); Barry Sparks, "Dick Radatz Still Stands Tall among Relievers," *BD* 43 (September 1984), pp. 82–83; Dan Shaughnessy, *The Curse of the Bambino* (New York, 1990); Robert Redmount, *The Red Sox Encyclopedia* (Champaign, IL, 1998); Bob Cairns, *Pen Men* (New York, 1993); Milton J. Shapiro, *Heroes of the Bullpen* (New York, 1967); Al Hirshberg, "The 'Monster' of the Red Sox," *Sport* 36 (October 1963), pp. 34–36ff.

Richard H. Gentile

RADBOURN, Charles Gardner "Charley," "Old Hoss" (b. December 11, 1854, Rochester, NY; d. February 5, 1897, Bloomington, IL), player, was nicknamed "Old Hoss" and ranked from 1882 to 1887 among the top four National Leaguers in complete games and innings pitched. The right-hander's 489 major league complete games rank seventh all-time while his 59 complete-game victories in 1884 established a major league record not likely to be surpassed. Radbourn received a grammar school education in

Bloomington, IL, where he had moved as an infant from Rochester, NY with his parents, English immigrants Charles Radbourn, a butcher, and Caroline (Gardner) Radbourn. Through professional baseball, Radbourn found escape from employment as a slaughterhouse butcher and railroad brakeman. In 1878, he barnstormed as pitcher and right fielder for the Peoria, IL Reds. The next year, he joined Dubuque, IA in the newly formed NWL.

Although signed to pitch for the Buffalo Bisons (NL) in 1880, Radbourn injured his arm and played only six games as outfielder and second baseman. He fared better the next year with the Providence Grays (NL), sharing pitching duties with Monte Ward* and winning 25 games. Replacing Ward as the Grays' workhorse, Radbourn from 1882 to 1884 pitched in over two-thirds of the team's championship games. His 140 wins accounted for 72 percent of the Grays' victories. In each of these years, he ranked either first or second in the NL in innings pitched, complete games, ERA, wins, and strikeouts. His 49 victories in 1883 set an NL record, which he shattered the next year.

Radbourn reached his peak in 1884. For the first half of the season, he shared the Grays' pitching with young Charlie Sweeney. Sweeney, however, was expelled from the NL for deserting the club in the middle of a game. Radbourn offered to take up the slack. During one stretch, he pitched 30 of 32 games (including 22 consecutive). He won 26 games, among them a then record 18 in succession. His 73 complete games and 678.2 innings pitched rank second in major league history to Will White's* 75 complete games and 680 innings pitched in 1879. Radbourn led the NL with a 1.38 ERA, a personal best, and 441 strikeouts, the fourth highest major league season total ever. His 59 pitching wins form one of baseball's most enduring records. Radbourn's pitching in 1884 brought Providence the NL championship. In baseball's first "world series" that October, he pitched and won all three games over the AA champion New York Metropolitans.

Changes in the pitching rules (Radbourn's famous leaping delivery was outlawed in 1885) and the wear and tear on his arm diminished Radbourn's effectiveness after 1884. Although winning at least 20 games five of the next six seasons, he pitched less often and saw his ERA rise and his winning percentage decline.

Providence folded following the 1885 season. Radbourn pitched from 1886 to 1889 for the Boston Red Stockings (NL), winning 78 and losing 80. Jumping in 1890 to the Boston Reds in the outlaw PL, he enjoyed his finest season since 1884 with 27 victories and helped Boston win the PL pennant. After pitching for the Cincinnati Reds (NL) in 1891, Radbourn retired from baseball with 309 major league wins and 195 losses.

Back home in Bloomington, Radbourn operated a pool hall/saloon purchased in 1887. He lost his sight in one eye in a hunting accident in 1894 and died less than three years later of paresis. He was survived by both parents, three brothers, and four sisters, his wife, Carrie, and his stepson, Charles Stanhope. In 1939, he was elected to the National Baseball Hall of Fame.

BIBLIOGRAPHY: Frank C. Bancroft, " 'Old Hoss' Radbourn," *BM* 1 (July 1908), pp. 12–14; Bloomington (IL) *Daily Pantagraph*, February 6, 1897; Sam Crane, "Charles Radbourn," New York *Journal*, January 12, 1912; Craig Carter, ed., *TSN Daguerreotypes*, 8th ed. (St. Louis, MO, 1990); Jack E. Harshman, "The Redbourn and Sweeney Saga," *BRJ* 19 (1990), pp. 7–9; Frederick Ivor-Campbell et al., eds., *Baseball's First Stars* (Cleveland, OH, 1996); Noel Hynd, *The Giants of the Polo Grounds* (New York, 1988); Frederick Ivor-Campbell, "1884: Old Hoss Redbourn and the Providence Grays," *TNP* 4 (Spring 1985), pp. 33–38; Harold Kaese, *The Boston Braves* (New York, 1948); John Thorn et al., eds., *Total Braves* (New York, 1996); Gary Caruso, *The Braves Encyclopedia* (Philadelphia, PA, 1995); Charles Radbourn file, National Baseball Library, Cooperstown, NY; *The Baseball Encyclopedia*, 10th ed. (New York, 1996); *SL*, 1884, February 13, 1897; Ted Sullivan, "Without an Equal," *TSN*, February 4, 1905.

                                                                     Frederick Ivor-Campbell

RADCLIFF, Raymond Allen "Rip" (b. January 19, 1906, Kiowa, OK; d. May 23, 1962, Enid, OK), player and manager, was of English descent. He was nicknamed by his father, who compared his sleeping ability to that of Rip Van Winkle. The 5-foot 10-inch, 170-pound left-hander, a high school graduate, began playing baseball professionally in 1928, winning minor league batting championships in 1930 with Selma, AL (SEL) and 1931 with Shreveport, LA (TL).

In 1934, Radcliff joined the Philadelphia Athletics (AL) for spring training, but Manager Connie Mack* optioned him to the Louisville, KY Colonels (AA). His .335 batting average there inspired the Chicago White Sox (AL) to purchase his contract. After hitting .268 in 14 games in 1934 and .286 as a rookie for the Chicago White Sox in 1935, Radcliff posted consecutive .335, .325, and .330 batting averages from 1936 to 1938. On July 18, 1936, 11 days after starting for the AL All-Stars, he enjoyed his best major league game with six hits in seven at-bats against the Philadelphia Athletics.

A shoulder injury triggered Radcliff's declining .264 batting average in 1939. The Chicago White Sox traded him that December to the St. Louis Browns (AL). In 1940, Radcliff hit .342 with the St. Louis Browns and shared the AL lead in hits with 200. The defending champion Detroit Tigers (AL) acquired him in May 1941 for $25,000. Other AL teams claimed the sale violated the "spirit" of the recently passed law forbidding intra-league trades or purchases (except on waivers) with last year's pennant-winner. The deal caused abolition of the rule.

Radcliff joined the U.S. Navy after the 1943 season, ending a 10-year AL career with a .311 batting average and 1,267 hits, and 533 RBI. He performed for the Chattanooga, TN Lookouts (SA) in 1946 and played first base while managing Greensboro, NC (CrL) in 1948. Radcliff, who married Jessie Haughton in September 1930 and had one son, Raymond, Jr., worked as a salesman for a road machinery company in Enid, OK.

BIBLIOGRAPHY: Warren Brown, *The Chicago White Sox* (New York, 1952); Richard Lindberg, *Sox* (New York, 1984); Bill Borst, ed., *Ables to Zoldak*, vol. 3 (St. Louis, MO, 1990); Bill Borst, *Still Last in the American League* (West Bloomfield, MI, 1992); Frederick G. Lieb, *The Detroit Tigers* (New York, 1946); Detroit (MI) *Free Press*, May 24, 1962; *TSN*, June 2, 1962; Rip Radcliff file, National Baseball Library, Cooperstown, NY; *WWIB*, 1935, 20th ed.

Lyle Spatz

RADCLIFFE, Alexander "Alec" (b. July 26, 1905, Mobile, AL; d. July 18, 1983, Chicago, IL), player, performed in the Negro Leagues from 1932 to 1947 and was one of eight children born to James Radcliffe, a construction worker, and Mary (Marsh) Radcliffe. His older brother, Ted,* was an East-West All-Star pitcher and catcher. His first wife, Narlean, had three children, while his second wife, Gladys, had four children.

The 6-foot 2-inch, 210-pound Radcliffe, a rangy third baseman with speed, mobility, and an accurate arm, was quick for his size and once stole home plate against Satchel Paige* in a 1944 contest to win the game. He also hit for power, capturing the NAL HR titles in 1944 and 1945.

Radcliffe began his professional baseball career with Cole's American Giants (NSL) in 1932. The majority of his career was spent with the Chicago, IL American Giants (NAL) from 1933 to 1939 and from 1941 to 1944. Brief stints came with the New York Cubans (NNL) in 1936, the Indianapolis, IN Clowns (NAL) in 1944 and 1945, and Memphis, TN Red Sox (NAL) in 1946. His exemplary career was ended with the semiprofessional Detroit Senators in 1947.

In his first pro season with Cole's American Giants, Radcliffe hit a HR off his brother Ted to defeat the Pittsburgh Crawfords, 1–0. In 1934, he made his first appearance at the East-West All-Star game en route to seven consecutive selections. Altogether, the right-handed hitter made 11 game appearances in East-West All-Star competition, hitting .341 in 44 at-bats. Radcliffe led All-Star players in hits (15) and ranked second in runs scored (7) and RBI (10).

Dave Malarcher,* Richard Lundy,* Ray Dandridge,* Judy Johnson,* and Radcliffe were considered the elite Negro League third basemen.

BIBLIOGRAPHY: *The Baseball Encyclopedia*, 10th ed. (New York, 1996); Larry Lester, interviews with Ted Radcliffe, December 1992 and January 1993; Larry Lester, interview with Margaret Hedgepath, February 1993; Kyle P. McNary, *Ted 'Double Duty' Radcliffe* (St. Louis Park, MN, 1994); James A. Riley, *The Biographical Encyclopedia of the Negro Baseball Leagues* (New York, 1994); Mike Shatzkin, ed., *The Ball-*

players (New York, 1990); Alexander Radcliffe file, National Baseball Library, Cooperstown, NY.

Larry Lester

RADCLIFFE, Theodore Roosevelt "Ted," "Double Duty" (b. July 7, 1902, Mobile, AL), player and manager, participated in the Negro Leagues from 1928 to 1950 and was one of eight children born to James Radcliffe, a construction contractor, and Mary (Marsh) Radcliffe. His brother Alec* was an East-West All-Star third baseman. He married Alberta Robinson and had one daughter, Shirley, who died in 1927 during childbirth. His nickname, "Double Duty," was given to him by New York sportswriter Damon Runyon (OS), who saw Radcliffe catch Satchel Paige* in one game and pitch a shutout in the nightcap of a 1932 doubleheader.

The chunky, 5-foot 9½-inch, 210-pound catcher started his 23-year professional career with the Detroit, MI Stars (NNL) in 1928. His much-traveled career included stops with the St. Louis, MO Stars (NNL) in 1930, Homestead, PA Grays (NNL) in 1931, 1933, 1936, and 1946, Pittsburgh, PA Crawfords (EWL) in 1932, Columbus, OH Blue Birds (NNL) in 1933, Brooklyn, NY Eagles (NNL) in 1935, Cincinnati, OH Tigers (NAL) in 1936 and 1937, Memphis, TN Red Sox (NAL) in 1938 and 1939, Chicago, IL American Giants (NAL) in 1941–1943, and 1949–1950, Birmingham, AL Black Barons (NAL) in 1942 and 1944–1945, Kansas City, MO Monarchs (NAL) in 1945, and several nonleague teams like the New York Black Yankees in 1933 and the Harlem Globetrotters in 1947.

Radcliffe appeared in six East-West All-Star Games (1937–1939, 1941, 1943–1944), with three as a catcher and three as a pitcher. He hit .308 in All-Star competition, including one HR, and recorded an All-Star victory in 1939. Against major league competition in nine exhibition games, he hit .376 in 29 at-bats. Radcliffe's lifetime batting average is listed at .282, with his win–loss pitching record at 53–33. In 1943, he was named the team's MVP as player–manager of the Chicago American Giants. Radcliffe's biggest thrill came in the 1944 East-West All-Star classic, when he hit a HR in the presence of his mother. He managed the Memphis Red Sox in 1938 and 1939 and the Chicago American Giants in 1949 and 1950. In 1952, he was selected to the Pittsburgh (PA) *Courier*'s all-time, all-star team as fourth team pitcher and third team catcher. Radcliffe, who has a great sense of humor, still attends reunions and other baseball events.

BIBLIOGRAPHY: *The Baseball Encyclopedia*, 10th ed. (New York, 1996); Larry Lester, interviews with Ted Radcliffe, December 1992 and January 1993; Kyle P. McNary, *Ted 'Double Duty' Radcliffe* (St. Louis Park, MN, 1994); Robert Obojski, "Negro League Player Starred as Pitcher and Catcher," *SCD* 24 (August 8, 1997), p. 90; Paul Post, " 'Double Duty' Radcliffe Has Fond Memories," *SCD* 21 (March 5, 1993), p. 82; James A. Riley, *The Biographical Encyclopedia of the Negro Baseball Leagues* (New

York, 1994); Mike Shatzkin, ed., *The Ballplayers* (New York, 1990); Ted Radcliffe file, National Baseball Library, Cooperstown, NY.

Larry Lester

RADER, Douglas Lee "Doug," "The Red Rooster," "Rojo" (b. July 30, 1944, Chicago, IL), player, scout, coach, and manager, participated in football, baseball, basketball, and ice hockey at Glenbrook High School and attended Illinois Wesleyan University for two years on a baseball and basketball scholarship. He also played semipro ice hockey in Peoria, IL under assumed names and worked out with the Chicago Black Hawks (NHL). After beginning professional baseball as a shortstop, Rader soon moved to third base. He won Gold Glove Awards for the Houston Astros (NL) from 1970 to 1974, leading the NL in fielding percentage in 1970 and 1975. The 6-foot 2-inch, 208-pound redhead, nicknamed "the Red Rooster" for his presumed resemblance to the Warner Brothers animated character Foghorn Leghorn, received as much attention for his practical jokes and other antics as for his playing ability. He played 11 major league seasons with the Houston Astros from 1967 to 1975, San Diego Padres (NL) in 1976 and 1977, and Toronto Blue Jays (AL) in 1977. A right-hander, he hit 155 career HR, drove in 722 runs, and compiled a .251 batting average.

When Rader was named the Houston Astros' manager in November 1982, Houston (TX) *Chronicle* baseball writer John Wilson remarked, "I'm quite sure that everybody who played with Doug probably found it a little surprising that he ended up a manager." Still, Rader possessed a serious side and regarded Ernest Hemingway as his favorite author. He piloted the Hawaii Islanders (PCL) in the San Diego Padres organization from 1980 through 1982. As the Texas Rangers (AL) manager from 1983 through May 1985, he often quarreled with players and the media. He coached with the Chicago White Sox (AL) in 1986, 1987, and 1997 and scouted for the California Angels (AL) in 1988 before managing the California Angels from 1989 to 1991. His best record as a manager came with the Angels' third-place finish of 91–71 in 1989. His career managerial record included 388 wins, 417 losses, and one tie.

Rader married Jeannette Becklin in 1967 and converted from Presbyterianism to Catholicism, the religion of his wife and mother in 1979. He and his wife have three children, Christine, Elizabeth, and Matthew, and reside in Stuart, FL.

BIBLIOGRAPHY: Doug Rader file, National Baseball Library, Cooperstown, NY; Thomas Aylesworth and Benton Minks, *The Encyclopedia of Baseball Managers* (New York, 1990); Phil Rogers, *The Impossible Takes a Little Longer* (Dallas, TX, 1991); Ron Fimrite, "He's Not Just a Wild and Crazy Guy," *SI* 59 (August 8, 1983), pp. 38–41; Peter Gammons, "He's an Angel Now," *SI* 71 (August 7, 1989), pp. 34–39; Steve Pate, "A Good Old Boy Rides the Ranger," *Sport* 74 (April 1983), pp. 47ff; Mike

Shatzkin, ed., *The Ballplayers* (New York, 1990); John Thorn et al., eds., *Total Baseball*, 5th ed. (New York, 1997); *WWIB*, 62nd ed., 1977.

Victor Rosenberg

RAINES, Timothy "Tim," "Rock" (b. September 16, 1959, Sanford, FL), player, is the son of Ned Raines, Sr., and Florence (Reynolds) Raines and attended Seminole High School in Sanford, FL. Raines emerged as one of the speediest, most daring base runners among the talented pool of fleet-footed triple-threat major league outfielders of the 1980s. Disappointment, injury, and substance-abuse problems have marked his career which has also been filled with constant media and fan allegations of his uninspired play and failure to fulfill his unlimited talent and potential. Raines first captured the attention of the baseball world as AA batting champion (.345) and *TSN* Minor League Player of the Year as a second baseman with the Denver Bears in 1980.

Bursting on the major league scene with the Montreal Expos (NL) in 1981, Raines stole a remarkable 71 bases in only 88 games, hit .304 in 313 at-bats, and finished a close second to Los Angeles Dodgers (NL) pitching star Fernando Valenzuela* for NL Rookie-of-the-Year honors. Four consecutive stolen base titles (1981–1984) came for the fleet-footed Raines, who had been converted to an outfield position upon his major league arrival in Montreal. Raines continued to dominate the base paths for his first six major league seasons, stealing over 70 bases each campaign. Raines enjoyed his finest all-around season in 1986, pacing the NL in both batting (.334) and on-base percentage (.415) and garnering a career-high 194 hits. Raines opted for free-agent status after his batting-title season, but quickly discovered that a baseball owners' collusion on free-agent signings left him without an offer. Raines was forced to return to the Montreal Expos lineup in May 1987 without participating in either spring training or minor league warm-up play. A dramatic return featured a HR in his first game and a second title for runs scored, despite his considerable missed playing time. His other milestone achievements have been recording career highs in steals (90) and runs scored (133) in 1983 and his record 85.2 percent success rate in over 900 stolen base attempts through 2,112 major league games. In February 1991, the Montreal Expos traded Raines to the Chicago White Sox (AL) for Ivan Calderon and Barry Jones. In 1993, Raines batted .306 to help the Chicago White Sox capture the NL West and hit .444 in the AL Championship Series against the Toronto Blue Jays. He holds the single series AL Championship Series record for most singles (10) and shares the mark for most hits (12). The New York Yankees (AL) acquired him in a December 1995 trade. He played limited roles in 1996, when the New York Yankees defeated the Atlanta Braves in the World Series, and 1997. He clouted a HR with three RBI in the AL Division Series loss to the Cleveland Indians in 1997. Raines batted .290 in 1998, when the New York Yankees set an AL record with 114 victories. He made limited appearances in the AL Division Series against the Texas Rangers and the AL Championship Series against the Cleveland Indians. In January 1999, the Oakland Athletics (AL) signed him as a free agent. He became a free agent in October 1999.

Through 1999, Raines has batted .295 with 2,561 hits, 419 doubles, 168 HR, 964 RBI, and 807 stolen bases. He appeared in the All-Star Game in each of his first seven (1981–1987) major league campaigns.

BIBLIOGRAPHY: Timothy Raines file, National Baseball Library, Cooperstown, NY; Peter C. Bjarkman, ed., *The Encyclopedia of Major League Baseball Team Histories National League* (Westport, CT, 1991); Ron Fimrite, "Don't Knock the Rock!" *SI* 60 (June 25, 1984), pp. 48–56; Peter Gammons, "Light Years Ahead of the Field," *SI* 65 (July 28, 1986), pp. 34–36; Phil Jasner, "Tim Raines: The Majors' New Base-Stealing Sensation," *BD* 48 (August 1981), pp. 20–22; Robert E. Kelly, *Baseball's Best* (Jefferson, NC, 1988); Hal Quinn, "Like a Thief in the Night," *Macleans* 96 (June 8, 1981), p. 38; Mike Shatzkin, ed., *The Ballplayers* (New York, 1990); *TSN Official Baseball Register*, 1998; D. Whitford, "The Last Laugh," *Sport* 78 (December 1987), pp. 16–18; Dan Turner, *The Expos Inside Out* (Toronto, Canada, 1983).

Peter C. Bjarkman

RAMSEY, Thomas A. "Toad," "Tode" (b. August 8, 1864, Indianapolis, IN; d. March 27, 1906, Indianapolis, IN), player, possibly threw baseball's first knuckle ball. As a teenager, Ramsey apprenticed as a bricklayer and played sandlot baseball. He accidentally sliced a tendon in the index finger of his left hand with a trowel. The injury failed to heal properly, preventing him from straightening his finger. The crooked digit enabled Ramsey to throw a ball that veered downward when it reached the plate. The "drop curve," his special pitch, proved almost unhittable. He soon graduated to semiprofessional baseball and joined Chattanooga, TN (SL) in 1885. Ramsey's trick pitch helped him strike out 16 batters in one game. The same season he reached the major leagues with the Louisville, KY Colonels (AA).

In 1886, Ramsey ranked among the best major league baseball pitchers. He won 38 games, lost 27 contests, and led the AA in complete games (66) and innings pitched (588.2). Ramsey almost duplicated these statistics in 1887, compiling a 37–27 record. He led the AA with 355 strikeouts, despite a rule change that allowed batters four strikes.

By 1888, Ramsey's pitching career began to unravel. Heavy alcohol consumption contributed to a deplorable 8–30 record, alienating his teammates. After Ramsey struggled to a 1–16 start in 1889, the Louisville Colonels sent him to the St. Louis Browns (AA). For the St. Louis Browns, Ramsey finished 3–1 in 1889 and 24–17 in 1890. Prior to the 1891 season, the St. Louis Browns released Ramsey after his shouting match with owner Chris Von der Ahe.* He appeared briefly in the minor leagues in 1891 and again in 1894.

Ramsey, whose nickname may have been a play on the name Tom, compiled a 114–124 major league career record with a 3.29 ERA. A terrible fielder, he made 107 errors in 452 chances. Ramsey eventually returned to Indianapolis, IN, where he resumed his bricklaying career and played baseball semiprofessionally. He worked as a bartender in an establishment owned by his brother, William. He died of pneumonia and was survived by his wife, Anna.

BIBLIOGRAPHY: *The Baseball Encyclopedia*, 10th ed. (New York, 1996); Peter J. Cava, Indiana-born major league player files, Peter J. Cava Collection, Indianapolis, IN; Alan Kaufman and James C. Kaufman, *The Worst Baseball Pitchers of All Time* (Jefferson, NC, 1993); Bill Madden, *The Hoosiers of Summer* (Indianapolis, IN, 1994); David Nemec, *The Beer and Whisky League* (New York, 1994); Philip Van Borries, *Legends of Louisville* (West Bloomfield, MI, 1993); Philip Van Borries, *Louisville Diamonds* (Paducah, KY, 1997); J. Thomas Hetrick, *Chris Von der Ahe and the St. Louis Browns* (Lanham, MD, 1999); Frederick G. Lieb, *The St. Louis Cardinals* (New York, 1945); Toad Ramsey file, National Baseball Library, Cooperstown, NY; James K. Skipper, *Baseball Nicknames* (Jefferson, NC, 1992); Robert Smith, *Baseball in the Afternoon* (New York, 1993); Robert Smith, *Heroes of Baseball* (New York, 1952); Robert L. Tiemann and Mark Rucker, eds., *Nineteenth Century Baseball Stars* (Kansas City, MO, 1989).

Peter J. Cava

RANDALL, Maxine Kline (b. September 16, 1929, North Adams, MI), player, starred as an AAGPBL pitcher. She grew up in Addison, MI, the daughter of German farmers, and had seven sisters and two brothers. In her small midwestern town, she played softball. At North Adams High School, Randall starred in basketball with a 23-point average and led her team to three straight undefeated seasons. Coach Lawrence Wilson took her to Fort Wayne for a baseball tryout with the AAGPBL. She reported to the Fort Wayne Daisies (AAGPBL) immediately after graduation in 1948.

The 5-foot 7-inch, 130-pound Randall began her seven-year AAGPBL career as an outfielder, utilizing her strong throwing arm. When all Fort Wayne's pitchers had been used one game that season, she was asked to pitch. The Fort Wayne Daisies won Randall's first two starts, blanking opponents. In 1947, Randall hurled a one-hitter. She pitched a 5–0 no-hitter against the Grand Rapids Chicks on June 12, 1949 and led the AAGPBL in victories with a 23–9 mark in 1950, making the All-Star team for the initial time. No AAGPBL hurler compiled more triumphs in a season. Randall's 18–4 record in 1951 earned her another All-Star selection. Randall made the All-Star team five of her seven seasons, relying primarily on a fastball. Fort Wayne excelled most of Randall's tenure, winning pennants with win–loss records in 1952, 1953, and 1954. The Fort Wayne Daisies never won the AAGPBL playoffs, but Randall pitched the first, fourth, and sixth games of the 1950 championship series. She was managed by AL star Jimmie Foxx* in 1952. She compiled a 19–7 record with six shutouts in 1952 and a 16–14 mark in 1953. In the AAGPBL's hitting-dominated last season in 1954, Randall led the AAGPBL in victories (18), games pitched (28), complete games (24), innings pitched (181), and shutouts (6) and recorded her second no-hitter on June 20 against the Grand Rapids Chicks.

Among the best AAGPBL overhand pitchers, Randall proved a tough competitor and consistent pitcher. She possessed good control of the fastball, change-up, and curve, walking only 389 batters in 1,518 career innings pitched. Her 116–65 win–loss lifetime pitching record included a cumulative 2.05 ERA. In three seasons, her ERA dropped below 2.00. One time, the five-foot seven-inch, 130-pound right-hander threw a 17-inning shutout. Following the AAGPBL's demise, she played four years with Bill Allington's All-Americans summer barnstorming team.

Randall married Robert Randall, whom she met while working for Jonesville (Automotive) Products in North Adams, in 1973. She lives on the family farm, only 10 miles from her birthplace. Randall played in the 1984 reunion game, where she hit a HR.

BIBLIOGRAPHY: Barbara Gregorich, *Women at Play* (San Diego, CA, 1993); Susan E. Johnson, *When Women Played Hardball* (Seattle, WA, 1994); AAGPBL files, Northern Indiana Historical Society, South Bend, IN; W. C. Madden, *The Women of the All-American Girls Professional Baseball League* (Jefferson, NC, 1997).

Dennis S. Clark

RANDOLPH, William Larry, Jr. "Willie" (b. July 6, 1954, Holly Hill, SC), player, coach, and executive, is the son of Willie Randolph, Sr., a construction worker, and Minnie Randolph and moved to Brooklyn, NY with his family as an infant. As a youth, he played stickball in the streets and baseball at Tilden High School. Several major league baseball teams scouted the infield prospect, who graduated in 1972 and was signed by the Pittsburgh Pirates (NL) in the seventh round of the June 1972 free agent draft. Assigned to Bradenton, FL (GCL) in 1972, Randolph spent subsequent minor league seasons at Charleston, SC (WCL) in 1973, Thetford, Canada Mines (EL) in 1974, and Charleston, WV (IL) in 1975. Upon joining the Pittsburgh Pirates in July 1975, he had led the IL in hitting. Pittsburgh traded the 5-foot 11-inch, 170-pound, right-handed–hitting second baseman to the New York Yankees (AL) in December 1975.

In his 1976 rookie season, Randolph hit .267, stole 37 bases, and quickly became known as a very smooth second baseman with a good arm and good range. His ability to turn the double play proved excellent. His career 1,547 double plays at second base was exceeded in major league history only by Nellie Fox* (1,619) and Bill Mazeroski* (1,706). Randolph in 1992 became the all-time leader in games played for a New York Yankee second baseman with 1,689 and shares the all-time single-game record for assists by a second baseman with 13, accomplished on August 25, 1976 in 19 innings against the Minnesota Twins. During that same game, he also established an AL single-game record for most chances accepted by a second baseman with 20. During his career, he led the AL in several categories. In 1979, Randolph topped AL second basemen with 846 total chances, 355 putouts, 478 assists, and 128 double plays. He also led the AL in 1984 with 112 double plays and 119 walks in 1980. Contemporaries respected Randolph as a student of the game. In 1986, Randolph and Ron Guidry* were named cocaptains of the New York Yankees. Often, he was mentioned as a possible future manager.

The Los Angeles Dodgers (NL) signed Randolph as a free agent in December 1988. In May 1990, the Oakland Athletics (AL) acquired him in a trade. The Milwaukee Brewers (AL) signed him as a free agent in April 1991, while the New York Mets (NL) obtained him as a free agent in December 1991. Six times Randolph made his leagues' All-Star team. In 1976, he became the first rookie listed on an All-Star ballot. He was selected, but could not play due to injury. His other All-Star team designations included the 1977, 1980, 1981, and 1987 AL All-Star squads and the 1989 NL aggregate. *TSN* chose him for second base on its 1977, 1980, and 1987 AL All-Star teams and 1980 AL Silver Slugger team.

Randolph's major league playing career ended after the 1992 season. He compiled a lifetime .276 batting average with 1,239 runs scored, 2,210 hits, 54 HR, 687 RBI, 271 stolen bases, and a .980 fielding average. He hit an aggregate .271 in the 1976, 1977, 1980, 1981, and 1990 AL Championship Series and 1975 NL Championship Series. His 1976, 1977, 1981, and 1990 World Series appearances led to a combined .181 batting average. He became an assistant general manager for the New York Yankees (AL) in 1993 and has coached there since 1994. Randolph and his wife, Gretchen, have four children, Taniesha, Chantre, Ciara, and Andre.

BIBLIOGRAPHY: John Dewan and Don Zminda, eds., *The Scouting Report, 1993* (New York, 1993); Mark Gallagher, *The Yankee Encyclopedia*, vol. 3 (Champaign, IL, 1997); Maury Allen, *Damn Yankee* (New York, 1980); Sparky Lyle and Peter Golenbock, *The Bronx Zoo* (New York, 1979); Dick Lally, *Pinstriped Summers* (New York, 1985); Jon Heyman, "Willie's Back," *Newsday*, April 14, 1993, pp. 132, 138; *Los Angeles Dodgers 1989 Media Guide; New York Mets 1992 Media Guide; New York Yankees 1998 Media Guide*; Phil Pepe, "Willie Randolph on the Way to Greatness," *BD* 39 (September 1980), pp. 60–61; Willie Randolph file, National Baseball Library, Cooperstown, NY; Seymour Siwoff, ed., *The 1993 Elias Baseball Analyst* (New York, 1993); John Thorn et al., eds., *Total Baseball*, 5th ed. (New York, 1997); *TSN Official Baseball Register*, 1993.

Robert J. Brown

RASCHI, Victor John Angelo "Vic," "The Springfield Rifle" (b. March 28, 1919, West Springfield, MA; d. October 14, 1988, Groveland, NY), player, was the son of northern Italian immigrants who settled first in Connecticut.

As a high school student in West Springfield, MA, he starred in track and field, basketball, and football. The New York Yankees (AL) scouted him at age 14 and signed Raschi to a contract that guaranteed him the opportunity to complete his college education. The 6-foot 1-inch, 205-pound Raschi attended the College of William and Mary in Williamsburg, VA, but left in 1941 to join the New York Yankees' farm team in Amsterdam, NY (CAL). He graduated from William and Mary in 1950 after 11 years of part-time study.

The New York Yankees promoted Raschi from the Newark, NJ Bears (IL) farm club in 1946 with Yogi Berra* and Bobby Brown.* Raschi compiled a 132–66 win–loss record and 3.72 ERA in a major league career that also included stints with the St. Louis Cardinals (NL) in 1954 and 1955 and the Kansas City Athletics (AL) in 1955. He led the AL in 1951 with 164 strike-outs and established a major league record for pitchers by driving in seven runs on August 4, 1953, helping defeat the Detroit Tigers, 15–0. According to Raschi, his biggest game came on the final day of the 1949 season when the Yankees and the Boston Red Sox shared first place in the AL. Raschi pitched a complete game in defeating Boston 5–3, enabling New York to win the AL pennant.

Raschi led the AL in games started twice and paced the AL in winning percentage (.724) with a 21–8 mark in 1950. From 1948 through 1951, he led the Yankees in victories. Raschi's Yankee .706 major league career win–loss percentage and 120–50 record ranked him second highest in club history. He was selected for the AL All-Star team four times (1948–1950, 1952), winning the 1948 game and starting the 1950 and 1952 contests.

In the fifth and final game of the 1949 World Series against the Brooklyn Dodgers, Raschi helped the Yankees win the title. This compensated for an earlier 1–0 loss in the second game. He triumphed in the first game of the 1950 World Series, having a 2-hit, 1–0 shutout against the Philadelphia Phillies. His other World Series victories included the sixth and final game against the New York Giants in 1951 and the second and sixth games over the Brooklyn Dodgers in 1952.

Raschi and Yankees General Manager George Weiss* usually quarreled over his salary. In February 1954, the Yankees sold Raschi's contract to the St. Louis Cardinals (NL) for a reported $85,000. Ed Lopat,* Allie Reynolds,* and Raschi formed the nucleus of the pitching staff that allowed the Yankees to win five straight World Series from 1949 to 1953. No other major league baseball team has ever matched that feat.

BIBLIOGRAPHY: Dom Forker, *The Men of Autumn* (Dallas, TX, 1989); Mark Gallagher, *The Yankee Encyclopedia*, vol. 3 (Champaign, IL, 1997); David Halberstam, *Summer of '49* (New York, 1989); Donald Honig, *Baseball Between the Lines* (New York, 1976); Sol Gittleman, "Raschi, Lopat, and Reynolds," *BRJ* 22 (1993), pp. 78–79; Walter LeConte, *The Ultimate New York Yankees Record Book* (New York, 1984); *NYT*, October 16, 1988, p. 34; George Sullivan and John Powers, *Yankees: An Illus-*

trated History (Englewood Cliffs, NJ, 1982); Robert W. Creamer, *Stengel: His Life and Times* (New York, 1984); Dave Anderson et al., *The Yankees* (New York, 1979); Peter Golenbock, *Dynasty* (Englewood, Cliffs, NJ, 1975); Tom Meany, *The Magnificent Yankees* (New York, 1952).

Arthur F. McClure

RAY, John Cornelius "Johnny" (b. March 1, 1957, Chouteau, OK), player, is the son of Ray Charles Ray, a drywall contractor, and Dorothy (Cade) Ray and attended Northeastern Oklahoma A&M University and the University of Arkansas. The Houston Astros (NL) drafted the 5-foot 11-inch, 189-pound second baseman, who switch hit and threw right-handed, in the 12th round in June 1979. Ray played under three minor league seasons with Sarasota, FL (GCL) and Daytona Beach, FL (FSL) in 1979, Columbus, GA (SL) in 1980, and Tucson, AZ (PCL) in 1981.

The Houston Astros traded Ray to the Pittsburgh Pirates (NL) in August 1981. Ray joined the Pittsburgh Pirates that month and spent the next six seasons with them. In 1982, he batted .281 with 182 hits in 162 games and led NL second basemen in chances, putouts, assists, and errors, becoming the first Pirate to win *TSN* NL Rookie of the Year honors. The disciplined gap hitter shared the NL lead in doubles with 38 in both 1983 and 1984. His best season with the Pittsburgh Pirates came in 1984, when he batted .312 with 173 hits and 67 RBI. In 1986, he hit .301 with 33 doubles and 78 RBI and tied a major league record for fewest errors by a second baseman with five.

In August 1987, the Pittsburgh Pirates traded Ray to the California Angels (AL). His major league pinnacle came in 1988, when he batted .306, established career highs with 184 hits, 42 doubles, and 83 RBI, and made the AL All-Star team. Ray played two more seasons with the California Angels and was released in December 1990. His professional baseball career ended with the Yakult, Japan Swallows (JCL) in 1991 and 1992.

In 10 major league seasons, Ray batted .290 with 1,502 hits, 294 doubles, 594 RBI, and 80 stolen bases. *TSN* named him on its NL Silver Slugger team in 1983 and on its AL All-Star team in 1988. The Chouteau, OK resident fanned just 329 times in 5,188 official major league at-bats. Ray, who is retired, married Tammy McNack on February 23, 1983 and has two children, Johnny, Jr., and Jasmine.

BIBLIOGRAPHY: Johnny Ray file, National Baseball Library, Cooperstown, NY; Johnny Ray to David L. Porter, February 9, 1998; *TSN Baseball Register*, 1990; Bob Smizik, *The Pittsburgh Pirates: An Illustrated History* (New York, 1990); John Thorn et al., eds., *Total Baseball*, 5th ed. (New York, 1997).

David L. Porter

REACH, Alfred James "Al" (b. May 25, 1840, London, England; d. January 14, 1928, Atlantic City, NJ), player, manager, and manufacturer, was the son of Benjamin Reach and Elizabeth (Dyball) Reach and entered baseball in 1855 with the newly formed Brooklyn, NY Eckford team. Reach joined the Philadelphia Athletics in 1865 at a $25 a week salary "for expenses," a guise to maintain the sport's amateur status. He thus became the first paid player in the game's history. He married Louise Betts on December 25, 1866 and had four children. The 5-foot 6-inch, 155-pound Reach played second base and outfield, was "clever" on the bases, and proved a remarkably hard-hitting left-handed batter. He played with the Philadelphia Athletics from 1865 through 1875 and managed Philadelphia the last two seasons. In the NA from 1871 to 1875 Reach compiled a .247 lifetime batting average in the dead ball era and was selected for the first All-America team chosen in 1876. In 80 games from 1871 to 1875, he scored 89 runs and made 97 hits. As a manager, he guided the Athletics to 33–22 and 53–20 marks in 1874 and 1875, respectively.

Reach continued to have an active interest in baseball. In 1876, he named and backed the new Philadelphia Phillies (NL) and did not sell his interest until 1903. He managed Philadelphia briefly to a 4–7 mark in 1890. During those decades, A. J. Reach & Company made him a millionaire. This venture began as a cigar store and gathering place for sportsmen, but was transformed into a sporting goods store and became one of the largest companies of its type. Reach's company specialized in manufacturing baseballs by using a machine he allegedly developed personally to wind them more tightly. It also became one of the first mail-order houses and regularly sent out catalogues in the 1880s. These successful ventures enabled him to pursue his baseball interests. In 1883 he began publishing the avidly read *Reach's Official Base Ball Guide*, which probably contributed to the early development of baseball's mania for records and statistics. His successful company came under the watchful gaze of the emerging sporting goods giant Spalding & Company. He was given $100,000 and an executive position in 1889, when his own company became a division of the Spalding business. Reach, who sold out in 1892, spent his later years helping to popularize baseball. He served in 1907–1908 on the National Commission, which established the definitive American roots of the game and enabled it to become the national pastime.

BIBLIOGRAPHY: Alfred Reach file, National Baseball Library, Cooperstown, NY; Frederick G. Lieb and Stan Baumgartner, *The Philadelphia Phillies* (New York, 1953); Rich Westcott and Frank Bilovsky, *The New Phillies Encyclopedia* (Philadelphia, PA, 1993); Gene Karst and Martin J. Jones, Jr., *Who's Who in Professional Baseball* (New Rochelle, NY, 1973); *DAB* 15 (1935), pp. 418–419; *The Baseball Encyclopedia*, 10th ed. (New York, 1996); Harold Seymour, *Baseball: The Early Years* (New York, 1960); Robert L. Tiemann and Mark Rucker, eds., *Nineteenth Century Stars* (Kansas City, MO, 1989); William J. Ryczek, *Blackguards and Red Stockings* (Jefferson, NC, 1992); William J. Ryczek, *When Johnny Comes Sliding Home* (Jefferson, NC, 1998); David

Q. Voigt, *American Baseball*, vol. 1 (Norman, OK, 1966); Douglass Wallop, *Baseball: An Informal History* (New York, 1969).

Charles R. Middleton

REARDON, Jeffrey James "Jeff," "The Terminator" (b. October 1, 1955, Dalton, MA), player, is one of six children of John T. Reardon, a security guard, and Marion (Stevens) Reardon, grew up in Dalton, and majored in history at the University of Massachusetts. The New York Mets (NL) signed the 6-foot, 205-pound right-hander in June 1977 and assigned the starting pitcher to Lynchburg, VA (CrL) in 1977 and Jackson, TX (TL) in 1978. New York converted him to a reliever at Tidewater, VA (IL) in 1979. Reardon split relief responsibilities for the New York Mets with Neil Allen from 1979 to 1981.

The Montreal Expos (NL) in May 1981 acquired Reardon, who compiled a career-best 2.06 ERA with 26 saves in 1982 and saved 44 games over the next two seasons. Manager Buck Rodgers designated Reardon the exclusive closer in 1985, when the bearded fastball pitcher led the major leagues with 41 saves, made the NL All-Star team, and was named *TSN* NL Fireman of the Year. Mitch Melnick, the Montreal Expos announcer, nicknamed him "The Terminator." In 1986, he saved 35 contests and repeated as an NL All-Star selection.

In February 1987, the Montreal Expos traded Reardon to the Minnesota Twins (AL). Reardon helped Minnesota capture the 1987 AL pennant with 31 saves, striking out 83 batters in 80.1 innings. His honors included winning the Twins' MVP Award and sharing AL Fireman of the Year accolades. Reardon saved two games and split two decisions in the AL Championship Series against the Detroit Tigers. The Minnesota Twins defeated the St. Louis Cardinals in the seven-game World Series, as Reardon hurled 4.2 scoreless innings and saved the decisive seventh game. Reardon in 1988 saved a career-high 42 games with a 2.47 ERA, making the AL All-Star team.

After Reardon saved 31 games in 1989, the Boston Red Sox (AL) signed him as a free agent that December. Reardon relied more on his curveball and accurate control. His best season with Boston came in 1991, when he saved 40 games and was selected to the AL All-Star team. Reardon in 1992 surpassed Rollie Fingers* as the all-time save leader with 342. In August 1992, the Boston Red Sox traded Reardon to the Atlanta Braves (NL). Reardon compiled a 3–0 record and a 1.15 ERA with three saves, helping Atlanta garner the NL West Division title. He recorded one win and one save in the NL Championship Series, when the Atlanta Braves defeated the Pittsburgh Pirates to take the NL pennant. Reardon struggled in the World Series, blowing two save opportunities against the Toronto Blue Jays. The Cincinnati Reds (NL) signed him as a free agent in January 1993 and used him primarily as a setup reliever. His major league career ended with the New York Yankees (AL) in 1994.

The quiet, unemotional Reardon, who seldom relieved for more than one inning, ranks fourth to Lee Smith,* Dennis Eckersley,* and John Franco* in career saves with 367. In 880 major league games spanning 16 seasons, he had 73 wins, 77 losses, a 3.16 ERA, and 877 strikeouts in 1,132.1 innings. From 1982 to 1992, no other major league reliever recorded at least 20 saves each season.

He and his wife, Phebe, have two sons, Jeffrey and Shane, and reside in Palm Beach Gardens, FL.

BIBLIOGRAPHY: Jeff Reardon file, National Baseball Library, Cooperstown, NY; Peter C. Bjarkman, ed., *Encyclopedia of Major League Baseball Team Histories American League* (Westport, CT, 1991); Jim Kaplan, "Saving Face in Montreal," *SI* 62 (June 24, 1985), pp. 58, 60; Jack Lang and Peter Simon, *The New York Mets* (New York, 1986); Dan Turner, *The Expos Inside Out* (Toronto, Canada, 1983); Steve Rushin, "The Pen Ultimate," *SI* 76 (June 8, 1992), pp. 54–57; Mike Shatzkin, ed., *The Ballplayers* (New York, 1990); *TSN Official Baseball Register*, 1995.

David L. Porter

REARDON, John Edward "Jack," "Beans" (b. November 23, 1897, Taunton, MA; d. July 31, 1984, Long Beach, CA), umpire, was the son of William Reardon, a cotton mill foreman and saloon co-owner, and Margarett M. Reardon. After his father died, his mother remarried in 1912 and moved to Los Angeles, CA. A high school dropout, Reardon apprenticed as a boiler-maker in the Southern Pacific Railroad shops. He acquired his unusual nick-name during noon pick-up baseball games as a shortened version of "Baked Beans," prompted by his Massachusetts heritage and accent. Although unskilled as a player, Reardon became a popular semiprofessional baseball arbiter in Southern California and began his professional umpiring career at age 22 with the Class B WCL in 1920. He advanced to the Class AA PCL in 1922 and debuted in the NL in 1926.

Besides umpiring the 1936, 1940, and 1948 All-Star games and the 1930, 1934, 1939, 1943, and 1949 World Series, Reardon experienced many memorable moments in his 24-year major league career. He made an unusual double-play call on August 15, 1926 at Ebbets Field when three Brooklyn Dodgers wound up simultaneously on third base, was present when Commissioner Kenesaw Mountain Landis* banished Joe Medwick* of the St. Louis Cardinals from the final game of the 1934 World Series, and umpired at home plate when Babe Ruth* of the Boston Braves hit his last three career HR at Forbes Field in Pittsburgh, PA on May 25, 1935. The cocky, combative, profane, 5-foot 8-inch, 145-pound Reardon projected a tough-guy image. Nevertheless, his friendly manner and infectious humor, hustle, and absolute honesty endeared him to fans, players, and managers. He readily admitted an incorrect call and rarely ejected players. Reardon evidenced his career-long feud with Bill Klem,* the NL's senior umpire, by refusing to use an inside chest protector and wearing a blue and white polka dot bow-tie instead of the preferred black four-in-hands. In accepting the 1970 Bill

Klem Award for meritorious service to baseball, Reardon quipped: "I must tell you that Klem hated my guts and I hated his guts."

The garrulous Reardon appeared in several movies with Mae West and did promotional work for Anheuser-Busch brewery, which in 1946 awarded him the Budweiser distributorship in Long Beach, CA. He retired after the 1949 World Series as the highest paid ($11,500) umpire in baseball and wrote a column, "The Umpire," for the NEA for several years.

Reardon married Marie Pickett on November 23, 1929. After she died, he married Nell Eugenia Schooler in 1954 and had two stepchildren. Reardon was immortalized along with Larry Goetz and Babe Pinelli* as the plate umpire in Norman Rockwell's famous April 23, 1949 *SEP* cover painting "Game Called Because of Rain."

BIBLIOGRAPHY: John Reardon file, National Baseball Library, Cooperstown, NY; U.S. Census: 1900, Massachusetts, vol. 12, ED 227, sheet 4, line 66; Larry R. Gerlach, ed., *The Men in Blue* (Lincoln, NE, 1994); James M. Gould, "A Man in a Blue Suit," *BM* 37 (July 1941), pp. 347–348, 382; *TSN*, August 13, 1984, p. 53.

Larry R. Gerlach

REDDING, Richard "Dick," "Cannonball Dick" (b. 1891, Atlanta, GA; d. 1948, Islip, NY), player and manager, excelled as a pitcher in the early black baseball leagues and was nicknamed "Cannonball Dick" because of his overpowering fastball. A superb pitcher who was compared to Walter Johnson,* the 6-foot 4-inch, 210-pound, right-handed Redding hurled his peak seasons with the New York Lincoln Giants between 1911 and 1915. He began pitching with the semipro Atlanta Depins as a youth. In 1911, the Philadelphia Giants recognized his ability and took him with them on tour. Later that season, Redding joined the New York Lincoln Giants and won 17 consecutive games for that outstanding team as a rookie. He performed at his peak as a fast-throwing pitcher in 1912, winning 43 games and losing 12 and pitching several no-hitters. Against the Jersey City, NJ Skeeters (EL), Redding hurled a perfect game with 17 strikeouts. Redding pitched against a team comprised of minor league players that same season and tossed a three-hitter with 24 strikeouts, a semipro baseball record. The Lincoln Giants ranked among the great teams in black history with John Henry Lloyd,* Spottswood Poles,* Louis Santop,* and the fine pitching duo of Smoky Joe Williams* and Redding. He compiled a 12–3 record with 101 strikeouts in 1914. In 1915, Redding won 20 consecutive games for the New York Lincoln Stars and defeated several teams made up of major league players. After playing with the Brooklyn Royal Giants in 1916, Redding in 1917 won 13 of 16 decisions for the Chicago American Giants.

After U.S. Army combat service in France during World War I, Redding joined the Atlantic City, NJ Bacharach Giants as a pitcher and manager through 1922. That winter Redding journeyed to Cuba for his fifth season, but enjoyed only average success there with an 18–23 overall record. Redding returned to the Brooklyn Royal Giants (ECL, ANL) in 1923 and pitched and managed there until 1932. The Royal Giants lacked the talent of the other league clubs and usually finished in last place. Redding was not considered a great manager, but players liked him and performed hard for him. The clean-cut, clean-living Redding proved easygoing and good natured and enjoyed life.

Credited with 30 career no-hitters, Redding pioneered the no-windup delivery and developed a very effective, crowd pleasing hesitation pitch long before it was popularized by Satchel Paige.* Redding showed the batter his back for a few seconds, balanced on his right foot, and then turned and fired his fastball toward the plate. He became ill with a "strange malady" in July 1948 and died in a mental hospital.

BIBLIOGRAPHY: John B. Holway, *Smoky Joe and the Cannonball* (Alexandria, VA, 1983); John B. Holway, *Blackball Stars* (Westport, CT, 1988); Robert W. Peterson, *Only the Ball Was White* (Englewood Cliffs, NJ, 1970); James A. Riley, *The All-Time All-Stars of Black Baseball* (Cocoa, FL, 1983); James A. Riley, *The Biographical Encyclopedia of the Negro Baseball Leagues* (New York, 1994).

John L. Evers

REED, Ronald Lee "Ron" (b. November 2, 1942, LaPorte, IN), baseball and basketball player, starred as a 6-foot 6-inch, 215-pound basketball forward for the University of Notre Dame from 1963 to 1966. He possessed a soft shooting touch, great leaping ability, and thrilled crowds with his thunderous dunks. Reed received honorable mention All America basketball honors after his senior year, ranking among the top rebounders and averaging 21.2 points per game. His 18.9 point, three-year scoring average ranked him second on the all-time Notre Dame list.

Reed enjoyed only mediocre success in college baseball, missing two campaigns because of academic difficulties and finishing 2–1 as a senior. He was bypassed in the baseball draft, but the Detroit Pistons (NBA) selected and signed him. The Pistons recommended him to General Manager John McHale* of the Atlanta Braves (NL). Reed spent 1965 with West Palm Beach, FL (FSL) and advanced rapidly through three leagues in 1966, winning 13 of his final 17 decisions. On the last day of the 1966 season, Reed hurled a three-hit victory for the Atlanta Braves against the Cincinnati Reds.

Reed joined around two dozen players combining professional baseball and basketball. This group included Dave Debusschere (IS), who coached him with the Detroit Pistons. Reed played two seasons with the Pistons as their sixth man before the Atlanta Braves required him to abandon the hardwood. In two NBA seasons, he averaged 8 points and 6.4 rebounds per game.

Reed made the NL All Star team in 1969, winning 18 games of 28 decisions that season. Reed bested Al Downing* of the Los Angeles Dodgers on April 8, 1974, when Hank Aaron* made baseball history by breaking Babe

Ruth's* career HR record. The Atlanta Braves traded Reed to the Philadel-phia Phillies (NL) in May 1975. Reed achieved his greatest success there after being converted to the bullpen by manager Danny Ozark.* He teamed with Tug McGraw* for eight seasons to give the Philadelphia Phillies an effective duo. The bullpen perfectly suited Reed's excellent control, big sweeping motion, and stamina to pitch 60 games a year. In 1979, Reed led the major leagues in relief victories with 13.

Reed pitched in six NL Championship Series (1969, 1976–1978, 1980, 1983) and two World Series (1980, 1983), saving the second game of the 1980 World Series against the Kansas City Royals. He retired after the 1984 season and ranks 27th on the all-time list for games with 751. The Lilburn, GA resident boasted a 146–140 win–loss record and 3.46 ERA with 103 saves and 515 relief appearances.

BIBLIOGRAPHY: Bill Ballew, "Ron Reed—Former Two Star Athlete Had Two Base-ball Careers," *SCD* 21 (May 13, 1994), pp. 148–149; Bill Madden, *The Hoosiers of Summer* (Indianapolis, IN, 1994); Ronald Reed file, National Baseball Library, Coop-erstown, NY; *The Baseball Encyclopedia*, 10th ed. (New York, 1996); *The Official NBA Encyclopedia* (New York, 1989); Gary Caruso, *The Braves Encyclopedia* (Philadelphia, PA, 1995); Allen Lewis, *The Philadelphia Phillies: A Pictorial History* (Virginia Beach, VA, 1981); Hal Bodley, *The Team That Wouldn't Die* (Wilmington, DE, 1981); Frank Dolson, *The Philadelphia Story* (South Bend, IN, 1981).

Cappy Gagnon

REESE, Harold Henry "Pee Wee," "The Little Colonel" (b. July 23, 1918, Ekron, KY; d. August 14, 1999, Louisville, KY), player, coach, and sports-caster, was the son of railroad detective Carl Reese. He grew up in Louisville, KY, attended Louisville public schools, and graduated from DuPont Manual High School. Reese, whose nickname bears no reference to his 5-foot 10-inch, 160-pound frame but rather because he was a marble-shooting cham-pion during his adolescent years, married Dorothy Walton on March 29, 1942 and had one daughter, Barbara, and one son, Mark. A .269 lifetime right-handed batter, Reese played shortstop for the Brooklyn Dodgers (NL) from 1940 to 1957 with time out from 1943 to 1945 for military service and the Los Angeles Dodgers (NL) in 1958. The captain of the famed "Boys of Summer," Reese held that star-filled team together. His National Baseball Hall of Fame plaque cites his "subtle leadership," "professional pride," and "easing acceptance of Jackie Robinson."*

Reese excelled with Brooklyn in many batting categories. He led all Dodg-ers in career stolen bases (231) and runs scored (1,317); ranked second in games played (2,107), hits (2,137), doubles (323), singles (1,612), and at-bats (7,911); placed fifth in triples (78) and RBI (868) and stood eighth in HR (122). With Los Angeles in 1958, he added 33 hits, 7 doubles, 2 triples, 4 HR, 21 runs scored, 17 RBI, and 1 stolen base. Reese became the focal point of a ceremony unique in baseball history. The Dodgers celebrated his birthday in 1955 with Pee Wee Reese Night. Before the game at Ebbets Field, the lights were turned out and over 33,000 fans lit candles and sang "Happy Birthday" to him.

He began his professional baseball career in 1938 and 1939 with the Louisville, KY Colonels (AA). In 1940, Brooklyn purchased the entire Louisville team just to secure Reese's services. The shortstop spanned two generations of Dodgers players, with his early teammates including Pete Reiser,* Fred "Dixie" Walker,* Fred Fitzsimmons,* player–manager Leo Durocher,* Hugh Casey,* Billy Herman,* Dolf Camilli,* and Cookie Lavagetto. His later teammates, subsequently nicknamed "The Boys of Summer," included Jackie Robinson,* Gil Hodges,* Roy Campanella,* Preacher Roe,* Carl Furillo,* Carl Erskine,* Don Newcombe,* and Billy Cox. After ending his playing career with Los Angeles in 1958, Reese served as a coach there in 1959. Although Brooklyn allegedly had offered him the managerial post twice, he preferred to continue solely as their shortstop and captain. Subsequently, Reese worked as an announcer on the Baseball Game of the Week with Dizzy Dean,* served as a banker, and owned a storm window business and bowling alley in Louisville. He was a manufacturing representative with the Hillerich and Bradsby Corporation, maker of Louisville Slugger baseball bats. Besides being elected to the National Baseball Hall of Fame in 1984, he also was inducted into the Brooklyn Dodgers Baseball Hall of Fame as a charter member on June 7, 1984. Reese served on the Veterans Committee of the National Baseball Hall of Fame and underwent major cancer surgery in 1997. He lived near Louisville, KY for six months and wintered in Florida.

BIBLIOGRAPHY: Harold Reese file, National Baseball Library, Cooperstown, NY; William F. McNeil, *The Dodgers Encyclopedia* (Champaign, IL, 1997); Richard Goldstein, *Superstars and Screwballs* (New York, 1991); Red Barber and Barney Stein, *The Rhubarb Patch* (New York, 1954); *Brooklyn Dodgers Yearbooks, 1947, 1949–1957*; Leo Durocher, *The Dodgers and Me* (New York, 1946); Ed Fitzgerald, ed., *The Story of the Brooklyn Dodgers* (New York, 1949); Harvey Frommer, *New York City Baseball* (New York, 1980); Peter Golenbock, *Bums* (New York, 1984); Roger Kahn, *The Boys of Summer* (New York, 1972); Rich Marazzi, "The 1955 Dodgers: A Team of Destiny," *SCD* 22 (April 28, 1995), pp. 134–135; Tommy Holmes, *The Dodgers* (New York, 1975).

Ronald L. Gabriel

REILLY, John Good "Long John" (b. October 5, 1858, Cincinnati, OH; d. May 31, 1937, Cincinnati, OH), player, was reared by relatives in Illinois following the death of his father, Frank A. Reilly, a river boat pilot, when he was about age four. He returned to Cincinnati after his mother, Ellen, married Henry Schafer, Jr., several years later. Reilly became an apprentice at Cincinnati's Strobridge Lithographing Company at age 14 and worked there as a commercial artist during and after his baseball years.

Reilly played first base for Cincinnati's semiprofessional Stars in 1879, remaining with the club when it entered the NL in 1880 as the Cincinnati Base Ball Association. The Cincinnati Reds were expelled from the NL that October. Reilly played for two Cincinnati semiprofessional teams in 1881 and spent 1882 with the independent New York Metropolitans. After the season, both the New York Gorhams (NL) and Cincinnati Red Stockings (AA) signed him. At a meeting of the rival leagues in February 1883, Reilly was awarded to Cincinnati and spent the remainder of his baseball career there.

The lanky 6-foot 3-inch, 178-pound right-hander often ranked among the AA's heaviest hitters. In 1883, he finished second in runs, hits, triples (tied), total bases, and slugging percentage. The next year, he led the AA with 11 HR and a .551 slugging average, shared first with 247 total bases, and placed second in hits, triples, and with a career-high .339 batting average. Reilly finished first in HR (13), total bases (264), RBI (103), and slugging percentage (.501) and second in hits and batting in 1888.

When Cincinnati moved to the NL as the Reds in 1890, Reilly's 26 triples set a league record. After a poor season in 1891, Reilly left baseball despite contract offers from several clubs. He continued at Strobridge Lithographing, where he was better paid, until 1932. Reilly never married.

In 1,142 major league games, Reilly batted .289 with 1,352 hits, 898 runs, 740 RBI, and a .438 slugging average. Modern statistics rate him below average in fielding, but his 10.12 putouts per game rank 10th all-time among first basemen.

BIBLIOGRAPHY: John Reilly file, National Baseball Library, Cooperstown, NY; Lee Allen, *The Cincinnati Reds* (New York, 1948); David Nemec, *The Beer and Whisky League* (New York, 1994); Floyd Connor and John Snyder, *Day-by-Day in Cincinnati Reds History* (West Point, NY, 1984); Bob Rathgeber, *Cincinnati Reds Scrapbook* (Virginia Beach, VA, 1982); Lonnie Wheeler and John Baskin, *The Cincinnati Game* (Wilmington, OH, 1988); David Ball, correspondence with Frederick Ivor-Campbell, 1994, 1997; Frederick Ivor-Campbell et al., eds., *Baseball's First Stars* (Cleveland, OH, 1996); David Nemec, *The Great Encyclopedia of 19th Century Major League Baseball* (New York, 1997); Preston D. Orem, *Baseball (1882) from the Newspaper Accounts* (Altadena, CA, 1967); *Spalding's Base Ball Guide*, 1880; John Thorn et al., eds., *Total Baseball*, 5th ed. (New York, 1997).

Frederick Ivor-Campbell

REISER, Harold Patrick "Pete," "Pistol Pete" (b. March 17, 1919, St. Louis, MO; d. October 25, 1981, Palm Springs, CA), player, coach, scout, and manager, had German and Irish roots and came from a family of 12 children. He attended Beaumont High School in St. Louis for two years. St. Louis Cardinals (NL) scouts began watching Reiser when he was only 12 years old. In 1934, 15-year-old Reiser lied about his age to attend a St. Louis Cardinals tryout camp. St. Louis Cardinals scout Charley Barrett signed him for $50 a month in 1937 and sent him to New Iberia, LA (EvL) to play shortstop. St. Louis Cardinals general manager Branch Rickey* administered 50 farm teams, holding over 1,000 players under contract. In 1938, Commissioner Kenesaw Mountain Landis* declared 100 Cardinals minor league players free agents. Rickey, who did not want to lose Reiser, asked longtime friend Larry MacPhail,* general manager of the Brooklyn Dodgers (NL), to sign Reiser, hide him in his farm system for a few years and then trade him back to the St. Louis Cardinals. MacPhail initially agreed, but when Reiser batted over .300 at Superior, WI (NoL) in 1938 and Elmira, NY (EL) in 1939 and 1940, he reneged on the agreement. MacPhail promoted Reiser to the Brooklyn Dodgers, where he batted .293 in 58 games over the last half of the 1940 season.

Reiser's first full season with the Brooklyn Dodgers remains legendary. Manager Leo Durocher* moved him from shortstop to the outfield. Reiser led the NL with 117 runs scored, 39 doubles, 17 triples, a .343 batting average, and a .558 slugging average and belted 14 HR. The 22-year-old was the youngest player to win a major league batting crown. Reiser, unfortunately, played with reckless abandon, shortening his career. In 1942, the switch-hitting Reiser batted .310, but fractured his skull when he crashed into a wall trying to catch St. Louis Cardinals outfielder Enos Slaughter's* drive. After serving in the U.S. Army cavalry from 1943 to 1945, the 5-foot 10½-inch, 185-pound Reiser batted .277 in 1946 and .309 in 1947 for the Brooklyn Dodgers. In 1946, he stole home seven times, establishing an NL record. Reiser was carried off the field nine times after slamming into walls, resulting in seven fractures or dislocations. One pitch hit him on the head, causing a cerebral blood clot. Nevertheless, he always maintained a joyful, optimistic disposition. Leo Durocher recalled, "Willie Mays* had everything. Pete Reiser had everything but luck." Sportswriter Red Smith (OS) noted, "There never was a ballpark big enough to contain his effort."

After Reiser played only 64 games in 1948, the Brooklyn Dodgers traded him to the Boston Braves (NL) that December. Reiser served as a reserve outfielder for the Braves in 1949 and 1950, signed with the Pittsburgh Pirates (NL) in 1951, and finished his major league career with the Cleveland Indians (AL) in 1952. Reiser also played for the NL squad in the 1941, 1942, and 1946 All-Star contests. He batted .214 in the 1941 and 1947 World Series against the New York Yankees. His 10-year major league career included 861 games, 786 hits, 473 runs, 58 HR, 368 RBI, and a .295 batting average.

Reiser compiled a record of 366 victories and 348 defeats managing Thomasville, GA (GFL), Kokomo, IN (ML), Green Bay, WI (3IL), Spokane, WA (PCL), and Dallas–Ft. Worth, TX (TL) from 1955 to 1959, in 1965, and in 1966. He served as a coach with the Los Angeles Dodgers (NL) from 1960 to 1964, the Chicago Cubs, where he rejoined manager Leo Durocher from 1966 to 1969 and 1972 to 1973, and the California Angels (AL) in 1970 and 1971.

Reiser, who married Patricia T. Hurst on March 29, 1942 and had two daughters, Sally and Shirley, enjoyed woodworking, cooking, ice skating, and golf. He recovered from a 1965 heart attack, but died 16 years later of respiratory problems.

BIBLIOGRAPHY: Stanley Cohen, *Dodgers! The First 100 Years* (New York, 1990); Peter Golenbock, *Bums* (New York, 1984); Donald Honig, *Baseball When the Grass Was Real* (New York, 1975); Rich Koster, "Pete Reiser: He Was the Original Mr. Hustle," *BD* 41 (April 1982), pp. 53–56; Kevin Nelson, *Greatest Stories Ever Told About Baseball Players* (New York, 1986); John Phillips, *Winners* (Cabin John, MD, 1987); Gary Caruso, *The Braves Encyclopedia* (Philadelphia, PA, 1995); Tommy Holmes, *The Dodgers* (New York, 1975); William F. McNeil, *The Dodgers Encyclopedia* (Champaign, IL, 1997); Richard Goldstein, *Superstars and Screwballs* (New York, 1991); Richard Goldstein, *Spartan Seasons* (New York, 1980); Frank Graham, *The Brooklyn Dodgers* (New York, 1945); Wil A. Linkugel and Edward J. Pappas, *They Tasted Glory* (Jefferson, NC, 1998); Danny Peary, ed., *Cult Baseball Players* (New York, 1990); Harold Reiser file, National Baseball Library, Cooperstown, NY; Richard Scheinin, *Field of Screams* (New York, 1994).

Frank J. Olmsted

RENNERT, Laurence Henry, Jr. "Dutch" (b. June 12, 1934, Oshkosh, WI), umpire, is the son of Laurence Rennert, Sr., and Viola Rennert and received his nickname not because of his German heritage but in honor of major league pitcher Emil "Dutch" Leonard.* A three-sport athlete in high school, Rennert briefly played semiprofessional baseball and football before attending the Al Somers Umpire School in 1957. He began his professional umpiring career in the Class D AlFL and advanced to the Class C PrL in 1958, Class B 3IL in 1959, Class AA SA in 1961, and Class AA TL in 1962. Although signing a major league contract after the 1964 season, he umpired in the Class AAA PCL from 1965 until being called up to the NL in September 1973.

Despite exemplary umpiring ability, Rennert found his promotion to the major leagues blocked by the prevailing preference for umpires at least 6 feet tall and 200 pounds. After 17 years in the minor leagues, the 5-foot 8-inch, 176-pound Rennert finally reached the majors when 5-foot 10-inch Al Barlick* became supervisor of NL umpires. A fan favorite, Rennert became the most colorful NL arbiter and used a booming voice and exaggerated motions, especially when calling strikes, to compensate for his relatively small stature. He also enjoyed the respect of the players, who, in a 1983 *NYT* poll, named him the best all-around NL umpire. In 19 full major league seasons, he umpired two All-Star Games (1979, 1984), six NL Championship Series (1977, 1981, 1982, 1986, 1988, 1990), and three World Series (1980, 1983, 1989).

Rennert, who suffered from an astigmatism and damaged knee cartilage, retired in January 1993 after 37 years of professional umpiring. "I always said," he explained, "if I didn't feel I was doing a 100 percent job, if I started slipping, that would be it for me." Rennert married Shirley Malchow in 1964 and has four children.

BIBLIOGRAPHY: "Interview: Laurence 'Dutch' Rennert," *Referee* 15 (April 1990), pp. 20–23; *Referee* 18 (April 1993), p. 16; Dutch Rennert file, National Baseball Library, Cooperstown, NY; *USAT*, January 11, 1993; R. L. Watt, "Memories," *Sport* 84 (July 1993), pp. 70–71.

Larry R. Gerlach

REULBACH, Edward Marvin "Ed," "Big Ed" (b. December 1, 1882, Detroit, MI; d. July 17, 1961, Glens Falls, NY), player, was the son of bookkeeper Edward J. Reulbach and Catherine M. (Paulus) Reulbach. He attended elementary school in Detroit and Manual Training High School in St. Louis, MO. He studied electrical engineering at the University of Notre Dame and pre-medicine at the University of Vermont without graduating from either institution. While starring on the mound for the Notre Dame baseball team, Reulbach played minor league baseball under assumed names. As "Lawson," he pitched three summers (1901–1903) for Sedalia, KS (MVL). As "Sheldon," he pitched for Montpelier, VT (GML) in 1904. Confused scouts thought that they were tracking three different pitchers. He was signed as Reulbach for the Chicago Cubs (NL) in May 1905 by George Huff, Illinois athletic director and former Dartmouth College catcher and football star.

The big 6-foot 1-inch, 190-pound right-hander pitched impressively from the outset. In 1905 he won 18 games, nine consecutively, and scored a 20-inning, 2–1, victory over the Philadelphia Phillies. In 29 starts, he achieved 28 complete games, 291.2 innings pitched, and a 1.42 ERA. On August 13, 1906, he married Mary Ellen "Nellie" Whelan. They had one son. Reulbach won 19 of 23 decisions and finished the season with a 12-game winning streak and a 1.65 ERA. For the first of three straight years, he compiled the NL top winning percentage (.826). Only Lefty Grove* has equalled this record. Reulbach enjoyed his finest season in 1908, winning 24 games, pitching 297.2 innings, and recording a 2.03 ERA. Nine wins came against the Brooklyn Superbas, two of them in a unique shutout doubleheader to tie an NL mark. At season's end, he pitched 44 consecutive shutout innings to help the Cubs edge past the New York Giants by a game to win the NL pennant.

In 1909, Reulbach recorded a 14-game winning streak on the way to 19 victories and a 1.78 ERA. He continued through 1912 with winning percentages above .600, but his ballooning ERA's indicated that his great years were past. After being traded to the Brooklyn Dodgers (NL) in July 1913, he compiled an 11–18 record the next season in 256 innings. He jumped to the FL in 1915, becoming the ace of the Newark Peppers staff. His 21 victories, however, reflected the FL's weakness rather than his arm's rejuvenation. He won seven of 13 decisions for the Boston Braves (NL) in 1916 and had one loss in 1917, when released to Providence, RI (IL).

Reulbach's career statistics confirm his pitching renown. His .632 winning percentage (182 victories against 106 defeats) place him 24th on the all-time list, his 2.28 ERA 10th. He completed 201 of 300 starts, hurled 40 shutouts, and struck out 1,137 batters. For 13 major league seasons, Reulbach's innings pitched exceeded his hits allowed. This superlative pitcher achieved modest World Series success and won two World Series decisions, including a scintillating one-hitter against the Chicago White Sox in 1906. In three other games, he was hit hard and removed.

A brainy pitcher, Reulbach threw perhaps the best curve in either league. Great contemporaries, including Mordecai "Three Finger" Brown* and Ed Walsh,* overshadowed him. For many, he became "the third best pitcher in Chicago" and its second "Big Ed." Reulbach served as founding director and secretary (1914–1915) of the short-lived Base Ball Players' Fraternity, organized to better working conditions, oppose contract abuses, and advise players with grievances. After leaving baseball, he worked for a piano manufacturer and operated a tire business which was bankrupted by the expenses of his son's long illness and eventual death. For two decades, he was associated with a construction company.

BIBLIOGRAPHY: "Daguerreotypes," *TSN*, October 12, 1939; John J. Evers with Hugh S. Fullerton, *Touching Second* (Chicago, IL, 1910); Cappy Gagnon, "Ed Reulbach Remembered," *BRJ* 11 (1982), pp. 77–79; J. Warren McEligot, "Ed Reulbach— A Sad, Quiet Man of 50," Chicago (IL) *Tribune*, December 29, 1932; *The Baseball Encyclopedia*, 10th ed. (New York, 1996); Edward Reulbach file, National Baseball Library, Cooperstown, NY; Harold Seymour, *Baseball: The Golden Age* (New York, 1971); David Quentin Voigt, *American Baseball*, vol. 2 (University Park, PA, 1983); Warren Brown, *The Chicago Cubs* (New York, 1946); Jim Enright, *Chicago Cubs* (New York, 1975); Warren Wilbert and William Hageman, *Chicago Cubs: Seasons at the Summit* (Champaign, IL, 1997); Eddie Gold and Art Ahrens, *The Golden Era Cubs, 1876–1940* (Chicago, IL, 1985); Frank Graham, *The Brooklyn Dodgers* (New York, 1945); Richard Goldstein, *Superstars and Screwballs* (New York, 1991).

A. D. Suehsdorf

REUSCHEL, Ricky Eugene "Rick," "Big Daddy" (b. August 16, 1949, Quincy, IL), player, is the son of George Reuschel and Geneva (Buss) Reuschel and grew up in rural downstate Illinois. Reuschel played baseball and basketball at Central High School in Camp Point, IL and pitched two years for the Western Illinois University baseball team. His 10–0 record and 1.29 ERA led Western Illinois to the IIAC championship in 1969. The Chicago Cubs (NL) made Reuschel a third-round draft choice in 1970, the same year that he compiled a 9–2 record for Huron, MI (NoL). He finished with an 8–4 win–loss mark and 2.31 ERA for San Antonio TX (TL) in 1971 and won nine games for Wichita, KS (AA) in 1972 before the Chicago Cubs promoted him in June. Over the next nine seasons, Reuschel anchored the Cubs' pitching staff and averaged 35 starts and 14 victories per season. His best year came in 1977, when he won 20 games, lost 10 decisions, and compiled a 2.79 ERA. Reuschel earned a spot on the NL All-Star team, hurling one scoreless inning in the mid-season classic. In June 1981, he was traded to the New York Yankees (AL) and helped the Bronx Bombers win the AL pennant that year. Reuschel underwent rotator cuff surgery in 1982 and spent most of the 1982–1983 seasons on the disabled list. The Yankees released him in June 1983. Reuschel was signed by the Chicago Cubs organization and sent to Quad Cities (ML) for rehabilitation. Chicago promoted him in late 1983, but recurring shoulder problems plagued him again in 1984. He pitched only sparingly for the 1984 Cubs, who left him off their post-season roster.

The 6-foot 3-inch, 230-pound right-hander signed as a free agent with the Pittsburgh Pirates (NL) in February 1985 and led their staff over the next two and a half seasons. In August 1987, Pittsburgh traded him to the San Francisco Giants (NL). Reuschel won five games during the final six weeks of the season, helping the Giants win the NL West title. He continued to pitch effectively, with 19 wins and 11 losses in 1988 and 17 wins and eight losses in 1989. He earned the starting berth for the NL All-Star team in 1989, allowing two runs and three hits in one inning. His major league career ended with the San Francisco Giants in 1991. In 19 major league seasons, Reuschel compiled a career 214–191 win–loss record and a 3.37 ERA. He appeared in four NL Championship Series games (1981, 1987, 1989) with a 1–2 overall record and in three World Series contests (1981, 1989) with a 0–1 record. Not an overpowering pitcher, he possessed excellent control and intelligent pitch selection. He was highly competitive, but quiet and reclusive with the press and public. Reuschel married Jill Darlene Perz in 1972. After their divorce, he wed Barbara Thompson in July 1988. They have a daughter and live in Butler, PA, where he engages in dairy farming. His brother, Paul, pitched in the major leagues with the Chicago Cubs and the Cleveland Indians (AL) between 1975 and 1979.

BIBLIOGRAPHY: *The Baseball Encyclopedia*, 10th ed. (New York, 1996); *Chicago Cubs Media Guide 1978*; Ricky Reuschel file, National Baseball Library, Cooperstown, NY; Eddie Gold and Art Ahrens, *The New Era Cubs, 1941–1985* (Chicago, IL, 1985); Chuck Greenwood, "Reuschel Resurrected Career Twice in Minors," *SCD* 25 (August 21, 1998), pp. 70–71; Jim Langford, *The Game Is Never Over* (South Bend, IN, 1980); Bob Smizik, *The Pittsburgh Pirates: An Illustrated History* (New York, 1990); Warren Wilbert and William Hageman, *Chicago Cubs: Seasons at the Summit* (Champaign, IL, 1997); Bob Kravitz, "Pittsburgh's Golden Oldie," *SI* 63 (July 15, 1985), pp. 62, 64; John Thorn et al., eds., *Total Baseball*, 5th ed. (New York, 1997); *TSN*, September 19, 1988, pp. 14–15; *TSN Official Baseball Register, 1992*; Jim Enright, *Chicago Cubs* (New York, 1975).

John E. Findling

REUSS, Jerry (b. June 19, 1949, St. Louis, MO), player and sportscaster, is the second of three sons of Melvin Reuss, a paint salesman, and Vi Reuss, who worked in interior decorating for Sears, Roebuck Company. Reuss pitched Ritenor High School in St. Louis to two Missouri State Baseball Championships before signing with the St. Louis Cardinals (NL) in 1967 for a $30,000 bonus. His minor league assignments in the Cardinals farm system included Sarasota, FL (GCL), Cedar Rapids, IA (ML), Little Rock-based Arkansas (TL), and Tulsa, OK (AA).

After winning 14 games for the St. Louis Cardinals in 1971, Reuss held out with Steve Carlton* for more money. Owner August A. Busch, Jr.* ordered Reuss traded in a disastrous April 1972 deal for St. Louis. The 6-foot 5-inch, 225-pound southpaw won 16 contests for the Houston Astros (NL) in 1973 and then was dispatched to the Pittsburgh Pirates (NL) for catcher Milt May in October 1973. Reuss conferred with a hypnotist to relax more on the mound and discover why he pitched well in some ballparks and poorly at Wrigley Field in Chicago and other stadiums. He sparkled for the Pirates with 18 victories and a 2.54 ERA in 1975 and a 14–9 record in 1976, but then faded in the 1977 and 1978 campaigns.

The Los Angeles Dodgers (NL) acquired Reuss in April 1979 for pitcher Rick Rhoden,* giving the dugout humorist new life. Reuss, the TSN 1980 Comeback Player of the Year, compiled 18 wins, a 2.52 ERA, a June 8–0 no-hitter against the San Francisco Giants, and an All-Star game victory. Reuss played instrumental roles in Dodger NL Western Division crowns in 1981, 1983, and 1985 and a 1981 World Series title against the New York Yankees.

After being disabled much of the 1986 season, Reuss limped through a 4–10 campaign with the Dodgers, Cincinnati Reds (NL), and California Angels (AL) in 1987. The aging two-time All Star visited the Chicago White Sox (AL) 1988 spring training camp as its only non-roster invitee and led the staff that year with 13 triumphs. He won nine of 18 decisions in 1989, being traded in July to the Milwaukee Brewers (AL). After being released by Milwaukee in November 1989, he appeared briefly for the Pittsburgh Pirates in 1990.

Reuss joined Milt Pappas* as only the second major league pitcher to record 200 wins without a 20-win season. Reuss earned a victory in the 1981 World Series, but lost all 7 decisions with a 5.45 ERA in the NL Championship Series. Reuss completed 22 major league seasons with 3,669.2 innings, 220 wins, 191 losses, 1,907 strikeouts, and a 3.64 ERA in 628 games. Reuss handled baseball telecasts for ESPN from 1991 through 1993, for the Los Vegas, NV Stars (PCL) in 1994 and 1995, and the California Angels (AL) since 1996.

BIBLIOGRAPHY: Jerry Reuss file, National Baseball Library, Cooperstown, NY; William F. McNeil, *The Dodgers Encyclopedia* (Champaign, IL, 1997); Richard L. Burtt, *The Pittsburgh Pirates, A Pictorial History* (Virginia Beach, VA, 1977); Tommy Lasorda and David Fisher, *The Artful Dodger* (New York, 1985); Bob Broeg, *Redbirds: A Century of Cardinals' Baseball* (St. Louis, MO, 1981); Charley Feeney, "Hypnotist's Finger

Drills Sharpen Reuss' Skills," *TSN*, May 24, 1975, p. 18; Zander Hollander, ed., *1989 Complete Handbook of Baseball* (New York, 1989); Stan Isle, "Reuss Engineers Deal," *TSN*, May 26, 1986, p. 32; Robert E. Kelly, *Baseball's Best* (Jefferson, NC, 1988); Eileen Kenny, interview with Frank Olmsted, November 15, 1989; John Kuenster, "Why Pennant Contenders Need Lefthanded Starting Pitchers," *BD* 41 (June 1982), pp. 15–19; Paul Burka, "Houston Astros," *TM* (December 1980), pp. 156–161, 264–271; Jerry Reuss, "The Game I'll Never Forget," *BD* 46 (September 1988), pp. 69–71; Bob Broeg and Jerry Vickery, *St Louis Cardinals Encyclopedia* (Grand Rapids, MI, 1998); Rich Marazzi, "Jerry Reuss," *SCD* 24 (January 17, 1997), pp. 68–69, (January 24, 1997), pp. 70–71; Stanley Cohen, *Dodgers! The First 100 Years* (New York, 1990); Morris Eckouse and Carl Mastro Cula, *This Date in Pittsburgh Pirates History* (New York, 1985).

Frank J. Olmsted

REYNOLDS, Allie Pierce "Superchief" (b. February 10, 1915, Bethany, OK; d. December 26, 1994, Oklahoma City, OK), player, ranked among the leading right-handed pitchers of the 1940s and early 1950s. The son of fundamentalist minister D. L. Reynolds, he was one-quarter Creek Indian and starred in track and field and football at Capitol High School in Oklahoma City, OK. Although entering Oklahoma A&M University on a track and field scholarship, he impressed coach Hank Iba (IS) while pitching batting practice and launched his baseball career in 1937. He also starred as one of the best football running backs in the MVC. Reynolds graduated in 1939 with a Bachelor of Science degree and was drafted by both the New York Giants (NFL) and Cleveland Indians (AL). In the Indians' minor league system at Springfield, OH (MAL), Cedar Rapids, IA (3IL), and Wilkes-Barre, PA (EL), he caught, played the outfield, and pitched.

After joining the Cleveland Indians (AL) in 1942, he won 51 games over the next four years and hurled 18 victories in 1945. Traded in October 1946 to the New York Yankees (AL) for popular second baseman Joe Gordon,* Reynolds became perhaps the mainstay of the Yankees pitching staffs of manager Bucky Harris* and Casey Stengel* in the world championship seasons of 1947, 1949, 1950, 1951, 1952, and 1953. From 1947 to 1954, he won 131 and lost only 60 and compiled 19 victories in 1947 and 20 triumphs in 1952. He also led the AL in strikeouts in 1943 and 1952, winning percentage in 1947, and shutouts in 1951 and 1952. The fastball pitcher overcame wildness to post an impressive 1,423 strikeouts in a 13-year major league career.

Reynolds did not reach the major leagues until age 27 and had to overcome several physical and psychological obstacles. Often bothered by bone chips in his pitching elbow, he suffered through a successful 17–6 season in 1949. The fans and press derided his inability to finish games that year and named the Yankees' best pitcher "Reynolds-Page." In the 1949 World Series opener against the Brooklyn Dodgers' formidable Don Newcombe,* he pitched a masterful 1–0 victory decided by a ninth-inning Tommy Henrich* HR. His World Series career proved outstanding, as his seven wins placed him with Red Ruffing* and Whitey Ford* among the most successful clutch pitchers in post-season history. In 1951, he joined Johnny VanderMeer* as one of only two pitchers at that time with two no-hitters in the same season (against the Cleveland Indians in July and Boston Red Sox in September, the latter game clinching the AL pennant).

Reynolds, a devout Methodist, retired after the 1954 season and served as chairman of the board of New Park Mid-Continental Drilling Company in Oklahoma City. He married Dale Jones in 1935 and had two sons and one daughter. During his major league career, he won 182 games, lost 107 contests, hurled 36 shutouts, and compiled a 3.30 ERA.

BIBLIOGRAPHY: Mark Gallagher, *The Yankee Encyclopedia*, vol. 3 (Champaign, IL, 1997); David Halberstam, *Summer of '49* (New York, 1989); Dom Forker, *The Men of Autumn* (Dallas, TX, 1989); Sol Gittleman, "Raschi, Lopat, and Reynolds," *BRJ* 22 (1993), pp. 78–79; Allie Reynolds file, National Baseball Library, Cooperstown, NY; Franklin Lewis, *The Cleveland Indians* (New York, 1949); John Thorn et al., eds., *Total Indians* (New York, 1996); John Phillips, *Winners* (Cabin John, MD, 1987); Dave Anderson et al., *The Yankees* (New York, 1979); Robert W. Creamer, *Stengel: His Life and Times* (New York, 1984); Harry Molter, *Famous American Athletes of Today*, 13th ser. (Boston, MA, 1953); *NYT*, December 28, 1994, D 18; Rich Westcott, *Diamond Greats* (Westport, CT, 1988); *The Baseball Encyclopedia*, 10th ed. (New York, 1996).

Leonard H. Frey

REYNOLDS, Carl Nettles (b. February 1, 1903, LaRue, TX; d. May 29, 1978, Houston, TX), player, coach, and scout, was the son of R. P. Reynolds and matriculated at LaRue High School. After graduating from Alexander College (now Lon Morris JC) in Jacksonville, TX in 1924, he earned a Bachelor's degree from Southwestern University in Georgetown, TX in 1926. Reynolds, Southwestern's first four-sport letterman, won eight letters in two years of football, basketball, track and field, and baseball competition.

Chicago White Sox (AL) scout Ray Largent discovered him by accident when following a Trinity University pitcher. The Chicago White Sox signed Reynolds in 1927 and optioned him to Palestine, TX (LSL), where he converted from shortstop to the outfield. The Chicago White Sox promoted him to the major leagues that September. Reynolds performed the next four seasons with the Chicago White Sox, becoming a starter in 1929. In 1930, he batted a career-high .359 and clouted three consecutive HR against the New York Yankees on July 2. The Chicago White Sox traded the 6-foot, 195-pound outfielder to the Washington Senators (AL) in December 1931. In July 1932, New York Yankees star catcher Bill Dickey* broke Reynolds' jaw after the latter charged into him standing up at home plate and was suspended for 30 days. The Washington Senators kept the Texan one season and traded him to the St. Louis Browns (AL) in December 1932. In December 1933, the Browns sent the right-handed outfielder to the Boston Red

Sox (AL). He patrolled the Fenway Park outfield for two seasons before rejoining the Washington Senators in 1935.

The Washington Senators optioned Reynolds to Minneapolis, MN (AA) after the 1936 campaign. The Chicago Cubs (NL) purchased his contract in September 1937 for their NL pennant stretch run, but a severe charley horse sidelined him that month. He went hitless in the 1938 World Series against the New York Yankees in his only post-season appearance. After remaining with the Chicago Cubs through 1939, he spent 1940 as a player–coach for Los Angeles, CA (PCL). In 13 major league seasons, Reynolds batted .302 with 1,357 hits, 80 HR, and 699 RBI.

Reynolds, who became a farmer and rancher in Wharton, TX, served on the Board of Directors of the Wharton Bank Trust Company, Wharton JC, and Caney Valley Memorial Hospital. The Southwestern University Sports Hall of Fame and Texas Sports Hall of Fame enshrined him in 1972. He married Ruth Dayvault and had two sons, Carl, Jr., and Robert.

BIBLIOGRAPHY: *The Baseball Encyclopedia*, 10th ed. (New York, 1996); J. R. Hillman, "Carl Reynolds," *SCD* 24 (November 28, 1997), pp. 154–155; Carl Reynolds file, National Baseball Library, Cooperstown, NY; Carl Reynolds file, Southwestern University, Georgetown, TX; Warren Brown, *The Chicago White Sox* (New York, 1952); Richard Lindberg, *Sox* (New York, 1984); Bill Borst, ed., *Ables to Zoldak*, vol. 3 (St. Louis, MO, 1980); Shirley Povich, *The Washington Senators* (New York, 1954); Frederick G. Lieb, *The Boston Red Sox* (New York, 1947); Eddie Gold and Art Ahrens, *The Golden Era Cubs, 1876–1940* (Chicago, IL, 1958).

John Hillman

RHINES, William Pearl "Billy" (b. March 14, 1869, Ridgway, PA; d. January 30, 1922, Ridgway, PA), player, was the son of George Washington Rhines, a lumberman, and Nancy Helen (Moore) Rhines. Rhines signed as a pitcher with Binghamton, NY (CL) in 1888 and moved later that season to Jersey City, NJ (CL). In 1889, he starred for Davenport, IA (CIL). The Cincinnati Reds, who joined the NL in 1890, acquired the 5-foot 11-inch, 168-pound, right-handed batter and thrower. Rhines, a rookie sensation at age 21, won 28 games and lost 17 with an NL-leading 1.95 ERA. Rhines pitched with the Cincinnati Reds the next two seasons, but his performance declined due to overwork and too much night life. Catcher Jerry Harrington joined him in carousing and fell under the harmful influence of Pete Browning,* receiving fines and suspensions. Rhines pitched only 12 games in 1892 before the Cincinnati Reds dropped him and performed in just five games for the Louisville Colonels (NL) in 1893.

The 1894 campaign saw Rhines demoted to the minor leagues with Grand Rapids, MI (WL). After pitching 58 games there, he returned to the Cincinnati Reds with a 19–10 mark in 1895. The following year, Rhines led the NL in ERA (2.45) at the longer pitching distance. Although Rhines finished 21–15 in 1897, the Cincinnati Reds released him. He joined the Pittsburgh

Pirates (NL) for his last two major league seasons and retired after 1899 to Ridgway, where he managed the home town team for several years. He also worked various jobs, including driving a taxi, and died in poverty after a long illness, leaving a wife and four children.

Rhines won 113 major league games, lost 103, and posted a 3.48 ERA in 1,891 innings. He used a distinctive submarine delivery, in which the ball was released below the knee and appeared to curve upward. Since this seemed physically impossible, some players asked him to demonstrate the pitch. They confirmed Rhines pitch actually curved upward. Rhines may have copied the pitching style of Jim McCormick.* Early 20th century star Joe McGinnity* modeled his delivery after that of Rhines. Ewell Blackwell* later employed a similar style.

BIBLIOGRAPHY: Lee Allen, *The Cincinnati Reds* (New York, 1948); Frederick Ivor-Campbell et al., eds., *Baseball's First Stars* (Cleveland, OH, 1996); *TSN*, February 10, 1921, p. 3, February 9, 1922, p. 3, February 16, 1922, p. 7; William Rhines file, National Baseball Library, Cooperstown, NY; Frederick G. Lieb, *The Pittsburgh Pirates* (New York, 1948); Bob Rathgeber, *Cincinnati Reds Scrapbook* (Virginia Beach, VA, 1982); Lonnie Wheeler and John Baskin, *The Cincinnati Game* (Wilmington, OH, 1988).

                                                                    William E. McMahon

RHODEN, Richard Alan "Rick" (b. May 16, 1953, Boynton Beach, FL), player, overcame a serious childhood illness to become a successful major league pitcher. Rhoden suffered from osteomyelitis, a bone disease that caused him to wear a leg brace and necessitated the removal of part of his left knee. Nevertheless, the 6-foot 3-inch, 195-pound right-hander developed into a fine athlete. The Los Angeles Dodgers (NL) selected Rhoden as their first-round (twentieth player taken overall) selection in the 1971 free agent draft.

After pitching in the minor leagues at Daytona Beach, FL (FSL), El Paso, TX (TL), and Albuquerque, NM (PCL), Rhoden debuted for the Los Angeles Dodgers in 1974. In 1976, Rhoden posted a 12–3 win–loss record with a 2.98 ERA and was named to the NL All-Star squad. The following year, he won a career-high 16 games, a figure he matched in 1987 while pitching for the New York Yankees (AL). Rhoden played in two NL Championship Series with the Los Angeles Dodgers (1977, 1978) without any decisions. He pitched in the 1977 World Series, where he was charged with one loss in two appearances against the New York Yankees. Working chiefly as a starting pitcher for the Los Angeles Dodgers, Rhoden won 42 games and lost 24. In April 1979, Los Angeles traded Rhoden to the Pittsburgh Pirates (NL) for pitcher Jerry Reuss.*

Rhoden's career with the Pittsburgh Pirates began inauspiciously when shoulder surgery forced him to miss almost the entire 1979 season and the first part of the 1980 season. Rhoden returned as the mainstay of the Pittsburgh Pirate staff in 1981 and started 193 games over six years for a talent-poor Pirate club that was further demoralized by a sensational drug scandal. He led the Pittsburgh Pirates in wins with nine in 1981, 14 in 1984, and 15 in 1986, being named to the 1986 All-Star team.

The Pittsburgh Pirates in November 1986 traded Rhoden to the New York Yankees for several players including Doug Drabek,* the 1990 NL Cy Young Award winner. Rhoden won 16 games for the New York Yankees in 1987, but believed that he was denied a place on that year's AL All-Star team because of frequent accusations that he scuffed the ball. The New York Yankees traded Rhoden to the Houston Astros (NL) in January 1989. Rhoden completed his 16-year major league career in 1989.

Rhoden compiled a major league career record of 151 wins and 125 losses for a .547 winning percentage and 3.59 ERA. Rhoden, quite an accomplished hitter, batted .238 with 181 hits and nine HR. Between 1984 and 1986, he won three NL Silver Slugger awards for pitchers.

An avid golfer and fisherman, Rhoden won the $22,500 1993 Celebrity Golf Classic at Brampton, Ontario, with a 2-under-par score of 214. Rhoden and his wife, Leslie, reside in Crescent City, FL with their son, Tanner.

BIBLIOGRAPHY: Rick Rhoden file, National Baseball Library, Cooperstown, NY; Tommy Lasorda and David Fisher, *The Artful Dodger* (New York, 1985); William F. McNeil, *The Dodgers Encyclopedia* (Champaign, IL, 1997); Stanley Cohen, *Dodgers: The First 100 Years* (New York, 1990); Bob Smizik, *The Pittsburgh Pirates: An Illustrated History* (New York, 1990); *The Baseball Encyclopedia*, 10th ed. (New York, 1996); *1981, 1985, 1986 Pittsburgh Pirates Yearbook*; Mike Shatzkin, ed., *The Ballplayers* (New York, 1990).

Frank W. Thackeray

RICE, Edgar Charles "Sam" (b. February 20, 1890, Morocco, IN; d. October 13, 1974, Rossmor, MD), player, was the son of farmers Charles Rice and Louise Christine (Newmyre) Rice. He attended Rhode Island Country School in Iroquois Country, IL, where classmates remembered him as a good athlete with exceptional speed. Rice married Beulah Stam on September 17, 1908, moved to Watseka, IL, and had two children. He played sandlot and town team baseball, but sought unsuccessfully for four years to become a pitcher with a CA team. In April 1912, Rice's entire family (parents, siblings, wife, and children) was killed in a tornado. Following this tragedy, he made some last attempts at local baseball, wandered the nation working odd jobs, and joined the U.S. Navy in 1913.

After playing baseball in the Navy during tours of Mexico and Cuba, Rice pitched for Petersburg, VA (VL) in 1914 and posted a 9–2 record. In 29 appearances in 1915, Rice compiled an 11–12 mark. The Washington Senators (AL) secured him as payment for a Petersburg debt to owner Clark Griffith.* The 5-foot 9-inch, 150-pound Rice saw limited action as a right-handed Washington pitcher, but enjoyed success as a pinch hitter in 1915 and 1916 and moved to right field. In 1917 Rice batted .302 and stole 35 bases. Rice served in the U.S. Army in 1918 and then started as the Senators' right fielder from 1919 through 1931. He saw only limited action the following three seasons and finished his career with the Cleveland Indians (AL) in 1934. He married his second wife, Mary Kendal on July 4, 1929 and retired with their daughter to his Maryland farm.

During his 20-year major league career, Rice posted a .322 batting average and retired only thirteen hits short of the magic 3,000 mark. In 2,404 games, the left-handed Rice slugged 498 doubles and 184 triples, scored 1,514 runs, knocked in 1,078 runs, walked 708 times, and stole 351 bases. He batted .302 in three World Series (1924, 1925, and 1933) and achieved immortality in the 1925 World Series, when he tumbled over a right field barrier and emerged with the ball in his glove. Although the umpire ruled the batter out, controversy raged for years. Rice was overshadowed by contemporaries Babe Ruth,* Ty Cobb,* and Lou Gehrig* and never earned over $18,000 a season. His achievements included having 200 or more hits in six different seasons, leading the AL in hits in 1924 and 1926 (216), and setting an AL record with 182 singles in 1925. Besides leading AL outfielders in putouts with 454 in 1920 and 385 in 1922, he paced the AL in stolen bases with 63 in 1920. Rice batted more than 600 times during eight different seasons and struck out only 275 times during 9,269 career at bats.

The durable, consistent Rice belatedly was elected to the National Baseball Hall of Fame by unanimous vote of the Veterans Committee in 1963. He remained active in baseball, making his last appearance at Cooperstown only months before his death. Rice, a gifted athlete, overcame tremendous odds of age, inexperience, and great personal tragedy to achieve success in professional baseball.

BIBLIOGRAPHY: Edgar Rice file, National Baseball Library, Cooperstown, NY; Shirley Povich, *The Washington Senators* (New York, 1954); Bill Madden, *The Hoosiers of Summer* (Indianapolis, IN, 1994); Martin Appel and Burt Goldblatt, *Baseball's Best: The Hall of Fame Gallery* (New York, 1977); Mary Lou LeCompte, correspondence with Thomas R. Heitz, Mary Lou LeCompte Collection, Austin, TX; *The Baseball Encyclopedia*, 10th ed. (New York, 1996); "Sam Rice, Hall of Fame Outfielder, Dies," *NYT*, October 15, 1974; Steve Wulf, "The Secrets of Sam," *SI* 79 (July 19, 1993), pp. 58–64; Morris Bealle, *The Washington Senators* (Washington, DC, 1947); Henry W. Thomas, *Walter Johnson* (Washington, DC, 1995); John Yost, "Edgar Charles 'Sam' Rice, Enterprise Profile," Newton County (IN) *Enterprise*, June 7, 1984, p. 9.

Mary Lou LeCompte

RICE, Harry Francis (b. November 22, 1901, Ware Station, IL; d. January 1, 1971, Portland, OR), player and manager, was an outstanding defensive outfielder who batted .299 with 48 HR and 506 RBI in 1,034 games over 10 major league seasons from 1923 to 1933. Born on a southern Illinois farm as the son of William Rice and Minnie M. (Benson) Rice, he sought an alternative to farm life after completing high school. His professional baseball career began at age 20 when he signed with Paris, KY (BGL). After Rice played with Danville, IL (3IL) and Tulsa, OK (TL), the St. Louis Browns (AL) purchased his contract in 1923.

The stocky, 5-foot 9-inch, 175 pounder, who batted left-handed and threw right-handed, played every position except pitcher for the St. Louis Browns. After batting .359 in 1925 and .313 in 1926, he slumped in 1927 and was traded to the Detroit Tigers (AL) that December. Rice enjoyed his finest seasons with the Detroit Tigers between 1928 and 1930, achieving career bests in stolen bases (20) in 1928, doubles (33) and runs scored (97) in 1929, and RBI (98) in 1930 and consistently batting .300 or better. He possessed one of the strongest throwing arms in baseball, rivaling Bob Meusel* of the New York Yankees. Rice finished his major league career as a reserve with the Washington Senators (AL) in 1931 and Cincinnati Reds (NL) in 1933. Between those stints, he batted .345 to lead the Minneapolis, MN Millers (AA) to an AA pennant.

During the Depression, Rice continued playing and managing in the minor leagues for the remainder of the 1930s. He played for Toronto, Canada (IL), Nashville, TN (SA), San Francisco, CA (PCL), Seattle, WA (PCL), and Portland, OR (PCL). Rice managed in the low minor leagues for four years at Evergreen, AL (AlFL), Cordele, GA (GFL), Deland, FL (FSL), and Fond du Lac, WI (WSL). Rice lived comfortably selling insurance during and after his playing career and died of bladder cancer.

BIBLIOGRAPHY: Harry Rice file, National Baseball Library, Cooperstown, NY; Frank C. Lane, "Harry Rice: The Versatile Star of the St. Louis Browns," *BM* 36 (March 1926), pp. 451–452; Frederick G. Lieb, *The Baltimore Orioles*: (New York, 1955); Bill O'Neal, *The American Association, 1902–1991* (Austin, TX, 1991); George Sullivan and David Cataneo, *Detroit Tigers* (New York, 1985); Bill Borst, ed., *Ables to Zoldak*, vol. 3 (St. Louis, MO, 1990); Bill Borst, *Still Last in the American League* (West Bloomfield, MI, 1992); Fred Smith, *995 Tigers* (Detroit, MI, 1981); Frederick G. Lieb, *The Detroit Tigers* (New York, 1946); Joe Falls, *Detroit Tigers* (New York, 1975).
William E. Akin

RICE, James Edward "Jim," "Ed" (b. March 8, 1953, Anderson, SC), player, was the best right-handed slugger for the Boston Red Sox (AL) since Jimmie Foxx* and is the fourth of nine children of True Temper Company supervisor Roger Rice and Julia Mae Rice. Nicknamed "Ed," Rice excelled as an all-around athlete at Westside and Hanna high schools in Anderson, SC. An All-State football player, he also attracted numerous major league baseball scouts. Shortly after Rice graduated, the Red Sox selected him in the first round of the June 1971 amateur draft. Rice signed with Boston shortly thereafter for a reported $45,000 bonus and began his professional career as an outfielder in 1971 at Williamsport, PA (NYPL). Rice played at Winter

Haven, FL (FSL) in 1972 and Bristol, CT (EL) in 1973, batting .317 to lead the EL. He moved up to Pawtucket, RI (IL) late in 1973 and enjoyed a superb season there in 1974. After winning the Triple Crown (25 HR, 93 RBI, .337 batting average), he was named *TSN* Minor League Player of the Year and IL MVP. In September 1974, Rice joined the Red Sox (AL).

In 1975, Rice and fellow rookie Fred Lynn* led the Red Sox to the AL pennant. Rice led the AL three times in HR (1977–1978, 1983), twice in RBI (1978, 1983) and slugging percentage (1977–1978), and once each in triples (1978) and hits (1978), and made the AL All-Star team eight times (1977–1980, 1983–1986). In his finest season, he in 1978 batted .315 and led the AL in games (163), at-bats (677), hits (213), triples (15), HR (46), RBI (139), total bases (406), and slugging percentage (.600). The same year, he was voted AL MVP. In 1986, Rice ranked fifth in the AL in batting (.324), fourth in RBI (110), tied for third in doubles (39), and tied for fifth in hits (200), helping the Red Sox capture the AL pennant and finishing third in the AL MVP balloting. Although batting only .161 in the AL Championship Series against the California Angels, he slugged two HR and one double and knocked in six runs. Rice batted .333 and made one double and one triple in the World Series, won by the New York Mets. He spent his entire major league career with the Boston Red Sox, retiring after the 1989 season. Rice's career totals included 2,452 hits, 1,249 runs scored, 373 doubles, 382 HR, 1,451 RBI, a .298 batting average, and a .502 slugging average. At Fenway Park through 1983, his effective totals included 153 HR, 535 RBI, .327 batting average, and .577 slugging percentage. Rice ranked among his era's best players, deserving of National Baseball Hall of Fame recognition. Rice, who married Corine Gilliard in 1972 and has one child, Chauncy, has coached for the Boston Red Sox since 1994.

BIBLIOGRAPHY: Jim Rice file, National Baseball Library, Cooperstown, NY; Anderson (SC) *Independent*, 1971–1983; Ron Fimrite, "An Ultrastrong Silent Type," *SI* 50 (April 9, 1979), pp. 53–61; John Benson et al., *Baseball's Top 100* (Wilton, CT, 1997); Peter Gammons, "Is It Twilight Time?" *SI* 68 (March 14, 1988), pp. 30–32; Robert E. Kelly, *Baseball's Best* (Jefferson, NC, 1988); Robert Redmount, *The Red Sox Encyclopedia* (Champaign, IL, 1998); Howard Liss, *The Boston Red Sox* (New York, 1982); Peter Golenbock, *Fenway* (New York, 1992); Dan Shaughnessy, *The Curse of the Bambino* (New York, 1990); Peter Gammons, *Beyond the Sixth Game* (Boston, MA, 1985); Dan Shaughnessy, *One Strike Away* (New York, 1987); *TSN Baseball Register*, 1990; R. Wetzsteon, "What's Eating Jim Rice," *Sport* 78 (June 1987), pp. 40–41.

                                                                    Clark Nardinelli

RICHARD, James Rodney "J. R." (b. March 27, 1950, Vienna, LA), player, is the son of Clayton Richard and Lizzie (Frost) Richard and attended Lincoln High School in Ruston, LA and Arizona State University for one semester. Richard was an outstanding right-handed fastball pitcher in the late 1970s. Although his promising career with the Houston Astros (NL) was cut short by a tragic stroke, he joined a select circle of lifetime 100-game winners who achieved a career winning percentage above .600. As a 6-foot 8-inch, 222-pound natural athlete from rural Louisiana with a blazing fastball once clocked at 100 miles per hour, he was selected first by the Houston Astros in the 1969 amateur draft and declined over 200 college basketball scholarships to sign a professional baseball contract. He debuted for the Houston Astros with a spectacular effort against the San Francisco Giants in April 1971, striking out 15 batters to tie Karl Spooner's record for most strikeouts in a first major league start. However, he received little opportunity to advance from the minor leagues over the next several seasons.

After winning only 11 games during his first four partial seasons (1971–1974) with the Astros, Richard emerged as a dominating NL hurler by 1976. He enjoyed his only 20-victory season in 1976 and followed with three consecutive 18-win seasons. He also cracked the benchmark of 300 strikeouts twice, leading the NL with 303 and 313 in 1978 and 1979, respectively. Richard's 2.71 ERA also furnished a NL standard during 1979. His sterling 1.90 ERA (along with a 10–4 record) seemed headed toward a second consecutive NL title when tragedy struck in mid-July of his tenth major league season. After Richard complained of a "dead arm" in July 1980, fans and the media criticized him for supposed malingering and possible drug abuse. He became dazed and disoriented during a July 14 game and was promptly placed on the disabled list. Subsequent medical examination revealed that an artery leading to his right arm was blocked, but doctors suspected no real danger. Richard was working out again on July 30 when he finally collapsed. Richard's stroke partially paralyzed his left side, although two operations and extensive therapy restored much of his strength and drastically improved his partially impaired speech.

In 10 major league seasons, Richard compiled a career 107–71 win–loss record with 1,493 strikeouts in 1,606 innings pitched, 19 shutouts, and a 3.15 ERA. The deeply religious Richard, who resides in Ruston, LA, turned to "a life of God" and sold automobiles once his baseball career had terminated. Perhaps more tragic than his lost pitching career was the racial prejudice and stereotyping among fans and the media alike that led his detractors to so readily suspect loafing and charge cowardice from so superb and dedicated an athlete. It took Richard's near death to convince others that his rapid slide in performance indeed had been due to a physical malady rather than any simple lack of desire and personal fortitude.

BIBLIOGRAPHY: J. R. Richard file, National Baseball Library, Cooperstown, NY; John Benson et al., *Baseball's Top 100* (Wilton, CT, 1997); Steve Bloedaw, "Headed for the Hall, Richard's Career Halted by Stroke," *SCD* 21 (December 9, 1994), p. 160; Bill Gilbert, "J. R. Richard's Aborted Career," *BRJ* 16 (1996), pp. 29–31; Paul Burka, "Houston Astros," *TM* (December 1980), pp. 156–161, 262–271; Wil A. Linkugel and Edward J. Pappas, *They Tasted Glory* (Jefferson, NC, 1998); R. Deutsch, "Catching up with J. Rodney Richard," *SI* 88 (March 23, 1998), p. 15; Pete Prisco,

"J. R. Richard at Peace with His New Lifestyle," *BD* 43 (December 1984), pp. 77–81; Ron Reid, "Sweet Whiff of Success," *SI* 49 (September 4, 1978), p. 66ff; Mike Shatzkin, ed., *The Ballplayers* (New York, 1990).

Peter C. Bjarkman

RICHARD, Ruth "Richy" (b. September 20, 1928, Argus, PA), player, is the daughter of a Pennsylvania farming family and starred as an AAGPBL catcher–outfielder. She learned how to catch while playing softball near Philadelphia.

Richard attended an AAGPBL tryout in Allentown, PA. The 5-foot 4-inch, 134-pound Richard, who batted left but threw right-handed, played eight seasons in the AAGPBL from 1947 to 1954. She spent 1947 as a right fielder with the Grand Rapids, MI Chicks (AAGPBL) and seven campaigns from 1948 through 1954 with the Rockford, IL Peaches (AAGPBL). Rockford won the AAGPBL championship in 1948 and 1949 with Richard behind the plate. She struggled at the plate, but starred defensively. Richard caught two no-hitters during the 1949 playoffs.

Richard batted .241 in 725 games during her AAGPBL career, collecting 608 hits, driving in 287 runners, and clouting 15 career HR. In 1950, she batted .251 and clouted a career-best, six doubles. Richard broke her ankle on the final day of the 1950 season and missed the playoffs, but Rockford still repeated as AAGPBL champions. Her batting averages of .284 in 1952 and .298 in 1954 ranked among the AAGPBL leaders. She clouted a career-high seven HR in 1954. Richard made the All-Star team six consecutive times between 1949 and 1954 as a catcher and committed only 134 errors in 3,407 total chances for a .961 career fielding percentage.

The most memorable experience of her sports career came in 1949 while on an AAGPBL tour of Central and South America. The AAGPBL team was welcomed by both government officials and commoners. In Nicaragua, they visited the presidential palace and were greeted by President Anastasio Samoza. After the demise of the AAGPBL, she toured summers with Bill Allington's All-Americans barnstorming team for four years. She worked in a factory and played amateur softball for a few seasons. Ametek employed her for 26 years until 1993. Richard, who never married, lives at her family homestead in Sellersville, PA, where she enjoys travel, hunting, fishing, and playing golf.

BIBLIOGRAPHY: AAGPBL files, Northern Indiana Historical Society, South Bend, IN; W. C. Madden, *The Women of the All-American Girls Professional Baseball League* (Jefferson, NC, 1997); Susan E. Johnson, *When Women Played Hardball* (Seattle, WA, 1994).

Dennis S. Clark

RICHARDS, Paul Rapier (b. November 21, 1908, Waxahachie, TX; d. May 4, 1986, Waxahachie, TX), player, coach, manager, and executive, was the son of Jesse T. Richards, a teacher, and Stella (McGowan) Richards. He caught with borderline major league ability, but proved one of his era's most intelligent, innovative managers and executives.

The 6-foot 1½-inch, 180-pound Richards began his baseball career as a third baseman and ambidextrous pitcher in high school in Waxahachie, TX. He began playing baseball professionally as an infielder, but became a catcher in 1930 partly because of his limited batting ability. After reaching the major leagues with the Brooklyn Dodgers (NL) in 1932, he caught for the New York Giants (NL) from 1933 to 1935 and Philadelphia Athletics (AL) in 1935. The Philadelphia Athletics sent Richards in 1936 to Atlanta, GA (SA), where he gained his first managerial experience from 1938 to 1942. In 1943, he returned to the major leagues as regular catcher and coach for the Detroit Tigers (AL). Richards' best season came in 1945, when he hit .256 and drove in the winning run against the Chicago Cubs in the seventh game of the World Series. In 523 career major league games, Richards batted .227 and knocked in 155 runs.

Richards returned to managing with Buffalo, NY (IL) in 1947 and piloted Seattle, WA (PCL) in 1950. His first major league managerial assignments came with the Chicago White Sox (AL) from 1951 to 1954 and Baltimore Orioles (AL) from 1955 to 1960. In both instances, he developed fast teams with strong pitching staffs and revived weak franchises. His inventions and innovations included the floppy catcher's mitt to handle knuckleball pitchers, the "Iron Mike" pitching machine, and the transfer of pitchers to the infield while a reliever faced one batter.

The Houston Colt .45s (NL) chose Richards as general manager on formation of the team in 1961. After remaining there through 1965, he then served as vice-president for baseball operations of the Atlanta Braves (NL) from 1967 to 1972. He also worked as sports columnist and for 12 years as part owner of the Waxahachie (TX) *Light*. He reluctantly consented to manage the Chicago White Sox in 1976 as a favor to Bill Veeck,* but eagerly desired to return to the front office. His major league managerial record included 923 wins and 901 losses for a .506 winning percentage. Richards served as the Chicago White Sox director of player development through 1980, once again forming an excellent corps of young pitchers which would help Chicago capture the 1983 Western Division championship. His last appointment involved consulting for the Texas Rangers (AL) in 1984 and 1985.

Richards married Margie Marie McDonald in February 1932 and had two daughters, Lou Redith, who died at age 6 in 1951, and Paula Del. Richards, an avid golfer, died on a fairway of the Waxahachie Country Club.

BIBLIOGRAPHY: Baltimore (MD) *Sun*, May 5, 1986; *The Baseball Encyclopedia*, 10th ed. (New York, 1996); Chicago (IL) *Sun-Times*, May 5, 1986; Chicago (IL) *Tribune*, May 5, 1986; Donald Honig, *The Man in the Dugout* (Lincoln, NE, 1995); Leonard Koppett, *The Man in the Dugout* (New York, 1993); Joseph M. Overfield, "Richards and Jethroe," *BRJ* 16 (1982), pp. 33–35; Thomas Aylesworth and Benton Minks, *The Encyclopedia of Baseball Managers* (New York, 1990); Frank Graham, *The New York Giants* (New York, 1952); Peter Williams, *When the Giants Were Giants* (Chapel Hill, NC, 1994); Fred Smith, *995 Tigers* (Detroit, MI, 1981); Frederick G. Lieb, *The Detroit Tigers* (New York, 1946); Joe Falls, *Detroit Tigers* (New York, 1975); Warren Brown, *The Chicago White Sox* (New York, 1952); Richard Lindberg, *Sox* (New York, 1984); Richard Lindberg, *Who's on Third?* (South Bend, IN, 1983); Ted Patterson, *The Baltimore Orioles* (Dallas, TX, 1995); James H. Bready, *Baseball in Baltimore* (Baltimore, MD, 1998); Paul Richards file, Waxahachie (TX) *Light*; Paul Richards file, National Baseball Library, Cooperstown, NY; Washington (DC) *Post*, May 5, 1986.

George W. Hilton

RICHARDSON, Abram Harding "Hardy," "Old True Blue" (b. April 21, 1855, Clarksboro, NJ; d. January 14, 1931, Utica, NY), player, batted .299 lifetime in 14 major league seasons from 1879 to 1892. He started his professional baseball career as a 5-foot 9-inch, 170 pounder with the independent Philadelphias in the mid–1870s. When that team disbanded in July 1876, Richardson joined the Binghamton, NY Crickets (IA) for two seasons. At Utica, NY in 1878, he married, attracted the attention of the baseball establishment by hitting .324, and was recognized by the New York *Clipper* as the best-fielding center fielder in baseball.

Richardson joined the Buffalo, NY Bisons (NL) in 1879 and soon became one of the game's best-known players. From 1879 to 1885, Richardson collaborated with Buffalo teammates Dan Brouthers,* Jack Rowe,* and Jim White* to form the "Big Four." The versatile Richardson played every position, shifting from third base (1879–1880) to the outfield (1881) to second base (1882–1885). His final three campaign with Buffalo saw him bat over .300 each season and field brilliantly at second base.

After having several fine clubs, Buffalo fell on hard times in 1885 both on the field and at the gate. In an unprecedented, successful move, the Detroit Wolverines (NL) purchased the entire Buffalo team for $7,000 to acquire the "Big Four." Detroit ascended to second place in 1886, when Richardson enjoyed his best campaign, leading the NL in hits (189) and HR (11) and batting a career-high .351. The Wolverines achieved their first NL title in 1887, as Richardson batted .328, and demolished the St. Louis Browns in the 1887 Temple Cup Series. Detroit plummeted quickly, however, and folded after the 1888 season.

Richardson and Brouthers were transferred to the Boston Red Stockings (NL) for 1889. The duo helped the Boston Reds (PL) take the 1890 championship, with the former leading the PL in RBI with 146 and batting a formidable .326 mark. When the PL folded, Brouthers and Richardson joined the Boston Reds (AA) and captured their third title in five years. Richardson ended his major league career with the Washington Senators (NL) and New York Giants (NL) in 1892.

Richardson operated a hotel in Utica, NY and worked for Remington Typewriter Company in Ilion, NY. He was survived by his widow and one daughter.

BIBLIOGRAPHY: Abram Richardson file, National Baseball Library, Cooperstown, NY; James M. DiClerico and Barry Pavelic, *The Jersey Game* (New Brunswick, NJ, 1991); Harold Kaese, *The Boston Braves* (New York, 1948); Joseph Overfield, *The 100 Years of Buffalo Baseball* (Kenmore, NY, 1985); Robert L. Tiemann and Mark Rucker, eds., *Nineteenth Century Stars* (Kansas City, MO, 1989).

William E. Akin

RICHARDSON, Robert Clinton, Jr. "Bobby" (b. August 19, 1935, Sumter, SC), player and coach, is the son of Robert Clinton Richardson, Sr., who owned and operated a marble and granite company, and Willie (Owens) Richardson. Although small for his age, Richardson acquired a love of baseball from his father and as a youth played for a team sponsored by the Salvation Army. By the time he began high school, he had won the second base position on his American Legion team by performing better than boys three or four years older. As a sophomore, he started at second base for his high school nine.

The 5-foot 9-inch, 160-pound Richardson did not hit with power but, as he related, "walked, bunted, and depended on my legs to get on base and keep moving." Scouts from a dozen major league teams followed him by his senior year. Within a few hours after his high school graduation in 1953, he signed with the New York Yankees (AL). He started his minor league career with Norfolk, VA (PiL), but was sent down to Olean, NY (PoL) and hit .412 there. He starred for Binghamton, NY (EL) in 1954 and Denver, CO (AA) the following year. He played briefly with the New York Yankees in 1955 and 1956, but did not stay in the major leagues until 1957. After spending two years in a reserve role, Richardson became the New York Yankees' regular second baseman in 1959 and won raves for his ability to cover ground, sure hands, and deft pivot play on double play balls. He also proved a timely hitter. The devout Baptist had begun to think of retirement before his 30th birthday to spend time working with children in Sumter, SC, where he maintained his off-season residence. He retired as a player after the 1966 season and subsequently coached baseball at the University of South Carolina, Coastal Carolina CC, and Liberty University in Lynchburg, VA. His 1975 and 1977 South Carolina squads finished second in the NCAA College World Series. In 1976, he was defeated in a bid for a seat in the U.S. House of Representatives. Richardson, who married Alice Elizabeth Dobson on June 8, 1956 and has five children, has been involved with FCA and serves as president of Baseball Chapel in Asheville, NC.

Richardson spent 10 full years with the New York Yankees, batting over .300 in 1959 and in 1962. In 1962, he led the AL in hits with 209 and finished second to teammate Mickey Mantle* in the AL MVP balloting. In the major leagues, Richardson had a .266 career batting average with 1,432 hits. He played in seven World Series, winning acclaim in 1960 by batting .367 with 12 RBI against the Pittsburgh Pirates and a gain in 1964 by getting 13 hits against the St. Louis Cardinals. In 1961, he tied a World Series record with nine hits against the Cincinnati Reds in a five-game series.

BIBLIOGRAPHY: Bobby Richardson file, National Baseball Library, Cooperstown, NY; Mark Gallagher, *The Yankee Encyclopedia*, vol. 3 (Champaign, IL, 1997); Dave Anderson et al., *The Yankees* (New York, 1979); Martin Appel, *Yesterday's Heroes* (New York, 1988); *CB* (1966), pp. 330–332; Dom Forker, *Sweet Seasons* (Dallas, TX, 1991); Gene Karst and Martin J. Jones, Jr., *Who's Who in Professional Baseball* (New Rochelle, NY, 1973); Tony Kubek and Terry Pluto, *Sixty-one* (New York, 1987); David Halberstam, *October 1964* (New York, 1994); Ralph Houk and Robert W. Creamer, *Season of Glory* (New York, 1988); Jack Orr, ed., *Baseball's Greatest Players Today* (New York, 1963); Paul Post, "After 30 Years, He's Still a Hit with Fans," *SCD* 24 (April 11, 1997), pp. 160–161; Bobby Richardson, *The Bobby Richardson Story* (Westwood, NJ, 1965).

Lloyd J. Graybar

RICHMOND, J. Lee (b. May 5, 1857, Sheffield, OH; d. October 1, 1929, Toledo, OH), player, was the son of Cyrus R. Richmond, a Baptist minister, and Eliza (Tinan) Richmond and first played baseball as a left-handed pitcher with Oberlin College of Ohio from 1873 to 1876. He enrolled at Brown University in 1876, performing the fall season as an outfielder. Richmond was elected class president, played on the school's first football team, and spent the next two seasons as a baseball outfielder and pitcher for Brown. Richmond labored in Brown's gymnasium the winter of 1878–1879, developing several curved deliveries. His devastating curves broke up and down rather than in and out and combined well with his rare left-handed delivery. Richmond, slight in stature at 5-feet 10-inches and 142 pounds, did not overpower hitters and consequently allied his unusual pitches with cunning, deception (including a change of pace), and strategy. He studied hitters and kept a book on them.

Richmond burst upon the baseball scene in 1879, leading his Brown University nine to the college championship and pitching a no-hitter in his professional debut. His composite record for the 1879 season included 47 wins and an above-.350 batting average. He pitched a second no-hitter later in the season and won his major league debut with the Boston Red Caps (NL).

Richmond signed with the Worcester Ruby Legs (NL) for a record $2,400 in 1880, perhaps making him sports' first "franchise player." He pitched the entire three-year history of the Worcester Ruby Legs franchise, accounting for 80 percent of the club's wins. He finished 32–32 in 1880 and 25–26 in 1881. He pitched for the Providence Grays (NL) in 1883 and briefly for the

Cincinnati Red Stockings (AA) in 1886. In six major league seasons, he compiled a 75–100 record and 3.06 ERA.

Richmond accounted for many "firsts" during his short major league career and hurled baseball's first perfect game, a 1–0 win over the Cleveland Blues on June 12, 1880. Since he played concurrently as an amateur and professional, baseball established the first rules barring professionals from participating with amateurs. These rules continue with virtually all sports worldwide. He struck out a record five consecutive batters in his first major league game and gave up the first grand-slam HR. Besides being the first hurler to win 20 games for a last-place team, he became the first pitcher to relieve and be relieved for an opposite-side hurler. His portside delivery led to the first platooning and popularized switch-hitting, strategies integral to every game today.

Richmond used baseball to finance his education and earned bachelor's and master's degrees from Brown University and his medical degree from the University of the City of New York (now NYU) while still in the game. For seven years, he played professional baseball in the summer and attended school in the winter. He ranked among the first collegians to play major league baseball and marked the first physician to do so.

After retiring from baseball in 1883, he returned to northeastern Ohio to practice medicine. He later gave up medicine for an education career spanning 40 years in Toledo, OH. He served as a teacher, orchestra leader, coach, and principal at Toledo high schools. At age 65, he "retired" to the University of Toledo to serve as Dean of Men. Richmond, a lifelong baseball fan and scratch golfer, married Mary Naomi Chapin and had three daughters.

BIBLIOGRAPHY: J. Lee Richmond file, National Baseball Library, Cooperstown, NY; *The Baseball Encyclopedia*, 10th ed. (New York, 1996); John Richmond Husman, "J. Lee Richmond's Remarkable 1879 Season," *TNP* 4 (Winter 1985), pp. 65–70; Martin Kaufman, ed., *Historical Journal of Massachusetts*, vol. 19 (Westfield, CT, 1991); Ronald A. Mayer, *Perfect!* (Jefferson, NC, 1991); Ronald A. Smith, *Sports & Freedom* (New York, 1988); R. A. Smith, "Lee Richmond, Brown University, and the Amateur-Professional Controversy in College Baseball," *NEQ* 64 (March 1991), pp. 82–99; Robert L. Tiemann and Mark Rucker, eds., *Nineteenth Century Stars* (Kansas City, MO, 1989).

John R. Husman

RICKEY, Wesley Branch "The Mahatma" (b. December 20, 1881, Flint, OH; d. December 9, 1965, Columbia, MO), player, manager, and executive, was the son of farmer Franklin Rickey and Emily (Braum) Rickey. A gifted student, Rickey worked his way through Ohio Wesleyan College and the University of Michigan Law School by teaching and coaching sports. He married Jane Moulton of Lucasville, OH in 1906 and had six children. As a mediocre catcher, Rickey played three seasons of minor league baseball at Terre

Haute, IN (3IL) and Le Mars, IA (ISDL) in 1903 and Dallas, TX (TL) in 1904 and 1905 and three major league seasons with the St. Louis Browns (AL) in 1905–1906 and the New York Highlanders (AL) in 1907. Injuries and tuberculosis ended his brief professional career in 1907. In 20 games, he batted .239 and knocked in 39 runs. His reputation as a coach returned the bespectacled, scholarly Rickey to the major leagues, where he became this century's most brilliant, innovative baseball executive. After joining the St. Louis Browns (AL) in 1913 as field manager and executive director, he acquired young players cheaply by negotiating working agreements with minor league teams. Under Rickey, the Browns finished with 139 wins and 179 losses from 1913 through 1915 and in the second division.

In 1916, Rickey joined the St. Louis Cardinals (NL) in the same dual capacity. Following World War I service as a major in the chemical warfare branch, Rickey returned in 1919 and shaped the lackluster St. Louis Cardinals into a perennial contender. Rickey served as Cardinals manager through early 1925 and guided the club to two third place finishes. During his ten-year managerial career, he posted 597 wins and 664 losses (.473 winning percentage). By building a network of minor league farm clubs, Rickey acquired and developed a steady flow of young talent. No major league rival matched the efficiency of the Cardinals' farm system, which included 33 teams by 1940. The system's productivity stemmed from tryout camps, brilliant teaching and evaluative techniques, and other Rickey innovations. During Rickey's tenure through 1942, the Cardinals won six NL pennants (1926, 1928, 1930–1931, 1934, 1942) and four world championships (1926, 1931, 1934, 1942). Rickey profited from his percentage on the sale of surplus players, which aroused the enmity of owner Sam Breadon.*

Fired by Breadon in 1942, Rickey became president and general manager of the Brooklyn Dodgers (NL) and built their superb farm system. By his bold, successful experiment of selecting Jackie Robinson* as the first black player to play in the majors in this century, he cornered the market on black and Hispanic players. Rickey's efforts made the Dodgers a perennial NL power and 1947 and 1949 NL champions. Rickey was forced out of his Dodgers post in 1950 by Walter O'Malley,* who sought full ownership of the club and resented Rickey's flamboyant leadership. Rickey signed a five-year contract as executive vice-president of the Pittsburgh Pirates (NL) and laid the groundwork for their 1960 world championship.

In 1959, the 77-year-old Rickey surfaced as president of the CntL. Although it did not become a major league, the CntL forced the established majors to expand and brought major league baseball to hitherto excluded urban centers. The author of *The American Diamond* (1965), Rickey was elected to the National Baseball Hall of Fame in 1967. Rickey's innovations as baseball executive, dominant role in the racial integration of organized baseball, and stimulus to the game's expansion place him among this century's most influential baseball leaders.

BIBLIOGRAPHY: Richard L. Burtt, *The Pittsburgh Pirates; A Pictorial History* (Virginia Beach, VA, 1977); Branch Rickey file, National Baseball Library, Cooperstown, NY; Howard Green, "Branch Rickey," *TNP* 16 (1996), pp. 104–106; Arnold Rampersad, *Jackie Robinson* (New York, 1997); Harvey Frommer, *Rickey & Robinson* (New York, 1982); Leonard Koppett, *The Man in the Dugout* (New York, 1993); Brad Herzog, *The Sports 100* (New York, 1995); David Lipman, *Mr. Baseball* (New York, 1966); Arthur Mann, *Branch Rickey* (Boston, MA, 1957); Robert Obojski, *Bush League* (New York, 1975); Branch Rickey and Robert Rieger, *The American Diamond* (New York, 1965); Jackie Robinson with Alfred Duckett, *I Never Had It Made* (New York, 1972); Tommy Holmes, *The Dodgers* (New York, 1975); Stanley Cohen, *Dodgers! The First 100 Years* (New York, 1990); Richard Goldstein, *Superstars and Screwballs* (New York, 1991); Peter Golenbock, *Bums* (New York, 1984); John Thorn and Jules Tygiel, "Signing Jackie Robinson," *TNP* 10 (1990), pp. 7–12; Wilfred Sheed, "Branch Rickey," *Sport* 77 (December 1986), pp. 29ff; John Thorn and Jules Tygiel, "The Signing of Jackie Robinson; The Untold Story," *Sport* 79 (June 1988), pp. 65–66; William McNeil, *The Dodgers Encyclopedia* (Champaign, IL, 1997); Jules Tygiel, *Baseball's Great Experiment: Jackie Robinson* (New York, 1983); Joseph J. Vecchione, ed., *The New York Times Book of Sports Legends* (New York, 1991); David Q. Voigt, *American Baseball*, vols. 2, 3 (University Park, PA, 1983); Murray Polner, *Branch Rickey* (New York, 1982).

David Q. Voigt

RIGHETTI, David Allan "Rags," "Snake" (b. November 28, 1958, San Jose, CA), player, is the son of Leo Righetti, a former minor league baseball player, and Sandra (Smith) Righetti and attended San Jose City College before signing with the Texas Rangers (AL) in 1977. Righetti spent most of the next four years in the minor leagues, impressing scouts with his live fastball and struggling with his control. In November 1978, the Texas Rangers traded him to the New York Yankees (AL). With Tulsa, OK (TL) in 1979, Righetti struck out 21 batters in one game.

In May 1981, the New York Yankees recalled the 6-foot 4-inch 195-pound left-handed Righetti from Columbus, OH (IL). He fared 8–4 with a 2.05 ERA in the strike-shortened campaign, won two games against the Milwaukee Brewers in the Eastern Division playoffs, and triumphed once against the Oakland Athletics in the AL Championship Series. Despite a mediocre World Series against the Los Angeles Dodgers, he won the AL Rookie of the Year award. After a lackluster 1982 campaign, Righetti blossomed in 1983, when he finished 14–8 with a 3.44 ERA, struck out 169 batters, and walked only 67. On July 4, 1983, he hurled a no-hitter against the Boston Red Sox.

In the off-season, the New York Yankees surprisingly cast off closer Rich Gossage* and assigned Righetti that role. He recorded 31 saves in 1984, 29 in 1985, and 46 in 1986, at the time a major league record. He became the New York Yankees all-time saves leader in 1987, but Yankees owner George Steinbrenner* criticized him for pitching poorly at the beginning of the season. He hurled erractically during the 1988 and 1989 seasons and again received Steinbrenner's criticism.

After a fine 1990 campaign in which Righetti saved 36 games, the San Francisco Giants signed him to a 4-year, $10 million contract. He pitched poorly for the San Francisco Giants, winning just 5 of 20 decisions, compiling a 4.61 ERA, and saving only 28 games in three seasons. The San Francisco Giants released him after the 1993 season.

Righetti began 1994 with the Oakland A's (AL), but was released and pitched in the minor leagues. The Toronto Blue Jays (AL) promoted him and released him after an August players' strike ended the 1994 season. He began 1995 at Nashville, TN (AA), but was recalled by the Chicago White Sox (AL) and returned to the regular rotation. He finished with a 3–2 record and retired at the season's end. In his major league career, Righetti compiled an 82–79 record with a 3.46 ERA. His 252 saves ranked highest among left-handers at his retirement.

Righetti married Kandice Lee Owen in 1989 and has triplets. He is currently involved with venture capital sporting goods firms and remains an avid amateur golfer.

BIBLIOGRAPHY: Robert Weir, Interview with David Righetti, June 1997; Jill Lieber, "The Relief Is Not So Sweet," *SI* 72 (April 16, 1990), pp. 70–73; New York *Post*, February 2, 1987, April 5, 1990, July 19, 1990; David Righetti file, National Baseball Library, Cooperstown, NY; "Dave Righetti," *Microsoft Complete Baseball* CD-ROM (Redmond, WA, 1994); *TSN*, September 6, 1985, October 13, 1986; Mark Gallagher, *The Yankee Encyclopedia*, vol. 3 (New York, 1997); Bob Cairns, *Pen Men* (New York, 1993); David Neft and Richard Cohen, eds., *The Sports Encyclopedia: Baseball 1997*, 17th ed. (New York, 1997).

                                                                    Robert E. Weir

RIGLER, Charles "Cy," "Charley" (b. May 16, 1882, Massillon, OH; d. December 21, 1936, Philadelphia, PA), athlete, umpire, coach, official, and administrator, was the son of John "Jack" Rigler and Emeline (Fisher) Rigler and worked as a machinist. The 6-foot 2-inch, 240-pound Rigler starred at tackle on the original semiprofessional football Massillon Tigers of 1903 and began umpiring local baseball games in 1904 when a knee injury forced his retirement from the gridiron. He never played baseball, but possessed a knack for umpiring. After umpiring from 1904 to 1906 in the Class B CL, he debuted as an NL arbiter on September 27, 1906 at the personal request of NL President Harry Pulliam.* Rigler temporarily quit umpiring in 1922 to concentrate on his off-season job of developing oil land leases for the East Ohio Gas Company, but gave up this financial security to return to the game he loved.

Rigler's 30-year career saw him umpire 62 games in 10 World Series (1910, 1912, 1913, 1915, 1917, 1919, 1921, 1925, 1928, 1930). He ranks second to Bill Klem* in World Series games umpired and is tied with Hank

O'Day* behind Klem for the most World Series assignments. Major league baseball selected Rigler to umpire the first All-Star game in 1933. Strangely, he called only two no-hit contests (1908, 1915) while working more than 6,150 games. His most famous call occurred during the 1925 World Series. After rushing to the outfield from second base, he ruled that Washington Senators (AL) outfielder Sam Rice* had caught a fly ball hit by Earl Smith of the Pittsburgh Pirates (NL). Rice had fallen out of sight into the stands. Rigler immediately urged the adoption of a six-umpire system for the World Series, but his recommendation was not adopted until 1947. Rice subsequently wrote a letter confirming Rigler's decision.

Rigler made his most enduring contribution to umpiring before reaching the major leagues. At an Evansville, IN game on April 30, 1905, he began the now universal custom of "indicating balls by the fingers of his left hand and strikes with the fingers of the right hand so everyone in the park could tell what he had called." Umpires quickly adopted the raised-arm technique, which is often incorrectly attributed to Klem. The "genial giant" remained one of baseball's most popular umpires, combining sound judgment with a keen understanding of human relations. He never used profanity, rarely ejected players or managers, and possessed a fine sense of humor, earning him the reputation as a "prize kidder" and ingenious prankster.

During the off-season, the talented, ambitious Rigler refereed football games, designed golf courses and baseball fields in the United States and Cuba, and served as an athletics adviser/director for several colleges and universities. Although never attending college, he obtained a degree at the University of Virginia Law School and passed the state bar exam. Rigler served as a part-time baseball and football coach at the University of Virginia, coaching pitcher Eppa Rixey* and arranging for him to sign with the Philadelphia Phillies (NL). NL officials barred umpires from "scouting" players after Rigler received a cash bonus from Philadelphia.

Rigler, who was injured severely in 1934 automobile accident, retired after the 1935 season. He succeeded O'Day as supervisor of NL umpires in December 1935, but died unexpectedly two weeks later following an operation for a brain tumor. Rigler married Nellie Evelyn Goodrich in 1910 and had two stepdaughters, Doris and Frances.

BIBLIOGRAPHY: Charles S. Dautel, correspondence and interviews with Larry R. Gerlach, February–March 1991; Evansville (IN) *Courier*, May 1, 1905; Dan Krueckeberg, "Take Charge Cy," *TNP* 4 (1985), pp. 7–11; Charles Rigler file, National Baseball Library, Cooperstown, NY; Charles Rigler file, *TSN* Archives, St. Louis, MO; Charles Rigler Scrapbook, Charles S. Dautel Collection, Lawrenceburg, IN.

Larry R. Gerlach

RIGNEY, William Joseph "Bill," "Specs" (b. January 29, 1918, Alameda, CA), player, manager, coach, scout, sportscaster, and executive, is the son of George Rigney, tile business owner, and Eleanor Rigney and graduated from

Oakland, CA High School. The 6-foot 1-inch, 183-pound bespectacled infielder, who batted and threw right-handed, idolized Mel Ott* and began his professional baseball career in 1938 with Spokane, WA (WIL). Rigney spent four more minor league seasons with Vancouver-Bellingham, WA (WIL) in 1939, Topeka, KS (WA) in 1940, and Oakland, CA (PCL) in 1938, 1939, 1941, and 1942.

After spending from 1943 to 1945 in the U.S. Navy, Rigney was a light-hitting infielder with the New York Giants (NL) from 1946 to 1953. His best season came as regular second baseman in 1947, when he batted .267 with career-highs in hits (142), doubles (24), HR (17), and RBI (59). He made the NL All-Star team in 1948 and performed as a utility infielder after 1949. Rigney hit .250 with one RBI in the 1951 World Series against the New York Yankees and .300 in 1952. In eight major league seasons, he batted .259 with 212 RBI in 654 games.

Rigney began his managerial career with Minneapolis, MN (AA) in 1954 and piloted the Millers to first place in 1955, earning *TSN* Minor League Manager of the Year honors. In 1956, he replaced Leo Durocher* as New York Giants manager. Rigney managed 18 years in the major leagues with the New York Giants in 1956 and 1957, San Francisco Giants (NL) from 1958 to 1960 and 1976, newly formed Los Angeles Angels (AL) from 1961 to 1964, California Angels (AL) from 1965 to 1969, and Minnesota Twins (AL) from 1970 to 1972. The San Francisco Giants blew the NL pennant in 1959, finishing third. In 1962, *TSN* named him Manager of the Year after he guided Los Angeles to third place with an 86–76 record. His best season came in 1970, when the Twins took the AL Western Division with a 98–64 mark. The Baltimore Orioles blanked the Twins, 3–0, in the AL Championship Series. Altogether, Rigney's teams compiled a 1,239–1,321 record and .484 winning percentage.

Rigney coached and scouted for the San Diego Padres (NL) in 1975, handled special assignments for the California Angels from 1978 to 1981, and has served as special assistant for the Oakland Athletics (AL) since 1983. The Alamo, CA resident married Paula Bruen in January 1944 and has three children, Bill, Jr., a baseball executive, Tom, and Lynn.

BIBLIOGRAPHY: Thomas Aylesworth and Benton Minks, *The Encyclopedia of Baseball Managers* (New York, 1990); Joe King, *The San Francisco Giants* (Englewood Cliffs, NJ, 1958); Mick Peters, *Giants Almanac* (Berkeley, CA, 1988); *TSN Baseball Register*, 1972; *WWA*, 37th ed. (1972–1973), p. 2652; Maury Allen, *Baseball* (New York, 1990); Frederick Freed, "Rigney at Second for the Giants," *NR* 117 (August 11, 1947), pp. 20–24; Noel Hynd, *The Giants of the Polo Grounds* (New York, 1988); Brent P. Kelley, *The Early All-Stars* (Jefferson, NC, 1997); Leonard Koppett, *The Man in the Dugout* (New York, 1993); Frank Graham, *The New York Giants* (New York, 1952); Steve Bitker, *The Original San Francisco Giants* (Champaign, IL, 1998); Ross Newhan, *The California Angels* (New York, 1982); Dave Mona and Dave Jarzyna, *Twenty-five Seasons* (Minneapolis, MN, 1986); Ed Linn, "Year of Decision for Bill Rigney," *SEP*

232 (June 25, 1960), pp. 25, 103–104; Robert Obojski, "Bill Rigney: 60 Years of Baseball Memories," *SCD* 24 (February 14, 1997), p. 140; E. M. Swift, "Up Against the Wall," *SI* 73 (October 29, 1990), pp. 82–84.

David L. Porter

RIJO, Jose Antonio (Abreau) (b. May 13, 1965, San Cristobal, DR), player, is 6-foot 3-inches and 215 pounds. The Dominican sports hero attended Colegio San Cristobal and married Rosie Marichal, daughter of the Dominican Republic's first native elected to the National Baseball Hall of Fame. They have two children, Jose, Jr., and Sascha, and reside in San Cristobal.

As a phenomenal young pitcher out of San Cristobal, Rijo signed with the New York Yankees (AL) in August 1980 and reported to Brandenton, FL (GCL) as a 16-year-old the next summer. Before turning age 19, he wore major league flannels as an opening day member of the 1984 New York Yankees. In December 1984, Rijo was traded with four other future major leaguers for Rickey Henderson* of the Oakland Athletics (AL). His next three seasons were divided between the Oakland bullpen and the Tacoma, WA (PCL) farm team. In December 1987, the Oakland A's traded Rijo to the Cincinnati Reds (NL) with Tim Birtsas for outfielder Dave Parker.*

Rijo began the 1988 season as a reliever for the Cincinnati Reds and led the NL with 29 appearances by early June. The midyear trade of Eric Rasmussen to the San Diego Padres moved Rijo into Cincinnati's rotation. A right-hander with good stuff and control, Rijo prospered as a starter. From 1988 through 1993, his cumulative ERA stood slightly over 2.50 or the lowest cumulative mark since legendary Lefty Grove's,* from 1926 to 1931. Rijo averaged fewer than two walks per nine innings over 211 innings in 1992 and from 1988 to 1995 tied Eppa Rixey* as Cincinnati's only pitchers to have winning seasons in their first eight campaigns with the Reds. In the 1990 World Series, he pitched 15.2 innings in Cincinnati's sweep over the Oakland A's. His two wins featured a 0.59 ERA and earned him World Series MVP accolades. He led the NL in strikeouts with 227 in 1993.

Between 1995 and 1997, Dr. James Andrews of Birmingham, AL performed five operations on Rijo's pitching elbow. The surgeries forced him to miss the 1996 and 1997 campaigns. To further his rehabilitation, he trained in Santo Domingo, DR with Pedro Martinez,* Ramon Martinez,* and other players. He attempted an unsuccessful comeback at spring training in 1998. Rijo compiled 111 wins, 87 losses, a .561 winning percentage, and a 3.16 ERA in 12 major league seasons. He made the 1994 NL All-Star team and was selected right-handed pitcher on *TSN* All-Star team for 1991.

BIBLIOGRAPHY: Donald Honig, *The Cincinnati Reds* (New York, 1992); Jose Rijo file, National Baseball Library, Cooperstown, NY; J. Crasnick, "One on One . . . with Jose Rijo," *Sport* 82 (July 1991), pp. 21–22; Tim Kurkjian, "Call It Rijo's Revenge," *SI* 73 (October 29, 1990), p. 24; *TSN Baseball Register*, 1998; *The Cincinnati Reds 1989 Media Guide*.

David Fitzsimmons

RIPKEN, Calvin Edwin, Jr. "Cal" (b. August 24, 1960, Havre de Grace, MD), player, is the second of four children of Calvin Ripken, Sr., and Viola Ripken and graduated in 1978 from Aberdeen High School, starring for its State Championship baseball team. His father, who played and managed minor league baseball, coached for (1976–1986, 1988–1992) and piloted (1987–1988) the Baltimore Orioles (AL), while his brother, Billy, performed at second base for Baltimore (1987–1992). The Baltimore Orioles drafted the 6-foot 4-inch, 220-pound Ripken in the second round in June 1978 and assigned the infielder to Bluefield, WV (ApL), Miami, FL (FSL), Charlotte, NC (SL), and Rochester, NY (IL) between 1978 and 1981. Ripken joined the Baltimore Orioles in August 1981 and began 1982 at third base. Manager Earl Weaver* shrewdly switched the excellent fielder to shortstop, where he played every inning from June 1982 to September 1987. Ripken earned AL Rookie of the Year honors in 1982, batting .264 with 28 HR and 93 RBI. The Baltimore Orioles lost the AL East title to the Milwaukee Brewers in the season finale.

Ripken garnered AL MVP and Major League Player of the Year accolades in 1983, helping the Baltimore Orioles dominate the AL East. He led the AL in runs scored (121), hits (211), and doubles (42), batting .318 with 27 HR and 102 RBI and topping AL shortstops in assists, total chances, and double plays. The Baltimore Orioles defeated the Chicago White Sox in the AL Championship Series, as Ripken hit .400, and nearly swept the Philadelphia Phillies in the World Series. The Baltimore Orioles struggled from 1984 through 1988. Ripken batted .304 with 27 HR and 86 RBI in 1984, hitting for the cycle against the Texas Rangers on May 6 and establishing a record for most assists by an AL shortstop (583). Ripken's 110 RBI in 1985 marked his second-highest run production. The Baltimore Orioles barely lost the 1989 AL East Division title to the Toronto Blue Jays, as Ripken became the first AL shortstop to register eight consecutive 20–HR campaigns. On June 12, 1990, he played his 1,308th straight game, attaining second on the all-time list and breaking Everett Scott's* record for most successive games at one position. He led AL shortstops in fielding percentage (.996) in 1990, setting major league shortstop marks for fewest errors (3) and most consecutive contests (95) without a miscue.

Ripken garnered a second AL MVP Award in 1991, the third player ever designated from a losing team. Ripken, the Major League Player of the Year and All-Star Game MVP, belted a three-run HR that sparked a 4–2 AL victory. He ranked second in HR (34), hits (210), doubles (46), and slugging percentage (.556), fourth in RBI (114), and sixth in batting average (.323). His 368 total bases and 85 extra base hits led the major leagues. Ripken earned his first Gold Glove Award, pacing AL shortstops in fielding percentage (.986), putouts, assists, total chances, and double plays. He also won the Gold Glove in 1992, but his offensive production plummeted. During the strike-shortened 1994 season, he batted .315 with 13 HR and 75 RBI.

On August 1, 1994, Ripken appeared in his 2,000th consecutive major league game.

Amid much fanfare, the 17-time AL All-Star broke Lou Gehrig's* 56-year-old record of 2,130 consecutive games on September 5, 1995. He received a 22-minute-long standing ovation and clouted a HR to help the Baltimore Orioles defeat the California Angels, 4–2. Ripken in 1996 batted .278 with 26 HR and 102 RR, helping the Baltimore Orioles capture the Wild Card. After batting .444 with two RBI in the AL Division Series against the Seattle Mariners, he hit .250 in the AL Championship Series against the New York Yankees. His .270 batting average helped the Orioles take the AL East in 1997. He batted .438 against the Seattle Mariners in the AL Division Series and .348 with one HR and three RBI against the Cleveland Indians in the AL Championship Series, but Baltimore failed again to reach the World Series.

Ripken sat out a game against the New York Yankees at Camden Yards on September 20, 1998, ending his major league record for most consecutive games played at 2,632. He apparently did not want to keep answering questions about when the streak would end. Despite injuries, he hit .340 with 18 HR and 57 RBI in 1999. On September 2, he became the 29th major leaguer to hit 400 HR. Through 1999, he has batted .278 with 2,992 hits, 571 doubles, 402 HR, and 1,571 RBI in 2,790 games. He holds the major league record for most HR by a shortstop with 345, 268 more than Ernie Banks.* He holds the AL record for most seasons leading shortstops in putouts (6) and has paced AL shortstops in double plays eight times, assists seven times, and total chances and fielding percentage four times. *TSN* honored him as AL All-Star team shortstop eight times (1983–1985, 1989, 1991, 1993–95) and as AL Silver Slugger team member eight times (1983–1986, 1989, 1991, 1993, 1994). *TSN* named him Sportsman of the Year in 1995. He made Major League Baseball's All-Century Team. The Reistertown, MD resident married Kelly Greer in 1987 and has one daughter, Rachel. The Aberdeen, MD City Hall houses the Ripken Museum featuring a bronze statue.

BIBLIOGRAPHY: John Benson et al., *Baseball's Top 100* (Wilton, CT, 1997); "Cal's 2,000," Baltimore (MD) *Sun*, July 31, 1994, pp. 1C, 12C, 13C; *CB* (1992), pp. 470–474; Ron Fimrite, "He's Done His Daddy Proud," *SI* 60 (April 2, 1984), pp. 34–36; Cal Ripken, Jr. file, National Baseball Library, Cooperstown, NY; H. Herman, "Count on Cal," *MH* 7 (June 1994), pp. 54–57; Hank Hersch, "One Big Rip-Roaring Family Affair," *SI* 66 (March 9, 1987), pp. 26–28; Richard Hoffer, "Sportsman of the Year," *SI* 83 (December 18, 1995), pp. 70–76; Tim Kurkjian, "Man of Iron," *SI* 83 (August 17, 1995), pp. 22–32; P. Richmond, "Local Hero," *GQ* 63 (May 1993), pp. 166–171; James H. Bready, *Baseball in Baltimore* (Baltimore, MD, 1998); Michael Stadnicki, "Ripken Museum a Dream Destination for Fans, Collectors," *SCD* 25 (December 25, 1998), pp. 74–75; Ted Patterson, *The Baltimore Orioles* (Dallas, TX, 1995); Robert E. Kelly, *Baseball's Best* (Jefferson, NC, 1988); Tim Kurkjian, "Rip on a Tear," *SI* 75 (July 29, 1991), pp. 24–26; Lois Nicholson, *Cal Ripken, Jr., A Quiet Hero* (Centreville, MD, 1993); Cal Ripken, Jr., with Mike Bryan, *The Only Way I Know* (New York, 1997); Cal Ripken, Jr., *Ripken* (New York, 1995); Peter Schmuck,

"A Matter of Record," *Sport* 83 (May 1992), pp. 22–24, 26–27; *TSN Official Baseball Register*, 1998; Tom Verducci, "Solitary Man," *SI* 78 (June 28, 1993), pp. 40-42; Ralph Wiley, "A Monumental Streak," *SI* 72 (June 18, 1990), pp. 70–74; *WWA*, 47th ed. (1992–1993), p. 2827.

David L. Porter

RIPPY, Benjamin Wesley. *See* Charles Wesley Jones.

RITCHEY, Claude Cassius "Little All Right" (b. October 5, 1873, Emlenton, PA; d. November 8, 1951, Emlenton, PA), player, was the son of Lucretia Anita Ritchey, a schoolteacher. He began his professional baseball career as an infielder with Franklin, PA in 1894, moving in 1895 to the Warren, OH Wonders (IOL) and 1896 to Buffalo, NY (EL). As a result of his excellent play, he was drafted by the major league Brooklyn Bridegrooms (NL) for the 1897 season. The Brooklyn Bridegrooms sold him to the Cincinnati Reds (NL) as a replacement for a player who had failed to report to that club. As a substitute infielder–outfielder, Ritchey played three positions with the Cincinnati Reds. The Louisville, KY Colonels (NL) acquired him in 1898 to play shortstop and switched him in midseason to second base, where he remained a fixture thereafter. As the starting second baseman for the Louisville Colonels in 1899, he hit .300 for the highest batting average of his major league career. After the Louisville franchise was transferred to the Pittsburgh Pirates (NL), Ritchey batted .292 in 1900, .296 in 1901, .277 in 1902, and .287 in 1903. His batting average steadily declined after that until he hit only .172 in 30 games for the Boston Doves (NL) in 1909, his final major league season. He finished with a 13-year major league career with a .273 batting average, 1,618 hits, and 673 RBI.

Ritchey's deft, quick play at second base, however, ranked him among the era's most valuable major league players. He and future National Baseball Hall of Fame shortstop Honus Wagner* provided a brilliant keystone combination, enabling the Pittsburgh Pirates to win three consecutive NL pennants from 1901 to 1903. The 5-foot 6½-inch, 167-pound Ritchey led or tied NL second basemen in fielding average in 1902, 1903 and from 1905 to 1907. With the exception of Nap Lajoie,* he compiled the highest major league fielding average (.960) at that position during the first decade of the 20th century. The rugged Ritchey also performed more games at second base (1,262) than any other player during this period and led NL second basemen in assists in 1903. Ritchey appeared in the first modern World Series that year against the Boston Pilgrims, establishing one-game fall classic records for most chances and assists at second base. His records endured for many years. He finished his major league career with a .957 fielding average.

Ritchey remained with the Pittsburgh Pirates until December 1906, when he was traded with Ginger Beaumont* and Pat Flaherty to the Boston Doves (NL) for second baseman Ed Abbaticchio. After playing 30 games with the

Boston Doves in 1909, he was released to Providence, RI (EL) and refused to report there. Louisville (AA) signed Ritchey in 1910, but he played only two weeks there. A broken arm, suffered while sliding into second base, ended his baseball career.

Subsequently, Ritchey was employed for many years as a laborer with the Quaker State Oil Refining Company in Emlenton. He married Sophia Augusta Bayer in 1902. Following their divorce in 1917, he wed Kathryn Ruth Kunselman in 1924. He had a daughter, Eleanor, by his first marriage, and three children, Jack, Lois, and Marian, by his second marriage.

BIBLIOGRAPHY: *The Baseball Encyclopedia*, 10th ed. (New York, 1996); Jack C. Braun, telephone interview with Jack Ritchey, October 4, 1993; Richard L. Burtt, *The Pittsburgh Pirates, A Pictorial History* (Virginia Beach, VA, 1977); Frederick G. Lieb, *The Pittsburgh Pirates* (New York, 1948); David Nemec and Pete Palmer, *1001 Fascinating Baseball Facts* (Stamford, CT, 1993); Claude Ritchey file, National Baseball Library, Cooperstown, NY; John Thorn et al., eds., *Total Baseball*, 5th ed. (New York, 1997); Bob Smizik, *The Pittsburgh Pirates: An Illustrated History* (New York, 1990); Frederick G. Lieb, *The Boston Braves* (New York, 1948); Gary Caruso, *The Braves Encyclopedia* (Philadelphia, PA, 1995).

Jack C. Braun

RIVERS, John Milton "Mickey," "Mick the Quick" (b. October 31, 1948, Miami, FL), player and coach, attended Miami-Dade CC and signed with the Atlanta Braves (NL) in June 1969. He dubbed himself "Mickey" after his idol, Mickey Mantle.* In September 1969, the Atlanta Braves traded Rivers to the California Angels (AL). He was promoted to the California Angels in September 1970 and split the next three seasons between the Angels and Salt Lake City, UT (PCL). Rivers became a California regular in 1974, when he batted .285, led the AL with 11 triples, and stole 30 bases. His 70 stolen bases in 1975 surpassed all AL players since 1915. He also defended his triples crown with 13. Nonetheless, the California Angels traded Rivers to the New York Yankees (AL) in December 1975.

Rivers possessed habits that endeared him to fans but exasperated managers and teammates. He limped to the plate like an arthritis patient and annoyed pitchers with his deliberate pre-batting rituals. Rivers wasted little time at the plate, walking only 266 times in 5,629 at-bats. He gave unflattering nicknames to teammates and opponents alike. Critics claimed he preferred the race track to the baseball diamond.

But speed made Rivers a superb center fielder and compensated for his lack of plate discipline. He only struck out 471 times and hit into just 44 double plays, the third best lifetime percentage for avoiding twin killings. In 1976, he hit .312, stole 43 bases, helped the New York Yankees win their first AL pennant since 1964, and was named the team's MVP.

In 1977, the New York Yankees won the World Series against the Los Angeles Dodgers. Rivers contributed significantly to the team's success and to the turmoil that writers dubbed the "Bronx Zoo." Although Rivers hit .326, some teammates considered the "injuries" that reduced his stolen bases to 22 imaginary. He drew numerous salary advances to cover alleged losses at the track and enjoyed baiting Reggie Jackson.* But Rivers hit .391 in the AL Championship Series and drove in the winning run against the Kansas City Royals in the deciding fifth game.

Tax and marital problems dogged Rivers in 1978. Manager Billy Martin* blasted him when his plate production dropped. The New York Yankees slumped in 1979 and traded the mercurial Rivers to the Texas Rangers (AL) in August.

In 1980, Rivers achieved career highs in batting (.333), runs (96), hits (210), doubles (32), and on-base percentage (.355). His 24-game hitting streak broke the Texas Rangers record. He also missed games for unspecified ailments, lobbied to be a DH, poked fun at his manager, asked to be returned to the Yankees, and drew numerous salary advances. Injuries robbed him of his speed, relegating him to part-time status after 1981. In 1985, the Texas Rangers released him. He finished with a .295 lifetime average, 61 HR, 499 RBI, 267 stolen bases, and a .982 fielding percentage.

In 1969, Rivers married Sheralyn Givens and had two children before their divorce. He also fathered a child born to Angela Martinez. The Miami resident worked with the Dade County Recreation Department helping youngsters and in 1995 served as a spring training coach and instructor for the New York Yankees.

BIBLIOGRAPHY: Franz Lidz, "Ol' Man Rivers," *SI* 72 (January 29, 1990), pp. 36–38; Mickey Rivers file, National Baseball Library, Cooperstown, NY; "Mickey Rivers," *Microsoft Complete Baseball*, CD-ROM (Redmond, WA, 1993); David Neft and Richard Cohen, eds., *The Sports Encyclopedia: Baseball 1997*, 17th ed. (New York, 1997); Ross Newhan, *The California Angels* (New York, 1982); Mark Gallagher, *The Yankee Encyclopedia*, vol. 3 (Champaign, IL, 1997); Reggie Jackson and Mike Lupica, *Reggie* (New York, 1984); Sparky Lyle and Peter Golenbock, *The Bronx Zoo* (New York, 1979); Phil Rogers, *The Impossible Takes a Little Longer* (Dallas, TX, 1991).

Robert E. Weir

RIXEY, Eppa, Jr. "Eppa Jephtha" (b. May 3, 1891, Culpeper, VA; d. February 28, 1963, Cincinnati, OH), player, was the son of banker Eppa Rixey, Sr., and Willie Alice (Walton) Rixey. He attended grade school in Culpeper and moved with his family at age 11 to Charlottesville, VA. He attended high school in Charlottesville and enrolled at the University of Virginia, where he played baseball. In 1912, the left-handed Rixey moved directly from college to the Philadelphia Phillies (NL) without playing in the minor leagues. From 1912 to 1920, he won 87 games and lost 103 for the Phillies. He joined the Cincinnati Reds (NL) in February 1921 and won 179 and lost 148 over the next 13 seasons. During his 21-year major league career, he compiled 266 wins and 251 losses for a 3.15 ERA. In the 1915 World Series, he lost his only decision to the Boston Red Sox.

Rixey appeared in 692 games, starting 553 and completing 290. He pitched 4,494.2 innings, gave up 4,633 hits, walked 1,082, struck out 1,350, and threw 37 shutouts. In relief appearances, he won 20, lost 17, and saved 14. These accomplishments place him among the most successful pitchers in baseball history. Rixey's 6-foot 5-inch, 210-pound frame, reliable pitching strength, and strange name made him a fan favorite. Although many references cite his full name as Eppa Jephtha (or Jeptha) Rixey, Jr., "Jephtha" was probably invented by a Cincinnati sportswriter. Rixey's 21 seasons set a longevity record among NL left-handers until Steve Carlton* broke it in 1986. In 1969, Cincinnati fans named Rixey the Reds' most outstanding left-hander. On October 29, 1924, he married Dorothy Meyers; they had two children. From his retirement until his death, Rixey managed a successful insurance business in Cincinnati, OH. He was elected to the National Baseball Hall of Fame in 1963, one month before his death.

BIBLIOGRAPHY: Eppa Rixey, Jr. file, National Baseball Library, Cooperstown, NY; Floyd Connor and John Snyder, *Day-by-Day in Cincinnati Reds History* (West Point, NY, 1984); Bob Rathgeber, *Cincinnati Reds Scrapbook* (Virginia Beach, VA, 1982); Connie Wheeler and John Baskin, *The Cincinnati Game* (Wilmington, OH, 1988); Martin Appel and Burt Goldblatt, *Baseball's Best: The Hall of Fame Gallery* (New York, 1977); Danny Diehl, "Eppa Rixey—Culpeper Baseball Hall of Fame," Culpeper (VA) *News,* July 21, 1983; Lee Allen, *The Cincinnati Reds* (New York, 1948); David Driver, "Eppa Rixey," *TNP* 15 (1995), pp. 85–87; Frederick G. Lieb and Stan Baumgartner, *The Philadelphia Phillies* (New York, 1953); Rich Westcott and Frank Bilovsky, *The New Phillies Encyclopedia* (Philadelphia, PA, 1993); Allen Lewis, *The Philadelphia Phillies: A Pictorial History* (Virginia Beach, VA, 1981); Allen Lewis and Larry Shenk, *This Date in Philadelphia Phillies History* (New York, 1979); Ritter Collett, *The Cincinnati Reds* (Virginia Beach, VA, 1976); Randy Hask and Linda Queen, "Eppa Jeptha Rixey" (photocopied), Culpeper High School, Culpeper, VA, n.d.; Gene Karst and Martin J. Jones, Jr., *Who's Who in Professional Baseball* (New Rochelle, NY, 1973); *The Baseball Encyclopedia,* 10th ed. (New York, 1996); Robert Weaver, correspondence with Guinn, August 26, 1983, Robert G. Weaver Collection, Petersburg, PA.

Robert G. Weaver

RIZZUTO, Philip Francis "Phil," "Scooter" (b. September 25, 1917, New York, NY), player and sportscaster, is the son of Fiero Francis Rizzuto, trolley car conductor, and Rose (Angotti) Rizzuto. He attended Richmond Hill (NY) High School, where he starred as a third baseman and football quarterback. Rizzuto dropped out of school at age 16 to play baseball and received his diploma in 1948 as special recognition of his diamond success. Paul Krichell, Rizzuto's high school baseball coach, arranged several tryouts for him. Brooklyn Dodgers (NL) manager Casey Stengel* rejected the short, 5-foot 6-inch, 150-pound Rizzuto and told him, "Go get a shoebox!" The New York Yankees (AL) signed him and assigned him to Bassett, VA (BSL) in 1937. With Kansas City, MO (AA) in 1939, the right-handed Rizzuto teamed with second baseman Jerry Priddy* to form "the Heavenly Twins." Teammate Billy Hitchcock nicknamed him "Scooter" for his swift motion from shortstop to second base. Rizzuto led the AA with 35 stolen bases and was named Minor League Player of the Year in 1940.

Rizzuto, who joined New York Yankees (AL) in 1941, married Cora Esselborn on June 24, 1943 and has three daughters. The deeply religious Rizzuto was plagued with sickness and injuries most of his career. He suffered many head injuries, the most serious being a 1946 beaning by Nelson Potter of the St. Louis Browns. Dizzy spells, ulcers, and malaria later developed from his U.S. Navy stint during World War II. In 1950, he hit .324 and was named the AL's MVP. He played in five All-Star games (1942, 1950–1953) and led AL shortstops in putouts (1942, 1950), assists (1952), fielding average (1949–1950), and double plays (1941–1942, 1952). An outstanding bunter, he paced the AL from 1949 to 1953 in sacrifice bunts.

With the Yankees through 1956, Rizzuto hit .273 in 1,661 games, made 1,588 hits, slugged 239 doubles, 62 triples, and 38 HR, scored 877 runs, knocked in 563 runs, and stole 149 bases. In nine World Series, he hit .246 in 52 games, made two HR, knocked in 8 runs, and walked 30 times. Rizzuto, who lives in Hillside, NJ, broadcast for the New York Yankees from 1956 to 1997. His infectious enthusiasm is evident in his characteristic expression, "Holy Cow." He was awarded a Doctor of Humane Letters honorary degree from Hofstra University in April 1995 and was elected to the National Baseball Hall of Fame in 1994.

BIBLIOGRAPHY: Maury Allen, *Baseball's 100* (New York, 1981); *CB* (July 1950), pp. 494–496; Dom Forker, *Sweet Seasons* (Dallas, TX, 1991); Dom Forker, *The Men of Autumn* (Dallas, TX, 1989); David Halberstam, *Summer of '49* (New York, 1989); Gene Karst and Martin J. Jones, Jr., *Who's Who in Professional Baseball* (New York, 1973); Brent P. Kelley, *Baseball Stars of the 1950s* (Jefferson, NC, 1993); Dave Anderson et al., *The Yankees* (New York, 1979); Tim Cohane, *Look* 14 (May 9, 1950), p. 80; Tim Cohane, "Scooter Is Still Scooting," *Look* 22 (August 5, 1958), pp. 31–32; Richard Marazzi and Len Fiorito, *Aaron to Zuverink* (New York, 1982); "Professor Rizzuto's Baseball Academy," *RD* (March 1953), pp. 26–28; Ira Berkow, "Too Small to Play, Right Size for Hall," *NYT Biographical Service* 25 (July 1994), pp. 1143–1145; Robert Obojski, " 'Joltin' Joe Goes Back to the Show," *SCD* 21 (December 9, 1994), pp. 156–157; Robert W. Creamer, *Stengel: His Life and Times* (New York, 1984); Mark Gallagher, *The Yankee Encyclopedia*, vol. 3 (Champaign, IL, 1997); Phil Rizzuto file, National Baseball Library, Cooperstown, NY; Joe Reichler, *Inside the Majors* (New York, 1952); Harold Rosenthal, *Lucky He's Still a Yankee* (New York, 1953); "Scooter Spared," *Time* (April 14, 1941), p. 14; Gene Shoor, *The Scooter* (New York, 1982); Joe Trimble, *Phil Rizzuto* (New York, 1951); *WWA*, 41st ed. (1980–1981), p. 2785; V. Ziegel, "Little Phil," *NY* 23 (December 24–31, 1990), p. 91.

William A. Borst

ROBERTS, Robin Evan (b. September 30, 1926, Springfield, IL), player and coach, was a sturdy right-handed pitching star for 19 major league seasons.

Roberts played with the Philadelphia Phillies (NL 1948–1961), Baltimore Orioles (AL 1962–1965), and Houston Astros (NL 1965–1966) and Chicago Cubs (NL 1966–1967). His father, Tom Roberts, a Welsh coal miner, and his mother, Sarah Roberts, came to the United States from England in 1921. One of five children, Roberts grew up in the Springfield, IL area and became interested in sports. An accomplished high school basketball player, he was offered a scholarship at Michigan State University. When World War II intervened, he served as a U.S. Army Air Force flying cadet (1944–1945).

After his discharge in 1945, Roberts enrolled at Michigan State University and earned a Bachelor of Science degree in physical education there. At Michigan State, his interest and talent in baseball began blossoming. He pitched two no-hitters, including one against the University of Michigan, then coached by former big league pitcher Ray Fisher. Fisher spent his summers managing the Montpelier, VT team in a semipro league that used college players who desired to have professional status. In 1946, Roberts began spending his summers with Fisher and within two years attracted the attention of major league scouts. Five clubs—the Boston Braves (NL), Philadelphia Phillies (NL), Boston Red Sox (AL), Detroit Tigers (AL), and New York Yankees (AL)—offered him contracts. The $25,000 bonus given by the Philadelphia Phillies proved the persuading factor. He was sent to Wilmington, DE, the Phillies' ISL farm team.

Roberts soon demonstrated that he pitched too well for the ISL. By the middle of June, he had started 11 games and compiled a 9–1 record. On June 17, 1948, he joined the Philadelphia Phillies. The next day, Roberts lost his first major league game, 2–0, to the Pittsburgh Pirates, but pitched well and allowed only five hits. In his next appearance, he defeated the Cincinnati Reds for his first major league victory. After a 7–9 record his first year, he finished 15–15 in 1949. In 1950 he achieved the first of six consecutive 20–win seasons, narrowly missing a seventh (19) in 1956. Roberts led the NL in games started six times, complete games, innings pitched and hits surrendered five times, wins four times, strikeouts twice, and shutouts once. Over the ensuing years, he amassed 286 career wins, 245 losses, and a 3.41 ERA.

Roberts starred as a pitcher on the 1950 NL pennant-winning Phillies "Whiz Kids." He earned the NL pennant-clinching win with his 20th win of the year in the final game against the Brooklyn Dodgers. In the World Series against the New York Yankees, he lost his only start by 2–1 in ten innings. Over the years, Roberts became a control pitcher, walking only 902 batters in 4,688.2 innings or an average of one every five to six innings. Since good control reduces the anxiety index, batters tagged him 502 times for HR, a major league record.

The years 1959–1960 saw a decline in his pitching effectiveness. His dismal 1–10 record in 1961 ended his usefulness to the Phillies. He was sold to the New York Yankees (AL) in October 1961 and trained with them in 1962. On May 21, the Baltimore Orioles (AL) picked him up. Roberts enjoyed over three good seasons with Baltimore, winning 42 and losing 36. When the Orioles released him in July 1965, he signed with the Houston Astros (NL) and logged a 5–2 record. A year later, he captured only three of eight decisions for the Astros before being released. Roberts completed his major league career with the Chicago Cubs (NL) in 1966, posting a 2–3 mark in 11 games. The following year (1967) was supposed to be a rehabilitation one with Reading, PA (EL), but persistent arm trouble ended his hopes of returning to the major leagues.

Roberts married Mary Ann Kaines in December 1949 and has four sons. He participated in the MLBPAA and made significant contributions to the welfare of players. Roberts won *TSN* Pitcher of the Year Award in 1952 and 1955. In 13 of his 19 years, he was elected as opening game pitcher. Roberts appeared in five All-Star games and was elected to the National Baseball Hall of Fame in 1976. He coached baseball at the University of South Florida and served as coordinator of minor league instruction for the Philadelphia Phillies in the late 1980s.

BIBLIOGRAPHY: Robin Roberts file, National Baseball Library, Cooperstown, NY; Rich Westcott and Frank Bilovsky, *The New Phillies Encyclopedia* (Philadelphia, PA, 1993); Frederick G. Lieb and Stan Baumgartner, *The Philadelphia Phillies* (New York, 1953); Allen Lewis, *The Philadelphia Phillies: A Pictorial History* (Virginia Beach, VA, 1981); Allen Lewis and Larry Shenk, *This Date in Philadelphia Phillies History* (New York, 1979); Martin Appel and Burt Goldblatt, *Baseball's Best: The Hall of Fame Gallery* (New York, 1977); Donald Honig, *Baseball Between the Lines* (New York, 1976); Robin Roberts and C. Paul Rogers III, *The Whiz Kids and the 1950 Pennant* (Philadelphia, PA, 1997); Harry Paxton, *The Whiz Kids* (New York, 1950); *The Baseball Encyclopedia*, 10th ed. (New York, 1996).

                                                                    Robert G. Weaver

ROBINSON, Brooks Calbert, Jr. (b. May 18, 1937, Little Rock, AR), player, coach, sportscaster, and executive, is the son of fireman Brooks Calbert Robinson, Sr., and Ethel Mae (Denker) Robinson. In 1955, he signed for a $4,000 bonus with the Baltimore Orioles (AL) immediately upon graduation from Little Rock Central High School. Although primarily a third baseman, Robinson also played second base and shortstop early in his career. He played a portion of four of his first five seasons (1955–1959) with minor league clubs in York, PA (PiL), San Antonio, TX (TL), and Vancouver, Canada (PCL). The balance of each season he played with the Baltimore Orioles. At 180 pounds, the 6-foot 1-inch Robinson slugged at least 20 HR on six occasions and 268 career HR. He batted over .300 and knocked in over 100 runs twice each. He won the AL's MVP Award in 1964, when he slugged 28 HR, led the AL with 118 RBI, and batted .317. In 2,896 games, he batted .267, made 2,848 hits, 482 doubles, and 68 triples, scored 1,232 runs, and knocked in 1,357 runs.

The right-handed Robinson became the premier AL third baseman for most of his career. He topped the AL's third basemen in fielding average from 1960 through 1964, 1966 through 1969, and in 1972 and 1975. Frequently, he also paced his position in assists and double plays. He ranks as the major league career leader at his position in total chances (9,165), double plays (618), assists (6,205), putouts (2,697), and fielding average (.971), and won twelve Gold Glove awards. Robinson participated in four World Series with the Orioles, helping them win world championships in 1966 over the Los Angeles Dodgers and in 1970 over the Cincinnati Reds. He starred in the 1966 and 1967 All-Star games, making three hits in the former and homering for the only AL run in the latter. Perennially Robinson made third base on the AL All-Star teams. In 1970, he was selected as Hickok Professional Athlete of the Year.

Robinson, who retired in 1977 after 23 major league seasons, ranks among the best third basemen in baseball history. In 1983, he was elected to the National Baseball Hall of Fame in his first year of eligibility. He coached for the Baltimore Orioles in 1977 and served as a television color analyst for Oriole games. He belongs to the board of directors of the National Baseball Hall of Fame and presides over the 2,500 member MLBPAA. He made Major League Baseball's All-Century Team. Robinson married Constance Louise Butcher in October 1960 and has three sons and one daughter.

BIBLIOGRAPHY: Brooks Robinson file, National Baseball Library, Cooperstown, NY; Brooks Robinson with Fred Baver, *Putting it All Together* (New York, 1971); Ted Patterson, *The Baltimore Orioles* (Dallas, TX, 1995); James H. Bready, *Baseball in Baltimore* (Baltimore, MD, 1998); Mike Bryan, "Baseball Lives," *SI* 70 (April 24, 1989), pp. 78ff; Thomas Boswell, *The Baseball Hall of Fame 50th Anniversary Book* (New York, 1988); *CB* (1973), pp. 361–363; *The Baseball Encyclopedia*, 10th ed. (New York, 1996); Gordon Beard, *Birds on the Wing* (Garden City, NY, 1967); Ted Patterson, *Day-by-Day in Orioles History* (New York, 1984); Lowell Reidenbaugh, *Baseball's Hall of Fame—Cooperstown* (New York, 1993); Donald Honig, *Baseball's Ten Greatest Teams* (New York, 1982); Brooks Robinson, "World Series: The Human Vacuum Cleaner," *SI* 83 (October 23, 1995), pp. 51–54; Rich Westcott, *Diamond Greats* (Westport, CT, 1988); C. Richard McKelvey, *Fisk's Homer, Willie's Catch and the Shot Heard 'Round the World* (Jefferson, NC, 1998); Jack Zanger, *The Brooks Robinson Story* (New York, 1967).

Stephen D. Bodayla

ROBINSON, Cornelius Randall "Neil," "Shadow" (b. July 7, 1908, Grand Rapids, MI), player, started his baseball career in 1934 with the Homestead, PA Grays (NNL), but a severe drinking problem limited his time. He signed with the Cincinnati Tigers in 1936 and launched his career with a robust .367 batting average. Two years later manager Ted "Double Duty" Radcliffe* took him to the Memphis, TN Red Sox (NAL). Memphis captured the first-half title in the NAL's 1938 split season. An All-Star outfielder with the Memphis Red Sox, he appeared in eight East-West All-Star games between 1938 and 1948. In the mid-season classic, the 5-foot 11-inch, 182 pounder hit .476 with an .810 slugging percentage and two crucial HR. His inside-the-park, three-run HR helped the West to a 5–4 victory in 1938, while his HR keyed the West's 4–2 victory in 1939. Prior to the 1939 contest, he was photographed with heavyweight boxing champion Joe Louis (IS). Louis threw out the ceremonial first ball.

Robinson stayed with the Memphis Red Sox for the remainder of his career through 1952, but his club never won another championship. In 1939, he led the NAL with 54 HR. Robinson also captured the 1940 HR title and played in the 1940–1941 PRWL. Upon his return to Memphis, he continued his consistent hitting in the middle of the batting order for the Red Sox. Robinson batted .314 in 1942 and .319 in 1944, finishing second in the NAL in both HR and stolen bases. After batting .303 in 1945, he recorded batting marks of .290, .333, .272, and .283 from 1947 to 1950. Although the NAL declined to minor league status in 1951, he played two more seasons with the Memphis Red Sox.

BIBLIOGRAPHY: *Afro-American*, 1934–1937; Chicago (IL) *Defender*, 1938–1949; Kansas City (MO) *Call*, 1938–1948; Memphis (TN) *Commercial Appeal*, 1938–1948; Robert W. Peterson, *Only the Ball Was White* (Englewood Cliffs, NJ, 1970); Philadelphia (PA) *Tribune*, 1934–1937; Pittsburgh (PA) *Courier*, 1934–1937; James A. Riley, *The All-Time All-Stars of Black Baseball* (Canton, GA 1983); James A. Riley, *The Biographical Encyclopedia of the Negro Baseball Leagues* (New York, 1994); James A. Riley, interviews with former Negro League players, James A. Riley Collection, Canton, GA; *The Baseball Encyclopedia*, 10th ed. (New York, 1996).

                                                                    James A. Riley

ROBINSON, Frank (b. August 31, 1935, Beaumont, TX), player, coach, manager, executive, and sportscaster, is the son of Frank and Ruth (Shaw) Robinson. One of ten children, Robinson attended school in Oakland, CA and excelled in baseball there. He played on the Oakland American Legion team, winners of consecutive national titles in 1949 and 1950. Following high school graduation in 1953, the right-handed Robinson signed with the Cincinnati Reds (NL) and played for Ogden, UT (PrL), Tulsa, OK (TL), and Columbia, SC (SAL) between 1953 and 1955. After joining the Reds in 1956, Robinson led the NL in runs scored and tied a major league record by hitting 38 HR as a rookie. In 1959, he batted for the cycle and belted three HR in one game. The 6-foot 1-inch, 194-pound Robinson, who was an outfielder–first baseman for Cincinnati from 1956 to 1965, won NL Rookie of the Year honors in 1956 and the NL MVP Award in 1961. Besides helping the Reds win the NL pennant in 1961, Robinson led the NL in slugging percentage (1960–1962) and runs scored, doubles, and on base percentage (1962).

Robinson was traded to the Baltimore Orioles (AL) in December 1965 and the next year became one of just 11 players to win baseball's Triple

Crown. He paced the AL in HR (49), RBI (122), and runs scored (122), and compiled a .316 batting average. He also led the AL in on base (.415) and slugging (.637) percentage. Selected as the AL's MVP, he became the only player to achieve this feat in both leagues. In 1970, Robinson tied a major league record by slugging grand slam HR in two successive times at bat. Robinson helped the Orioles win four AL pennants (1966, 1969–1971) and two world championships (1966, 1970) and was selected as the MVP in the 1966 World Series. In 26 World Series games, Robinson collected 23 hits, 8 HR, 14 RBI, and a .250 batting average. Robinson performed in 11 All-Star games and was named the MVP in the 1971 classic. He belted a two-run HR for the AL, making him the only player in All-Star competition to hit a HR for each league. After playing with the Los Angeles Dodgers (NL) in 1972, California Angels (AL) in 1973, and Cleveland Indians (AL) in 1974, Robinson in 1975 was chosen Indians player–manager and became the first black major league manager. Replaced in 1977, he then piloted Rochester, NY (IL) in 1978 and coached for the Baltimore Orioles (1979–1980). He was named manager of the San Francisco Giants (NL) in 1981 and guided them to third place in 1982, earning NL Manager of the Year honors, but was dismissed during the 1984 season. Robinson coached for the Baltimore Orioles from 1985 through 1987 and piloted them from 1988 through 1991. His highest finish (second place) came in 1989, when his club compiled an 87–75 record. As a major league manager, he piloted his teams to 680 wins and 751 losses. He served as assistant to the general manager of the Baltimore Orioles from 1992 to 1995 and as a color analyst for Fox-TV Sports.

In his 21-year major league playing career, Robinson batted at least .300 nine times, knocked in 100 or more runs six times, clouted 30 or more HR eleven times, belted two or more HR in one game 54 times, and scored at least 100 runs eight times. On the all-time major league lists, Robinson ranks high in nearly all statistical categories. He played in 2,808 games (15th), scored 1,829 runs (10th), and collected 2,943 hits (24th), 528 doubles (22nd), 72 triples, 586 HR (4th), 1,812 RBI (15th), and 5,373 total bases (8th). Robinson received 1,420 bases on balls (19th), struck out 1,532 times (17th), compiled a .537 slugging average (20th), and batted .294 lifetime. Robinson married Barbara Ann Cole in 1961 and has one son, Frank Kevin, and one daughter, Michelle. The co-author of *My Life in Baseball*, Robinson in 1982 was elected to the National Baseball Hall of Fame and became only the 13th player to achieve this honor in the first year of eligibility.

BIBLIOGRAPHY: Frank Robinson file, National Baseball Library, Cooperstown, NY; John Benson, *Baseball's Top 100* (Wilton, CT, 1997); Donald Honig, *The Power Hitters* (St. Louis, MO, 1989); David L. Porter, ed., *African-American Sports Greats* (Westport, CT, 1995); Phil Jackman, "Orioles' Rivals Celebrating the Departure of F. Robby," *TSN*, December 18, 1971, p. 50; Frank Robinson and Berry Stainback, "Fighting the Baseball Blackout," *Sport* 79 (July 1988), pp. 66–67; Frank Robinson and Berry Stainback, *Extra Innings* (New York, 1988); Lowell Reidenbaugh, *Baseball's*

Hall of Fame—Cooperstown (New York, 1993); Donald Honig, *The Cincinnati Reds* (New York, 1992); Jim Brosnan, *Pennant Race* (New York, 1962); Bob Rathgeber, *Cincinnati Reds Scrapbook* (Virginia Beach, VA, 1982); Ted Patterson, *The Baltimore Orioles* (Dallas, TX, 1995); Larry Moffi and Jonathan Kronstadt, *Crossing the Line* (Jefferson, NC, 1994); John Thorn et al., eds., *Total Indians* (New York, 1996); Jack Torry, *Endless Summers* (South Bend, IN, 1995); Terry Pluto, *The Curse of Rocky Colavito* (New York, 1994); Nick Peters, *Giants Almanac* (Berkeley, CA, 1988); Donald Honig, *Baseball's Ten Greatest Teams* (New York, 1982); James H. Bready, *Baseball in Baltimore* (Baltimore, MD, 1998), Ted Patterson, *Day by Day in Orioles History* (New York, 1984); Roslyn A. Mazur, "Frank Robinson Inspires Oriole Magic," *TNP* 11 (1992), pp. 77–79; John Thom, *Champion Batsman of the 20th Century* (Los Angeles, CA, 1992); *TSN Official Baseball Record Book 1998* (St. Louis, 1998); *TSN Official Baseball Register 1991.*

John L. Evers

ROBINSON, Jack Roosevelt "Jackie" (b. January 31, 1919, Cairo, GA; d. October 24, 1972, Stamford, CT), player and all-around athlete, was the first black to play baseball in the modern major leagues and the youngest child of sharecropper Jerry Robinson and Mallie (McGriff) Robinson. After his father deserted the family in 1920, his mother moved her five children to Pasadena, CA. Robinson's athletic versatility allowed him to escape an impoverished life. After excelling at track and field, baseball, football, basketball, and tennis at Muir Technical High School, the 5-foot 11½-inch, 195-pound right-hander starred in baseball at Pasadena JC and in baseball, basketball, and football at UCLA. In 1941, financial pressures forced Robinson to leave UCLA without earning a degree. After playing professional football briefly, he enlisted in the U.S. Army in 1942 and the next year was commissioned a second lieutenant. Robinson's opposition to racial discrimination led to a court martial for insubordination and subsequent acquittal. In November 1944, he was honorably discharged.

Robinson's stellar play as a $400-a-month second baseman with the 1945 Kansas City, MO Monarchs of the segregated NAL excited the interest of Clyde Sukeforth, who scouted the black major leagues for Brooklyn Dodgers (NL) president Branch Rickey.* A brilliant baseball innovator, Rickey knew that the changing social climate must soon end major league baseball's segregation policy. Despite hostile colleagues, Rickey signed Robinson to a Dodgers contract and made him a *cause célèbre* in integrating major league baseball. In 1946, Robinson paced the IL in batting and led the Montreal, Canada Royals (IL) to the Little World Series championship. After promotion to the Brooklyn Dodgers in 1947, Robinson played first base and maintained a docile posture amidst controversy surrounding his presence. By batting .297 and leading the NL in stolen bases (29), Robinson won Rookie of the Year honors and helped the Dodgers win the NL pennant. In 1949, he captured the NL batting championship (.342) and the NL's MVP Award as a second baseman. The admission of other black players enabled pathfinder Robinson to change his docile posture. An aggressive team leader and perennial All Star, he outspokenly advocated integrated baseball. His sallies against continuing discrimination caused some to label him a troublemaker.

From 1947 to 1956 with the Dodgers, he compiled a .311 batting average and helped his club win six NL pennants (1947, 1949, 1952–1953, 1955–1956) and a world title (1955). In 1962, sportswriters voted him into the National Baseball Hall of Fame. In 1,382 major league games, he made 1,518 hits, slugged 273 doubles, 54 triples, and 137 HR, scored 947 runs, knocked in 734 runs, and stole 197 bases. From 1956 to 1972, Robinson pursued business interests and fought for broader participation and civil rights for black Americans. As a vice-president of Chock Full o' Nuts Company, he hired many blacks. Four semi-autobiographical books appeared disclosing Robinson's changing views of his quest to integrate baseball. Robinson concluded that he had done little for himself and his people as a black man "who never had it made" in a white world. When Robinson died of heart disease in 1972, he was afforded a hero's funeral. Robinson was extolled as an authentic All-American "who made a memorable impact for good in his country and his time." The nationally acclaimed pathfinder paved the way for black American and dusky Hispanic players, whose batting feats dominated baseball's early expansion era. In February 1946 he married Rachel Isum of Los Angeles; they had three children, two of whom survived him. On April 15, 1997, major league baseball celebrated the 50th anniversary of Robinson's debut with the Dodgers and officially retired his uniform number 42 from baseball. He made Major League Baseball's All-Century Team and ranked 15th among ESPN's top century athletes.

BIBLIOGRAPHY: Maury Allen, *Jackie Robinson* (New York, 1987); David Falkner, *Great Time Coming* (New York, 1995); Brad Herzog, *The Sports 100* (New York, 1995); Tot Holmes, *Jackie 1947* (Gothenburg, NE, 1997); Roger Kahn, *The Boys of Summer* (New York, 1972); David Halberstam, "Jackie Robinson," *Sport* 77 (December 1986), pp. 10–14; Roger Kahn, "The Ten Years of Jackie Robinson," *Sport* 82 (October 1991), pp. 67–69; Jack Robinson and Alfred Duckett, *Breakthrough to the Big Leagues* (New York, 1965); Arnold Rampersad, *Jackie Robinson* (New York, 1997); Jack Robinson with Alfred Duckett, *I Never Had It Made* (New York, 1972); Jack Robinson with Bill Roeder, *Jackie Robinson* (New York, 1950); Jack Robinson and Carl T. Rowan, *Wait Till Next Year* (New York, 1960); Jack Robinson and Wendell Smith, *Jackie Robinson* (New York, 1948); Jackie Robinson with Charles Dexter, *Baseball Has Done It* (Philadelphia, PA, 1964); Rachel Robinson with Lee Daniels, *Jackie Robinson* (New York, 1996); Sharon Robinson, *Stealing Home* (New York, 1996); Barbara Carlisle Bigelow, ed., *Contemporary Black Biography*, vol. 6 (Detroit, MI, 1994); Larry Moffi and Jonathan Kronstadt, *Crossing the Line* (Jefferson, NC, 1994); Roger Angell, "Designated Hero," *NY* 73 (September 15, 1997), pp. 82–88; S. E. Hyman, "The Other Jackie Robinson," *NLe* 80 (April 21, 1997), pp. 8–16; R. Jerome, "Man on Fire," *PW* 47 (April 28, 1997), pp. 71–74; B. Kashatus, "Baseball's Noble Experiment," *AHI* 32 (March/April 1997), pp. 32–37; W. Leavy, "The 50th Anniversary of the Jackie Robinson Revolution," *Ebony* 52 (April 1997), pp. 87–90; A. S. Young, "Jackie Robinson Remembered," *Ebony* 52 (February 1997), pp. 103ff; Frank Deford, "Crossing the Bar," *Newsweek* 129 (April 14, 1997), pp. 52–55; John Thorn and Jules Tygiel, "The Signing of Jackie Robinson, the Untold Story," *Sport* 79 (June 1988); pp. 65–66; Roger Kahn, "Jackie Robinson" in *The Baseball Hall of Fame 50th Anniversary Book* (New York, 1988); John Thorn and Jules Tygiel, "Signing Jackie Robinson," *TNP* 10 (1990), pp. 7–12; William F. McNeil, *The Dodgers Encyclopedia* (Champaign, IL, 1997); Richard Goldstein, *Superstars and Screwballs* (New York, 1991); Peter Golenbock, *Bums* (New York, 1984); Stanley Cohen, *Dodgers! The First 100 Years* (New York, 1990); Tommy Holmes, *The Dodgers* (New York, 1975); John Thom, *Champion Batsman of the 20th Century* (Los Angeles, CA, 1992); Jules Tygiel, *Baseball's Great Experiment* (New York, 1983); David Q. Voigt, *American Baseball*, vol. 3 (University Park, PA, 1983); Jackie Robinson file, National Baseball Library, Cooperstown, NY.

David Q. Voigt

ROBINSON, Wilbert "Uncle Robbie" (b. June 29, 1863, Boston, MA; d. August 8, 1934, Atlanta, GA), player, coach, manager, and executive, was the son of butcher Henry Robinson and Lucy Robinson and the younger brother of Fred Robinson, who played with the Cincinnati Outlaw Reds (UA) in 1884. "Uncle Robbie," a Falstaffian figure with sound baseball knowledge, attended only the first few grades of the Hudson, MA public schools. Robinson's limited education hampered him as a baseball manager. As pilot of the Brooklyn Robins (NL) in the 1920s, Robinson removed Oscar Roettger from his lineup because he could not spell his name.

The 5-foot 8½-inch, 215-pound right-hander began his professional baseball career with the Philadelphia Athletics (AA) in 1886 and caught with the Athletics until 1890, when he joined the Baltimore Orioles (AA). He stayed with the Baltimore Orioles when the team moved to the NL the following season. With manager Ned Hanlon's* team, Robinson befriended John McGraw.* In February 1900, the Orioles traded both players to the St. Louis Cardinals (NL). Robinson in 1901 returned to Baltimore, now in the AL under player–manager McGraw, and played there through the 1902 season. In 1902, he managed the Baltimore Orioles to a 22–54 record. During the 1903 and 1904 seasons, Robinson caught for Baltimore, MD (EL). A broken hand forced him to retire at age 40.

His impressive National Baseball Hall of Fame (1945) statistics include his batting .273 in 1,371 games, making 1,388 hits, slugging 212 doubles, 51 triples, and 18 HR, scoring 637 runs, knocking in 722 runs, and stealing 196 bases. He hit at least .300 four times, peaking with .353 in 109 games in 1894. On June 19, 1892, Robinson set a major league record (since tied by Pittsburgh's Rennie Stennett) by making hits in all seven at-bats in a nine-inning game. After working seven years in his father's butcher shop, Robinson joined the New York Giants (NL) as a coach under McGraw. Robinson coached them from 1911 to 1913, but a bitter argument with manager McGraw over a missed sign caused him to join the Brooklyn Robins (NL) as manager in 1914.

Robinson managed the Robins 18 seasons, guiding his players to NL pennants in 1916 and 1920 and to a 1,399–1,398 (.500 winning percentage) career mark. Since Robinson was one of the most popular Brooklyn figures ever, the team was renamed the Robins in 1914. Robinson excelled at developing pitching talent, but proved a very lax disciplinarian. His players played cards or caroused all night and openly read newspapers on the bench. Robinson hoped to eliminate stupid plays by instituting the "Bonehead Club," but became its first and last member when he posted the wrong lineup card. In 1915, Robinson set the tone for the "Daffy Dodgers" by boasting that he could catch a baseball thrown from a plane. Madcap Casey Stengel* substituted a grapefruit that exploded on impact, causing Robinson to think momentarily that he had been killed.

Robinson served as the president of the Brooklyn Dodgers from 1926 to 1929 and held a similar post with the Atlanta, GA Crackers (SA) from 1933 until his death from a stroke in 1934. His first wife died in the early 1890s. He married Mary O'Rourke in the mid-1890s and had one daughter and two sons.

BIBLIOGRAPHY: Noel Hynd, *The Giants of the Polo Grounds* (New York, 1988); Charles C. Alexander, *John McGraw* (New York, 1988); James H. Bready, *Baseball in Baltimore* (Baltimore, MD, 1998); Peter Golenbock, *Bums* (New York, 1984); William F. McNeil, *The Dodgers Encyclopedia* (Champaign, IL, 1997); Tommy Holmes, *The Dodgers* (New York, 1975); Stanley Cohen, *Dodgers! The First 100 Years* (New York, 1990); Frank Graham, *The Brooklyn Dodgers* (New York, 1945); Richard Goldstein, *Superstars and Screwballs* (New York, 1991); Thomas Aylesworth and Benton Minks, *The Encyclopedia of Baseball Managers* (New York, 1990); Wilbert Robinson file, National Baseball Library, Cooperstown, NY; Frederick Ivor-Campbell et al., eds., *Baseball's First Stars* (Cleveland, OH, 1996); Gene Karst and Martin J. Jones, Jr., *Who's Who in Professional Baseball* (New Rochelle, NY, 1973); Jack Kavanagh, "An Appreciation of Uncle Robbie," *TNP* 12 (1997), pp. 88–90; Tom Knight, "Uncle Robbie and Hugh Casey," *BRJ* 22 (1993), pp. 105–106; Craig Carter, ed., *TSN Daguerreotypes*, 8th ed. (St. Louis, MO, 1990); *NYT*, August 9, 1934, p. 17; August 10, 1934, p. 22; August 12, 1934, p. 22.

William A. Borst

ROBINSON, William Edward "Eddie" (b. December 15, 1920, Paris, TX), player and executive, is of Scotch-Irish descent. After attending Paris High School and Paris JC for a year. Robinson began his professional baseball career as a first baseman with Valdosta, GA (GFL) in 1939 and 1940 and spent the 1941 season with Elmira. NY (EL). The 6-foot 2-inch, 210 pounder blossomed as a power hitter with the Baltimore, MD Orioles (IL) in 1942 and appeared briefly with the Cleveland Indians (AL) that year.

Robinson, who hit left-handed and threw right-handed, rejoined the Baltimore Orioles in 1946 after serving three years in the U.S. Navy, batting .318 with 34 HR and 123 RBI. In eight games with the Cleveland Indians, he hit .400 with three HR.

Robinson made the Cleveland Indians roster in 1947 and assumed first base duties. In 1948, he teamed with Larry Doby* to give the Indians left-handed punch to augment right-handers Ken Keltner,* Joe Gordon,* and player–manager Lou Boudreau.* The Cleveland Indians won the AL pennant in a memorable one-game playoff with the Boston Red Sox and defeated the Boston Braves in the World Series, as Robinson hit .300 with six hits. Owner Bill Veeck* traded Robinson to the Washington Senators (AL) in December 1948 for smooth-fielding first sacker Mickey Vernon* and pitcher Early Wynn.* Robinson provided the struggling Washington Senators with offensive power in 1949, but was traded to the Chicago White Sox (AL) in a six-player deal in May 1950.

With the Chicago White Sox, Robinson knocked in 117 runs in 1951 and 104 runs in 1952. He produced career highs in HR (29) and RBI (117) in 1951 and doubles (37) and batting average (.296) in 1952, but the Chicago White Sox sent him to the Philadelphia Athletics in January 1953 for first baseman Ferris Fain,* a smooth-fielding, two-time AL batting champion. Robinson batted in 102 runs in 1953. In December 1953, however, he was traded to the New York Yankees (AL). The New York Yankees expected Robinson to replace Johnny Mize* as a part-time first baseman and pinch-hitter. Robinson excelled as a pinch-hitter in 1954 and 1955, batting .667 with two hits in the World Series against the victorious Brooklyn Dodgers. In June 1956, he was sent to the Kansas City Athletics (AL). His major league career ended in 1957 with the Detroit Tigers (AL), Cleveland Indians, and the Baltimore Orioles (AL).

Robinson, who married Elayne Elder in 1943 and Bette Jane Farlow in 1955, joined the Baltimore Orioles as field director in 1957. He held front-office positions with the Houston Astros (NL) and Atlanta Braves (NL) and served as director of player personnel for the Texas Rangers (AL). In 13 major league seasons, Robinson batted .268 with 1,146 hits, 172 doubles, 172 HR, and 723 RBI.

BIBLIOGRAPHY: Eddie Robinson file, National Baseball Library, Cooperstown, NY; *WWIB, 1951,* 36th ed.; *Who's Who in the Big Leagues, 1955*; Rich Marazzi and Len Fiorito, *Aaron to Zuverink* (New York, 1982); Franklin Lewis, *The Cleveland Indians* (New York, 1949); Russell Schneider, *The Boys of Summer of '48* (Champaign, IL, 1998); John Phillips, *Winners* (Cabin John, MD, 1987); Shirley Povich, *The Washington Senators* (New York, 1954); Warren Brown, *The Chicago White Sox* (New York, 1952); Richard Lindberg, *Who's on Third?* (South Bend, IN, 1983).

Lloyd J. Graybar

RODRIGUEZ, Ivan (Torres) "Pudge" (b. November 27, 1971, Manati, PR), player, is the son of Jose Rodriguez, Sr., and attended Lina Padron Rivera High School in Vega Baja, PR, where he played baseball. The Texas Rangers (AL) organization signed him on July 27, 1988 at age 16. Rodriguez's first professional baseball season came in 1989 with Gastonia, NC (SAL), where he led SAL catchers in assists with 96. In 1990, he paced Charlotte, FL (FSL) in batting (.287) and RBI (55) and led the FSL's catchers in putouts (727) and chances (842).

Rodriguez batted .274 with Tulsa, OK (TL) in 1991 before being promoted to the Texas Rangers. At 8:30 am on June 20, he married Maribel Rivera in Tulsa, OK. That afternoon, Rodriguez helped the Texas Rangers defeat the Chicago White Sox, 7–3, in Chicago, IL. His two-run single in the ninth inning and throwing out of two Chicago base runners trying to steal proved pivotal. He started 81 of the Rangers' 102 remaining games in 1991, becoming the youngest major league regular since 18-year-old Robin Yount* in 1974. The right-handed hitter batted .264 in 88 games in 1991.

In 1992, Rodriguez hit .260 with eight HR and made his first AL All-Star team. His 15 errors led AL catchers. The following year, the 5-foot 9-inch, 205-pound Rodriguez belted 10 HR and batted .273. He in 1993 became the seventh youngest player to start an All-Star game, doubling in two at-bats. In 1994, Rodriguez led AL catchers with a .298 batting average and belted 16 HR. He caught all 10 innings in the AL's 8–7 loss in the 1994 All-Star Game, getting two hits.

Rodriguez again paced AL receivers with a .303 batting average in 1995. He made 32 doubles and 12 HR to accompany his team-leading batting average and led AL catchers with 67 assists. His .437 percent success rate in throwing out runners trying to steal paced the AL for the third time. His third best season came in 1996, when he batted .300 with 19 HR, 86 RBI, and a career-best in doubles (47). In 1997, he batted .313 with 20 HR. In 1998, he recorded a .321 batting average, 21 HR, and 91 RBI, helping the Rangers win their second AL West crown in three seasons. Rodriguez batted .375 in the 1996 AL Division Series against the New York Yankees, but New York Yankee pitchers limited him to one hit in the 1998 AL Division Series. He earned AL MVP honors in 1999 and attained career bests with a .332 batting average, 35 HR, and 113 RBI, as Texas again won the AL West. He hit .250 in the AL Division Series. Through 1999, he has batted .300 with 361 doubles, 144 HR, 621 RBI, and a .989 fielding percentage. From 1992 through 1999, Rodriguez has earned Gold Gloves and appeared in All-Star Games. Since 1994, he has made the *TSN* All-Star and AL Silver Slugger teams.

Rodriguez has played several seasons of Puerto Rican winter ball garnering MVP honors in the 1993 PRWL All-Star Game. In 1995, he started the Ivan Rodriguez Charitable Fund to aid underprivileged children with cancer. He and his wife have two children, Ivan and Amanda.

BIBLIOGRAPHY: Ivan Rodriguez file, National Baseball Library, Cooperstown, NY; Tim Kurkjian, "Short Hops (Rangers' Dean Palmer and Ivan Rodriguez)," *SI* 74 (June 24, 1991), p. 68; Tim Kurkjian, "Another Day at the Office (Texas Ranger Catcher Ivan Rodriguez)," *SI* 75 (July 1, 1991), pp. 53–55.

David A. Goss

ROE, Elwin Charles "Preacher" (b. February 26, 1915, Ashflat, AR), player, enjoyed a sparkling, abbreviated major league career as a crafty left-handed moundsman with the St. Louis Cardinals (NL), Pittsburgh Pirates (NL), and Brooklyn Dodgers (NL) and became one of few major league pitchers to win over 100 games and finish with a career-long winning percentage above .600. His first four regular seasons came with the Pittsburgh Pirates during the World War II years after making a brief one-game appearance with the St. Louis Cardinals in 1938. The 6-foot 2-inch, 170-pound Roe suffered a 34–47 win–loss mark at Pittsburgh, falling to a dismal 4–15 ledger in 1947. His unpromising major league start was rescued in December 1947, however, when Roe was traded with Billy Cox and Gene Mauch* to the Brooklyn Dodgers for veteran outfielder Dixie Walker.*

With booming Brooklyn Dodgers bats behind him and a newly acquired sense of the pitching craft, Roe completely transformed his career with a sterling 93–37 win–loss record over his next seven campaigns. His "career season" came in 1951, when Roe logged a sparkling 22–3 record for an NL best .880 winning percentage. Roe, thus, established a still-existing record for winning percentage among NL pitchers with over 20 victories and earned *TSN* honors as NL Pitcher of the Year. His final 1954 campaign marked the only Dodgers season in which Roe failed to post a winning record or achieve double-digit victory figures. The only time Roe lost at least 10 games in a single summer came in the 1950 campaign, when he won 19 of 30 games and compiled a 3.30 ERA. Roe also paced the NL in winning percentage (.714) with a 15–6 state with the Dodgers in 1949 and in strikeouts (148) with the Pittsburgh Pirates in 1945. In three career World Series appearances against the New York Yankees (1949, 1952–1953), Roe posted a 2–1 mark in five games, earned the Dodgers' only victory in the 1949 World Series, and recorded a complete-game, 5–3 triumph in Game 3 of the 1952 classic. In 12 major league seasons, Roe compiled a 127–84 slate, .602 winning percentage, and 3.43 ERA. After retiring into the grocery store business in West Plains, MO, Roe stirred considerable controversy with a candid 1955 *SI* article where he openly admitted to utilizing the outlawed spitball delivery as a main weapon of his crafty pitching arsenal.

BIBLIOGRAPHY: Preacher Roe file, National Baseball Library, Cooperstown, NY; Frederick G. Lieb, *The Pittsburgh Pirates* (New York, 1948); Richard L. Burtt, *The Pittsburgh Pirates, A Pictorial History* (Virginia Beach, VA, 1977); William F. McNeil, *The Dodgers Encyclopedia* (Champaign, IL, 1997); Richard Goldstein, *Superstars and Screwballs* (New York, 1991); Peter Golenbock, *Bums* (New York, 1984); Stanley

Cohen, *Dodgers! The First 100 Years* (New York, 1990); Tommy Holmes, *The Dodgers* (New York, 1975); Roger Kahn, *The Boys of Summer* (New York, 1971); Rick Marazzi and Len Fiorito, *Aaron to Zuverink* (New York, 1982); Mike Shatzkin, ed., *The Ballplayers* (New York, 1990); Ira L. Smith, *Baseball's Famous Pitchers* (New York, 1954).

Peter C. Bjarkman

ROGAN, Wilbur "Bullet Joe" (b. July 28, 1889, Oklahoma City, OK; d. March 4, 1967, Kansas City, MO), player, manager, and umpire, was of African-American descent. The 5-foot 7-inch, 180-pound right-hander became a versatile performer, starring as a hitter and pitcher as did National Baseball Hall of Famers Martin Dihigo* and Babe Ruth.* Rogan grew up in Kansas City, MO and began his career there as a catcher for Fred Palace's Colts in 1908. He also performed for the black Kansas City, MO Giants before joining the U.S. Army in the autumn of 1911. Rogan remained in the service through 1919 primarily with units in the Philippines, Honolulu, and the American Southwest, but pitched for the All-Nations baseball team and Los Angeles White Sox (CWL) in 1917.

Rogan honed and exhibited his baseball skills in the Army and was recommended to J. L. Wilkinson,* white owner of the Kansas City, MO Monarchs (NNL) by Pittsburgh Pirates (NL) outfielder Casey Stengel.* He joined Kansas City in 1920 and remained there through 1938. Long before Don Larsen,* Rogan employed a quick no-wind-up delivery. His nearly sidearm motion propelled him to the pinnacle then attainable for a black baseball player. Rogan's pitches included a blazing fastball, resulting in his nickname, "Bullet Joe." Rogan compiled 106 regular season wins and 44 losses against top black competition and an 8–3 post-season mark from 1920 through 1930.

Rogan, an excellent hitter, often batted cleanup for powerful Monarchs teams and posted batting averages of .351, .416, .412, .366, .314, .330, .353, .341, and .311 between 1922 and 1930. He also posted win–loss marks of 13–6, 12–8, 16–5, 15–2, 12–4, 15–6, and 9–3 from 1922 through 1929. His .325 batting mark in the 1924 Negro World Series and .500 and .583 batting averages in the 1925 and 1926 NNL Championship Series gave him an incredible .410 standard in post-season competition. In 25 games against white major leaguers, Rogan hit .329. During Rogan's tenure, Kansas City claimed NNL titles in 1923, 1924, 1925, and 1929. The Monarchs added the NAL crown in 1937 and split a pair of black World Series with the Philadelphia Hilldale Club in 1924 (won) and 1925 (lost). The 1926 unit, managed by Rogan, captured the NNL first half, but lost the Championship Series to the second half winner and eventual black world champion Chicago American Giants.

Rogan exhibited knowledgeable, capable leadership while captaining Army teams, managed with a military-like manner, and piloted the 1929 champions. He participated in the 1936 East-West (Negro) All-Star Game. Rogan's personal qualities ranged from being easygoing, jolly, quiet, gentlemanly, and free with advice to being arrogant, uncooperative, and demanding of his players. The trim, square-shouldered Rogan possessed slim legs and hips and a soldierly bearing. After retirement from the Monarchs, he umpired NAL games through 1946, worked in the Kansas City post office, and lived quietly with his wife on their farm by a lake until his death.

BIBLIOGRAPHY: Janet Bruce, *The Kansas City Monarchs* (Lawrence, KS, 1985); John B. Holway, *Bullet Joe and the Monarchs* (Alexandria, VA, 1984); John B. Holway, *Blackball Stars* (Westport, CT, 1988); James A. Riley, *The Biographical Encyclopedia of the Negro Baseball Leagues* (New York, 1994).

Merl F. Kleinknecht and John B. Holway

ROGERS, Stephen Douglas "Steve" (b. October 26, 1949, Jefferson City, MO), player, graduated from Glendale High School in Springfield, MO in 1967 and attended the University of Tulsa. At Tulsa, he pitched splendidly with a four-year record of 31 wins and five losses and won the 1971 Jack Charvat Award as the top amateur athlete in the American Southwest. Rogers, who was selected to the College World Series All-Star team in 1971, earned a Bachelor of Science degree in petroleum engineering.

The 6-foot 1-inch, 175-pound right-handed pitcher, who batted right-handed, was selected by the New York Yankees (AL) in the 60th round of the free agent draft in June 1967 and by the Montreal Expos (NL) in the secondary phase of the free agent draft in June 1971. In 1971, he pitched for Winnipeg, Canada (IL), winning only two games and losing 10 decisions. The following year for Peninsula, VA (IL), he won two games and lost six.

Rogers appeared in 17 games for the Montreal Expos (NL) in 1973 after spending the early part of that season with Quebec City, Canada (EL) and Peninsula. With the Montreal Expos, he compiled 10 wins and 5 losses in 1973. His entire major league career was spent with the Montreal Expos, where he won 15 of 37 decisions in 1974 and 11 of 23 in 1975 with a 3.29 ERA. He triumphed only seven times while dropping 17 in 1976. In 1977, he pitched 301.2 innings in 40 games, winning 17 games and losing 16. He struck out 206 batters while boasting a 3.10 ERA. In 1978, he hurled 219 innings, won 13 decisions and lost 10, and compiled a 2.47 ERA. He again recorded 13 victories while dropping 12 in 1979 and won 16 times while losing 11 with a 2.98 ERA in 1980.

After winning 12 and losing eight decisions in 1981, Rogers triumphed 19 times with eight setbacks and a 2.40 ERA in 1982. In 1983 he won 17, lost 12, and recorded 146 strikeouts with a 3.22 ERA. He struggled in his final season, taking only two of eight decisions in 1985. In 13 major league seasons with the Montreal Expos, he pitched in 399 games, won 158 contests, and lost 152 decisions with a career 3.17 ERA and 1,621 strikeouts.

Rogers led the NL in sacrifice hits (20) and shutouts (5) in 1983, ERA (2.40) in 1982, and complete games (14) in 1980 and shared the NL lead in shutouts (5) in 1979. He was selected *TSN* NL Rookie Pitcher of the Year in 1973 and right-handed pitcher on the *TSN* NL All-Star team in 1982. In the NL East Division Series with the Philadelphia Phillies in 1981, Rogers won two games and lost none with a 0.51 ERA. In the NL Championship Series that year against the Los Angeles Dodgers, he split two decisions with a 1.80 ERA.

Rogers pitched in three All-Star Games (1978, 1979, 1982), winning the 1982 contest and compiling an impressive 1.29 ERA. He was named to NL All-Star teams in 1974 and 1983, but did not play.

Rogers married Barbara Boduarchuk of Winnipeg, Canada on September 16, 1972 and has three children, Colleen, Stephen Jason, and Geoffrey Douglas. For hobbies, the Tulsa, OK resident collects coins and Indian arrowheads, plays golf, and enjoys working crossword puzzles.

BIBLIOGRAPHY: Stephen Rogers file, National Baseball Library, Cooperstown, NY; Stan W. Carlson, letter to Montreal Expos Public Relations, October 1993; *Montreal Expos Media Guide*, 1985; *TSN Baseball Register*, 1986; Dan Turner, *The Expos Inside Out* (Toronto, Canada, 1983); Brodie Snyder, *The Year the Expos Finally Won Something!* (Toronto, Canada, 1981); Peter C. Bjarkman, ed., *Encyclopedia of Major League Baseball Team Histories National League* (Westport, CT, 1991).

Stan W. Carlson

ROLFE, Robert Abial "Red" (b. October 17, 1908, Penacook, NH; d. July 8, 1969, Guilford, NH), player, coach, manager, and administrator, was selected by Ed Barrow* as the all-time best New York Yankee (AL) third baseman and by Connie Mack* as the greatest team baseball player. Rolfe began his baseball career as a shortstop for Penacook High School and Exeter Academy and starred for Jeff Tesreau's* Dartmouth College baseball teams from 1929 through 1931, leading the Big Green to the first EL title in 1930. At Dartmouth, he also participated in musical and campus governmental groups.

Rolfe signed a professional baseball contract with the New York Yankees (AL) in 1931 and was assigned to Albany, NY (EL) in 1932 and Newark, NJ (IL) in 1933 before advancing to New York in 1934. New York Yankees manager Joe McCarthy* shifted Rolfe to third base, where he quietly starred from 1935 to 1942 with the awesome Yankees AL pennant winners of 1936 to 1939, 1941, and 1942. Rolfe, who posted a major league career .289 regular season batting average and .284 World Series batting average, made 1,394 hits in 1,175 games, slammed 257 doubles, and scored 942 runs. A four-time .300 batter (1935–1936, 1938–1939), Rolfe enjoyed his greatest season in 1939 when he demonstrated a .329 batting mark and led the AL in runs scored (139), hits (213), and doubles (46). He also paced the NL in triples (15) in 1936. An intestinal disorder prompted his retirement after the 1942 season.

Rolfe then coached baseball (56 wins and 17 losses) and basketball (48 wins and 28 losses) at Yale University from 1942 to 1946. After returning to the New York Yankees as a coach in 1946, he coached the Toronto Huskies (NBA) to a 17–27 mark in the 1946–1947 campaign and then joined the Detroit Tigers (AL) as director of their farm system in 1947 and 1948 and as manager from 1949 to 1952. His managerial mark with the Tigers included 278 wins and 256 losses as well as AL Manager of the Year honors in 1950, when he achieved a second-place finish. From 1954 to 1967, Rolfe served as athletic director at Dartmouth College. The era of Dartmouth's football greatness began with Rolfe's hiring of Bob Blackman as head coach in 1955.

Following intestinal surgery in 1967, Rolfe retired to Laconia, NH. The 5-foot 11-inch, 170-pound, left-handed hitter impressed others with his glove skills and an accurate throwing arm and was named to the AL All-Star team for four consecutive seasons from 1937 through 1940. He led AL third basemen in fielding in 1935 and 1936. A major league record was set by Rolfe when he scored in 18 consecutive games in 1939. Rolfe married Maude Isabel Africa in October 1934. Dartmouth's baseball field was named for Rolfe in 1969.

BIBLIOGRAPHY: Red Rolfe file, National Baseball Library, Cooperstown, NY; Mark Gallagher, *The Yankee Encyclopedia*, vol. 3 (Champaign, IL, 1997); Dave Anderson et al., *The Yankees* (New York, 1979); Joe Falls, *Detroit Tigers* (New York, 1975); William M. Anderson, *The Detroit Tigers* (South Bend, IN, 1996); Fred T. Smith, *Tiger Tales and Trivia* (Lathrup Village, MI, 1988); Thomas Aylesworth and Benton Minks, *The Encyclopedia of Baseball Managers* (New York, 1990); *The Baseball Encyclopedia*, 10th ed. (New York, 1996); Dartmouth College Sports Information Bureau, Hanover, NH; Frank Graham, *The New York Yankees* (New York, 1943); New York Yankees Sports Information Bureau.

                                                                    Leonard H. Frey

ROMMEL, Edwin Americus "Eddie" (b. September 13, 1897, Baltimore, MD; d. August 26, 1970, Baltimore, MD), player, coach, manager, and umpire, was a son of merchant Frederick Rommel and German-born Louisa Rommel. Most baseball record books state his middle name as "Americus," but Rommel wrote it as "Aloysious" when completing a questionnaire. After attending Baltimore Public School No. 94 and playing sandlot baseball, he began professionally in 1916 with a Seaford, DE independent team. The pitcher entered organized baseball with a 12–15 win–loss record for Newark, NJ (IL) in 1918. He participated in spring training in 1919 with the New York Giants (NL) and was returned to Newark, where he compiled an impressive 22–15 mark and pitched a no-hit game. Manager Connie Mack* saw him hurl and bought him for the Philadelphia Athletics (AL). He pitched for the Athletics from 1920 through 1932, winning 171 games, losing 119 contests, allowing 3.54 earned runs in 2,556.1 innings, and playing in two World Series. His best seasons came in 1922 and 1925 with 27–13 and 21–10 marks, respectively. Rommel led the AL three times in relief victories and twice in games won, games lost, and appearances. He coached for the Philadelphia Athletics in 1933 and 1934 and managed Richmond, VA (PiL) briefly in 1935 before a salary dispute prompted his resignation.

At Newark, NJ, Rommel initially specialized with the spitball. When the talkative, 6-foot 2-inch, 197-pound right-hander realized that the spitter would be banned shortly, he developed a new mainstay. A Baltimore friend showed him how to throw the knuckler. Rommel perfected his delivery of it so well that he is regarded as the first great knuckleball pitcher. A better than average hitting pitcher, he batted .199 during his major league career and became an excellent bunter. Subsequently he umpired in the NYPL in 1936 and the IL in 1937 before the AL purchased his contract. He umpired in the AL for 22 years from 1938 through 1959, during which time he participated in two World Series and six All-Star games and demonstrated fairness and an ability to get along with the players.

The lifetime Baltimore, MD resident married Emma Elizabeth Fahey in September 1922 and had one son, Edwin A. Jr. and one daughter, Patricia Ruth. Rommel, whose hobbies included golf and bowling, became an outstanding duck pin bowler. After leaving baseball, Rommel in 1959 became an aide to Maryland's Governor Millard Tawes.

BIBLIOGRAPHY: Dan Daniel, "Batters Going Batty from Butterflies," *TSN*, June 12, 1936; *NYT*, August 28, 1970; *The Baseball Encyclopedia*, 10th ed. (New York, 1996); Eddie Rommel file, National Baseball Library, Cooperstown, NY; *TSN Baseball Register, 1958*; *TSN*, April 25, 1940, February 29, 1956, September 12, 1970, May 22, 1971; Frederick G. Lieb, *Connie Mack* (New York, 1945); Connie Mack, *My 66 Years in the Big Leagues* (Philadelphia, PA, 1950); Jerome C. Romanowski, *The Mackmen* (Upper Darby, PA, 1979); Jerry Sulecki, "Eddie Rommel's Last Win," *BRJ* 27 (1998), pp. 103–104.

Frank V. Phelps

ROOT, Charles Henry "Charlie," "Chinski" (b. March 17, 1899, Middletown, OH; d. November 5, 1970, Hollister, CA), player, manager, and coach, was of German descent, grew up in southwestern Ohio, and attended grammar school. At age 22, he became a professional baseball player. The 5-foot 10½-inch, 190-pound right-hander married Dorothy Hartman in May 1918 and had two children. After pitching for Terre Haute, IN (3IL) in 1922–1923, he compiled an 0–4 record for the St. Louis Browns (AL) in 1923. At Los Angeles, CA (PCL), he enjoyed 20-plus victory seasons in 1924 and 1925 and returned to the major leagues.

From 1926 through 1941, Root pitched for the Chicago Cubs (NL) and led the NL once each in total wins (26), games pitched (48), and innings pitched (309) in 1927, winning percentage (.760) in 1929, shutouts (4) in 1930, and relief wins (4) in 1931. In his outstanding single-game achievement, he pitched the NL pennant clincher in 1938 to help the Cubs edge the Pittsburgh Pirates. He ended his major league career with 201 triumphs, 160 losses, and a .557 winning percentage and became the only Cubs pitcher to win over 200 games. In 632 major league games, he pitched 3,197.1 innings, struck out 1,459 batters, hurled 21 shutouts, and compiled a 3.59 ERA.

Unfortunately, Root is chiefly remembered for his World Series catastrophes. In four starts, he lost three times and surrendered seven HR to National Baseball Hall of Fame sluggers. In the 1929 World Series, he started the famous fourth game that saw the Philadelphia Athletics rally for a 10-run inning to defeat the Cubs. Moreover, he surrendered Babe Ruth's* fabled "Called Shot" HR on October 1, 1932. Ruth always claimed forecasting the homer, but Root vehemently denied it.

During World War II, Root pitched in the minor leagues at Hollywood, CA (PCL) from 1942 to 1944 and at Columbus, OH (AA) in 1945. He pitched a few more games at Columbus, OH in 1946 and at Billings, MT (PrL) in 1948. Root managed in the minor leagues at Hollywood, CA (PCL) in 1943 and 1944; Columbus, OH (AA) in 1945 and 1946; Billings, MT (PrL) in 1948; Des Moines, IA (WL) in 1950; and Eau Claire, WI (NoL) in 1954. He coached with Hollywood, CA (PCL, 1949), the Chicago Cubs (1951–1953), and the Milwaukee Braves (NL, 1956–1957). He died on his ranch near Hollister, CA.

BIBLIOGRAPHY: Charley Root file, National Baseball Library, Cooperstown, NY; Warren Brown, *The Chicago Cubs* (New York, 1946); Jim Enright, *Chicago Cubs* (New York, 1975); Warren Wilbert and William Hageman, *Chicago Cubs: Seasons at the Summit* (Champaign, IL, 1997); Eddie Gold and Art Ahrens, *The Golden Era Cubs, 1876–1940* (Chicago, IL, 1985); *NYT*, November 6, 1970; *TSN*, November 21, 1970, October 18, 1982.

Lowell L. Blaisdell

ROSE, Peter Edward "Charlie Hustle" (b. April 14, 1941, Cincinnati, OH), player and manager, is one of four children of bank cashier Harry "Pete" Rose and La Verne (Bloebaum) Rose. His father, an outstanding semipro athlete in the Cincinnati area, began encouraging his son at age three to participate in sports. Rose became so absorbed in sports that he required an extra year to finish at Western Hills High School. Although he weighed under 150 pounds by graduation in 1960, Rose was offered a football scholarship from Ohio's Miami University. He declined, hoping to play professional baseball. Only the Baltimore Orioles (AL) and his hometown Cincinnati Reds (NL) expressed interest in him. Buddy Bloebaum, Rose's uncle and a Reds scout, persuaded the Reds to offer Rose a modest bonus, arguing that men in their family matured late. Phil Seghi, the Reds official who signed him, recalled that Rose demonstrated "purpose and desire and dedication and ambition. . . . He wanted to make it and he made it, but it wasn't easy."

Assigned to Geneva, NY (NYPL), the switch-hitting Rose struggled his first year in organized baseball. Despite batting only .277 and failing to sparkle at second base, he still moved up two notches in the Reds' minor league system. Off-season work lifting crates for the Railway Express Agency in Cincinnati helped Rose mature physically. During his next two minor league seasons, the 5-foot 11-inch, 190-pound Rose averaged well over .300. In 1963, Rose became the Reds' second baseman. Whitey Ford* nicknamed him "Charley Hustle" upon seeing him run to first base in a spring training camp after drawing a base on balls. Rose acquired the habit from hearing his father praise the aggressive play of Enos Slaughter.* Rose married Karolyn Ann Englehardt in January 1964 and had two children before their 1980 divorce. In April 1984, he wed Carol Woliung; they have one child.

Although his .273 batting average earned him NL Rookie of the Year honors in 1963, Rose still exhibited fielding deficiencies going to his right and making the double play pivot. Rose slumped badly at the plate the first half of 1964 and was benched in August. After returning to the starting lineup, he hit well and raised his season's batting average to .269. Off-season drills and playing Venezuelan winter ball developed Rose into a star. In 1965, he hit over .300 for the first of 15 seasons. Besides leading the NL with 209 hits, he exhibited good power for a leadoff man with 35 doubles, 11 triples, and 11 HR. Never more than adequate at second base, Rose in 1967 demonstrated his versatility and team spirit by shifting to the outfield. As an outfielder in 1968 and 1969, he won consecutive NL batting titles with .335 and .348 averages. His third batting title came in 1973, when he hit .338 and was named the NL's MVP. He led the NL in hits seven times, doubles five times, runs scored and fielding percentage four times, and on-base percentage once.

Although the Reds rarely contended during Rose's first six seasons, stars Tony Perez,* Johnny Bench,* and Joe Morgan* joined Rose on a hard-hitting team he dubbed "The Big Red Machine." Rose started for the Reds in the 1970, 1972, 1975, and 1976 World Series at right field, left field, and third base and was selected 1975 World Series MVP. He played first base for the Philadelphia Phillies (NL) in the 1980 and 1983 World Series. *TSN* named him its Player of the Decade for the 1970s.

Rose remains the only player to appear in over 500 major league games at five different positions (second base, left field, right field, third base, and first base) and made NL All Star at each. Rose, remembered chiefly for his hustle, thrilling head-first slides, and numerous batting records in 24 major league seasons through 1986, played with the Cincinnati Reds (1963–1978, 1984–1986), Philadelphia Phillies (1979–1983), and Montreal Expos (NL 1984). He had joined the Phillies as a free agent December 1978. He reached 2,000 hits on June 19, 1973, having become the Reds' all-time hit leader the previous year. On May 5, 1978, he became the 13th and youngest player to achieve 3,000 hits. On August 10, 1981, Rose broke Stan Musial's* NL record of 3,630 hits. In 1982 he climbed past Hank Aaron* into second place behind Ty Cobb* on the all-time hit list.

Rose's batting average steadily declined, but he kept in good shape, never smoked, drank only occasionally, and kept his weight at or below 200 pounds. After joining the Montreal Expos (NL) as a free agent in January 1984, Rose opened the season in left field, hit well, and made his 4,000th hit against the Philadelphia Phillies on April 13. In August 1984, Montreal traded Rose to become player–manager of the struggling Cincinnati Reds. Although the front office emphasized that he would be a manager first and player second, Rose's homecoming electrified the Cincinnati team and city. He played first base in his first three games as manager, pounding out eight hits. The crowds gave him numerous standing ovations. He concentrated on managing thereafter, but still raised his batting average to .286 by season's end. On September 11, 1985, Rose singled in the first inning off Eric Show of the San Diego Padres for his 4,192nd hit to break Cobb's longstanding major league mark. In 1985, Rose batted .264 and supplied 6 game-winning hits. Rose's qualities of leadership also made him a successful manager. After piloting the Reds to a 19–22 mark in 1984, he guided Cincinnati to an 89–72 record and a surprising second place finish in the Western Division in 1985. *TSN* named Rose Man of the Year for his 1985 achievements. Rose guided the Reds to an 86–76 record and another second place Western Division finish in 1986, but slumped to a career-low .219 batting average and retired as a player.

His major league playing career brought remarkable achievements. Rose ranks first in major league career games played (3,562), at-bats (14,053), singles (3,217), and hits (4,256), second in doubles (746), fourth in runs scored (2,165), and sixth in total bases (5,754). Ten times he made over 200 hits in a season to set a major league record. In each of his first 23 major league seasons, he made at least 100 hits to establish another record. Rose incredibly made over 1,000 hits after reaching age 38. The lifetime .303 batter and Ty Cobb remain the only players to have amassed 4,000 hits. Rose was selected 17 times to the NL All-Star Squad (1965, 1967–1971, 1973–1982, 1985). His own words best summarize his career: "I've been the most consistent player of my generation. There are a lot of players better than me, but I do the same thing day in and day out, year in and year out."

Rose managed the Cincinnati Reds to second place in the NL Western Division with an 84–78 record in 1987 and remained as pilot through most of the 1989 season, compiling an overall 412–373 win–loss record and .525 winning percentage. In 1989, Commissioner A. Bartlett Giamatti suspended Rose from baseball for life for gambling activities. Rose served five months in prison in 1990 for income tax evasion and still remains ineligible for induction into the National Baseball Hall of Fame. He made Major League Baseball's All-Century Team.

BIBLIOGRAPHY: Si Burick, "200 Grounders a Day!" *BD* 24 (July 1965), pp. 79–80; *CB* (1975), pp. 361–363; Dwight Chapin, "Pete Rose Alias—Charlie Hustle," *BD* 28

(May 1969), pp. 51–52; Ron Fimrite, "Pete's Out to Prove He Can Pull His Weight," *SI* 60 (February 13, 1984), pp. 42–47; M. S. Goodman, "Pete Rose Longs to Rise Again," *PW* 36 (September 2, 1991), pp. 47ff; Pete Harmon to Lloyd J. Graybar, August 25, 1983, February 22, 1984; Reuben Katz to Lloyd J. Graybar, January 14, 1984, February 10, 1984; Pete Rose file, National Baseball Library, Cooperstown, NY; J. Kaplan, "Pete Rose," *Sport* 77 (December 1986), pp. 125–143; J. Levine, "Restoring the Rose," *Forbes* 145 (June 25, 1990), pp. 146ff; Bill Libby, *Pete Rose* (New York, 1972); Mike Lupica, "Goooood Morning, Cooperstown," *Esquire* 118 (September 1992), pp. 135ff; Jill Lieber and C. Neff, "Deeper and Deeper," *SI* 72 (February 12, 1990), pp. 50ff; Jack Mann, "Joe Hustle May Bring Flag to the Reds," *SI* 23 (September 20, 1965), pp. 114–115; *NYT*, June 20, 1973, May 6, 1978, August 11, 1981, June 23, 1982; *NYT Biographical Service* 24 (February 1993), pp. 298–300; Rick Reilly, "A Rose Is a Rose," *SI* 79 (August 16, 1993), pp. 30–36; James Reston, Jr., *Collision at Home Plate* (New York, 1991); Thomas Aylesworth and Benton Minks, *The Encyclopedia of Baseball Managers* (New York, 1990); John Thom, *Champion Batsman of the 20th Century* (Los Angeles, CA, 1992); Pete Rose as told to Dick Kaplan, "Memories of My Dad," *Sport* 51 (April 1971), pp. 16, 18, 52–53; Pete Rose with Bob Hertzel, *Charlie Hustle* (Englewood Cliffs, NJ, 1975); Pete Rose and Roger Kahn, *Pete Rose: My Story* (New York, 1989); Floyd Conner and John Snyder, *Day-by-Day in Cincinnati Reds History* (West Point, NY, 1984); Bob Hertzel, *The Big Red Machine* (Englewood Cliffs, NJ, 1976); Bob Rathgeber, *Cincinnati Reds Scrapbook* (Virginia Beach, VA, 1982); Robert H. Walker, *Cincinnati and the Big Red Machine* (Bloomington, IN, 1988); Lonnie Wheeler and John Baskin, *The Cincinnati Game* (Wilmington, OH, 1988); Richard Scheinin, *Field of Screams* (New York, 1994); Michael Sokolove, *Hustle: The Myth, Life, and Lies of Pete Rose* (New York, 1990); George Will, *Bunts* (New York, 1998); *TSN*, January 30, 1984, p. 38; Steve Wulf, "For Pete's Sake, Look Who's Back," *SI* 61 (August 27, 1984), pp. 16–22; Elliot Asinof, "Pete Rose Can't Lose," *Sport* 80 (April 1989), pp. 54–56; G. J. Church, "Why Pick on Pete?" *Time* 134 (July 10, 1989), pp. 16–21; P. Jordan, "War of the Roses," *GQ* 59 (April 1989), pp. 274–279; Robert E. Kelly, *Baseball's Best* (Jefferson, NC, 1988).

Lloyd J. Graybar

ROSEBORO, John Junior "Johnny," "Gabby" (b. May 13, 1933, Ashland OH), player and coach, is the son of John Roseboro, Sr., a mechanic, and Ceul Roseboro and graduated in 1951 from Ashland High School, where he played baseball and football. He attended Central State College in Wilberforce, OH on a football scholarship. The Brooklyn Dodgers (NL) signed the 5-foot 11-inch, 190-pound, left-handed–hitting catcher in 1952 and optioned him to Sheboygan, WI (WSL). After spending part of the 1953 season with Great Falls, MT (PrL), Roseboro was drafted in the U.S. Army. He returned to the Brooklyn Dodgers organization in 1955 with Pueblo, CO (WL) and Cedar Rapids, IA (3IL). In 1956, he hit .273 with 25 HR and 78 RBI for Montreal, Canada (IL).

After playing 48 games for Montreal in 1957, Roseboro joined the Brooklyn Dodgers. In January 1958, Brooklyn catcher Roy Campanella* was paralyzed in an automobile accident. Roseboro became the starting Los Angeles Dodger catcher and held the position for a decade. In November 1967, the Los Angeles Dodgers traded Roseboro, Bob Miller, and Ron Perranoski* to the Minnesota Twins (AL) for Zoilo Versalles* and Jim "Mudcat" Grant.* The Minnesota Twins released him after the 1969 season. Roseboro ended his major league playing career with the Washington Senators (AL) in 1970 and rejoined the Los Angeles Dodgers as a minor league hitting instructor in 1977 and 1978, minor league catching instructor in 1988, and roving catcher instructor from 1989 to 1992.

Roseboro's major league career featured a .249 batting average with 548 RBI, 104 HR, and 67 stolen bases. In the 1959, 1963, 1965, and 1966 World Series, he batted just .157 with seven RBI and one HR. He made the NL All-Star team in 1958, 1961, and 1962 and the AL All-Star squad in 1969 and earned Gold Gloves in 1961 and 1966. Roseboro led NL catchers in putouts (848) and passed balls (14) in 1959, double plays (10) in 1960, games (125), putouts (877), double plays (16), and chances (933) in 1961, putouts (842) and errors (14) in 1962, and putouts (904) in 1966. In 1961, he established NL marks for putouts and chances accepted in a season. In the 1963 World Series against the New York Yankees, Roseboro set records for most putouts in a four-game series (43) and nine-inning game (18). He married Geraldine Fraime in August 1956 and had three children, Shelley, Stacy, and Jaime. After their divorce, he married Barbara Fouch.

BIBLIOGRAPHY: *Los Angeles Dodgers 1966 Media Guide; The Baseball Encyclopedia*, 10th ed. (New York, 1996); Larry Moffi and Jonathan Kronstadt, *Crossing the Line* (Jefferson, NC, 1994); John Roseboro file, National Baseball Library, Cooperstown, NY; John Roseboro with Bill Libby, *Glory Days with the Dodgers* (New York, 1978); *TSN Complete Baseball Record Book*, 1998; William F. McNeil, *The Dodgers Encyclopedia* (Champaign, IL, 1997); Walter Alston with Jack Tobin, *A Year at a Time* (Waco, TX, 1976); Peter C. Bjarkman, *Baseball's Great Dynasties: The Dodgers* (New York, 1990); Tommy Holmes, *The Dodgers* (New York, 1975); Stanley Cohen, *Dodgers! The First 100 Years* (New York, 1990).

Robert J. Brown

ROSEN, Albert Leonard "Al," "Flip" (b. February 29, 1924, Spartanburg, SC), player and executive, is the son of Louis Rosen and Rose (Levine) Rosen. At the age of seven, Rosen saw his father for the last time because of his parents' divorce. His mother worked as a saleswoman to support the family. Rosen grew up in Miami, FL and graduated in 1941 from Florida Military Academy in St. Petersburg, FL, where he played baseball. After attending the University of Florida and the University of Miami from 1941 to 1943, he served in the U.S. Navy during World War II. The 1947 University of Miami graduate entered professional baseball the same year with Thomasville, NC (NCL) and was promoted to Kansas City, MO (AA) in 1948.

The 24-year-old Rosen reached the major leagues in 1948, playing briefly for the World Series Champion Cleveland Indians (AL). After the Cleveland Indians traded longtime third baseman Ken Keltner* to the Boston Red Sox (AL) in 1950, Rosen started for the Indians the next seven seasons. Rosen's rookie season saw him hit .287 with an AL-best 37 HR and 116 RBI. The muscular, rugged, 5-foot 10-inch, 180-pound Rosen quickly emerged as the leading power hitter for the perennial AL pennant contenders. His best season came in 1953, when he nearly won the triple crown and was named the AL's MVP. Rosen's 43 HR and 145 RBI led the AL, but he lost the batting title to Mickey Vernon* on the last day of the season by less than .001 with a .336 mark. He also led the AL with 115 runs scored and a .613 slugging average. The next year produced similar results until Rosen suffered a broken finger. The Indians had moved Rosen to first base for a hot-hitting rookie third baseman who soon faded. One of his greatest sports moments came in 1954, when he hit two HR in the All-Star Game played in Cleveland. Overall, he competed in four All-Star contests. Rosen ended the Indians' record-breaking, NL pennant-winning 1954 season with a .300 batting average, 24 HR, and 102 RBI. Rosen never reached those numbers again, as injuries continued to plague him. He retired after the 1956 season, having batted .267 with only 15 HR and 61 RBI. His major league career batting average of .285 included 192 HR and 717 RBI.

After working two decades as an investment broker, Rosen returned to baseball in 1977 as president of the New York Yankees (AL). From 1980 to 1985, he served as president and general manager of the Houston Astros (NL). He enjoyed success as president and general manager of the San Francisco Giants (NL) from 1986 through 1992. The Giants appeared in the 1987 and 1989 NL Championship Series and were swept by the Oakland A's in the 1989 World Series.

Rosen has wed twice, marrying Teresa Ann Blumberg in 1952. She died in 1970, leaving him with three children. Rosen subsequently married Rita (Kallman), with whom he has two stepchildren, and resides in Rancho Mirage, CA.

BIBLIOGRAPHY: John Benson et al., *Baseball's Top 100* (Wilton, CT, 1997); Cleveland (OH) *Plain Dealer*, October 20, 1976, May 25, 1978, July 24, 1988; Erwin Lynn, *The Jewish Baseball Hall of Fame* (New York, 1987); Al Rosen file, National Baseball Library, Cooperstown, NY; David S. Neft et al., *The Sports Encyclopedia: Baseball*, 17th ed. (New York, 1997); Albert Rosen, letters to James N. Giglio, December 29, 1989, June 5, 1990; John Thorn et al., *Total Indians* (New York, 1996); John Phillips, *Winners* (Cabin John, MD, 1987); Bruce Dudley, *Bittersweet Season* (Annapolis, MD, 1995); Mark Gallagher, *The Yankee Encyclopedia*, vol. 3 (Champaign, IL, 1997).

James N. Giglio

ROUSH, Edd J. "Eddie" (b. May 8, 1893, Oakland City, IN; d. March 21, 1988, Bradenton, FL), player and coach, was one of twin sons of farmer William C. Roush and Laura (Herrington) Roush and began his baseball career in 1909 as a high school student with the hometown semipro Walk-Overs. After two years at Oakland City Baptist College, he turned professional in 1912 with Evansville, IN (KL). He earned a nine-game tryout with the Chicago White Sox (AL) in 1913 and the following year joined the Indianapolis Hoosiers of the new FL. With a $225 monthly salary, he considered himself wealthy enough to marry his Oakland City sweetheart, Essie Mae Swallow, on April 27, 1914; they had one child. After the FL collapsed, Roush and leading hitter Benny Kauff* were acquired by the New York Giants (NL) in December 1915. John McGraw* mistakenly kept Kauff and included Roush in the July 1916 deal that sent Christy Mathewson* to the Cincinnati Reds (NL).

The 5-foot 11-inch, 190-pound Roush, a remarkably consistent hitter and a nonpareil in center field, soon became Cincinnati's most popular player. The left-handed wrist hitter shifted his stance with the pitch, rarely struck out (once every 33 at-bats), and sprayed line drives to all fields. Of these, 29 were inside-the-park HR. Swinging the NL's heaviest bat (48 ounces), he won the NL batting championship in 1917 (.341) and 1919 (.321), and lost out in 1918 to Zack Wheat* by .002 points (.335 to .333). From 1921 through 1923, his batting averages varied only a single point: .352, .352, and .351. Twice, he led the NL with 27-game hitting streaks. In a June 1927 doubleheader, he made five singles, one double, and two HR in 12 at-bats. Afield, the left-hander made notable long sprints and circus catches of seemingly sure extra-base hits. "Oh, what a beautiful and graceful outfielder that man was," teammate Rube Bressler* reminisced. Many experts considered Roush the equal of Tris Speaker,* although the "Gray Eagle" possessed a better arm.

Roush was traded back to the Giants (NL) in February 1927 for George Kelly* and returned to the Cincinnati Reds (NL) for his final year in 1931. In 13 of his 18 major league seasons, he hit over .300. Roush batted .323 lifetime and hit 182 triples to place 17th on the all-time list. He hit 10 or more triples 11 times and in 1924 led the NL with 21. He also enjoyed 11 seasons with 20 or more doubles, including an NL-leading 41 in 1923. He also paced the NL with a .455 slugging percentage in 1918. In 1,967 games, he made 2,376 hits, 339 doubles, 182 triples, and 68 HR; scored 1,099 runs, knocked in 981 runs, and stole 268 bases.

Above all, Roush possessed a strong mind and a keen sense of his own value. He held out frequently for a better contract and to avoid spring training. He considered it foolish to risk injury (or the charley horse, to which he was prone) in meaningless games and always kept in condition. "All that fella has to do," Manager Pat Moran* once said, "is wash his hands, adjust his cap, and he's in shape to hit." When his salary terms were not met, however, he stubbornly sat out most of the 1922 season at Cincinnati and all of the 1930 season at New York. After one year (1938) as a Cincinnati Reds coach, he retired to Oakland City, IN, independently wealthy from shrewd investments in blue-chip stocks. In 1962, he was voted into the National Baseball Hall of Fame.

BIBLIOGRAPHY: John Thom, *Champion Batsman of the Twentieth Century* (Los Angeles, CA, 1992); Frank Graham, *The New York Giants* (New York, 1952); Donald Honig, *The Cincinnati Reds* (New York, 1992); Lonnie Wheeler and John Baskin, *The Cincinnati Game* (Wilmington, OH, 1988); Tom Meany, *Baseball's Greatest Teams* (New York, 1949); Ritter Collett, *The Cincinnati Reds* (Virginia Beach, VA, 1976); Floyd Connor and John Snyder, *Day-by-Day in Cincinnati Reds History* (West Point, NY, 1984); Edd Roush file, National Baseball Library, Cooperstown, NY; Bill Madden, *The Hoosiers of Summer* (Indianapolis, IN, 1994); Bob Rathgeber, *Cincinnati Reds Scrapbook* (Virginia Beach, VA, 1982); Lee Allen, *The Cincinnati Reds* (New York, 1948); Lee Allen and Tom Meany, *Kings of the Diamond* (New York, 1965); Noel Hynd, *The Giants of the Polo Grounds* (New York, 1988); *NYT Biographical Service* 19 (March 1988), p. 335; W. K. Zinsser, "A Visit to Edd Roush," *AS* 58 (Winter 1989), pp. 113–116; Lawrence S. Ritter, *The Glory of Their Times* (New York, 1966); Joseph M. Wayman, "Roush's Ruled-out Batting Title, 1918," *BRJ* 22 (1993), pp. 9–10.

David L. Porter

ROWE, John Charles "Jack" (b. December 8, 1856, Harrisburg, PA; d. April 25, 1911, St. Louis, MO), player and manager, began his professional baseball career in 1879 with Rockford, IL and joined the Buffalo Bisons (NL) later that season. Rowe overshadowed his older brother, Dave, an outfielder and utility player during the 1880s. During the 1880–1885 seasons, the versatile Rowe became Buffalo's regular catcher and a promising infielder. The accomplished 5-foot 8-inch, 170-pound, left-handed batter twice topped the .300 mark for the Buffalo Bisons. During 1882, NL pitchers never struck him out in 308 plate appearances.

When the Buffalo Bisons left the NL after the 1885 season, Rowe accompanied Dan Brouthers,* Hardy Richardson,* and Jim White* of the celebrated "Big Four" in joining the Detroit Wolverines (NL). He became the Detroit Wolverines' reliable shortstop, helping the 1887 team win the NL championship and defeat the St. Louis Browns in the World Series. After Detroit dropped out of the NL in 1888, Rowe and White successfully held out for part of their $7,000 purchase price before joining the Pittsburgh Alleghenys (NL) in 1889. The following year, Rowe and White joined the Buffalo Bisons (PL) as players and part owners. The PL collapse ended Rowe's major league career. During 12 major league seasons, Rowe batted .286 and fielded .882 in 1,044 games. His 11 triples led the NL in 1881, while his .943 fielding paced NL catchers in 1884 and his .901 fielding led the PL shortstops in 1890.

Rowe spent the 1891 season with Lincoln, NE (WA) and ended his playing career in 1893 with Buffalo, NY (EL). From 1896 to 1898, he managed Buffalo (EL), developing future stars Chick Stahl,* Claude Ritchey,* and Jack Barry.* His all red-headed 1897 outfield reportedly inspired writer Zane Grey's popular novel, *The Red-Headed Outfield*.

Rowe owned a cigar store in Buffalo, NY and later resided with his daughter, Helen, in St. Louis, MO. He also was survived by his wife and son, Henry.

BIBLIOGRAPHY: John Thorn et al., eds., *Total Baseball*, 5th ed. (New York, 1997); Robert L. Tiemann and Mark Rucker, eds., *Nineteenth Century Stars* (Kansas City, MO, 1989); John Rowe file, National Baseball Library, Cooperstown, NY; Jerry Lansche, *Glory Fades Away* (Dallas, TX, 1991); David Q. Voigt, *American Baseball*, vol. 1 (University Park, PA, 1983).

David Q. Voigt

ROWE, Lynwood Thomas "Schoolboy" (b. January 11, 1910, Waco, TX; d. January 8, 1961, El Dorado, AR), player, coach, manager, and scout, starred as a hurler in the 1930s and rivaled Dizzy Dean* in sports coverage. He grew up in El Dorado, AR, where his father, a circus trapeze performer, had moved the family. Rowe attended El Dorado High School, performing well in basketball, football, track and field, and golf. Since baseball was not offered there, he learned that sport on the sandlots and in semiprofessional leagues. At age 14, the tall youth pitched a one-hit game in an adult church league. His lifelong nickname, "Schoolboy," was launched in a banner headline in the town newspaper.

The Detroit Tigers (AL) signed the 6-foot 4½-inch, 210-pound right-hander in 1931 and assigned him to Beaumont, TX (TL), where he won 19 decisions and lost seven games in 1932. The Detroit Tigers promoted him in 1933, but used him sparingly until new manager–catcher Mickey Cochrane* took charge of the talented hurler in 1934. Rowe won 24 contests and lost eight games, leading the Tigers to the 1934 AL pennant. He triumphed 16 consecutive times to tie the AL record held by Smoky Joe Wood,* Walter Johnson,* and Lefty Grove.* Rowe pitched brilliantly in a 12-inning, 3–2 victory over the St. Louis Cardinals in the second game of the 1934 World Series, but lost the sixth contest, 4–3. St. Louis won that fall classic in seven games. He recorded 19 triumphs in 1935, as the Tigers repeated as the AL titlists. Detroit also captured the 1935 World Series against the Chicago Cubs, with Rowe contributing one win and two losses.

Nineteen victories followed in 1936, but Rowe developed a sore arm and missed much of the 1937 season. On June 2, 1938, he was optioned to Beaumont, TX to strengthen his arm and finished 12–2 there. Upon returning to Detroit in 1939, he led the AL in winning percentage (.842) with a 16–3 mark. The Tigers captured the AL pennant in 1940, but Rowe lost two games to the Cincinnati Reds in the World Series. He was sold to the Brooklyn Dodgers (NL) in April 1942 and the Philadelphia Phillies (NL) in March 1943. After making a comeback with a 14–8 record for a seventh-place team in 1943, he then departed for two years of U.S. Naval service. He again pitched well for the second division Phillies from 1946 to 1949 and helped develop young hurlers Robin Roberts* and Curt Simmons.*

One of the best hitting pitchers of his era, Rowe belted 18 HR and enjoyed a career .263 batting average. He led the NL with 15 pinch hits in 1943 and compiled a career 3.87 ERA. His 158–101 win–loss record exceeded his team's win–loss percentage by a remarkable 86 points. After serving as a player–manager for Williamsport, PA (EL) in 1951, he worked for the Detroit Tigers (AL) as a coach in 1954 and 1955 and then as a scout until his death of a heart attack. In October 1934 he married Edna Mary Skinner, who became a familiar figure at Detroit games. Her husband often shouted from the mound, "How'm I doin' Edna?"

BIBLIOGRAPHY: Herbert J. Hoffman, "Schoolboy Rowe and the 1934 Tigers," *TNP* 17 (1997), pp. 62–66; Frederick G. Lieb, Necrology, *TSN*, January 18, 1961; Jimmy Powers, "Schoolboy Rowe—Ideal Athlete," New York *Daily News*, August 25, 1934; Allen Lewis, *The Philadelphia Phillies: A Pictorial History* (Virginia Beach, VA, 1981); Rich Westcott and Frank Bilovsky, *The New Phillies Encyclopedia* (Philadelphia, PA, 1993); Fred Smith, *995 Tigers* (Detroit, MI, 1981); Frederick G. Lieb and Stan Baumgartner, *The Philadelphia Phillies* (New York, 1953); Lynwood Rowe file, National Baseball Library, Cooperstown, NY; *TSN Baseball Register, 1949*; J. Alva Waddell, "Milestones in the Life of the Famous Schoolboy," *TSN*, November 11, 1934; Frederick G. Lieb, *The Detroit Tigers* (New York, 1946); Joe Falls, *Detroit Tigers* (New York, 1975); William M. Anderson, *The Detroit Tigers* (South Bend, IN, 1996).

L. Robert Davids

ROWLAND, Clarence Henry "Pants" (b. February 12, 1879, Platteville, WI; d. May 17, 1969, Chicago, IL), player, manager, umpire, scout, owner, and executive, grew up in Dubuque, IA. As a youngster, he worked as a hotel bellhop and first came into contact with the professional baseball players for Dubuque's (3IL) team. One of these players, upon learning Rowland's first name, thought it inappropriate and started calling him "Pants." The nickname remained.

Rowland's professional baseball career began in 1903 as a catcher with Dubuque, IA (3IL). After being injured or ill much of the 1904–1906 seasons, he caught for and managed Dubuque in 1907 and 1908. Following brief stints with Aberdeen, SD (NoL), Jacksonville, IL (Ind), and Winnipeg, Canada (NoL) over the next two seasons, he returned to Dubuque as the owner–manager from 1911 to 1913. In 1914, he managed Peoria, IL (3IL), transforming a losing team into a contender. League president Al Tierney recommended Rowland to owner–president Charles Comiskey* for the vacant Chicago White Sox (AL) managerial post. In December 1914, Rowland was appointed to the job. Critics sneered at Comiskey for "digging a manager out of the bushes," but Rowland soon proved his mettle.

Rowland guided the Chicago White Sox from 1915 to 1918, winning 339 games and losing 247 for a .578 winning percentage. Chicago finished third in 1915 and second in 1916 before winning the AL pennant with a 100–54 record in 1917. His 1917 Chicago White Sox prevailed in the World Series, defeating manager John McGraw's* New York Giants, 4–2. A sixth-place finish in 1918 cost Rowland his job. He was replaced for the turbulent, scandal-ridden 1919 season by "Kid" Gleason.*

Rowland's exit from the baseball scene remained brief. He managed Milwaukee, WI (AA) in 1919 and moved on to Columbus, OH (AA) for a three-year stint as pilot from 1920 to 1922. In 1923, his career took an unusual twist. Rowland became an AL umpire, a post he held for five years. He later managed Nashville, TN (SA), scouted for the Chicago Cubs (NL), and presided over the PCL from 1944 to 1954. He eased into his twilight years as executive vice president of the Chicago Cubs and ended his long, colorful baseball career with the Cubs as an honorary vice president, the title that he held at his death.

BIBLIOGRAPHY: *The Baseball Encyclopedia*, 10th ed. (New York, 1996); Clarence Rowland file, National Baseball Library, Cooperstown, NY; Warren Brown, *The Chicago White Sox* (New York, 1952); Gustav Axelson, *Commy* (Chicago, IL, 1919); Richard Lindberg, *Sox* (New York, 1984); Thomas Aylesworth and Benton Minks, *The Encyclopedia of Baseball Managers* (New York, 1990).

David S. Matz

RUCKER, George Napoleon "Nap" (b. September 30, 1884, Crabtree, GA; d. December 19, 1970, Alphabetta, GA), player and scout, was a successful baseball pitcher during the pre-1920 "dead ball" era. His parents were John Rucker, a farmer, and Sara (Embree) Rucker. Rucker, who obtained an eighth-grade grammar school education, married Edith Wood on October 1, 1911 and had a daughter, Anne. Rucker stood 5-feet 10-inches, weighed 190 pounds, threw left-handed, and batted right-handed.

Rucker began baseball professionally with Atlanta, GA (SL) in 1904 and pitched for Augusta, GA (SAL) in 1905 and 1906. His major league career lasted exactly a decade from 1907 to 1916, entirely with the weak-hitting Brooklyn Superbas-Dodgers-Robins (NL). Rucker pitched very well and remains a classic example from the pre-free agent age of how restriction to an inferior team could mar a hurler's record. In Rucker's first eight years with Brooklyn, the Superbas-Dodgers-Robins did not once finish in the first division or reach a .500 winning percentage and averaged a sixth-place finish. In his major league career, Rucker exactly split 268 decisions and compiled an individual winning percentage 58 points above his team. He possessed an outstanding fastball until 1913, when he hurt his arm. In his last three years with the Brooklyn Robins-Dodgers, he pitched cleverly but less effectively with a slower ball. Charles Ebbets,* the club owner, admired Rucker for his cooperative attitude and friendly disposition.

Despite his lowly teams, Rucker finished five seasons among the NL's pitching leaders in various pitching categories. He led the NL in innings pitched (320.1) in 1910 and won 22 games in 1911. Rucker also paced the NL in complete games (27) in 1910 and shutouts (6) in 1910 and 1912. On September 5, 1908, he pitched a no-hit game against the Boston Doves, striking out 14 batters and allowing no bases on balls. On July 14, 1909, he permitted only two hits, struck out 16 batters, and walked three. He achieved an admirable 2.42 career ERA, struck out 1,217 batters in 2,375.1 innings, and hurled 38 shutouts. Brooklyn won the NL pennant in Rucker's last year, when his arm had given out. He made a token two-inning appearance in one game of the 1916 World Series against the Boston Red Sox (AL), not permitting a run.

Rucker scouted for the Brooklyn Robins-Dodgers from 1919 to 1934 and 1939 to 1940. Subsequently, back in Georgia, he farmed, operated a wheat and corn mill, and served as mayor of Roswell, water commissioner, and umpire of local baseball games.

BIBLIOGRAPHY: *The Baseball Encyclopedia*, 10th ed. (New York, 1996); *DAB*, Supp. 8 (New York, 1988), pp. 558–559; William F. McNeil, *The Dodgers Encyclopedia* (Champaign, IL, 1997); Richard Goldstein, *Superstars and Screwballs* (New York, 1991); Frank Graham, *The Brooklyn Dodgers* (New York, 1945); Tommy Holmes, *The Dodgers* (New York, 1975); Stanley Cohen, *Dodgers! The First 100 Years* (New York, 1990); *NYT*, December 21, 1970; Nap Rucker file, National Baseball Library, Cooperstown, NY.

Lowell L. Blaisdell

RUDI, Joseph Oden "Joe" (b. September 7, 1946, Modesto, CA), player, is the son of Norwegian-born parents and overcame the objections of his father, who told him that "in Norway young men worked hard learning to be shipbuilders or fishermen or engineers and didn't waste time fooling with bats and balls." Six feet tall by age 11, he lettered in football, wrestling, and baseball at Thomas Downey High School in Modesto and declined football scholarships to Stanford University and Baylor University.

After entering professional baseball in 1964 with Wytheville, GA (ApL), Rudi reached the major leagues with the Kansas City Athletics (AL) in 1967 and made the major leagues permanently in 1969. The right-hander possessed a strong work ethic and benefited from the hitting instruction of Charlie Lau.* He led the AL in hits in 1972 with 181, doubles in 1974 with 39, and triples in 1972 with nine. Rudi was better known for his fielding, winning Gold Glove Awards from 1974 through 1976 and making spectacular catches. His game-saving catch of a drive by Denis Menke* of the Cincinnati Reds against the wall in the ninth inning of the second game of the 1972 World Series provided his greatest thrill in baseball.

With the often strife-torn championship teams of the Oakland Athletics in the early 1970s, Rudi remained above the fray. Pitching coach Bill Posedel, who spent over four decades in professional baseball, described him as "the nicest guy I've ever met since I've been in baseball." Teammate Reggie Jackson* referred to him as the "nicest guy in the league—underrated, under-paid, a self-made ballplayer and the best left fielder in the American League." Manager Dick Williams* affirmed that "a manager would like to have 25 Joe Rudis on his ball club." The San Francisco (CA) *Chronicle* started a trend by referring to him as "Gentleman Joe." Rudi became outspoken only when moved to first base at the start of the 1975 season. He returned to left field in 1976 and won another Gold Glove Award.

In 1976, Rudi and pitcher Rollie Fingers* were sold by Oakland owner Charlie Finley* to the Boston Red Sox (AL) because they were about to become free agents. Commissioner Bowie Kuhn* vetoed the sale as against the best interests of baseball. Rudi signed a four-year, $2.09 million contract with the California Angels (AL) in November 1976, but injuries prevented him from fulfilling expectations. He finished his major league career with the Boston Red Sox in 1981 and Oakland A's in 1982, compiling 179 HR, 810 RBI, and a .264 batting average in 16 major league seasons. An AL All-Star in 1972, 1974, and 1975, Rudi played in the AL Championship Series from 1971 to 1975 and in the World Series from 1972 to 1974. He batted .300 with 21 hits in the World Series and never made an error in 125 post-season chances.

Rudi married his childhood sweetheart, Sharon Howell, on May 9, 1966. They have two sons, Michael and Scott, and a daughter, Heather Jo Ann, and reside in Baker, OR.

BIBLIOGRAPHY: Joe Rudi file, National Baseball Library, Cooperstown, NY; Steve Ames, "Joe Rudi: The A's [sic] Unheralded Star," *BD* 32 (March 1973), pp. 25–29; Phil Elderkin, "Joe Rudi: Oakland's Mr. Nobody," *BD* 33 (December 1974), pp. 90–92; Ron Fimrite, "The Man Who'd Never Bite a Dog," *SI* 41 (September 2, 1974), pp. 23–24; Peter Gammons, "Joe Rudi—He's Under-Rated No Longer," *BD* 34 (September 1975), pp. 29–31; Lawrence Linderman, "Don't Tell Anyone, But Joe Rudi's Becoming a Star," *Sport* 53 (October 1972), pp. 72–73; Bruce Markusen, *Baseball's Last Dynasty* (New York, 1998); Ross Newhan, *The California Angels* (New York, 1982); Mike Shatzkin, ed., *The Ballplayers* (New York, 1990); John Thorn et al., eds., *Total Baseball*, 5th ed. (New York, 1997); *WWIB*, 1982, 67th ed.

Victor Rosenberg

RUDOLPH, Richard "Dick," "Baldy" (b. August 25, 1887, New York, NY; d. October 20, 1949, Bronx, NY), player, coach, manager, and owner, was born in Manhattan and grew up in the Bronx. Of German descent, he attended Morris High School and Fordham University. The Fordham student pitched several minor league baseball games, thus ending his college eligibility. Ed Barrow* signed Rudolph for the Toronto, Canada Maple Leafs (EL) in 1907. He pitched for Toronto until 1913, making the International League Hall of Fame.

In 1913, Rudolph threatened to leave baseball unless he was sold to a major league club. He had pitched four games for the New York Giants (NL) in 1910 and 1911, but Manager John McGraw* considered the 5-foot 9-inch, 160-pound right-hander too small to pitch in the major leagues.

Nevertheless, the Boston Braves (NL) purchased his contract in May 1913, and he won 14 games. He helped pitch the 1914 "Miracle Braves" to the NL pennant and a stunning four-game World Series sweep of the Philadelphia Athletics. Rudolph, a spitballer and staff ace, compiled a 26–10 record with a 2.35 ERA and 11-game winning streak. He won the opening game of the World Series, 7–1, and the fourth game, 3–1. Rudolph followed with 22 wins in 1915 and 19 victories in 1916, but his arm deteriorated after hurling more than 300 innings for three successive seasons. He coached for the Boston Braves from 1921 to 1927, pitching briefly in 1922, 1923, and 1927. His 13 major league seasons featured a 121–108 mark and 2.66 ERA.

Rudolph served as president and manager of Waterbury, CT (EL) in 1928, but the team encountered financial difficulties. Rudolph, who had married Alice Craig on October 8, 1912 and had two daughters, Marion and Ethel, worked as a sales representative and as a licensed undertaker after leaving baseball. Diabetes forced him to retire in 1945, but he coached the freshman Fordham baseball team in 1948.

BIBLIOGRAPHY: Frank Graham, *McGraw of the Giants* (New York, 1944); Frank Graham, *The New York Giants* (New York, 1952); Harold Kaese, *The Boston Braves* (New York, 1948); Frederick G. Lieb, *Connie Mack* (New York, 1945); Boston (MA) *Globe*, October 22, 1949; *NYT*, October 22, 1949; *TSN*, November 2, 1949; Dick Rudolph file, National Baseball Library, Cooperstown, NY; Gary Caruso, *The Braves Encyclopedia* (Philadelphia, PA, 1995); Al Hirshberg, *Braves, the Pick and the Shovel* (Boston, MA, 1948).

Lyle Spatz

RUEL, Herold Dominic "Muddy" (b. February 20, 1896, St. Louis, MO; d. November 13, 1963, Palo Alto, CA), player, coach, manager, and executive, caught in major league baseball for 19 years and was the son of George Ruel and Maria (Gallagher) Ruel. Nicknamed "Muddy" from his condition after a childhood game, he graduated from Washington University and its law school. Although among his era's most intelligent, well-educated players, he labeled catchers' equipment "the tools of ignorance."

The St. Louis Browns (AL) signed Ruel out of local semiprofessional baseball in 1910. He played only 10 games in 1915 for the St. Louis Browns and caught sparingly for the New York Yankees (AL) from 1917 to 1920. After spending 1921 and 1922 as regular catcher for the Boston Red Sox (AL), he was traded to the Washington Senators (AL) in February 1923 and gained his greatest reputation there. Between 1923 and 1930, he hit over .300 three seasons and established himself as the preferred receiver of Walter Johnson.* Although only 5 feet 8 inches and 150 pounds, Ruel caught regularly for Washington's 1924 and 1925 AL champions and scored the winning run in the final game of the 1924 World Series against the New York Giants. He did not start after 1928 and played short stints as bullpen catcher and *de facto* coach with the Boston Red Sox, Detroit Tigers (AL) and St. Louis

Browns from 1931 to 1933, ending his active career with the Chicago White Sox (AL) in 1934. In 1,468 major league games, he batted .275 with 1,242 hits and 534 RBI.

Ruel remained with the Chicago White Sox as pitching coach from 1934 through 1945 and was widely expected to replace Jimmy Dykes* as manager. He instead became special assistant to Commissioner A. B. Chandler,* a position well suited to his legal training. Ruel had been admitted to the Missouri bar in 1923 and to practice before the United States Supreme Court in 1925. Although practicing for a St. Louis law firm in off-seasons, he considered law as secondary to baseball.

After Ruel spent 1946 in the Commissioner's office, the St. Louis Browns selected him manager for the 1947 season. Ruel, who long had held managerial ambitions, took the job, but the St. Louis Browns finished last with a 59–95 record. He had acrimony with the ownership and was discharged after the season. He coached for the Cleveland Indians (AL) from 1948 to 1950 and directed their farm clubs in 1951. He directed farm clubs for the Detroit Tigers in 1952 and 1953, being promoted to general manager from 1954 to 1956 and assistant to the president in 1957. Ruel retired to Palo Alto, CA, where he died of a heart attack while driving. He married Dorothea Werter in December 1938 and had two sons and two daughters.

BIBLIOGRAPHY: Thomas Aylesworth and Benton Minks, *The Encyclopedia of Baseball Managers* (New York, 1990); Frank Graham, *The New York Yankees* (New York, 1943); Frederick G. Lieb, *The Boston Red Sox* (New York, 1947); Morris Bealle, *The Washington Senators* (New York, 1947); Henry W. Thomas, *Walter Johnson* (Washington, DC, 1995); Bill Borst, *Still Last in the American League* (West Bloomfield, MI, 1992); Bill Borst, ed., *Ables to Zoldak*, vol. 3 (St. Louis, MO, 1990); *The Baseball Encyclopedia*, 10th ed. (New York, 1996); Warren Brown, *The Chicago White Sox* (New York, 1952); Shirley Povich, *The Washington Senators* (New York, 1954); *TSN*, November 23, 1963, p. 32; Herold Ruel file, National Baseball Library, Cooperstown, NY.

George W. Hilton

RUETHER, Walter Henry "Dutch" (b. September 13, 1893, Alameda, CA; d. May 16, 1970, Phoenix, AZ), player, manager, and scout, initially attracted the interest of major league scouts as a 19-year-old, left-handed pitcher for St. Ignatius College (later the University of San Francisco). On March 10, 1913, he limited the Chicago White Sox (AL) to one run and one hit in an exhibition game. After accepting a $500 signing bonus from the Pittsburgh Pirates (NL), he hurled in 1914 for Vancouver, Canada (PCL). He joined the major leagues three years later with the Chicago Cubs (NL).

Ruether saw little action in the first half of the 1917 season and was waived in July to the Cincinnati Reds (NL). With the Cincinnati Reds in 1919, he enjoyed probably the best of his 11 major league campaigns. His 19 victories, 1.82 ERA, and NL-leading .760 winning percentage helped Cincinnati capture the NL pennant. The 6-foot 1½-inch, 180-pound Ruether started the first game of the 1919 World Series against the Chicago White Sox, defeating Eddie Cicotte,* 9–1. Disappointment followed upon discovering that his well-pitched game apparently resulted as much from a lack of effort on the part of his opponents as from his own pitching skill. In December 1920, Cincinnati traded him to the Brooklyn Robins (NL).

Ruether also performed well in 1922 with a career-best 21 victories for the Brooklyn Robins. He was sold to the Washington Senators (AL) in December 1924 and won 18 games there in 1925 before finishing his career with the 1927 New York Yankees (AL). His record with the powerful 1927 World Series Champion Yankees included 13 victories, six losses, and a 3.38 ERA.

Lifetime, Ruether won 137 major league games, lost 95 decisions, boasted a 3.50 ERA, hurled 155 complete games, and notched 18 shutouts. Ruether, a good hitter, occasionally played first base and pinch hit. His only appearance in the 1925 World Series against the New York Giants came as a pinch batter. He managed several minor league clubs and also scouted, giving him 56 years in baseball.

BIBLIOGRAPHY: Lee Allen, *The Cincinnati Reds* (New York, 1948); *The Baseball Encyclopedia*, 10th ed. (New York, 1996); Walter Ruether file, National Baseball Library, Cooperstown, NY; Ritter Collett, *The Cincinnati Reds* (Virginia Beach, VA, 1976); Floyd Connor and John Snyder, *Day-by-Day in Cincinnati Reds History* (West Point, NY, 1984); Tom Meany, *Baseball's Greatest Teams* (New York, 1949); Bob Rathgeber, *Cincinnati Reds Scrapbook* (Virginia Beach, VA, 1982); Lonnie Wheeler and John Baskin, *The Cincinnati Game* (Wilmington, OH, 1988); Frank Graham, *The Brooklyn Dodgers* (New York, 1945); William F. McNeil, *The Dodgers Encyclopedia* (Champaign, IL, 1997); Richard Goldstein, *Superstars and Screwballs* (New York, 1991); Shirley Povich, *The Washington Senators* (New York, 1954).

David S. Matz

RUFFING, Charles Herbert "Red" (b. May 3, 1904, Granville, IL; d. February 17, 1986, Mayfield Heights, OH), player, manager, coach, and scout, grew zup in the coal-mining area of north-central Illinois and was the son of German-born John Ruffing, a coal miner, and Frances Ruffing. The burly redhead attended Nakomis, IL schools and played first base for his father's Nakomis mine team at age 15, when he lost three toes because a mining car ran over his left foot. Unable to run well thereafter, he switched to the mound and became a premier pitcher. He married Pauline Mulholland on October 6, 1934. After starring on local teams, he signed a professional contract in 1923 with Danville, IL (3IL). He won 12 games and lost 16 at Danville and posted a 4–7 record for Dover, DE (ESL) in 1924 before being purchased by the Boston Red Sox (AL). Ruffing appeared in 8 games without decision to launch his 17-year major league career. The hard-throwing right-hander won 273 games and lost 225 for the Red Sox (1924–1930), New York

Yankees (AL, 1930–1942, 1945–1946), and Chicago White Sox (AL, 1947). He lost the entire 1943 and 1944 seasons to military service and was released by Chicago in July 1947.

The 6-foot 2-inch, 210-pound Ruffing hardly seemed destined for the National Baseball Hall of Fame after his six years with Boston. By the 1930 season, he had won just 36 games against 96 losses for a .289 winning percentage, and had twice lost over 20 games. In May 1930, he was traded to the New York Yankees (AL) for outfielder Cedric Durst and $50,000. "I was so tickled to death I couldn't wait 'till I got there," Ruffing recalls. Boston had finished last in the AL five consecutive years. In 1930, Ruffing finished with a 15–8 mark. After going 18–7 and leading the AL in strikeouts with 190 in 1932, the fastballer competed in his first World Series. Against the Chicago Cubs, he notched the first of his seven World Series wins and struck out 10 batters. From 1936 through 1939, he relied on his fastball and pinpoint control. Ruffing won 20, 20, 21, and 21 games these seasons and led the AL with a 21–7 mark and .750 winning percentage in 1938. From 1937 through 1939, he compiled a 4–0 mark in World Series games.

After winning 14 of 21 games in 1942, Ruffing was drafted into the U.S. Army. Upon his return in 1945, he won seven of 10 decisions. Sparingly used in 1946 because of a broken kneecap, he finished 5–1 before the Yankees released him in September. Ruffing signed with the Chicago White Sox (AL) primarily as a pinch hitter and completed his career in 1947 with three wins and five losses. By age 37, Ruffing had earned 258 career wins and had a postwar 15–9 mark. Most experts, along with Ruffing, believe that his military stint cost him a 300-win career. For his career, Ruffing appeared in 624 games, pitched 4,344 innings (over 200 for 13 consecutive seasons), compiled a 273–225 record (.548 winning percentage), and recorded a 3.80 ERA. He finished with 45 shutouts, once leading the AL. From 1930 to 1942, he and Lefty Gomez* won 408 games to make them the third best righty–lefty duo in history. In 10 World Series games, he finished 7–2 (.778 winning percentage) with a 2.63 ERA in 85.2 innings.

The competitive Ruffing ranked among the outstanding batters for pitchers, with a lifetime .269 batting average, 521 hits (third among pitchers), and a season batting average high of .364 in 1930. His 36 lifetime HR ranked third behind Wes Ferrell* (38) and Bob Lemon* (37). He slugged five HR in 1936, including two on June 7. In 1939, he supplemented his 21 wins with a .307 batting average. His 58 pinch hits rank second among pitchers, while his 273 RBI remain unsurpassed.

After retiring as a pitcher, Ruffing managed in the minor leagues, scouted, and coached for the Chicago White Sox, Cleveland Indians (AL), and New York Mets (NL). (He served as Casey Stengel's* first pitching coach.) He suffered a stroke in 1973 and was confined to a wheelchair in his Cleveland home thereafter. Bill Dickey,* the Yankees' great catcher, called Ruffing the best pitcher he ever caught. Yankees manager Joe McCarthy* named Ruffing, Gomez, and Spud Chandler* as his best pitchers ever. Ruffing, who made *TSN* Major League All Star teams in 1937, 1938, and 1939, was selected for the National Baseball Hall of Fame in 1967 and is honored in the BRS Museum in Nokomis, IL.

BIBLIOGRAPHY: Red Ruffing file, National Baseball Library, Cooperstown, NY; Maury Allen, *Baseball's 100* (New York, 1981); Dave Anderson et al., *The Yankees* (New York, 1979); Mark Gallagher, *The Yankee Encyclopedia*, vol. 3 (Champaign, IL, 1997); Frank Graham, *The New York Yankees* (New York, 1943); Daniel Okrent and Harris Lewine, eds., *The Ultimate Baseball Book* (Boston, MA, 1981); Paul Green, "Red Ruffing," *SCD* 11 (September 28, 1984), pp. 114–116; Cindy Landage and Janna Seiz, "Museum Named after Baseball HOFers," *SCD* 25 (May 1, 1998), p. 135; Lowell Reidenbaugh, *Baseball's Hall of Fame—Cooperstown* (New York, 1993); Frederick G. Lieb, *The Boston Red Sox* (New York, 1947); Howard Liss, *The Boston Red Sox* (New York, 1982); Dan Shaughnessy, *The Curse of the Bambino* (New York, 1990); Peter Golenbock, *Fenway* (New York, 1992); Robert Redmount, *The Red Sox Encyclopedia* (Champaign, IL, 1998).

                                                                 Douglas G. Simpson

RUNNELLS, James Edward. *See* James Edward Runnels.

RUNNELS, James Edward "Pete" (b. James Edward Runnells, January 28, 1928, Lufkin, TX; d. May 20, 1991, Pasadena, TX), player, manager, and coach, was the son of Pete Runnells and played semiprofessional baseball before graduating from high school. After enlisting in the U.S. Marine Corps, the 6-foot, 170-pound Runnels played third base for the San Diego Naval Air Station until discharged in 1948. Runnels, who married Betty Ruth Hinton on October 29, 1949, entered Rice Institute in 1948, but joined the St. Louis Cardinals (NL) for their 1949 spring training camp. The Cardinals assigned him to Albany, GA (GFL) and Winston-Salem, NC (CrL). Runnels, who threw right-handed and batted left-handed, left the Cardinals organization and signed with Chickasha, OK (SSL) in 1949, leading the circuit with a .372 batting average. The following year, he batted .330 with Texarkana, TX (BStL). The Washington Senators (AL) purchased Runnels and sent him to Chattanooga, TN (SA), where he batted .356 in 1951.

A line drive hitter, Runnels played with the Washington Senators from midseason of 1951 through 1957, Boston Red Sox (AL) between 1958 and 1962, and Houston Colt .45s (NL) in 1963 and 1964. He performed at virtually every infield position, playing over 600 games at both first base and second base. In 1958, he batted .322 with 183 hits and finished runner-up in the batting race to teammate Ted Williams.* Runnels credited Williams for making him a consistent .300 hitter. After batting .314 in 1959, he topped the AL the next year with a .320 mark and hit .317 in 1961. His best season came in 1962, when he regained the batting crown with a .326 batting average and made 183 hits. An outstanding defensive infielder, Runnels paced all AL second baseman in fielding in 1960 and performed the same feat at first base the next year. On June 23, 1957, he tied an AL record by starting three double plays in a game at third base.

In 14 major league seasons, Runnels hit .291 in 1,799 games with 1,854 hits, 876 runs scored, 282 doubles, 64 triples, 49 HR, 630 RBI, and 37 stolen bases. Besides batting above .300 and hitting at least 20 doubles six times, he tied a major league mark with nine hits in a doubleheader on August 30, 1960. Runnels played in the 1959, 1960, and 1962 All-Star games for the AL squad, becoming the first player to execute an unassisted double play in the summer classic and slugging a pinch hit HR in the 1962 contest. He coached for the Boston Red Sox in 1965 and 1966 and guided Boston to an 8–8 mark in 1966 as interim manager. Following his retirement from baseball, Runnels returned with his wife and children to Texas and became co-director of a children's camp and co-owner of a sporting goods store in Pasadena. Runnels was elected in 1982 to the Texas Sports Hall of Fame and three years later to the Texas Baseball Hall of Fame.

BIBLIOGRAPHY: Pete Runnels file, National Baseball Library, Cooperstown, NY; Paul Green, "SCD Interviews Pete Runnels," *SCD* 12 (August 16, 1985), pp. 112–113, 117, 120–134; Al Hirshberg, "Secrets of a Batting Champion," *SEP* 234 (April 22, 1961), pp. 30, 113–114; Gene Karst and Martin J. Jones, Jr., *Who's Who in Professional Baseball* (New Rochelle, NY, 1973); *NYT*, May 21, 1991, p. D–21; Robert Redmount, *The Red Sox Encyclopedia* (Champaign, IL, 1998); John Thom, *Champion Batsman of the 20th Century* (Los Angeles, CA, 1992); Shirley Povich, *The Washington Senators* (New York, 1954); Howard Liss, *The Boston Red Sox* (New York, 1952); Dan Shaughnessy, *The Curse of the Bambino* (New York, 1990); Peter Golenbock, *Fenway* (New York, 1992); *The Baseball Encyclopedia*, 10th ed. (New York, 1996).

                                                                    John L. Evers

RUPPERT, Jacob, Jr. "Colonel" (b. August 5, 1867, New York, NY; d. January 13, 1939, New York, NY), executive, was the son of brewery owner Jacob Ruppert and Anna (Gillig) Ruppert. His father founded the Ruppert Brewery in 1867 and built it into a successful enterprise. The younger Ruppert graduated from Columbia Grammar School and was accepted at the Columbia School of Mines, but never attended there. After entering the family business at age 19, Ruppert became general superintendent four years later. He assumed the brewery presidency upon his father's death in 1915 and invested heavily and successfully in real estate. Ruppert's wealth placed him in the highest New York City social circles, in which he moved with ease. Although he never married, the outgoing Ruppert entertained often and continually was seen in the company of women. Ruppert also pursued politics. A colonel with the Seventh Regiment of the New York National Guard, he served as an aide-de-camp on the staff of New York Governor David B. Hill. Ruppert carried the designation "Colonel" as his preferred title to his death. After leaving the governor's staff, the Democrat represented New York City's fifteenth district in the U.S. Congress for four terms from 1899 to 1907.

Ruppert followed baseball closely since boyhood. Upon the advice of John McGraw,* he and Tillinghast Huston purchased the New York Yankees (AL) in 1914 for $450,000. In 1918, Ruppert lured Miller Huggins* from the St. Louis Cardinals (NL) to manage the New York Yankees. The following year, Ruppert and Huston bought Babe Ruth* from the Boston Red Sox (AL) for $100,000 and a $350,000 loan secured by the mortgage on Fenway Park. Ed Barrow,* who was hired as general manager in 1920, assembled the Yankees dynasties of the next two decades. Ruppert operated the Yankees from a distance, letting Huggins and Barrow conduct daily operations. The famous Yankee pinstripes were designed by Ruppert, who thought they made the bulky Ruth look slimmer. During Ruppert's reign, the Yankees introduced uniform numbers corresponding to the player's slot in the batting order. In 1919, Boston Red Sox pitcher Carl Mays* jumped to the Yankees. After Red Sox owner Harry Frazee sold Mays' contract to the Yankees, AL president Ban Johnson* voided the sale and suspended Mays. Ruppert secured a court injunction against Johnson's action and was joined by other rebellious AL owners. One year later, new baseball commissioner Judge Kenesaw Mountain Landis* assumed Johnson's power.

In 1919, Ruppert bought a plot of land directly across the Harlem River from the Polo Grounds for $600,000. Yankee Stadium was built there in 1922 and opened for play the next year. Yankee Stadium, which became "The House that Ruth Filled," was built by Ruppert and Huston for $2,500,000 and held 62,000 spectators. Ruppert contracted phlebitis in April 1938 and died nine months later in his New York City apartment. One of his last visitors was Babe Ruth.

BIBLIOGRAPHY: Jacob Ruppert file, National Baseball Library, Cooperstown, NY; *BDAC* (Washington, DC, 1961), p. 1,549; Robert Creamer, *Babe* (New York, 1974); *DAB*, Suppl. 2, pp. 589–590; Mark Gallagher, *The Yankee Encyclopedia*, vol. 3 (Champaign, IL, 1997); Dave Anderson et al., *The Yankees* (New York, 1979); Frank Graham, *The New York Yankees* (New York, 1943); *NCAB*, vol. 29 (New York, 1941), p. 489.

Robert E. Jones

RUSIE, Amos Wilson "The Hoosier Thunderbolt" (b. May 30, 1871, Mooresville, IN; d. December 6, 1942, Seattle, WA), player, excelled as a right-handed pitcher and married May Smith in 1890. His wife predeceased him by two months, leaving one daughter, Mrs. C. E. Spalding. Rusie generally was considered the best NL pitcher from 1891 through 1899, being ranked even better than Cy Young.* Nicknamed "The Hoosier Thunderbolt," he resembled Walter Johnson* by throwing a blinding fastball. Manager Connie Mack,* who saw the major fastball hurlers through Bob Feller,* and John McGraw* both labeled Rusie the fastest moundsman ever. New

York catcher Richard Buckley admitted adding lead wrapped in a handkerchief and a sponge when handling Rusie's pitches. The 6-foot 1-inch, 210 pounder, however, considered the outdrop his favorite pitch. Elected to the National Baseball Hall of Fame in 1977, he remarkably finished all but 35 of his 427 starts.

Rusie quit Indianapolis, IN public schools early to work in a factory and played outfield for an Indianapolis city league team. Rusie joined his hometown Indianapolis Hoosiers (NL) team in 1889 and accompanied the club when the franchise shifted the next season to New York. He became the ace of the New York Giants (NL) staff with 94 wins over the next three years. His walks (289, 262, and 267) and strikeouts (341, 337, and 304) usually paced the NL from 1890 through 1892. He pitched New York's first no-hitter on July 31, 1891 against the Brooklyn Bridegrooms and led the NL in shutouts (6) that year. The pitching mound was moved from 50 feet to 60 feet, six inches from home plate partly because of Rusie. He set several single-season marks in 1893 by starting 52 games, completing 50 contests, pitching 482 innings, and walking 218 batters. Rusie also led the NL in hits surrendered (451), strikeouts (208), and shutouts (4). He beaned Hughie Jennings,* who was feared dead, and was hit by a line drive leaving him partially deaf.

In 1894 Rusie led the New York Giants to the NL championship by winning 36 contests, including 26 of his last 30 decisions, and two Temple Cup games. Rusie paced the NL in victories, ERA (2.78), games started (50), walks (200), strikeouts (195), and shutouts (3). Rusie's win total dropped to 23 in 1895, but he still topped the NL in strikeouts (201) and shutouts (4). New York fined Rusie $200 for breaking training rules, a claim the latter vigorously denied. When New York asked Rusie to accept a $600 pay cut, the hurler sat out the 1896 season and then sued the Giants for $5,000 in damages and his release. The other owners raised the $5,000 to settle out of court, keeping the reserve clause intact.

In 1897, Rusie won 28 games for New York and led the NL with a 2.54 ERA. During a creditable 20-victory 1898 season, he hurt his arm picking William Lange* of the Chicago Colts off first base. Rusie remained out of baseball two years, during which time he drank heavily. In December 1900, the Giants traded Rusie to the Cincinnati Reds (NL) for rights to Christy Mathewson.* Rusie's arm injury and heavy drinking aborted his attempted comeback with Cincinnati in 1901. He then retired, having won at least 20 games each of his eight seasons with the Giants and setting the record for most walks allowed (1,707). The latter record stood until after World War II. Overall, Rusie won 246, lost 174, completed 393 of 427 starts, struck out 1,950 batters in 3,778.2 innings, hurled 30 shutouts, and compiled a 3.07 ERA.

Rusie worked in a Muncie, IN paper and pulp mill for three years, engaged in fresh water pearling in Vincennes, IN, and held a steamfitting job

in Seattle, WA from 1911 to 1921. John McGraw hired him as superintendent of the Polo Grounds in New York in 1921 and kept him there through
the 1928 season. In 1929, Rusie moved to Seattle for health reasons and
opened a small chicken ranch in Auburn, WA. He lived in Seattle until his
death.

BIBLIOGRAPHY: Craig Carter, ed., *TSN Daguerreotypes*, 8th ed. (St. Louis, MO,
1990); Noel Hynd, *The Giants of the Polo Grounds* (New York, 1988); Frederick Ivor-
Campbell et al., eds., *Baseball's First Stars* (Cleveland, OH, 1996); Bill Madden, *The
Hoosiers of Summer* (Indianapolis, IN, 1994); Frank Graham, *The New York Giants*
(New York, 1952); James P. Hardy, Jr., *The New York Giants Baseball Club* (Jefferson,
NC, 1996); Fred Stein and Nick Peters, *Giants Diary* (Berkeley, CA, 1987); New
York *Herald Tribune*, December 8, 1942; *The Baseball Encyclopedia*, 10th ed. (New
York, 1996); Lowell Reidenbaugh, *Baseball's Hall of Fame—Cooperstown* (New York,
1993); Seattle (WA) *Sunday Times*, June 9, 1929, p. 5; *TSN*, December 28, 1939;
Amos Rusie file, National Baseball Library, Cooperstown, NY.

David B. Merrell

RUSSELL, William Ellis "Bill," "Ropes" (b. October 21, 1948, Pittsburg, KS),
player, coach, and manager, is the son of Warren Russell and Fern (Epple)
Russell and was a 6-foot, 175-pound basketball player in high school. Since
his high school did not field a baseball team, he was surprised when the Los
Angeles Dodgers (NL) drafted him in 1966. The Los Angeles Dodgers promoted him as an outfielder in 1969, but returned him to Spokane, WA
(PCL) in 1970 and converted him to an infielder. The Los Angeles Dodgers
summoned him permanently in 1971. Russell started at shortstop in every
1973 game, playing in the longest continuously intact major league infield
with Steve Garvey,* Davey Lopes,* and Ron Cey.*

Although not a power hitter or run producer, Russell proved a clutch
performer by hitting behind runners, bunting, and executing the hit-and-
run play. He led the NL in intentional walks (25) in 1974 and ran bases
intelligently, swiping 167 career bases. Defensively, he led NL shortstops in
double plays (102) in 1977.

Russell's appearances included three All-Star Games (1973, 1976, 1980),
five NL Championship Series (1974, 1977–1978, 1981, 1983), and four
World Series (1974, 1977–1978, 1981). He established an NL Championship Series record for most singles in a four-game series (7) in 1974 and
drove in the winning run in the tenth inning of the final game of the 1978
NL Championship Series against the Philadelphia Phillies to give the Los
Angeles Dodgers consecutive NL titles. Russell set a mark for most assists
by a shortstop in a six-game World Series (26) in 1981 against the New
York Yankees and shares the record for making hits in each game of a six-
game World Series against the New York Yankees in 1978.

In 1980 his right index finger was shattered by a pitch, nearly ending his
career. Russell credits his remarkable recovery and adjustment in 1981 to

his faith in God. He batted .263 with 1,926 hits, 293 doubles, and 627 RBI in his 18-year major league career spanning 2,181 games. His entire professional career came with the Los Angeles Dodgers, for whom he contributed as a utilityman and inspirational role model in his final three campaigns. Upon Russell's retirement, the Los Angeles Dodgers hired him as a coach from the 1987 through 1991 seasons. The Los Angeles Dodgers won the 1988 World Series over the Oakland Athletics. Russell managed Albuquerque, NM (PCL) in 1992 and 1993 and coached the Los Angeles Dodgers (NL) from 1994 to 1996, when he replaced Tommy Lasorda* as manager. He guided the Los Angeles Dodgers to a 49–37 record and second place NL West finish in 1996 before being swept by the Atlanta Braves in the NL Division Series. The Los Angeles Dodgers again finished second with an 88–74 record in 1997, but Russell was fired in June 1998 after the club started 36–38. Through June 1998, he compiled a 173–149 record for a .537 winning percentage. He managed the Orlando, FL Rays to a title in 1999 and joined the Tampa Bay Devil Rays as third base coach that November. He and his wife, Mary Anne, have two daughters and live in Tulsa, OK.

BIBLIOGRAPHY: Bill Russell file, National Baseball Library, Cooperstown, NY; *The Baseball Encyclopedia*, 10th ed. (New York, 1996); Gene Karst and Martin J. Jones, Jr., *Who's Who in Professional Baseball* (New Rochelle, NY, 1973); Lawrence S. Ritter and Donald Honig, *The Image of Their Greatness* (New York, 1979); *The Scouting Report* (New York, 1985); John Thorn et al., eds., *Total Baseball*, 5th ed. (New York, 1997); *TSN Official Baseball Register, 1998*; William F. McNeil, *The Dodgers Encyclopedia* (Champaign, IL, 1997); Tommy Lasorda and David Fisher, *The Artful Dodger* (New York, 1985); Peter C. Bjarkman, *Baseball's Great Dynasties: The Dodgers* (New York, 1990); Tommy Holmes, *The Dodgers* (New York, 1975); Stanley Cohen, *Dodgers! The First 100 Years* (New York, 1990).

Gaymon L. Bennett

RUTH, George Herman, Jr. "Babe," "The Sultan of Swat," "The Bambino" (b. February 6, 1895, Baltimore, MD; d. August 16, 1948, New York, NY), player and coach, became the most celebrated baseball player and perhaps America's leading all-time sports hero. Ruth was the son of saloon-keeper George Herman Ruth and Katherine (Shamborg) Ruth. Frustrated by young George's incorrigible behavior, his parents committed him at age seven to St. Mary's Industrial School for Boys. Ruth learned sports and a trade there. By 1914 Ruth's remarkable prowess as a left-handed pitcher prompted Jack Dunn,* owner of the Baltimore, MD Orioles (IL), to adopt and sign him. With the Orioles, he received the nickname "Babe." After being sold in 1914 to the Boston Red Sox (AL), he helped Boston win the 1915 and 1916 world championships. During six seasons with the Red Sox, Ruth compiled a brilliant 89–46 win–loss pitching record and set a record for scoreless innings pitched in World Series play. In 163 career major league games as a pitcher, he compiled a 94–46 record, completed 107 of 148 starts, struck out 488 batters, pitched 17 shutouts, and compiled a 2.28 ERA. Ruth's slugging prowess, however, persuaded manager Ed Barrow* to assign him to outfield duty. In 1919, the 6-foot 2-inch, 215-pound left-hander set a major league record with 29 HR, ushering in a long-distance hitting style still prevalent in major league offenses.

Baseball fans were electrified in January 1920 when the Red Sox sold Ruth to the New York Yankees (AL) for $125,000 and a $350,000 loan. Since the amount set a record, the sale enhanced the fame of both Ruth and the Yankees. From 1920 until his release in 1934, the New York media treated Ruth as a national celebrity. The New York superstar led the Yankees to seven AL pennants (1921–1923, 1926–1928, 1932) and four World Series titles. The AL's HR king 12 times, Ruth belted 60 HR in 1927 to set a then record for a 154-game season. His 714 career HR were unsurpassed until 1974. Since Ruth also compiled a lifetime .342 batting average, many experts rated him the sport's best offensive player. In 2,503 major league games, he made 2,873 hits, 506 doubles, and 136 triples, scored 2,174 runs, knocked in 2,213 runs, walked 2,056 times, and compiled a .690 slugging average. His fielding and earlier pitching success made him perhaps the sport's most versatile player.

Ruth became the most highly touted player ever. Besides having vast popularity, he earned enormous annual salaries and large endorsement incomes. Ruth was paid $80,000 for the 1930 season and reportedly received $2 million during his 22-year major league career. Although he spent much in high living, prudent advice from investment counsellors enabled him to live comfortably in retirement. Ruth's lofty salaries helped raise earnings of other stars. As baseball's leading celebrity, Ruth christened newly built Yankee Stadium in April 1923 by blasting a HR on the day it opened. The structure was soon dubbed "the house that Ruth built." As "the Babe," "the Sultan of Swat," and "the Bambino," he became the most photographed and heralded hero of his day. Like his Homeric feats, his misdeeds and off-the-field promotions and excesses only enhanced his image.

When Ruth retired in 1935, his undisciplined reputation kept him from being selected a manager. After leaving the Yankees, he played briefly in 1935 for the Boston Braves (NL) and also coached for the Brooklyn Dodgers (NL) in 1938. For the remainder of his life, he remained popular with baseball fans. In 1936, he was voted a charter member of the newly established National Baseball Hall of Fame. His popular mystique made him the stuff of enduring legends. In 1946, Ruth headed the Ford Motor Company's junior baseball program. In 1969, a panel of sportswriters named him the most famous figure in American sports history. He also was named the greatest baseball figure of the first half of the 20th century. Ruth died of cancer in New York City. The nation mourned his passing, as 100,000 people viewed his bier as it rested in the rotunda of Yankee Stadium. Twice married (to waitress Helen Woodford, who died in 1929, and then to actress-model Claire Merritt Hodgson in 1929), Ruth brought up two adopted daughters. Ruth was named AP Baseball Player of the Century, made Major League Baseball's All-Century Team, and ranked second among ESPN's top century athletes.

BIBLIOGRAPHY: Babe Ruth file, National Baseball Library, Cooperstown, NY; Bob Considine, *The Babe Ruth Story* (New York, 1948); Robert W. Creamer, *Babe: The Legend Comes to Life* (New York, 1974); Howard Liss, *The Boston Red Sox* (New York, 1982); Dan Shaughnessy, *The Curse of the Bambino* (New York, 1990); Peter Golenbock, *Fenway* (New York, 1992); Frederick G. Lieb, *The Boston Red Sox* (New York, 1947); Robert Redmount, *The Red Sox Encyclopedia* (Champaign, IL, 1998); Dan Valenti, *Clout: The Top Home Runs in Baseball History* (Lexington, MA, 1989); George Vecsey, "Babe Ruth," in *The Baseball Hall of Fame 50th Anniversary Book* (New York, 1988); Frank Graham, *The New York Yankees* (New York, 1943); Waite Hoyt, *Babe Ruth as I Knew Him* (New York, 1948); Kerry Keane et al., *The Babe in Red Stockings* (Champaign, IL, 1997); Brent P. Kelley, *In the Shadow of the Babe* (Jefferson, NC, 1995); Joseph J. Vecchione, ed., *The New York Times Book of Sports Legends* (New York, 1991); Donald Honig, *The Power Hitters* (St. Louis, MO, 1989); Noel Hynd, *The Giants of the Polo Grounds* (New York, 1988); Dorothy Ruth Pirone and Chris Martins, *My Dad, the Babe, Growing Up with an American Hero* (Boston, MA, 1988); Lawrence S. Ritter, *The Babe: A Life in Pictures* (Boston, MA, 1988); Louis J. Leisman, *I Was with Babe Ruth at St. Mary's* (Baltimore, MD, 1956); Dave Anderson et al., *The Yankees* (New York, 1979), B. Locke, "The Babe: What Would It Be Like If Babe Ruth Played Today," *Sport* 83 (May 1992), pp. 30–35; Tom Meany, *Babe Ruth* (New York, 1947); Lawrence Ritter and Mark Rucker, *The Babe: A Life in Pictures* (New York, 1989); John G. Robertson, *The Babe Chases 60* (Jefferson, NC, 1999); Claire M. Ruth with Bill Slocum, *The Babe and I* (New York, 1959); E. M. Scahill, "Did Babe Ruth Have a Comparative Advantage as a Pitcher?" *JEE* 21 (Fall 1990), pp. 402–410; Marshall Smelser, *The Life that Ruth Built* (New York, 1975); Ken Sobol, *Babe Ruth and the American Dream* (New York, 1974); David Q. Voigt, *American Baseball*, vol. 2 (University Park, PA, 1983); Christy Walsh, *Adios to Ghosts* (New York, 1937); Kal Wagenheim, *Babe Ruth: His Life and Legend* (Burlington, VT, 1990); Martin Weldon, *Babe Ruth* (New York, 1948).

David Q. Voigt

RYAN, James Edward "Jimmy" (b. February 11, 1863, Clinton, MA; d. October 26, 1923, Chicago, IL), player and manager, attended Holy Cross College and joined Bridgeport, CT (EL) in 1885 as a left-handed–throwing baseball shortstop and outfielder. Ryan, who batted right-handed, joined the Chicago White Stockings (NL) late that season. He became manager Cap Anson's* regular right fielder in 1886, hitting .306 in 84 games and helping Chicago win its second straight NL pennant. When Chicago lost a postseason "World Series" to the St. Louis Browns (AA), disappointed owner Albert Spalding* sold several front-line players, including Michael "King" Kelly,* pitcher Jim McCormick,* and outfielders Abner Dalrymple* and George Gore.*

The fleet-footed, 5-foot 9-inch, 162-pound Ryan was moved to center field, where he starred for the next three seasons (1887–1889) by averaging 68 hits, 124 runs, and 51 stolen bases per season. In 1888, he led the NL in hits (182), doubles (33), HR (16), total bases (283), and slugging percentage (.515) and finished second to Anson in batting (.332). Ryan jumped to Charles Comiskey's* Chicago Pirates in the short-lived PL in 1890, but returned as the White Stockings' center fielder in 1891. He remained in the Chicago outfield for the next decade, switching from center field to the right field to make room for promising newcomer Bill Lange* in 1894 and then moving to left field in 1898. Ryan hit over .300 in six consecutive seasons (1894–1899), including a career-high .361 in 1894.

When Ryan slumped to a .277 batting average in 1900, the Chicago White Stockings released him. He signed with St. Paul, MN (WL), where he hit .323 in 108 games as a player-manager in 1901. He returned to the major leagues for the 1902–1903 seasons as an outfielder for the Washington Senators (AL) and finished his pro baseball career managing Colorado Springs, CO (WL) in 1904. Ryan stayed in Chicago, where he worked many years in the assessor's office and later as a deputy in the sheriff's office. He also managed the Rogers Parks, an amateur baseball club on Chicago's near north side, and played on the team until he was 51 years old. Ryan, who later served as a deputy sheriff, died suddenly of heart failure at his Chicago home.

In 18 major league seasons, Ryan appeared in 2,012 major league games, collected 2,502 hits, made 451 doubles, 157 triples, and 118 HR, scored 1,642 runs, knocked in 1,093 runs, and compiled a .306 batting average. Although best known for his outfield play, he occasionally played the infield and compiled a lifetime 6–1 mark as a pitcher in 24 games. Ryan made five hits in one game on five separate occasions and four extra-base hits in a game twice. He batted for the cycle in 1888 and 1891 and scored six runs in a July 1894 game. He batted first throughout most of his career and led off 22 games with HR, high on the all-time list.

BIBLIOGRAPHY: Jimmy Ryan file, National Baseball Library, Cooperstown, NY; Art Ahrens, "An Assist for Jimmy Ryan," *BRJ* 12 (1983), pp. 66–70; Adrian C. Anson, *A Ballplayer's Career* (Chicago, IL, 1900); Jim Enright, *Chicago Cubs* (New York, 1975); Eddie Gold and Art Ahrens, *The Golden Era Cubs, 1876–1940* (Chicago, IL, 1985); Albert G. Spalding, *Base Ball* (New York, 1911); Warren Brown, *The Chicago Cubs* (New York, 1946); Chicago *Daily Tribune*, October 30, 1923; Craig Carter, ed., *TSN Daguerreotypes*, 8th ed. (St. Louis, MO, 1990); Joseph L. Reichler, *The Great All-Time Baseball Record Book* (New York, 1981); *The Baseball Encyclopedia*, 10th ed. (New York, 1996), Robert L. Tiemann and Mark Rucker, eds., *Nineteenth Century Stars* (Kansas City, MO, 1989); Warren Wilbert and William Hageman, *Chicago Cubs: Seasons at the Summit* (Champaign, IL, 1997); David Q. Voigt, *American Baseball*, vol. 1 (Norman, OK, 1966).

Raymond D. Kush

RYAN, Lynn Nolan (b. January 31, 1947, Refugio, TX), player and executive, is the son of oil field supervisor Lynn Nolan Ryan and Mary (Haneal) Ryan. Ryan grew up in the small town of Alvin, TX, where he idolized Sandy Koufax.* A star right-handed pitcher at Alvin High School, he appeared in 24 of the team's 36 games during his senior year. He attended Alvin JC from

1966 to 1969, married childhood sweetheart Ruth Elise Holdruff on June 26, 1967, and has one son, Reid. His son is an executive in the Houston Astros (NL) organization.

An eighth round selection by the New York Mets (NL) in 1965, Ryan pitched in the minor leagues for Marion, SC (ApL) in 1965; Greenville, NC (WCL) and Williamsport, PA (EL) in 1966; and Winter Haven, FL (FSL) and Jacksonville, FL (IL) in 1967. He reached the major leagues to stay in 1968 with a record-setting fastball, a devastating curve, and, in his own words, without "the slightest idea where the ball was going." Ryan's wildness led the Mets to trade him to the California Angels (AL) for infielder Jim Fregosi* in December 1971. Ryan spent the 1972 through 1979 campaigns with the California Angels. The Houston Astros (NL) signed him as a free agent in November 1979. Ryan pitched for the Astros from 1980 through 1988 and joined the Texas Rangers (AL) as a free agent in December 1988. His final major league season came with Texas in 1994.

The handsome, 6-foot, 2-inch, 190-pound Ryan emerged as the premier power pitcher in a period boasting several all-time leading strikeout pitchers. Ryan reached a new plateau against the Oakland A's on August 22, 1989, when he became the first pitcher ever to record 5,000 lifetime strikeouts. He struck out Ricky Henderson* of the Oakland A's in the fifth inning to break the 5,000 barrier.

Ryan, the only pitcher to have three straight seasons with at least 300 or more strikeouts (1972–1974), remains the only hurler to have pitched seven no-hit games (against the Kansas City Royals [AL] and Detroit Tigers [AL] in 1973, Minnesota Twins [AL] in 1974, Baltimore Orioles [AL] in 1975, Los Angeles Dodgers [NL] in 1981, Oakland A's [AL] in 1990, and Toronto Blue Jays [AL] in 1991). On July 31, 1990, he defeated the Milwaukee Brewers to become the 20th major league 300-game winner. He also established major league marks for the most games with 15 or more strikeouts (19) and 10 or more strikeouts (213) and most seasons with 300 or more strikeouts (6). He set the AL record for the most seasons with 200 or more strikeouts (10). He holds the major league records for the most seasons played and pitched (27), most walks allowed (2,795), and most strikeouts (5,714). No hurler threw more pitches in the game's long history. Ryan led the AL in strikeouts nine times (1972–1974, 1976–1979, 1989–1990) and in walks six times (1972–1974, 1976–1978). He topped the NL in ERA twice (1981, 1987), walks twice (1980, 1982), and strikeouts twice (1987–1988). The fascination with Ryan's numbers was perhaps underscored best by the numerous attempts to clock the speed of his fastball (at least 100.9 miles per hour), despite considerable evidence that his sharp-breaking curveball produced many of his strikeouts. Ryan was selected for the AL All-Star team in 1972, 1973, 1975, 1979, and 1989 and for the NL All-Star team in 1981 and 1985.

Ryan's records failed to evoke universal praise because critics stressed his .526 win–loss percentage and paucity of 20-victory seasons (1973 and 1974) and questioned whether he was more show than substance. Ryan expressed his own disappointment that, despite being a key figure in three division championships (California Angels, 1979, and Houston Astros, 1980, 1986), his only World Series experience had come early in his career with the New York Mets in 1969.

During 27 major league seasons, Ryan won 324, lost 292, struck out 5,714 batters in 5,387 innings, and compiled a 3.19 ERA. He owns four ranches, raises cattle, owns two banks, and established the Nolan Ryan Foundation and Nolan Ryan Scholarship Fund for Alvin, TX. He was elected to the Texas Baseball Hall of Fame in 1987 and the National Baseball Hall of Fame in 1999. Ryan, an assistant to the president of the Texas Rangers since 1999, made Major League Baseball's All-Century Team.

BIBLIOGRAPHY: John Benson et al., *Baseball's Top 100* (Wilton, CT, 1997); Bob Brill, "Nolan Ryan: National Hero and Businessman," *SCD* 21 (April 15, 1994), p. 60; Ron Fimrite, "Bringer of the Big Heat," *SI* 42 (June 16, 1975), pp. 32–33; Ron Fimrite, "A Great Hand with Old Cowhide," *SI* 65 (September 29, 1986), pp. 84–88; Ron Fimrite, "Speed Trap for an Angel," *SI* 41 (September 16, 1974), pp. 98ff; Richard Hoffer, "Armed and Still Dangerous," *GQ* 58 (May 1988), pp. 246–249; Robert E. Kelly, *Baseball's Best* (Jefferson, NC, 1988); Robert Grayson, "The Class of '99," *SCD* 25 (December 25, 1998), pp. 80–81; Scott Kelnhofer, "Ryan Is on Cooperstown's Doorstep," *SCD* 25 (November 27, 1998), pp. 72–73; William Leggett, "Angel Who Makes the Turnstiles Sing," *SI* 38 (May 14, 1973), pp. 26–27, 32–33; Brent Kelley, "Nolan Ryan? In My Bullpen," *BRJ* 21 (1992), pp. 49–52; Joe Mangeno, "Nolan Ryan: Tough Luck Great?" *BRJ* 21 (1992), pp. 46–48; Leigh Montville, "Citizen Ryan," *SI* 74 (April 15, 1991), pp. 120–129; *NYT Biographical Service* 24 (March 1993), pp. 434–435; Steve Rushin, "As Big as All Texas," *SI* 73 (August 13, 1990), pp. 18–21; Ross Newhan, *The California Angels* (New York, 1982); Rich Coberly, *The No Hit Hall of Fame* (Newport Beach, CA, 1985); Phil Rogers, *The Impossible Takes a Little Longer* (Dallas, TX, 1991); Nolan Ryan and Harvey Frommer, *Throwing Heat* (New York, 1988); Nolan Ryan and Jerry B. Jenkins, *Miracle Man: Nolan Ryan* (Boston, MA, 1993); Stanley Cohen, *A Magic Summer* (San Diego, CA, 1988); Joseph Durso, *Amazing: The Miracle of the Mets* (New York, 1970); Jack Lang and Peter Simon, *The New York Mets* (New York, 1986); Nolan Ryan with Steve Jacobsen, *Nolan Ryan Strikeout King* (New York, 1975); Nolan Ryan with Bill Libby, *Nolan Ryan* (New York, 1977); Nolan Ryan with Joe Torre, *Pitching and Hitting* (New York, 1977); "Ryan Records Special K," *TSN*, July 22, 1985, p. 6; Ruth Ryan, *Covering Home* (Waco, TX, 1995); *TSN Baseball Register, 1995*; "Throwing Smoke," *Time* 105 (June 2, 1975), pp. 37–38; Nick Trujillo, *The Meaning of Nolan Ryan* (College Station, TX, 1994).

James W. Harper

S

SABERHAGEN, Bret William (b. April 11, 1964, Chicago Heights, IL), player, is the son of Robert Saberhagen. The 6-foot 1-inch, 190-pound pitcher bats and throws right-handed and attended Cleveland High School in Reseda, CA. Saberhagen, selected by the Kansas City Royals (AL) in the 19th round of the free agent draft in June 1982, pitched in 1983 for Fort Myers, FL (FSL), winning 10 games and losing five decisions. He finished the 1983 season with Jacksonville, FL (SL), producing a 6–2 win–loss record.

In 1984, Saberhagen began an eight-season stint with the Kansas City Royals (AL), recording 10 victories and 11 setbacks. He won 20 games and lost only six in 1985. After winning only seven contests and dropping 12 in 1986, he compiled 18 victories against only 10 losses the next season. In 1988, his record slipped to 14 triumphs and 16 losses. Saberhagen enjoyed his best major league season in 1989, winning 23 games against only six setbacks. He led the AL in victories, winning percentage (.793), complete games (12), ERA (2.16), and innings pitched (262.1). In 1990, he triumphed only five times while dropping nine. The 1991 campaign saw him win 13 games and lose only eight. In December 1991, the Kansas City Royals traded him to the New York Mets (NL). With the Mets, he took only three games and dropped five decisions in 1992, being on the disabled list twice. He compiled a 7–7 record and 3.29 ERA for the last-place New York Mets in 1993 and a superb 14–4 mark and 2.74 ERA during the strike-shortened 1994 season, pacing the NL with a .778 winning percentage. In July 1995, the Mets traded Saberhagen to the Colorado Rockies (NL). He spent the entire 1996 season on the disabled list and joined the Boston Red Sox (AL) in December 1996. Saberhagen compiled 15–8 record with a 3.96 ERA, helping Boston win the Wild Card in 1998. His 10.6 record and 2.95 ERA aided Boston's Wild Card win in 1999.

Saberhagen, *TSN* AL Pitcher of the Year in 1985 and 1989, was named right-handed pitcher on the *TSN* All-Star team in 1985 and 1989. The

BBWAA voted him the AL Cy Young Award, the top pitching honor, in both 1985 and 1989, while *TSN* named him the Comeback Player of the Year in 1987 and the AL Gold Glove recipient as a pitcher in 1989. On August 26, 1991, Saberhagen pitched a 7–0, no-hit victory against the Chicago White Sox. He hurled in the AL Championship Series in 1984 and 1985 without any decisions. Saberhagen pitched in the 1987 and 1990 All-Star Games and was credited with the AL victory in 1990. He won two games for the victorious Kansas City Royals against the St. Louis Cardinals in the 1985 World Series. He lost his only start with a 3.86 ERA against the Cleveland Indians in the 1998 AL Division Series. He struggled with one loss in the AL Division Series and lost his only decision with a 1.50 ERA in the AL Championship Series.

In 11 AL seasons, Saberhagen won 135 games and lost 93 contests for a 3.31 ERA. In four NL seasons he won 31 of 53 games. His major league career included 1,605 strikeouts and a 3.33 ERA with 151 victories and 107 losses. Saberhagen and his former wife, Janeane, have three children, Drew, Daulton William, and Brittany. His hobbies are golf and boating.

BIBLIOGRAPHY: John Benson et al., *Baseball's Top 100* (Wilton, CT, 1997); Peter Gammons, "Return of the Royal Nonesuch," *SI* 66 (June 8, 1987), pp. 28–29; *NYT Biographical Service* 22 (December 1991), pp. 1354–1355; *NYT Biographical Service* 25 (February 1994), pp. 337–338; *New York Mets Media Guide*, 1994; *TSN Official Baseball Register*, 1998; Bret Saberhagen file, National Baseball Library, Cooperstown, NY; Alan Eskew, *A Royal Finish* (Chicago, IL, 1985); Ken Young, *Cy Young Award Winners* (New York, 1994).

Stan W. Carlson

SAIN, John Franklin "Johnny" (b. September 25, 1917, Havana, AR), player and coach, is the son of John Sain, a mechanic, and Eva Sain and graduated from Havana High School in 1935. He entered professional baseball in 1936 and was selected an All-Star pitcher in the NEAL in 1938 and 1939. Sain married Doris McBride on October 1, 1945 and has four children, John, Jr., Sharyl, Randy, and Rhonda. He served in the U.S. Navy from 1943 through 1945 as a test pilot.

Sain began his major league career with the Boston Braves (NL) in 1942 and became one of the best known pitchers in Braves history. The 6-foot 2-inch, 195 pounder won 20 or more games four times for Boston and recorded an NL-leading 24 victories in 1948, when Boston captured the NL pennant. The Braves possessed only three proven starters, Warren Spahn,* Sain, and Vernon Bickford. Sain and 15-game winner Spahn invented the phrase "Spahn and Sain and pray for rain," which became part of baseball folklore. During Sain's career, only Bob Feller* of the Cleveland Indians and Spahn completed a greater percentage of games started. Sain finished 245 (59 percent) of his 412 starts.

Sain outdueled Feller, 1–0, in the opening game of the 1948 World Series. The game against the Cleveland Indians remains controversial because umpire Bill Stewart (IS) missed the call on a pickoff play at second base involving the Braves' Phil Masi, who scored the game's only run. Sain struck out the entire side in one inning in the 1948 All-Star game, one of only seven pitchers to accomplish that feat. In 1947, he won 21 games, batted .346, and became one of only 29 20-game winners in the game's history to hit over .300 in the same season.

In August 1951, the New York Yankees (AL) purchased Sain for $50,000. Sain's exploits as a relief pitcher helped the Yankees win AL pennants from 1951 through 1953. In May 1955, New York traded Sain to the Kansas City Athletics (AL). Altogether, Sain won 139 contests, lost 116 games, and split four World Series decisions. He compiled identical 1–1 World Series records with the Braves and the Yankees. His regular season and World Series ERAs were 3.49 and 2.64, respectively. He was selected to two NL and one AL All-Star teams, appearing only in the 1947 and 1948 games for the NL.

Subsequently, Sain served as a pitching coach for several major league teams and as a minor league pitching instructor. His coaching assignments included the Kansas City Athletics (AL) in 1959, New York Yankees (AL) from 1961 through 1963, Minnesota Twins (AL) in 1965 and 1966, Detroit Tigers (AL) from 1967 through 1969, Chicago White Sox (AL) from 1971 through 1975, and Atlanta Braves (NL) in 1977, 1985, and 1986. A respected and innovative pitching coach, he considered coaching the 1968 Detroit Tigers pitching staff to an AL pennant and World Series title over the St. Louis Cardinals as his most memorable achievement. Denny McLain's* 31 regular season victories and Mickey Lolich's* three World Series triumphs paced the Tigers' staff. Retired, he resides in Oakbrook, IL.

BIBLIOGRAPHY: Peter Golenbock, *Dynasty* (Englewood Cliffs, NJ, 1975); Ralph Houk and Robert W. Creamer, *Season of Glory* (New York, 1988); Dave Anderson et al., *The Yankees* (New York, 1979); Mark Gallagher, *The Yankee Encyclopedia*, vol. 3 (Champaign, IL, 1997); Bob Cairns, *Pen Men* (New York, 1993); Gary Caruso, *The Braves Encyclopedia* (Philadelphia, PA, 1995); Mark Onigman, *This Date in Braves History* (New York, 1982); Al Hirshberg, *Braves, the Pick and Shovel* (Boston, MA, 1948); Harold Kaese, *The Boston Braves* (New York, 1948); John Sain file, National Baseball Library, Cooperstown, NY; Brent P. Kelley, *The Case For: Those Overlooked by the Baseball Hall of Fame* (Jefferson, NC, 1992); Tony Kubek and Terry Pluto, *Sixty-one* (New York, 1987); *The Baseball Encyclopedia*, 10th ed. (New York, 1996); Dom Forker, *The Men of Autumn* (Dallas, TX, 1989); *NYT*, May 21, 1952, March 11, 1953; New York *World Telegram*, August 6, 1947, September 21, 1948; John Sain, interview with Albert J. Figone, September 2, 1989; Rich Westcott, *Masters of the Diamond* (Jefferson, NC, 1994); John Thorn et al., eds., *Total Braves* (New York, 1996); Dixie Tourangeau, "Spahn, Sain, and the '48 Braves," *TNP* 17 (1998), pp. 17–20.

Albert J. Figone

ST. AUBIN, Helen Callaghan Candaele "Cally" (b. March 13, 1923, Vancouver, Canada; d. December 8, 1992, Lompoc, CA), player, was the daughter of Albert Callaghan, a truck driver, and Hazel (Terryberry) Callaghan and had two brothers and three sisters. Her older sister, Margaret, played second base and third base in the AAGPBL from 1944 to 1951 and teamed with her at Fort Wayne, IN. At King Edward High School in Vancouver, the sisters participated in track and field, basketball, lacrosse, volleyball, soccer and field hockey. Helen greatly admired baseball star Lou Gehrig.* She and her sister played softball for the Vancouver Western Mutuals and performed at the 1943 World Series Softball Tournament at Detroit, MI, where the AAGPBL recruited them.

The 5-foot 1-inch 115-pound St. Aubin, who batted and threw left-handed, played in the outfield and hit better than her sister. Nicknamed "Cally," she played for the Minneapolis, MN Millerettes (AAGPBL) in 1944, Fort Wayne, IN Daisies (AAGPBL) in 1945, 1946, 1948, and Kenosha, WI (AAGPBL) in 1949. For Fort Wayne in 1945, she shared the AAGPBL crown with a .299 batting average and for HR (3). She also led the AAGPBL in hits (122), total bases (336), and doubles (17). She loved stealing bases. St. Aubin possessed an amazing sense of timing and excellent acceleration, pilfering 112 bases her rookie season and 114 stolen bases in 1946. In 495 career games, she amassed 419 stolen bases. Her impressive .940 fielding average reflected her solid, reliable outfield skills. In six AAGPBL seasons, she batted .256 with 449 hits and 117 RBI.

St. Aubin married Robert Candaele after the 1946 season and had five sons. Her youngest son, Casey, played major league baseball for the Montreal Expos (NL), Houston Astros (NL), and Cleveland Indians (AL). No other offspring of AAGPBL players made the major leagues. Her son Kelly wrote *A League of Their Own*, the inspiration and source for Penny Marshall's successful full-length 1992 movie.

St. Aubin nearly died during a night game in 1946. "She stepped up to bat and experienced excruciating abdominal pain, so bad that the team called a doctor out of the stands. Although the doctor declared there were nothing wrong, Helen had to be rushed to the hospital, where a tubal pregnancy was correctly diagnosed. Because the hospital couldn't reach Robert Candaele, Helen's sister and teammate, Margaret Callaghan, had to give permission to operate."

St. Aubin described AAGPBL life on the road: "After a double-header, we'd shower, get dressed, travel all night in the bus, get to our hotel at 8 or 9 in the morning, shower, play two games of baseball in 110 degrees of heat, then do it all over again the next day." She retired after the 1949 season to bring up her young family. After divorcing Robert Candaele, she married Ron St. Aubin. The British Columbia Softball Hall of Fame enshrined her. She also appears in the AAGPBL Gallery at the National Baseball Hall of Fame.

BIBLIOGRAPHY: Scott A.G.M. Crawford, telephone interview with Margaret Callaghan Maxwell, April 19, 1996; Helen St. Aubin, "This Mother Could Hit," *PW* 28 (August 17, 1987), pp. 77–78ff; AAGPBL file, Northern Indiana Historical Society,

South Bend, IN; Tim Wiles, National Baseball Hall of Fame, Cooperstown, NY, letter to Scott A.G.M. Crawford, December 14, 1995; Scott A.G.M. Crawford, telephone conversations with Dottie Collins, AAGPBLPA, February 1996; Barbara Gregorich, *Women at Play* (San Diego, CA, 1993); W. C. Madden, *The Women of the All-American Girls Professional Baseball League* (Jefferson, NC, 1997); *NYT*, December 11, 1992, p. D-19; Gai I. Berlage, *Women in Baseball* (Westport, CT, 1994).

Scott A.G.M. Crawford

SALLEE, Harry Franklin "Slim" (b. February 3, 1885, Higginsport, OH; d. March 22, 1950, Higginsport, OH), player, married Catherine Roberts at Darnell, AR and entered organized baseball in 1904 with Springfield, IL (3IL). The 6-foot 3-inch, 180-pound, left-handed pitcher sat out much of the 1905 season with an injury and returned to action in 1906 with the Birmingham, AL Barons (CSL). After posting 17 wins for Birmingham in 1906 and 22 triumphs the next year with Williamsport, PA (TSL), he joined the St. Louis Cardinals (NL) for the 1908 season. His three wins that campaign included a 2–0 masterpiece against Christy Mathewson* of the New York Giants.

Sallee remained with the St. Louis Cardinals until July 1916, winning 81 games from 1911 through 1915. His next stop came with the New York Giants (NL), which were managed by John McGraw.* Sallee enjoyed a fine season in 1917, triumphing 18 times, dropping only seven decisions, and posting a sparkling 2.17 ERA while helping the Giants take the NL title. In March 1919, the Cincinnati Reds (NL) selected Sallee on waivers. For the NL pennant–winning Cincinnati Reds, he enjoyed his best campaign with 21 wins, four shutouts, and a 2.06 ERA. He won the second game of the 1917 World Series against the Chicago White Sox for his only fall classic victory. Like many of his teammates, he expressed shock and surprise upon discovering that the White Sox were alleged to have thrown the 1919 World Series. Sallee's pitching career declined sharply after 1919, causing him to be waived to the New York Giants in September 1920 and to leave major league baseball the following season. He won 174 major league games and lost 143 contests lifetime with 25 shutouts and a 2.56 ERA.

Sallee and his wife owned an ice plant, restaurant, and gas station in Higginsport, OH. Unfortunately, an Ohio River flood swept away all their holdings, nearly bankrupting them. They recovered from the disaster and eventually purchased another restaurant, "Slim's Cafe," which they operated until Sallee's death.

BIBLIOGRAPHY: Bob Broeg, *Redbirds: A Century of Cardinals' Baseball* (St. Louis, MO, 1981); Bob Broeg and Jerry Vickery, *St. Louis Cardinals Encyclopedia* (Grand Rapids, MI, 1998); Noel Hynd, *The Giants of the Polo Grounds* (New York, 1988); Charles C. Alexander, *John McGraw* (New York, 1988); Frank Graham, *The New York Giants*; Elliot Asinof, *Eight Men Out* (New York, 1963); Ritter Collett, *The Cincinnati Reds* (Virginia Beach, VA, 1976); Lee Allen, *The Cincinnati Reds* (New York, 1948); Tom Meany, *Baseball's Greatest Teams* (New York, 1949); *The Baseball Encyclopedia*, 10th ed.

(New York, 1996); Frederick G. Lieb, *The St. Louis Cardinals* (New York, 1945); Harry Sallee file, National Baseball Library, Cooperstown, NY; A. D. Suehsdorf and Richard J. Thompson, "Slim Sallee's Extraordinary Year," *BRJ* 19 (1990), pp. 10–14.

David S. Matz

SAMS, Doris "Sammye" (b. February 2, 1927, Knoxville, TN), player, is the daughter of Robert Sams, a salesman and semipro outfielder, and Pauline (Moore) Sams and had two elder brothers. Her father and grandfather, a semipro pitcher, both enjoyed playing baseball and taught her their skills. As a young child, Sams kept active and athletic. She thrived on horseshoe tossing, marbles, and other competitions and especially enjoyed winning a yo-yo championship at school. She started competitive softball at age 11 in 1938 and performed well at softball, tennis, and badminton in high school. She helped her softball team capture the state tournament for eight consecutive years and tried out for the AAGPBL in Knoxville, TN in 1946.

The 5-foot 9-inch, 145-pound Sams, who batted and threw right-handed, starred as an AAGPBL pitcher–outfielder from 1946 to 1953. She played for the Muskegan, MI Lassies (AAGPBL) from 1946 to 1949 and finished her baseball career with the Kalamazoo, MI Lassies (AAGPBL) from 1950 to 1953. She proved an effective sidearm pitcher and batted .274 as an outfielder her rookie season.

"Sammye," a stellar performer, made the AAGPBL All Star team six times, including as a pitcher from 1947 to 1950 and as an outfielder in 1951 and 1952. She shared the batting championship in 1949 with a .279 average and won the HR title in 1952 with 12. On August 18, 1947, Sams pitched a perfect game against the Fort Wayne, IN Daisies. Only two perfect games had been hurled in the AAGPBL previously. Her 11–4 record and league-best .733 winning percentage helped the Lassies capture their first pennant. She compiled the best fielding percentage among pitchers and the second best ERA at 0.98. She batted .280 with 41 RBI. In 1948, she finished 18–10 with a club record 59 RBI. The following season, she led the AAGPBL with 114 hits, compiled a 15–10 record, and paced pitchers in fielding. Sams batted above .300 for the first time in 1950 and hit .306 as just an outfielder in 1951. In 1952, she batted .314 and shared best fielding percentage honors. Her most special baseball memories involved winning MVP awards in 1947 and 1949. "Off the baseball field I sometimes felt awkward. On the diamond I felt full of confidence. I enjoyed every moment of every game and even now, as I look back, I remember myself as being a natural," she observed. Her career included a .290 batting average, 22 HR, and 286 RBI.

Sams worked as a computer operator for the Knoxville Utility Board from 1954 to 1979. Although enjoying the 1992 movie *A League of Their Own*, she considers it only 60 percent true. Sams enjoys golf and the movie *The Sound of Music*. "I've always felt happy singing. When we travelled on our baseball buses, I remember a group of us developing a regular program of Irish folk songs."

The Knoxville, TN resident, who remains single, was inducted into the Tennessee Sports Hall of Fame in 1970 and the Knoxville Hall of Fame in 1982 and appears in the AAGPBL Gallery at the National Baseball Hall of Fame in Cooperstown, NY. Only Sams and Jean Faut Eastman* won two AAGPBL MVP titles. The Knoxville (TN) *Journal* observed, "Miss Sams, [was] probably the most versatile distaff athlete in the state's history."

BIBLIOGRAPHY: Scott A.G.M. Crawford, telephone interview with Doris Sams, April 15, 1996; AAGPBL files, Northern Indiana Historical Society, South Bend, IN; Tim Wiles, National Baseball Library, Cooperstown, NY, letter to Scott A.G.M. Crawford, December 14, 1995; Scott A.G.M. Crawford, telephone conversations with Dottie Collins, AAGPBLPA, February 1996; Barbara Gregorich, *Women at Play* (San Diego, CA, 1993); W. C. Madden, *The Women of the All-American Girls Professional Baseball League* (Jefferson, NC, 1997); Gai I. Berlage, *Women in Baseball* (Westport, CT, 1994).

Scott A.G.M. Crawford

SAMUEL, Juan Milton (b. December 9, 1960, San Pedro de Marcoris, DR), player and coach, is the son of Jorge Samuel and Jane Samuel and attended high school in Licey, PR. The Philadelphia Phillies (NL) signed the 5-foot 11-inch, 185-pound second baseman, who batted and threw right-handed, as a free agent in April 1980. Samuel spent nearly four seasons in the minor leagues with Central Oregon (NWL) in 1980, Spartanburg, SC (SAL) in 1981, Peninsula, VA (CrL) in 1982, and Reading, PA (EL) and Portland, OR (PCL) in 1983. After joining the Philadelphia Phillies in 1983, he appeared briefly in the National League Championship Series against the Los Angeles Dodgers and the World Series against the Baltimore Orioles.

Samuel started at second base for the Philadelphia Phillies from 1984 to 1989. In 1984, he set a NL record by batting 701 times, led the NL in triples (19), and established career-highs with 191 hits and 72 stolen bases. No major league rookie had stolen as many bases. Samuel made the NL All-Star team and finished behind Dwight Gooden* in the NL Rookie of the Year balloting. His best season with the Philadelphia Phillies came in 1987, when he batted .272, set career-highs with 28 HR and 100 RBI, led the NL with 15 triples, and made the NL All-Star team. *TSN* named him to its All-Star and Silver Slugger teams. He tied a major league record by leading the NL in strikeouts from 1984 to 1987 and stole at least 30 bases eight straight seasons. He led NL second basemen in putouts and errors three times and chances and double plays once.

The Philadelphia Phillies traded Samuel to the New York Mets (NL) for Lenny Dykstra* and Roger McDowell in June 1989. Six months later, the New York Mets shipped him to the Los Angeles Dodgers (NL) for Alejandro Pena and Mike Marshall. Samuel batted .271 in 1991 and singled in the

All-Star Game, but the Los Angeles Dodgers released him in July 1992. He finished 1992 with the Kansas City Royals (AL), spent 1993 with the Cincinnati Reds (NL), and played the next two campaigns with the Detroit Tigers (AL), batting a career-high .309 in 1994. In September 1995, the Detroit Tigers returned him to the Kansas City Royals. From January 1996 to November 1998 he played with the Toronto Blue Jays (AL).

In 16 major league seasons, Samuel batted .259 with 1,578 hits, 287 doubles, 161 HR, and 703 RBI. He struck out 1,442 times, walked only 440 times, and stole 396 bases. In January 1999, the Detroit Tigers named him an assistant coach. The San Pedro de Marcoris, DR resident married Mery Del Rosario in March 1985 and has one child, Neomy.

BIBLIOGRAPHY: Juan Samuel file, National Baseball Library, Cooperstown, NY; *TSN Baseball Register*, 1999; *Toronto Blue Jays Media Guide*, 1998; Rich Westcott and Frank Bilovsky, *The New Phillies Encyclopedia* (Philadelphia, PA, 1993).

David L. Porter

SANDBERG, Ryne Dee "Ryno" (b. September 18, 1959, Spokane, WA), player and coach, excelled as an all-around sports star at Spokane's North Central High School. He earned All-City honors in basketball and baseball and was selected All-State in football. Drafted by the Philadelphia Phillies (NL) in 1978, Sandberg played four years in their farm system before appearing in 13 major league games with Philadelphia at the end of the 1981 season. The Philadelphia Phillies traded Larry Bowa* and Sandberg to the Chicago Cubs (NL) for Ivan DeJesus in January 1982, marking one of the great trades in Chicago Cubs history.

Despite making only one hit in his first 32 at-bats in his rookie year, Sandberg ended the 1982 season with a .271 batting average and a club record of 103 runs scored. His 32 stolen bases established a Cubs record for third basemen. The Chicago Cubs switched him to second base in 1983, resulting in his emergence as a premier NL player and fan favorite. A smooth-fielding, power-hitting player, the 6-foot, 185-pound, right-handed Sandberg established many records in the following decade. He became the first second baseman in major league history to win nine Gold Glove Awards and holds the major league record for 123 consecutive errorless games from June 21, 1989 to May 17, 1990 at his position, involving 584 chances. During his major league career, he enjoyed 15 streaks of at least 30 errorless games. He led NL second basemen four times in fielding percentage. The modest Sandberg commented, "I've worked at it. It hasn't come easy." He shares the major league career record of highest fielding percentage by a second baseman with .989.

Sandberg in 1990 became the first second baseman since Rogers Hornsby* in 1925 to lead the NL in HR, hitting 40 HR. The same season, he became only the third player in major league history to hit 40 HR and steal 25 bases.

No other second baseman in major league history previously had reached the 30 HR plateau in consecutive seasons. His .309 batting average in 1993 marked the fifth time in his Chicago Cubs career that he surpassed .300. From 1984 to 1993, Sandberg appeared in 10 consecutive All-Star Games.

Sandberg helped lead the Chicago Cubs to two NL East titles. The first came in 1984, when he achieved his best batting average with .314 and played 61 consecutive games without an error. Sandberg's efforts won him the 1984 NL MVP Award. Sandberg retired in June 1994 after slumping to a career-low .238 batting mark. Sandberg returned to the Chicago Cubs in 1996 and retired again in September 1997. In October 1998, the Chicago Cubs named him an instructor. With the Cubs 16 years, Sandberg ranked among the team's top 10 in many categories. These included stolen bases (344), HR (282), hits (2,386), and RBI (1,061). He had a .285 career batting average and holds the major league record for most HR by a second baseman with 277. Sandberg married Cindy White and had two children before their divorce. He married his second wife, Margaret, in 1995 and resides in Phoenix, AZ.

BIBLIOGRAPHY: John Benson et al., *Baseball's Top 100* (Wilton, CT, 1997); Ryne Sandberg file, National Baseball Library, Cooperstown, NY; *CB* 55 (November 1994), pp. 50–53; *1994 Chicago Cubs Information Guide; Chicago Cubs Vineline* (December 1990, May 1991, December 1992); Ryne Sandberg and Barry Rozner, *Second to Home* (Chicago, IL, 1995); Steve Rushin, "City of Stars," *SI* 77 (July 27, 1992), pp. 62–66; S. Rosenbloom, "Mr. Cub, '90s Style," *Sport* 82 (June 1991), pp. 67–71; Eddie Gold and Art Ahrens, *The New Era Cubs, 1941–1985* (Chicago, IL, 1985); Ryne Sandberg and Fred Machell, *Ryno* (Chicago, IL, 1985); Warren Wilbert and William Hageman, *The Chicago Cubs: Seasons at the Summit* (Champaign, IL, 1997); *TSN Official Baseball Register*, 1998.

Duane A. Smith

SANDERS, Alexander Bennett "Ben," "Big Ben" (b. February 16, 1865, Catharpen, VA; d. August 29, 1930, Memphis, TN), player, grew up in Prince William County, VA and initially played baseball for Roanoke College. The 6-foot 1-inch, 200-pound right-hander turned professional in 1886 as a reserve outfielder for Nashville, TN (SL). During 1887, he pitched regularly for Altoona, PA (PSL) and Canton, OH (OSL).

In 1888, manager Harry Wright* of the Philadelphia Phillies (NL) signed Sanders. Sanders initially found major league hitters difficult to face and was moved to the outfield. By mid-season, however, he found his form and rivaled Charles Buffinton* as the Philadelphia Phillies' best pitcher. Sanders' rookie season comprised his best major league campaign, as he won 19 games against 10 losses with a glittering 1.90 ERA in 275.1 innings. He led the NL with eight shutouts and struck out 121 batters while walking just 33. In 1889 with the Philadelphia Phillies, Sanders again won 19 games, but lost 18 and his ERA almost doubled to 3.55. The 1890 season found Sanders jumping to the Philadelphia Quakers (PL), where he finished 19–8 in a backbreaking 346.2 innings.

After the 1890 season, Sanders matriculated at Vanderbilt University in engineering. When the PL disbanded in late 1890, Sanders was apportioned to the Philadelphia Athletics (AA). The Philadelphia Athletics paid him $4,000 for a truncated season. Sanders insisted that his contract be built around his college schedule, compiling an 11–5 record for the Philadelphia Athletics with a 3.79 ERA in 1891. An arm injury relegated him to the outfield in late August. In the spring 1892, Sanders graduated from Vanderbilt and signed with the Louisville Colonels (NL). For a ninth place club, he finished 12–19 mark with a respectable 3.22 ERA. A no-hit game on August 22 against the Baltimore Orioles highlighted his only losing major league season.

In 1892, Sanders retired from baseball and moved to Chicago to work for an engineering company designing the Chicago elevated railway. In 1894, he returned to Louisville, KY and founded his own engineering firm. Rumors persisted for several years that Sanders was working out and contemplating a return to major league baseball, but he never did.

Sanders, a reserved, serious man, refused to play baseball on Sunday. The control pitcher allowed only 297 walks in five major league seasons. His one drawback remained poor fielding, especially of bunts. His awkward delivery left him with his back toward the batter. During his major league career, he garnered 80 wins against 70 losses with a 3.24 ERA. He appeared in 168 games, striking out 468 batters in 1,385 innings and tossing 14 shutouts. Sanders, who batted .271 with five HR, married Mary Mayes and had three children, Edward, A.B. Jr., and Mary.

BIBLIOGRAPHY: Alexander Sanders file, National Baseball Library, Cooperstown, NY; Joe Klein, "Alexander Bennett Sanders," unpublished manuscript, 1996; *Commercial Appeal*, August 31, 1930, sec. 7, p. 7; John Thorn et al., eds., *Total Baseball*, 5th ed. (New York, 1997); Frederick G. Lieb and Stan Baumgartner, *The Philadelphia Phillies* (New York, 1953); Rich Westcott and Frank Bilovsky, *The New Phillies Encyclopedia* (Philadelphia, PA, 1993).

                                                                                 John H. Ziegler

SANDERSON, Scott Douglas (b. July 22, 1956, Dearborn, MI), player, is the son of John A. N. Sanderson and Jane (Klein) Sanderson and graduated from Glenbard North High School in Northbrook, IL, where he played baseball, football, and basketball. Sanderson, a two-time high school All-State baseball selection, graduated in 1977 from Vanderbilt University with majors in business, finance, and history. He pitched for the U.S. International team in 1975 and performed in the Pan-American Games in 1976. He and his wife, Cathleen, have one son, Patrick, and one daughter, Erica.

The Kansas City Royals (AL) selected the 6-foot 5-inch, 192-pound right-handed pitcher in the June 1974 draft, but did not sign him. In June 1977,

Sanderson signed with the Montreal Expos (NL). He spent his first professional baseball season at West Palm Beach, FL (FSL) and divided the 1978 campaign between Memphis, TN (SL) and Denver, CO (AA). After hurling only 28 minor league games, Sanderson joined the Montreal Expos in 1978. He pitched from 1978 to 1983 with the Montreal Expos, compiling a 56–47 record. On December 7, 1983, Sanderson was traded twice. The Montreal Expos traded him to the San Diego Padres (NL), who shipped him to the Chicago Cubs (NL). Sanderson hurled for the Chicago Cubs from 1984 to 1989 aside from brief rehabilitation assignments with Lodi, CA (CaL) in 1984 and Peoria, IL (ML) and Des Moines–based Iowa (AA) in 1988. He posted a 42–42 mark for the Cubs and appeared in two games in the 1984 and 1989 NL Championship Series with no decisions.

The Chicago Cubs granted Sanderson free agency following the 1989 season. Sanderson signed in December 1989 with the Oakland Athletics (AL), where in 1990 he won 17 games and lost 11 and was selected to the AL All-Star team. He led Oakland to the 1990 World Series, appearing twice with no decisions against the Cincinnati Reds. The Oakland A's sold Sanderson in December 1990 to the New York Yankees (AL), where he recorded a 28–21 mark the next two seasons. Sanderson paced the 1991 New York Yankees pitching staff in wins, complete games, shutouts, innings pitched, and strikeouts. On May 2, 1992, he tied the major league record for most HR allowed in one inning (4). When the New York Yankees defeated the Milwaukee Brewers (AL) on May 30, 1992, Sanderson became just the tenth pitcher in history to defeat all 26 major league clubs. After being granted free agency, he split the 1993 season between the California Angels (AL) and San Francisco Giants (NL) with 11 wins and 13 losses. The Chicago White Sox (AL) signed him for the 1994 campaign, which featured eight wins and four losses. He hurled for the California Angels (AL) in 1995 and 1996, winning just one game before retiring in May 1996.

Sanderson's 19 major league seasons include a 163–143 record and a 3.84 ERA. He pitched in 472 games, completed 43 of 407 starts, tossed 14 shutouts, and recorded five saves. Sanderson surrendered 2,590 hits, 1,209 runs, 1,093 earned runs, and 625 bases on balls and struck out 1,611 batters in 2,561.2 innings.

BIBLIOGRAPHY: Scott Sanderson file, National Baseball Library, Cooperstown, NY; *Chicago White Sox Media Guide*, 1994; Eddie Gold and Art Ahrens, *The New Era Cubs, 1941–1985* (Chicago, IL, 1985); Dan Turner, *The Expos Inside Out* (Toronto, Canada, 1983); *TSN Official Baseball Register*, 1997; *USAT*, October 4, 1995, p. 7C.

John L. Evers

SANFORD, John Stanley "Jack" (b. May 18, 1929, Wellesley Hills, MA), player, is the son of Frederick Sanford, a stationary engineer, and Margaret Sanford and graduated in 1947 from Wellesley High School, where he played baseball. The Philadelphia Phillies (NL) signed Sanford in 1947, but wildness and a temper impeded his progress. The 5-foot 11½-inch, 196-pound fast ball pitcher, who batted and threw right-handed, spent seven minor league seasons, with Bradford, PA (NYPL) and Dover, DE (ESL) in 1948, Americus, GA (GFL) in 1949, Wilmington, DE (ISL) in 1950, Schenectady, NY (EL) in 1951 and 1952, Baltimore, MD (IL) in 1953, and Syracuse, NY (IL) in 1954. After serving nearly two years in the U.S. Army, he joined the Philadelphia Phillies in September 1956.

Sanford, who developed an effective curve ball, hurled twelve full major league seasons from 1957 through 1968. The BBWAA named him NL Rookie of the Year in 1957, when he enjoyed a 19–8 record with a 3.08 ERA, led the NL with a career-high 188 strikeouts, and made the NL All-Star team. He tied a Phillies record by fanning 13 Chicago Cubs in June 1957. After Sanford slumped in 1958, the Philadelphia Phillies traded him to the San Francisco Giants (NL). He compiled a 15–12 record and career-best 3.16 ERA in 1959 and recorded 25 victories the next two years, pacing the NL with six shutouts in 1960.

Sanford's best major league season came in 1962, when he sparked the Giants to the NL pennant with a 24–7 mark and 3.43 ERA. Besides recording 16 consecutive triumphs, he established career bests in victories and winning percentage (.774). Sanford boasted an impressive 1.93 ERA in the World Series against the New York Yankees, but lost two of three decisions. After blanking New York on three hits in Game 2, he struck out 10 Yankees in the Game 5 setback and lost a 1–0 heartbreaker in the finale.

Sanford led the NL with 42 starts in 1963, but right shoulder surgery sidelined him part of 1964. In August 1965, the San Francisco Giants sold him to the California Angels (AL). He compiled a 13–7 record and 3.83 ERA in 1966, pacing AL relievers with 12 victories. In June 1967, the California Angels traded Sanford to the Kansas City Athletics (AL). He retired following that season with a 137–101 mark and 3.69 ERA, and 1,182 strikeouts in 2,049.1 innings. After coaching for the Cleveland Indians (AL) in 1968 and 1969, he scouted for the Baltimore Orioles (AL) from 1977 through 1987 and worked as a golf professional. The West Palm Beach, FL resident married Patricia Reynolds in January 1955 and has three children, Laura, John, Jr., and Nancy.

BIBLIOGRAPHY: John Sanford file, National Baseball Library, Cooperstown, NY; Allen Lewis, *The Philadelphia Phillies: A Pictorial History* (Virginia Beach, VA, 1981); Rich Westcott and Frank Bilovsky, *The New Phillies Encyclopedia* (Philadelphia, PA, 1993); David Plaut, *Chasing October* (South Bend, IN, 1994); Nick Peters, *Giants Almanac* (Berkeley, CA, 1988); Harry T. Paxton, "Baseball's Oldest Youngster," *SEP* 230 (March 29, 1958), pp. 27, 74–76; "Thrower," *Newsweek* 50 (September 2, 1957), pp. 84–85; *TSN Baseball Register*, 1968.

David L. Porter

SANGUILLEN, Manuel de Jesus (Magan) "Manny" (b. March 21, 1944, Colon, Panama), player, graduated from Abel Bravo High School in Panama, where he excelled in basketball, soccer, and track and field. The Pittsburgh Pirates (NL) signed the 6-foot, 193-pound catcher as a free agent in October 1964. He spent less than four minor league seasons with Batavia, NY (NYPL) in 1965, Raleigh, NC (CrL) in 1966, and Columbus, OH (IL) from 1966 through 1968, seeing limited action with the Pittsburgh Pirates (NL) in 1967.

The popular, enthusiastic, deeply religious Sanguillen caught with the Pittsburgh Pirates from 1968 through 1976, hitting over .300 four times. He finished third in the NL with a .325 batting average in 1970 to help the Pittsburgh Pirates win the NL East, but struggled in the NL Championship Series against the Cincinnati Reds. Sanguillen batted .319 with a career-high 81 RBI in 1971 and made the NL All-Star team. After the Pittsburgh Pirates defeated the San Francisco Giants in the NL Championship Series, he hit .379 with 11 hits to lift the Pirates over the Baltimore Orioles in the World Series. He even edged out perennial selection Johnny Bench* on *TSN* and AP All-Star teams.

Sanguillen's batting average dropped below .300 in 1972, but he repeated on the NL All-Star team. He enjoyed his best NL Championship Series with a .313 batting average, one HR, and two RBI against the Cincinnati Reds. The Pittsburgh Pirates won another NL East title in 1974 and lost to the Los Angeles Dodgers in the NL Championship Series. Sanguillen ranked third in the NL with a career-best .328 batting average in 1975 and again made the NL All-Star team, but struggled in the NL Championship Series against the Cincinnati Reds.

In an unusual November 1976 transaction the Pittsburgh Pirates sent Sanguillen to the Oakland A's (AL) for manager Chuck Tanner.* Sanguillen spent only one season with Oakland, leading the A's in hits. The Pittsburgh Pirates reacquired him in April 1978. His playing time steadily diminished during his final three major league seasons, but his dramatic ninth inning pinch single gave Pittsburgh a 3–2 victory over the Baltimore Orioles in Game 2 of the 1979 World Series.

During 13 major league seasons, Sanguillen batted .296 with 1,500 hits and 585 RBI. The smiling, talkative Pittsburgh, PA resident seldom struck out or walked. Blessed with a strong arm, he demonstrated exceptional agility, unusual speed, and durability. Sanguillen helped start a baseball program at Pan American Bible School. He and his wife, Kathy, have two children, Manuel, Jr. and Sarah.

BIBLIOGRAPHY: Manuel Sanguillen file, National Baseball Library, Cooperstown, NY; Joel Cohen, *Manny Sanguillen* (New York, 1975); Ron Fimrite, "Two Catchers Cut from Royal Cloth," *SI* 36 (June 26, 1972), pp. 31–32, 35; Ray Blount, "Now Playing Right: Manny Sanguillen," *SI* 38 (March 19, 1973), pp. 28–29; "Manny's

Task," *Newsweek* 81 (April 2, 1973), pp. 55, 57; *Pittsburgh Pirates Media Guide*, 1980; *TSN Baseball Register*, 1981; Richard L. Burtt, *The Pittsburgh Pirates, A Pictorial History* (Virginia Beach, VA, 1977); Morris Eckhouse and Carl Mastrocola, *This Date in Pittsburgh Pirates History* (New York, 1980); Lou Sahadi, *The Pirates* (New York, 1980); Bob Smizik, *The Pittsburgh Pirates: An Illustrated History* (New York, 1990).

David L. Porter

SANTIAGO, Benito (Rivea) "Benny" (b. March 25, 1965, Ponce, PR), player, is the son of Isabel Santiago and grew up in low income Santa Isabel, PR. His father, a truck driver, died of cancer when Benito was just an infant. Santiago, who was brought up by an uncle and aunt, hurled nine no-hitters as a youth. He attended John F. Kennedy High School in Ponce, dropping out at age 16. Santiago and his wife, Bianco, had one daughter, Benny Beth, and one son, Benito, Jr., before their separation.

In September 1982, the San Diego Padres (NL) signed the 6-foot 1-inch, 182-pound right-handed catcher as a free agent. Santiago progressed through the Padres organization with Miami, FL (FSL) in 1983, Reno, NV (CaL) in 1984, Beaumont, TX (TL) in 1985, and Las Vegas, NV (PCL) in 1986. The San Diego Padres promoted him in September 1986 to the parent roster, for whom he batted .290 in 17 games.

Santiago dramatically improved San Diego Padres fortunes in 1987 as a 22 year old rookie, catching more games (146) than any other receiver. He earned NL Rookie of the Year honors, recording a career-high .300 batting average with 18 HR and 79 RBI. Only one other San Diego Padres catcher had batted .300 in a season. In August and September 1987, he batted safely in 34 consecutive games. The streak, the longest in the senior circuit in a decade, established the major league record for a rookie. His post-season honors included *TSN* Silver Slugger and All-League teams, the Clyde McCullough Award as Padres Rookie of the Year, and Outstanding Puerto Rican Athlete in the US.

Santiago caught for the San Diego Padres through the 1992 season. Although his batting average plunged to .248 in 1988, he made *TSN* Silver Slugger team and won his first Gold Glove. Eight runners were picked off base by the San Diego Padres catcher, who threw out 45 percent of the runners trying to steal and led major league catchers with 78 assists. The 1989 season brought Santiago more honors, as he was named starting catcher for the NL All-Stars, earned a second Gold Glove, and made *TSN* NL All-Star team. He picked off 16 runners, but struggled offensively. A broken arm sidelined him for part of the 1990 season. He batted .267 with 17 HR and a career-high 87 RBI in 1991, leading NL catchers in assists. Santiago slumped to a .250 batting average in 1992, his final season with the San Diego Padres.

In December 1992, the Florida Marlins, NL signed Santiago as a free agent. He spent two season with the Florida Marlins, pacing NL catchers in assists in 1994. He spent the 1995 campaign with the Cincinnati Reds (NL), batting .286 during the regular season and .231 in the NL Championship Series against the Atlanta Braves. In January 1996, the Philadelphia Phillies (NL) signed him as a free agent to replace Darren Daulton.* He belted a career-best 30 HR with 85 RBI in 1996 and joined the Toronto Blue Jays (AL) as a free agent in December 1996. Injuries suffered in an automobile accident sidelined him most of the 1998 season. Santiago joined the Chicago Cubs (NL) as a free agent in December 1998. The Cubs released him in November 1999.

Through the 1999 season, the Davie, FL resident has batted .260 with 170 HR and 677 RBI in 1,358 games. Defensively, he recorded 721 assists through 1998. Santiago made the NL All-Star team four consecutive seasons from 1989 to 1992. His exceptional throwing arm enabled him to pick runners off base, throw runners out attempting to steal, and prevent many runners from scoring from second base on singles.

BIBLIOGRAPHY: Tom Friend, "The Honeymoon's Over," *Sport* 83 (August 1992), pp. 49–53; Franz Lidz, "Benito Finito at 34 Games," *SI* 67 (October 12, 1987), pp. 26–27; Bruce Newman, "Man with the Golden Gun," *SI* 74 (February 17, 1991), pp. 60–62, 64–65; David L. Porter, interview with Benito Santiago, July 21, 1989; *San Diego Padres 1992 Media Guide*; Benito Santiago file, National Baseball Library, Cooperstown, NY; *WWA*, 48th ed. (1994), p. 3016.

David L. Porter

SANTO, Ronald Edward "Ron" (b. February 25, 1940, Seattle, WA), player and sportscaster, is of Italian-Swedish descent, graduated from high school in Seattle, and starred in baseball in secondary school. He married Judy Lynn Scott in January 1960 and has two sons. The 6-foot, 190-pound right-hander possessed an excellent build for a third baseman. After entering professional baseball at age 19, Santo spent the 1959 season at San Antonio, TX (TL). Santo began 1960 at Houston, TX (AA), but joined the Chicago Cubs (NL) in late June. He spent 14 seasons with the Chicago Cubs and played more games at third base than any other Bruin. By a wide margin, he became the team's hardest-hitting third baseman.

During his career, Santo tied for the NL lead in triples once (13 in 1964), and led in bases on balls four times (1964, 1966–1968) and on base percentage twice (1964, 1966). Repeatedly he ranked among the first five in RBI, HR, total bases, and slugging average. Defensively, he led NL third basemen seven consecutive seasons in assists, eight times in total chances, six times in double plays, twice in games played, and once in fielding percentage. Santo ranks ninth lifetime in assists and tenth in single-season assists. Besides standing sixth in career games (2,130) and fifth in assists (4,581) at the hot corner, he ranks fifth in lifetime total chances (6,853), and seventh in double plays (395). He won five consecutive Gold Gloves defensively. Santo batted .285 in seven All-Star games and compiled a .277 lifetime batting average. In 2,243 major league games, he made 2,254 hits, 365 doubles,

67 triples, and 342 HR, scored 1,138 runs, knocked in 1,331 runs, walked 1,108 times, and stole 35 bases. During Santo's career, the Cubs came close to winning the championship only in 1969 and 1970 and never played in a World Series. Santo moved crosstown to the Chicago White Sox (AL) in December 1973 and played one season there. In retirement, he prospered as an executive in the oil trucking business from 1975 to 1991 and has announced for the Chicago Cubs since 1990.

BIBLIOGRAPHY: Leo Durocher, *Nice Guys Finish Last* (New York, 1975); Eddie Gold and Art Ahrens, *The New Era Cubs, 1941–1985* (Chicago, IL, 1985); Brent P. Kelley, *The Case For: Those Overlooked by the Baseball Hall of Fame* (Jefferson, NC, 1992); Ron Santo file, National Baseball Library, Cooperstown, NY; Jim Langford, *The Game Is Never Over* (South Bend, IN, 1980); Ron Santo and Randy Minkoff, *Ron Santo* (Chicago, IL, 1993); *TSN*, November 8, 1961, January 16, 1965, December 13, 1974; Warren Wilbert and William Hageman, *Chicago Cubs: Seasons at the Summit* (Champaign, IL, 1997); Jim Enright, *Chicago Cubs* (New York, 1975); Art Ahrens and Eddie Gold, *Day-by-Day in Chicago Cubs History* (West Point, NY, 1982).

Lowell L. Blaisdell

SANTOP, Louis Loftin "Top," "Big Bertha" (b. Louis Loftin, January 17, 1890, Tyler, TX; d. January 6, 1942, Philadelphia, PA), player, batted left-handed and became the first of the great Negro League sluggers. Nicknamed "Big Bertha" after the monstrous German siege gun of World War I, the gigantic 6-foot 5-inch catcher, who weighed 245 pounds, switched his last name to Santop for baseball games. After beginning professionally in 1909 with the Fort Worth, TX Wonders, he played the following year with Sol White's* Philadelphia Giants and teamed with husky rookie "Cannonball Dick" Redding* to form the famous kid battery. From 1911 through 1914, Santop caught for the powerful New York Lincoln Giants and combined with "Smoky Joe" Williams* to form one of the all-time greatest batteries. Redding later joined the Lincoln Giants, giving Santop two premier fastball pitchers to handle. From 1911 to 1914, he batted .470, .422, .429, and .455.

Santop performed through 1926 for several teams, including the Brooklyn Royal Giants from 1914 to 1919, Chicago American Giants in 1915, New York Lincoln Stars in 1915 and 1916, and Philadelphia Hilldale Daisies from 1917 to 1926, and served in the U.S. Navy in 1918 and 1919. From 1922 to 1926, he played exclusively for Ed Bolden's Hilldale Daisies (ECL) and then left black baseball. He batted .358, .364, and .389 from 1922 to 1924. During his career, he caught in Black World Series in 1915 for the New York Lincoln Stars and in 1921, 1924, and 1925 for the Hilldale Daisies. Philadelphia defeated the Chicago American Giants for the 1921 title and the Kansas City, MO Monarchs in the 1925 classic, while the 1915 set ended in a draw between the Stars and American Giants. Santop's best series came in a losing effort in 1924, when he batted .333 in nine games versus the Monarchs.

The gruff-voiced Santop often boasted to opposing pitchers about how far he would belt their deliveries and occasionally predicted his HR. In 1912, he hit one ball over a 485-foot fence in Elizabeth, NJ in the dead ball era. At Philadelphia's Shibe Park on October 12, 1920, Babe Ruth* led a semipro team against the Hilldale Daisies. Santop outperformed Ruth with a double and two singles in four at-bats against Carl Mays* of the New York Yankees and Slim Harriss of the Philadelphia Athletics. Ruth made no hits in three official at-bats and walked once, as the Hilldale Daisies won 5–0.

Although best remembered for his power, Santop consistently batted for high averages. He proved a durable, strong-armed catcher, occasionally played the outfield, and once caught a doubleheader with a broken thumb. His widow, Mrs. Eunice Taylor, described Santop as fiery and added, "But if you didn't rub his fur the wrong way, he was a lovely person." Santop's fine talent and showboat tendencies made him a top crowd drawer and earned him a salary of around $450–$500 a month in his prime. He broadcast for radio station WELK in Philadelphia, participated in local politics, and tended bar.

BIBLIOGRAPHY: John B. Holway, "Louis Santop, The Big Bertha," *BRJ* 8 (1979), pp. 93–97; John B. Holway, *Baseball Stars* (Westport, CT, 1988); Robert W. Peterson, *Only the Ball Was White* (Englewood Cliffs, NJ, 1970); James A. Riley, *The Biographical Encyclopedia of the Negro Baseball Leagues* (New York, 1994).

John B. Holway and Merl F. Kleinknecht

SAUER, Henry John "Hammering Hank" "Hank," (b. May 17, 1917, Pittsburgh, PA), player, scout, and coach, attended Bellevue High School and was one of the most popular Chicago Cubs (NL) players in the 1950s. Sauer appeared briefly in 1941, 1942, and 1945 in the major leagues with the Cincinnati Reds (NL) and enjoyed several solid minor league seasons before making the major leagues permanently in 1948. After starting slowly the next year, he and Frank Baumholtz were traded in June to Chicago in one of Chicago's best deals. With the Cubs, the 6-foot 4-inch, 200-pound, right-handed Sauer emerged as a genuine star and HR slugger. His best all-around campaign came in 1952, when he led the NL in HR (37) and RBI (121) and was named the NL's MVP. His two-run HR won the rain-shortened All-Star game for the NL. Sauer, the first Cub to hit three HR in a game, accomplished the feat on August 28, 1950 and June 11, 1952 against Curt Simmons* of the Philadelphia Phillies. In 1954, clouted a career-high 41 HR.

Never a strong outfielder, the slow Sauer played left field. The Chicago Cubs acquired Ralph Kiner* in June 1953 and moved Sauer to right field. Sauer remained a popular favorite, but Baumholtz worked hard trying to cover the vast field territory between his two lumbering teammates. The Cubs experienced lean years and traded Sauer in March 1956 to the St. Louis Cardinals (NL). In seven years as a Cub, Sauer slugged 197 HR.

In October 1956, Sauer signed as a free agent with the New York Giants (NL). His last good season came in 1957 with 26 HR. He hit into a triple play when the Chicago Cubs defeated the San Francisco Giants (NL), 5–4, on April 27, 1958. He worked for the San Francisco Giants as a coach in 1959 and as a scout from 1960 through 1992. Chicago fans of the 1950s never forgot their hero. When Sauer appeared in an old-timers' game in 1977, he was given packets of tobacco in a scene reminiscent of the day they had honored him on August 22, 1954. The Millbrae, CA resident married Esther Tavel on December 29, 1940 and had two children, Betty and Henry, Jr. In 15 major league seasons, Sauer batted .266, made 1,278 hits, slugged 200 doubles and 288 HR and knocked in 876 runs. The IL Hall of Fame inducted him.

BIBLIOGRAPHY: Hank Sauer file, National Baseball Library, Cooperstown, NY; Art Ahrens and Eddie Gold, *Day by Day in Chicago Cubs History* (West Point, NY, 1982); Eddie Gold and Art Ahrens, *The New Era Cubs, 1941–1985* (Chicago, IL, 1985); Jim Langford, *The Game Is Never Over* (South Bend, IN, 1980); Robert Obojski, "Former NL Slugger Hank Sauer Interviewed," *SCD* 21 (April 22, 1994), p. 131; Jim Enright, *Chicago Cubs* (New York, 1975); Warren Wilbert and William Hageman, *Chicago Cubs: Seasons at the Summit* (Champaign, IL, 1997); Warren Brown, *The Chicago Cubs* (New York, 1952); Steve Bitker, *The Original San Francisco Giants* (Champaign, IL, 1998).

                                                                              Duane A. Smith

SAX, Stephen Louis "Steve" (b. January 29, 1960, Sacramento, CA), player and sportscaster, is the younger brother of former major leaguer Dave Sax and attended James Marshall High School in West Sacramento, CA. The Los Angeles Dodgers (NL) drafted the 5-foot 11-inch, 189-pound infielder, who batted and threw right-handed, in the ninth round in June 1978. He spent under four minor league seasons with Lethbridge, Canada (PrL) in 1978, Clinton, IA (ML) in 1979, Vero Beach, FL (FSL) in 1980, and San Antonio, TX (TL) in 1981, earning TL MVP honors. He joined the Los Angeles Dodgers for 31 games in 1981, briefly appearing in the NL Championship Series against the Montreal Expos and World Series against the New York Yankees.

Sax starred for the Los Angeles Dodgers from 1982 through 1988, making the 1982, 1983, and 1986 NL All-Star teams. He replaced Davey Lopes* at second base in 1982, earning BBWAA NL Rookie of the Year honors. Besides batting .282, Sax set a Dodger rookie record with 49 stolen bases and led the Dodgers with 88 runs and 180 hits. In NL Championship Series, he batted .250 against the Philadelphia Phillies in 1983 and .300 with three doubles and one RBI against the St. Louis Cardinals in 1985. His best season with the Los Angeles Dodgers came in 1986, when he established career-highs in batting average (.332), hits (210), and doubles (43) and made *TSN* All-Star and Silver Slugger teams. Sax enjoyed a 25 game hitting streak in

September 1986, missing the NL batting title by just two points. In 1988, he hit .267 with three RBI against the New York Mets in NL Championship Series and .300 in the World Series against the Oakland A's.

In November 1988, the New York Yankees (AL) signed Sax as a free agent. Sax enjoyed his second best major league season in 1989. Besides leading AL second basemen in fielding percentage (.987), he batted .315 with 205 hits. In 1991, Sax batted .304 with 198 hits and clouted a career-high 10 HR. The New York Yankees traded him to the Chicago White Sox (AL) in January 1992. After playing two seasons there, he ended his major league career with the Oakland A's (AL) in 1994.

In 14 major league seasons, Sax batted .281 with 1,949 hits, 550 RBI, and a .978 fielding percentage. An enthusiastic, energetic, aggressive player, he stole 40 or more bases six times. The Fair Oaks, CA resident married Debbie Graham and has two children, Lauren and John. He serves as a baseball analyst for Fox-Sports.

BIBLIOGRAPHY: Steve Sax file, National Baseball Library, Cooperstown, NY; Steve Sax, *Sax* (Chicago, IL, 1986); Ira Berkow, "For Steve Sax, Christmas in July," *NYT Biographical Service*, July 1982, p. 912; M. Martinez, "Taking a Defensive Stand," *NYT Biographical Service*, May 1990, pp. 440–441; Wayne Coffey, "Baseball's Baby Boom," *Sport* 73 (September 1982), pp. 54–56; Danny Knobler, "Baseball's Best Leadoff Hitters," *Sport* 81 (July 1990), pp. 40–42, 44–45; *TSN Baseball Register*, 1995; William F. McNeil, *The Dodger Encyclopedia* (Champaign, IL, 1997); Mark Gallagher, *The Yankee Encyclopedia*, vol. 3 (Champaign, IL, 1997); Tommy Lasorda and David Fisher, *The Artful Dodger* (New York, 1985); Stanley Cohen, *Dodgers! First 100 Years* (New York, 1990); Peter C. Bjarkman, *Baseball's Great Dynasties: The Dodgers* (New York, 1990).

David L. Porter

SCALES, George Walter (b. August 16, 1900, Talledega, AL; d. April 15, 1976, Los Angeles, CA), player and manager, was the son of Joseph Scales and attended Talladega College, playing shortstop on the baseball team. Scales excelled as a player in the NNL, ECL, ANL, CUWL, and PRWL. He began his professional baseball career in 1919 with the black Montgomery, AL Grey Sox and joined the St. Louis, MO Giants (NNL) in 1921. Scales played second base for the New York Lincoln Giants (ECL) from 1923 through 1929 and the Homestead, PA Grays (ANL) from 1929 through 1931. Other stops included the Homestead Grays (NNL), New York Black Yankees (NNL), and Baltimore, MD Elite Giants (NNL) through 1948. He managed the Birmingham, AL Black Barons (NAL) in 1952.

Scales attracted attention as an intelligent, team-oriented performer and became a successful manager with the New York Black Yankees (NNL), Baltimore Elite Giants (NNL), Ponce, PR (PRWL), and Santurce, PR (PRWL). He managed a record six PRWL championship teams, piloting

Ponce to PRWL titles in the 1941–1942, 1942–1943, 1943–1944, 1944–1945, and 1946–1947 campaigns and guiding Santurce to the 1950–1951 PRWL crown. In the NNL, Scales helped prepare eventual Brooklyn Dodgers (NL) stars Roy Campanella* and Jim Gilliam* for major league stardom.

Scales, a 5-foot 11-inch, 195-pound, right-handed line-drive hitter with a good eye, produced a .299 batting average with 112 hits in 375 at-bats during three CWL seasons. He batted .313 in 25 Negro League seasons. He performed for an All-Star team that Satchel Paige* took to the Dominican Republic to represent the island's ruler Generalisimo Rafael Trujillo in 1937 and hit .295 for the Estrellas Orientales. As a part-time player, Scales posted NNL marks of .300 in 1944 and .309 in 1945. Defensively, Scales normally held down second or third base, but also played some outfield, shortstop and first base. Although lacking range, he studied opposing batters and used positioning and a strong arm as defensive assets.

Scales's talents earned him All-Star recognition in 1929 as the premier ANL keystoner and in 1934 as Cum Posey's* black All-American third baseman. In the twilight of his career, he pinch-hit in the 1943 East–West All-Star Game. In 1952, Scales was ranked fourth best black second baseman of all time by a Pittsburgh (PA) *Courier* poll behind Jackie Robinson,* Bill Monroe,* and Bingo Demoss.* After retiring from baseball, he worked as a stockbroker.

BIBLIOGRAPHY: John B. Holway, *Blackball Stars* (Westport, CT, 1988); NNL Statistics, 1944, 1945, Merl F. Kleinknecht Collection; Robert W. Peterson, *Only the Ball Was White* (Englewood Cliffs, NJ, 1970); James A. Riley, *The All-Time All-Stars of Black Baseball* (Cocoa, FL, 1983); James A. Riley, *Biographical Encyclopedia of the Negro Baseball Leagues* (New York, 1994); Pepe Seda, *Don Q Base Ball Cues* (Ponce, PR, 1970).

                                                                          Merl F. Kleinknecht

SCHALK, Raymond William "Ray," "Cracker" (b. August 12, 1892, Harval, IL; d. May 19, 1970, Chicago, IL), player, manager, and scout, was a durable catcher with the Chicago White Sox (AL) for 17 years. Despite his slender 5-foot 9-inch, 155-pound frame, Schalk caught at least 100 games for 12 seasons, including 11 in succession. Schalk worked briefly as a printer in Litchfield, IL and started playing baseball when invited to catch for his Litchfield, IL town team. Before joining the Chicago White Sox in 1912, he played professionally at Taylorville, IL (IiML) in 1911 and Milwaukee, WI (AA) in 1911 and 1912. He never attained a .300 season and hit only 12 HR before ending his 18-year major league career in 1929 with the New York Giants (NL). Exceptional defensively, Schalk became one of the game's all-time best catchers and compiled numerous records. He holds major league catching standards for most years leading in fielding (5) and putouts (9), most double plays (226), and most assists in one league (1,811). Schalk tied major league marks by making three assists in one inning and leading in chances accepted the most years (8). His records included being the only catcher to handle four no-hit games: those by Jim Scott* and Joe Benz in 1914, Ed Cicotte* in 1917, and Charley Robertson (perfect game) in 1922.

Besides being credited as the first receiver to back up plays at first and third base, Schalk even made putouts at second base. He played on Chicago's 1917 world championship team and on the 1919 "Black Sox" squad, but was not involved in the scandal. Schalk batted .286 in 14 World Series games. Behind the plate in 1,726 games, Schalk played in 1,762 games, collected 1,345 hits, scored 579 runs, drove in 594 runs, and compiled a .253 batting average.

Schalk managed the White Sox to fifth place in 1927, but was fired when Chicago faltered the next year. As a major league mentor, he compiled a 102–125 mark. He managed minor league teams in Buffalo, NY (IL) from 1932 to 1937 and in 1950, Indianapolis, IN (AA) from 1938 to 1939, and Milwaukee, WI (AA) in 1940. His Buffalo teams won the IL playoffs in 1933 and 1936. Schalk, who later scouted for the Chicago Cubs (NL), operated a bowling establishment in Chicago, IL, served as an assistant baseball coach for 18 years at Purdue University, and directed the baseball program for Mayor Richard Daley's Chicago Youth Foundation. Schalk, who married Lavina Graham on October 25, 1916 and had at least one daughter, Mrs. Pauline Brinxon, in 1955 was elected to the National Baseball Hall of Fame and is honored in the BRS Museum in Nokomis, IL.

BIBLIOGRAPHY: Ray Schalk file, National Baseball Library, Cooperstown, NY; Cindy Landage and Janna Seiz, "Museum Named after Baseball HOFers," *SCD* 25 (May 1, 1998), p. 135; Elliot Asinof, *Eight Men Out* (New York, 1963); Warren Brown, *The Chicago White Sox* (New York, 1952); Richard Lindberg, *Sox* (New York, 1984); Richard Lindberg, *Who's on Third?* (South Bend, IN, 1983); Victor Luhrs, *The Great Baseball Mystery* (Cranbury, NJ, 1966); Lowell Reidenbaugh, *Baseball's Hall of Fame—Cooperstown* (New York, 1993); *TSN*, June 6, 1970, p. 44; Craig Carter, ed., *TSN Daguerreotypes*, 8th ed. (St. Louis, MO, 1990).

John L. Evers

SCHANG, Walter Henry "Wally" (b. August 22, 1889, South Wales, NY; d. March 6, 1965, St. Louis, MO), player and manager, joined the major leagues with the Philadelphia Athletics (AL) in 1913. Schang, who spent his childhood on a farm and received very little formal education, rode a horse seven miles to board a train to play for his semiprofessional team. His older brother, Bobby, who later played for three seasons with the Pittsburgh Pirates (NL) and the St. Louis Cardinals (NL), had broken his finger. Wally was inserted into the lineup of the semipro club even though he had never caught before.

Schang spent the 1912 season with Buffalo, NY (IL) and was drafted by Connie Mack's* Philadelphia Athletics in 1913. Albert "Chief" Bender* gave Schang his start, asking manager Mack to let "the kid catch me." Schang played in the 1913 World Series against the New York Giants and became the first switch-hitter to hit a HR from each side of the plate in the same game. Shang also showed adeptness at drawing walks and hit .300 or better six times. The *Reach Guide* in 1915 called Schang "one of the most sensational catchers in recent years." He possessed a great arm and enjoyed success as a switch-hitting batter. He started as a right-handed batter, but became a switch-hitter because right-handers bothered him with curveballs. His best season came in 1926, when he hit .330 with the St. Louis Browns (AL). Schang once engaged in a celebrated fight with Babe Ruth* on a train while playing with the New York Yankees (AL). Although an excellent catcher, he still holds the record for the most errors at that position since 1900, with 215 miscues. The 5-foot 10-inch, 180 pounder made eight assists in a 1929 game, throwing out six runners who were attempting to steal.

Schang played with five different major league teams during 19 seasons. In December 1917, the Philadelphia Athletics traded Schang, Amos Strunk,* and Joe Bush* to the Boston Red Sox (AL) for three players and $60,000. The Boston Red Sox in December 1920 sent Schang, Waite Hoyt,* and two other players to the New York Yankees (AL), as owner Harry Frazee unloaded his stars for Muddy Ruel,* Del Pratt,* and two others. After five seasons in a Yankees uniform, Schang was sent to the declining St. Louis Browns (AL) in March 1926 for George Mogridge* and an undisclosed amount of cash. In 1927, Schang's brother, Bobby, caught three games for the rival St. Louis Cardinals (NL). In December 1929, the St. Louis Browns traded him back to the Philadelphia Athletics for Sammy Hale. His major league career ended with 30 appearances for the Detroit Tigers (AL) in 1931.

In 19 major league seasons, Schang played in 1,842 games and caught 1,435 contests. He batted .284 and made 1,506 hits, his best batting average (.330) coming with the St. Louis Browns in 1926. His slugging percentage that season ascended to an incredible .516. Schang slugged 264 career doubles, 90 triples, and 59 HR, scored 769 runs, recorded 710 RBI, 849 walks, and 573 strikeouts, and stole 121 bases.

Schang played in six World Series with three different teams (Philadelphia Athletics, 1913–1914; Boston Red Sox, 1918; New York Yankees, 1921–1923), one of few players appearing on three different clubs to capture World Series titles. His World Series record included 27 hits, a .287 batting average, one HR, 11 walks, and 20 strikeouts in 32 games.

Schang managed several minor league teams, including Joplin, MO (WA) in 1934 and Muskogee, OK (WA) in 1935. He piloted Three Rivers, Canada (ProL) in 1940 and Owensboro, KY (KL) in 1942, batting .500 in seven games at age 52 the same year. Schang resided with his wife, Dorothy, on a Dixon, MO farm.

BIBLIOGRAPHY: Bill Borst, *Still Last in the American League* (West Bloomfield, MI, 1992); Mark Gallagher, *The Yankee Encyclopedia*, vol. 3 (Champaign, IL, 1997); Frank Graham, *The New York Yankees* (New York, 1943); Robert Redmount, *The Red Sox*

Encyclopedia (Champaign, IL, 1998); Frederick G. Lieb, *Boston Red Sox* (New York, 1947); Jerome C. Romanowski, *The Mackmen* (Upper Darby, PA, 1979); Wally Schang file, National Baseball Library, Cooperstown, NY; Connie Mack, *My 66 Years in the Big Leagues* (Philadelphia, PA, 1950); Frederick G. Lieb, *Connie Mack* (New York, 1945); Bill Borst, ed., *Ables to Zoldak*, vol. 3 (St. Louis, MO, 1990); Al Hirshberg, *Baseball's Greatest Catchers* (New York, 1966); Bill James, *The Bill James Historical Baseball Abstract* (New York, 1986); Gene Karst and Martin J. Jones, Jr., *Who's Who in Professional Baseball* (New Rochelle, NY, 1973); Jim Sargent, "Wally Schang: Baseball's Greatest Forgotten Catcher," *OTBN* 6 (July 1994).

William A. Borst

SCHILLING, Curtis Montague "Curt" (b. November 14, 1966, Anchorage, AK), player, graduated from Shadow Mountain High School in Phoenix, AZ and attended Yavapai College in Prescott, AZ. In January 1986, the Boston Red Sox (AL) selected the 6-foot 4-inch, 226-pound pitcher, who bats and throws right-handed, in the second round of the free agent draft. Schilling spent six minor league seasons with Elmira, NY (NYPL) in 1986, Greensboro, NC (SAL) in 1987, New Britain, CT (EL) and Charlotte, NC (SL) in 1988, Rochester, NY (IL) in 1989 and 1990, and Tucson, AZ (PCL) in 1991.

In July 1988, the Boston Red Sox traded Schilling to the Baltimore Orioles (AL). Between 1988 and 1990, he dropped six of seven decisions for Baltimore. The Baltimore Orioles traded him to the Houston Astros (NL) in January 1991. After compiling a 3–5 record in 1991, he was sent to the Philadelphia Phillies (NL) in April 1992.

Schilling anchored the Philadelphia Phillies staff for much of the decade. In 1992, he finished 14–11 with a career-best 2.35 ERA and hurled a 2–1 one-hit victory over the New York Mets on September 9. The Philadelphia Phillies won the NL East in 1993, as Schilling enjoyed a 16–7 mark with a 4.02 ERA. He allowed only three earned runs while fanning 19 Atlanta Braves in 16 innings, earning 1993 NL Championship Series MVP honors. Schilling set two NL Championship Series records in Game 1, striking out five consecutive Atlanta Braves to start the contest. In the 1993 World Series against the Toronto Blue Jays, he split two decisions with a 3.52 ERA. Injuries sidelined him portions of the next three seasons.

Schilling's best major league season came in 1997, when he finished fifth in the NL Cy Young Award balloting. He recorded a career-high 17 wins for a Phillies club that won just 68 games. Schilling lost just 11 decisions with a 2.97 ERA, making the NL All-Star team. His career-best 319 strikeouts in 254.1 innings paced the NL, as he set a NL record single season record for most strikeouts by a right-hander. On September 1, Schilling fanned a career-high 16 New York Yankees. He began the 1998 season brilliantly, outdueling Greg Maddux* of the Atlanta Braves, 2–1 and 1–0, in April. In 1998, he finished 15–14 with a 3.25 ERA and struck out 300 batters in 268.2 innings. Despite injuries, he posted a 15–6 mark with a 3.54 ERA in 1999.

Through 1999, Schilling has compiled a 100–85 record with a 3.38 ERA, 13 shutouts, 1,571 strikeouts, and only 454 walks in 1,691.2 innings. Schilling, who contemplated becoming a history teacher, possesses excellent control with a 95–98 mph fast ball. He married Shonda Brewer in November 1992 and has two children, Gehrig and Gabriella.

BIBLIOGRAPHY: G. Callahan, "Fast and in Your Face," *SI* 88 (February 2, 1998), pp. 78–82; Curt Schilling file, National Baseball Library, Cooperstown, NY; *TSN Baseball Register*, 1999; Rich Westcott and Frank Bilovsky, *The New Phillies Encyclopedia* (Philadelphia, PA, 1993).

David L. Porter

SCHMIDT, Frank Elmer. *See* Frank Elmer Smith.

SCHMIDT, Michael Jack "Mike" (b. September 27, 1949, Dayton, OH), player, became the greatest power hitter in Philadelphia Phillies (NL) history. The only son of Jack Schmidt and Lois Schmidt, managers of a restaurant at a popular Dayton swim club, he has one sister, Sally. After graduating from Fairview High School in Dayton in 1967, Schmidt won a baseball scholarship to Ohio University. After a sluggish start, Schmidt eventually established Ohio University single-season hitting records for runs scored (45), HR (10), and walks (38) and was named College All-America his senior year. After graduating in 1971 with a Bachelor of Arts degree in business administration, he was selected in the second round of the free agent draft by Phillies scout Tony Lucadello. At Reading, PA (EL), he batted only .211 with 8 HR and 31 RBI in 1971. An excellent 1972 season followed with Eugene, OR (PCL), where Schmidt hit .291 with 26 HR and 91 RBI. Following promotion to the Phillies (NL) in September 1972, he shared third base with Cesar Tovar in 1973 and experienced a frustrating year. He showed signs of defensive brilliance and power (18 HR), but struck out 136 times and hit only .196.

The 6-foot 2-inch, 200-pound right-hander blossomed in 1974 and won three consecutive HR titles (36, 38, 38). Altogether, he led the NL in HR 8 seasons (1974–1976, 1980–1981, 1983–1984, 1986), breaking Ralph Kiner's* record. Schmidt also paced the NL five times in slugging average, four times in RBI, walks, and strikeouts, and once in runs scored. Schmidt's 548 career HR rank him seventh all-time. He clouted more career HR (509) than any other third basemen. Schmidt hit 48 HR in 1980, the most in major league history by a third basemen. Schmidt's defensive brilliance earned him ten Gold Gloves, second among third basemen to Brooks Robinson.* Defensively, he made 2,836 putouts, 5,193 assists, and 328 errors for a .961 fielding percentage. Schmidt slugged four HR in a game against the Chicago Cubs in April 1976, the first in the NL to accomplish that dramatic feat since Willie Mays* in 1965.

Schmidt, the NL MVP Award winner in 1980, 1981, and 1986, led the Phillies to the 1980 World Series title over the Kansas City Royals and captured the World Series MVP Award. In 1983 he helped lead Philadelphia to the World Series, but managed only one hit as the Baltimore Orioles won the title. Along with 548 HR, Schmidt has 1,595 RBI and a .267 lifetime batting mark. He averaged a HR 6.5 percent of his times at bat to stand tenth on the all-time list. Schmidt made the NL All-Star team in 1974, 1976–1977, 1979–1984, 1986 and 1987 and holds most Phillies slugging records, including being first in round trippers, walks, extra-base hits, total bases, and strikeouts, and second in RBI. Schmidt lives in Jupiter, FL with his wife, Donna, and two children, Jessica and Jonathan. He operates Mike Schmidt's Restaurant in Philadelphia and was elected to the National Baseball Hall of Fame in 1995. He made Major League Baseball's All-Century Team. His hobbies include golf and collecting toy trains.

BIBLIOGRAPHY: Barbara Walter and Mike Schmidt, *Always on the Offense* (New York, 1982); Allen Lewis and Larry Shenk, *This Date in Philadelphia Phillies History* (New York, 1979); Allen Lewis, *The Philadelphia Phillies: A Pictorial History* (Virginia Beach, VA, 1981); Frank Dolson, *The Philadelphia Story* (South Bend, IN, 1981); Rich Westcott and Frank Bilovsky, *The New Phillies Encyclopedia* (Philadelphia, PA, 1993); Hal Bodley, *The Team That Wouldn't Die* (Wilmington, DE, 1981); Donald Honig, *The Power Hitters* (St. Louis, MO, 1989); Robert E. Kelly, *Baseball's Best* (Jefferson, NC, 1988); Robert Obojski, "Retired Phillies Great Mike Schmidt Interviewed," *SCD* 21 (July 22, 1994), pp. 100–101; Frederick G. Lieb and Stan Baumgartner, *The Philadelphia Phillies* (Philadelphia, PA, 1953); John P. McCarthy, *Baseball's All-Time Dream Team* (Cincinnati, OH, 1994); *NYT Biographical Service* 20 (May 1989), pp. 502–503; John Benson et al., *Baseball's Top 100* (Wilton, CT, 1997); Stan Hochman, *Mike Schmidt* (New York, 1983); G. Waggoner, "Master of Swat," *Esquire* 107 (May 1987), pp. 139–140; D. Whitford, "Mike Schmidt Loves Baseball Seriously," *Sport* 77 (July 1986), pp. 56–58; D. Whitford, "The Unhappiness of Mike Schmidt," *GQ* 62 (July 1982), pp. 62ff; Jim Wright, *Mike Schmidt* (New York, 1979).

John P. Rossi

SCHOENDIENST, Albert Fred "Red" (b. February 2, 1923, Germantown, IL), player, coach, and manager, is one of seven children of Joseph Schoendienst and Mary Schoendienst. His father, a coal miner and farmer, played semipro baseball. Nicknamed "Red" because of his freckles and fiery hair, Schoendienst left New Baden School at age 14, worked at odd jobs, and in 1939 joined the Civilian Conservation Corps. After a staple became embedded in his left eye, he started switch-hitting to favor his bad eye. He was employed as a civilian clerk at Scott Air Force Base when St. Louis Cardinals (NL) scout Joe Mathes signed him. After playing for Union City, TN (KL) and Albany, GA (GFL) in 1942, he hit .337 for Rochester, NY in 1943 and was named the IL's MVP.

The 6 foot, 170 pound Schoendienst played the outfield for the St. Louis Cardinals (NL) in 1945, but switched to second base the next season. For many years, he formed a great hitting tandem with roommate and close friend Stan Musial.* In the 1950 All-Star Game, he slugged the game-winning HR off Ted Gray of the Detroit Tigers in the 14th inning. Schoendienst was elected to 10 NL All-Star teams and five of *TSN* All-Star teams. He was traded to the New York Giants (NL) in a multiplayer deal in June 1956 and to the Milwaukee Braves (NL) in June 1957 for Ray Crone, Bobby Thomson,* and Danny O'Connell. He spent the 1959 season mostly on the disabled list, as his right lung was removed. After the Braves released him in 1960, he spent the next three seasons with the St. Louis Cardinals as a player–coach and made 22 pinch hits in 1963. His career record included a .289 batting average in 2,216 games, 2,449 hits, 427 doubles, 78 triples, 84 HR, 1,223 runs scored, 89 stolen bases, and 773 RBI. He led the NL in stolen bases with 26 in 1945, in doubles with 43 in 1950, and in hits with 200 in 1957. His fielding records included the most years at second base (17) and the most seasons leading second basemen in fielding average (6). In 1948, the right-handed fielder tied a record with six doubles in a double header.

He managed the St. Louis Cardinals longer than anyone else, piloting the club from 1965 to 1976 and for portions of 1980 and 1990. His teams won 1,041 games and lost 955 for a .522 winning percentage. In his two World Series as manager, St. Louis defeated the Boston Red Sox in 1967 and lost to the Detroit Tigers in 1968. After coaching with the Oakland Athletics (AL) in 1977 and 1978, he coached with the St. Louis Cardinals from 1979 to 1995. In 1989, he was elected to the National Baseball Hall of Fame. He married Mary Eileen O'Reilly on September 20, 1947 and has four children. His one son, Kevin, played in the Chicago Cubs (NL) organization.

BIBLIOGRAPHY: Red Schoendienst file, National Baseball Library, Cooperstown, NY; Bob Broeg, *Redbirds: A Century of Cardinals' Baseball* (St. Louis, MO, 1981); Bob Broeg and Jerry Vickery, *St. Louis Cardinal's Encyclopedia* (Grand Rapids, MI, 1998); Bob Broeg, "Red Loves to Take Charge," *SEP* 223 (July 22, 1950), p. 223–228; Hal Butler, *Sports Heroes Who Wouldn't Quit* (New York, 1973); *CB* 25 (1964), pp. 22–23; Tim Cohane, "Glue That Made Milwaukee Famous," *Look* 22 (May 2, 1958), pp. 74–76; David Craft et al., *Redbirds Revisited* (Chicago, IL, 1990); Gene Karst and Martin J. Jones, Jr., *Who's Who in Professional Baseball* (New Rochelle, NY, 1973); Leonard Koppett, *The Man in the Dugout* (New York, 1993); Harry Molter, *Famous American Athletes* (New York, 1982); *NYT*, November 18, 1957; Thomas Aylesworth and Benton Minks, *The Encyclopedia of Baseball Managers* (New York, 1990); Rob Rains, *The St. Louis Cardinals* (New York, 1992); Bob Buege, *The Milwaukee Braves: A Baseball Eulogy* (Milwaukee, WI, 1988); Gary Caruso, *The Braves Encyclopedia* (Philadelphia, PA, 1995); Red Schoendienst with Rob Rains, *Red: A Baseball Life* (Champaign, IL, 1998).

William A. Borst and Frank J. Olmsted

SCHROEDER, Dorothy "Dottie" (b. April 11, 1928, Champaign, IL; d. December 8, 1996, Champaign, IL), player, was the daughter of a German farmer and local postmaster and had an older brother, Walter, and a twin brother, Don. Her father managed a semipro team. The Schroeders moved from their family farm to Sadorus, IL when she was nine years old. She played baseball with her brothers and father in Sadorus. She played on a fast-pitch 4-H softball team in 1939 and joined the Illinois Commercial College team in 1940. Schroeder read about the new AAGPBL in a Chicago *Tribune* advertisement, and became the AAGPBL youngest player at age 15 in 1943. Her parents insisted on close supervision before permitting her to join the AAGPBL.

The 5-foot 7-inch, 150-pound, perennial All-Star shortstop, played in the AAGPBL with the South Bend, IN Blue Sox (1943–1945), Kenosha, WI Comets (1945–1947), Fort Wayne, IN Daisies (1947–1952), and Kalamazoo, MI Lassies (1953–1954). In 1943, she batted only .188, led the AAGPBL shortstops in fielding and stole 312 bases. She pilfered 70 bases in 1944. Her South Bend 1943 team and Fort Wayne 1952 squad produced the best regular season records. She made her first All-Star team in 1952 and was named Daisies MVP. In her final season, the Kalamazoo Lassies won the 1954 AAGPBL championship playoffs. She doubled twice in the final title game. Schroeder holds the AAGPBL records for the most games played (1,249), RBI (431), at-bats (4,129), walks (696), and strikeouts (566). During her career, she batted .211, scored 571 runs on 870 hits, and clouted 42 HR with 431 RBI. She ranks second in career hits, and third in career HR, leading AAGPBL shortstops three times in fielding. When the AAGPBL switched to overhand pitching, her hitting improved. Her best offensive seasons came in the last two AAGPBL years, when she hit .285 and a career-high .304 and made the All-Star team both times. In 1954, she also clouted a career-high 17 HR and drove in 65 runs in only 98 games. After the AAGPBL folded, the friendly, witty Schroeder toured with Bill Allington's All-Americans for four summers.

Schroeder, the only woman to play in all 12 AAGPBL seasons, personified the family background and ideals that the AAGPBL founders attempted to cultivate. As a 15-year-old farm girl from central Illinois, she attended the first AAGPBL tryout camp in St. Louis, MO and the final tryouts in Chicago, IL. The tan, healthy looking Schroeder, with a single, long, gray-blond braid flowing down her back, was probably the most photographed AAGPBL player. Her picture appeared on the cover of *Parade Magazine* in August 1948. A defensive star, she made 2,579 putouts and 3,376 assists for a .913 fielding average during her career. Major league manager Charlie Grimm* once said, "Dottie would be worth $50,000 if she was a man."

Schroeder, who never married, lived in Champaign, IL, and worked for Collegiate Cap & Gown Company for 36 years until retiring in 1993. She attended St. Paul's Lutheran Church in nearby Sadorus and sang in the choir. She is one of the few AAGPBL players pictured individually in the National Baseball Hall of Fame.

BIBLIOGRAPHY: "AAGPBL Star Dottie Schroeder," *SCD* 24 (January 10, 1997), p. 10; Barbara Gregorich, *Women at Play* (San Diego, CA, 1993); Susan E. Johnson, *When Women Played Hardball* (Seattle, WA, 1994); AAGPBL files, Northern Indiana Historical Society, South Bend, IN; W. C. Madden, *The Women of the All-American Girls Professional Baseball League* (Jefferson, NC, 1997); Jim Sargent, "Dottie Schroeder," *SCD* 24 (April 25, 1997), p. 180.

Dennis S. Clark

SCHULTE, Frank "Wildfire" (b. September 17, 1882, Cohocton, NY; d. October 2, 1949, Oakland, CA), player, married Mabel Kirby on June 26, 1911. Schulte's baseball career began as a teenager with various semiprofessional and town teams in New York and Pennsylvania. His father heartily disapproved of Schulte's interest in baseball and even offered him $1,000 to quit the game, and the latter's refusal reputedly caused some tension in the Schulte household. Nevertheless, Schulte signed in 1902 with Syracuse, NY (NYSL) and launched his 15-year major league career in 1904 with the Chicago Cubs (NL).

The 5-foot 11-inch, 170-pound Schulte, a solid, dependable outfielder, consistently produced respectable, if unspectacular, seasons. He batted .281 during the Cubs' fabulous 1906 season, leading the NL with 13 triples. In 1910, Schulte's 10 HR paced the NL. Although batting just .300 in 1911, he won the Chalmers MVP Award that year. Schulte's power statistics may have influenced the MVP selection, for he led the NL in HR (21), RBI (107), and slugging percentage (.534).

Schulte, a left-handed batter and right-handed thrower, stole 233 bases lifetime and ranks third in steals of home plate with 22. Only Ty Cobb* and George J. Burns* accomplished that feat more times. Schulte participated in the 1906, 1907, 1908, and 1910 World Series with the Chicago Cubs, accumulating 25 hits and a .309 batting average. Brief stints for the Pittsburgh Pirates (NL) in 1916 and 1917, Philadelphia Phillies (NL) in 1917, and Washington Senators (AL) in 1918 preceded his retirement. Lifetime, Schulte batted .270 and produced 288 doubles, 124 triples, and 92 HR.

Schulte's nickname came from his racehorse, Wildfire. He kept the horse during the baseball season in Chicago, IL, where he frequently entered it in races at the Windy City Speedway. During the winter months, he took Wildfire with him to Syracuse, NY.

BIBLIOGRAPHY: *The Baseball Encyclopedia*, 10th ed. (New York, 1996); Warren Brown, *The Chicago Cubs* (New York, 1946); Eddie Gold and Art Ahrens, *The Golden Era Cubs, 1876–1940* (Chicago, IL, 1985); Jim Enright, *Chicago Cubs* (New York, 1975); Warren Wilbert and William Hageman, *Chicago Cubs: Seasons at the Summit* (Champaign, IL, 1997); Art Ahrens and Eddie Gold, *Day-by-Day in Chicago Cubs History* (West Point, NY, 1982); Frank Schulte file, National Baseball Library, Cooperstown, NY; Abbot Solomon, *Baseball Records Illustrated* (Secaucus, NJ, 1988).

David S. Matz

SCHUMACHER, Harold Henry "Prince Hal" (b. November 23, 1910, Hinckley, NY; d. April 21, 1993, Cooperstown, NY), player, joined the New York Giants (NL) as a pitcher in 1931 shortly after leaving the St. Lawrence University campus. After only five weeks of minor league seasoning at Bridgeport, CT (EL) and Rochester, NY (IL), he debuted with the New York Giants on April 15, 1931. The 6-foot, 190-pound right-hander became a starting pitcher in 1933 and helped the New York Giants win an unexpected World Series Championship against the Washington Senators. His fondest baseball memory came in the summer of 1933 when the entire Giants team accompanied him to his delayed graduation. He enjoyed his best years from 1933 to 1935, triumphing 61 times over the period. He compiled a career 158–121 win–loss record and a commendable 3.36 ERA. One of his era's best hitting pitchers, he slugged 15 career HR and belted 6 HR in 1934.

Schumacher excelled in the 1935 All-Star game and achieved a 2–2 record in three World Series. His most important win came in the 1936 World Series, when he defeated the powerful New York Yankees, 5–4, in 10 innings. In a must-win situation, he gave the New York Giants a characteristically noble performance. Although allowing 10 hits, he struck out 10 batters, mostly in clutch situations. The upstate New Yorker's trademarks included an exceptional sinker and bulldog determination. Schumacher's arm-wrenching delivery resulted in arm problems, which plagued him for most of his career and required a postseason operation in 1938.

After retiring as a player in 1946, Schumacher helped found the Adirondack Bat Company in his hometown of Dolgeville, NY. He and his wife, Alice (Sullivan) Schumacher, had three children. After retiring as executive vice president of the Adirondack Bat Company in 1967, he and his wife split residences between Dolgeville and the South.

BIBLIOGRAPHY: Hal Schumacher file, National Baseball Library, Cooperstown, NY; *NYT Biographical Service* 24 (April 1993), p. 547; Noel Hynd, *The Giants of the Polo Grounds* (New York, 1988); Frank Graham, *The New York Giants* (New York, 1952); Peter Williams, *When the Giants Were Giants* (Chapel Hill, NC, 1994); Hal Schumacher, letter to Fred Stein, May 12, 1989; Fred Stein, *Under Coogan's Bluff* (Glen Shaw, PA, 1978); Fred Stein and Nick Peters, *Giants Diary* (Berkeley, CA, 1987); John Thorn et al., eds., *Total Baseball*, 5th ed. (New York, 1997).

Fred Stein

SCORE, Herbert Jude "Herb" (b. June 7, 1933, Rosedale, NY), player and sportscaster, starred as a 6-foot 2-inch, 185-pound, left-handed pitcher with a superb fastball for the Cleveland Indians (AL) in the mid–1950s. His baseball career was altered drastically and probably shortened when he was struck in the right eye by a line drive hit by Gil McDougald* of the New York Yankees in the first inning of a night game in Cleveland, OH on May 7, 1957. The ball hit the top of Score's right eyebrow, his cheek bone, and his nose. Sportswriter Til Ferdenzi described this incident as one of the most tragic events affecting a pitcher in major league baseball history: "I heard the crack of the bat, and the sickening thud as the blur of a baseball struck Herb Score. Score went down as if he had been shot. Blood poured from his right eye. His mouth was ajar." Score recovered to pitch again the next season and did not lose sight in his eye, but his effectiveness was diminished.

The Cleveland Indians signed Score as a "bonus baby" for a reported $50,000 in 1955. Before joining the Cleveland Indians, Score was selected TSN 1954 Minor League Player of the Year at Indianapolis, IN (AA). In 1954, Score set an AA record for strikeouts (330 in 251 innings) and paced the AA in wins (22) and ERA (2.62). During his first two major league seasons, Score compiled a 36–19 win–loss record and became the first pitcher ever to lead the AL in strikeouts during his first two major league seasons. He incredibly struck out 508 batters in 476.2 innings. The remainder of his major league career from 1958 to 1962 saw Score win only 17 games, lose 26 decisions, and strike out 290 batters in 345.2 innings. In April 1960, Cleveland traded Score to the Chicago White Sox (AL). His eight-year major league career included 55 wins, 46 losses, a 3.36 ERA, 11 shutouts, and 837 strikeouts in 858.1 innings pitched. Score handled color television commentary for the Cleveland Indians from 1964 through 1967. He replaced Jimmy Dudley as radio play-by-play announcer for the Cleveland Indians in 1968 and served in that capacity through 1997. His shout, "Stwike Thwee!" became something of a Cleveland institution. He married Nancy McNamara in July 1957. He was involved in a serious automobile accident in New Philadelphia, OH in October 1998.

BIBLIOGRAPHY: *The Baseball Encyclopedia*, 10th ed. (New York, 1996); John Benson et al., *Baseball's Top 100* (Wilton, CT, 1997); Jim Brosnan, *Great Rookies of the Major Leagues* (New York, 1966); William Furlong, "The Rebuilding of Herb Score," *Sport* 31 (January 1961), pp. 44–45; Donald Honig, *Baseball Between the Lines* (New York, 1976); Bruce Jacobs, *Baseball Stars of 1956* (New York, 1956); Gene Karst and Martin J. Jones, Jr., *Who's Who in Professional Baseball* (New Rochelle, NY, 1973); Wil A. Linkugel and Edward J. Pappas, *They Tasted Glory* (Jefferson, NC, 1998); Robert Liston, *The Pros* (New York, 1968); Jack Newcombe, *Fireballers* (New York, 1964); Robert Obojski, "Score Completes 32nd Year as Indians Broadcaster," *SCD* 22 (November 24, 1995), pp. 130–131; John Phillips, *Winners* (Cabin John, MD, 1987); John Thorn et al., eds., *Total Indians* (New York, 1996); Jack Torry, *Endless Summers* (South Bend, IN, 1995); Jimmy Olsen, "The Private Ordeal of Herb Score," *SI* 15 (August 7, 1961), pp. 25–27; Herbert Score file, National Baseball Library, Cooperstown, NY; Curt Smith, *Voices of the Game* (South Bend, IN, 1987).

                                                                James K. Skipper, Jr.

SCOTT, George Charles, Jr. "Boomer," "Peatuck" (b. March 23, 1943, Greenville, MS), player, manager, and coach, is the son of George C. Scott, Sr., and in 1962 graduated from Coleman High School in Greenville, where he averaged 35 points per game as a basketball forward and guard and starred in baseball and football. Approximately 150 colleges and universities offered Scott athletic scholarships. The Boston Red Sox (AL) signed the 6-foot 2-inch, 215-pound, right-handed third baseman as a free agent in May 1962. Scott spent the 1962 campaign at Olean, NY (NYPL), 1963 at Wellsville, NY (NYPL), and 1964 at Winston-Salem, NC (CrL) and earned MVP honors in 1965 at Pittsfield, MA (EL), leading the EL in batting average, hits, doubles, HR, and RBI. In 1966 Scott joined the Boston Red Sox, pacing AL batters in strikeouts (152) and setting an AL record for most intentional walks given to a rookie (13).

Scott, who resides in Greenville, played mostly at first base during his major league career and batted .268 with 306 doubles, 60 triples, 271 HR, and 1,051 RBI. The Boston Red Sox traded Scott in October 1971 to the Milwaukee Brewers (AL). In December 1976, Milwaukee returned Scott to the Boston Red Sox for first baseman Cecil Cooper.* Scott ended his major league career in 1979 with the Kansas City Royals (AL) and New York Yankees (AL).

Brilliant fielding and enormous power distinguished Scott's performance. The agile Scott fielded .990 lifetime and made *TSN* AL All-Star fielding team eight times (1967–1968, 1971–1976), a record for AL first basemen. Besides topping AL first basemen in total chances and fielding percentage in 1974, Scott paced AL first basemen three times in putouts (1966–1967, 1974), assists (1974–1976), and double plays (1966–1967, 1974) and twice in errors (1967, 1977). Offensively, Scott led AL batters in total bases twice (1973, 1975), knocked in at least 80 runs seven times, and hit at least 20 HR six times. In 1967, Scott batted .303 with 19 HR and 82 RBI to help the Red Sox win the AL pennant. His best season came in 1973, when he batted a career-high .306 and knocked in 107 runs. The 1975 season saw Scott lead the AL in RBI (109), share the AL crown in HR (36), and hit 26 doubles. The RBI and HR marked career bests. Scott appeared in the 1967 World Series against the St. Louis Cardinals and in the 1966, 1975, and 1977 All-Star Games, slugging a two-run HR in the 1977 classic. Scott managed in the MEL two seasons and helped organize recreational baseball leagues in Mississippi. He coached baseball at Foxbury, MA CC five years and managed the Massachusetts Mad Dogs of the Independent Northeast League in 1997.

BIBLIOGRAPHY: George Scott file, National Baseball Library, Cooperstown, NY; Peter Golenbock, *Fenway* (New York, 1992); Howard Liss, *The Boston Red Sox* (New York, 1982); Dan Shaughnessy, *The Curse of the Bambino* (New York, 1990); Roy Blount, Jr., "Sometimes the Ball Just Takes a Funny Bounce," *Esquire* 88 (August 1977), pp. 17–18; Jack Lautier, *Fenway Voices* (Camden, ME, 1990); Robert Redmount, *The Red Sox Encyclopedia* (Champaign, IL, 1998); Paul Post, "The Boomer," *SCD* 24 (August 1, 1997), p. 96; Ken Coleman and Dan Valenti, *The Impossible Dream Remembered* (Lexington, MA, 1987); Bill McSweeney, *The Impossible Dream* (New York, 1968); Carl Yastrzemski with Al Hirshberg, *Yaz* (New York, 1968); John

Thorn, et al., eds., *Total Baseball*, 5th ed. (New York, 1997); Richard Topp, letter to David L. Porter, February 3, 1990; *TSN Official Baseball Register*, 1967–1980.

David L. Porter

SCOTT, James "Death Valley Jim" (b. April 23, 1888, Deadwood, SD; d. April 7, 1957, Palm Springs, CA), player and umpire, was the son of George Scott, who worked for the U.S. government, and Kitty (Wilson) Scott and attended Wesleyan College in Lincoln, NE. The 6-foot 1-inch, 235-pound pitcher, who threw and batted right-handed, was nicknamed "Death Valley" or "Death Valley Jim" because his name resembled Walter Scott, the original "Death Valley Scott."

Scott began his professional baseball career with Oskaloosa, IA (IoSL) in 1907, where he compiled a 20–11 mark. In 1908, he finished 25–18 for Wichita, KS (WA). Scott made his major league debut in 1909 with the Chicago White Sox (AL) and pitched there throughout his nine-year major league career. One reporter compared him to teammate Ed Walsh,* the future National Baseball Hall of Fame pitcher. Scott, however, did not attain Walsh's level of success. He won 20 games with a 1.90 ERA and AL-leading 38 starts in 1913, but also paced the AL with 20 losses. His best season came in 1915, when he fared 24–11 with a 2.03 ERA. Scott hurled a nine-inning no-hitter against the Washington Senators on May 14, 1914, but lost the game, 1–0, on two hits in the 10th inning. He also fanned six straight batters on June 22, 1913 against the St. Louis Browns, tying the then AL record for consecutive strikeouts. His overall record for the Chicago White Sox featured 107 wins, 113 losses, and a 2.30 ERA.

After marrying Harriet B. Cook on November 17, 1917, Scott joined the military during 1918. He was only the second major league player to enlist following Hank Gowdy.* In 1919, Scott returned to baseball as a minor leaguer. He compiled a 94–65 mark for San Francisco, CA (PCL) from 1919 through 1924, enjoying a 23–14 record in 1920 and 25–9 slate in 1922. Scott pitched for New Orleans, LA (SA) from 1925 to 1927, with 31 wins and 33 losses. Scott umpired in the SA in 1928 and 1929 and the NL during the 1930–1931 seasons, finishing his career back in the SA in 1932.

Scott, who worked as a movie technician in Hollywood, CA, had one son, James Scott Jr., who played minor league baseball. He died of heart failure at age 68.

BIBLIOGRAPHY: James Scott file, National Baseball Library, Cooperstown, NY; Warren Brown, *The Chicago White Sox* (New York, 1952); Richard Lindberg, *Sox* (New York, 1984); Richard Lindberg, *Who on Third?* (South Bend, IN, 1983); *TSN Official Baseball Guide*, 1958; *TSN Baseball Register*, 1948.

Michael J. McBride

SCOTT, Lewis Everett "Deacon," "Scotty" (b. November 19, 1892, Bluffton, IN; d. November 2, 1960, Fort Wayne, IN), player, starred as a defensive shortstop and formerly held the major league record for most consecutive games played. The son of Louis Scott and Minnie (Keeper) Scott, he had two brothers, William and Walter, and a sister, Alice. Measles kept Scott home during his first week of school, but he never missed another day of classes. He later applied that same work ethic in the major leagues.

Scott joined the Boston Red Sox (AL) in 1914 and replaced Charlie Wagner at shortstop. The 5-foot 8-inch rookie, who weighed 148 pounds, posed little threat offensively but his fielding and bunting skills made him an asset. Scott's quiet manner earned him the nickname "Deacon."

Scott played for AL pennant-winning Boston Red Sox teams in 1915, 1916 and 1918. After World War I, however, the Boston Red Sox faded. Boston owner Harry Frazee began peddling star players to finance his theatrical ventures. In December 1921, 11 months after selling Babe Ruth* to the New York Yankees (AL), Frazee traded Scott to the same club in a six-player deal.

Scott performed for New York Yankees AL pennant winners in 1922 and 1923 and led AL shortstops in fielding from 1912 to 1923. He began a consecutive game streak on June 20, 1916 with the Boston Red Sox. By 1923, the skein had reached over 1,000 games. A general team slump ended Scott's consecutive games streak in 1925. That year, the New York Yankees finished an unaccustomed seventh. Manager Miller Huggins* benched Scott on May 6 to shake up his team. Scott's streak of 1,307 consecutive games lasted until Lou Gehrig* broke it in 1933.

In June 1925, the New York Yankees sold Scott to the Washington Senators (AL). The Washington Senators finished first to give Scott his sixth pennant-winning team, but he did not play in the World Series. He split the 1926 season between the Chicago White Sox (AL) and Cincinnati Reds (NL) before leaving the major leagues with a .249 career batting average in 1,654 games. Scott batted only .156 in 27 World Series contests.

Scott played briefly in the minor leagues before returning to Fort Wayne, IN, where he operated several bowling alleys. An avid kegler, he won numerous city and state titles and bowled 300 over 50 times. Scott married Gladys Watts and had one son, L. Everett Jr.

BIBLIOGRAPHY: *The Baseball Encyclopedia*, 10th ed. (New York, 1996); Peter J. Cava, Indiana-born Major League Player files, Peter J. Cava Collection, Indianapolis, IN; Peter J. Cava and Paul Sandin, "First 'Iron Man' Was Long-Time Resident of City," Fort Wayne (IN) *Journal Gazette*, September 6, 1995, pp. 1–2B; Everett Scott file, National Baseball Library, Cooperstown, NY; Leo Trachtenberg, "The Durable Deacon," *YM* 58 (December 17, 1992), pp. 38–39, 41; Bill Madden, *The Hoosiers of Summer* (Indianapolis, IN, 1994); Frederick G. Lieb, *The Boston Red Sox* (New York, 1947); Howard Liss, *The Boston Red Sox* (New York, 1982); Robert Redmount, *The Red Sox Encyclopedia* (Champaign, IL, 1998); Frank Graham, *The New York Yankees* (New York, 1943); Dave Anderson et al., *The Yankees* (New York, 1979); Mark Gallagher, *The Yankee Encyclopedia*, vol. 3 (Champaign, IL, 1997).

Peter J. Cava

SCOTT, Michael Warren "Mike" (b. April 26, 1955, Santa Monica, CA), player, is the son of Warren Scott, a Chevron employee, and Kathy Scott, North American Rockwell employee. Scott served as team captain and made all-league in both baseball and basketball at Hawthorne, CA High School. As a senior, he won nine and lost one with a 0.67 ERA, pitched a no-hitter, and led his league with four HR. Scott attended Pepperdine University in Malibu, CA for three years, posting a career 26–14 record and 2.09 ERA and making All WCAC all three years. He set Pepperdine records for career wins, strikeouts (232), and innings pitched (343.2). The United States College All-Star team defeated the Japanese College All-Stars in 1975, as Scott won once and allowed two runs in 11 innings. After finishing 1–0 for the United States in the 1975 Pan American Games, he was selected 37th in the June 1976 free agent draft as the New York Mets' (NL) second round choice. Scout Roger Jongewaard of the New York Mets signed him to his first professional contract.

Scott pitched in 1976 and 1977 for Jackson, TX (TL), leading the TL in wins (14) and innings pitched (187) in 1977. He performed for Tidewater, VA (IL) for all or parts of the 1977 to 1980 seasons, finishing 8–4 in 1979 and 13–7 in 1980. Scott won his first major league appearance on April 24, 1979 for the New York Mets against the San Francisco Giants, compiling 1–3 and 1–1 marks in 1979 and 1980. After having losing seasons for the New York Mets in 1981 and 1982, he was traded to the Houston Astros (NL) for Danny Heep in December 1982. With the Houston Astros, he fared 10–6 in 1983 and 5–11 in 1984.

The Houston Astros wanted Scott to add another pitch and hired former pitcher Roger Craig* to teach him the split-fingered fastball prior to the 1985 season. Scott improved to 18–8 that campaign with a 3.29 ERA. Scott's best season came in 1986, when his 18–10 record led the Houston Astros to a Western Division crown. His 2.22 ERA, 275.1 innings pitched, and 306 strikeouts that season paced the NL. He shared the NL lead in shutouts with five and struck out at least nine batters in 19 games, hurling a 13-strikeout no-hitter against the San Francisco Giants on September 25 to clinch the Western Division title. In the fifth inning on September 3, Scott tied the major league record for most strikeouts in an inning (4). He won the NL Cy Young Award and hurled two complete game victories against the New York Mets in the NL Championship Series, fanning 19 and allowing only eight hits and one walk in 18 innings. He matched the NL Championship Series records for most complete games and most strikeouts in a game (14). The Houston Astros lost the NL Championship Series, but Scott was named the MVP.

Scott finished 16–13 (3.23 ERA) in 1987, 14–8 (2.92 ERA) in 1988, and 20–10 (3.10 ERA) in 1989, sharing the NL lead in games started (36) in 1987 and leading the NL in victories (20) in 1989. In 1990, he slipped to a 9–13 record with a 3.81 ERA. Scott underwent surgery on his right shoulder before the 1991 season, but rotator-cuff pain limited him to two starts. He retired after the 1991 season with a 124–108 career won–lost record, a 3.54 ERA, and 1,469 strikeouts. The 6-foot 3-inch, 215-pound Scott appeared in the 1986 and 1987 All-Star Games, allowing one run in three innings, and was selected for the 1989 midseason classic.

Scott and his wife, Vicki, have two daughters, Kimberlee and Kelsey. His parents were honored on August 5, 1990, as the Little League Parents of the Year for their work in the Hawthorne, CA Little League program.

BIBLIOGRAPHY: Mickey Scott file, National Baseball Library, Cooperstown, NY; Ron Fimrite, "No Wonder He's Hot," *SI* 66 (January 12, 1987), pp. 92–102; Donald Honig, *The New York Mets* (New York, 1986); Jack Lang and Peter Simon, *The New York Mets* (New York, 1986); Ken Young, *Cy Young Award Winners* (New York, 1994); Pat Jordan, "Mike Scott Got a Grip on the Split-Fingered Fastball and Threw His Career a Nice Curve," *PW* 28 (July 6, 1987), pp. 45–47; M. Moran, "Unlikely Star Makes His Mark on Baseball," *NYT Biographical Service* 17 (October 1986), pp. 1253–1254; Dave Nightengale, "Scott Speaks off the Cuff," *TSN* (August 28, 1989), pp. 11–13.

David A. Goss

SEAVER, George Thomas "Tom," "Tom Terrific" (b. November 17, 1944, Fresno, CA), player and sportscaster, is the son of Charles Seaver, a 1932 Walker Cup golfer, and Betty (Cline) Seaver. In 1962, the 5-foot 9-inch, 160-pound senior compiled a 6–5 record for Fresno High School and received no baseball offers. After a stint in the U.S. Marine Corps and experience with the semipro Alaska Goldpanners, he had gained 3 inches and 30 pounds by 1965 and starred for the University of Southern California. He eventually earned a Bachelor's degree in public relations there in 1974.

The Los Angeles Dodgers (NL) drafted Seaver in 1965, but did not offer him a contract. When the Atlanta Braves (NL) made him an offer with a reported $40,000 bonus in February 1966, Commissioner William Eckert* nullified the contract by claiming that it violated the "college rule." Ironically, at the same time, the NCAA declared him ineligible. Eckert then made him available to any team willing to match the Braves' offer. When three teams indicated their interest, the New York Mets (NL) won the right to sign him in a drawing. He signed for a $50,000 bonus and pitched for Jacksonville, FL (IL).

After an impressive spring in 1967, the Mets promoted the 6-foot 1-inch, 210-pound right-hander. Seaver enjoyed a winning season on a losing ballclub. Two years later, "Tom Terrific" led the "Amazin' Mets" to the World Series with a major league leading 25–7 record. He was rewarded with a record $100,000-plus annual salary after only five seasons. Seaver proved the mainstay on the New York pitching staff from 1967 to 1977, providing almost one-quarter of the Mets' victories. He led the NL in wins three times with 25 in 1969, 22 in 1975, and 14 in 1981 and in strikeouts five times, establishing major league records for most seasons (10) registering 200 or more strikeouts (including a record nine in a row from 1968 to 1976). In 1970, he tied the then major league record of 19 strikeouts in one game and established the mark for most consecutive strikeouts (10). Three times, he paced the NL in ERA, with his 1.76 in 1971 and 2.08 in 1973 being major league bests. He hurled 46 shutouts in his first 11 seasons, topping the NL with seven in 1977.

In 1967, Seaver was honored as NL Rookie of the Year. He was named *TSN* NL Pitcher of the Year in 1969 and 1975 and won the Cy Young Award three times—in 1969, 1973, and 1975. He was named to the NL All-Star team 12 times—nine as a Met—and pitched the Mets to NL titles in 1969 and 1973 and a World Series championship in 1969. After a dispute with the Mets ownership, Seaver was traded in June 1977 to the Cincinnati Reds (NL). He spent six seasons in Cincinnati, where his five shutouts and .727 winning percentage in 1979 topped the NL and his .875 win–loss percentage in 1981 led the major leagues. On June 10, 1978, he pitched a 4–0 no hitter against the St. Louis Cardinals. In December 1982, Seaver was traded back to the Mets ostensibly to play out his career in Shea Stadium. When the Mets left Seaver unprotected during the 1984 free agent compensation draft, however, the Chicago White Sox (AL) selected him. In his first season with the White Sox, he led all Chicago starters with 15 wins and posted a 3.95 ERA. In 1985 he again paced the White Sox staff with a 16–11 mark and a 3.17 ERA. On August 4, 1985, he became the 17th major league pitcher to win 300 games by defeating the New York Yankees, 4–1. On October 4, 1985, he struck out seven Seattle Mariners to pass Gaylord Perry* for third place in all-time strikeouts. Chicago traded Seaver on June 28, 1986 to the Boston Red Sox (AL) for center fielder–third baseman Steve Lyons. Seaver started 16 games for the AL pennant winning Red Sox, but a knee injury prevented him from participating in either the AL Championship Series or World Series.

In 20 major league seasons, Seaver compiled a 311–205 win–loss mark for a .603 winning percentage and a 2.86 ERA. He hurled 61 career shutouts (7th best) and struck out 3,640 batters (4th best). In 4,782.2 innings, he surrendered only 1,390 walks. Seaver threw a 98-mile-an-hour fastball as a rookie, although never labeled a fireballer. He succeeded with superb pitch selection and placement, claiming that on a good day all but five pitches in a game were on target. Seaver pioneered training with weights for arm strength and pitching speed and developed a mechanically perfect delivery by eliminating unnecessary motion and using his entire body.

Although the picture of concentration on the mound and refined in public, Seaver was fun-loving and prankish in the clubhouse. He is a family man who enjoys reading, hunting, fishing, golfing, traveling, and playing bridge. The co-author of two baseball books, he has succeeded in many business and broadcasting ventures. He served as a color television analyst for the

New York Yankees (AL) in 1992 and 1993 and the New York Mets since 1995 and was elected to the National Baseball Hall of Fame in 1992. He and his wife, Nancy, have two daughters and live in Greenwich, CT.

BIBLIOGRAPHY: John Benson et al., *Baseball's Top 100* (Wilton, CT, 1997); *CB* (1970), pp. 384–386; Murray Chass, "Compensation System Showing Flaws," *TSN*, February 6, 1984, p. 40; Frank Deford, "Behind the Fence," *SI* 55 (July 27, 1981), pp. 50–64; Joseph Durso, "The Ordeal of George Thomas Seaver," *SR* 2 (April 19, 1975), pp. 12–13; Ron Fimrite, "They're the Talks of Their Town," *SI* 65 (July 14, 1986), pp. 22–24; "How the Franchise Went West," *Time* 109 (June 27, 1977), p. 49; Joe Jares, "The Mets Find a Young Phenom," *SI* 26 (June 26, 1967), pp. 64–66; Pat Jordan, "Tom Terrific and His Mystic Talent," *SI* 37 (July 24, 1972), pp. 22–31; Pat Jordan, "Tom Seaver," *Sport* 78 (December 1987), pp. 95–97; Robert E. Kelly, *Baseball's Best* (Jefferson, NC, 1988); *NYT Biographical Service* 19 (July 1988), pp. 838–839; William Leggett, "Sportsman of the Year," *SI* 31 (December 22, 1969), pp. 32–37; Melissa Ludtke Lincoln, "TV Radio Making Another Kind of Pitch," *SI* 49 (September 18, 1978), p. 50; J. Maura, "Mound Olympus," *PT* 25 (July/August 1992), pp. 22–23; *The Baseball Encyclopedia*, 10th ed. (New York, 1996); Gene Schoor, *Seaver* (Chicago, IL, 1986); Stanley Cohen, *A Magic Summer* (San Diego, CA, 1988); Dennis D'Agostino, *This Date in New York Mets History* (New York, 1981); Donald Honig, *The New York Mets* (New York, 1986); Jack Lang and Peter Simon, *The New York Mets* (New York, 1986); Bob Rathgeber, *Cincinnati Reds Scrapbook* (Virginia Beach, VA, 1982); Robert H. Walker, *Cincinnati and the Big Red Machine* (Bloomington, IN, 1988); *TSN Official Baseball Register, 1981*; *Washington Post*, April 19, 1985, p. E7; Ken Young, *Cy Young Award Winners* (New York, 1994).

Gaymon L. Bennett

SEITZER, Kevin Lee (b. March 26, 1962, Springfield, IL), player, is the son of Clifford Seitzer and starred in baseball at Eastern Illinois University, where he earned a Bachelor of Science degree in industrial electronics. In 1983, the Kansas City Royals (AL) selected him in the 11th round of the June free agent draft. He compiled three .300-plus seasons as a minor leaguer before debuting with the Kansas City Royals in September 1986.

Seitzer became the Kansas City Royals' regular third baseman in 1987 and enjoyed a spectacular rookie campaign with a .323 batting average, 15 HR, and 83 RBI and led the AL with 207 hits. He made the AL All-Star team and finished second in the AL's Rookie of the Year balloting behind Mark McGwire.* Seitzer's productivity declined in 1988, but he still hit .304. Unfortunately, he also led AL third basemen in errors for the second consecutive year.

The right-handed Seitzer enjoyed two more respectable seasons before being slowed by injuries. In April 1991, he landed on the disabled list with a broken wrist. Knee problems also limited his playing time, as he finished the season batting .265 in only 234 at-bats. Seitzer underwent arthroscopic surgery on both knees in the off-season and was released by the Kansas City Royals. The Milwaukee Brewers (AL) signed him, for whom he hit .270 with

71 RBI in 1992. Seitzer also improved his fielding, recording the fewest errors among AL third basemen in 1992.

In February 1993, Seitzer signed with the Oakland A's (AL) as a free agent. In July 1993, however, he refused an assignment to an Oakland A's farm team and again became a free agent. The 5-foot 11-inch, 193-pound infielder returned to the Milwaukee Brewers later that month. Although hamstring problems limited his playing time in 1994, Seitzer enjoyed a solid year in 1995 with a .311 batting average, five HR, and 69 RBI. In July 1995, he played in his second All-Star game. Despite injury problems and three serious beanings, which have required him to wear a protective mask, Seitzer remained a potent offensive threat. After Seitzer batted .316 with 12 HR and 62 RBI in 1996, the Milwaukee Brewers traded him to the Cleveland Indians (AL) that August. He helped the Cleveland Indians win the AL Central Division and batted .294 with four RBI in the AL Division Series against the Baltimore Orioles. In 1997, Seitzer went hitless in just nine combined at-bats in the AL Division Series against the New York Yankees, the AL Championship Series against the Baltimore Orioles, and the World Series against the Florida Marlins. The Indians released him in October 1997.

In 12 major league seasons he batted .295 with 1,557 hits, 74 HR, and 613 RBI. Seitzer, a committed Christian, resides in Overland Park, KS, with his wife, Lisa, and two children.

BIBLIOGRAPHY: Kevin Seitzer file, National Baseball Library, Cooperstown, NY; John Garrity, "Here Come the Young Lions," *SI* 67 (July 26, 1987), p. 48; "Kevin Seitzer," *Microsoft Complete Baseball* CD-ROM (Redmond, WA, 1994); Kevin Seitzer, "Fear Strikes Back," *SI* 82 (July 24, 1995), p. 118.

Kent M. Krause

SELBACH, Albert Karl "Kip" (b. March 24, 1872, Columbus, OH; d. February 17, 1956, Columbus, OH), player, was the son of Charles Selbach and Maria Selbach and married Nina G. Roberts in 1894. The stocky 5-foot 7-inch, 190-pound Selbach was signed as a catcher for Chattanooga, TN (SL) at age 21. His old-world German parents had refused to let him sign until he turned age 21. His Chattanooga mentor, Gus Schmelz, became manager of the Washington Senators (NL) the next year and took Selbach along. Since the Washington Senators already possessed catcher James McGuire,* Selbach became a left fielder and spent 13 years in the major leagues at that position. He also occasionally played in the infield.

In 1899, Selbach shifted to the Cincinnati Reds (NL). Cincinnati Reds owner John T. Brush, also part owner of the New York Giants (NL), transferred Selbach to the latter franchise in February 1900. Selbach in 1902 jumped to the Baltimore Orioles (AL) when John McGraw* offered him a higher salary. When the Baltimore Orioles franchise was dissolved, Selbach was awarded to the Washington Senators (AL) and played there in 1903 and part of 1904. The Boston Pilgrims (AL), which won the 1904 AL pennant, acquired him that July. In the midseason of 1906, Selbach was sold to Providence, RI (EL) due to his declining skills. He finished his professional baseball career with Harrisburg, PA (TSL) from 1907 to 1910.

Selbach, who hit .300 or better seven times, compiled a career .293 batting average and knocked in 779 runs during 13 major league seasons. His 1,803 career hits included 299 doubles and 149 triples. Selbach belted at least 11 triples nine times and 20 or more doubles in 10 seasons. On June 9, 1896, Selbach made six hits in seven trips to the plate against the Cincinnati Reds. His fellow outfielders added five hits each to set a single-game record of 16 hits for an outfield. A speedy base runner despite his stout build, Selbach stole 334 career bases and reached a pinnacle of 49 stolen bases in 1896. Selbach, who excelled as a leadoff man and defensive outfielder, was known for dallying at the plate and then sticking his wad of gum on the bottom of his cap when he finally was ready to hit. Selbach also became a championship bowler and in 1896 organized the first bowling team in Columbus. In 1903, he teamed with Herman Collins to win the American Bowling Congress doubles title. Subsequently, Selbach owned and operated two bowling alleys in Columbus.

BIBLIOGRAPHY: Albert Selbach file, National Baseball Library, Cooperstown, NY; Morris Bealle, *The Washington Senators* (Washington, DC, 1947); Frank Graham, *The New York Giants* (New York, 1952); Robert Redmount, *The Red Sox Encyclopedia* (Champaign, IL, 1998); Gene Karst and Martin J. Jones, Jr., *Who's Who in Professional Baseball* (New Rochelle, NY, 1973); Frederick G. Lieb, *The Boston Red Sox* (New York, 1947); *NYT*, February 18, 1946; Shirley Povich, *The Washington Senators* (New York, 1954); John Thorn et al., eds., *Total Baseball*, 5th ed. (New York, 1997); Robert L. Tiemann and Mark Rucker, eds., *Nineteenth Century Stars* (Kansas City, MO, 1989).

Ralph S. Graber

SELEE, Frank Gibson (b. October 26, 1859, Amherst, NH; d. July 5, 1909, Denver, CO), player, manager, and executive, was the second of three children of Methodist-Episcopal clergyman Nathan P. Selee and Annie Marie (Cass) Selee. The Selees moved to Melrose, MA, when Frank was still an infant. He attended local public schools and belonged to the town's Alpha baseball club. His professional baseball career began in 1884, when he left a job with the Waltham Watch Company to organize a town entry in the MasL. Although "without any practical experience as a manager or player," Selee wrote that he raised a capital fund of $1,000, played some outfield, and quickly found his métier as manager. He managed Haverhill, MA (NEL) in 1885–1886, and made his "real start in baseball" in 1887 with Oshkosh, WI (NWL), where he won his first pennant. The following year, the NWL became the WA. Selee shifted to Omaha, NE (WA) and in 1889 won another pennant.

In 1890, the Boston Beaneaters (NL) signed Omaha's ace right-hander Kid Nichols* and hired Selee as manager. Undaunted by the loss of 10 Beaneaters to the Boston Reds (PL), Selee combined the remaining loyalists with shrewd acquisitions from other leagues to finish first. Over the next nine years, he managed the Boston Beaneaters to five NL pennants (1891–1893, 1897–1898), won 774 games, and lost only 451 contests for a .632 percentage. His 1892 and 1898 teams became the first clubs to win over 100 games in one NL season. The 1894 powerhouse finished third, but set the major league single-season record of 1,222 runs scored. Seven regulars tallied over 100 runs each for a team that was never shut out in 132 games and clouted 103 HR. No other major league club between 1884 and 1920 hit over 100 HR in a season.

As a master of inside baseball, Selee made his reputation. He favored the hit-and-run, the strategically stolen base, and signals to deploy his team defensively. In a rowdy era, he proved "modest and retiring," "courteous and mild-mannered." He represented an emerging breed of manager, who directed his team from the bench and knew baseball without having been a star player. His eye for talent was so keen that he supposedly could "tell a ball player in his street clothes." The Boston years demonstrated his skill in player selection and development. Fred Tenney,* a left-handed college-educated catcher, was switched to first base and taught to execute the game's first 3–6–3 double plays. Jimmy Collins,* a minor league outfielder, became a National Baseball Hall of Fame third baseman. Six other Hall of Famers played for Selee in Boston, while four others did in Chicago. Two potential stars he supposedly rejected, however, were Honus Wagner* and Napoleon Lajoie.*

After a fifth place finish in 1901 and three years without a pennant, Boston released Selee. The sixth place Chicago Cubs (NL) promptly signed him. Undertaking again to create a new team, Selee raised the Cubs a notch in 1902. Frank Chance,* a catcher and part-time outfielder, was shifted to first base, while third baseman Joe Tinker,* acquired from Portland, OR (PNL), moved to shortstop. Johnny Evers,* an infielder from Troy, NY (NYSL), joined the team on Labor Day and became the second baseman. On September 15, the Tinker-Evers-Chance combination made its first double play.

The Cubs advanced to third place in 1903 and finished second in 1904. Selee added "Wildfire" Schulte* and persuaded the St. Louis Cardinals (NL) to accept an aging pitcher and second-string catcher for Mordecai "Three Finger" Brown.* In May 1905 Ed Reulbach* was signed. After 90 games that season, the Cubs' management shifted to Frank Chance. The never robust Selee was gravely ill with tuberculosis and was given an indefinite leave of absence to regain his health. He moved to Denver, CO, bought an interest in the Pueblo, CO Indians (WL), and served as club president from mid–1906 to June 1907. He also became a partner in a Denver hotel.

He was buried in Melrose, MA, where he had operated a clothing store with Sidney Farrar, one-time first baseman for the Philadelphia Quakers (NL and PL) and father of the great operatic soprano, Geraldine Farrar. In 16 years as major league manager, Selee won 1,284 games and lost 862 for a .598 winning percentage, the fourth highest in baseball history. None of his teams ever finished lower than fifth. With the Cubs, he developed teams winning pennants from 1906 to 1908 and in 1910 for Chance. Survived by his wife May, he had no children. In 1999, the Veterans Committee elected him to the National Baseball Hall of Fame.

BIBLIOGRAPHY: Lee Allen, *The National League Story* (New York, 1961); Thomas Aylesworth and Benton Minks, *The Encyclopedia of Baseball Managers* (New York, 1990); Chicago *Tribune*, July 29, 1905, July 6, 1909; Cincinnati *Enquirer*, July 7–8, 12, 1909; Allison Danzig and Joe Reichler, *The History of Baseball* (Englewood Cliffs, NJ, 1959); Denver *Republican*, July 9, 1909, p. 9; Denver *Times*, July 9, 1909, p. 8; John L. Evers with Hugh S. Fullerton, *Touching Second* (Chicago, IL, 1910); Ralph Hickok, *Who Was Who in American Sports* (New York, 1971); Harold Kaese, *The Boston Braves* (New York, 1948); Frederick G. Lieb, *The Baseball Story* (New York, 1950); Melrose (MA) *Free Press*, July 9, 16, 1909, February 9, 1912; Pueblo (CO) *Chieftain*, March 26, May 25, July 6, 1909; *The Baseball Encyclopedia*, 10th ed. (New York, 1996); Joseph L. Reichler, ed., *The Baseball Trade Register* (New York, 1984); Frank G. Selee, "Twenty-one Years in Baseball," *BM* 8 (December 1911), pp. 53–56; Harold Seymour, *Baseball: The Early Years* (New York, 1960); Harold Seymour, *Baseball: The Golden Age* (New York, 1971); *Spalding's Official Base Ball Guide, 1906* (New York, 1906); *SL*, August 5, 12, 19, 26, 1905, June 8, 1907, July 24, 1909; A. D. Suehsdorf, "Frank Selee: Dynasty Builder," *TNP* 4 (Winter 1985), pp. 35–41; Robert L. Tiemann and Mark Rucker, eds., *Nineteenth Century Stars* (Kansas City, MO, 1989); Eddie Gold and Art Ahrens, *The Golden Era Cubs, 1876–1940* (Chicago, IL, 1985); Al Hirshberg, *Braves, the Pick and the Shovel* (Boston, MA, 1948); Gary Caruso, *The Braves Encyclopedia* (Philadelphia, PA, 1995); Warren Brown, *The Chicago Cubs* (New York, 1946); Jim Enright, *Chicago Cubs* (New York, 1975); David Quentin Voigt, *American Baseball*, vol. 1 (University Park, PA, 1983); Frank Selee file, National Baseball Library, Cooperstown, NY.

A. D. Suehsdorf

SELIG, Allan H. "Bud" (b. July 30, 1934, Milwaukee, WI), owner and acting commissioner, is the son of Ben Selig, a Ford dealership owner, and Marie Selig, a grade school teacher. Selig received a Bachelor of Science degree from the University of Wisconsin in Madison in 1956 and served in the U.S. Army from 1956 to 1958. Marie Selig, an avid baseball fan, turned her son's interest to the sport and encouraged his dreams of playing professionally. After his father's death, Selig assumed the ownership and presidency of Selig Executive Leasing Company in West Allis, WI. Although only 25 years old, he prospered in the automobile business and became the first public investor in the Milwaukee Braves (NL) baseball team. He sold his Milwaukee Braves' stock when the team relocated to Atlanta in 1966.

Selig assembled a group of investors to bid for an expansion AL club, but was bitterly disappointed when the franchises were awarded to Kansas City, MO and Seattle, WA for the 1969 season. He continued seeking an expansion team or troubled franchise that might relocate. One week before the start of the 1970 season, Selig purchased the bankrupt Seattle Pilots for $10.8 million, moved the team to Milwaukee, and christened it "the Brewers." Selig became club president, earning the respect of major league owners with his responsible fiscal management and ability to show profits in one of the smallest major league markets. The Milwaukee Brewers usually ranked at or near the bottom in total team payroll.

Selig married Suzanne Lappin Steinman in 1977. They have two daughters, Sari and Wendy. He was named UPI 1978 Major League Executive of the Year. In 1984, he headed the committee that selected Peter Ueberroth (OS) major league baseball commissioner. Selig, who chaired Major League Baseball's Players Relations Committee in the 1980s and served on the Executive Council from 1992 to 1998, led the movement to oust Baseball Commissioner Faye Vincent.* Vincent's plan to reorganize baseball from four to six divisions angered some owners. Although adamantly refusing a permanent position as commissioner, Selig became interim commissioner when Vincent resigned in September 1992.

Negotiations on a new labor agreement between owners and players in 1994 left Selig in an awkward position. He long advocated the need for revenue sharing to assist small market teams, caps on player salaries, and an end to player salary arbitration, which he believed primarily caused salary escalation. As acting commissioner, he needed to guide baseball through bitter negotiations. Yet as an owner, he was not a disinterested party. Many saw this as a conflict of interest. He took a hard line on labor issues and held the 28 owners together during the endless rounds of negotiations. On August 11, 1994, the MLPAA called a strike against the AL and NL. With 52 days remaining on the schedule, the owners cancelled the remainder of the regular season and the World Series. The labor impasse threatened the 1995 season, as owners sought replacement players for spring training before an agreement was reached. Some media personnel and many fans blamed the labor turmoil on Selig.

Owners attempted to bring fans back to major league parks by adding another round of playoffs featuring a wild card team in 1996 and interleague play in 1997. With the Tampa Bay, FL Devil Rays (AL) and Arizona Diamondbacks (NL) beginning play in 1998, Selig faced the challenge of realignment of the NL and AL to foster geographic rivalries, generate more television revenue, and curb travel. Selig favored a radical realignment that would have 15 current teams switch leagues creating divisions of teams in relative proximity to one another. His plan received strong opposition from numerous owners. Ultimately, the Milwaukee Brewers shifted to the NL, Tampa Bay joined the AL East, Detroit shifted to the AL Central, and Arizona joined the NL West. Selig still considered his role interim, but the owners appointed him permanent commissioner in July 1998. He eliminated the titles of AL and NL presidents and supervised the replacement of 22 veteran umpires. Selig also sits on the Board of Directors of the Green Bay Packers (NFL) team and numerous other business, civic, and charitable boards. His numerous honors include the 1989 August A. Busch, Jr. Award for long and meritorious service to baseball, Pro Urbe Award for community service, 1990 Humanitarian Award with his wife, Suzanne, and the Anti-Defamation League's World of Difference Award for 1994.

BIBLIOGRAPHY: Roger Angell, "Hardball," *TNY* 70 (October 17, 1994), pp. 65–76; CQ Researcher Staff, "The Business of Sports," *CQR* 5 (February 10, 1995), pp. 121–140; Louise Mooney Collins and Geri Speace, eds., *Newsmakers* (New York, 1995); *Milwaukee Brewers 1989 Official Yearbook*; Richard O'Brien and Kostya Kennedy, "The Buddy System," *SI* 84 (May 6, 1996), p. 22; Daniel Okrent, *Nine Innings* (New York, 1985); Bud Selig file, National Baseball Library, Cooperstown, NY; Tom Verducci, "Brushback," *SI* 82 (April 10, 1995), pp. 60–62, 67; Tom Verducci, "Making Small Talk: How Small Market Teams Led by a Car Dealer Got Control of Baseball and Drove It to a Strike," *SI* 81 (September 26, 1994), pp. 20, 22–24.

Frank J. Olmsted

SELKIRK, George Alexander "Twinkletoes" (b. January 4, 1908, Huntsville, Canada; d. January 19, 1987, Ft. Lauderdale, FL), player, manager, scout, and executive, spent 50 years in baseball and most notably replaced slugger Babe Ruth* in the New York Yankees (AL) lineup. He was born to parents of Scottish extraction. His father, a funeral director, moved the family to Rochester, NY when George was only five years old. Selkirk gained fame in football at Rochester Technical High School, acquiring the nickname "Twinkletoes" for running on his toes.

The Rochester, NY Red Wings (IL) signed him to a professional baseball contract as a catcher in 1927 and sent him to Cambridge, MD (ESL), where he became an outfielder. The 6-foot 1-inch, 182-pound Selkirk, who batted left-handed and threw right-handed, spent nine seasons in the minor leagues before the New York Yankees summoned him in August 1934. His other minor league stops included Rochester, NY, Jersey City, NJ (IL), Toronto, Canada (IL), Columbus, OH (AA), and Newark, NJ (IL).

Selkirk played parts of nine seasons from 1934 to 1942 with the New York Yankees. Six of those teams won AL pennants, with Selkirk playing in 22 World Series games. On August 12, 1934, Babe Ruth played his last game for the New York Yankees in left field. Selkirk took Ruth's normal right field position. The New York Yankees regarded Selkirk so highly that they assigned him Ruth's fabled uniform number 3. Selkirk wore the number throughout his career.

Selkirk's best seasons came in 1936 and 1939, when he made the AL All-Star teams. In 1936, he drove in 107 runs and batted .308. In 1939, he posted career highs of 21 HR, 103 runs, and 103 walks, batted .306 with 101 RBI, and led AL outfielders with a .989 fielding percentage. His batting average dropped abruptly the next three seasons. He joined the U.S. Air Corps in 1943 following his major league playing career.

After World War II, Selkirk managed in the minor leagues for 11 seasons with Newark, NJ, Binghamton, NY (EL), Kansas City, MO (AA), Toledo, OH (AA), and Wichita, KS (AA). His 1953 Toledo club won an AA pennant. Selkirk moved from the dugout to baseball administration in 1956. After being supervisor of player personnel for the Kansas City Athletics (AL) from 1956 to 1961, he served as general manager of the expansion Washington Senators (AL) from 1962 to 1969. Selkirk retired to Ft. Lauderdale, FL with his wife, Norma Fox, whom he had married in June 1931. He scouted for the New York Yankees from 1970 until 1977.

The Canadian Baseball Hall of Fame inducted Selkirk among its first members. During his nine major league seasons, he batted .290 with 108 HR and 576 RBI.

BIBLIOGRAPHY: George Selkirk file, National Baseball Library, Cooperstown, NY; Dave Anderson et al., *The Yankees* (New York, 1979); Frank Graham, *The New York Yankees* (New York, 1943); Mark Gallagher, *The Yankee Encyclopedia*, vol. 3 (Champaign, IL, 1997); William Humber, *Cheering for the Home Team* (Toronto, Canada, 1983); *NYT*, January 20, 1987, p. B-7; Randy Schultz, "George Selkirk Recalls the Yankees of Old," *BD* 41 (September 1982), pp. 65–66ff.

William E. Akin

SEMINICK, Andrew Wasil "Andy" (b. September 12, 1920, Pierce, WV), player, coach, manager, and scout, is the son of a Russian coal miner. The squat 5-foot 11-inch, 187-pound right-hander is the youngest of 10 children. He moved with his family to Muse, PA near Pittsburgh and attended Cecil High School. Seminick joined his father in the mines for two years but pursued baseball after straining his back.

Seminick signed a baseball contract with scouts Pie Traynor* and Leo Mackey of the Pittsburgh Pirates (NL) organization in 1940 and shuttled around the minor leagues for four years. The Philadelphia Phillies (NL) acquired him in 1943 after his successful season at Knoxville, TN (SA). Seminick briefly appeared with the Philadelphia Phillies in 1943, 1944, and 1945 and became Philadelphia's starting catcher in 1946. Besides hitting .264, he drove in 52 runs and led all NL catchers in HR with 12. Defensively, he paced NL catchers in double plays in 1946 and passed balls in 1947.

Seminick remained the Philadelphia Phillies regular catcher for six seasons, guiding a young pitching staff in 1950 to the Phillies' first NL pennant in 35 years. His best campaigns came in 1949 and 1950, when he hit 24 HR and drove in 68 runs. In 1950, Seminick also batted a career high .288. A broken bone in his foot handicapped him in the 1950 World Series against the New York Yankees, as he hit just .182.

The Philadelphia Phillies traded Seminick to the Cincinnati Reds (NL) in December 1951. He started behind the plate for the Cincinnati Reds in 1952 and 1953, hitting 33 HR over the two seasons. Seminick returned to the Philadelphia Phillies in April 1955, completing his major league career as a reserve catcher there in 1957. He led NL catchers with a .994 fielding percentage in 1955.

Seminick coached with the Philadelphia Phillies in 1957, 1958, and from 1967 to 1969 and managed in their farm system from 1959 to 1966 and again from 1970 to 1972, piloting Elmira, NY (NYPL), Miami, FL (FSL), Williamsport, PA (EL), Des Moines, IA (WL), Macon, GA (SL), Chattanooga, TN (SL), Reading, PA (EL), and Eugene, OR (PCL). He also served as a minor league instructor and scouted for the Philadelphia Phillies from 1983 through 1985. Seminick started the athletic program at Florida Institute of Technology in Melbourne, FL and belongs to the Sunshine State Conference Hall of Fame. The Melbourne, FL resident married Gussie Irene Anderson on August 14, 1941 and has one son, Andrew. He is the first active member of the Russian Orthodox Church to make the major leagues.

During his 15 year major league career, Seminick batted .243 with 164 HR and 495 RBI. He belted three HR, including two in one inning, on June 2, 1949 against the Cincinnati Reds.

BIBLIOGRAPHY: Allen Lewis, *The Philadelphia Phillies: A Pictorial History* (Virginia Beach, VA, 1981); Rich Marazzi, "Interview with a Whiz Kid: Andy Seminick," *SCD* 25 (July 31, 1998), pp. 80–81; *SCD* 25 (August 7, 1998), pp. 80–81; Harry Paxton, *The Whiz Kids* (New York, 1950); Robin Roberts and C. Paul Rogers III, *The Whiz Kids and the 1950 Pennant* (Philadelphia, PA, 1997); Rich Westcott and Frank Bilovsky, *The New Phillies Encyclopedia* (Philadelphia, PA, 1993); Frederick G. Lieb and Stan Baumgartner, *The Philadelphia Phillies* (New York, 1953).

John P. Rossi

SERRELL, William C. "Bonnie," "Barney," "El Grillo" (b. March 9, 1922, Dallas, TX), player, grew up with his mother and five siblings after his father left to find work in industrialized northern cities. In 1933, the family was reunited in Chicago, IL. Serrell left high school before graduation and developed his baseball skills on Chicago's sandlots. In 1941, he joined Rube Foster's* Chicago American Giants (NAL) as one of the club's four third basemen. The slender 5-foot 11-inch, 160-pound Serrell in 1942 joined the Kansas City Monarchs (NAL), where he established himself as black baseball's premier second baseman of the 1940s. His strong, accurate arm, great range, and consistent fielding earned him the nickname "The Vacuum Cleaner." Serrell, who possessed good speed and batted left-handed, proved a good contact hitter with respectable power. He batted .376 in 1942 and .556 to lead the champion Monarchs to a World Series sweep of the Homestead, PA Grays (NNL).

Serrell was inducted into military service before the 1943 season, but returned to the Kansas City Monarchs after suffering a skin rash. He spent the 1943–1944 seasons with the Kansas City Monarchs, batting .297 and .321 respectively. In 1944, he participated in his only East-West All-Star game and made two hits. Serrell jumped to the MEL, where he batted .313, .272, .264, and .289 with Tampico, Mexico from 1945 to 1948 and appeared in All-Star games his first two seasons. When Serrell left for Mexico, the Kansas City Monarchs replaced their star second baseman with Jackie Robinson.* Of the two players, Serrell was considered the better performer. The Brooklyn Dodgers' (NL) signing of Robinson in 1947 left Serrell extremely hurt. Serrell also did not know about a second military induction notice. Upon returning to the United States in 1949, he was heavily fined for failure to appear for a second physical examination.

Serrell returned to the Kansas City Monarchs for the 1949–1950 seasons, hitting .282 and .319, and played winter ball in Cuba and Puerto Rico. After starting 1951 with the Monarchs, Serrell batted .302 with Yakima, WA (WeIL) and .243 with the San Francisco Seals (PCL). In 1952, Serrell batted .380 with Nuevo Laredo, Mexico (MEL). He hit .323, .350, .333, .326, and .299 the next five seasons and twice led the MEL in hits (128, 132) and triples (13, 11) in 1953–1954. Serrell batted .330 and .265 in winter ball in Mexico in 1957 and 1958 before ending his career by hitting .376 with Nogales-Juarez, Mexico (AMeL) in 1958. Serrell married a Mexican and has resided near Nogales, where he worked as a laborer.

BIBLIOGRAPHY: Janet Bruce, *The Kansas City Monarchs* (Lawrence, KS, 1985); Dick Clark and Larry Lester, eds., *The Negro Leagues Book* (Cleveland, OH, 1994); Phil Dixon, *The Negro Baseball Leagues* (Mattituck, NY, 1992); John B. Holway, *Black Diamonds* (Westport, CT, 1989); Neil Lanctot, *Fair Dealing and Clean Playing* (Jefferson, NC, 1994); William Serrell file, National Baseball Library, Cooperstown, NY; William Serrell file, Negro Leagues Baseball Museum, Kansas City, MO; Robert Peterson, *Only the Ball Was White* (New York, 1970); Mark Ribowsky, *A Complete History of the Negro Leagues, 1884 to 1955* (New York, 1995); James A. Riley, *The Encyclopedia of the Negro Baseball Leagues* (New York, 1994).

Jerry J. Wright

SEVEREID, Henry Levai "Hank" (b. June 1, 1891, Story City, IA; d. December 17, 1968, San Antonio, TX), player, manager, coach, and scout, was the son of Lars Severeid, a stone mason, and Maria (Ness) Severeid, both Norwegian immigrants. After spending eight years in the local grade school, he worked full-time to help support the family. Severeid, taught to play baseball by his older brothers, caught for the Story City semiprofessional team before turning professional with the Burlington, IA Pathfinders (CA) in 1909 and the Ottumwa, IA Packers (CA) in 1910. His excellent performance as a catcher and hitter prompted the Cincinnati Reds (NL) to purchase his contract.

The Cincinnati Reds used Severeid so sparingly from 1911 through 1913 that he requested assignment to the Louisville, KY Colonels (AA) to allow him to catch regularly. After he batted .317 in 143 games, Louisville traded him to the St. Louis Browns (AL). A right-handed hitter and thrower, the 5-foot, 175-pound quiet Severeid starred for St. Louis from 1915 to June 1925. The St. Louis Browns then traded him to the Washington Senators (AL). The exceptionally strong, durable, sure-handed, hard-throwing Severeid excelled in handling pitchers. He caught at least 100 games eight different seasons and batted above .300 each year from 1921 through 1925. In 1921 Browns' home games, Severeid reputedly threw out 51 of 53 runners attempting to steal. In July 1926, the injury-riddled New York Yankees (AL) bought him at the waiver price. In the 1926 World Series against the St. Louis Cardinals, the veteran receiver batted .273 and caught all seven games.

Severeid caught for the Sacramento, CA Senators (PCL) and Hollywood, CA Stars (PCL) from 1927 to 1931 and served as catcher-manager for the Wichita Falls, TX Spudders (TL), Longview, TX Browns (TL), San Antonio, TX Missions (TL), and Galveston, TX Buccaneers (TL) from 1932 to 1937 except 1936, when he managed the Omaha, NE Robin Hoods (WL). His subsequent positions involved being a coach for the Syracuse, NY Chiefs (IL) in 1938, scout for the Cincinnati Reds (NL) from 1938 to 1940, manager for the Durham, NC Bulls (PiL) in 1941, scout for the Chicago Cubs (NL) in 1942, and scout for the Boston Red Sox (AL) from 1943 to 1968.

Severeid served in the U.S. Army Tank Corps in 1918 and reached France just before World War I ended. He married Adele Bertha Messmer in December 1920. They had three daughters, Jane, June, and Joan. Utilizing his thorough knowledge of baseball mechanics and tactics, Severeid collaborated with Charles E. "Al" Chapman on a 1941 textbook, *Play Ball! Advice to Young Ballplayers*. Although using a hefty 48-ounce bat, he batted .289 during his 15-year major league career. Severeid made 1,245 hits with 539 RBI in 1,390 major league games, seldom striking out. Exclusive of World Series contests, he caught 2,358 professional baseball games. These included 1,225 major league and 1,133 minor league contests.

BIBLIOGRAPHY: Jerry E. Clark, *Anson to Zuber* (Omaha, NE, 1992); Hank Severeid file, National Baseball Library, Cooperstown, NY; Des Moines (IA) *Register*, March 26, 1962; "Hank Severeid, Catcher Noted for His Durability," *TSN*, January 4, 1969, p. 52; John Thorn et al., eds., *Total Baseball*, 5th ed. (New York, 1997); Bill Borst, ed., *Ables to Zoldak*, vol. 3 (St. Louis, MO, 1990); Bill Borst, *Still Last in the American League* (West Bloomfield, MI, 1992); Roger A. Godin, *The 1922 St. Louis Browns* (Jefferson, NC, 1991); Mark Gallagher, *The Yankee Encyclopedia*, vol. 3 (Champaign, IL, 1997).

Frank V. Phelps

SEWELL, James Luther "Luke" (b. January 5, 1901, Titus, AL; d. May 14, 1987, Akron, OH), player, coach, and manager, was the son of Jabez Wesley Sewell and Susan (Hannon) Sewell and the brother of baseball players Joe Sewell* and Tommy Sewell. The 5-foot 9-inch, 160-pound Sewell, who batted and threw right-handed, originally signed with the Cleveland Indians (AL) after his 1921 graduation from the University of Alabama, where he had starred in football and baseball. After performing briefly with Columbus, OH (AA) and Indianapolis, IN (AA), he stayed in the major leagues. He played with the Cleveland Indians through 1932, primarily as a catcher. In January 1933, the Cleveland Indians traded him to the Washington Senators (AL) for Roy Spencer. Sewell appeared in all five games of the 1933 World Series against the victorious New York Giants. The Washington Senators traded Sewell to the St. Louis Browns (AL) in January 1935. The same day, St. Louis sold him to the Chicago White Sox (AL). The Chicago White Sox sent him to the Cleveland Indians in December 1938. His playing career ended in 1939 (except for token appearances with the 1942 St. Louis Browns). Sewell played 1,630 major league games, 1,562 behind the plate. He compiled a .259 lifetime batting average and batted in 696 runs on 1,393 hits, mostly singles. A good, alert, defensive catcher, Sewell once made a double play at second base by trapping two base runners in a rundown. He caught no-hit games by Wes Ferrell,* Vern Kennedy, and Bill Dietrich.

Sewell's most noteworthy achievements came as a manager. In May 1941, Sewell replaced Fred Haney as St. Louis Browns manager. He guided the 1942 Browns to a third-place finish and the 1944 St. Louis Browns to their only AL pennant, edging the Detroit Tigers and the New York Yankees on the last day of the season. After leading two games to one, the St. Louis Browns lost the 1944 World Series in six games to the rival St. Louis Cardinals. The St. Louis Browns finished third in 1945 and dropped to seventh place in 1946, causing Sewell's dismissal. After spending two years in business, he was hired as a coach by the Cincinnati Reds (NL) in 1949 and replaced manager Bucky Walters* for the final three games. He managed the Cincinnati Reds to sixth-place finishes in 1950 and 1951 and seventh-place in 1952. In 10 years as a major league manager, Sewell compiled a 606–644 mark for a .485 winning percentage. From 1953 to 1955, he managed the Toronto, Canada Maple Leafs (IL). Sewell joined an unsuccessful group in Seattle, WA seeking a major league franchise. Sewell left baseball permanently and pursued business interests in the Akron, OH area. He married Edna Ridge on August 14, 1926.

BIBLIOGRAPHY: Thomas Aylesworth and Benton Minks, *The Encyclopedia of Baseball Managers* (New York, 1990); Bill Borst, *Still Last in the American League* (West Bloomfield, MI, 1992); Franklin Lewis, *The Cleveland Indians* (New York, 1949); Shirley Povich, *The Washington Senators* (New York, 1954); Warren Brown, *The Chicago White Sox* (New York, 1952); Bill Borst, ed., *Ables to Zoldak*, vol. 3 (St. Louis, MO, 1990); William B. Mead, *Even the Browns* (Chicago, IL, 1978); Richard Goldstein, *Spartan Seasons* (New York, 1980); *The Baseball Encyclopedia*, 10th ed. (New York, 1996); Donald Honig, *The Man in the Dugout* (Lincoln, NE, 1995); Robert Obojski, *Bush League* (New York, 1975); Joseph L. Reichler, ed., *The Great All-Time*

Baseball Record Book (New York, 1981); James Luther Sewell file, National Baseball Library, Cooperstown, NY.

Horace R. Givens

SEWELL, Joseph Wheeler "Joe" (b. October 9, 1898, Titus, AL; d. March 6, 1990, Mobile, AL), baseball and football player, coach, and scout, was the son of Jabez Wesley Sewell and Susan (Hannon) Sewell and one of three brothers to play professional baseball. James Luther "Luke" Sewell* caught for several major league teams and managed the St. Louis Browns to the AL pennant in 1944, while Thomas played briefly for the Chicago Cubs (NL) in 1927. Sewell attended the Wetumpka, AL public schools and enrolled at the University of Alabama in 1916 to study medicine. At Alabama, Sewell played football and baseball with his brother Luke and Riggs Stephenson.* During this period, Alabama won four SIAA baseball championships and compiled a 58–17 overall win–loss record.

With one year (1918) out for military service, Sewell graduated from Alabama in 1920 and began his professional baseball career with New Orleans, LA (SA). His contract was purchased later that year by the Cleveland Indians (AL) because their shortstop, Ray Chapman,* had died from being beaned by New York Yankees pitcher Carl Mays.* The 5-foot 9-inch, 155-pound shortstop and later third baseman played for Cleveland through 1930 and the New York Yankees (AL) for the 1931–1933 seasons. Besides playing in 1,103 consecutive games, he compiled a .312 career batting average. Famous for his bat control, the left-handed swinging and right-handed throwing Sewell proved the hardest hitter in baseball history to strike out. In 1925, 1929, and 1933, he batted over 500 times each season and struck out only four times. In 7,132 career at-bats, Sewell struck out only 114 times, made 2,226 hits, scored 1,141 runs, and knocked in 1,055 runs. He led the AL in doubles with 45 in 1924 and led shortstops three times in fielding percentage.

Sewell married Willie Veal on December 31, 1921 and had three children, Joseph, Jr., James, and Mary Sue. Following his playing days, Sewell coached for the Yankees (1934–1935) and scouted for both the Indians (1952–1962) and the New York Mets (NL, 1963). He operated a hardware store in Tuscaloosa, AL for several years and worked in public relations with a local dairy. At the behest of Alabama football coach Paul "Bear" Bryant (FB), Sewell in 1964 became head Crimson Tide baseball coach. Alabama won the 1968 SEC championship, earning him SEC Coach of the Year honors. He was elected to the Alabama Sports Hall of Fame in 1970 and the National Baseball Hall of Fame in 1977.

BIBLIOGRAPHY: *CB* (1944), pp. 606–609; L. Robert Davids, "Sewell Was a Real Fox at the Plate," *BRJ* 5 (1976), pp. 123–127; Frank Graham, *The New York Yankees* (New York, 1943); Mark Gallagher, *The Yankee Encyclopedia*, vol. 3 (New York, 1997); Lowell Reidenbaugh, *Baseball's Hall of Fame-Cooperstown* (New York, 1993); Cecil Hurt, "Hall of Famer Joe Sewell," *Bama* (April 1981), pp. 24–25; Gene Karst and Martin J. Jones, Jr., *Who's Who in Professional Baseball* (New Rochelle, NY, 1973); *NYT Biographical Service* 21 (March 1990), p. 234; Franklin Lewis, *The Cleveland Indians* (New York, 1949); Joseph L. Reichler, *The Great All-Time Baseball Record Book* (New York, 1981); *The Baseball Encyclopedia*, 10th ed. (New York, 1996); Joseph Sewell file, National Baseball Library, Cooperstown, NY; John Thorn et al., eds., *Total Indians* (New York, 1996).

Horace R. Givens

SEWELL, Truett Banks "Rip" (b. May 11, 1907, Decatur, AL; d. September 3, 1989, Plant City, FL), player, manager, and coach, was the fifth of six children of Charles Sewell, a streetcar conductor, and Eleanor (Banks) Sewell, who was of Scotch-Irish descent. A distant cousin of major league players Joe Sewell* and Luke Sewell,* he graduated from Alabama Military Institute and attended Vanderbilt University for one year. In 1931, he began his professional baseball career with Raleigh, NC (PiL). His other minor league stops included Toronto, Canada (IL), Beaumont, TX (TL), Seattle, WA (PCL), Toledo, OH (AA), Louisville, KY (AA), and Buffalo, NY (IL). He hurled briefly for the Detroit Tigers (AL) in 1932 and joined the Pittsburgh Pirates (NL) at age 31 in 1938.

Sewell usually won more games than he lost for mediocre Pittsburgh Pirate teams from 1939 through 1945. He finished with a 16–5 win–loss slate in 1940 and won 14 games while losing an NL-leading 17 contests in 1941. On December 7, 1941, he suffered severe wounds in the abdomen, thighs, legs, and feet in a hunting accident. Several pellets remained in his right foot. Sewell, who possessed only an average fastball and curve, was forced to alter his delivery because of his injury. The "blooper" or "eephus" pitch, a change-up that arched 25 feet in the air, became his trademark. Employing the pitch occasionally, Sewell won 17 games in 1942 and 21 contests in both 1943 and 1944, leading the NL in victories and with 25 complete games in 1943. Free-swinging batters hated the "blooper," but spectators loved it. His most famous moment came in the 1946 All-Star Game. With the AL already leading 8–0, Ted Williams* of the Boston Red Sox hit Sewell's "blooper" pitch for a three-run HR at Fenway Park. Sewell always claimed that he never served up another HR with that pitch. Hitters had to supply nearly all the impetus on the "blooper."

Sewell helped dissuade the Pittsburgh Pirates from striking in the late summer of 1946, when Boston labor attorney Robert Murphy attempted to organize major league players. His major league career ended after the 1949 season, although he compiled a combined 19–4 record during his final two campaigns. Overall, the 6-foot 1-inch, 180-pound right-hander won 143 contests, lost 97 decisions, hurled 137 complete games, compiled a lifetime 3.48 ERA, and made the NL All-Star team three times (1943–1944, 1946).

Sewell managed in the minor leagues from 1950 to 1955 and coached for the Pittsburgh Pirates in 1948 and Kansas City Athletics (AL) in 1956.

After retiring from baseball, Sewell worked as a salesman for the Carl W. Lindell Oil and Chemicals Distributorship until 1972. He suffered circulation disorders resulting from the hunting accident. Although both his legs were amputated in 1972, Sewell remained active and even played golf a year later while using artificial limbs. Sewell, who married Margaret Abbott on October 14, 1936 and had two sons, retired to Plant City, FL.

BIBLIOGRAPHY: *The Baseball Encyclopedia*, 10th ed. (New York, 1996); Donald Honig, *Baseball When the Grass Was Real* (New York, 1975); Frederick G. Lieb, *The Pittsburgh Pirates* (New York, 1948); *NYT*, September 5, 1989, p. B-6; Truett Sewell file, National Baseball Library, Cooperstown, NY; Margaret A. Sewell, interview with Luther W. Spoehr, February 16, 1990; *TSN*, September 18, 1989, p. 56; Bob Smizik, *The Pittsburgh Pirates: An Illustrated History* (New York, 1990); Rich Westcott, *Masters of the Diamond* (Jefferson, NC, 1994); Richard L. Burtt, *The Pittsburgh Pirates, A Pictorial History* (Virginia Beach, VA, 1977).

Luther W. Spoehr

SEYBOLD, Ralph Orlando "Socks" (b. November 23, 1870, Washingtonville, OH; d. December 22, 1921, Greensburg, PA), player, held the AL season HR record with 16 for 17 years until slugger George "Babe" Ruth* hit 29 HR in 1919. Seybold, originally from extreme eastern Ohio, came to Jeannette, PA, a glass manufacturing town, where he started his baseball career in 1890 with the Grays. After playing locally, he began his professional career with Easton, PA (ESL) in 1894 and played his first major league game with the Cincinnati Reds (NL) on August 20, 1899. From 1901 until a broken leg ended his career in 1908, the 5-foot 11-inch, 175-pound right-handed outfielder and occasional first baseman played for manager Connie Mack's* Philadelphia Athletics (AL). Mack had brought Seybold, whom he described as "the sturdiest and most serviceable of players," with him from the WA.

Seybold's major league career included 997 games, 1,085 hits, 218 doubles, 54 triples, 51 HR, 556 RBI, and a .294 batting average. His 16 HR in 1902, the second AL season, also led the major leagues. He also led the major leagues with 45 doubles in 1903 and attained his highest batting average with .334 in 1901. In the 1905 World Series against the New York Giants, he hit only .125 in five games. Seybold batted safely in 27 consecutive games in 1901 and three times surpassed a .300 batting average and 90 RBI. He finished second in the AL in RBI in 1907 (97) and fourth in 1902 (92). Although not considered adept defensively, he made two unassisted double plays from the outfield in 1907.

Seybold returned to his home town of Jeannette, PA after his professional baseball career and managed an industrial semiprofessional baseball team. He was serving as the steward at the Jeannette Eagles Club at the time of his death, which resulted from a broken neck when his car went over a bank along the Lincoln Highway near Greensburg, PA.

BIBLIOGRAPHY: Ralph Seybold file, National Baseball Library, Cooperstown, NY; Greensburg (PA) *Morning Review*, December 23, 1921; *History of Jeannette* (Jeannette, PA, 1976); Mike Shatzkin, ed., *The Ballplayers* (New York, 1990); John Thorn et al., eds., *Total Baseball*, 5th ed. (New York, 1997); Frederick G. Lieb, *Connie Mack* (New York, 1945); Connie Mack, *My 66 Years in the Big Leagues* (Philadelphia, PA, 1950); Jerome C. Romanowski, *The Mackmen* (Upper Darby, PA, 1979).

                                                                  Robert B. Van Atta

SEYMOUR, James Bentley "Cy" (b. December 9, 1872, Albany, NY; d. September 20, 1919, New York, NY), player, was the son of a carpenter and first gained notice in baseball with the Ridgefield AC of Albany, NY. He pitched for Plattsburg, NY in 1895 and Springfield, MA (EL) in 1896 before joining the New York Giants (NL) late in 1896. Seymour's pitching wildness and strong hitting caused him to switch to the outfield. After jumping to the Chicago White Stockings (AL) in late 1900, Seymour joined the Baltimore Orioles (AL) in 1901. He moved during July 1902 to the Cincinnati Reds (NL), where he hit over .300 every year through 1905. In July 1906, the New York Giants (NL) purchased his contract for $10,000. Although a solid performer the next four years, he did not achieve the level he had established at Cincinnati. In 1908, he misplayed into a triple a long fly ball hit by Chicago's Joe Tinker* in the playoff game for the NL pennant, resulting in three runs scored. He played for Baltimore, MD (EL) in 1910–1911, Newark, NJ (IL) in 1912, and the Boston Braves (NL), Buffalo, NY (IL), and Newark (IL) in 1913.

A left-handed pitcher, the 6-foot, 200-pound Seymour compiled 61 wins and 56 losses in 140 appearances. He led the NL in strikeouts in 1897, but also paced the NL in walks in 1897, 1898, and 1899. Seymour appeared in 1,333 major league games as an outfielder. A left-handed batter, he hit .303 in 16 major league seasons, with 1,723 hits, 229 doubles, 96 triples, 52 HR, 799 RBI, and 222 stolen bases. In 1905, he hit .377 to defeat Honus Wagner* for the NL batting championship. Seymour's 219 hits, 40 doubles, 21 triples, 121 RBI, and .559 slugging percentage also led the NL. Seymour, who married, became one of the few major leaguers to convert successfully from pitcher to everyday player. He proved a notable member of baseball's supporting cast at the turn of the 20th century.

BIBLIOGRAPHY: James Seymour file, National Baseball Library, Cooperstown, NY; Lee Allen, *The Cincinnati Reds* (New York, 1948); Frank Graham, *The New York Giants* (New York, 1952); *The Baseball Encyclopedia*, 10th ed. (New York, 1996); Bob Rathgeber, *Cincinnati Reds Scrapbook* (Virginia Beach, VA, 1982); Noel Hynd, *The Giants of the Polo Grounds* (New York, 1988); James D. Hardy, Jr., *The New York Giants Baseball Club* (Jefferson, NC, 1996); Floyd Conner and John Snyder, *Day-by-Day in Cincinnati Reds History* (West Point, NY, 1984); Ray Robinson, *Matty: An*

American Hero (New York, 1993); Charles C. Alexander, *John McGraw* (New York, 1988).

Luther W. Spoehr

SHAFFER, George "Orator" (b. 1852, Philadelphia, PA; d. unknown), player, batted left-handed and threw right-handed. After playing amateur baseball in Philadelphia, the 5-foot 9-inch, 165 pounder played outfield with Hartford, CT (NA) and the Mutuals of New York (NA) in 1874. He spent 1875 with the Philadelphia Athletics (NA) and 1876 with the independent Columbus, OH Buckeyes. Shaffer participated in the NL the next several seasons, appearing with the Louisville Greys in 1877, Indianapolis Hoosiers in 1878, Chicago White Stockings in 1879, Cleveland Blues from 1880 to 1882, and Buffalo Bisons in 1883. He batted .338 in 1878 and .304 in 1879. Shaffer shifted to the St. Louis Maroons (UA) in 1884 and, along with Fred Dunlap,* led the St. Louis Maroons to an easy championship. Besides pacing the UA in doubles with 40, he finished second in runs, hits, total bases, bases on balls, and slugging percentage and ranked third in triples and batting average.

Shaffer's career declined thereafter. He rejoined the NL when the St. Louis Maroons were admitted in 1885, but struggled and finished the campaign with the Philadelphia Athletics (AA). After being released in early 1886, Shaffer spent the next four seasons in the minor leagues. He played for Atlanta, GA in 1886, Lincoln, NE in 1887, Des Moines, IA in 1888, and Detroit, MI in 1889. A .460 batting average highlighted his 1887 WL season. At age 38, Shaffer received one more chance to play in the major leagues because of expansion to three major leagues in 1890. He rejoined the Philadelphia Athletics, teaming with his 20-year old brother, Taylor. The rest of Shaffer's life remains a mystery. During 11 major league seasons, he batted .283 with 974 hits and 308 RBI.

Shaffer, one of the era's best right fielders, often threw batters out at first base. His nickname "Orator" derived from his habit of talking to himself on the field, as he gave himself private pep talks to maintain his enthusiasm.

BIBLIOGRAPHY: Frederick Ivor-Campbell et al., eds., *Baseball's First Stars* (Cleveland, OH, 1996); New York *Clipper*, January 22, 1882; John Montgomery Ward, *Base-Ball* (Philadelphia, PA, 1888); George Shaffer file, National Baseball Library, Cooperstown, NY; William J. Ryczek, *Blackguards and Red Stockings* (Jefferson, NC, 1992).

Frederick Ivor-Campbell and William E. McMahon

SHANTZ, Robert Clayton "Bobby" (b. September 26, 1925, Pottstown, PA), player, was one of the shortest pitchers in major league baseball at 5-feet 6-inches. Shantz worked in a sawmill after graduating from Pottstown High School and played on a semiprofessional baseball team near Philadelphia. The Philadelphia Phillies (NL) scouted Shantz in 1947, but deemed him too short for the major leagues. The Philadelphia Athletics (AL), however, offered him a professional baseball contract. Although doubtful of his own potential, Shantz was encouraged by his parents, Wilmer Shantz and Ruth Shantz. The 139 pound left-hander reported to Lincoln, NE (WL), where he won 18 games in 1948.

The following season, Shantz hurled nine innings of no-hit relief in his major league debut for Connie Mack's* Philadelphia Athletics and finished his rookie campaign with a 6–8 win–loss record. Batters hit Shantz hard his sophomore season, but he settled into an 18–10 groove in 1951. He helped himself at bat and with his prowess in the field. Many baseball authorities considered him the best fielding pitcher of his era and labeled him "the fifth infielder." Eight Gold Gloves for fielding excellence adorn his mantel.

In 1952, no major league pitcher performed better. Shantz worked the corners, changed speeds, and employed occasional knuckleballs en route to a sparkling 24–7 season. He led the AL in wins and winning percentage (.774), finished second in complete games (27), and placed third in shutouts (5), ERA (2.48), and strikeouts (152). In his only All-Star appearance, Shantz hurled an inning of relief and struck out Whitey Lockman,* Jackie Robinson,* and Stan Musial.* The favorite game of his career was a 1952 battle with the New York Yankees, in which Shantz pitched 14 innings and won, 2–1. Shantz, voted 1952 AL MVP, was hit by pitcher Walt Masterson of the Washington Senators in his last start and broke his left wrist in two places.

Shantz tore muscles in his left shoulder during his first start in 1953 and recorded only 13 triumphs over his final four seasons with the Athletics. In 1954 and 1955, his brother, Billy, often caught his games. After joining the New York Yankees (AL) in February 1957, a rejuvenated Shantz led the AL with a 2.45 ERA. For four seasons, he proved an invaluable reliever with the New York Yankees. Shantz remained a steady fireman with the Pittsburgh Pirates (NL), Houston Colt 45s (NL), St. Louis Cardinals (NL), Chicago Cubs (NL), and Philadelphia Phillies (NL) until his retirement in 1964. He finished his major league career with 119 victories, 99 setbacks, 48 saves, 1,072 strikeouts, and a 3.38 ERA in 537 games. Shantz, who resides in Ambler, PA, operated a dairy bar and bowling alley with Joe Astroth for 22 years and enjoys playing golf nearly every day at a course managed by Curt Simmons.* He married Shirley Vogel of Lincoln, NE in January 1950 and has three sons and one daughter.

BIBLIOGRAPHY: Donald Honig, *Baseball Between the Lines* (New York, 1976); Gene Karst and Martin J. Jones, Jr., *Who's Who in Professional Baseball* (New Rochelle, NY, 1973); Rich Marazzi and Len Fiorito, *Aaron to Zuverink* (New York, 1982); Peter Golenbock, *Dynasty* (New York, 1975); Rich Marazzi, "Bobby Shantz Proves a Popular Autograph Guest at Sports Fest '98," *SCD 25* (July 17, 1998), pp. 110–111; Bobby Shantz file, National Baseball Library, Cooperstown, NY; Connie Mack, *My 66 Years in the Big Leagues* (Philadelphia, PA, 1950); Bob Cairns, *Pen Men* (New York, 1993); Dave Masterson and Tim Boyle, *Baseball's Best: The MVPs* (Chicago,

IL, 1985); Chuck McAnulla, "Bobby Shantz: 1952 AL MVP Collects Memories," *SCD* 25 (April 3, 1998), pp. 166–167; Robert Obojski, "Bobby Shantz: 1952 A.L. MVP Interviewed," *SCD* 21 (August 19, 1994), p. 154; Mark Gallagher, *The Yankee Encyclopedia*, vol. 3 (Champaign, IL, 1997); Bob Broeg and Jerry Vickery, *St. Louis Cardinals Encyclopedia* (Grand Rapids, MI, 1998); Bobby Shantz, correspondence with Frank Olmsted, January 7, 1990; Rich Westcott, *Diamond Greats* (Westport, CT, 1988); Dom Forker, *Sweet Seasons* (Dallas, TX, 1991).

Frank J. Olmsted

SHAWKEY, James Robert "Sailor Bob," "Bob the Gob" (b. December 4, 1890, Sigel, PA; d. December 31, 1980, Syracuse, NY), player, coach, and manager, was the second of four children of farmer John W. Shawkey and Sarah C. Shawkey, attended a country schoolhouse and spent one year at Slippery Rock Teachers College. He married Anna Blauser around 1910, had one daughter, and later wed Gertrude Weiler Killian on December 12, 1943. Shawkey's nautical nicknames derived from his year of service in the U.S. Navy aboard the battleship *Arkansas* during World War I. He pitched for Bloomsburg, PA (MtnsL) in 1910 and worked as a tool dresser in the Pennsylvania oil fields. The following year, he left a job as fireman for the Pennsylvania Railroad and entered professional baseball with Harrisburg, PA (TSL).

After signing with the Philadelphia Athletics (AL) in 1913, Shawkey won 16 games in 1914 and lost the fourth game of the World Series sweep by Boston's "Miracle Braves." When Connie Mack* began breaking up his team, Shawkey was dealt to the New York Yankees (AL) in July 1915 and promptly became their pitching ace. He won 168 of his 196 major league victories for the Yankees, including 24 in 1916 and 20 each in 1919, 1920, and 1922. During 15 major league seasons, he lost 150 games, completed 197 of 333 starts, struck out 1,360 batters in 2,937 innings, hurled 33 shutouts, and compiled a 3.09 ERA. He led the AL with 8 shutouts in 1916 and 5 shutouts in 1919, 10- and 11-game winning streaks in 1919 and 1920, and a 2.45 ERA in 1920. During his career, he pitched a Yankees record seven 1–0 victories. He also achieved 15 strikeouts against the Athletics in 1919 and won one of four decisions in five World Series. In 1923 he pitched and won the first game played at Yankee Stadium, hitting the park's second HR. (Babe Ruth* blasted the first.) He surrendered an AL-leading 17 HR during that season.

A strong, confident, 5-foot 11-inch, 168-pound right-hander, Shawkey exhibited an unassuming manner and a mild temperament and wore a distinctive red-sleeved sweatshirt under his uniform. After his playing career ended in 1927 with Montreal, Canada (IL), he returned to the New York Yankees as coach in 1929 and manager in 1930. Dismissed after a third place finish, he managed Jersey City, NJ (IL) in 1931, Scranton, PA (NYPL) in 1932–1933, Newark, NJ (IL) in 1934–1935, Watertown, NY (BL) in 1947, and

Tallahassee, FL (GFL) in 1949. He served as a pitching coach in the Pittsburgh Pirates (NL) and Detroit Tigers (AL) farm systems and baseball coach at Dartmouth College between 1952 and 1956.

BIBLIOGRAPHY: Bob Shawkey file, National Baseball Library, Cooperstown, NY; Robert W. Creamer, *Babe: The Legend Comes to Life* (New York, 1976); Dan Daniel, New York *Telegram*, October 13, 1929; Dartmouth College Sports Information Department, Hanover, NH; Mark Gallagher, *The Yankee Encyclopedia*, vol. 3 (Champaign, IL, 1997); Donald Honig, *The Man in the Dugout* (Lincoln, NE, 1995); Gene Karst and Martin J. Jones, Jr., *Who's Who in Professional Baseball* (New Rochelle, NY, 1973); Ronald G. Liebman, "Winning Streaks by Pitchers," *BRJ* 7 (1978), pp. 35–42; Paul MacFarlane, ed., *TSN Daguerreotypes of Great Stars of Baseball* (St. Louis, MO, 1981); John Mosedale, *The Greatest of All: The 1927 New York Yankees* (New York, 1975); *NYT*, January 4, 1981, p. 26; *The Baseball Encyclopedia*, 10th ed. (New York, 1996); Lawrence S. Ritter, *The Glory of Their Times* (New York, 1966); Bob Shawkey, "The Veteran of the Yankee Hurling Staff" (interview) *BM* 37 (July 1926), p. 349; A. D. Suehsdorf, telephone interview with Mrs. Dorothy Shawkey Hitchcock, December 20, 1983; Dave Anderson et al., *The Yankees* (New York, 1979); Frank Graham, *The New York Yankees* (New York, 1943); Leo Trachtenberg, *The Wonder Team* (Bowling Green, OH, 1995).

A. D. Suehsdorf

SHECKARD, Samuel James Tilden "Jimmy" (b. November 23, 1878, Upper Chanceford Township, PA; d. January 15, 1947, Lancaster, PA), player, coach, and manager, was of German descent and was born on a farm in York County near Columbia in southeastern Pennsylvania. Sheckard only attended grammar school and wed Cora Seicrest. In May 1922, he married Frances Ewes. The 5-foot 9-inch, 175-pound Sheckard entered professional baseball in 1896 at age 17 with Portsmouth, VA (VL). After spending the next season at Brockton, MA (NEL), he joined the Brooklyn Bridegrooms-Superbas (NL) in late 1897. He played outfield with Brooklyn through 1905 except for a one-year stint with the Baltimore Orioles (NL) in 1899 and a brief time in 1902 when the latter city was in the AL. He performed from 1906 to 1912 with the Chicago Cubs (NL), split the 1913 campaign between the St. Louis Cardinals (NL) and Cincinnati Reds (NL), and finished his career in 1914 as player-manager for Cleveland, OH (AA). In 1917, he served as coach for the Chicago Cubs.

The left-handed batting and right-handed throwing Sheckard, a fine base runner, clever, coaxing batter, and skillful outfielder and thrower, led the NL in stolen bases with 77 in 1899 and 67 in 1903. He paced the NL in triples (19) and total bases (299) in 1901, runs scored (121) and bases on balls (147) in 1911 and (122) in 1912. His 147 walks in 1911 remained the NL record until 1945. In 1903, he led the NL in HR (9). He also paced the NL in slugging percentage (.534) in 1901 and on base percentage (.434) in 1911. For his career, Sheckard batted .274 with 2,084 hits, 354 doubles, 136 triples, 56 HR, 1,296 runs scored, 813 RBI, 1,135 walks, and 465 stolen bases. A fine fielder, he participated in 14 double plays in 1899, made 36 assists in 1903, and led outfielders in putouts in 1902.

Sheckard played for the great 1906–1910 Chicago Cubs squads. The superlative 1906 team lost the World Series in six games to the Chicago White Sox partly because Sheckard made no hits in 21 at-bats and hit only one ball out of the infield. Sheckard, however, performed better in the Cubs' 1907 and 1908 World Series triumphs and drove in the winning run in the lone 1910 Cubs victory against the Philadelphia Athletics. Ill luck subsequently dogged Sheckard, who lost his modest savings in the stock market crash. He later worked as a physical laborer, delivered milk, and held a filling station job. His death came from being struck by a car.

BIBLIOGRAPHY: Jimmy Sheckard file, National Baseball Library, Cooperstown, NY; Tommy Holmes, *The Dodgers* (New York, 1975); William F. McNeil, *The Dodgers Encyclopedia* (Champaign, IL, 1997); Warren Brown, *The Chicago Cubs* (New York, 1946); Jim Enright, *Chicago Cubs* (New York, 1975); Warren Wilbert and William Hageman, *Chicago Cubs: Seasons at the Summit* (Champaign, IL, 1997); Eddie Gold and Art Ahrens, *The Golden Era Cubs, 1876–1940* (Chicago, IL, 1985); Frank Graham, *The Brooklyn Dodgers* (New York, 1945); Richard Goldstein, *Superstars and Screwballs* (New York, 1991); Stanley Cohen, *Dodgers! The First 100 Years* (New York, 1990); Gregg Dubbs, "Jim Sheckard in the Dead-Ball Era," *BRJ* 9 (1980), pp. 134–139; *NYT*, January 16, 1947; Philadelphia *Bulletin*, January 15, 1947; Philadelphia *Inquirer*, January 16, 1947.

Lowell L. Blaisdell

SHEELY, Earl Homer "Whitey" (b. February 12, 1893, Bushnell, IL; d. September 16, 1952, Seattle, WA), player, is the father of Hollis "Bud" Sheely, who caught in 101 games over three seasons for the Chicago White Sox (AL) in the early 1950s. Sheely enjoyed a distinguished major league career with a lifetime .300 batting average in 1,234 games spanning nine seasons. He spent the first seven seasons as the Chicago White Sox regular first baseman, appearing in 938 games. He held the team record for games played at that position until Frank Thomas* surpassed it in 1997. Sheely, a 6-foot 3½-inch, 195 pounder, batted and threw right-handed.

In the winter of 1920–1921, following the Grand Jury proceedings against eight White Sox members accused of throwing the 1919 World Series, owner Charles Comiskey* purchased the entire infield of the Salt Lake City, UT (PCL). Of those imported from Utah, Sheely alone enjoyed a successful major league career. The 28 year old rookie made so favorable an exhibition game impression on manager Kid Gleason* that the White Sox traded first baseman Shano Collins,* who had batted .305 in 1920, and outfielder Nemo Leibold to the Boston Red Sox (AL) for Hall of Fame outfielder Harry Hooper.* Gleason's confidence in Sheely was immediately rewarded with a .304 batting average, 11 HR, and 95 RBI.

Although slow afoot, Sheely proved a solid, sometimes spectacular performer for the Chicago White Sox beyond his 37th birthday. He proved tough to strike out, fanning less than five times out of each 100 at-bats. He also ranks among the Chicago White Sox top ten all time leaders in doubles (207), RBI (582), and career putouts and assists for a first baseman. In 1925 Sheely clouted 43 doubles, not surpassed on the team until Floyd Robinson belted 45 in 1962. Sheely played with the Pittsburgh Pirates (NL) in 1929 and batted .273 for the Boston Braves (NL) in 1931, his final major league season. His career featured just 48 HR, but 747 RBI.

BIBLIOGRAPHY: Richard Lindberg, *Sox* (New York, 1984); Richard Lindberg, *Who's on Third?* (South Bend, IN, 1983); Warren Brown, *The Chicago White Sox* (New York, 1952); *The Baseball Encyclopedia*, 10th ed. (New York, 1996).

David Fitzsimmons

SHEFFIELD, Gary Antonian (b. November 18, 1968, Tampa FL), player, is the son of Betty Jones and nephew of major league pitcher Dwight Gooden.* He played in the Little League World Series and graduated from Hillsborough High School in Tampa. The Milwaukee Brewers (AL) selected the shortstop as the sixth overall pick in the June 1986 free agent draft. Sheffield batted .365 and led the PrL with 71 RBI at Helena, MT in 1986. The next season for Stockton, CA, he topped the CaL with 103 RBI and amassed 39 errors at shortstop. Sheffield divided the 1988 campaign between El Paso, TX (TL) and Denver, CO (AA), slugging 28 HR with 119 RBI, and earning *TSN* Minor League Player of the Year accolades. He added four HR and 12 RBI in a September trial with Milwaukee.

In 1989, Sheffield batted .247 with the Brewers, platooning at shortstop with Bill Spiers. The following year, he moved to third base and batted .294. In 1991, his batting average plummeted 100 points. The Brewers traded the 5-foot 11-inch, 205-pound Sheffield to the San Diego Padres (NL) in a five player March 1992 transaction. The right-handed third baseman compiled a career high .330 batting average and clubbed 33 HR with 100 RBI, winning *TSN* Comeback Player of the Year, Major League Player of the Year, and Silver Slugger Awards and finishing third in the 1992 NL MVP voting.

San Diego dealt Sheffield to the Florida Marlins (NL) in June 1993 for three young pitchers. Despite playing with a sore right shoulder, he finished with 20 HR and a .294 batting average. Sheffield, the initial player from a first year expansion team to start in an All-Star game, homered off Mark Langston* in his first All-Star at-bat. He was rewarded with a four-year, $22.4 million contract extension. After moving to the outfield in 1994, he suffered a bruised rotator cuff muscle and yet managed 27 HR in only 87 games. He batted .324 in only 63 games because of torn ligaments in his thumb. On September 18, 1995, Sheffield made three hits with two HR and seven RBI in a 13–10 loss to the Philadelphia Phillies, giving him eight consecutive hits in two games. He produced MVP numbers in 1996 with 118 runs, 42 HR, 120 RBI, 142 walks, and a .314 batting average, being named to the *TSN* Silver Slugger team and finishing seventh in the MVP voting. In April 1997, Sheffield received a $61 million, six year contract extension with Florida. Although starting slowly in 1997, he batted .250 with 21 HR and 71 RBI to help the Marlins capture a Wild Card spot. His .444 batting average, doubles, and HR boosted Florida in the NL Division Series against the San Francisco Giants. He clouted one HR in the NL Championship Series against the Atlanta Braves and batted .292 in the World Series with a double, HR, and five RBI in Game 3 against the Cleveland Indians. In a blockbuster May 1998 trade, the Los Angeles Dodgers (NL) acquired him from the Florida Marlins. Sheffield batted .302 with 22 HR and 85 RBI in 1998 and .301 with 34 HR and 101 RBI in 1999.

Sheffield creates a great combination of power, contact hitting, and speed and has performed better defensively in the outfield. His baseball talent seems unlimited if he can avoid off-field problems. In 1995, Sheffield claimed a former girlfriend tried to set him up by reporting he carried drugs on a plane. None were found. Fearing he was being stalked, he hired bodyguards later that year. Sheffield sued a former girlfriend for writing bad checks, while she countersued him for false imprisonment. A female acquaintance was accused in a plot to kill Sheffield's mother, but denied involvement and passed a polygraph test. In October 1995, Sheffield was shot in the left shoulder by a supposed carjacker. He feuded publically with Marlins' general manager Dave Dombrowski and hired a public relations firm to give him a public image makeover. Through the 1999 season, his major league career included 1,345 hits, 241 doubles, 236 HR, 779 runs scored, 807 RBI, 156 stolen bases, and a .290 batting average in 1,308 games.

Sheffield, who has never married, is a devoted father to his three children, Ebony, Carissa and Gary, Jr. Each child has a different mother.

BIBLIOGRAPHY: Gary Sheffield file, National Baseball Library, Cooperstown, NY; Dave Rosenbaum, *If They Don't Win It's a Shame* (Tampa, FL, 1998); John Dewan, ed., *The Scouting Report: 1994* (New York, 1994); Mark Eisenbath, "Top Sheff: New Contract, New Attitude Put the Spotlight on Sheffield," St. Louis (MO) *Post-Dispatch*, May 1, 1997, pp. D-1, 6; B. Keidan and W. Ladson, "Compadres," *Sport* 84 (March 1993), pp. 58–61; Bill Koenig, "Main Marlin," *USAT Baseball Weekly*, March 25, 1997, pp. 10–12; *San Diego Padres 1993 Media Guide*; Marc Topkin, "Gary Sheffield Sets His Sights on a Banner Year," *BD* 56 (June 1977), pp. 66–67.

Frank J. Olmsted

SHELLENBACK, Frank Victor "Shelly" (b. December 16, 1898, Joplin, MO; d. August 17, 1969, Newton, MA), player, coach, manager, and scout, spent over 50 years in baseball. His chief fame came as a minor league pitcher with a 295–178 win–loss mark in 19 PCL seasons after the spitballer was barred from the major leagues. In childhood, he moved to Hollywood, CA with his parents, Albert and Caroline (Nolte) Shellenback, and played baseball at Hollywood High School. After attending Santa Clara University briefly, he pitched for a semiprofessional mining baseball league around Ely, NV in 1916 and worked as an ore assayer. The Chicago White Sox (AL) signed Shellenback, who pitched for Providence, RI (IL) and Milwaukee, WI (AA) in 1917. Following three games with Minneapolis, MN (AA) in 1918, the 6-foot 3-inch, 195-pound right-hander joined the Chicago White Sox and compiled a 9–12 win–loss record and creditable 2.66 ERA. He also saw military duty in aviation during World War I. In 1919, a slow 1–3 start with the Chicago White Sox brought his reassignment to Minneapolis. Shellenback's major league career ended at age 20. After pitching for Vernon, CA (PCL) in 1920, he was not protected on the White Sox roster or on the "certified" exempt list when the major leagues barred "trick" deliveries in December.

With the spitball as his best pitch, Shellenback remained in the PCL from 1920 to 1938 with Vernon (1920–1924), Sacramento, CA (1925), Hollywood, CA (1926–1935), and San Diego, CA (1936–1938). His 295 victories (including a 27–7 slate in 1931), 361 complete games, and 4,185 innings remain PCL records, earning him a niche in the PCL's Hall of Fame. Besides batting well, he won 15 straight games in 1931 and 33 out of 34 decisions during the 1930–1931 seasons. Shellenback's career minor league win–loss mark of 315–192 places him with Joe Martina, Bill Thomas, Sam Gibson, and Willard Mains among the best right-handers ever.

Shellenback managed the last-place Hollywood club in 1935 and was retained by owner H. W. "Bill" Lane when the franchise shifted to San Diego in 1936. During his three seasons with the Padres, San Diego compiled a 284–247 overall mark. Shellenback won a PCL playoff championship in 1937, helped develop second baseman Bobby Doerr,* and converted Ted Williams* from a pitcher to an outfielder. Shellenback served as a pitching coach for the St. Louis Browns (AL) in 1939, Boston Red Sox (AL) from 1940 to 1944, and Detroit Tigers (AL) in 1946 and 1947. Following a brief management stint with Minneapolis (AA) in 1947, he coached for the New York Giants (NL) from 1948 to 1955. He remained with the New York Giants and San Francisco Giants as an adviser and scout until his death. Shellenback married Elizabeth Taylor on January 17, 1922 and had six children.

BIBLIOGRAPHY: *Minor League Baseball Stars* (Cooperstown, NY, 1978); Frank Shellenback file, National Baseball Library, Cooperstown, NY; John Thorn et al., eds., *Total Baseball*, 5th ed. (New York, 1997); *TSN*, August 30, 1969, p. 46; *TSN Baseball Register*, 1940; Warren Brown, *The Chicago White Sox* (New York, 1952).

                                                                    James D. Smith III

SHERDEL, William Henry "Wee Willie," "Sherry" (b. August 15, 1896, McSherrystown, PA; d. November 14, 1968, McSherrystown, PA), player, was of German descent and graduated from Penn Township Elementary School. He was scouted and signed by St. Louis Cardinals (NL) general manager Branch Rickey.* Although winning just six of 18 decisions, Sherdel compiled a respectable 2.71 ERA for the error-prone 1918 St. Louis Cardinals. Rickey assumed field manager duties in 1919 and used Sherdel mostly in relief for the next three seasons. After Rickey moved him to the starting rotation, Sherdel recorded 17 victories in 1922 and 15 triumphs in 1923. In 1924, however, Rickey returned Sherdel to the bullpen. Rogers Hornsby,* who succeeded Rickey as manager in July 1925, reinserted Sherdel into the starting corps. Sherdel triumphed 15 times and led the NL with a .714 winning percentage in 1925. From 1925 to 1928, he performed in a solid St. Louis Cardinals rotation with Jesse Haines,* Grover Alexander,* and Flint Rhem. Sherdel's 16 victories in 1926 helped the St. Louis Cardinals to their first NL pennant. His finest season came in 1928, when he established a record 21 wins for a Cardinals left-hander and attained career highs of 20 complete games and 248.2 innings to lead the St. Louis Cardinals to another pennant. He led NL hurlers in saves three times, including 1927 and 1928. The upbeat Sherdel twice batted over .300, often singing or whistling on the mound. Not overpowering, he relied on control and tempted batters with his "slow ball" pitch.

Sherdel experienced tough luck in the World Series. In the 1926 classic, Herb Pennock* of the New York Yankees outdueled him, 2–1, in Game 1 and 3–2 in 10 innings in Game 5. The 1928 World Series again pitted the St. Louis Cardinals against the New York Yankees. Sherdel surrendered three runs in the 4–1 first game loss to Waite Hoyt.* In the final game, St. Louis led, 2–1, in the seventh inning when Sherdel struck out Babe Ruth* on a quick-pitch. Unfortunately, Commissioner Kenesaw Mountain Landis* had outlawed the quick-pitch delivery for the World Series. Ruth, allowed another pitch, and Lou Gehrig* both clouted HR to defeat Sherdel again. In Sherdel's four World Series starts, the St. Louis Cardinals scored only seven runs.

Sherdel prevailed in only 10 of 25 decisions, allowing a club record 129 earned runs for southpaws in 1929. In June 1930, the St. Louis Cardinals traded him to the Boston Braves (NL) for pitcher Burleigh Grimes.* Sherdel spot started and relieved for the Boston Braves in 1930 and 1931. The St. Louis Cardinals reclaimed Sherdel in May 1932, but he retired after just three games.

On the St. Louis Cardinals' All-Time list, Sherdel ranks third in appearances (465) and fourth in victories (153), innings pitched (2,450), complete games (144), and seasons pitched (14). His major league career totals included 165 wins, 146 defeats, 159 complete games, 839 strikeouts, 11 shutouts, a 3.72 ERA, and 2,709.1 innings in 514 games. He clouted nine HR with a career .223 batting average.

Sherdel married Marguerite Ethel Strasbaugh on November 24, 1919 and worked as a steward at Hanover, PA Moose Home #227.

BIBLIOGRAPHY: Charles Alexander, *Rogers Hornsby* (New York, 1995); Bob Broeg, *Redbirds: A Century of Cardinals' Baseball* (St. Louis, MO, 1981); Bob Broeg and Jerry Vickery, *St. Louis Cardinals Encyclopedia* (Grand Rapids, MI, 1998); Frederick G. Lieb, *The St. Louis Cardinals* (New York, 1945); Gary Caruso, *The Braves Encyclopedia* (Philadelphia, PA, 1995); Rob Rains, *The St. Louis Cardinals* (New York, 1992); Mike Shatzkin, ed., *The Ballplayers* (New York, 1990); William Sherdel file, National Baseball Library, Cooperstown, NY; *The Baseball Encyclopedia*, 10th ed. (New York, 1996).

Frank J. Olmsted

SHERIDAN, John F. (b. 1852, Decatur, IL; d. November 2, 1914, San Jose, CA), player, umpire, and scout, moved with his family to San Francisco, CA at a young age and began a promising baseball career in 1884 as a second baseman for the Renos, a local semiprofessional club. He hurt his arm while playing for Chattanooga, TN (SL) and Rochester, NY (NYSL) in 1885 and umpired occasionally in both leagues while unable to play. He became a professional umpire in the CL in 1886, jumping to the major leagues with the PL in 1890. He umpired the next year in the AA, which merged with the NL in 1892. His next umpiring stints came in the WL in 1894 and 1895 and in the NL in 1896 and 1897. He rejoined the WL in 1898 and shifted with it to the AL in 1901. The WL was renamed the AL in 1900 and began operating as a major league in 1901. On May 31, 1901, Sheridan recorded the first forfeit in AL history when he awarded a game to the Detroit Tigers. The Baltimore Orioles, irate over a close play at home plate, refused to take the field for the bottom of the ninth inning despite leading, 5–4. He umpired five games in each of four World Series (1905, 1907, 1908, 1910), and handled contests in 1913 for Charles Comiskey's* around-the-world touring All-Stars. Sheridan, the era's senior and highest-paid umpire, earned an annual $6,000 salary. A severe sunstroke forced his retirement after the 1914 season, when he became the first umpire scout in major league history.

Sheridan personified the transition of umpiring from the single- to the two-man system and from the contentiousness of the late 19th century to the professionalism of the early 20th century. AL players and managers acknowledged him as "the best umpire." Sporting a walrus mustache, the tall, debonair, and rather eccentric Sheridan earned universal respect with his engaging personality, firm decisions, and restraint in ejections. The diplomatic disciplinarian showed remarkable tolerance of fan and player abuse and often socialized with spectators and players. Sheridan, one of the few major league umpires who lived in California, occasionally voiced civic boosterism when emphasizing a called third strike: "Strike three! San Jose, California! The Garden Spot of America!" A close friend of AL President Ban Johnson,* he helped increase league support of umpires and attract quality new men to the staff. Sheridan, role model and tutor for the younger umpires, shunned the chest protector and shin guards and wore only a mask behind the plate. He initiated the technique of working from a crouch instead of standing upright when calling balls and strikes. National Baseball Hall of Fame umpires Billy Evans (AL)* and Bill Klem (NL)* considered Sheridan the greatest umpire in major league history. A bachelor, Sheridan operated a mortuary in San Jose, CA with his brother during the off-season.

BIBLIOGRAPHY: John F. Sheridan file, National Baseball Library, Cooperstown, NY; John F. Sheridan file, *TSN* Archives, St. Louis, MO; John F. Sheridan, "Umpiring for the Big Leagues," *BM* 1 (May 1908), pp. 9–12; *TSN*, December 3, 1908, November 5, 1914.

Larry R. Gerlach

SHIBE, Benjamin Franklin "Ben" (b. 1838, Philadelphia, PA; d. January 14, 1922, Philadelphia, PA), executive, joined Connie Mack* in helping establish the Philadelphia Athletics (AL) in 1901. Shibe, a horse car driver in Philadelphia, became an enthusiastic baseball fan in the late 1800s. Although unable to play because of a leg injury that required him to wear a steel brace, he helped develop baseball equipment. A flair for making baseballs led him in 1882 to join the sporting goods firm of Alfred J. Reach.* Shibe later developed the two-piece baseball cover and invented the cork center baseball. Shibe's partnership with Reach established his fortune, estimated at over $1 million by his death.

When Ban Johnson* formed the AL in 1901, he approached Shibe about establishing a team in Philadelphia. In partnership with field manager Mack, Shibe effectively directed business operations for the new team and saw the Athletics dominate the first decade of the AL. From 1901 to 1914, the Athletics won 6 AL pennants, 3 World Series titles, and finished in second place twice. In 1909, he played an instrumental role in moving the Athletics to the modern Shibe Park. He also became one of the first baseball executives to adopt the scoreboard, enabling fans in all parts of the stadium to follow the game. Shibe served as president of the Athletics until his death, two years after involvement in a serious automobile accident. Shibe, whose wife predeceased him, left four children, Thomas, John, Mrs. Frank MacFarlane, and Mrs. George Reach. His son Thomas (1866–1936) served as vice-president and later president of the Athletics and chief officer of the Reach Company.

BIBLIOGRAPHY: Benjamin Shibe file, National Baseball Library, Cooperstown, NY; Connie Mack, *My 66 Years in the Big Leagues* (Philadelphia, PA, 1950); Philadelphia *Bulletin*, January 15, 1922, February 17, 1936; Philadelphia *Inquirer*, January 14, 1922; Philadelphia *Public Ledger*, January 15, 1922, February 17, 1936; Philadelphia *Record*, February 17, 1936; Frederick G. Lieb, *Connie Mack* (New York, 1945); Jerome C. Romanowski, *The Mackmen* (Upper Darby, PA, 1979); Bruce Kuklick, *Shibe Park and Urban Philadelphia* (Princeton, NJ, 1991).

John P. Rossi

SHINDLE, William "Billy" (b. December 5, 1860, Gloucester, NJ; d. June 3, 1936, Lakeland, NJ), player and manager, was a son of Frederick Shindle, mayor of Gloucester City in 1883, and Sarah (Whitehead) Shindle and attended elementary school in Gloucester City. Shindle developed his baseball skills playing with local amateur teams and entered professional baseball with the Wilmington, DE Blue Hens (EL) in 1885. After the Wilmington franchise disbanded in June, Shindle finished the season as third baseman with Norfolk, VA (EL). In 1886, he signed with the Utica, NY Pent-Ups (IL). When Utica won the championship, Shindle attracted major league attention. Consequently, the Detroit Wolverines (NL) acquired him and used him for seven games during October 1886. The following year, he could not dislodge the veteran Deacon White* from his third base position and played in only 22 games. In the spring of 1888, manager Ned Hanlon* of the Baltimore Orioles (AA) purchased his contract and installed him at the hot corner. Shindle led the AA third basemen with a .922 fielding average. The righthanded batter and thrower hit only .208 in 1888, but raised his batting average to .314 for the Baltimore Orioles in 1889.

Shindle jumped to the Philadelphia Quakers (PL) in 1890, batting a career-high .324. When the PL disbanded, he was assigned to the Philadelphia Phillies (NL) and played shortstop regularly in 1891. In 1892 and 1893, he returned to third base for the Baltimore Orioles (NL). During January 1894, manager Ned Hanlon traded Shindle and outfielder George Treadway to the Brooklyn Bridegrooms (NL) for veteran Dan Brouthers* and unheralded rookie Willie Keeler.* The 5-foot 8½-inch, 155-pound Shindle played adequately as Brooklyn's third baseman from 1894 through 1898. He performed as captain and third baseman three seasons for the Hartford, CT (EL) Indians and as manager following Bill Barnie's death in July 1900.

An excellent fielder, Shindle demonstrated good range, threw strongly and accurately, and showed speed on the bases. During his 13-year major league career, he batted .269 with 992 runs, 1,561 hits, and 318 stolen bases in 1,422 games. He was elected in 1977 to the Gloucester Sports Hall of Fame.

BIBLIOGRAPHY: Gloucester City (NJ) *News*, June 11, 1936, p. 1; New York *Clipper*, July 20, 1889, p. 311; William Shindle file, National Baseball Library, Cooperstown, NY; John Thorn et al., eds., *Total Baseball*, 5th ed. (New York, 1997); James H. Bready, *Baseball in Baltimore* (Baltimore, MD, 1998); Frank Graham, *The Brooklyn Dodgers* (New York, 1945); William F. McNeil, *The Dodgers Encyclopedia* (Champaign, IL, 1997).

Frank V. Phelps

SHIVELY, Twila (b. March 20, 1922, Decatur, IL; d. November 30, 1999, Douglas, MI), player, was the daughter of Glenn Shively, a truck driver, and Eva (Bryant) Shively and grew up in a rural east central Illinois community. She had one brother and began playing softball at age eight. She joined an organized softball league at age 13. Since Steinmetz High School in Chicago offered no structured athletic opportunities for young women, Shively played "make-up games of soccer, baseball, and basketball during recess and after school." An AAGPBL scout signed her for $75 a week after seeing her play in an amateur softball league in Chicago. She had received only $16 a week at Hydrox.

The 5-foot 6-inch, 128-pound Shively, who batted and threw right-handed, played first base and the outfield for the Grand Rapids, MI Chicks (AAGPBL) from 1945 to 1947, Chicago Colleens (AAGPBL) in 1948, and Peoria, IL Redwings (AAGPBL) from 1948 to 1950. In 1946, she led Grand Rapids in runs scored with 78 and stole 75 bases. A good defensive player, Shively participated on the 1947 championship Grand Rapids team. Her career highlight came in 1950, when she belted a game winning grand slam HR for Peoria in the ninth inning. In 614 career AAGPBL games, she batted .200 with 429 hits, 166 RBI and 255 stolen bases. A broken ankle, suffered while sliding, shortened her playing career.

Shively earned a Bachelor's degree in physical education at Illinois State College in Normal, IL and completed a Masters degree in physical education at Indiana University. Her teaching career at Washington High School in South Bend, IN, spanned 30 years and included softball and volleyball coaching.

Shively's hobbies involved golf, hiking, and aerobics. She admired aviatrix Emelia Earhart and held a student aviation license in the early 1950s. Shively noted, "If I had had the money I would have become a serious and competitive flyer." She enjoys being a numismatist and exercises regularly by swimming laps.

As an AAGPBL player, Shively liked travelling to new places. "It really was such fun because you were always with a group of friends," she added. Shively enjoyed *A League of Their Own*, the 1992 Hollywood feature film on the Rockford Peaches. "It's my favorite movie," she stated.

Shively appears in the AAGPBL Gallery at the National Baseball Hall of Fame in Cooperstown, NY and was elected to the Chicago Baseball Hall of Fame.

BIBLIOGRAPHY: Scott A.G.M. Crawford, telephone interview with Twila Shively, April 15, 1996; AAGPBL files, Northern Indiana Historical Society, South Bend, IN; Tim Wiles, National Baseball Hall of Fame, Cooperstown, NY, letter to Scott A.G.M. Crawford, December 14, 1995; W. C. Madden, *The Women of the All-American Girls Professional Baseball League* (Jefferson, NC, 1997); Scott A.G.M. Crawford, telephone conversations with Dottie Collins, AAGPBLPA, February 1996.

                                                      Scott A.G.M. Crawford

SHOCKCOR, Urbain Jacques. *See* Urban James Shocker.

SHOCKER, Urban James (b. Urbain Jacques Shockcor, August 22, 1890, Cleveland, OH; d. September 9, 1928, Denver, CO), player, was one of the last legal spitball pitchers. He never suffered a losing season and achieved a .615 winning percentage in a 13-year major league career with the St. Louis Browns (AL) and New York Yankees (AL).

Originally a catcher, Shocker first played professional baseball in 1913 for Windsor, Canada (BL). The speed and accuracy of his throws prompted his conversion to the mound. He won 39 games in two years for Ottawa, Canada (CAL) and was bought by the New York Yankees in 1916 for $750. After Shocker enjoyed an impressive option season with Toronto, Canada (IL), the New York Yankees recalled him and traded him to the St. Louis Browns in January 1918. New manager Miller Huggins* sent the 5-foot 10-inch, 170-pound Shocker and four other players to the St. Louis Browns for Del Pratt,* Eddie Plank,* and cash.

The deal marked a rare miscalculation by the 5-foot 6-inch, 140-pound Huggins. Between 1919 and 1924, Shocker ranked among the premier AL hurlers, contributing 120 of the Browns' 465 victories. In four of those six seasons, he won 20 or more games. His 27 triumphs in 1921 and 24 victories in 1922, when the Browns lost the AL pennant by one game, topped the AL. In 1924, he won a doubleheader from the Chicago White Sox, winning 6–2 in both games. A right-hander of medium build, Shocker never overpowered batters and yet pitched two 300-inning seasons with up to 30 complete games. His most elegant statistics, however, reflect the intelligence and finesse of his pitching. He achieved ERAs under 3.00 while allowing under two walks and seven hits per nine innings.

Shocker possessed a sharp eye for batters' weaknesses and exploited them with a wide assortment of curves. A crook in the top joint of his ring finger, the result of spearing a ball while still a catcher, imparted a break to his throws. He bluffed the spitball often, but rarely used it more than half dozen times per game.

Shocker's most flamboyant moment came in 1923, when he refused to take an eastern road trip because the St. Louis Browns would not allow his wife to accompany him. Fined $1,000 and suspended, he appealed to Commissioner Kenesaw Mountain Landis.* Longtime baseball executive Bob Quinn, then the Browns' secretary, acted as intermediary, getting Shocker's fine rescinded and salary paid.

In December 1924, the New York Yankees reacquired him for Joe Bush,* Milt Gaston, and Joe Giard. After compiling a 12–12 record for the seventh-place 1925 Yankees, Shocker earned 19 wins in 1926 and 18 victories in 1927. Lifetime, he achieved 187 triumphs against 117 losses and a 3.17 ERA. He retired suddenly in April 1928 ostensibly to operate his St. Louis, MO radio shop. Death came within months due to an overstrained "athlete's heart."

BIBLIOGRAPHY: Bill Borst, ed., *Ables to Zoldak*, vol. 3 (St. Louis, MO, 1990); Bill Borst, *Still Last in the American League* (West Bloomfield, MI, 1992); Mark Gallagher *The Yankee Encyclopedia*, vol. 3 (Champaign, IL, 1997); Roger A. Godin, *The 1922 St. Louis Browns* (Jefferson, NC, 1991); Frank Graham, *The New York Yankees* (New York, 1943); Lee Trachtenberg, *The Wonder Team* (Bowling Green, OH, 1995); Bill James, *Historical Baseball Abstract* (New York, 1986); John Mosedale, *The Greatest of*

All: The 1927 New York Yankees (New York, 1975); Urban Shocker file, National Baseball Library, Cooperstown, NY; John Thorn et al., eds., *Total Baseball*, 5th ed. (New York, 1997).

                                                                                A. D. Suehsdorf

SHOLLENBERGER, Fern "Shelly" (b. May 18, 1923, Hamburg, PA; d. June 12, 1977, Leesport, PA), player, was the daughter of Alvas Shollenberger, a machinist, and Fannie (Young) Shollenberger and grew up with three brothers and one sister. Her brother, Kenneth, recalled that sporting activity was hugely popular in the household. Shollenberger often played basketball and baseball with her brothers and idolized Babe Ruth.* At Hamburg High School, she participated energetically in every available sport and starred in basketball and baseball.

The 5-foot 4-inch, 125 pounder, who batted and threw right-handed, played outfield and eventually third base for the Kenosha, WI Giants (AAGPBL) from 1946 to 1951. From 1952 to 1954, Shollenberger performed for the Kalamazoo, MI Lassies (AAGPBL). Nicknamed "Shelly," she starred for the 1954 playoff champion Kalamazoo Lassies. She made 77 hits in 1946, 106 hits in 1950, 89 hits in 1954 and stole 35 bases as a rookie. She led AAGPBL third basemen in fielding from 1949 through 1951. The 1950, 1951, 1952, and 1954 campaigns saw her selected to the AAGPBL All-Star team. Shollenberger's best batting average (.268) came her final season in 1954, when she recorded career highs in HR (8) and RBI (58). During nine AAGPBL seasons, she batted .221 with 725 hits, 231 RBI, and 167 stolen bases and compiled a .942 fielding average as one of the AAGPBL's best third basemen.

After graduating from Hamburg High School, Shollenberger worked as an office secretary. She was married briefly, but had no children. Shollenberger returned home to care for her parents and loved watching baseball and basketball games. She and her father were killed in an automobile accident.

Her brother, Kenneth, pictured her as absolutely crazy about sports. "She had a wonderful nine year career as a pro. She loved every aspect of baseball. Even the poor pay did not affect her. I never heard her complain. Baseball meant everything to her."

BIBLIOGRAPHY: Scott A.G.M. Crawford, telephone interview with Kenneth Shollenberger, April 5, 1996; AAGPBL files, Northern Indiana Historical Society, South Bend, IN; Tim Wiles, National Baseball Hall of Fame, Cooperstown, NY, letter to Scott A.G.M. Crawford, December 14, 1995; W. C. Madden, *The Women of the All-American Girls Professional Baseball League* (Jefferson, NC, 1997); Scott A.G.M. Crawford, telephone conversation with Dottie Collins, AAGPBLPA, February 1996.

                                                                            Scott A.G.M. Crawford

SIEBERN, Norman Leroy "Norm" (b. July 26, 1933, St. Louis, MO), player and scout, performed as an outfielder and first baseman for six major league clubs from 1956 through 1968. Besides batting .272 lifetime, he slugged 132 HR, drove in 636 runs, compiled a .992 career fielding percentage and won several Gold Gloves.

When growing up in Wellston, near St. Louis, Siebern loitered outside of Sportsman's Park for a glimpse at his St. Louis Cardinals heroes. He starred as a fine high school and sandlot baseball player and was offered several professional baseball contracts after graduation from high school. Siebern's father, a milkman, wanted him to attend college. Siebern enrolled in Southwest Missouri State College from 1951 to 1953, playing minor league baseball with McAlester, OK (SSL), Joplin, MO (WA), and Birmingham, AL (SL). In 1954 and 1955, he served in the U.S. Army. He split the 1956 season shuttling between Denver (AA) and the talent-laden New York Yankees (AL), who owned his major league rights. Siebern fractured his kneecap after playing 54 games with the New York Yankees in 1956 and was optioned to Denver for the 1957 season. He led the AA in batting average, runs scored, hits, doubles, and triples. *TSN* named him its Minor League Player of the Year for 1957.

The 6-foot 2-inch, 200-pound Siebern, who batted left and threw right, joined the New York Yankees for the 1958 season, hitting .300 with 14 HR, and 55 RBI. He also won a Gold Glove, although always having trouble with the Yankee Stadium outfield. Siebern misjudged two fly balls in Game 4 of the 1958 World Series against the Milwaukee Braves, costing the New York Yankees the contest. Some fans scapegoated him as New York fell behind in the World Series three games to one, but the Yankees rallied to win the fall classic.

During 1959, manager Casey Stengel* platooned Siebern. By then, rising star Elston Howard* received more playing time. Siebern competed in a crowded outfield with Howard, Hank Bauer,* Mickey Mantle,* and Enos Slaughter.* His hitting declined slightly for the third place Yankees.

In December 1959, Siebern, Bauer, Marv Throneberry, and Don Larsen* were traded to the Kansas City Athletics (AL) for Roger Maris,* in a transaction that changed baseball history. Siebern converted to first base, marking a bright spot on otherwise dismal Kansas City Athletics teams. His best season came in 1962, when he made the AL All-Star squad, hit .308, clouted 25 HR, and drove in 117 runs in 162 games. In four seasons with the Kansas City Athletics, Siebern never batted under .272. From 1960 through 1963, he averaged 19 HR and 92 RBI.

Nonetheless, the Kansas City Athletics traded Siebern to the Baltimore Orioles (AL) for Jim Gentile* and cash in November 1963. In 1964, his wife, Elizabeth, had a very difficult childbirth and his mother died. Replacing the flamboyant power-hitting Gentile in Baltimore proved burdensome. Siebern hit only .245 with 12 HR and 56 RBI, but led the AL in walks with 106 and made the AL All-Star squad. He raised his batting average to .256 for 1965. His productivity declined, however, causing him to lose his first-base job to

John "Boog" Powell.* The Baltimore Orioles traded Siebern to the California Angels (AL) in December 1965. He played for the San Francisco Giants (NL) until sold to the Boston Red Sox (AL) in July 1967 and retired during the 1968 campaign.

Siebern, who married Elizabeth Vigil in October 1958 and has several children, scouted for the Atlanta Braves (NL) and Kansas City Royals (AL) and operated insurance agencies in Missouri and Naples, FL.

BIBLIOGRAPHY: Norm Siebern file, National Baseball Library, Cooperstown, NY; "Norm Siebern," *Microsoft Complete Baseball* CD-ROM (Redmond, WA, 1994); Dom Forker, *Sweet Seasons* (Dallas, TX, 1991); John C. Hawkins, *This Date in Baltimore Orioles and St. Louis Browns History* (New York, 1983); Peter Golenbock, *Dynasty: The New York Yankees, 1949–1964* (Englewood Cliffs, NJ, 1975); Walter LeConte, *The Ultimate New York Yankees Record Book* (New York, 1984); *New York Yankees Yearbook,* 1958; Ted Patterson, *The Baltimore Orioles* (Dallas, TX, 1995); *The Baseball Encyclopedia,* 10th ed. (New York, 1996).

Robert E. Weir

SIEBERT, Richard Walther "Dick," "The Chief" (b. February 19, 1912, Fall River, MA; d. November 9, 1978, Minneapolis, MN), player, coach, and sportscaster, was the son of Edward Siebert, a Lutheran minister, and Carolyn (Krato) Siebert. Siebert began his baseball career at Concordia High School and Concordia JC in St. Paul, MN. He attended Concordia Seminary in St. Louis, MO in 1931–1932 to train for the ministry and earned a bachelor's degree from the University of Minnesota in 1934. The 6-foot, 170-pound left-hander began professional baseball with Waynesboro, PA (BRL) in 1929 as a pitcher. A sore arm forced him to switch to first base, a position he played in the minor leagues at Dayton, OH (CL, MAL), York, PA (NYPL), Albany, NY (IL), Buffalo, NY (IL), Indianapolis, IN (AA), and Columbus, OH (AA). Siebert played briefly with the Brooklyn Dodgers (NL) in 1932 and 1936 and St. Louis Cardinals (NL) in 1937 and 1938. He became the regular first baseman for the Philadelphia Athletics (AL) under the legendary manager Connie Mack* in 1938 and played over 100 games in each of the next seven seasons there, batting .334 in 1941. During the off-season, he coached basketball at Concordia JC. In 1,035 major league games, he made 1,104 hits and compiled a .282 career batting average. Siebert appeared in the 1942 All-Star game and was selected again in 1945, but wartime restrictions canceled the latter contest. In October 1945, the Philadelphia Athletics traded him to the St. Louis Browns (AL). Contract troubles ended his professional baseball career. His most memorable moment was breaking up a developing no-hit game by Bob Feller* of the Cleveland Indians.

After Siebert served one year as a sportscaster for radio station WTCN in Minneapolis, the University of Minnesota hired him as head baseball coach. Minnesota won nine WC titles, including three consecutive crowns from 1958 to 1960 and 1968 to 1970. Three NCAA national baseball titles (1956, 1960, 1964) were captured by Siebert's clubs. He served as ACBC president, was named College Baseball Coach of the Year in 1956 and 1960, and developed several future major league stars including Paul Molitor,* David Winfield,* and Paul Giel.* His greatest coaching thrills included a sensational come-from-behind win over the University of Southern California in the finals of the 1960 NCAA national championships and the stellar performance of his 1964 amazing title team. The University of Minnesota named the baseball field in his honor. He married Marie Schoening on November 10, 1934.

BIBLIOGRAPHY: Dick Siebert file, National Baseball Library, Cooperstown, NY; *The Baseball Encyclopedia*, 10th ed. (New York, 1996); Stan W. Carlson, Spectator Club program biography of Dick Siebert (Minneapolis, MN, 1973); Richard Siebert, letter to Stan W. Carlson, August 1989. *TSN Baseball Register, 1940*; University of Minnesota, Media Release, 1989; Frederick G. Lieb, *Connie Mack* (New York, 1945); Connie Mack, *My 66 Years in the Big Leagues* (Philadelphia, PA, 1950); Jerome C. Romanowski, *The Mackmen* (Upper Darby, PA, 1979).

Stan W. Carlson

SIEBERT, Wilfred Charles, III "Sonny" (b. January 14, 1937, St. Marys, MO), player and coach, is the son of Wilfred Siebert, Jr., a National Lead Company worker, and Fern Rose (Gross) Siebert. Siebert, who received the nickname "Sonny" from his parents, grew up in St. Louis, MO and graduated from Bayless High School. He attended the University of Missouri in Columbia for three years, starring in basketball with an 18-point per game average. Siebert also played shortstop and first base at Missouri and signed a professional baseball contract after his junior year with the Cleveland Indians (AL) for a $35,000 bonus. The 6-foot 3-inch, 200-pound Siebert played right field at Burlington, NC (CrL) and Batavia, NY (NYPL) in 1958 and at Minot, ND (NoL) in 1959 before the St. Louis Hawks (NBA) basketball club drafted him. Siebert, however, decided to remain in professional baseball.

In 1960, Siebert returned to Burlington as a pitcher and won eight of 15 decisions. He hurled for Salt Lake City, UT (PCL) and Reading, PA (EL) in 1961. The right-hander blossomed at Charleston, WV (IL) in 1962, winning 15 games and losing eight. After spending another year of seasoning at Jacksonville, FL (IL) in 1963, Siebert won seven and lost nine decisions for the Cleveland Indians (AL) in 1964. His record included a respectable 3.23 ERA and 144 strikeouts in 156 innings. In 1965 and 1966, he produced 16–8 records for the Cleveland Indians. The hard-throwing Siebert in 1965 struck out a career-high 191 batters, including 15 Washington Senators in one game. In his next start against the Washington Senators on June 10, 1966, he hurled a 2–0 no-hitter in outdueling Phil Ortega. Siebert pitched two perfect innings in the 1966 All-Star Game. His .667 winning percentage paced the AL in 1966.

Despite winning only 10 of 22 decisions in 1967, Siebert recorded a career-best 2.38 ERA. On September 13, 1967, he matched the Chicago White Sox's Gary Peters* with 11 innings of shutout pitching and allowed only four base runners. The Cleveland Indians finally won, 1–0, in 17 innings. Siebert hurled 23 consecutive scoreless innings over three starts. He surrendered only 145 hits in 206 innings and compiled a 2.97 ERA in 1968, but won only a dozen games.

In April 1969, the Cleveland Indians dealt Siebert to the Boston Red Sox (AL). Siebert immediately became a mainstay of their rotation, winning 14 in 1969, 15 in 1970, and 16 in 1971. In 1971, he batted .266 and belted six HR. On September 2, 1972, he pitched a 3–0 shutout over the Baltimore Orioles and smashed solo and two–run HR off Pat Dobson. He recalled "missing a third home run when my drive tailed foul by a few feet." Siebert remains the last AL pitcher to hit two HR in a game.

In May 1973, the Boston Red Sox sold Siebert's contract to the Texas Rangers (AL). After a difficult 7–12 campaign, Siebert returned to his St. Louis hometown in 1974 and split 16 decisions with the Cardinals (NL). On September 11, 1974, Siebert won the second-longest game in major league history, holding the New York Mets (NL) scoreless in the 23rd, 24th, and 25th innings. The St. Louis Cardinals scratched out a 4–3 victory, after which Siebert went "out with Cards' announcer Jack Buck [OS] and several players for New York cheesecake at 5 or 6 AM." Siebert divided the 1975 season between the San Diego Padres (NL) and Oakland Athletics (AL), winning seven and losing six. The power pitcher, who relied on a 90-mph-plus fastball, said, "My best success came against the power hitters and I had the most trouble with the punch and judy hitters." His major league career included 399 games, 140 wins, 114 losses, 16 saves, 1,512 strikeouts, and 21 shutouts. In 2,152 innings, Siebert yielded only 1,919 hits. He also hit 12 HR.

Siebert subsequently attended Northeast Missouri State University in Kirksville and Southern Illinois University at Edwardsville, serving the latter as pitching coach. Siebert owned a Baskin-Robbins ice cream parlor and St. Louis (MO) *Post-Dispatch* and *Suburban Journal* newspaper routes until 1994. From 1984 to 1993, Siebert served as a pitching instructor throughout the San Diego Padres (NL) farm system. The Padres employed him as pitching coach in 1994 and 1995. He has served as a pitching coach in the Colorado Rockies (NL) organization since 1996.

Siebert married Carol Ann Buckner on June 28, 1958 and has four children, Scott, Steve, a former middle infielder in the San Diego Padres and Chicago White Sox (AL) farm systems, Sherri, and Sandi. He still makes St. Louis his home.

BIBLIOGRAPHY: Gary Herron, "Sonny Siebert Was Almost a Two-Sport Player," *SCD* 24 (July 18, 1997), pp. 132–133; Jack Torry, *Endless Summers* (South Bend, IN, 1995); Terry Pluto, *The Curse of Rocky Colavito* (New York, 1994); Robert Redmount, *The Red Sox Encyclopedia* (Champaign, IL, 1998); Ellery H. Clark, Jr., *Boston Red Sox* (Hicksville, NY, 1975); Bob Broeg and Jerry Vickery, *St. Louis Cardinals Encyclopedia* (Grand Rapids, MI, 1998); Rich Marazzi and Len Fiorito, *Aaron to Zipfel* (New York, 1985); Jeff Miller, *Down to the Wire* (Dallas, TX, 1992); Frank J. Olmsted, interview with Sonny Siebert, October 24, 1993; Mike Shatzkin, ed., *The Ballplayers* (New York, 1990); Sonny Siebert file, National Baseball Library, Cooperstown, NY; Rick Spiritosanto, "Sonny Siebert Recalls When He Put End to Marathon Game," *BD* 45 (August 1987), pp. 31–32.

Frank J. Olmsted

SIERRA, Ruben Angel (Garcia) (b. October 6, 1965, Rio Piedras, PR), player, is the son of Ruben Sierra, Sr., a taxi driver who died in 1970, and Petra Sierra, a hospital cleaner. He and his wife, Janette, have two children, Neysha and Ruben, Jr. Scout Orlando Gomez signed him for the Texas Rangers (AL) in November 1982.

A powerful switch hitter, the 6-foot 1-inch, 200-pound Sierra was lauded as "the next Clemente" and wore his number in the major leagues. In 1986, he joined the Texas Rangers and clouted 16 HR, including HR from both sides of the plate. The right-handed right fielder led the AL in assists (17), double plays (6), sacrifice flies, and at-bats (643) in 1987. He also drove in 109 runs, scored 97 runs, hit 30 HR, and set a Rangers record for extra base hits with 69.

After driving in 91 runs in 1988, Sierra the next season led the AL in triples (14), total bases (350), slugging percentage (.543), and RBI (119). He batted .306 with 29 HR and 101 runs scored, breaking his own Rangers record with 75 extra base hits. *TSN* named him as its AL Player of the Year and to its AL All-Star and AL Silver Slugger teams. He received 228 MVP votes that year, trailing Robin Yount* by 28 votes.

In April 1990, Sierra hit his 100th career HR at age 24. His HR declined from 29 to 16, but he still produced 96 RBI. The 1991 campaign saw him produce a career best 203 hits and 44 doubles and produce 116 RBI. Contract quarrels with the Texas Rangers management prompted his trade to the Oakland A's (AL) for Jose Canseco* in August 1992. In the 1992 AL Championship Series against the Texas Rangers, he hit .333 with one HR. During the 1993 and 1994 seasons, he averaged over 20 HR and 100 RBI.

The Oakland A's traded Sierra to the New York Yankees (AL) for Danny Tartabull* in July 1995. Sierra finished that campaign with 19 HR and 86 RBI and clouted two HR with five RBI in the AL Division Series against the Seattle Mariners. He was traded to the Detroit Tigers (AL) in July 1996 and Cincinnati Reds (NL) in October 1996. Sierra spent one month with the Toronto Blue Jays (AL) in 1997 and joined the Chicago White Sox (AL) in January 1998.

In 10 major league seasons through 1997, Sierra batted .269 with 235 HR and 1,036 RBI. He made the AL All-Star team in 1989, 1991, 1992, and 1994.

BIBLIOGRAPHY: *TSN*, July 31, 1989; A. Murphy, "Rising to the Top of the Game," *SI* 62 (April 16, 1990), pp. 60–63; *USAT Baseball Weekly*, March 10, 1992; Ruben Sierra file, National Baseball Library, Cooperstown, NY; Rick Weinberg, "Texas Terror," *Sport* 83 (May 1992), pp. 38–40.

Thomas H. Barthel

SIEVERS, Roy Edward "Squirrel" (b. November 18, 1926, St. Louis, MO), player and manager, is the son of William "Skinny" Sievers, who had been given an unsuccessful tryout with the Detroit Tigers (AL) baseball club, and Anna (Hirt) Sievers. He was born near Sportsman's Park, the home of the St. Louis Browns (AL) and St. Louis Cardinals (NL). Ducky Medwick* was his favorite ballplayer, as Sievers learned to hit by watching him bat with the St. Louis Cardinals.

Sievers signed a professional baseball contract with the St. Louis Browns directly from Beaumont High School in St. Louis, where he also had starred in basketball. Scout Jack Fournier* signed him on the recommendation of St. Louis Browns executives Bill De Witt and Charley De Witt, who had seen him play only one game in 1946. Fournier offered just a pair of spikes for the future AL Rookie-of-the-Year star. Fournier convinced Sievers that he could advance rapidly through the St. Louis Browns system.

After graduating from high school, Sievers entered military service as a private at Fort Knox, KY. In 1947, Sievers joined Hannibal, MO (CA). His other minor league stops included Elmira, NY (EL) and Springfield, IL (3IL) in 1948. Sievers in 1949 became the first AL player to win the Rookie of the Year Award by hitting .306 with 16 HR and 91 RBI for the St. Louis Browns. He married Donna Colburn in November 1949 and has two sons and one daughter.

Several debilitating injuries hampered Sievers' career. In 1951 he fell on his right shoulder, seriously limiting his throwing ability. The St. Louis Browns sent him to San Antonio, TX (TL) for rehabilitation that season. The St. Louis Browns traded Sievers to the Washington Senators (AL) for outfielder Gil Coan in February 1954.

It took Sievers only four seasons to become the greatest right-handed slugger in Washington Senators history, as he consistently hit at least 21 HR each season there. In 1957 the 6-foot 1½-inch, 204-pound slugger won two-thirds of the triple crown with 42 HR and 114 RBI, finishing third in the AL MVP race that year. Failure to win the batting title denied him the triple crown. That season, he tied Ken Williams'* AL record when he hit a HR in his sixth consecutive game to win a game in the 17th inning. In a night given in his honor that season, he received a station wagon and became so emotional that he openly wept on Vice-President Richard M. Nixon's shoulder. Nixon always considered him one of his favorite ball players.

In April 1960, the Senators traded him to the Chicago White Sox (AL) for Earl Battey,* Don Mincher,* and $150,000. He clouted 28 HR and 27 HR in 1960 and 1961, respectively, batting .295 each season. In November 1961, the Chicago White Sox traded him to the Philadelphia Phillies (NL) for John Buzhardt and Charley Smith. Sievers started the season with the 1964 Phillies team, which collapsed in the stretch run and lost the pennant to the St. Louis Cardinals. During July 1964 he was sold back to the Washington Senators, now an expansion AL franchise. Sievers closed out his active major league career the following season.

During his 17-year major league career Sievers played first base or outfield in 1,887 games, compiled a .267 batting average, drove in 1,147 runs, and slugged 318 HR. He drove in 100 or more runs in four seasons and made the AL All-Star team in 1956, 1957, 1959, and 1961. He managed two seasons in the minor leagues at Williamsport, PA (EL) in 1967 and Memphis, TN (SL) in 1968. In 1986, the St. Louis resident was inducted into the St. Louis Browns Historical Society Hall of Fame.

BIBLIOGRAPHY: Roy Sievers file, National Baseball Library, Cooperstown, NY; Bill Borst, *Last in the American League* (St. Louis, MO, 1978); Bill Borst, *We Could Have Finished Last Without You* (St. Louis, MO, 1986); Bill Borst, ed., *Ables to Zoldak*, vol. 3 (St. Louis, MO, 1990); Bill Borst, *Still Last in the American League* (West Bloomfield, MI, 1992); Lee Heiman et al., *When the Cheering Stops* (New York, 1990); Peter C. Bjarkman, ed., *Encyclopedia of Major League Baseball Team Histories American League* (Westport, CT, 1991); Richard Lindberg, *Sox* (New York, 1984); Richard Lindberg, *Who's on Third?* (South Bend, IN, 1983); Rich Westcott and Frank Bilovsky, *The New Phillies Encyclopedia* (Philadelphia, PA, 1993); Gene Karst and Martin J. Jones, Jr., *Who's Who in Professional Baseball* (New Rochelle, NY, 1973); Larry Moffi, *This Side of Cooperstown* (Iowa, City, IA, 1996); David Tracy, *Tracy at the Bat* (New York, 1950).

William A. Borst

SIMMONS, Aloysius Harry "Al," "Bucketfoot Al" (b. Aloysius Harry Syzmanski, May 22, 1902, Milwaukee, WI; d. May 26, 1956, Milwaukee, WI), player, was the son of Polish immigrants and was nicknamed "Old Bucketfoot." He grew up in Milwaukee, briefly attended Stevens Point Teachers College, and played semipro baseball for a Juneau, WI team. The Milwaukee, WI Brewers (AA) signed him in 1922 and farmed him to Aberdeen, SD (DL), where he hit .365 in 99 games. After Simmons batted .360 in 1923 for Shreveport, LA (TL), the Brewers recalled him for the team's final 24 games. His .398 batting average impressed manager Connie Mack,* who bought him for the Philadelphia Athletics (AL). Simmons played every game in 1924 for Philadelphia and received much derision for his strange batting stance. A right-handed hitter and thrower, he pointed his left foot almost straight down the third base line. But Mack refused to alter the stance, as the rookie hit .308 and batted in 102 runs. Simmons hit over .300 in 14 major league seasons, including 11 consecutive ones.

Simmons, who stood 6 feet tall and weighed about 200 pounds, possessed a very strong throwing arm and twice led the AL outfielders in fielding average. But he was best known for his heavy hitting and high batting average. In 2,215 major league games, he made 2,927 hits and slugged 539 doubles, 149 triples, and 307 HR. Besides knocking in 1,827 runs, he compiled a career .334 batting average and .535 slugging percentage. He led the AL in hitting twice (.381 in 1930, .390 in 1931) and finished second two times. His career peak .392 batting average in 1927 ranked second behind Harry Heilmann's* .398. He led the AL in hits twice (253 in 1925 and 216 in 1932) and in RBI (157) in 1929. Although never leading in HR, he in 1930 slugged 36 HR and 41 doubles among his 211 hits. In 1929, he was chosen the AL's MVP.

During Simmons' nine seasons with Philadelphia, the Athletics always contended and won three consecutive AL pennants (1929–1931). In those three World Series, Simmons hit .333 in 18 games and batted in 17 runs. His .364 batting average in 1930 paced both teams, while his HR and single in the seventh inning of the dramatic fourth game of the 1929 World Series helped the Philadelphia Athletics overcome an 8–0 Chicago Cubs lead. The Athletics won that World Series, 4 games to 1, defeated the St. Louis Cardinals, 4–2, in 1930, and lost to the Cardinals, 4–3, in 1931. Simmons also played one game in the 1939 World Series for the Cincinnati Reds (NL). His 253 hits in 1925 perhaps represented his greatest baseball achievement.

After the 1932 season, manager Mack began reducing his expenses by selling his stars. Simmons was sold to the Chicago White Sox (AL) in September and batted .331 in 1933 and .344 and 1934. After his batting average declined to .267 in 1935, he was traded that December to the Detroit Tigers (AL) and enjoyed a fine year there. Nearing the end of his career, he was sold to the Washington Senators (AL) in April 1937, Boston Braves (NL) in December 1938, Cincinnati Reds (NL) in August 1939, Philadelphia Athletics (AL) in 1940, and Boston Red Sox (AL) in 1943. Simmons, who ended his playing career with Philadelphia (AL) in 1944, was elected to the National Baseball Hall of Fame in 1953. Simmons coached for the Philadelphia Athletics (AL) from 1940 to 1942 and 1944 to 1948 and Cleveland Indians (AL) in 1950. He married Doris Lynn Reader of Chicago in August 1934 and had one son, John, before their subsequent divorce. Simmons died of a heart attack.

BIBLIOGRAPHY: Al Simmons file, National Baseball Library, Cooperstown, NY; Lee Allen, *The American League Story* (New York, 1962); Martin Appel and Burt Goldblatt, *Baseball's Best: The Hall of Fame Gallery* (New York, 1980); John Benson et al.,

Baseball's Top 100 (Wilton, CT, 1997); Warren Brown, *The Chicago White Sox* (New York, 1952); Donald Honig, *Baseball's Ten Greatest Teams* (New York, 1982); Frederick G. Lieb, *Connie Mack* (New York, 1945); Connie Mack, *My 66 Years in the Big Leagues* (Philadelphia, PA, 1950); Jerome C. Romanowski, *The Mackmen* (Upper Darby, PA, 1979); Richard Lindberg, *Sox* (New York, 1984); Frederick G. Lieb, *The Detroit Tigers* (New York, 1946); Joe Falls, *Detroit Tigers* (New York, 1975); Fred Smith, *995 Tigers* (Detroit, MI, 1981); Richard Lindberg, *Who's on Third?* (South Bend, IN, 1983); *LD* 116 (December 23, 1933), p. 26; *NYT*, September 22, 1927, June 3, 1930, August 11, 1934, May 27–28, 1956; Lowell Reidenbaugh, *Baseball's Hall of Fame-Cooperstown* (New York, 1993).

                                                                           Thomas L. Karnes

SIMMONS, Curtis Thomas "Curt" (b. May 19, 1929, Egypt, PA), player and coach, is the son of Lawrence Simmons and Hattie Simmons and was scouted by a dozen major league clubs at Whitehall High School in Egypt, PA. Simmons accepted a $60,000 bonus from the Philadelphia Phillies (NL) and struck out 197 batters in only 147 innings in 1947 for Wilmington, DE (ISL). The 18-year-old southpaw finished the 1947 season with his major league debut in the Philadelphia Phillies' finale, tossing a 5-hit, 9-strikeout victory over the New York Giants. By 1949, the 5-foot 11-inch Simmons was heralded as "a second Rube Waddell"* by Herb Pennock* and as the possessor of the best curveball since Bob Feller* by some sportswriters. On September 23, 1951, Simmons married Dorothy Elsie Ludwig. They have three children, Thomas, Timothy, and Susan.

His 17 wins helped the 1950 Phillies capture their first NL pennant since 1915. Immediately after the regular season, he was drafted into the military and missed the World Series against the New York Yankees. He was discharged in 1952, and returned to win 14 games and hurl a NL-leading 6 shutouts. In 1953, 27 consecutive Boston Braves were retired by Simmons in a game after a leadoff single. Simmons's career survived a lawn mower accident that took part of a toe, but arm trouble slowed him in 1958 and limited him to 10 innings in 1959. The St. Louis Cardinals (NL) acquired him in May 1960, when he was selected Cardinals Comeback Player of the Year. In 1961, he ranked third in the NL in ERA (3.13), batted .303, and led the NL in yielding most unearned runs. His 15 wins and team-leading 2.48 ERA powered the Cardinals into second place in 1963. One stretch saw Simmons spin 28 straight scoreless frames. His finest season came in 1964, when the 35-year-old workhorse pitched 244 innings, won 18 decisions, and lost only nine decisions. The Cardinals captured the 1964 World Series over the New York Yankees.

Simmons finished his 20-year major league career with the Chicago Cubs (NL) and the California Angels (AL) in 1967. His major league career totals included 193 wins, 183 losses, 1,697 strikeouts, 36 shutouts, and a 3.54 ERA in 569 games. Simmons served as a part-time pitching instructor in the Phillies minor league system and manages a golf course near his home in Prospectville, PA.

BIBLIOGRAPHY: Bob Broeg, *Redbirds: A Century of Cardinals' Baseball* (St. Louis, MO, 1981); Gene Karst and Martin J. Jones, Jr., *Who's Who in Professional Baseball* (New Rochelle, NY, 1973); Brent P. Kelley, *Baseball Stars of the 1950s* (Jefferson, NC, 1993); David Halberstam, *October 1964* (New York, 1994); Rich Marazzi and Len Fiorito, *Aaron to Zuverink* (New York, 1982); Harry Paxton, *The Whiz Kids* (New York, 1950); Robin Roberts and C. Paul Rogers III, *The Whiz Kids and the 1950 Pennant* (Philadelphia, PA, 1997); Rich Westcott and Frank Bilovsky, *The New Phillies Encyclopedia* (Philadelphia, PA, 1993); Frederick G. Lieb and Stan Baumgartner, *The Philadelphia Phillies* (New York, 1953); Allen Lewis, *The Philadelphia Phillies: A Pictorial History* (Virginia Beach, VA, 1981); Rob Rains, *The St. Louis Cardinals* (New York, 1992); Bob Broeg and Jerry Vickery, *St. Louis Cardinals Encyclopedia* (Grand Rapids, MI, 1998); Curt Simmons file, National Baseball Library, Cooperstown, NY; *St. Louis Cardinals 1960 Yearbook; St. Louis Cardinals 1961 Yearbook.*

Frank J. Olmsted

SIMMONS, Ted Lyle "Simba" (b. August 9, 1949, Highland Park, MI), player, scout, and executive, is the son of Finis Simmons, owner, trainer, and occasional driver of harness horses. After graduating from Southfield (MI) High School, Simmons attended the University of Michigan and Wayne State University. Simmons in 1970 married Maryane Ellison, the daughter of his Little League baseball coach. They have two sons, John and Mathew, and reside in Chesterfield, MO. Simmons idolized Al Kaline,* the Detroit Tigers' outstanding outfielder, and became a switch-hitter at age 13. At Southfield High School, he was named MVP in baseball, All-League in basketball, and All-State in football. Despite football scholarship offers from several universities, the 6-foot, 200-pound Simmons instead signed a $50,000 baseball contract as a free agent with the St. Louis Cardinals (NL) in June 1967.

Simmons divided his first professional baseball season in 1967 between Sarasota, FL (GCL) and Cedar Rapids, IA (ML). He won both Rookie of the Year and MVP honors with Modesto, CA (CaL) in 1968. The following year, he advanced to Tulsa, OK (AA) and won another MVP Award. In his first full major league season, Simmons batted .304 in 1971 for the St. Louis Cardinals. He hit above .300 six other times and attained a personal high .332 mark in 1975, finishing second in the NL. Besides hitting 20 or more HR at least six seasons, he drove in at least 100 runs three times.

During 10 years as a regular with the Cardinals (1971–1980), Simmons was primarily a catcher but occasionally played first base, third base, and the outfield. A line drive hitter who seldom struck out, he set NL records for most hits by a catcher in a season (188 in 1975) and most career HR by a switch-hitter (172). He was named to six midseason All-Star teams and three *TSN* All-Star teams as a National Leaguer. The right-handed throwing Simmons led the NL three times in total chances, twice each in intentional walks, assists, and putouts, and once in fielding percentage. Conversely, he paced the NL three times in passed balls and once in grounding into double plays.

In December 1980, Simmons was traded to the Milwaukee Brewers (AL). Simmons played in one World Series (1982) with Milwaukee, hitting two HR, and in two All-Star games (1981, 1983). With the Brewers, he was a DH, catcher, first baseman, and third baseman. He was traded to the Atlanta Braves (NL) in March 1986 and retired following the 1988 season. In 21 major league seasons, he batted .285 in 2,456 games with 1,074 runs, 2,472 hits, 483 doubles, 47 triples, 248 HR, and 1,389 RBI.

He served as director of player development for the St. Louis Cardinals from 1989 through 1992, senior vice president and general manager for baseball operations for the Pittsburgh Pirates (NL) in 1993, and special assignment scout for the Cleveland Indians (AL) from 1994 through 1999. The San Diego Padres named him vice president of player development and scouting in September 1999.

BIBLIOGRAPHY: Ted Simmons file, National Baseball Library, Cooperstown, NY; Rob Rains, *The St. Louis Cardinals* (New York, 1992); Bob Broeg and Jerry Vickery, *St. Louis Cardinals Encyclopedia* (Grand Rapids, MI, 1998); Bob Broeg, "A Batting Title in Store for Ted Simmons?" *BD* 37 (May 1978), pp. 38–40; Jim Brosnan, *The Ted Simmons Story* (New York, 1977); Mac Hoffman, "Ted Simmons—Finally out of the Shadows," *SW* 18 (August 1979), pp. 16, 80; Zander Hollander, ed., *The Complete Handbook of Baseball, 1979, 1984* (New York, 1979, 1984); Robert E. Kelly, *Baseball's Best* (Jefferson, NC, 1988); *1983 Milwaukee Brewers Media Guide*; *TSN Official Baseball Register, 1984*; *WWA*, 42nd ed. (1982–1983), p. 3081; Alexander Wolff, "Playing by Her Own Rules," *SI* 67 (July 6, 1987), pp. 38–39; *Milwaukee Brewers 1989 Official Yearbook*.

Thomas D. Jozwik

SINGLETON, Kenneth Wayne "Ken" (b. June 10, 1947, New York, NY), player and sportscaster, grew up in Mount Vernon, NY and became a New York Giants (NL) fan. An admirer of Willie Mays* and Willie McCovey,* he learned to be a switch-hitter to imitate them in sandlot games. After entering Hofstra University on a baseball and basketball scholarship in 1966, he was drafted by the New York Mets (NL) in 1967 as their first choice and given a $10,000 bonus. Singleton, who threw right-handed, played outfield and first base in the minor leagues at Winter Haven, FL (FSL), Raleigh-Durham, NC (CrL), Visalia, CA (CaL), Jacksonville, FL (IL), and Memphis, TN (TL) from 1967 through 1970, ending that portion of his career at Tidewater, VA (IL).

Singleton was called up to the New York Mets in 1970 and traded in April 1972 to the Montreal Expos (NL). Singleton played outfield for Montreal from 1972 through 1974 and led the Expos in runs, hits, and doubles in 1972. From 1975 to 1984, he performed in the outfield and as DH with the Baltimore Orioles (AL). After leading Baltimore in hitting in 1975 and 1976, he earned a five-year contract, at that time the longest ever given to an Oriole. He won Baltimore's MVP Award in 1975. In 1977, he hit .328 to break the modern Orioles single-season batting average record. The 6-foot 4-inch, 210-pound Singleton always hit with considerable power. Upon entering the NL, he was thought to have the potential to become the strongest HR hitter since Mickey Mantle.* An intelligent hitter with a sharp eye, he consistently compiled one of the highest on-base percentages in the majors. Like most power hitters, however, he struck out frequently.

Singleton's career never prospered to full expectations. He played with noncontending teams in the early 1970s and consequently remained relatively unknown. By the late 1970s, his fielding career declined partly due to arm trouble. Surgical removal of a bone chip in December 1977 helped Singleton, but his speed slowed further. His DH role prolonged his career, making him a valued team member. During 15 major league seasons, he compiled a .282 batting average with 985 runs, 2,029 hits, 317 doubles, 25 triples, 246 HR, and 1,065 RBI. Singleton appeared in the 1979 and 1983 World Series, batting .357 and making 10 hits against the Pittsburgh Pirates in 1979. Singleton and his wife, Colette, have one son, Matthew. Singleton served as sportscaster for the Montreal Expos from 1992 through 1995 and for the New York Yankees (AL) since 1997.

BIBLIOGRAPHY: Ken Singleton file, National Baseball Library, Cooperstown, NY; Ron Fimrite, "Looking for an Argument? Then Name Your MVP," *SI* 51 (September 24, 1979), pp. 20–22ff; Larry Keith, "Beat Feet but Eyes Right," *SI* 47 (July 25, 1977), pp. 38ff; *NYT*, July 25, 1970, March 23, 1971; *Who's Who Among Black Americans* (Northbrook, IL, 1978); Jack Lang and Peter Simon, *The New York Mets* (New York, 1986); Dan Turner, *The Expos Inside Out* (Toronto, Canada, 1983); Ted Patterson, *The Baltimore Orioles* (Dallas, TX, 1995); James H. Bready, *Baseball in Baltimore* (Baltimore, MD, 1998); Ted Patterson, *Day-by-Day in Orioles History* (West Point, NY, 1984).

Charles R. Middleton

SISLER, George Harold "Gorgeous George" (b. March 24, 1893, Manchester, OH; d. March 26, 1973, Richmond Heights, MO), player, manager, coach, and scout, came from a prominent Ohio family and was the son of Cassius Sisler, a coal mine manager, and Mary (Whipple) Sisler. His parents graduated from Hiram College, while an uncle served as mayor of Akron, OH. Sisler graduated from the University of Michigan in 1915 with a bachelor's degree in mechanical engineering. When Branch Rickey* served as the Michigan baseball coach, Sisler became his first outstanding find. As a star pitcher, Sisler reputedly compiled an incredible 50–0 mark for the Wolverines. The 5-foot 10½-inch, 170-pound Sisler possessed excellent coordination and speed and proved a superb athlete. Upon his graduation, several major league clubs wanted him for their parent rosters.

Although sought by the Pittsburgh Pirates (NL), he signed with the St.

Louis Browns (AL) and played under manager Rickey. Like Babe Ruth,* he began as a left-handed pitcher and compiled a 5–6 lifetime record. His decisions included 2–1 and 1–0 wins over Washington Senators standout Walter Johnson* and one loss to the fellow National Baseball Hall of Famer. Sisler, a great left-handed batter, soon was converted to a first baseman. He hit .407 in 1920 and .420 in 1922, the latter equaling Ty Cobb's* highest AL batting percentage. Besides holding the major league record for single-season hits (257 in 1920), he won the AL batting championship in his two .400-plus years. He led the AL in hits (257) in 1920 and (246) in 1922, total bases in 1920, triples (18) in 1921 and 1922, runs scored (134) in 1922, and stolen bases in 1918 (45), 1921 (35), 1922 (51), and 1927 (27). In 1922 he compiled a 41-game hitting streak, exceeded only by Joe DiMaggio* and Pete Rose* in this century. The same year he won the AL MVP Award. Sisler's lifetime .340 batting average over 15 major league seasons ranks him 14th among all hitters. In 2,055 major league games, he made 2,812 hits, 425 doubles, 164 triples, 102 HR, 1,284 runs scored, 1,175 RBI, and 375 stolen bases. In 1939, he was named to the National Baseball Hall of Fame.

The agile, hard-throwing Sisler made a fine first baseman. He led AL first basemen in assists six times, including a one-season record in 1920 (140), and paced the NL once. Sisler ranks third in lifetime assists at his position (1,529). Unfortunately, Sisler missed the entire 1923 season due to a severe sinus infection. Although he hit well thereafter, eye trouble prevented him from achieving his previous greatness. From 1924 through 1927, he served reluctantly as the Browns player–manager and compiled a 218–241 (.475 winning percentage) mark. After very brief service with the Washington Senators (AL) in 1928, Sisler played from May 1928 through 1930 for the Boston Braves (NL) and ended his major league career there. He played one season each in the minor leagues with Rochester, NY (IL) and Shreveport, LA–Tyler, TX (TL), managing briefly in the latter location.

Sisler led an exemplary life, neither drinking nor smoking. Comedian W. C. Fields, a baseball fan, admired Sisler's play. When Sisler refused a drink poured by Fields, the comedian responded, "Even the perfect ball player isn't perfect in everything." Sisler married Kathleen Holznagle in 1916 and had three sons and one daughter. Sons Dick and Dave achieved prominence as major league players, while George, Jr. served as IL president. George, Sr. later served under old mentor Rickey as scout and batting instructor for the Brooklyn Dodgers (NL, 1943, 1946–1950) and Pittsburgh Pirates (NL, 1951–1966), engaged in printing and sporting goods enterprises, and supervised the National Semi-Professional Baseball Tournament.

BIBLIOGRAPHY: George Sisler file, National Baseball Library, Cooperstown, NY; John Benson et al., *Baseball's Top 100* (Wilton, CT, 1997); *DAB*, Supp. 9 (1971–1975), pp. 729–730; Paul Greenwell, "The 1922 Browns-Yankees Pennant Race," *BRJ* 6 (1977), pp. 68–73; Ronald G. Liebman, "George Sisler the Pitcher," *BRJ* 8 (1979), pp. 94–98; *NYT*, March 27, 1973; Lowell Reidenbaugh, *Baseball's Hall of*

Fame-Cooperstown (New York, 1993); Thomas Aylesworth and Benton Minks, *The Encyclopedia of Baseball Managers* (New York, 1990); Bill Borst, ed., *Ables to Zoldak*, vol. 3 (St. Louis, MO, 1990); Bill Borst, *Still Last in the American League* (West Bloomfield, MI, 1992); Roger A. Godin, *The 1922 St. Louis Browns* (Jefferson, NC, 1991); Harold Kaese, *The Boston Braves* (New York, 1948); Al Hirshberg, *Braves, the Pick, and the Shovel* (Boston, MA, 1948); Gary Caruso, *The Braves Encyclopedia* (Philadelphia, PA, 1995); *TSN*, April 14, 1973.

Lowell L. Blaisdell

SKOWRON, William Joseph "Moose," "Bill" (b. December 18, 1930, Chicago, IL), player, was described by former New York Yankees (AL) manager Ralph Houk* as "a quiet, hardworking guy who would do anything for anybody" and "a good all-around player." Skowron, the grandson of Polish immigrants, was nicknamed "Moose" after his paternal grandfather gave him a haircut short enough to remind young Skowron's friends of the bald Italian dictator, Mussolini.

Skowron's father, a sanitation department worker, played semiprofessional baseball. His mother hoped that her son would enter the priesthood. Skowron attended Chicago's Weber High School on a basketball scholarship and Purdue University on a football scholarship, kicking for the Hank Stram (FB)-coached Boilermakers football squad. Under the same celebrated coach, Skowron played shortstop on Purdue's baseball team, set a BTC record by batting .500 one season, and also earned all-American status. Skowron, who signed a professional baseball contract with the New York Yankees in 1951, split that season as a third baseman and outfielder with Binghamton, NY (EL) and Norfolk, VA (PiL). He led the PiL with a .334 batting average. With the Kansas City Blues (AA) the following season, the right-handed Skowron hit .341 and topped the AA with 31 HR and 134 RBI.

After capturing Minor League Player of the Year honors, Skowron in 1954 began a nine-year stint as a first baseman with the New York Yankees. In 1958, he led AL first baseman with a .993 fielding percentage. His .309 batting average in 1960, along with 28 HR and 108 RBI in 1961, marked personal major league highs. Skowron later contended that his "biggest highlight was just putting on a Yankee uniform. Everybody on the team felt the same way. Nobody wanted to get traded."

The New York Yankees traded the 6-foot, 200-pound Skowron to the Los Angeles Dodgers (NL) in November 1962. The trade haunted the Yankees during the 1963 World Series, when Skowron hit .385 to help lead Los Angeles to a four-game sweep over New York. The Los Angeles Dodgers sold Skowron to the Washington Senators (AL) in December 1963. Skowron subsequently played for the Chicago White Sox (AL) from July 1964 to May 1967 and California Angels (AL) in 1967. His .282 lifetime major league batting average included 1,566 hits, 243 doubles, and 211 HR. He hit .293 and clouted 8 HR in World Series games and played in five All-Star contests during an injury-riddled career. Skowron, who married Virginia Lou Holm-quist on June 14, 1952, worked for Crosstown Trucking in Chicago and operated Call Me Moose restaurant and sports bar in East Cicero, IL.

BIBLIOGRAPHY: Bill Skowron file, National Baseball Library, Cooperstown, NY; Dave Anderson et al., *The Yankees* (New York, 1979); Charles Dexter, "Memo to N. L. Pitchers: Watch Out for the Moose!" *BD* 22 (March 1963), pp. 55–60; Mark Gallagher, *50 Years of Yankee All-Stars* (New York, 1984); Peter Golenbock, *Dynasty* (Englewood Cliffs, NJ, 1975); Ralph Houk and Robert W. Creamer, *Season of Glory* (New York, 1988); Tony Kubek and Terry Pluto, *Sixty-one* (New York, 1987); *New York Yankees Yearbook, 1962*; Robert Obojski, *All-Star Baseball Since 1933* (New York, 1980); Robert Obojski, "Ex-Yankee Stars Are Still Teaming Up," *SCD* 25 (May 15, 1998), pp. 38–39; Dom Forker, *Sweet Seasons* (Dallas, TX, 1991); *WWIB, 1962*, 47th ed.; Fluffy Saccucci, "Call Me Moose," *SCD* 23 (December 20, 1996), p. 156; Mark Gallagher, *The Yankee Encyclopedia*, vol. 3 (Champaign, IL, 1997); Robert W. Creamer, *Stengel: His Life and Times* (New York, 1984); Mike Shatzkin, ed., *The Ballplayers* (New York, 1990); Bill Skowron, "Memoirs of a Moose," *PW* 28 (September 14, 1987), pp. 103–104ff; Bill Skowron, interview with Thomas D. Jozwik, June 5, 1987; John Tullius, *I'd Rather Be a Yankee* (New York, 1986).

Thomas D. Jozwik

SLAUGHTER, Enos Bradsher "Country" (b. April 27, 1916, Roxboro, NC), player, manager, and coach, is the son of farmer Zadok Slaughter and Lonnie (Gentry) Slaughter. He graduated from Bethel Hill High School (NC) in 1934, married five times, and had five daughters. After signing with the St. Louis Cardinals (NL) in 1934, he played outfield the next year with Martinsville, VA (BSL). At Columbus, GA (SAL) in 1936, he hit .325 and led the SAL in triples. In 1937 with Columbus, OH (AA), he paced the AA with 245 hits, 147 runs scored, and a .382 batting average.

From 1938 through 1953 (except for 1943–1945, spent in military service), Slaughter played with the St. Louis Cardinals. Besides having an accurate rifle arm from right field, the right-handed throwing Slaughter made many thrilling catches. With the Cardinals, Slaughter, a left-handed hitter, made 2,064 hits and compiled a .305 composite batting average. Slaughter twice led the NL in triples (17 in 1942, 13 in 1949), double plays by an outfielder (1939 and 1940), and assists (18 in 1939, 23 in 1946). He paced the NL once each in fielding percentage (.996 in 1953), hits (188 in 1942), doubles (52 in 1939), and RBI (130 in 1946). After being traded to the New York Yankees (AL) in April 1954, Slaughter batted only .248. He split the 1955 season between the Yankees and the Kansas City Athletics (AL), hitting .315. In August 1956, he returned to the Yankees and helped New York win the AL pennant and the World Series. Against the Brooklyn Dodgers, he made seven hits, scored six runs, and belted a game-winning three-run HR. He split the 1959 season with New York (AL) and the Milwaukee Braves (NL) before leaving the major leagues.

During his 19-year major league career, Slaughter made 2,383 hits, including 413 doubles, 148 triples, and 169 HR, and compiled a .453 slugging and .300 batting average. In 2,380 games, he scored 1,247 runs, knocked in 1,304 runs, and walked 1,018 times. Over five World Series, he hit .291. The 10-time All-Star made two hits, scored two runs, batted in one tally, and made a diving catch in the NL's 5–1 victory in 1953. *TSN* named Slaughter to their 1942 and 1946 Major League All-Star teams. His career highlight came in Game 7 of the 1946 World Series, when he scored the winning run from first base on a double to left center field against the Boston Red Sox. Nicknamed "Country," Slaughter hustled constantly and played back-alley baseball. Manager Eddie Dyer* called Slaughter "a professional who plays like one of those starry-eyed amateurs." In 1985, Slaughter belatedly was selected for the National Baseball Hall of Fame. He served as player–manager in 1960 with Houston, TX (AA) and in 1961 with Raleigh, NC (CrL). From 1971 to 1977, he coached baseball at Duke University. Slaughter raises tobacco on a Roxboro, NC farm and lives in his self-built home.

BIBLIOGRAPHY: Enos Slaughter file, National Baseball Library, Cooperstown, NY; Martin Appel, *Yesterday's Heroes* (New York, 1988); Mark Gallagher, *The Yankee Encyclopedia*, vol. 3 (Champaign, IL, 1993); Peter Golenbock, *Dynasty* (New York, 1975); Bob Broeg and Jerry Vickery, *St. Louis Cardinals Encyclopedia* (Grand Rapids, MI, 1998); Rob Rains, *The St. Louis Cardinals* (New York, 1992); Bob Broeg, *Redbirds: A Century of Cardinals' Baseball* (St. Louis, MO, 1981); Frederick G. Lieb, *The St. Louis Cardinals* (New York, 1945); Jack Drees, *Where Is He Now?* (Middle Village, NY, 1973); Donald Honig, *Baseball Between the Lines* (New York, 1976); Ralph Knight and Bob Broeg, "Country Keynotes the Cards," *SEP* 219 (May 17, 1947), pp. 23ff; Daniel Okrent and Harris Lewine, eds., *The Ultimate Baseball Book* (Boston, MA, 1979); Enos Slaughter and Kevin Reid, *Country Hardball: The Autobiography of Enos Slaughter* (New York, 1991); Rich Westcott, *Diamond Greats* (Westport, CT, 1988).

John E. DiMeglio

SMALLEY, Roy Frederick, III (b. October 25, 1952, Los Angeles, CA), player and sportscaster, is the son of Roy Smalley, Jr., a major league shortstop for 11 seasons, and Jolene Smalley. His uncle, Gene Mauch,* managed for a long time in the major leagues and also played infield there for nine seasons. A graduate of Westchester (CA) High School, Smalley attended Los Angeles CC and studied philosophy at the University of Southern California. His honors included playing in two NCAA College World Series Championships, being twice selected All-PEC and being named on the 1973 NCAA All-America baseball squad. He played for Anchorage, AK in 1972 and Boulder, CO in 1973 and was chosen a National Baseball Congress All-American each season. The U.S. College All-Star member competed in Japan in 1972 and the United States in 1973, earning Series MVP honors in 1973. The 6-foot 1-inch, 182-pound, right-handed shortstop married Christine Sherry on January 14, 1978. They have three children, Jeffrey and identical twins, Catherine and Laura.

The Texas Rangers (AL) chose Smalley number 1 in the January 1974 draft. The Texas Rangers traded him to the Minnesota Twins (AL) in June 1976, when he led the major leagues with 25 sacrifice bunts. A power-hitting infielder, Smalley led all major league shortstops in HR in the 1978 and 1979 seasons. His honors included being the Minnesota Twins' MVP and Most Improved Player in 1978. In 1979 he set a major league record for shortstops with 144 double plays and an AL record with 572 assists, making All-Star shortstop. Smalley was sidelined much of the 1981 season with a lower back problem and was traded to the New York Yankees (AL) in April 1982. The New York Yankees sent him to the Chicago White Sox (AL) in July 1984. Smalley returned to the Minnesota Twins in February 1985. After being sold to the Chicago White Sox in February 1988, he retired. His major league career totals included a .257 batting average, 1,454 hits, 163 HR, and 694 RBI. He lives in Edina, MN, where he was executive director for the 1991 International Special Olympics. He handled color television commentary for the Minnesota Twins in 1995 and for ESPN in 1997.

BIBLIOGRAPHY: Roy Smalley III file, National Baseball Library, Cooperstown, NY; *The Baseball Encyclopedia*, 10th ed. (New York, 1996); Los Angeles (CA) *Times*, May 6, 1975, August 11, 1979, April 10, 1988; *Minnesota Twins Media Guide, 1987*; Dave Mona and Dave Jarzyna, *Twenty-five Seasons* (Minneapolis, MN, 1986); Mark Gallagher, *The Yankee Encyclopedia*, vol. 3 (Champaign, IL, 1997); Omaha (NE) *World Herald*, June 14, 1973; Roy Smalley III, interview with Albert J. Figone, September 29, 1989; *TSN*, April 4, 1981, p. 38.

Albert J. Figone

SMILEY, John Patrick (b. March 17, 1965, Phoenixville, PA), player, is a 6-foot 4-inch, 210-pound, left-handed pitcher who graduated in 1983 from Perkiomen Valley High School in Graterford, PA. Smiley, a tall, thin hurler with fine control, was selected by the Pittsburgh Pirates (NL) in the 12th round of the June 1983 free-agent draft. His first professional baseball assignments came with the Bradenton, FL Pirates (GCL) in 1983 and Macon, GA (SAL) in 1984. Smiley split the 1985 season between Prince William, VA (CrL) and Macon and spent 1986 twirling for Prince William, primarily in relief, earning 14 saves. In four minor league seasons, he posted 15 wins and 29 losses in 107 games.

Smiley joined the Pittsburgh Pirates late in September 1986, appearing in 12 games and gaining his first major league victory. He relieved in 63 contests as a Pittsburgh Pirates rookie in 1987 before joining the starting rotation the following season. Smiley hurled for the Pirates through 1991, compiling a 60–42 record. His best campaign came in 1991, when he triumphed 20 times while losing just eight times for a .714 winning percentage. He led the NL hurlers in winning percentage. Smiley's 20 victories equalled the Atlanta Braves' Tom Glavine* for the NL lead. He appeared in one 1990 NL Championship Series game against the Cincinnati Reds and lost two 1991 NL Championship Series games to the Atlanta Braves.

The Pittsburgh Pirates traded Smiley to the Minnesota Twins (AL) in March 1992 for pitcher Denny Neagle and outfielder Midre Cummings. Smiley led Minnesota Twins pitchers with 241 innings pitched and 163 strikeouts while recording a 16–9 record. After spending one season with the Minnesota Twins, he signed with the Cincinnati Reds (NL) in December 1992.

In his first season with the Cincinnati Reds, Smiley posted a 3–9 record until elbow surgery sidelined him. After having an 11–11 slate in 1994, he stood at 9–1 with a 3.06 ERA at mid-season in 1995. Smiley fared only 3–4 the remainder of the 1995 season with the Reds and hurled one game each in the 1995 NL Division Series against the Los Angeles Dodgers and NL Championship Series against the Atlanta Braves without a decision. He made the NL All-Star team in 1991 and 1995 and hurled one-hit complete game victories against the Montreal Expos in 1988 and the New York Mets in 1991. Smiley was traded to the Cleveland Indians (AL) in July 1997, but missed the 1998 season with an injury. The Indians assigned him to Buffalo, NY (IL) in November 1998.

In 12 major league seasons through 1999, Smiley has compiled a 126–103 won–lost record and a 3.80 ERA. He has appeared in 361 games, completing 28 of 280 starts and pitching 8 shutouts. Smiley has surrendered 1,842 base hits, 888 runs, and 496 walks while striking out 1,284 batters in 1,907.2 innings pitched.

BIBLIOGRAPHY: John Smiley file, National Baseball Library, Cooperstown, NY; Zander Hollander, ed., *The Complete Handbook of Baseball* (New York, 1994); *TSN Official Baseball Register*, 1998.

John L. Evers

SMITH, Alphonse Eugene "Al," "Fuzzy" (b. February 7, 1928, Kirkwood, MO), player, is the son of William Grant Smith, a St. Louis city worker, and Inez (Mere) Smith and the youngest of 12 children. He graduated from Douglas High School in Webster Grove, MO at age 17. Smith, a phenomenal high school football player, scored nine touchdowns in one game and received All-State honors as a single wing tailback. The University of Mississippi scouted him until learning he was of African-American descent. He also excelled as an AAU and Golden Gloves boxing champion.

Smith declined an opportunity to join the Detroit Lions (NFL) football club and entered professional baseball following graduation. Cleveland Buckeyes (NAL) general manager Wilbur Hayes signed him. Smith's mother signed the contract because he was too young. Smith batted .300 with the Cleveland Buckeyes in 1948. The Cleveland Indians (AL) signed him that summer and sent him to Wilkes-Barre, PA (EL).

After batting .316 with Wilkes-Barre in 1948, Smith paced the EL with 17 triples while hitting .311 and scoring 112 runs in 1949. He spent the next two seasons with San Diego, CA (PCL) and joined Indianapolis, IN (AA) in 1952. Smith split the 1953 campaign with Indianapolis and the Cleveland Indians and assumed the Tribe's left field and leadoff duties in 1954.

In 1955 Smith ranked among major league baseball's premier players, as he topped the AL with 123 runs scored, hit .306, won the Cleveland Indians' Man of the Year honors, and finished third in AL MVP voting. He remained with the Cleveland Indians through the 1957 campaign. Smith played for the Chicago White Sox (AL) from 1958 through 1962 and Baltimore Orioles (AL) in 1963, completing his major league career in 1964 with the Boston Red Sox (AL) and Cleveland Indians. Smith's major league career bests included a .315 batting average in 1960 and 28 HR and 93 RBI in 1961. He stroked AL pitching for a .272 batting average, 164 HR, and 676 RBI in 1,517 games over 12 major league seasons. The right-handed, 6-foot, 190 pounder primarily played outfield, but also performed in the infield.

Smith played for three NAL/AL pennant winners. He started at shortstop for the 1947 Cleveland Buckeyes, managed by Quincy Trouppe,* and in left field for the 1954 Cleveland Indians and 1959 Chicago White Sox, both piloted by Al Lopez.* He performed for the AL in the 1955 and 1960 All-Star games.

Smith married Mildred Corbin on February 14, 1956. They have two sons and two daughters. He attended St. Louis University and operated the Chicago Parks Department baseball program from from 1966 through 1981. Smith, an accomplished golfer who shoots in the low eighties, resides in Chicago, IL and was enshrined in the Ohio Baseball Hall of Fame in 1993.

BIBLIOGRAPHY: Al Smith file, National Baseball Library, Cooperstown, NY; Martin Appel, *Yesterday's Heroes* (New York, 1988); Dick Clark and Larry Lester, *The Negro Leagues Book* (Cleveland, OH 1994); Cleveland (OH) *Call & Post*, 1946–1948; Thomas C. Eakin, *Ohio Baseball Hall of Fame Official Publication* (Shaker Heights, OH, 1993); Lee Heiman et al., *When the Cheering Stops* (New York, 1990); Brent P. Kelley, "Al Smith," *SCD* 22 (November 17, 1995), pp. 160–162; Rich Marazzi, "Al Smith was the Consummate Lead Off Man for the Indians and White Sox," *SCD* 23 (September 27, 1996), pp. 96–97; Larry Moffi and Jonathan Kronstadt, *Crossing the Line* (Jefferson, NC, 1994); John Phillips, *Winners* (Cabin John, MD, 1987); Bruce Dudley, *Bittersweet Season* (Annapolis, MD, 1995); Richard Lindberg, *Sox* (New York, 1984); Richard Lindberg, *Who's on Third?* (South Bend, IN, 1983); Al Smith, telephone conversation with Merl F. Kleinknecht, May 1994; Al Smith, letter to Merl F. Kleinknecht, July 1994.

Merl F. Kleinknecht

SMITH, Carl Reginald "Reggie" (b. April 2, 1945, Shreveport, LA), player and coach, grew up in southern California and graduated from Centennial High School, where he starred in baseball and football. A natural right-handed hitter, Smith was converted to switch-hitting by his high school coach. The young shortstop, sought by several major league teams, signed with the Minnesota Twins (AL) in 1963. At Wytheville, VA (ApL) in 1963, he displayed a strong, inaccurate arm at shortstop. Following the 1963 season, he was drafted by the Boston Red Sox (AL) and played third base in 1964 at Reading, PA (EL) and Waterloo, IA (ML). In 1965, Smith became the regular center fielder for Pittsfield, MA (EL). At Toronto, Canada (IL) in 1966, he won the IL batting championship with a .320 average.

Smith joined the AL pennant-winning Boston Red Sox in 1967 and hit .250 in the World Series against the St. Louis Cardinals. He batted over .300 for the Red Sox in 1969, 1970, and 1973 before being traded in October 1973 to the St. Louis Cardinals (NL). After hitting over .300 the next two seasons with St. Louis, he was sent to the Los Angeles Dodgers (NL) in June 1976. In 1977 and 1978, Smith set an NL record for HR (61) by a switch-hitter over two consecutive seasons. His 17 HR on the road in 1977 established an NL mark for a switch-hitter. Smith belted a career-high 32 HR in 1977 and joined Steve Garvey,* Dusty Baker,* and Ron Cey* in making the Dodgers the first major league club in history to have at least four players hitting 30 or more HR. During 1980, Smith batted a career-high .322 for Los Angeles. A severe shoulder injury diminished his playing time in 1979, 1980, and 1981 and limited him to playing first base and pinch-hitting. After hitting only .200 in 1981, Smith was released by the Dodgers. He batted .284 with the San Francisco Giants (NL) in 1982. In December 1982, Smith signed with the Tokyo, Japan Giants (JCL).

In 17 major league seasons, Smith batted over .300 seven times, led the AL in doubles twice (1968, 1971), paced the NL in on base percentage in 1977, and hit .247 in four World Series. His final three World Series came in 1977, 1978, and 1981 against the New York Yankees. The 6 foot, 185 pound outfielder compiled a lifetime .287 batting average, 2,020 hits, and 1,092 RBI. Smith's 314 career HR rank second only to Mickey Mantle* among switch-hitters. In 1,987 major league games, he scored 1,123 runs, hit 363 doubles, and stole 137 bases. A fine defensive outfielder, he possessed one of the best throwing arms in baseball. He coached for the Los Angeles Dodgers from 1994 to 1998. Smith married Ernestine Mary Alexander on September 6, 1964 and has two children, Carl Reginald, Jr., and Nicole La Shann.

BIBLIOGRAPHY: Tommy Lasorda and David Fisher, *The Artful Dodger* (New York, 1985); William F. McNeil, *The Dodgers Encyclopedia* (Champaign, IL, 1997); *Los Angeles Dodgers 1981 Media Guide*; *The Baseball Encyclopedia*, 10th ed. (New York, 1996); Reggie Smith file, National Baseball Library, Cooperstown, NY; *TSN Official Baseball Record Book*, 1998; Harry Xanthakos, "Smith's Bat Keeps Cards in Contention," *BS* (September 1974), pp. 26, 28, 38; Howard Liss, *The Boston Red Sox* (New York, 1982); Ken Coleman and Dan Valenti, *The Impossible Dream Remembered* (Lexington, MA, 1987); Al Hirshberg, *What's the Matter with the Red Sox?* (New York, 1973); Bill

McSweeney, *The Impossible Dream* (New York, 1968); Bob Broeg and Jerry Vickery, *St. Louis Cardinals Encyclopedia* (Grand Rapids, MI, 1998).

Robert J. Brown

SMITH, Charles "Chino" (b. 1903, Greenwood, SC; d. January 16, 1932), player, was ranked by pitcher Satchel Paige* as one of the two greatest Negro League hitters. The compact, scrappy, 5-foot 6-inch, 168-pound Smith excited fans and intimidated pitchers. Nicknamed "Chino" because of a slant across his eyes, he rocketed through the black baseball world like a meteor in his brief, bright career. The left-handed batter and right-handed fielder excelled as a defensive outfielder and gained most notoriety as a hitter. A line drive spray hitter, the keen-eyed Smith rarely struck out. The supremely confident slugger hit virtually all pitches and displayed no major batting weaknesses.

As a young adult, Smith worked summers as a redcap in New York's Pennsylvania Station and played second base on their baseball team. He performed in 1924 with the Philadelphia Giants and the next three seasons with the Brooklyn Royal Giants (ECL), recording .341, .326, and .439 batting averages. After joining the New York Lincoln Giants (ANL) in 1929, Smith the next year hit two HR and one triple in the first game played by blacks in Yankee Stadium. He teamed with John Beckwith,* John Henry Lloyd,* Norman "Turkey" Stearnes,* Clint Thomas,* and Clarence "Fats" Jenkins (IS) on the powerful Lincoln Giants and compiled superior marks batting third in the lineup. In an abbreviated career from 1924 to 1930, Smith batted .423 lifetime in regular season play and exhibitions against major leaguers and .335 in the CUWL. In 1929, he also belted 23 HR and led the ANL in hitting (.464) and HR. Smith enjoyed his best season in 1930 and then died, possibly from yellow fever. Baseball historians wonder what Smith would have accomplished if he had enjoyed a long career.

BIBLIOGRAPHY: John B. Holway, "Charlie 'Chino' Smith," *BRJ* 7 (1978), pp. 63–67; John B. Holway, *Blackball Stars* (Westport, CT, 1988); Robert W. Peterson, *Only the Ball Was White* (Englewood Cliffs, NJ, 1970); James A. Riley, *The All-Time All-Stars of Black Baseball* (Cocoa, FL, 1983); James A. Riley, *The Biographical Encyclopedia of the Negro Baseball Leagues* (New York, 1994); James A. Riley, interviews with former Negro Leagues players, James A. Riley Collection, Canton, GA.

James A. Riley

SMITH, David Stanley, Jr. "Dave" (b. January 21, 1955, Richmond, CA), player and coach, is the son of David Smith, Sr. and graduated from Poway High School. The 6-foot 1-inch, 195-pound right-handed pitcher attended San Diego State University.

The Houston Astros (NL) selected Smith in the eighth round of the 1976 free agent draft. He compiled a 5–5 record for Covington, WV (ApL) in 1976. Smith split the 1977 season between Cocoa, FL (FSL) and Columbus,

GA (SL), finishing 7–5 and 3–5, respectively. In 1978, he returned to Columbus and posted 10 wins and 13 losses. The Houston Astros assigned Smith to Charleston, WV (IL), where he won seven and lost eight in 1979.

The relief pitcher, who debuted with the Houston Astros in April 1980, hurled 11 seasons in Houston, becoming their all-time leader in saves (199) and games pitched (563). The Chicago Cubs (NL) signed Smith to a free agent contract in December 1990. He hurled two seasons in Chicago, retiring with a 53–53 career mark.

Smith appeared in 609 major league games, recording 216 saves, striking out 548 batters, and posting a career 2.67 ERA. He made post-season appearances in the 1980 NL Championship Series and 1986 NL Championship Series and in the 1981 NL Division Series, posting a 1–1 mark. Smith made the 1986 and 1990 NL All-Star squads, hurling two-thirds of an inning in 1990. He served as a pitching coach for Las Vegas, NV (PCL) in 1998 and for the San Diego Padres (NL) since 1999.

BIBLIOGRAPHY: Dave Smith file, National Baseball Library, Cooperstown, NY; *The Baseball Encyclopedia*, 10th ed. (New York, 1996); A. Keteyian, "Flight 45 from Houston Has Arrived," *SI* 64 (June 23, 1986), p. 70; A. Keteyian, "Tossed on the Waves," *SI* 67 (December 14, 1987), p. 36; Peter C. Bjarkman, ed., *Encyclopedia of Major League Baseball Team Histories National League* (Westport, CT, 1991); Mike Shatzkin, ed., *The Ballplayers* (New York, 1990); *TSN Official Baseball Register*, 1993.

John Hillman

SMITH, Edward Mayo (b. January 17, 1915, New London, MO; d. November 24, 1977, Boynton Beach, FL), player, manager, and scout, was the son of Frederick Smith, a farmer and butcher, and Eva (Lake) Smith. Smith, an only child, moved with his parents to Lake Worth, FL, at age 11 and performed as a multi-talented athlete at Lake Worth High School. Upon graduation in 1933, he rejected college scholarship offers to sign with the Toronto, Canada (IL) baseball club for a $500 bonus. Toronto converted him from third base to the outfield, where he developed into a fine fielder. Smith compiled solid, unspectacular minor league statistics between 1933 and 1944 mainly with Toronto and Buffalo, NY (IL) until leading the IL with a .340 batting average in 1944.

In November 1944, the Philadelphia Athletics (AL) drafted Smith. Before reporting to spring training, however, he was stricken with rheumatic fever and was bed-ridden for three months. He played 73 games for the Philadelphia Athletics in 1945, hitting just .212 in his only major league season. The Philadelphia Athletics traded Smith to Portland, OR (PCL) after the 1945 season. Smith played for Jim Turner,* who advised New York Yankees (AL) general manager George Weiss* that the veteran possessed managerial promise. Smith began his managerial career in 1949 as a player–manager with Amsterdam, NY (CAL) and piloted successfully in the New York Yankee organization through 1954, winning pennants with Norfolk, VA (PiL) in 1951–1952.

Smith, a knowledgable, low-key manager, remained comparatively unknown until named Philadelphia Phillies (NL) manager after the 1954 season. After producing one fourth and two fifth place finishes, he was fired in July 1958 because Philadelphia was en route to a last place finish. The Cincinnati Reds (NL) hired him as manager for 1959, but released him in July with the Reds struggling at 35–46. He super scouted for the New York Yankees from 1959 through 1966 until hired to pilot the Detroit Tigers (AL). Smith enjoyed success with the Detroit Tigers, producing two second place finishes and a World Series championship in 1968. The Detroit Tigers rallied from a 3 to 1 deficit to defeat the St. Louis Cardinals. Smith's daring gamble in playing center fielder Mickey Stanley at shortstop throughout the series belied his reputation as a cautious manager. A sub-.500 season in 1970 led to his firing. Smith compiled a 662–612 win–loss mark in nine seasons, winning 52 percent of his games.

Smith married Louise Otto on March 10, 1940. They had two children. He lived leisurely with his wife at their Boynton Beach, FL home after 1970, golfing and fishing. He scouted the Baltimore Orioles for the Oakland A's (AL) prior to the 1971 AL Division playoffs.

BIBLIOGRAPHY: Mayo Smith file, National Baseball Library, Cooperstown, NY; Thomas Aylesworth and Benton Minks, *The Encyclopedia of Baseball Managers* (New York, 1990); Rich Westcott and Frank Bilovsky, *The New Phillies Encyclopedia* (Philadelphia, PA, 1993); Allen Lewis, *The Philadelphia Phillies: A Pictorial History* (Virginia Beach, VA, 1981); Joe Falls, *Detroit Tigers* (New York, 1975); Jerry Green, *Year of the Tiger* (New York, 1969); George Sullivan and David Cataneo, *Detroit Tigers* (New York, 1985); William M. Anderson, *The Detroit Tigers* (South Bend, IN, 1996); Edgar Williams, "Here's Who Is Mayo Smith," *BD* 13 (April 1955), pp. 31–38; Si Burick, "Adversity Molded Mayo Smith as Pilot," *BD* 17 (February 1959), pp. 67–71; Donald Honig, *The Man in the Dugout* (Lincoln, NE, 1995); David Pietrusza, *Baseball's Canadian-American League* (Jefferson, NC, 1990); *NYT*, November 27, 1977; *TSN*, December 10, 1977.

                                                                    Edward J. Tassinari

SMITH, Elmer Ellsworth "Mike" (b. March 23, 1868, Pittsburgh, PA; d. November 3, 1945, Pittsburgh, PA), player, began his professional baseball career in 1886 as a pitcher with Nashville, TN (SL). After Smith played only 10 games there, the Cincinnati Red Stockings (AA) promoted the 5-foot 11-inch, 178-pound southpaw. Smith finished the 1886 campaign with a mediocre 4–4 record. The next season, 19-year-old Smith posted an astounding 34–17 record and completed 49 games. The young fastballer, along with veteran hurler Tony Mullane,* who compiled a 31–17 mark, helped pace the Cincinnati Red Stockings to a strong second-place finish. In 1888, Smith's record fell to 22–17 due largely to a recurring sore shoulder.

Thoughout the next season, the ailment limited Smith to a disappointing 9–12 record.

The Cincinnati Red Stockings, fearing that Smith's pitching career was finished, released him in October 1889. Smith went back to the minor leagues for the 1890 and 1891 seasons and hit a composite .320 as an out-fielder and occasional pitcher for Kansas City, MO (WA). In 1892, Smith returned to the major leagues with the hometown Pittsburgh Pirates (NL). He remained the Pirates' regular left fielder through the 1897 season, aver-aging a .325 batting average and 160 hits per year. His best season came in 1893, when he batted .346 with 179 hits, 121 runs, and 103 RBI. His strong performance, coupled with the hitting of Jake Beckley* and Jake Stenzel,* helped the Pittsburgh Pirates to an impressive 81–48 record and a second-place finish in the 12-team NL. After the 1897 season, the Pittsburgh Pirates traded Smith to the Cincinnati Reds. In 1898, his solid .342 batting average helped Buck Ewing's* Reds finish in third place with a 92–60 mark. Smith was sold in June 1900 to the New York Giants (NL), where he played the rest of the season. He split duty between the Pittsburgh Pirates (NL) and Boston Beaneaters (NL) in 1901. For the next five seasons, Smith bounced around the minor leagues with Kansas City, MO (AA) in 1902, Minneapolis, MN (AA) in 1903, Kansas City, MO (AA) and Ilion, NY (NYSL) in 1904, Scranton, PA (NYSL) in 1905, and Binghamton, NY (NYSL) in 1906.

During his 14-year major league career, Smith compiled a .310 batting average, 663 RBI, and 136 triples among his 1,454 hits. On the mound, he won 75 of 132 decisions for a .568 winning percentage and completed 122 of 136 games started. In 1887, he led all AA hurlers with a 2.94 ERA. He resided his entire life in Pittsburgh and worked in the iron and steel mills. His wife died of tuberculosis in 1889.

BIBLIOGRAPHY: *The Baseball Encyclopedia*, 10th ed. (New York, 1996); Craig Carter, ed., *TSN Daguerreotypes*, 8th ed. (St. Louis, MO, 1990); Elmer Ellsworth Smith file, National Baseball Library, Cooperstown, NY; John Thorn et al., eds., *Total Baseball*, 5th ed. (New York, 1997); Robert L. Tiemann and Mark Rucker, eds., *Nineteenth Century Stars* (Kansas City, MO, 1989); David Nemec, *The Beer and Whisky League* (New York, 1994); Lee Allen, *The Cincinnati Reds* (New York, 1949); Frederick G. Lieb, *The Pittsburgh Pirates* (New York, 1948).

Raymond D. Kush

SMITH, Frank Elmer (b. Frank Elmer Schmidt, October 28, 1879, Pitts-burgh, PA; d. November 3, 1952, Pittsburgh, PA), player and coach, was a powerful, erratic, early 20th-century pitcher for the Chicago White Sox (AL). Smith, the son of German immigrants, attended Grove City College and coached baseball there around 1902. He entered professional baseball with independent Erie, PA in 1901 and Raleigh, NC (NCL) in 1902. At Birmingham, AL (SA) in 1903, he took advantage of his huge shoulder and back muscles to become an iron man. He frequently pitched with only a day of rest, crafting a 31–18 record.

Chicago White Sox owner Charles A. Comiskey* acquired Smith for the 1904 season. Smith toiled for an outstanding pitching staff during the remainder of the decade, joining Ed Walsh,* "Doc" White,* Frank Owen, and Nick Altrock. He finished 16–9 in 1904 and 19–13 in 1905, but struggled to a 5–5 mark in the team's World Championship 1906 season. He did not appear in the World Series, thus missing his only opportunity. Comiskey considered Smith inconsistent on the mound and a malcontent off the field. Smith continually threatened to leave the "Hitless Wonders" for his off-season profession as a piano mover or to become a professional boxer. After being knocked out of the box three times consecutively, the inconsistent hurler threw a no-hit game against the Detroit Tigers on September 6, 1905. He pitched a second no-hitter on September 20, 1908, defeating the Philadelphia Athletics, 1–0, to join Cy Young* and Christy Mathewson* as the only then active pitchers to have two such masterpieces.

Smith's best years came from 1907 to 1909 with 23–10, 16–17, and 25–17 marks. In 1909, he led the AL in appearances (51), complete games (37), innings pitched (365), and strikeouts (117). He started 1910 effectively, but characteristically slumped. Smith was traded to the Boston Red Sox (AL) for Harry Lord in mid-August and pitched ineffectively there. He produced a 10–14 record with a weak Cincinnati Reds (NL) team in 1911, but spent 1912 and 1913 with Montreal, Canada (IL). He finished his major league career with the Baltimore Terrapins (PL) and Brooklyn Tip-Tops (FL) in 1914 and 1915. Overall, he won 139 games and lost 111 decisions with a 2.59 ERA and 1,051 strikeouts in 2,273 innings.

Smith, a lifelong resident of Pittsburgh, was survived by his wife, Rena (Shriner) Smith and their son, Frank "Bud" Smith.

BIBLIOGRAPHY: Warren Brown, *The Chicago White Sox* (New York, 1952); Richard Lindberg, *Sox* (New York, 1984); Richard Lindberg, *Who's on Third?* (South Bend, IN, 1983); *The Baseball Encyclopedia*, 10th ed. (New York, 1996); Pittsburgh *Press*, November 4, 1952, p. 25; *NYT*, November 5, 1952, p. 27; Frank Elmer Smith file, National Baseball Library, Cooperstown, NY.

George W. Hilton

SMITH, Hilton Lee (b. February 27, 1912, Giddings, TX; d. November 18, 1983, Kansas City, MO), player and scout, was the son of school teacher John Smith and Mattie Smith. Smith's amateur career began in 1927, when he played town ball with his father. He attended Prairie View A&M (TX) College for two years and pitched there his final year. After pitching for the semi-pro Austin, TX Senators in 1931, the right-hander hurled for the Monroe, LA Monarchs (NSL) from 1932 to 1935. He married Louise Humphrey in 1934 and had two children, Hilton and DeMorris. In 1935 and 1936, Smith compiled a 5–0 record on semi-pro teams in the National Baseball

Congress tournament in Wichita, KS. During the fall of 1936, he barn-stormed with the Kansas City Monarchs (NAL).

Smith, who threw one of the best curveballs in Negro baseball, joined the Kansas City Monarchs full time in 1937 and pitched a perfect game in his NAL debut against the Chicago American Giants. Reputedly the equal of Satchel Paige,* Smith compiled an unofficial 129–28 ledger from 1937 through 1942 and 161–32 record for the Monarchs in NAL play from 1937 to 1948. A sore arm limited his effectiveness in 1943 and 1944. Counting non-league games, he won at least 20 games every season from 1937 to 1948. An excellent hitter, he played many games in the outfield and occasionally batted fourth. Smith, an intelligent pitcher, enjoyed great success against major league players. He shut out an All-Star team with Bob Feller* and Johnny Mize* in 1937, and in 1946 beat Feller's All-Star team 3–2. The next spring in Caracas, Venezuela, he pitched five scoreless innings against the New York Yankees, missing only Joe DiMaggio.*

In two CUWL seasons (1937–1938 and 1939–1940), Smith won 10 games and lost 5. He pitched six consecutive East-West All-Star games from 1937 to 1942 and triumphed in the 1938 game, striking out 13 batters to tie Satchel Paige for second place on the All-Star list. He won one game in both the 1942 and 1946 Negro World Series. Smith in 1945 recommended Jackie Robinson* to the Monarchs after having played with him in the CUWL. He declined an offer to play in the Brooklyn Dodgers (NL) organization in 1946 and finished his pro career in 1948 with Kansas City. After two semi-pro seasons in Fulda, MN, he taught, coached, and worked for Armco Steel in Kansas City, MO as a foreman until 1978. He served as an associate scout for the Chicago Cubs (NL) at the time of his death. Smith, a superlative Negro League pitcher, played in the generation immediately preceding the entrance of blacks into organized baseball. He joined others establishing the excellence of Negro League baseball and paving the way for integration of the major leagues.

BIBLIOGRAPHY: Terry A. Baxter, correspondence with Jose Figueroda, 1984, Cuban League statistics, Terry A. Baxter Collection, Cedar Rapids, IA; Terry A. Baxter, telephone interview with Monte Irvin, 1984; Terry A. Baxter, telephone interview with John "Buck" O'Neill, 1984; Terry A. Baxter, telephone interview with Mrs. Hilton Smith, 1984; Terry A. Baxter, telephone interview with Quincy Troupe, 1984; Janet Bruce, *The Kansas City Monarchs* (Lawrence, KS, 1985); John Holway, "They Made Me Survive," *TSN* (July 18, 1981); John Holway, *Voices from the Great Black Baseball Leagues* (New York, 1975); "Monarchs' Hilton Smith Dies at 71," Kansas City (MO) *Star*, November 20, 1983; National Baseball Congress, *Official Baseball Annual* (Wichita, KS, 1957); James A. Riley, *The All-Time All-Stars of Black Baseball* (Cocoa, FL, 1983); James A. Riley, *Biographical Encyclopedia of the Negro Baseball Leagues* (New York, 1994); Donn Rogosin, *Invisible Men: Life in Baseball's Negro Leagues* (New York, 1983); Quincy Troupe, *Twenty Years Too Soon* (Los Angeles, CA, 1977).

Terry A. Baxter

SMITH, Lee Arthur, Jr. (b. December 4, 1957, Jamestown, LA), player, is the son of Lee Smith, Sr. and trained in the Chicago Cubs' (NL) farm system at Pompano Beach, FL (FSL) Midland, TX (TL), and Wichita, KS (AA). His minor league record did not achieve excellence until the right-hander switched to relief pitching in 1978. A tall, powerful fastballer, the 6-foot 5-inch, 220-pound Smith broke into the major leagues in 1980 with a 2–0 record in 18 relief appearances for the Chicago Cubs.

Smith used no trick pitches when coming out of the bull pen. He simply reared back and dared the batters to hit his fastball. In eight seasons with the Cubs, Smith struck out 644 batters in 682 innings. He blossomed as a relief pitcher in 1983, when he led the NL with 29 saves and enjoyed a 1.65 ERA. No previous NL reliever posted 30 or more saves in four consecutive seasons. His 1986 season seemed typical, with nine wins and 31 saves in 66 games. Smith did not walk a batter in 40 appearances and shut out the opposition in 45 games, retiring the first batter 70 percent of the time. He compiled a post-season 0–1 record for the Cubs.

In December 1987, Chicago traded Smith to the Boston Red Sox (AL). Although the "closer" and ace of their bull pen, Smith saved fewer games in the next two seasons. He recorded only 25 saves in 64 games in 1989, but struck out 96 batters in 70.2 innings. In May 1990, Boston traded Smith to the St. Louis Cardinals (NL) for Tom Brunansky.* Smith in 1991 set an NL record for saves (47), breaking Bruce Sutter's* 1984 mark of 45. Smith, who compiled a 6–3 record and 2.34 ERA, participated in 63 percent of his club's 84 victories. He was named to the NL All-Star team in 1983, 1987, and 1991 through 1993 and to the AP 1991 Major League All Star team. He led the NL with 43 saves in 1992 and compiled 43 saves for St. Louis in 1993. In August 1993, the New York Yankees (AL) acquired him. The Baltimore Orioles (AL) signed him as a free agent in January 1994. Smith led the AL with 33 saves and made the AL All-Star team. His last productive season came with the California Angels (AL) in 1995 with 37 saves and his final AL All-Star team selection. He split the 1996 campaign between the California Angels and Cincinnati Reds (NL) and spent 1997 with the Montreal Expos (NL). In 1998, Smith pitched in the Kansas City Royals (AL) organization and then retired. In 18 major league seasons, he compiled a 71–92 win–loss record with 478 saves, 1,251 strikeouts in 1,290 innings pitched, and a 3.03 ERA. He holds the major league career record for most saves (478), the NL career record for most saves (347), the Chicago Cubs record for most saves (180), and the St. Louis Cardinals record for most saves (160). He was named *TSN* Co-Fireman of the Year in 1983 and 1992, NL Fireman of the Year in 1991, and AL Fireman of the Year in 1994. Smith married Diane Sanders.

BIBLIOGRAPHY: Lee Smith file, National Baseball Library, Cooperstown, NY; Eddie Gold and Art Ahrens, *The New Era Cubs, 1941–1985* (Chicago, IL, 1985); *1984 Chicago Cubs Media Guide*; *1987 Chicago Cubs Media Guide*; *TSN Official Baseball Reg-*

ister, 1998; W. Ladson, "The Intimidator," *Sport* 83 (June 1992), pp. 48–50; Warren Wilbert and William Hageman, *Chicago Cubs: Seasons at the Summit* (Champaign, IL, 1997); Bob Broeg and Jerry Vickery, *St. Louis Cardinal Encyclopedia* (Grand Rapids, MI, 1998); Rob Rains, *The St. Louis Cardinals* (New York, 1992).

Duane A. Smith

SMITH, Lonnie "Skates" (b. December 22, 1955, Chicago, IL), player, is the son of Willie Smith and Beleven Smith. He graduated from Centennial High School in Compton, CA and played Connie Mack* baseball with Ozzie Smith* in Compton. The Philadelphia Phillies (NL) selected the outfielder as the third overall pick in the June 1974 free agent draft. He batted .286 at Auburn, NY (NYPL) in 1974 and led the WCL with 150 hits, 114 runs, and 56 stolen bases at Spartanburg, SC the next season. From 1976 to 1979, the 5-foot 9-inch, 170-pound right-handed–swinging Smith compiled a .307 batting average at Oklahoma City, OK (AA), with 171 stolen bases and 393 runs scored. He also led AA outfielders four straight years in errors, however. After late season appearances with the Philadelphia Phillies in 1978 and 1979, Smith made the Phillies as an extra outfielder in 1980. In 100 games, he batted .339 with 33 stolen bases and was named *TSN* and *BD* Rookie of the Year. After hitting .324 as a utility player for the 1981 Philadelphia Phillies, Smith was involved in a three-way trade with the Cleveland Indians (AL) and St. Louis Cardinals (NL) in November 1981.

Smith, the catalyst St. Louis Cardinals skipper Whitey Herzog* needed, scored an NL leading 120 runs, stole a career-high 68 bases, and batted .307 as a starter in 1982. He stole five bases in a game against the San Francisco Giants and starred in the Cardinals' World Series Championship over the Milwaukee Brewers, being named the St. Louis BBWAA's 1982 Man of the Year. Smith batted .321 in 1983, but spent a month in drug rehabilitation from cocaine use. When his batting average slipped to .250 the following season, the Cardinals traded him to the Kansas City Royals (AL) for outfielder John Morris in May 1985. He hit .287 for the Kansas City Royals in 1986, but divided the 1987 campaign between Kansas City and Omaha, NE (AA).

The Atlanta Braves (NL) signed Smith as a free agent in 1988 and optioned him to Richmond, VA (IL) for much of the year. With Dale Murphy* as their only established outfielder in 1989, the Atlanta Braves gave the left field job to Smith. Smith responded with career highs of 21 HR and 79 RBI, batting .315, leading the NL with a .420 on base percentage, and making only two errors. He batted .305 in 1990, but an Atlanta outfield of Ron Gant,* Dave Justice,* and Otis Nixon pushed him into a utility role by 1992. Smith appeared with the Pittsburgh Pirates (NL) in 1993 and completed his major league career as a DH for the Baltimore Orioles (AL) in 1993 and 1994.

Smith remains the only player to perform in the League Championship

Series and World Series with four different teams, including the Philadelphia Phillies in 1980, St. Louis Cardinals in 1982, Kansas City Royals in 1985, and Atlanta Braves in 1991 and 1992. In 26 League Championship games, Smith batted .284. He hit .277 in 32 World Series games, playing on World Championship clubs in 1980 when the Philadelphia Phillies defeated the Kansas City Royals, in 1982 when the St. Louis Cardinals downed the Milwaukee Brewers, and in 1985 when the Kansas City Royals triumphed over the Cardinals. The 1985 World Series proved especially sweet for Smith, as he batted .333 against his recent teammates.

Smith sustained a 17-year major league career with his bat, making legendary misplays defensively. His nickname "Skates" came because he seemingly slipped around the outfield as if he were on skates and fielded only .964 lifetime. Some accused him of attention lapses, failure to hustle, and cautious defensive play. Smith's major league career included 1,488 hits, 909 runs, 98 HR, 533 RBI, 370 stolen bases and a .288 batting average in 1,613 games.

He and his wife, Pearl (Jeter) Smith, have a daughter, Jaritza, and a son, Eric, and live in Atlanta, GA.

BIBLIOGRAPHY: Lonnie Smith file, National Baseball Library, Cooperstown, NY; R. Demak, "Some Kind of Comeback," *SI* 71 (August 7, 1989), p. 52; David Falkner, "The Comeback of Lonnie Smith," *NYT Biographical Service* 20 (July 1989), pp. 700–701; John Dewan, ed., *The Scouting Report: 1990* (New York, 1990); John Granville, "Lonnie Smith: He's a Catalyst for the Cardinals," *BD* 41 (September 1982), pp. 75–76; Vince Kerrigan, "Lonnie and Ozzie: The Cardinals' Talented Smiths," *BD* 41 (December 1982), pp. 18–20; Mike Shatzkin, ed., *The Ballplayers* (New York, 1990); Jim Toomey, *St. Louis Cardinals 1984 Media Guide* (St. Louis, MO, 1984); Rich Westcott and Frank Bilovsky, *The New Phillies Encyclopedia* (Philadelphia, PA, 1993); Allen Lewis, *The Philadelphia Phillies: A Pictorial History* (Virginia Beach, VA, 1981); Hal Bodley, *The Team That Wouldn't Die* (Wilmington, DE, 1981); Frank Dolson, *The Philadelphia Story* (South Bend, IN, 1981); Bob Broeg and Jerry Vickery, *St. Louis Cardinals Encyclopedia* (Grand Rapids, MI, 1998); Rob Rains, *The St. Louis Cardinals* (New York, 1992); Gary Caruso, *The Braves Encyclopedia* (Philadelphia, PA, 1995).

Frank J. Olmsted

SMITH, Osborne Earl "Ozzie," "Wizard," "The Oz" (b. December 26, 1954, Mobile, AL), player and sportscaster, grew up in the Watts section of Los Angeles, CA. His father worked as a sandblaster and truckdriver, while his mother was employed as a nurse's aide. Smith, one of six children, played baseball with Eddie Murray* at Locke High School in Watts. He attended California Polytechnic University in San Luis Obispo on an academic scholarship and played shortstop on their baseball team. Smith and his wife, Denise, have two sons, Ozzie, Jr., and Dustin.

Smith debuted in professional baseball with Walla Walla, WA (NWL) in 1977 after being selected by the San Diego Padres (NL) in the free-agent draft. He led the NWL in games played, runs scored, and fielding average at shortstop while batting .303. This success vaulted him to the starting shortstop position with the San Diego Padres the next season. Smith performed well in his rookie campaign, playing exciting defense and batting .258 with 40 stolen bases. In 1979, his glovework grew still better. A disastrous 0 for 32 start at the plate left Smith in a slump from which he never fully recovered, as he finished with a .211 batting average. In 1980, Smith stole 57 bases and set a major league record with 621 assists at shortstop. The previous mark, set by Glenn Wright* in 1924, was believed to be unreachable by most baseball experts. Smith's relationship with Ray Kroc and Joan Kroc, owners of the Padres, was never warm and suffered in yearly contract disputes. In 1981 Smith led the NL shortstops in assists and fielding average, but struggled with a .222 batting average.

Despite Smith's fielding prowess at shortstop, the San Diego Padres began shopping for a better hitting shortstop. The St. Louis Cardinals (NL) hoped to trade shortstop Garry Templeton,* a consistent .300 hitter who had worn out his welcome with manager Whitey Herzog* and Cardinals fans with his temper. The Smith-for-Templeton trade finally was sealed in February 1982. Smith gave the Cardinals the type of defense on Busch Stadium astroturf that St. Louis needed to win. Sportswriters, sportscasters, and players described Smith as "poetry in motion," "a combination of baseball and ballet," and "an acrobat on astroturf." Baseball peers regarded him as the best contemporary defensive shortstop and perhaps the best ever. He played on 12 consecutive NL All-Star teams from 1981 through 1992 and also made the 1994 through 1996 squads and was awarded an unprecedented 12th straight Gold Glove at shortstop in 1991, leading the NL in assists eight times. Defensively, he compiled a career .978 fielding percentage and made only 281 errors in 2,573 games. In 1991 Smith made only eight errors, breaking Larry Bowa's* 1972 mark of nine for 150 or more games. The 5-foot 10-inch, 155-pound switch-hitter developed into a fine hitter with the Cardinals, reaching a career high .303 batting average with 104 runs scored in 1987. Smith, consistently one of the toughest NL batters to strike out, batted .303 in four NL Championship Series and slumped to a combined .173 in the 1982, 1985, and 1987 World Series with St. Louis.

In 19 major league seasons through 1996, Smith batted .262, scored 793 runs, and stole 580 bases. He has announced for the St. Louis Cardinals since 1997 and replaced Mel Allen (OS) as host of the syndicated television show "This Week in Baseball." He was one of the most popular players in St. Louis Cardinals history and remains very active in civic projects.

BIBLIOGRAPHY: *CB* (February 1997), pp. 44–47; J. Coplon, "The Secret on My New Success," *Sport* 78 (November 1987), pp. 50–51ff; Craig Davis, "Ozzie Smith: Baseball's Most Graceful Fielder of Them All," *BD* 42 (July 1983), pp. 80–82; Peter C. Bjarkman, ed., *Encyclopedia of Major League Baseball Team Histories National League* (Westport, CT, 1991); Ozzie Smith file, National Baseball Library, Cooperstown, NY; Robert Grayson, "An *SCD* Interview with the Wizard Ozzie Smith," *SCD* 25

(December 25, 1998); Ron Fimrite, "No. 1 in His Field," *SI* 67 (September 28, 1987), pp. 60–69; Tom Hultman, "Smith Still the Wizard of Oz," *SCD* 24 (July 11, 1997), pp. 130–131; Barry Jacobs, "The Wizardry of Ozzie Smith," *SEP* 255 (May/June 1983), pp. 64–65; Vince Kerrigan, "Lonnie and Ozzie, the Cardinals' Talented Smiths," *BD* 41 (December 1982), pp. 18–20; Rob Rains, *The St. Louis Cardinals* (St. Louis, MO, 1992); David L. Porter, ed., *African-American Sports Greats* (Westport, CT, 1995); Bob Broeg and Jerry Vickery, *St. Louis Cardinals Encyclopedia* (Grand Rapids, MI, 1998); Ozzie Smith with Rob Rains, *Wizard* (Chicago, IL, 1988); *St. Louis Cardinals 1988 Official Scorebook*.

Frank J. Olmsted

SMOLTZ, John Andrew (b. May 15, 1967, Detroit, MI), player, is the son of John Smoltz, an usher at Tiger Stadium and a professional accordion player, and Mary Smoltz. His second cousin, Charlie Gehringer,* made the National Baseball Hall of Fame as a second baseman for the Detroit Tigers (AL). Smoltz, an accordion-playing prodigy, won regional contests before quitting at age seven. He grew up in Lansing, MI and graduated in 1985 from Waverly High School, where he made All-State in baseball and basketball. Smoltz played on the Junior Olympic baseball team and in the National Sports Festival.

The Detroit Tigers (AL) picked the 6-foot 3-inch, 185-pound right-handed pitcher in the 22nd round of the 1985 free agent draft. Smoltz pitched for Lakeland, FL (FSL) in 1986 and Glens Falls, NY (EL) in 1987. In August 1987, the Detroit Tigers traded him to the Atlanta Braves (NL) for pitcher Doyle Alexander.* He finished 1987 with Richmond, VA (IL). A *BA* poll of IL managers named him the top prospect in the IL in 1988, when he won 10 and lost only five with a 2.79 ERA and 115 strikeouts in 135.1 innings for Richmond. After the Atlanta Braves called him up, Smoltz prevailed only two of nine times for the remainder of 1988. He showed signs of great potential in 1989, with 12 wins, 11 losses, and a 2.94 ERA for a weak Atlanta team. The 22 year old became the youngest Atlanta Braves pitcher ever chosen for the All-Star game, but was the losing pitcher.

The Atlanta Braves, sparked by a nucleus of talented young players, became a powerful team over the next several years. Smoltz pitched well but was often overshadowed by fellow pitchers Tom Glavine* and, beginning in 1993, Greg Maddux.* He won 14 and lost 11 in 1990 and compiled a 14–13 record in 1991, as the Atlanta Braves won the NL pennant. Smoltz pitched the clinching game for the Western Division title and won two more decisions, including the deciding contest, of the NL Championship Series against the Pittsburgh Pirates. In Atlanta's losing effort against the Minnesota Twins in the World Series, he surrendered only two runs in 14.1 innings and pitched a shutout through 7.1 innings in the seventh game without a decision.

In 1992, Smoltz won 15 and lost 12, lowered his ERA to a career-best 2.85, and led the NL with 35 starts, as the Braves again captured the NL pennant and lost the World Series. During the 1992 season, he led the NL with 215 strikeouts and tied Warren Spahn's* franchise record with 15 strikeouts in a 9-inning game. Smoltz again triumphed twice in the NL Championship Series against the Pittsburgh Pirates and was named the series MVP, setting a series record for most career strikeouts (46). In the World Series against the Toronto Blue Jays, Smoltz won one game and pitched well. Although Smoltz cemented his reputation as a "big game" pitcher, the Atlanta Braves lost the World Series. He won 15 games and lost 11 in 1993, but the the Philadelphia Phillies defeated the Braves in the NL Championship Series. He was named to the NL All-Star team in both 1992 and 1993.

In the strike-shortened 1994 season, Smoltz struggled to a record of six victories and 10 defeats. An elbow injury rendered his forkball useless. He underwent surgery to remove bone spurs and chips in September and started the 1995 season tentatively. But his arm strengthened as he learned to throw a change-up more effectively. Smoltz finished the 1995 campaign with 12 victories, only seven defeats, a 3.18 ERA, and 193 strikeouts in 192.2 innings. But he did not pitch well against the Colorado Rockies in the NL Division Series or the Cincinnati Reds in the NL Championship Series, and gave up four earned runs in just 2.1 innings in the Braves' World Series victory over the Cleveland Indians.

In 1996, Smoltz pitched more aggressively and with less concern about making every pitch perfect. After losing his first start, he then won his next 11 decisions on his way to 24 victories against only eight defeats. Smoltz recorded 276 strikeouts and only 55 walks in 253.2 innings. When the Braves captured the NL Division Series against the Los Angeles Dodgers, he won a complete-game victory in his only start. Against the St. Louis Cardinals in the NL Championship Series, he allowed only two runs in eight innings in the Game 1 victory, and pitched seven shutout innings to help the Braves win Game 5. The Atlanta Braves lost the World Series to the New York Yankees. Smoltz won Game 1, but lost Game 5 despite giving up no earned runs in eight innings. He in 1996 made the NL All-Star team and won the NL Cy Young Award. In 1997, he compiled a 15–12 record with a 3.02 ERA and 241 strikeouts in 256 innings and struck out 11 batters to clinch the NL Division Series against the Houston Astros. Although fanning nine batters in six innings, Smoltz lost Game 3 of the NL Championship Series against the Florida Marlins. In 1998 his 17–3 mark and 2.90 ERA helped the Atlanta Braves capture another NL East crown and secure their highest victory total in franchise history. He allowed only one run and picked up the victory in Game 1 of the NL Division Series against the Chicago Cubs, but was not involved in any decisions in both starts against the San Diego Padres in the NL Championship Series. He won 11 of 19 decisions with a 3.19 ERA in 1999, as Atlanta repeated as NL East titlists. He finished 1–0 with a 5.14 ERA in the NL Division Series, 1–0 with a 5.74 ERA and one save in the NL Championship Series, and 0–1 with a 3.86 ERA in the World Series. In post-season play, he has won 13 of 17 decisions.

Smoltz, once described as the "Ringo" among the Braves' "Fab Four" starting rotation of Steve Avery, Glavine, and Maddux, now assumes a more prominent role. Bearded and intense, he no longer broods. Smoltz has reached the top of his profession. Through 1999, he has compiled 157 wins and only 113 losses with a 3.35 ERA and 2,098 strikeouts in 2,414.1 innings. He and his wife, Dyan, live in Duluth, GA, and have two children, John, Jr., and Rachel.

BIBLIOGRAPHY: John Smoltz file, National Baseball Library, Cooperstown, NY; Gary Caruso, *The Braves Encyclopedia* (Philadelphia, PA, 1995); Tom Glavine with Nick Cafardo, *None But the Braves* (New York, 1996); P. M. Johnson, "Smoke Signals," *Sport* 87 (November 1996), pp. 74–76; W. Plummer, "Faith Hurler," *PW* 46 (July 15, 1996), pp. 173–174; John Thorn et al., eds., *Total Braves* (New York, 1996); Tom Verducci, "Eye Opener," *SI* 84 (June 10, 1996), pp. 47–49, 55; *TSN Baseball Guide, 1998*; *TSN Baseball Register, 1998*.

Luther W. Spoehr

SNIDER, Edwin Donald "Duke," "Silver Fox" (b. September 19, 1926, Los Angeles, CA), player, scout, manager, and sportscaster, is the son of naval shipyard worker Ward Snider and Florence (Johnson) Snider. The elder Snider, a former semipro player, nicknamed his 6-year-old son "Duke" because he acted like royalty. He also taught his right-handed child to bat left-handed because most baseball parks favored southpaws. Snider starred at Compton High School in football and baseball and signed with the Brooklyn Dodgers (NL) in 1944 for $750. At Newport News, VA (PiL), Snider in 1944 led the PiL in doubles and HR and began a lifetime problem hitting southpaw curveball pitchers.

The petulant 6-foot, 179-pound Snider joined the Brooklyn Dodgers in 1947 following two years in the U.S. Navy, including 11 months on a submarine in the Pacific. After hitting only .241, Snider was farmed out to St. Paul, MN (AA) and hit .316 there. He was recalled by the Dodgers to help in their NL pennant fight. Although ineligible to play against the New York Yankees, he received a $1,000 World Series share. Snider split the 1948 season between the Dodgers and the Montreal, Canada Royals (IL), often swinging at balls out of the strike zone and having problems with left-handed curveball pitchers. With Brooklyn in 1949, he led the NL in strikeouts with 92.

During the 1952 World Series, Snider made ten hits against the New York Yankees and tied the existing record by slugging four HR. He duplicated this feat against the New York Yankees in 1955, leading Brooklyn to its only World Series championship. In 1955, he led the NL for the third consecutive year in runs scored (126) and paced both leagues with 136 RBI. Nicknamed the "Silver Fox" because his hair had turned prematurely gray, he hit at least 40 HR each season from 1953 through 1957. He slugged three HR in single games on May 30, 1950 and June 1, 1955 and set an NL mark (since broken) of 11 World Series HR. *TSN* named Snider the Major League

Player of the Year in 1955 and selected him for its All-Star team in 1950 and 1952–1955. Snider played on the NL All-Star team in 1950, 1952–1956, and 1963, batting .273 composite. In 2,143 career major games, Snider made 2,116 hits, scored 1,259 runs, slugged 358 doubles, 85 triples, and 407 HR, knocked in 1,333 runs, struck out 1,237 times, and batted .295. He was elected to the National Baseball Hall of Fame in 1980.

After ending his active career with the New York Mets (NL) in 1963 and San Francisco Giants (NL) in 1964, Snider scouted for the Los Angeles Dodgers (1965), managed Spokane, WA (PCL) in 1965, and piloted Kennewick, WA (NWL), in 1966. After scouting for the Los Angeles Dodgers in 1967 and 1968 and for the San Diego Padres (NL) in 1969, he managed Alexandria, LA (TL) in 1972. He served as a batting instructor with the Montreal Expos (NL) in 1974–1975 and served as one of their regular announcers for many years. The Fallbrook, CA resident married Beverly Null on October 25, 1947 and has one son and one daughter.

BIBLIOGRAPHY: John Benson et al., *Baseball's Top 100* (Wilton, CT, 1997); Bill Borst, *The Brooklyn Dodgers* (St. Louis, MO, 1982); *CB* (1956), pp. 590–591; Donald Honig, *Mays, Mantle, Snider* (New York, 1987); Duke Snider file, National Baseball Library, Cooperstown, NY; Roger Kahn, *The Boys of Summer* (New York, 1972); Richard Goldstein, *Superstars and Screwballs* (New York, 1991); Roger Kahn, "I Play Baseball For Money, Not Fun," *Collier's* 137 (May 25, 1956), p. 42; Gene Karst and Martin J. Jones, Jr., *Who's Who in Professional Baseball* (New Rochelle, NY, 1973); Tim Cohane, "He Reaches for Greatness," *Look* 19 (June 28, 1955), pp. 107, 590–591; Craig Carter, ed., *TSN Daguerreotypes*, 8th ed. (St. Louis, MO, 1990); *NYT*, March 27, 1953, June 7, 1955; "Duke or Willie? A Vote for Snider," *SI* 2 (June 27, 1955), p. 17; Peter Golenbock, *Dynasty* (New York, 1984); Tommy Holmes, *The Dodgers* (New York, 1975); Rich Marazzi, "1955: 'The Boys of Summer' Have Their October," *SCD* 22 (May 5, 1995), pp. 160–162; Duke Snider with Bill Gilbert, *The Duke of Flatbush* (New York, 1988); William F. McNeil, *The Dodgers Encyclopedia* (Champaign, IL, 1997).

William A. Borst

SOCKALEXIS, Louis M. "Chief" (b. October 24, 1871, Old Town, ME; d. December 24, 1913, Burlington, ME), player and manager, was the son of American Indians Francis P. Sockalexis and Frances (Sockabeson) Sockalexis and grew up at Indian Island, Old Town, ME, the Penobscot tribe reservation. Sockalexis, whose father worked as a guide, excelled in all sports. After playing semipro baseball in Maine and upstate New York, he enrolled at Holy Cross College in Worcester, MA. Michael "Doc" Powers, who had played summer baseball with Sockalexis, knew that the stocky Indian could strengthen the Holy Cross baseball program. Sockalexis, who batted left-handed and threw right-handed, helped the Crusaders become among the best baseball teams in the eastern United States. In February 1897, Sockalexis joined Powers in moving to the University of Notre Dame and quickly became the team's best athlete.

After approximately one month at South Bend, IN, Sockalexis borrowed money from Notre Dame to travel by train to Cleveland and signed professionally with the Cleveland Spiders (NL) baseball team. Sockalexis, the first Native American professional athlete, quickly proved an outstanding hitter and a marvelous fielder with a strong, accurate throwing arm and tremendous crowd appeal. At each city the Spiders played, he was greeted with derisive "war whoops" that turned to cheers because of his adept field play. In 1897, right fielder Sockalexis batted third in the lineup and only twice went without a hit in two consecutive games. His batting average never dropped below .300 after the seventh game of the season and rose to .386 on May 17.

In four consecutive games before July 4, Sockalexis compiled 11 hits in 21 at-bats. On July 4, however, Sockalexis engaged in a night of protracted drinking and could not play for two days. Upon returning to the lineup, he made two hits in each of his next three games. Sockalexis, however, began to stumble in the outfield and made errors attributed to his being intoxicated. In mid-July, Cleveland manager Patsy Tebeau* began assigning players to check on Sockalexis so that he would not get drunk. Sockalexis sneaked out of his second floor hotel room one night and jumped or fell to the ground, severely injuring his ankle. He played one game a few weeks later, was benched for another month, and made two more outfield errors in his final game. During 1897, he batted .338, made 94 hits, and knocked in 42 runs in 66 games. *SL* observed: "Much of the stuff written about his dalliance with grape juice and his trysts with palefaced maidens is purely speculation. . . . Too much popularity has ruined Sockalexis by all accounts. It is no longer a secret that the Cleveland management can no longer control Sockalexis."

The Cleveland Spiders still held out hope for Sockalexis for the 1898 season. Unfortunately, he returned to his old ways and batted only .224 in 21 games. Seven similar games in 1899 finished his major league baseball career. In 94 career games, he batted .313 with 115 hits and 55 RBI. The single Sockalexis drifted to minor league teams in New England, occasionally umpired, and worked as a woodsman near the reservation until dying in 1913 of chronic alcoholism. Two years later, a contest was held to rename the Cleveland baseball team. The Indians, a team nickname when Sockalexis was playing, was selected. His exploits during a short stay with Cleveland still inspired the Indians two decades later. More than 80 years later, the team nickname remains.

BIBLIOGRAPHY: Lew Sockalexis file, National Baseball Library, Cooperstown, NY; Jay Feldman, "Rise and Fall of Louis Sockalexis," *BRJ* 15 (1986), pp. 39–42; Harry Grayson, *They Played the Game* (New York, 1945); John Thorn et al., eds., *Total Indians* (New York, 1996); J. Thomas Hetrick, *The Misfits* (Jefferson, NC, 1991); John Phillips, *The Spiders—Who Was Who* (Cabin John, MD, 1991); Franklin Lewis, *The Cleveland Indians* (New York, 1949); *The Baseball Encyclopedia*, 10th ed. (New

York, 1996); *SL* (April, August, September 1897); Robert L. Tiemann and Mark Rucker, eds., *Nineteenth Century Stars* (Kansas City, MO, 1989).

                                                                   Cappy Gagnon

SODEN, Arthur Henry (b. April 23, 1843, Framingham, MA; d. August 13, 1925, Lake Sunapee, NH), owner and executive, was one of the original owners of the Boston Red Caps (NL) franchise and originated baseball's reserve clause. Soden, the son of Samuel Soden, a book publisher, and Ferona Soden, grew up and was educated in rural Massachusetts, and began playing baseball there. Soden, who served in the Civil War and married Mary Simpson, started his own roofing business in Boston, MA in 1867 and operated the company for 50 years. In 1874, Soden accompanied a Boston baseball team on a tour of England, the first international tour by an American baseball club.

In 1876, Soden purchased shares in the Boston Red Caps baseball club in the newly formed NL and expressed immediate interest in club affairs. Two years later, Soden obtained a controlling interest in the Boston Red Caps and became club president. The Red Caps-Beaneaters lost money for five seasons despite finishing in second place, causing Soden to assume tight control over club finances. He cut players' salaries, made players work the turnstiles before games, booked the team into third-rate hotels to cut travel expenses, charged players' wives full ticket prices, and removed the press box to accommodate more seats for fans. Soden's response to baseball's falling economy typified club owners' views on overpaid and pampered players.

Despite his tight-fisted reign, Soden's Beaneaters excelled on the field, especially in the 1890s. His clubs won eight NL championships, including five in the 1890s, and finished second four times from 1876 to 1900. His teams featured stellar managers Frank Selee* and Harry Wright* and National Baseball Hall of Famers Jimmy Collins,* Hugh Duffy,* and Tom McCarthy.*

Soden's lasting influence on baseball remained his proposal for a "reserve clause." The NL adopted the reserve clause in 1879 to prevent bidding wars for players, allowing NL clubs to keep control of players and preventing other teams from signing them. The NL clubs also agreed not to play games with any teams or leagues violating this rule. Although the reserve clause was ruled illegal in 1974 and paved the way for free agency, players initially viewed the clause as a status symbol. Soden resigned from baseball ownership in 1906, but retained his stock in the Boston club and managed his roofing business until 1917.

BIBLIOGRAPHY: Arthur Soden file, National Baseball Library, Cooperstown, NY; Charles Alexander, *Our Game* (New York, 1991); *CAB* Supp., vol. 11 (New York, 1928); Paul Dickson, *The Dickson Baseball Dictionary* (New York, 1989); Frederick Ivor-Campbell et al., eds., *Baseball's First Stars* (Cleveland, OH, 1996); Harold Kaese, *The Boston Braves* (New York, 1948); Gary Caruso, *The Braves Encyclopedia* (Philadelphia, PA, 1995); *NYT*, August 15, 1925, p. 7; Harold Seymour, *Baseball: The Early Years* (New York, 1960).

Brian L. Laughlin

SOMERS, Charles W. (b. October 13, 1868, Newark, OH; d. June 29, 1934, Put-In-Bay, OH), executive, was one of the AL's founding fathers and the son of businessman Joseph Hook Somers and Philenia M. Somers. He married Mae (Gilbert) Somers and had one daughter, Dorothy (Somers) Clarke. In 1900, at age 31, he and John F. Kilfoyle organized and financed the Cleveland Blues in Ban Johnson's* new AL. Somers' father disapproved of his son's involvement with "such a foolish and unprofitable thing as baseball" and suggested that it would be more worthwhile if Charles devoted his energies to the J. H. Somers Coal Company. Despite his father's protests, young Somers continued his involvement in the fledgling AL by bankrolling the Cleveland franchise and holding financial interests in the Philadelphia Athletics, Boston Pilgrims (president, 1901–1904), and Chicago White Stockings clubs. The shy Somers, who served as AL vice-president from 1901 through 1916, avoided the glare of publicity.

Somers proved instrumental in signing several established NL stars, including Nap Lajoie,* Bill Bernhard, and Elmer Flick,* for his Cleveland Blues. He also helped bring into organized baseball Ernest S. Barnard,* who succeeded Johnson as AL president. In 1913, Somers purchased the New Orleans, LA Pelicans (SA) and again remained in the background. He selected A. J. Heinemann, who had been merely an office clerk, as club president. But Somers possessed a gift for recognizing and developing administrative talent, and Heinemann became an excellent president. Three years later, Somers' fortunes declined. Since his Cleveland club struggled on the field and at the gate, he sold the team in 1916 to James Dunn. Contemporary reports indicate that Somers lost much money in the last few years that he owned the franchise.

Somers still maintained control over the New Orleans Pelicans, although few people knew it, and allowed Heinemann free rein to run the club. When Heinemann died suddenly, Somers assumed a more active role in June 1930. Once again, he delegated much authority and responsibility to new president Larry Gilbert. Somers received less publicity and acclaim than magnates Johnson, Charles Comiskey,* and Clark Griffith,* but his influence, wealth, and business acumen played an equally important part in the development of baseball in the early 20th century.

BIBLIOGRAPHY: Cleveland *Plain Dealer*, June 29, 1934; Franklin Lewis, *The Cleveland Indians* (New York, 1949); Frederick G. Lieb, *The Boston Red Sox* (New York, 1947); Robert Redmount, *The Red Sox Encyclopedia* (Champaign, IL, 1998); George E. Condon, *Cleveland* (Garden City, NY, 1967); J. M. Murphy, "Napoleon Lajoie: Modern Baseball's First Superstar," *TNP* 7 (Spring 1988), pp. 1–79; Charles Somers file, National Baseball Library, Cooperstown, NY; *NYT*, June 30, 1934.

David S. Matz

SOSA, Samuel Peralta "Sammy" (b. Samuel Peralta Montero, November 12, 1968, San Pedro de Macoris, DR), player, is the son of Bautista Montero and Lucretia Montero Sosa and has two brothers and two sisters. His father died when Samuel was only seven years old. He became Sosa when his mother remarried. Sosa grew up in poverty and received very little formal education, selling oranges to help his family. He also learned to play baseball, using a folded-over milk carton as a glove. He and his wife, Sonia, have two daughters, Keysha and Kenia, and two sons, Samuel, Jr. and Michael.

The 6-foot, 200-pound right fielder, who bats and throws right-handed, was signed by Texas Rangers (AL) scout Omar Minaya for $3,500 as a non-drafted free agent in July 1985. Minaya liked Sosa's speed and throwing arm. Sosa spent slightly over three minor league seasons with the Gulf Coast, FL Rangers (GCL) in 1986, Gastonia, NC (SAL) in 1987, Charlotte, FL (FSL) in 1988, and briefly with Oklahoma City, OK (AA) and Vancouver, Canada (PCL) in 1989. In July 1989, the Texas Rangers traded Sosa to the Chicago White Sox (AL) in a five player transaction.

Sosa split his rookie 1989 season between the Texas Rangers and Chicago White Sox, batting .257 with four HR and 13 RBI in 58 games. He struggled offensively the next two seasons with the Chicago White Sox, leading AL outfielders in errors in 1991. His major league career blossomed after the Chicago Cubs (NL) acquired him in March 1992. He clouted 33 HR with 93 RBI and a career-high 36 stolen bases in 1993 and batted .300 with 25 HR and 70 RBI in the strike-shortened 1994 season. In 1995, Sosa belted 36 HR with 119 RBI in 144 games, making the NL All-Star Team, *TSN* All-Star team, and *TSN* Silver Slugger team. He also led NL outfielders in errors.

Sosa showed remarkable power for his size. He batted .273 with 40 HR and 100 RBI in 124 games in 1996, but missed the balance of the season with a broken hand. In 1997, he clouted 36 HR with 119 RBI. His banner season came in 1998, when he helped the Chicago Cubs win the Wild Card and won the NL MVP and *TSN* Player of the Year awards. He demonstrated more patience at the plate, walking a career-high 73 times. Sosa batted .308 with 198 hits, 66 HR, and 158 RBI and made the NL and *TSN* All-Star teams and *TSN* Silver Slugger team. He led the NL in runs scored (152), RBI, and total bases (414) and finished second to Mark McGwire* of the St. Louis Cardinals in HR and slugging percentage (.648). Sosa also paced the NL in strikeouts for the second consecutive season. He clouted 20 HR in June, setting a major league record for most HR in a calendar month. Sosa produced the second most HR for a single season in major league history, finishing just four behind Mark McGwire. His historic HR chase with McGwire captivated a nation and reinvigorated the sport, which had slumped since the 1994 player strike. He gestured to his mother after hitting each HR, blowing a kiss and tapping his heart. Atlanta Braves pitchers limited him to two hits in the 1998 NL Division Series. In 1999, he led the NL in total bases (397), ranked 2nd in HR (63) and 3rd in RBI (141) and slugging percentage (.635), and struck out 171 times. He and McGwire became the only major leaguers to hit at least 60 HR in two consecutive seasons. *TSN* selected him to its NL All-Star (for the third time) and Silver Slugger Teams.

In 11 major league seasons, Sosa has batted .267 with 1,413 hits, 336 HR, 941 RBI, and 224 stolen bases. He twice has clouted at least 30 HR and stolen 30 bases in a season, a feat no other Chicago Cub has accomplished. The popular Sosa, in the fourth year of a $42.5 million, four-year contract, wears uniform number 21 to honor Roberto Clemente.* The San Pedro de Macoris, PR resident gives generously to charities, including hospitals, schools, and hurricane relief.

BIBLIOGRAPHY: *USAT*, August 7, 1998, pp. A–1, 2; George Castle, *Clearing the Vines* (Champaign, IL, 1998); "Sammy Sosa," *A&E Biography*, September 26, 1998; Leif Schreiber, *Race for the Record* (New York, 1998); Gary Smith, "Heaven and Hell," *SI* 89 (December 21, 1998), pp. 54–72; George Vecsey et al., *McGwire and Sosa* (New York, 1998); *Slammin' Sammy Sosa* (Tulsa, OK, 1998); *TSN Baseball Register*, 1999; John Thorn et al., eds., *Total Baseball*, 5th ed. (New York, 1997).

David L. Porter

SOUTHWORTH, William Harrison "Billy" (b. March 9, 1893, Harvard, NE; d. November 15, 1969, Columbus, OH), player and manager, began his professional baseball career with Portsmouth, OH (OSL) in 1912 for $5 a day. The 5-foot 9-inch, 170-pound Southworth, who batted left-handed and threw right-handed, played outfield with Portsmouth into 1913, Toledo, OH (AA) in 1913, Cleveland, OH (AA) in 1914–1915, Portland, OR (PCL) in 1915–1916, and Birmingham, AL (SA) in 1917–1918. After brief trials with the Cleveland Indians (AL) in 1913 and 1915, Southworth performed in the major leagues as an NL outfielder with the Pittsburgh Pirates (1918–1920), Boston Braves (1921–1923), New York Giants (1924–June 1926), and St. Louis Cardinals (June 1926–1929). Southworth hit .300 or better six times and shared the NL lead in triples with 14 in 1919. He enjoyed his greatest playing day on September 24, 1926, when he hit a two-run HR against his former manager, John McGraw,* and the New York Giants to put the Cardinals into first place. The Cardinals won the NL pennant and defeated the formidable New York Yankees in a seven-game World Series. In 13 major league seasons, Southworth compiled a lifetime .297 batting average with 1,296 hits, 173 doubles, 91 triples, 52 HR, 661 runs scored, 561 RBI, and 138 stolen bases in 1,192 games.

After piloting successfully at Rochester, NY (IL) in 1928, Southworth the next year was named St. Louis Cardinals manager. Since the Cardinals faltered, however, Southworth returned as Rochester pilot in July 1929 and managed there through the 1932 season. After serving as a coach with the New York Giants (NL) in 1933, he managed at Asheville, NC (PiL) in 1935–1936, Memphis, TN (SA) from July 1936 through 1938, and Rochester, NY (IL) in 1939–1940. Southworth, who married Mabel Stemen on January 7, 1934, replaced Ray Blades as Cardinal manager in June 1940. He piloted the Cardinals six seasons, winning three consecutive NL pennants (1942–1944) and World Series titles over the 1942 New York Yankees and 1944 St. Louis Browns. In 1943, the Cardinals lost the World Series to the New York Yankees. Southworth, named *TSN* Manager of the Year in 1941 and 1942, signed with the Boston Braves (NL) as manager in 1945 while still under contract to the Cardinals. Cardinals owner Sam Breadon* permitted Southworth to join the Braves only after Eddie Dyer* agreed to manage St. Louis. In 1948 Southworth piloted the Braves to their first NL pennant in 34 years, but Boston lost the World Series to the Cleveland Indians in six games. Southworth, who managed Boston until removed during the 1951 season, compiled 1,044 wins and only 704 losses for a .597 winning percentage (5th) in 13 major league seasons as manager.

BIBLIOGRAPHY: Noel Hynd, *The Giants of the Polo Grounds* (New York, 1988); Billy Southworth file, National Baseball Library, Cooperstown, NY; John P. Carmichael, *My Greatest Day in Baseball* (New York, 1946); Ed Fitzgerald, *The National League* (New York, 1952); Brent P. Kelley, *The Case For: Those Overlooked by the Baseball Hall of Fame* (Jefferson, NC, 1992); Frederick G. Lieb, *The St. Louis Cardinals* (New York, 1945); Bob Broeg, *Redbirds! A Century of Cardinals' Baseball* (St. Louis, MO, 1981); Rob Rains, *The St. Louis Cardinals* (New York, 1992); *NYT*, November 16, 1969; Bob Broeg and Jerry Vickery, *St. Louis Cardinals Encyclopedia* (Grand Rapids, MI, 1998); John Thorn et al., eds., *Total Braves* (New York, 1996); Harold Kaese, *The Boston Braves* (New York, 1948); Al Hirshberg, *Braves, the Pick and the Shovel* (Boston, MA, 1948); Gary Caruso, *The Braves Encyclopedia* (Philadelphia, PA, 1995); Frederick G. Lieb, *The Pittsburgh Pirates* (New York, 1948).

                                                                        Edward J. Walsh

SPAHN, Warren Edward (b. April 23, 1921, Buffalo, NY), player, coach, manager, and scout, attended Park High School in Buffalo and by age 15 played for three teams six days a week. Spahn's life was greatly influenced by his father, Edward Spahn, a wallpaper salesman who taught him the fundamentals of pitching. After signing with the Boston Braves (NL) in 1940, the 6-foot 183-pound Spahn began his professional career as a left-handed pitcher for Bradford, PA (PoL). The next season, Spahn hurled for Evansville, IN (3IL) and led the 3IL in victories. After a short stay with Boston, Spahn was sent to Hartford, CT (EL) to complete the 1942 season. He served in the U.S. Army (1943–1946) and was cited for bravery with the engineers in Germany. Following his discharge, Spahn excelled in his first full major league season in 1947 by winning 21 games, losing 10, and pacing NL pitchers in ERA (2.33).

Spahn pitched for the Boston Braves in 1942 and from 1946 to 1952 and Milwaukee Braves from 1953 through 1964 after the franchise was switched. In 1965, he finished his major league career with the New York Mets (NL) and San Francisco Giants (NL). During his 21-year pitching tenure, Spahn established major league records for most seasons winning 20 or more games by a left-handed pitcher (13), most years leading in games won (8), most consecutive years pacing the NL in complete games (7), most career games won by a left-handed pitcher (363), most career strikeouts by a left-handed pitcher (2,583, since broken), and most consecutive years with at least 100 strikeouts (17). He established NL records, some since broken, for most career shutouts by a left-handed pitcher (63), most career games started (665), most seasons with at least 100 strikeouts (17), most seasons pitching for one team (20), and most career games pitched (750). Spahn also paced NL pitchers in strikeouts (1949–1952), innings pitched (1947, 1949, 1958–1959), ERA (1947, 1953, 1961), and complete games (1949, 1951, 1957–1963), and led or tied for the league lead in shutouts (1947, 1959, 1961).

Spahn pitched no-hit victories against the Philadelphia Phillies in September 1960 and San Francisco Giants in April 1961. At age 42, he posted a 23–7 record for his final big season. The good-hitting Spahn clouted 35 lifetime HR, an NL record for pitchers. Named by *TSN* as outstanding NL pitcher (1953, 1957–1958, 1961) and Major League Pitcher of the Year (1961), Spahn won the Cy Young Award as the best major league pitcher (1957). Combining with Johnny Sain* and Lew Burdette,* Spahn helped lead the Braves to three NL pennants (1948, 1957–1958) and one world championship (1957). In eight World Series games, Spahn won four and lost three. He pitched in seven All-Star games and was the NL's winning pitcher in the 1953 classic.

Elected to the National Baseball Hall of Fame in 1973, Spahn ranks near the top of the all-time major league lists for pitchers in nearly every category. Spahn compiled 363 victories (5th) and 245 losses (11th), started 665 games (11th), pitched in 750 games (28th), and completed 382 games (19th). He pitched 5,243.2 innings (8th), allowed 4,830 hits (7th), and 2,016 runs (16th), issued 1,434 bases on balls (12th), struck out 2,583 batters (16th), recorded 20 or more victories 13 times (3rd), and compiled a career 3.09 ERA.

After hurling a few games in Mexico City, Mexico, Spahn managed at Tulsa, OK (PCL) from 1967 to 1970. His Tulsa Oilers captured a PCL championship (1968) and finished second (1969–1970) when the franchise was switched to the AA. In 1971, he scouted and handled minor league pitching instruction for the St. Louis Cardinals (NL). He served as pitching coach for the Cleveland Indians (AL) in 1972 and 1973 and a minor league pitching instructor for the California Angels (AL) from 1978 to the early 1980s. Spahn operates a 2,800 acre cattle ranch near Hartshorne, OK and does promotional work for the Borden Company. He married Lorene Southard in August 1946 and has one son, Gregory. The craftiest pitcher of his day, Spahn overcame knee surgery three times to return to the mound. A master of control, he consistently placed pitches and continually kept batters off stride. Besides having an excellent fastball, curve, and change of pace, Spahn developed the screwball and slider. He made Major League Baseball's All-Century Team.

BIBLIOGRAPHY: Tom Meany, *Milwaukee's Miracle Braves* (New York, 1957); Bob Buege, *The Milwaukee Braves: A Baseball Eulogy* (Milwaukee, WI, 1988), Gary Caruso,

The Braves Encyclopedia (Philadelphia, PA, 1995); Al Hirshberg, *Braves, the Pick and the Shovel* (Boston, MA, 1948); Harold Kaese, *The Boston Braves* (New York, 1948); John Thorn et al., eds., *Total Braves* (New York, 1996); Warren Spahn file, National Baseball Library, Cooperstown, NY; John Benson et al., *Baseball's Top 100* (Wilton, CT, 1997); Bob Broeg, *Super Stars of Baseball* (St. Louis, MO, 1971); Robert Obojski, "Warren Spahn, Winningest Lefty of Them All," *SCD* 22 (December 15, 1995), p. 80; *TSN Official Baseball Record Book, 1998*; *TSN Official Baseball Register, 1973*; Dixie Toupangeau, "Spahn, Sain, and the '48 Braves," *TNP* 17 (1998), pp. 17–20.

John L. Evers

SPALDING, Albert Goodwill "Al" (b. September 2, 1850, Byron, IL; d. September 9, 1915, San Diego, CA), player, manager, owner, and manufacturer, was the son of James Spalding and Harriet Spalding, attended Byron, IL and Rockford, IL public schools, and completed his formal education at the Rockford Commercial College. His father owned substantial property and trained horses. He married Josie Keith of Boston in 1875 and had one son. After her death in 1899, he married Mrs. Elizabeth Meyer Churchill in 1901. During baseball's first half century, no other individual so dominated the sport as player, owner, and business entrepreneur. A product of the Illinois prairies, Spalding pitched well for the Forest City Club of Rockford in the 1860s and then joined the Boston Red Stockings (NA) in 1871, leading them to four consecutive NA championships from 1872 to 1875. From 1871 to 1875, he compiled an amazing 204–53 won–lost record (.794 winning percentage) and became baseball's first 200-game winner. Spalding twice won over 50 decisions in a season, with 52–16 and 54–5 marks in 1874 and 1875, respectively. Spalding also compiled 38–8 and 41–14 won–lost records in 1872 and 1873. An excellent batter, he made 455 hits in 284 games and hit .323 from 1871 to 1875.

"The champion pitcher of the world" surprised the baseball community by jumping in 1876 to the Chicago White Stockings (NL). During that season, the right-hander won 47 of 59 decisions for a 1.75 ERA, batted .312, and managed his club to the championship. He hurled shutouts in his first two appearances and threw eight for the season. This represented the last hurrah for the crafty 6-foot 1-inch, 170-pound "gentlemanly and effective pitcher," who played rarely thereafter and retired following the 1878 season. In the NL, he won 48, lost 12 (.800 winning percentage), boasted a 1.78 ERA, and completed 53 of 61 starts. He played mainly first base and some second base in 1877 and batted .256. From 1876 to 1878, he appeared in 127 games, made 158 hits, 21 doubles, and 8 triples, scored 83 runs, and knocked in 79 runs.

Spalding already had charted another career. The Chicago *Tribune* announced his opening in February 1876 of a "large emporium in Chicago, where he will sell all kinds of baseball goods and turn his place into the headquarters for the Western Ball Clubs." His company, eventually named

A. G. Spalding & Brothers, emerged as the generation's dominant sporting goods firm. The NL gave Spalding exclusive authority to supply its official baseballs and to publish *Spalding's Official Base Ball Guide*. Spalding proved a skilled businessman, capitalizing on his fame as a ballplayer to promote his company. His favorite motto, "Everything is possible to him who dares," guided his company's growth. With a fierce drive to succeed, Spalding became a captain of industry and developed as tight a monopoly as Andrew Carnegie and other business leaders. With superior organization, imagination, and ruthlessness, he virtually eliminated competition.

While developing and expanding his business, Spalding served from 1882 to 1891 as president of the Chicago White Stockings (NL, eventually renamed the Cubs). A hard worker, he sought to improve baseball's image around ballparks by reducing rowdiness and eliminating gamblers' influence. He even hired detectives to check up on his players, creating a Chicago press and public upheaval in the 1880s. When the PL was formed in 1890, Spalding led the fight against it and probably saved the NL from extinction by helping crush the rival league. A skillful diplomat and first-rate organizer, Spalding promoted baseball's interests nationally and internationally and simultaneously furthered his own sporting goods enterprises. He in 1874 arranged a tour of England and Ireland for two baseball teams and in 1888–1889 led the first world baseball tour. His Chicago team and a squad of "All Star" players performed at such widely separated stops as Australia, Egypt, Italy, and England. Although it did not succeed financially, the latter tour publicized baseball and Spalding's company abroad.

By 1900, Spalding was acknowledged as the "Father of Baseball" and of the NL. Spalding's classic baseball history, *America's National Game* (1911), further enhanced his reputation and provided the best comprehensive early examination of the sport. His compulsion to prove that baseball's origins were American led him to advance the myth that Abner Doubleday founded the sport at Cooperstown, NY in 1839. Since Spalding recorded games played before 1839 in his book, he personally may not have believed the myth.

An all-around sportsman, Spalding was selected American commissioner for the 1900 Olympic games in Paris, France and later received the rosette of the Legion of Honor from France for his work. Upon his death, the *NYT* praised his versatile ability as a player, positive genius as a manager, exceptional executive ability, and personal magnetism. These qualities held organized baseball together throughout its "earlier tribulations." In 1939, he was elected to the National Baseball Hall of Fame. Spalding's plaque acclaimed him as the "organizational genius of baseball's pioneer days" and a star pitcher.

BIBLIOGRAPHY: Arthur Bartlett, *Baseball and Mr. Spalding* (New York, 1951); *Baseball Player*, 1869–1877; Brad Herzog, *The Sports 100* (New York, 1995); Noel Hynd, *The Giants of the Polo Grounds* (New York, 1988); Frederick Ivor-Campbell et al., eds.,

Baseball's First Stars (Cleveland, OH, 1996); Eddie Gold and Art Ahrens, *The Golden Era Cubs, 1876–1940* (Chicago, IL, 1985); Peter Levine, *A. G. Spalding and the Rise of Baseball* (New York, 1985); Daniel Pearson, *Baseball in 1889* (Bowling Green, OH, 1993); Warren Brown, *The Chicago Cubs* (New York, 1946); Jim Enright, *Chicago Cubs* (New York, 1975); Harold Seymour, *Baseball: The Early Years* (New York, 1960); Robert Smith, *Pioneers of Baseball* (Boston, MA, 1978); Albert G. Spalding, *America's National Game* (New York, 1911); Albert G. Spalding Collection, New York Public Library; Albert Spalding file, National Baseball Library, Cooperstown, NY; David Quentin Voigt, *American Baseball*, vol. 1 (Norman, OK, 1966); Warren Wilbert and William Hageman, *Chicago Cubs: Seasons at the Summit* (Champaign, IL, 1997).

Duane A. Smith

SPEAKER, Tristram E. "Tris," "The Gray Eagle," "Spoke" (b. April 4, 1888, Hubbard, TX; d. December 8, 1958, Lake Whitney, TX), player, manager, executive, and sportscaster, was the son of merchant Archie Speaker and homemaker Nancy Jane (Peer) Speaker and married Mary Frances Cudahy on January 15, 1925. Speaker, who exhibited dedication, desire for athletic perfection, and self-confidence, steadfastly recognized his potential before others became believers and was outspoken when exposed to criticism. Nick-named "The Gray Eagle," he worked as a telegraph linesman and cow puncher as a youth and excelled as an all-around athlete in high school. In 1906, 18-year-old Speaker began his professional baseball career as a pitcher–right fielder for Cleburne, TX (NTL) and batted .268. In 1907 this franchise was transferred to Houston (TL), where he raised his batting average to .314. After the Boston Red Sox (AL) bought his contract in August 1907 for $750, Speaker hit just .158 in seven games. Boston did not send Speaker a 1908 contract, but he paid his own expenses to their Little Rock, AR training camp. Boston left him with the Little Rock club in lieu of ground rent payment with $500 purchase rights to him. After leading the SA in batting that year with .350, Speaker rejoined Boston (AL) and hit .224 in 31 games.

With the Red Sox from 1909 to 1915, Speaker became an AL star. The winner of the Chalmers Award in 1912, he helped the Red Sox capture world championships in 1912 and 1915 and made 197 assists from 1909 to 1915 as center fielder in the superb "Duffy" Lewis*–Speaker–Harry Hooper* trio. During the winter of 1915–1916, Boston owner Joe Lannin proposed cutting Speaker's salary from $11,000 to $9,000. The furious Speaker held out and was traded in April 1916 to the Cleveland Indians (AL) for two players and $50,000. With Cleveland for 11 seasons, he batted .354 and frequently led the Indians in offensive categories. He paced the AL six times in doubles, including four consecutive from 1920 to 1923, with Cleveland. As Cleveland manager, he compiled a 617–520 won–lost mark (.543 winning percentage) from 1919 through 1926. In 1920 he led Cleveland to its first AL pennant and world championship, defeating the Brooklyn Robins (NL), five games to two. Following a delayed scandal over a questionable 1919 AL game, AL president Ban Johnson* in late 1926 persuaded managers Speaker and Ty Cobb* of the Detroit Tigers to resign. Speaker ended his major league career with one season each for the Washington Senators (AL) and Philadelphia Athletics (AL). After spending 1929 and early 1930 as manager–player of Newark, NJ (IL), he served as a broadcaster and briefly as part-owner and manager of Kansas City, MO (AA).

A major leaguer for 22 years, Speaker still leads the majors in career doubles (792), outfield assists (449), and double plays (139) and paces the AL in outfield putouts (6,788). The eight-time AL leader in doubles ranks fifth in major league hits (3,514), fifth in batting average (.345), sixth in triples (222), eighth in runs scored (1,882), and ninth in both total bases and extra-base hits (1,133). Of his 3,514 career hits, 68 percent were singles, 23 percent doubles, 6 percent triples, and 3 percent (117) HR. Speaker knocked in 1,529 runs, walked 1,381 times, struck out only 220 times, and stole 432 bases. In 1937, he was elected to the National Baseball Hall of Fame. Speaker, whose plaque correctly cites him as "the greatest centerfielder of his day," made an outstanding impact on the development of his position, batting, and base running skills. Defensively, he quickly determined the eventual direction and distance of fly balls when a hitter's bat made contact with the ball. His great speed and accurate estimates frequently enabled him to get a jump on the ball. He deliberately played shallow, helping him set a major league outfield record for double plays. An extremely versatile batter, he used aggressiveness, speed, and deception on the base paths.

BIBLIOGRAPHY: Tris Speaker file, National Baseball Library, Cooperstown, NY; Mark Alvarez, "Say It Ain't So, Ty: The Cobb-Speaker Scandal," *TNP* 14 (1994), pp. 21–28; John Benson et al., *Baseball's Top 100* (Wilton, CT, 1997); *Boston Red Sox Media Guide, 1984*; Ellery H. Clark, Jr., *Boston Red Sox: 75th Anniversary History* (Hicksville, NY, 1975); Ellery H. Clark, Jr., Red Sox Analytical Letter Collection, correspondence with Harry Hooper, "Duffy" Lewis, Ellery H. Clark, Jr., Collection, Annapolis, MD; Ellery H. Clark, Jr., *Red Sox Fever* (Hicksville, NY, 1979); Ellery H. Clark, Jr., *Red Sox Forever* (Hicksville, NY, 1977); Ellery H. Clark, Jr., interviews, Everett Scott, September 1924; Tris Speaker, June 1926, June 1927; Bill Carrigan, May 1928; Marty McHale, May 1950; Ray Collins, July 1950; "Duffy" Lewis, June 1973, August 1974; Marty McHale, "A Closeup of Tris Speaker," Ellery Clark Collection, Annapolis, MD; A. W. Laird, *Ranking Baseball's Elite* (Jefferson, NC, 1990); Frederick G. Lieb, *The Boston Red Sox* (New York, 1947); Howard Liss, *The Boston Red Sox* (New York, 1982); Dan Shaughnessy, *The Curse of the Bambino* (New York, 1990); Robert Redmount, *The Red Sox Encyclopedia* (Champaign, IL, 1998); Thomas Aylesworth and Benton Minks, *The Encyclopedia of Baseball Managers* (New York, 1990); Franklin Lewis, *The Cleveland Indians* (New York, 1949); John Thorn et al., eds., *Total Indians* (New York, 1996); *The Baseball Encyclopedia*, 10th ed. (New York, 1996).

Ellery H. Clark, Jr.

SPEIER, Chris Edward (b. June 28, 1950, Alameda, CA), player, coach, and manager, starred in interscholastic basketball and baseball. At the University of California–Santa Barbara, Speier's baseball teammates voted him Most Inspirational Player. The San Francisco Giants (NL) drafted him in 1969. After spending only one season in the minor leagues, the 20-year-old short-stop joined the San Francisco Giants in 1971. He and his wife, Aletha, were married in October 1972 and have four children, Justin, Erika, Luke, and Travis. Justin pitched briefly for the Chicago Cubs (NL) and Atlanta Braves.

The 6-foot 1-inch, 175-pound Speier enjoyed a solid 1971 campaign, helping the San Francisco Giants reach their first NL Championship Series against the Pittsburgh Pirates and making the Topps All-Star Rookie team. During his first five seasons, the fiery shortstop averaged 11 HR, 62 RBI, and .254 at the plate. He made the NL All-Star team from 1972 through 1974 and led NL shortstops in fielding in 1975. The San Francisco Giants dealt Speier to the Montreal Expos (NL) in April 1977 after his sub-par 1976 campaign and contract dispute. Speier started at shortstop for the Montreal Expos from 1977 to 1982 and was one of only a few Expos to live the entire year in Quebec. His daughter, Erika, sang the Canadian national anthem in French before one home game.

Speier rode the bench during 1983 and 1984, dividing the latter campaign between the Montreal Expos, St. Louis Cardinals (NL), and Minnesota Twins (AL). In 1985, his career revived with the Chicago Cubs (NL) as a valuable utility player. He rejoined the San Francisco Giants in December 1986 and belted 11 HR, his best since 1973. His last two seasons were injury plagued, keeping him out of the 1989 World Series against the Oakland A's.

Speier retired following the 1989 campaign after playing 2,260 major league games, ranking him among the top 100 of all-time. A true genera-tional bridge, he teamed with both Willie Mays* and Will Clark.* The solid, if not unspectacular, offensive player lasted nearly two decades in the major leagues because of his defensive skills. During 19 major league seasons, he batted .246 with 1,759 hits, 112 HR, and 720 RBI. He served as a minor league instructor for the San Francisco Giants and the Chicago Cubs and in 1999 managed Tucson, AZ. In November, the Milwaukee Brewers named him third base coach.

BIBLIOGRAPHY: Eddie Gold and Art Ahrens, *The New Era Cubs, 1941–1985* (Chi-cago, IL, 1985); "Chris Speier," *Microsoft Complete Baseball*, CD-ROM (Redmond, WA, 1994); Chris Speier file, National Baseball Library, Cooperstown, NY; Dan Turner, *The Expos Inside Out* (Toronto, Canada, 1983); Larry Powell, "Former All-Star Chris Speier Understands the Cyclical Nature of the Game . . . and of Life," *SCD* 22 (October 27, 1995), p. 156; Nick Peters, *Giants Almanac* (Berkeley, CA, 1988); "They're Neither Too Old Nor Too Young," *SI* 30 (April 1973), pp. 26, 31.

Chad Israelson

SPENCE, Stanley Orvil "Stan" (b. March 20, 1915, South Portsmouth, KY; d. January 9, 1983, Kinston, NC), player, was a 5-foot 10½-inch 180 pounder who played baseball for the CKAL. Boston Red Sox (AL) scout Fred Hunter walked onto the field during a game delay to persuade Spence to sign professionally. Hunter brought the contract to the garage where

Spence worked and saw him lifting the front end of a car so blocks could be set. Hunter declared, "He was as strong as a bull." Spence, however, spent the 1940–1941 seasons on the Boston Red Sox bench because Ted Williams,* Dom DiMaggio,* and Lou Finney held the outfield jobs. "I'm as good a center-fielder," Spence insisted, "as Dom DiMaggio." In December 1941, the Boston Red Sox traded Spence to the Washington Senators (AL). Bucky Harris,* Senators' manager, said, "He always looks like a .300 hitter to me, whatever his average."

Spence performed better in Washington than at Boston. He enjoyed his best major league season in 1942, hitting .323 in 149 games and leading the AL with 15 triples. His defensive ability, however, drew more notice, as the left-handed-throwing Spence owned "the most feared arm in the league." Spence made the 1942, 1944, 1946, and 1947 AL All-Star teams, playing in the last three. In 1944, he batted .316 with a career-high 100 RBI. The high, hard pitch did not intimidate him at bat. "Those battles at the plate," Spence remarked, "are a lot of fun." Spence made life miserable for the St. Louis Browns especially. In a seven-game series with St. Louis from August 22 through 25, 1943, he made 14 hits in 27 at-bats with six HR. On June 1, 1944, Spence produced hits in all six at-bats. He ended with 11 hits in 21 at-bats for the entire series at Sportsman's Park in St. Louis, where "I just feel at home." He spent 1945 with the U.S. Navy.

Upon returning to the Washington Senators, Spence hit .292 in 152 games in 1946 and then fell to .279 in 1947. The Washington Senators returned him to the Boston Red Sox for a disappointing 1948 season. He batted just .235 in 1948 and then was traded in May 1949 to his "favorite" team, the St. Louis Browns. Spence's final major league season in 1949 resulted in a .240 batting average. The St. Louis Browns sent him to the minor leagues, selling him to Los Angeles, CA (PCL). Spence protested the deal, calling it "raw" because it deprived him of a 10th major league season and a lifetime pension. In nine major league seasons, he batted .282 with 95 HR and 575 RBI.

Spence married Mildred Virginia Harper on October 15, 1938. In retirement, he owned and operated the Southern Equipment Company in Kinston, NC. During the final game of the 1949 season, this writer witnessed Spence's last major league at-bat, ironically in Sportsman's Park. Spence lined a pinch single on the first pitch, a solid hit from a solid performer.

BIBLIOGRAPHY: Stanley Spence file, National Baseball Library, Cooperstown, NY; Frederick G. Lieb, *The Boston Red Sox* (New York, 1947); Robert Redmount, *The Red Sox Encyclopedia* (Champaign, IL, 1998); Morris Bealle, *The Washington Senators* (Washington, DC, 1947); Shirley Povich, *The Washington Senators* (New York, 1954); Bill Borst, ed., *Ables to Zoldak*, vol. 3 (St. Louis, MO, 1990); *The Baseball Encyclopedia*, 10th ed. (New York, 1996); Tommy Fitzgerald, "Signed between Putouts," *BD* 6 (August 1947); "Hats Off," *TSN*, September 2, 1943; Frank O'Brien, "Spence on Sit-Down over Sale to Angels," *TSN*, February 15, 1950; John B. Old, "Spence Misses a Game on Phony Phone Call," *TSN*, May 10, 1950; Frank "Buck" O'Neill,

"Hitting 'Em Where They Can't Get 'Em, Spence's Explanation for St. Louis Streak," *TSN*, June 8, 1944; Shirley Povich, "The Spence Is Terrific," *BD* 3 (October 1944); Shirley Povich, "This Morning," Washington (DC) *Post*, August 23, 1944; John Thorn et al. eds., *Total Baseball*, 5th ed. (New York, 1997).

William J. Miller

SPLITTORFF, Paul William, Jr. "Splitt" (b. October 8, 1946, Evansville, IN), player and sportscaster, is the son of Paul Splittorff, Sr. He participated in basketball and baseball at Arlington Heights (IL) High School and Morningside College in Sioux City, IA, where he received a Bachelor of Science degree in business administration. In 1967, Splittorff pitched for the victorious U.S. baseball team in the Pan American games. The Kansas City Royals (AL) selected him in the 22nd round of the June 1968 free agent draft. Splittorff hurled for Corning, NY (NYPL) that year. In 1969 and 1970, the 6-foot 3-inch, 210-pound left-hander pitched for the Omaha, NE Royals (AA). In September 1970, he became the first player originally signed by Kansas City to make it to the Royals major league roster.

Splittorff began 1971 at Omaha, but rejoined the Kansas City Royals in May. He lost nine of 17 decisions, but led Kansas City Royals' starters with a 2.69 ERA. Splittorff recorded 12 wins and 12 losses in 1972 and in 1973 became the first pitcher in Royals' history to register 20 victories. He relied on knowledge of opposing batters and excellent control rather than overpowering pitches. His fortunes reversed in 1974, when he finished 13–19 with a 4.10 ERA. Skipper Whitey Herzog* moved the bespectacled southpaw to the bullpen for a time in 1975. Besides improving his ERA substantially, Splittorff won nine, lost 10, and gained his only career save. On August 3, 1975, he hurled the finest game of his career with a 5–0 one-hitter against the Oakland A's, and retired 26 consecutive batters. Splittorff also fashioned 25 and 24 scoreless inning streaks. In 1976, he ended 11–8 and pitched twice in the AL Championship Series against the New York Yankees, winning his only decision and producing a 1.93 ERA.

Splittorff led the AL with a .727 winning percentage in 1977, when he triumphed 16 of 22 times. He tossed a one-hitter against the Milwaukee Brewers, helping the Royals record a franchise best 102 victories. He added another win in the AL Championship Series, which Kansas City again lost to the New York Yankees. In 1978, Splittorff won 19 games and attained a career high 38 starts, 262 innings, and 13 complete games. He started once in the 1978 AL Championship Series, captured by the New York Yankees for the third straight year. Splittorff led Kansas City Royals hurlers in games started (35), innings (240), wins (15), and losses (17) in 1979. He recorded 14 victories the next season and pitched in the 1980 AL Championship Series. The Kansas City Royals swept the New York Yankees. Splittorff relieved once in the 1980 World Series, won by the Philadelphia Phillies in six games. He struggled around the .500 mark in 1981 and 1982 with ERAs above 4.00, but won 13 of 21 decisions in 1983. The fan favorite and very popular clubhouse player was bothered by back problems and retired in July 1984.

With Splittorff in the rotation from 1971 to 1983, the Kansas City Royals finished first four times and second six times in the AL West. His major league career record included 166 victories, 143 losses, one save, 17 shutouts, 1,057 strikeouts, and a 3.81 ERA in 2,554.2 innings spanning 429 games. He holds the Kansas City Royals' team records for wins and innings pitched.

He and his wife, Lynn (Litterick) Splittorff, have a daughter, Jennifer, and son, Jamie, and live in Blue Springs, MO. Splittorff became involved in real estate and will receive deferred salary from the Royals until 2004. He serves as a television color analyst for the Kansas City Royals.

BIBLIOGRAPHY: Mike Fish, "Splittorff's Retirement Severs Another Link to Club's Past," Kansas City (MO) *Times*, July 2, 1984, pp. C-1, 7; Zander Hollander, *The Complete Handbook of Baseball*, 10th ed. (New York, 1980); Kansas City Royals, *Grandslam* (Kansas City, MO, 1976, 1979, 1982); Paul Splittorff file, National Baseball Library, Cooperstown, NY; Sid Bordman, *Expansion to Excellence* (Marcelline, MS, 1981); John Garrity, *The George Brett Story* (New York, 1981).

Frank J. Olmsted

STAHL, Charles Sylvester "Chick" (b. January 10, 1873, Avilla, IN; d. March 28, 1907, West Baden, IN), player and manager, was the sixth of nine children of Reuben Stahl, a carpenter, and Barbara (Stadtmiller) Stahl. Player–manager Garland "Jake" Stahl was not related. Nicknamed "Chick," Stahl was meagerly educated at Fort Wayne, IN schools and concentrated early on baseball. A left-handed 5-foot 10-inch 160 pounder, he pitched for the semiprofessional Fort Wayne Pilsners and moved to the outfield because of his formidable hitting skills. His swift progress included stops at Roanoke, VA (VL) in 1895, Buffalo, NY (EL), where he hit .337 in 1896, and the powerful Boston Beaneaters (NL) in 1897. The right fielder became a Boston fan favorite, batting a career high .354 and .308 in the NL pennant-winning 1897 and 1898 seasons, .351 in 1899, and .295 in 1900. In 1900, he led NL outfielders in fielding percentage.

Stahl joined his close friend, Jimmy Collins,* in jumping to the Boston Pilgrims of the newly formed AL in 1901. The Boston Pilgrims switched him to center field, where he resumed his stout hitting with a .303 mark in 1901 and a .323 batting average in 1902. Injuries limited Stahl to 77 games with a .274 batting average in 1903, but his .303 led all Pilgrim hitters to help Boston down the Pittsburgh Pirates in the first-ever World Series. The Boston Pilgrims again finished first in 1904, as Stahl hit a solid .290 and led the AL in triples with 19. This gave him a unique record as the only performer ever to play twice for Boston pennant winners in two leagues.

After slipping to fourth in 1905, the Boston Pilgrims plummeted to the cellar in 1906. Stahl batted .286 and assumed managerial duties for the final

40 games after Boston owner John I. Taylor, exasperated by the Pilgrims' collapse, suspended Collins.

In November 1906, Stahl married Julia Harmon, thereby removing himself from prominence as one of baseball's eligible bachelors. During the winter, he tried unsuccessfully to persuade Taylor to reinstate Collins. He pleaded a lack of managerial temperament and ambition but took the team, now named the Boston Red Sox, to spring training in 1907. In late March 1907, he resigned abruptly as manager and agreed to serve as field captain. Three days later, in a West Baden, IN hotel room prior to an exhibition game, he drank a fatal dose of carbolic acid. Shocked speculation persisted as to the reason for Stahl's aberrant death, although longtime Indiana friends were not surprised. Throughout his life, Stahl was plagued by bouts of depression and at least twice had threatened suicide.

In 1,304 major league games spanning a decade, Stahl batted .305 with 1,546 hits, 219 doubles, 118 triples, and 622 RBI. His .961 fielding average included 159 outfield assists.

BIBLIOGRAPHY: *The Baseball Encyclopedia*, 10th ed. (New York, 1996); Cincinnati (OH) *Enquirer*, March 29, 1907; Fort Wayne (IN) *Journal Gazette*, December 22, 1906, March 29–31, 1907; Harold Kaese, *The Boston Braves* (New York, 1948); Gary Caruso, *The Braves Encyclopedia* (Philadelphia, PA, 1995); Frederick G. Lieb, *The Boston Red Sox* (New York, 1947); Howard Liss, *The Boston Red Sox* (New York, 1982); Robert Redmount, *The Red Sox Encyclopedia* (Champaign, IL, 1998); Charles Stahl file, National Baseball Library, Cooperstown, NY; Glenn Stout, "The Manager's Endgame," *BoM*, November 1987, p. 134; Dick Thompson, "And in an Unrelated Development . . . The 'Brothers' Stahl Weren't," *TF*, November 1987; *TSN*, April 6, 1907.

A. D. Suehsdorf

STALEY, Gerald Lee (b. August 21, 1920, Brush Prairie, WA), player, enjoyed success as an NL starting pitcher and AL relief pitcher and is the son of Adelbert Randolph Staley, a lumberman, and Clementine (Steelman) Staley. Although 6 feet and 195 pounds, the right-handed Staley combined a sinker and knuckleball with excellent control. After pitching for Boise, ID (PrL) in 1941 and 1942, he spent three years in military service and entered the major leagues with the St. Louis Cardinals (NL) in 1947. Staley reached his peak from 1951 to 1953 with 19, 17, and 18 victories, respectively. After finishing 7–13 in 1954, he was dealt to the Cincinnati Reds (NL) and won five of 13 decisions in 1955. The Cincinnati Reds waived him in September to the New York Yankees (AL). Staley's tenure with the New York Yankees marked the nadir of his career, as he made just two appearances in 1955 and one in 1956. The Chicago White Sox (AL) acquired him on waivers in May 1956. After starting 10 games that season, he appeared exclusively as a relief pitcher. With outstanding reliever Omar Lown, Staley helped the Chicago White Sox win the 1959 AL pennant. He could warm up on as little as six pitches and made an AL-leading 67 appearances. Due to Staley's control, batters expected his first pitches to be strikes and usually swung at his first or second delivery. On September 22, 1959, Staley relieved Bob Shaw against the Cleveland Indians and got Vic Power* to ground out on a single sinker ball, clinching the AL pennant for the White Sox. In the 1959 World Series, he lost one game on a HR by Gil Hodges* of the Los Angeles Dodgers. In 1960 Staley had a remarkable 13–8 record for a reliever in 64 appearances. He pitched ineffectively in 1961 for the Chicago White Sox, Kansas City Athletics (AL), and Detroit Tigers (AL). Staley ended his major league career with 134 victories, 111 defeats, and a 3.70 ERA in 640 games, 186 as a starting pitcher.

Staley, who married Shirle A. Lockert in May 1947 and had two sons and a daughter, worked off-seasons in the family's lumber mill. He served 17 years as Superintendent of the Clark County Parks & Recreation Department in Vancouver, WA.

BIBLIOGRAPHY: *The Baseball Encyclopedia*, 10th ed. (New York, 1996); Bob Broeg, *Redbirds! A Century of Cardinals' Baseball* (St. Louis, MO, 1981); Bob Broeg and Jerry Vickery, *St. Louis Cardinals Encyclopedia* (Grand Rapids, MI, 1998); Richard Lindberg, *Sox* (New York, 1984); Richard Lindberg, *Who's on Third?* (South Bend, IN, 1983); David Condon, *The Go-Go Chicago White Sox* (New York, 1960); *WWIB*, 46th ed., 1961; Brent P. Kelley, *Baseball Stars of the 1950s* (Jefferson, NC, 1993); Bob Vandenberg, *Sox: From Lane and Fain to Zisk and Fisk* (Chicago, IL, 1982); Gerald Staley file, National Baseball Library, Cooperstown, NY; Gerald Staley, letter to George W. Hilton, January 1996.

George W. Hilton

STALLINGS, George Tweedy "The Miracle Man," "Chief," "The Edison of Baseball" (b. November 17, 1867, Augusta, GA; d. May 13, 1929, Haddock, GA), player, manager, and executive, was the son of a Confederate officer and graduated in 1886 from Virginia Military Institute, where he caught for the baseball team. Although originally planning to be a doctor, Stallings was signed to a professional baseball contract by manager Harry Wright* of the Philadelphia Phillies (NL) in 1887. His brief major league career as a player included only the Brooklyn Bridegrooms (NL) 1890 and Philadelphia Phillies (NL) in 1897 and 1898, resulting in only two hits and a .100 batting average. Of the 43 years Stallings spent in baseball, 36 involved managing. He compiled an 879–898 career major league record in 13 seasons. Stallings' early managerial stints came with the Philadelphia Phillies in 1897 and 1898 and Detroit Tigers (AL) in their maiden 1901 season. He piloted the New York Highlanders (AL) to a second place finish in 1910 in his second year with the club.

Boston Braves (NL) owner James Gaffney hired Stallings to revive his moribund franchise in 1913. Stallings promptly fired lackadaisical players, preferring guts over talent. His decision initially seemed suspect, as the stumbling 1914 Braves stood in last place on July 18. But led by shortstop

Rabbit Maranville,* second baseman Johnny Evers,* outfielder Joe Connelly, and pitchers Dick Rudolph,* Bill James, and Lefty Tyler,* the torrid Boston Braves dominated their remaining schedule. Boston surged into first place past John McGraw's* New York Giants on September 8, winning 34 of their last 44 games and taking the NL pennant by 10½ games. Although the Boston Braves were 2–1 underdogs to manager Connie Mack's* Philadelphia Athletics, the self-confident Stallings disdained scouting the Athletics. He declared that Boston would sweep the World Series in a record four games. The "Miracle Braves" stunned the Athletics and America with four straight victories, highlighting Stallings' career.

Stallings never won another major league pennant, although managing the Boston Braves through 1920. He retired to his plantation until 1924, when he bought into the Rochester, NY franchise (IL). After selling his interest in the Rochester club in 1927, Stallings invested in and managed Montreal, Canada (IL) in 1928. Heart trouble cut his career short in Montreal.

Stallings possessed a schizoid personality. At the ballpark, he acted profane, volatile, and wildly superstitious. At his plantation, Meadowmire, in Haddock, GA, however, the fastidious grandee remained charming and dignified in speech and dress. Players often took pay cuts to perform for the superb motivator despite his legendary temper. Stallings introduced major innovations, two platooning his outfield and instituting hour-long skull sessions forcing players to acknowledge individual mental and physical errors. He never fined ballplayers, believing it better to treat them as adults. Stallings shamelessly manipulated players, however, if he believed that such treatment would improve team or player performance. He married three times to Mie Belle White, Eunice, and Bertha Elizabeth Thorp and had two sons, George Vernon and George Tweedy, Jr.

BIBLIOGRAPHY: George Stallings file, National Baseball Library, Cooperstown, NY; Thomas Aylesworth and Benton Minks, *The Encyclopedia of Baseball Managers* (New York, 1990); Frederick G. Lieb and Stan Baumgartner, *The Philadelphia Phillies* (New York, 1953); Rich Westcott and Frank Bilovsky, *The New Phillies Encyclopedia* (Philadelphia, PA, 1993); Frederick G. Lieb, *The Detroit Tigers* (New York, 1946); Harold Kaese, *The Boston Braves* (New York, 1948); Al Hirshberg, *Braves, the Pick and Shovel* (Boston, MA, 1948); Gary Caruso, *The Braves Encyclopedia* (Philadelphia, PA, 1995); *TSN*, May 16, 1929; Warren Brown, "George Stallings Introduced Platooning," *BD* 30 (February 1971), pp. 76–80; *NYT*, May 14, 1929; Frank C. Lane, "The Miracle Man," *BM* 14 (February 1915), pp. 57–66; Atlanta (GA) *Constitution*, May 14, 1929; Charles Einstein, ed., *The Fireside Book of Baseball* (New York, 1956); Edwin Pope, *Baseball's Greatest Managers* (Garden City, NY, 1960); Mike Shatzkin, ed., *The Ballplayers* (New York, 1990); George T. Stallings, "The Miracle Man's Own Story," *Collier's* 54 (November 28, 1914), pp. 7–8, 24.

                                                                  John H. Ziegler

STANKY, Edward Raymond "The Brat," "Muggsy" (b. September 3, 1916, Philadelphia, PA; d. June 6, 1999, Fairhope, AL), player, coach, and manager, attended high school in the Philadelphia area and began his professional baseball career as a second baseman in the Philadelphia Athletics (AL) system. His minor league stops included Greenville, MS (EDL) in 1935, Williamsport, PA (NYPL), and Portsmouth, OH (MAL) in 1936, Williamsport in 1937, and Portsmouth, VA (PiL) from 1937 to 1939. In 1939 Philadelphia sold him to Macon, GA (SAL). He married Myrtle Dickie Stock, the daughter of manager Milton Stock, in April 1942. He performed for Milwaukee, WI (AA) in 1942 and was called up the following year by Milwaukee's parent team, the Chicago Cubs (NL).

The 5-foot 8-inch, 160-pound, right-handed Stanky played with five different NL teams over an 11-year major league career. These clubs included the Chicago Cubs, 1943–1944; Brooklyn Dodgers, 1944–1947; Boston Braves, 1948–1949; New York Giants, 1950–1951; and St. Louis Cardinals, 1952–1953. He appeared in the 1947, 1948, and 1951 World Series, was selected to the NL All-Star team in 1947, 1948, 1950, and 1951, and batted .268 lifetime. Not a power hitter, he stroked only 29 HR among 1,154 hits. He possessed an excellent eye for the strike zone, however, three times leading the NL in walks and twice in on base percentage. His 996 career walks rank among the top 100 on the all-time list, while his ratio of one walk per 18.8 at-bats remains fourth best among all players.

Stanky became player–manager of the St. Louis Cardinals in 1952 and performed that dual role for two more years. After spending the 1956 season piloting the Minneapolis, MN Millers (AA), he coached for the Cleveland Indians (AL) in 1957 and 1958. He then moved to the front office as director of minor league operations for the St. Louis Cardinals from 1959 to 1964 and the New York Mets (NL) in 1965 and 1966. He then managed the Chicago White Sox (AL) from 1966 to 1968 before retiring from major league baseball. In 1977, he piloted the Texas Rangers (AL) for a one-game stint. His career major league managerial record totaled 467 wins and 435 losses with no league championships.

In 1969, the University of South Alabama hired Stanky as coach. In 14 seasons there (1969–1979, 1981–1983), he proved highly successful. His teams compiled a 488–193 win–loss record, won three SBC titles, and appeared in the NCAA College World Series five times. The feisty, inspirational team leader earned his nickname, "The Brat," during his years with the Brooklyn Dodgers, which were then managed by the fiery Leo Durocher.* He was a member of the Alabama Sports Hall of Fame and the University of South Alabama Athletic Hall of Fame and lived in Mobile, AL.

BIBLIOGRAPHY: Eddie Stanky file, National Baseball Library, Cooperstown, NY; Thomas Aylesworth and Benton Minks, *The Encyclopedia of Baseball Managers* (New York, 1990); Eddie Gold and Art Ahrens, *The New Era Cubs, 1941–1985* (Chicago, IL, 1985); Richard Goldstein, *Superstars and Screwballs* (New York, 1991); Peter Golenbock, *Bums* (New York, 1984); William F. McNeil, *The Dodgers Encyclopedia* (Champaign, IL, 1997); Gary Caruso, *The Braves Encyclopedia* (Philadelphia, PA,

1995); John Thorn et al., eds., *Total Braves* (New York, 1996); Rob Rains, *The St. Louis Cardinals* (New York, 1992); Bob Broeg, *Redbirds! A Century of Cardinals' Baseball* (St. Louis, MO, 1981); Bob Broeg and Jerry Vickery, *St. Louis Cardinals Encyclopedia* (Grand Rapids, MI, 1998); Richard Lindberg, *Sox* (New York, 1984); Richard Lindberg, *Who's on Third?* (South Bend, IN, 1983); *The Baseball Encyclopedia*, 10th ed. (New York, 1996); *CB* (1951), pp. 604–606; Mobile (AL) *Press-Register*, April 29, 1989; John Thorn et al., eds., *Total Baseball*, 5th ed. (New York, 1997).

John E. Findling

STANLEY, Robert William "Bob," "Steamer," "Bigfoot" (b. November 10, 1954, Portland, ME), player, is the son of Herbert M. Stanley, a lobster fisherman and vendor, and moved to Kearney, NJ at two years old. An all-around athlete, Stanley made All-County in basketball and All-State as a pitcher in baseball at Kearney High School. The Los Angeles Dodgers (NL) drafted him in 1973, but he declined their $4,000 bonus offer to enter Newark State College (now Kean College). After spending a month at college, he left to pitch professionally. The right-handed Stanley was selected first by the Boston Red Sox (AL) in the secondary phase of the January 1974 draft and was signed by Boston Red Sox scout Matt Sczesny for $4,000.

After an unimpressive 6–6 record and 4.60 ERA at Elmira, NY (NYPL) in 1974, Stanley finished just 5–17 with a 2.93 ERA at Winter Haven, FL (FSL) in 1975. He was promoted to Bristol, CT (EL) in 1976 and enjoyed a banner season with 15 wins, only six losses and a 2.66 ERA, leading the EL with 13 complete games. In 1977, he made the substantial jump from Class AA to the Boston Red Sox.

Stanley, whose 6-foot 4-inch, 225-pound frame and sinking fastball reminded many of Don Drysdale,* alternated between starting and relieving as a rookie and compiled an 8–7 record and 3.99 ERA. In 1978, when the Boston Red Sox lost the AL East to the New York Yankees in a playoff game, he finished 15–2 (13–2 in relief) with 10 saves and a 2.60 career-best ERA. A 16–12 mark and 3.99 ERA followed as a starter in 1979. Stanley set an AL one-season record of 168.1 innings pitched in relief in 1982, enjoying a 12–7 record with a 3.10 ERA and 14 saves and contributing to 30 of his team's 89 victories. He earned 33 saves in 1983 and 22 saves in 1984. Stanley's record as a major league starter, middle reliever, and closer established him as one of the most versatile major league pitchers.

Stanley, whose first-year major league salary was $19,500, signed a contract in 1981 for $1.8 million over four years. In 1984, agent Bob Woolf negotiated a new five-year deal worth over $1 million a year for Stanley. From 1985 through 1989, he won only 27 of 60 games with an overall 4.06 ERA and became the target of booing fans at Fenway Park. The booing intensified after Stanley's ninth-inning wild pitch in the pivotal sixth game loss in the 1986 World Series. The Boston Red Sox dropped the World Series to the New York Mets in seven games. After experiencing a disastrous

4–15 mark and 5.01 ERA as a starter in 1987, Stanley rebounded with respectable 6–4 and 5–2 records as a reliever in his last two major league seasons. He retired following the 1989 season, finishing his 13-year career with 115 victories, 97 losses (85–61 in relief) and a 3.64 ERA. An AL All-Star in 1979 and 1982, he remains the Red Sox all-time leader in saves (132) and games pitched (637). Only nine others have played at least a decade exclusively for the Boston Red Sox.

Stanley, who has pursued the landscaping and sporting goods businesses in the Boston area, lives in Wenham, MA. In November 1997, he joined the St. Lucie, FL Mets (FSL) as pitching coach. He married Joan Mathers and has three children, Kristen, Kyle, and Kerri. Stanley and his wife work in behalf of the Jimmy Fund, which supports children's cancer research, and other local charities.

BIBLIOGRAPHY: Bob Stanley file, National Baseball Library, Cooperstown, NY; *The Baseball Encyclopedia*, 10th ed. (New York, 1996); Will Anderson, *Was Baseball Really Invented in Maine?* (Portland, ME, 1992); Peter Golenbock, *Fenway* (New York, 1984); Howard Liss, *The Boston Red Sox* (New York, 1982); Peter Gammons, *Beyond the Sixth Game* (Boston, MA, 1985); Dan Shaughnessy, *One Strike Away* (New York, 1987); Robert Redmount, *The Red Sox Encyclopedia* (Champaign, IL, 1998); *Boston Red Sox 1988 Media Guide*; Jim Kaplan, "Stanley Has the Steam," *SI* 58 (April 25, 1983), pp. 66ff; Todd Balf, "The Mourning After," *Sport* 78 (March 1987), pp. 32–34; Curtis Wilkie, "Another Fine Mess, Stanley," *Boston Globe Magazine* (October 25, 1987), pp. 16ff; Steve Fainaru, "Sox Win One and Lose Two: Stanley and Rice Check Out," *Boston Globe*, September 26, 1989, pp. 65ff.

Richard H. Gentile

STARGELL, Wilver Dornel "Willie," "Pops" (b. March 6, 1940, Earlsboro, OK), player, coach, and executive, is the son of William Stargell and Verlene Stargell and moved as a small boy with his family to Oakland, CA, where he starred in baseball, basketball, and track and field at Encinal High School. He played baseball briefly at Santa Rosa JC before the Pittsburgh Pirates (NL) signed him for a $1,200 bonus in 1958. After four minor league seasons with Roswell, NM (SpL) in 1959, Grand Forks, ND (NoL) in 1960, Asheville, NC (SAL) in 1961, and Columbus, OH (IL) in 1962, Stargell joined the Pirates in 1962 and remained with Pittsburgh for 21 seasons.

Stargell played the outfield primarily through 1974, but shifted permanently to first base in 1975. A feared slugger, Stargell hit 475 HR to rank high on the all-time list with Stan Musial.* He compiled a .282 lifetime batting average and drove in 1,540 runs. In 2,360 major league games, he made 2,232 hits, 423 doubles, 1,195 runs scored, and 1,936 strikeouts, second on the all-time list. Stargell's HR output might have been considerably higher had he not played much of his career in spacious Forbes Field in Pittsburgh. During 62 seasons of major league play at Forbes Field, only 18 HR were hit completely out of the stadium; Stargell slugged seven of those.

After the Pirates moved to Three Rivers Stadium, Stargell led the NL with 48 HR in 1971 and 44 HR in 1973.

Stargell helped the Pirates win six NL Eastern Division championships in the 1970s and NL pennants and World Series titles in 1971 and 1979. In 1979, the 38-year-old Stargell provided on- and off-field leadership that enabled the underdog Pirates to win the World Series over the Baltimore Orioles. As "Pops" of the Pirate "Family," Stargell hit .281 with 32 HR in 1979 and shared the NL's MVP Award with Keith Hernandez* of the St. Louis Cardinals. He batted .455 and hit two HR in the Pirates' sweep of the Cincinnati Reds in the NL Championship Series. In the World Series against the Baltimore Orioles, Stargell hit .400 and slugged three HR, including a decisive two-run HR in the seventh game.

Used primarily as a pinch hitter his last two campaigns, Stargell retired as an active player following the 1982 season and rejoined the Pirates as a coach in 1985. Stargell coached for the Atlanta Braves (NL) from 1986 through 1988 and served as a batting instructor in their minor league system for several years. Since 1994, he has served as special assistant to the general manager for the Pittsburgh Pirates. He participated in various civic and charitable activities, serving as chair of an organization of athletes raising money for research on sickle-cell anemia. Stargell and his wife, Dolores, have three children. A dangerous power hitter, fierce competitor, and clubhouse leader, Stargell excelled as one of baseball's greatest left-handed sluggers. In 1988, he was elected to the National Baseball Hall of Fame.

BIBLIOGRAPHY: John Benson et al., *Baseball's Top 100* (Wilton, CT, 1997); Ron Fimrite, "Two Champs from the City of Champions," *SI* 51 (December 14, 1979), pp. 36–42; Arnold Hano, "Willie Stargell and the Beautiful Challenge," *Sport* 15 (August 1971), pp. 61–70; Donald Honig, *The Power Hitters* (St. Louis, MO, 1989); Hank Nauer, "Willie Stargell: The Pride of Pittsburgh," *SEP* 7 (May/June 1980), pp. 29–38; Bob Smizik, *The Pittsburgh Pirates: An Illustrated History* (New York, 1990); Lou Sahadi, *The Pirates* (New York, 1980); David L. Porter, ed., *African-American Sports Greats* (Westport, CT, 1995); Willie Stargell and Tom Bird, *Willie Stargell* (New York, 1984); Richard L. Burtt, *The Pittsburgh Pirates: A Pictorial History* (Virginia Beach, VA, 1977); Willie Stargell file, National Baseball Library, Cooperstown, NY.

Fred M. Shelley

STARK, Albert "Dolly" (b. November 4, 1897, New York, NY; d. August 24, 1968, New York, NY), athlete, umpire, coach, and sportscaster, was born on Manhattan's Lower East Side and was only eight years old when his father died. Stark spent almost two years in an orphanage. As a youth, he subsequently pushed a peddler's cart to help his mother, Augusta, support a family of five children. Family financial responsibilities forced him to leave high school short of graduation.

An outstanding athlete, the slightly built 5-foot 10-inch, 115-pound infielder signed with the New York Yankees (AL) and spent several years in the minor leagues. He did not reach the major leagues, but received a spring training trial with the Washington Senators (AL) in 1920. He played professional basketball during the off-season and coached varsity basketball and freshman baseball from 1923 to 1935 at Dartmouth College. In 1923, he began umpiring regional college baseball games and soon turned professional. After Stark umpired in the Class B EL in 1927, the NL promoted him the next season.

Agility, keen vision, impeccable judgment, and mental alertness made Stark a "natural" umpire. The protégé of Bill Klem,* who once called Stark "the best I ever saw," he was named in 1935 as the best NL umpire by a *TSN* player's poll. The next year, appreciative fans gave him an automobile during "Dolly Stark Day" at the Polo Grounds in New York. He umpired one All-Star game (1934) and 13 contests in two World Series (1931, 1935). An energetic, active umpire, Stark introduced the practice of physically following a runner around the bases.

The intense, high-strung, and ultrasensitive Stark's umpiring skills were offset by his inability to handle the emotional pressures and loneliness of the job or the vicious, often anti-Semitic, abuse of fans and players. He resigned twice (1929, 1930) and spent the 1936 season broadcasting Philadelphia Athletics (AL) and Philadelphia Phillies (NL) games because of a salary dispute. A bad knee sidelined him for part of the 1940 season. He retired in 1942 after severely aggravating his knee injury in spring training.

After leaving umpiring, Stark engaged in the textile industry, stocks and bonds, and radio and television. His tragic personal life included spending huge sums of money caring for both his blind mother and his emotionally ill sister, who committed suicide. A December 1952 marriage to Betsy Lee ended in divorce four years later. His resources depleted, he began living on unemployment compensation in 1964 while residing in a hotel. His unusual nickname derived from Monroe "Dolly" Stark, who played with the Brooklyn Superbas (NL) from 1910 to 1912.

BIBLIOGRAPHY: Clifford Bloodgood, "Bearing Down on Every Pitch," *BM* 49 (August 1932), pp. 401–402, 430; Harold C. Burr, "Fate Hounds This Ump," *BM* 69 (June 1942), pp. 309–310, 329; Harold U. Ribalow and Meir Z. Ribalow, *Jewish Baseball Stars* (New York, 1984); *NYT*, August 26, 1968; Albert Stark file, National Baseball Library, Cooperstown, NY; Albert Stark file, *TSN* Archives, St. Louis, MO; Albert Stark, "How to Get the Thumb," *BD* 11 (November 1952), pp. 11–14.

Larry R. Gerlach

START, Joseph "Joe," "Old Reliable" (b. October 14, 1842, New York, NY; d. March 27, 1927, Providence, RI), player, enjoyed a three-decade baseball career and became a national hero in the 1860s as a power hitter. Of Dutch-American parents, Start attended the Bedford Avenue and Monroe Street Elementary School. A first baseman practically his entire career, the 5-foot

9-inch, 165-pound left-hander joined the Enterprise Club of Brooklyn, NY in 1860 at age 17. He played there with John Chapman* for two seasons until both moved to the mighty Brooklyn Atlantics in 1862. For Brooklyn from 1862 to 1870, Start enjoyed his strongest seasons. He batted third, fourth, and fifth, helping the Atlantics win championships in 1865 and 1866. Start jumped to the New York Mutuals in 1871, a charter member of the new NA, baseball's first professional league. The same year, he married Angeline Creed.

The first available statistical records of Start's accomplishments appeared in the NA. During five full seasons, he compiled a .295 batting average, scored 264 runs, and made 387 hits in 273 games, and peaked in 1871 with a .360 batting percentage. He remained with the New York Mutuals when the NL was formed in 1876. Start batted .332 with the Hartford, CT Dark Blues (1877) and .351 with the Chicago White Stockings (1878), leading the NL in at-bats (285) and hits (100). He joined the Providence, RI Grays in 1879 and helped them to the NL championship that year and in 1884. He remained with Providence through 1885, hitting .319 in 1879, .328 in 1881, and .329 in 1882, and finished his playing career with the Washington Statesmen (NL) in 1886. During 11 NL seasons, Start hit .300 in 798 games. Before retiring at age 44, he collected 1,031 hits, scored 590 runs, and knocked in 357 runs, switching from a power to a percentage hitter. He belted 107 doubles, 55 triples, and seven HR and walked 150 times. Start, who later became an innkeeper in Lakewood, RI, was one of the few early stars to participate in the pre-professional, NA, and young NL eras.

BIBLIOGRAPHY: Preston D. Orem, *Baseball, 1845–1881* (Altadena, CA, 1961); *The Baseball Encyclopedia*, 10th ed. (New York, 1996); Joe Start file, National Baseball Library, Cooperstown, NY; Robert L. Tiemann and Mark Rucker, eds., *Nineteenth Century Stars* (Kansas City, MO, 1989); William J. Ryczek, *When Johnny Came Sliding Home* (Jefferson, NC, 1998); William Ryzcek, *Blackguards and Red Stockings* (Jefferson, NC, 1992); Eddie Gold and Art Ahrens, *The Golden Era Cubs, 1876–1940* (Chicago, IL, 1985).

Mark D. Rucker

STAUB, Daniel Joseph "Rusty" (b. April 1, 1944, New Orleans, LA), player, coach, scout, and sportscaster, owns Rusty Staub's Restaurant in New York City. Staub, a bachelor who batted left and threw right, is 6-feet 2-inches tall and weighs 190 pounds. In 1961, Staub was named Louisiana Scholastic Athlete of the Year and an All-State selection in basketball and baseball at Jesuit High School in New Orleans. At age 17, Staub signed his first professional contract with the Houston Colt .45's (NL) organization in 1961. He started in 1963 at outfield for Houston. In January 1969, the red-orange haired Staub was traded to the Montreal Expos (NL), where he became the first baseball hero in the expansion team city and was dubbed "Le Grand Orange" by the fans.

After joining the New York Mets (NL) in April 1972, Staub established several records. In the 1973 NL Championship Series against the Cincinnati Reds, he set records for most HR in a series (3) and most HR in two consecutive innings (2). During the 1973 World Series against the Oakland A's, Staub tied a record by reaching base safely five times in one game, batted .423, drove in six runs, and became one of 42 players to get four hits in one game. Two years later, Staub became the first Met to drive in over 100 runs in a season. He was traded to the Detroit Tigers (AL) in December 1975. As a Tiger, Staub in 1978 was voted the AL's Outstanding DH by batting .273 and knocking in 121 runs in 162 games. After brief stints with the Montreal Expos (NL) in 1979 and the Texas Rangers (AL) in 1980, Staub finished his major league career with the New York Mets from 1981 through 1985.

In 1983, he made 24 pinch hits, compiled a .296 batting average, and tied major league pinch hit records with 8 consecutive hits and 25 RBI. In 1984, at age 40, Staub again led the NL pinch hitters in hits and RBI. He became only the second player to hit major league HR as a teenager and 40-year-old.

Staub, one of a few dozen players in major league history to amass over 4,000 total career bases, played in five straight All-Star games with the NL (1967–1971) and was voted an AL starter in 1976. Staub, who retired following the 1985 season, scored 1,189 runs, made 2,716 hits, slugged 499 doubles, 47 triples, and 292 HR, knocked in 1,466 runs, and batted .279. In 1986, the New York Mets (NL) named him a spring training instructor, special scout, talent evaluator, and announcer. He also serves as a vice president of the MLBPAA.

BIBLIOGRAPHY: Roger Angell, "My Summer Vacation," *NY* 60 (May 7, 1984), pp. 74–120; Larry Keith, "He's Still Le Grand Orange," *SI* 49 (August 21, 1978), pp. 58–59; "Le Grand Orange," *NY* 64 (June 2, 1989), pp. 18–19; Mark Mulvoy, "In Montreal They Love Grand Orange," *SI* 33 (July 6, 1970), pp. 38–39; *New York Mets 1984 Information Guide* (New York, 1984); *NYT*, February 13, 1982; *The Baseball Encyclopedia*, 10th ed. (New York, 1996); Gary Ronberg, "Houston's Boy Is Now a Man," *SI* 27 (August 14, 1967), pp. 54–56; *TSN Official Baseball Register, 1985*; Rusty Staub file, National Baseball Library, Cooperstown, NY; Peter C. Bjarkman, ed., *Encyclopedia of Major League Baseball Team Histories National League* (Westport, CT, 1991); Dan Turner, *The Expos Inside Out* (Toronto, Canada, 1983); Jack Lang and Peter Simon, *The New York Mets* (New York, 1986); Donald Honig, *The New York Mets* (New York, 1986); John Robertson, *Rusty Staub of the Expos* (Scarborough, Canada, 1971).

Leslie Eldridge

STEARNES, Norman "Turkey" (b. May 8, 1901, Nashville, TN; d. September 4, 1979, Detroit, MI), player, was the son of Will Stearnes and Mary (Everett) Stearnes and pitched for the Pearl High School baseball team. Following his father's death, Stearnes left school to work at age 15 and played baseball in his spare time. Stearnes performed with the Nashville, TN Elite Giants (NSL) in 1920, Montgomery, AL Grey Sox (NSL) in 1921, and Memphis, TN Red Sox (NSL) in 1922, when Bruce Petway* of the Detroit Stars (NNL) recruited him. Since Stearnes desired to finish school and needed full-time employment, he accepted the Detroit offer. In 1923 the 6-foot 1-inch, 170-pound, switch-hitting outfielder began working for the Briggs Manufacturing Company and playing for the Detroit Stars (NNL). He quickly was recognized as an outstanding outfielder by slugging 35 HR in 1923 and 50 HR in 1924 and remained with Detroit through the 1931 season. Although they usually contended during those years, the Detroit Stars finished at the top only in the first half of the 1930 season and were defeated that year by the St. Louis Stars for the NNL pennant.

After the Depression terminated the NNL, Stearnes performed for several other clubs over the next decade. He played briefly for the New York Lincoln Giants (ANL) in 1930 and then patrolled the outfield for Cole's Chicago American Giants (NSL) from 1932 to 1935, the Philadelphia Stars (NNL) in 1936, and the Chicago American Giants (NAL) in 1938 under manager Dave Malarcher.* Stearnes learned there to bunt, something the free-swinging power hitter hitherto had not done very often. At Chicago, Stearnes teamed with "Steel Arm" Davis and Nat Rogers to form one of the better outfields in black baseball. He returned to the Detroit Stars (NAL) in 1937 and slugged 35 HR, performing with "Cool Papa" Bell* and Davis in the outfield. Stearnes, who finished his playing career with the Kansas City Monarchs (NAL) in 1940 and 1941 and Detroit Black Sox in 1942, played winter ball in California and Cuba. Stearnes clearly ranked among the best outfielders of his time, batting .359 with 185 HR and seven HR titles in his Negro League career. He batted .351 in exhibitions against the major leaguers. He performed well enough during the 1930s to play center field in four of the first five East-West Negro All-Star games (1933–1935, 1937). After quitting baseball, Stearnes worked until 1964 in the rolling mills of Detroit, married Nettie MacArthur on May 8, 1946, and had two children.

BIBLIOGRAPHY: Richard Bak, *Turkey Stearnes and the Detroit Stars* (Detroit, MI, 1994); William Brashler, *Josh Gibson* (New York, 1978); John B. Holway, *Voices from Great Black Baseball Leagues* (New York, 1975); John B. Holway, *Blackball Stars* (Westport, CT, 1988); Robert W. Peterson, *Only the Ball Was White* (Englewood Cliffs, NJ, 1970); James A. Riley, *The Biographical Encyclopedia of the Negro Baseball Leagues* (New York, 1994); Donn Rogosin, *Invisible Men: Life in Baseball's Negro Leagues* (New York, 1983); Norman "Turkey" Stearnes file, National Baseball Library, Cooperstown, NY.

Douglas D. Martin

STEINBRENNER, George Michael, III (b. July 4, 1930, Rocky River, OH), sports owner, executive, and football coach, is the son of Henry G. Steinbrenner II, a rigid German disciplinarian, fierce business and sports competitor, and owner of the Kinsman Marine Transit Company, and Rita (Haley) Steinbrenner. He succeeded his father as head of Kinsman and merged it with his own American Ship Company.

At Culver Military Academy in Indiana, Steinbrenner excelled as a multi-sports athlete and was selected to the Culver Athletic Hall of Fame. His later athletic accomplishments were limited to serving as assistant football coach at Northwestern University in 1955 and Purdue University from 1956 to 1967, both BTC schools.

Steinbrenner graduated from Williams College with a Bachelor's degree in English in 1952 and participated as a hurdler on the school's track and field team. He pursued a Masters degree in physical education at Ohio State University in 1954 and 1955 and married Elizabeth Joan Zieg in May 1956. They have four children, Henry III, Jennifer, Jessica, and Harold. In 1960, Steinbrenner acquired the Cleveland Pipers (ABL) against his family's wishes. The Pipers went bankrupt two years later.

Steinbrenner led a group of unsuccessful investors seeking to buy the Cleveland Indians (AL). The New York Yankees (AL), owned by CBS, became available for sale. On January 3, 1973, Steinbrenner appeared at a press conference in the Bronx to announce that he was coleader of a syndicate buying the New York Yankees for $10 million. Steinbrenner did not plan to be active in the day-to-day operations of the club.

On August 30, 1974, Steinbrenner pleaded guilty to making illegal campaign contributions to Richard Nixon's presidential election campaign and was fined $15,000. President Ronald Reagan later pardoned him. Three months later, baseball commissioner Bowie Kuhn* suspended him from the New York Yankees for 15 months for conduct "not in the best interests of baseball." During this exile, others close to the game suspected him of still running the team.

After the suspension, Steinbrenner in 1975 hired Billy Martin* to manage the New York Yankees. The appointment marked the first of five tours by Martin as pilot of the New York club. Since 1975, Steinbrenner has changed New York Yankees managers 21 times. The New York Yankees finished first in the East AL nine times and won the World Series over the Los Angeles Dodgers in 1977 and 1978, Atlanta Braves in 1996 and 1999, and San Diego Padres in 1998. New York also appeared in the 1981 World Series, losing to the Los Angeles Dodgers.

Steinbrenner remains heavily involved in civic and community causes and holds four honorary doctoral degrees. He founded the Silver Shield Foundation, which provides college education for children of New York City policemen and fire-fighters who died in the line of duty. He chaired the U.S. Olympic program. Since February 1989, he has served as vice president of USOC. Steinbrenner also owns the Tampa Bay Lightning, an expansion NHL franchise. Steinbrenner's controversies with several New York Yankee players have caused him to be called the "most hated man in baseball."

BIBLIOGRAPHY: Dick Shaap, *Steinbrenner!* (New York, 1982); Dick Lally, *Pinstriped Summers* (New York, 1985); Dave Anderson et al., *The Yankees* (New York, 1979); George Steinbrenner file, National Baseball Library, Cooperstown, NY; *The Baseball Encyclopedia*, 10th ed. (New York 1996); Mark Gallagher, *The Yankee Encyclopedia*, vol. 3 (New York, 1997); Jill Lieber, "Will the Boss Behave Himself?" *SI* 78 (March 1, 1997), pp. 18–21; *New York Yankees 1994 Information Guide*; Bill Madden, "The Big Payback," *Sport* 84 (March 1993), pp. 52–57; Bill Madden and Moss Klein, *Damned Yankees* (New York, 1990); George Steinbrenner, letter to Stan W. Carlson, December 10, 1992; John Thorn et al., eds., *Total Baseball*, 5th ed. (New York, 1997); George Will, "The Most Hated Man in Baseball," *Newsweek* 116 (August 6, 1990), pp. 52–59; *WWA*, 47th ed. (1992–1993), p. 3332.

Stan W. Carlson

STEINFELDT, Harry M. "Steinie" (b. September 29, 1877, St. Louis, MO; d. August 17, 1914, Bellevue, KY), player, grew up in Fort Worth, TX, where his parents moved when he was five years old. Steinfeldt originally aspired a theatrical career, but displayed considerable ability in Fort Worth's amateur baseball leagues and entered the professional baseball ranks. In June 1895, he joined Houston, TX (TL) as an infielder. When the team disbanded a month later, Steinfeldt signed with Fort Worth, TX (TL) for the rest of the season. He started 1896 with Fort Worth, but joined the Galveston, TX (TL) squad when that team folded. For the season, Steinfeldt batted .320 and led TL second basemen with 573 chances and a .931 fielding average. In 1897, Detroit, MI (WL) drafted Steinfeldt and made him a third baseman. For Detroit, he hit .322 and compiled an .869 fielding average. Contemporaries considered him the first and perhaps only third sacker to wear shinguards. The 5-foot 9½-inch, 180-pound right-handed infielder was drafted by the Cincinnati Reds (NL) after the 1897 season and debuted there in April 1898.

From 1898 through 1901, Steinfeldt played second base, shortstop, and third base for the Cincinnati Reds. Although possessing a strong arm and dependable glove, he committed an NL-high 49 errors in 1902 during his first season as the regular third baseman. Steinfeldt enjoyed his finest season for the Cincinnati Reds in 1903, batting .312 and leading the NL in doubles with 32. A leg injury hampered his play in 1904 and resulted in just a .244 batting average, but he rebounded the next season to bat .271.

In March 1906, the Cincinnati Reds traded Steinfeldt to the Chicago Cubs (NL) to replace Doc Casey at third base. He worked well with the future National Baseball Hall-of-Fame double-play combination of shortstop Joe Tinker,* second baseman Johnny Evers,* and first baseman Frank Chance.* In his first season with the Chicago Cubs, Steinfeldt batted a team-high .327, stole 29 bases, and led the NL in hits (176), RBI (83), and fielding percentage (.954) at third base. The Chicago Cubs won the NL pennant with a major league record 116 wins. He batted .250 in the 1906 World Series, as the Chicago Cubs lost to the crosstown Chicago White Sox in six games. Steinfeldt's batting average dropped to .266 in 1907, but he drove in a club-high

70 runs, led NL third basemen with a .967 fielding percentage, and helped spark the Chicago Cubs to another NL flag. In the 1907 World Series, he batted a team-high .471 with eight hits. The Cubs triumphed over the Detroit Tigers to capture their first World Series.

Before the 1908 campaign, the Chicago Cubs signed Steinfeldt to a three-year contract. He batted just .241 in 1908, but continued his dependable work at third base and helped the Chicago Cubs again triumph over Detroit in the World Series. In the five World Series games, Steinfeldt collected only four hits. He batted .252 in each of the next two campaigns, as the Chicago Cubs finished in second place in 1909 and captured another NL pennant in 1910. In the 1910 World Series against the Detroit Tigers, Steinfeldt managed just two hits.

In March 1911, a bitter contract dispute with the Chicago Cubs caused Steinfeldt's sale to St. Paul, MN (AA). When he refused to report, the Chicago Cubs traded him to the Boston Rustlers (NL). A broken finger and other ailments limited him to only 19 games. Steinfeldt retired to Bellevue, KY, where his health deteriorated. He spent time in a local sanitarium and died at age 36, being survived by his wife of 20 years. In 14 major league seasons, he batted .267 with 1,576 hits, and 762 RBI in 1,646 games.

BIBLIOGRAPHY: Chicago (IL) *Daily Tribune*, August 18, 1914; Eddie Gold and Art Ahrens, *The Golden Era Cubs, 1876–1940* (Chicago, IL, 1985); Harry M. Steinfeldt file, National Baseball Library, Cooperstown, NY; John Thorn et al., eds., *Total Baseball*, 5th ed. (New York, 1997); Warren Brown, *The Chicago Cubs* (New York, 1946); Jim Enright, *Chicago Cubs* (New York, 1975); Warren Wibert and William Hageman, *Chicago Cubs: Seasons at the Summit* (Champaign, IL, 1997); Lee Allen, *The Cincinnati Reds* (New York, 1948).

Raymond D. Kush

STELZLE, Jacob Charles. *See* Jacob Charles Stenzel.

STENGEL, Charles Dillon "Casey," "Dutch," "The Old Professor" (b. July 30, 1890, Kansas City, MO; d. September 29, 1975, Glendale, CA), player and manager, was the son of Irish-German Louis Stengel of Kansas City. Nicknamed "Dutch" and later "Casey," he attended Woodland Grade School, starred in baseball, football, and basketball at Central High School, and spent three years studying dentistry at Western Dental College. In 1910, he quit his studies and signed for $75 a month as an outfielder for Kankakee, IL (NoA). When the NoA disbanded that July, he played with Shelbyville–Maysville, KY (BGL), batting .223 and fielding .987. For Aurora, IL (WIL) in early 1911, he nearly won the batting title with a .352 average and led the WIL in stolen bases. The left-handed Stengel in 1912 performed with Montgomery, AL (SL) and was purchased by the Brooklyn Robins (NL) for $300.

Stengel played 17 games with Brooklyn in 1912, debuting with hits in all four at-bats. He batted .316 during that short season and compiled a .284 mark over 14 NL seasons as an outfielder with the Brooklyn Robins (1912–1917), Pittsburgh Pirates (1918–1919), Philadelphia Phillies (1920–July 1921), New York Giants (July 1921–1923), and Boston Braves (1924–1925). He hit .316 in 126 games in 1914, achieved career highs of 141 hits, 73 RBI, and 69 runs scored with the Brooklyn Robins in 1917, and hit .364 in his first World Series in 1916. After being traded in January 1918 to the Pittsburgh Pirates (NL), he hit .246 and fielded .957. He was dealt in September 1919 to the Philadelphia Phillies (NL) and in July 1921 to John McGraw's* New York Giants. His 1922 batting average reached a career-high .368 mark. He batted .339 in 1923 for the Giants and starred in the 1922 and 1923 World Series. He hit .400 in the 1922 fall classic and .417 in the 1923 World Series against the New York Yankees, winning two 1923 games with crucial HR. Stengel was traded to the Boston Braves in November 1923 and played his last two major league seasons there. In 1,277 major league games, he compiled 1,219 hits, 182 doubles, 89 triples, 60 HR, 575 runs scored, 535 RBI, and 131 stolen bases.

Stengel managed Worcester, MA (EL) in 1925 and the Toledo, OH Mudhens (AA) from 1926 to 1931 and coached with the Brooklyn Dodgers (NL) in 1932 and 1933. When the Dodgers fired pilot Max Carey* in 1934, Stengel began his major league managerial career. He endured nine barren years with Brooklyn and the Boston Braves (NL). After 1936, the Dodgers paid him to sit out the fourth year of his contract. Hired by the Boston Braves in 1938, he experienced six struggling years. The Braves finished fifth in 1938, seventh the next three seasons, and sixth in 1942. Stengel, who resigned in 1943, was hired the next year by Bill Veeck* as manager of the Milwaukee, WI Brewers (AA). After finishing first there, he managed his hometown Kansas City, MO Blues (AA) in 1945 and Oakland, CA (PCL) from 1946 to 1948. On October 13, 1948, he signed to manage the New York Yankees (AL) for $25,000 and succeeded Bucky Harris.* General manager George Weiss* had tried for years to bring Stengel to the Yankees. Stengel recorded an unprecedented 10 AL pennants and seven World Series titles in 12 years. From 1949 to 1953, the Yankees won five straight AL pennants in Stengel's first five years. His 1954 Yankees won 103 games, but finished eight games behind the Cleveland Indians. New York won AL pennants from 1955 through 1958 and in 1960, winning the World Series in 1956 and 1958.

Stengel rewrote managing rules. When the Yankees suffered 11 injuries in 1949, he skillfully platooned his players, followed intuition, gambled on percentages, and abruptly became "The Old Professor." After being released in 1960 by the Yankees, he returned to Oakland as a millionaire and served as a bank director. From 1962 to 1965, Stengel managed the New York Mets (NL) to four tenth place finishes. In 25 years as a major league manager, Stengel compiled 1,905 wins and 1,842 losses (.508 winning percentage). He was elected to the National Baseball Hall of Fame in 1966 and saw his uniform number, 37, retired by the Yankees and the New York Mets. He married Edna Lawson on August 16, 1924, and had no children. Stengel, who died of cancer, may have held more public affection than any other baseball figure since Babe Ruth.*

BIBLIOGRAPHY: Ira Berkow and Jim Kaplan, *The Gospel According to Casey* (New York, 1992); Casey Stengel file, National Baseball Library, Cooperstown, NY; Robert W. Creamer, "Casey Stengel—An Appreciation," *SI* 43 (October 13, 1975), p. 41; Robert W. Creamer, *Stengel: His Life and Times* (New York, 1984); Joseph Durso, *Casey: Mr. McGraw* (St. Louis, MO, 1989); Frank Deford, *Casey on the Loose* (New York, 1989); David Halberstam, *Summer of '49* (New York, 1989); Noel Hynd, *The Giants of the Polo Grounds* (New York, 1988); Mark Gallagher, *The Yankee Encyclopedia*, vol. 3 (Champaign IL, 1997); Leonard Koppett, *The Man in the Dugout* (New York, 1993); Red Smith, "Leave Him to the Angels," *NYT*, January 18, 1981; Joseph J. Vecchione, ed., *The New York Times Book of Sports Legends* (New York, 1991); Dom Forker, *The Men of Autumn* (Dallas, TX, 1989); Dom Forker, *Sweet Seasons* (Dallas, TX, 1991); Dave Anderson et al., *The Yankees* (New York, 1979); Peter Golenbock, *Dynasty* (New York, 1975); Richard Goldstein, *Superstars and Screwballs* (New York, 1991); William F. McNeil, *The Dodger Encyclopedia* (Champaign, IL, 1997); Frank Graham, *The Brooklyn Dodgers* (New York, 1945); Harold Kaese, *The Boston Braves* (New York, 1948); Gary Caruso, *The Braves Encyclopedia* (Philadelphia, PA, 1995); John Thorn et al., eds., *Total Braves* (New York, 1996); Thomas Aylesworth and Benton Minks, *The Encyclopedia of Baseball Managers* (New York, 1990).

Arthur F. McClure

STENZEL, Jacob Charles "Jake" (b. Jacob Charles Stelzle, June 24, 1867, Cincinnati, OH; d. January 6, 1919, Cincinnati, OH), player, was born of German parents and changed his name to Stenzel when he ran away from home to play professional baseball. He began his professional baseball career in 1887 as a catcher in the TSL. With Wheeling, WV (TSL), he batted a resounding .373 in 1887. Wheeling shifted him in 1888 to the outfield, where he played for the remainder of his career. The 5-foot 10-inch, 168-pound right-hander slumped badly with a .213 batting average in 1888 and moved to the West Coast. Following two seasons with Portland, OR (PNL) and an unsuccessful trial with the Chicago White Stockings (NL) in 1890, he regained his batting eye in 1891 while hitting .351 for Spokane, WA (PNL).

Stenzel's major league career was confined to the 1890s. Although spending portions of nine seasons with five NL teams, he performed regularly for only five campaigns. He joined the Pittsburgh Pirates (NL) in 1892 and peaked in the 1894 to 1897 seasons at the plate, batting .360 overall and averaging 120 runs scored, 104 RBI and 60 stolen bases. In one 1894 contest against the Boston Beaneaters, he hit two HR in one inning. Two years later, against the same club, he became the first Pittsburgh player to make six hits in one game. Four peak seasons saw him feature batting averages above .350, on-base percentages over .400, and slugging averages over .480. His brilliant accomplishments, however, were overshadowed by several contemporary outfielders, who were later selected to the National Baseball Hall of Fame.

The Baltimore Orioles (NL) acquired Stenzel for Steve Brodie* in 1897. Stenzel played centerfield between Willie Keeler* and Joe Kelley,* appearing on his only championship team. Besides hitting .353, he led the NL with 43 doubles, finished second in stolen bases with 69, contributed 116 RBI for second place on the Orioles after Kelley, and scored 113 runs. In the 1897 Temple Cup Series, Baltimore claimed the NL championship by defeating the Boston Beaneaters, four games to one. Stenzel compiled an impressive .381 batting average and seven runs in that series.

Stenzel's career declined rapidly after 1897. After Stenzel started slowly in 1898, Baltimore shipped him to the last-place St. Louis Browns (NL). Stenzel failed to regain his batting stroke, causing St. Louis to release him in 1899. He played a few games with his hometown Cincinnati Reds (NL) in 1899, but was not signed the following year. His marriage to a Cincinnati woman produced one son, William, and one daughter. Stenzel owned and operated a restaurant opposite Redland Field in Cincinnati from 1900 to 1917 and then worked as a night watchman until his death.

During his short major league career, Stenzel compiled a lofty .339 batting average with 1,024 hits, 533 RBI, and 292 stolen bases. Nevertheless, Stenzel has received little recognition because his brief career overlapped with so many better hitting outfielders.

BIBLIOGRAPHY: Jacob Stenzel file, National Baseball Library, Cooperstown, NY; Richard L. Burtt, *The Pittsburgh Pirates, A Pictorial History* (Virginia Beach, VA, 1977); James H. Bready, *Baseball in Baltimore* (Baltimore, MD, 1998); Bill Felber, "Hit'er Up Again Boston!" *BH* 2 (Winter 1987/1988), pp. 20–31; Frederick G. Lieb, *The Baltimore Orioles* (New York, 1955); Frederick G. Lieb, *The Pittsburgh Pirates* (New York, 1948); Frederick Ivor-Campbell et al., eds., *Baseball's First Stars* (Cleveland, OH, 1996).

William E. Akin

STEPHENS, Vernon Decatur "Junior," "Buster" (b. October 23, 1920, McAlister, NM; d. November 3, 1968, Long Beach, CA), player, ranked among the leading power hitters and shortstops of the 1940s and early 1950s. His father, a farmer and WL umpire, moved the family to Long Beach, CA in the early 1920s. Stephens grew up in an athletic environment with baseball and basketball, but weighed under 100 pounds and was too small for high school competition. After a regimen of body building and swimming, he developed rapidly as a star baseball shortstop in American Legion play. In 1936 he tentatively was signed by the St. Louis Browns (AL) organization while studying journalism at Long Beach JC. He reported to Springfield, IL

(3IL) and spent four seasons in the minor leagues. As a minor leaguer, he batted .290 and fielded brilliantly but erratically.

Stephens joined the St. Louis Browns (AL) in 1942 and starred immediately with a .294 batting mark and 92 RBI. Browns manager Luke Sewell* claimed that he never saw a player develop as rapidly as Stephens. During the next five years with St. Louis, Stephens batted around .290 with impressive RBI statistics, showed a formidable throwing arm, and was named to the AL All-Star teams in 1943–1944, 1946, and 1948. He led the AL with 24 HR and a .961 fielding percentage in 1945. An early knee injury exempted him from military service. In 1944, he helped the Browns capture their first AL pennant by leading the AL with 109 RBI. Traded in November 1947 with Jack Kramer to the Boston Red Sox (AL), Stephens starred in a potent lineup that included Ted Williams,* Bobby Doerr,* Johnny Pesky* and Dom DiMaggio.* Batting behind Williams, he averaged 35 HR and 145 RBI the next three years and tied for the AL lead in RBI with 159 in 1949 and 144 in 1950. After an injury-shortened 1952 season, he divided 1953 between the Chicago White Sox (AL) and the St. Louis Browns (AL) and 1954 and 1955 between the Baltimore Orioles (AL) and the Chicago White Sox.

The 5-foot 10-inch, 180-pound Stephens was renowned for his clutch hitting and frequent brilliance afield. At Boston, his hitting ranked second to Williams in one of the most lethal batting orders in major league history. In 1,720 major league games, he made 1,859 hits, 307 doubles, 247 HR, and 1,174 RBI, and batted .286. He married Bernice Hood in 1940 and had two sons, Vernon III and Ronald, and one daughter, Wendy.

BIBLIOGRAPHY: Vernon Stephens file, National Baseball Library, Cooperstown, NY; Robert Redmount, *The Red Sox Encyclopedia* (Champaign, IL, 1998); Howard Liss, *The Boston Red Sox* (New York, 1982); Jack Lautier, *Fenway Voices* (Camden, ME, 1990); Dan Shaughnessy, *The Curse of the Bambino* (New York, 1990); Richard Lindberg, *Who's on Third?* (South Bend, IN, 1983); *The Baseball Encyclopedia*, 10th ed. (New York, 1996); David Halberstam, *Summer of '49* (New York, 1989); Brent P. Kelley, *The Case For: Those Overlooked by the Baseball Hall of Fame* (Jefferson, NC, 1992); Bill Borst, ed., *Ables to Zoldak*, vol. 3 (St. Louis, MO, 1990); Bill Borst, *Still Last in the American League* (West Bloomfield, MI, 1992); Richard Goldstein, *Spartan Seasons* (New York, 1980); Frederick G. Lieb, *The Baltimore Orioles* (New York, 1955); William B. Mead, *Even the Browns* (Chicago, IL, 1978); Frank Waldman, *Famous American Athletes of Today*, 11th series (Boston, MA, 1949).

                                                                   Leonard H. Frey

STEPHENSON, Jackson Riggs "Old Hoss" (b. January 5, 1898, Akron, AL; d. November 15, 1985, Tuscaloosa, AL), baseball and football player and manager, attended high school in Guntersville, AL, graduated from the University of Alabama with a Bachelor of Science degree in 1921, and served one year (1918) in the U.S. Army. At Alabama, Stephenson made All-SC football squads his junior and senior years and in 1920 was named All-SC fullback. Baseball became Stephenson's primary sport at Alabama, where he played shortstop from 1918 to 1920 with lifelong friend Joe Sewell.* In 1921 the 5-foot 10-inch, 185-pound Stephenson signed a contract for $300 a month with the Cleveland Indians (AL) and expected to join the Indians after the college season. Stephenson, however, was called up by Cleveland before opening day to replace the injured Bill Wambsganss* at second base.

Although a great hitter, the right-handed Stephenson proved only a mediocre infielder and possessed a weak arm due to a boyhood accident. Cleveland manager Tris Speaker* in 1925 optioned Stephenson to Kansas City, MO (AA) to become an outfielder, but Kansas City traded him the same year to Indianapolis, IN (AA) for Johnny Hodapp. When Louisville manager Joe McCarthy* became the Chicago Cubs pilot in 1926, he quickly obtained Stephenson. With Stephenson in left, Lewis "Hack" Wilson* in center, and Kiki Cuyler* in right, the Cubs (NL) wielded one of the hardest hitting outfields of all time. Stephenson played outfield nine years for Chicago and helped the Cubs win NL pennants in 1929 and 1932, but Chicago lost the World Series in 1929 to the Philadelphia Athletics and in 1932 to the New York Yankees. Stephenson led Cubs batters in the 1932 World Series with a .444 average and hit .316 in the 1929 World Series.

During the regular season, Stephenson compiled batting averages of .362 in 1929 and .367 in 1930 for Chicago. Although not considered a long-ball hitter, he led the NL in doubles in 1927 with 46. Stephenson had a .336 career batting average with 773 RBI, 714 runs scored, 1,515 hits, 321 doubles, and only 247 strikeouts in 4,508 at-bats in 14 major league seasons. After being released by the Cubs, Stephenson joined Indianapolis, IN (AA) in 1935 and Birmingham, AL (SA) as player–manager in 1936 and 1937. His Birmingham team finished third in 1936 and won the SA playoffs, defeating Nashville and New Orleans. He managed Helena, AL (CSL) in 1938 and Montgomery, AL (SEL) in 1939 before retiring from baseball. Stephenson married Norma Chadwick on January 10, 1934 and had one daughter.

BIBLIOGRAPHY: Gene Karst and Martin J. Jones, Jr., *Who's Who in Professional Baseball* (New Rochelle, NY, 1973); Laurie Kiely, "A Football Star Turned Baseball Pro," *Bama* (March 1983), pp. 23–25; Franklin Lewis, *The Cleveland Indians* (New York, 1949); Warren Brown, *The Chicago Cubs* (New York, 1946); Jim Enright, *Chicago Cubs* (New York, 1975); Eddie Gold and Art Ahrens, *The Golden Era Cubs, 1876–1940* (Chicago, IL, 1985); Warren Wilbert and William Hageman, *Chicago Cubs: Seasons at the Summit* (Champaign, IL, 1997); Joseph L. Reichler, *The Great All-Time Baseball Record Book* (New York, 1981); *The Baseball Encyclopedia*, 10th ed. (New York, 1996); Riggs Stephenson file, National Baseball Library, Cooperstown, NY.

Horace R. Givens

STEWART, David Keith (b. February 19, 1957, Oakland, CA), player, executive, and coach, is of African-American descent and the son of David Stewart, Jr., and Nathalie Helen (Dixon) Stewart. He grew up within walking distance of the Oakland Coliseum and starred in three sports at Oakland's St. Elizabeth High School. Stewart also attended Merritt College in Oakland and California State University at Hayward, CA.

Stewart's professional baseball career was launched at Bellingham, WA (NWL) in 1975 and included stints with the Los Angeles Dodgers (NL) in 1978 and 1981 to 1983, Texas Rangers (AL) from 1983 to 1985, and the Philadelphia Phillies (NL) in 1985 and 1986 prior to his achieving stardom with the Oakland Athletics (AL). The Oakland Athletics signed Stewart, the Philadelphia Phillies having released him in the spring of 1986 with a mediocre 30–35 major league record.

Stewart's dedication, self-confidence, and hard work finally paid dividends when he became an outstanding pitcher for the Oakland Athletics. He helped spur the Oakland Athletics' drive to three consecutive AL pennants from 1988 through 1990 and their 1989 World Series triumph over the San Francisco Giants.

From 1987 through 1990, Stewart proved baseball's outstanding pitcher. He topped the AL in games started each season while earning 20, 21, 21, and 22 victories. His 20 triumphs paced the AL in 1987. He also led the major leagues in complete games and innings pitched in 1988 and 1990, hurling the most shutouts (4) the latter season. No other major league pitcher won 20 games three times during the 1980s.

The talented 6-foot-2-inch, 200-pound right-hander possessed an overpowering fastball and outstanding forkball among his repertoire of pitches. Stewart proved especially dominant in the spring and during postseason play. His early season accomplishments included four straight opening day triumphs (1988–1991) and a 16–0 mark in April from 1988 through 1990. He holds the record for most wins in League Championship Series competition with a perfect 8–0 log.

Stewart participated on the Los Angeles Dodgers' 1981 World Series winner, the Oakland Athletics' 1989 World's Champions, 1988 and 1990 AL pennant winners, 1992 AL West titlist, and the Toronto Blue Jays 1993 World Series Champions. His honors included being named to the 1988 *TSN* AL All-Star team and selected MVP of the 1989 World Series and 1990 and 1993 AL Championship Series. Stewart's greatest honor may have come in 1993 when the Baseball Assistance Team awarded him the Bart Giamatti Award for exceptional community service.

Stewart, who won 116 games while losing 71 contests for the Oakland Athletics from 1986 to 1992, married Vanessa McKinney on July 8, 1977 and has a daughter. Stewart signed an $8.5 million contract with the Toronto Blue Jays (AL) and compiled a 12–8 mark in 1993 and 7–8 slate in 1994. His major league career ended with the Oakland Athletics in 1995. In 16 major league seasons, he boasted 168 wins, 129 losses, a 3.95 ERA, and 1,741 strikeouts in 2,629 innings. He served as special assistant to the general manager of the Oakland Athletics in 1996 and assistant general manager of the San Diego Padres (NL) in 1997. He served as Padre pitching coach in 1998, helping improve the team ERA markedly. The San Diego Padres won the NL West and defeated the Houston Astros in the NL Division Series and Atlanta Braves in the NL Championship Series before losing the World Series to the New York Yankees. In October 1998, the Toronto Blue Jays appointed him assistant general manager and as director of player personnel in December 1999.

BIBLIOGRAPHY: Peter C. Bjarkman, ed., *Encyclopedia of Major League Baseball Team Histories American League* (Westport, CT, 1991); Rich Westcott and Frank Bilovsky, *The New Phillies Encyclopedia* (Philadelphia, PA 1993); David Stewart file, National Baseball Library, Cooperstown, NY; Ron Fimrite, "The A's New Stew Can Do," *SI* 67 (October 5, 1987), pp. 69–70; Dwight Chapin, "Throwing Smoke," *SSBM* 51 (1991), pp. 30, 40; Peter Gammons, "The A's Ace of an Ace," *SI* 68 (May 16, 1988), pp. 30–31; Peter Gammons, "A Hero Lives Here," *SI* 71 (November 6, 1989), pp. 28–31; "The 1989 World Series MVP," *Sport* 81 (February 1990), p. 98; R. Kroichick, "From the Scrap Heap to the Penthouse ... Dave Stewart," *Sport* 82 (July 1991), p. 55; National Baseball Hall of Fame, questionnaire completed by David Stewart, 1981; *The 1994 Information Please Sports Almanac* (Boston, MA, 1993); *TSN Baseball Guides*, 1988–1994; *TSN Official Baseball Register*, 1993; *USAT*, January 27, 1993; *USAT Baseball Weekly*, January 27, 1993; February 9, 1993; Steve Wulf, "Dave Stewart," *SI* 79 (December 27, 1993–January 3, 1994), p. 80.

                                                                        Merl F. Kleinknecht

STIEB, David Andrew "Dave," "Sir David" (b. July 22, 1957, Santa Ana, CA), player, is the son of Peter Stieb and Patricia (Meeler) Stieb and attended Oak Grove High School in San Jose, CA and San Jose City College. He later studied at Southern Illinois University, where he played varsity baseball. The 6-foot, 180-pound Stieb ranked among the most dominant AL right-handed pitchers of the 1980s and was the winningest pitcher in the first two decades of the Toronto Blue Jays (AL) expansion franchise. A six-time AL All-Star and 1985 AL ERA leader (2.48), Stieb held or holds most Blue Jays pitching records. These included single-season standards for ERA (2.48), wins (18), strikeouts (198), complete games (19), shutouts (5), and innings pitched (288.1). He still holds career marks for innings pitched (2,873), wins (175), strikeouts (1,658), shutouts (30), and complete games (103). Originally a most promising outfielder, Stieb was converted to a pitcher by Blue Jays management at the Class A minor league level in 1978 because of his lively arm and excellent fielding abilities, but his penchant for sulking and fits of anger sometimes distracted him. Stieb became the first winning hurler ever for the expansion Toronto Blue Jays in 1981 with an 11–10 mark and in 1982 was named *TSN* AL Pitcher of the Year.

After a poor performance in 1986, Stieb embraced born-again Christianity and returned to the mound with a new dedication and vigor for the 1987 campaign. Stieb became one of the most intimidating pitchers in the Junior Circuit from 1988 to 1990. Stieb completed the 1988 campaign in spectacular fashion, throwing near-no-hitters in his final two starts. Both master-pieces were spoiled with two outs in the ninth inning, the first at Cleveland against the Indians and the second at home versus the Baltimore Orioles. Well-placed singles through the infield on the potential last pitch blocked baseball immortality and left Stieb tantalizingly short of a club-first no-hit effort. The hard-luck string continued when the flame-throwing right-hander barely missed another no-hitter against the New York Yankees in Toronto in August 1989. Yankees rookie Roberto Kelly slapped a two-strike double with two outs in the ninth inning, ending a perfect game effort. By season's end, however, Stieb had led the Toronto Blue Jays to a second Eastern Division title in five summers and had won a club-high 17 contests for the fourth time. Stieb enjoyed his best season in 1990, with an 18–6 mark and 2.93 ERA. On September 2, 1990, he hurled a no-hitter against the Cleveland Indians. A herniated disc and sciatic pains sidelined Stieb for most of the 1991 season. The Toronto Blue Jays captured the Eastern Di-vision title, but missed Stieb's pitching leadership in the AL Championship Series against the Minnesota Twins. Stieb struggled thereafter, missing the last two months of the 1992 season. He retired after pitching briefly for the Chicago White Sox (AL) in 1993. He made a comeback with the Toronto Blue Jays in 1998, compiling a 1–2 record in 19 appearances. In 16 major league seasons, Stieb compiled a 176–137 win–loss mark with 1,669 strike-outs, 30 shutouts, and a 3.44 ERA.

BIBLIOGRAPHY: Dave Stieb file, National Baseball Library, Cooperstown, NY; Peter C. Bjarkman, *The Toronto Blue Jays* (New York, 1990); Ron Fimrite, "A Rare Bird: The Natural," *SI* 58 (May 16, 1983), pp. 48–52; Mike Shatzkin, ed., *The Ballplayers* (New York, 1990); Dave Stieb with Kevin Boland, *Tomorrow I'll Be Perfect* (New York, 1986).

                                                              Peter C. Bjarkman

STIRNWEISS, George Henry "Snuffy" (b. October 26, 1918, New York, NY; d. September 15, 1958, Newark Bay, NJ), player and manager, was the son of Andrew Stirnweiss, a police officer, and Sophie (Daly) Stirnweiss and starred in several sports at Fordham Prep School. He graduated in 1940 from the University of North Carolina, where he became the first player to captain both the football and baseball teams. A star gridiron running back in 1938 and 1939, Stirnweiss declined a chance to play professional football for the Chicago Cardinals (NFL) and signed instead with the New York Yankees (AL) baseball club. He played for Norfolk, VA (PiL) in 1940 and Newark, NJ (IL) from 1940 to 1942. Gastric ulcers and severe hay fever kept him out of military service during World War II.

The speedy 5-foot 8-inch, 175-pound second baseman enjoyed his best seasons with the New York Yankees in 1944 and 1945, batting .319 and an AL-leading .309. His 1945 batting average marked the lowest to win an AL title since 1905. Stirnweiss made three hits on the final day to edge Tony

Cuccinello* for the AL Crown. He led the AL in hits (205, 195), triples (16, 22), stolen bases (55, 33), and runs scored (125, 107) both years, paced the AL with a .476 on base percentage in 1945, and finished third in the 1945 voting for AL MVP. Stirnweiss was traded to the St. Louis Browns (AL) in June 1950 and to the Cleveland Indians (AL) in April 1951. He finished his major league career in 1952, compiling a .268 career batting average with 989 hits, 604 runs scored, 68 triples, and 134 stolen bases in 1,028 games. Stirnweiss played in the 1946 All-Star game and the 1943, 1947, and 1949 World Series, batting .250 in nine games. He managed Schenectady, NY (EL) in 1954 and Binghamton, NY (EL) in 1955 before joining the Caldwell and Company freight business. Stirnweiss drowned after a train ran off a bridge into Newark Bay, being survived by his wife, Jane, and six children.

BIBLIOGRAPHY: Dave Anderson et al., *The Yankees* (New York, 1979); Tim Cohane, "Yankee Bandit: Stirnweiss," *BD* 4 (July 1945), pp. 34–35; Dan Daniel, "Snuffy's Winning Bat Drive No. 1 Individual Feat," *TSN*, November 29, 1945, p. 3; Charles Dexter, "Bronx Express: Snuffy Stirnweiss," *Collier's* 112 (July 17, 1943), p. 30; Mark Gallagher, *The Yankee Encyclopedia*, vol. 3 (Champaign, IL, 1997); Peter Golenbock, *Dynasty* (New York, 1975); Dom Forker, *The Men of Autumn* (Dallas, TX, 1989); Robert W. Creamer, *Stengel: His Life and Times* (New York, 1984); Bill Borst, ed., *Ables to Zoldak*, vol. 3 (St. Louis, MO, 1990); John Phillips, *Winners* (Cabin John, MD, 1987); George Stirnweiss file, National Baseball Library, Cooperstown, NY.

Jim L. Sumner

STIVETTS, John Elmer "Jack," "Happy Jack" (b. March 31, 1868, Ashland, PA; d. April 18, 1930, Ashland, PA), player, won over 200 games as a pitcher and batted near .300 during an 11-year major league career. Stivetts, the son of coal miner Adam Stivetts and Ameila (Cooper) Stivetts, attended the Ashland public school for eight years, worked around the anthracite mines, and pitched for the town baseball team. He first played professionally for York, PA and Allentown, PA (CL) and in 1889 signed with the major league St. Louis Browns (AA). The 6-foot 2-inch, 185-pound right-hander displayed exceptional skill at the plate and on the mound and often was used at other positions to take advantage of his powerful hitting. As a rookie in 1889, Stivetts appeared in 26 games, won 12, lost seven, struck out 143 batters, and led the AA with a 2.25 ERA. The following year, he finished among the AA's top five pitching and batting leaders. His 27 victories and 289 strikeouts placed him fourth and second, respectively, in those categories. He hit seven HR to tie for third place in the final standings. Besides improving to 33 wins and an AA-leading 259 strikeouts in 1891, Stivetts also hit .305, drove in 54 runs, and again clouted 7 HR.

With the demise of the AA, Stivetts in 1892 signed with the Boston Beaneaters, the defending NL champions and one of the decade's dominant teams. Stivetts strengthened an already formidable pitching staff led by Charles "Kid" Nichols,* a perennial 30-game winner. In his first NL season,

Stivetts recorded 35 victories and batted .296. On August 6, 1892, he became the first Boston Beaneater pitcher to hurl a no-hit, no-run game when he blanked the Brooklyn Bridegrooms, 11–0. He also hurled a five-inning no-hitter against the Washington Senators on October 15 in a game shortened to allow the Boston team to catch a train.

Behind the pitching of Stivetts and 35-game winner Nichols, Boston clinched the second half pennant in the NL experimental split season schedule. A post-season playoff between Boston and first half leader Cleveland Spiders decided the overall championship. In the opening game, Stivetts dueled Cy Young* through 11 scoreless innings before darkness ended the contest. The two faced each other again in Game 3, with Stivetts emerging the winner. He triumphed again in the fifth game, as Boston swept to the championship without defeat. Injuries, along with difficulties adjusting to the new pitching distance of 60-feet 6-inches, hampered Stivetts in 1893. Although dropping to 20 victories, he batted .297 to help Boston capture its third consecutive NL pennant. Stivetts came back in 1894 to win 26 games and bat .328, with career highs in HR (8) and RBI (64). He recorded 17 and 22 wins and .190 and .344 batting averages, respectively, the next two seasons. After 1896, Stivetts pitched less and played most often in the outfield. He batted a career-high .367 in 1897 and .252 the following season, as Boston won two more NL pennants.

Stivetts was sold to the Cleveland Spiders (NL) in 1899 and ended his major league career with a 0–4 pitching mark. Cleveland compiled the worst win–loss record (20–134) in major league history that season. After retiring from baseball, Stivetts returned to Ashland, PA, where he worked as a carpenter and umpired local baseball games. Stivetts married Margaret Ann Thomas in June 1886 and had five daughters and one son.

As a pitcher, Stivetts compiled a 203–132 lifetime win–loss record and one of the best win–loss percentages (.606) of the pre–1900 era. He registered 1,223 strikeouts, completed 278 of his 333 starts, and had a 3.74 ERA. For three consecutive years (1890–1892), he pitched over 400 innings and completed over 40 starts. Stivetts batted .297 lifetime with 35 HR, including 20 as a pitcher. He made 592 hits, including 84 doubles and 46 triples, and knocked in 357 runs. On three occasions, he slugged two HR in a single game. He belted three HR as a pinch hitter, becoming the first pitcher to accomplish this feat. Considered among the fastest throwers of his time, Stivetts also ranks among the greatest hitting pitchers in major league history and showed extraordinary versatility by playing every position except catcher. The friendly, good-natured Stivetts won the admiration of teammates and fans through his dedication, selflessness, and hard work on the field.

BIBLIOGRAPHY: J. Thomas Hetrick, *Misfits!* (Jefferson, NC, 1991); David Nemec, *The Beer and Whisky League* (New York, 1994); J. Thomas Hetrick, *Chris Von der Ahe and the St. Louis Browns* (Lanham, MD, 1999); Harold Kaese, *The Boston Braves* (New York, 1948); Gary Caruso, *The Braves Encyclopedia* (Philadelphia, PA, 1995);

John Phillips, *The Spiders—Who Was Who* (Cabin John, MD, 1991); Gene Karst and Martin J. Jones, Jr., *Who's Who in Professional Baseball* (New Rochelle, NY, 1973); Providence (RI) *Journal*, April 20, 1930; John Stivetts file, National Baseball Library, Cooperstown, NY; Robert L. Tiemann and Mark Rucker, eds., *Nineteenth Century Stars* (Kansas City, MO, 1989); George V. Tuohey, comp., *A History of the Boston Base Ball Club* (Boston, MA, 1897).

Joseph Lawler (Nicoteri)

STOCK, Milton Joseph "Milt" (b. July 11, 1893, Chicago, IL; d. July 16, 1977, Montrose, AL), player, coach, and executive, was a reliable-hitting, slick-fielding third baseman for four major league clubs, but gained notoriety for a coaching error on the final day of the 1950 season. The Philadelphia Phillies (NL) and Brooklyn Dodgers (NL) were vying for the NL pennant. When Brooklyn Dodgers third-base coach Stock waved Cal Abrams home, Philadelphia's Richie Ashburn* threw him out. The Philadelphia Phillies won the NL pennant, while Stock lost his coaching job.

Luckily, Stock's baseball career contained compensating highlights. An indifferent student perhaps because of his partial deafness, he left St. Ignatius College in 1911 at age 17 and signed a professional baseball contract with the New York Giants (NL). The shortstop spent the 1911 to 1913 seasons in the minor leagues with Fond du Lac, WI (WIL), Buffalo, NY (EL), and Mobile, AL (SA) before making the New York Giants in 1914. Although Stock hit .263 and fielded well, the New York Giants traded him to the Philadelphia Phillies (NL) in January 1915. He played a utility role on the 1915 NL pennant-winners, but batted only .118 against the victorious Boston Red Sox in the World Series. Stock remained a fixture in the Phillies infield through 1918.

The Philadelphia Phillies traded Stock to the St. Louis Cardinals (NL) in January 1919, convinced that the 5-foot 8-inch, 154-pound third baseman would not be a good hitter. Although never hitting for power, he became a fine spray hitter with St. Louis and batted over .300 for four consecutive seasons from 1919 to 1922. Stock was traded to the Brooklyn Robins (NL) in April 1924. The 1925 season saw him bat a career high .328 with 202 hits, including 164 singles. His major league playing career ended shortly after a 1926 preseason collision with Lou Gehrig* of the New York Yankees. In 14 major league seasons, Stock batted .289, collected 1,806 hits, scored 839 runs, had 696 RBI, and rarely struck out.

Stock served as player–manager for Mobile, AL (SA) from 1926 through 1928 and Dallas, TX (TL) in 1929. He also piloted Knoxville, TN (SA) in 1931, Beckley, WV (MAL) in 1934, Monessen, PA (PSA) in 1935, Macon, GA (SA) from 1938 to 1942, and Portsmouth, VA (PiL) in 1943. Stock served as president of Mobile, AL (SEL) in 1932 and of Quincy, IL (ML) in 1933. Eddie Stanky,* who played for Macon, subsequently married Stock's daughter, Myrtle. Stock coached for the Chicago Cubs (NL) from 1944 through 1948, Brooklyn Dodgers (NL) in 1949 and 1950, and Pittsburgh Pirates (NL) in 1951 and 1952. He married Myrtle McNamara in December 1915.

BIBLIOGRAPHY: Rich Westcott and Frank Bilovsky, *The New Phillies Encyclopedia* (Philadelphia, PA, 1993); "Milton Stock," *Microsoft Complete Baseball*, CD-ROM (Redmond, WA, 1994); Allen Lewis and Larry Shenk, eds., *This Date in Philadelphia Phillies History* (New York, 1979); Danny Peary, ed., *We Played the Game* (New York, 1994); *The Baseball Encyclopedia*, 10th ed. (New York, 1996); Milton Stock file, National Baseball Library, Cooperstown, NY; Allen Lewis, *The Philadelphia Phillies: A Pictorial History* (Virginia Beach, VA, 1981); Frederick G. Lieb and Stan Baumgartner, *The Philadelphia Phillies* (New York, 1953); Frederick G. Lieb, *The St. Louis Cardinals* (New York, 1945); Bob Broeg, *Redbirds! A Century of Cardinals' Baseball* (St. Louis, MO, 1981); Bob Broeg and Jerry Vickery, *St. Louis Cardinals Encyclopedia* (Grand Rapids, MI, 1998); Charles C. Alexander, *Rogers Hornsby* (New York, 1995); Richard Goldstein, *Superstars and Screwballs* (New York, 1991); Peter Golenbock, *Bums* (New York, 1984); William F. McNeil, *The Dodgers Encyclopedia* (Champaign, IL, 1997).

Robert E. Weir

STONE, George Robert "Silent" (b. September 3, 1877, Lost Nation, IA; d. January 5, 1945, Clinton, IA), player, executive, and owner, was the son of Samuel Stone and Hannah Stone and attended Coleridge, NE schools. He played baseball for Laurel, NE, Hartington, NE, Bloomfield, NE and Pierce, NE town teams, building a local reputation as "the kid who could hit a mile." After playing for an Onowa, IA team in a local tournament, Stone was signed by Omaha, NE (WL) in 1902 and loaned to Peoria, IL (3IL) the same season. Peoria sold the 5-foot 9-inch, 175-pound left-hander to the Boston Pilgrims (AL), who optioned Stone to Milwaukee, WI (WL) in 1903 and 1904 after he twice went hitless as a pinch hitter in 1903.

In January 1905, the Boston Pilgrims sold Stone to the Washington Senators (AL). Washington sent him the same day to the St. Louis Browns (AL) for star Jesse Burkett.* In his first full major league season in 1905, the left fielder batted .296 and led the AL in plate appearances with 632 and hits, 187. The 1906 campaign marked the banner year for Stone, who edged star Nap Lajoie* for the AL batting title with a .358 average. He again led the AL in total bases (288), on base percentage (.417), and slugging average (.501). Stone's second best season came in 1907, as he hit .320 with a .399 slugging average. The offensive stalwart played regularly four full seasons with the St. Louis Browns and appeared in only 83 games in 1909. In 1911, the St. Louis Browns released Stone to Milwaukee.

Stone worked in Coleridge, NE as a banker until 1940, when he opened a bowling alley in Clinton, IA. He had looked forward to beginning a business in Coleridge and had worked there as a retail clerk in the off season. Stone became part owner and president of the Lincoln, NE (WL) baseball franchise in 1916, but sold out in 1917. He married high school sweetheart Pearl Moore in 1906. His son, Vean, became a physician and worked at a station hospital in New Guinea.

A fierce competitor, Stone often slid into first base to beat out infield grounders. Off the field, the quiet, well-spoken, polite Nebraskan enjoyed reading and playing the violin. In seven major league seasons, Stone appeared in 848 games with 984 hits, a .301 batting average, and a .396 slugging average. He made 106 doubles, 68 triples, and 23 HR with 268 RBI and 132 stolen bases.

BIBLIOGRAPHY: Gene Karst and Martin J. Jones, Jr., *Who's Who in Professional Baseball* (New Rochelle, NY, 1973); *TSN*, January 11, 1945; George Stone file, National Baseball Library, Cooperstown, NY; Clinton (IA) *Herald*, January 5, 1945; Coleridge (IA) *Blade*, January 11, 1945; Mike Shatzkin, ed., *The Ballplayers* (New York, 1990); Jerry E. Clark, *Anson to Zuber* (Omaha, NE, 1992); Bill Borst, ed., *Ables to Zoldak*, vol. 3 (St. Louis, MO, 1990); John Thom, *Champion Batsman of the 20th Century* (Los Angeles, CA, 1992); Bill Borst, *Still Last in the American League* (West Bloomfield, MI, 1992); Frederick G. Lieb, *The Baltimore Orioles* (New York, 1955).

John H. Ziegler

STONE, John Thomas "Johnny," "Rocky" (b. October 10, 1905, Lynchburg, TN; d. November 30, 1955, Shelbyville, TN), player, batted left-handed and threw right-handed, stood 6-feet 1-inch, and weighed 178 pounds. He first attracted attention as a star baseball player at Maryville (TN) College, from which he graduated with a bachelor's degree in 1928. Stone captained the 1927 Maryville squad to a 16–5 record and victories over the University of Michigan and the University of Tennessee and the 1928 team to a 15–2 mark. He married Ruth C. Ellis on January 11, 1933 and had two children, John, Jr. and Susanne. After entering professional baseball, Stone divided his playing time as an outfielder with Evansville, IN (3IL), Toronto, Canada (IL), and the Detroit Tigers (AL) in 1928 and 1929. Stone became an outfield fixture with Detroit from 1930 through December 1933 and the Washington Senators (AL) from 1934 until tuberculosis ended his major league career in mid–1938. Stone unfortunately never played with an AL pennant–winner or gained acclaim otherwise. Although hitting .341 in 1936 and .330 in 1937 with Washington, he did not earn an All-Star game selection or rank among the first five hitters. His best batting accomplishment comprised finishing second in triples in 1935 (18) and 1937 (15), with half his games played in mammoth Griffith Stadium. For his 11 year major league career, Stone batted .310 with 268 doubles, 105 triples, and 77 HR. He recuperated from tuberculosis and returned to his native environs, engaging in the milk-processing and distribution business.

BIBLIOGRAPHY: *The Baseball Encyclopedia*, 10th ed. (New York, 1996); Ellie Koella, Development and Alumni Relations, Maryville College, Maryville, TN, letter to Lowell Blaisdell, April 1990; Craig Carter ed., *TSN Daguerreotypes*, 8th ed. (St. Louis,

MO, 1990); John Stone file, National Baseball Library, Cooperstown, NY; John Thorn, "John Stone's Batting Streak," *BRJ* 21 (1992), pp. 61–62; Frederick G. Lieb, *The Detroit Tigers* (New York, 1946); Joe Falls, *Detroit Tigers* (New York, 1975); Fred Smith, *995 Tigers* (Detroit, MI, 1981); Morris Bealle, *The Washington Senators* (Washington, DC, 1947); Shirley Povich, *The Washington Senators* (New York, 1954).

Lowell L. Blaisdell

STONE, Steven Michael "Steve" (b. July 14, 1947, Euclid, OH), player and sportscaster, is the son of Paul Stone, an insurance salesman, and Dorothy Stone. Like his mother, Stone became a restauranteur. He carefully learned the business in several Chicago eateries and then opened restaurants in Scottsdale, AZ, where he resides. On June 21, 1970, Stone married Nancy Nathanson. The couple divorced in 1972.

Stone attended Kent State University from 1965 to 1971, competing on the baseball, volleyball, and bowling teams. New York Yankees star Thurman Munson* caught him at Kent State. After signing with the San Francisco Giants (NL) in 1969, Stone returned to Kent State following his first minor league season and graduated the next year with a Bachelor's degree in history and government.

After averaging a strikeout per inning in the minor leagues, the 5-foot 10-inch, 175-pound right-handed Stone joined the San Francisco Giants in 1971. Arm troubles prompted his trade to the Chicago White Sox (AL) in November 1972 and forced him to become a control pitcher. Stone, dealt uptown to the Chicago Cubs (NL) in December 1973, enjoyed his first two winning seasons in 1974 and 1975. After slumping in 1976 when suffering a shoulder injury, he rebuilt his shoulder through concentrated weight training. The Chicago White Sox again acquired him in November 1976. He won 27 games over the next two seasons and signed a lucrative four-year contract with the Baltimore Orioles (AL).

His solid 1979 season concluded with five straight wins and a World Series appearance against the Pittsburgh Pirates. Stone exploded for an AL-leading 25 wins and .781 winning percentage in 1980, winning the AL Cy Young Award. He credited his sudden success to discontinuing the weight training, which had reduced the flexibility in his shoulder; working with Oriole pitching coach Ray Miller, who taught him to work faster between pitches and use only two pitches early in the game; and concentrating more on the mental aspects of pitching.

Stone's major league career again fell victim to arm problems in 1981, when he appeared in only 15 games. After winning just four contests, he retired after the 1981 season with a 107–93 lifetime record and 3.97 ERA. He returned to Chicago to become a Cubs broadcaster, restauranteur, and author.

BIBLIOGRAPHY: Eddie Gold and Art Ahrens, *The New Era Cubs, 1941–1985* (Chicago, IL, 1985); Ray Kennedy, "Hold the Twinkies Flambé," *SI* 52 (June 16, 1980), pp. 47ff; Robert Markus, "How Steve Stone Turned into a Big Winner," *BD* 39 (November 1980), pp. 66–69; Leigh Montville, "The First to Be Free," *SI* 72 (April 16, 1990), pp. 98–108; Steve Stone file, National Baseball Library, Cooperstown, NY; Nick Peters, *Giants Almanac* (Berkeley, CA, 1988); Richard Lindberg, *Who's on Third?* (South Bend, IN, 1983); Ken Young, *Cy Young Award Winners* (New York, 1994); Ted Patterson, *The Baltimore Orioles* (Dallas, TX, 1995); Ken Nigro, "Over-30s Find Good Life," *TSN*, August 23, 1980, pp. 3ff; Steve Stone with Nolan Anglum, *Teach Yourself to Win* (Chicago, IL, 1991).

Allen E. Hye

STONEHAM, Charles (b. July 5, 1876, Jersey City, NJ; d. January 6, 1936, Hot Springs, AR), owner and executive, played a major role administering the New York Giants (NL). Stoneham married Margaret Leonard and had four children, Horace, Mary, Jane, and Russell. An altar boy as a youth, Stoneham became a runner for a major stockbroker and then a stock sales-man. New York Curb Exchange activity represented a far cry from his church duties, but could mean millions in earnings for an industrious person. In 1913, he established Charles A. Stoneham and Company with a sizeable portion of his earnings. The balance, including some accumulated earnings, was spent in 1919 when he, John McGraw,* and New York City magistrate Francis McQuade formed a syndicate to purchase the New York Giants from the estate of John T. Brush.* The three simultaneously purchased numerous Cuban properties, including a racetrack, casino, and newspaper in Havana. After the company disbanded in 1921, the syndicate encountered legal diffi-culties. In 1923, Stoneham was indicted on charges of perjury and mail fraud because of activities involving his Cuban holdings and stock transfers for company customers. He was cleared of the mail fraud charges, but found guilty of perjury in 1925 and fined heavily. During the nearly three-year ordeal, Stoneham was pressured constantly to leave the baseball arena by both newspapermen and other owners. Stoneham, who had paid $1 million for his 1,300 shares, intended to keep them and pass them on to his son.

BIBLIOGRAPHY: Alvin Dark and John Underwood, *When in Doubt, Fire the Manager* (New York, 1980); Charles Einstein, *Willie Mays* (New York, 1979); Frank Graham, *The New York Giants* (New York, 1952); Russ Hodges, *My Giants* (Garden City, NY, 1963); Noel Hynd, *The Giants of the Polo Grounds* (New York, 1988); Leo Durocher, *Nice Guys Finish Last* (New York, 1975); Fred Stein and Nick Peters, *Giants Diary* (Berkeley, CA, 1987); Charles Stoneham file, National Baseball Library, Coopers-town, NY; *NYT*, January 7, 9–11, 16, 1936, April 2, 16, 1936, January 9, 1990, p. D-23.

Alan R. Asnen

STONEHAM, Horace (b. April 27, 1903, Newark, NJ; d. January 7, 1990, Scottsdale, AZ), owner and executive, figured prominently in administering the New York Giants. He attended prep school at Loyola, Hunter, and Pawling and graduated from Fordham University, where he played both baseball and hockey. Stoneham worked at a California copper mine and married Valleda Pyke in April 1924. Stoneham, who had three children, Mary, Horace, Jr., and Peter, became involved in the Giants' administrative organization in 1929. When his father, Charles Stoneham,* contracted Brights disease, Horace assumed more daily operational responsibility in the front office. By the time Charles died in 1936, Horace had already performed his father's duties for nearly a year. On January 16, 1936, Horace was voted president and part-owner of the Giants and became the youngest owner in baseball history. Charles was considered a sharp-witted, often ruthless businessman, who frequented after-hours gambling clubs on nightly free-spending binges. By contrast, Horace seemed overly sentimental, too close to the game, and too business-minded, and limited his gambling to very risky, often criticized trades.

Horace, one of the few owners in history to concentrate on baseball as an interest and business, joined Bill Terry* in building the Giants minor league system and held the same commitment to his farm club and Polo Grounds customers. When Willie Mays* was advanced to the major leagues in 1951, Stoneham used a full page in the Minneapolis, MN papers to apologize to the Millers (AA) fans for his action. Earlier Stoneham had promised that Mays would stay at the Triple A level club for another year. During the late 1940s and early 1950s, Stoneham proved instrumental among the owners in bringing black and Latin American talent into organized baseball. After his NL team swept the Cleveland Indians in the 1954 World Series, Stoneham was named *TSN* Executive of the Year. Despite this success on the field, Stoneham lost money at the gate. Nevertheless, he rejected a $1 million offer by August Busch* of the St. Louis Cardinals for Mays in 1956. Financial insecurity, the changing baseball market in New York, and numerous other factors convinced Stoneham to move his team initially to Minneapolis, where he had a ready-made, baseball-hungry audience. He was talked out of this location by Brooklyn Dodgers executive Walter O'Malley,* who desperately needed a California rival to accompany his own team's move to Los Angeles. Business and baseball did not treat Stoneham very well after the Giants' move to San Francisco, CA. Despite further expansion on the West Coast, a new stadium, and some truly awesome baseball talent, he regularly lost large sums of money on the franchise. Stoneham, who refused to sell the team to Labatts Brewery of Toronto, sold the San Francisco Giants in 1976 to local real estate magnate Robert Lurie. Both Charles and Horace were seldom seen or heard except during spring training, watching all the games from their offices rather than from the field. After selling the Giants, Stoneham retired from public life.

BIBLIOGRAPHY: Alvin Dark and John Underwood, *When in Doubt, Fire the Manager* (New York, 1980); Charles Einstein, *Willie Mays* (New York, 1979); Frank Graham, *The New York Giants* (New York, 1952); Russ Hodges, *My Giants* (Garden City, NY,

1963); Noel Hynd, *The Giants of the Polo Grounds* (New York, 1988); Leo Durocher, *Nice Guys Finish Last* (New York, 1975); Fred Stein and Nick Peters, *Giants Diary* (Berkeley, CA, 1987); Horace Stoneham file, National Baseball Library, Coopers-town, NY; *NYT*, January 7, 9–11, 16, 1936, April 2, 16, 1936, January 9, 1990, p. D-23.

Alan R. Asnen

STOTTLEMYRE, Melvin Leon, Sr. "Stott," "Mel" (b. November 13, 1941, Hazelton, MO), player and coach, was a 6-foot 1-inch, 190-pound right-handed pitcher and spent his entire major league pitching career with the New York Yankees (AL) from 1964 to 1974. He married Jean Mitchell of Yakima, WA, in November 1962 and has three children. For Richmond, VA in 1964, he led the IL in ERA (1.42) with a 13–3 win–loss record and was named *TSN* Minor League Player of the Year. Stottlemyre mastered control rather than developing a variety of pitches. He specialized in throwing an effective sinker and strove to keep the ball low and on the corners, never becoming a power pitcher. His quiet, confident temperament proved ideal.

The New York Yankees summoned Stottlemyre for the 1964 AL stretch drive. Stottlemyre responded with a 9–3 win–loss performance and defeated Bob Gibson* of the St. Louis Cardinals, 8–3, in the second game of the first World Series he ever saw. "Stottlemyre is the best pitcher we have," commented one grateful Yankee executive about the young hurler. Stottlemyre's future campaigns fulfilled his promise. Three 20-game victory seasons over the next decade included a career best 21–12 mark and 2.45 ERA in 1968 and four All-Star Game appearances. He once held the major league record (272) for most consecutive starting assignments. Stottlemyre led the AL in complete games in 1965 and 1969 and innings pitched in 1965. His final major league career totaled a 164–139 win–loss slate (.541 winning percentage), a 2.97 ERA, and 40 shutouts, ranking him second among all-time Yankees pitchers.

A shoulder injury contributed to Stottlemyre's lackluster 6–7 season in 1974. The Yankees in March 1975 abruptly released Stottlemyre, ending his major league career. The Seattle Mariners (AL) made him their pitching coach from 1977 to 1981. Manager Dave Johnson* brought him to the New York Mets (NL) as a pitching coach in 1984. He coached for the New York Mets through 1993, the Houston Astros (NL) in 1994 and 1995, and the New York Yankees since 1996. The New York Yankees won the 1996, 1998, and 1999 World Series and compiled the second most victories in major league history with 114 in 1998. Stottlemyre's playing career witnessed some significant batting achievements, including his five hits versus the Washington Senators on September 6, 1964, and his inside-the-park grand-slam HR against the Boston Red Sox on July 20, 1965. His son, Mel, Jr., pitched for the Kansas City Royals (AL) in 1990, while his son, Todd, pitches for the Arizona Diamondbacks (NL).

BIBLIOGRAPHY: *The Baseball Encyclopedia*, 10th ed. (New York, 1996); Charles Dexter, "Young Mel of Mabton," *BD* 23 (December-January 1965), pp. 85–90; Brent P. Kelley, *The Case For: Those Overlooked by the Baseball Hall of Fame* (Jefferson, NC, 1992); Mel Stottlemyre file, National Baseball Library, Cooperstown, NY; Dom Forker, *Sweet Seasons* (Dallas, TX, 1991); Peter Golenbock, *Dynasty* (New York, 1975); Dave Anderson et al., *The Yankees* (New York, 1979); David Halberstam, *October 1964* (New York, 1994); Mark Gallagher, *The Yankee Encyclopedia*, vol. 3 (Champaign, IL, 1997); *The 1989 Mets Information Guide*, p. 23; *TSN*, May 3, 1969, April 19, 1975; *TSN Baseball Register, 1975*; *TSN Baseball Register, 1989*.

William J. Miller

STOVEY, George Washington (b. 1866, Williamsport, PA; d. March 22, 1936, Williamsport, PA), player and umpire, was of mixed parentage with a white father and a black mother whose names and backgrounds are unknown. He stood approximately 6 feet tall, weighed about 165 pounds, and threw left-handed. He played amateur baseball in the early 1880s until joining the all-black Cuban Giants of Trenton, NJ in 1886. After pitching just one game, he jumped to Jersey City, NJ (IL) in a "daring midnight raid." Stovey won 30 games for Jersey City that season, holding opposing batters to an unbelievably low .167 batting average. In a heartbreaking loss against Bridgeport, CT, he struck out 22 batters.

Stovey's fine career was marred by racial controversy. At the end of the 1886 season, the New York Giants (NL) almost signed Stovey. Since virulent racist, highly influential Cap Anson* of the Chicago White Stockings (NL) vigorously opposed Stovey's signing, the New York Giants bowed to Anson's wishes. Stovey enjoyed his best season in 1887 while pitching for Newark. He dominated the IL with a 34–15 win–loss record, a victory mark unlikely to be broken. He also participated in a historic first that season when he and catcher Fleet Walker* formed organized baseball's first all-African-American battery. Stovey became a cause célèbre in July 1887, when his Newark team was scheduled to play an exhibition with Anson's Chicago White Stockings. Anson refused to let his White Stockings play Newark if Stovey pitched against them. This incident may have led to the erection of organized baseball's color line. Stovey's contract with Newark was not renewed for the following year. Stovey played for Worcester, MA (NEL), Troy, NY (NYSL), and in 1891 for one of the all-time great black teams, the New York Gorhams. His baseball career ended with the New York Cuban Giants in 1893. In six seasons of organized baseball, he registered 60 wins, 40 losses and a 2.17 ERA.

At the height of Stovey's career, a Binghamton, NY newspaper described him as "the fellow with the sinister fin who has such a knack of tossing up balls that they appear as large as an alderman's opinion of himself, but you can't hit with a cellar door."

Stovey returned to his native Williamsport, working as a laborer in a sawmill, possibly as a barber, and in other odd jobs. Stovey kept involved in baseball, playing intermittently with local amateur teams until his early fifties. He also umpired frequently, his judgment being respected. Williamsport's African-American community highly respected Stovey and his athletic accomplishments in his youth. Most baseball historians regard Stovey as the greatest African-American pitcher of the 19th century. Stovey, a bachelor, died destitute at age 70.

BIBLIOGRAPHY: Binghamton (NY) *Leader*, quoted in the Newark (NJ) *Journal*, July 29, 1887; Cleveland (OH) *Gazette*, May 13, 1892; *SL*, February 23, 1887; Lou Hunsinger, Jr., "George W. Stovey," *TNP* 14 (1994), pp. 80–82; James A. Riley, *The Biographical Encyclopedia of the Negro Baseball Leagues* (New York, 1994); Noel Hynd, *The Giants of the Polo Grounds* (New York, 1988); Trenton (NJ) *True American*, February 23, 1887; Williamsport (PA) *Grit*, March 29, 1936.

                                                    Louis E. Hunsinger, Jr.

STOVEY, Harry Duffield (b. Harry Duffield Stowe, December 20, 1856, Philadelphia, PA; d. September 20, 1937, New Bedford, MA), player, was the son of watchman John Stowe and Lizzie Stowe. His father was descended from bellmaker and foundry owner Charles Stowe, who recast the Liberty Bell after it had been cracked. When Stowe began playing professional baseball, he changed his name to Stovey so that his mother, who forbade him to play, would not see his name in the newspapers. Although he had little formal education, Stovey became one of his era's most articulate, knowledgeable players. In 1876 the right-handed, 5-foot 11½-inch, 180-pound Stovey began his pro baseball career as a pitcher for the old Defiance Club of Philadelphia, PA. Two years later, he played first base for Frank Bancroft's New Bedford, MA Clam-Eaters. He married Mary L. Walker in 1879 and had three children.

Noted for his gentlemanly behavior, Stovey in 1880 started his major league career as an outfielder–first baseman for the Worcester, MA Ruby Legs (NL). After Worcester disbanded in 1882, Stovey played from 1883 to 1889 for the Philadelphia Athletics (AA) and joined the Boston Reds of the short-lived PL in 1890. The NL and AA quarreled over the ownership of Stovey and Louis Bierbauer,* resulting in a twelve-club NL. When the Board of Control ruled that the Boston Beaneaters (NL) club owned the rights to Stovey, he signed in 1891 with the Beaneaters. The Boston team experienced financial problems. Stovey's skills faded, causing his release in June 1892. Stovey played with the Baltimore Orioles (NL) until August 1893, when the Brooklyn Bridegrooms (NL) signed him. After playing briefly for Michael "King" Kelly's* Allentown, PA (PSL) in 1894, he finished his playing career that same year as captain of New Bedford, MA (NEL). Stovey joined the New Bedford police force in 1895 and served as captain from 1915 until his retirement in 1923.

A swift base runner and power hitter in the dead ball era, Stovey also exhibited a strong arm. Stovey led the AA in doubles (31) in 1883, in triples four times (1880, 1884, 1888, and 1891), in runs scored four times (1883–1885, 1889), and in RBI (119) in 1889. The first player to wear sliding pads, he led base stealers of his era and reached a career high 97 in 1890 for Boston. Besides allegedly circling the bases in 14 seconds in 1891, he led the AA once and the PL once in stolen bases. The solid HR hitter led or tied for most HR in a season five times and belted a career-high 19 in 1889. Stovey slugged three triples in games on August 18, 1884 and July 21, 1892. In 1888, he showed his strong arm in a distance-throwing contest sponsored by the Cincinnati *Enquirer*, finishing second to Ned Williamson* with a throw of 123 yards, 2 inches. A premier performer of the pre–1900 era, Stovey became the first player to combine speed with both power and batting average. He batted .289 lifetime, hit 122 career HR, and stole 509 bases (after 1886). In 1,486 major league games, he made 1,771 hits, 347 doubles, and 174 triples, and scored 1,492 runs. Stovey played on championship teams in three major leagues: the AA, PL, and NL.

BIBLIOGRAPHY: Harry Stovey file, National Baseball Library, Cooperstown, NY; Gene Karst and Martin J. Jones, Jr., *Who's Who in Professional Baseball* (New Rochelle, NY, 1973); Lew Lipset, " 'Grandpa' was Harry Stovey," *TNP* 4 (Winter 1985), pp. 84–85; New Bedford (MA) *Standard-Times*, September 20, 1937, October 1, 1982; New York *Clipper*, August 7, 1880; Harold Seymour, *Baseball: The Early Years* (New York, 1960); George V. Tuohey, *A History of the Boston Base Ball Club* (Boston, MA, 1897); David Nemec, *The Beer and Whisky League* (New York, 1994); Robert L. Tiemann and Mark Rucker, eds., *Nineteenth Century Stars* (Kansas City, MO, 1989); Harold Kaese, *The Boston Braves* (New York, 1948); David Quentin Voigt, *American Baseball*, vol. 1 (Norman, OK, 1966).

                                                                    Ralph S. Graber

STOWE, Harry Duffield. *See* Harry Duffield Stovey.

STRAWBERRY, Darryl Eugene "Straw" (b. March 12, 1962, Los Angeles, CA), player, is the son of Henry Strawberry, a post office employee, and Ruby Strawberry and grew up in Los Angeles. He played basketball and baseball at Crenshaw High School, from which he graduated in 1980. In his senior year, he ranked among the most scouted baseball prospects in the nation. The New York Mets (NL), who had the first overall pick in the June 1980 major league draft, selected Strawberry and signed him for a $200,000 bonus. The 6-foot 6-inch, 215-pound left-handed–hitting outfielder was assigned to Kingsport, TN (ApL) in 1980. After spending the 1981 season at Lynchburg, VA (CrL), he batted .283 for Jackson, TX (TL) in 1982 with a TL-leading 34 HR, .602 slugging average, and 100 bases on balls. Strawberry was named the TL MVP and played for a Caracas, Venezuela, team in the winter of 1982.

After playing 16 games in 1983 for Tidewater, VA (IL), Strawberry was promoted to the New York Mets and compiled a .257 batting average with 74 RBI, 26 HR, and a .512 slugging average. He was named NL Rookie of the Year and *TSN* NL Rookie Player of the Year. Strawberry, blessed with tremendous power, hit at least 26 HR every year in his first nine NL seasons. During this period, he belted a major league-leading 280 HR. Good speed enabled him to join the 30/30 club in 1987, when he hit 39 HR and stole 36 bases. Teammate Howard Johnson* also accomplished the same feat in 1987, making them the first pair of 30/30 teammates in major league history. In 1988, Strawberry led the NL with 39 HR and a .545 slugging percentage. The glare of the spotlight constantly focused on Strawberry, who had been dubbed "The Black Ted Williams*'" since high school. He found that his actions on and off the field were carefully scrutinized. Spectators in the stands frequently chanted "Darryl" in unison.

The Los Angeles Dodgers (NL) signed Strawberry as a free agent in November 1990. After appearing in 139 games in 1991, he played in only 43 games in 1992 and 32 games in 1993. A herniated disk eventually required an operation. The San Francisco Giants (NL) signed Strawberry in June 1994 after the Dodgers released him because of substance abuse problems. From 1984 to 1991, he made eight straight NL All-Star teams. *TSN* selected him for its NL All-Star teams in 1988 and 1990 and as an outfielder on its NL Silver Slugger team in 1988 and 1990. Strawberry shares two NL Championship Series records, recording the most strikeouts (12, 1986) and most at-bats (30, 1988). In these two appearances, he hit a combined .269 with three HR and 11 RBI. During his only World Series, he hit .208 with one HR and one RBI for the 1986 World Championship Mets against the Boston Red Sox.

Strawberry is divorced and has two children, Darryl, Jr., and Diamond. In December 1994, he was indicted for not reporting over $500,000 in income from sports autograph shows. Two months later, he was suspended for 60 days for violating major league baseball's drug policy and the terms of his aftercare program. The San Francisco Giants released him the next day. The New York Yankees (AL) organization signed Strawberry in June 1995. He saw limited action with New York in 1995 and batted .435 in 29 games for St. Paul, MN (NoL) in 1996 before rejoining the Yankees that July. Strawberry hit .417 with three HR and five RBI in the AL Championship Series against the Baltimore Orioles, but struggled in the World Series against the Atlanta Braves. Injuries sidelined him most of the 1997 season. He clouted 24 HR with 57 RBI as the New York Yankees set an AL record with 114 victories in 1998. Strawberry underwent surgery for colon cancer in October 1998 and batted .327 in limited action in 1999. He hit .333 in the AL Division and Championship Series and in the World Series, hitting 2 HR with 4 RBI in AL postseason play. Through 1999, he batted .259 with 335 HR, 990 RBI, 1,401 hits, and 221 stolen bases.

BIBLIOGRAPHY: Mike Lupica, "A Swing and a Prayer," *Esquire* 116 (October 1991), pp. 69–70ff; R. Hoffer, "Try, Try Again," *SI* 80 (March 14, 1994), pp. 38–40; *Los Angeles Dodgers 1994 Media Guide*; William Nack, "The Perils of Darryl," *SI* 60

(April 23, 1984), pp. 32–39; David L. Porter, ed., *African-American Sports Greats* (Westport, CT, 1995); S. Ostler, "The Sport Q & A: Darryl Strawberry," *Sport* 82 (June 1991), pp. 32–38; Richard J. Brenner, *Roger Clemens, Darryl Strawberry* (New York, 1989); Mike Lupica, "The Strawberry Statement," *Esquire* 109 (April 1988), pp. 65ff; Ralph Wiley, "Doc and Darryl," *SI* 69 (July 11, 1988), pp. 70–74; Seymour Siwoff, ed., *The 1992 Elias Baseball Analyst* (New York, 1992); Darryl Strawberry, *Darryl* (New York, 1992); Jack Lang and Peter Simon, *The New York Mets* (New York, 1986); Davey Johnson and Peter Golenbock, *Bats* (New York, 1986); Donald Honig, *The New York Mets* (New York, 1986); Darryl Strawberry and Don Gold, *Hard Learnin'* (New York, 1990); Darryl Strawberry file, National Baseball Library, Cooperstown, NY; John Thorn et al., eds., *Total Baseball*, 5th ed. (New York, 1997); *TSN Official Baseball Register*, 1998; Tom Verducci, "The High Price of Hard Living," *SI* 82 (February 27, 1995), pp. 16–24.

Robert J. Brown

STREET, Charles Evard "Gabby," "Old Sarge" (b. September 30, 1882, Huntsville, AL; d. February 6, 1951, Joplin, MO), player, manager, coach, and sportscaster, was of English descent and attended Huntsville secondary schools. After signing with the Cincinnati Reds (NL) in 1903, Street caught for Hopkinsville, KY (KL) in 1903 and Terre Haute, IN (CL) in 1904 and appeared in 11 games for the Cincinnati Reds in 1904. He began the 1905 season as the Cincinnati Reds third string catcher. The Cincinnati Reds sold the 5-foot 11-inch, 183-pound right-handed receiver to the Boston Red Sox (AL) in June 1905, but reacquired him eight weeks later. Street spent the next two seasons with San Francisco, CA (PCL), demonstrating good defensive skills and little offensive promise. He joined the Washington Senators (AL) in 1908 and caught Walter Johnson* the next four seasons. Street never batted above .222 with the Washington Senators, but his 924 chances accepted in 1909 set an AL record. After catching an extremely high pop foul, he was approached about catching a baseball dropped from the 555-foot-high Washington Monument. On a sunny, windy day, Street caught the thirteenth ball dropped.

The Washington Senators traded Street to the New York Highlanders (AL) in December 1911. After playing only 29 games with the New York Highlanders (AL) in 1912, Street caught for Chattanooga, TN (SL) in 1913 and 1914 and Nashville, TN (SL) from 1915 to 1917. He served as a sergeant in the U.S. Army 30th engineers regiment in France in 1918 and 1919 and was sprayed by shrapnel during the battle at Saint-Mihiel. He caught for Nashville, TN in 1919 and served as player–manager at Suffolk, VA (VL) in 1920 and 1921, Joplin, MO (WA) in 1922 and 1923, Muskogee, OK, (WA) in 1924 and 1925, Augusta, GA (SAL) in 1926, Columbia, SC (SAL) in 1927, and Knoxville, TN (SAL) in 1928.

Street joined the St. Louis Cardinals as a coach in 1929 and won his only game as interim manager. In 1930, he became the fifth Cardinals manager in five years and led the St. Louis Cardinals to the NL pennant, but the Philadelphia Athletics defeated them in the six game World Series. Many

St. Louis Cardinals observers consider the 1931 team, piloted by Street, as the best in franchise history. National Baseball Hall of Famers Jim Bottomley,* Frankie Frisch,* Chick Hafey,* Jesse Haines,* and Burleigh Grimes* played for that team. St. Louis won 101 games, 13 games ahead of the New York Giants, and defeated Connie Mack's* Philadelphia Athletics in the seven game World Series. With essentially the same team the next season, however, Street's St. Louis Cardinals plummeted to seventh place. With the team at 46–45, Frisch replaced Street in July 1933. As manager, Street was respected by his players and masterfully relieved clubhouse tension. He lived up to his nickname, "Gabby," telling countless stories about baseball and World War I. Dizzy Dean* recalled, "He always shared the troubles of his players."

Street managed San Francisco, CA (PCL) in 1934–1935 and St. Paul, MN (AA) in 1936–1937. He joined the St. Louis Browns (AL) as a coach in July 1937 and managed them to seventh place in 1938. His major league managerial record included 365 victories, 332 defeats, and five ties. As a major league player, he batted .208 with 312 hits, 98 runs, 105 RBI, and two HR in 504 games.

Street, who married Lucinda Chandler on November 10, 1923, appeared at Ray Doan's Original All-Star Baseball School in Jackson, MS, and broadcast St. Louis Cardinals games.

BIBLIOGRAPHY: Charles C. Alexander, *Rogers Hornsby* (New York, 1995); David Cataneo, *Baseball Legends and Lore* (New York, 1997); Rob Rains, *The St. Louis Cardinals* (New York, 1992); Mike Shatzkin, ed., *The Ballplayers* (New York, 1990); *TSN Baseball Register*, 1940; Charles Street file, National Baseball Library, Cooperstown, NY; Morris Bealle, *The Washington Senators* (Washington, DC, 1947); Shirley Povich, *The Washington Senators* (New York, 1954); Henry W. Thomas, *Walter Johnson* (Washington, DC, 1995); Frederick G. Lieb, *The St. Louis Cardinals* (New York, 1945); Bob Broeg, *Redbirds! A Century of Cardinals' Baseball* (St. Louis, MO, 1981); Bob Broeg and Jerry Vickery, *St. Louis Cardinals Encyclopedia* (Grand Rapids, MI, 1998); Robert Gregory, *Diz* (New York, 1992).

Frank J. Olmsted

STRONG, T. R. "Ted" (b. January 2, 1917, South Bend, IN; d. 1951, Chicago, IL), player, excelled as a versatile athlete by starring in baseball with the Kansas City, MO Monarchs, (NAL) from 1937 through 1942 and in 1946 and 1947 and performing for basketball's original Harlem Globetrotters. The 6-foot 6-inch 210 pounder, an ideal baseball player, possessed all the tools required for stardom and proved outstanding in all phases of the game. Defensively, he was an accomplished right fielder with an exceptionally strong arm. Offensively, the switch-hitter demonstrated good power from both sides of the plate.

The talented Strong was selected to five East-West All-Star teams during a six-year interval from 1937 to 1942, missing only the 1940 season when playing in Mexico. He started at three different positions (shortstop, first base, and outfield) and compiled a career .313 All-Star batting average. His first two All-Star appearances came as a member of the Indianapolis, IN ABCs (NAL), while all other appearances were with the Kansas City Monarchs.

In his last two All-Star seasons, Strong batted .319 in 1941 and .345 in 1942 with good power. The latter year marked the Kansas City Monarchs' fourth consecutive NAL pennant since Strong joined the team and the initiation of World Series play between the NNL and the NAL. The Kansas City Monarchs swept the Homestead, PA Grays, as Strong hit .316 with a HR.

Following the 1942 World Series, Strong entered military service for three years and returned to help the Kansas City Monarchs capture the 1946 NAL pennant. A pull-hitter, he led the NAL in both HR (7) and RBI (45) while batting .287. He and Satchel Paige* missed the last two games of the World Series against the Newark, NJ Eagles (NNL) under circumstances that are unclear.

During the 1940 season, he played with Nuevo Laredo, Mexico (MEL) and batted .332 with a .603 slugging percentage. After leaving the Kansas City Monarchs, he played with the Indianapolis, IN Clowns (NAL) in 1948, Minot, ND (MkL) in 1950, and the Chicago American Giants (NAL) in 1951.

BIBLIOGRAPHY: Janet Bruce, *The Kansas City Monarchs* (Lawrence, KS, 1985); Chicago (IL) *Defender*, 1937–1948; Robert W. Peterson, *Only the Ball Was White* (Englewood Cliffs, NJ, 1970); James A. Riley, *The All-Time All-Stars of Black Baseball* (Cocoa, FL, 1983); James A. Riley, *The Biographical Encyclopedia of the Negro Baseball Leagues* (New York, 1994); James A. Riley, interviews with former Negro League players, James A. Riley Collection, Canton, GA; Mike Shatzkin, ed., *The Ballplayers* (New York, 1990).

James A. Riley

STRUNK, Amos Aaron "Dutchie" (b. January 22, 1889, Philadelphia, PA; d. July 22, 1979, Lianerch, PA), player, was the son of Amos Strunk, a wood carver, and Amanda Strunk, both of German ancestry. Strunk, who grew up in Philadelphia's Strawberry Mansion neighborhood, starred in baseball at Central High School and Blaine School. He joined the Anderson, SC Electricians (CarA) in 1908 after graduating from Blaine School, but quickly jumped to the outlaw Shamokin, PA club. Strunk's sparkling performances at Shamokin impressed manager Connie Mack* of the Philadelphia Athletics (AL). Mack signed Strunk upon the recommendation of Lave Cross,* former Philadelphia Athletics third baseman.

Strunk spent most of 1909 with the Milwaukee, WI Brewers (AA), but appeared in 11 games for the Philadelphia Athletics. A wrenched knee sidelined him for all but 16 games in the 1910 regular season, but he batted .278

for the injured Rube Oldring in the World Series against the Chicago Cubs. Strunk started in the Philadelphia Athletics' outfield from 1911 through 1917 and was traded in December 1917 to the Boston Red Sox (AL) in a six-player transaction. Despite frequent leg and ankle injuries, he performed regularly as an AL outfielder until 1922. The Philadelphia Athletics reacquired him from the Boston Red Sox in a June 1919 trade and waived him to the Chicago White Sox (AL) in July 1920. Strunk's playing time gradually diminished as his speed declined. In August 1924, the Chicago White Sox waived him to the Philadelphia Athletics. After spending 1925 with the Shamokin, PA Shammies (NYPL), he became a successful stock broker in Philadelphia. He married Ethel Kennedy in October 1915. They had no surviving children.

The 5-foot 11½-inch, 175-pound Strunk, who batted and threw left-handed, batted .284 with 1,418 hits and 185 stolen bases in 1,512 major league games spanning 17 seasons. His best offensive seasons came when he batted .305 in 1913, .316 in 1916, and .332 in 1921. Strunk, possibly the swiftest AL runner at his peak, proved an exceptionally gifted center fielder and left fielder with vast range, a sure glove, and strong, accurate throwing arm. He led the AL in fielding percentage in 1912, 1914, 1917, and 1918 and batted just .200 overall in the 1910, 1911, 1913, 1914, and 1918 World Series.

BIBLIOGRAPHY: John Dell, "Whatever Happened to Amos Strunk?" Philadelphia (PA) *Inquirer*, June 25, 1973; Amos Strunk file, National Baseball Library, Cooperstown, NY; John Thorn et al., eds., *Total Baseball*, 5th ed. (New York, 1997); Edgar Williams, "Amos Strunk, 89, Outfielder for Pennant-Winning Athletics," Philadelphia (PA) *Inquirer*, July 27, 1979; Frank Yuetter, "Amos Strunk Won Baseball Fame after 'Jumping' S. Carolina Team," Philadelphia (PA) *Bulletin*, March 3, 1958; Frederick G. Lieb, *Connie Mack* (New York, 1945); Connie Mack, *My 66 Years in the Big Leagues* (Philadelphia, PA, 1950); Jerome C. Romanowski, *The Mackmen* (Upper Darby, PA, 1979); Frederick G. Lieb, *The Boston Red Sox* (New York, 1947); Robert Redmount, *The Red Sox Encyclopedia* (Champaign, IL, 1998); Warren Brown, *The Chicago White Sox* (New York, 1952); Richard Lindberg, *Sox* (New York, 1984).

Frank V. Phelps

STUART, Richard Lee "Dick," "Stu," "Dr Strangeglove" (b. November 7, 1932, San Francisco, CA), player, is the son of a dry cleaner of Scotch-Irish ancestry and graduated from high school in 1951. After signing with the Pittsburgh Pirates (NL), he played for Modesto, CA (CaL). He batted .313 with 31 HR, 121 RBI, and 115 runs scored for Billings, MT (PrL) in 1952 and spent 1953 and 1954 in military service. In 1955, Stuart played briefly for New Orleans, LA (SL) and the Mexico City Tigers (MEL) and then clouted 32 HR in 101 games for Billings. In 1956, he became just the ninth minor leaguer to hit more than 60 HR. He clouted 66 HR with 158 RBI in 141 games for Lincoln, NE (WL). Stuart played briefly for Hollywood, CA

(PCL) and Atlanta (SL) in 1957 and then belted 31 HR in 97 games for Lincoln. He led the PCL in HR and RBI in 1958 when the Pittsburgh Pirates summoned him in July. The Pittsburgh Pirates surged to second place, their best finish in years. Stuart hit 16 HR in just 254 at-bats, but made 16 errors at first base.

The 6-foot 3-inch, 210-pound first baseman, who batted and threw right-handed, epitomized the "good-hit, no-field" player. In 1959, Stuart batted .297, hit 27 HR in 397 at-bats, knocked in 97 runs, and made 22 errors at first base in 118 games. In 1960, the Pirates won the NL pennant for the first time since 1927. Stuart hit 23 HR and frequently was replaced at first base in the late innings by Rocky Nelson. The Pittsburgh Pirates defeated the New York Yankees in a seven-game World Series, but Stuart struggled. Stuart enjoyed perhaps his best year in 1961, batting .301 with 35 HR and 117 RBI. Although fanning a league-leading 121 times, he made the NL All-Star team. After he slumped to .228 with only 16 HR in 1962, the Pittsburgh Pirates traded him to the Boston Red Sox (AL) that November. Fenway Park ideally suited Stuart's swing, as he clouted 42 HR with an AL-leading 118 RBI in 1963. But he also made an AL-leading 29 errors, reviving his nickname "Dr. Strangeglove." Reliever Dick Radatz* commented that Stuart's license plate should read "E-3," as the latter led his league's first basemen in errors every year from 1958 through 1964.

Stuart clouted 33 HR with 114 RBI in 1964. The Boston Red Sox traded him to the Philadelphia Phillies (NL) that November. He hit only .234 with 28 HR and 95 RBI for the Philadelphia Phillies and was dealt in February 1966 to the New York Mets (NL). Stuart batted only .218 in 31 games before being released in July, and signed with the Los Angeles Dodgers (NL). He hit .264 in just 38 games for the Los Angeles Dodgers, mainly as a pinch-hitter, and went hitless in his two World Series at-bats. The Los Angeles Dodgers were swept in four games by the Baltimore Orioles (AL).

In 1967, Stuart became one of the first American players to play in Japan and batted .280 with 33 HR for the Taiyo, Japan Whales (JCL). After playing for the Taiyo Whales again in 1968, he joined the California Angels (AL) in 1969. He hit just one HR in 51 at-bats, and finished his career with Phoenix (PCL).

In 10 major league seasons, Stuart batted .264 with 1,055 hits, 228 HR, 157 doubles, and 743 RBI. No other player hit more than 200 HR in both the minor and major leagues. The colorful, outgoing slugger, who remained popular with fans wherever he went, was described by sportswriter Larry Merchant as having "an amazing ego, a quick wit, a sharp eye for what is happening and a delightful faculty for self-mockery." Stuart once said, "When I'm at first, it's like Tinker* to Evers* to take a Chance.*"

Stuart, who sold insurance in Greenwich, CT, married Lois Morano on May 31, 1958 and has two sons. He now lives in Redwood City, CA.

BIBLIOGRAPHY: Dick Stuart file, National Baseball Library, Cooperstown, NY; Myron Cope, "An Irrepressible Egotist," *SEP* 235 (April 28, 1962), pp. 65–66ff; Robert W. Creamer, "Old Stonefingers—Best Show around Boston in Years," *SI* 19 (September 2, 1963), pp. 42ff; Arthur Daley, "Dick Stuart: The Pirates' Daredevil Dick," *BD* 18 (May 1959), pp. 13–15; Arnold Hano, "Dick Stuart: Man and Showman," *Sport* 37 (June 1964), pp. 56–67; Mark Harris, "The Man Who Hits Too Many Home Runs," *Life* 43 (September 2, 1957), pp. 85–86ff; Bill Liston, "Dick Stuart: The Pirates Held Me Back," *Sport* 35 (June 1963), pp. 30–32ff; Larry Merchant, "The Impact of Belinsky and Stuart on the Phillies," *Sport* 39 (June 1965), pp. 32–33ff; Larry Merchant, "What's Happening to Dick Stuart?" *Sport* 34 (August 1962), pp. 18–19ff; Jack Orr, "The Unabashed Dick Stuart," *Sport* 28 (September 1959), pp. 20–21ff; Richard L. Burtt, *The Pittsburgh Pirates, A Pictorial History* (Virginia Beach, VA, 1977); John T. Bird, *Twin Killing: The Bill Mazeroski Story* (Birmingham, AL, 1995); Jim O'Brien, *Maz and the 1960 Bucs* (Pittsburgh, PA, 1994); Dick Groat and Bill Surface, *The World Champion Pittsburgh Pirates* (New York, 1961); Howard Liss, *The Boston Red Sox* (New York, 1982); Jack Lautier, *Fenway Voices* (Camden, ME, 1990); Robert Redmount, *The Red Sox Encyclopedia* (Champaign, IL, 1998); Peter Golenbock, *Fenway* (New York, 1992); Rich Westcott and Frank Bilovsky, *The New Phillies Encyclopedia* (Philadelphia, PA, 1993).

Luther W. Spoehr

SUHR, August Richard "Gus," "Goose" (b. January 3, 1906, San Francisco, CA), player and manager, is the fourth son of August Richard Suhr and Elise (Nobmann) Suhr, both of German descent. He played baseball at Polytechnic High School and signed with the San Francisco, CA Seals (PCL) in 1925. The San Francisco Seals optioned him to Quincy, IL (3IL) for the 1925 season and recalled him in 1926. Suhr played some second base and shortstop before assuming his natural first base position in 1929. For the San Francisco Seals in 1929, he played every inning of a 202-game season, recorded 299 hits (including 51 HR), drove in 177 runs, batted .381, and scored a PCL-leading 196 runs. After playing in 588 of 589 games for the San Francisco Seals between 1927 and 1929, he joined the Pittsburgh Pirates (NL) in 1930.

Suhr, who threw right-handed and batted left-handed, enjoyed a superb rookie season in 1930, batting .286 with 17 HR, 14 triples, 93 runs, and 107 RBI. His 107 RBI rank sixth for modern NL rookies. On April 29, 1930, he walked five times to tie a single game major league record. Suhr slumped to .211 in an injury-riddled 1931 season, but returned to the regular lineup on September 11. He established an NL record for consecutive games played with 822, still the ninth-longest of all time. His streak ended on June 4, 1937, when he took himself out of the lineup after his mother's death.

Noted as a smooth fielder, Suhr set an NL record with 70 consecutive errorless games at first base. The 6-foot, 180 pounder also possessed surprising speed, clouting more triples (110) than any other major leaguer between

1930 and 1938. His best season came in 1936, when he hit .312 with 33 doubles, 12 triples, 11 HR, and 118 RBI, and made the NL All-Star team.

In July 1939, the Pittsburgh Pirates traded Suhr to the Philadelphia Phillies (NL). The Philadelphia Phillies released him in 1940. He finished the 1940 season with Montreal, Canada (IL) and returned to the San Francisco Seals from 1943 through 1945. In 1948, he managed in the minor leagues.

During his major league career, Suhr batted .279 with 1,446 hits, 288 doubles, 114 triples, and 818 RBI. He walked 718 times, while striking out only 433 times. Suhr held his own in a hitter's era despite being overshadowed at first base by Johnny Mize* and Jim Bottomley.* With infielders Pie Traynor* and Arky Vaughan,* he gave the Pirates defensive stability and offensive punch.

Suhr married Helen Hart in December 1930 and had two children, one of whom played professional baseball briefly. He worked in a brewery until 1969 and now lives in Millbrae, CA.

BIBLIOGRAPHY: Gus Suhr file, National Baseball Library, Cooperstown, NY; Brent Kelley, "Gus Suhr: National League Iron Horse," *SCD* 21 (May 27, 1994), pp. 210–211; Brent P. Kelley, *In the Shadow of the Babe* (Jefferson, NC, 1995); Frederick G. Lieb, *The Pittsburgh Pirates* (New York, 1948); Richard L. Burtt, *The Pittsburgh Pirates: A Pictorial History* (Virginia Beach, VA, 1977); Bob Smizik, *The Pittsburgh Pirates: An Illustrated History* (New York, 1990); Morris Eckhouse and Carl Mastrocola, *This Date in Pittsburgh Pirates History* (New York, 1980); Rich Westcott and Frank Bilovsky, *The New Phillies Encyclopedia* (Philadelphia, PA, 1993); Lee Pacini, "Gus Suhr Recalls the 'Good Old Days,'" *BD* 41 (June 1982), pp. 87–90; Luther W. Spoehr, interview with Gus Suhr, December 18, 1997.

Luther W. Spoehr

SUMMERS, William Reed "Bill" (b. November 10, 1895, Harrison, NJ; d. September 12, 1966, Upton, MA), umpire, was the son of Scottish immigrants John Summers and Jenny (Reed) Summers. He grew up in Woonsocket, RI and quit school in the seventh grade to work with his father in a textile mill to help support the family. Since boxing was his favorite sport, he fought professionally as a 135-pound lightweight under the names of Marty Winters and Marty Summers. He quit the ring in April 1917 after marrying Mary Ellen Van Riper, with whom he had eight children. His umpiring career began in 1913, when he was called from the stands to officiate a high school game after the regular umpire failed to appear. Summers, initially relying upon his reputation as a fighter to control the game, quickly earned a reputation for accurate, authoritative decisions and for the next eight years umpired local amateur and industrial league games. He became a professional umpire upon losing his job as a policeman following the famous 1919 Boston, MA police strike. After a season in the independent BVL, he joined the EL in 1921 and spent 10 years in that Class A circuit before advancing to the AA IL during the 1931 season. In 1933, Summers finally reached the major leagues at the relatively advanced age of 37.

A protégé of Bill McGowan,* Summers quickly emerged as one of the AL's finest umpires and was assigned in 1936 to both the All-Star Game and World Series in only his fourth year. He was selected in 1948 to umpire the one-game AL playoff between the Boston Red Sox and the Cleveland Indians. In 1950, he was appointed to represent AL umpires on the committee that rewrote and recodified the rule book. Summers, especially adept at calling balls and strikes, earned the respect of players and managers for his levelheaded, even-tempered style of umpiring and experienced far fewer on-field confrontations than most umpires. Summers ranks near the top in career service for major league umpires, his 27 seasons exceeded by only 12 arbiters. He and Al Barlick* worked the most All-Star Games at seven (1936, 1941, 1946, 1949, 1952, 1955, and 1959). Only three umpires surpassed his eight World Series assignments (1936, 1939, 1942, 1945, 1948, 1951, 1955, and 1959).

Summers, a popular after-dinner speaker, retired after the 1959 season. He worked for AL president Joe Cronin* as a goodwill ambassador for baseball, giving lectures and conducting clinics at American military bases around the globe.

BIBLIOGRAPHY: *NYT*, September 13, 1966; *TSN*, September 24, 1966; Bill Summers file, National Baseball Library, Cooperstown, NY; Bill Summers with Tim Cohane, "Baseball Boors I Have Known," *Look* 24 (July 5, 1960), pp. 65–69, 71.

Larry R. Gerlach

SUNDBERG, James Howard "Jim," "Sunny" (b. May 18, 1951, Galesburg, IL), player and sportscaster, is the son of Howard William Sundberg and Shirley Grace (Riggle) Sundberg and graduated in 1969 from Galesburg (IL) High School, where he lettered in basketball and baseball. In the June 1969 draft, the right-handed Sundberg was chosen by the Oakland A's (AL). He attended the University of Iowa, helping lead the Hawkeyes to the 1972 BTC championship and an NCAA College World Series appearance. The Texas Rangers (AL) selected Sundberg in the June 1972 draft and the secondary phase of the June 1973 draft. He began his professional baseball career in 1973 with Pittsfield, MA (EL), where he batted .298 and led EL catchers in fielding (.994).

The 6-foot, 190-pound Sundberg, who was known throughout his career for his excellent defensive skills, made his major league debut in 1974 for the Texas Rangers (AL) with a .247 batting average in 132 games. In 10 seasons with the Rangers from 1974 to 1983, he averaged .253 and 45 RBI offensively and led AL catchers in numerous defensive categories. These included double plays (1974, 1976), assists (1975–1978, 1980–1981), total chances (1975–1980), and fielding percentage (1976–1979).

In December 1983, the Texas Rangers traded Sundberg to the Milwaukee Brewers (AL). In 1984, Sundberg hit .261 and again led AL catchers in fielding. He was sent to the Kansas City Royals (AL) in January 1985 and helped them defeat the Toronto Blue Jays in the AL Championship Series with six RBI and the St. Louis Cardinals in the World Series with six walks and six runs scored. In 1986, he led AL catchers in fielding for the sixth time. Kansas City sent him in March 1987 to the Chicago Cubs (NL), where he saw limited duty through July 1988. He then signed with the Texas Rangers (AL) and ended his major league career there in 1989.

Sundberg appeared in the 1974, 1978, and 1984 All-Star games and remains the only major league catcher to win six consecutive Gold Glove awards, accomplishing that feat from 1976 through 1981. In 1979, he set new AL records for catchers by making only four errors and registering a .995 fielding percentage. Sundberg ranks in fourth place behind Carlton Fisk,* Bob Boone,* and Gary Carter* in career games behind the plate. In 1,962 games spanning 16 major league seasons, Sundberg hit .248 with 95 HR and 624 RBI. Sundberg married Janet Naugle on July 3, 1971. They have three children, Aaron, Audra, and Briana, and live in Arlington, TX, where Sundberg works as a television broadcaster for Texas Rangers games.

BIBLIOGRAPHY: *Chicago Cubs Media Guide, 1988*; Zander Hollander, ed., *The Complete Handbook of Baseball, 1979* (New York, 1979); James Sundberg file, National Baseball Library, Cooperstown, NY; John Thorn et al., eds., *Total Baseball*, 5th ed. (New York, 1997); *TSN*, August 21, 1989; Phil Rogers, *The Impossible Takes a Little Longer* (Dallas, TX, 1991); Alan Eskew, *A Royal Finish* (Chicago, IL, 1985).

Raymond D. Kush

SUTCLIFFE, Richard Lee "Rick" (b. June 21, 1956, Independence, MO), player, coach, and sportscaster, is the son of Richard Sutcliffe and Louise (Vearout) Sutcliffe and graduated from Van Horn High School. He married Robin Ross and has one daughter. The 6-foot 7-inch, 239-pound, right-handed pitcher broke into professional baseball with Bellingham, WA (NWL), producing a 10–3 record in 1974. Following a 10–11 campaign with 121 strikeouts for Waterbury, CT (EL) in 1976, he pitched one game for the Los Angeles Dodgers (NL). Sutcliffe spent the next two seasons with Albuquerque, NM (PCL). A 13–6 record in 1978 put him in the major leagues to stay.

After finishing 17–10 with the Los Angeles Dodgers in 1979, Sutcliffe earned NL Rookie of the Year honors. Following two sub-par years with the Dodgers, he was traded to the Cleveland Indians (AL) in December 1981. Sutcliffe finished 14–8 and led the AL with an 2.96 ERA in 1982 and 17–8 in 1983. After his slow 4–5 start in 1984, the Cleveland Indians traded Sutcliffe to the Chicago Cubs (NL). He compiled a 16–1 mark to win the NL Cy Young Award, leading the Chicago Cubs to an Eastern Division championship. His .941 winning percentage paced the NL. Sutcliffe split two decisions as the San Diego Padres defeated the Chicago Cubs in the NL Championship Series. After signing a five-year, $10.5 million contract, he established the Sutcliffe Foundation that contributed to many Chicago charities and social agencies.

The following season, injuries sidelined him for the first time. Sutcliffe spent three times on the disabled list in an 8–8 season. An off season in 1986 at 5–14 preceded three fine seasons. In 1987, he led the NL with 18 victories and was named *TSN*'s Pitcher of the Year and Comeback Player of the Year. He also received the prestigious Roberto Clemente Award for humanitarian service and won the Lou Gehrig Award.

Sutcliffe won 13 games in 1988 and finished 16–11 in 1989. On July 29, 1988, he stole home plate, becoming the first Chicago Cubs pitcher to accomplish that feat since 1919. Sutcliffe pitched with pain throughout both seasons. He appeared in the 1989 NL Championship Series against the San Francisco Giants. A torn rotator cuff required surgery, limiting his 1990 season to just five games. Despite the various physical problems, Sutcliffe enjoyed a 6–5 season in 1991. The Baltimore Orioles (AL) signed him as a free agent in December 1991. His last successful campaign came in 1992 with a 16–15 record and league leading 32 starts. He was named the AL Comeback Player of the Year. After signing with the St. Louis Cardinals (NL) in January 1994, Sutcliffe, who retired in 1995 with a 171–139 record, a 4.08 ERA, and 1,679 strikeouts in 2,697.2 innings, made the 1983 AL All-Star team and the 1987 and 1989 NL All-Star Teams. The San Diego Padres (NL) hired him as a minor league pitching coach in 1996. He has served as a broadcaster for the San Diego Padres and ESPN since 1997.

BIBLIOGRAPHY: Richard Sutcliffe file, National Baseball Library, Cooperstown, NY; Eddie Gold and Art Ahrens, *The New Era Cubs, 1941–1985* (Chicago, IL, 1985); Jack Torry, *Endless Summers* (South Bend, IN, 1995); Terry Pluto, *The Curse of Rocky Colavito* (New York, 1994; Warren Wilbert and William Hageman, *Chicago Cubs: Seasons at the Summit* (Champaign, IL, 1997); Ted Patterson, *The Baltimore Orioles* (Dallas, TX, 1995); *TSN Baseball Register*, 1994; *Chicago Cubs Information Guide*, 1991; *Chicago Cubs Vineline*, December 1991; *Wrigley Field between the Vines* (January 1996).
                                                                    Duane A. Smith

SUTTER, Howard Bruce (b. January 8, 1953, Lancaster, PA), player, is the son of Howard Sutter, retired manager of a Farm Bureau warehouse in Mt. Joy, PA, and Thelma Sutter. Sutter and his wife, Jamye, and their three sons reside in Kennesaw, GA. After graduation from Donegal High School in Mt. Joy in 1972, he entered organized baseball that year with two games for Bradenton, FL (GCL). The 6-foot 2-inch, 190 pound right-hander pitched for Quincy, IL (ML) in 1973, Key West, FL (FSL) and Midland, TX (TL) in 1974, Midland in 1975, and Wichita, KS (AA) in 1976 in the Chicago Cubs minor league system. The Chicago Cubs (NL), impressed with his strikeout–walk ratio, summoned him early in the 1976 season as a relief pitcher. He popularized a baffling "out" pitch, his split-finger fastball. Sutter appeared in 661 major league games without making a start. During 12 major league seasons, he posted 300 saves and 68–71 won–lost record, struck out 861 batters in 1,042 innings pitched, and compiled a 2.83 ERA.

In December 1980, the St. Louis Cardinals (NL) obtained Sutter in a trade with the Cubs. The trade paid dividends for the Cardinals in 1982, when Sutter pitched in 70 games and led the NL with 36 saves. St. Louis won the NL and World Series titles, helped by Sutter's two saves and one win against the Milwaukee Brewers. Sutter, selected for the NL All-Star team five successive seasons and in 1984, won the 1978 and 1979 games and was credited with saves in 1980 and 1981. Besides leading the NL in saves four consecutive years through 1982 and five times altogether, Sutter received the Rolaids Relief Pitcher of the Year Award for the NL and was selected *TSN* All-Star Fireman of the Year in 1979, 1981–1982, and 1984. In 1979, 37 saves and six victories earned Sutter the NL Cy Young Award. On September 8, 1977, he struck out the side on nine pitches to the the major league record. In 1984, he tied the then major league record for the most saves (45) in a season. Sutter in December 1984 joined the Atlanta Braves (NL) as a free agent. He underwent elbow surgery at the end of the 1985 season and saw limited action in 1986 and 1988 before retiring as a player.

BIBLIOGRAPHY: Chicago *Tribune*, 1976–1980; *The Baseball Encyclopedia*, 10th ed. (New York, 1996); Eddie Gold and Art Ahrens, *The New Era Cubs, 1941–1985* (Chicago, IL, 1985); Rob Rains, *The St. Louis Cardinals* (New York, 1992); Bruce Sutter file, National Baseball Library, Cooperstown, NY; Bob Cairns, *Pen Men* (New York, 1993); Ken Young, *Cy Young Award Winners* (New York, 1994); Warren Wilbert and William Hageman, *Chicago Cubs: Seasons at the Summit* (Champaign, IL, 1997); Bob Broeg and Jerry Vickery, *St. Louis Cardinals Encyclopedia* (Grand Rapids, MI, 1998); *St. Louis Cardinals Yearbook, 1984*; St. Louis (MO) *Post Dispatch*, 1980–1984; *TSN Official Baseball Register, 1989*; Don Weiskoff, "Keep 'Em Close," *Athletic Journal* 64 (January 1984), pp. 40–47.

Emil H. Rothe

SUTTLES, George "Mule" (b. March 2, 1901, Brockton, LA; d. 1968, Newark, NJ), player and manager, starred in black baseball during a career spanning over one-quarter of a century. The powerfully built right-hander stood 6-feet 3-inches and weighed 215 pounds. He worked in the coal mines of Birmingham, AL and played semipro baseball on mining teams. Nicknamed "Mule," Suttles began his baseball career in 1923 as a first baseman with the Birmingham Black Barons and entered the top echelon of black baseball when the Black Barons joined the NNL in 1924. He spent 1926 through 1931 with the St. Louis Stars (NNL) and 1932 with the doomed EWL's Washington Pilots and Detroit Wolves. He performed in the NNL with the Chicago American Giants (1933–1935) and Newark Eagles (1936). Suttles also played with the Newark Eagles in the NNL from 1937 through 1940 and 1942 through 1944. He spent the 1941 NNL season with the New York Black Yankees and winters playing in California and Cuba.

Although not considered a talented defensive player, Suttles ranked among the most feared black league sluggers with a .338 career batting average in Negro League play. Suttles batted .432 with 26 HR and a 1.000 slugging percentage in 1926 and .384 with a .837 slugging percentage in 1930. He hit .396 with 36 HR in 1936 and .420 with 26 HR in 1938. A .325 batter in the 1933–1934 CWL, he paced the loop with 14 HR in 42 games. In 27 contests against white major leaguers, he hit .374 with 7 HR and a .670 slugging average. Suttles participated in five East-West (Negro League) All-Star games, starting for the West in 1933, 1934, 1935, and for the East in 1937 and 1939. His two All-Star homers included a game-winning blow off National Baseball Hall of Famer Martin Dihigo* in 1935 with two on and two out in the bottom of the eleventh to produce a dramatic 11–8 West victory. He posted robust All-Star .412 batting and incredible .883 slugging averages.

The 1928, 1930, and 1931 St. Louis Stars captured NNL titles, while the Chicago American Giants made disputed NNL title claims with the Pittsburgh Crawfords in 1933 and the Philadelphia Stars in 1934. Suttles managed the Newark Eagles to an 18–14 mark in a short 1943 NNL season. Teammates included Hall of Famers James "Cool Papa" Bell,* Monte Irvin,* Raymond Dandridge,* Larry Doby,* and Willie Wells,* and star Biz Mackey.* He retired in Newark, NJ and died of cancer.

BIBLIOGRAPHY: Chicago *Defender*, September 29, October 6, 13, 1928, September 20, 27, 1930, September 15, 22, 1934; John B. Holway, *Blackball Stars* (Westport, CT, 1988); Robert W. Peterson, *Only the Ball Was White* (Englewood Cliffs, NJ, 1970); Philadelphia *Tribune*, October 4, 1934; Pittsburgh *Courier*, October 4, 1934; James A. Riley, *All-Time All-Stars of Black Baseball* (Cocoa, FL, 1983); James A. Riley, *The Biographical Encyclopedia of the Negro Baseball Leagues* (New York, 1994); James Overmyer, *Effa Manley and the Newark Eagles* (Metuchen, NJ, 1993); Art Rust, Jr., *Get That Nigger off the Field* (New York, 1976).

Merl F. Kleinknecht

SUTTON, Donald Howard "Don" (b. April 2, 1945, Clio, AL), player and sportscaster, pitched for the Los Angeles Dodgers (1966–1980, 1988) and Houston Astros (1981–1982) of the NL and for the Milwaukee Brewers (1982–1984), Oakland A's (1985), and California Angels (1985–1987) of the AL. After signing with the Los Angeles Dodgers on September 11, 1964, the right-handed Sutton began his professional baseball career with Santa Barbara, CA (CaL) in 1965. He posted an 8–1 mark with a 1.50 ERA in 10 games there and quickly was promoted to Albuquerque, NM (TL) where he led the TL in winning percentage (.714) and was named its Player of the

Year. Aside from two games at Spokane, WA (PCL) in 1968, Sutton joined the Dodgers' starting rotation of Sandy Koufax,* Don Drysdale,* and Claude Osteen* in 1966, compiled a 12–12 record, and struck out 209 batters in 225.2 innings. He was named *TSN* Rookie Pitcher of the Year, helping the Dodgers win the NL pennant.

The 6-foot 1-inch, 190-pound Sutton excelled as a Dodger. At his retirement, he ranked first on the all-time Dodger lists for regular season games pitched (550), innings pitched (3,815), strikeouts (2,696), shutouts (52), wins (233), and for NL Championship Series innings (32.2), strikeouts (17), and wins (3). In 1976, his only season as a 20-game winner, he compiled a 21–10 record and was named right-handed pitcher on *TSN* NL All-Star team. Sutton led the NL in ERA (2.21) in 1980, games started (40) in 1974, shutouts (9) in 1972, earned runs allowed (118) in 1970, and balks (3) in 1968. From 1966 to 1969, he lost 13 consecutive games to the Chicago Cubs to set a major league record for consecutive losses to a single opponent. Sutton struck out at least 100 batters in 21 seasons from 1966–1986, establishing a major league record for most consecutive years accomplishing that feat. Although never pitching a no-hitter, he hurled an NL record five career one-hit games. In a game against the Cincinnati Reds on May 27, 1980, Sutton surrendered a record three consecutive HR in the third inning to Ken Griffey, Sr.,* George Foster,* and Dan Driessen.* Sutton, high on the all-time strikeout-to-walk ratio list, never hit a major league HR. He joined the Houston Astros (NL) as a free agent on December 4, 1980. During their successful AL pennant drive of 1982, the Milwaukee Brewers acquired Sutton in August for three players. In December 1984, Milwaukee traded him to the Oakland A's (AL).

Oakland sent him to the California Angels (AL) in September 1985. On June 18, 1986, Sutton pitched a three hitter for his 300th career major league victory in a 5–1 triumph over the Texas Rangers at Anaheim, CA. The 41-year-old right-hander became the 19th pitcher to win 300 major league games. He signed with the Los Angeles Dodgers (NL) as a free agent in January 1988, for his final major league season. In NL Championship Series play, Sutton won the first and deciding fourth game of Los Angeles' successful 1974 series against the Pittsburgh Pirates and pitched a complete-game victory in Game 2 of the Dodgers' triumphant 1977 series against the Philadelphia Phillies. Sutton's only NL Championship Series loss came in Game 3 of the 1978 series against the Phillies. Sutton's win in Game 3 of the 1982 AL Championship Series helped the Brewers defeat the California Angels. Sutton pitched well in relief in the 1986 AL Championship Series against the Boston Red Sox, but was not involved in any decision.

Sutton posted an overall record of 2–3 in World Series competition, winning Game 2 of the 1974 World Series against the Oakland A's and Game 5 of the 1977 World Series for Los Angeles against the New York Yankees. His World Series losses came in Games 3 and 6 of the 1978 World Series against the New York Yankees and in Game 6 of the 1982 World Series against the St. Louis Cardinals. Sutton, who did not appear in the 1966 World Series, compiled a World Series 5.26 ERA. He pitched for the NL All-Star team in 1972, 1973, 1975, and 1977. In his only All-Star Game decision, Sutton started and won the 1977 game at Yankee Stadium and considers this game the highlight of his career. Sutton struck out seven and did not allow a run in eight composite All-Star innings.

In 23 major league seasons, Sutton compiled a 324–256 win–loss record with a 3.26 ERA. He ranks fifth on the all-time strikeout list (3,574), tenth in shutouts (58), third in games started (756) and seventh in innings pitched (5,002.2). Sutton was originally signed with the Dodgers in 1965 for $7,500 by scout Monte Basgall. As a free agent in 1980, Sutton received a $500,000 bonus to sign a $700,000 annual three-year contract with the Houston Astros (NL). His father Howard Sutton, a Florida tenant farmer, works as a construction company superintendent, while his mother, Lillian, is a postmistress. Sutton attended Gulf Coast JC, Mississippi College, Whittier College, and the University of Southern California, leaving 30 credits short of a degree. Sutton, who met his wife, Patti, an interior decorator, in 1967, has one son, Daron, and one daughter, Staci. He has served as a color analyst for the Atlanta Braves (NL) on WTBS since 1989 and was elected to the National Baseball Hall of Fame in 1998.

BIBLIOGRAPHY: Don Sutton file, National Baseball Library, Cooperstown, NY; John Benson et al., *Baseball's Top 100* (Wilton, CT, 1997); Ron Bergman, "Don Sutton," *USAT*, September 19, 1985, p. 9C; Ron Fimrite, "Blood on the Dodger Blue," *SI* 49 (September 4, 1978), pp. 24–25; Robert Grayson, "Don Sutton; Cooperstown Was Always the Goal," *SCD* 25 (August 7, 1998), pp. 120–121; Tommy Lasorda and David Fisher, *The Artful Dodger* (New York, 1985); Peter C. Bjarkman, *Baseball's Great Dynasties: The Dodgers* (New York, 1990); Tommy Holmes, *The Dodgers* (New York, 1975); William F. McNeil, *The Dodgers Encyclopedia* (Champaign, IL, 1997); *Milwaukee Brewers 1989 Official Yearbook*; Jeff Everson, *This Date in Milwaukee Brewers History* (Appleton, WI, 1987); Mickey Herskowitz, "Houston Bets a Fortune That Don Can Break the Jinx," *Sport* 72 (June 1981), pp. 26–32; Tot Holmes, *Dodgers Blue Book*, 1983; Robert E. Kelly, *Baseball's Best* (Jefferson, NC, 1988); *The Baseball Encyclopedia*, 10th ed. (New York, 1996); Sue Reilly, "Don and Patti Sutton Were Striking Out Till They Got Help—And Now They're Safe at Home," *PW* 17 (April 5, 1982), pp. 89–93; Don Sutton, "The Game I'll Never Forget," *BD* 43 (November 1984), pp. 25–27; *TSN Official Baseball Dope Book, 1983*; *TSN Official Baseball Guide, 1989*; *TSN Official World Series Records, 1982*.

Jack P. Lipton

SUTTON, Ezra Ballou (b. September 17, 1850, Palmyra, NY; d. June 20, 1907, Braintree, MA), player, played amateur baseball in Rochester, NY and began his 20-year professional baseball career in 1870 at age 19 as third baseman for Forest City of Cleveland. He remained with the Forest City club when it joined the NA, baseball's first professional league, in its inaugural 1871 season. He led third baseman in fielding percentage in 1871. After Forest City folded in August 1872, Sutton signed with the Athletics of Philadelphia (NA, NL) and played there four years. The Chicago White Stockings signed him for the first NL season in 1876, but he broke the contract and remained in Philadelphia when the Athletics offered him more money. After the 1876 season, Sutton signed with the Boston Red Stockings (NL) and played his final 12 major league years with the Red Stockings and the Beaneaters.

Although primarily a third baseman, Sutton also played shortstop and the other infield and outfield positions. The 5-foot 8½-inch, 153-pound right-hander possessed a strong, accurate throwing arm, although statistics show him somewhat below average as a fielder. He batted cross-handed early in his career and switched to a standard grip as the quality of major league pitching improved. After hitting .311 over his first six major league seasons from 1871 through 1876, he dropped to a .255 batting average in his first five years with the Boston Red Stockings and then rebounded from 1883 through 1885 with his three finest seasons. In 1883, he hit .324 and ranked among the top four NL hitters in hits, triples, runs, slugging average, and RBI. The Boston Beaneaters surprised forecasters by winning the 1883 NL pennant. Sutton's 162 hits tied for the NL lead in 1884, while his .346 batting average ranked third. He also paced NL third basemen in fielding percentage. His .313 batting average in 1885 dropped him out of the upper echelons, but his 143 hits shared fourth in the NL.

Sutton batted .277 for the Boston Beaneaters in 1886 and .304 in 1887. After hitting only .218 in 28 games in 1888, he finished the season with minor league Rochester, NY (IA). After playing a year with minor league Milwaukee, WI (WA) in 1889, Sutton retired from the game. With his base-ball earnings, he had bought an interest in a Palmyra, NY concern (variously identified as an ice plant, grist mill, or sawmill) in 1886. The business, how-ever, failed in 1890, the same year Sutton experienced the onset of locomotor ataxia, a gradual paralysis that incapacitated him by 1902. His wife, Susie, whom he had married in 1871, died in January 1906 of burns suffered six weeks earlier. A lamp had exploded, igniting her dress in front of the helpless Sutton. Sutton was hospitalized in Rochester, NY that April and was later moved to hospitals in Boston and Braintree, MA to be closer to his baseball friends before his death. Two children predeceased him. He was survived by a daughter, Georgia, and two elder brothers. In 1,263 major league games, Sutton batted .294. His 1,574 hits included 227 doubles, 97 triples, and 25 HR.

BIBLIOGRAPHY: William J. Ryczek, *Blackguards and Red Stockings* (Jefferson, NC, 1992); Ezra Sutton file, National Baseball Library, Cooperstown, NY; John Thorn et al., eds., *Total Baseball*, 5th ed. (New York, 1997); Robert L. Tiemann and Mark Rucker, eds., *Nineteenth Century Stars* (Kansas City, MO, 1989); Frederick G. Lieb and Stan Baumgartner, *The Philadelphia Phillies* (New York, 1953); Rich Westcott and Frank Bilovsky, *The New Phillies Encyclopedia* (Philadelphia, PA, 1993); Harold Kaese, *The Boston Braves* (New York, 1948); Gary Caruso, *The Braves Encyclopedia* (Philadelphia, PA, 1995); George V. Tuohey, comp., *A History of the Boston Base Ball Club* (Boston, MA, 1897).

Frederick Ivor-Campbell

SYZMANSKI, Aloysius Harry. *See* Aloysius Harry Simmons.

Branch Rickey

Unless otherwise credited, all photographs appearing in this volume are courtesy of the National Baseball Hall of Fame Library, Cooperstown, NY.

Cal Ripkin, Jr.

(Photo credit: National Baseball Hall of Fame Library, Cooperstown, NY; courtesy of Lou Sauritch)

Brooks Robinson

Frank Robinson

Amos Rusie

Babe Ruth

Nolan Ryan

Ryne Sandberg

Mike Schmidt

Tom Seaver

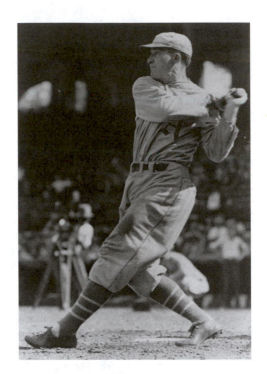

Al Simmons

Ozzie Smith

Warren Spahn

A. G. Spalding

Tris Speaker

Willie Stargell

Frank Thomas

Pie Traynor

Honus Wagner

Ed Walsh

Hoyt Wilhelm

Ted Williams

Dave Winfield

Carl Yastrzemski

Cy Young

Robin Yount

T

TABOR, James Reubin "Jim," "Rawhide" (b. November 5, 1916, New Hope, AL; d. August 22, 1953, Sacramento, CA), player, entered the University of Alabama in the fall of 1935 and played freshman baseball and basketball. In 1937, Boston Red Sox (AL) scout Fred Hunter signed him for $4,000. Tabor left school to join the Boston Red Sox farm team at Little Rock, AR (SA), where he quickly gained national fame by hitting a grandslam HR in an exhibition game against Bob Feller* of the Cleveland Indians.

Tabor batted .295 for the pennant-winning Little Rock Travelers in 1937 and .330 for the Minneapolis, MN Millers (AA) in 1938 before the Red Sox promoted him that September to replace injured third baseman Pinky Higgins.* The right-hander's .316 batting average in 19 games so impressed Manager Joe Cronin* that he traded Higgins. On July 4, 1939, Tabor enjoyed his greatest performance, with two grandslam HR in the second game of a doubleheader against the Philadelphia Athletics at Shibe Park. Tabor belted a third HR in that game and slugged another in the opener. His 21 HR in 1940 and 101 RBI in 1941 marked career highs. Tabor married Irene Bryan on July 14, 1940 and had two children, Virginia and James. Nicknamed "Rawhide" for his aggressive style of play, the 6-foot 2-inch, 175 pounder often was benched, fined, or suspended for training-rules violations. The erratic thrower led AL third basemen in errors from 1939 to 1943.

Tabor entered the U.S. Army following the 1944 season and was discharged in December 1945. The Boston Red Sox sold him to the Philadelphia Phillies (NL) for $25,000 in January 1946. He played two seasons with the Philadelphia Phillies, finishing his nine-year major league career with a .270 batting average, 104 HR, and 598 RBI in 1,005 games. After spending three seasons in the PCL, mostly with Sacramento, Tabor worked for a construction company there. He died of a heart attack.

BIBLIOGRAPHY: Frederick G. Lieb, *The Boston Red Sox* (New York, 1947); *The Boston Globe*, August 23, 1953; *The Philadelphia Inquirer*, August 23, 1953; *TSN*, September 2, 1953; Jim Tabor file, National Baseball Library, Cooperstown, NY; Howard Liss, *The Boston Red Sox* (New York, 1982); Dan Shaughnessy, *The Curse of the Bambino* (New York, 1990); Robert Redmount, *The Red Sox Encyclopedia* (Champaign, IL, 1998); Rich Westcott and Frank Bilovsky, *The New Phillies Encyclopedia* (Philadelphia, PA, 1993).

Lyle Spatz

TANANA, Frank Daryl (b. July 3, 1953, Detroit, MI), player, is the son of Frank Richard Tanana, a former minor league outfielder, and pitched for the California Angels (AL), Boston Red Sox (AL), Texas Rangers (AL), and Detroit Tigers (AL). An All-State baseball and basketball player at Detroit Catholic Central High School, Tanana signed with the California Angels as their first selection in the June 1971 free-agent draft and as the 13th player selected overall. The 6-foot 3-inch, 195-pound left-hander pitched just 47 games in the minor leagues before the Angels promoted him in 1973. The TL chose Tanana Pitcher of the Year that same season, as he posted a 16–6 win–loss record and 2.71 ERA for El Paso, TX. He led the TL with 15 complete games, 206 innings pitched, and 197 strikeouts before compiling a 2–2 record and 3.08 ERA for California in 1973.

Tanana's first full major league season saw him record 14 wins and 180 strikeouts in 1974 to earn *TSN* Rookie Pitcher of the Year Award. He led the AL with 269 strikeouts, including a career-high 17 versus the Texas Rangers, in 1975, and posted 261 strikeouts in 1976 and 205 strikeouts in 1977. He was named to *TSN* and AL All-Star teams both seasons and the AL team in 1978.

Tanana in 1979 helped California clinch its first division title with a victory over the Kansas City Royals on September 25. He recorded a 3.60 ERA in his only 1979 AL Championship Series appearance against the Baltimore Orioles. His final season with California in 1980 resulted in an 11–12 record and 4.15 ERA.

In January 1981, California traded Tanana, Jim Dorsey, and Joe Rudi* to the Boston Red Sox for Fred Lynn* and Steve Renko. The Texas Rangers signed him as a free agent in January 1982. He lost an AL-high 18 games, but the Rangers scored two runs or less in 15 of his 30 starts. In 1984 Tanana was named Texas Rangers Pitcher of the Year, posting 15 victories to match the club record for left-handers. He paced the AL in balks in 1978 and shared the AL lead in balks in 1984.

The Texas Rangers traded the struggling Tanana to the Detroit Tigers in June 1985. He finished that season with a 10–7 mark and 3.34 ERA for Detroit, pitching the only one-hitter of his career on August 29 against the Milwaukee Brewers. Tanana tossed a six-hit, 1–0 shutout against the Toronto Blue Jays to clinch the 1987 AL Eastern Division title for Detroit, but lost his only decision and compiled a 5.06 ERA in the 1987 AL Champion-ship Series against the Minnesota Twins. His 2,000th career strikeout came that season on July 12 against Gary Pettis of the California Angels.

Tanana won his first five 1988 starts, the first Tiger to accomplish that feat since Steve Gromek* in 1954. He triumphed 14 times in 1988 and 10 times in 1989, giving him at least 10 victories for the 6th straight campaign and 12th time in his 16-year career. Tanana compiled 13 victories in both 1991 and 1992, his final seasons with Detroit. His major league career ended in 1993 with the New York Mets (NL) and New York Yankees (AL). In 21 major league seasons, he owned a 240–236 win–loss record, a 3.66 ERA, 2,773 strikeouts in 4,188 innings pitched, and 34 shutouts. He holds the AL record for most HR allowed (422) and pitched over 4,000 innings in the AL. He and his wife, Cathy Ann (Mull), have four children, Lauren, Jillian, Karin, and Erin.

BIBLIOGRAPHY: Frank Tanana file, National Baseball Library, Cooperstown, NY; *The Baseball Encyclopedia*, 10th ed. (New York, 1996); Columbus (OH) *Dispatch*, May 19, 1980, p. D–2; *Detroit Tigers Media Guide* 1989; *TSN Complete Baseball Record Book, 1998; TSN Official Baseball Register, 1994*; Fred T. Smith, *Tiger Tales and Trivia* (Lathrup Village, MI, 1988); Richard Bak, *A Place for Summer* (Detroit, MI, 1998); Ross Newhan, *The California Angels* (New York, 1982); Phil Rogers, *The Impossible Takes a Little Longer* (Dallas, TX, 1990); William M. Anderson, *The Detroit Tigers* (South Bend, IN, 1996); Sparky Anderson and Don Ewald, *Sparky* (New York, 1990).

William A. Sutton and Robert S. Butcher

TANNEHILL, Jesse Niles (b. July 14, 1874, Dayton, KY; d. September 22, 1956, Dayton, KY), player, manager, and umpire, spent most of his life in the Dayton area. His younger brother, Lee, played infield for 10 seasons with the Chicago White Sox (AL). The 5-foot 8-inch, 150-pound left-handed pitcher proved a steady performer and hurled a 6–0 no-hit victory for the Boston Pilgrims (AL) over the Chicago White Sox on August 17, 1904. After compiling a 1–0 mark with the Cincinnati Reds (NL) in 1894, Tannehill enjoyed outstanding seasons with Richmond, VA (VL) in 1895 and 1896 before joining the Pittsburgh Pirates (NL) in 1897. From 1898 to 1902, he won 25, 24, 20, 18, and 20 games, respectively, for the Pirates. Tannehill helped Pittsburgh win NL pennants in 1901 and 1902 with spark-ling 2.18 and 1.95 ERAs and led the NL in ERA (1901). In 1903, he joined teammate John Chesbro* in jumping to the New York Highlanders (AL) for more money. Tannehill compiled a mediocre 15–15 record, while the Pirates won a third straight NL pennant.

In December 1903 the Highlanders traded Tannehill to the Pilgrims (AL) for Thomas Hughes. At Boston, he won 21 games in 1904, 22 in 1905, and 13 in 1906. In July 1908, he and Robert Unglaub were traded to the Wash-ington Senators (AL) for Casey Patten. Tannehill compiled a 1–1 mark for Washington in 1909 and left the major leagues except for one appearance with the Cincinnati Reds (NL) in 1911. He journeyed around the minor leagues with Minneapolis, MN (AA) in 1910, Birmingham, AL (SA) and Montgomery AL (SA) in 1911, South Bend, IN (CL) and Chillicothe, OH (OSL) in 1912, and St. Joseph, MO (WL) in 1913. In 15 major league seasons, Tannehill garnered 197 wins (117 in the NL) and 117 losses, completed 263 of 320 starts, struck out 940 batters, walked only 477 hitters in 2,750.1 innings, hurled 34 shutouts, and compiled a 2.79 ERA. A lifetime .256 batter, he occasionally played the outfield early in his career. After his playing days, Tannehill managed at Portsmouth, VA (VL) in 1914 and Topeka, KS (SWL) in 1923 and umpired in the OSL in 1916, IL in 1917, and WL in 1920.

BIBLIOGRAPHY: Jesse Tannehill file, National Baseball Library, Cooperstown, NY; Paul MacFarlane, ed., *TSN Daguerreotypes of Great Stars of Baseball* (St. Louis, MO, 1968); Robert Redmount, *The Red Sox Encyclopedia* (Champaign, IL, 1998); Frederick G. Lieb, *The Pittsburgh Pirates* (New York, 1948); Richard L. Burtt, *The Pittsburgh Pirates, An Illustrated History* (Virginia Beach, VA, 1977); Frank Graham, *The New York Yankees* (New York, 1943); Frederick G. Lieb, *The Boston Red Sox* (New York, 1947); *The Baseball Encyclopedia*, 10th ed. (New York, 1996).

David B. Merrell

TANNER, Charles William, Jr. "Chuck" (b. July 4, 1929, New Castle, PA), player, manager, and executive, is the son of Charles Tanner, Sr., a Pennsylvania Railroad brakeman and conductor, and Anna (Baka) Tanner and graduated in 1946 from Shenango High School, where he played three sports. The Boston Braves (NL) signed the 6-foot, 185-pound outfielder, who batted and threw left-handed, in June 1946. He spent nine minor league seasons with Evansville, IN (3IL) in 1946, Owensboro, KY (KL) in 1946–1947, Eau Claire, WI (NoL) in 1947–1948, Pawtucket, RI (NEL) in 1948, Denver, CO (WL) in 1949–1950, Atlanta, GA (SL) from 1951–1954, Milwaukee, WI (AA) in 1952, and Toledo, OH (AA) in 1953.

In 1955, Tanner made his major league debut with the Milwaukee Braves (NL). On April 12, 1955, he became only the third pinch hitter and fifth player in major league history to homer on the first major league pitch he ever saw. His eighth inning HR came off Gerald Staley* of the Cincinnati Reds. Tanner spent eight major league seasons with the Milwaukee Braves from 1955–1957, Chicago Cubs (NL) in 1957–1958, Cleveland Indians (AL) in 1959–1960, and Los Angeles Angels (AL) in 1961–1962, batting .261 with 21 HR and 105 RBI in 396 games. He was optioned to Minneapolis, MN (AA) in 1959, Toronto, Canada (IL) in 1960–1961, and Dallas–Fort Worth, TX (TL) in 1961–1962.

Tanner made greater impact as a minor and major league manager. He piloted Davenport, IA–based Quad Cities (ML) in 1963–1964, El Paso, TX (TL) in 1965–1966 and 1968, Seattle, WA (PCL) in 1967, and Hawaii (PCL) in 1969–1970, winning Manager of the Year honors in 1968 and 1970. In

September 1970, he replaced Don Gutteridge as manager of the Chicago White Sox (AL). The master motivator–strategist exhibited contagious enthusiasm and communicated well with players. Tanner helped transform the Chicago White Sox from 1970 through 1975 and received *TSN* Co-Manager of the Year honors in 1972 for guiding Chicago to second place in the AL West with an 87–67 record. In 1976, his Oakland A's (AL) finished runner up in the AL West. In November 1976, the Oakland A's traded him to the Pittsburgh Pirates (NL).

Tanner's best managerial stint came with the Pittsburgh Pirates from 1977 through 1985. Powerful, speedy Pittsburgh placed second in the NL East in 1977, 1978, and 1983 and won the NL East with a 98–64 record in 1979, sweeping the Cincinnati Reds in the NL Championship Series and overcoming a 3–1 deficit to defeat the Baltimore Orioles in the World Series. Tanner, who ended his managerial career with the Atlanta Braves (NL) from 1986 to 1988, compiled a major league record of 1,352 wins and 1,381 losses. Since 1992, he has served as special assistant to baseball operations for the Milwaukee Brewers (AL, NL).

Tanner married Barbara Weiss in 1950 and has four sons, Mark, Gary, Brent, and Bruce. Mark and Bruce pitched in professional baseball.

BIBLIOGRAPHY: Leonard Koppett, *The Man in the Dugout* (New York, 1993); *TSN Baseball Register*, 1988; Chuck Tanner file, National Baseball Library, Cooperstown, NY; Chuck Tanner, letter to David L. Porter, March 20, 1998; Thomas Aylesworth and Benton Minks, *The Encyclopedia of Baseball Managers* (New York, 1990); Bob Buege, *The Milwaukee Braves: A Baseball Eulogy* (Milwaukee, WI, 1988); Richard Lindberg, *Who's on Third?* (South Bend, IN, 1983); Richard Lindberg, *Sox* (New York, 1984); Bob Vanderberg, *Sox: From Lane and Fain to Zisk and Fisk* (Chicago, IL, 1982); Bob Smizik, *The Pittsburgh Pirates: An Illustrated History* (New York, 1990); Lou Sahadi, *The Pirates* (New York, 1980); Gary Caruso, *The Braves Encyclopedia* (Philadelphia, PA, 1995); *Atlanta Braves Media Guide*, 1987; Chuck Wills and Pat Wills, *Beyond Home Plate* (Ocala, FL, 1993).

David L. Porter

TARTABULL, Danilo (Mora) "Danny," "Bull" (b. October 30, 1962, San Juan, PR), player, is the son of José Tartabull, a major league baseball player, and Antonia Maria Mora, both Cuban-born. He married Kellie Van Kirk and has three children, Danica, Danny Jr., and Zachary. Tartabull played baseball and basketball for Carol City High School in Miami, FL, making All-Florida at second base as a senior. His 1979 American Legion team won the national title and the National Sports Festival gold medal.

The Cincinnati Reds (NL) selected Tartabull in the third round of the 1980 draft. He was named Player of the Year in 1981 with Tampa, FL (FSL), leading the FSL in batting. The Seattle Mariners (AL) picked him in the January 1983 compensation draft. He earned the MVP award with Calgary, Canada (PCL) in 1985, his 43 HR leading professional baseball. Tartabull moved from infield to outfield during his fine rookie season with the Seattle Mariners in 1986, producing 96 RBI and 25 HR. In December 1986, the Seattle Mariners traded him to the Kansas City Royals (AL), the team of his father's greatest successes. The 6-foot 1-inch, 204 pounder's outstanding 1991 season included leading the major leagues in slugging percentage (.593), pacing the Royals with a .316 batting average, 100 RBI, and 31 HR, and playing in the All-Star Game.

Tartabull averaged .290 at the plate with 25 HR and 85 RBI during his five seasons with the Kansas City Royals. He signed in December 1992 with the New York Yankees (AL), hoping to gain recognition he believed was long deserved. In July 1995, the New York Yankees traded him to the Oakland A's (AL). The Chicago White Sox (AL) acquired him in January 1996. In February 1997, the Philadelphia Phillies (NL) signed him as a free agent. He spent nearly the entire 1997 season on the disabled list and retired following the 1997 campaign.

Tartabull remained a dangerous, productive hitter, but injuries often shortened his appearances and limited his speed and fielding ability. His use as a DH increased markedly. In the 1987, 1991, and 1993 seasons, he combined at least 31 HR with at least 100 RBI. He compiled a .273 career batting average, a .497 slugging percentage, 925 RBI, and 262 HR, including 11 grand slams.

BIBLIOGRAPHY: Danny Tartabull file, National Baseball Library, Cooperstown, NY; http://www.chisox.com/roster/, May 1996; Tim Kurkjian, "Raging Bull," *SI* 75 (August 5, 1991), pp. 36–37; Bruce Newman, "Bright Light, New City," *SI* 76 (March 23, 1992), pp. 56–61; *White Sox Media Guide*, 1996; Rick Weinberg, "One-on-One: Danny Tartabull," *Sport* 83 (May 1992), pp. 18–20; Mark Gallagher, *The Yankee Encyclopedia*, vol. 3 (Champaign, IL, 1997).

John T. English

TAYLOR, Antonio Nemesio (Sanchez) "Tony" (b. December 19, 1935, Central Alara, Cuba), player and coach, ranked among the most popular Philadelphia Phillies (NL) of the last half century. The fine second baseman was signed by the New York Giants (NL) in 1954 and drafted by the Chicago Cubs (NL) after spending four seasons in the minor leagues. He led the EvL in triples in 1954 and the NoL in stolen bases in 1955.

The 5-foot 9-inch, 169 pounder began his major league career with the Chicago Cubs in 1958, batting just .235 but showing signs of promise. After hitting .280 in 1959, he was traded to the Philadelphia Phillies in May 1960 for first baseman Ed Bouchee and pitcher Don Cardwell.

Taylor played 12 seasons for the Philadelphia Phillies, mostly as a second baseman and occasional third baseman. He quickly became a fan favorite because of his hustle and alert style of play. In 1963 Taylor batted .281 with 180 hits while scoring a career-high 102 runs and pacing NL second baseman with a .986 fielding percentage for the rapidly improving Philadelphia

Phillies. He remained Philadelphia's regular second baseman until being traded in June 1971 to the Detroit Tigers (AL). Taylor helped the Detroit Tigers win the 1972 Eastern Division title as a part time player and pinch hitter. He batted only .133 with two doubles in the AL Championship Series against the Oakland A's. Taylor returned to the Philadelphia Phillies in 1974 and finished his career there as a pinch hitter in 1976. He led all NL pinch hitters with 17 hits in 1974 and with 54 at-bats in 1975.

Taylor retired after the 1976 season and served as a coach for the Philadelphia Phillies from 1977 to 1980 and in 1988 and 1989. During 19-year major league seasons, he batted .261 with 2,007 hits, 298 doubles, and 1,005 runs scored. A fine base runner, he stole 234 bases.

Taylor married Nilda Martinez in February 1960. They had two children, Elizabeth and Tony Jr., before their divorce. He resides in Broussard, Canada and joined the Florida Marlins as coach in 1999.

BIBLIOGRAPHY: Eddie Gold and Art Ahrens, *The New Era Cubs, 1941–1985* (Chicago, IL, 1985); Larry Moffi and Jonathan Kronstadt, *Crossing the Line* (Jefferson, NC, 1994); Allen Lewis, *The Philadelphia Phillies: A Pictorial History* (Virginia Beach, VA, 1981); Frank Dolson, *The Philadelphia Story* (South Bend, IN, 1981); Fred Smith, *995 Tigers* (Detroit, MI, 1981); Rich Westcott and Frank Bilovsky, *The New Phillies Encyclopedia* (Philadelphia, PA, 1993).

John P. Rossi

TAYLOR, Benjamin H. "Ben" (b. July 1, 1888, Anderson, SC; d. January 24, 1953, Baltimore, MD), player and manager, was the son of a Methodist minister and youngest of four brothers significant in Negro League history. His oldest brother, Charles,* became one of the greatest black managers and a vice-president of the NNL. A second brother, John, pitched with a half dozen clubs before World War I, while his brother "Candy Jim" played third base and managed 16 different teams from 1904 through 1948. Taylor began his professional baseball career as a pitcher with the Birmingham, AL Giants in 1908 and 1909 and with the St. Louis Giants in 1911 and 1912 as a pitcher–first baseman and reached his prime with the Indianapolis, IN ABC's (NNL) from 1914 through 1918 and 1920. The ABC's, sponsored by the American Brewing Company, ranked among the top teams of that era. The club featured Ben's brother Jim, Oscar Charleston,* and Dave Malarcher* and was managed by Ben's oldest brother, Charles.

After Charles died in 1922, Taylor joined the powerhouse Chicago American Giants (NNL), one of black baseball's most enduring franchises. Taylor's career spanned the entire period between World Wars I and II. Taylor also played for and/or managed the Washington Potomacs (ECL) in 1923 and 1924, Harrisburg, PA Giants (ECL) in 1925, Baltimore Black Sox (ECL) from 1926 through 1928, Atlantic City, NJ Bacharach Giants (ANL) in 1929, Baltimore Stars in 1933, Brooklyn Eagles (NNL) in 1935, Washington Black Senators (NNL) in 1938, and New York Cubans (NNL) in 1940 before retiring. Taylor, who batted .334 lifetime, already had reached the twilight of his career when the annual East-West Game became a feature of black baseball. Although not playing in the annual game, Taylor apparently umpired the first game in 1933. Contemporaries remember Taylor as a sterling fielder and excellent hitter who threw and batted left-handed. He was considered about the best first baseman in black baseball prior to Buck Leonard's* arrival. Taylor managed Leonard with the Baltimore Stars and taught him how to play first base. He operated a pool room and printed game programs and scorecards for Baltimore Elite Giants games.

BIBLIOGRAPHY: William Brashler, *Josh Gibson* (New York, 1978); John B. Holway, *Voices from the Great Black Baseball Leagues* (New York, 1975); Robert W. Peterson, *Only the Ball Was White* (Englewood Cliffs, NJ, 1970); James A. Riley, *The Biographical Encyclopedia of the Negro Baseball Leagues* (New York, 1994); Paul Debono, *The Indianapolis ABCs* (Jefferson, NC, 1997); Donn Rogosin, *Invisible Men: Life in Baseball's Negro Leagues* (New York, 1983).

Douglas D. Martin

TAYLOR, Charles Isham "C. I." (b. January 20, 1875, SC; d. February 23, 1922, Indianapolis, IN), player, manager, and executive, was the son of a Methodist minister and the oldest of four baseball brothers, attended Clark College in Atlanta, GA, and served in the U.S. Army during the Spanish-American War. Taylor became manager of the Birmingham, AL Giants in 1904 and moved the team in 1910 to West Baden, IN as the Sprudels. He shifted the franchise in 1914 to Indianapolis, IN, where it was sponsored by the American Brewing Company and christened the ABC's. Under Taylor's tutelage, the Indianapolis ABC's ranked among the premier teams in black professional baseball. The club became financially sound and usually traveled by railroad. In 1920 Taylor put the ABC's into the fledging NNL, the first black major baseball circuit to survive its baptismal season. The NNL endured until the Depression ended it in 1932. Taylor served as NNL vice-president from its inception until his death and perhaps left his greatest legacy with his pioneering efforts for this league.

Taylor, of impeccable reputation and appearance, was considered gentlemanly, honest, fair, strict, and a good teacher. Players benefitting from his tutorship included Bingo DeMoss,* Dave Malarcher,* Dizzy Dismukes,* National Baseball Hall of Famer Oscar Charleston,* and his brothers Ben,* James, and Johnny Taylor. The 1916 ABC's, probably his greatest team, defeated Rube Foster's* Chicago American Giants five games to four in the Negro World Series. Earlier that season, Indianapolis bested the top eastern club, the New York Lincoln Stars, in four or five games. Taylor ranked among the three greatest black baseball managers.

BIBLIOGRAPHY: Chicago *Defender*, September 2, October 28, November 4, 1916; Leon Hardwick and Effa Manley, *Negro Baseball* (Chicago, IL, 1976); Indianapolis

Freeman, September 2, 16, October 28, November 4, 1916; Indianapolis *Star*, July 24–26, 28, August 28–31, October 23–25, 27, 30, 1916; Robert W. Peterson, *Only the Ball Was White* (Englewood Cliffs, NJ, 1970); James A. Riley, *The All-Time All-Stars of Black Baseball* (Cocoa, FL, 1983); James A. Riley, *The Biographical Encyclopedia of the Negro Baseball Leagues* (New York, 1994); Paul Debono, *The Indianapolis ABCs* (Jefferson, NC, 1997).

Merl F. Kleinknecht

TAYLOR, John W. "Jack" (b. January 14, 1874, New Straightville, OH; d. March 4, 1938, Columbus, OH), player, starred as an early 20th-century major league pitcher. The 5-foot 10-inch, 170-pound Taylor threw and batted right-handed. Taylor first pitched professionally for Milwaukee, WI (WL) in 1897 and most of 1898. He advanced to the Chicago Orphans (NL) in late 1898 and pitched for the Chicago Orphans-Cubs through 1903. Chicago traded Taylor in December 1903 to the St. Louis Cardinals (NL), for whom he hurled in 1904, 1905, and through July 1906. Taylor returned to the Chicago Cubs (NL) for the remainder of that season and 1907, thus ending his decade-long major league career.

With a 97 percent ratio in completing 278 of 286 major league starts, Taylor retains the highest complete game ratio of all long-term starting pitchers. He ranked as one of the NL's better pitchers, tying for the NL lead in complete games (39) in 1902 and finishing among the leaders several other years. Taylor also remained high in innings pitched different seasons. He led the NL retroactively in ERA in 1902 with a low 1.33 and won 20 or more games four times. Taylor holds a unique record of having completed every game he started for four straight years from 1902 to 1905, hurling 139 consecutive complete games. This streak included an 18-inning, 2–1 loss on June 24, 1904. For his major league career, he won 152 games, lost 139 decisions, and compiled a 2.66 ERA with 19 shutouts and 657 strikeouts in 2,617 innings.

Taylor's rash personality, a penchant for alcohol, and a tendency to gamble aroused suspicions of his honesty and probably prevented him from realizing a longer, more eminent career. Some suspected him of losing games deliberately in the first Chicago City Series in 1903 between the Chicago White Sox and the Chicago Cubs and, at the instigation of gamblers, dropping a contest to the Pittsburgh Pirates on July 30, 1904. At hearings, Taylor effectively refuted both charges. Backing came from fellow players and St. Louis Cardinals owner Frank D. Robison, who regarded him as unfairly maligned. By contrast, Chicago Cubs owner James S. Hart disliked Taylor and had planned to trade him well before he grew suspicious of his pitching in the 1903 Chicago City Series. Aside from being fined for pitching while inebriated in the Pittsburgh game, Taylor was fully exonerated. His serious threat to sue baseball ownership probably contributed to his acquittal.

BIBLIOGRAPHY: Arthur R. Ahrens, "Jack Taylor, King of the Iron Men," *BRJ* 5 (1976), pp. 92–95; Warren Brown, *The Chicago Cubs* (New York, 1946); Eddie Gold and Art Ahrens, *The Golden Era Cubs, 1876–1940* (Chicago, IL, 1985); Frederick G. Lieb, *The St. Louis Cardinals* (New York, 1945); Jim Enright, *Chicago Cubs* (New York, 1975); Warren Wilbert and William Hageman, *Chicago Cubs: Seasons at the Summit* (Champaign, IL, 1997); Bob Broeg, *Redbirds: A Century of Cardinals' Baseball* (St. Louis, MO, 1981); Bob Broeg and Jerry Vickery, *St. Louis Cardinals Encyclopedia* (Grand Rapids, MI, 1998); *The Baseball Encyclopedia*, 10th ed. (New York, 1996); Lowell L. Blaisdell, "Trouble and Jack Taylor," *TNP* 16 (1996), pp. 132–136; New York *Tribune*, January 18, 1905, February 14–15, 1905; *NYT*, June 25, 1904, July 30, 1904, January 10, 1905, February 14–16, 1905; St. Louis (MO) *Post-Dispatch*, January 6, 1905, January 11, 1905, January 13, 1905, February 14, 1905, February 16, 1905; Jack Taylor file, National Baseball Library, Cooperstown, NY.

Lowell L. Blaisdell

TEBBETTS, George Robert "Bird," "Birdie" (b. November 10, 1911, Burlington, VT; d. March 24, 1999, Manatee, FL), player, manager, executive, and scout, was the son of Charles Tebbetts, a salesman, and Elizabeth (Ryan) Tebbetts. An aunt nicknamed him, "Bird," remarking that he had "lips just like a bird!" After influenza killed his father, Tebbetts moved with his mother, sister, and brother to Nashua, NH, in 1917. At Nashua High School, Tebbetts made All-State in football and starred in basketball and baseball. The Detroit Tigers (AL) signed the catcher and paid him $200 a month while he attended Providence College on a baseball scholarship. After earning a Bachelor's degree in philosophy in 1934, Tebbetts played for Bedford, MA (NEL) in 1934, Springfield, IL (3IL) in 1935, and Beaumont, TX (TL) in 1935 and 1936.

Tebbetts caught for the Detroit Tigers from September 1936 to 1947 except for U.S. Army service from 1943 to 1945. The 5-foot 11-inch, 200-pound right-hander, one of the smartest, most dedicated catchers, handled pitchers astutely and intimidated opponents with his high-pitched shriek. The witty, scrappy Tebbetts led AL catchers in assists (1939–1941) and made the AL All-Star team in 1941 and 1942. He batted .296 in 1940, as the Tigers won the AL pennant and lost the World Series to the Cincinnati Reds. In May 1947 the Detroit Tigers traded Tebbetts to the Boston Red Sox (AL), where he batted .280 in 1948 and a career-high .310 in 1950. Boston nearly won AL pennants in 1948 and 1949, seasons that Tebbetts made the AL All-Star team. The Boston Red Sox in December 1950 sent Tebbetts, who sold insurance during the off-season, to the Cleveland Indians (AL) after he publicly criticized teammates. Tebbetts retired following the 1952 campaign, having batted .270 with 1,000 hits and 469 RBI in 14 major league campaigns.

Tebbetts, an excellent teacher, managed Indianapolis, IN (AA) in 1953 and the Cincinnati Reds (NL) from 1954 through 1958. The 1956 Reds, featuring sluggers Frank Robinson,* Ted Kluszewski,* and Wally Post,* finished only two games behind the Brooklyn Dodgers, as *TSN* named Tebbetts NL Manager of the Year. Tebbetts, vice president of the Milwaukee Braves (NL) from 1959 until September 1961, piloted Milwaukee in 1961 and 1962 and the Cleveland Indians (AL) from 1963 through 1966. Tebbetts's clubs compiled a 748–705 win–loss record over 11 major league seasons. Scouting assignments followed with the New York Yankees (AL) from 1975 to 1982, Cleveland Indians (AL) from 1983 to 1988, Baltimore Orioles (AL) from 1989 to 1992, and Florida Marlins (NL) in 1993.

Tebbetts married Mary Hartnett in October 1950 and had three daughters, Susan, Elizabeth, and Patricia. Boston fans in 1969 voted him the Red Sox all-time catcher. Tebbetts served on the Veterans Committee of the National Baseball Hall of Fame.

BIBLIOGRAPHY: "A Game of Inches," *Time* 70 (July 8, 1957), pp. 42–47; Robert Creamer, "The Three Worlds of Birdie Tebbetts," *SI* 6 (February 25, 1957), pp. 60–66; Jack Torry, *Endless Summers* (South Bend, IN, 1995); Terry Pluto, *The Curse of Rocky Colavito* (New York, 1994); Gary Caruso, *The Braves Encyclopedia* (Philadelphia, PA, 1995); Bob Buege, *The Milwaukee Braves: A Baseball Eulogy* (Milwaukee, WI, 1988); Bob Rathgeber, *Cincinnati Reds Scrapbook* (Virginia Beach, VA, 1982); John Phillips, *Winners* (Cabin John, MD, 1987); David Halberstam, *Summer of '49* (New York, 1989); Dan Shaughnessy, *The Curse of the Bambino* (New York, 1990); Thomas Aylesworth and Benton Minks, *The Encyclopedia of Baseball Managers* (New York, 1990); Al Hirshberg, *Baseball's Greatest Catchers* (New York, 1966); Ed Linn, "The Man in the Dugout," *Sport* 17 (September 1954), pp. 50–60; Harry T. Paxton, "Can He Lift the Redlegs Out of the Rut?" *SEP* 226 (May 22, 1954), p. 31; Birdie Tebbetts, "I'd Rather Catch," *Atlantic* 184 (September 1949), pp. 45–48; Birdie Tebbetts, letter to David L. Porter, August 11, 1993; *TSN Official Baseball Register*, 1963; Birdie Tebbetts file, National Baseball Library, Cooperstown, NY; Frederick G. Lieb, *The Detroit Tigers* (New York, 1946); Joe Falls, *Detroit Tigers* (New York, 1975); Fred Smith, *995 Tigers* (Detroit, MI, 1981); Howard Liss, *The Boston Red Sox* (New York, 1982); Robert Redmount, *The Red Sox Encyclopedia* (Champaign, IL, 1998).

David L. Porter

TEBEAU, Oliver Wendell "Patsy," "Pat" (b. December 5, 1864, St. Louis, MO; d. May 15, 1918, St. Louis, MO), player and manager, joined his brother, George Tebeau, as a major league player. The scrappy competitor played second base with St. Joseph, MO (WL) in 1886 and Denver, CO (WL) in 1887. The Chicago White Stockings (NL) purchased him in 1887, inserting him at third base in 20 games. Minor league stints followed with Minneapolis, MN (WA) and Omaha, NE (WA) in 1888.

Before the 1889 season, the Cleveland Spiders (NL) signed him. In 1890 the right-handed Tebeau switched to the Cleveland Infants (PL) franchise, leading third basemen in putouts (204) and fielding average (.872) while batting .298. The Cleveland Spiders re-signed him in 1891 and assigned him managerial duties at midseason. In the split 1892 season, Cleveland captured the second-half championship before losing to the Boston Beaneaters in the playoff series. After sharing third base and first base responsibilities in 1893, he played mostly at first base in 1894. Authorities considered the 5-foot 8-inch, 163 pounder small for the position, but he paced NL first basemen in fielding average with .994 in 1897. Under Tebeau, Cleveland finished second in 1894 and defeated the champion Baltimore Orioles, four games to one, in the Temple Cup Series.

The Cleveland Spiders owners bought the St. Louis Cardinals (NL) franchise and shipped manager Tebeau and his best players, including Cy Young,* there. The 1899 St. Louis Cardinals enjoyed a winning season, but Tebeau angrily resigned in 1900 after 92 games. Tebeau claimed that the owners were preparing the newly acquired John McGraw* to replace him.

Although not achieving greatness, Tebeau batted at least .300 for three seasons and hit .279 lifetime with 1,290 hits and 196 doubles. As a feisty manager, Tebeau made his mark. Tebeau's teams nearly always attained winning records and finished with a 726–583 win–loss mark for a .555 winning average. His clubs regularly led the NL in bases on balls, manufacturing runs with stolen bases and hit-and-run plays. Tebeau, who was estranged from his wife, Kate, and had two children, shot himself at his saloon.

BIBLIOGRAPHY: Thomas Aylesworth and Benton Minks, *The Encyclopedia of Baseball Managers* (New York, 1990); J. Thomas Hetrick, *The Misfits!* (Jefferson, NC, 1991); John Phillips, *The Spiders—Who Was Who* (Cabin John, MD, 1991); Franklin Lewis, *The Cleveland Indians* (New York, 1949); Bob Broeg, *Redbirds: A Century of Cardinals' Baseball* (St. Louis, MO, 1981); Bob Broeg and Jerry Vickery, *St. Louis Cardinals Encyclopedia* (Grand Rapids, MI, 1998); *The Baseball Encyclopedia*, 10th ed. (New York, 1996); Gene Karst and Martin J. Jones, Jr., *Who's Who in Professional Baseball* (New Rochelle, NY, 1973); Frederick G. Lieb, *The St. Louis Cardinals* (New York, 1944); Richard Scheinin, *Field of Screams* (New York, 1994); Ira L. Smith, *Baseball's Famous First Basemen* (New York, 1956); Oliver Wendell Tebeau file, National Baseball Library, Cooperstown, NY; John Thorn et al., eds., *Total Baseball*, 5th ed. (New York, 1997); Robert L. Tiemann and Mark Rucker, eds., *Nineteenth Century Stars* (Kansas City, MO, 1989).

Gaymon L. Bennett

TEKULVE, Kenton Charles "Kent," "Teke" (b. March 5, 1947, Cincinnati, OH), player, coach, and sportscaster, established a major league record for most games (1,050) as a relief pitcher in an NL career spanning from 1974 until 1989. Injuries sidelined the toothpick-slender, durable right-hander only five days in 1981 and 19 days in 1988 during his entire major league career. The son of Henry Tekulve, he moved at age five with his family to Hamilton, OH. Tekulve graduated from Hamilton Catholic High School, where he played basketball and baseball and earned a bachelor's degree in physical education from Marietta (OH) College. After pitching for Marietta, he signed his first professional baseball contract at age 22 and joined Geneva, NY (NYPL). The 6-foot 4-inch, 175-pound right-hander relieved for Salem, VA (CL), Waterbury, CT (EL), Sherbrooke, Canada (EL), and Charleston,

WV (IL). His Pittsburgh Pirates (NL) debut came on May 20, 1974. He pitched for the Pittsburgh Pirates until being traded to the Philadelphia Phillies (NL) in April 1985 and ended his major league career with the Cincinnati Reds (NL) in 1989. He replaced "Goose" Gossage* as the Pirates closer in November 1977 when the latter signed as a free agent with the New York Yankees.

In 15 major league seasons, Tekulve pitched in 1,050 games and ranked third only to Dennis Eckersley* and Hoyt Wilhelm.* His major league records included most games and most consecutive appearances as a relief pitcher (1,050). He established NL marks for most games pitched, most games finished (638), and most innings by a relief pitcher (1,436.1). The unorthodox sidearmer compiled a career 94–90 win–loss record, 184 saves, and a 2.85 ERA, surrendering 491 bases on balls while striking out 779 batters.

Tekulve, a member of the NL 1980 All-Star team who used a slider and sinker, led the NL in pitching appearances in four campaigns (1978–1979, 1982, 1987) and made a career-high 94 appearances for the Pirates in the 1979 world championship season. The all-time Pirates leader in saves (158) broke Elroy Face's* NL record of 846 games pitched on September 16, 1986. Tekulve pitched in both the 1975 and 1979 NL Championship Series and the 1979 World Series. His most memorable moment came when he secured the last out of the 1979 World Series. He made a then World Series record three saves, striking out 10 Baltimore Orioles in 9.1 innings. No previous reliever in major league history had pitched over 1,000 consecutive games without making a start.

Tekulve, who married Linda Taylor on October 30, 1976, has four children and resides in Pittsburgh, PA. He has served as a special assignment pitching coach for the Pittsburgh Pirates from 1990 to 1992 and a color television analyst for the Philadelphia Phillies since 1993.

BIBLIOGRAPHY: *The Baseball Encyclopedia*, 10th ed. (New York, 1996); Hal McCoy, "An Unnoticed Milestone," *TSN*, May 1, 1989; *Phillies Reports, 1986–1987*; Rich Westcott and Frank Bilovsky, *The New Phillies Encyclopedia* (Philadelphia, PA, 1993); John Thorn et al., eds., *Total Baseball*, 5th ed. (New York, 1997); *TSN Baseball Register*, 1990; *TSN*, May 10, 1980; Lou Sahadi, *The Pirates* (New York, 1980); Chuck Wills and Pat Wills, *Beyond Home Plate* (Ocala, FL, 1993); Bob Cairns, *Pen Men* (New York, 1993); Richard L. Burtt, *The Pittsburgh Pirates: A Pictorial History* (Virginia Beach, VA, 1977); Bob Smizik, *The Pittsburgh Pirates: An Illustrated History* (New York, 1990).

Robert B. Van Atta

TEMPLE, John Ellis (b. August 8, 1927, Lexington, NC; d. January 9, 1994, Anderson, SC), player, coach, and sportscaster, was the son of J. Lester Temple and briefly attended Catawba College in 1946. The fiery infielder, whose competitive drive made him a fan favorite, possessed a hot temper which made him combative with umpires, managers, teammates, and even official scorers. After serving in the United States Navy during the latter part of World War II, Temple signed with the Cincinnati Reds (NL) in 1948 and progressed through their minor league chain with Morganton, NC (WCL) in 1948, Ogden, UT (PrL) in 1949, Columbia, SC (SAL) in 1950, and Tulsa, OK (TL) in 1951 and 1952. He batted a league-leading .400 in 1949 and paced the TL with 180 hits in 1951.

Temple made the major leagues in 1952 and became the Cincinnati Reds' regular second baseman in 1954. He batted at least .284 every season from 1954 through 1959 and made the 1956, 1957, and 1959 NL All-Star teams. Temple, who led the NL in bases on balls in 1957 with 94, was traded to the Cleveland Indians (AL) in December 1959 and spent the 1960 and 1961 seasons there, making the 1961 AL All-Star team. He played with the Baltimore Orioles (AL) in 1962 and Houston Astros (NL) in 1962 and 1963. Temple served as player-coach with the Cincinnati Reds in his final 1964 season, which was marred by a late-season fight with fellow coach Reggie Otero. Altogether, he batted .284 with 1,484 hits, 208 doubles, and 140 stolen bases in 1,420 major league games.

Temple worked as sports director for KHOU-TV in Houston TX, but several business ventures left him in financial and legal difficulties. He moved to his wife's hometown of Columbia, SC, where he served as a state government official for a brief period. He had met Rebekah Sheely while playing minor league baseball in Columbia and married her on September 5, 1950 in a ballpark ceremony. They had one child, Michael. Temple died of pancreatic cancer.

BIBLIOGRAPHY: John Temple file, National Baseball Library, Cooperstown, NY; Walter Bingham, "Temple's Temper," *SI* 12 (April 18, 1960), pp. 67–70; Furman Bisher, "Roughneck at Second Base," *Sport* 29 (January 1960), pp. 36–39; *NYT*, January 12, 1994, p. B6; Harry T. Paxton, "The Redlegs' Miraculous Twins," *SEP* 234 (August 3, 1957), pp. 22–23; Al Silverman, "A Lot Depends on Temple," *Sport* 29 (May 1960), pp. 18–20; Edgar Williams, "The Temple in Cincinnati," *BD* 13 (July 1954), pp. 53–60; Ritter Collett, *The Cincinnati Reds* (Virginia Beach, VA, 1976); Peter C. Bjarkman, *Baseball's Great Dynasties: The Reds* (New York, 1991); Bob Rathgeber, *Cincinnati Reds Scrapbook* (Virginia Beach, VA, 1982); Terry Pluto, *The Curse of Rocky Colavito* (New York, 1994); Jack Torry, *Endless Summers* (South Bend, IN, 1995).

Jim L. Sumner

TEMPLETON, Garry Lewis (b. March 24, 1956, Lockney, TX), player and manager, is the son of Spiavia Templeton, an infielder in the Negro Leagues, and Otella (William) Templeton. His brother, Kenneth Templeton, played outfield in the Oakland Athletics (AL) organization. Templeton signed out of Santa Anna (CA) High School for a $40,000 bonus as the St. Louis Cardinals' (NL) first draft choice in June 1974. After having numerous well-

fielding but weak-hitting shortstops, St. Louis yearned for offensive production from that position. Templeton immediately was tutored in switch-hitting
in 1974 at Sarasota, FL (GCL) and St. Petersburg, FL (FSL). He developed
proficiency from both sides of the plate and batted .401 with Little Rock–
based Arkansas (TL) after his promotion at midseason 1975 from St. Petersburg. Templeton batted .321 with Tulsa, OK (AA) in 1976 and was called
up by the St. Louis Cardinals. He finished the 1976 season by batting .291
in 53 games for St. Louis as starting shortstop. From 1976 to 1981, Templeton batted .305 for the Cardinals; led the NL in triples in 1977, 1978,
and 1979; made over 100 hits from each side of the plate in 1979; and
reached a personal-high 34 stolen bases in 1978. The 5-foot 11-inch, 185-
pound Templeton led NL shortstops in errors from 1978 to 1980, but was
exciting afield and displayed excellent range. Templeton and his wife,
Glenda, have two sons, Garry II and Gerome, and one daughter, Genae. He
has another daughter, Sharmine, from a previous marriage.

   Templeton's temper tantrums and sulking irked St. Louis Cardinals manager Whitey Herzog.* Tensions culminated in August 1981, when Templeton made obscene gestures to the St. Louis fans who had booed him for
obvious lackluster play. Herzog suspended him and sent Templeton in February 1982 to the San Diego Padres (NL) for shortstop Ozzie Smith.*

   Templeton improved defensively at shortstop with the Padres from 1982
to 1989, but never approached his St. Louis offensive production. Age
brought maturity and leadership ability for Templeton, who was made Padres team captain in 1987. In May 1991, the Padres traded Templeton to
the New York Mets (NL) for Tim Teufel. He ended his major league career
following that season.

   Templeton was selected for the NL All-Star squad in 1977, 1979, and
1982, but declined to attend the 1979 game because he was not voted the
starting shortstop. In 1984, he batted .333 in the NL Championship Series
against the Chicago Cubs and .316 in the World Series against the Detroit
Tigers. In 16 major league seasons, Templeton batted .271 with 2,096 hits,
893 runs, 70 HR, 728 RBI, and 242 stolen bases in 2,079 games. He managed Cedar Rapids, IA (ML) in 1998 and Erie, PA in 1999.

BIBLIOGRAPHY: Bob Broeg, *Redbirds: A Century of Cardinals' Baseball* (St. Louis, MO,
1981); Chris Cobbs, "How Garry Templeton Emerged as Leader of the Padres,"
BD 44 (July 1985), pp. 37–39; Whitey Herzog and Kevin Horrigan, *White Rat* (New
York, 1987); Garry Templeton file, National Baseball Library, Cooperstown, NY;
Rob Rains, *The St. Louis Cardinals* (New York, 1992); Bob Broeg and Jerry Vickery,
St. Louis Cardinals Encyclopedia (Grand Rapids, MI, 1998); Peter C. Bjarkman, ed.,
Encyclopedia of Major League Baseball Team Histories National League (Westport, CT,
1991); Ozzie Smith with Rob Rains, *Wizard* (Chicago, IL, 1988); George Vass,
"There's Usually a Market for Controversial Players," *BD* 41 (July 1982), pp. 51–
54; Steve Wulf, "All My Padres," *SI* 70 (April 5, 1989), pp. 42–50; Steve Wulf,

"You've Got to Hand It to the Padres," *SI* 61 (October 15, 1984), pp. 28–34; Jack McKeon with Tom Friend, *Jack of All Trades* (Chicago, IL, 1988); Dick Williams and Bill Plaschke, *No More Mr. Nice Guy* (San Diego, CA, 1990).

Frank J. Olmsted

TENACE, Fury Gene (b. Fiore Gino Tennaci, October 10, 1946, Russelton, PA), player and coach, graduated from Valley Local High School in Lucasville, OH and was selected by the Kansas City Athletics (AL) in the 11th round of the June 1965 draft. The 6-foot, 195-pound Tenace, who batted and threw right-handed, spent six minor league seasons as an outfielder–catcher with Shelby, TN (WCL) in 1965, Leesburg, FL (FSL) in 1966 and 1967, Peninsula, VA (CrL) in 1967 and 1968, Birmingham, AL (SL) in 1969, and Des Moines–based Iowa (AA) in 1970. He batted .305 in 38 games for the Oakland Athletics (AL) in 1970 and played on five consecutive AL West titlists. Tenace became a regular catcher in August 1972 and was moved to first base in 1973, when he batted .259 with 24 HR. His best season with the Oakland A's came in 1975, when he batted .255 with a career-high 29 HR and 87 RBI.

Tenace knocked in the decisive run in Oakland's 2–1 victory over the Detroit Tigers in Game 5 of the 1972 AL Championship Series and sparked the Athletics over the Cincinnati Reds in the 1972 World Series, batting .348 with four HR and nine RBI. In the A's 3–2 victory in Game 1, he became the first player to homer in his first two World Series at-bats. Tenace clouted a three run HR in the Game 5 loss and drove in two runs in Oakland's 3–2 clinching victory in Game 7. The World Series MVP, he set a record for the highest slugging percentage (.913) and tied a mark for the most HR in a seven-game series. In 1973, Tenace tied a World Series mark by walking 11 times against the New York Mets. He batted .228 with four HR and 12 RBI in four World Series.

In December 1976, the San Diego Padres (NL) signed Tenace as a free agent. His best season with the San Diego Padres came in 1979, when he led NL catchers with a .998 fielding percentage and batted .263 with 20 HR and 67 RBI. The San Diego Padres sent him to the St. Louis Cardinals (NL) in an 11 player, December 1980 transaction. He played a utility role with the St. Louis Cardinals and ended his major league career with the Pittsburgh Pirates (NL) in 1983.

Altogether, Tenace batted .241 with 1,060 hits, 201 HR, and 674 RBI in 1,555 major league games spanning 15 seasons. Despite his low batting average, he reached base nearly 40 percent of the time. Tenace drew over 100 walks six seasons, leading the AL with 110 in 1974 and the NL with 125 in 1977. He coached the Houston Astros (NL) in 1986 and 1987 and Toronto Blue Jays (AL) from 1990 through 1997. He married Linda Osmeyer in December 1967 and has three children, Stacey, Merinda, and Gina.

BIBLIOGRAPHY: Gene Tenace file, National Baseball Library, Cooperstown, NY; Ron Fimrite, "A Hero Finds There's No One for Tenace," *SI* 38 (April 2, 1973), pp. 71–72, 75–76; Bruce Markusen, *Baseball's Last Dynasty* (New York, 1998); Jack McKeon with Tom Friend, *Jack of All Trades* (Chicago, IL, 1988); Rob Rains, *The St. Louis Cardinals* (New York, 1992); Louis Sabin, *Record Breakers of the Major Leagues* (New York, 1974); Donald Honig, *October Heroes* (New York, 1979); *TSN Baseball Register*, 1984.

David L. Porter

TENER, John Kinley (b. July 25, 1863, County Tyrone, Ireland; d. May 19, 1946, Pittsburgh, PA), player and executive, was the son of George Evans Tener and Susan (Wallis) Tener and had nine brothers and sisters. The Teners immigrated to the United States and settled in Pittsburgh, where John was orphaned at age nine. The 6-foot 4-inch, 180-pound, right-handed Tener played amateur baseball from 1881 to 1885 and began his professional career the latter year with the Baltimore Orioles (AA). After hurling with Haverhill, MA (NEL) in 1886, he was signed by Cap Anson* in 1887 and pitched the next two seasons for the Chicago White Stockings (NL). In 1889, he started 30 games, won 15 decisions, lost 15 contests, hurled one shutout, and batted .273. When the BPBP was organized in 1885, Tener became one of its most influential members. In 1890 he joined the Pittsburgh Burghers (PL), but compiled a disappointing 3–11 mark in 14 starts and left baseball to pursue a banking career. As a major league pitcher, Tener finished 25–31, struck out 174 batters, walked 200, surrendered 552 hits in 506 innings pitched, and threw two shutouts.

A banker until his retirement in 1930, the Republican represented Pittsburgh in the U.S. Congress from 1909 to 1911 and served one term as governor of Pennsylvania from 1911 to 1915. Although chosen NL president in 1913, he served only part-time until his term as governor expired. He held the NL presidency until 1918, initiating the splitting of World Series receipts and handling the Scott Perry case. Tener proposed sharing World Series player receipts with the other first-division teams, thus averting a players' strike. In 1918 Philadelphia Athletics (AL) pitcher Perry was awarded by Tener and Garry Herrmann of the National Commission to the Boston Braves (NL), who originally had signed him. After the AL obtained an injunction against the Commission's action, Tener resigned in protest. As president, Tener also negotiated the breakup of the FL. After leaving baseball, he served on the boards of several Pittsburgh businesses and frequently attended Pittsburgh Pirates (NL) games. Tener married Harriet J. Day in 1889. After her death in 1935, he married Leone Evans in 1936 and again became a widower the next year.

BIBLIOGRAPHY: John Tener file, National Baseball Library, Cooperstown, NY; *BDAC* (Washington, DC, 1961); Glenn Dickey, *The History of National League Base-*

ball (New York, 1982); Richard C. Gallagher, "John Tener's Brilliant Career," *BRJ* 19 (1990), pp. 36–38; *NYT*, May 20, 1946; *The Baseball Encyclopedia*, 10th ed. (New York, 1996).

Robert E. Jones

TENNACI, Fiore Gino. *See* Fury Gene Tenace.

TENNEY, Frederick "Fred" (b. November 26, 1871, Georgetown, MA; d. July 3, 1952, Boston, MA), player and manager, was among the first college graduates to enter major league baseball. After graduating from Brown University in June 1894, the 5-foot, 9-inch, 155-pound Tenney was signed by the injury-riddled Boston Beaneaters (NL) and became one of the few left-handed catchers in major league history. From 1894 through 1896, Tenney caught in 68 games and played the outfield in 94 contests for Boston. After shifting to first base in 1897, he joined Jimmy Collins,* Herman Long,* and Bobby Lowe* to form one of baseball's most famous infields. Tenney performed for the Boston Beaneaters and Boston Doves 14 consecutive seasons, including the 1905–1907 campaigns as player–manager. In December 1907, the Boston Doves traded him to the New York Giants (NL) in one of the biggest exchanges in major league baseball history. Tenney was released by the Giants in 1910 and completed the season with Lowell, MA (NEL) as player–manager. He returned to Boston in 1911 as their player–manager, compiling a .263 batting average in 102 games at age 39. He retired from baseball after managing Newark, NJ (IL) in 1916, batting .318 in 16 games.

The intelligent, competitive Tenney was unrivaled at fielding a bunt and cutting the runner down at second base by perfecting the "first to second to first" double play. Tenney and Christy Mathewson* developed the "quick pitch" to hold runners close to first base, but the strategy was eliminated when the balk rule was initiated. Tenney, who threw and batted left-handed, batted .294 in 1,994 major league games with 2,231 hits, 1,278 runs scored, 270 doubles, 77 triples, 22 HR, 688 RBI, and 285 stolen bases. He hit above .300 six full seasons and made six hits in a May 31, 1897 contest. Tenney's best season came in 1899, when he batted a career-high .347, collected 209 base hits, made 17 triples, and scored 115 runs. He led the NL with 566 at-bats (1897) and 101 runs scored (1908) and paced in putouts (1905, 1907–1908), assists (1898, 1901–1907), and fielding average (1902) at first base. He held the NL record for most assists (1,363) at first base and the major league mark for most years leading the league in assists (8). Tenney, who married Bessie Berry on October 21, 1895, enjoyed little success as Boston's manager (1905–1907, 1911). Under Tenney, Boston won only 202 of 606 games and finished in seventh and eighth place twice. After leaving baseball, Tenney wrote articles for a newspaper syndicate, operated a shoe store, managed Newark, NJ (IL) in 1916, and prospered in the insurance industry.

BIBLIOGRAPHY: Fred Tenney file, National Baseball Library, Cooperstown, NY; Frank Graham, *The New York Giants* (New York, 1952); Ray Robinson, *Matty: An American Hero* (New York, 1993); Gene Karst and Martin J. Jones, Jr., *Who's Who in Professional Baseball* (New Rochelle, NY, 1973); Paul MacFarlane, ed., *TSN Daguerreotypes of Great Stars of Baseball* (St. Louis, MO, 1971); *The Baseball Encyclopedia*, 10th ed. (New York, 1996); Ira L. Smith, *Baseball's Famous First Basemen* (New York, 1956); Noel Hynd, *The Giants of the Polo Grounds* (New York, 1988); Robert L. Tiemann and Mark Rucker, eds., *Nineteenth Century Stars* (Kansas City, MO, 1989); George V. Tuohey, comp., *A History of the Boston Base Ball Club* (Boston, MA, 1897); Harold Kaese, *The Boston Braves* (New York, 1948); Gary Caruso, *The Braves Encyclopedia* (Philadelphia, PA, 1995).

John L. Evers

TERRY, William H. "Adonis" (b. August 7, 1864, Westfield, MA; d. February 24, 1915, Milwaukee, WI), player, was the son of Joseph Terry, a Southwick, MA carpenter. He launched his professional baseball career with the Brooklyn, MA Grays (ISA) in 1883 and began his major league career with the fledgling Brooklyn Trolley-Dodgers (AA) in 1884. In eight seasons with Brooklyn, the 5-foot, 11½-inch, 190-pound right-hander won 126 games. His 22 victories in 1889 and 26 triumphs in 1890 helped the Bridegrooms accomplish the unprecedented feat of winning consecutive pennants in two major leagues, namely the AA and NL. He also hurled AA no-hitters against the 1886 St. Louis Browns and the 1888 Louisville Colonels.

Terry, admiringly nicknamed "Adonis" by Brooklyn fans, left the Bridegrooms for Pittsburgh Pirates (NL) in 1892 and won 30 games over the next two seasons. The Chicago Colts (NL) signed him in 1894. He won 41 games spanning the next three campaigns, logging a 21–14 mark in 1895. The versatile Terry, who also played the outfield and the four infield positions, ended his 14-year major league career with Chicago in 1897. Altogether, he owned a 197–196 pitching record with a 3.73 ERA and batted .249 in 667 major league games.

Terry joined the Milwaukee (WL) team in 1897 and promoted minor league baseball there until his death. An avid bowler, Terry served on the executive committee of the AmBC and operated a bowling center in Milwaukee. He was survived by his wife, son, William, and daughter, Cecilia.

BIBLIOGRAPHY: John Thorn et al., eds., *Total Baseball*, 5th ed. (New York, 1997); William H. Terry file, National Baseball Library, Cooperstown, NY; Richard Gentile, telephone interview, July 1996; Richard Goldstein, *Superstars and Screwballs* (New York, 1991); Frank Graham, *The Brooklyn Dodgers* (New York, 1945); Stanley Cohen, *Dodgers: The First 100 Years* (New York, 1990); Frederick Ivor-Campbell et al., eds., *Baseball's First Stars* (Cleveland, OH, 1996); Warren Brown, *The Chicago Cubs* (New York, 1946); Jerry Lansche, *Glory Fades Away* (Dallas, TX, 1991); Eddie Gold and Art Ahrens, *The Golden Era Cubs, 1876–1940* (Chicago, IL, 1985); Tommy Holmes, *The Dodgers* (New York, 1975); William E. McNeil, *The Dodgers Encyclopedia* (Champaign, IL, 1997); Daniel M. Pearson, *Base Ball in 1889* (Bowling Green, OH, 1993); Robert L. Tiemann, *Dodger Classics* (St. Louis, MO, 1983); David Q. Voigt, *Baseball: An Illustrated History* (University Park, PA, 1987); David Nemec, *The Beer and Whisky League* (New York, 1994).

David Q. Voigt

TERRY, William Harold "Bill," "Memphis Bill" (b. October 30, 1898, Atlanta, GA; d. January 9, 1989, Jacksonville, FL, player, manager, and executive, was the son of William Thomas Terry, a grain businessman, and Bertha Elizabeth (Blackman) Terry and attended school through eighth grade in Atlanta. He lived with his mother after his parents separated and unloaded freight cars in a railroad yard. He married Elvena Snead of Memphis, TN in November 1916 and had three sons, William, Jr., Roy, and Ken, and one daughter, Marjorie. After pitching for local Atlanta teams, Terry began his professional baseball career with Newnan, GA (GAL) in 1915. He pitched for Newnan in 1915 and played with Shreveport, LA (TL) in 1916–1917. Terry left organized baseball in 1918 to work with the Standard Oil Company of Memphis, but pitched for the company's semipro team. He remained with Standard Oil Company of Memphis until 1922, when owner Tom Watkins of Memphis, TN (SA) recommended him to New York Giants manager John McGraw.* McGraw was more impressed with Terry's hitting than his left-handed pitching and assigned him to Toledo, OH (AA). Now a full-time first baseman, the left-handed, 6-foot 1-inch, 200-pound Terry hit .377 for Toledo in 1923 and joined the Giants (NL) that September.

Terry, a straightaway hitter, drove balls to all parts of the field rather than aiming for the nearby right field stands at the Polo Grounds. After hitting a mediocre .239 for the Giants in 1924, he batted .319 in 1925. In 1927, he compiled the first of six consecutive seasons with at least 100 runs scored and batted in and the first of ten straight seasons batting over .300. Nicknamed "Memphis Bill," he enjoyed his best year in 1930 by batting .401 and tying the NL record for hits with 254. No NL player has topped the 254 hits or .400 mark since. Terry won the NL's MVP Award in 1930 despite the Giants' third place finish. Besides compiling an outstanding .341 lifetime batting average in 14 major league seasons, he led first basemen in fielding percentage twice and was the premier NL first baseman most of his playing career. In 1,721 major league games, he compiled 2,193 hits, 373 doubles, 112 triples, 154 HR, 1,120 runs scored, 1,078 RBI, and 56 stolen bases.

Terry's brilliance as a player was complemented by his successful reign as New York Giants manager from June 1932 through the 1941 season. Mc-Graw, although having a personality conflict with Terry and not on speaking terms with him for two years, recommended him as his managerial successor. Through several successful trades and clever defensive field strategy, Terry moved the Giants from a sixth place finish in 1932 to a surprise NL pennant and World Series victory over the Washington Senators in 1933. With superb pitching by Carl Hubbell* and powerful hitting by Mel Ott,* Terry's

Giants won NL pennants again in 1936 and 1937. The Giants were defeated in the World Series both years by overpowering New York Yankees teams. The Giants finished third in 1938 and slipped to the second division from 1939 through 1941, after which Ott replaced Terry as manager. As Giants manager from 1932 to 1941, Terry compiled 823 wins, 661 losses, and a .555 winning percentage. Terry served one season as the Giants' farm system director and left the major leagues permanently. He became president of the SAL in 1954, but quit that post four years later for a full-time business career.

The very bright, purposeful Terry speculated in oil after leaving the Giants in 1942 and operated a profitable automobile dealership in Memphis. Terry opened a larger dealership in Jacksonville, FL in 1949 and participated in Jacksonville civic and religious affairs. Always blunt and businesslike, Terry clashed continually with sportswriters during his managerial career. After his belated election to the National Baseball Hall of Fame in 1954, he was asked for his reaction upon becoming a baseball immortal. Miffed over having waited so long for his election, Terry characteristically responded, "I have nothing to say."

BIBLIOGRAPHY: Martin Appel and Burt Goldblatt, *Baseball's Best: The Hall of Fame Gallery* (New York, 1977); Gordon Forbes, "Bill Terry: The Strong Willed Giant," *Sport* 39 (May 1965), pp. 66–67ff; Frank Graham, *McGraw of the Giants* (New York, 1944); Arnold Hano, *Greatest Giants of Them All* (New York, 1967); Noel Hynd, *The Giants of the Polo Grounds* (New York, 1988); *NYT*, January 10, 1989, p. B-6; Robert C. McConnell, "Bill Terry as Pitcher," *BRJ* 18 (1989), pp. 53–54; Fred Stein, *Under Coogan's Bluff* (Glyddon, MD, 1979); Fred Stein and Nick Peters, *Day by Day in Giants History* (Berkeley, CA, 1987); Bill Terry file, National Baseball Library, Cooperstown, NY; Charles C. Alexander, *John McGraw* (New York, 1988); Frank Graham, *The New York Giants* (New York 1952).

Fred Stein

TESREAU, Charles Monroe "Jeff" (b. March 5, 1889, Silver Mine, MO; d. September 24, 1946, Hanover, NH), player and coach, pitched semiprofessional baseball after completing high school in Missouri and hurled in the minor leagues for Austin, TX (TL), Houston, TX (TL) and Shreveport, LA (TL). The St. Louis Browns (AL) and Detroit Tigers (AL) declined to sign him, but the New York Giants (NL) recruited him in 1910. After being optioned to Toronto, Canada (IL), Tesreau made his major league debut with the New York Giants on April 12, 1912.

In his rookie season, Tesreau compiled a 17–7 win–loss record and led NL pitchers with a 1.96 ERA. His 3–0 no-hitter came against the Philadelphia Phillies on September 6. In the 1912 World Series, New York Giants manager John McGraw* gave the brilliant right-handed spitball specialist the honor of pitching the opening game against the Boston Red Sox. Boston bested Tesreau, 4–3. Tesreau won only one of four decisions in three World Series.

The 6-foot 2-inch, 220-pound Tesreau contributed a 22–13 win–loss performance in 1913, helping the Giants repeat as NL pennant winners. Tesreau nearly hurled another no-hitter on May 16, 1914, holding the Pittsburgh Pirates hitless until there were two outs in the ninth inning. Tesreau enjoyed his best season in 1914 with a 26–10 mark and led NL pitchers with eight shutouts. After having a 19–16 record for the last-place Giants in 1915, he lost much of his effectiveness. His relatively short major league career ended with the 1918 season. He compiled a fine career 115–72 win–loss mark and 2.43 ERA.

Tesreau became baseball coach at Dartmouth College in 1919. Under Tesreau's guidance, Dartmouth won the EIL title several times. He became a popular campus figure during his 27 year coaching career. Tesreau held other baseball positions after the collegiate seasons ended, serving as a coach for the Chicago White Sox (AL) in 1928 and managing local Vermont independent teams. Tesreau, who married Helen Blake on October 16, 1913, fathered twin sons. One son starred as a pitcher and all-around athlete at Dartmouth College.

BIBLIOGRAPHY: Jeff Tesreau file, National Baseball Library, Cooperstown, NY; Noel Hynd, *The Giants of the Polo Grounds* (New York, 1988); Frank Graham, *The New York Giants* (New York, 1952); Frank Graham, *McGraw of the Giants* (New York, 1944); Charles C. Alexander, *John McGraw* (New York, 1988); Ray Robinson, *Matty: An American Hero* (New York, 1993); Fred Stein and Nick Peters, *Giants Diary* (Berkeley, CA, 1987); John Thorn et al., eds., *Total Baseball*, 5th ed. (New York, 1997); *TSN*, October 2, 1946, p. 38.

Fred Stein

TETTLETON, Mickey Lee (b. September 16, 1960, Oklahoma City, OK), player, graduated from Southeast High School in Oklahoma City and attended Oklahoma State University. The Oakland A's (AL) drafted the 6-foot 2-inch, 212-pound catcher, who switch hit and threw right-handed, in the fifth round in June 1981. Tettleton played under four minor league seasons with Modesto, CA (CaL) from 1981 to 1983 and Albany-Colonie, NY (EL) in 1984 before joining the Oakland A's for 33 games in 1984. He spent the next three seasons as an often injured reserve catcher with the Oakland A's before being released in March 1988.

In April 1988, Rochester (NY) signed Tettleton as a free agent. He joined the Baltimore Orioles (AL) that May as a catcher and DH and made the AL All-Star team and *TSN* All-Star and Silver Slugger teams in 1989. He batted .258 with 26 HR and 65 RBI in 1990, but set a major league single-season record for switch hitters by striking out 160 times.

In January 1991, the Baltimore Orioles traded Tettleton to the Detroit Tigers (AL). Tettleton's most productive seasons came with the Detroit Tigers. He clouted 31 HR with 89 RBI in 1991, 32 HR with 83 RBI in 1992, and 32 HR with a career-high 110 RBI in 1993, making *TSN* All-Star and

Silver Slugger teams in 1991 and 1992. In 1992, Tettleton led AL batters with 122 walks and AL catchers with a .996 fielding percentage. Two years later, he made the AL All-Star team for the second time.

The Texas Rangers (AL) signed Tettleton as a free agent in April 1995 and used him as an outfielder, first baseman, DH, and catcher. He clouted 32 HR with 78 RBI in 1995 and 24 HR with 83 RBI in 1996, but struggled in the AL Championship Series against the New York Yankees. Injuries prompted him to retire in July 1997.

During 14 major league seasons, Tettleton batted .241 with 210 doubles, 245 HR, 732 RBI, and a .990 fielding percentage. Although striking out frequently, he combined power with plate discipline, walked often, and recorded high on base and slugging percentages. He and his wife, Sylvia, have two children, Tyler and Jessica, and reside in Pauls Valley, OK.

BIBLIOGRAPHY: Mickey Tettleton file, National Baseball Library, Cooperstown, NY; Steve Rushin, "Cereal Killer at Large," *SI* 70 (June 12, 1989), p. 82; *TSN Baseball Register*, 1998; Ted Patterson, *The Baltimore Orioles* (Dallas, TX, 1995); William M. Anderson, *The Detroit Tigers* (South, Bend, IN, 1996); Richard Bak, *A Place for Summer* (Detroit, MI, 1998); Sparky Anderson with Dan Ewald, *They Call Me Sparky* (Chelsea, MI, 1998).

David L. Porter

THIGPEN, Robert Thomas "Bobby" (b. July 17, 1963, Tallahassee, FL), player, graduated from Aucilla Christian Academy in Monticello, FL, where he played football, basketball, and baseball. After graduating from Seminole CC, Thigpen starred in baseball with Will Clark* and Rafael Palmiero* at Mississippi State University. The Chicago White Sox (AL) drafted the 6-foot 3-inch, 222-pound outfielder–pitcher, who batted and threw right-handed, in the fourth round in June 1985. He climbed to the major leagues in under two seasons after hurling for Niagara Falls, NY (NYPL) and Appleton, WI (ML) in 1985 and Birmingham, AL (SL) in 1986.

Thigpen never saw a major league game until joining the Chicago White Sox in 1986 and remained with them until 1993, becoming the club's ace reliever. After faring 2–0 with a 1.77 ERA his rookie year, he compiled a 7–5 mark with a 2.73 ERA and 16 saves in 1987. Thigpen recorded 34 saves in both 1988 and 1989, striking out 109 cumulative batters. His best season came in 1990, when he set a major league record with 57 saves and led the AL with 77 appearances. Thigpen shattered Dave Righetti's* four-year-old single season save record by 11. Although winning only four of 10 decisions, he possessed a sparkling 1.83 ERA and struck out a career-high 70 batters in 88.2 innings. Thigpen made the AL-Star team and was named *TSN* AL Fireman of the Year. He finished 7–5 with a 3.49 ERA and 30 saves in 1991. After saving 22 games in 1992, he was converted to set-up man for the Chicago White Sox in 1993.

In August 1993, the Chicago White Sox traded Thigpen to the Philadel-

THOMAS, CLINTON CYRUS

phia Phillies (NL). After compiling a 3–1 record, he made two brief appearances in the NL Championship Series against the Atlanta Braves and blanked the Toronto Blue Jays in 2.2 innings in the World Series. His major league career ended with the Seattle Mariners (AL) in 1994.

In nine major league seasons, Thigpen compiled a 31–36 win–loss record with a 3.43 ERA and 201 saves. The Monticello, FL resident struck out 376 batters in 568.2 innings and induced batters to hit ground balls. He married Keri Keesler and has one son, Robert Alan.

BIBLIOGRAPHY: Robert Thigpen file, National Baseball Library, Cooperstown, NY; *TSN Baseball Register*, 1995; George Castle, "Beers with Bobby Thigpen," *Sport* 82 (March 1991), pp. 25–26; Bob Cairns, *Pen Men* (New York, 1993).

David L. Porter

THOMAS, Clinton Cyrus "Clint," "Hawk" (b. November 25, 1896, Greenup, KY; d. December 3, 1990, Charleston, WV), player, excelled as a left-handed power hitting outfielder in the Negro Leagues. The son of janitor James Thomas and Lutie Thomas and the oldest of eight children, he quit school in eighth grade and journeyed to Columbus, OH in 1910. Thomas, who played amateur baseball there, worked in a restaurant and grocery store and joined the U.S. Army in World War I. After his discharge, he returned to Columbus and played semipro baseball with the Bowers Easters in 1919. Thomas began his professional career as a second baseman in 1920 with the Brooklyn Royal Giants and played in 1921 with the Columbus, OH Buckeyes (NNL). After he joined the Detroit Stars (NNL) in 1922, manager Bruce Petway* moved him to the outfield. Nicknamed "Hawk" because of his great range, he worked that winter at the Ford Plant in Detroit, MI.

After jumping to the new ECL, Thomas played seven years with the Philadelphia Hilldale Daisies and hit .373 in 1923, .363 in 1924, and .351 in 1925. He played in both the 1924 and 1925 Negro World Series, helping Hilldale win the 1925 ECL title with his excellent fielding. He batted .306 in 1926 led the ECL with 23 stolen bases and barnstormed against the Philadelphia Athletics, reportedly slugging his 28th HR of the season off Eddie Rommel.* Thomas, an exceptional base stealer, batted .310 in six seasons in Cuba between 1923 and 1931. He hit .335 in the 1925–1926 season against Adolfo Luque,* Fred Fitzsimmons,* Jesse Petty, and other major league pitchers. Thomas worked as a truck driver for Ballantine Scotch when not playing winter ball.

Thomas moved to the Atlantic City, NJ Bacharach Giants (ANL) in 1929 and jumped to the New York Lincoln Giants in 1930, hitting .351 as a leadoff hitter and playing in the NNL playoffs against the Homestead, PA Grays. He played against major leaguers Tony Lazzeri,* Earl Averill,* and Lefty Gomez* in California in the 1932–1933 winter season and tripled and stole home in 1934 to defeat Dizzy Dean* and his All Stars, 1–0. Thomas later worked four years as a guard at the Brooklyn, NY Navy Yard, as a custodian for the West Virginia Department of Mines, and as a staff supervisor for the state senate. He married Ellen Odell (Smith) Bland in 1963 and had no children. Called the black Joe DiMaggio* by Monte Irvin,* Thomas combined speed, power, and superb defensive skills. Thomas and others proved that black players could compete against major league baseball players, paving the way for the ensuing integration.

BIBLIOGRAPHY: Terry A. Baxter, correspondence with Jorge Figueroda, 1984, Cuban League statistics, Terry A. Baxter Collection, Cedar Rapids, IA; Terry A. Baxter, telephone interview with Monte Irvin, 1984; Terry A. Baxter, telephone interview with Clint Thomas, 1984; Pat Hemlepp, "Clint Thomas Was That Good," Ashland (KY) *Daily Independent*, July 5, 1979, p. 15; James A. Riley, *The All-Time All-Stars of Black Baseball* (Cocoa, FL, 1983); Donn Rogosin, *Invisible Men: Life in Baseball's Negro Leagues* (New York, 1983); *TSN*, February 8, 1978; *NYT*, December 6, 1990, p. D-20; James A. Riley, *The Biographical Encyclopedia of the Negro Baseball Leagues* (New York, 1994).

                                                                Terry A. Baxter

THOMAS, Frank Edward, Jr. "The Big Hurt" (b. May 27, 1968, Columbus, GA), player, is the son of Frank Thomas, Sr., a textile worker and bail bondsman, and Charlie Mae Thomas and graduated from Columbus High School, where he excelled in baseball, football, and basketball. His high school won the State Championship twice. Thomas hoped to attend college on a baseball scholarship, but received no offers. He accepted a football scholarship to Auburn University instead and played tight end there. Thomas also made the Auburn baseball team and clouted 21 HR as a freshman in 1987. He batted .385 in 1988 and .403 in 1989 and was selected for the *TSN* 1989 All-America College baseball team.

The Chicago White Sox (AL) chose the 6-foot 5-inch, 270-pound Thomas in the June 1989 free agent draft as the seventh player selected. He spent fewer than two seasons in the minor leagues, batting a combined .296 with the Gulf Coast, FL White Sox (GCL) and Sarasota, FL (FSL) in 1989 and .323 with Birmingham, AL (SL) in 1990. After being promoted to Chicago in 1990, he batted .330 for the White Sox in 60 games.

From 1991 to 1998, no one inflicted more damage on AL pitchers than Thomas. He recorded more than 100 runs scored, 100 RBI, and 100 walks each year, including the strike-shortened 1994 season. No other player has accomplished that feat in his first eight full seasons. Thomas blasted at least 40 HR in 1993, 1995, and 1996 and led the AL with 46 doubles in 1992 and a .347 batting average in 1997. The righthanded first baseman batted .308 or above and compiled on base percentages of .426 or better each season from 1991 through 1997. In 1995, pitchers walked him intentionally an AL record 29 times. He demonstrated great discipline at the plate, exhibiting very modest strikeout totals for a power hitter with a large strike zone.

Thomas made the AL All-Star team from 1993 through 1997. In 1993, he batted .353 in the AL Championship Series against the triumphant Toronto Blue Jays. He also set a Championship Series record by being walked 10 times. Thomas has worked hard to improve his defensive skills, but remains only average at first base.

Thomas, voted AL MVP in 1993 and 1994, was selected by *TSN* for its AL Silver Slugger teams in 1991, 1993, and 1994 and was named *TSN* Major League Player of the Year in 1993. He enters the 2000 season with 1,564 hits, 968 runs, 1,031 RBI, 1,076 bases on balls, and a .320 batting average in 1,371 major league games. Thomas saw better pitches to hit after Albert Belle,* signed as a free agent in November 1996, batted behind him in 1997 and 1998. He agreed to a $29 million contract extension from 1995 to 1998 with options for about $7 million per year in 1999 and 2000. He ranked 4th in batting average (.320) in the 1990s.

Thomas makes his family his top priority and married Elise Silver, whom he first met at spring training in 1991. The Rochester, NY Red Wings (IL) play in Silver Stadium, named for her great uncle Maury Silver. They have a son, Sterling, and a daughter, Sloan. Thomas takes care of the financial needs of his parents and siblings and actively supports various charities.

BIBLIOGRAPHY: Steve Aschburner, "Frank Thomas of the White Sox Puts Big Hurt on Opposing Pitchers," *BD* 52 (December 1993), pp. 34–37; Frank E. Thomas, Jr. file, National Baseball Library, Cooperstown, NY; John Benson et al., *Baseball's Top 100* (Wilton, CT, 1997); *CB Yearbook* (1994), pp. 593–596; John Dewan, ed., *The Scouting Report 1994* (New York, 1994); D. Dieffenbach and D. Howerton, "The Strike Zone," *Sport* 87 (May 1996), pp. 26–30; Zander Hollander, ed., *1996 Complete Handbook of Baseball* (New York, 1996); J. Howard, "Frankly Speaking," *Sport* 83 (April 1992), pp. 41–43; T. Keegan, "The Big Hurt," *Sport* 85 (May 1994), pp. 54–57; Rocky Landsverk, "The Responsibilities of a Hero," *SCD* 23 (October 4, 1996), pp. 24–25; Skip Myslenski, "Perfectly Frank," *Chicago Tribune*, August 7, 1994, sec. 3, pp. 1, 8–9; David L. Porter, ed., *African-American Sports Greats* (Westport, CT, 1995); Rick Reilly, "The Big Heart," *SI* 81 (August 8, 1994), pp. 16–22; Steve Rushin, "No Doubting Thomas," *SI* 75 (September 16, 1991), pp. 30–32ff; Steve Wulf, "The Big Hurt," *SI* 79 (September 13, 1993), pp. 40–43.

Frank J. Olmsted

THOMAS, Frank Joseph, Jr. (b. June 11, 1929, Pittsburgh, PA), player, is the second of four children of Frank Thomas, Sr. (b. Branislas Tumas in Lithuania), a hospital laundry foreman, and Anna (Pavlick) Thomas, who was of Slavic descent. Thomas, who planned to become a priest, attended Mt. Carmel College Seminary in Niagara Falls, Canada for four and a half years and played football, basketball, and baseball there. In 1947, the Pittsburgh Pirates (NL) signed Thomas for $3,200. He played outfield in 1948 with Tallahassee, FL (GFL) and in 1949 with Davenport, IA (3IL), Waco, TX (BStL), and Tallahassee, where he hit .326. He performed with Charleston, SC (SAL) and New Orleans, LA (SA) in 1950 and New Orleans in 1951, briefly appearing with the Pittsburgh Pirates in the latter campaign. In 1952, he led the SA in hits, runs, total bases, RBI (131), and HR (35) and hit .303 for New Orleans before rejoining the Pittsburgh Pirates.

The following year, Thomas played mostly in the outfield and set a Pirates rookie record with 30 HR. He switched to third base in 1956 and also appeared at first base in 1957. Although a competent, versatile fielder, Thomas became best known as a right-handed power hitter in Pittsburgh's vast Forbes Field. The 6-foot 3-inch, 200 pounder pulled everything he could reach. His finest campaign came in 1958, when he hit 35 HR and drove in 109 tallies. He made the NL All-Star team in 1954, 1955, and 1958.

In January 1959, Thomas was traded to the Cincinnati Reds (NL). A lingering thumb injury, suffered late in the 1958 season, limited his HR production to 12 in 1959. Cincinnati traded Thomas to the Chicago Cubs (NL) in December 1959. In May 1961, Chicago sent him to the Milwaukee Braves (NL). With the expansion New York Mets (NL) in 1962, he hit 34 HR and produced 94 RBI. In August 1964, New York traded him to the Philadelphia Phillies (NL). Thomas helped Philadelphia's pennant drive until fracturing his thumb while sliding in early September. After being waived by the Phillies in 1965, Thomas was acquired by the Houston Colt 45s (NL) in July 1965 and was traded to the Milwaukee Braves two months later. His major league career ended with the Chicago Cubs in 1966, with Thomas having produced 286 major league career HR, 262 doubles, 962 RBI, 894 strikeouts, and a .266 batting average.

Thomas, who married Dolores Marie Wozniak on January 20, 1951, and had eight children, worked as a recruiter for ICM School of Business in Pittsburgh until retiring in 1984.

BIBLIOGRAPHY: Martin Appel, *Yesterday's Heroes* (New York, 1988); Richard L. Burtt, *The Pittsburgh Pirates, A Pictorial History* (Virginia Beach, VA, 1977); Bob Smizik, *The Pittsburgh Pirates, An Illustrated History* (New York, 1990); Eddie Gold and Art Ahrens, *The New Era Cubs, 1941–1985* (Chicago, IL, 1985); Jimmy Breslin, *Can't Anybody Here Play This Game?* (New York, 1963); Donald Honig, *The New York Mets* (New York, 1986); Jack Lang and Peter Simon, *The New York Mets* (New York, 1986); Frank Dolson, *The Philadelphia Story* (South Bend, IN, 1981); *The Baseball Encyclopedia*, 10th ed. (New York, 1996); Frank J. Thomas, Jr. file, National Baseball Library, Cooperstown, NY; Frank J. Thomas, interview with Luther W. Spoehr, December 19, 1989.

Luther W. Spoehr

THOMAS, James Gorman, III "Stormin Gorman" (b. December 12, 1950, Charleston, SC), player, is the son of James Gorman Thomas II and Gladys (Altman) Thomas and graduated from James Island High School in Charleston, earning 14 letters in four sports. Thomas was the first player signed in 1969 by the expansion Seattle Pilots (AL), who became the Milwaukee Brewers (AL) in 1970. The 6-foot 3-inch, 210-pound, right-handed batter led the

ML with 31 HR at Danville, IL (ML) in 1971 and the TL with 26 HR at San Antonio, TX (TL) in 1972. Although belting 51 HR with Sacramento, CA (PCL) in 1974, he hit just .187 in 1973, .261 in 1974, .179 in 1975 and .198 in 1976 with the Milwaukee Brewers. Thomas hit 36 HR for Spokane, WA (PCL) in 1977 and was traded that October to the Texas Rangers (AL).

The Milwaukee Brewers reacquired Thomas in February 1978. Manager George Bamberger, who liked his power and aggressive play, installed him as starting center fielder. Thomas produced 32 HR and 86 RBI. In 1979, he led the AL with 45 HR while driving in 123 runs. Thomas shared the HR title with Reggie Jackson* at 39 and knocked in 112 runs in 1982, as the Brewers slugged 216 HR and won the AL pennant. In the World Series against the St. Louis Cardinals, he batted only .115 with three RBI.

In a surprise move, the Milwaukee Brewers traded Thomas to the Cleveland Indians (AL) in June 1983. The Cleveland Indians sent him to the Seattle Mariners (AL) in December 1983. He injured his right shoulder the following season, but made a remarkable recovery from rotator cuff surgery. Thomas returned as a DH in 1985 to set a Seattle Mariners record with 32 HR and was named *TSN* Comeback Player of the Year. He returned in July 1986 to the Milwaukee Brewers, where he remained a tremendous fan favorite, to close out his major league career.

A notorious clubhouse prankster, the colorful, irascible Thomas gave 100 percent both on and off the field. The free-swinger led the AL in strikeouts in 1979 (175) and 1980 (170) and HR percentage in 1978 (7.1) and 1979 (8.1). He hit three HR against the Oakland A's on April 11, 1985. During his 13-year major league career, Thomas batted .225 with 1,051 hits, 212 doubles, 268 HR, 681 runs scored, and 782 RBI in 1,435 games. He was named an outfielder on *TSN* AL All-Star team in 1982.

Thomas, divorced from his first wife, has two children, Kelly and Justin. He married Rolanne Cardwell Wiggens in February 1996 and lives in Dousman, WI. He operates Gorman's Grill at Milwaukee County Stadium during Brewers home games.

BIBLIOGRAPHY: J. Gorman Thomas file, National Baseball Library, Cooperstown, NY; Chuck Carlson, *True Blue* (Dallas, TX, 1993); M. Sullivan, ed., *The Scouting Report* (New York, 1986); Anthony Cotton, "Gorman Is Always Stormin," *SI* 51 (September 19, 1979), pp. 90–93; *Milwaukee Brewers Media Guide*, 1981; Craig Carter, ed., *TSN Daguerreotypes*, 8th ed. (St. Louis, MO, 1990); *The Baseball Encyclopedia*, 10th ed. (New York, 1996); Peter C. Bjarkman, *Encyclopedia of Major League Baseball Team Histories: American League* (Westport, CT, 1991).

Edward J. Pavlick

THOMAS, Roy Allen (b. March 24, 1874, Norristown, PA; d. November 20, 1959, Norristown, PA), player and coach, was a gifted outfielder for the Philadelphia Phillies (NL), Pittsburgh Pirates (NL), and Boston Doves (NL) from 1899 to 1911. He spent his most productive years with the Philadelphia

Phillies between 1899 and 1907, joined the Pittsburgh Pirates in April 1908, moved to the Boston Doves in February 1909, and briefly returned to the Philadelphia Phillies in 1910 and 1911.

The 5-foot 11-inch, 150-pound Thomas was a superb defensive fielder and remains, next to Richie Ashburn,* the best leadoff hitter in the history of the Philadelphia franchise. He led the NL in on base percentage in 1902 and 1903 and walks for seven seasons, averaging better than 100 a campaign from 1899 to 1907. He also paced the NL in runs scored in 1900 with 132 and averaged over 100 tallies between 1899 and 1907. The steady outfielder led the NL in total chances from 1903 to 1905.

A lifetime .290 hitter, Thomas batted over .300 five times and reached a career high .327 average in 1903. Only 160 of his 1,537 career hits were extra-base hits. A remarkable 89.6 percent of his hits were singles, a commentary on the nature of dead ball hitting. Among modern hitters, only Maury Wills* and Nelson Fox* approached this percentage. Perhaps Thomas' most unusual contribution to baseball comprised his indirect responsibility for changing the foul-strike rule. He shrewdly fouled off balls, which then did not count as strikes, in order to gain a walk. Thomas's strategy incensed manager Ned Hanlon* of the Brooklyn Superbas. In 1901 Hanlon suggested the rule change, which made any foul ball not caught on a fly a strike unless the batter had two strikes on him.

Thomas, a graduate of the University of Pennsylvania, later coached college baseball at his alma mater and at Haverford College and engaged in the coal delivery business in Philadelphia. He and his wife, Bessie, had four children and resided in Norristown, PA.

BIBLIOGRAPHY: Roy Thomas file, National Baseball Library, Cooperstown, NY; Frederick G. Lieb and Stan Baumgartner, *The Philadelphia Phillies* (New York, 1953); Ralph C. Moses, "Roy Thomas," *TNP* 15 (1995), pp. 41–42; Allen Lewis, *The Philadelphia Phillies, A Pictorial History* (Virginia Beach, VA, 1981); Rich Westcott and Frank Bilovsky, *The New Phillies Encyclopedia* (Philadelphia, PA, 1993); Norristown (PA) *Times*, November 21, 1959; John Thorn et al., eds., *Total Baseball*, 5th ed. (New York, 1997).

John P. Rossi

THOMPSON, Henry Curtis "Hank" (b. December 8, 1925, Oklahoma City, OK; d. September 30, 1969, Fresno, CA), player, was the son of Ollie Thompson, a laborer, and Annie (Coats) Thompson, a cook and domestic. One of seven children, Thompson often skipped school to play sandlot baseball. After chronic truancy and a suspected theft, Thompson was sent to a Texas reform school in 1937. Upon being released, he joined a Dallas, TX black baseball team. He had begun to drink by age 15 and eventually became an alcoholic.

In 1942, Thompson joined the Kansas City, MO Monarchs (NNL) and batted .314 as right fielder. After being drafted into the U.S. Army, he spent two years with a combat engineering unit and fought in the Battle of the Bulge. Following his discharge, he returned to the Kansas City Monarchs and barnstormed with the Satchel Paige* All Stars against Bob Feller's* All Stars in the autumn of 1946.

Thompson and teammate Willard Brown* joined the St. Louis Browns (AL) on July 17, 1947. St. Louis management hoped they would help the Browns and attract black fans. Since the St. Louis Browns continued to struggle and draw poorly at home, Thompson and Brown were released after one month. Thompson batted .256 in 27 games.

With the Kansas City Monarchs, Thompson batted .344 in 1947 and .375 in 1948 as an infielder and outfielder. En route to spring training in 1948, he shot and killed a man who had threatened him with a knife. Thompson was briefly jailed for murder and then released on a $5,000 bond, with the case being dismissed as justifiable homocide.

Between 1946 and 1949, Thompson starred with Havana, Cuba (CUWL). On June 9, 1949, he married Maria Quesada. Thompson and Monte Irvin* were purchased by the New York Giants (NL) in 1949 and promoted that July from Jersey City, NJ (IL). Thompson played with the New York Giants through 1956. The versatile player with a strong arm, speed and power batted .267 with 129 HR and 482 RBI in 933 games. In the 1954 World Series against the Cleveland Indians, he hit .364 and set a record with seven walks in four games. He batted .302 and clouted 26 HR with 86 RBI in 1954.

Alcohol, injuries and domestic problems prompted Thompson's retirement from baseball in 1957. On July 13, 1963, after several prior arrests, Thompson held up a Houston, TX liquor store and was quickly apprehended. He pled guilty to robbery and was sentenced to 10 years imprisonment. After being paroled in 1966, Thompson worked as a playground director for the Fresno, CA Recreation Department.

BIBLIOGRAPHY: Hank Thompson file, National Baseball Library, Cooperstown, NY; James A. Riley, *The Biographical Encyclopedia of the Negro Baseball Leagues* (New York, 1994); Dick Clark and Larry Lester, eds., *The Negro Leagues Book* (Cleveland, OH, 1994); Larry Moffi and Jonathan Kronstadt, *Crossing the Line* (Jefferson City, NC, 1994); Dwight Chapin, "Henry Thompson Looks Back to Days of Baseball Glory," *BD* 28 (September 1969), pp. 45–48; Hank Thompson with Arnold Hano, "How I Wrecked My Life—How I Hope to Save It," *Sport* 40 (December 1965), pp. 46–51, 95–98; *The Baseball Encyclopedia*, 10th ed. (New York, 1996); *TSN*, July 23, 30, August 6, 13, 20, September 3, 1947, October 18, 1969; Bill Borst, ed., *Ables to Zoldak*, vol. 3 (St. Louis, MO, 1990); Janet Bruce, *The Kansas City Monarchs* (Lawrence, KS, 1985); Frank Graham, *The New York Giants* (New York, 1952); Noel Hynd, *The Giants of the Polo Grounds* (New York, 1988); Leo Durocher, *Nice Guys Finish Last* (New York, 1975); Thomas Kieran, *The Miracle of Coogan's Bluff* (New York, 1975); Fred Stein and Nick Peters, *Giants Diary* (Berkeley, CA, 1987); Roy Robinson, *The Home Run Heard 'Round the World* (New York, 1991).

Edward J. Tassinari

THOMPSON, Jason Dolph (b. July 6, 1954, Hollywood, CA), player, graduated from Apple Valley High School and studied business for three years at California State University, Northridge. The Detroit Tigers (AL) selected the 6-foot 3-inch, 210-pound first baseman, who batted and threw left-handed, in the fourth round of the June 1975 draft. He played only 79 minor league games with Montgomery, AL (SA) in 1975 and Evansville, IN (AA) in 1976 before joining the Detroit Tigers.

Thompson started at first base with the Detroit Tigers from 1976 to May 1980, clouting 14 HR in his first 16 games. In 1977, he batted .270 with career highs in HR (31) and RBI (105) and made the AL All-Star team. Tiger Stadium suited Thompson well, as he belted two HR over the right field roof against the New York Yankees in 1977. Defensively, he led AL first basemen in chances (1,712) and putouts (1,599). In 1978, Thompson batted .287 with 26 HR and 96 RBI, led AL first basemen in double plays (153), and repeated as an AL All-Star.

In May 1980, the Detroit Tigers traded Thompson to the California Angels (AL). He batted a career-high .288 with 21 HR and 90 RBI that season, including .317 with 17 HR and 70 RBI in 102 games after joining the California Angels to share Angel MVP honors with Bobby Grich.* In April 1981, the Pittsburgh Pirates (NL) acquired him from the California Angels. Thompson spent from 1981 through 1985 with the Pittsburgh Pirates. His best season there came in 1982, when he batted .284 with 31 HR and 101 RBI and made the NL All-Star team. He became just the third Pirate to draw 100 walks and drive in 100 runs the same season. In 1984, Thompson led NL first basemen in chances (1,425), putouts (1,337), and errors (14). His major league career ended with the Montreal Expos (NL) in 1986.

In 11 major league seasons, Thompson batted .261 with a .369 on-base percentage, 1,253 hits, 204 doubles, 208 HR, 782 RBI, 816 walks, and a .992 fielding percentage. Besides ranking among major league leaders in walks and on base percentage, he became just the eighth major leaguer to hit over 30 HR in a season in both leagues. Thompson, elected to the Sports Hall of Fame at California State University, Northridge in 1982, homered in every major league stadium. He and his wife, Bernadette, have one son, Matthew, and reside in Orchard Lake, MI.

BIBLIOGRAPHY: Jason Thompson file, National Baseball Library, Cooperstown, NY; *TSN Baseball Register*, 1987; *Pittsburgh Pirates Media Guide*, 1985; Joe Falls, *The Detroit Tigers: An Illustrated History* (New York, 1989); Fred Smith, *995 Tigers* (Detroit, MI, 1981); William M. Anderson, *The Detroit Tigers* (South Bend, IN, 1996); Richard Bak, *A Place for Summer* (Detroit, MI, 1998); George Sullivan and David Cataneo, *Detroit Tigers* (New York, 1985); Bob Smizik, *The Pittsburgh Pirates: An Illustrated History* (New York, 1990).

David L. Porter

THOMPSON, Samuel Luther "Sam," "Big Sam," "The Marvel" (b. March 5, 1860, Danville, IN; d. November 7, 1922, Detroit, MI), player, was scouted on Danville sandlots by Indianapolis, IN minor league manager Dan O'Leary. Thompson worked as a carpenter and roofer while playing amateur baseball. O'Leary had heard about a Danville player who "never does anything but hit home runs." Thompson began his professional baseball career with Evansville, IN (NWL) in 1884 and starred the next year for Indianapolis, IN (WL). Bill Watkins, manager of the 1884 Indianapolis Hoosiers (AA) entry, also saw Thompson play. After becoming manager of the 1885 Detroit Wolverines (NL), Watkins recommended that Detroit purchase Thompson's contract and kept him as a reserve. When regular left fielder Gene Moriarty sustained an injury, Watkins used Thompson. Since the 6-foot 2-inch, 207-pound Thompson was much larger than his contemporaries, Watkins could not find a uniform large enough to fit "Big Sam." Thompson, looking like a man in a boy's outfit, hit a triple his first time at bat. Thompson's trousers split in the seat as he rounded second base, while the cuffs came up to his knees. He combined color and skill, making him among the gaslight era's most popular players.

In 1886, the left-handed Thompson became an NL star by hitting .310 and driving in 89 runs. Although hitting a career-high .407 in 1894, he enjoyed his best year in 1887 when he batted .372 and led the NL with 203 hits, 23 triples, 166 RBI, and a .571 slugging percentage. He and Detroit first baseman Dan Brouthers* comprised the best power tandem in baseball and spearheaded Detroit's 1887 championship season. A HR hitter in the deadball era, he was nicknamed "The Marvel" for his fielding and slugging skills. Thompson often crashed through the low white fence at Recreation Park to make one-handed catches after long runs, possessed a fine throwing arm, and became the first outfielder to throw to home plate on the bounce.

When the Detroit Wolverines dissolved in 1888, Thompson was sold to the Philadelphia Phillies (NL). Thompson twice led the NL in HR, with 20 in 1889 and 18 in 1895, and finished his career in 1898 there. His 127 career HR remained a major league record until Babe Ruth* broke it in 1921. Thompson also led the NL in hits three times (203 in 1887, 172 in 1890, 222 in 1893), RBI twice (166 in 1887, 165 in 1895) and slugging averages twice (.571 in 1884, .654 in 1895). Thompson, who settled in Detroit in 1899, became a real estate agent, dabbled in Republican party politics, and served as a trusted adviser and confidant to Detroit Tigers general manager and part-owner Frank Navin.* From 1900 to 1907, he starred as an outfielder for the Detroit AC. The great fan favorite, whose team occasionally outdrew the Detroit Tigers, retired in his prime.

During September 1906, the injury-riddled Detroit Tigers persuaded Thompson to play the final eight games of the season. His appearance against the Chicago White Sox, then engaged in a close pennant race with the New York Highlanders, was criticized by New York manager Clark Griffith.* Griffith contended that the Tigers, by inserting a 46-year-old player into the lineup, were giving the AL championship to the White Sox.

Although Chicago swept the Detroit series, Thompson patrolled the outfield with rookie Ty Cobb* and veteran Sam Crawford.* He experienced trouble hitting the spitter, a pitch not used in his day. Thompson batted .226 and showed flashes of his old form at season's end. In Thompson's final appearance, fans packed Bennett Park to see him play rather than the second division Tigers. Thompson, who treated them with a triple that drove in two runs, stated that baseball had not changed much from the 1880s to 1906. During 15 major league seasons, Thompson compiled 1,979 hits, 340 doubles, 160 triples, 1,256 runs scored, 1,299 RBI, 229 stolen bases, and .331 batting and .505 slugging averages.

Thompson regularly attended Tigers games and stayed close to his 1887 Detroit teammates, for whom he arranged a reunion in 1907. Despite being stronger and larger than most players, he did not bully them. The modest Thompson likened his HR to bunts compared to Ruth's blasts. Thompson's contemporaries, however, claimed that he could have matched Ruth with a livelier ball. Thompson's self-deprecatory humor, colorful playing style, and immense skills made him Detroit's most popular 19th-century athlete.

BIBLIOGRAPHY: Samuel Thompson file, National Baseball Library, Cooperstown, NY; Jerrold Casway, "The Best Outfield Ever?" *BRJ* 27 (1998), pp. 3–7; Detroit Baseball Club Letterbooks, vol. 1, Ernie Harwell Collection, Detroit Public Library, Detroit, MI; Detroit *News*, September 1906, November 8, 1922; Frederick Ivor-Campbell et al., eds., *Baseball's First Stars* (Cleveland, OH, 1996); Joe Falls, *Detroit Tigers* (New York, 1975); William M. Anderson, *The Detroit Tigers* (South Bend, IN, 1996); Daniel Pearson, *Base Ball in 1889* (Bowling Green, OH, 1993); Frederick G. Lieb and Stan Baumgartner, *The Philadelphia Phillies* (New York, 1953); Allen Lewis, *The Philadelphia Phillies: A Pictorial History* (Virginia Beach, VA, 1981); Rich Westcott and Frank Bilovsky, *The New Phillies Encyclopedia* (Philadelphia, PA, 1993); Bill Madden, *The Hoosiers of Summer* (Indianapolis, IN, 1994); Frederick G. Lieb, *The Detroit Tigers* (New York, 1946); John Lodge, *I Remember Detroit* (Detroit, MI, 1928).

                                                              Anthony J. Papalas

THOMSON, Robert Brown "Bobby," "Flying Scot" (b. October 25, 1923, Glasgow, Scotland), player, made baseball history with one swing of his bat on October 3, 1951. The New York Giants (NL) and the Brooklyn Dodgers (NL) had finished the 1951 regular season in a tie. Both clubs had won a game apiece in the three-game playoff. In the deciding game, the Dodgers led, 4–2, with two outs in the last of the ninth inning. Thomson turned the NL pennant race around with an exciting HR off Ralph Branca. Sports fans voted this dramatic comeback the most memorable sports event of the past 50 years.

He is the son of James Thomson, a professional soldier, and Elizabeth Thomson and came to Staten Island, NY at age two. The youngest of six children, he graduated from Curtis High School. Thomson signed with the New York Giants after high school and appeared briefly with Rocky Mount,

NC (BSL) and Bristol, VA (ApL) before entering the U.S. Army. He played outfield for Jersey City, NJ (IL) in 1946. The rangy 6-foot 2-inch, 180-pound youngster with the deceptively fast, loping stride became the Giants' regular center fielder in 1947, hitting .283 with 29 HR. He recorded more than 100 RBI in four seasons during the 1949–1953 period before being traded to the Milwaukee Braves (NL) in February 1954. Hampered by a serious ankle injury, he never regained his earlier effectiveness while playing with the Milwaukee Braves from 1954 through June 1957, the New York Giants from June 1957 through April 1958, the Chicago Cubs (NL) from April 1958 through December 1959, and the Boston Red Sox (AL) and the Baltimore Orioles (AL) in 1960. Thomson compiled a .270 career batting average with 1,026 RBI, 267 doubles, and 264 HR.

The personable "Flying Scot" possessed all the tools to be a baseball superstar except, by his own admission, the flaming drive. He remains more enthusiastic about his successful post playing career in marketing with a major paper company than he does about his earlier fame. Thomson married Elaine May (Coley) Thomson in December 1952. They had three children before her death from cancer in 1993. Thomson resides in Watchung, NJ.

BIBLIOGRAPHY: Bobby Thomson file, National Library, Cooperstown, NY; Ira Berkow, "Thomson's 1950 Homer Still Going," *NYT Biographical Service* 18 (July 1987), pp. 1213–1214; Lee Heiman et al., *When the Cheering Stops* (New York, 1990); Russ Hodges and Al Hirshberg, *My Giants* (Garden City, NY, 1963); Noel Hynd, *The Giants of the Polo Grounds* (New York, 1988); Richard McKelvey, *Fisk's Homer, Willie's Catch and the Shot Heard 'Round the World* (Jefferson, NC, 1998); Harry Molter, ed., *Famous Athletes of Today*, 13th series (Boston, MA, 1953); *1984 San Francisco Giants Yearbook*; Bob Buege, *The Milwaukee Braves: A Baseball Eulogy* (Milwaukee, WI, 1988); Gary Caruso, *The Braves Encyclopedia* (Philadelphia, PA, 1995); T. S. O'Connell, "The Man Who Fired 'The Shot Heard 'Round the World' Had an All-Star Career That Seems Largely Overlooked," *SCD* 21 (July 1994), pp. 160–164; Ray Robinson, *The Home Run Heard 'Round the World* (New York, 1991); Bobby Thomson, letter to Fred Stein, May 14, 1989; John Thorn et al., eds., *Total Baseball*, 5th ed. (New York, 1997); Dan Valenti, *Clout: The Top Home Runs in Baseball History* (Lexington, MA, 1989); Rich Westcott, *Diamond Greats* (Westport, CT, 1988); Fred Stein and Nick Peters, *Giants Diary* (Berkeley, CA, 1987); Eddie Gold and Art Ahrens, *The New Era Cubs, 1941–1985* (Chicago, IL, 1985); Bobby Thomson et al., *The Giants Win the Pennant! The Giants Win the Pennant!* (New York, 1991); Frank Graham, *The New York Giants* (New York, 1952); Thomas Kieran, *The Miracle at Coogan's Bluff* (New York, 1975).

Fred Stein

THORNTON, Andre "Andy," "Thor," "Thunder" (b. August 13, 1949, Tuskegee, AL), player, is the son of Harold Thornton and Arcola (Williams) Thornton and played baseball at Phoenixville, PA High School, where he led his team to the Middle Atlantic title and played in the 1965 Babe Ruth World Series. The Philadelphia Phillies (NL) in 1967 signed Thornton, who made his professional debut with Huron, MI (NoL). During the next four and one-half seasons (interrupted by brief stints in the National Guard), he played first base, third base, and the outfield for minor league teams at Eugene, OR (NWL) in 1968, Spartanburg, SC (WCL) in 1969, Peninsula, VA (CrL) in 1970, Reading, PA (EL) in 1971, and Eugene, OR (PCL) in 1972. In June 1972, the Atlanta Braves (NL) acquired him in a trade and assigned him to Richmond, VA (IL), where he played until May 1973. The Atlanta Braves traded Thornton to the Chicago Cubs (NL) for Joe Pepitone* and cash. The Chicago Cubs sent Thornton to their Wichita, KS (AA) affiliate. He made his major league debut with the Chicago Cubs in July 1973.

The 6-foot 3-inch, 200-pound Thornton, who hit and threw right-handed, played in 106 games for the Chicago Cubs in 1974. The next season, he fractured his right wrist in spring training and missed the first month. Nevertheless, he still hit .293 and belted 18 HR. The Chicago Cubs traded Thornton in May 1976 to the Montreal Expos (NL), which dealt him to the Cleveland Indians (AL) that December. As the Indians' regular first baseman from 1977 through 1979, he posted impressive slugging figures and average 29 HR and 89 RBI. In June 1979 Thornton was presented with the ninth annual Roberto Clemente* Award, given to the player who best exemplifies the game through his playing ability, sportsmanship, character, and community involvement. During spring training in 1980, Thornton suffered torn knee ligaments and cartilage and was sidelined for the entire season. The next year saw him limited to only 69 games, as a broken hand and a badly sprained thumb twice put him on the disabled list.

In 1982, Thornton rebounded with a "career year," in which he batted .273 with 32 HR and 116 RBI and won *TSN* 1982 AL Comeback Player of the Year Award. For the 1983 and 1984 seasons, he continued as the Cleveland Indians' regular first baseman. In 1984, he walloped a career-high 33 HR and earned a spot on *TSN* AL Silver Slugger team. Thornton became Cleveland's DH during the 1985 and 1986 seasons, averaging nearly 20 HR and 77 RBI. Thornton retired after the 1987 season to devote his time and energy to the Board of Christian Family Outreach and other business interests. In his 14-year major League career, Thornton played in 1,565 games, hit .254, and collected 253 HR and 895 RBI. He participated in the 1982 and 1984 All-Star Games, but never played in a League Championship Series or World Series.

Thornton attended Cheyney State College and Nyack College. He and his wife, Gertrude, were married in 1970 and had two children, Andre, Jr., and Theresa. In 1977, Thornton's wife and daughter were killed in an automobile accident on the Pennsylvania Turnpike. He later married Gail Jones, with whom he had two sons, Jonathan and Andy.

BIBLIOGRAPHY: *Chicago Cubs Official Press, Radio, and TV Roster Book*, 1974, 1975, 1976; Craig Carter, ed., *TSN Daguerreotypes*, 8th ed. (St. Louis, MO, 1990); Eddie Gold and Art Ahrens, *The New Era Cubs, 1941–1985* (Chicago, IL, 1985); Robert E.

Kelley, *Baseball's Best* (Jefferson, NC, 1988); John Thorn et al., eds., *Total Baseball*, 5th ed. (New York, 1997); Andre Thornton file, National Baseball Library, Cooperstown, NY; *TSN Baseball Guide*, 1981, 1982; Jack Torry, *Endless Summers* (South Bend, IN, 1995); Terry Pluto, *The Curse of Rocky Colavito* (New York, 1994); John Thorn et al., *Total Indians* (New York, 1996); *TSN Official Baseball Register*, 1988.

Raymond D. Kush

TIANT, Luis Clemente Vega, Jr. "Louie" (b. November 23, 1940, Marianao, Cuba), player and coach, remains the third-winningest Latin American pitcher in major league history behind Dennis Martinez* and Juan Marichal* and owned a lifetime 229–172 win–loss record and 3.30 ERA over 19 major league seasons. He authored more strikeouts (2,416) than any other Latin American hurler in major league history. The steady 6-foot, 180-pound right-hander, who pitched for the Cleveland Indians, Minnesota Twins, Boston Red Sox, New York Yankees, and California Angels in the AL and Pittsburgh Pirates (NL), also descends from noble baseball lineage. He is the son of Luis Tiant, Sr., and Isabel (Vega) Tiant. Luis, Sr., had starred as a masterful left-handed Negro League hurler with the Cuban Stars and New York Cubans throughout the 1930s and 1940s. The elder Tiant, a herky-jerky junkball and screwball pitcher with a memorable pickoff move, drew national attention in 1975 when Cuban dictator Fidel Castro allowed the Cuban baseball legend to briefly visit the United States to see his son pitch for the Boston Red Sox against the Cincinnati Reds in the 1975 World Series.

Although not joining the Boston Red Sox until the second decade of his career, Tiant quickly became one of the most colorful, popular players in Red Sox history during an eight-year tenure there in the 1970s. The indelible Tiant image remains that of a balding, overweight starter who fostered a reputation as an incorrigible clubhouse prankster, and baffled hitters on the mound with his rocking, twisting delivery and an assortment of release points for his taunting fastball. Tiant enjoyed four 20-win seasons, including three with the Boston Red Sox, and 13 double-digit victory campaigns, but never led the Junior Circuit in either victories or innings pitched (despite numerous workhorse years). He paced the AL with nine shutouts and 1.60 ERA while compiling a 21–9 win–loss record in 1968 for Cleveland in his best season. The following summer, Tiant slumped to a 9–20 ledger, a 3.71 ERA, and the AL lead in both defeats and walks allowed (129). In December 1969, the colorful Cuban hurler was dealt to the Minnesota Twins. He started swiftly in 1970 with six straight wins before being sidelined by a hairline fracture in his shoulder, an injury from which he recovered slowly. The Minnesota Twins released him in April 1971. In 1972, Tiant was named AL Comeback Player of the Year with the Boston Red Sox. Over the next seven seasons, Tiant won at least 12 games with Boston each summer, averaged 17 victories a campaign, and compiled an outstanding .620 winning percentage with 121 victories and 74 losses. One of the truly outstanding hurlers of the 1970s, Tiant is best remembered for the eccentric cigar puffing and heavy Spanish accent which made him an instant national media celebrity during 1975 AL Championship Series and World Series play. In November 1978, the New York Yankees signed him as a free agent. Tiant spent 1981 with the Pittsburgh Pirates and 1982 with the California Angels. Tiant served as a pitching coach in the Los Angeles Dodgers (NL) organization from 1993 through 1996 and the Chicago White Sox (AL) organization since 1997. He was elected to the Boston Red Sox Hall of Fame in 1997. He married Maria del Refugio Navarro in August 1961 and has three children, Luis, Isabel, and Danny.

BIBLIOGRAPHY: Arnold C. Bailey, "Former Pitching Star Luis Tiant Profiled," *SCD* 24 (October 17, 1997), pp. 140–141; Peter C. Bjarkman, *Baseball with a Latin Beat* (Westport, CT, 1991); Bill Liston, "The Comeback Saga of Luis Tiant," *BD* 34 (July 1975), pp. 40–43; Mike Shatzkin, ed., *The Ballplayers* (New York, 1990); Jack Torry, *Endless Summers* (South Bend, IN, 1996); Terry Pluto, *The Curse of Rocky Colavito* (New York, 1994); Howard Liss, *The Boston Red Sox* (New York, 1982); Peter Golenbock, *Fenway* (New York, 1992); Dan Shaughnessy, *The Curse of the Bambino* (New York, 1990); Robert Redmount, *The Red Sox Encyclopedia* (Champaign, IL, 1998); Luis Tiant file, National Baseball Library, Cooperstown, NY; Luis Tiant and Joe Fitzgerald, *El Tiante—The Luis Tiant Story* (New York, 1976).

Peter C. Bjarkman

TIERNAN, Michael Joseph "Mike," "Silent Mike" (b. January 21, 1867, Trenton, NJ; d. November 9, 1918, New York, NY), player, was the son of an Irish laborer, grew up near the Trenton State Prison, and played for the Athletic Juniors. The renowned ice skater and track star ran the 100 yard dash in slightly under ten seconds. He debuted as a pitcher at age 17 with Williamsport, PA and struck out 15 batters in an exhibition game against the NL champion Providence Grays. Providence manager Frank Bancroft,* impressed with Tiernan's performance, observed the teenager from the grandstand after the fourth inning. Nicknamed "Silent Mike," the 5-foot 11-inch, 165-pound Tiernan disliked publicity and was reserved on the field even when disagreeing with the umpire.

Tiernan, who batted and threw left-handed, began his professional baseball career in 1885 with Trenton, NJ (EL) and led the EL in hitting with .390 at Jersey City, NJ in 1886. From 1887 to 1889, he played outfield for the New York Giants (NL) and batted .287 as a 20-year-old rookie. The versatile, durable Tiernan batted well, demonstrated power in the dead ball era, ran swiftly, and fielded well. In 1,476 career major league games, he batted .311, made 1,834 hits, slugged 256 doubles, 162 triples, and 106 HR, scored 1,313 runs, knocked in 851 runs, stole 428 bases, and compiled a .463 slugging average. Tiernan surpassed the .300 mark at the plate seven times, including a stellar .369 performance in 1896.

Tiernan led the NL in HR in 1890 (13) and 1891 (16), in runs scored (147) in 1889, in slugging percentage in 1890 (.495), and in walks (96) in 1889. Besides pacing NL outfielders defensively in 1888 and 1889, he stole 428 career bases and recorded a season-high 56 stolen bases in 1890. On June 15, 1887, he made two triples, three singles, and walked once and tied an NL record by scoring six runs against the Philadelphia Phillies. Hall of Famers Amos Rusie* and Kid Nichols* were engaged in a scoreless duel in the bottom of the 13th inning on May 12, 1890, when Tiernan clouted a long HR off Nichols to end what news accounts termed the finest game ever played. After retiring from baseball, Tiernan operated a cafe in New York City. He died of tuberculosis.

BIBLIOGRAPHY: Mike Tiernan file, National Baseball Library, Cooperstown, NY; Gene Karst and Martin J. Jones, Jr., *Who's Who in Professional Baseball* (New Rochelle, NY, 1973); Randolph Linthurst, "Silent Mike Tiernan Belongs in the Hall of Fame," *TrM* (April 1975), pp. 30–31; Craig Carter, ed., *TSN Daguerreotypes*, 8th ed. (St. Louis, MO, 1990); Eugene C. Murdock, "The Pre-1900 Batting Stars," *BRJ* 2 (1973), pp. 75–78; Robert L. Tiemann and Mark Rucker, eds., *Nineteenth Century Stars* (Kansas City, MO, 1989); James M. Dclerico and Barry Pavelec, *The Jersey Game* (New Brunswick, NJ, 1991); Noel Hynd, *The Giants of the Polo Grounds* (New York, 1988); Frank Graham, *The New York Giants* (New York, 1952); James D. Hardy, Jr., *The New York Giants Baseball Club* (Jefferson, NC, 1996); Fred Stein and Nick Peters, *Giants Diary* (Berkeley, CA, 1987).

B. Randolph Linthurst

TINKER, Joseph Bert "Joe" (July 27, 1880, Muscotah, KS; d. July 27, 1948, Orlando, FL), player, manager, and executive, was the son of Samuel Tinker and Elizabeth (Williams) Tinker, attended Kansas City, KS public schools, and played semipro baseball for the Coffeyville, KS team in 1899. Tinker, who married Ruby Rose Menown and had three sons and one daughter, later wed Suzanne Chabot in 1942. He began his professional baseball career as a shortstop with Denver, CO (WL) and Great Falls-Helena, MT (MtSL), in 1900 and Portland, OR (PNL) in 1901. The next year, he joined the Chicago Cubs (NL).

From 1902 to 1912, the 5-foot 10-inch, 175-pound right-hander achieved fame with the Cubs as a member of the Tinker to John Evers* to Frank Chance* double play combination, immortalized in poetry by Franklin P. Adams. Although the trio executed relatively few double plays, Tinker played solidly on offense and defense and performed well on the 1906–1908 and 1910 NL championship teams. Despite his .262 career batting average, the aggressive, spirited Tinker excelled as a clutch hitter and batted exceptionally well against pitcher Christy Mathewson.* Tinker hit .350 in 1902 and over .400 in 1908 against the New York Giants hurler. On July 28, 1910, he tied a major league record by stealing home twice in one game. In 1,804 major league games, he made 1,687 hits, 263 doubles, 114 triples, 774 runs, 782 RBI, 336 stolen bases, and a .353 slugging percentage.

In December 1912, the Cubs traded Tinker to the Cincinnati Reds (NL). Tinker managed the Reds to a 64–89 record and seventh place finish and clashed with owner Garry Herrmann* over his salary. He was sold to the Brooklyn Dodgers (NL) for $25,000 in December 1913, but demanded $10,000 of the sale price. Since neither club complied, Tinker became the first "name" player to join the newly formed FL in 1914. He served as player–manager of the Chicago Whales (FL) and led the team in 1915 to a first place finish. With the demise of the FL, the Chicago Cubs hired Tinker in 1916 as team manager. Tinker piloted the Cubs to a 67–86 mark and fifth place finish. As a major league manager, Tinker recorded 304 wins and 308 losses (.497 winning percentage).

In 1917 Tinker joined Columbus, OH (AA) as manager and president and left the field two years later exclusively for the front office. Tinker bought controlling interest in the Orlando, FL Gulls (FSL) in 1921, managing the club that year and serving as its vice-president in 1923. He also briefly managed Buffalo, NY (IL) and Jersey City, NJ (IL) and scouted several years for the Chicago Cubs. During the 1920s, he made and subsequently lost a fortune in Florida real estate. Tinker owned an Orlando billiard parlor and bar and invested in the stadium (Tinker Field) where the Cincinnati Reds trained. Although surviving a serious illness in 1936, he later developed diabetes and lost a leg. On his sixty-eighth birthday, he succumbed to respiratory complications. With Evers and Chance, he was elected to the National Baseball Hall of Fame in 1946.

Tinker, minimally involved in the "Merkle* Boner" 1908 game against the New York Giants, hit a triple to decide the playoff game in October 1908 for the NL pennant. Tinker belted the only HR of the 1908 World Series against the Detroit Tigers, the first fall classic round tripper in Cubs history. Although first acquired as a third baseman, Tinker was shifted against his will by Cubs manager Frank Selee* to shortstop. Baseball's first holdout, he demanded a $1,000 raise and sat out part of the 1909 season until settling for $200. Tinker's quarrel with second baseman Evers over the payment of a taxicab fare resulted in the two not speaking to each other for nearly three years. An advocate of the hit-and-run play, Tinker often supported progressive changes in baseball and proved instrumental in the abolition of the spitball from the AA and the major leagues.

BIBLIOGRAPHY: Joe Tinker file, National Baseball Library, Cooperstown, NY; Warren Brown, *The Chicago Cubs* (New York, 1946); Glenn Dickey, *History of National League Baseball* (New York, 1980); Jim Enright, *Chicago Cubs* (New York, 1975); G. F. Fleming, *The Unforgettable Season* (New York, 1982); Ralph Hickok, *Who Was Who in American Sports* (New York, 1971); Gene Karst and Martin J. Jones, Jr., *Who's Who in Professional Baseball* (New Rochelle, NY, 1973); Craig Carter, ed., *TSN Daguerreotypes*, 8th ed. (St. Louis, MO, 1990); National Biographical Society, *Who's Who in American Sports* (Washington, DC, 1928); *NYT*, July 17, 28, 31, 1948; *The Baseball Encyclopedia*, 10th ed. (New York, 1996); Lowell Reidenbaugh, *Baseball's Hall of Fame—Cooperstown* (New York, 1993); Warren Wilbert and William Hageman, *Chicago Cubs: Seasons at the Summit* (Champaign, IL, 1997); Thomas Aylesworth and Benton Minks, *The Encyclopedia of Baseball Managers* (New York, 1990); Eddie Gold and Art Ahrens, *The Golden Era Cubs, 1876–1940* (Chicago, IL, 1985); Lee Allen, *The Cincinnati Reds* (New York, 1948).

Alan R. Asnen and John E. Findling

TITUS, John Franklin "Silent John," "Tight Pants" (b. February 21, 1876, St. Clair, PA; d. January 8, 1943, St. Clair, PA), player, was the son of Theodore Titus, a police officer, and Agnes Titus, an English immigrant. He grew up in St. Clair and enlisted in the U.S. Army in 1898 to serve during the Spanish-American War. At a Savannah, GA Army camp, Titus developed his baseball for the St. Clair Athethic Association and Pottsville, PA semiprofessional teams.

The 5-foot 9-inch, 156-pound Titus, who batted and threw left-handed, entered organized baseball in 1903 at the relatively late age of 27. A spectacular debut with the Concord, NH Mariners (NEL) saw him hit .407 in 30 games and prompted his sale to the Philadelphia Phillies (NL). He batted .286 in 72 contests as Philadelphia's left fielder. In 1904, the Philadelphia Phillies inserted newly acquired Sherry Magee* in left field, shifted Titus to right field, and kept Roy Thomas* in center field. The especially gifted outfield served the Philadelphia Phillies exceptionally well until the departure of Thomas in 1908. After breaking an ankle sliding into home plate in May 1911, Titus never regained his normal running speed. In June 1912, the Philadelphia Phillies traded him to the Boston Braves (NL) for outfielder Roy Miller. In September 1913, the Boston Braves released Titus to the Kansas City, MO Blues (AA). A pitch fractured his skull in early 1914, but he still hit .343 in 96 games. He retired after one more season with Kansas City.

Titus, a reticent, capable outfielder, rarely swung at pitches outside the strike zone. For his 11-year NL career, he batted .282, well above the average for players of his era, and made 1,401 hits in 1,402 games. His best offensive seasons came when he batted .308 in 1905 and .309 in 1912. His trademark idiosyncrasies included a magnificent handlebar mustache, a toothpick protruding from his mouth while batting (a target never dislodged by pitchers trying to do so), cashing salary checks only at season's end (upsetting club bookkeepers), and, invariably, wearing a derby "as well as a vest adorned by a heavy gold chain . . . even in the hot summer months." He in September 1915 married next door neighbor, 17-year-old Ethel Stone, who survived him. They had no surviving children.

BIBLIOGRAPHY: Bill Dooly, "Toothpick Undoing of John Titus," *TSN*, January 1943; John H. Gruber, "Nine Years with the Phillies and Always an Outfield Star,"

Philadelphia (PA) *Public Ledger*, March 28, 1915; John Titus file, National Baseball Library, Cooperstown, NY; John Thorn et al., eds., *Total Baseball*, 5th ed. (New York, 1997); Gary Caruso, *The Braves Encyclopedia* (Philadelphia, PA, 1993); Frederick G. Lieb and Stan Baumgartner, *The Philadelphia Phillies* (New York, 1953); Allen Lewis, *The Philadelphia Phillies: A Pictorial History* (Virginia Beach, VA, 1981); Rich Westcott and Frank Bilovsky, *The New Phillies Encyclopedia* (Philadelphia, PA, 1993).

Frank V. Phelps

TOBIN, John Thomas "Jack" (May 4, 1892, St. Louis, MO; d. December 10, 1969, St. Louis, MO), player, manager, coach, and scout, attended St. Malachy's Elementary School for eight years. He signed a professional baseball contract with Houston, TX (TL), but never reported and was released. After joining the St. Louis Terriers (FL) as an outfielder in 1914, he hit .270 that inaugural season and led the FL with 184 hits in 1915. Tobin played briefly with the St. Louis Browns (AL) in 1916 after Phil Ball, owner of the now defunct Terriers, purchased the club. At Salt Lake City, UT (PCL), Tobin in 1917 paced the PCL in runs scored (149) and hits (265) and was reacquired before the 1918 season by the Browns. From 1919 through 1923, the 5-foot 8-inch, 142-pound left-hander teamed with Ken Williams* and "Baby Doll" Jacobson* to form one of baseball's most prolific outfields. For those five seasons, the outfield trio each hit at least .300. The streak ended in 1924, when the right fielder Tobin slipped to .299.

An adroit bunter, Tobin in February 1926 was traded with Joe Bush* to the Washington Senators (AL) for Win Ballou and Tom Zachary.* In July 1926, Tobin joined the Boston Red Sox (AL). He retired after the 1927 campaign. Tobin later managed Bloomington, IL (3IL) in 1930 and coached and scouted for the St. Louis Browns (AL) from 1944 through 1951. Tobin's major league career statistics included a .309 batting average, 1,906 hits, 936 runs scored, 294 doubles, 99 triples, 64 HR, 581 RBI, and 147 stolen bases in 1,619 games. He hit .300 or better seven times, his best mark being .352 in 1921. He made at least 200 hits four times and ranked among the AL leaders in runs scored and total bases. Tobin's two grand slam HR off Walter Johnson* gave him his greatest thrill. The best drag bunter in baseball history, he was elected to the All-Time St. Louis team in 1957. He married Loretta Sack on March 4, 1914 and had one daughter.

BIBLIOGRAPHY: Jack Tobin file, National Baseball Library, Cooperstown, NY; Bill Borst, *Last in the American League* (St. Louis, MO, 1976); Gene Karst and Martin J. Jones, Jr., *Who's Who in Professional Baseball* (New York, 1973); Craig Carter, ed., *TSN Daguerreotypes*, 8th ed. (St. Louis, MO, 1990); Bill Borst, ed., *Ables to Zoldak*, vol. 3 (St. Louis, MO, 1990); Bill Borst, *Still Last in the American League* (West Bloomfield, MI, 1992); Roger A. Godin, *The 1922 St. Louis Browns* (Jefferson, NC, 1991); Frederick G. Lieb, *The Baltimore Orioles* (New York, 1955); Frederick G. Lieb, *The Boston Red Sox* (New York, 1947); Robert Redmount, *The Red Sox Encyclopedia* (Champaign, IL, 1998).

William A. Borst

TONEY, FRED

TONEY, Fred (b. December 11, 1888, Nashville, TN; d. March 11, 1953, Nashville, TN), player, entered professional baseball as a pitcher in 1908 with the Class D Winchester, KY Hustlers (BGL). On May 10, 1909, the 21-year-old Toney incredibly fired a 17-inning no-hitter for Winchester against the Lexington, KY Colts (BGL). The Hustlers won the contest in the bottom of the 17th inning on a single, a two-base throwing error, and a suicide squeeze. Toney played for Winchester again in 1910 and signed later that year with the Chicago Cubs (NL).

Toney spent the next three seasons with the Chicago Cubs, hurling only 130 innings. Although liking Cubs manager Frank Chance,* he disliked the browbeating personality of Chance's successor, Johnny Evers.* Toney pitched for Louisville, KY (AA) before returning to the major leagues with the Cincinnati Reds (NL) for the 1915 season. His impressive victory totals included 17 games that year, 14 contests in 1916, and 24 games in 1917.

The 1917 season marked Toney's best in the major leagues. Under easygoing manager Christy Mathewson,* Toney posted career highs in wins (24), innings pitched (339.2), games started (42), complete games (31), and shutouts (7), and recorded an impressive 2.20 ERA. On May 2, 1917, he faced Chicago's Hippo Vaughn.* Both hurlers pitched hitless, runless baseball for nine straight innings for the only nine inning double no-hitter in major league history. In the top of the tenth inning, Cincinnati manufactured a run. Toney retired the Cubs in the bottom of the tenth inning to preserve both his victory and the no-hitter.

In July 1918 Toney joined the New York Giants (NL) under manager John McGraw.* His 52 triumphs from 1919 to 1921 included 21 victories in the Giants' World Series championship 1921 season. Toney faltered in 1922 and was traded to the Boston Braves (NL) that July. Boston sold him to the St. Louis Cardinals (NL) in October 1922 for his final major league season. During his 12-year career he won 139 of 241 decisions and posted a 2.69 ERA. The 6-foot 1-inch, 195-pound, ponderous, husky right-hander, called by writers the "man who walks like a bear," retired to a farm near his native Nashville, TN and was employed by the sheriff's office.

BIBLIOGRAPHY: Lee Allen, *The Cincinnati Reds* (New York, 1948); *The Baseball Encyclopedia*, 10th ed. (New York, 1996); Warren Brown, *The Chicago Cubs* (New York, 1946); Eddie Gold and Art Ahrens, *The Golden Era Cubs, 1876–1940* (Chicago, IL, 1985); Peter C. Bjarkman, *Baseball's Great Dynasties: The Reds* (New York, 1991); Bob Rathgeber, *Cincinnati Reds Scrapbook* (Virginia Beach, VA, 1982); Charles Einstein, ed., *The Fireside Book of Baseball* (New York, 1956); Lonnie Wheeler and John Baskin, *The Cincinnati Game* (Wilmington, OH, 1998); Noel Hynd, *The Giants of the Polo Grounds* (New York, 1988); Frank Graham, *The New York Giants* (New York, 1952); Fred Toney file, National Baseball Library, Cooperstown, NY.

David S. Matz

TOPPING, Daniel Reid, Sr. "Dan" (b. June 11, 1912, Greenwich, CT; d. May 18, 1974, Miami, FL), baseball and football executive, owned the New York

Yankees (AL) baseball team for 22 years. The son of Henry J. Topping and Rhea (Reid) Topping, he became heir to a family fortune made in the tin and steel industries. He attended the Hun School in Lawrenceville, NJ and Wharton School of Finance at the University of Pennsylvania. Topping entered professional sports as a football executive, hiring Dr. Jock Sutherland (FB) in 1940 for $17,500 to coach the Brooklyn Dodgers (NFL). After World War II, Topping shifted his interest to the New York Yankees (AAFC), but concentrated on baseball when the AAFC folded in 1949.

His association with the New York Yankees baseball club began in the U.S. Marines during World War II. In 1945, Leland S. (Larry) MacPhail, Sr.,* Del E. Webb,* and Topping purchased the Bronx Bombers from the heirs of Jacob Ruppert* for $2.8 million. Two years later, Topping joined Webb in buying out MacPhail and became president. Not a baseball expert, Topping knew his limitations and let general manager George M. Weiss* and field manager Casey Stengel* conduct daily operations. Stengel won nine AL pennants and seven World Series before finishing third in 1959. After the Yankees lost a heartstopping World Series to the Pittsburgh Pirates in 1960, Topping announced a new mandatory retirement policy and dismissed the 70-year-old Stengel and the 65-year-old Weiss.

The New York Yankees captured four straight AL championships under managers Ralph Houk* and Yogi Berra,* but the Yankees fortunes had begun to decline after the 1960 firings. Yankees superstars had aged, while the amateur draft and expansion cut into the club's domination of player development. During the 1964 season, Topping and Weiss sold 80 percent of the club's stock to CBS for $11.2 million. Topping later faced a congressional inquiry into a possible antitrust violation. Two years later, Topping severed his official connections with the New York Yankees and retired to a Florida yacht. The father of nine children, Topping was married six times—to Theodora Boettger in 1932, actress Arline Judge in 1937, Olympic gold medal figure skater Sonja Henie in 1940, actress Kay Sutton in 1946, Alice Lowther in 1952, and Charlotte Ann Lillard in 1957.

BIBLIOGRAPHY: Dave Anderson et al., *The Yankees* (New York, 1979); Mark Gallagher, *The Yankee Encyclopedia*, vol. 3 (Champaign, IL, 1997); Peter Golenbock, *Dynasty* (New York, 1995); Dom Forker, *The Men of Autumn* (Dallas, TX, 1989); Dom Forker, *Sweet Seasons* (Dallas, TX, 1991); Robert W. Creamer, *Stengel: His Life and Times* (New York, 1984); Frank Graham, *The New York Yankees* (New York, 1943); *NYT*, October 1960, February 19, 1965, May 20, 1974; *TSN*, January 3, 1962, pp. 4, 5, 16; Dan Topping file, National Baseball Library, Cooperstown, NY.

John David Healy

TORGESON, Clifford Earl "The Earl of Snohomish" (b. January 1, 1924, Snohomish, WA; d. November 8, 1990, Everett, WA), player, was known as a "walking man" and idolized baseball star Earl Averill* as a youth. Torgeson, the son of a carpenter, signed out of high school and began his professional baseball career with Wenatchee, WA (WIL) in 1942 and served from 1943 to 1945 in the armed forces. In his major league rookie season, the left-handed–hitting and –throwing first baseman batted .281 for the Boston Braves (NL) in 1947 with 16 HR, 11 stolen bases (fifth highest in the NL), and a .403 on-base percentage. On May 30, 1947, he tied a major league record for first basemen by playing the entire game without a putout.

In 1948, the Boston Braves captured the NL flag. Torgeson, who played mostly against right-hand pitching, tied for fourth in the NL in walks (81) and ranked fifth in stolen bases (19). He led all batters in the Boston Braves' six-game World Series loss to the Cleveland Indians with a superlative .389 average. Torgeson missed most of 1949 with a shoulder injury, but rebounded in 1950 with his best year. He batted .290 with 23 HR, an NL-leading 120 runs scored, 119 walks (third), 15 stolen bases (fourth), and a .412 on-base percentage. In 1951, he hit .263 and again finished among NL leaders in walks (102) and stolen bases (20).

After spending the 1952 campaign with the Boston Braves, the 6-foot 3-inch, 180-pound Torgeson was traded to the Philadelphia Phillies (NL) in February 1953, sold to the Detroit Tigers (AL) in June 1955, and sent to the Chicago White Sox (AL) in June 1957. Torgeson started the 1959 season as the regular first baseman for the AL champion "Go Sox" and drew 62 walks in only 277 official at-bats, but was replaced in August by newly acquired Ted Kluszewski.* Torgeson made only one official at-bat (plus a walk, of course) in the Chicago White Sox's World Series loss to the Los Angeles Dodgers. Torgeson continued with the Chicago White Sox as a reserve player in 1960 and early 1961 and ended his major league career with a brief stint on the mighty 1961 New York Yankees (AL).

Although Torgeson's batting average over his five-team, 15-year career was just .265, he proved a good clutch hitter and fine base runner. Torgeson literally walked his way into the record books. His .387 major league on-base percentage ranked among the hundred highest ever achieved and tied that of Willie Mays.* His ratio of 16.47 walks per 100 at-bats ranks the 14th highest in major league history.

Torgeson, who married Norma Syverson in March 1946 and had one daughter, Christine, and one son, Andy, enjoyed basketball, golf, and bowling. He worked as a lumber company salesman and supervisor of logging operations in Everett, WA, following his retirement from baseball.

BIBLIOGRAPHY: Earl Torgeson file, National Baseball Library, Cooperstown, NY; Harold Kaese, *The Boston Braves* (New York, 1948); Rich Lindberg, *Who's on Third?* (South Bend, IN, 1983); David Condon, *The Go-Go Chicago White Sox* (New York, 1960); Harold Kaese, "It's Now or Never for Torgeson," *Sport* 12 (May 1952), pp. 34–35, 93–95; Rich Marazzi and Len Fiorito, *Aaron to Zuverink* (New York, 1982); David Neft et al., *The Sports Encyclopedia: Baseball* (New York, 1993); *NYT*, November 11, 1990, p. 40; John Thorn et al., eds., *Total Baseball*, 5th ed. (New York, 1997); *TSN Official Baseball Register*, 1961; Al Hirshberg, *Braves, the Pick and the Shovel*

(Boston, MA, 1948); Gary Caruso, *The Braves Encyclopedia* (Philadelphia, PA, 1995); Rich Westcott and Frank Bilovsky, *The New Phillies Encyclopedia* (Philadelphia, PA, 1993); Joe Falls, *Detroit Tigers* (New York, 1975); Fred Smith, *995 Tigers* (Detroit, MI, 1981).

Sheldon L. Appleton

TORRE, Joseph Paul, Jr. "Joe" (b. July 18, 1940, Brooklyn, NY), player, manager, and sportscaster, is the youngest of five children born to Joseph Paul Torre, Sr. and Margaret Torre and grew up in a baseball family. His father scouted for the Milwaukee Braves (NL) and the Baltimore Orioles (AL), while his older brother, Frank, played first base for the Milwaukee Braves (1956–1960) and Philadelphia Phillies (NL, 1962–1963).

A star third baseman at St. Francis Prep School, Torre began his professional baseball career as a catcher because of a tendency to put on weight. An all-star performance in his first season with Eau Claire, WI (NoL) led to his promotion to the Milwaukee Braves for the last two weeks of the 1960 season. He began the 1961 season at Louisville, KY (AA), but hit .342 in the first 27 games and returned to the major leagues. He played for 18 NL league seasons, with the Milwaukee Braves (1960–1965), Atlanta Braves (1966–1968), St. Louis Cardinals (1969–1974), and New York Mets (1975–1977).

An excellent fielder who could hit for power and average, the 6-foot 2-inch, 215-pound Torre also proved a versatile and consistent performer. Primarily a catcher with the Milwaukee Braves and Atlanta Braves, he divided playing time after 1971 between first and third base. His best year was 1971, the only season he played exclusively at third. Named NL MVP, he led the major leagues in batting average (.363), hits (230), RBI (137), total bases (352), and putouts by a third baseman. Remarkably, he went hitless in only 28 of 161 games. Selected to the NL All-Star team nine times (1963–1967, 1970–1973), the right-handed Torre compiled major league career totals of 2,209 games played, 2,342 hits, 344 doubles, 252 HR, 996 runs scored, 1,185 RBI, .452 slugging percentage, and .297 batting average.

In May 1977, Torre became manager of the New York Mets. He was fired in October 1981 after five losing seasons (286–420, .405 winning percentage), which saw the Mets finish no higher than fifth place. He then was hired by the Atlanta Braves, which in 1982 won the Western Division title and lost to the St. Louis Cardinals in the NL Championship Series. Despite leading the Atlanta Braves to second place finishes in 1983 and 1984, Torre was released as manager after the 1984 season.

He managed the St. Louis Cardinals (NL) from August 1990 to June 1995 to a 351–354 overall record and a second place NL East finish in 1991. He has piloted the New York Yankees (AL) since 1996, when he earned *TSN* Sportsman of the Year and BBWAA Co-AL Manager of the Year honors and participated in his first World Series. After winning the AL East with a 92–70 record in 1996, the New York Yankees defeated the Texas Rangers in the AL Division Series, the Baltimore Orioles in the AL Championship

Series, and the Atlanta Braves, 4–2, in the World Series. The New York Yankees finished second in the AL East with a 96–66 record in 1997, but lost to the Cleveland Indians in the Division Series. Torre won AP and BBWAA AL Manager of the Year honors, as the New York Yankees set an AL record for victories with a 114–48 win–loss record. The New York Yankees swept the Texas Rangers in the AL Division Series, defeated the Cleveland Indians in six games in the AL Championship Series, and swept the San Diego Padres in the World Series. He missed the first 36 games of 1999 because of prostate cancer. His club repeated as AL East titlists with a 98–64 record and won the AL Division, AL Championship, and World Series. His managerial record for 18 seasons through 1999 included 1,273 wins, 1,236 losses, and a .507 winning percentage.

Torre married Diane Romaine in 1968. They have three children: Christina Lynn, Loren from Diane's previous marriage, and Michael from his previous marriage to Jacqueline Ann Reed. He also served as a television broadcaster with the California Angels (AL) in the late 1980s.

BIBLIOGRAPHY: *CB* (1972), pp. 430–433; Joe Torre file, National Baseball Library, Cooperstown, NY; *CB* (May 1997), pp. 51–54; R. Jerome, "Torre, Torre, Torre!" *PW* 46 (November 11, 1996), pp. 52–56; Tom Verducci, "Crowd Pleasers," *SI* 89 (November 2, 1998), pp. 46–56; Mark Gallagher, *The Yankee Encyclopedia*, vol. 3 (Champaign, IL, 1997); Bob Buege, *The Milwaukee Braves: A Baseball Eulogy* (Milwaukee, WI, 1988); Gary Caruso, *The Braves Encyclopedia* (Philadelphia, PA, 1995); Bob Broeg, *Redbirds: A Century of Cardinals' Baseball* (St. Louis, MO, 1981); Rob Rains, *The St. Louis Cardinals* (New York, 1992); Donald Honig, *The New York Mets* (New York, 1986); Jack Lang and Peter Simon, *The New York Mets* (New York, 1986); Thomas Aylesworth and Benton Minks, *The Encyclopedia of Baseball Managers* (New York, 1990); Gene Karst and Martin J. Jones, Jr., *Who's Who in Professional Baseball* (New Rochelle, NY, 1973); *NYT*, June 3, 1976, June 1, 1977, October 5, 21, 1981, October 2, 1984; *NYT Biographical Service* 27 (September 1996), pp. 1336–1339; *The Baseball Encyclopedia*, 10th ed. (New York, 1996); *TSN Official Baseball Register, 1998*; *TSN*, November 7, 28, 1981, October 22, 1984; Tom Verducci, "Regular Joe," *SI* 85 (October 28, 1996), pp. 40–44; Bob Broeg and Jerry Vickery, *St. Louis Cardinals Encyclopedia* (Grand Rapids, MI, 1998).

Larry R. Gerlach

TORREZ, Michael Augustine "Mike" (b. August 28, 1946, Topeka, KS), player, is of Mexican-American descent and grew up in a poor Topeka neighborhood. Torrez, whose father worked as a switchman for a railroad company, has seven brothers and sisters. After attending Topeka High School for three years, he served in the U.S. Marines Reserves from 1965 to 1971. He married his second wife Danielle Gagnon, a fashion model, on October 26, 1974. They had a son, Iannick, before their 1980 divorce.

At age 17, Torrez signed with the St. Louis Cardinals (NL) and played three seasons in the minor leagues. On September 10, 1967, the 6-foot 5-inch, 220-pound right-handed pitcher made his major league debut. Torrez pitched between 1967 and 1984 for the St. Louis Cardinals (1967–1970), Montreal Expos (NL, 1971–1974), Baltimore Orioles (AL, 1975), Oakland Athletics (AL, 1976–1977), New York Yankees (AL, 1977), Boston Red Sox (AL, 1978–1982), and New York Mets (NL, 1983–1984). During his major league career, he won 185 games, lost 160 decisions, and compiled a 3.96 ERA. Torrez won at least 15 games each season from 1974 to 1979. An occasionally wild pitcher, he led the league in walks three times and averaged 80–90 walks a year. His wildness may have accounted for his several trades.

Under Orioles manager Earl Weaver* and pitching coach George Bamberger, Torrez added a curve ball to his explosive fast ball. He enjoyed his best season with a 20–9 mark in 1975 and led the AL with a .690 winning percentage. His April 1976 trade to the Oakland A's brought Reggie Jackson* to the Baltimore Orioles. The following year, Torrez helped the New York Yankees win the AL pennant with seven straight wins in July and August and hurled two complete-game victories against the Los Angeles Dodgers in the World Series. He pitched Game 6, in which Reggie Jackson hit three HR to secure the World Series win for New York. In 1978, Torrez hurled the one-game playoff for the Boston Red Sox against the New York Yankees for the East Division title. In the seventh inning, his three run HR pitch to Bucky Dent cost the Boston Red Sox the game and AL pennant. After being traded to the New York Mets in January 1983, Torrez lost an NL high 17 games while winning only 10. His second start with the New York Mets in 1984 resulted in a wild pitch, which hit and shattered the bones around the eye of Houston Astros shortstop Dickie Thon. Torrez signed with the Oakland A's in July 1984 and retired after 2.1 innings.

BIBLIOGRAPHY: Mike Torrez file, National Baseball Library, Cooperstown, NY; Danielle Gagnon Torrez and Ken Lizotte, *High Inside* (New York, 1983); Mike Shatzkin, ed., *The Ballplayers* (New York, 1990); "Mike Torrez," Microsoft Complete Baseball, CD-ROM (Redmond, WA, 1994); Bob Broeg and Jerry Vickery, *St. Louis Cardinals Encyclopedia* (Grand Rapids, MI, 1998); Dan Turner, *The Expos Inside Out* (Toronto, Canada, 1983); Bruce Markusen, *Baseball's Last Dynasty* (New York, 1998); Mark Gallagher, *The Yankees Encyclopedia*, vol. 3 (Champaign, IL, 1997); Howard Liss, *The Boston Red Sox* (New York, 1982); Peter Golenbock, *Fenway* (New York, 1992); Dan Shaughnessy; *The Curse of the Bambino* (New York, 1990); Robert Redmount, *The Red Sox Encyclopedia* (Champaign, IL, 1998); Jack Lang and Peter Simon, *The New York Mets* (New York, 1986).

Lowell D. Smith

TORRIENTE, Christobal (b. 1895, Cuba; d. 1938, New York, NY), player, was a powerful 5-foot 10-inch, 190-pound Cuban star in the NNL throughout the 1920s. He batted and threw from the left side and made all his teams successful with his presence. Despite being coveted by the white major leagues, the light-skinned Torriente's kinky hair kept him confined to black teams.

Torriente began his American career in 1913 with Tinti Molina's Cuban Stars. After stints in 1913, 1916, and 1917 with J. L. Wilkinson's* All-Nations team, Torriente joined Rube Foster's* Chicago American Giants in 1918. Chicago captured the first three NNL pennants from 1920 to 1922, with Torriente proving a vital cog. Torriente remained with the American Giants through 1925, spent 1926 with the Kansas City, MO Monarchs (NNL), and performed in 1927 and 1928 with the Detroit, MI Stars (NNL). Torriente's baseball career also included stints with the Gilkerson's Union Giants in 1930, the Atlanta, GA Black Crackers in 1932, and Cleveland, OH Cubs in 1932.

Torriente's lifetime NNL batting average was .333. Torriente generally ranked among the leaders in batting average, extra base hits, and stolen bases, capturing the NNL hitting crown with .412 in 1923. Torriente also won two CUWL batting titles in his native Cuba with .387 in 1913–1914 and .360 in 1919–1920. He led the CUWL with 48 hits in 1914–1915, 56 hits in 1915–1916, 61 hits in 1922–1923, and 15 stolen bases in 1922–1923.

Torriente played 13 CUWL seasons, competing with the best white and black players who chose to perform there. He compiled a .352 career batting average in Cuba, collecting 463 hits in 1,316 at-bats covering 358 games. His hits included 62 doubles, 39 triples, and 18 HR for 657 total bases and a .499 slugging average. He also stole 107 bases. Torriente's highest CUWL mark, a .402 batting average in 1915–1916, nearly took the batting title, but Eusaquio Pedroso hit a superb .413 that year. Torriente starred on CUWL championship teams with Almendares in 1913–1914, 1915–1916, and 1919–1920, and with Havana in 1921, 1926, and 1927. Torriente, remembered among the black leagues' greatest outfielders, is included on most All-Time Negro League teams. He normally patrolled center field but occasionally became a portside third baseman and compiled a 15–5 win–loss career record as an NNL pitcher. Torriente entered the Cuban Baseball Hall of Fame in 1939. He died an impoverished, lonely alcoholic, but his body was returned to Havana in hero's fashion, draped with the Cuban flag.

BIBLIOGRAPHY: Janet Bruce, *The Kansas City Monarchs* (Lawrence, KS, 1985); John Holway, "Cristobal Torriente," *BHR* (1981), pp. 72–74; John B. Holway, *Blackball Stars* (Westport, CT, 1988); Robert W. Peterson, *Only the Ball Was White* (Englewood Cliffs, NJ, 1970); Angel Torres, *La Historia del Beisbol Cubano* (Los Angeles, CA, 1976); James A. Riley, *The Biographical Encyclopedia of the Negro Baseball Leagues* (New York, 1994); Christobal Torriente's CUWL Career Record, Raymond Gonzalez Collection, Hialeah, FL; Christobal Torriente file, National Baseball Library, Cooperstown, NY.

Merl F. Kleinknecht

TRAMMELL, Alan Stuart "Tram" (b. February 21, 1958, Garden Grove, CA), player and coach, led the fine Detroit Tigers (AL) teams of the mid–1980s. As a youth, the southern California native drew strike zones on garage doors and spent many hours practicing throws and sneaking into ballparks to watch games. The Detroit Tigers selected the high school baseball and basketball star in the second round of the June 1976 draft. After playing shortstop with Bristol, CT (EL) and Montgomery, AL (SL) in 1976, he was named SL MVP the next year at Montgomery and first combined there with second baseman Lou Whitaker.* The two later became the longest-running double-play combination in major league history. Trammell joined the Detroit Tigers at the end of the 1977 campaign.

In 1984, the 6-foot, 175-pound, right-handed–hitting shortstop sparked the Detroit Tigers to a sensational 35–5 start by hitting .403 in April. Despite suffering a shoulder injury, he finished the 1984 season with a .314 batting average and his fourth Gold Glove award in five years. He hit .364 in the AL Championship Series against the Kansas City Royals and .450 with two HR and six RBI for the World Series victors against the San Diego Padres, winning the World Series MVP award. Trammell formed the heart of a less gifted 1987 Detroit Tigers team, which barely won the AL Eastern Division title by sweeping its last seven games. That year, Trammell recorded 205 hits and batted .343 with 28 HR, 105 RBI (a record for Tigers shortstops), and 21 stolen bases, and finished second to George Bell* for AL MVP. He batted .329 with 60 RBI in 1993.

Trammell hit at least .300 in seven seasons was selected Tiger of the Year three times, AL All-Star shortstop six times, and AL Comeback Player of the Year (1983), and ranked among the top ten in Detroit Tigers history in career games played (2,293), hits (2,365), runs (1,231), doubles (412), and stolen bases (236). In 20 major league seasons with the Tigers through 1996, Trammell batted .285 with 185 HR and 1,003 RBI. He has served as first base, outfield, and base-running coach for the Detroit Tigers from 1997 through 1999 and the Padres since 2000.

Trammell married Barbara Leverett, his high school sweetheart, on February 21, 1978. Their three children include Lance, named after then-teammate Lance Parrish,* Kyle, and Jade Lynn.

BIBLIOGRAPHY: Detroit Tigers, *The Press Guide, 1989*, pp. 64–65, 93–111; George Sullivan and David Cataneo, *Detroit Tigers* (New York, 1985); Sparky Anderson and Dan Ewald, *Sparky* (New York, 1990); Richard Bak, *A Place for Summer* (Detroit, MI, 1998); Sparky Anderson with Dan Ewald, *They Call Me Sparky* (Chelsea, MI, 1998); Robert E. Kelly, *Baseball's Best* (Jefferson, NC, 1988); Tim Lee, "Alan Trammell," *SCD* 23 (May 31, 1996), pp. 162–163; William M. Anderson, *The Detroit Tigers* (South Bend, IN, 1996); Sparky Anderson and Dan Ewald, *Bless You Boys* (Chicago, IL, 1984); Joe Falls, *The Detroit Tigers: An Illustrated History* (New York, 1989); Fred T. Smith, *Tiger Tales and Trivia* (Lathrup Village, MI, 1988); John Thorn et al., eds., *Total Baseball*, 5th ed. (New York, 1997); Alan Trammell file, National Baseball Library, Cooperstown, NY.

Sheldon L. Appleton

TRAUTMAN, George McNeal (b. January 11, 1890, Bucyrus, OH; d. June 24, 1963, Columbus, OH), player, coach, manager, club official, and administrator, served as president and treasurer of the NAPBL from 1947 through 1962. After pitching from 1905 to 1908 for Bucyrus High School, Trautman played varsity football, basketball, and baseball at Ohio State University from 1909 through 1913 and formed a battery with noted politician John W. Bricker.

Following graduation, the red-haired hurler studied at Harvard University Graduate School in physical education and served as athletic director at Camp Sheridan, AL with the rank of army captain. He spent two years as coach and athletic director at Fostoria, OH High School and served until 1929 in the Ohio State physical education department. Besides being head basketball coach, he was an assistant athletic director under longtime associate Lynn St. John (IS) and joined the National Intercollegiate Wrestling Rules Committee. Trautman in 1929 became director of conventions and publicity for the Columbus, OH Chamber of Commerce and helped bring the 1931 Ryder Cup golf matches to the Scioto CC. At Ohio State, he had directed the U.S. Open golf championship tournament at Scioto in 1926. He received a lifetime honorary membership from the American Bowling Congress for promoting its annual meet at Columbus in 1933.

In 1933 he succeeded Leland MacPhail, Sr.,* as president of the Columbus, OH Red Birds (AA), then the top minor league baseball circuit. Under Trautman's direction, the St. Louis Cardinals farm club won AA pennants his first and second years and remained in contention with profitable attendance. He served as AA president from 1936 to 1944 and became general manager of the Detroit Tigers (AL) under owner Walter O. Briggs.* As executive vice-president, he was asked to fulfill only assignments strictly related to his job and disliked having visitors or callers.

In 1946, the minor leagues made Trautman a virtually unanimous choice to replace ailing Judge William Bramham of Durham, NC as their president. Trautman promptly moved the minor league headquarters from Durham to Columbus, took along several key staffers, and presided over the greatest growth of professional baseball. By 1949, the minor leagues expanded to 59 leagues and 448 teams. The tremendous growth of major league farm systems and the mass signing of young players returning from World War II military service spurred the increase. Trautman, however, believed that much of the expansion was irresponsible and doomed to failure because television competed heavily with minor league baseball. Towns without strong financial structures for their teams and well-developed promotion programs lost their club franchises. The number of leagues and franchises steadily declined, causing detractors to predict doom for the minors.

Trautman in 1957 launched the strongest promotion program devised for pro-sports to that time. He organized a promotional staff, headed by former wire services sportswriter Carl Lundquist and including field representatives Eddie Stumpf, G. E. Gilliland, Warren LeTarte, and Bob Frietas. They traveled throughout the minor league empire, devising promotional projects to bring fans back to the ballparks. Despite a continuing reduction in leagues and clubs, Trautman's plan stabilized the minor league structure. Trautman had assured the future of the minors when illness forced him to resign as president in 1962.

BIBLIOGRAPHY: George Trautman file, National Baseball Library, Cooperstown, NY; *American League 1946 Official Red Book* (Chicago, IL, 1946); Columbus (OH) *Dispatch*, June 25, 1963; Columbus (OH) *Dispatch Sunday Magazine*, April 1, 1962; *TSN Official Baseball Guide, 1964*; *Seventy Nights in a Ball Park* (Columbus, OH, 1958); George M. Trautman, *The Story of Minor League Baseball* (Columbus, OH, 1952).

Carl Lundquist

TRAVIS, Cecil Howell (b. August 8, 1913, Riverdale, GA), player and scout, is the son of James Travis and Ada (Collinsworth) Travis. Travis, who married Helen Hubbard in September 1942 and has three sons, began his professional baseball career by playing 10 games for Chattanooga, TN (SA) in 1931. After enjoying excellent seasons there in 1932 and 1933, he joined the Washington Senators (AL) in September 1933. In his first major league game, he made five consecutive hits to equal the record set in 1894 by Fred Clarke* of the Louisville Colonels (NL). The next year, he won the regular third base job and batted .319.

With the exception of nearly four years in the U.S. Army during World War II, Travis played regularly with the Washington Senators until the 1947 season. He was switched to shortstop in 1936, later alternated between shortstop and third base, and played at times in the outfield. After the 1941 season, he joined the U.S. Army. He spent 10 months with the 76th Infantry Division fighting in Belgium and Germany and suffered badly frozen feet in the Battle of the Bulge. He rejoined the Washington Senators for 15 games in 1945 and remained there until his retirement during the 1947 season. His ailing feet prevented him from regaining his prewar greatness. He scouted for the Washington Senators from 1948 to 1955.

Travis's 12 major league seasons saw him bat .314 with 1,544 hits, 665 runs, 265 doubles, 78 triples, 27 HR, and 657 RBI. He hit over .300 in eight seasons and achieved his best batting average (.359) in 1941, the same year he led the AL in hits (218). He produced 20 or more doubles in nine seasons. Defensively, Travis led third basemen in double plays (29) in 1936 and shortstops in double plays (113) in 1938. His record makes him a worthy candidate for the National Baseball Hall of Fame. If his baseball career had not been shortened by military service, his achievements would have been even greater. An aggressive, clean player respected by both teammates and opponents, Travis resides on a 60-acre farm in Riverdale, GA.

BIBLIOGRAPHY: Marty Appel, *Yesterday's Heroes* (New York, 1988); Ron Fimrite, "A Call to Arms," *SI* 75 (Fall 1991), pp. 98–102; Donald Honig, *Baseball Between the Lines* (New York, 1976); John Hillman, "Making the Pitch for Cecil Travis in the

Hall of Fame," *SCD* 22 (July 7, 1995), p. 166; Gene Karst and Martin J. Jones, Jr., *Who's Who in Professional Baseball* (New Rochelle, NY, 1973); Shirley Povich, *The Washington Senators* (New York, 1954).

Ralph S. Graber

TRAYNOR, Harold Joseph "Pie" (b. November 11, 1899, Framingham, MA; d. March 16, 1972, Pittsburgh, PA), player, manager, sportscaster, and scout, was one of eight children of James H. Traynor, an Irish printer, and Lydia (Matthews) Traynor, an English native. He moved to Somerville, MA at age five and completed his education at Bingham School in Somerville. He may have received his nickname, "Pie," for his favorite childhood food or when his father one day declared that the dirty boy resembled pied type. Traynor began working as a messenger and office boy at age 12 and tried to enlist during World War I, but was rejected and became a freight car checker. He started his professional baseball career as a shortstop with Portsmouth, VA (VL) in 1920 and was purchased by the Pittsburgh Pirates (NL). After one minor league season at Birmingham, AL (SA), he joined the Pirates permanently in 1922.

Although originally a shortstop, Traynor the next 12 years became baseball's finest third baseman. The slightly over 6-foot, 170-pound right-hander lined many extra-base hits to right field and right center field and made 2,416 major league career hits, including 371 doubles, 164 triples, and 58 HR. Traynor also batted .320 lifetime, drove in over 100 runs seven times, scored 1,183 runs, knocked in 1,273 runs, and stole 158 bases. He batted .293 in the 1925 World Series against the Washington Senators and 1927 World Series against the New York Yankees. Traynor used his speed in the field, where his range and throwing arm were legendary. It was often said that a player "doubled down the third base line, but Traynor threw him out." He exhibited daring base running and led the NL in triples (19) in 1923, but his aggressiveness shortened his career. While trying to score in a 1934 game against the Philadelphia Phillies, he slid and reached back for home plate. The catcher landed on Traynor's right arm, injuring it. Traynor played little more than a season after that.

In 1934, Traynor became the Pirates' manager. His 1938 Pirates narrowly lost the NL pennant to the Chicago Cubs on Gabby Hartnett's* famous "homer in the gloaming." He was asked to resign after the 1939 season, having posted a 457–406 (.530 winning percentage) career record. Traynor, who married Eva Helmer of Cincinnati, OH in January 1931 and had no children, moved to Cincinnati after leaving baseball. Although he never learned to drive, Traynor sold cars there. He returned to Pittsburgh as a sports commentator for radio station WKQV in 1944 and held that job for 22 years. He also became a part-time Pirates scout and instructor (1940–1972), frequently received speaking invitations, and did commercial endorsements. The elegant, articulate Traynor was beloved for his good humor and gentle disposition.

In the 1920s, John McGraw* termed Traynor "the greatest team player in baseball today." Upon Traynor's induction into the National Baseball Hall of Fame in 1948, Branch Rickey* lauded him as "a mechanically perfect third baseman, a man of intellectual worth on the field of play." During baseball's 1969 centennial celebration, he was named the greatest third baseman in baseball history. Traynor helped baseball's star shine brightly during sports' golden age between the world wars.

BIBLIOGRAPHY: Pie Traynor file, National Baseball Library, Cooperstown, NY; Thomas Aylesworth and Benton Minks, *The Encyclopedia of Baseball Managers* (New York, 1990); Bob Broeg, *Super Stars of Baseball* (St. Louis, MO, 1971); *DAB*, supp. 9 (1970–1975), pp. 805–806; Lowell Reidenbaugh, *Baseball's Hall of Fame-Cooperstown* (New York, 1993); Frederick G. Lieb, *The Pittsburgh Pirates* (New York, 1948); Richard L. Burtt, *The Pittsburgh Pirates, A Pictorial History* (Virginia Beach, VA, 1977); Bob Smizik, *The Pittsburgh Pirates: An Illustrated History* (New York, 1990).

Luther W. Spoehr

TRENT, Theodore "Ted," "Highpockets," "Big Florida" (b. December 17, 1903, Jacksonville, FL; d. January 10, 1944, Chicago, IL), player, pitched for St. Augustine, FL in 1924 and Bethune-Cookman College in 1925–1926. After hurling for the West Palm Beach, FL Giants in 1926, he performed in the Negro Leagues from 1927 to 1939. Trent, the ace pitcher for the champion St. Louis, MO Stars (NNL), led the Stars to championships in 1928, 1930, and 1931. The long-legged pitcher relied on his roundhouse curveball and nasty slider. Trent's best year came in 1928, when he compiled a 21–2 win–loss record and led the Stars in innings pitched, strikeouts, complete games, and shutouts. He compiled marks of 15–11 in 1927, 12–8 in 1929, and 12–2 in 1930 for St. Louis. The 6-foot 3-inch, 185-pound Trent appeared in four East-West All-Star Games from 1934 to 1937 and started for the West squad in 1934 and 1937 with no decisions.

After leading the St. Louis Stars to a 1931 NNL championship, Trent defeated an All-Star major league team composed of "Babe" Herman,* Bill Terry,* Hack Wilson,* and brothers Paul Waner* and Lloyd Waner.* National Baseball Hall of Famer Terry, who had batted over .400 the previous year, struck out four times against the tall right-hander. Trent defeated the major leagues, 8–6, striking out 16 batters.

Trent's career included appearances with the Detroit, MI Wolves (EWL) in 1932, Washington, DC Pilots (EWL) in 1932, Kansas City, MO Monarchs (NSL) in 1932, New York Black Yankees in 1933 and 1934, and Chicago, IL American Giants (NAL) from 1933 to 1939. Chicago played as an independent team in 1936, when he posted a 29–5 mark. Overall, Trent compiled a 94–49 win–loss Negro League record, triumphing in 66 percent of his decisions over 13 years. He suffered from tuberculosis and excessive drinking, dying at age 40.

BIBLIOGRAPHY: Chicago (IL) *Defender*, July 28, 1934; John B. Holway, *Blackball Stars* (Westport, CT, 1988); James A. Riley, *The Biographical Encyclopedia of the Negro Baseball Leagues* (New York, 1994); Mike Shatzkin, ed., *The Ballplayers* (New York, 1990).

                                                                      Larry Lester

TRESH, Thomas Michael "Tom" (b. September 20, 1937, Detroit, MI), player, is the son of Mike Tresh, baseball player and coach, and Doris (Mills) Tresh and learned baseball at an early age from his father, a veteran major league catcher. A star scholastic athlete, Tresh attended Central Michigan University for one year and signed with the New York Yankees (AL) for $30,000 in January 1958. The powerful, switch-hitting shortstop advanced through the New York Yankees organization between 1958 and 1961 and batted .315 as MVP with Richmond, VA (IL) in 1961. After joining the New York Yankees that September, Tresh won the shortstop job over Phil Linz in 1962. Tresh batted .286 with 20 HR and 93 RBI, winning the AL Rookie of the Year award. When regular shortstop Tony Kubek* returned from military service in August, Tresh performed well in left field. In the 1962 World Series against the San Francisco Giants (NL), he batted .321 with a three-run HR in Game 5 and a game saving catch in Game 7.

Tresh played in the major leagues throughout the 1960s. The consummate team player performed in the outfield and at shortstop and third base. He batted .277 in 18 World Series games, clouting four HR with 13 RBI. In 1965, Tresh hit .279 with 26 HR and 74 RBI. On June 6, 1965, he belted three consecutive HR against the Chicago White Sox. The member of the 1962 and 1963 All Star teams led AL outfielders with a .996 fielding percentage in 1964 and won an outfield Gold Glove in 1965.

After a sub-par 1966 season, Tresh suffered torn knee ligaments in a 1967 spring training game. He played at the request of team management and further damaged his knee, shortening his career. Despite two subsequent operations, Tresh never recovered his old skills. The Detroit Tigers (AL) acquired him in June 1969, but he was released in 1970. In 1,192 major league games, he batted .245 with 153 HR and 530 RBI.

Tresh received his Bachelor's degree from Central Michigan University after attending classes off-season for 12 years and worked for the university in various administrative positions for 14 years. He later served as assistant coach of the university baseball team. Tresh has developed and marketed an innovative device, Slide-Rite, to teach proper sliding technique.

On December 29, 1961, Tresh married Cheryl Lynne Tefft. Following their divorce, he remarried. An avid fisherman, hunter and golfer, Tresh resides with his wife, Sandi, in Mt. Pleasant, MI.

BIBLIOGRAPHY: Tom Tresh file, National Baseball Library, Cooperstown, NY; Lee Heiman et al., *When the Cheering Stops* (New York, 1990); Mark Gallagher, *The Yankee Encyclopedia*, vol. 3 (Champaign, IL, 1997); Phil Pepe, "Tom Tresh: A Study in Versatility," *Sport* 35 (February 1963), pp. 56–59, 80–82; Dave Sabaini, "Tom Tresh and His Baseball Legacy," *SCD* 16 (February 3, 1989), pp. 158–161; Robert Obojski, "Tom Tresh Discusses Career in Pinstripes," *SCD* 18 (November 29, 1991), p. 160; Fluffy Saccucci, "1962 AL Rookie of the Year Profiled," *SCD* 23 (January 16, 1996), p. 189; Dom Forker, *Sweet Seasons* (Dallas, TX, 1991); Peter Golenbock, *Dynasty* (New York, 1975); Dave Anderson et al., *The Yankees* (New York, 1979); *TSN*, December 8, 1962; *The Baseball Encyclopedia*, 10th ed. (New York, 1996); John Thorn et al., *Total Baseball*, 5th ed. (New York, 1997).

Edward J. Tassinari

TRIANDOS, Gus Constantine (b. July 30, 1930, San Francisco, CA), player, coach, and scout, was a 6-foot 3-inch, 220-pound catcher who threw and batted right-handed and is one of three children of Peter Triandos and Helen (Mourgas) Triandos. Triandos married Evelyn Moore on January 12, 1952 and has three children. Of Greek descent and handsome physique, he played baseball and basketball at Mission High School in the San Francisco Bay Area.

Triandos left school to sign with the New York Yankees (AL) organization as a first baseman, but the Yankees also played him at third base and catcher. In November 1954, the New York Yankees traded him to the Baltimore Orioles (AL) in a huge 16-player exchange. Triandos played first base for the Orioles, but manager Paul Richards* found him a more capable starting receiver by 1956. For the next eight seasons, Triandos combined real HR power with catching. Most clubs usually sacrificed hitting for defense with catchers. An appreciative Richards, a former receiver, observed, "Gus is the best catcher in either major league." Triandos' most memorable game occurred on September 2, 1958, when knuckleball pitcher Hoyt Wilhelm* threw a no-hitter against the New York Yankees. Triandos' 30th HR of the season provided the 1–0 victory and tied Yogi Berra* for the AL season HR record for catchers. Richards designed a special glove, larger than the standard catcher's mitt with a deeper pocket and more flexibility, to handle Wilhelm's difficult knuckler.

Triandos led the Orioles in HR and RBI from 1955 to 1958 and made the AL All-Star team from 1957 through 1959. The admiring Baltimore media lauded him as the "Golden Greek of Chesapeake," while a street in a Baltimore suburb was named Triandos Drive. Triandos considered the arms of youthful Orioles pitchers Milt Pappas,* Chuck Estrada, Jack Fisher, and Steve Barber as the best he ever saw. He was traded to the Detroit Tigers (AL) in November 1962 and sent with Jim Bunning* to the Philadelphia Phillies (NL) in December 1963. Triandos caught Bunning's perfect game against the New York Mets in June 1964, his second most memorable contest. No major leaguer had caught no-hitters in both leagues previously.

He completed his major league career in 1965 with the Houston Astros (NL). During his 13-year major league career, Triandos batted .244 with 167 HR and 608 RBI and compiled a .987 fielding percentage. After helping coach baseball at the University of California, he briefly scouted for the Los Angeles Dodgers (NL) and owns the Diamond Mailing Service in San Jose, CA. Baltimore Orioles fans considered Triandos a model of diligent, determined dedication.

BIBLIOGRAPHY: John Thorn et al., eds., *Total Baseball*, 5th ed. (New York, 1997); *The Baseball Encyclopedia*, 10th ed. (New York, 1996); David S. Neft et al., eds., *The Sports Encyclopedia: Baseball*, 16th ed. (New York, 1996); Mike Shatzkin, ed., *The Ballplayers* (New York, 1990); John F. Steadman, "Tender Moment for Triandos Family," *Baltimore News-Post*, June 15, 1959, p. 21; Frank Finch, "Knuckler Had Gus on Ropes," *Los Angeles Times*, January 25, 1960, p. 2; Rich Marazzi, "Lumbering Gus Triandos Was an All-Star Catcher for Some Top-Flight Clubs," *SCD* 24 (April 4, 1997), pp. 80–81; Gus Triandos file, National Baseball Library, Cooperstown, NY; Ted Patterson, *The Baltimore Orioles* (Dallas, TX, 1995); James H. Bready, *Baseball in Baltimore* (Baltimore, MD, 1998); Fred Smith, *995 Tigers* (Detroit, MI, 1981); Ralph Bernstein, *The Story of Jim Bunning* (Philadelphia, PA, 1965); Rich Westcott and Frank Bilovsky, *The New Phillies Encyclopedia* (Philadelphia, PA, 1993); *TSN*, May 6, 1953, p. 31, August 26, 1953, pp. 1–2, June 10, 1959, pp. 5–6, March 23, 1963, pp. 7–8; *TSN Baseball Register, 1965*.

William J. Miller

TRILLO, Jesus Manuel Marcano "Manny" (b. December 25, 1950, Carapito, Venezuela), player and coach, is the son of Ismael (Marcano) Trillo and attended Colegio Libertador Bolivar, Maturin, in Munagas, Venezuela. He was signed by the Philadelphia Phillies (NL) in 1968. After playing shortstop and second base with Huron, MI (NoL), he was drafted by the Oakland A's (AL) organization in 1969. The lanky, 6-foot 1-inch, 160-pound infielder progressed through Oakland's farm system with a "great field, no hit" reputation before joining the A's briefly in 1973 and 1974. The Oakland A's traded him to the Chicago Cubs (NL) in October 1974.

Chicago Cubs fans criticized the trade that sent the popular Billy Williams* to Oakland, but Trillo proved an excellent acquisition. After Trillo hit .248 with 70 RBI and 55 runs scored in 1975, Chicago baseball writers named him the Chicago Cubs Rookie of the Year. He starred defensively for the Chicago Cubs with spectacular play and a strong arm and hit dangerously in the clutch.

After spending four seasons with the Chicago Cubs, Trillo was traded to the Philadelphia Phillies (NL) in February 1979. He starred with the Philadelphia Phillies in the 1980 NL Championship Series, batting .381 against the Houston Astros and being selected MVP. The Philadelphia Phillies defeated the Kansas City Royals in the 1980 World Series. Trillo also won Gold Gloves as the NL's best fielding second baseman from 1979 to 1982.

From 1984 to 1989, Trillo suffered many injuries and became a baseball gypsy with the Cleveland Indians (AL) in 1983, Montreal Expos (NL) in 1983 and 1984, and San Francisco Giants (NL) in 1984 and 1985. He returned to the Chicago Cubs from 1986 to 1988 and finished his major league career with the Cincinnati Reds (NL) in 1989. Trillo played second base for most of his major league career, but played all infield positions and became a skillful pinch hitter. During his major league career, he batted .263 with 1,562 hits and 571 RBI and fielded .981 in 1,780 games. Trillo in 1982 and 1983 became the first player to start consecutive All-Star Games in different leagues. He returned to the Chicago Cubs organization in 1996 as hitting coach for Williamsport, PA (NYPL), his first coaching assignment with a major league club. Trillo is divorced with three daughters and a son.

BIBLIOGRAPHY: Manuel Trillo file, National Baseball Library, Cooperstown, NY; *Chicago Cubs Poster Books and Informational Guide*, 1976, 1978, 1996; Eddie Gold and Art Ahrens, *The New Era Cubs, 1941–1985* (Chicago, IL, 1985); *The Baseball Encyclopedia*, 10th ed. (New York, 1996); Jim Langford, *The Game Is Never Over* (South Bend, IN, 1980); Rich Westcott and Frank Bilovsky, *The New Phillies Encyclopedia* (Philadelphia, PA, 1993); Hal Bodley, *The Team That Wouldn't Die* (Wilmington, DE, 1981); Frank Dolson, *The Philadelphia Story* (South Bend, IN, 1981); Allen Lewis, *The Philadelphia Phillies: A Pictorial History* (Virginia Beach, VA, 1981).

Duane A. Smith

TROSKY, Harold Arthur, Sr. "Hal" (b. Harold Arthura Troyavesky, Sr., November 11, 1912, Norway, IA; d. June 18, 1979, Cedar Rapids, IA), player and coach, was of German ancestry. Trosky compiled excellent statistics as a Cleveland Indians (AL) first baseman during the 1930s and became one of the most emotionally enigmatic performers of his era. By mid–1939, Trosky, a hard-hitting, 6-foot 2-inch, 207-pound left-handed slugger, was considered second only to Hank Greenberg* at his AL position. He starred in baseball at Norway High School. Cleveland scout Cy Slapnicka discovered him batting corncobs against the side of a barn. Trosky played outfield at Cedar Rapids-Dubuque, IA (MOVL) in 1931 and at Quincy, IL (3IL) and Burlington, IA (MOVL), in 1932. After spending 1933 at Toledo, OH (AA), he hit .295 in 11 games for the Indians in September. In 1934, the right-handed first baseman hit .330 with 35 HR and 142 RBI for a spectacular rookie season. He fell victim to a sophomore slump with a .271 batting average, 26 HR, and 113 RBI. In 1936, Trosky enjoyed a dream year with a .343 batting average, 42 HR, and a major league leading 162 RBI. He continued a first-rate performance in 1937 and 1938, improving his fielding, learning to hit to left field, and hitting 32 and 19 HR. In 1939, however, Trosky participated in a player rebellion against manager Ossie Vitt. In the "Cleveland Crybabies" incident, Trosky complained that the press singled him out as team captain and for his Russian-sounding name. A series of unexplained illnesses and migraine headaches forced him to drop out of baseball for various periods after the 1941 season. Trosky spent the World War II years in a factory and on a farm and attempted comebacks in 1944 and 1946 with the Chicago White Sox (AL). He left a solid 11-year major league record of 1,561 hits, 331 doubles, 58 triples, 228 HR, a lifetime .302 batting average, and 1,012 RBI. Trosky, who scouted for the Chicago White Sox in 1947 and 1948 and sold real estate in Cedar Rapids, married Lorraine Glenn in November 1933 and had one son, Harold Jr., who played professional baseball.

BIBLIOGRAPHY: Jerry E. Clark, *Anson to Zuber* (Omaha, NE, 1992); John Thorn et al., eds., *Total Indians* (New York, 1996); Bob Feller with Bill Gilbert, *Now Pitching Bob Feller* (New York, 1990); Morris Eckhouse, *Day-by-Day in Cleveland Indians History* (New York, 1983); Lawrence S. Katz, *Baseball in 1939* (Jefferson, NC, 1995); Franklin Lewis, *The Cleveland Indians* (New York, 1949); Hal Trosky, Sr. file, National Baseball Library, Cooperstown, NY.

Eric Solomon

TROUPPE, Quincy Thomas (b. December 25, 1912, Dublin, GA; d. August 10, 1993, Creve Coeur, MO), player, manager, and scout, was the youngest of 10 children born to Charles Trouppe, a Georgia sharecropper, and Mary Trouppe. The Trouppes moved when Quincy was a youngster to Compton Hill in south St. Louis, MO, where Charles was employed by the American Car Foundry. Trouppe attended Vashon High School, located across from the home park of the St. Louis Stars (NNL). He served as the St. Louis Stars' batboy while playing for the Tom Powell American Legion Post 77 and later enrolled at Lincoln University of Missouri.

A 6-foot 3-inch, 200-pound catcher, Trouppe began nearly a quarter century in professional baseball in 1931 with the NNL Champion St. Louis Stars. He also played for the Detroit, MI Wolves–Homestead, PA Grays (EWL) in 1932 and the racially mixed Bismarck, ND Cubs (Independent) from 1933 to 1936, catching for Satchel Paige* and Hilton Smith.* Injuries sidelined Trouppe for the 1937 season, but he returned with the Indianapolis, IN ABCs (NAL) in 1938 and spent six years in the MEL from 1939 to 1944. In 1936, Trouppe also won an amateur boxing championship.

Trouppe excelled as an All-Star player and championship manager in the Negro Leagues, MEL, and Latin American Winter Leagues. His Negro League play led to five East-West All-Star Game appearances (1938, 1945–1948) and a .311 career batting average, including a pinnacle .352 mark with the 1947 Cleveland, OH Buckeyes (NAL). During a three-year stint with the Buckeyes, Trouppe managed the Cleveland Buckeyes to NAL championships in 1945 and 1947 and the 1945 Black World Series crown. The 1947 titlists fielded future major leaguers Vibert Clarke, Sam Jethroe,* Sam Jones,* Al Smith,* and Trouppe. Trouppe played for the Chicago, IL American Giants (NAL) in 1948 and posted a .342 batting average with 10 HR. He hit .282 for Drummondville, Canada (CaPL) in 1949 prior to returning to the MEL for the 1950 and 1951 schedules. His eight MEL campaigns produced a .304 batting mark and three MEL All-Star Game appearances (1943, 1944, 1950). He managed Jalisco, Mexico (MEL) to the top regular season record with a 50–34 win–loss mark and the 1950 second half title, before losing in the MEL Championship Series. He also played winter ball in Colombia, Cuba, Puerto Rico, and Venezuela. Trouppe topped the 1941–1942 PRWL with 57 RBI and managed Caguas, PR to the 1947–1948 PRWL championship. He made the Negro Leagues All-Star team, along with Roy Campanella,* Jethroe, and Jackie Robinson,* which performed in Caracas, Venezuela following the 1945 regular season.

The switch-batting Trouppe performed in eight leagues in seven nations prior to getting the opportunity to play in recognized organized baseball at age 39 with the Cleveland Indians (AL) organization. During the 1952 season, he appeared in six contests with Cleveland and in 84 games with their Indianapolis, IN (AA) farm club.

Trouppe married Dorothy Smith in 1938, but they divorced in 1943. He wed Myralin Donaldson in 1952, and was divorced in 1957. The first marriage produced two sons, while the second produced one daughter. Trouppe, who moved to Los Angeles, CA, married Bessie Cullen in 1962 and owned and operated a restaurant there. He also scouted for the St. Louis Cardinals (NL) and resided in St. Louis, MO at his death. His autobiography, *20 Years Too Soon*, was published in 1977.

BIBLIOGRAPHY: *The Baseball Encyclopedia*, 10th ed. (New York, 1996); Pedro Treto Cisneros, *Enciclopedia del beisbol Mexicano* (Mexico City, Mexico, 1992); Cleveland (OH) *Call & Post*, 1945–1947; Merritt Clifton, *Disorganized Baseball* (Brigham, Quebec, 1982); Rafael Costas, *Enciclopedia beisbol Ponce Leons 1938–1987* (Santo Domingo, DR, 1989); Larry Moffi and Jonathan Kronstadt, *Crossing the Line* (Jefferson, NC, 1994); G. B. Mijares and E. D. Rangel, *El beisbol en Caracas* (Caracas, Venezuela, 1967); *Official Negro American League Statistics*, 1945–1948; James A. Riley, *The Biographical Encyclopedia of the Negro Baseball Leagues* (New York, 1994); Pepe Seda, *Don Q Baseball Cues* (Ponce, Puerto Rico, 1970); Quincy Trouppe, *20 Years Too Soon* (Los Angeles, CA, 1977).

Merl F. Kleinknecht

TROUT, Paul Howard "Dizzy" (b. June 29, 1915, Sandcut, IN; d. February 28, 1972, Harvey, IL), player and sportscaster, blossomed in the same greater–Terre Haute, IN milieu that produced baseball pitching greats Mordecai Brown,* Art Nehf,* and Tommy John.* He married Pearl Ortmann on September 27, 1939 and had 10 children. One son, Steven, pitched in the major leagues from 1978 to 1989 with only moderate success.

The 6-foot 2-inch, 195-pound Trout started his professional baseball career at Terre Haute, IN (3IL) in 1935. He advanced to Indianapolis, IN (AA) at the season's end and pitched there in 1936. After hurling for Toledo, OH (AA) in 1937 and early 1938, he enjoyed an outstanding campaign with

Beaumont, TX (TL). He spent 13 successive seasons with the Detroit Tigers (AL) from 1939 until 1952 and reached stardom during the mid–1940s. Detroit traded him in June 1952 to the Boston Red Sox (AL), where he finished the season. He tried a comeback with the Baltimore Orioles (AL) in 1957, but that attempt lasted for only two appearances. His accomplishments included sharing the AL leadership in wins in 1943 (20) and ranking among the top five the same year in innings (246.2) and games pitched (44), complete games (30), and ERA (2.48), placing second in total wins (27) in 1944, and either tying for or pacing the AL in shutouts with 5 in 1943 and 7 in 1944. During the Tigers' AL pennant–winning 1945 season, he pitched six times and won four decisions in nine days from September 8 to 16. For his career, Trout won 170 contests and lost 161 decisions with a 3.23 ERA. He appeared in the 1940 and 1945 World Series, defeating the Chicago Cubs in the fourth game of the 1945 fall classic, losing two games, and compiling a very low 1.72 ERA.

Trout, who used a colorful red bandana to mop his brow frequently while on the mound, liked a whiskey and Coca Cola for relaxation. Subsequently, Trout broadcast Detroit Tigers games. In 1959, owner Bill Veeck* hired Trout as his driver and as chief promotional representative for the Chicago White Sox (AL). He served as the "straight man" in the frequent tours that the pair made around the "rubber-chicken" circuit. A free-wheeling raconteur, Trout became very popular and continued in his promotional capacity after Veeck sold the club. Cancer gradually debilitated Trout's health and eventually proved fatal.

BIBLIOGRAPHY: Larry Amman, "Newhouser and Trout in 1944," *BRJ* 12 (1983), pp. 18–21; *The Baseball Encyclopedia*, 10th ed. (New York, 1996); Frederick G. Lieb, *The Detroit Tigers* (New York, 1946); Paul Trout file, *TSN* Archives, St. Louis, MO; Paul Trout file, National Baseball Library, Cooperstown, NY; Joe Falls, *Detroit Tigers* (New York, 1975); Fred Smith, *995 Tigers* (Detroit, MI, 1981); William M. Anderson, *The Detroit Tigers* (South Bend, IN, 1996); George Sullivan and David Cataneo, *Detroit Tigers* (New York, 1985); *TSN Official Baseball Register*, 1953.

Lowell L. Blaisdell

TROYAVESKY, Harold Arthura, Sr. *See* Harold Arthur Trosky, Sr.

TRUCKS, Virgil Oliver "Fire" (b. April 26, 1919, Birmingham, AL), player, coach, and scout, was a right-handed pitcher. Trucks, one of the 13 children of Oliver T. and Lula (Belle) Trucks, graduated from high school. He married Mamie Aitken in July 1936 and had three children before their divorce. He married twice more, having two children by his second wife.

At 6 feet, 210 pounds, the burly Trucks performed numerous spectacular pitching feats. He began his professional baseball career at Andalusia, AL (AlFL) in 1938, winning 25 games, pitching two no-hitters, and striking out 418 batters. He divided the 1939 campaign between Alexandria, LA (EL) and Beaumont, TX (TL) and returned to Beaumont in 1940, pitching a seven-inning no-hitter. Trucks hurled for Buffalo, NY (IL) in 1941 and lost a game that marked his fourth no-hitter. In September 1941, he appeared once with the Detroit Tigers (AL).

Trucks spent eight full seasons from 1942 through 1952 with the Detroit Tigers. He lost the entire 1944 campaign and nearly all of the 1945 season in wartime naval service. Trucks also missed the greater part of 1950, having suffered a sore arm following a 1–0 extra-inning victory against Ned Garver* of the St. Louis Browns. With the weak last-place Tigers in 1952, Trucks pitched 1–0 no-hit games against the Washington Senators on May 15 and the New York Yankees on August 25. He divided the 1953 season between the St. Louis Browns (AL) and Chicago White Sox (AL), winning 20 games. He hurled for the Chicago White Sox in 1954 and 1955, returned to the Detroit Tigers in 1956, pitched for the Kansas City Athletics (AL) in 1957 and 1958, and joined the New York Yankees in June 1958. In 1959, he retired after appearing in a few games for Miami, FL (IL).

Trucks attained several of the AL's top five pitching categories, leading the AL in strikeouts (153) in 1949, sharing the lead in shutouts in 1949 (6) and 1954 (5), and placing fourth in wins in 1953. In his only World Series appearance, Trucks achieved a complete game victory in the second contest for the eventually triumphant Detroit Tigers over the Chicago Cubs in 1945. During his major league career he won 177 games and lost 135 decisions for a .567 winning percentage and 3.39 ERA.

Trucks coached for the Pittsburgh Pirates (NL) in 1963 and Buffalo, NY (IL) in 1970 and scouted for the Seattle Pilots (AL) in 1969. He also worked as a sales representative and in public relations, sailing on the S.S. *Norway* cruise ship as a sports celebrity. His honors include election to both the Alabama and Michigan Sports Halls of Fame.

BIBLIOGRAPHY: Virgil Trucks file, National Baseball Library, Cooperstown, NY; Frederick G. Lieb, *The Detroit Tigers* (New York, 1946); Joe Falls, *Detroit Tigers* (New York, 1975); Fred Smith, *995 Tigers* (Detroit, MI, 1981); William M. Anderson, *The Detroit Tigers* (South Bend, IN, 1996); Bill Borst, *Still Last in the American League* (West Bloomfield, MI, 1992); *The Baseball Encyclopedia*, 10th ed. (New York, 1996); Bill Borst, ed., *Ables to Zoldak*, vol. 3 (St. Louis, MO, 1990); Paul MacFarlane, ed., *TSN Daguerreotypes of Great Stars of Baseball* (St. Louis, MO, 1968); Larry Moffi, *This Side of Cooperstown* (Iowa City, IA, 1996); Richard Lindberg, *Who's on Third?* (South Bend, IN, 1983); Virgil Trucks file, *TSN* Archives, St. Louis, MO; Virgil Trucks, letter to Lowell L. Blaisdell, July 25, 1989; Rich Westcott, *Masters of the Diamond* (Jefferson, NC, 1994).

Lowell L. Blaisdell

TUCKER, Thomas Joseph "Tommy," "Foghorn," "Noisy Tom" (b. October 28, 1863, Holyoke, MA; d. October 22, 1935, Montague, MA), player and coach, began his professional baseball career in 1884 with nearby Springfield,

MA (MSA) and played for Newark, NJ (EL) in 1885 and 1886. A switch-hitting first baseman throughout his career, Tucker made his major league debut with the original Baltimore Orioles (AA) in 1887 and compiled a .275 batting average with 85 stolen bases and an AA-leading 1,346 putouts. After raising his batting average to .287 the next season, he enjoyed his finest year in 1889 and led the AA in both hits (196) and batting average (.372). His .372 batting mark that season remains the highest ever for a switch-hitter. In three seasons with the Baltimore Orioles, he batted a composite .311 and averaged 175 hits.

The 5-foot 11-inch, 165-pound Tucker played from 1890 through 1896 with the Boston Beaneaters (NL), managed by Frank Selee,* and helped the Beaneaters win three consecutive NL pennants from 1891 through 1893. During his seven years in Boston, Tucker averaged 146 hits and 92 runs scored and batted a respectable .288. The Boston Beaneaters sold Tucker early in the 1897 season to the Washington Senators (NL), where he hit .338 in 93 games. Tucker split duty between the Brooklyn Bridegrooms (NL) and St. Louis Cardinals (NL) in 1898 and finished his major league career in 1899 with the hapless Cleveland Spiders (NL), who lost a record 120 games. Returning to his native New England, Tucker played minor league baseball for Springfield, MA (EL) in 1900, New London, CT (CtSL) in 1901, and Meriden, CT (CtSL) in 1902. Nicknamed for his boisterous and flamboyant style as a base coach, he was once assaulted by Philadelphia, PA fans after leading his Boston Beaneaters teammates in game-stalling tactics in hopes of a rainout. In his 13-year major league career, Tucker, who threw right-handed, batted .290 with 1,882 hits, 1,084 runs, and 352 stolen bases. He scored more than 100 runs in five seasons and led his league in being hit by pitched balls on five occasions. Tucker tied a major league record with four doubles on July 22, 1893. On July 15, 1897, he collected six hits in six at-bats for the Washington Senators in a game against the Cincinnati Reds. A flashy first baseman, he made dazzling one-handed scoops with his small glove at a time when using two hands was the conventional method.

BIBLIOGRAPHY: *The Baseball Encyclopedia*, 10th ed. (New York, 1996); Boston (MA) *Evening Transcript*, October 22, 1935; Craig Carter, ed., *TSN Complete Baseball Record Book* (St. Louis, MO, 1992); J. Thomas Hetrick, *Misfits! The Cleveland Spiders in 1899* (Jefferson, NC, 1991); John Phillips, *The Spiders—Who Was Who* (Cabin John, MD, 1991); John Thorn et al., eds., *Total Baseball*, 5th ed. (New York, 1997); Robert L. Tiemann and Mark Rucker, eds., *Nineteenth Century Stars* (Kansas City, MO, 1989); Thomas Tucker file, National Baseball Library, Cooperstown, NY; David Nemec, *The Beer and Whisky League* (New York, 1994); Daniel Pearson, *Base Ball in 1889* (Bowling Green, OH, 1993); James H. Bready, *Baseball in Baltimore* (Baltimore, MD, 1998); George V. Touhey, *A History of the Boston Base Ball Club* (Boston, MA, 1897);

Harold Kaese, *The Boston Braves* (New York, 1948); Gary Caruso, *The Braves Encyclopedia* (Philadelphia, PA, 1995).

Raymond D. Kush

TUDOR, John Thomas "Tute" (b. February 2, 1954, Schenectady, NY), player and coach, is the son of Metton Tudor and the grandson of George Robinson, a minor league baseball player. He graduated from Peabody, MA Veterans Memorial High School. Tudor, the MVP in baseball at North Shore CC in Beverly, MA in 1973, received a bachelor's degree in criminal justice at Georgia Southern College in Statesboro, GA in 1978. The Boston Red Sox (AL) signed Tudor in January 1976. The 6-foot, 185-pound left-hander pitched for Winston-Salem, NC (CrL), Bristol, CT (EL), and Pawtucket, RI (IL) from 1976 to 1980, winning 33 and losing 28.

After being called up in September 1979, Tudor returned to the Boston Red Sox at midseason in 1980 and posted eight wins and five losses with a 3.02 ERA. He won 13 games each in 1982 and 1983. In December 1983, Tudor was traded to the Pittsburgh Pirates (NL) for outfielder Mike Easler. In 1984, he captured 12 of 23 decisions for the last-place Pittsburgh Pirates. In December 1984, the Pittsburgh Pirates swapped Tudor to the St. Louis Cardinals (NL) for outfielder George Hendrick* and catcher Steve Barnard.

The 1985 season began in a disappointing manner, as Tudor dropped seven of eight decisions. Dave Bettencourt, Tudor's high school catcher, watched a televised St. Louis Cardinals game, however, and noticed a flaw in the southpaw's motion. He phoned his old friend, who immediately corrected it and built one of the finest pitching stretches in baseball history. From June through season's end, Tudor won 20 of 21 decisions. He hurled 10 shutouts, a record for Cardinals southpaws. Tudor's four-month streak included a one-hitter, a two-hitter, and two three-hitters. He opened September with three straight shutouts and 31 consecutive scoreless innings. Tudor finished the season with a career-best 1.93 ERA, being named to the *TSN*, UPI, and AP All-Star teams. Dwight Gooden,* however, edged him out for the NL Cy Young Award. Tudor defeated the Los Angeles Dodgers in an NL Championship Series game and triumphed twice over the Kansas City Royals in the World Series, before yielding five runs in the St. Louis Cardinals' seventh-game loss.

After enjoying a 13–7 season in 1986, he missed half of the 1987 campaign when New York Mets catcher Barry Lyons fell into the St. Louis dugout chasing a foul ball and broke Tudor's knee. Tudor returned in August 1987, ending with 10 wins and two losses. Tudor began the 1988 campaign on the disabled list with a sore elbow. The St. Louis Cardinals traded Tudor to the Los Angeles Dodgers (NL) in August 1988 for outfielder Pedro Guerrero.* Tudor underwent surgery on his left elbow during the off-season and pitched in only six games in 1989. He made one appearance with the Los

Angeles Dodgers in the 1988 NL Championship Series against the New York Mets and one in the 1988 World Series against the Oakland Athletics.

Tudor returned to the St. Louis Cardinals as a free agent in December 1989, winning 12, losing 4, and compiling a 2.40 ERA in 1990 despite spending time on the disabled list. His 62–26 win–loss record with the St. Louis Cardinals produced a .705 winning percentage, the highest in team history for a hurler with at least 50 decisions. He was employed as a minor league pitching instructor for the St. Louis Cardinals in 1991 and 1992, the Philadelphia Phillies (NL) in 1993 and 1994, and the Texas Rangers (AL) since 1995.

Tudor, who married Gail Norgard on November 12, 1988 and resides in Peabody, MA, enjoys playing ice hockey and scuba diving.

BIBLIOGRAPHY: Peter Gammons, *Beyond the Sixth Game* (Boston, MA, 1985); Peter Golenbock, *Fenway* (New York, 1992); Robert Redmount, *The Red Sox Encyclopedia* (Champaign, IL, 1998); Rob Rains, *The St. Louis Cardinals* (New York, 1992); Bob Broeg and Jerry Vickery, *St. Louis Cardinals Encyclopedia* (Grand Rapids, MI, 1998); Peter Gammons, "John Tudor: His Competitive Fire Burned Brightly in '85," *BD* 45 (January 1986), pp. 65–67; Peter Gammons, "How Long Will It Last?" *SI* 72 (May 21, 1990), pp. 78–80ff; Joe Henderson, "John Tudor: The Man and the Image," *BD* 45 (August 1986), pp. 48–55; Kip Ingle and Brian Bartow, *St. Louis Cardinals 1990 Media Guide* (St. Louis, MO, 1990); Dan Schlossberg, *Baseball Stars, 1986* (Chicago, IL, 1986); Mike Shatzkin, ed., *The Ballplayers* (New York, 1990); John Tudor file, National Baseball Library, Cooperstown, NY.

                                                              Frank J. Olmsted

TURLEY, Robert Lee "Bob," "Bullet Bob" (b. September 19, 1930, Troy, IL), player, is the son of Delbert Turley and Henrietta Turley, packing house workers. On the evening that his class graduated from East Side High School in East St. Louis, IL, he began his professional baseball career with Bellville, IL (IlSL).

Turley began his major league career with the St. Louis Browns (AL) from 1951 to 1953, spending most of the 1952 and 1953 seasons in the military. In 1954, the St. Louis Browns moved to Baltimore and became the Orioles (AL). The shift agreed with the 6-foot 2-inch, 215-pound right-handed power pitcher, who won 14 games and lost 15 for a seventh-place team. He also led the AL with 185 strikeouts and 181 walks. Turley reached his peak performance from 1955 to 1962 with the New York Yankees (AL). In November 1954, the Yankees acquired him in a massive 18-player deal. From 1955 through 1957, Turley won 38 decisions and lost 23 games and helped the New York Yankees win AL pennants each of those seasons.

In 1958, Turley enjoyed the best campaign of his career. His 21–7 record marked the best in the AL, as he led the AL in games won, winning percentage (.750), walks (128), and complete games (19). He easily won the AL Cy Young Award and performed well during the World Series against the

Milwaukee Braves. Although lasting less than one inning in Game 2, Turley hurled a five-hit shutout in Game 5, recorded a save in Game 6, and won the deciding Game 7 with a six-inning relief stint. He was named the World Series MVP and drove away with the Corvette, awarded by *Sport* magazine. "That was the kind of year everyone dreams about," he recalled.

But the dream proved short-lived. Turley pitched four more years for the New York Yankees with mixed success, recording marks of 8–11 in 1959 and 9–3 in 1960. He in 1960 developed bone chips in his arm, which began to limit his effectiveness. In October 1962, the New York Yankees sold Turley to the Los Angeles Angels (AL). In 1963, Turley pitched for both the Los Angeles Angels and Boston Red Sox (AL) with little success. He retired following that season with a 12 year major league career record of 101 wins, 85 losses, and 3.64 ERA.

Turley became a successful securities salesperson and worked in insurance management for A. L. Williams. He founded his own company, Primerica Financial Services, in 1977. He married Clare Weaver in April 1952 and lives in Naples, FL. They have five grown children.

BIBLIOGRAPHY: Bob Turley file, National Baseball Library, Cooperstown, NY; C. Robert Barnett, interview with Bob Turley, August 17, 1996; Tony Kubek and Terry Pluto, *Sixty-one* (New York, 1987); Brent P. Kelley, *They Too Wore Pinstripes* (Jefferson, NC, 1998); Rich Marazzi, " '55 Yankees Gather for Reunion Show in Flushing," *SCD* 22 (May 26, 1995), pp. 130–131; Ralph Houk and Robert W. Creamer, *Season of Glory* (New York, 1988); Dom Forker, *Sweet Seasons* (Dallas, TX, 1991); Mark Gallagher, *The Yankee Encyclopedia*, vol. 3 (Champaign, IL, 1997); Dave Anderson et al., *The Yankees* (New York, 1979); Rich Marazzi and Len Fiorito, *Aaron to Zuverink* (New York, 1982); *TSN Baseball Register*, 1960; *The Baseball Encyclopedia*, 10th ed. (New York, 1996).

C. Robert Barnett

TURNER, James Riley "Jim," "Milkman Jim" (b. August 6, 1903, Antioch, TN; d. November 29, 1998, Nashville, TN), player, coach, and manager, was a 6-foot, 185-pound pitcher who attended Antioch High School and played amateur and semiprofessional baseball. His parents were Charles Gray Turner and Hattie Mae Turner. His nickname came from his off-season dairy business. Turner, dedicated to hard work and eager to learn, entered professional baseball with Paris, TN (KL) in 1923 and began a slow climb to the major leagues as a right-handed pitcher. Scouts, looking for the live arm and great fastball, often passed him over. Turner relied on control and intelligence, advancing slowly. Turner admitted, "I was in the minors 14 years . . . a long, hard haul." General manager Bob Quinn* of the Boston Bees (NL) purchased Turner in 1936 from Indianapolis, IN (AA).

Nonetheless, the 34-year-old Turner astounded everyone in 1937 with a 20–11 mark and an NL-leading 2.38 ERA, being the first rookie hurler to win 20 games since Grover Cleveland Alexander* in 1911. He also led NL hurlers in complete games (24) and shutouts (5). Without overpowering speed, Turner "cut corners," threw the batter off stride, and forced a hitter "to bite at bad ones." He pitched for the NL in the 1938 All-Star Game. A subpar season followed, however, causing him to be traded in December 1939 to the Cincinnati Reds (NL). Turner helped the Cincinnati Reds win an NL pennant and World Series against the Detroit Tigers in 1940 with a 14–7 mark and 2.89 ERA. After being traded to the New York Yankees (AL) in July 1942, he appeared in the World Series that year against the St. Louis Cardinals. A relief pitcher through 1945, he mastered the art of pitching low balls to make the batter hit grounders and threw strikes. His 10 saves in 1945 paced the AL. He won 287 games altogether, including a 69–60 win–loss record and 3.22 ERA in nine major league seasons.

After managing two minor league clubs, Turner returned to the New York Yankees as pitching coach in 1949. Manager Casey Stengel,* who had piloted Turner in Boston, recalled the latter's dedication and intelligence. The Yankees' skipper relied considerably on Turner, stating, "I've got to talk to Jim." Turner's supervision of their staff paid off with five consecutive World Series titles from 1949 to 1953. He left the New York Yankees after 11 seasons following 1959 and became pitching coach for the Cincinnati Reds from 1961 to 1965 under manager Fred Hutchinson.* His major league career climaxed in a final term as pitching coach with the New York Yankees from 1966 to 1973 under manager Ralph Houk.* Altogether, he played or coached in 13 World Series and spent a record 51 consecutive years in professional baseball.

Young pitchers appreciated Turner's realistic approach and ability to communicate. Turner stressed "condition and control." During spring training, he considered running essential to strengthen arms and legs and believed that an athlete could not really play himself into shape. As for control, Turner remarked, "You keep on throwing until you get it." He believed only hard work would suffice and deemed mastery of the fastball, curve, and change-up was necessary. "Jim always talks sense," Houk observed.

Turner married Annie Pauline Sanford on October 2, 1926 and had two daughters. He was elected to the Tennessee Sports Hall of Fame and regularly attended New York Yankees' and Cincinnati Reds' old-timer's games and Nashville, TN Sounds (SA) baseball club contests. Turner remained grateful to baseball for his 51 consecutive seasons to which he contributed his dedication, intelligence, and compatibility.

BIBLIOGRAPHY: Martin Appel, *Yesterday's Heroes* (New York, 1988); Jim Turner file, National Baseball Library, Cooperstown, NY; Harold Kaese, *The Boston Braves* (New York, 1948); Al Hirshberg, *The Braves, the Pick, and the Shovel* (Boston, MA, 1948); *The Baseball Encyclopedia*, 10th ed. (New York, 1996); Lee Allen, *The Cincinnati Reds* (New York, 1948); Bob Rathgeber, *Cincinnati Reds Scrapbook* (Virginia Beach, VA, 1982); Ritter Collett, *The Cincinnati Reds* (Virginia Beach, VA, 1976); Gary Caruso, *The Braves Encyclopedia* (Philadelphia, PA, 1995); Mark Gallagher, *The Yankee Ency-*

clopedia, vol. 3 (Champaign, IL, 1997); Peter Golenbock, *Dynasty* (New York, 1975); Dom Forker, *The Men of Autumn* (Dallas, TX, 1989); Dom Forker, *Sweet Seasons* (Dallas, TX, 1991); Bill Corum, "Turner: Yankee Man Behind the Scenes," New York *Journal-American*, March 13, 1952; L. H. Gregory, "A Pitcher's Face Tells the Story," *BD* 7 (July 1948); Joe King, "Turner's Success Speeds Trend to Pitching Coaches," *TSN*, July 9, 1958; Ed Rumill, "A Turn with Turner," *BM* 41 (September 1945); Fred Russell, "Milkman Jim Starts 48th Season over Same Route," *TSN*, February 28, 1970; Paul Shannon, "Jim Turner, 20 Game Winner for the Bees," *TSN*, March 10, 1938; Joseph M. Sheehan, "Sophomore Pitchers Help Yankee Flag Drive," *NYT*, August 31, 1956; J. G. Taylor Spink, "Milkman Puts Cream in Marse Joe's Coffee," *TSN*, June 14, 1945; J. G. Taylor Spink, "Professor Turner's Tips on Twirling," *TSN*, April 7, 1954; John Thorn et al., eds., *Total Baseball*, 5th ed. (New York, 1997); Joe Trimble, "Fireman Jim Turner Rescues Yankees," New York *Daily News*, June 10, 1945.

William J. Miller

TYLER, George Albert "Lefty" (b. December 14, 1889, Derry, NH; d. September 29, 1953, Lowell, MA), player and umpire, pitched on two NL championship teams, the 1914 Boston Braves and the 1918 Chicago Cubs. In 12 major league seasons between 1910 and 1921, he won 127 games and lost 116 decisions with a 2.95 ERA.

Born into an Irish-Catholic family, he was the son of John F. Tyler and Martha J. (McCannon) Tyler. He pitched and his brother, Fred, caught for local amateur teams, St. Anselm College, and the semiprofessional Derry Athletics. Tyler entered professional baseball with Lowell, MA (NEL) in 1909. After winning 19 games in 1910, he joined the Boston Braves (NL). He married Lillian D. McCarthy while pitching in Lowell.

Tyler pitched from 1910 to 1917 for the Boston Braves. Never the club's ace, he still won 92 games as a rotation workhorse. He led the NL in complete games in 1913, but also paced the NL with 22 losses in 1912. In 1914, the Boston Braves surprised the baseball world by capturing the NL pennant and upsetting the Philadelphia Athletics in the World Series. The 6-foot, 175-pound, left-handed Tyler contributed 16 wins and a 2.79 ERA that season. In the third game of the World Series, he pitched the first 10 innings. The Boston Braves removed him for a pinch-hitter and won the game in 12 innings.

In January 1918, the Boston Braves traded Tyler to the Chicago Cubs (NL). The deal paid quick dividends for the Chicago Cubs, as Tyler compiled a 19–8 record with a 2.00 ERA. In the 1918 World Series, Tyler pitched three games. He defeated Joe Bush* in Game 2 and drove in two runs in a 3–1 victory. In Game 4, Tyler dueled with Babe Ruth* before being lifted for a pinch hitter in the seventh inning. Game 6 saw him lose another tightly pitched game, 2–1, to Carl Mays,* as the Chicago Cubs lost the World Series to the Boston Red Sox. Tyler's baseball career quickly faded following his World Series heroics. A sore arm limited him to a 2–2 record in 1919. Disappointing seasons followed in 1920 and 1921. After umpiring in the NEL and EL through 1932, he worked for the New England Power Co. until a fatal heart attack.

BIBLIOGRAPHY: William Basel, "The Troubled World Series of 1918," *YM* 54 (May 1990), pp. 40ff; Warren Brown, *The Chicago Cubs* (New York, 1946); Harold Kaese, *The Boston Braves* (New York, 1948); Joe Overfield, "How Losing an Exhibition Sparked Miracle Braves," *BD* 20 (May 1961), pp. 83–85; Al Hirshberg, *Braves, the Pick and the Shovel* (Boston, MA, 1948); Gary Caruso, *The Braves Encyclopedia* (Philadelphia, PA, 1995); Eddie Gold and Art Ahrens, *The Golden Era Cubs, 1876–1940* (Chicago, IL, 1985); Jim Enright, *Chicago Cubs* (New York, 1975); Warren Wilbert and William Hageman, *Chicago Cubs: Seasons at the Summit* (Champaign, IL, 1997).

William E. Akin

U

UHLE, George Ernest "The Bull" (b. September 18, 1898, Cleveland, OH; d. February 26, 1985, Lakewood, OH), player, coach, and scout, grew up in Cleveland and attended Cleveland West High School for two years. Uhle pitched for the Cleveland East Views, Dubsky Furnitures, and Standard Parts before the Cleveland Indians (AL) signed him to a $1,500 contract in 1919. During his rookie season, he compiled a 10–5 win–loss record with a 2.91 ERA. The 6-foot, 190-pound right-hander hurled for the Cleveland Indians from 1919 to 1928, Detroit Tigers (AL) from 1929 to April 1933, New York Giants (NL) from April until July 1933, and New York Yankees (AL) from July 1933 to 1934. Uhle pitched for Toledo, OH (AA) in 1934, returned to the Cleveland Indians in 1936, and finished his career with Buffalo, NY (IL) in 1938 and 1939.

In 10 seasons with Cleveland, Uhle won 147 games and lost only 118 decisions. He led the AL in victories and innings pitched in 1923 and 1926, in games started, games completed, and hits surrendered twice, and in shutouts and walks once. Three times, Uhle won over 20 games. His best season came in 1926, when he compiled 27 victories, allowed only 2.83 earned runs per games, struck out 159 batters, and led the AL with a .711 winning percentage. In the 1920 World Series against the Brooklyn Robins, Uhle pitched in two games without a decision and allowed one hit and struck out three batters in three innings. Uhle claimed credit for developing the slider while throwing batting practice to Harry Heilmann* of the Detroit Tigers. He hurled 20 innings of a 21-inning 1929 game and outdueled Ted Lyons* of the Chicago White Sox for the victory, but his arm never recovered from the strain.

In 17 major league seasons, Uhle won 200 games, lost 166 contests, and compiled a 3.99 ERA. In 513 appearances, he won 10 or more games 10 times, allowed 3,417 hits and 1,635 runs in 3,119.2 innings pitched, issued

966 bases on balls, struck out 1,135 batters, and hurled 21 shutouts. New York Yankees slugger Babe Ruth* considered Uhle the most difficult pitcher to hit and slugged only two HR off him. An excellent batter, Uhle frequently pinch hit and belted nine career HR. Uhle hit three doubles in one game and drove in six runs in another contest. He clouted a grand slam HR in 1921 and two years later became one of only 17 AL pitchers ever to win 20 games and compile a batting average over .300. Uhle won 26 games that year and batted .361, third best ever for AL pitchers. His 52 hits in 1923 (equalled by Wes Ferrell* in 1935) were the most made by a pitcher in one season, while his 393 career hits rank him sixth on the all-time list. Uhle compiled a .289 career batting average, second only to Ruth's .304 career mark among pitchers.

Uhle served as coach for the Cleveland Indians in 1937, Buffalo, NY (IL) in 1938 and 1939, Chicago Cubs (NL) in 1940, and Washington Senators (AL) in 1944, and as scout for the Brooklyn Dodgers (NL) in 1941 and 1942. Uhle married Helen Schultz on October 20, 1920 and had two sons and one daughter. Following his retirement from baseball, he was employed as a manufacturer's representative for steel and aluminum companies in Bay Village, OH.

BIBLIOGRAPHY: Franklin Lewis, *The Cleveland Indians* (New York, 1949); Richard Bak, *Cobb Would Have Caught It* (Detroit, MI, 1991); Frederick G. Lieb, *The Detroit Tigers* (New York, 1976); Joe Falls, *Detroit Tigers* (New York, 1975); Fred Smith, *995 Tigers* (Detroit, MI, 1981); Gene Karst and Martin J. Jones, Jr., *Who's Who in Professional Baseball* (New Rochelle, NY, 1973); Craig Carter, ed., *TSN Daguerreotypes*, 8th ed. (St. Louis, MO, 1990); Joseph L. Reichler, *The Great All-Time Baseball Record Book* (New York, 1981); *The Baseball Encyclopedia*, 10th ed. (New York, 1996); George Uhle file, National Baseball Library, Cooperstown, NY.

John L. Evers and Harry A. Jebsen, Jr.

V

VALENZUELA, Fernando (Anguamea) (b. November 1, 1960, Navojoa, Mexico), player, is the youngest of nine children born to farmers Avelino Valenzuela and Hemeregilda (Anguamea) Valenzuela and grew up in Etcho-huaquila, Mexico. Valenzuela at age 13 began to play organized baseball with his seven brothers on the local town club. In 1976, his professional baseball career commenced in the rugged MEL. He played with numerous clubs, including Los Mayos de Navojoa. Los Angeles Dodgers (NL) scout Mike Brito in 1978 signed Valenzuela, who ascended through their minor league chain the next two years. Valenzuela eventually debuted with the Los Angeles Dodgers on September 15, 1980 against the Atlanta Braves. The Mexican lefty dazzled hitters with his screwball and did not allow an earned run in 17.2 innings pitched that year.

Valenzuela captured the national spotlight in 1980, when the rookie opened that campaign with eight consecutive victories. During that remarkable streak, he tossed seven complete games, hurled five shutouts, and boasted a 0.50 ERA. The young left-hander also became a folk hero, particularly to the large Mexican American community in the Los Angeles area. In June 1981, President Ronald Reagan invited him to a White House luncheon during a visit by Mexican president Jose Lopez de Portillo. Valenzuela on December 28, 1981 married Linda Burgos, a Merido, Mexico, schoolteacher. They have three children, Ricardo, Fernando, Jr., and Linda. The southpaw completed his strike-shortened 1981 "dream season" as the NL leader in complete games (11), shutouts (8), innings pitched (192.1), and strikeouts (180). For his efforts, he won both the NL Cy Young* and NL Rookie of the Year Awards. No major leaguer prior to that time had ever accomplished such a feat.

Valenzuela continued to pitch quality baseball throughout the 1980s. He led the NL in games won (21) and complete games (20) in 1986 and again paced the NL in complete games (12) in 1987. Valenzuela's durability also became his trademark, as the screwball artist averaged 255 innings pitched per season between 1981 and 1987. He also appeared in six consecutive All-Star Games from 1981 to 1986. Valenzuela, beset with arm troubles, was released by the Los Angeles Dodgers in March 1991 and joined the California Angels (AL) that May, but lasted only a few games. After a year's MEL stint, however, Valenzuela reemerged in the major leagues for the 1993 season with the Baltimore Orioles (AL). That year, the left-hander finished with an 8–10 win–loss record. In 1994, Valenzuela compiled a 10–3 record with the Jalisco, Mexico Cowboys of the MEL and appeared in eight games for the Philadelphia Phillies (NL).

In April 1995, the San Diego Padres (NL) signed him. He finished 8–3 in 1995 and 13–8 with a 3.62 ERA in 1996, helping the Padres win the NL West. Valenzuela split 1997 between the San Diego Padres and St. Louis Cardinals (NL), winning only two of 14 decisions. The St. Louis Cardinals released him in July 1997. He subsequently pitched in the MEL. His 17 major league seasons included a 173–153 win–loss record, 31 shutouts, 2,074 strikeouts in 2,930 innings, and a 3.54 ERA.

BIBLIOGRAPHY: Fernando Valenzuela file, National Baseball Library, Cooperstown, NY; Tony Castro, "Something Screwy Going on Here," *SI* 63 (July 8, 1985), pp. 31–37; K. Gurnick, "Valenzuela Masterly Amid Dodger Mishaps," *NYT Biographical Service* 17 (August 1986), pp. 1019–1021; Robert Heuer, "Etchohuaquila: Tracing Fernando's Roots," *TSN*, June 13, 1981; William F. McNeil, *The Dodgers Encyclopedia* (Champaign, IL, 1997); Tommy Lasorda and David Fisher, *The Artful Dodger* (New York, 1985); Peter C. Bjarkman, *Baseball's Great Dynasties: The Dodgers* (New York, 1990); Stanley Cohen, *Dodgers! The First 100 Years* (New York, 1990); Mike Littwin, *Fernando* (Los Angeles, CA, 1981); Robert E. Kelly, *Baseball's Best* (Jefferson, NC, 1988); F. Paramo, "Sport Interview," *Sport* 77 (July 1986), pp. 19ff; Eddie Rivera, "In America, Only in the Land of Opportunity . . . Could a Kid from Anywhere Go to Sleep a Pauper and Wake Up a Millionaire," *IS* 9 (June 1987), pp. 45–47, 50–52; Ken Young, *Cy Young Award Winners* (New York, 1994).

Samuel O. Regalado

VALO, Elmer William (b. March 5, 1921, Ribnik, Czechoslovakia; d. July 19, 1998, Palmerton, PA), player, scout, manager, and coach, spent 20 years in the major leagues as an outfielder best known for steady batting, fearless crashing into walls, and excellent pinch hitting.

Until age six, Valo lived on a Czechoslovakian farm. He never saw a baseball until his parents, Joseph Valo and Catherine Valo, moved to the United States. His father worked in Palmerton, PA. Valo starred in baseball at Palmerton High School and played with numerous teams in the Palmerton and anthracite coal regions.

Although still in high school, Valo in 1938 was signed by Connie Mack* of the Philadelphia Athletics (AL). After Valo graduated in 1939, Philadelphia optioned him to Federalsburg, MD (ESL) and recalled him late in the season. In 1940, he played for Wilmington, DE (ISL). After leading the ISL with a .364 batting average, he played six games for the Athletics. Valo divided the 1941 campaign between Wilmington and the Philadelphia Athletics and remained with the Athletics from 1942 to 1956, spending 1943 to 1945 in military service and moving with the franchise to Kansas City, MO in 1955. The Philadelphia Phillies (NL) signed him in May 1956 and traded him to the Brooklyn Dodgers (NL) in April 1957. In 1958, the Dodgers franchise moved to Los Angeles. Valo began the 1959 season with the Seattle, WA Rainiers (PCL) and finished the campaign with the Cleveland Indians (AL). In 1960, he played eight games with the New York Yankees (AL) and joined the Washington Senators (AL) in May. Valo moved with that franchise to Minnesota as the Twins for the 1961 season, making it the third club he played for that shifted its franchise. He began 1961 with the Minnesota Twins, but was released after 33 games and rejoined the Philadelphia Phillies. After the 1961 campaign, he retired as a player.

The solidly built 5-foot 10-inch, 190-pound line-drive hitter, who hit left-handed and threw right, batted .282 with 1,420 hits, including 228 doubles, 73 triples, and 58 HR in 1,806 major league games. He scored 768 runs, batted in 601 runs, and drew 942 walks. On May 1, 1949 Valo hit two triples with the bases loaded against the Washington Senators. The valuable pinch hitter batted safely 90 times in 386 appearances. Defensively, Valo possessed a strong arm and often collided with the wall while catching deep fly balls. His collisions led to broken ribs and shoulder injuries.

Valo coached two years for the Cleveland Indians (AL), managed two seasons in the Cleveland Indians' farm system, and worked in public relations and scouted for the Philadelphia Phillies until 1982. The Palmerton resident married Anna Zelienka on November 8, 1941 and had four children.

BIBLIOGRAPHY: Martin Appel, *Yesterday's Heroes* (New York, 1988); "Elmer Valo, 77," *SCD* 25 (August 21, 1998), p. 12; Frederick G. Lieb, *Connie Mack* (New York, 1945); Rich Marazzi, "Elmer Valo Hustled His Way to a 20-Year Career," *SCD* 21 (October 7, 1994), pp. 140–141; Connie Mack, *My 66 Years in the Big Leagues* (Philadelphia, PA, 1950); Jerome C. Romanowski, *The Mackmen* (Upper Darby, PA, 1979); *TSN Baseball Register*, 1961; Rich Westcott, *Diamond Greats* (Westport, CT, 1988); Elmer Valo file, National Baseball Library, Cooperstown, NY.

Ralph S. Graber

VANCE. Clarence Arthur "Dazzy" (b. March 4, 1891, Orient, IA; d. February 16, 1961, Homosassa Springs, FL), player, was the son of A. T. Vance and Sarah (Ritchie) Vance and grew up on farms in Iowa and Nebraska. His famous nickname derived from an often used childhood phrase, "Ain't that a daisy." Vance, however, pronounced the last word "dazzy." After graduating from rural Hastings, NE High School, Vance played professionally for Red Cloud, NE (NeSL) in 1912, but did not reach the major leagues permanently until 1922. After pitching briefly for the Pittsburgh Pirates (NL) in 1915 and New York Yankees (AL) in 1915 and 1918, he won his first major league game at age 31 in 1922. The 6-foot 2-inch, 200-pound right-hander had developed an exaggerated leg kick, which caused him control problems throughout his minor league career. Upon finding his control, however, Vance became the premier NL pitcher.

In his rookie season with the second division Brooklyn Robins (NL), Vance won 18 games and led the NL in strikeouts. He walked only 840 career batters and compiled 2,045 career strikeouts, pacing the NL in that category seven consecutive seasons. He topped the NL three times in ERA, four times in shutouts, and twice in victories and complete games. He threw a no-hit game against the Philadelphia Phillies in 1925 as well as one-hit games in 1923 and 1925. Although pitching for a habitual second division club, he won 197 games and lost only 140 decisions with 29 shutouts and a 3.24 ERA. He hurled for the Robins from 1922 to 1932, performed with the St. Louis Cardinals (NL) from 1933 through June 1934, the Cincinnati Reds (NL) the remainder of 1934, and finished his career with the Brooklyn Dodgers (NL) in 1935. He appeared in the 1934 World Series with the triumphant St. Louis Cardinals against the Detroit Tigers.

Vance won the initial NL MVP Award in 1924, leading the NL with 28 victories, 305 complete games, 262 strikeouts, and a 2.16 ERA. He outpolled Rogers Hornsby,* who that year had set a major league record with a .424 batting average, because one voter failed to place the latter on the ballot. Vance used the award to negotiate a highly publicized three-year contract worth $47,500 from Brooklyn owner Charles Ebbets.* By the end of the 1920s, Vance became the highest paid major league pitcher and achieved spectacular success despite playing on the erratic Dodgers. Managed by Wilbert Robinson* and led by Babe Herman* and Vance, the Dodgers were known for bizarre behavior, eccentric plays, and inconsistent baseball. The fun-loving, gregarious Vance earned the respect of his fellow players. During the land boom of the 1920s, Vance invested in Florida real estate. Following retirement from baseball in 1935, he managed his extensive realty operations and operated a hunting and fishing lodge around Homosassa Springs, FL. In 1955, he was elected to the National Baseball Hall of Fame.

BIBLIOGRAPHY: Joseph Cardello, "Dazzy Vance in 1930," *BRJ* 25 (1996), pp. 127–130; Jerry E. Clark, *Anson to Zuber* (Omaha, NE, 1992); Frank Graham, *The Brooklyn Dodgers* (New York, 1945); Richard Goldstein, *Superstars and Screwballs* (New York, 1991); Robert E. Hood, *The Gashouse Gang* (New York, 1978); Tommy Holmes, *The Dodgers* (New York, 1975); Peter C. Bjarkman, *Baseball's Great Dynasties: The Dodgers* (New York, 1990); William F. McNeil, *The Dodgers Encyclopedia* (Champaign, IL, 1997); Stanley Cohen, *Dodgers! The First 100 Years* (New York, 1990); *NYT*, February 17, 1961; *The Baseball Encyclopedia*, 10th ed. (New York, 1996); Lowell Reidenbaugh, *100 Years of National League Baseball* (St. Louis, MO, 1976); Harold Seymour, *Baseball: The Golden Age* (New York, 1971); Arthur Vance file, National Baseball Library,

Cooperstown, NY; Arthur Vance with Furman Bisher, "I'd Hate to Pitch Nowadays," *SEP* 228 (August 20, 1955), pp. 27ff.

Harry A. Jebsen, Jr.

VAN HALTREN, George Edward Martin "Rip" (b. March 30, 1866, St. Louis, MO; d. September 29, 1945, Oakland, CA), player, manager, umpire, and scout, grew up in Oakland, CA, where his family had moved when he was three years old. Van Haltren gained prominence in the San Francisco Bay area in 1886 while pitching and playing outfield for the amateur Greenhood and Morans, under the management of Colonel T. P. Robinson. He began his professional career the following year with the Chicago White Stockings (NL), managed by Cap Anson.* In his first season, the left-handed Van Haltren was used as a utility outfielder and spot starting pitcher. He compiled an 11–7 record with 18 complete games, sharing mound duties with the redoubtable John Clarkson* and Mark Baldwin.*

In 1888 the 5-foot 11-inch, 170-pound left-hander divided his time between the mound and the outfield, posting a mediocre 13–13 pitching record and batting a respectable .283. Given the regular left field position the next year, he hit .309 as part of a skillful outfield trio that included Jimmy Ryan* in center field and High Duffy* in right field. In 1890 Van Haltren jumped to the Brooklyn Wonders of the ill-fated PL, where he played the outfield and posted a 15–10 record in 28 games as a pitcher. He played with the Baltimore Orioles (AA) in 1891, managing the team for the last week of the season. Van Haltren remained as player–manager when Baltimore shifted to the NL in 1892, but was relieved of managerial duties after the Orioles opened with a dismal 1–14 record. He was traded to the Pittsburgh Pirates (NL) for outfielder Joe Kelley* in September 1892 and hit .338 in 1893 as the Pirates starting center fielder.

In 1894 Van Haltren signed with the New York Giants (NL) and became a fixture in center field. From 1894 through 1901, Van Haltren averaged 185 hits, 115 runs scored, and a composite .327 batting mark. He led the NL in triples (21) in 1896, at-bats (654) in 1898, and stolen bases (45) in 1900. In 1902, he broke his leg while sliding and missed most of the season. In 1903, he lost the starting center field job to Roger Bresnahan* and was sent to Seattle, WA (PCL) at the end of the year by New York Giants manager John McGraw.* With Seattle in 1904, Van Haltren knocked out 253 hits and led the PCL with a robust 941 at-bats.

In 1905, Oakland, CA Oaks (PCL) owner Cal Ewing signed the 39-year-old Van Haltren as player-manager. As a regular Oaks outfielder for the next four years, he averaged 184 hits in over 187 games per season. He was released by Ewing in June 1909 and finished the year as a PCL umpire. He scouted for Pittsburgh Pirates (NL) owner Barney Dreyfuss* for two years (1910–1911) and umpired in the NWL in 1912.

In 17 major league seasons, Van Haltren played in 1,984 games, collected

2,532 hits, scored 1,639 runs, and batted .316. As a pitcher, he started 68 games, completed 65, and finished with a 40–31 record and 4.05 ERA. In 1887, he set a major league record as a rookie hurler by walking 16 batters in one game. The following season, he pitched a six-inning no-hitter to defeat the Pittsburgh Alleghenys, 1–0. In 1901, Van Haltren roomed with Giants rookie Christy Mathewson* and helped the young hurler develop into one of the game's finest pitchers.

BIBLIOGRAPHY: Fred Stein and Mike Peters, *Giants Diary* (Berkeley, CA, 1987); James D. Hardy, Jr., *The New York Giants Baseball Club* (Jefferson, NC, 1996); Frank Graham, *The New York Giants* (New York, 1946); Frederick G. Lieb, *The Pittsburgh Pirates* (New York, 1948); Eddie Gold and Art Ahrens, *The Golden Era Cubs, 1876–1940* (Chicago, IL, 1985); George Van Haltren file, National Baseball Library, Cooperstown, NY; Warren Brown, *The Chicago Cubs* (New York, 1946); Craig Carter, ed., *TSN Daguerreotypes*, 8th ed. (St. Louis, MO, 1990); *The Baseball Encyclopedia*, 10th ed. (New York, 1996); San Francisco *Chronicle*, October 3, 1945; Robert L. Tiemann and Mark Rucker, eds., *Nineteenth Century Stars* (Kansas City, MO, 1989); David Quentin Voigt, *American Baseball*, vol. 1 (Norman, OK, 1966).

                                                                              Raymond D. Kush

VAN SLYKE, Andrew James "Andy," "Slick" (b. December 21, 1960, Utica, NY), player, starred as an All-America in baseball at New Hartford High School, where his father, Jim, served as principal. The St. Louis Cardinals (NL) selected the 6-foot 2-inch, 195-pound outfielder in the first round (the sixth player taken overall) of the June 1979 free agent draft. Van Slyke, who batted left-handed and threw right-handed, debuted for the St. Louis Cardinals in June 1983 and was named the Cardinals Rookie of the Year by the St. Louis BBWAA chapter. In 1986, Van Slyke led the St. Louis Cardinals in HR (13) and total bases (189) and shared the team lead in RBI (61).

The following year, the St. Louis Cardinals traded Van Slyke to the Pittsburgh Pirates (NL). A fixture in center field, the witty, talkative Van Slyke utilized his speed and a strong, accurate arm to win five consecutive Rawlings Gold Glove Awards from 1988 to 1992. Van Slyke's offensive skills also impressed the baseball world. In 1988, Van Slyke hit .288 with 101 runs scored, 25 HR, 100 RBI, 30 stolen bases, and an NL-leading 15 triples. Van Slyke was named to his first NL All-Star team, while *TSN* selected him NL Player of the Year and also placed him on its Silver Slugger team.

Van Slyke sparked the Pittsburgh Pirates to three consecutive NL East titles from 1990 to 1992. In 1992, Van Slyke led the major leagues in multi-hit games (65) and the NL in doubles (45), shared the NL lead in hits (199), finished second in the NL batting race (.324), and ranked third in the NL in runs scored (103), total bases (310), and triples (12). He made both the 1992 and the 1993 NL All-Star teams and batted .310 in his injury-shortened 1993 season. Despite these impressive statistics, Van Slyke performed poorly in four NL Championship Series, hitting only .202 with one HR and 10 RBI. He appeared in the NL Championship Series against the Los Angeles Dodgers in 1985, Cincinnati Reds in 1990, and Atlanta Braves in 1991 and 1992. In the 1985 World Series against the Kansas City Royals, Van Slyke made only one hit.

Van Slyke, who married Lauri Griffiths in 1983, has three sons, A. J., Scott, and Jared, and lives in Chesterfield, MO. In 1987, 1988, and 1992, the popular Van Slyke won the Roberto Clemente Award, an award presented annually by the Pittsburgh BBWAA chapter to the Pirate who best exemplifies the standard of excellence established by the late Pittsburgh star. The Pittsburgh Pirates released him in October 1994. His final major league season came in 1995 with the Baltimore Orioles (AL) and Philadelphia Phillies (NL). In 13 major league seasons, Van Slyke batted .274 with 293 doubles, 91 triples, 164 HR, and 792 RBI in 1,658 games.

BIBLIOGRAPHY: Andy Van Slyke file, National Baseball Library, Cooperstown, NY; Rob Rains, *The St. Louis Cardinals* (New York, 1992); Bob Broeg and Jerry Vickery, *St. Louis Cardinals Encyclopedia* (Grand Rapids, MI, 1998); Bob Smizik, *The Pittsburgh Pirates: An Illustrated History* (New York, 1990); *The Baseball Encyclopedia*, 10th ed. (New York, 1996); B. Chastain, "Beers with . . . Andy Van Slyke," *Sport* 80 (April 1989), pp. 19–20; *The Official Major League Baseball 1992 Stat Book*, p. 228; *Pittsburgh Pirates 1994 Record and Information Guide*; Steve Rushin, "Playing for Laughs," *SI* 77 (September 21, 1992), pp. 56–64; Mike Shatzkin, ed., *The Ballplayers* (New York, 1990); Ralph Wiley, "Slick Can Play," *SI* 70 (April 1989), pp. 56–58.

Frank W. Thackeray

VANDER MEER, John Samuel "Johnny," "Double No-Hit," "The Dutch Master" (b. November 2, 1914, Prospect Park, NJ; d. October 6, 1997, Tampa, FL), player and manager, was the son of Dutch immigrants Jacob Vander Meer, a stone mason, and Catherine (Vander Wall) Vander Meer. The young left-hander started pitching in a church league near his hometown of Midland Park, NJ. The Brooklyn Dodgers (NL) signed him at age 17 and sent him to Dayton, OH (MAL) in 1933. An error in his transfer papers brought him in 1934 to Scranton, PA (NYPL), an affiliate of the Boston Braves (NL). Scranton shipped him in 1936 to Nashville, TN (SA), where he attracted the attention of Brooklyn Dodgers vice-president Larry MacPhail, Sr.* MacPhail optioned him to Durham, NC (PiL) for most of the 1936 season. Vander Meer won 19 decisions at Durham striking out a PiL-leading 295 batters (including 20 hitters in one game), and posting a 2.65 ERA.

Named *TSN* 1936 Minor League Player of the Year, Vander Meer was purchased for $10,000 by the Cincinnati Reds (NL) and made his major league debut in April 1937. In 19 games that season, he compiled a modest 3–5 win–loss record and 3.86 ERA in 84 innings. Cincinnati inserted Vander Meer with Paul Derringer* and Bucky Walters* in the 1938 Reds' starting rotation. Vander Meer blossomed under the tutelage of manager Bill McKechnie.* Vander Meer, who possessed a blazing fastball and often erratic control, became an overnight celebrity in mid-June as the only major league pitcher to hurl two consecutive no-hit, no-run games (3–0 against the Boston Braves on June 11 and 6–0 against the Brooklyn Dodgers on June 15). The second no-hitter, which was pitched in Brooklyn's Ebbets Field, highlighted the first night game ever played in New York City. Vander Meer finished the 1938 campaign with a 15–10 win–loss record and 3.12 ERA and won nine consecutive games. In one six-game stretch, opponents recorded only three runs and 18 hits off Vander Meer.

In 1939, Vander Meer's record fell to a 5–9 mark and disappointing 4.67 ERA. An injury-filled 1940 season saw him divide his time between Indianapolis, IN (AA) and Cincinnati and post a 3–1 record in 10 games with the Reds. For the next three seasons from 1941 through 1943, Vander Meer led the Cincinnati Reds' pitching corps with a combined 49–41 win–loss record, 60 complete games, and a sparkling 2.71 ERA and paced the NL in strikeouts (202, 186, 174) each season. After a two-year stint in the U.S. Navy during World War II, he returned to the Cincinnati Reds. He pitched for Cincinnati from 1946 through 1949, averaging 28 starts per season and notching an overall 41–50 win–loss mark. The Cincinnati Reds sold him in February 1950 to the Chicago Cubs (NL), where he posted a 3–4 record in 32 games. He appeared in one game for the Cleveland Indians (AL) in 1951 before his retirement. In 13 major league seasons, he compiled 119 wins, 121 losses; 30 shutouts, a 3.44 ERA, and a .496 winning percentage.

During his major league career, the 6-foot 1-inch, 190-pound Vander Meer achieved seven 1–0 wins. He was the NL starting and winning pitcher in the 1938 All-Star Game, allowing one hit in three innings, and also was selected to the NL All-Star squad in 1939, 1942, and 1943. He remains one of only six hurlers since 1900 to lead the NL in strikeouts for three or more consecutive seasons. Vander Meer worked 20 years as a field manager for Schlitz Brewery and resided in Tampa, FL. He managed in the Cincinnati Reds farm system for six seasons. His wife, Lois Louise (Stewart) Vander Meer, whom he married on October 12, 1940, died in 1988. The Vander Meers had two daughters, Shirley and Evelyn. In 1996, the Johnny Vander Meer Museum opened in Midland Park, NJ. He died of an abdominal aneurysm.

BIBLIOGRAPHY: John P. Carmichael, ed., *Who's Who in the Major Leagues, 1939, 1940, 1941* (Chicago, IL, 1939, 1940, 1941); Chicago (IL) *Tribune*, June 17, 1938; Cleveland (OH) *Press*, June 16, 1938; Donald Honig, *Baseball Between the Lines* (New York, 1976); Harold (Speed) Johnson, ed., *Who's Who in the Major Leagues, 1937* (Chicago, IL, 1937); Joseph L. Reichler, *The Great All-Time Baseball Record Book* (New York, 1981); Joe Reichler and Ben Olan, eds., *Baseball's Unforgettable Games* (New York, 1960); Fluffy Saccucci, "Former Reds Pitcher Johnny Vander Meer 'Dutch

Master' Hurled Back-to-Back No-Hitters," *SCD* 23 (November 29, 1996), pp. 140–141; Ritter Collett, *The Cincinnati Reds* (Virginia Beach, VA, 1976); John Thorn et al., eds., *Total Baseball*, 5th ed. (New York, 1997); John Vander Meer file, National Baseball Library, Cooperstown, NY; Rich Westcott, *Diamond Greats* (Westport, CT, 1988); Lee Allen, *The Cincinnati Reds* (New York, 1948); Bob Rathgeber, *Cincinnati Reds Scrapbook* (Virginia Beach, VA, 1982); Peter C. Bjarkman, *Baseball's Great Dynasties: The Reds* (New York, 1990); Floyd Connor and John Snyder, *Day-by-Day in Cincinnati Reds History* (West Point, NY, 1984); Clayton B. Crosley, "A Conversation with Johnny Vander Meer," *BRJ* 27 (1998), pp. 69–70.

Raymond D. Kush

VAUGHAN, Joseph Floyd "Arky" (b. March 9, 1912, Clifty, AR; d. August 30, 1952, Eagleville, CA), player, was the son of farmers who moved to California when Vaughan was small. He played baseball the year round with his brothers and performed for his high school and local teams. After being signed by the Pittsburgh Pirates (NL) in 1931, Vaughan hit .338 with 21 HR and 81 RBI for Wichita, KS (WL). He married Margaret Allen in October 1931 and replaced an injured Pittsburgh Pirates shortstop a month into the 1932 season. In 1932, he batted .318 in 129 games for Pittsburgh and led the NL in errors. For the next nine years, he remained Pittsburgh's regular shortstop. Although his fielding improved, he made the most impact at the plate. Honus Wagner,* Pirates coach and Vaughan's roommate on road trips, facilitated the latter's development. In his best season (1935), Vaughan led the NL with a .385 batting average, a .491 on-base percentage, a .607 slugging average, and 97 walks and produced career highs in hits (192), HR (19), and RBI (99). *TSN* named Vaughan to the NL All-Star team and as NL MVP. Overall, Vaughan hit .324 for a Pittsburgh Pirates squad invariably finishing out of contention.

Vaughan batted .364 in seven All-Star games (1934–1935, 1937, 1939–1942) and enjoyed his finest performance in the 1941 classic, making three hits and becoming the first player to belt two HR in an All-Star game. Despite Vaughan's heroics and four RBI, the NL lost the game on a widely publicized ninth-inning HR by Ted Williams.* In December 1941, Pittsburgh traded Vaughan to the Brooklyn Dodgers (NL), where he played third base and batted .277 in 1942. The following year, he divided his time between third base and shortstop, batted .305, and led the NL in stolen bases. The "Newsom Revolt," which involved a dispute over an alleged spitter, caused Vaughan and others to confront Dodgers manager Leo Durocher.* Vaughan voluntarily retired at the end of the 1943 season, but returned in 1947 when Durocher was suspended from baseball. Vaughan performed well as a part-time outfielder and pinch hitter in 1947, hitting .325 overall and .385 as a pinch hitter to help the Dodgers win the NL pennant. He doubled once in the 1947 World Series loss to the New York Yankees. For the Dodgers in 1948, Vaughan batted a career-low .244 and was released. He hit .288 as an outfielder for the San Francisco, CA Seals (PCL) in 1949 and then retired from baseball to live with his family on their Surprise Valley ranch in California. Vaughan drowned in a sudden storm while fishing in August 1952 and was survived by his wife and four children.

Vaughan ranked among the leading NL hitters in the 1930s and proved an adequate defensive player, pacing NL shortstops in putouts in 1936, 1938, and 1939, assists in 1936, 1938, and 1939, and fielding percentage in 1940. During 14 major league seasons, he led the NL in runs scored three times (1936, 1940, 1943), triples three times (1933, 1937, 1940), on base percentage three times and stolen bases once (1943). During his major league career, Vaughan batted .318, produced 2,103 hits, 356 doubles, 128 triples, 96 HR, 926 RBI, and 118 stolen bases, scored 1,173 runs, and struck out only 276 times. His performance faded into obscurity partly because his best years came with a non–pennant-winning team outside a major media center and because he was a quiet person. In 1985, the Veterans Committee belatedly elected Vaughan to the National Baseball Hall of Fame.

BIBLIOGRAPHY: Stanley Cohen, *The Dodgers! The First 100 Years* (New York, 1990); Richard Goldstein, *Superstars and Screwballs* (New York, 1991); William F. McNeil, *The Dodgers Encyclopedia* (Champaign, IL, 1997); Tommy Holmes, *The Dodgers* (New York, 1995); Frank Graham, *The Brooklyn Dodgers* (New York, 1945); Bob Smizik, *The Pittsburgh Pirates, An Illustrated History* (New York, 1990); Richard L. Burtt, *The Pittsburgh Pirates, A Pictorial History* (Virginia Beach, VA, 1977); Frederick G. Lieb, *The Pittsburgh Pirates* (New York, 1948); John Thom, *Champion Batsman of the 20th Century* (Los Angeles, CA, 1992); Arky Vaughan file, National Baseball Library, Cooperstown, NY; Peter Golenbock, *Bums* (New York, 1984); John Benson et al., *Baseball's Top 100* (Wilton, CT, 1997); Leo Durocher, *The Dodgers and Me* (Chicago, IL, 1948); Craig Carter, ed., *TSN Daguerreotypes*, 8th ed. (St. Louis, MO, 1990); *NYT*, August 31, 1952; *The Baseball Encyclopedia*, 10th ed. (New York, 1996).

Douglas D. Martin

VAUGHN, James Leslie "Hippo" (b. April 9, 1888, Weatherford, TX; d. May 29, 1966, Chicago, IL), player, was one of eight children of stonemason Thomas H. Vaughn and Josephine S. Vaughn. He completed elementary school in Weatherford and played his first professional baseball with Temple, TX (TL) in 1906. In 1908, he shuttled among three teams and was sold by Macon, GA (SAL) to the New York Highlanders (AL). He pitched only two innings for the Highlanders and was optioned to Macon in 1909. After tossing no-hitters at Macon and Louisville, KY (AA), he was recalled for the 1910 season by the Highlanders. He contributed 13 wins and a 1.83 ERA in 1910, but slumped to an 8–10 mark and 4.39 ERA a year later. He was waived to the Washington Senators (AL) in June 1912 and traded two months later to Kansas City, MO (AA). In August 1913, he was traded to the Chicago Cubs (NL) and won five of six decisions in seven starts.

In his first full NL season (1914), the 26-year-old, 6-foot 4-inch, 215-pound Vaughn proved slow afoot (hence "Hippo") and a hard-throwing left-hander with solid pitching skills. He finished with a 21–13 record in 293.2 innings pitched and compiled a 2.05 ERA. Vaughn, who won 20 and 17 games the next two years, married Edna Coburn DeBold on February 11, 1916 and had one son. In 1917, he registered the first of three consecutive 20-win seasons and hurled the most extraordinary game of his career. On a cold midweek May 2 afternoon at Chicago, IL, he engaged in a nine-inning, double no-hit duel with Fred Toney* of the Cincinnati Reds. In the tenth inning, the Reds scored on a single, an outfield error, and a topped hit down the third base line. With no play at first base, Vaughn tried unsuccessfully to scoop the ball to the catcher with his glove hand. Vaughn struck out 10, while Toney fanned only three, two in the bottom of the tenth, to preserve the victory. For the year, Vaughn's record included 23 wins, 13 losses, 295.2 innings pitched, and 195 strikeouts.

Vaughn's peak season came in 1918, when his NL-leading 22 victories helped the Cubs win their only NL pennant between 1910 and 1929. Aside from his games won, he led the NL in games started (33), innings pitched (290.1), strikeouts (148), shutouts (8), and ERA (1.74). Against the mostly right-handed Boston Red Sox in the World Series, the Cubs started only left-handers. Vaughn, who won one game and lost two by a run each, achieved four World Series records. Besides hurling three complete games in six days, he tied marks for most innings pitched in a six-game World Series (27), total chances (17), and putouts (6). His 1.00 ERA remains among the best in World Series history. In 1919, Vaughn won 21 games and again led the NL in innings pitched (306.2) and strikeouts (141). He also made a remarkable steal of home against the New York Giants. He won 19 decisions in 1920, but slumped to 3–11 in his final season in 1921. His major league career totals included 178 wins, 137 losses, a respectable 41 shutouts, 1,416 strikeouts, and a 2.49 ERA. He played semipro baseball with a Fairbanks-Morse Company team at Beloit, WI and with Chicago's Logan Squares and Mills until age 47. He contemplated a comeback with the Cubs, but only pitched batting practice. He also worked as an assembler for a refrigeration products company.

BIBLIOGRAPHY: Jim Langford, *The Game Is Never Over* (South Bend, IN, 1980); Warren Wilbert and William Hageman, *Chicago Cubs: Seasons at the Summit* (Champaign, IL, 1997); Eddie Gold and Art Ahrens, *The Golden Era Cubs, 1876–1940* (Chicago, IL, 1985); Jim Enright, *Chicago Cubs* (New York, 1975); Warren Brown, *The Chicago Cubs* (New York, 1946); Charles Einstein, ed., *The Fireside Book of Baseball* (New York, 1956); Lee Allen, *The Cincinnati Reds* (New York, 1948); Chicago *Sun-Times*, May 30, 1966; Chicago *Tribune*, May 3, 1917, p. 13; May 30, 1966, pp. 1, 4; Leonard Gettelson, "Pitchers Stealing Home," *BRJ* 5 (1976), pp. 12–14; Craig Carter, ed., *TSN Daguerreotypes*, 8th ed. (St. Louis, MO, 1990); *The Baseball Encyclopedia*,

10th ed. (New York, 1996); Lawrence S. Ritter, *The Glory of Their Times* (New York, 1966); James Vaughn file, National Baseball Library, Cooperstown, NY.

A. D. Suehsdorf

VAUGHN, Maurice Samuel "Mo" (b. December 15, 1967, Norwalk, CT), player, is a 6-foot 1-inch, 240-pound first baseman who bats left-handed and throws right-handed. Vaughn is the son of Leroy Vaughn, a school administrator, and Shirley Vaughn, an elementary school teacher, and remains single. He graduated from Trinity Pawling Prep School in Pawling, NY in 1986 and attended Seton Hall University for three years. Vaughn broke the Seton Hall Pirates record with 28 HR as a freshman and compiled a three-year .417 batting average, setting a school career record with 57 HR and 218 RBI. The three-time All America was named BEaC Player of the Decade and was inducted into the Seton Hall Athletic Hall of Fame in January 1996.

The Boston Red Sox (AL) selected Vaughn in the first round of the June 1989 free-agent draft. He spent his first professional baseball season with New Britain, CT (EL) and joined Pawtucket, RI (IL) in 1990, ranking second in the IL in slugging percentage (.539) and fourth in batting average (.295) and HR (22) and being named the team's MVP. Vaughn started 1991 with Pawtucket and joined the Boston Red Sox in June, posting a .260 batting average in 74 games. He played in 39 games with Pawtucket the following season and returned to the Boston Red Sox, where he batted .234 in 113 games.

Vaughn enjoyed an excellent first full major league season in 1993, compiling a .297 batting average and a career-high 34 doubles. The Boston Red Sox best offensive performer in 1994, he batted .310 with a .576 slugging percentage and .408 on base percentage and led AL first basemen with 103 double plays. Although pacing the AL by striking out 150 times in 1995, Vaughn batted .300, clouted 39 HR and shared the AL lead in RBI (126). Vaughn also led AL first basemen with 1,368 total chances, 128 double plays, and 1,262 putouts. He spearheaded the Red Sox to the 1995 AL Division Series, where they lost to the Cleveland Indians. Cleveland pitchers held him hitless in 14 times at bat. In 1996, Vaughn enjoyed his best overall season and established career-highs in runs (118), hits (207), HR (44), and RBI (143). The 1997 campaign saw him bat .315 with 35 HR with 96 RBI. His .337 batting average, 205 hits, 40 HR, 115 RBI, and .591 slugging percentage helped Boston capture the Wild Card in 1998. He finished second in batting average and hits. In Game 1 of the AL Division Series, he clouted two HR and tied a postseason record with seven RBI against the Cleveland Indians. Altogether, he batted .412 with two doubles, two HR, and seven RBI in the AL Division Series. In November 1998, the California Angels (AL) signed him to an $80 million, six-year contract. He batted .281 with 33 HR and 108 RBI in 1999. He played in the All-Star game in 1995 and was named first baseman on *TSN* AL All-Star and Silver Slugger teams that same year. Vaughn collected his third consecutive Thomas A. Yawkey Award as team MVP and edged Cleveland's Albert Belle* to capture the AL's MVP award. In 1996, he received the Bart Giamatti Award for outstanding community service.

In nine major league seasons, through 1999, Vaughn has scored 691 runs and made 1,312 hits in 1,185 games. He has compiled a .301 batting average with 219 doubles, 10 triples, 263 HR (including 6 grand slam clouts) and produced 860 RBI while recording 565 walks, 1,081 strikeouts, and 28 stolen bases.

BIBLIOGRAPHY: Mo Vaughn file, National Baseball Library, Cooperstown, NY; *Boston Red Sox Media Guide*, 1998; Gerry Callahan, "Sox Appeal," *SI* 83 (October 2, 1995), pp. 42–44, 47–48; Nicholas Dawidoff, "They're Hungry for Mo," *SI* 74 (April 1, 1991), p. 51; D. Dieffenbach, "Hitting It with Mo Vaughn," *Sport* 87 (May 1996), pp. 86–87; D. Dieffenbach, "Mo Vaughn's Prize," *Sport* 87 (July 1996), pp. 79–81; Ed Lucas and Paul Post, "Slugging Cousins," *SCD* 25 (October 23, 1998), pp. 120–121; Michael J. Mahoney, " 'Hit Dog' Becomes Red Sox Team Leader," *SCD* 24 (October 3, 1997), p. 144; A. Moir and D. Christy, "The Role Model," *Forbes* 153 (March 14, 1994), pp. 58–62; W. Leavy, "Baseball's Two of a Kind," *Ebony* 51 (July 1996), pp. 100–102; Robert Redmount, *The Red Sox Encyclopedia* (Champaign, IL, 1998); *TSN Official Baseball Register*, 1998.

John L. Evers

VEACH, Robert Hayes "Bobby" (b. June 29, 1888, Island, KY; d. August 7, 1945, Detroit, MI), player, was one of three sons of coal miner Mark Veach and Sally Veach, both of Irish descent. He moved to Herrin, IL as a youth. Without graduating from high school, he entered professional baseball as a pitcher with Kankakee, IL (NoA) in 1910. Since Veach lacked speed and base-running ability, he was not considered a major league prospect. At Peoria, IL (3IL) in 1911, he batted .297 and was converted to an outfielder. St. Louis Browns (AL) scout Charlie Barrett, who had joined the Peoria club as fundamentals coach, gave Veach specialized instruction. In 1912, Veach batted .285 for Indianapolis, IN (AA) and .342 in 23 games for the Detroit Tigers (AL). Veach became a mainstay in left field for the Tigers from 1913 through 1923 and combined with center fielder Ty Cobb* and right fielders Sam Crawford* (1913–1917) and Harry Heilmann* (1918–1923) to give Detroit one of the most potent outfields in AL history. He was sold in January 1924 to the Boston Red Sox (AL) and was traded in May 1925 to the New York Yankees (AL). Veach was sold to the Washington Senators (AL) in August 1925 and pinch-hit in the 1925 World Series against the New York Giants. After playing from 1926 through 1929 for Toledo, OH (AA), he ended his baseball career with Jersey City, NJ (IL) in 1930.

Baseball historian Robert Creamer remarked that Veach is "surely one of the least remembered of the really fine hitters." Besides batting .310 lifetime, he led the AL twice in doubles (1915, 1919), once each in triples (1919) and hits (1919), and three times in RBI (1915, 1917–1918). Veach enjoyed his best season in 1919, when his 191 hits, 45 doubles, and 17 triples paced the AL and his .355 batting average placed second to roommate Cobb's .384 mark. His 2,063 major league hits included 393 doubles, 147 triples, and 64 HR. He also stole 195 bases and scored 953 runs, while driving in 1,166 tallies. In one 12-inning game in 1920, he batted six for six and clouted a double, triple, and HR.

The 5-foot 11-inch, 160-pound Veach had gray eyes and dark hair, threw right-handed, and batted left-handed. Fred Lieb (OS) described him as "a phlegmatic chap who lacked Cobb's inspirational qualities, but packed a terrific punch for his size." In 1921, Tigers manager Cobb allegedly tried to "put more fire into Bobbie" by ordering Heilmann to "ride" Veach all season long. Veach hit .338 and developed a lasting resentment of Heilmann, but Cobb apparently never admitted his role in the scheme.

Veach married Ethel Clare Spiller on January 22, 1910 and had four sons. After leaving baseball, he became a coal dealer in Detroit, MI and proved instrumental in persuading the Detroit Tigers to sign infielder Charlie Gehringer* of Fowlerville, MI. Veach brought Gehringer to Detroit for a tryout under the watchful eye of manager Cobb, who signed him instantly. Veach died after a long illness. Although overshadowed by Cobb, he proved a consistently outstanding performer and made substantial contributions to the Detroit teams of the World War I era.

BIBLIOGRAPHY: Robert Veach file, National Baseball Library, Cooperstown, NY; Charles C. Alexander, *Ty Cobb* (New York, 1984); Richard Bak, *Ty Cobb: His Tumultuous Life and Times* (Dallas, TX, 1994); Joe Falls, *Detroit Tigers* (New York, 1975); Fred Smith, *995 Tigers* (Detroit, MI, 1981); William M. Anderson, *The Detroit Tigers* (South Bend, IN, 1996); George Sullivan and David Cateneo, *Detroit Tigers* (New York, 1985); Robert W. Creamer, *Babe: The Legend Comes to Life* (New York, 1974); Detroit *Free Press*, December 30, 1943, August 7, 1945; Brent P. Kelley, *The Case For: Those Overlooked by the Baseball Hall of Fame* (Jefferson, NC, 1992); Frederick G. Lieb, *The Detroit Tigers* (New York, 1946); *The Baseball Encyclopedia*, 10th ed. (New York, 1996); *TSN*, June 1913.

David S. Matz and Luther W. Spoehr

VEALE, Robert Andrew, Jr. "Bob" (b. October 28, 1935, Birmingham, AL), player and coach, is the second of 14 children of Robert Andrew Veale, Sr., a workman for Tennessee Coal and Iron Company who pitched briefly for the Homestead, PA Grays (NNL), and Olie Belle (Ushry) Veale of African-American descent. Veale graduated from Holy Family High School in Birmingham, where he participated in baseball and basketball. He attended St. Benedict's College in Atchison, KS for three years, playing basketball and baseball there. He served in the U.S. Marine Corps Reserve from 1959 to 1962 and received a medical discharge for a knee injury.

The Pittsburgh Pirates (NL) signed Veale in 1958 and assigned the pitcher in 1958 to Las Vegas, NV (CaL), in 1959 to Wilson, NC (CrL), and in 1960 and 1961 to Columbus, OH (IL). After starting the 1962 season with Columbus, he was called up to the Pittsburgh Pirates in April. From 1964 through 1970, he was the mainstay of the Pittsburgh Pirates' staff and never pitched less than 200 innings a year. The imposing 6-foot 6-inch, 212-pound bespectacled left-hander proved an imposing figure on the mound. He consistently ranked among NL leaders in both strikeouts and walks, leading the NL in both categories in 1964 and in walks in 1965, 1967, and 1968. Veale won 16 or more games four times, with 18 victories in 1964 marking his personal best. Despite finishing 13–14 in 1967, he compiled a 2.05 ERA. The Pittsburgh Pirates sold Veale in September 1972 to the Boston Red Sox (AL), where he served as a relief pitcher until his retirement following the 1974 season. Overall, Veale won 120 games (116 with Pittsburgh) and lost 95 (91 with Pittsburgh) with a 3.07 ERA. In 1,926 major league innings, he surrendered 1,684 hits, struck out 1,703 batters, and walked 858. His 7.96 strikeouts per nine innings ranks sixth on the all-time list.

After retiring as an active player, Veale worked as a pitching coach in the Atlanta Braves (NL) farm system for 10 years and for another year in the New York Yankees (AL) system. He lives in Birmingham, AL with his wife, Eredean, and has one daughter. Veale and Sandy Koufax* were the hardest-throwing left-handers of the 1960s. With Koufax, Don Drysdale,* Bob Gibson,* Juan Marichal,* and others, Veale excelled in the "Age of the Pitcher."

BIBLIOGRAPHY: Richard L. Burtt, *The Pittsburgh Pirates, A Pictorial History* (Virginia Beach, VA, 1977); Leo Heiman et al., *When the Cheering Stops* (New York, 1990); Bob Smizik, *The Pittsburgh Pirates: An Illustrated History* (New York, 1990); Luther Spoehr, interview with Bob Veale, August 17, 1993; Bob Veale file, National Baseball Library, Cooperstown, NY; Rich Westcott, *Diamond Greats* (Westport, CT, 1988); Morris Eckhouse and Earl Mastrocola, *This Date in Pittsburgh Pirates History* (New York, 1980); Robert Redmount, *The Red Sox Encyclopedia* (Champaign, IL, 1998).

Luther W. Spoehr

VEECK, William Louis, Jr. "Bill" (b. February 9, 1914, Chicago, IL; d. January 2, 1986, Chicago, IL), college football player, sports executive, scout, and sportscaster, was the son of baseball executive William Louis Veeck and Grace (DeForest) Veeck. His father served as president of the Chicago Cubs (NL) from 1919 to 1933. Following grammar school, Veeck attended Phillips Academy in Andover, MA; Hinsdale, IL High School, where he played blocking back on the football team; and Los Alamos, NM Ranch School. Although he failed to graduate from high school, Veeck attended Kenyon College after passing entrance examinations. He played football for the Lords until his father's death in 1933, when he joined the Chicago Cubs as office boy and learned the complete operation of a baseball franchise. He worked in the Chicago Cubs' advertising agency, operated the commissary, handled ushers and ticket sellers, and conducted tryout schools for high school players. Veeck also worked in the concession stands, directed park maintenance, and in 1940 became club treasurer and assistant secretary. He attended night school at Northwestern University to study accounting and business law and Lewis Institute for designing and blueprint reading.

Veeck owned his first team at age 28 and brought fun and excitement into the game with innovative promotional gimmicks. He operated five clubs, including three major league and two minor league teams. In three cities, his teams won pennants and broke attendance records. In 1941, Veeck and Charlie Grimm* purchased the Milwaukee, WI Brewers (AA) and made the team a highly successful franchise with three AA pennants from 1943 to 1945. Veeck was named *TSN* Minor League Executive of the Year in 1942. After joining the U.S. Marine Corps in 1944, he was wounded and later had to have his leg amputated. Veeck sold the Brewers following the 1945 season and purchased the Cleveland Indians (AL) as part of a 10-man syndicate. Cleveland's attendance soared to a remarkable 2,620,627 in 1948, when the Indians won the AL flag and the World Series under player–manager Lou Boudreau.* The same year, Veeck was named Major League Executive of the Year. Veeck signed Larry Doby,* the first AL black player, in 1947 and recruited Satchel Paige* the next year to pitch for the Indians. After selling his interest in the Indians, Veeck purchased the St. Louis Browns (AL) in July 1951. He could not advance the Browns financially and sold his interest in 1953, when the franchise was moved to Baltimore as the Orioles. His finest promotional stunt came on August 29, 1951, when he sent midget Eddie Gaedel to bat in a game against the Detroit Tigers (AL).

Baseball owners considered him a maverick and prevented Veeck from purchasing the Philadelphia Athletics (AL) in 1954 and the Detroit Tigers (AL) in 1956. He formed a public relations firm in Cleveland, OH and scouted for the Cleveland Indians before operating a minor league franchise in Miami, FL (IL) for one season. After announcing sports for NBC-TV in 1957 and 1958, Veeck in March 1959 purchased the Chicago White Sox (AL). Chicago won the AL pennant Veeck's first year and set another attendance record. The White Sox had not won a pennant since 1919, the year of the "Black Sox" scandal. Veeck helped design Comiskey Park for the comfort and convenience of the fans. His promotions included placing players' names on the backs of uniforms and installing exploding scoreboards, which were touched off by HR hit by the home team. Veeck later sold his interest in the Chicago White Sox and served as president of Suffolk Downs race track in Boston, MA. Veeck again purchased the Chicago White Sox in 1976 and operated the franchise until 1980, when failing health forced him to sell the club. The co-author of *Veeck as in Wreck, The Hustler's Handbook*, and *Thirty Tons a Day*, Veeck married Eleanor Raymond on December 8, 1935 and had three children. After their divorce in 1949, he married Mary Frances Ackerman on April 29, 1950; they had six children. In 1991, he was elected to the National Baseball Hall of Fame.

BIBLIOGRAPHY: *CB* (1948), pp. 645–647; Bob Vanderberg, *Sox: From Lane and Fain to Zisk and Fisk* (Chicago, IL, 1982); Richard Lindberg, *Sox* (New York, 1984); Richard Lindberg, *Who's on Third?* (South Bend, IN, 1983); Gerald Eskenazi, *Bill Veeck: A Baseball Legend* (New York, 1988); David Condon, *The Go-Go Chicago White Sox* (New York, 1960); Bill Veeck, *The Hustler's Handbook* (New York, 1965); David Kaiser, *The Epic Season* (Amherst, MA, 1998); Russell Schneider, *The Boys of Summer of '48* (Champaign, IL, 1998); Franklin Lewis, *The Cleveland Indians* (New York, 1949); John Thorn et al., eds., *Total Indians* (New York, 1996); Bill Veeck file, National Baseball Library, Cooperstown, NY; *CB* (1986), pp. 644–645; Brad Herzog, *The Sports 100* (New York, 1995); Joseph J. Vecchione, *The New York Times Book of Sports Legends* (New York, 1991); Hank Greenberg, "Unforgettable Bill Veeck," *RD* 129 (July 1986), pp. 67–72; David Jordan et al., "A Baseball Myth Exploded," *TNP* 17 (1998), pp. 3–13; Bill Veeck with Ed Linn, *Veeck as in Wreck* (New York, 1989); *WWA*, 43rd ed. (1984–1985).

John L. Evers

VENTURA, Robin Mark (b. July 14, 1967, Santa Maria, CA), player, attended Righetti High School in Santa Maria, where he twice won all-state honors in baseball. He attended Oklahoma State University, developing into one of the greatest collegiate players in baseball history. The 6-foot 1-inch, 198-pound third baseman, who bats left and throws right, hit .469 his freshman year in 1986 and was selected *BA's* Freshman of the Year. During his sophomore year, Ventura batted .428 with 21 HR and 110 RBI. In his final season, he hit .391 with 26 HR and 96 RBI. His .459 batting average during the 1987 NCAA College World Series marked the highest in College World Series history. Ventura's greatest collegiate success perhaps came in 1987, when he hit safely in 58 consecutive games.

Ventura's stellar play earned him numerous awards, including a three-time All-America selection. In 1987, *BA* named him College Player of the Year. In 1988 he received the Dick Howser Trophy as college baseball's outstanding player and the Golden Spikes Award, college baseball's equivalent of the Heisman Trophy. *BA* designated him the College Player of the Decade and as third baseman for its All-Time College All-Star team. Ventura played on the 1988 United States Olympic team, batting .409 and leading the squad to a gold medal.

In June 1988, the Chicago White Sox (AL) signed Ventura as their first-round selection in the free agent draft and 10th player taken overall. After an All-Star season at Birmingham, AL (SL) in 1989, Ventura joined the Chicago White Sox in 1990 and made the Topps Major League Rookie All-Star team. In 1991, he won the first of three consecutive Rawlings Gold Glove Awards. Besides winning AL Player of the Month honors for July 1991, he knocked in 100 runs. Ventura was selected for the AL All-Star squad in 1992 and earned TSN Gold Gloves in 1996 and 1998. He batted .200 with five RBI against the Toronto Blue Jays in the 1993 AL Championship series. His best season came in 1996, when he attained career highs in runs (96) and HR (34), hit 105 RBI, and earned another Gold Glove. A fractured ankle sidelined him for most of the 1997 season. In December

1998, the New York Mets (NL) signed him to a $32 million, four-year contract. In 1999, his .301 batting average, 32 HR, and 120 RBI helped New York win the Wild Card. He batted .214 with 1 RBI in the NL Division Series and .120 with 1 RBI in NL Championship Series. He hit a game-winning grand slam in the 15th inning of Game 5 but was credited with only a single as teammates mobbed him before reaching second base. Through the 1999 season, he has batted .277 with 203 HR and 861 RBI. He won another Golden Glove and made the USA Baseball All-Time Team.

He and his wife, Stephanie (Habbard) Ventura have two children, Rachel and Madison, and reside in Santa Maria, CA. Ventura participated in Chicago's Children's Memorial Hospital and the United Way.

BIBLIOGRAPHY: L. T. Bessone, "A Hollywood Homer," *SI* 72 (May 21, 1990), p. 97; *The Baseball Encyclopedia*, 10th ed. (New York, 1996); *Chicago White Sox 1998 Media Guide*; Robin Ventura file, *TSN* archives, St. Louis, MO; Robin Ventura file, National Baseball Library, Cooperstown, NY.

Frank W. Thackeray

VERNON, James Barton "Mickey" (b. April 22, 1918, Marcus Hook, PA), player, coach, and manager, graduated from Eddystone High School and attended Villanova College for one year. He married Elizabeth Firth on March 14, 1941 and had one child, Gay. A 6-foot 2-inch, 170-pound, left-handed batting and throwing first baseman, he ranked among the most productive, consistent major league players and in 1969 was voted the Washington Senators (AL) All-Time first baseman. Vernon began his professional baseball career with Easton, MD (ESL) in 1937. After hitting .328 with Greenville, SC (SAL) in 1938, he batted .343 for Springfield, MA (EL) in 1939 and finished that season with the Washington Senators. He played most of the 1940 campaign at Jersey City, NJ (IL) before returning permanently to the major leagues in late September.

Vernon started at first base for the Washington Senators from 1941 through 1943, spent 1944 and 1945 in military service, and rejoined the Senators in 1946. After performing three years with Washington, he was traded in December 1948 to the Cleveland Indians (AL). Vernon played with the Indians in 1949 and 1950 and returned to the Washington Senators in June 1950 for six more seasons. He spent the 1956 and 1957 campaigns with the Boston Red Sox (AL) as a part-time first baseman and rejoined the Cleveland Indians in 1958. Before retiring as a player, he performed briefly with the Milwaukee Braves (NL) in 1959 and the Pittsburgh Pirates (NL) in 1960.

Vernon twice led the AL in batting with .353 in 1946 and .337 in 1953, paced AL hitters in doubles in 1946 (51), 1953 (43), and 1954 (33), and batted over .300 in 1955 and 1956. In 2,409 major league games, he netted 2,495 hits, 1,196 runs scored, 490 doubles, 120 triples, 172 HR, and 1,311 RBI, batted .286, and compiled a .428 slugging percentage. A seven-time AL All Star, Vernon led AL first basemen in putouts three times, assists once, and fielding average four times. He ranks third on the all-time major league list in games played by a first baseman (2,237), seventh in putouts (19,808) and chances (21,467), and first in double plays (2,044). Besides establishing a major league record for most assists by a first baseman in a season (155, since broken) in 1949, he holds AL records for most career games and putouts. He participated in ten double plays in an August 18, 1943 doubleheader, made two unassisted double plays in a game on May 29, 1946, and led AL first basemen in double plays in 1941, 1953, and 1954.

President Dwight D. Eisenhower's favorite player, Vernon remains one of the few major leaguers to perform in four different decades. Vernon managed the Washington Senators to a 61 win, 100 loss, ninth place finish in 1961 and 60–101 tenth place finish in 1962. The Senators stood in last place with a 14–26 mark in 1963 when he was replaced by Gil Hodges.* Vernon managed Vancouver, Canada (PCL) from 1966 through 1968, Richmond, VA (IL) in 1969 and 1970, and Manchester, NH (EL) in 1971. The Wallingford, PA resident also coached for the Pittsburgh Pirates (NL) in 1960 and 1964, St. Louis Cardinals (NL) in 1965, Montreal Expos (NL) in 1977 and 1978 and New York Yankees (AL) in 1982; worked as a minor league batting instructor for the Kansas City Royals (AL) in 1973 and 1974 and Los Angeles Dodgers (NL) in 1975 and 1976; and scouted for the New York Yankees in 1986 and 1987.

BIBLIOGRAPHY: Donald Honig, *Baseball Between the Lines* (New York, 1976); Mickey Vernon file, National Baseball Library, Cooperstown, NY; Gene Karst and Martin J. Jones, Jr., *Who's Who in Professional Baseball* (New Rochelle, NY, 1973); Brent P. Kelley, *Baseball Stars of the 1950s* (Jefferson, NC, 1993); Jack Lautier, *Fenway Voices* (Camden, ME, 1990); Craig Carter, ed., *TSN Daguerreotypes*, 8th ed. (St. Louis, MO, 1990); *The Baseball Encyclopedia*, 10th ed. (New York, 1996); *TSN Official Baseball Record Book, 1997* (St. Louis, MO, 1997); David Hartley, *Washington's Expansion Senators 1961–1997* (Germantown, MD, 1998); Thomas Aylesworth and Benton Minks, *The Encyclopedia of Baseball Managers* (New York, 1990); Robert Redmount, *The Red Sox Encyclopedia* (Champaign, IL, 1998); Shirley Povich, *The Washington Senators* (New York, 1954); Morris Bealle, *The Washington Senators* (Washington, DC, 1947); John Phillips, *Winners* (Cabin John, MD, 1987); Rich Westcott, *Diamond Greats* (Westport, CT, 1988).

Jack R. Stanton

VINCENT, Francis Thomas, Jr. "Fay" (b. May 29, 1938, Waterbury, CT), executive, grew up in Waterbury as the son of Francis T. Vincent, Sr. and Alice (Lynch) Vincent. After graduating from the Hotchkiss School, he entered Williams College and sustained a serious spinal injury that permanently restricted his mobility. Vincent graduated with a Bachelor of Arts degree from Williams College in 1960 and earned a law degree from Yale University in 1963. He married Valerie McMahon in July 1965 and has three children, Anne, William, and Edward.

Vincent specialized in securities law, spending 15 years with New York and Washington, DC firms and a brief stint with the Securities and

Exchange Commission. In 1978, Columbia Pictures appointed him president. When Columbia Pictures was acquired by the Coca-Cola Company in 1982, Vincent headed its entertainment division. He held this post until 1987, when the division's declining earnings prompted his resignation.

The affluent Vincent had resumed his legal career when his friend A. Bartlett Giamatti,* the newly appointed commissioner of major league baseball, persuaded him to become the sport's first deputy commissioner. During Giamatti's brief six-month incumbency in 1989, Vincent drafted the agreement that banned player Pete Rose* from the game. Upon Giamatti's death in September 1989, Vincent was officially elected commissioner and was contracted to serve the remaining years of Giamatti's five-year term.

Vincent's three stormy years as commissioner were marked by steadily eroding relations with his club owner employers. His early decision to delay the 1989 World Series for 10 days, owing to the earthquake that disrupted play between the San Francisco Giants and Oakland Athletics, was generally applauded. Vincent's subsequent efforts to function as an activist commissioner, however, evoked increasing resentment from some owners.

In March 1990, Vincent angered several owners by seeking to end the labor dispute involving the owners locking the players out of spring training camps. Vincent persuaded the owners to reopen the camps, but his role in negotiating the basic agreement that followed was criticized by some owners and by the MLPA. The MLPA faulted him for refusing to discipline owners after an arbitrator found the latter guilty of collusion against free agent players during the 1985–1989 period. Owners in 1991 criticized Vincent's negotiations, which ended a brief umpires' strike, for conceding too much to the umpires. The owners in 1992 named Richard Ravitch to be their chief negotiator and paid him a higher salary than that of Vincent.

In 1992 Vincent's rulings sought to make the game a more cohesive industry, but widened the rift with the owners. After the NL owners voted to expand by admitting the Colorado Rockies and Florida Marlins, Vincent in June ended the owners' impasse over the division of entry fees and the stocking of new teams with players. He ruled that both major leagues must supply players and must share in the division of the $190 million entry fees paid by the new clubs. Vincent's preemptory ruling angered owners in both leagues. His decision to allow a Japanese corporation to become the principal owner of the Seattle Mariners (AL) club angered those AL owners who wanted the franchise moved to another city. Vincent, acting on the advice of some NL owners, ordered the NL to realign its two divisions on more logical geographical lines. The Chicago Cubs, however, in August won a federal court injunction against his ruling.

Vincent's decision on the realignment issue precipitated the owners' action to oust him from his post. On September 7, 1992, a two-thirds majority of major league owners voted no confidence in him and demanded his resignation. Although insisting that his contract prevented his dismissal until the 1994 expiration of his contract, Vincent resigned in September 1992.

Following Vincent's resignation, the owners assumed full control of the game. For over two years, an executive council of owners took control. Bud Selig,* the principal owner of the Milwaukee Brewers (AL), functioned as interim commissioner. An owners' search committee continued to ponder the choice of a new commissioner, while the ousted Vincent wrote a book on 15 people he was privileged to meet during his lifetime. Vincent served on the board of directors of the New York Mets (NL) in 1994.

BIBLIOGRAPHY: Fay Vincent file, National Baseball Library, Cooperstown, NY; *CB Yearbook* (1991), pp. 588–593; T. Callahan, "Baseball's Unlikely Champion," *U.S. News & World Report* 109 (October 15, 1990), pp. 97ff; Roger Cohn, "Nothing But Curve Balls," *NYT Magazine*, June 3, 1990, pp. 34, 56–58; Ray Corliss, "Fay Vincent Gets Beaned," *Time* 140 (September 14, 1992), p. 61; John Feinstein, *Play Ball* (New York, 1993); Richard Hoffer, " 'Take Care of the Game,' " *SI* 76 (March 2, 1992), pp. 46–48ff; *NYT Biographical Service* 21 (June 1990), pp. 525–527; Michael Knisley, "Friends or Foes?" *TSN*, September 21, 1993, pp. 11–12; Mike Lupica, "Welcome to Hardball City," *Esquire* 115 (June 1991), pp. 38ff; Jerome Holtzman, *The Commissioners* (New York, 1998); Richard Sandomir, "Twists of Fate," *Sports Inc.*, February 27, 1989; John Thorn et al., eds., *Total Baseball*, 5th ed. (New York, 1997); George Vecsey, "Fay Vincent Speaks from Exile," *NYT*, June 23, 1993; Tom Verducci, "Have You Seen This Man?" *SI* 79 (July 5, 1993), pp. 38–41; Steve Wulf, "A Man in Command," *SI* 71 (October 30, 1989), pp. 30–32.

David Q. Voigt

VIOLA, Frank John, Jr. (b. April 19, 1960, East Meadow, NY), player, is the son of Frank Viola, Sr., a radio station comptroller, and Helen (Weindler) Viola, graduated from East Meadow High School and attended St. John's University of New York, where he pitched the Redmen to the 1980 NCAA College World Series and a 1981 NCAA appearance. In the 1981 NCAA Northeast regional tournament, he bested Ron Darling* of Yale University, 1–0, in 12 innings.

The Minnesota Twins (AL) drafted the 6-foot 4-inch, 210-pound Viola in the second round in June 1981 and assigned the meticulous, tempestuous left-hander to Orlando, FL (SL) in 1981 and Toledo, OH (IL) in 1982. Viola debuted with the Minnesota Twins in 1982 and struggled through two consecutive losing seasons. He won 18 games in 1984 and 1985 and 16 contests in 1986, leading the AL in games started (37). The Minnesota Twins suffered losing seasons from 1982 through 1986 before capturing the West Division title in 1987. After developing among the best change-ups in the AL, Viola in 1987 compiled a 17–10 record and 2.90 ERA and did not lose a game at the Metrodome after May 22. Minnesota upset the Detroit Tigers in the 1987 AL Championship Series, as Viola won Game 4. The

Minnesota Twins defeated the St. Louis Cardinals in the 1987 World Series, with Viola garnering MVP honors. Viola took Game 1, 10–1, lost Game 4, 7–2, and triumphed in Game 7, 4–2, striking out 16 batters in 19.1 innings.

In 1988 Viola enjoyed his best major league season, earning the AL Cy Young Award and *TSN* AL Pitcher of the Year honors. He led the AL in victories (24) and winning percentage (.774), while losing only six decisions. Viola, who finished third in the AL with 193 strikeouts and a career-best 2.64 ERA, hurled two innings to earn credit for the victory in the All-Star Game. His 93 victories from 1984 through 1988 paced all major league pitchers. In July 1989, the Minnesota Twins traded Viola to the New York Mets for five players. Viola won 20 of 32 decisions with a 2.67 ERA in 1990, leading the NL in starts (35) and innings pitched (249.2) and being named *TSN* NL All-Star left-hander. Viola, a consistent control artist, made the NL All-Star team in 1990 and 1991. In January 1992, the Boston Red Sox (AL) signed him as a free agent. Viola compiled a 13–12 record in 1992 and an 11–18 mark in 1993, but was released in October 1994. He lost his only decision for the Cincinnati Reds (NL) in 1995 and ended his major league career with the Toronto Blue Jays (AL) in 1996. In 15 major league seasons, he recorded 176 victories, 150 losses, a 3.73 ERA, 16 shutouts, and 1,844 strikeouts in 2,816.1 innings.

The Longwood, FL resident married Kathy Daltas of Roseville, MN and has two children, Frankie and Brittany.

BIBLIOGRAPHY: Peter Gammons, "Concerto for Viola and Twins," *SI* 67 (November 2, 1987), pp. 32–33; Peter Gammons, "Near Perfect Pitch," *SI* 69 (August 22, 1988), pp. 44–46, 56, 58–59; Robert Redmount, *The Red Sox Encyclopedia* (Champaign, IL, 1998); E. Pooley, "Sports," *NY* 23 (September 10, 1990); p. 122–123; Larry Powell, "Frank Viola Wants Another World Series Ring," *SCD* 21 (May 20, 1994), p. 190; T. Rogers, "Viola Reaps His Rewards," *NYT Biographical Service* 18 (October 1987), pp. 1132–1133; Frank Viola, Jr. file, National Baseball Library, Cooperstown, NY; Dave Mona and Dave Jarzyna, *Twenty-five Seasons* (Minneapolis, MN, 1986); Ken Young, *Cy Young Award Winners* (New York, 1994); Mike Shatzkin, ed., *The Ballplayers* (New York, 1990); *TSN Official Baseball Register*, 1997.

David L. Porter

VIRDON, William Charles "Bill," "Quail" (b. June 9, 1931, Hazel Park, MI), player, manager, scout, instructor, and coach, is the second child and only son of Charles Neles Virdon, a laborer of English descent, and Bertha (Marley) Virdon, of English and German ancestry. After Virdon graduated from West Plains High School in West Plains, MO in 1949 and attended Drury College for one semester, the New York Yankees (AL) signed him and sent him to Independence, MO (KOML) and Kansas City, MO (AA) in 1950. His other minor league assignments included Norfolk, VA (PiL) in 1951, Binghamton, NY (EL) in 1952, and Kansas City, MO and Birmingham, AL

(SA) in 1953. The New York Yankees traded Virdon in April 1954 to the St. Louis Cardinals (NL) organization, where he starred for Rochester, NY (IL) and led the IL in hitting.

With the St. Louis Cardinals in 1955, Virdon hit .281 with 17 HR and was named NL Rookie of the Year. In May 1956, the St. Louis Cardinals traded him to the Pittsburgh Pirates (NL). The left-handed–hitting, right-handed–throwing, quiet, intense, and bespectacled center fielder provided steady offense and superb defense, highlighted by several spectacular catches in the 1960 World Series. He also hit the ball that struck New York Yankees shortstop Tony Kubek* in the throat in the seventh inning of the seventh game, helping ignite a classic five-run Pirates rally. The 6-foot, 185 pounder retired after the 1965 season, but made a brief six-game comeback in 1968. His major league career record included a .267 batting average, 1,596 hits, and 502 RBI.

Virdon managed in the New York Mets (NL) system in 1966 at Williamsport, PA (EL) and in 1967 at Jacksonville, FL (IL) and coached the Pittsburgh Pirates under managers Larry Shepard and Danny Murtaugh* from 1968 to 1971. He managed the Pirates to the NL Eastern Division title in 1972, but was fired abruptly during the 1973 NL pennant race. He piloted the New York Yankees (AL) to a second-place finish in 1974 and garnered AL Manager of the Year honors. Billy Martin* replaced Virdon as Yankees manager during the 1975 season. The Houston Astros (NL) hired Virdon as pilot 17 days later and won the NL Western Division title in 1980 and the second half of the split 1981 season under him. He piloted the Houston Astros through 1982 and the Montreal Expos (NL) in 1983 and 1984. Overall, his major league clubs won 995 games and lost 921 contests for a .519 winning percentage. He worked for the Pittsburgh Pirates from 1984 through 1995, coaching in 1986 and from 1992 through 1995 and as a scout and minor league instructor. Virdon has coached for the Houston Astros (NL) since 1997.

Virdon married Shirley Shemwell on November 17, 1951 and has three daughters. Virdon lives in Springfield, MO, where he is a director of Landmark Bank.

BIBLIOGRAPHY: Paul Burka, "Houston Astros," *TM* (December 1980), pp. 156–161, 264–271; Richard L. Burtt, *The Pittsburgh Pirates, A Pictorial History* (Virginia Beach, VA, 1977); Bob Smizik, *The Pittsburgh Pirates: An Illustrated History* (New York, 1990); Jim O'Brien, *Maz and the 1960s Bucs* (Pittsburgh, PA, 1994); Bob Broeg and Jerry Vickery, *St. Louis Cardinals Encyclopedia* (Grand Rapids, MI, 1998); Rob Rains, *The St. Louis Cardinals* (New York, 1992); Thomas Aylesworth and Benton Minks, *The Encyclopedia of Baseball Managers* (New York, 1990); *The Baseball Encyclopedia*, 10th ed. (New York, 1996); Chuck Greenwood, "Virdon Has Lived the American Dream," *SCD* 22 (September 29, 1995), pp. 160–161; Dick Groat and Bill Surface, *The World Champion Pittsburgh Pirates* (New York, 1961); Leonard Koppett, *The Man in the Dugout* (New York, 1993); John Thorn et al., eds., *Total Baseball*, 5th ed. (New York, 1997); Bill Virdon file, National Baseball Library, Cooperstown, NY; Bill Virdon, letter to Luther W. Spoehr, January 17, 1990.

Luther W. Spoehr

VON DER AHE, Christian Frederick Wilhelm "Der Poss Bresident" (b. October 7, 1851, Hille, Germany; d. June 7, 1913, St. Louis, MO), owner and manager, came to St. Louis, MO in 1870 to make his fortune and opened a combination grocery and saloon on the corner of Grand and St. Louis Avenues. Although understanding very little about baseball, "der Poss Bresident" associated thirsty customers with the game. With John Peckington, Al Spink,* and other area businessmen, Von der Ahe formed the Sportsman's Park Association. This group founded the AA, a new league in direct competition with the established NL. The first AA game was played in 1882.

When Von der Ahe hired veteran Charles Comiskey* to manage his St. Louis Brown Stockings (AA) franchise in 1883, he started realizing his dreams. From 1885 through 1888, the Brown Stockings won four AA pennants and compiled a 1–2–1 record in the World Series against the NL. Von der Ahe, who thrived on ceremony, treated his players and fans with regal affection during prosperous times. He often transported his players to Sportsman's Park in open carriages pulled by white steeds and spent a fortune taking his fans on the road during the World Series. He ceremoniously took the game's receipts each day to the bank in a wheelbarrow, flanked by armed guards.

When Comiskey left the Brown Stockings during the Brotherhood War in 1890 for a year and permanently to manage the Cincinnati Red Stockings (NL) in 1892, Von der Ahe's team started declining. Von der Ahe, an early-day Bill Veeck,* made the game more of a sideshow than the main attraction with merry-go-rounds, beer gardens, and artificial lakes. Baseball's P. T. Barnum wanted to make Sportsman's Park the "Coney Island of the West." During the next few years, Von der Ahe suffered numerous personal and business reverses. He managed the Brown Stockings in a few games from 1895 to 1897 to a 3–14 record. Two divorces, a terrible fire on April 16, 1898, unwise real estate deals, and his kidnapping by officials of the Pittsburgh Pirates over his dispute with pitcher Mark Baldwin* forced Von der Ahe out of baseball. He sold the team to attorney G. A. Gruner, who represented Frank and Stanley Robison. Von der Ahe slipped into obscurity and became a charity case for the St. Louis Cardinals (NL), who played a benefit in his honor in 1908. He married Emma Hoffmann on March 3, 1870 and had one son. He later wed Della Wells, who divorced him in 1898, and finally Anna Kaiser, who survived him.

BIBLIOGRAPHY: Chris Von der Ahe file, National Baseball Library, Cooperstown, NY; Bill Borst, *Last in the American League* (St. Louis, MO, 1976); Bill Borst, *Baseball*

Through a Knothole (St. Louis, MO, 1980); Robert Egenreither, "Chris Von der Ahe," *BRJ* 18 (1989), pp. 27–31; J. Thomas Hetrick, *Chris Von der Ahe and the St. Louis Browns* (Lanham, MD, 1999); Noel Hynd, *The Giants of the Polo Grounds* (New York, 1988); Frederick G. Lieb, *The St. Louis Cardinals* (New York, 1945); Missouri *Republican*, January 19, 1913; Daniel Peterson, *Base Ball in 1889* (Bowling Green, OH, 1993); Richard Scheinin, *Field of Screams* (New York, 1994); Bob Broeg and Jerry Vickery, *St. Louis Cardinals Baseball* (Grand Rapids, MI, 1998); St. Louis (MO) *Post Dispatch*, June 6, 1913; Robert L. Tiemann and Mark Rucker, eds., *Nineteenth Century Stars* (Kansas City, MO, 1989); Bill Nemec, *The Beer and Whisky League* (New York, 1994); Bob Broeg, *Redbirds: A Century of Cardinals' Baseball* (St. Louis, MO, 1981); Rob Rains, *The St. Louis Cardinals* (New York, 1992).

William A. Borst

VOSMIK, Joseph Franklin "Joe" (b. April 4, 1910, Cleveland, OH; d. January 27, 1962, Cleveland, OH), player, manager, and scout, was the son of Joseph Vosmik and Anna (Klecan) Vosmik, both of Bohemian ancestry. His father worked as a sawman for the Reliance Electric Company. After attending a local grade school, Vosmik played sandlot ball because his Cleveland East Tech High School fielded no baseball team. After playing for Rotbart Jewelers in 1928, the blond, stocky 6-foot, 185-pound right-hander signed a Cleveland Indians (AL) contract and joined their Class D Frederick, MD (BRL) farm team in 1929. He batted .397 in Class B baseball at Terre Haute, IN (3IL) in 1930.

On the second day of the Cleveland Indians' 1931 season, Vosmik became the starting left-fielder and batted five for five at Cleveland's League Park. The line drive hitter finished the year with a .320 batting average. For the next six seasons, he and Earl Averill* became one of the best outfield duos of all time. In 1932, he led AL outfielders with a .986 fielding percentage. After hitting .341 in 1934, Vosmik led the AL in batting the next year until Buddy Myer* of Washington topped his .348 batting average by less than one-hundredth of a point in the last game. The same season, Vosmik led the AL in hits (216), doubles (47), and triples (20). At the 1935 All-Star Game in Cleveland, fans gave him a two-minute standing ovation when he came to the plate. Vosmik married Sally Joanne Okla in November 1936 and had three children, Joseph Robert, Larry Earl, and Karen.

After Vosmik experienced an off year in 1936, the Cleveland Indians traded him to the St. Louis Browns (AL) in January 1937. He hit .325 for St. Louis that year and .324 for the Boston Red Sox (AL) in 1938, when he paced the AL in hits (201). Plagued by chronic leg problems, he finished his major league career with the Brooklyn Dodgers (NL) in 1940–1941 and Washington Senators (AL) in 1944. Vosmik, who played with Louisville, KY (AA) in 1941 and Minneapolis, MN (AA) from 1942 to 1944, retired in 1944 with a major league lifetime .307 batting average, 1,682 hits, 335 doubles, 92 triples, 65 HR, 818 runs scored, and 874 RBI.

Vosmik made his managerial debut with the Cleveland Indians' farm team in Tucson, AZ (ArTL) in 1947. After some managerial success at Dayton, OH (CL) in 1948 and Oklahoma City, OK (TL) in 1949 and 1950, he ended his baseball career at Batavia, NY (PoL) in 1951 and as a Cleveland Indians (AL) scout in 1951 and 1952 because of health problems. Never happy out of baseball, he spent his last years as a department store salesman and died after an operation for lung cancer. The quiet, easygoing Vosmik ranks among the most popular all-time Cleveland Indians players.

BIBLIOGRAPHY: Joe Vosmik file, National Baseball Library, Cooperstown, NY; Bill Borst, ed., *Ables to Zoldak*, vol. 3 (St. Louis, MO, 1990); Frederick G. Lieb, *The Boston Red Sox* (New York, 1947); Robert Redmount, *The Red Sox Encyclopedia* (Champaign, IL, 1998); William F. McNeil, *The Dodgers Encyclopedia* (Champaign, IL, 1997); Cleveland *News*, March 20, 1935, January 18, 1937, February 17, 1940, July 5, 1941, March 9, 1943, January 1, 1948, January 16, 1956; Cleveland *Plain Dealer*, January 28, 1962; Cleveland *Press*, January 27, 1962; Franklin Lewis, *The Cleveland Indians* (New York, 1949); John Thorn et al., eds., *Total Indians* (New York, 1996); Emily Yusek, letter to James N. Giglio, June 18, 1984.

James N. Giglio

VOYCE, Inez "Lefty" (b. August 16, 1924, Rathbun, IA), player, is the ninth of ten children born to Sidney Voyce, the superintendent of a coal mine, and Grace (Thomas) Voyce and had five brothers and four sisters. Voyce began playing sandlot baseball with her brothers at age five and listened to the Chicago Cubs (NL) over radio. At Seymour, IA High School, she played on the girls' basketball and softball teams. Prior to her professional baseball stint Voyce enlisted as an apprentice in the Navy. She served as a secretary to the legal officer at Hunters' Point Naval Base in San Francisco, CA, attaining the rank of second class yeoman. Voyce would have stayed in the armed forces if the AAGPBL had not beckoned. Her military career lasted 21 months. She first heard about the AAGPBL while in the Navy and tried out in Los Angeles, CA.

The 5-foot 6-inch, 148-pound Voyce, who batted and threw left-handed, played first base and pitched for the South Bend, IN Blue Sox (AAGPBL) in 1946 and for the Grand Rapids, MI Chicks from 1947 to 1953 (AAGPBL). She helped the Chicks win one pennant and two championships. In 1949, she batted .257 and led the AAGPBL with three HR and 316 total bases. Her most successful season came in 1952, when she batted .295 with 115 hits and 10 HR. The AAGPBL suspended her for 10 games in 1952 for hitting umpire Al Stover. "While winning was nice," Voyce reminisced, "the real thrill was the level of competition. I hated not playing." Voyce disliked the long night-time travelling, recalling bus trips from Racine, WI to Grand Rapids, MI that ended around dawn. Her eight year AAGPBL career included a .256 batting average, 28 HR, 422 RBI, and 168 stolen bases. Although one of the best power hitters and first basemen, she never made an All-Star team. She led first basemen three times in fielding and compiled a .961 fielding percentage.

Voyce's career highlight came against the Rockford, IL Peaches, when she doubled with two runners on base. Voyce recalled, "I never could hit well against lefties. Then, to my astonishment Rockford sent in their ace pitcher, the right handed Lois Florreich.* I thumped that ball really hard, I got a double . . . and we won."

Voyce, who is single, enjoys *The Wizard of Oz* and considers *A League of Their Own* as far-fetched. The film, however, forever changed the lives of AAGPBL participants. "Overnight, from being unknown we became famous," she chuckled.

Following her baseball career, she worked as officer manager for an electronic wire and cable business until 1990. She bowled very competitively, has golfed twice a week for 30 years and enjoys yard chores and gardening. The Santa Monica, CA resident belongs to the AAGPBL Gallery at the National Baseball Hall of Fame in Cooperstown, NY.

BIBLIOGRAPHY: Scott A.G.M. Crawford, telephone interview with Inez Voyce, April 17, 1996; AAGPBL files, Northern Indiana Historical Society, South Bend, IN, February 16, 1996; Tim Wiles, National Baseball Hall of Fame, Cooperstown, NY, letter to Scott A.G.M. Crawford, December 14, 1995; W. C. Madden, *The Women of the All-American Girls Professional Baseball League* (Jefferson, NC, 1997); Scott A.G.M. Crawford, telephone conversations with Dottie Collins, AAGPBLPA, February 1996.

Scott A.G.M. Crawford

VUCKOVICH, Peter Dennis "Pete" (b. October 27, 1952, Johnstown, PA), player and coach, is the son of Lazo Vuckovich, a Pennsylvania steel mill worker, and Betty Jane (Gjurich) Vuckovich. Vuckovich played football and baseball at Conemaugh, PA Valley High School and was selected baseball MVP twice. He made all-conference three times at Clarion State Teachers College in Pennsylvania. The Chicago White Sox (AL) chose the 6-foot 4-inch, 220-pound right-hander in the third round of the June 1974 free agent draft. He divided the 1974 season between Appleton, WI (ML) and Knoxville, TN (SL), winning three of eight decisions and striking out better than a hitter per inning. Vuckovich won 11 and lost four at Denver, CO (AA) in 1975, earning a September promotion to the Chicago White Sox. In 1976, he worked mostly in middle relief, splitting four decisions and winning five of seven starts. In November 1976, the Toronto Blue Jays (AL) selected Vuckovich in the AL expansion draft. He triumphed seven times, lost seven, and saved eight as the Blue Jays closer. In a rare start on June 23, Vuckovich pitched the first shutout in Toronto Blue Jays history in a 2–0 victory over Jim Palmer* of the Baltimore Orioles.

In December 1977, the Toronto Blue Jays traded Vuckovich to the St. Louis Cardinals (NL). St. Louis boasted 20 game winner Bob Forsch,* but possessed little other starting pitching. After struggling at 1–4 in relief, Vuc-kovich finished 11–8 when Cardinals skipper Ken Boyer* inserted him into the starting rotation. His 2.54 ERA led the St. Louis Cardinals staff and ranked third best in the NL for 1978. Vuckovich did not possess an over-powering fastball, but used a sharp-breaking slider, curveball, good control and a distracting three-quarters delivery to keep batters off stride. His size and angry glare from the mound further intimidated hitters. Vuckovich led St. Louis Cardinals hurlers with 233 innings pitched and 15 victories in 1979 and with 222.1 innings and 12 wins in 1980.

Whitey Herzog,* newly appointed St. Louis Cardinals manager and gen-eral manager, traded Vuckovich, catcher Ted Simmons,* and relief ace Rollie Fingers* to the Milwaukee Brewers (AL) for four players. In the strike-shortened 1981 season, Vuckovich won 14 of 18 decisions to help the Brew-ers capture the AL Eastern Division. He led AL hurlers in victories and with a .778 winning percentage. He won one game in the AL Division Series, but the New York Yankees defeated Milwaukee in five games. In 1982, Vuc-kovich won 18 games and lost only six, pacing AL hurlers in winning per-centage (.750), leading the Brewers to the AL Eastern Division title, and netting the AL Cy Young Award. He lost one start and had no decision in a second start in the AL Championship Series, but the Milwaukee Brewers defeated the California Angels for the AL pennant. Vuckovich lost his only World Series decision to the St. Louis Cardinals, who triumphed in seven games.

After mid-September 1982, Vuckovich pitched with a sore shoulder. Ro-tator cuff surgery cost him almost the entire 1983 season. Vuckovich re-turned in August and made three starts before a hamstring injury sidelined him for the remainder of the year. The shoulder kept him on the disabled list all of 1984. Vuckovich came back in 1985 and seemed on track after the All Star break, when his shoulder became painful again. He struggled thereafter, finishing with a 6–10 record and a 5.51 ERA. Vuckovich refused a demotion to the minor leagues and sat out 1986 until agreeing to report to Vancouver, Canada (PCL) in August. After compiling a 1.26 ERA in six starts at Vancouver, he was recalled to Milwaukee in September and won just two of six decisions. The Milwaukee Brewers released Vuckovich in October 1986. Vuckovich's major league career included 1,455.1 innings, 93 wins, 69 defeats, 10 saves, 882 strikeouts, and a 3.66 ERA in 286 games.

Vuckovich, who married Anna Kuzak in 1975 and has a son, Louis, served as director of player personnel for the Pittsburgh Pirates (NL) and became their pitching coach in 1997.

BIBLIOGRAPHY: Peter Vuckovich file, National Baseball Library, Cooperstown, NY; Peter Gammons, "He Doesn't Look Pretty, But He Wins," *BD* 42 (May 1983), pp. 25–27; Don Kausler, Jr., "Pete Vuckovich of the Brewers Silences His Critics," *BD* 41 (May 1982), pp. 51–53; John Mehno, "Pete Vuckovich: He Has Something to Prove in 1984," *BD* 43 (April 1984), pp. 97–98; Marybeth Sullivan, ed., *The Scouting Report: 1986* (New York, 1986); Jim Toomey, *Cardinals 1979* (St. Louis, MO, 1979); Ken Young, *Cy Young Award Winners* (New York, 1994); Rob Rains, *The St. Louis Cardinals* (New York, 1992); Bob Broeg, *Redbirds: A Century of Cardinals' Baseball* (St. Louis, MO, 1981); Bob Broeg and Jerry Vickery, *St. Louis Cardinals Encyclopedia* (Grand Rapids, MI, 1998); Jeff Everson, *This Date in Milwaukee Brewers History* (Appleton, WI, 1987); *Milwaukee Brewers 1983 Official Yearbook; Milwaukee Brewers 1989 Official Yearbook*; Peter C. Bjarkman, ed., *Encyclopedia of Major League Baseball Team Histories American League* (Westport, CT, 1981).

Frank J. Olmsted

W

WADDELL, George Edward "Rube" (b. October 13, 1876, Bradford, PA; d. April 1, 1914, San Antonio, TX), player, was born into a poor farm family and received little formal education. At age 18, he began pitching for the Butler, PA town team and quickly achieved stardom. In 1896, he pitched semi-pro baseball for Franklin, PA and won all four games for the Homestead, PA AC in a series against Duquesne County. Waddell earned $100 for this feat and signed a $500 contract with the Louisville, KY Colonels (NL) franchise. Waddell's first major league seasons proved uneventful and erratic largely because he possessed little discipline. He participated in two games for Louisville before jumping the Colonels in 1898 to pitch for Detroit, MI (WL) and for semipro Chatham, Canada. In 1899, he finished with a 26–8 mark for Columbus, OH/Grand Rapids, MI (WL) and won seven of nine decisions for the Louisville Colonels at the season's end. Waddell pitched for the Pittsburgh Pirates (NL) in 1900, when the Louisville and Pirates organizations merged. He compiled an impressive 2.37 ERA and 130 strikeouts before leaving the Pirates in July. Milwaukee, WI (WL) skipper Connie Mack* acquired Waddell, but the latter pitched so well for the AL club that Pittsburgh demanded his return. After coming back to the Pittsburgh Pirates in 1901, he was sold to the Chicago Orphans (NL) in May. The 1902 season began with Waddell at Los Angeles, CA (PCL), where he pitched well and became very popular. He agreed to join the Philadelphia Athletics (AL), but it required two Pinkerton detectives to bring him eastward to manager Connie Mack's new club.

Waddell's years with Philadelphia marked the most stable period in his career. In four of six seasons with the Athletics, the 6-foot 1½-inch, 196-pound left-hander won over 20 games (24–7 in 1902, 21–16 in 1903, 25–19 in 1904, 27–10 in 1905). Waddell led the AL in strikeouts from 1902 through 1907 and paced the major leagues in that category all those years except 1907. In 1905, he combined with Eddie Plank,* Chief Bender,* and Andrew Coakley for 88 victories and led the AL with a superb 1.48 ERA as Philadelphia won the AL pennant. Waddell's 27 wins led the club even though he missed the last four weeks of the season and the World Series. Waddell and Plank together won 267 games for Philadelphia from 1902 through 1907, accounting for 56 percent of the team's victories. Mack sold Waddell to the St. Louis Browns (AL) in October 1907 for $5,000. When the teams met the next season, Waddell struck out a then record 16 Philadelphia Athletics. Waddell recorded 19 victories and a 1.89 ERA for the Browns that year, but his performance declined in 1909 and 1910. Waddell in 1910 joined Newark, NJ (EL), where he compiled a 5–3 record. In 1911, he finished with a 20–17 mark for Minneapolis, MN (AA) and befriended club owner Joe Cantillon. The following year, Waddell compiled a 12–6 slate with Minneapolis and then stayed that winter at the Cantillon home near Hickman, KY. Floodwaters broke a nearby dike, threatening the community. Waddell stood shoulder deep in the swirling water for hours helping to repair the dike, but caught a severe cold from which he never recovered. A very sick Waddell slumped to 3–9 in 1913 with Virginia, MN (NoL). Cantillon paid for Waddell's admission to a tuberculosis sanitarium in San Antonio, TX where the latter died.

Nicknamed "Rube," Waddell became one of the greatest major league pitchers ever. He possessed an excellent fastball, a deep-biting curve, and superb control. In 13 major league seasons, he won 193 games and lost 143 for a .574 winning percentage, compiled a 2.16 ERA, and struck out 2,316 batters and walked only 803 hitters in 2,961.1 innings. He never pitched a no-hitter, but defeated Cy Young,* 4–2, in a 20-inning game on July 4, 1905. In a remarkable 1900 doubleheader, he won both the 17-inning first game and the second game, 1–0. Waddell, remembered for his antics and carefree attitude toward discipline, missed games to go fishing, attend fires, play marbles, wrestle alligators, and tend bar. Married three times, he spent time in jail for missing alimony payments, drank too much, and could not manage money. Although the stories that he sat his outfielders down and then struck out the side in major league games are false, Waddell did this several times in exhibition contests. The legendary Waddell was admitted to the National Baseball Hall of Fame in 1946.

BIBLIOGRAPHY: Rube Waddell file, National Baseball Library, Cooperstown, NY; Martin Appel and Burt Goldblatt, *Baseball's Best: The Hall of Fame Gallery* (New York, 1977); John Benson, *Baseball's Top 100* (Wilton, CT, 1997); Eric Duchess, *Rube Waddell: Butler's Outrageous Southpaw* (Slippery Rock, PA, 1998); Noel Hynd, *The Giants of the Polo Grounds* (New York, 1988); Donald Honig, *The American League* (New York, 1983); Craig Carter, ed., *TSN Daguerreotypes*, 8th ed. (St. Louis, MO, 1990); Connie Mack, *My 66 Years in the Big Leagues* (Philadelphia, PA, 1950); Tom Meany, *Baseball's Greatest Players* (New York, 1955); Pete Palmer, "Rube Wadden in 1902," *BRJ* 8 (1979), pp. 98–100; Frank G. Lieb, *The Pittsburgh Pirates* (New York, 1948);

Joseph L. Reichler, *The Baseball Trade Register* (New York, 1984); *The Baseball Encyclopedia*, 10th ed. (New York, 1996); Joe Scott, "Rube Waddell," *TNP* 10 (1990), pp. 72–74; Ken Smith, *Baseball's Hall of Fame* (New York, 1978); Philip Van Borries, *Legends of Louisville* (West Bloomfield, MI, 1993); Frederick G. Lieb, *Connie Mack* (New York, 1945); Jerome C. Romanowski, *The Mackmen* (Upper Darby, PA, 1979); Bill Borst, ed., *Ables to Zoldak*, vol. 3 (St. Louis, MO, 1990); Bill Borst, *Still Last in the American League* (West Bloomfield, MI, 1992).

Douglas D. Martin

WAGNER, Audrey (b. December 27, 1927, Bensenville, IL; d. date and place unknown), player, grew up in Illinois and starred as an AAGPBL outfielder. Wagner played in the AAGPBL for seven seasons from 1943 through 1949 with the Kenosha, WI Comets. She collected 627 hits, including 55 triples, and drove in 297 runs in 694 games. Wagner, who compiled a .254 career batting average, demonstrated good speed with 246 stolen bases and possessed a strong throwing arm. She compiled a .951 career fielding percentage and 90 career assists from the outfield, including a season high 23. The Kenosha Comets won half-season crowns in both 1943 and 1944, but never won an AAGPBL championship. Wagner batted .230 with 43 RBI in 1943 and led the AAGPBL with nine triples in 1945. When the AAGPBL switched to sidearm pitching in 1946, she batted .281 and led the AAGPBL with 15 doubles. From 1945 through 1947, the Kenosha Comets finished near the bottom of the standings.

Wagner led the AAGPBL in HR in 1946 with nine and 1947 with seven, and shared the title in 1949 with three. She made the All-Star team in 1947, when she batted .305 to rank second in the AAGPBL. Wagner also led the AAGPBL with 119 hits, 25 doubles, and 53 RBI. The next season, she led the AAGPBL in hitting with a .312 mark and with 130 hits in 117 games. The 5-foot 7-inch, 145-pound right-handed batter also drove in 56 runs, recorded 14 triples, and was named an All-Star for the second time. The Kenosha Comets finished the 1948 season with a modest 61–64 record, but Wagner was selected AAGPBL Player of the Year for her outstanding individual performance. Her performance declined considerably in 1949, but her 55 career triples rank third in AAGPBL history. Wagner attended medical school and became a doctor.

BIBLIOGRAPHY: AAGPBL files, Northern Indiana Historical Society, South Bend, IN; Susan E. Johnson, *When Women Played Hardball* (Seattle, WA, 1994); W. C. Madden, *The Women of the All-American Girls Professional Baseball League* (Jefferson, NC, 1997); Frank G. Menke, *The All-Sports Record Book* (New York, 1950).

Dennis S. Clark

WAGNER, John Peter "Honus," "Hans," "The Flying Dutchman" (b. February 24, 1874, Mansfield, PA; d. December 6, 1955, Carnegie, PA), player, manager, and coach, was elected to the National Baseball Hall of Fame in

1936. Although having a thick chest, huge shoulders, bowed legs, and long arms, the 5-foot 11-inch, 200-pound Wagner exhibited great speed. His speed and German heritage resulted in his nickname, "The Flying Dutchman." From 1895 at Steubenville, OH (ISL), Mansfield, OH (OSL), Adrian, MI (MISL), and Warren, OH (IOL) to 1913, Wagner never batted below .300. He entered the major leagues with the Louisville, KY Colonels (NL) in 1897 and played with the Colonels through the 1899 season. With the Pittsburgh Pirates (NL) from 1900 through 1917, the right-handed batting and throwing Wagner led the NL in batting average eight times (1900, 1903–1904, 1906–1909, 1911) and won successive batting titles from 1906 to 1909. Besides leading or tying twice for the NL lead in hits (1908, 1910) and runs scored (1902, 1906), he paced the NL five times in RBI (1901–1902, 1908–1909, 1912). Wagner also led the NL seven times in doubles, three times in triples, five times in stolen bases, four times in on base percentage and six times in slugging percentage. With a .327 career batting average, .391 on base percentage, and .466 slugging average in 10,430 at-bats (10th all-time), he compiled 1,736 runs scored, 3,415 hits (7th), 640 doubles (8th), 252 triples (3rd), 101 HR, 1,732 RBI, and 722 stolen bases (10th). Wagner, one of baseball's greatest shortstops, exhibited outstanding fielding ability and leadership.

In the winter of 1899–1900, the NL was reduced from 12 to eight teams. Louisville Colonels owner Barney Dreyfuss* became Pittsburgh Pirates club president and brought Wagner with him. With Wagner batting an NL leading .381 in 1900, Pittsburgh started dominating the NL. The Pirates won NL pennants from 1901 to 1903 and in 1909, the year Forbes Field opened. In 1909, the Pirates defeated the Detroit Tigers in a seven-game World Series to atone for their 1903 World Series loss to the Boston Pilgrims. Wagner outhit Ty Cobb* .333 to .231 and stole four more bases than Cobb. During that World Series, Cobb attempted to steal second base. Cobb allegedly yelled to Wagner, " 'Hey, Kraut Head, I'm comin' down on the next pitch.' I told him to come ahead. George Gibson,* our catcher, laid the ball perfect, right in my glove and I stuck it on Ty as he came in. I guess I wasn't too easy about it, cause it took three stitches to sew up his lip."

When Dreyfuss fired manager Jimmy Callahan in 1917, Wagner directed the club to one win in five games in early July. Wagner resigned, stating, "I never was cut out to be a manager." Although finishing the year as a player, the 43-year-old Wagner then retired after 22 major league seasons. Subsequently, Wagner coached baseball and basketball at Carnegie Tech (now Carnegie-Mellon University) in Pittsburgh not far from Forbes Field and served as sergeant-at-arms for the Pennsylvania Legislature. Along with Pirates third baseman Pie Traynor,* he owned a sporting goods store in downtown Pittsburgh, PA. From 1933 to 1951, Wagner served as a Pirates coach.

Wagner, one of five sons and four daughters of coal miner Peter Wagner and Katrina (Wolf) Wagner, began working at age 12 in the coal mines and steel mills of western Pennsylvania and also was employed as a barber. He married Bessie Baine Smith on December 30, 1916 and had two daughters, Betty and Virginia "Jennie." He learned to play every position while performing on a sandlot team with his four brothers. New York Giants manager John J. McGraw* remarked, "While Wagner was the greatest shortstop, I believe he could have been the number one player at any position he might have selected. That's why I vote him baseball's foremost all-time player." Wagner made Major League Baseball's All-Century Team.

BIBLIOGRAPHY: John P. Carmichael, *My Greatest Day in Baseball* (New York, 1951); Dennis DeValeria and Jeanne Burke DeValeria, *Honus Wagner: A Biography* (New York, 1996); Ed Fitzgerald, *The National League* (New York, 1952); Frederick G. Lieb, *The Pittsburgh Pirates* (New York, 1948); Richard L. Burtt, *The Pittsburgh Pirates: A Pictorial History* (Virginia Beach, VA, 1977); William Hageman, *Honus: The Life and Times of a Baseball Hero* (Champaign, IL, 1996); Arthur D. Hittner, *Honus Wagner: The Life of Baseball's 'Flying Dutchman'* (Jefferson, NC, 1996); *NYT*, December 6, 1955; John Thom, *Champion Batsman of the 20th Century* (Los Angeles, CA, 1992); Bob Smizik, *The Pittsburgh Pirates: An Illustrated History* (New York, 1990); Honus Wagner file, National Baseball Library, Cooperstown, NY; John P. McCarthy, *Baseball's All-Time Dream Team* (Cincinnati, OH, 1994); Jimmy Powers, *Baseball Personalities* (New York, 1949); *The Reach Official American League Baseball Guide, 1910*; Lowell Reidenbaugh, *Baseball's Hall of Fame-Cooperstown* (New York, 1993); A. D. Suehsdorf, "Honus Wagner's Rookie Year," *TNP* 6 (Winter 1987), pp. 11–17; Philip Von Borries, *Legends of Louisville* (West Bloomfield, MI, 1993); Joseph J. Vecchione, *The NYT Book of Sports Legends* (New York, 1991).

                                                                                    Edward J. Walsh

WAGNER, Leon Lamar "Daddy Wags" (b. May 13, 1934, Chattanooga, TN), player, is the son of Eugene Wagner, a foundry worker, and Hattie Lee (Foster) Wagner. Wagner's family moved to Detroit, MI when he was eight years old and later to suburban Inkster, MI. At Inkster High School, he played baseball and football and worked evenings at an automobile plant. He attended Tuskegee, AL Institute for three semesters, but left school to work in Detroit.

Wagner played semiprofessional baseball on weekends and attracted the attention of local scouts. The Philadelphia Phillies (NL) gave him a tryout and liked his power, but that organization's lack of African-American players led him elsewhere. New York Giants (NL) scout Ray Lucas signed Wagner for $175 in 1954. Wagner amassed terrific power statistics in the minor leagues between 1954 and 1956, producing 51 HR, 166 RBI, and a .318 batting average with Danville, VA (CrL) in 1956. After military service in 1957, he batted .318 with Phoenix, AZ (PCL) in 1958. He hit .317 with 13 HR for the San Francisco Giants (NL) in 1958, but struggled in 1959 and was traded to the St. Louis Cardinals (NL) that December. After slumping in 1960, he was optioned to Rochester, NY (IL). Rochester traded him to

Toronto, Canada (IL) in January 1961. Wagner joined the expansion Los Angeles Angels (AL) in April, hitting his stride with 91 HR from 1961 to 1963 and making the AL All Star team in 1962 and 1963. He made two singles and belted a two-run HR, being named MVP in the second 1962 All Star game. The same season, his career-high 37 HR and 107 RBI helped keep the Los Angeles Angels in the AL pennant race until mid-September.

The Los Angeles Angels traded Wagner to the Cleveland Indians (AL) in December 1963. With the Cleveland Indians, his production steadily declined and his always erratic fielding worsened. On May 4, 1966, Wagner and shortstop Larry Brown collided while chasing a pop fly. Brown suffered double skull fractures and convulsions and nearly died, while Wagner incurred lesser injuries. Wagner was traded to the Chicago White Sox (AL) in June 1968 and played briefly with the San Francisco Giants in 1969, finishing his baseball career with Phoenix in 1969 and 1970. In 1,352 major league games, he hit .272 with 211 HR and 799 RBI.

The flamboyant crowd favorite Wagner married Sherry Stewart on October 17, 1959 and had one daughter. On October 30, 1965, he married Doris Jean Hudson. The Pasadena, CA resident performed several minor roles in television and film, including "A Woman Under the Influence," and "The Bingo Long Traveling All-Stars and Motor Kings," and worked as a car salesman.

BIBLIOGRAPHY: Leon Wagner file, National Baseball Library, Cooperstown, NY; "The Has Been Who Became a Star," *Ebony* 18 (October 1963), pp. 102–104, 106–108; Edward Kiersh, *Where Have You Gone, Vince DiMaggio?* (New York, 1983); Braven Dyer, "Daddy Wags Demolished Tribe Hurlers," *TSN*, December 21, 1963, pp. 3–4; Jackie Robinson, *Baseball Has Done It* (Philadelphia, PA and New York, 1964); Frank Graham, "The Making of an Outfielder," *BD* 22 (February 1963), pp. 65–66; Larry Moffi and Jonathan Kronstadt, *Crossing the Line* (Jefferson, NC, 1994); Ross Newhan, *The California Angels* (New York, 1982); Terry Pluto, *The Curse of Rocky Colavito* (New York, 1994); *The Baseball Encyclopedia*, 10th ed. (New York, 1996); John Thorn et al., *Total Baseball*, 5th ed. (New York, 1997); Jack Torry, *Endless Summers* (South Bend, IN, 1995).

Edward J. Tassinari

WAGONER, Betty Ann (b. July 17, 1930, Lebanon, MO), baseball and basketball player and coach, is the daughter of Irvin Wagoner, a farmer and plumber, and Irene (Martley) Wagoner and had one brother and one sister. From the outset, she loved competitive sports. In elementary and junior high school, Wagoner joined boys' softball and baseball teams. She attended Bolivar High School, where she played softball and basketball and admired baseball star Stan Musial* and basketball star Bob Pettit (IS). She wrote the AAGPBL asking for a tryout after reading about the league in a *Life* magazine article and was drafted as an outfielder.

The 5-foot 2-inch, 110-pound Wagoner, who batted and threw left-handed, pitched and played outfield with the Muskegan, MI Lassies

(AAGPBL) in 1948 and South Bend, IN Blue Sox (AAGPBL) from 1949 until the league disbanded in 1954. In 1948, her .278 batting average ranked fifth in the AAGPBL. She led the AAGPBL with 87 walks in 1949 and made the All-Star team in 1950, when she batted .296 in 106 games, scored 61 runs, and made career-bests with 115 hits and 11 doubles. Her career highlights included winning the AAGPBL 1951 Championship and reaching the 1952 playoffs. She batted .272 in 1951 and .295 with a 5–2 record as a pitcher in 1952. In 1954, she hit a career-best .320 in 48 games.

In the May 1949 issue of *Calling All Girls*, actress June Allyson ranked Wagoner among the top teenagers in her profession. During seven AAGPBL seasons, Wagoner batted .271 with 609 hits and 191 RBI and compiled a 13–22 win–loss record with a 3.68 ERA. In August 1957, the Allington All American All-Star team broke with tradition by playing a nostalgic game against a team of former AAGPBL members, including Wagoner, at South Bend, IN.

"I just loved to play competitive sports," disclosed Wagoner. "My most vivid memory was playing in the outfield and being mesmerized by Jean Faut Eastman* who pitched a perfect no hitter." Her disappointment in giving up professional baseball was eased by her transition into women's basketball. She served as player–coach of the South Bend Rockettes, who won National Championships from 1954 to 1960. In each of these seasons, she was named the MVP and made the All Star Team.

Wagoner, who remains single, worked 32 years until 1986 for the Bendix Company, a brake and steering manufacturer. *Gone with the Wind* is her favorite book and Charlton Heston's *Ten Commandments* her favorite film. She enjoys competitive bowling and likes reading, televised sports, and yard work. The South Bend, IN resident belongs to the AAGPBL Gallery at the National Baseball Hall of Fame in Cooperstown, NY.

BIBLIOGRAPHY: Scott A.G.M. Crawford, telephone interview with Betty Wagoner, April 24, 1996; AAGPBL files, Northern Indiana Historical Society, South Bend, IN; Tim Wiles, National Baseball Hall of Fame, Cooperstown, NY, letter to Scott A.G.M. Crawford, December 14, 1995; Scott A.G.M. Crawford, telephone conversations with Dottie Collins, AAGPBLPA, February 1996; Gai I. Berlage, *Women in Baseball: The Forgotten History* (Westport, CT, 1994); W. C. Madden, *The Women of the All-American Girls Professional Baseball League* (Jefferson, NC, 1997).

Scott A.G.M. Crawford

WALBERG, George Elvin "Rube" (b. July 27, 1896, Pine City, MN; d. October 27, 1978, Tempe, AZ), player and scout, was the son of Samuel Walberg and Anna Christine Walberg, of Swedish descent, and broke into professional baseball with the Portland, OR Beavers (PCL) in 1922. The New York Giants (NL) acquired Walberg that fall, but waived him after just two appearances in 1923. The Philadelphia Athletics (AL) claimed him and kept him the rest of the 1923 season.

Following an excellent year with Milwaukee, WI (AA) in 1924, Walberg became a mainstay of the Philadelphia Athletics pitching staff from 1925 to 1933. He alternated between starting and relieving assignments his first two seasons in Philadelphia, but became mostly a starter in 1927. Although the 6-foot 1½-inch, 190-pound, hard-throwing left-hander struggled with control problems throughout his career, he became Philadelphia's number three starter behind Lefty Grove* and George Earnshaw.

Walberg helped pitch the Philadelphia Athletics to three consecutive AL pennants from 1929 through 1931, winning 18, 13, and 20 games, respectively. He pitched in five World Series games, winning one against the Chicago Cubs in 1929 and losing one against the St. Louis Cardinals in 1930. Despite leading the AL with 291 innings pitched in 1931, Walberg hurled only one inning in the 1931 World Series against the St. Louis Cardinals. He won 17 games for the second-place Philadelphia Athletics in 1932.

In December 1933, Manager Connie Mack* dismantled a great Philadelphia Athletics team by trading Walberg, Grove, and second baseman Max Bishop* to the Boston Red Sox (AL). The Philadelphia Athletics acquired pitcher Bob Kline and infielder Rabbit Warstler, and received $125,000 from Boston's Tom Yawkey.* After spending four mediocre seasons with the Boston Red Sox through 1937, Walberg retired with a 155–141 lifetime record, 4.16 ERA, and 1,031 walks and 1,085 strikeouts in 2,644 innings. He opened a tavern in the Philadelphia, PA area and scouted for the Philadelphia Athletics before moving to Florida in 1948. Walberg, who married Lillian Estelle Cunnington in 1923 and had two children, George and Nancy, moved to Tempe, AZ in 1973.

BIBLIOGRAPHY: Frederick G. Lieb, *Connie Mack* (New York, 1945); Philadelphia (PA) *Inquirer*, October 28, 1978; Rube Walberg file, National Baseball Library, Cooperstown, NY; *WWIB*, 1933, 18th ed.; Connie Mack, *My 66 Years in the Big Leagues* (Philadelphia, PA, 1950); Jerome C. Romanowski, *The Mackmen* (Upper Darby, PA, 1979); Frederick G. Lieb, *The Boston Red Sox* (New York, 1947); Howard Liss, *The Boston Red Sox* (New York, 1982); Robert Redmount, *The Red Sox Encyclopedia* (Champaign, IL, 1998).

Lyle Spatz

WALKER, Clarence William "Tillie" (b. September 4, 1887, Telford, TN; d. September 20, 1959, Unicoi, TN), player, umpire, and manager, excelled as a hard-hitting, hard-throwing outfielder and made a smooth transition from dead ball to lively ball in 1920. The son of eastern Tennessee farmers Nelson Walker and Florence Walker, he attended Washington County schools and Washington College of Knoxville, TN. He began his minor league baseball career with Spartanburg, SC (CrA) in 1910. Walker, a 5-foot 11-inch, 165-pound outfielder with an exceptionally strong right arm, also pitched several games. In 1911, Walker's power hitting and CrA-leading .390 batting av-

erage persuaded the Washington Senators (AL) to purchase him. In his ma-
jor league debut on June 10, he hit a single, double, and triple in four at-bats
against the Chicago White Sox. He batted .278 in 1911, but manager Clark
Griffith* sold him in October 1912 to the St. Louis Browns (NL). The St.
Louis Browns sold him to Kansas City, MO (AA) before the 1913 season to
sharpen his skills. In 1913, Walker hit 21 triples for Kansas City and led the
AA in slugging average. After the St. Louis Browns (AL) reacquired him,
Walker began making his mark as one of the strongest throwing outfielders
in baseball. In 1914, he set a club record by hitting in 27 consecutive games
and recorded 30 assists in 1914 to take over the AL leadership from Tris
Speaker.* He also paced the AL with 27 assists in 1915. The Boston Red
Sox (AL) traded Speaker to the Cleveland Indians and acquired Walker from
St. Louis in April 1916. After spending two seasons with the Boston Red
Sox, he was traded in January 1918 to the Philadelphia Athletics and shared
the AL lead with Babe Ruth* by hitting 11 HR in 1918. The Philadelphia
Athletics had become the AL doormat, as Connie Mack* had sold his stars.
Walker provided them with the only power they could muster for the next
several years. He adjusted well to the lively ball era, as his HR totals soared
from 10 in 1919 to 17 in 1920, 23 in 1921, and 37 in 1922. Walker's 98 HR
over five years ranked second to that of Ruth, while his 37 HR in 1922
marked the fourth highest total achieved up to that time. Only Ruth, Rogers
Hornsby,* and Ken Williams* had hit more HR.

The Philadelphia Athletics unfortunately finished no higher than seventh
place while leading the AL in HR, causing Mack to consequently downplay
the long ball. Walker, who also had slowed down defensively, saw only limited duty in 1923, his last major league season. He led the AL a record four
times in assists and compiled 222 career assists in 1,348 outfield games. He
recorded a career .281 batting average and produced 118 HR and 679 RBI.
Walker played several more years in the minor leagues, leading the SAL in
HR with 33 in 1928 at age 40. He umpired in the ApL in 1938 and 1939
and managed Erwin, TN (ApL) in 1940. Walker then worked 14 years as a
highway patrolman. Walker's marriage, which produced one son and two
daughters, ended in divorce in the 1920s. His nickname, "Tillie," which is
carried on his tombstone, reportedly came from the quick, short steps he
took while walking.

BIBLIOGRAPHY: Bill Borst, ed., *Ables to Zoldak*, vol. 3 (St. Louis, MO, 1990); Bill
Borst, *Still Last in the American League* (West Bloomfield, MI, 1992); Frederick G.
Lieb, *The Baltimore Orioles* (New York, 1955); Robert Redmount, *The Red Sox En-
cyclopedia* (Champaign, IL, 1998); Connie Mack, *My 66 Years in the Big Leagues* (Phil-
adelphia, PA, 1950); Jerome C. Romanowski, *The Mackmen* (Upper Darby, PA, 1979);
Erwin (TN) *Record*, September 23, 1959; F. C. Lane, "One Reason Why the Browns
Are Winning," *BM* 13 (September 1914), pp. 73–76; Frederick G. Lieb, *Connie Mack*
(New York, 1945); John B. Sheridan, "Pride Made C. Walker Great," St. Louis

(MO) *Globe Democrat*, June 21, 1914; Clarence Walker file, National Baseball Library, Cooperstown, NY; "Walker Has Big Day," Washington (DC) *Post*, June 11, 1911.

L. Robert Davids

WALKER, Fred "Dixie," "The People's Cherce" (b. September 24, 1910, Villa Rica, GA; d. May 17, 1982, Birmingham, AL), player, coach, and manager, performed as an outfielder for the New York Yankees (AL, 1931–1936), Chicago White Sox (AL, 1936–1937), and Detroit Tigers (AL, 1938–July 1939), and Brooklyn Dodgers (NL, July 1939–1947) and Pittsburgh Pirates (NL, 1948–1949). Nicknamed "Dixie," he became one of the most popular players in Brooklyn Dodgers history and earned the label "The People's Cherce" for his consistent clutch fielding and hitting. His father, Ewart Gladstone "Dixie" Walker, pitched for the Washington Senators (AL) from 1909 to 1912, while his uncle, Ernie Walker, played outfield for the St. Louis Browns (AL) from 1913 to 1915. His mother, Flossie (Vaughn) Walker, was a homemaker. The left-handed hitting and right-handed throwing Dixie and his brother, Harry, combined for a .303 career batting average and became one of only six brother combinations in baseball history to surpass the .300 lifetime level.

Walker, a .306 career major league batter and .270 lifetime pinch-hitter, led the AL with 16 triples in 1937, won the NL batting title in 1944 with a .357 average, and led the NL with 124 RBI in 1945. On April 30, 1939, he scored five runs in one game. He participated in .300-hitting outfields with Rip Radcliff* and Mike Kreevich* on the 1937 Chicago White Sox and with Pete Reiser* and Joe Medwick* on the 1942 Brooklyn Dodgers. Not a power hitter, Walker slugged a career-high 15 HR in 1933. Although hitting only nine HR in 1946, he drove in 116 runs. During his 18-year major league career, he compiled 2,064 hits, 376 doubles, 96 triples, 105 HR, 1,037 runs scored, 1,023 RBI, 817 walks, and 59 stolen bases.

Walker played in the 1941 and 1947 World Series for the Brooklyn Dodgers and in the 1943–1944 and 1946–1947 All-Star games. In 1943 and 1947, he joined his brother, Harry, on the NL All-Star team. In 1944 *TSN* named him to its major league All-Star team. After retiring as a player, Walker managed in the minor leagues at Atlanta, GA (SA) in 1950–1952, Houston, TX (TL) in 1953–1954, Rochester, NY (IL) in 1955–1956, and Toronto, Canada (IL) in 1957–1959, coached for the St. Louis Cardinals (NL, 1953, 1955) and Milwaukee Braves (NL, 1963–1965), scouted for the Milwaukee Braves (1960–1962) and Atlanta Braves (NL, 1966–1968), and served as a batting instructor in the Los Angeles Dodgers organization (NL, 1968–1978).

At a Waldorf-Astoria luncheon in 1943, Walker, Carl Hubbell* of the New York Giants, and Joe Gordon* of the New York Yankees were "auctioned off" for pledges toward War Bonds. Walker drew a $11,250,000 bid from a Brooklyn social club. In late 1943, Walker, Stan Musial,* and other major leaguers visited U.S. military troops in the Aleutian Islands.

Walker began his professional baseball career at age 12, earning $5 a game by playing on a semipro Calvert, AL team managed by his father. Walker batted .401 for Greenville, SC (SAL) in 1930, when the New York Yankees bought him in midseason for a then record $25,000. Unfortunately, he suffered serious injuries throughout his career. When the Brooklyn Dodgers purchased Walker from the Detroit Tigers, many baseball followers considered his career finished. After home state Alabamans pressured him not to play with Jackie Robinson,* Walker wrote Dodgers' president W. Branch Rickey* asking to be traded. Walker, born in a log cabin, was a high school dropout. He married Estelle Shea in May 1936. Tragedy struck at the height of his career on May 23, 1940, when his daughter, Mary Ann, died from double pneumonia. The mild Walker, who spoke in a slow, high-pitched southern drawl, died of cancer.

BIBLIOGRAPHY: Dixie Walker file, National Baseball Library, Cooperstown, NY; *SEAL*, vol. 1 (1981–1985), pp. 830–832; John Thom, *Champion Batsman of the 20th Century* (Los Angeles, CA, 1992); Mark Gallagher, *The Yankees Encyclopedia*, vol. 3 (Champaign, IL, 1997); Frank Graham, *The New York Yankees* (New York, 1943); Craig Carter, *TSN Official Baseball Dope Book* (St. Louis, MO, 1983); Stanley Frank, "Nobody Wanted Him but the Fans," *SEP* 214 (February 14, 1942), pp. 27ff; Sam Goldaper, "Dixie Walker, Dodger Star of the 1940s, Dead at 71," *NYT*, May 18, 1982; Tot Holmes, *Dodgers Blue Book* (Los Angeles, CA, 1983); William F. McNeil, *The Dodger Encyclopedia* (Champaign, IL, 1997); Stanley Cohen, *Dodgers! The First 100 Years* (New York, 1990); Tommy Holmes, *The Dodgers* (New York, 1975); Peter Golenbock, *Bums* (New York, 1984); Fred Smith, *995 Tigers* (Detroit, MI, 1981); Jack Kavanagh, "Dixie Walker—'The Peepul's Cherce,'" *BRJ* 22 (1993), pp. 80–83; Richard Goldstein, *Superstars and Screwballs* (New York, 1991); William B. Mead, *Even the Browns* (Chicago, IL, 1978); *The Baseball Encyclopedia*, 10th ed. (New York, 1996); *TSN Official Baseball Guide, 1983*.

Jack P. Lipton

WALKER, Gerald Holmes "Gee" (b. March 19, 1908, Gulfport, MS; d. March 20, 1981, Whitfield, MS), player, became a leading hitter in the 1930s and was a brother of major leaguer "Hub" Walker. After attending the University of Mississippi, the 5-foot 11-inch, 188-pound right-hander entered organized baseball in 1928 with Fort Smith, AR (WA). He progressed rapidly through the minor leagues, joining the Detroit Tigers (AL) in 1931. He quickly developed into a hard hitter, but proved an erratic outfielder and a reckless baserunner with an incorrigible tendency to be caught off base. Walker's flamboyant base running made him the despair of some managers, but a great favorite of Detroit Tigers fans. When manager Mickey Cochrane* polled his players in 1934 whether Walker should be retained, the Tigers voted almost unanimously in the outfielder's favor. Walker enjoyed his finest years in Detroit, hitting .300 or more in five of seven seasons. He played on the Detroit Tigers' championship teams of 1934 and 1935, but was limited mainly to pinch hitting in the World Series. When Walker was traded to the Chicago White Sox (AL) in December 1937, Tigers fans uttered the greatest protest the club had ever experienced.

Walker, mainly a singles hitter, was well suited to the spacious Comiskey Park. Although his performance in Chicago nearly equalled his play in Detroit, he never achieved his earlier popularity partly because he had been traded for the well-liked Fred "Dixie" Walker.* Walker was traded to the Washington Senators (AL) in December 1939, Cleveland Indians (AL) in December 1940, and Cincinnati Reds (NL) in March 1942. Despite arthritis, he played with the Reds throughout World War II and was released at the end of the 1945 season. In 15 major league seasons, Walker played in 1,784 games, made 1,991 hits, 399 doubles, 76 triples, and 124 HR, scored 954 runs, batted in 997 runs, and stole 223 bases. He achieved a lifetime .294 batting average. Walker, of English ancestry, married Grace McLain on November 14, 1930 and later sold real estate in Mississippi and Florida.

BIBLIOGRAPHY: Gerald Walker file, National Baseball Library, Cooperstown, NY; *The Baseball Encyclopedia*, 10th ed. (New York, 1996); *WWIB, 1945*, 30th ed.; Frederick G. Lieb, *The Detroit Tigers* (New York, 1946); Joe Falls, *Detroit Tigers* (New York, 1975); Fred Smith, *995 Tigers* (Detroit, MI, 1981); George Sullivan and David Cataneo, *Detroit Tigers* (New York, 1985); David M. Anderson, *The Detroit Tigers* (South Bend, IN, 1996); Warren Brown, *The Chicago White Sox* (New York, 1952); Richard Lindberg, *Sox* (New York, 1984); Franklin Lewis, *The Cleveland Indians* (New York, 1949).

George W. Hilton

WALKER, Larry Kenneth Robert, Jr. (b. December 1, 1966, Maple Ridge, Canada), player, rose from an unlikely prospect to a prominent NL outfielder. Walker is one of four sons of Larry Walker, Sr., who manages a building supply store, and Mary Walker and attended Maple Ridge Senior Secondary School. Walker's first taste of professional baseball came with the Utica, NY Blue Sox (NYPL) in 1985. Scouts considered him a long shot to succeed because he lacked developmental experience. "In Canada, as a kid, we'd play 10 baseball games a year," Walker disclosed. "Baseball just wasn't big. The weather was against it." He spent 1986 with Burlington, IA (ML) and West Palm Beach, FL (FSL), 1987 with Jacksonville, FL (SL), and 1989 with Indianapolis, IN (AA).

Walker reached the major leagues with the Montreal Expos (NL) in 1989, batting just .170 in 20 games. The 6-foot 2-inch, 205-pound left-hander, a Canadian-born player on a Canadian-based club, quickly blossomed into a star outfielder and a power-hitting threat. Walker started in the Montreal Expos outfield in 1990, batting .241 and belting 19 HR. A reliable defensive player, he made just four errors in 265 chances. In 1991, Walker's offensive output continued to improve. His batting average climbed to .290. Although his HR production declined slightly to 16, his slugging average rose from .434 to .458, largely because he connected for 30 doubles. During 1992, Walker became a legitimate NL star. He clouted 23 HR and batted .301. Walker committed just two errors and was awarded a Gold Glove. He also made *TSN*'s NL Silver Slugger and All-Star teams in 1992 and earned a second Gold Glove in 1993. Walker appeared in the 1992 All-Star Game, making a hit in his lone at-bat.

By 1994, Walker had become Montreal's biggest headliner. A Canadian publication noted, "Students of the game now regard him as the Expos' best position player since Andre Dawson.*'" The cost-conscious Montreal Expos, however, refused to meet Walker's large salary demands. After the strike-shortened 1994 season, he signed with the Colorado Rockies (NL) as a free agent. In 1995, he batted .306 with 36 HR and 101 RBI and clouted one HR with three RBI in the NL Division Series against the Atlanta Braves. On May 21–22, 1996, Walker broke an NL mark for most consecutive extra base hits with two doubles, three triples, and a HR against the Pittsburgh Pirates. Walker's feat tied a major league record for most extra base hits in consecutive games. *TSN* named him to its NL All-Star and Silver Slugger teams from 1997 through 1999 and awarded him Gold Gloves those seasons. His best season came in 1997, when he led the NL with a career-high 49 HR and recorded career bests with a .366 batting average, 143 runs scored, 208 hits, 46 doubles, 130 RBI, and 33 stolen bases. He made the NL All-Star team and became the first Canadian-born player and Colorado Rockie to win the NL MVP award. Walker led the NL in batting (.363) in 1998, finishing third in on-base percentage (.445) and slugging percentage (.630). In 1999, he paced the NL in batting (a career-high .379), on-base percentage (.458), and slugging percentage (.710), making his 4th NL All-Star Team. His home town of Maple Ridge, Canada has named a youth baseball park after him. Through the 1999 season, Walker has batted .312 with 1,431 hits, 304 doubles, 262 HR, and 855 RBI. He and his wife, Christa, have one daughter, Brittany.

BIBLIOGRAPHY: *CB* (May 1998), pp. 57–59; A. Finlayson, "The Dreams of Summer," *Macleans* 99 (September 8, 1986), pp. 6ff; Gare Joyce, "Yerrr Out!," *SN* 109 (October 1994), pp. 71–74; Leigh Montville, "The Accidental Ballplayer," *SI* 78 (April 5, 1993), pp. 78–80; Leigh Montville, "Southern Exposure," *SIC* 1 (April 5, 1993), pp. 70–75; *The Baseball Encyclopedia*, 10th ed. (New York, 1996).

John G. Robertson

WALKER, Moses Fleetwood "Fleet" (b. October 7, 1856, Mt. Pleasant, OH; d. May 11, 1924, Cleveland OH), player, was the fourth of five children of minister or doctor Moses Walker and Caroline Walker and became the major league's first black baseball performer. Between 1878 and 1882, Walker attended Oberlin College and the University of Michigan Law School. Although catching for both baseball teams, he earned degrees from neither school. In the summer of 1883, "Walker" joined Toledo, OH (AA) ostensibly to earn money to complete his education. Walker, however, pursued a professional baseball career with the Toledo Blue Stockings (in 1884 the AA became a major league, making Walker the first black major leaguer), Cleveland, OH (WL, 1885), Waterbury, CT (EL, 1885–1886), Newark, NJ (IL, 1887), Syracuse, NY (IL, 1888–1889), and Terre Haute, IN (1890). During these seven years, Walker compiled mediocre statistics, never hit above .279, and often had among the worst league fielding averages. The right-hander proved a strong-armed, erratic catcher in a bare-handed era and a fair hitter with good speed.

Walker's tenure in white leagues came in years of increasing separatist sentiment and was plagued by racial harassment. In both 1883 and 1887, Cap Anson* refused to allow his Chicago White Stockings (NL) to play against Walker. Baseball fans in the southern cities of Louisville, KY and Richmond, VA occasionally threatened Walker, while the press in cities of opposition teams wrote negative, tauntingly racist accounts. Nevertheless, Walker rejected playing for all-Negro teams. Although involved in the Sunday baseball controversy and affected by the political vigilance his younger brother, Welday, brought to the black cause, Walker increased his political activity following his retirement from baseball.

In 1908, he and Welday edited a newspaper, *The Equator*, and opened a Steubenville, OH office for Liberian emigration. Walker's treatise, *Our Home Colony*, comprised a bitter, oversimplified history of the Negro race, urging American blacks to return to Africa. Despite his baseball career, his ventures in hotel and theater ownership, and his sophisticated, articulate nature, Walker suffered from the myth of black incapability, the nearly systematic exclusion of blacks from the economic market, and the continuing futile preoccupation of some with the possibility for African colonization. Walker outlived both of his wives, Arabella Taylor and Edna Jane Mason, the first of whom bore him three sons.

BIBLIOGRAPHY: Ocania Chalk, *Pioneers of Black Sport* (New York, 1975); Noel Hynd, *The Giants of the Polo Grounds* (New York, 1988); R. Giancaterino, "1884: Moses Fleetwood Walker," *AV* 8 (June/July 1993), pp. 25–26; Robert W. Peterson, *Only the Ball Was White* (Englewood Cliffs, NJ, 1970); James A. Riley, *The Biographical Encyclopedia of the Negro Baseball Leagues* (New York, 1994); Robert L. Tiemann and Mark Rucker, eds., *Nineteenth Century Stars* (Kansas City, MO, 1989); Moses Fleetwood Walker, *Our Home Colony* (Steubenville, OH, 1908); Moses Fleetwood Walker file, National Baseball Library, Cooperstown, NY; Moses Fleetwood Walker papers, Oberlin College Archives, Oberlin, OH; Carl F. Wittke, "Oberlinian First Negro Player in Major Leagues," *OAB*, 1946; David Zang, *Fleet Walker's Divided Heart* (Lincoln, NE, 1995).

David W. Zang

WALKER, William Curtis "Curt" (b. July 3, 1896, Beeville, TX; d. December 9, 1955, Beeville, TX), player, was the son of N. B. Walker and Emma

Walker and graduated from Beeville High School in 1914. A versatile athlete, he won the state tennis doubles championship as a high school senior. Walker attended Southwestern University in Georgetown, TX two years before serving in World War I. He began his professional baseball career with Houston, TX (TL) in 1919 and also played that season with Augusta, GA (SAL). The New York Yankees (AL) gave him a one game trial in September 1919.

The 5-foot 9-inch, 170-pound outfielder returned to Augusta in 1920 and earned a major league trial that September with the New York Giants (NL). Walker made the New York Giants roster in 1921, but was traded that July to the Philadelphia Phillies (NL). Walker started for the Philadelphia Phillies the next two seasons, batting a career-high .337 in 1923. In May 1924, the Philadelphia Phillies traded Walker to the Cincinnati Reds (NL). He started in the outfield with the Cincinnati Reds for the rest of his major league tenure through 1928. A fractured skull, suffered in August 1928, almost killed Walker. Chicago Cubs shortstop Woody English* hit him with a ball above his right ear while attempting to turn a double play. The throw knocked Walker unconscious, but he suffered no after-effects.

The left handed hitting Walker batted .304 as a major leaguer with 1,475 hits, including 235 doubles, 117 triples, and 64 HR. He shares the major league record for hitting two triples in one inning against the Boston Braves in 1927. His professional baseball career concluded with Indianapolis, IN (AA) in 1931 and 1932. Following his father's death, he returned to Beeville and joined his brother, Jesse, in operating the Walker Funeral Home. The licensed embalmer worked at the funeral home until selling it in 1946. Walker in 1954 was elected Justice of the Peace and held that position until his death. He died of a cerebral hemorrhage following a stroke.

BIBLIOGRAPHY: *The Baseball Encyclopedia*, 10th ed. (New York, 1996); Curtis Walker file, National Baseball Library, Cooperstown, NY; Frederick G. Lieb and Stan Baumgartner, *The Philadelphia Phillies* (New York, 1953); Rich Westcott and Frank Bilovsky, *The New Phillies Encyclopedia* (Philadelphia, PA, 1993); Lee Allen, *The Cincinnati Reds* (New York, 1948), Floyd Connor and John Snyder, *Day-by-Day in Cincinnati Reds History* (West Point, NY, 1984); Bob Rathgeber, *Cincinnati Reds Scrapbook* (Virginia Beach, VA, 1982).

John Hillman

WALLACE, Roderick John "Bobby," "Rhody" (b. November 4, 1873, Pittsburgh, PA; d. November 3, 1960, Torrance, CA), player, coach, manager, scout, and umpire, was the son of John Wallace of Scottish descent and attended the First Ward Elementary School in Millvale, PA. As a teenager, he worked in his brother-in-law's food store in Millvale and pitched for semipro baseball teams in western Pennsylvania. In 1894, the Franklin, PA semipro team signed Wallace for $45 per month. Wallace then joined the Cleveland, OH Spiders (NL). The 5-foot 8-inch right-hander compiled 12–

14 and 10–7 records with the Spiders in 1895 and 1896 before moving to third base and hitting .339 in 1897.

After being sent to the St. Louis Cardinals (NL) in 1899, Wallace moved to shortstop. From 1899 to 1901 with the Cardinals, he fielded well and once hit over .300. He jumped to the St. Louis Browns (AL) in 1902, received a $6,500 advance, and signed a five-year, no-trade, $32,500 contract, making him the day's highest paid player. He married June Mann on August 8, 1906. From 1902 to 1910, Wallace ranked as the premier AL shortstop, led in assists and putouts three times, and fielding average twice. He reluctantly became player–manager of the St. Louis Browns in 1911, but quit after a last place finish that year and a 12–27 start in 1912. A broken hand in 1912 and severe burns in 1914 greatly limited his playing time.

Wallace became an AL umpire in June 1915, but rejoined the St. Louis Browns in August 1916. He started the 1917 campaign managing Wichita, KS (WL), signed with the St. Louis Cardinals following his June release, and completed a 25-year major league career in 1918 by playing 32 games for the Cardinals. His career totals included 2,309 hits, 391 doubles, 143 triples, 34 HR, 1,057 runs scored, 1,121 RBI, 211 stolen bases, and a .268 batting average in 2,383 games. Although Wallace owns no single-season or career offensive records, he ranks in or near the top ten for career chances (11,130), assists (6,303), putouts (4,142), assists per game (3.5), and chances per game among shortstops (5.7). He compiled a win–loss 24–22 record and 3.89 ERA as a pitcher and a 62–154 mark as manager of the Browns and the 1937 Cincinnati Reds (NL). Wallace also managed Muskogee, OK (SWL) in 1921, scouted for the Chicago Cubs (NL) in 1924, coached with the Cincinnati Reds in 1926, and scouted for Cincinnati from 1927 to 1937 and 1938 until his death. Wallace, who enjoyed billiards and golf in his later years, was elected to the National Baseball Hall of Fame in 1953.

BIBLIOGRAPHY: Martin Appel and Burt Goldblatt, *Baseball's Best: The Hall of Fame Gallery* (New York, 1977); Bill Borst, *The Pride of St. Louis: A Cooperstown Gallery* (St. Louis, MO, 1984); Lowell Reidenbaugh, *Baseball's Hall of Fame-Cooperstown* (New York, 1993); J. Thomas Hetrick, *The Misfits!* (Jefferson, NC, 1991); John Phillips, *The Spiders—Who Was Who* (Cabin John, MD, 1991); Frederick G. Lieb, *The St. Louis Cardinals* (New York, 1945); Bob Broeg, *Redbirds: A Century of Cardinals' Baseball* (St. Louis, MO, 1981); Bob Broeg and Jerry Vickery, *St. Louis Cardinals Encyclopedia* (Grand Rapids, MI, 1998); Bill Borst, ed., *Ables to Zoldak*, vol. 3 (St. Louis, MO, 1990); Bill Borst, *Still Last in the American League* (West Bloomfield, MI, 1992); Frederick G. Lieb, *The Baltimore Orioles* (New York, 1955); Thomas Aylesworth and Benton Minks, *The Encyclopedia of Baseball Managers* (New York, 1990); Lee Allen, *The Cincinnati Reds* (New York, 1948); Ken Smith, *Baseball's Hall of Fame*, rev. ed. (New York, 1970); Roderick Wallace file, National Baseball Library, Cooperstown, NY.

Frank J. Olmsted

WALLACH, Timothy Charles "Tim" (b. September 14, 1957, Huntington Park, CA), player, is the son of Richard Wallach and attended University

High School in Irvine, CA, Saddlebrook JC, and California State University-Fullerton, where he was named 1979 NCAA College Baseball Player of the Year. The 6-foot 3-inch, 202-pound right-handed–hitting third baseman began his professional baseball career with Memphis, TN (SL) in 1979 after the Montreal Expos (NL) drafted him in the first round. In 1980, the Montreal Expos summoned him from Denver, CO (AA). Wallach clouted a HR in his first official major league at-bat. On October 10, 1980, he married Lori Jeannette Bickford.

The Montreal Expos used Wallach sparingly during 1981. After the Montreal Expos traded third baseman Larry Parrish* to the Texas Rangers in March 1982, Wallach replaced him and ended that season with 28 HR and 97 RBI. He also earned Player of the Month honors that May. His offensive production dropped the next two seasons, but he led NL third basemen with 151 putouts in 1983. Wallach made the NL All-Star team in 1984 and led NL third basemen in games, putouts, assists, total chances, and double plays.

The 1985 season brought Wallach his first Gold Glove, another NL All-Star team designation, and an initial *TSN* Silver Slugger team selection. Wallach's 1987 campaign produced career highs in batting average (.298), doubles (42), and RBI (123). He paced the NL in doubles, set a club record in RBI, made the NL All-Star team for the third time, and won both Montreal Expos and *SI* Player of the Year honors. In 1988, Wallach earned his second Gold Glove and led NL third basemen with 124 putouts. Wallach, who repeated as Montreal Expos Player of the Year in 1989, won his third Gold Glove in 1990 and made the NL All-Star team both years. In 1991, he led NL third basemen with a .968 fielding percentage and made only 14 errors.

In December 1992, the Montreal Expos traded their career leader in games, at-bats, hits, doubles, RBI, total bases, and third base fielding percentage to the Los Angeles Dodgers (NL) for Tim Barker. The California Angels (AL) acquired him in December 1995, but he returned to the Los Angeles Dodgers in July 1996. He retired following the 1996 season with a .257 batting average, 2,085 hits, 432 doubles, 260 HR, 1,125 RBI, and a .959 fielding percentage. He appeared in the 1981, 1995, and 1996 NL Division Series and the 1981 NL Championship Series against the Los Angeles Dodgers.

BIBLIOGRAPHY: Tim Wallach file, National Baseball Library, Cooperstown, NY; Dan Turner, *The Expos Inside Out* (Toronto, Canada, 1983); Peter C. Bjarkman, *Encyclopedia of Major League Baseball Team Histories National League* (Westport, CT, 1991); William F. McNeil, *The Dodgers Encyclopedia* (Champaign, IL, 1997).

Chad Israelson

WALSH, Edward Augustine "Ed," "Big Ed" (b. May 14, 1881, Plains, PA; d. May 26, 1959, Pompano Beach, FL), player, manager, coach, and umpire, became the greatest practitioner of the legal spitball. Walsh was the youngest of 13 children of Irish immigrant Michael Walsh, an anthracite miner in the Wilkes-Barre, PA area. He attended parochial schools for five years and then worked in the mines, developing exceptional arm and shoulder muscles. After establishing a local reputation in amateur and semipro baseball, Walsh entered organized baseball with Wilkes-Barre, PA (PSL) in 1902 and progressed to Meriden, CT (CtL). He married Rosemary Carney, an ice cream vendor at the ballpark there, in 1904. His son, Edward, pitched for the Chicago White Sox (AL) from 1928 to 1932.

The 6-foot 1-inch, 193-pound right-hander won 20 composite games at Meriden, CT and Newark, NJ (EL) in 1903, but scouting reports indicated that he possessed little beyond a fastball. Consequently, Charles A. Comiskey* drafted him for the Chicago White Sox (AL) for only $750. At spring training in 1904, he learned the spitball from Elmer Striklett and encountered difficulty controlling the pitch for two years. He mastered the pitch by 1906 and compiled a 17–13 record to help the White Sox win the AL pennant in spite of the team's .230 batting average. When the White Sox upset the Chicago Cubs in the 1906 World Series, Walsh won two games.

In 1907 Walsh blossomed as one of baseball's leading pitchers, winning 24 of 42 decisions. Walsh, who threw four variants of the spitball and possessed an impressive fastball, later said, "I had such control of my spitter that I could hit a tack on a wall with it." In 1908, he pitched a modern record 464 innings, won 40 games (the second highest in modern baseball), lost 15 decisions, threw 42 complete games, and recorded 11 shutouts. In a futile effort to win the AL pennant, he pitched in the season's last seven games. On September 29, he won both complete games of a doubleheader for the second time in his career. He lost a four-hit shutout, 1–0, on a passed ball, while his opponent, Addie Joss* of the Cleveland Naps, pitched a perfect game. Walsh won 15 games in 1909 and 18 contests in 1910, but returned to peak form with 27–18 in 1911 and 27–17 in 1912. He pitched his only no-hit game on August 27, 1911, defeating the Boston Red Sox, 5–0. Walsh hurled his best in the 1912 City Series, recording four complete games, two relief appearances, and two of the White Sox' four victories.

At spring training in 1913, Walsh strained his arm throwing a medicine ball. After years of overwork, the arm remained weak and tired rather than sore. With the White Sox through 1916, he won only 13 more games and lost his effectiveness. Never paid more than $6,000 by the penurious Comiskey, Walsh refused a $75,000 offer for three seasons in the FL because he could not certify his arm as sound. He last appeared in four games for the Boston Braves (NL) in 1917, losing one decision. His lifetime record was 195–126 and a 1.82 ERA, the lowest in major league history. Walsh completed 250 of 315 starts, struck out 1,736 batters in 2,964.1 innings, and hurled 57 shutouts (11th best). He led the NL five times in games pitched and saves, four times in innings pitched, three times in games started and shutouts, twice in ERA, games completed, and strikeouts, and once in winning percentage.

Walsh's subsequent career proved mainly unsuccessful. He managed Bridgeport, CT (EL) in 1920, umpired for the AL in 1922, and coached for the Chicago White Sox from 1923 to 1925 and 1928 to 1930. In 1926, he served as baseball coach at Notre Dame University and used his sons, Edward Arthur and Robert, as pitchers. He left baseball and lived in Meriden, CT until 1957, when an arthritic condition caused him to move to Florida. In 1946, Walsh was elected to the National Baseball Hall of Fame.

BIBLIOGRAPHY: Edward Walsh file, National Baseball Library, Cooperstown, NY; Warren Brown, *The Chicago White Sox* (New York, 1952); Jerry Holtzman, "Big Ed Walsh, 77, Former White Sox Star, Gets Day to Remember at Comiskey Park," *TSN*, July 2, 1958; Richard Lindberg, *Who's on Third?* (South Bend, IN, 1983); Richard Lindberg, *Sox* (New York, 1984); G. F. Fleming, *The Unforgettable Season* (New York, 1981); Frederick G. Lieb, "Hall of Famer Ed Walsh Dies," *TSN*, June 3, 1959; Craig Carter, ed., *TSN Daguerreotypes*, 8th ed. (St. Louis, MO, 1990); *The Baseball Encyclopedia*, 10th ed. (New York, 1996); *Spalding's Official Baseball Record, 1913* (New York, 1913).

George W. Hilton

WALTERS, William Henry, Jr. "Bucky" (b. April 19, 1909, Philadelphia, PA; d. April 20, 1991, Abington, PA), player, coach, and manager, was the eldest of seven children of telephone employee William Henry Walters and Mildred (Scheetz) Walters. Nicknamed "Bucky," like his father, Walters left Germantown High School his sophomore year to become an electrician and entered professional baseball in 1929 with High Point, NC (PiL). He married June Caroline Yoast on December 21, 1931 and had three children.

During his 19-year major league career, the 6-foot 1-inch, 180-pound Walters switched from a journeyman third baseman from 1931 to 1934 to become one of the era's premier right-handed pitchers. After playing for seven minor league teams and having indifferent seasons with the Boston Braves (NL) in 1931 and 1932 and Boston Red Sox (AL) in 1933 and 1934, he was sold to the Philadelphia Phillies (NL) in June 1934. Manager Jimmie Wilson,* who had acquired Johnny Vergez to play third base, urged that Walters move to the mound. The quiet, adaptable Walters possessed a strong arm and a cool head and threw a sinking fastball and sharp-breaking slider that he learned from Chief Bender.* A willing worker, he hurled 3,104.2 innings in 15 NL seasons and completed 242 (61 percent) of 398 games started, the sixth best all-time record.

After being the NL's losingest pitcher in 1936 (21 games), he became an immediate winner with the Cincinnati Reds (NL). The Reds traded catcher Virgil Davis,* pitcher Al Hollingsworth, and $55,000 for him in June 1938. In his best season (1939), he topped the NL in wins (27), innings pitched (319), complete games (31), and ERA (2.29), and tied for the lead in strikeouts (137). He batted .325 and was voted the NL MVP. Six times, he made the NL All-Star team.

During his major league career, he won 198 games and lost 160 (.553

winning percentage), compiled a 3.30 ERA, hurled 42 shutouts, and struck out 1,107 batters. The adroit fielder ranks fifth in double plays for a pitcher (76) and is one of few NL pitchers to steal home. As a hitter, he compiled a .243 batting average, made 477 hits, 99 doubles, 16 triples, and 23 HR, scored 227 runs, knocked in 234 runs, and stole 12 bases. He lost two games to the New York Yankees in the 1939 World Series, but won two contests in the 1940 World Series triumph over the Detroit Tigers.

Walters managed the Cincinnati Reds for parts of the 1948 and 1949 seasons to a composite 81–123 win–loss record (.397 winning percentage) and ended his pitching career in 1950 with the Boston Braves (NL). He served as a pitching coach with the Boston Braves and Milwaukee Braves (NL) from 1950 until 1955 and New York Giants (NL) in 1956 and 1957. After retiring from baseball, he worked several years as the public relations representative of a small Philadelphia metal-working company. His only regret is not having succeeded as a major league infielder: "I liked to play every day."

BIBLIOGRAPHY: Lee Allen, *The Cincinnati Reds* (New York, 1948); Leonard Gettelson, "Pitchers Stealing Home," *BRJ* 5 (1976), pp. 12–14; Donald Honig, *Baseball When the Grass Was Real* (New York, 1977); Gene Karst and Martin J. Jones, Jr., *Who's Who in Professional Baseball* (New Rochelle, NY, 1973); Paul MacFarlane, ed., *TSN Daguerreotypes of Great Stars of Baseball* (St. Louis, MO, 1981); *NYT*, April 24, 1991, p. D-25; Martin Quigley, *The Crooked Pitch* (Chapel Hill, NC, 1984); *The Baseball Encyclopedia*, 10th ed. (New York, 1996); A. D. Suehsdorf, telephone interview, William Walters, Jr., August 18, 1983, July 9, 1984; Ritter Collett, *The Cincinnati Reds* (Virginia Beach, VA, 1976); Thomas Aylesworth and Benton Minks, *The Encyclopedia of Baseball Managers* (New York, 1990); Gary Caruso, *The Braves Encyclopedia* (Philadelphia, PA, 1995); Rich Westcott, *Diamond Greats* (Westport, CT, 1988); Robert Redmount, *The Red Sox Encyclopedia* (Champaign, IL, 1998); Frederick G. Lieb and Stan Baumgartner, *The Philadelphia Phillies* (New York, 1953); Allen Lewis, *The Philadelphia Phillies: A Pictorial History* (Virginia Beach, VA, 1981); Rich Westcott and Frank Bilovsky, *The New Phillies Encyclopedia* (Philadelphia, PA, 1993); Peter C. Bjarkman, *Baseball's Great Dynasties: The Reds* (New York, 1991); Bob Rathgeber, *Cincinnati Reds Scrapbook* (Virginia Beach, VA, 1982).

David L. Porter

WANER, Lloyd James "Little Poison" (b. March 16, 1906, Harrah, OK; d. July 22, 1982, Oklahoma City, OK), player and scout, was nicknamed "Little Poison" and began his career in a way similar to older brother Paul.* He was the son of Ora Lee Waner and Etta Lenora (Beavers) Waner, both from prosperous farming families who had migrated from Germany to Oklahoma during the land rush of 1889. Lloyd graduated from high school in nearby Oklahoma City and attended the State Teachers' College (East Central Oklahoma State) in Ada, OK for over two years while playing amateur and semipro baseball. He signed a professional baseball contract with the San Francisco, CA Seals (PCL) but became a free agent after the 1925 season when the Seals failed to pay a $2,500 bonus within a 90-day time limit. Upon the recommendation of his brother Paul, the Pittsburgh Pirates (NL) signed Lloyd and assigned him to Columbia, SC (SAL). At Columbia, Waner hit .345 and was named SAL MVP in 1926.

Waner started in center field for Pittsburgh in 1927 and teamed with brother Paul to help lead the Pirates to the NL pennant. During the 1927 season, he finished third in the NL with a .355 batting average and second to Paul in hits with 223. His 198 singles set a modern major league record, while his 133 runs scored paced the NL. During the 1927 World Series against the New York Yankees, Lloyd made six hits, batted .400, and scored five runs. Like brother Paul, Waner never participated in another World Series.

Waner's greatest attributes were his exceptional speed and keen eye at the plate. Al Lopez,* National Baseball Hall of Famer, manager, and roommate, remarked, "Infielders would have to play him differently. He had unbelievable speed for those days. I don't know if he was the reason why, but soon after he came up, you started hearing about teams looking for fast ball players." According to former Pirate Frank Gustine, Lloyd claimed that "the ball looked bigger than it was." During Waner's 18-year major league career, he struck out only 173 times and ranked among the all-time best leadoff hitters.

Waner's career highlights, mostly from his 14 seasons with the Pittsburgh Pirates, included setting a major league record for putouts in a doubleheader by a center fielder (18, on August 25, 1935), being selected to the 1938 NL All-Star team, having a .316 career batting average, and being elected to the National Baseball Hall of Fame in 1967. His major league career totals included 2,459 hits, 281 doubles, 118 triples, 27 HR, 1,201 runs scored, and 598 RBI.

Waner, traded by the Pittsburgh Pirates to the Boston Braves (NL) in May 1941, also played with the Cincinnati Reds (NL), Philadelphia Phillies (NL), and Brooklyn Dodgers (NL). He returned in 1944 to the Pittsburgh Pirates, where he finished his major league career the next year. Upon retirement, he scouted for the Pittsburgh Pirates from 1946 to 1949 and Baltimore Orioles (AL) in 1955 and worked as a field clerk for Oklahoma City, OK from 1950 through 1967. Waner, who married Frances Mae Snyder on September 17, 1929, had two children, Lloyd, Jr., and Lydia. He died after a long bout of emphysema.

BIBLIOGRAPHY: Lloyd Waner file, National Baseball Library, Cooperstown, NY; *SEAL*, vol. 1 (1981–1985), pp. 837–839; Lee Allen, "Memory Can Play Some Tricks," *CCo* (May 8, 1965); Frederick G. Lieb, *The Pittsburgh Pirates* (New York, 1948); Richard L. Burtt, *The Pittsburgh Pirates, A Pictorial History* (Virginia Beach, VA, 1977); Bob Smizik, *The Pittsburgh Pirates: An Illustrated History* (New York, 1990); Dan Donovan, "Little Lloyd Waner, A Baseball Giant, Dies," Pittsburgh *Press*, July 23, 1982; Dan Donovan, "Lloyd Waner, Brother Paul Were Poison to

Pitchers," Pittsburgh *Press*, June 19, 1981; Donald Honig, *The October Heroes* (New York, 1970); Daniel Okrent and Harris Lewine, eds., *The Ultimate Baseball Book* (Boston, MA, 1981); Joseph L. Reichler, *The Great All Time Baseball Record Book* (New York, 1981); Lawrence S. Ritter, *The Glory of Their Times* (New York, 1966); Regis M. Stefanik, "Little Poison," Pittsburgh *Post Gazette*, July 23, 1982; *TSN*, February 18, 1967; *NYT*, July 23, 1982; St. Louis *Post Dispatch*, July 26, 1982.

William A. Sutton

WANER, Paul Glee "Big Poison" (b. April 16, 1903, Harrah, OK; d. August 29, 1965, Sarasota, FL), player, coach, and manager, was the son of Ora Lee Waner and Etta Lenora (Beavers) Waner, both from prosperous farming families who had migrated from Germany to Oklahoma during the land rush of 1889, and brother of star major leaguer Lloyd Waner.* He spent the majority of his baseball career with the Pittsburgh Pirates (NL) and also played with the Boston Bees/Braves (NL), Brooklyn Dodgers (NL), and New York Yankees (AL). Nicknamed "Big Poison," Waner starred as a hard-hitting outfielder for the Pittsburgh Pirates. He began his professional baseball career at age 20 with the San Francisco, CA Seals (PCL) in 1923. Previously, Waner had graduated from high school in Oklahoma City, OK in 1921 and had attended the State Teachers' College in Ada, OK, for two years in hopes of becoming a teacher and ultimately a lawyer. As a college student, he played baseball on various Oklahoma amateur and semipro teams. Waner began his professional baseball career as a pitcher, but his hitting proficiency caused San Francisco manager Dots Miller to move him to the outfield. After finishing the 1923 season there with a .369 batting average, he impressed major league clubs by collecting 209 hits and 97 RBI in 1924. San Francisco asked for $100,000, a price many clubs considered excessive for the small 5-foot 8-inch, 153-pound Waner. When Waner batted .401 and collected 280 hits in 1925, the Pittsburgh Pirates (NL) purchased him.

During his rookie year (1926), Waner hit .336, led the NL with a .413 on base percentage, and persuaded the Pittsburgh Pirates to sign his younger brother Lloyd. Paul said of Lloyd, "He's a better player than me." Lloyd joined the Pirates the next season (1927) and teamed with Paul to help lead Pittsburgh to the NL pennant. In 1927, Waner led the NL in batting with a .380 batting average, 237 hits and 131 RBI, the latter two setting club records. He also hit .333 and knocked in three runs that year in his only World Series appearance, but the Pirates were swept four games to zero by what many consider the greatest all-time team, the 1927 New York Yankees. Waner's forte remained hitting, as he again led the NL in batting average in 1934 and 1936, and compiled a lifetime .333 batting average over 20 major league seasons.

Despite his small stature, the speedy Waner collected 3,152 career major league hits, ranks tenth all-time in career doubles (605) and triples (191), and made 200 or more hits eight seasons. Waner also scored 1,627 runs, knocked in 1,309 runs, walked 1,091 times, struck out only 376 times, and stole 104 bases. The 5,611 hits made by Paul and Lloyd Waner exceed those of the five Delahanty brothers and three DiMaggio brothers. Waner also was selected a four-time NL All Star (1933–1935, 1937) and proved a talented and very colorful player. Although wearing glasses off the field, he was too vain to wear them on the field and admitted that he could not read the scoreboard from his right field position. Nevertheless, he maintained that "the baseball was as big as a grapefruit" when hitting. Waner also became a legendary drinker and apparently found drinking beneficial to his baseball career. Heavy drinking partially caused the numerous shifts toward the end of his playing career. According to his brother Lloyd, "Paul thought you played best when you relaxed and drinking was a good way to relax." When Pirates management asked Waner to give up drinking in 1938 because Pittsburgh considered themselves contenders for the pennant, he agreed and hit only .280. This marked the only year in his Pirates career that he failed to hit .300.

Waner was married twice, to Corrine Moore on June 10, 1927 and to Mildred Arnold Carroll on June 12, 1953. His first marriage produced one son. After retiring as an active player, he managed Miami, FL (IL) in 1946, and served terms as a batting coach for the Milwaukee Braves (NL) in 1957, St. Louis Cardinals (NL) in 1958 and 1959, and for the Philadelphia Phillies (NL) in 1960 and from 1965 until his death. He also operated a batting practice range in Sarasota, FL. In 1952, Waner was elected to the National Baseball Hall of Fame.

BIBLIOGRAPHY: Paul Waner file, National Baseball Library, Cooperstown, NY; *DAB*, supp. 7 (1961–1965), pp. 768–769; Frederick G. Lieb, *The Pittsburgh Pirates* (New York, 1948); Richard L. Burtt, *The Pittsburgh Pirates: A Pictorial History* (Virginia Beach, VA, 1977); Bob Smizik, *The Pittsburgh Pirates: An Illustrated History* (New York, 1990); Dan Donovan, "Holdout Paul Waner Was Big Poison to N.L.," Pittsburgh *Press*, June 12, 1981; Victor Debs, Jr., *Still Standing After All These Years* (Jefferson, NC, 1997); Daniel Okrent and Harris Lewine, eds., *The Ultimate Baseball Book* (Boston, MA, 1981); Joseph L. Reichler, *The Great All Time Baseball Record Book* (New York, 1981); Lawrence S. Ritter, *The Glory of Their Times* (New York, 1966).

William A. Sutton

WARD, John Montgomery "Monte" (b. March 3, 1860, Bellefonte, PA; d. March 4, 1925, Augusta, GA), player, manager, and executive, was the son of tobacconist James Ward and Ruth (Hall) Ward. A gifted student and athlete, Ward attended Pennsylvania State College and in 1887 received both Bachelor's and law degrees from Columbia University. Ward married actress Helen Dauvray in 1887, but divorced her three years later. Neither this marriage nor a later one to Katharine Waas produced any offspring. At age 18, Ward joined the Providence, RI Grays (NL) midway through the

1878 season, compiled a 22–13 win–loss record as a pitcher and led the NL with a 1.51 ERA. The following year, his 47–19 pitching mark carried the Grays to the NL pennant. The 5-foot 9-inch, 165-pound right-hander paced the NL in wins, pitching percentage (.712), and strikeouts (239). After Ward posted a 39–24 record in 1880, injuries shortened his pitching career. In seven NL seasons, Ward compiled a 164–102 record (.617 winning percentage), hurled 24 shutouts and a perfect game, and registered a 2.10 ERA (4th best). He completed 244 of 261 starts and struck out 920 batters.

After being sold to the New York Gothams (NL) in the fall of 1882, Ward played infield and became a star shortstop. Ward, who retired in 1894, batted .275 lifetime with 2,104 hits, 231 doubles, 96 triples, 26 HR, 1,408 runs scored, 867 RBI, and 540 stolen bases after 1886. The left-handed batting Ward led the NL in stolen bases in 1887 (111) and 1892 (88). An able tactician and leader, he managed the New York Gothams in 1884 and captained the New York Giants to world championships in 1888 and 1889. He served as player–manager of the Brooklyn Wonders (PL) in 1890 and of the Brooklyn Bridegrooms (NL) in 1891–1892. After returning to the New York Giants (NL) as player–manager (1893–1894), he led the New York Giants to a Temple Cup victory in 1894. As manager, he compiled a 412–320 record (.563 winning percentage) over six seasons.

The most memorable action of Ward's 17-year major league career came with his leadership in the cause of players' rights. His strong opposition to the reserve clause and other monopolistic practices of baseball club owners led Ward to organize and preside over the BPBP. From 1886 to 1888, Ward's attacks on the reserve clause appeared in *Lippincott's, Cosmopolitan,* and other magazines and rallied major league players to the cause of reform. When the owners refused to deal with the Brotherhood and unilaterally imposed a salary limitation plan in 1889, Ward organized the PL in 1890 to challenge the established majors. The Brotherhood provided star players and planted teams in most NL cities. Ward consequently confronted the established majors with a formidable challenge. Although the PL outdrew its major league rivals, financial losses of $400,000 forced the PL financiers to surrender. The victory enabled owners to maintain control over major league players until the 1960s.

Retiring after the 1894 season, Ward became a leading corporate lawyer in New York City. He maintained an interest in baseball, representing players against owners and running unsuccessfully for the NL presidency in 1909. Ward served as president of the Boston Rustlers-Braves in 1911 and 1912 and as business manager of the Brooklyn Tip-Tops (FL) in 1913. An expert golfer, Ward founded and was the first president of the Long Island Golf Association. He authored *Base Ball: How to Become a Player* and was elected to the National Baseball Hall of Fame in 1964.

BIBLIOGRAPHY: John Montgomery Ward file, National Baseball Library, Cooperstown, NY; Cynthia Bass, "The Making of a Baseball Radical," *TNP* 2 (Fall 1982), pp. 63–65; Larry Bowman, "Baseball's Intriguing Couple," *TNP* 18 (1998), pp. 69–

72; Lee Lowenfish, "The Later Years of John M. Ward," *TNP* 2 (Fall 1982), pp. 66–69; Lee Lowenfish and Tony Lupien, *The Imperfect Diamond* (New York, 1980); Ronald A. Mayer, *Perfect!* (Jefferson, NC, 1991); Daniel Pearson, *Base Ball in 1889* (Bowling Green, OH, 1993); Francis C. Richter, *A Brief History of Baseball* (Philadelphia, PA, 1909); Albert G. Spalding, *America's National Game* (New York, 1911); David Stevens, *Baseball's Radical for All Seasons: A Biography of John Montgomery Ward* (Lanham, MD, 1998); David Quentin Voigt, *American Baseball*, vol. 1 (University Park, PA, 1983); David Quentin Voigt, *America Through Baseball* (Chicago, IL, 1976); David Quentin Voigt, *The League That Failed* (Lanham, MD, 1998); Noel Hynd, *The Giants of the Polo Grounds* (New York, 1988); Frederick Ivor-Campbell et al., eds., *Baseball's First Stars* (Cleveland, OH, 1996); Frank Graham, *The New York Giants* (New York, 1952); James D. Hardy, Jr., *The New York Giants Base Ball Club* (Jefferson, NC, 1996); Fred Stein and Nick Peters, *Giants Diary* (Berkeley, CA, 1987); Richard Goldstein, *Superstars and Screwballs* (New York, 1991); William F. McNeil, *The Dodgers Encyclopedia* (Champaign, IL, 1997); Thomas Aylesworth and Benton Minks, *The Encyclopedia of Baseball Managers* (New York, 1990); John M. Ward, *Base Ball: How to Become a Player* (Philadelphia, PA, 1888); John M. Ward, "Is the Base Ball Player a Chattel?" *LM* 40 (August 1887).

David Q. Voigt

WARFIELD, Francis Xavier "Frank," "Weasel" (b. 1895, Indianapolis, IN; d. July 24, 1932, Pittsburgh, PA), player, manager, and executive, excelled as a defensive second baseman and championship manager in the Negro Leagues. The 5-foot 7-inch, 160-pound right-hander normally batted second, utilizing his skills as a place hitter, bunter, and speedy base runner.

Warfield's baseball career began in 1914 with the St. Louis Giants. He played for the St. Louis Giants through 1916 except for a 1915 stint with the Indianapolis ABCs. After returning to the Indianapolis ABCs for the 1917 and 1918 seasons, he split the 1919 campaign with the Dayton, OH Marcos and Detroit Stars and then remained with the Detroit Stars (NNL) through 1922.

Warfield's talents as both a player and manager fully blossomed with the Hilldale Daisies (ECL) of Philadelphia from 1923 through 1928. He piloted the Hilldale Daisies to the 1924 ECL pennant and was named the ECL's all-star keystoner. Warfield led the Hilldale Daisies to their third consecutive ECL flag in 1925 and a Black World Series title against the Kansas City Monarchs (NNL).

The Hilldale Daisies traded Warfield to the Baltimore Black Sox (ANL) in 1929. He again filled the player–manager role superbly, as the Baltimore Black Sox won the ANL title in the circuit's only season. The Baltimore Black Sox featured one of baseball's greatest infields with first baseman Jud Wilson,* Warfield, shortstop Dick Lundy,* and third baseman Oliver Marcelle.* Warfield remained with the Baltimore Black Sox through 1931 and served as a player, field manager, and business manager for the Washington Pilots until his sudden death from a heart attack in 1932.

Warfield was extolled as a gentleman, leader, and player with keen intelligence, respectful demeanor, and high ideals by Cum Posey,* Oscar Charleston,* Dizzy Dismukes,* and Gus Greenlee.* Although long respected for his competitive nature and winning ways, Warfield was viewed with enmity and fear.

Warfield, who possessed a fiery temper and carried a knife, died in Pittsburgh's Hotel Bailey allegedly after a brief illness. The recognized money flasher and womanizer was accompanied by a young lady and reportedly bleeding when his death occurred. Another time he bit off part of teammate Marcelle's nose in a gambling-related struggle.

Warfield batted .264 in Negro League play. He hit .342 for the 1924 Hilldale Daisies and .304 in four CUWL seasons. The clutch performer sparked the Hilldale's 1925 World Series triumph with timely hitting, crafty base running, and flawless defense despite batting .261. In 16 World Series contests, Warfield hit .250 and fielded .982 in 1924 and 1925. He knew the ingredients to win and employed them.

BIBLIOGRAPHY: *Chicago Defender*, 1924–1925; Dick Clark and Larry Lester, *The Negro Leagues Book* (Cleveland, OH, 1994); Paul Debono *The Indianapolis ABCs* (Jefferson, NC, 1997); Bill Madden, *Hoosiers of Summer* (Indianapolis, IN, 1994); *The Baseball Encyclopedia*, 10th ed. (New York, 1996); *Philadelphia Tribune*, 1924; *Pittsburgh Courier*, 1924, July 30, 1932; James A. Riley, *The Biographical Encyclopedia of the Negro Baseball Leagues* (New York, 1994).

Merl F. Kleinknecht

WARNEKE, Lonnie "Lon," "The Arkansas Hummingbird" (b. March 28, 1909, Mount Ida, AR; d. June 23, 1976, Hot Springs, AR), player and umpire, grew up in Mount Ida, 50 miles from Hot Springs. In 1928 the lean, lanky, 6-foot 2-inch, 180-pound, right-handed pitcher traveled to Houston, TX (TL) for his first professional baseball tryout with the St. Louis Cardinals' (NL) farm club. After an impressive showing, he joined Laurel, MS (CSL). Unsuccessful there, he left the Cardinals' organization and posted a 16–10 record in 1929 for Alexandria, LA (CSL).

Alexandria sold Warneke for $100 in 1930 to the Chicago Cubs (NL), where he made his major league debut early that season and joined Reading, PA (IL). He returned to the majors permanently in 1931 and proved a mainstay in the Cubs' starting rotation for the next five seasons, compiling a 98–55 record and .641 winning percentage. The most popular Cubs pitcher since Mordecai Brown,* Warneke appeared in the 1932 World Series against the New York Yankees and in the 1935 fall classic against the Detroit Tigers. In the 1935 World Series, he made three appearances, pitched a four-hit shutout in the opening game, and compiled a 0.54 ERA in 16.2 innings.

Despite his popularity with Cubs fans, Warneke was traded to the St. Louis Cardinals (NL) for Rip Collins* and Roy Parmelee in October 1936. He spent the next five and one-half seasons with the Cardinals, posting an 83–52 record (.615 winning percentage). In 1941, he pitched the major leagues' only no-hitter, a 2–0 shutout over the Cincinnati Reds at Crosley Field. Warneke was nicknamed the "Arkansas Hummingbird" by a St. Louis (MO) *Post-Dispatch* writer impressed with his lively fastball and darting form of delivery. The Cardinals in July 1942 sold him back to the Chicago Cubs, where he played until entering military service after the 1943 season. Following World War II, he pitched in nine games for the 1945 NL pennant-bound Chicago Cubs and then retired. In 15 major league seasons, he compiled a 192–121 win–loss record (.613 winning percentage) with a 3.18 ERA.

After his playing career, the modest, taciturn Warneke rejected major league coaching and minor league managing offers for the more secure occupation of umpiring. With help from Cubs owner Philip K. Wrigley,* he began umpiring in 1946 with the PCL and joined the NL three years later. He spent the next seven seasons from 1949 to 1955 as an NL arbiter, umpiring in the 1952 All-Star game and 1954 World Series.

Following the 1955 season, Warneke returned to his native Arkansas to pursue farming and politics. He in 1962 was elected a Garland County judge to mediate civil cases and served in that position until retiring for health reasons ten years later. He died of a heart attack, survived by his wife Erma Charlyne (Shannon) Warneke, whom he had married in February 1933, and one son and one daughter.

During his playing career, Warneke ranked among the game's best lowball pitchers and most skilled fielders at his position. A three-time 20-game winner for the Chicago Cubs (1932, 1934, and 1935), he pitched four shutouts in five different seasons (1932, 1933, 1936, 1938, and 1941), averaged over 17 wins per season from 1932 through 1941, and handled his final 227 fielding chances from 1938 through 1945 without an error. He hurled four innings in the first major league All-Star Game at Comiskey Park in Chicago, IL in 1933, slugging a triple in his only at-bat and scoring the first NL run in All-Star history. Warneke also appeared in the 1934 and 1936 All-Star games and remains the only major leaguer to have played and umpired in both an All-Star game and a World Series.

BIBLIOGRAPHY: Lon Warneke file, National Baseball Library, Cooperstown, NY; Eddie Gold and Art Ahrens, *The Golden Era Cubs, 1876–1940* (Chicago, IL, 1985); Jim Enright, *Chicago Cubs* (New York, 1975); Warren Wilbert and William Hageman, *Chicago Cubs: Seasons at the Summit* (Champaign, IL, 1997); Frederick G. Lieb, *The St. Louis Cardinals* (New York, 1945); Bob Broeg, *Redbirds: A Century of Cardinals' Baseball* (St. Louis, MO, 1981); Bob Broeg and Jerry Vickery, *St. Louis Cardinals Encyclopedia* (Grand Rapids MI, 1998); Warren Brown, *The Chicago Cubs* (New York, 1946); Paul MacFarlane, ed., *TSN Daguerreotypes of Great Stars of Baseball* (St. Louis, MO, 1981); *The Baseball Encyclopedia*, 10th ed. (New York, 1996); St. Louis (MO) *Post-Dispatch*, June 24, 1976; *TSN*, July 10, 1976.

Raymond D. Kush

WASHINGTON, Claudell (b. August 31, 1954, Los Angeles, CA), player, is the brother of minor league baseball player Don Washington and graduated in 1972 from Berkeley, CA High School, where he played basketball rather than baseball. The Oakland A's (AL) signed the 6-foot 2-inch, 195-pound outfielder, who batted and threw left-handed, for $3,000 in July 1972. Washington spent under three minor league seasons with Coos Bay-North Bend, OR (NWL) in 1972, Burlington, IA (ML) in 1973, and Birmingham, AL (SL) in 1974 before joining the A's at age 19.

Washington, a confident line drive hitting speedster, remained with the Oakland A's through 1976. In 1974, he batted .273 with one RBI in the AL Championship Series against the Baltimore Orioles and played all three outfield positions while hitting .571 in the World Series against the Los Angeles Dodgers. Washington established career highs with a .308 batting average, 182 hits, and 40 stolen bases as starting left fielder in 1975 and made the AL All-Star team. In the 1975 AL Championship Series, he batted .250 against the Boston Red Sox.

The journeyman played with six other major league clubs. In March 1977, the Oakland A's traded him to the Texas Rangers (AL). After batting .284 for the Texas Rangers in 1977, he was dealt to the Chicago White Sox (AL) in May 1978. He clouted a career-high 33 doubles for the Chicago White Sox in 1979 and was sent to the New York Mets (NL) in June 1980. The Atlanta Braves (NL) acquired Washington as a free agent in November 1980. He spent over five seasons with the Atlanta Braves, attaining career-highs with 80 RBI in 1982 and 17 HR in 1984. Washington, NL Player of the Month in September 1982, batted .333 in the NL Championship Series against the St. Louis Cardinals. He also doubled in the 1984 All-Star game. In June 1986, the Atlanta Braves traded Washington to the New York Yankees (AL). After Washington batted .308 with 64 RBI in 1988, the California Angels (AL) signed him as a free agent in January 1989. His major league career ended with the New York Yankees in 1990.

During 17 major league seasons, Washington batted .278 with 1,884 hits, 164 HR, 824 RBI, and 312 stolen bases. He also hit .281 in three Championship Series, .571 in one World Series, and .667 in two All-Star games. The Fairfield, CA resident belted three HR on July 14, 1979 against the Detroit Tigers and on June 22, 1980 against the Los Angeles Dodgers. Only sluggers Babe Ruth* and Johnny Mize* had accomplished that feat in both major leagues.

BIBLIOGRAPHY: Claudell Washington file, National Baseball Library, Cooperstown, NY; *TSN Baseball Register*, 1990; "Make Way for Washington," *Time* 106 (July 21, 1975), pp. 47–48; Bruce Markusen, *Baseball's Greatest Dynasty* (New York, 1998); Richard Lindberg, *Who's on Third?* (South Bend, IN, 1983); Gary Caruso, *The Braves Encyclopedia* (Philadelphia, PA, 1995).

David L. Porter

WATSON, Robert Jose "Bob," "Bull" (b. April 10, 1946, Los Angeles, CA), player, coach, and executive, grew up with his grandparents near the Watts district of Los Angeles. He attended the 28th Street Grade School and graduated in 1964 from Fremont High School in Los Angeles, where he played baseball with future major leaguers Bobby Tolan and Willie Crawford. He also attended Los Angeles Harbor College and attained sergeant rank in the U.S. Marine Corps. He and his wife, Carol, have two children, Keith and Kathy.

On January 31, 1965, Watson signed as a catcher with the Houston Astros (NL) and played with Salisbury, NC (WCL). He batted .302 at Cocoa, FL (FSL) in 1966. After trials with Houston in 1966, 1967, and 1968, Watson hit .408 in 61 games for Oklahoma City, OK (AA) in 1969 and returned permanently to the major leagues. From 1970 through 1978, the 6-foot 2-inch, 205-pound Watson proved the heart of the Astros offense at first base and in the outfield. The right-handed slugger hit .312 or better four times from 1972 to 1976 and powered career highs in 1977 of 22 HR and 110 RBI.

On May 4, 1978, Watson scored the millionth run in major league history. After his slow start in 1979, Houston dealt him to the Boston Red Sox (AL) in June for pitchers Pete Ladd and Bob Sprowl. In 84 games at Boston, Watson batted .337 with 13 HR. Granted free agency, he signed with the New York Yankees (AL) in November 1979, and hit .307 as the regular first baseman in 1980. In his only World Series, Watson powered the 1981 Yankees with two HR, seven RBI, and a .318 batting average against the Los Angeles Dodgers. The Yankees traded Watson in April 1982 to the Atlanta Braves (NL) for pitcher Scott Patterson. From 1982 to 1984, he served as the Braves' main pinch hitter. Watson retired as a player in October 1984. His major league career totals for 19 seasons included 1,826 hits, 307 doubles, 184 HR, 989 RBI, and a .295 batting average. Watson hit for the cycle in both major leagues and played on the NL All-Star team in 1973 and 1975. After serving as minor league batting instructor for the Oakland A's (AL) from 1986 through 1988, he worked with the Houston Astros (NL) as assistant general manager from 1989 through 1993 and as general manager in 1994 and 1995. Watson, who has battled prostate cancer, held vice president and general manager positions with the New York Yankees (AL) from 1996 to 1998. Watson, active in a church started by former major league pitcher Dave Roberts, enjoys fishing and listening to music in his free time.

BIBLIOGRAPHY: Paul Burka, "Houston Astros," *TM* (December 1980), pp. 156–161, 264–271; Peter C. Bjarkman, ed., *Encyclopedia of Major League Baseball Team Histories: National League* (Westport, CT, 1981); Robert Redmount, *The Red Sox Encyclopedia* (Champaign, IL, 1998); Zander Hollander, ed., *The Complete Handbook of Baseball, 1976* (New York, 1976); Zander Hollander, ed., *The Complete Handbook of Baseball, 1977* (New York, 1977); Irv Kaze, "Bob Watson, N.L. Player of the Month," *National League Press-Radio-TV Information*, San Francisco, CA, June 12, 1975; Harry Shattuck, " 'As You Were,' Virdon Tells Astro Infield," *TSN*, March 24, 1979, p. 38; Harry Shattuck, "Watson Asking Astros for Trade," *TSN*, October 21, 1978, p. 14;

Bob Watson file, National Baseball Library, Cooperstown, NY; Mark Gallagher, *The Yankees Encyclopedia*, vol. 3 (Champaign, IL, 1997); Gary Caruso, *The Braves Encyclopedia* (Philadelphia, PA, 1995); Bob Watson with Russ Pate, *Survive to Win* (Chicago, IL, 1997); Chuck Wills and Pat Wills, *Beyond Home Plate* (Ocala, FL, 1993); Steve Wulf, "Bob Watson," *SI* 79 (October 18, 1993), p. 74.

Frank J. Olmsted

WEAVER, Betty. *See* Betty Weaver Foss.

WEAVER, Earl Sydney (b. August 14, 1930, St. Louis, MO), player, coach, manager, scout, and sportscaster, is the son of dry cleaning shop proprietor Earl Milton Weaver and Ethel Genieve (Wakefield) Weaver and played second base at Beaumont High School in St. Louis. Despite his small size and mediocre talents, the 5-foot 7-inch, 160-pound, right-hander impressed five professional baseball clubs and signed with the St. Louis Cardinals (NL) in 1948. He played second base with West Frankfort, IL (ISL) in 1948, St. Joseph, MO (WA) in 1949, Winston-Salem, NC (CrL) in 1950, Houston, TX (TL) and Omaha, NE (WL) in 1951 and 1952, Omaha in 1953, and Denver, CO (WL) in 1954. In 1955, the St. Louis Cardinals sold him to the Pittsburgh Pirates (NL) New Orleans, LA (SA) farm club. Weaver began managing a year later while playing for Montgomery, AL-Knoxville, TN (SAL). He served as player–manager at Fitzgerald, GA (GFL) in 1957 and then experienced a steady, methodical rise in the Baltimore Orioles farm system. His clubs included Dublin, GA (GFL) in 1958, Aberdeen, SD (NoL) in 1959, Fox Cities, WI (3IL) in 1960 and 1961, Elmira, NY (EL) from 1962 through 1965, and Rochester, NY (IL) in 1966 and 1967.

Under Weaver, Rochester won the IL pennant in 1966 and tied for first place in 1967 when the Redwings lost a one-game playoff. In 1961, he directed the Orioles' minor league central spring training camp and designed an instructional program of techniques and fundamentals for every club in the Baltimore organization below the Class AAA level. Harry Dalton, former director of player personnel and general manager with the Orioles, persuaded the Baltimore organization to hire and promote Weaver and refuted critics who claimed that Weaver was "a push-button manager." Dalton later stated, "Weaver set a plan of instruction in 1961 when he was 31 years old which we've barely changed to this day. [He is] the most knowledgeable, most methodical, most careful manager in baseball. Push button manager? He built the machine and installed all the buttons." In 1968 Weaver joined the Baltimore Orioles as a coach and replaced Hank Bauer* later that season as manager.

From 1968 through 1982 and 1985 through 1986, Weaver guided the Orioles to a .583 winning percentage, a 1,480–1,060 win–loss mark (10th best in major league history), four AL pennants (1969–1971, 1979), one world championship (1970), and five 100-victory seasons (exceeded only by Joe McCarthy's* six). A brilliant, highly motivated, aggressive manager, Weaver made unprecedented use of computers and charts. He developed a system that combined scouting reports with data on how to pitch and defend against opposing batters and on the success of Orioles batters against opposing pitchers. The resulting information was employed in consultation with his coaches to best use all 25 players on his roster and only expect players to execute within their abilities and limitations, a lesson he learned early in his career. Weaver's other innovations, including the development of a training manual for the entire Orioles' organization, solid pitching staffs, and sound offensive philosophy, brought new life to the Baltimore organization. His intense habit of winning, developed early in his minor league playing career, made him the most ejected manager in the majors with at least 91 dismissals from games and four suspensions. In 1985, he was ejected from both games of a doubleheader.

Weaver wed Marianna Osgood in 1964, a year after his 14-year marriage to Jane Johnston ended in divorce. By his first marriage, Weaver has three children, Michael, Rhonda, and Theresa. He also has a stepdaughter from his present wife's first marriage. Weaver initially retired from managing in 1982 and became a television analyst, Orioles consultant, and scout. In June 1985, he replaced Joe Altobelli* as Baltimore manager and guided the Orioles to a 53–52 mark. The Orioles finished in last place with a 73–89 mark in 1986. Weaver suffered his first losing season as a major league manager, and he resigned at the end of the season. In 1996, he was elected to the National Baseball Hall of Fame.

BIBLIOGRAPHY: James H. Bready, *Baseball in Baltimore* (Baltimore, MD, 1998); Thomas Aylesworth and Benton Minks, *The Encyclopedia of Baseball Managers* (New York, 1990); Robert Grayson, "Wearing a Path to Cooperstown," *SCD* 23 (August 9, 1996), pp. 80–81; Leonard Koppett, *The Man in the Dugout* (New York, 1993); Ed Linn, "Earl of Baltimore: He's a Mouthful," *Sport* 71 (July 1980), pp. 32–36; Los Angeles *Times*, October 11, 1982, p. 13; Mike Lupica, "That's Earl, Folks," *Esquire* 111 (May 1989), pp. 53–54; Jim Palmer and Jim Dale, *Together We Were Eleven Foot Nine* (Kansas City, MO, 1996); *The Baseball Encyclopedia*, 10th ed. (New York 1996); *TSN*, July 26, 1982, p. 2; Earl Weaver and Terry Pluto, *The Earl of Baltimore* (New York, 1982); Earl Weaver and Berry Stainback, *It's What You Learn After You Know It All That Counts* (New York, 1982); Earl Weaver and Berry Stainback, *Winning* (New York, 1972); Earl Weaver file, National Baseball Library, Cooperstown, NY; Ted Patterson, *The Baltimore Orioles* (Dallas, TX, 1995).

Albert J. Figone

WEAVER, George Daniel "Buck" (b. August 18, 1890, Pottstown, PA; d. January 31, 1956, Chicago, IL), player, remains perhaps the finest third baseman of his era and arguably the most tragic victim of the Chicago White Sox (AL) scandal. The son of an ironworker, he played semiprofessional baseball at shortstop as a youth. The Philadelphia Phillies (NL) signed him in 1910 for $125 a month and later sold him to the Chicago White Sox. Ostensibly a replacement for aging Lee Tannehill,* Weaver was sent to San Francisco, CA (PCL) to sharpen his hitting and correct his scattergun throwing arm. The Chicago White Sox recalled him in 1912. The 5-foot 11-inch, 170-pound Weaver played shortstop for four full seasons, led the AL in miscues three times, and earned the nickname "Error-a-Day." In 1916, he split shortstop duties with Zeb Terry and played his first 85 games at third base. In his nine-year major league career, however, he was positioned there for only 427 games compared to 822 contests at shortstop.

Weaver's reputation as a hot-corner marvel cannot be justified by his statistics and may have derived primarily from his verve. He loved baseball, as shown in his ever-present smile, dash, dedication, and purity of style. He played a shallow third base, challenging the hitters. Star hitter Ty Cobb* even quit bunting in his direction. Defensively, Weaver was equalled or surpassed by Oscar Vitt,* Larry Gardner,* and Frank Baker.*

Originally a right-handed batter, Weaver became a switch hitter. He was not notable for hitting the long ball or for driving in runs, but earned the third spot in the Chicago White Sox lineup. His career .272 batting average and .355 slugging average were respectable. Weaver's best year statistically came in 1920, when he compiled 208 hits and a .331 batting average in 151 games. He performed ably at shortstop in Chicago's 1917 World Series victory over the New York Giants, but failed to disclose his "guilty knowledge" of the conspiracy to throw the 1919 World Series to the Cincinnati Reds. Despite a .324 batting average and errorless fielding at third, he was banished from organized baseball for life. He operated a drugstore with his brother for many years and then became a pari-mutuel clerk at a Chicago, IL racetrack. He never stopped believing himself innocent and petitioned tirelessly for reinstatement. By his death, commissioners Kenesaw Mountain Landis,* Albert B. "Happy" Chandler,* and Ford Frick* had rejected his pleas.

BIBLIOGRAPHY: Charles C. Alexander, *Ty Cobb* (New York, 1984); Eliot Asinof, *Eight Men Out* (New York, 1963); *The Baseball Encyclopedia*, 10th ed. (New York, 1996); Warren Brown, *The Chicago White Sox* (New York, 1952); Harold Seymour, *Baseball: The Golden Age* (New York, 1971); Irving M. Stein, *The Ginger Kid: The Buck Weaver Story* (Carmel, IN, 1992); Harvey Frommer, *Shoeless Joe and Ragtime Baseball* (Dallas, TX, 1992); John Thorn et al., eds., *Total Baseball*, 5th ed. (New York, 1997); George "Buck" Weaver file, National Baseball Library, Cooperstown, NY; Richard Lindberg, *Sox* (New York, 1984); Victor Luhrs, *The Great Baseball Mystery* (Cranbury, NJ, 1966); Dan Gutman, *Baseball Babylon* (New York, 1992); Daniel E. Ginsburg, *The Fix Is In* (Jefferson, NC, 1995).

A. D. Suehsdorf

WEAVER, Joanne "Jo," "Jo the Jolter," "The Little" (b. December 19, 1935, Metropolis, IL), player, was the youngest of three sisters who played on the

Magnovox softball team. She tried out for the AAGPBL in Missouri and was drafted at age 14 and performed in the AAGPBL from 1951 until its demise after the 1954 season. Weaver joined the Fort Wayne, IN Daisies (AAGPBL) with her sisters, Betty* and Jean, in 1950, but saw little playing time because of her age. She spent 1950 developing her baseball skills with Fort Wayne and joined the regular lineup in 1951, batting .276 in 48 games. Weaver played outfield four seasons with the Fort Wayne Daisies, but won primary acclaim for her superb hitting and speed. She won three consecutive AAGPBL batting titles with averages of .344 in 1952, .346 in 1953, and .429 in 1954, the highest professional baseball batting average of the 20th century. No professional baseball player has batted over .400 since. She helped Fort Wayne win its first pennant and made the All-Star team. Her fielding ability gradually improved. Weaver again made the All-Star team in 1953, as Fort Wayne won another pennant. In 1954, Weaver led the AAGPBL with 254 total bases, 109 runs scored, 143 hits, and 79 stolen bases and again made the All-Star team. The AAGPBL reduced the size of the ball from 10 inches to major league size midway through the 1954 season. Weaver set a league record by clouting 29 HR. Her speed made her a good outfielder, too. She was named the AAGPBL's MVP in 1954, helping Fort Wayne win another pennant. In 329 games, she batted .359 with 438 hits, 52 doubles, 17 triples, 29 HR, 109 runs scored, 87 RBI, 79 stolen bases, and a .932 fielding average. Weaver played several seasons with the Bill Allington All-Americans, who toured against men's semiprofessional clubs across the nation. The team operated under Bill Allington, the winningest AAGPBL manager and coach. She completed high school in Metropolis and worked 30 years for Essex in Fort Wayne, IN. She retired to an Illinois farm in 1987.

BIBLIOGRAPHY: Gai Berlage, *Women in Baseball* (Westport, CT, 1994); Merrie Fidler, "The Development and Decline of the All-American Girls Baseball League, 1943–54," MA thesis, University of Massachusetts, Amherst, MA, 1976; Susan Johnson, *When Women Played Hardball* (Seattle, WA, 1994); W. C. Madden, *The Women of the All-American Girls Professional Baseball League* (Jefferson, NC, 1997); AAGPBL files, Northern Indiana Historical Society, South Bend, IN.

Leslie Heaphy

WEIMER, Jacob "Tornado Jake" (b. November 29, 1873, Ottumwa, IA; d. June 19, 1928, Chicago, IL), player and scout, was one of six children of Adam Weimer, a farmer, and Mary (Davis) Weimer and began his professional baseball career in 1895 as a left-handed pitcher with Burlington, IA (WA). For the next seven seasons, the 5-foot 11-inch, 175-pound Weimer toiled in the minor leagues. With Kansas City, MO (WL), he led WL pitchers in winning percentage in 1901 and 1902.

In 1903 manager Frank Selee* signed Weimer to play with the Chicago Cubs (NL). After winning his first game in 1903, Weimer posted a 20–8 win–loss record and 2.30 ERA and led all NL hurlers by holding opposing hitters to a .225 batting average. Even more effective the following year, he notched a 20–14 slate and career-best 1.91 ERA and limited opposing batters to a .204 average. Rumors started that the Pittsburgh Pirates wanted to acquire him for $12,000. In 1905, Weimer compiled an 18–12 record and 2.26 ERA. Manager Frank Chance,* who replaced the ailing Selee, traded Weimer and Hans Lobert* to the Cincinnati Reds (NL) in March 1906 for pitcher Orval Overall* and third baseman Harry Steinfeldt.* The trade helped the Chicago Cubs to win the next three NL pennants.

Weimer's 20–14 mark and 2.22 ERA led the second division Cincinnati Reds' pitching staff in 1906. Despite his fine 2.40 ERA over the next two seasons, Weimer won only 19 games and lost 21. The Cincinnati Reds released him after the 1908 season. Weimer ended his major league career after a brief tryout with the 1909 New York Giants (NL). In seven major league seasons, he compiled a 97–69 win–loss record with a 2.23 ERA and a .213 batting average. The tough pitcher held batters to a .227 batting average and yielded only 14 HR. After walking 104 batters in his rookie season, Weimer issued only 389 free passes thereafter.

Weimer worked as a buyer and butcher at the Chicago Stockyards. For several years, he continued to pitch semiprofessional baseball in Chicago, coached the Chicago Loyola Academy team, and scouted for the New York Giants. One of his Loyola players, Fred Lindstrom,* starred at third base for the New York Giants. Weimer, who married Laura Trumbull, a Chicago, IL teacher, in 1904 and had three children, died of peritonitis.

BIBLIOGRAPHY: Jacob Weimer file, National Baseball Library, Cooperstown, NY; John Thorn et al., eds., *Total Baseball*, 5th ed. (New York, 1997); Lee Allen, *The Cincinnati Reds* (New York, 1948); David Q. Voigt, *American Baseball*, vol. 2 (University Park, PA, 1983); Jerry Clark, *From Anson to Zuber* (Omaha, NE, 1992); John Fieberg, FAX clippings, June 25, 1996; Rich Topp, letter to David Voigt, July 1, 1996; David Stevens, letter to David Voigt, June 26, 1996; Warren Brown, *The Chicago Cubs* (New York, 1946); Jim Enright, *Chicago Cubs* (New York, 1975); Eddie Gold and Art Ahrens, *The Golden Era Cubs, 1876–1940* (Chicago, IL, 1985); Warren Wilbert and William Hageman, *Chicago Cubs: Seasons at the Summit* (Champaign, IL, 1997); Floyd Connor and John Snyder, *Day-by-Day in Cincinnati Reds History* (West Point, NY, 1984); Bob Rathgeber, *Cincinnati Reds Scrapbook* (Virginia Beach, VA, 1982).

David Q. Voigt

WEISS, George Martin (b. June 23, 1895, New Haven, CT; d. August 13, 1973, Greenwich, CT), executive, began a 59-year career in baseball administration managing his New Haven high school baseball team and then attended Yale University from 1914 to 1916. Weiss, whose parents, Conrad Weiss and Anna Weiss, owned a grocery store, organized a semipro team that used Ty Cobb* and other major league stars on their days off. When his promotions overshadowed the local EL team, he bought the minor league franchise with borrowed money and at age 24 became the youngest owner in organized baseball. For nine years, his EL club played in Weiss Park, ranked among the best in the minor leauges, and sent many players to the major leagues.

Weiss displayed his talents as general manager of the Baltimore, MD Orioles (IL) from 1929 to 1931 by reviving the ailing team through player sales. His Baltimore success impressed New York Yankees (AL) owner Jacob Ruppert,* who hired Weiss in 1932. Weiss was instructed to develop a farm system modeled on clubs already organized by Branch Rickey* to train young baseball players for the St. Louis Cardinals (NL). A tireless worker, Weiss assembled a premier farm system that sent Joe DiMaggio,* Charlie Keller, and other stars to the New York Yankees. During the 15 years Weiss directed the Yankees farm system, New York won nine AL pennants and eight world championships and sold an estimated $2 million worth of players to other teams. Weiss married Boston sculptor Hazel Wood in 1937 and brought up a foster son, Allen Wood III.

As Yankees general manager from 1948 through 1960, Weiss built a dynasty that won 10 AL pennants and seven World Series in 13 seasons, and a record five straight championships from 1949 to 1953. He hired Casey Stengel,* whom some regarded as a clown, to manage the New York Yankees from 1949 through 1960 and provided Stengel with Mickey Mantle,* Yogi Berra,* Whitey Ford,* and other stars. The coldly efficient Weiss kept the Yankees on top with a superior farm system and skillful trades. In a 17-player swap with the Baltimore Orioles (AL) in November 1954, he acquired pitchers Bob Turley* and Don Larsen.* In December 1959, he shrewdly engineered a deal with the Kansas City Athletics (AL) for slugger Roger Maris.* With uncanny ability, the Yankees boss plucked veterans from NL rosters. Johnny Mize* came from the New York Giants (NL) in August 1949 and Enos Slaughter* from the St. Louis Cardinals (NL) in April 1954 to help in AL pennant drives. Many players resented Weiss' hard bargaining on salaries, while others criticized his reluctance to use black players. The shy, conservative Weiss won a record four Major League Executive of the Year Awards and was elected to the National Baseball Hall of Fame in 1971.

After being retired by the Yankees in 1960, Weiss became president of the expansion New York Mets (NL) in 1961. Besides hiring Stengel to manage the Mets, he built an organization that in 1969 produced the first pennant and world championship for an expansion club. Weiss retired from the Mets in 1966, but remained an advisor for the club until 1971. Sportswriter Red Smith (OS) rated Weiss the "greatest baseball executive who ever lived."

BIBLIOGRAPHY: George Weiss file, National Baseball Library, Cooperstown, NY; Dave Anderson et al., *The Yankees* (New York, 1979); Frank Graham, *The Yankees* (New York, 1943); Dom Forker, *The Men of Autumn* (Dallas, TX, 1989); Dom Forker, *Sweet Seasons* (Dallas, TX, 1991); Robert W. Creamer, *Stengel: His Life and Times* (New York, 1984); Mark Gallagher, *The Yankee Encyclopedia*, vol. 3 (Champaign, IL, 1997); David Halberstam, *Summer of '49* (New York, 1989); Donald Honig, *The New York Mets* (New York, 1986); Peter Golenbock, *Dynasty* (Englewood Cliffs, NJ, 1975); Leonard Koppett, *The New York Mets* (New York, 1970); New York *Daily News*, August 14, 1972; *NYT*, August 14, 1972; Lowell Reidenbaugh, *Baseball's Hall of Fame-Cooperstown* (New York, 1993); Jack Lang and Peter Simon, *The New York Mets* (New York, 1986); David Quentin Voigt, *American Baseball*, vol. 3 (University Park, PA, 1983); Harold Rosenthal, ed., *Baseball Is Their Business* (New York, 1952).

Joseph E. King

WELCH, Michael Francis "Mickey," "Smiling Mickey" (b. July 4, 1859, Brooklyn, NY; d. July 30, 1941, Concord, NH), player, learned the fundamentals of baseball on the streets and sandlots of Brooklyn. Welch, a 5-foot 8-inch, 160-pound, right-handed pitcher, left home at age 18 to pitch for the Poughkeepsie, NY Volunteers. Nicknamed "Smiling Mickey," Welch became the third of major league pitchers to attain 300 victories. Welch began his professional baseball career with Auburn, NY (NA) and Holyoke, MA (NA) in 1878 and 1879. Upon joining the Troy, NY Haymakers (NL) in 1880, Welch won 34 games and pitched 574 innings. He lacked tremendous speed, but utilized an effective curveball, change of pace, and screwball. The durable Welch pitched a double victory over the Cleveland Blues (NL) in 1881 and hurled complete games in his first 105 league starts. In 1883, the Troy franchise transferred to New York and became the Gothams. Welch hurled the first game at the original Polo Grounds on May 1 and pitched over 400 innings that season. The next year, he completed 62 of 65 starts and struck out 345 batters. On August 28, 1884, Welch established a major league record by striking out the first nine Cleveland Blues batters to face him.

In 1885, the New York Gothams became the Giants. Between July 18 and September 4, Welch won 17 consecutive games and hurled 4 shutouts and 4 one-run games. The 44-game winner compiled a 1.66 ERA and led the NL with an .800 winning percentage. During the next two seasons, Welch won 55 games. Welch and Tim Keefe* in 1888 accounted for 61 of the Giants' 84 victories and pitched the Giants to their first NL pennant. In a post-season series against the St. Louis Browns (AA), the Giants won six of 10 games and Welch split two decisions. By winning 17 of their last 20 games in 1889, the Giants repeated as NL champions and defeated the Brooklyn Bridegrooms (AA) in the post-season series. Welch won 22 games the next two seasons. After one game in 1892, he was sent to the Giants farm club at Troy, NY and terminated his active career there. After retirement, Welch moved to Holyoke, MA and served for a long time as steward of the Elks Club. He returned to New York in 1912, when John McGraw* offered him a job at the Polo Grounds.

Elected to the National Baseball Hall of Fame in 1973, Welch ranks high on the all-time major league lists for pitchers in several departments. In 13 major league seasons, he posted 20 or more victories nine times (3rd) and at least 30 wins four times (4th), hurled 41 shutouts, and recorded a 2.71 lifetime ERA. He won 307 games (18th), lost 210 (34th), started 549 games (23rd), completed 525 games (6th) and pitched 4,802 innings (14th). Welch surrendered 4,588 hits (11th) and 2,548 runs (4th), issued 1,297 bases on balls (29th), and struck out 1,850 batters.

BIBLIOGRAPHY: Mickey Welch file, National Baseball Library, Cooperstown, NY; Gene Karst and Martin J. Jones, Jr., *Who's Who in Professional Baseball* (New Rochelle, NY, 1973); Craig Carter, ed., *TSN Daguerreotypes*, 8th ed. (St. Louis, MO, 1990); Lowell Reidenbaugh, *Baseball's Hall of Fame-Cooperstown* (New York, 1993); Noel Hynd, *The Giants of the Polo Grounds* (New York, 1988); Frank Graham, *The New York Giants* (New York, 1952); James D. Hardly, Jr., *The New York Giants Base Ball Club* (Jefferson, NC, 1996); Fred Stein and Nick Peters, *Giants Diary* (Berkeley, CA, 1987); Frederick Ivor-Cambell, *Baseball's First Stars* (Cleveland, OH, 1996).

John L. Evers

WELCH, Robert Lynn "Bob" (b. November 3, 1956, Detroit, MI), player, is the youngest of three children of Rupert Welch and Loraine (Mungle) Welch and grew up in the Detroit suburb of Ferndale, MI. The three-sport athlete at Hazel Park High School pitched for Eastern Michigan University and, as a freshman, helped the Hurons make the 1975 NCAA College World Series.

The number-one draft choice of the Los Angeles Dodgers (NL) in 1977, Welch signed for a $55,000 bonus and pitched for San Antonio, TX (TL) in 1977. He started the 1978 season at Albuquerque, NM (PCL), but joined the Los Angeles Dodgers on June 20. Welch capped his rookie 7–4 season by earning a win in the NL Championship Series against the Philadelphia Phillies and striking out New York Yankees slugger Reggie Jackson* to save the second game in the World Series. The New York Yankees won the World Series, 4–2.

The 6-foot 3-inch, 190-pound right-hander battled problems with alcohol and his pitching arm in 1979, slipping to a 5–6 record. He pioneered major league baseball's drug and alcohol treatment efforts by committing himself to The Meadows, a rehabilitation facility in Wickenburg, AZ during the off-season. He posted a 14–9 win–loss record with a 3.29 ERA and earned All-Star recognition in 1980, becoming the Los Angeles Dodgers' steadiest pitcher over the next seven seasons. He in 1983 recorded the NL third-best ERA (2.65) and in 1985 finished with a 14–4 record and a 2.31 ERA. In his last season with the Los Angeles Dodgers, he compiled a 15–9 record with a 3.22 ERA and led the NL with four shutouts.

The Los Angeles Dodgers traded Welch to the Oakland Athletics (AL) in December 1987. He developed a split-finger pitch to complement his fastball and curveball, compiling 17–9 and 17–8 records the next two seasons.

His career season came in 1990, when his 27–6 record and .818 winning percentage paced the major leagues and his 238 innings placed third in the AL. Besides pitching in his second All-Star Game, he won the AL Cy Young Award and led the Oakland Athletics to the World Series. Oakland lost the fall classic to the Cincinnati Reds in four games. His major league career ended with the Oakland Athletics in 1994.

Welch appeared in eight League Championship Series, four each for Los Angeles and Oakland, and five World Series, two for the Dodgers and three for the Athletics. In 17 major league seasons, he compiled a 211–146 win–loss record for a .591 winning percentage and 3.47 ERA. He struck out 1,969 batters while walking only 1,034 for nearly a 2:1 strikeouts-to-walks ratio. As a National Leaguer, he batted .151 with a high of .243 in 1980.

Welch resides in Scottsdale, AZ with his wife, Mary Ellen, and their two sons.

BIBLIOGRAPHY: Robert Welch file, National Baseball Library, Cooperstown, NY; Tommy Lasorda and David Fisher, *The Artful Dodger* (New York, 1985); William F. McNeil, *The Dodgers Encyclopedia* (Champaign, IL, 1997); Peter C. Bjarkman, *Baseball's Great Dynasties: The Dodgers* (New York, 1990); Stanley Cohen, *Dodgers! The First 100 Years* (New York, 1990); *The Baseball Encyclopedia*, 10th ed. (New York, 1996); Ron Fimrite, "One Pitch at a Time," *SI* 73 (September 17, 1990), pp. 58–63; Robert E. Kelly, *Baseball's Best* (Jefferson, NC, 1988); Joe McDonnell, "Bob Welch Sets Goals for '84 Season," *BD* 43 (May 1984), pp. 48–53; Mike Shatzkin, ed., *The Ballplayers* (New York, 1990); John Thorn et al., eds., *Total Baseball*, 5th ed. (New York, 1997); George Vecsey, "Bob Welch: Young, Talented and an Alcoholic," *NYT Biographical Service* 11 (April 1980), pp. 626–628; Bob Welch and George Vecsey, *Five O'Clock Comes Early* (New York, 1986).

Gaymon L. Bennett

WELLS, Willie "El Diablo" (b. August 10, 1908, Austin, TX; d. January 22, 1989, Austin, TX), player and manager, is the son of a delivery man. He graduated from Anderson High School and attended Sam Houston College. The premier Negro League shortstop from the late 1920s until the mid–1940s, Wells moved from the Texas sandlots to the Negro Leagues and played winter ball in Mexico, Cuba, and Puerto Rico. After leading the San Antonio, TX Black Aces against barnstorming Negro League teams in Texas, Wells joined the St. Louis Stars (NNL) in 1924. The slick-fielding shortstop overcame initial difficulties at the plate to lead the NNL in batting with .368 in 1929 and .404 in 1930. When the Stars disbanded after the 1931 season, Wells played with the Detroit Wolves (EWL) in 1932, Homestead, PA Grays (NNL) in 1932, Kansas City Monarchs (NAL) in 1932 and 1934, Chicago American Giants (NAL) from 1933 to 1935 (NAL), New York Black Yankees (NNL) in 1945 and 1946, Newark, NJ Eagles (NNL) from 1936 to 1939, 1942 and 1945, Indianapolis Clowns in 1947 (NAL), and Memphis Red Sox (NAL) in 1944 and 1948.

In the late 1930s, Wells performed with the Newark Eagles' "million dollar infield." Wells, who played in eight East-West classics, compiled a career .334 batting average in the Negro Leagues and hit .392 against major leaguers in exhibition games. In the 1940s, the 5-foot 7-inch, 160-pound Wells played and managed in Mexico, and was nicknamed "El Diablo." Wells also managed the Newark Eagles in 1942 and Birmingham Black Barons in 1954. He was ranked among the best managers the Negro Leagues produced and is considered the first professional player to use a batting helmet, having fashioned one out of a hardhat after he was knocked unconscious in a 1942 game against the Baltimore Elite Giants (NNL).

Wells had two children, Thelma and Willie Jr. He worked in New York City in a delicatessen for 13 years and moved back to Austin, TX in 1973 to care for his aging mother. In 1997, he was elected to the National Baseball Hall of Fame. He spoke for many Negro Leaguers when he wrote to the Pittsburgh *Courier* to explain why he had left the Newark Eagles in 1943 to play for Vera Cruz, Mexico (MEL):

Not only do I get more money playing here, but I live like a king. . . . I am not faced with the racial problem. . . . We live in the best hotels, we eat in the best restaurants. . . . We don't enjoy such privileges in the U.S. I didn't quit Newark and join some other team in the United States. I quit and left the country. . . . I've found freedom and democracy here, something I never found in the United States. . . . Here, in Mexico, I am a man.

BIBLIOGRAPHY: John B. Holway, "Willie Wells," *BRJ* 17 (1988), pp. 50–53; John B. Holway, "The Black Cal Ripken Willie Wells," *SCD* 24 (April 18, 1997), p. 134; *NYT*, January 25, 1989, p. D–27; Robert W. Peterson, *Only the Ball Was White* (Englewood Cliffs, NJ, 1970); James A. Riley, *The Biographical Encyclopedia of the Negro Baseball Leagues* (New York, 1994); Willie Wells file, National Baseball Library, Cooperstown, NY; James Overmyer, *Effa Manley and the Newark Eagles* (Metuchen, NJ, 1994); Donn Rogosin, *Invisible Man: Life in Baseball's Negro Leagues* (New York, 1983).

                                                                Robert L. Ruck

WENDELSTEDT, Harry Hunter, Jr. (b. July 27, 1938, Baltimore, MD), umpire, is the son of Harry Wendelstedt, Sr., a truck driver, and Elizabeth J. (Lusby) Wendelstedt. After graduating from Kenwood High School in 1957, he spent two years in the U.S. Marine Corps and attended Essex CC in Baltimore and the University of Maryland. In 1962, Wendelstedt was the top-ranked student in the Al Somers Umpire School and began his professional umpiring career in the Class D GFL. Displaying remarkable agility and excellent judgment, the 6-foot 2-inch, 230 pounder rapidly advanced to the Class A NWL in 1963, the Class AA TL in 1964, the Class AAA IL in 1965, and the NL in 1966.

Wendelstedt, who retired in 1998 as senior NL umpire after 33 seasons, worked four All-Star games (1968, 1976, 1983, 1992), eight NL Championship Series (1970, 1972, 1977, 1981, 1982, 1988, 1990), and five World Series (1973, 1980, 1986, 1991, 1995), and the NL's first Division Series in 1995. He umpired at home plate on April 22, 1970, when Tom Seaver* of the New York Mets tied the then major league record for strikeouts by fanning 19 San Diego Padres and 10 consecutively to end the game. His most controversial call occurred in a game between the Los Angeles Dodgers and the San Francisco Giants on May 30, 1968. With the bases loaded and no outs in the ninth inning, Los Angeles Dodgers pitcher Don Drysdale* hit Dick Dietz. Wendelstedt, however, called a ball instead because the San Francisco Giants catcher did not try to avoid the pitch. Drysdale then retired the side without yielding a run, thus tying the major league record for consecutive shutouts (5) and keeping his scoreless inning streak alive. He subsequently set new marks for consecutive shutouts (6) and scoreless innings (58.2).

Wendelstedt made major contributions to the umpiring profession off the field. He served four terms as the first president of the MLUA (from 1970 to 1974) and helped train a generation of minor and major league umpires as an instructor at the Somers School, which he purchased in 1977 and renamed the Harry Wendelstedt School for Umpires. In 1975, Wendelstedt and the other umpires in his crew publicly repudiated the unflattering and unfair account of them in Lee Gutkind's *The Best Seat in Baseball, But You Have to Stand!*

Wendelstedt married Cheryl Maher in 1970 and has two children. His son, Harry Hunter III, umpires in the minor leagues.

BIBLIOGRAPHY: Harry Wendelstedt, Jr. file, National Baseball Library, Cooperstown, NY; Maury Allen, *Baseball* (New York, 1990); Mark Mulvoy, "The Giants Find It Tough," *SI* 26 (June 10, 1968), pp. 28–31; Lee Gutkind, *The Best Seat in Baseball, But You Have to Stand!* (New York, 1975); " 'Foul' Yells Wendelstedt Over New Book," *TSN*, May 10, 1975; "Book Singes Unwary Umpires," *TSN*, July 26, 1975; *Harry Wendelstedt School for Umpires* 15 (Ormond Beach, FL, 1991).

Larry R. Gerlach

WERBER, William Murray "Bill" (b. June 20, 1908, Berwyn, MD), player, is the son of Waldemar Werber and Margaret (Sefton) Werber and spent 11 major league seasons as a slick-fielding third baseman, shortstop, and outfielder. The well-educated Werber graduated in 1930 from Duke University, where he made All-America as a guard on the Blue Devils' basketball team in the 1929–1930 season. The 5-foot 11½-inch, 170-pound shortstop hit .400 his senior year for the Duke baseball team and signed in 1930 with the New York Yankees (AL), who had financed three years of his college education. The Yankees optioned Werber that year to Albany, NY (EL), where he was named the team's MVP. He entered Georgetown University Law School that fall, but concentrated on playing baseball the following spring.

He had married Kathryn Potter on September 16, 1929, already had a son, the first of three children, and needed the money. Werber progressed rapidly through the minor leagues with Toledo, OH (AA) and Newark, NJ (IL) in 1931 and Buffalo, NY (IL) in 1932.

Werber joined the New York Yankees as a utility infielder in 1933, but could not dislodge Frank Crosetti* at shortstop. New York sold Werber to the Boston Red Sox (AL) in May 1933. The Boston Red Sox bought Lyn Lary* to play shortstop in 1934 and shifted Werber to third base, where he remained for most of his major league career. He stayed with the Boston Red Sox until being traded in December 1936 to the Philadelphia Athletics (AL) for Pinky Higgins.* Werber broke a toe in 1935 and underwent an operation following the season to repair it, but it bothered him for the rest of his career. Although Werber played 45 games in the outfield for Boston, the Philadelphia Athletics used him almost exclusively at third base. He clashed with Connie Mack,* the Athletics owner–manager, about salary and was sold to the Cincinnati Reds (NL) in March 1939 for $25,000. Werber helped the Cincinnati Reds capture NL pennants in 1939 and 1940 and played well in World Series losses to the New York Yankees and Detroit Tigers. When Werber's batting average fell in 1941, the Cincinnati Reds sold him in December 1941 to the New York Giants (NL). He retired, however, to work full time in the insurance business his father had started in 1904.

In 1,295 major league games, the line-drive hitting Werber batted .271 and collected 1,363 hits, including 271 doubles, 50 triples, and 78 HR. Besides driving in 539 runs and scoring 875 runs, he rarely struck out, received 701 walks, and led the AL in stolen bases in 1934, 1935, and 1937. In two World Series, he hit .326 in 11 games. Werber remains the only major-league player to hit four consecutive doubles in one game in each league, accomplishing the feat with the Boston Red Sox in 1935 and Cincinnati Reds in 1940.

Werber inherited his father's insurance business in Hyattsville, MD and became a millionaire. In 1972, he handed the insurance business to his son and retired to Naples, FL. An English major at Duke, Werber wrote three books: a history of his family, an account of his hunting experiences, and *Circling the Bases*, his privately published autobiography.

BIBLIOGRAPHY: Bill Werber file, National Baseball Library, Cooperstown, NY; Lee Allen, *The Cincinnati Reds* (New York, 1948); Donald Honig, *Baseball Between the Lines* (New York, 1976); Brent P. Kelley, "Bill Werber—The Reds' Winning Edge," *SCD* 21 (June 17, 1994), pp. 184–187; Brent P. Kelley, *In the Shadow of the Babe* (Jefferson, NC, 1995); Frederick G. Lieb, *The Boston Red Sox* (New York, 1947); Robert Redmount, *The Red Sox Encyclopedia* (Champaign, IL, 1998); Connie Mack, *My 66 Years in the Big Leagues* (Philadelphia, PA, 1950); Jerome C. Romanowski, *The Mackmen* (Upper Darby, PA, 1979); Frederick G. Lieb, *Connie Mack* (New York, 1945); William Werber, *Circling the Bases* (n.p., n.d.); Rich Westcott, *Masters of the*

Diamond (Jefferson, NC, 1994); *TSN Baseball Register*, 1941; Ritter Collett, *The Cincinnati Reds* (Virginia Beach, VA, 1976); Bob Rathgeber, *Cincinnati Reds Scrapbook* (Virginia Beach, VA, 1982).

Ralph S. Graber

WERDEN, Percival Wherrit "Perry," "Moose" (b. July 21, 1865, St. Louis, MO; d. January 9, 1934, Minneapolis, MN), player, manager, and umpire, was the most renowned 19th-century minor league slugger. The son of William Werden and Sarah (Wherrit) Werden, he attended St. Louis schools. Werden left his pie delivery wagon for a semiprofessional baseball game with the Libertys in 1882 and hit two HR. After playing with the Libertys through 1883, he posted a 12–1 win–loss pitching record for the major league St. Louis Maroons (UA) in 1884. After the UA collapsed, the 6-foot 2-inch, 210-pound right-hander blossomed as a first baseman with Memphis, TN (SL), a slugger with Lincoln, NE (WL), and a .393 batter with Topeka, KS (WL) and Des Moines, IA (NWL) in 1887. In 1888, Werden led the SL in HR (5) and stolen bases (65) at New Orleans, LA (SL). At Toledo, OH, he paced the 1889 IA in batting average (.394) and the 1890 major league AA in triples (20). The next season, he recorded 104 RBI for the famed Baltimore Orioles (AA). With the St. Louis Cardinals (NL) the next two campaigns, he paced the NL in triples (29) in 1893. St. Louis released Werden in favor of National Baseball Hall-of-Famer Roger Connor.*

Werden's move to Minneapolis, MN (WL) created a folk hero. The Athletic Park home field helped him bat .417 with 42 HR in 1894. The following season, he improved to a WL-leading .428 batting average and 241 hits. His record 45 HR, which was later broken by Babe Ruth,* included a 4-HR game on July 23. In 1897, Werden batted .302 in his final major league season with the Louisville, KY Colonels (NL), but manager Fred Clarke* regarded his behavior as too boisterous. Werden batted .282 lifetime in seven major league seasons. Back in Minneapolis, a broken kneecap erased his 1898 season. Weight and further injury problems ensued. Werden led the newly named minor league AA in doubles and HR in 1900. Subsequent minor league stops from Fargo, ND (NoL) to Vicksburg, MS (CSL) marked his gradual decline through 1906.

Still a colorful gate attraction, Werden umpired (AA, 1907; NoL chief, 1913–1914; DL chief, 1920–1922), coached (Indianapolis, IN [AA, 1908]), and managed especially "Werden's All Stars," engaging black and other teams across the Midwest. A divorce from his wife, Mary, proved difficult, but Werden's .341 minor league batting average and 166 HR (broken in 1922) secured his place as an early legend.

BIBLIOGRAPHY: *Minor League Baseball Stars* (Cooperstown, NY, 1978); Raymond Nemec, "The Performance and Personality of Perry Werden," *BRJ* 6 (1977), pp. 127–132; Robert L. Tiemann and Mark Rucker, eds., *Nineteenth Century Stars* (Kansas City, MO, 1989); Perry Werden file, National Baseball Library, Cooperstown, NY; Frederick G. Lieb, *The St. Louis Cardinals* (New York, 1945); Bob Broeg and Jerry Vickery, *St. Louis Cardinals Encyclopedia* (Grand Rapids, MI, 1998); J. Thomas Hetrick, *Chris Von der Ahe and the St. Louis Browns* (Lanham, MD, 1999).

James D. Smith III

WERTZ, Victor Woodrow "Vic" (b. February 9, 1925, York, PA; d. July 7, 1983, Detroit, MI), player, was a 6-foot, 185-pound, hard-hitting, left-handed outfielder–first baseman primarily for the Detroit Tigers (AL), Cleveland Indians (AL), St. Louis Browns (AL), and Boston Red Sox (AL) from 1947 to 1963 and became legendary for a hit he did not get. In the eighth inning of the first game of the 1954 World Series against the New York Giants, Wertz batted for the Cleveland Indians with two teammates on base, no outs, and the game tied, 2–2. He lofted a long, 460-foot fly ball off New York Giants reliever Don Liddle to center field in the Polo Grounds. Wertz claimed that it was the hardest ball he ever hit, but New York Giants center fielder Willie Mays* chased the ball down and made an over-the-shoulder catch with his back to the infield. The New York Giants won that game, 5–2, and swept the 1954 World Series. Wertz expressed bitter disappointment over the catch, which has been replayed on film every year around World Series time. Wertz always maintained that he would rather be remembered for that play than totally forgotten.

This incident overshadows the fact that Wertz batted .277 lifetime with 266 HR, 289 doubles, and 1,178 RBI in 17 major league seasons. His career highlights included making 20 or more HR six times, 20 or more doubles eight times, 100 or more RBI five times, seven RBI in two consecutive innings in 1947, seven HR in five consecutive games in 1950, eight hits and a .500 batting average in the 1954 World Series, and four doubles in one game in 1956. Wertz entered the major leagues with the Detroit Tigers in 1947 after spending 1942 at Winston-Salem, NC (PiL), 1943 and 1946 at Buffalo, NY (IL), and three years in U.S. military service from 1943 to 1945. He was traded to the St. Louis Browns (AL) in August 1952, accompanied the franchise shift to the Baltimore Orioles (AL) in 1954, and was sent to the Cleveland Indians (AL) in June 1954. Wertz was stricken with a non-paralytic form of polio in August 1955, but made a miraculous recovery in time for the 1956 season. In December 1958, Cleveland traded him to the Boston Red Sox (AL). He returned to the Detroit Tigers in September 1961 and finished his major league career with the Minnesota Twins (AL) in 1963.

Wertz, who married Lucille Carroll Caleel in May 1952 and had two sons, worked as a beer distributor in the Detroit, MI area. His civic activities included raising money for the March of Dimes and Special Olympics.

BIBLIOGRAPHY: *The Baseball Encyclopedia*, 10th ed. (New York, 1996); Gene Karst and Martin J. Jones, Jr., *Who's Who in Professional Baseball* (New Rochelle, NY, 1973); Hal Lebovitz, "Vic Wertz Finds Out: Everybody Loves a Hero," *Sport* 18 (March 1955), pp. 28–29; Willie Mays, "My Greatest Catches," in Haskell Cohen, ed., *Willie*

Mays Baseball (New York, 1963); Lynall Smith, "Tiger Tune Has New Wertz," *BD* 16 (November 1947), pp. 25–27; John Thorn et al., eds., *Total Indians* (New York, 1996); Robert Redmount, *The Red Sox Encyclopedia* (Champaign, IL, 1998); Victor Wertz file, National Baseball Library, Cooperstown, NY; Joe Falls, *Detroit Tigers* (New York, 1975); William M. Anderson, *The Detroit Tigers* (South Bend, IN, 1996); Fred Smith, *995 Tigers* (Detroit, MI, 1981); Bill Borst, ed., *Ables to Zoldak*, vol. 3 (St. Louis, MO, 1990); Bill Borst, *Still Last in the American League* (West Bloomfield, MI, 1992); Frederick G. Lieb, *The Baltimore Orioles* (New York, 1955); Morris Eckhouse, *Day-by-Day in Cleveland Indians History* (New York, 1983); John Phillips, *Winners* (Cabin John, MD, 1987); Bruce Dudley, *Bittersweet Season* (Annapolis, MD, 1995).

James K. Skipper, Jr.

WEST, Samuel Filmore "Sammy" (b. October 5, 1904, Gladewater, TX; d. November 23, 1985, Lubbock, TX), player and coach, was an AL outfielder who batted and threw left-handed. The 5-foot 10½-inch, 175-pound West married Grace Cross on February 23, 1930.

West began his professional baseball career in 1923 as an outfielder with Roswell, NM in the four-team PPVL. The 1924 and 1925 campaigns were spent at Sulphur Springs, TX (ETL) and part of the 1925 season at Long-view, TX (ETL). Most synopses of his career erroneously state that West played in 1925 at Muskogee, OK or Monroe, LA, and was born at Longview, TX. He was promoted to Birmingham, AL (SL) in late 1925 and enjoyed an outstanding stint there in 1926 despite a severe beaning. In 1927, he reached the major leagues with the Washington Senators (AL).

West spent six seasons from 1927 to 1932 with the Washington Senators, played for the St. Louis Browns (AL) from 1933 to June 1938, and rejoined the Washington Senators from June 1939 through 1941. Although ready to retire, West answered Jimmy Dykes's* request to play for the Chicago White Sox (AL) in 1942. The first player shortage occurred that year due to World War II. The 1942 season deprived West of a lifetime .300 average. In 1,753 major league games, West batted .299 with 1,838 hits, 347 doubles, 101 triples, 75 HR, and 838 RBI.

On his arrival in the major leagues, West received special instruction on center-field play from the great Tris Speaker.* He became skilled defensively, leading AL outfielders in putouts in 1932 and 1935 and fielding percentage in 1928 and 1935, and sharing the AL lead in assists in 1929. His outstanding batting feat came when he made hits in all six at-bats on April 13, 1933. West missed playing in a World Series, but appeared in the first All-Star game in 1933 as a defensive substitute for Babe Ruth.* He also appeared in the 1934 and 1937 All-Star games.

West entered the military service during World War II and served as a physical education instructor at Reese Air Force Base in Lubbock, TX from 1942 to 1945. He returned to the Washington Senators as coach from 1947 through 1949 and operated a sporting goods store in Lubbock, TX for many years.

BIBLIOGRAPHY: Morris Bealle, *The Washington Senators* (Washington, DC, 1947); Shirley Povich, *The Washington Senators* (New York, 1954); Bill Borst, ed., *Ables to Zoldak*, vol. 3 (St. Louis, MO, 1990); Bill Borst, *Still Last in the American League* (West Bloomfield, MI, 1992); Frederick G. Lieb, *The Baltimore Orioles* (New York, 1955); *The Baseball Encyclopedia*, 10th ed. (New York, 1996); C. Taylor Spink, comp., *TSN Daguerreotypes of Great Stars of Baseball* (St. Louis, MO, 1961); Samuel West file, National Baseball Library, Cooperstown, NY; Samuel West, taped interview with Lowell L. Blaisdell, August 23, 1982, Southwest Collection, Texas Tech University, Lubbock, TX.

Lowell L. Blaisdell

WEYHING, August "Gus," "Cannonball" (b. September 29, 1866, Louisville, KY; d. September 4, 1955, Louisville, KY), player, manager, and umpire, grew up in the Louisville area and married Mamie J. Gehrig, cousin of baseball star Lou Gehrig,* on January 9, 1901. His younger brother, John, pitched briefly with the Cincinnati Red Stockings (AA) and Columbus Buckeyes (AA) in 1888 and 1889. The 5-foot 10-inch, 145-pound right-hander began his professional baseball career with a brilliant 19–3 won–lost record at Richmond, VA (VL) in 1885, striking out 187 batters and walking only 39. The following year, Weyhing slipped to a 12–17 mark with Charleston, SC (SL), but remained a control pitcher. In 1887, he reached the major leagues with the Philadelphia Athletics (AA), won 26 games and lost 28, and allowed a remarkable 465 hits and 338 runs. The next year, Weyhing posted a 28–18 record for Philadelphia and hurled a 4–0 no-hitter against the Kansas City Cowboys (AA) on July 31. In 1889, he compiled 30 wins, four shutouts, and 213 strikeouts in 449 innings.

In 1890 Weyhing won 30 games after jumping with second baseman Lou Bierbauer* to the Brooklyn Wonders of the new PL. When the PL folded, Weyhing rejoined Philadelphia and notched career highs of 31 victories and 219 strikeouts in 1891. He was left without a team after that season when the AA ceased operation. Weyhing and teammates Lave Cross* and Bill Hallman* remained in Philadelphia in 1892 and signed with the Phillies (NL). Weyhing won 32, 23, and 16 games for the Phillies from 1892 to 1894 before the strain of over 3,200 innings in eight seasons and the increased pitching distance from 50 to 60½ feet told on his performance. Weyhing struggled through an 8–21 season in 1895 with the Philadelphia Phillies, Pittsburgh Pirates (NL), and Louisville Colonels (NL) and temporarily retired in 1896 after pitching poorly in five starts for Louisville.

In 1898, the Washington Senators (NL) lured Weyhing from retirement. In two seasons, he compiled a 32–47 record and averaged nearly 350 innings per year. He finished his major league career with the Brooklyn Superbas (NL) and St. Louis Cardinals (NL) in 1900 and the Cleveland Blues (NL) and Cincinnati Reds (NL) in 1901. Weyhing completed the 1901 season with a 14–6 record at Grand Rapids, MI (WL). In 1902 and 1903, he recorded a composite 29–29 mark with Memphis, TN (SL), Atlanta, GA (SL), and Little Rock, AR (SL). Weyhing spent the 1910 season in the TL as manager of the Tulsa, OK club and as an umpire. He pitched 4,324.1 innings, started 503 games, won 264 games, lost 232 decisions, and ranks 11th in career major league complete games (448). Although walking nearly as many batters as he struck out and surrendering over one hit per inning, Weyhing won 23 or more games seven consecutive years and pitched over 400 innings five times. He compiled a career 3.89 ERA and struck out 1,665 batters. Weyhing, one of few ballplayers to perform in four major leagues, later operated a cigar store tavern and worked as a night watchman in Louisville, KY.

BIBLIOGRAPHY: Gene Karst and Martin J. Jones, Jr., *Who's Who in Professional Baseball* (New Rochelle, NY, 1973); Frederick G. Lieb and Stan Baumgartner, *The Philadelphia Phillies* (New York, 1953); Rich Westcott and Frank Bilovsky, *The New Phillies Encyclopedia* (Philadelphia, PA, 1993); Shirley Povich, *The Washington Senators* (New York, 1954); Craig Carter, ed., *TSN Daguerreotypes*, 8th ed. (St. Louis, MO, 1990); Robert L. Tiemann and Mark Rucker, eds., *Nineteenth Century Stars* (Kansas City, MO, 1989); David Nemec, *The Beer and Whisky League* (New York, 1994); Daniel Pearson, *Base Ball in 1889* (Bowling Green, OH, 1993); August Weyhing file, National Baseball Library, Cooperstown, NY.

Frank J. Olmsted

WHEAT, Zachariah Davis "Zack," "Buck" (b. May 23, 1888, Hamilton, OH; d. March 11, 1972, Sedalia, MO), player, was the son of farmer and stockyard worker Basil C. Wheat and Julia (Davis) Wheat, grew up on a farm near Bonanza, OH and moved with his family to Kansas City, KS at age 14. After playing semipro baseball in Enterprise, KS (KSL), he performed at Shreveport, LA (TL) in 1908 and Mobile, AL (SL) in 1909. In 1909, a Brooklyn Superbas (NL) scout signed him to a contract. From August 1909 through 1926, the 5-foot 10-inch, 170-pound, right-handed thrower served as a regular left fielder for the Brooklyn Superbas, Dodgers, and Robins. Since Wheat wore a 5½-inch shoe, however, he frequently suffered ankle injuries.

Known for his line drives, the soft-spoken left-handed batter made 2,884 major league hits, compiled a lifetime .317 batting average, and was never ejected from a game. In 2,410 major league games, he made 476 doubles, 172 triples, and 132 HR, scored 1,289 runs, knocked in 1,248 runs, and stole 205 bases. Although hitting .375 in both 1923 and 1924, he won only one NL batting title with a .335 mark in 1918. Wheat enjoyed above all playing in the 26-inning, 1–1 tie between the Brooklyn Robins and the Boston Braves in 1920. After batting .324 in a part-time capacity for the Philadelphia Athletics (AL) in 1927, he ended his career the next year with the Minneapolis, MN Millers (AA). Wheat three times made more than 200 hits in a season, played in more games (2,322) than any Brooklyn Dodger in history, and led the NL in slugging percentage (.461) in 1916.

Wheat spent off-seasons at his 162 acre farm near Polo, MO until depression conditions forced him to sell the property. He also had owned a bowling and billiards parlor in Kansas City, MO and joined the Kansas City, MO police force. In April 1936, Wheat was seriously injured in a patrol car accident and left the police force. Upon doctors' orders, Wheat settled on the Lake of the Ozarks at Sunrise Beach near Versailles, MO. Except during World War II, Wheat resided at Sunrise Beach and operated a fishing camp there until the 1950s. In 1959, he was elected unanimously to the National Baseball Hall of Fame.

Wheat married Daisy Forsith in 1912 and had one son, Zachary, and one daughter, Mary. His wife died in November 1959. Once described by Branch Rickey* as the best outfielder Brooklyn ever had, Wheat batted over .300 13 of his 18 years with the Dodgers. He died while living with his daughter.

BIBLIOGRAPHY: Zack Wheat file, National Baseball Library, Cooperstown, NY; *The Baseball Encyclopedia*, 10th ed. (New York, 1996); *DAB*, supp. 9 (1971–1975), pp. 857–858; Frank Graham, *The Brooklyn Dodgers* (New York, 1945); Richard Goldstein, *Superstars and Screwballs* (New York, 1991); Stanley Cohen, *Dodgers! The First 100 Years* (New York, 1990); William F. McNeil, *The Dodgers Encyclopedia* (Champaign, IL, 1997); Tommy Holmes, *The Dodgers* (New York, 1975); Kansas City (MO) *Star*, March 13, 1972; Lowell Reidenbaugh, *Baseball's Hall of Fame-Cooperstown* (New York, 1993).

Arthur F. McClure

WHITAKER, Louis Rodman, Jr. "Sweet Lou" (b. May 12, 1957, Brooklyn, NY), player, is the son of Louis Rodman Whitaker, Sr., whom he never knew. Whitaker's mother, restaurant worker M. R. Williams, took him to Virginia when he was two years old. Whitaker first played baseball in an organized youth league at age 10. At Martinsville High School, the left-handed–hitting, right-handed–throwing Whitaker proved a better pitcher than infielder.

Bill Lajoie, later general manager of the Detroit Tigers (AL), personally scouted Whitaker, who was the team's fifth selection in the June 1975 draft. Whitaker spent his entire career with the Detroit Tigers organization, including Bristol, CT (EL) in 1975, Lakeland, FL (FSL) in 1976 (being named FSL MVP), and Montgomery, AL (SL) in 1977. At Montgomery, second baseman Whitaker first teamed with shortstop Alan Trammell.* They later formed the longest-running double-play combination in major league history. Whitaker joined the Detroit Tigers briefly in September 1977.

In 1978, the 5-foot 11-inch, 160-pound Whitaker was named AL Rookie of the Year. The outstanding second baseman with a notably strong arm led the AL in fielding in 1982 and 1991 and won three Gold Glove and four *TSN* Silver Slugger Awards. An AL All-Star team selection each year from 1983 through 1986, he hit .500 with one HR and four RBI in those games. The 1983 campaign saw him record 206 hits, bat .320 for third best in the

AL, and be voted Tiger of the Year. In 1985 Whitaker belted 21 HR, including one over the right field roof, to set a record for Tigers' second basemen. Whitaker broke his own mark with 28 HR in 1989, when he was again named Tiger of the Year. He batted .301 in 1994 and retired as a player after the 1995 season. In 19 major league seasons, he compiled a career .276 batting average and ranks among the top 10 Tigers in hits (2,369), games played (2,390), doubles (420), and runs scored (1,386). He hit 244 HR, knocked in 1,084 runs, and stole 143 bases.

Whitaker played a key role on the Tigers' 1984 World Championship team and its 1987 Eastern Division titlists, scoring 13 runs in the 13 AL Championship Series and World Series games. He married Crystal Mc-Creary on November 21, 1979 and has three daughters, Asia, Sarah, and Angela.

BIBLIOGRAPHY: Detroit Tigers, *The Press Guide*, 1995; Robert E. Kelly, *Baseball's Best* (Jefferson, NC, 1988); John Thorn et al., eds., *Total Baseball*, 5th ed. (New York, 1997); Louis Whitaker, Jr. file, National Baseball Library, Cooperstown, NY; Louis Whitaker, Jr., letter to Sheldon Appleton, June 1989; William M. Anderson, *The Detroit Tigers* (South Bend, IN, 1996); Sparky Anderson, *Bless You Boys* (Chicago, IL, 1984); Joe Falls, *The Detroit Tigers: An Illustrated History* (New York, 1989); Fred T. Smith, *Tiger Tales and Trivia* (Lathrup Village, MI, 1988), George Sullivan and David Cataneo, *Detroit Tigers* (New York, 1985); Sparky Anderson and Dan Ewald, *Sparky* (New York, 1990); Richard Bak, *A Place for Summer* (Detroit, MI, 1998); Sparky Anderson with Dan Ewald, *They Call Me Sparky* (Chelsea, MI, 1998).

Sheldon L. Appleton

WHITE, Chaney "Reindeer," "Liz" (b. n.d., Dallas, TX; d. 1965, Philadelphia, PA), player, starred as an outfielder for the Atlantic City, NJ Bacharach Giants (ECL) during the 1920s. He possessed excellent speed and allegedly circled the bases in 14 seconds on a sprained ankle. The hard-nosed, aggressive White terrorized on the bases with his spikes-high slide, earning him a reputation as a "dirty" ballplayer. White, who threw left-handed and batted right-handed, displayed great range defensively and fielded well, but exhibited a weak arm. He batted a composite .347 for three CUWL campaigns, and .302 over an 18-year Negro League career.

White played with a Dallas-Fort Worth, TX team before joining the Philadelphia Hilldale Daisies in 1919. He remained with the Hilldale Daisies through 1922 except for a brief stint with Rube Foster's* Chicago American Giants (NNL) in 1920. He joined the Atlantic City Bacharach Giants in 1923 when the ECL was organized, hitting .385, .352 and .358 in his first three seasons there despite suffering from leg injuries. The Atlantic City Bacharach Giants captured consecutive ECL pennants in 1926 and 1927, but lost both World Series to the NNL Champion Chicago American Giants. White stole five bases in six attempts in the 1926 World Series, and batted .338 and .357 the next two seasons.

With no league in the east in 1930, White joined the Homestead, PA Grays. He left Homestead before the end of the 1930 season, however, and returned to the Hilldale Daisies. When both the EWL and the Hilldale Daisies folded in 1932, White switched to the Baltimore Black Sox for the remainder of the season. He joined Webster McDonald's* Philadelphia Stars in 1933. The Philadelphia Stars won the NNL pennant the next season and defeated the Chicago American Giants in the playoff for the Championship. White closed his baseball career with the New York Cubans (NNL) in 1936. In 1953, John Henry Lloyd* selected White as the left fielder on his all-time team for a national magazine.

BIBLIOGRAPHY: *The Afro-American*, 1920–1936; *The Atlantic City Daily Press*, 1926–1927; *The Chicago Defender*, 1920–1935; Robert W. Peterson, *Only the Ball Was White* (Englewood Cliffs, NJ, 1970); *The Philadelphia Tribune*, 1920–1936; *The Pittsburgh Courier*, 1923–1936; James A. Riley, *The All-Time All-Stars of Black Baseball* (Cocoa, FL, 1983); James A. Riley, *The Biographical Encyclopedia of the Negro Baseball Leagues* (New York, 1994); James A. Riley, interviews with former Negro League players, James A. Riley Collection, Canton, GA; Mike Shatzkin, ed., *The Ballplayers* (New York, 1990); *The Baseball Encyclopedia*, 10th ed. (New York, 1996).

James A. Riley

WHITE, Devon Markes (b. December 29, 1962, Kingston, Jamaica), player, moved to New York City at age nine and starred in basketball and baseball at Park West High School. The California Angels (AL) selected the 6-foot 2-inch, 190-pound switch-hitting outfielder, who throws right-handed, in the sixth round of the June 1981 draft. White spent six minor league seasons with Idaho Falls, ID (PrL) in 1981, Danville, IL (ML) in 1982, Peoria, IL (ML) and Nashua, NH (EL) in 1983, Redwood, CA (CaL) in 1984, Midland, TX (TL) in 1985, and Edmonton, Canada (PCL) in 1985 and 1986. He briefly appeared with the California Angels in 1985 and 1986, batting .500 in the 1986 AL Championship Series loss to the Boston Red Sox.

White played outfield with the California Angels from 1987 through 1990, winning Gold Gloves in 1988 and 1989. Besides recording career-highs with 24 HR and 87 RBI in 1987, he led AL outfielders in chances and assists. On September 9, 1989, White tied a major league record by stealing three bases in one inning against the Boston Red Sox. He has clouted HR from both sides of the plate twice and stole a career-high 44 bases in 1989, making the AL All-Star team.

The California Angels traded White to the Toronto Blue Jays (AL) in December 1990. His best seasons came with the Toronto Blue Jays, as he won five consecutive Gold Gloves from 1991 to 1995 and led AL outfielders in chances and putouts in 1991 and 1992. In 1991, White batted .282 during the regular season and .364 in the AL Championship Series loss to the Minnesota Twins. He hit .348 with two doubles and two RBI in the 1992 AL Championship Series against the Oakland A's and .231 in the World

Series triumph over the Atlanta Braves. In 1993, White batted .273 with career highs of 116 runs scored and 42 doubles and doubled in a run in the All-Star game. In the 1993 AL Championship Series against the Chicago White Sox, he batted .444 and tied a single series record with 12 hits. His power surge helped the Toronto Blue Jays defeat the Philadelphia Phillies in the World Series, as he batted .292 with three doubles, two triples, one HR, and seven RBI. The Florida Marlins (NL) signed him as a free agent in November 1995. His grand slam HR helped the Florida Marlins clinch the 1997 NL Division Series against the San Francisco Giants. After hitting only .190 in the NL Championship Series against the Atlanta Braves, he batted .242 with three doubles, a triple, and two RBI in the World Series triumph against the Cleveland Indians. In November 1997, the expansion Arizona Diamondbacks (NL) acquired White. White batted .279 in 1998, leading Arizona with 32 doubles, 22 HR, and 85 RBI. The Los Angeles Dodgers (NL) signed him as a free agent in November 1998.

In 15 major league seasons through 1999, White has batted .263 with 1,784 hits, 348 doubles, 68 triples, 190 HR, 813 RBI, 325 stolen bases, and a .985 fielding percentage. The Gilbert, AZ resident ranks fourth all-time with 29 leadoff HR and holds the career record for highest Championship Series batting average with a .392 mark. He and his wife, Colleen, have two children, Thaddeus and Davellynn.

BIBLIOGRAPHY: Devon White file, National Baseball Library, Cooperstown, NY; Matthew Toll, "Devon White," *SI* 67 (July 13, 1987), pp. 44–45; *TSN Baseball Register*, 1998; *Florida Marlins Media Guide*, 1997; John Kochmis, ed., *A Series to Remember* (San Francisco, CA, 1993); Dave Rosenbaum, *If They Don't Win It's a Shame* (Tampa, FL, 1998).

David L. Porter

WHITE, Frank, Jr. (b. September 4, 1950, Greenville, MS), player, coach, and manager, is the son of Frank White, Sr., and Daisie Vestula (Mitchell) White and attended Lincoln High School. The school was located one block from Municipal Stadium, where the Kansas City Athletics (AL) played and where the Kansas City Royals (AL) performed their first four seasons from 1969 to 1972. He participated in football and basketball because Lincoln High School did not field a baseball team, but performed baseball in the Connie Mack* and Ban Johnson* Leagues in Kansas City. The Kansas City Royals selected White to participate in their baseball academy at a Municipal Stadium tryout in 1973. White was the first graduate invited to the Royals' spring training camp. White, a 5-foot 11-inch, 190-pound right-handed second baseman, progressed quickly through the Royals' minor league system, showing good batting and outstanding defensive skills at Sarasota, FL (GCL) in 1971, San Jose, CA (CaL) and Jacksonville, FL (SL) in 1972, and Omaha, NE (AA) in 1973. He and his wife, Gladys, have two children, Frank III and Adrianne.

From 1973 to 1975, White played a reserve role with the Kansas City Royals behind Cookie Rojas at second base and Fred Patek at shortstop. In 1976, manager Whitey Herzog* benched Rojas in favor of White. White led AL second basemen in fielding average in 1977, 1983, and 1988 and won an unprecedented eighth AL Gold Glove at second base in 1987. In 1977, he established a Royals club record of 62 consecutive errorless games at second base. At age 38, White completed the 1988 season with only four errors in 150 games at second base. He recorded the sixth highest career fielding average (.984) at second base in major league history.

White also developed into a consistent hitter, reaching a major league career high .298 batting average in 1982. White's better than average speed enabled him to steal 20 or more bases in three seasons. An excellent bunter, White began to demonstrate power late in his major league career. White belted more HR (78) between 1984 and 1987 than he had in the previous 11 seasons. On August 19, 1986, he drove in seven runs against the Texas Rangers to tie a Royals' club record. White was voted MVP in the 1980 AL League Championship Series, batting .545 against the New York Yankees. He hit .244 in six AL Championship Series, but batted only a combined .170 for the 1980 and 1985 World Series against the Philadelphia Phillies and St. Louis Cardinals. A five-time AL All-Star, he pinch-hit a game-winning HR in the 1986 All-Star game.

White retired following the 1990 season and managed in the Boston Red Sox (AL) organization through 1993. After coaching for the Boston Red Sox from 1994 through 1996, he has coached for the Kansas City Royals since 1998. He ranked second to George Brett* for most seasons played in Royals history (18) and games played (2,324). He made 2,006 hits, with 912 runs scored, 160 HR, 886 RBI, 178 stolen bases, and a .255 batting average.

BIBLIOGRAPHY: Frank White, Jr. file, National Baseball Library, Cooperstown, NY; John Dewan, ed., *The Scouting Report: 1990* (New York, 1990); Whitey Herzog and Kevin Horrigan, *White Rat* (New York, 1987); Zander Hollander, ed., *The Complete Handbook of Baseball, 1987* (New York, 1987); Kansas City Royals, *Grandslam 1976*; Kansas City Royals, *Grandslam 1982*; Sid Bordman, *Expansion to Excellence* (Marcelline, MS, 1981); Alan Eskew, *A Royal Finish* (Chicago, IL, 1985); Peter C. Bjarkman, ed., *Encyclopedia of Major League Baseball Team Histories American League* (Westport, CT, 1991).

Frank J. Olmsted

WHITE, Guy Harris "Doc" (b. April 9, 1879, Washington, DC; d. February 19, 1969, Silver Spring, MD), player and executive, was the seventh son of a seventh son in an affluent Washington, DC family and a left-handed pitcher with outstanding control. He was the youngest of nine children of George White, who owned the only iron foundry in the nation's capital, and Marian Adelaide (Harris) White. White attended Georgetown University and earned a dental degree in 1902. After playing semipro baseball, he signed with the Philadelphia Phillies (NL) for $1,200 before the 1901 season. In the 1901 and 1902 NL seasons, White won 30 games and lost 33 contests.

White jumped to the Chicago White Sox (AL) in 1903 and quickly became the team's leading left-hander by relying on a fastball, sinker, and superb control. On September 6, 1903, the 6-foot 1-inch, 150-pound White pitched a ten-inning one-hit game. During a pennant race with the New York Highlanders and Boston Pilgrims in September 1904, he hurled an AL record five consecutive shutouts. He helped pitch the White Sox to the 1906 world championship, winning 18 games during the regular season as well as the final World Series game. White enjoyed his best season with a 27–13 mark in 1907, the only time he won 20 or more games. His 27 triumphs paced the AL. After White hurled 18 victories in 1908, his performance declined. He remained with the White Sox through 1913, winning 159 and losing 123, with 45 shutouts. During 13 major league seasons, he compiled a 189–156 mark (.548 winning percentage), completed 262 of 363 starts, struck out 1,384 batters in 3,041 innings, hurled 45 shutouts, and had a 2.39 ERA. Although never before pitching in the minor leagues, he ended his baseball career with two seasons (1914–1915) at Venice, CA (PCL) and Vernon, CA (PCL).

White practiced dentistry in the off-season only until 1906. A favorite of the White Sox management, he once designed the team's home uniform, composed songs to lyrics by Ring Lardner (OS), and performed them in vaudeville. After his active career, White owned TL franchises at Dallas, TX in 1917–1918 and Waco, TX in 1919. He returned to Washington, DC to teach physical education at Central High School, from which he had graduated, and became baseball and basketball coach and athletic director at Wilson Teachers College. White's wife, Iva Josephine Martin, whom he had met in high school, died in 1955. The couple had one son, Martin, and one daughter, Marian Palmer White, with whom the pitcher lived in his final years.

BIBLIOGRAPHY: Guy White file, National Baseball Library, Cooperstown, NY; Washington, DC *Evening Star*, February 19, 1969; George W. Hilton, correspondence with Martin Harris White, August 25, 1984, September 14, 1984; Gene Karst and Martin J. Jones, Jr., *Who's Who in Professional Baseball* (New Rochelle, NY, 1973); Craig Carter, ed., *TSN Daguerreotypes*, 8th ed. (St. Louis, MO, 1990); *TSN*, March 8, 1969; Rich Westcott and Frank Bilovsky, *The New Phillies Encyclopedia* (Philadelphia, PA, 1993); Warren Brown, *The Chicago White Sox* (New York, 1952); Richard Lindberg, *Sox* (New York, 1984); Richard Lindberg, *Who's on Third?* (South Bend, IN, 1983).

George W. Hilton

WHITE, James Laurie "Deacon" (b. December 7, 1847, Caton, NY; d. July 7, 1939, Aurora, IL), player, manager, and club owner, was the son of farmer James S. White and brother of major league pitcher William H. White* and attended Country Day School in Caton, NY. On April 24, 1871, he married Marium Van Arsdale of Caton. After her death, he wed Alice Force Thurber of Caton and was survived by a daughter, Grace Watkins of Aurora, IL. White, who learned baseball from a Civil War veteran, began to play amateur baseball in 1866 with the Caton town team and in 1867 with the Monitor club of nearby Corning, NY. In 1868, he joined the semipro Forest City team of Cleveland, OH as a catcher. The 5-foot 11-inch, 175-pound White became a full-fledged professional in 1871, when the Cleveland Forest Citys became a charter member of the NA, baseball's first professional league. When the Forest Citys played the Fort Wayne, IN Kekiongas (NA) on May 4, 1871, White became the first player to bat in a recognized major league game. The left-handed–batting and right-handed–throwing White made the first hit and first extra-base hit, a double, and became the initial player extinguished in a double play.

After the 1872 season, White moved to the Boston Red Stockings (NA) and gained recognition there as a member of the famed Big Four, including Al Spalding,* Ross Barnes,* and Cal McVey.* From 1871 to 1875, he made 447 hits and batted .347 in 261 games in the NA. Boston won a fourth straight championship in 1875, but the Big Four shocked the baseball world by signing with the Chicago White Stockings (NL) for the 1876 season. As Spalding's battery mate in 1876, White helped lead the White Stockings to a championship by batting .343, catching all but three games, and pacing the NL with 60 RBI. The versatile White joined the Boston Red Caps (NL) for the 1877 season at first base, third base, outfield, and catcher, and led the NL with 103 hits, a .387 batting average, .545 slugging average, 11 triples, and 49 RBI. After the 1877 season, White and his brother, Will, moved to the Cincinnati Reds (NL). White managed the club to a 9–9 record, but was replaced during the season by McVey and continued as a player there during the 1879 and 1880 seasons.

In 1881 White joined the Buffalo Bisons (NL) and won greater fame as a third baseman, outfielder, and occasional catcher. At Buffalo, he played with baseball legends Jim Galvin,* Jim O'Rourke,* and Dan Brouthers,* and formed part of a second Big Four with Brouthers, Hardy Richardson,* and Jack Rowe.* Late in the 1885 season, all Buffalo players were sold to the Detroit Wolverines (NL) in baseball's first mass player sale. White led Detroit to a second place finish in 1886 and an NL pennant in 1887. After the 1888 season, 40-year-old White was sold to the Boston Beaneaters (NL) and then shipped to the Pittsburgh Alleghenys (NL). He and teammate Jack Rowe, meanwhile, had purchased the Buffalo, NY franchise (IA). Pittsburgh, however, refused to release White and Rowe from their playing contracts and threatened to have the Buffalo club expelled if the pair attempted to play there. The stalemate continued until the middle of the 1889 season, when White and Rowe finally reported to Pittsburgh. When the PL was formed in 1890, Rowe and White surfaced as part-owners of the Buffalo

Bisons. At age 42, White batted .260 in 122 games for the Bisons. The PL collapsed after just one season, ending White's long baseball career. During 15 NL seasons, he played in 1,299 games, batted .303, and compiled 1,619 hits, 217 doubles, 73 triples, 18 HR, 849 runs scored, and 756 RBI.

White continued to live in Buffalo, NY, working for his brother, Will, as an optician and later operating a livery stable and garage. Around 1910, he moved to Aurora, IL and lived there until his death. An anomaly in a hard-bitten era of baseball history, he never drank, smoked, or swore, carried his Bible with him on the road, and attended church regularly. To White's great distress, he was never elected to the National Baseball Hall of Fame.

BIBLIOGRAPHY: Lee Allen, *The Cincinnati Reds* (New York, 1948); Arthur Bartlett, *Baseball and Mr. Spalding* (New York, 1951); Craig Carter, ed., *TSN Daguerreotypes*, 8th ed. (St. Louis, MO, 1990); Joseph M. Overfield, "James 'Deacon' White," *BRJ* 4 (1975), pp. 1–11; Frederick G. Lieb, *The Detroit Tigers* (New York, 1946); Gary Caruso, *The Braves Encyclopedia* (Philadelphia, PA, 1995); George Tuohey, comp., *A History of the Boston Base Ball Club* (Boston, MA, 1897); Eddie Gold and Art Ahrens, *The Golden Era Cubs, 1876–1940* (Chicago, IL, 1985); Warren Brown, *The Chicago Cubs* (New York, 1946); Harold Kaese, *The Boston Braves* (New York, 1948); William J. Ryczek, *Blackguards and Red Stockings* (Jefferson, NC, 1992); Robert L. Tiemann and Mark Rucker, eds., *Nineteenth Century Stars* (Kansas City, MO, 1989); James L. White file, National Baseball Library, Cooperstown, NY.

Joseph M. Overfield

WHITE, King Solomon "Sol" (b. June 12, 1868, Bellaire, OH; d. August 1955, New York, NY), player, manager, coach, official, and sportswriter, attended Wilberforce University from 1886 to 1890. His professional baseball career began as a third baseman in 1887 with the Pittsburgh Keystones of the League of Colored Baseball Clubs, but that league disbanded after one week. He joined the Wheeling, WV Green Stockings (OSL), where he batted .371. White played five seasons in official baseball with the New York Gorhams (MSL) in 1889, the Cuban Giants representing York, PA (EIL) in 1890, Ansonia, CT (CTL) in 1891, and Fort Wayne, IN (WEIL) in 1895. The outstanding hitter posted batting averages of .324 in 1889, .356 in 1890, .375 in 1891, and .385 in 1895 for a career .356 in organized baseball.

White played the bulk of his career with all-black teams, including the Pittsburgh Keystones (1887, 1892); New York Gorhams (1889); Cuban Giants (1889–1891, 1893–1894); New York Big Gorhams (1891); Adrian, MI, Page Fence Giants (1895); Cuban X Giants (1896–1899, 1901); Chicago Columbia Giants (1900); Philadelphia Giants (1902–1909); Brooklyn Royal Giants (1910); and New York Lincoln Giants (1911). White helped win the 1890 EIL championship. White became a successful manager and helped Walter Schlichter organize the Philadelphia Giants in 1902. Many premier black players eventually joined the Philadelphia Giants, which White piloted to the summit of black baseball from 1904 through 1907. Published records show 507 wins and 173 losses for Philadelphia from 1902 through 1906. Philadelphia played the Cuban X Giants for the World Colored Championship in 1903 and 1904, losing the former series five games to two and winning the latter two games to one. Challenges issued to the top white major league teams remained unanswered.

In 1907 White released his *History of Colored Baseball*, an invaluable historical source covering the pioneering years of black baseball through 1906. Unfortunately, his later efforts to publish an updated *History of Colored Baseball* failed. White retired from baseball in 1912, but returned as secretary of the infant Columbus, OH Buckeyes (NNL) in 1920. He left the Buckeyes to manage the Cleveland, OH Browns (NNL) in 1924 and spent his last year in baseball coaching for the 1926 Newark, NJ Stars (ECL). Subsequently, the learned, studious White penned a column for the New York *Amsterdam News*.

The right-handed second baseman, who stood 5 feet 7 inches and weighed 170 pounds, eventually played every position except pitcher as a professional. White possessed a calm, quiet nature, although admitting to being intense as a player. His efforts as a performer, leader, pioneer, and chronicler gave the multitalented White a unique place in baseball history.

BIBLIOGRAPHY: Ocania Chalk, *Pioneers of Black Sport* (New York, 1975); John B. Holway, *Blackball Stars* (Westport, CT, 1988); Robert W. Peterson, *Only the Ball Was White* (Englewood Cliffs, NJ, 1970); Pittsburgh (PA) *Courier*, March 12, 1927; James A. Riley, *The Biographical Encyclopedia of the Negro Baseball Leagues* (New York, 1994); Robert L. Tiemann and Mark Rucker, eds., *Nineteenth Century Stars* (Kansas City, MO, 1989); Jerry Malloy, comp., *Sol White's History of Colored Baseball with Documents on the Early Black Game, 1886–1936* (Lincoln, NE, 1996); Sol White file, National Baseball Library, Cooperstown, NY.

Merl F. Kleinknecht

WHITE, Roy Hilton (b. December 27, 1943, Los Angeles, CA), player and coach, performed for the New York Yankees (AL) from 1965 through 1979. White, the son of Marcus White, an artist and sculptor, and Margaret White, grew up in Compton, CA and attended Centennial High School and Compton JC.

White began his professional baseball career in the New York Yankees farm system with Greensboro, NC (CrL) in 1962 as a second baseman. In 1963, he proved his offensive abilities by posting a .309 batting average and leading the CrL in runs scored (117). Defensively, he paced second basemen in errors (33). White culminated two Columbus, GA (SL) campaigns in 1965 with the circuit best in runs scored (103), hits (168), total bases (279), and triples (14). His defensive woes continued, however, as he topped the circuit's keystoners with 27 errors. A composite minor league .956 fielding average in four seasons as a second sacker prompted the Yankees to find a defensive post better suited to his abilities. The New York Yankees promoted White for parts of the 1965 season. He batted a career-high .343 with Spokane, WA (PCL) in 1967 before returning permanently to the New York Yankees. After being given trials as a third baseman, White became a sure-handed, full-time outfielder for the New York Yankees in 1968.

His gentlemanly demeanor and consistent play brought a touch of dignity to the once-powerful New York Yankees, as the club struggled in the late 1960s. White, ever the consummate team player, set an AL standard with 17 sacrifice flies in 1971. He played the full slate of 162 games in 1970 and 1973. White posted a perfect 1.000 fielding average in 1971 and paced the AL in bases on balls (99) in 1972 and runs scored (104) in 1976.

White proved instrumental in the New York Yankees' return to glory, helping them win three consecutive AL pennants from 1976 to 1978 and garner World Series triumphs over the Los Angeles Dodgers the latter two seasons. He hit .316 in 14 AL Championship Series contests and .244 in 12 World Series encounters.

White, one of many successful switch-batters to don the New York Yankees pinstripes, posted a .271 batting average with 300 doubles, 160 HR, and 758 RBI in 15 major league seasons and made the 1969 and 1970 AL All-Star squads. The 5-foot 10-inch 170 pounder achieved his best major league batting average as a regular with .296 in 1970 and belted 22 HR.

White married Linda Hoxie on December 12, 1966 and has two children, Loreena and Reade. He coached for the New York Yankees in 1983, 1984, and 1986 and has served as a minor league instructor for the Yankees since 1996. White who has been enshrined in the New Jersey Sports Hall of Fame, resides in Oradell, NJ and operates his own baseball camps and clinics.

BIBLIOGRAPHY: Roy White file, National Baseball Library, Cooperstown, NY; *The Baseball Encyclopedia*, 10th ed. (New York, 1996); *1978 New York Yankees Yearbook*; Questionnaire completed by Roy White, 1993; *TSN Official Baseball Register, 1980*; Dave Anderson et al., *The Yankees* (New York, 1979); Mark Gallagher, *The Yankee Encyclopedia*, vol. 3 (Champaign, IL, 1997); Reggie Jackson and Mike Lupica, *Reggie* (New York, 1984); Dick Lally, *Pinstriped Summers* (New York, 1985); Sparky Lyle and Peter Golenbock, *The Bronx Zoo* (New York, 1979).

                                                              Merl F. Kleinknecht

WHITE, William DeKova "Bill" (b. January 28, 1934, Lakewood, FL), player, sportscaster, and executive, became the first black to announce major league baseball games when he joined the New York Yankees (AL) broadcast team in 1971 after playing 13 major league seasons for four different teams and became the first black to head a professional sports league in 1989. After growing up in Warren, OH, White attended Hiram College as a premedical student and graduated with a bachelor's degree in general science. He interrupted his studies to earn money for medical school, becoming a professional baseball player in 1953. His minor league teams included Danville,

VA (CrL) in 1953, Sioux City, IA (WL) in 1954, and Dallas, TX (TL) in 1955.

After starting the 1956 season with Minneapolis, MN (AA), White joined the New York Giants (NL) in May and hit a HR in his first at-bat. He spent one season with the New York Giants, served one year in the U.S. Army, and then was traded to the St. Louis Cardinals (NL) in March 1959. White remained seven seasons with the Cardinals, becoming the premier fielding first baseman of the decade and winning seven consecutive Gold Glove Awards from 1960 through 1966. He batted over .300 and drove in over 100 runs during four of his 13 seasons. His .286 major league career batting average included 1,706 hits, 278 doubles, 65 triples, 202 HR, and 870 RBI. On July 17–18, 1961, he collected a remarkable 14 hits in 18 at-bats during consecutive doubleheaders. He was traded with Bob Uecker and Dick Groat* to the Philadelphia Phillies (NL) in October 1965 and spent three seasons there. The 1969 campaign saw him used mainly as a pinch-hitter for the St. Louis Cardinals. During his major league career, he was selected six times as an NL All-Star.

After broadcasting in St. Louis, MO, and Philadelphia, PA, White joined Phil Rizzuto* in 1971 as part of the New York Yankees (AL) broadcast team on WPIX-TV and handled CBS-Radio national broadcasts. In 18 years as a Yankees broadcaster, White made outspoken, critical comments when he believed it was necessary and shared his solid baseball knowledge with the audience. The Rizzuto-White team constituted one of the most knowledge-able broadcasting teams ever, combining 13 years each of major league playing experience. The two men worked together effectively.

On February 3, 1989, White left broadcasting to become an NL executive. He was chosen unanimously to become the 13th NL President and officially replaced Angelo Bartlett Giamatti,* who became Commissioner, on April 1, 1989. Other black candidates had included Joe Morgan;* Simon Gourdine, former NBA Deputy Commissioner; and Gilroye Griffin, Jr., a business executive. White became the highest ranking black executive of a professional sports league. White's selection was applauded and celebrated by black notables and the baseball establishment, all of whom recognized his strong character and principles and his record of commitment to racial integration and equality. Leonard Coleman replaced White as NL president in March 1994.

White, who married Mildred Alberta Hightower on November 20, 1956, had five children before obtaining a divorce.

BIBLIOGRAPHY: Dave Anderson, "Bill White Keeps Fighting His Way," *NYT*, February 5, 1989; *The Baseball Encyclopedia*, 10th ed. (New York, 1996); "Bill White the National League's New Boss," *Ebony* 44 (May 1989), pp. 44ff; T. Callahan, "Baseball Picks a Pioneer," *Time* 133 (February 13, 1989), p. 76; Curt Smith, "Baseball's Angry Man," *NYT Magazine* (October 13, 1991), pp. 28–31; Murray Chass, "White Will Accept Offer to Head National League," *NYT*, February 3, 1989; Joseph Durso, "A

Symbol of Change: William DeKova White," *NYT*, February 4, 1989; Steve Gelman, "Bill White—'A Man Must Say What He Thinks Is Right,' " *Sport* 38 (July 1964), pp. 52–61; "It's Great to Be Traded," *Ebony* 14 (October 1959), pp. 46–48; L. B. Randolphe, "Bill White: National League President," *Ebony* 47 (August 1992), pp. 52ff; Bill White file, National Baseball Library, Cooperstown, NY; Michael LaBlanc, ed., *Contemporary Black Biography*, vol. 1 (Detroit, MI, 1994), pp. 243–245; Larry Moffi and Jonathan Kronstadt, *Crossing the Line* (Jefferson, NC, 1994); David L. Porter, ed., *African-American Sports Greats* (Westport, CT, 1995); Bob Broeg, *Redbirds: A Century of Cardinals' Baseball* (St. Louis, MO, 1981); Rob Rains, *The St. Louis Cardinals* (New York, 1992); Bob Broeg and Jerry Vickery, *St. Louis Cardinals Encyclopedia* (Grand Rapids, MI, 1998); Allen Lewis, *The Philadelphia Phillies: A Pictorial History* (Virginia Beach, VA, 1981); Rich Westcott and Frank Bilovsky, *The New Phillies Encyclopedia* (Philadelphia, PA, 1993); Bill Shannon, *All-Time Greatest Who's Who in Baseball: 1872–1990* (New York, 1990); Curt Smith, *Voices of the Game* (South Bend, IN, 1987).

Douglas A. Noverr

WHITE, William Henry "Will," "Whoop-La" (b. October 11, 1854, Caton, NY; d. August 31, 1911, Port Carling, Canada), player and manager, was the son of farmer James S. White and brother of baseball player James L. White.* After attending Country Day School in Caton, NY, he graduated in 1890 from the College of Ophthalmics in Corning, NY. White married Hattie L. Holmes in December 1875 and had one daughter, Katherine (White) Shull. The 5-foot 9½-inch, 175-pound White learned to pitch from his brother, Jim, as a Caton teenager. By age 17, the right-hander had mastered the curveball and could curve a ball around a post in the ground. He began his professional baseball career in 1877 by joining brother Jim with the Boston Red Caps (NL) and won two of three decisions. He and his brother moved in 1878 to the Cincinnati Reds (NL), where he became one of the NL's hardest working pitchers with 30 wins and 21 losses. In 1879 and 1880, he compiled 43–31 and 18–42 records, respectively. White led NL pitchers in games (76), games started (75), complete games (75), innings pitched (680), and hits surrendered (676) in 1879.

This hard work hurt his arm and White pitched only two games with the Detroit Wolverines (NL) in 1881. Upon joining the Cincinnati Red Stockings (AA) in 1882, however, he resumed his almost daily mound trips. From 1882 to 1885, he recorded 40–12, 43–22, 34–18, and 18–15 marks. In 1882, he paced the AA in wins, winning percentage (.769), complete games (52), innings pitched (480), and shutouts (8). The next year, he led the AA in wins (43), ERA (2.09), and shutouts (6). In 1884 he also managed the Cincinnati Red Stockings, but resigned at midseason with a 44–27 win–loss record. White claimed that he did not have the temperament or personality to be a baseball manager. After experiencing arm trouble again late in the 1885 season, White appeared in just three games the next season and retired. During 10 major league seasons, he won 229 games and lost 166 contests for a remarkable .580 winning percentage, completed 394 of 401 starts, and recorded 36 shutouts. White struck out 1,041 batters and walked only 496 in 3,542.2 innings and compiled a 2.28 ERA (10th best). He made his final professional appearance in 1889 with Buffalo NY (IA), compiling a 6–12 record.

White grew up near the glassmaking center of Corning, NY, and became the first major league player to wear glasses on the field. He founded the Buffalo Optical Company in 1893. At his Port Carling summer home in the Lake Muskoka region of Ontario, Canada White, a non-swimmer, was teaching a young niece to swim when he suffered a heart seizure in the water and drowned. The deeply religious White helped found and was chief benefactor of Christ Mission in his adopted city of Buffalo.

BIBLIOGRAPHY: Lee Allen, *The Cincinnati Reds* (New York, 1948); Buffalo (NY) *Courier*, August 31–September 2, 1911; Buffalo (NY) *Evening News*, August 31–September 2, 1911; Buffalo (NY) *Morning Express*, August 31, September 1, 2, 1911; Craig Carter, ed., *TSN Daguerreotypes*, 8th ed. (St. Louis, MO, 1990); Bob Rathgeber, *Cincinnati Reds Scrapbook* (Virginia Beach, VA, 1982); David Nemec, *The Beer and Whisky League* (New York, 1994); *The Baseball Encyclopedia*, 10th ed. (New York, 1996); Robert L. Tiemann and Mark Rucker, eds., *Nineteenth Century Stars* (Kansas City, MO, 1989).

Joseph M. Overfield

WHITEHILL, Earl Oliver "The Earl" (b. February 7, 1900, Cedar Rapids, IA; d. October 22, 1954, Omaha, NE), player, coach, and executive, learned baseball on the sandlots of Cedar Rapids. Cy Slapnicka, a Cedar Rapids native, NL pitcher, and scout who later discovered Bob Feller,* recommended Whitehill to the Detroit Tigers (AL). In 1919, Tigers manager Hugh Jennings* optioned Whitehill to Des Moines, IA (WL). From 1920 through 1923, Whitehill hurled for Birmingham, AL (SA), and Columbia, SC (SAL). At the end of the 1923 season, new Detroit Tigers manager Ty Cobb* promoted Whitehill to the parent club. He created a sensation by winning his two decisions and posting a 2.73 ERA. In 1924, he led the Detroit Tigers with 17 wins and only nine losses to help Detroit stay in or near first place in July and August and proved especially effective against the New York Yankees. Before a then-record 43,000 spectators at Navin Field in Detroit, MI he shut out the New York Yankees on August 4. Two days later, he defeated New York again to put the Tigers in first place.

In the spring of 1925, Whitehill experienced arm trouble and sought the services of Bonesetter Reese in Youngstown, OH. Due to Whitehill's slow start, Cobb wanted him to throw curves and trick pitches. On occasion, Whitehill proved effective with his "junk" pitches. Umpire Pants Rowland* repeatedly checked the ball for a foreign substance on June 11 when Whitehill defeated Walter Johnson* and the Washington Senators, 7–2. Whitehill proved a disappointment in 1925, however, winning only 11 of 22 decisions.

Cobb, who had promised Detroit fans an AL pennant in 1925, held White-hill largely responsible for the club's lackluster showing and wanted him to rely on off-speed pitches. On several occasions, Cobb rushed in from center field to the mound and gave Whitehill a public scolding for throwing a fastball. The feisty, outspoken Whitehill once retorted, "I like my fastball." The enraged "Georgia Peach" did not speak to Whitehill for nearly two years, conveying messages through a coach and giving him only a few minutes' notice about pitching assignments.

Whitehill, who was delighted when Cobb was fired as Detroit Tigers manager after the 1926 season, did not fulfill his great potential. Under manager George Moriarty, he won 16, lost 14 and posted a 3.36 ERA in 1927 and won 11, lost 16, and compiled a 4.31 ERA in 1928. From 1929 to 1932, he won 60 and lost 56 for Tigers manager Bucky Harris.* Although Whitehill was not much better than a .500 pitcher for Detroit, Washington Senators (AL) owner Clark Griffith* considered him one of the game's best hurlers. Whitehill proved particularly adept at vanquishing the New York Yankees, a team Griffith needed to beat consistently to win the AL pennant. In December 1932 Griffith made one of his best deals by trading veteran pitcher Fred Marberry* and rookie Carl Fischer to Detroit for Whitehill. Whitehill led the Senators to the AL pennant in 1933 and enjoyed his best season with 22 wins, eight losses, and a 3.33 ERA. He proved a formidable competitor, once challenging Yankees outfielder Ben Chapman* to a fight. Whitehill was suspended for five days for the altercation, but won the ad-miration and respect of the Washington fans and players. He pitched the third game and home opener of the 1933 World Series. Before President Franklin D. Roosevelt and a large congressional delegation, he shut out the New York Giants on five hits. The 4–0 victory was the Washington Senators only Series win.

Whitehill slumped to a 14–11 record in 1934, as the Washington Senators dropped into the second division. In four years with Washington, he won 64 decisions and lost 43. Since Whitehill's fastball was no longer effective, Griffith traded him to the Cleveland Indians (AL) in December 1936. Whitehill won 17 and lost 16 for Cleveland the next two years and ended his major league career in 1939 with a 4–7 record for the Chicago Cubs (NL). Altogether, Whitehill won 218 games, lost 185 decisions, walked 1,431 batters in 3,564.2 innings, hurled 16 shutouts, and boasted a 4.36 ERA. A workhorse, he averaged over 30 starts a year during the peak of his career. The 5-foot 9½-inch, 175-pound left-hander possessed an extraordinary fast-ball.

Whitehill, an extremely handsome player and elegant dresser possessing a lordly manner, was nicknamed "The Earl" and was a notorious lady's man until his marriage to Violet Linda Oliver on November 23, 1925. Mrs. Whitehill, a model, became famous as the Sun Maid and is pictured on that firm's package of raisins. After his playing career, he coached for the Cleveland Indians (AL) in 1941, Philadelphia Phillies (NL) in 1943, and Buffalo, NY Bisons (IL) in 1944. Upon leaving baseball, Whitehill became a public relations director for the A. G. Spalding* Sporting Goods Company and was killed in an automobile accident while representing the company.

BIBLIOGRAPHY: Jerry E. Clark, *Anson to Zuber* (Omaha, NE, 1992); Joe Falls, *Detroit Tigers* (New York, 1975); Fred Smith, *995 Tigers* (Detroit, MI, 1981); William M. Anderson, *The Detroit Tigers* (South Bend, IN, 1996); Morris Bealle, *The Washington Senators* (Washington, DC, 1947); Charles C. Alexander, *Ty Cobb* (New York, 1984); Franklin Lewis, *The Cleveland Indians* (New York, 1949); Detroit *News*, 1923–1932; Frederick G. Lieb, *The Detroit Tigers* (New York, 1946); Shirley Povich, *The Washington Senators* (New York, 1954); *TSN*, November 3, 1954.

Anthony J. Papalas

WHITNEY, Arthur Carter "Pinky" (b. January 2, 1905, San Antonio, TX; d. September 1, 1987, Center, TX), player, began his professional baseball career with the Cleveland Indians (AL) organization in 1925. Before Whitney appeared in a major league game, Cleveland optioned him to Decatur, IL (3IL). After spending the 1926 season at Decatur, Whitney was traded to New Orleans, LA (SA). His .339 batting average there in 1927 inspired the Philadelphia Phillies (NL) to draft him. In 1928, he won the starting position as the Philadelphia Phillies' third baseman and became one of the top NL players at that spot. He batted .301 his first season and recorded 200 hits for the 1929 Philadelphia Phillies, the only team in NL history to have four players reach 200 or more hits in a season. In 1930, he enjoyed his best major league season with 207 hits and a .342 batting average. On June 17, 1933, the financially strapped Philadelphia Phillies traded Whitney and Hal Lee to the Boston Braves (NL) for two players and cash. The Boston Braves made Whitney unhappy by playing him at second base frequently and shortstop occasionally. Whitney consequently welcomed the trade that returned him to the Philadelphia Phillies in April 1936. Whitney retired after the 1939 season and returned to the San Antonio, TX area, where he operated bowling alleys and worked as a public relations representative of Lone Star Brewery. He was named to the South Texas Sports Hall of Fame.

In 1,539 major league games spanning 12 seasons, Whitney batted .295, with 1,701 hits, 303 doubles, 56 triples, 93 HR, and 927 RBI. He hit .300 or better four times, recording a high of .342 in 1930. He hit 26 or more doubles six times, drove in 100 or more runs four seasons, scored 696 runs, and drew 400 walks. He was selected for the 1936 All-Star Game, hitting .333 in that contest.

Although playing all the infield positions, Whitney saw action mainly at third base with 1,358 games. He led NL third basemen in putouts three times, in assists four years, and in double plays and fielding average three times.

Whitney was survived by his wife, Harriet, one son, and one daughter.

BIBLIOGRAPHY: Pinky Whitney file, National Baseball Library, Cooperstown, NY; Gary Caruso, *The Braves Encyclopedia* (Philadelphia, PA, 1995); Rich Westcott and Frank Bilovsky, *The New Phillies Encyclopedia* (Philadelphia, PA, 1993); Harold Kaese, *The Boston Braves* (New York, 1948); Allen Lewis, *The Philadelphia Phillies: A Pictorial History* (Virginia Beach, VA, 1981); Frederick Lieb and Stan Baumgartner, *The Philadelphia Phillies* (New York, 1953); San Antonio (TX) *Express-News*, September 2, 1987; *TSN*, September 21, 1987.

Ralph S. Graber

WHITNEY, James Evans "Grasshopper Jim" (b. November 10, 1857, Conklin, NY; d. May 21, 1891, Binghamton, NY), player, was reared in Binghamton, NY, and played with his brother, Charlie, for independent professional baseball clubs in the mid–1870s. Nicknamed "Grasshopper Jim" for his distinctive walk, he entered organized baseball with Binghamton, NY (IA) in 1878 and played for Omaha, NE (NWL) in 1879 and the Knickerbockers of San Francisco, CA (CaL) in 1880.

In his first major league season with the 1881 Boston Red Stockings (NL), Whitney led NL pitchers in innings pitched (552.1) and shared the NL lead in wins (31) and complete games (57). His 33 losses for the weak-hitting Boston Red Stockings also led the NL. In 1882, the 6-foot 2-inch, 172-pound left-handed batter and right-handed hurler ranked among NL leaders both in hitting and pitching. His .323 batting average placed fifth in the NL, while his .382 on base percentage and .510 slugging average ranked third. Pete Palmer's statistical assessment in *Total Baseball* rates Whitney's 1882 batting performance the third best ever by a major league pitcher. Whitney also posted a winning 24–21 record as pitcher, finishing among the NL's top five in innings pitched, complete games, and strikeouts.

In 1883, Whitney married a Miss Haddock and enjoyed his finest season. Missing only two of the Boston Beaneaters' (NL) games, he performed in the outfield when not pitching. Whitney batted .281 and compiled a career-best .638 winning percentage with a 37–21 pitching record, propelling the Boston Beaneaters to the NL pennant. His personal-best 345 strikeouts, along with his average 6.04 strikeouts per nine innings, led the NL. The fastballer's accuracy also gave him the first of five straight NL titles in fewest walks per nine innings. Only one other major league pitcher, Walter Johnson* of the 1920 Washington Senators, led his league in most strikeouts and fewest walks per nine innings the same season.

Whitney enjoyed another winning season with a 23–14 mark in 1884, although illness limited him to 66 games altogether and 38 as pitcher. His 1885 record fell to 18–32, an NL high in losses. He was signed for 1886 by the new Kansas City Cowboys (NL) franchise. He endured his worst season there, again losing 32 games while winning only 12. His ERA ballooned to 4.49, two full points above his average for first five major league seasons.

When the Kansas City Cowboys dropped from the NL after just one year,

Whitney signed with the Washington Senators (NL) and compiled an impressive 24–21 record for the seventh-place club in 1887. The next year, however, he slipped to an 18–21 mark with Washington. The 1889 season found him with the Indianapolis, IN Hoosiers (NL). After a 2–7 start with Indianapolis, he finished the season with minor league Buffalo, NY (IA). Whitney returned to the major leagues with the Philadelphia Athletics (AA) in 1890, compiling a 2–2 record. The tuberculosis, which killed him a year later, already had begun to damage his health.

In 10 major league seasons, Whitney posted a 191–204 win–loss record and 2.97 ERA in 3,496.1 innings. His 550 games included 413 pitching appearances and 377 complete games in 396 starts.

BIBLIOGRAPHY: James Whitney file, National Baseball Library, Cooperstown, NY; Gary Caruso, *The Braves Encyclopedia* (Philadelphia, PA, 1995); Harold Kaese, *The Boston Braves* (New York, 1948); Paul MacFarlane, ed., *Daguerreotypes of Great Stars of Baseball* (St. Louis, MO, 1981); John Thorn et al., eds., *Total Baseball*, 5th ed. (New York, 1997); Robert L. Tiemann and Mark Rucker, eds., *Nineteenth Century Stars* (Kansas City, MO, 1989); Shirley Povich, *The Washington Senators* (New York, 1954); Morris Bealle, *The Washington Senators* (Washington, DC, 1947).

Frederick Ivor-Campbell

WICKWARE, Frank "Red Ant" (b. 1888, Coffeyville, KS; d. November 2, 1967, Schenectady, NY), player, ranked among the premier players in the preleague days of Negro baseball. Wickware, a right-handed pitcher, was known for his blazing fastball and his propensity for winning clutch games. His baseball career began in 1909 with the Dallas Giants and in 1910 he moved to Rube Foster's* Chicago Leland Giants. Wickware joined legends Frank "Pete" Duncan,* Pat Dougherty,* Pete Hill,* Grant "Home Run" Johnson,* John Henry Lloyd,* Andrew Payne, and Bruce Petway.* The Leland Giants, called by Foster his greatest team ever, compiled an incredible 123–6 win–loss record that season, with Wickware taking 18 of 19 decisions.

After spending three seasons with the Leland Giants, Wickware moved to the Mohawk Giants of Schenectady, NY. The semiprofessional team, owned by Bill Wernecke, a General Electric factory worker and former semiprofessional outfielder, arranged a game against the All-Americans, led by future National Baseball Hall of Fame pitcher Walter "Big Train" Johnson.* Wernecke selected Wickware to pitch the October 1913 contest, despite having legends Walter Ball* and "Smoky Joe" Williams* on his pitching staff. After five and one-half innings, the game was called on account of darkness. Wickware outdueled Johnson, 1–0. Wickware faced Johnson twice more, splitting the decisions. In 1912, he led the CUWL with 10 wins against four losses and hurling 11 complete games for his team, Fe, which won only 14 games.

Wickware's barnstorming career included stays with the Chicago American Giants (1911–1912, 1914–1921), Brooklyn Royal Giants (1913), Louisville White Sox (1914), Indianapolis ABCs (1916), Detroit Stars (1919), Chicago Giants (NNL) in 1921, and New York Lincoln Giants in 1925.

In 1925, police charged Wickware with the homicide of 27-year-old Ben Adair of New York City. Wickware, however, was cleared of all charges due to lack of evidence. His overall greatness was recognized in a 1952 poll by the Pittsburgh (PA) *Courier*, which selected him to their fourth all-time, all-star team for Negro League players. He served as a manager in New Bedford, MA in 1930.

BIBLIOGRAPHY: Chicago (IL) *Defender*, May 23, 1925; Frank Keetz, "When 'The Big Train' Met 'The Red Ant,' " *BRJ* 20 (1991), pp. 63–65; James A. Riley, *The Biographical Encyclopedia of the Negro Baseball Leagues* (New York, 1994); Mike Shatzkin, ed., *The Ballplayers* (New York, 1990).

Larry Lester

WILHELM, James Hoyt (b. July 26, 1923, Huntersville, NC), player, was an extremely durable relief pitcher and hurled effectively in the major leagues until age 49. One of 11 children in a family of tenant farmers, he attended high school in Cornelius, NC. Wilhelm learned to throw the knuckleball there, enabling him to enjoy a very long major league career. After reading about Emil "Dutch" Leonard's* knuckleball in a newspaper, he soon made it his most effective pitch. During his 18th major league season (1969), he said, "I don't even try to fool anybody. I just throw the knuckleball 85 to 90 percent of the time. You don't need variations, because the damn ball jumps around so crazily, it's like having a hundred pitches." After high school, he pitched three seasons for Mooresville, NC (NCSL) and then served three years in the armed forces during World War II. Four more minor league seasons followed, during which he was used primarily as a starting pitcher. He married Patti Reeves in September 1951 and has three children, Patti, Pam, and Jim.

At the relatively advanced age of 28, Wilhelm made the New York Giants (NL) roster in the spring of 1952 and hit a HR in his first major league at-bat. Converted by manager Leo Durocher* to relief pitching, Wilhelm in 1952 became the first rookie to lead the NL in both ERA (2.43) and winning percentage (.833). He also led the NL appearances in 1952 (71) and 1953 (68) and in relief wins in 1952 (15) and 1954 (12), helping the Giants win the NL pennant. When he paced the AL in ERA (2.19) in 1959 with the Baltimore Orioles (AL), he became one of few pitchers to so lead both major leagues. On September 20, 1958, he hurled a no-hit, no-run game against the New York Yankees. During 1958, 1959 and 1960 with Baltimore, he made the majority of his 52 major league starts. His 1,070 pitching appearances comprised a major league record until Jesse Orosco broke it in 1999. During 21 major league seasons, he won 143 games and lost 122 (.540 winning percentage) for a 2.52 ERA. Wilhelm struck out 1,610 batters in 2,254.1 innings, won 123 games in relief, and compiled 227 saves.

Wilhelm pitched for nine major league teams. His clubs included the New York Giants (NL), 1952–1956; St. Louis Cardinals (NL), 1957; Cleveland Indians (AL), 1957–1958; Baltimore Orioles (AL), 1958–1962; Chicago White Sox (AL), 1963–1968; California Angels (AL), 1969; Atlanta Braves (NL), 1969–1971; Chicago Cubs (NL), 1970–1971; and Los Angeles Dodgers (NL), 1971–1972. Since his knuckleball proved even more difficult to catch than to hit, his catchers repeatedly led the league in passed balls. When Wilhelm pitched with Baltimore, manager Paul Richards* developed a special large catcher's mitt to reduce the number of passed balls considerably. A 1965 rule, however, limited the size of the mitt. Ted Williams* considered Wilhelm one of the five toughest pitchers he faced "strictly for his knuckleballs. Wilhelm has a sure-strike knuckler, then a real good knuckler, then with two strikes, an utterly unhittable knuckler, dancing in your face. The closest thing to an unhittable ball I ever saw." In 1985, he became the first relief pitcher elected to the National Baseball Hall of Fame. Wilhelm served as a minor league pitching coach and scout for two decades for the New York Yankees (AL).

BIBLIOGRAPHY: Richard Lindberg, *Who's on Third?* (South Bend, IN, 1983); Richard Lindberg, *Sox* (New York, 1984); Ted Patterson, *The Baltimore Orioles* (Dallas, TX, 1995); Fred Stein and Nick Peters, *Giants Diary* (Berkeley, CA, 1987); Leo Durocher, *Nice Guys Finish Last* (New York, 1975); Noel Hynd, *The Giants of the Polo Grounds* (New York, 1988); Hoyt Wilhelm file, National Baseball Library, Cooperstown, NY; *CB* (1971), pp. 441–443; "King of the Flutter," *Newsweek* 73 (April 21, 1969), p. 127; Tom Meany and Tommy Holmes, *Baseball's Best* (New York, 1964); Larry Powell, "Hoyt Wilhelm: Master of the Knuckleball," *SCD* 23 (June 21, 1996), p. 164; Bob Cairns, *Pen Men* (New York, 1993); Martin Quigley, *The Crooked Pitch* (Chapel Hill, NC, 1984); Joseph L. Reichler, *Thirty Years of Baseball's Greatest Moments* (New York, 1974); Lou Sabin, *Record Breakers of the Major Leagues* (New York, 1974); Hoyt Wilhelm, "So I Escaped from the Bullpen," *SEP* 232 (August 1, 1959), pp. 25, 58, 60.

Leverett T. Smith, Jr.

WILKINSON, James Leslie (b. 1874, Perry, IA; d. August 21, 1964, Kansas City, MO), executive, was a Negro League baseball pioneer and team owner from 1909 through 1948. Wilkinson, the son of the president of Algona Normal College, grew up in Des Moines, IA and suffered an injury as a young man that ended his baseball playing career. He managed the All Nations team, sponsored by a Des Moines firm. Wilkinson's team, which included players of several nationalities and even a young woman, barnstormed through small towns of prairie America and large cities against top semipro and black clubs. Blacks comprised the best players on the team.

When the NNL was formed in 1920, the white Wilkinson assembled the Kansas City Monarchs. After the NNL collapsed in 1931, Wilkinson made the Monarchs a barnstorming club. He guided the Monarchs from the beginning of the NAL in 1937 until 1948, two years before the NAL disbanded. The powerful Monarchs captured ten NNL or NAL pennants from 1920 through 1948, winning in 1923, 1925, 1929, 1937, 1939–1942, and 1946. Wilkinson initiated the first interleague Negro World Series with the ECL in 1924. Kansas City competed in four Negro World Series, defeating the Philadelphia Hilldale Daisies in 1924 and sweeping the Washington, DC Homestead Grays in 1942. The Hilldale Daisies won a 1925 rematch, while the Newark, NJ Eagles triumphed in 1946.

Wilkinson helped pioneer night baseball, being among the first to use lights. As others installed permanent lights in scattered minor league parks, he first installed portable lighting on the beds of trucks in 1930. The initial $50,000 system proved so successful that it was paid for during the team's spring training tour of the Southwest. The Kansas City Monarchs eventually sent more players (27) into the major leagues than any other black team. These stars included Jackie Robinson,* Satchel Paige,* Hank Thompson,* Elston Howard,* and Ernie Banks.*

Wilkinson traveled with the team, while his wife operated an antique shop in Kansas City, MO. He loved baseball and treated his players well, with the Monarchs traveling by rail and bus and staying in the best available hotels. Bonuses were distributed liberally when available. Wilkinson, respected for his honesty, often conducted business with a handshake. Ailing and nearly blind, he sold his interest in the Monarchs to Tom Baird in 1948.

BIBLIOGRAPHY: Janet Bruce, *The Kansas City Monarchs* (Lawrence, KS, 1985); Jerry E. Clark, *Anson to Zuber* (Omaha, NE, 1992); John B. Holway, "The Gift of Light: J. L. Wilkinson," John B. Holway Collection, Springfield, VA; John B. Holway, *Blackball Stars* (Westport, CT, 1988); James A. Riley, *The Biographical Encyclopedia of the Negro Baseball Leagues* (New York, 1994).

                                                              John B. Holway and Merl F. Kleinknecht

WILLIAMS, Billy Leo "Sweet Swinging" (b. June 15, 1938, Whistler, AL), player and coach, is the son of Frank Williams and Jesse Mary Williams. He was educated in Whistler public schools, married Shirley Ann Williams on February 25, 1960, and has four daughters. Williams broke full-time into the Chicago Cubs (NL) lineup in 1961 with a .278 batting average and 25 HR, and won NL Rookie of the Year honors. His illustrious career included 1,117 consecutive games, at the time an NL record.

Signed directly out of high school by Chicago, Williams performed briefly with the Chicago Cubs in 1959 and 1960. He played for Ponca City, OK (SSL), in 1956 and 1957, Pueblo, CO (WL) and Burlington, IA (3IL) in 1958, San Antonio, TX (TL) and Fort Worth, TX (AA) in 1959, and Houston, TX (AA) in 1960. The modest and unassuming Williams, who batted left and threw right-handed, formed with Ernie Banks* and Ron Santo* the nucleus of Cubs power throughout the decade. Although playing on unsuccessful Chicago Cubs teams until the late 1960s, Williams batted .312 and

.315 in 1964–1965 and contributed 33 and 34 HR those seasons. The latter year, he topped the Cubs in every offensive category.

As the Cubs improved in the late 1960s, the 6-foot 1-inch, 175-pound Williams spearheaded the offense. He tied a major league record by hitting five HR in two consecutive games in September 1968 and collected 10 hits in 14 at-bats. When the Cubs astonished fans by almost winning an NL pennant in 1969, Williams batted .293 and broke the NL record for consecutive games. The Cubs faltered that year and resumed their familiar lackluster performance as also-rans in the 1970s. Williams, however, responded with three consecutive .300 seasons and in 1972 won the batting average (.333) and slugging percentage (.606) championships. In 1970, Williams batted .322 and led the NL with 205 hits and 137 runs. An outfielder throughout his career, Williams also played first base during his last three seasons with the Cubs. In October 1974, Williams was traded to the Oakland A's (AL) and spent two seasons there, mostly as a DH.

A .290 batting average, 2,711 hits, 426 HR, and 1,475 RBI distinguish Williams' 18-year major league career. He also recorded 434 doubles, 88 triples, 1,410 runs, 1,045 walks, 1,046 strikeouts, and a .492 slugging percentage. Williams ranks in the top ten among all-time Cubs hitters in every category except batting average. The six-time NL All-Star also earned numerous other honors, including being named *TSN* Major League Player of the Year in 1972. Following his retirement, he became a major league batting instructor for the Chicago Cubs and Oakland A's. Williams coached for the Chicago Cubs in 1986 and 1987 and since 1992 and has served as vice president of the MLPAA. He was elected to the National Baseball Hall of Fame in 1987.

BIBLIOGRAPHY: Art Ahrens and Eddie Gold, *Day by Day in Chicago Cubs History* (West Point, NY, 1982); Bruce Markusen, *Baseball's Last Dynasty* (New York, 1998); Warren Wilbert and William Hageman, *Chicago Cubs: Seasons at the Summit* (Champaign, IL, 1997); Jim Enright, *Chicago Cubs* (New York, 1975); Jim Langford, *The Game Is Never Over* (South Bend, IN, 1980); Billy Williams with Irv Haag, *Billy: The Classic Hitter* (Chicago, IL, 1974); Billy Williams file, National Baseball Library, Cooperstown, NY; "Billy Williams Joins His Friends in the Hall," *Jet* 71 (February 2, 1987), pp. 46–47; *Chicago Cubs Media Guide, 1998*; Eddie Gold and Art Ahrens, *The New Era Cubs, 1941–1985* (Chicago, IL, 1985); Jeff Guinn, *Sometimes a Fantasy* (Fort Worth, TX, 1994); Larry Moffi and Jonathan Kronstadt, *Crossing the Line* (Jefferson, NC, 1994); David L. Porter, ed., *African-American Sports Greats* (Westport, CT, 1995); *The Baseball Encyclopedia*, 10th ed. (New York, 1996).

Duane A. Smith

WILLIAMS, Claude Preston "Lefty" (b. March 9, 1893, Aurora, MO; d. November 4, 1959, Laguna Beach, CA), player, began his professional baseball career with Nashville, TN (SA) in 1912 and pitched for Salt Lake City, UT (PCL) before joining the Detroit Tigers (AL) in 1913. The left-handed Williams spent two seasons with the Detroit Tigers, appearing in only six games. After a one-year hiatus, he returned to the major leagues in 1916 with the Chicago White Sox (AL). He pitched for the Chicago White Sox for five years before being suspended from baseball for life because of his involvement in the Black Sox scandal.

During his major league career, Williams won 82 games, lost 48 decisions, and posted a 3.13 ERA. The 5-foot 9-inch 160 pounder served in the military during part of the 1918 season, starting only 14 contests that year. His best seasons included 1919, when he finished 23–11 and led the AL in starts with 40, and 1920, when he ended 22–14. In the 1917 World Series, he allowed one earned run on two hits in one inning. During the 1919 World Series against the Cincinnati Reds, Williams lost all three of his starts. Gamblers reportedly telephoned him the night before the final game of the series and warned him that his wife and child would be harmed unless he contrived to lose the game. He allowed four runs in the first inning of that game, retiring only one batter before exiting.

Little is known of Williams' life after his suspension from baseball. He and his wife, Lyria, lived in Laguna Beach, CA.

BIBLIOGRAPHY: Eliot Asinof, *Eight Men Out* (New York, 1963); Harvey Frommer, *Shoeless Joe and Ragtime Baseball* (Dallas, TX, 1992); Mike Shatzkin, ed., *The Ballplayers* (New York, 1990); *NYT*, November 7, 1959; John Thorn et al., eds., *Total Baseball*, 5th ed. (New York, 1997); *The Baseball Encyclopedia*, 10th ed. (New York, 1996); Warren Brown, *The Chicago White Sox* (New York, 1952); Richard Lindberg, *Sox* (New York, 1984); Richard Lindberg, *Who's on Third?* (South Bend, IN, 1983); Victor Luhrs, *The Great Baseball Mystery* (Cranbury, NJ, 1966); Dan Gutman, *Baseball Babylon* (New York, 1992); Daniel E. Ginsburg, *The Fix Is In* (Jefferson, NC, 1995); Claude Williams file, National Baseball Library, Cooperstown, NY.

John E. Findling

WILLIAMS, Fred C. "Cy" (b. December 21, 1887, Wadena, IN; d. April 23, 1974, Eagle River, WI), player, was the son of farmer Oscar Williams and Anna (Mead) Williams, both of Irish descent. Although a very small town, Wadena produced two well-known baseball figures born within a three-month period: Williams and pitcher–outfielder Otis "Doc" Crandall.* A 6-foot 2-inch, 180 pounder, Williams acquired the common nickname "Cy" and matriculated at the University of Notre Dame in 1908. He excelled as a track and field hurdler, vaulter, and sprinter, played for the football team, and won acclaim as a center fielder in baseball. Williams, who married Vaida Glenne Perkins on December 24, 1913 and had two sons and two daughters, impressed the Chicago Cubs' (NL) management in an exhibition game. Upon graduating from Notre Dame with a Bachelor's degree in architecture in 1912, the left-handed Williams immediately joined the Chicago Cubs as an outfielder. During 1915, he began playing regularly and slugged 13 HR. He shared the NL lead with 12 HR in 1916, but was traded to the Philadelphia Phillies (NL) in December 1917 for Dode Paskert. Since Paskert already had reached the twilight of his career, this trade ranked among the worst in Cubs history.

In 1920, Williams hit .325 for Philadelphia and belted 15 HR for the NL lead. He batted over .300 five of the next six seasons and slugged at least 12 HR for nine consecutive campaigns, quite a feat considering that Babe Ruth* had just popularized the long ball. Williams enjoyed his best year in 1923 with 41 round trippers and 114 RBI and tied Ruth for the major league HR title. In 1927, at age 38, he belted 30 HR for his fourth NL title and produced 98 RBI. The effective outfielder also led the NL with 29 assists in 1921.

Since Williams usually pulled the ball, NL managers defensed him extremely deep and definitely toward right field to produce the first Williams shift. Over 20 years later, this term became a household word when Cleveland Indians manager Lou Boudreau* developed a similar maneuver for Boston Red Sox slugger Ted Williams.* Williams served under 14 different managers, including the entire Joe Tinker,* John Evers,* and Frank Chance* double play combination, in his first 14 major league seasons. During his final three seasons, he excelled as one of the top major league pinch hitters.

Williams led the NL in career HR with 251 until Rogers Hornsby* surpassed him and held the NL left-handed HR record until Mel Ott* broke it. His other records included most career pinch hit HR (11); most NL HR through May 31 (18, 1923); most HR during May (15, 1923); most years leading and sharing the lead in HR (6); and most years leading or sharing the lead in HR on the road (5). In 2,002 career major league games, he batted .292 with 1,981 hits, 306 doubles, 1,024 runs scored, 1,005 RBI, and 115 stolen bases. After retiring to his several-hundred acre Wisconsin farm, he worked in the construction business. Some of the finest buildings in northeastern Wisconsin stand as a tribute to his architectural capabilities. Although a left-handed athlete, he was an accomplished right-handed artist.

BIBLIOGRAPHY: Fred Williams file, National Baseball Library, Cooperstown, NY; Jim Enright, *Chicago Cubs* (New York, 1975); Eddie Gold and Art Ahrens, *The Golden Era Cubs, 1876–1940* (Chicago, IL, 1985); Allen Lewis, *The Philadelphia Phillies: An Illustrated History* (Virginia Beach, VA, 1981); Allen Lewis and Larry Shenk, *This Date in Philadelphia Phillies History* (New York, 1979); Frederick G. Lieb and Stan Baumgartner, *The Philadelphia Phillies* (Philadelphia, PA, 1953); Rich Westcott and Frank Bilovsky, *The New Phillies Encyclopedia* (Philadelphia, PA, 1993); Warren Brown, *The Chicago Cubs* (New York, 1946); Brent P. Kelley, *The Case For: Those Overlooked by the Baseball Hall of Fame* (Jefferson, NC, 1992).

Cappy Gagnon

WILLIAMS, James Thomas "Jimmy," "Buttons," "Home Run" (b. December 20, 1876, St. Louis, MO; d. January 16, 1965, St. Petersburg, FL), player and scout, was a 5-foot 9-inch, 175-pound infielder associated with baseball for 40 years. He started in baseball primarily as a third baseman with Pueblo, CO (WA) in 1895–1896, Leadville, CO (WA) and Albuquerque, NM (WA) in 1896, and Kansas City, MO (WA) in 1897. Kansas City sold him to the Pittsburgh Pirates (NL) in 1899 as a third baseman under managers Bill Watkins and Patsy Donovan.* Williams excelled that year with a career-high .355 batting average, and led the NL in triples (27) and putouts (251). Nicknamed "Home Run," he belted a career-high nine HR as a rookie. Under a new manager, Fred Clarke,* however, his batting average dropped to just .264 in 1900. The 1900 season, Williams' last as a full-time third baseman, saw the Pirates rise to second place. Williams shifted permanently to second base with the Baltimore Orioles in the new AL in 1901, batting a healthy .317 and leading the new circuit with 21 triples under distinguished manager John McGraw.* Now established at his new position, he hit .313 the next year, again paced the junior circuit in three baggers with 21, and made six hits in the August 25 game. The Baltimore Orioles in 1903 shifted their franchise to New York as the Highlanders, managed by the "Old Fox," Clark Griffith.*

Williams was stationed at second base regularly. His batting suffered with the New York Highlanders, ranging from .267 in 1903 to .277 in 1906, while his HR production there peaked at six in 1905. The New York Highlanders traded Williams in February 1908 to the St. Louis Browns (AL), managed by Jim McAleer. Williams, infielder Hobe Ferris, and outfielder Danny Hoffman were sent to the St. Louis Browns for pitcher Fred Glade and outfielder Charlie Hemphill. Williams spent his last two major league seasons with the St. Louis Browns, hitting .236 in 1908 and just .195 the following year. Defensively, he proved a steady, far-ranging second baseman most of his career. For his 11 major league seasons, he compiled a .275 batting average with 1,507 hits, 49 HR, and 796 RBI.

The St. Louis Browns sold Williams to the minor league Minneapolis Millers (AA), where he played from 1910 through 1916. Although never a star, Williams, nevertheless, epitomized the dedicated professional. After remaining out of baseball until 1930, he scouted for the Cincinnati Reds (NL) from 1930 through 1935. Williams married Nan M. Smith on December 5, 1900.

BIBLIOGRAPHY: James Williams file, National Baseball Library, Cooperstown, NY; James H. Bready, *Baseball in Baltimore* (Baltimore, MD, 1998); Frederick G. Lieb, *The Baltimore Orioles* (New York, 1955); *The Baseball Encyclopedia*, 10th ed. (New York, 1996); "James Thomas Williams," *TSN* file, St. Louis, MO; "James Thomas ('Home Run') Williams, 88," *TSN*, January 31, 1965; Mike Shatzkin, ed., *The Ballplayers* (New York, 1990); John Thorn et al., eds., *Total Baseball*, 5th ed. (New York, 1997); Frederick G. Lieb, *The Pittsburgh Pirates* (New York, 1948); Richard L. Burtt, *The Pittsburgh Pirates: An Illustrated History* (Virginia Beach, VA, 1977); Frank Graham, *The New York Yankees* (New York, 1943); Mark Gallagher, *The Yankee Encyclo-*

pedia, vol. 3 (New York, 1997); Bill Borst, ed., *Ables to Zoldak*, vol. 3 (St. Louis, MO, 1990); Bill Borst, *Still Last in the American League* (West Bloomfield, MI, 1992).

William J. Miller

WILLIAMS, Joseph "Joe," "Smoky Joe," "Cyclone" (b. April 6, 1886, Seguin, TX; d. March 12, 1946, New York, NY), player, was born to an Indian mother and black father and was a lanky, hawk-nosed, 6-foot 5-inch, 200-pound right-hander. His fastball, which exploded out of an easy overhand motion, earned him the nicknames "Smoky Joe" and "Cyclone." Williams, whose heritage forced him to pitch under baseball's color ban, pitched with the black San Antonio, TX Bronchos from 1907 through 1909 and entered big time black baseball in 1910 with the Chicago Leland Giants. He pitched for the New York Lincoln Giants (ECL) from 1911 through 1923, spent 1924 with Brooklyn's Royal Giants (ECL), and performed from 1925 through 1932 on Cum Posey's* Homestead Grays (ANL). He then retired to tend bar in Harlem until his death.

The 1913 New York Lincoln Giants and the 1930 and 1932 Homestead Grays claimed the eastern championship of black baseball, but the ECL did not operate during these years. The 1930 Grays won a championship series over the Lincoln Giants, six games to four. Although the aging Williams struggled throughout the series, he bested Bill Holland* in Game 5, 7–3, and allowed no runs over the final six innings. Best known for the fastball, he possessed a full repertoire of pitches and displayed pinpoint control. His low chuckle was the closest the even-tempered Williams ever came to questioning an umpire's call.

Limited published records attest to Williams' skills. He compiled a 12–2 mark against major black competition and a 41–3 record against all competition, including semipro teams, in 1914. With Rube Foster's* Chicago American Giants on a western tour in the spring of 1912, he compiled a 9–1 mark and victories over every PCL team except Portland, OR. In the CUWL for three seasons, he produced a 22–15 career log. His 10–7 mark in 1911–1912 paced the CUWL in wins. He also spent winters in Florida waiting tables and pitching.

Williams made his biggest impression by compiling a 20–7 mark against white major league competition in scattered exhibitions throughout his career. Two losses came at age 45, while two others were by 1–0 margins. He hurled 10 shutouts against the white stars, including two against the 1912 NL champion New York Giants and another against the 1915 NL titlist Philadelphia Phillies. His other legendary games included two contests for which only eyewitness accounts are available: a no-hit, 20-strikeout contest against the 1917 New York Giants lost on a tenth-inning error, and a 1–0 conquest over Walter Johnson.* Other victims included New York Highlanders (now Yankees), Buffalo, NY Bisons (FL), and various All-Star aggregations. National Baseball Hall of Famers Grover Cleveland Alexander,* Chief Bender,* Waite Hoyt,* and Rube Marquard* were outhurled by Williams. Usually at least ten batters were fanned by Williams in these games.

His masterpieces against major black competition included a 1909 shutout of the Chicago Leland Giants and a 1919 no-hit victory over Cannonball Redding.* In 1930, he struck out 27 Kansas City Monarchs and surrendered just one hit under the lights in a 12-inning victory. The following year he hurled a two-hitter against the NNL champion St. Louis Stars, featuring James "Cool Papa" Bell,* "Mule" Suttles,* and Willie Wells.* In semi-pro competition, he struck out 21 hitters in Philadelphia, PA in 1920 and 25 batters in a 1924 loss to the powerful Brooklyn Bushwicks in 12 innings and tossed another no-hitter in 1928 against Akron, OH Tire. Williams became a "Stage Door Johnny" during his New York years. He married a pretty Broadway showgirl, Beatrice, in 1922 in New York. He proved popular with fans and drew large crowds, with his age often exaggerated to augment the mystique surrounding his legend. In 1952, the Pittsburgh *Courier* polled a panel of black veterans and sportswriters on black baseball's greatest pitcher. Williams won the honor by edging Satchel Paige,* 20 votes to 19. He was enshrined in the National Baseball Hall of Fame in 1999.

BIBLIOGRAPHY: Joe Williams file, National Baseball Library, Cooperstown, NY; John M. Coates, "Smoky Joe Williams," *BHR* (1981), pp. 46–47; John B. Holway, *Smoky Joe and the Cannonball* (Alexandria, VA, 1983); John B. Holway, *Blackball Stars* (Westport, CT, 1988); Robert W. Peterson, *Only the Ball Was White* (Englewood Cliffs, NJ, 1970); David L. Porter, ed., *African-American Sports Greats* (Westport, CT, 1995); James A. Riley, *The Biographical Encyclopedia of the Negro Baseball Leagues* (New York, 1994).

Merl F. Kleinknecht and John B. Holway

WILLIAMS, Kenneth Roy "Ken" (b. June 28, 1890, Grants Pass, OR; d. January 22, 1959, Grants Pass, OR), player, began his professional career in 1913 as an outfielder–third baseman at Regina, Canada (WCaL) and played for Edmonton, Canada (WCaL) and Spokane, WA (NWL) in 1914. His contract was purchased by the Cincinnati Reds (NL) in 1915. After two part-time seasons with Cincinnati, he was returned to the minor leagues for 1916–1917 with Spokane (NWL) and Portland, OR (PCL). He returned to the major leagues as an outfielder in 1918 with the St. Louis Browns (AL). After spending most of that year in military service, he hit .300 for the Browns in 1919. He played regularly with St. Louis through the 1927 season and was sold in December 1927 to the Boston Red Sox (AL), where he spent his last two major league seasons. The New York Yankees (AL) signed Williams in January 1930 perhaps because of a salary battle with Babe Ruth,* but he spent that year and 1931 at Portland (PCL) to finish his organized baseball career.

Williams' best major league season came in 1922, when his 39 HR and

155 RBI topped the AL and the St. Louis Browns lost a close pennant race to New York. He finished second in the AL in HR in 1921, 1923, and 1925, and surpassed the 100 RBI mark in 1921 and 1925 with 117 and 105. One of the earliest sluggers in the lively ball era, Williams averaged 24 HR per season from 1921 to 1927. He hit below .300 only once from 1919 through 1929, peaking at .357 in 1923, and averaged .319 for his major league career. In 1,397 games, Williams made 1,552 hits, 285 doubles, 196 HR, 860 runs, 913 RBI, 154 stolen bases, and a .530 slugging percentage. In 1922, he hit three HR in Game 1 on April 22, two HR in one inning on August 7 and HR in six consecutive games from July 28 to August 2. Williams suffered a severe beaning in a game against the Cleveland Indians in 1925, the same year he led the AL with a .613 slugging percentage. A left-handed–hitting, right-handed–throwing outfielder, the 6-foot, 170-pound Williams married Edith Wilkerson in June 1919. He suffered from a heart condition and died at his home.

BIBLIOGRAPHY: Ken Williams file, National Baseball Library, Cooperstown, NY; Craig Carter, ed., *TSN Daguerreotypes*, 8th ed. (St. Louis, MO, 1990); *The Baseball Encyclopedia*, 10th ed. (New York, 1996); *TSN*, January 30, 1959; Frederick G. Lieb, *The Baltimore Orioles* (New York, 1955); Bill Borst, ed., *Ables to Zoldak*, vol. 3 (St. Louis, MO, 1990); Bill Borst, *Still Last in the American League* (West Bloomfield, MI, 1992); Roger A. Godin, *The 1922 St. Louis Browns* (Jefferson, NC, 1991); Frederick G. Lieb, *The Boston Red Sox* (New York, 1947); Robert Redmount, *The Red Sox Encyclopedia* (Champaign, IL, 1998).

Phillip P. Erwin

WILLIAMS, Matthew Derrick "Matt" (b. November 28, 1965, Bishop, CA), player, is the son of Arthur Williams and Sarah (Griffith) Williams and grew up in Big Pine, CA and Carson City, NV. His grandfather, Bartholomew Griffith, played major league baseball from 1922 to 1924. Williams graduated from Carson City, NV High School in 1983 and earned a baseball scholarship to the University of Nevada–Las Vegas, where he made All-America at shortstop his junior year and majored in broadcasting.

The San Francisco Giants (NL) selected the 6-foot 2-inch, 216-pound Williams, who bats and throws right-handed, in the first round as the third overall pick in the June 1986 draft. After dividing 1986 between Everett, WA (NWL) and Clinton, IA (ML), he split the next three campaigns between Phoenix, AZ (PCL) and the San Francisco Giants. He batted .300 with two HR and a record nine RBI in the 1989 NL Championship Series against the Chicago Cubs, but fared poorly in the World Series against the Oakland A's.

Williams starred with the San Francisco Giants at third base from 1990 to 1996. He batted .277 with 33 HR and led the NL with a career-high 122 RBI in 1990, made the NL All-Star team. After clouting 34 HR in 1991, Williams won NL Comeback Player of the Year honors with 38 HR and 110 RBI in 1993. In the strike-shortened 1994 season, he belted a career-best, NL-leading 43 HR with 96 RBI in just 115 games. Although Williams batted a career-high .336 and made the NL All-Star team in 1995, injuries sidelined him much of the season. In 1996, Williams batted .302 and again was selected to the NL All-Star team. The San Francisco Giants traded him to the Cleveland Indians (AL) in November 1996.

Williams helped the Cleveland Indians win the 1997 AL Central Division with a .263 batting average, 32 HR, and 105 RBI. Although struggling in the AL Championship Series against the Baltimore Orioles, he starred in the World Series against the Florida Marlins with a .385 batting average, one HR, and three RBI in a losing cause. In December 1997, the Cleveland Indians traded him to the expansion Arizona Diamondbacks (NL) so he could be nearer his children. He clouted 22 HR with 71 RBI in 1998. In 1999, William ranked second with 142 RBI, batted .303, and hit 35 HR, helping Arizona take the NL West. He hit .375 in the NL Division Series and made the NL All-Star Team.

Through the 1999 season, Williams batted .268 with 334 HR and 1,050 RBI. His honors included making *TSN* All-Star and Silver Slugger teams and earning Gold Gloves in 1990, 1993, and 1994, as he led NL third basemen in double plays in 1990, 1992, and 1993, total chances in 1990 and 1994, putouts in 1991, and assists in 1994. The Paradise Valley, AZ resident married his wife, Tracie, in July 1989, and had three children, Alysha, Jacob, and Rachel, before their 1997 divorce.

BIBLIOGRAPHY: Matt Williams file, National Baseball Library, Cooperstown, NY; *TSN Baseball Register*, 1998; Rick Weinberg, "A Lasting Impression: Giants Slugger Matt Williams' Battles to Be the Best," *Sport* 83 (September 1992), pp. 64–67; Ron Fimrite, "The Strong Silent Type," *SI* 81 (July 25, 1994), pp. 30–32, 37; Kelly Whiteside, "Big Matt Attack," *SI* 82 (June 5, 1995), pp. 32–35; Chuck Greenwood, "Blast Off," *SCD* 22 (December 15, 1995), p. 100.

David L. Porter

WILLIAMS, Phillip. *See* Phillip Williams Cockrell.

WILLIAMS, Richard Hirschfield "Dick" (b. May 7, 1929, St. Louis, MO), player, manager, and executive, ranked among the most successful, controversial major league managers since 1967, when he led the Boston Red Sox to an AL pennant and a near victory in the World Series against the St. Louis Cardinals. The Red Sox had finished ninth in the previous season.

The son of Harvey Williams and Kathryn Louise (Rohde) Williams, he grew up a rabid baseball fan. After his family moved to southern California in the early 1940s, he starred at Pasadena JC (high school division) in baseball, basketball, and football and made the 1947 All-California baseball team as an outfielder. Drafted by the Brooklyn Dodgers (NL) in 1947, Williams played in Santa Barbara, CA (CaL) and Fort Worth, TX (TL) before reaching the major leagues in 1951. Thereafter, he played outfield for the Brooklyn Dodgers and their Montreal, Canada (IL) and St. Paul, MN (AA) farms until 1956, when he was sold to the Baltimore Orioles (AL). After an injury to his throwing arm impaired his effectiveness, he spent the next eight seasons moving among the Baltimore Orioles, Cleveland Indians (AL), Kansas City Athletics (AL), Houston Astros (NL), and Boston Red Sox (AL). His .260 major league batting average included 1,023 games, 768 hits, 70 HR, and 331 RBI.

As manager of the Boston Red Sox' Toronto, Canada (IL) farm team, Williams quickly displayed his skills by taking the Toronto Maple Leafs to the IL playoff championships in 1965 and 1966. He was promoted to pilot the Boston Red Sox and won AL Manager of the Year laurels for his 1967 victory. After the fourth and third place finishes with Boston in 1968 and 1969, he was hired by Charles Finley* in 1971 to manage the Oakland A's (AL). In three seasons with the A's, he won the AL West title in 1971 and AL pennants and World Series championships in 1972 and 1973. Oakland defeated the Cincinnati Reds and New York Mets in the 1972 and 1973 World Series, respectively. Williams resigned after 1973 to protest Finley's policies and managed the California Angels (AL) for the 1974–1976 seasons, finishing sixth twice and fourth once in the AL West. He joined the Montreal Expos (NL) in 1977 and piloted them to two second place finishes in the NL East (1979 and 1980). He was replaced by Jim Fanning late in 1981, the Expos' NL East championship year. In 1982, he joined the San Diego Padres (NL) as manager and recorded two fourth places, one third place, and one NL pennant (1984). After coming back from a two-game deficit to top the Chicago Cubs in the NL Championship Series, San Diego lost to the Detroit Tigers, 4–1, in the World Series. Williams resigned as San Diego manager in February 1986 and joined the Seattle Mariners (AL) that May. He piloted the struggling Mariners to second division finishes in 1986 and 1987 and was fired in May 1988.

Williams, the only major league manager other than Bill McKechnie* to win pennants with three different teams, compiled 1,571 wins and 1,451 losses for a .520 winning percentage in 21 major league seasons. He led the AL All-Stars three times (1968, 1973–1974) and the NL All-Stars once (1985). Williams married Norma Musato in October 1954 and has two sons and one daughter. Williams, who lives in Henderson, NV, has served with the New York Yankees (AL) as an adviser and consultant since 1996.

BIBLIOGRAPHY: Dick Williams file, National Baseball Library, Cooperstown, NY; *CB* (1973), pp. 437–439; Peter Golenbock, *Fenway* (New York, 1992); Donald Honig, *The Man in the Dugout* (Lincoln, NE, 1995); Leonard Koppett, *The Man in the Dugout* (New York, 1993); Jack Lautier, *Fenway Voices* (Camden, ME, 1990); Dan Shaughnessy, *The Curse of the Bambino* (New York, 1990); Bruce Markusen, *Baseball's Last Dynasty* (New York, 1998); Ross Newhan, *The California Angels* (New York, 1982); Dan Turner, *The Expos Inside Out* (Toronto, Canada, 1983); Peter C. Bjarkman, *Encyclopedia of Major League Baseball Team Histories National League* (Westport, CT, 1991); Thomas Aylesworth and Benton Minks, *The Encyclopedia of Baseball Managers* (New York, 1990); Peter Golenbock, *Bums* (New York, 1984); Peter Liss, *The Boston Red Sox* (New York, 1982); Robert Redmount, *The Red Sox Encyclopedia* (Champaign,

IL, 1998); San Diego Padres Public Relations Department, San Diego, CA; Dick Williams, *No More Mr. Nice Guy* (San Diego, CA, 1990).

Leonard H. Frey

WILLIAMS, Theodore Samuel "Ted," "The Splendid Splinter," "The Thumper," "The Kid," "The Big Guy," "Teddy Ballgame" (b. August 30, 1918, San Diego, CA), player, manager, and coach, is the eldest of two sons born to Samuel Steward Williams and May (Venzer) Williams. His father, variously described as a photographer and a "wanderer," played no significant role in the household. Williams grew up under the influence of his mother, an imperious personality who spent more time promoting the Salvation Army than caring for the family. As he later recalled of his youth, "The thing a kid remembers is that he never saw his mother or father very much." Williams grew up on the playgrounds and graduated from Herbert Hoover High School in San Diego, where he excelled at baseball but not academics. In 1936 at age 17, he signed with the newly organized San Diego, CA Padres (PCL) and was nicknamed "The Kid." The Boston Red Sox (AL) bought his contract from the Padres after the 1937 season and sent him to Minneapolis, MN (AA), where he led the AA in 1938 in batting average (.366), HR (43), runs scored (130), and RBI (142).

Williams was promoted to the Boston Red Sox in 1939 and, in his first season, hit .327, led the AL in RBI (145) and was named Outstanding Rookie of the Year. In 1941, he hit .406 to become the first major league player since 1930 to surpass .400, the youngest ever to break the mark, and the last player to achieve that feat. He hit .388 in 1957 at age 39 to become the oldest player to win a batting title, an achievement repeated the next year with a .328 batting average. With uncanny eyesight, exceptionally quick wrists, and an intelligent understanding of both hitting and pitching, the 6-foot 3-inch, 205-pound Williams was the premier batter of his generation. When he retired in 1960 after 19 seasons with Boston, he achieved career rankings that still stand—second in walks (2,019) and slugging percentage (.634) and sixth in batting average (.344). Other career totals include 2,292 games, 2,654 hits, 525 doubles, 521 HR, 1,798 runs scored, 1,839 RBI, and a mere 709 strikeouts. He led the AL 12 times in on base percentage, eight times in slugging percentage and walks, six times in batting average and runs scored, four times in HR and RBI, and twice in doubles.

Selected the AL MVP in 1946 and 1949, Williams, who hit left-handed but threw right-handed, was named to every AL All-Star team from 1940 to 1960 except for his years in military service. His most notable All-Star achievements came in 1941, when he hit a game-winning HR off Claude Passeau* in the ninth inning, and in 1946, when he turned in the greatest offensive performance in All-Star history by scoring four runs and driving in five more on four hits in four at-bats. Two of his hits were HR, one being the first ever hit off Rip Sewell's* famous "ephus" or "blooper" pitch. Williams was voted into the National Baseball Hall of Fame in 1966.

His relative greatness as a hitter is uncertain because he lost nearly five prime seasons as a pilot in the U.S. Marine Corps during World War II (1943–1945) and the Korean War (1952–1953). Nonetheless, his record clearly shows that he ranks second only to Babe Ruth* for a combination of power and batting average. His batting average probably would have been much higher had he hit to left field instead of stubbornly hitting into the strength of variations of the Williams shift. This defensive alignment, devised in 1946 by Cleveland Indians player–manager Lou Boudreau,* placed three infielders between first and second base.

Williams had a tempestuous relationship with Boston sportswriters and fans because of his candor, tactlessness, temper, and perfectionism. His stormy relations with the press probably cost him deserved recognition inasmuch as he was denied the AL MVP designation the year he hit .406 and the two seasons he won the Triple Crown (1942 and 1947). Yet umpires universally regarded him as a gentleman on the field. His fundraising efforts on behalf of the Jimmy Fund for Children's Cancer Hospital in Boston, MA endeared him to millions off the field.

Upon retiring in 1960, appropriately after hitting a HR in Fenway Park in his last time at bat, he served as chairman of the Ted Williams Sports Advisory Staff endorsing outdoor and recreational equipment for Sears & Roebuck and pursued his hobbies of hunting and fishing. He briefly emerged from his baseball "exile" to manage the Washington Senators (AL) from 1969 to 1971 and Texas Rangers (AL) in 1972. His best and only winning season came in 1969, when the Senators compiled a 86–76 record to finish fourth in the AL. Unable to relate well to modern players who lacked his talent and determination, he concluded his managerial career with 273 wins and 364 losses for a .429 winning percentage. Williams has served as batting instructor during spring training for the Red Sox and has achieved international acclaim as an expert fisherman. Williams, who serves on the Veterans Committee of the National Baseball Hall of Fame, suffered strokes in 1993 and 1995. His Ted Williams Museum in Florida was dedicated in February 1995. He made Major League Baseball's All-Century Team and ranked 16th among ESPN's top century athletes

Williams married and divorced Doris Soule, Lee Howard, and Dolores Wettach. He has two children, a daughter, Bobby Jo, and a son, John Henry.

BIBLIOGRAPHY: Robert Redmount, *The Red Sox Encyclopedia* (Champaign, IL, 1998); Ted Williams file, National Baseball Library, Cooperstown, NY; Dan Shaughnessy, *The Curse of the Bambino* (New York, 1990); Howard Liss, *The Boston Red Sox* (New York, 1982); Frederick G. Lieb, *The Boston Red Sox* (New York, 1947); John Benson et al., *Baseball's Top 100* (Wilton, CT, 1997); David Halberstam, *Summer of '49* (New York, 1989); Donald Honig, *The Power Hitters* (St. Louis, MO, 1989); P. Blandford, "Last Time Up," *AH* 41 (April 1990), pp. 30–31; Lawrence Baldassaro, ed., *The Ted*

Williams Reader (New York, 1991); *NYT Biographical Service* 25 (May 1994), pp. 780–781; *CB* (1947), pp. 685–687; Richard Ben Cramer, *Ted Williams: The Seasons of the Kid* (New York, 1990); Kit Crissey, "The Splendid Splinter's Splendid Finish," *TNP* 11 (1992), pp. 52–54; Ross Forman, "A Chat With the Best Hitter Who Ever Lived," *SCD* 22 (June 30, 1995), pp. 80–82; Peter Golenbock, *Fenway* (New York, 1992); John Holway, *The Last .400 Hitter* (Dubuque, IA, 1992); Jack Lautier, *Fenway Voices* (Camden, ME, 1990); James S. Kunen, "Last of the .400 Hitters," *NYT Magazine*, May 12, 1974, pp. 22–25; Ed Linn, *Hitter: The Life and Turmoils of Ted Williams* (San Diego, CA, 1993); Ed Linn, *Ted Williams* (Chicago, IL, 1961); *NYT*, January 21, July 26, 1966, February 14, 22, 1969, October 1, 2, 1972, August 10, 1982; Jim Prime and Bill Nowlin, *Ted Williams: A Tribute* (Indianapolis, IN, 1998); John P. McCarthy, *Baseball's All-Time Dream Team* (Cincinnati, OH, 1994); *The Baseball Encyclopedia*, 10th ed. (New York, 1996); *TSN Baseball Register, 1961*; Rich Westcott, *Diamond Greats* (Westport, CT, 1988); Richard Ben Cramer, "What Do You Think of Ted Williams, Now?" *Esquire* 105 (June 1986), pp. 74–76; John Updike, "Ted Williams," *Sport* 77 (December 1986), pp. 56–57; Glenn Stout and Dick Johnson, *Ted Williams: A Portrait in Words and Pictures* (New York, 1991); S. L. Price, "Rounding Third," *SI* 85 (November 25, 1996), pp. 92–96; John Underwood, "Ted Williams at Midstream," *SI 55* (June 29, 1981), pp. 66–82; John Updike, "Hub Fans Bid Kid Adieu," *NY* 36 (October 22, 1960), pp. 109ff; Ted Williams and Jim Prime, *Ted Williams' Hit List* (Indianapolis, IN, 1996); Michael Seidel, *Ted Williams: A Baseball Life* (Chicago, IL, 1991); Ted Williams and John Underwood, *My Turn at Bat* (New York, 1988); Ted Williams and John Underwood, *The Science of Hitting* (New York, 1971); Dan Valenti, *Clout! The Top Home Runs in Baseball History* (Lexington, MA, 1989).

Larry R. Gerlach

WILLIAMSON, Edward Nagle "Ned" (b. October 24, 1857, Philadelphia, PA; d. March 3, 1894, Hot Springs, AR), player, is rated as the finest third baseman of the 1880s. The son of a middle-class awning manufacturer, the lifetime Episcopalian enjoyed a more respectable reputation than most players, even though liking a drink and cards. A sportswriter described the 5-foot 11-inch 170 pounder as a "perfect physical machine." In 1875, he started the season with the amateur Shibe Club in Philadelphia, joined a semiprofessional club in Burlington, NJ, and caught for Braddock, PA. The following summer, he caught and played third base for the independent professional Neshannock Club of New Castle, PA and concluded the season with the Aetnas of Detroit. He hit poorly with the Allegheny Club of Pittsburgh (IL) in 1877, but fielded well enough for the Indianapolis Hoosiers (NL) to sign him for 1878.

The Chicago White Stockings (NL) established baseball's first real dynasty, capturing five NL titles in the 1880s. Williamson joined Chicago in 1879 and remained an integral part of the White Stockings and the Chicago Colts until his retirement in 1891. He teamed with Adrian "Cap" Anson,* Fred Pfeffer,* and Tommy Burns to form the famous "Stonewall Infield," the finest of the 19th century. Williamson played third base through 1885, being rated the best of his era at that position. He possessed a powerful, accurate arm, perhaps the strongest in baseball. In 1886, he switched positions with shortstop Burns. The Chicago White Stockings repeated as NL champion in 1886, but did not win again with Williamson at shortstop.

Williamson's most lasting fame came as a hitter. A right-handed batter with power to the opposite field, he was perfectly suited for Lakefront Park in Chicago. In 1883, the right field fence there was moved in to only 200 feet from home plate. Due to the short dimension, balls hit over this fence were declared ground-ruled doubles. The same year, Williamson belted an NL record 49 doubles. In 1884, the ground rules were changed to allow balls hit over the short fence to count as HR. Williamson continued to drive balls over the fence, hitting 25 before the season ended. Away from Lakefront Park, he hit only two HR. Williamson's 27 HR stood as a major league record until Babe Ruth* clouted 29 in 1919.

An injury Williamson received on A. G. Spalding's* "Around the World Tour" in the spring of 1889 shortened his baseball career. He injured his leg badly playing in Paris, France and blood poisoning complicated his recovery. In limited playing time in 1889, Williamson hit only .237. The following year, his batting average dropped to a feeble .195. Despite Williamson's disappointing ending, Chicago White Stockings manager Anson remembered Williamson as "the greatest all-around ball player the country ever saw."

Williamson opened a saloon in Chicago. He and his wife, Nettie Jean, appeared comfortable and respectable. When his health declined, however, doctors diagnosed his illness as dropsy. He traveled to Hot Springs, AR in January 1894, hoping that the mineral baths would improve his condition. He died there at age 36.

BIBLIOGRAPHY: Ned Williamson file, National Baseball Library, Cooperstown, NY; Warren Brown, *The Chicago Cubs* (New York, 1946); Jim Enright, *Chicago Cubs* (New York, 1975); Albert Spalding, *America's National Game* (New York, 1911); Eddie Gold and Art Ahrens, *The Golden Era Cubs, 1876–1940* (Chicago, IL, 1985); Warren Wilbert and William Hageman, *Chicago Cubs: Seasons at the Summit* (Champaign, IL, 1997); Peter Levine, *A. G. Spalding and the Rise of Baseball* (New York, 1985); Art Ahrens and Eddie Gold, eds., *Day-by-Day in Chicago Cubs History* (New York, 1982); Adrian C. Anson, *A Ball Player's Career* (Chicago, IL, 1900); Robert L. Tiemann and Mark Rucker, eds., *Nineteenth Century Stars* (Kansas City, MO, 1989); Jerry Lansche, *Glory Fades Away* (Dallas, TX, 1991); John J. O'Malley, "The Great Pennant Race of 1885," *BRJ* 6 (1977), pp. 81–87.

William E. Akin

WILLIS, Victor Gazaway "Vic" (b. April 12, 1876, Cecil County, MD; d. August 3, 1947, Elkton, MD), player, completed high school in Wilmington, DE, married Mary J. Minnis on February 8, 1900, and had two children, Victor, Jr., and Gertrude. In 1895, Willis entered professional baseball with

Harrisburg, PA (PSL). After winning 10 games in 1896 and 21 contests in 1897 with Syracuse, NY (EL), he trained with the Boston Beaneaters (NL) in the spring of 1898. From 1898 to 1905, Willis proved the mainstay of the Boston pitching staff with his excellent curveball. He won 52 games his first two seasons on strong Boston teams featuring Hugh Duffy,* Billy Hamilton,* and Kid Nichols.* On August 7, 1899, he hurled a 7–1 no-hitter against the Washington Senators. In 1899 and 1901, he paced the NL in shutouts with 5 and 6, respectively. Besides recording 27 wins, 45 complete games, and 410 innings in 1902, Willis led the NL in 1902 in losses (20), appearances (51), games started (46), games completed, innings pitched, hits surrendered (372), and strikeouts (225). In 1903, the contracts of Willis and 15 other players were disputed between the NL and AL. Since Willis' contract was awarded to the NL, he remained with Boston, compiling a 12–18 record in 1903. He led the NL with 25 and 29 losses the next two seasons with the now dismal Beaneaters. Willis paced the NL with 39 complete games in 1904 and 340 hits surrendered in 1905.

In December 1905, Willis was traded to the Pittsburgh Pirates (NL) for infielder Dave Brain and two minor league players. The 6-foot 2-inch, 185-pound right-hander rebounded with four outstanding years for the Pirates, winning 89 games, averaging over 300 innings per year, and compiling a sparkling 1.73 ERA in 1906. Willis hurled in the 1909 World Series, as the Pirates defeated the Detroit Tigers in seven games. He pitched 6.1 innings in relief in the second game and started the sixth game, but lasted just five innings and suffered the loss. Willis finished his career with the 1910 St. Louis Cardinals (NL), winning nine of 21 decisions. His major league career totals included 249 victories, 205 defeats, 3,996 innings pitched, 388 complete games in 471 starts, 1,651 strikeouts, 50 shutouts, and a 2.63 ERA. After retiring from baseball, Willis operated a hotel in Newark, DE. In 1995, the Veterans Committee elected Willis to the National Baseball Hall of Fame.

BIBLIOGRAPHY: Stephen Cunerd, "Vic Willis," *BRJ* 18 (1989), pp. 55–57; Dennis De Valeria and Jeanne Burke De Valeria, *Honus Wagner: A Biography* (New York, 1996); William Hageman, *Honus: The Life and Times of a Baseball Hero* (Champaign, IL, 1996); Arthur D. Hittner, *Honus Wagner: The Life of Baseball's "Flying Dutchman"* (Jefferson, NC, 1996); Bob Broeg and Jerry Vickery, *St. Louis Cardinals Encyclopedia* (Grand Rapids, MI, 1998); Gene Karst and Martin J. Jones, Jr., *Who's Who in Professional Baseball* (New Rochelle, NY, 1973); Craig Carter, ed., *TSN Daguerreotypes*, 8th ed. (St. Louis, MO, 1990); Brent P. Kelley, *The Case For: Those Overlooked by the Baseball Hall of Fame* (Jefferson, NC, 1992); *TSN Official World Series Records, 1903–1978*; Victor Willis file, National Baseball Library, Cooperstown, NY; John Thorn et al., eds., *Total Braves* (New York, 1996); Harold Kaese, *The Boston Braves* (New York, 1948); Gary Caruso, *The Braves Encyclopedia* (Philadelphia, PA, 1995); Mark Onigman, *This Date in Braves History* (New York, 1982); Frederick G. Lieb, *The Pittsburgh Pirates* (New York, 1948); Richard L. Burtt, *The Pittsburgh Pirates: A Pic-*

torial History (Virginia Beach, VA, 1977); Bob Smizik, *The Pittsburgh Pirates: An Il-lustrated History* (New York, 1990).

Frank J. Olmsted

WILLS, Maurice Morning "Maury," "The Mouse" (b. October 2, 1932, Washington, DC), player, coach, manager, and sportscaster, played in the minor leagues for nine years with stops at Hornell, NY (PoL) in 1951–1952, Pueblo, CO (WL) in 1953–1954 and 1956, Miami, FL (FIL) in 1953, Fort Worth, TX (TL) in 1955, Seattle, WA (PCL) in 1957, and Spokane, WA (PCL) in 1958–1959. Although primarily a shortstop and third baseman, Willis actually played all nine positions. After an unsuccessful spring training tryout with the Detroit Tigers (AL) in 1951, the fleet-footed Wills played with the Los Angeles Dodgers (NL) from 1959 to 1966. In December 1966, he was traded to the Pittsburgh Pirates (NL) for Gene Michael and Bob Bailey.* Wills performed for two full seasons in 1967 and 1968 for the Pirates before the Montreal Expos (NL) selected him in the expansion draft. In June 1969, the Expos traded Wills and Manny Mota* to the Los Angeles Dodgers for Ron Fairly* and Paul Popovich. Wills played with Los Angeles through the 1972 season and was released at age 40.

Wills stole 104 bases in 1962, breaking the major league record (96) established by Ty Cobb* in 1915. Wills' record subsequently was broken by Lou Brock* (118 in 1974) and Rickey Henderson* (130 in 1982). Wills, Brock, Henderson, and Vince Coleman* remain the only players in major league history to steal over 100 bases in one season. Wills revolutionized baseball by reintroducing the stolen base as a major offensive weapon and refining the "science" of base stealing. Before Wills led the NL a record six consecutive seasons (1960–1965) in stolen bases, Willie Mays* had paced the NL in 1959 with only 27 steals. As Dodgers captain and leadoff hitter in the mid-1960s, Wills sparked a team that relied heavily upon speed and pitching. When he reached base during his prime, sellout crowds at Dodger Stadium often spontaneously chanted "Go, Maury, Go." Wills also established a major league record for leading the NL seven years (1961–1963, 1965–1966, 1968–1969) in being caught stealing. The 5-foot 11-inch, 170-pound Wills, nicknamed "The Mouse," lacked power and hit only 20 career HR. He led the NL in singles a record four years (1961, 1962, 1965, 1969), in at-bats twice (1961–1962), and in triples (10) in 1962.

In 1962 Wills was named NL MVP and Major League Co-Player of the Year with teammate Don Drysdale.* He was selected as shortstop on *TSN* NL All-Star team in 1961, 1962, and 1965 and on *TSN* NL All-Star fielding team in 1961 and 1962. Wills also won the Gold Glove Award in 1961 and 1962. When the Dodgers and San Francisco Giants ended the 162-game 1962 season in a tie and played a three-game playoff, he established a major league record by appearing in all 165 games. As of the end of the 1986 season, the switch-hitting, right-handed–throwing Wills ranked among the top ten on the all-time Dodgers lists for career games (1,593), at-bats (6,156), runs scored (876), and hits (1,732). Wills, the all-time Dodgers leader in stolen bases with 490, batted .281 lifetime with 2,134 hits, 177 doubles, 71 triples, 1,067 runs scored, 458 RBI, and 586 stolen bases in 1,942 games.

Wills played in four World Series with the Los Angeles Dodgers (1959, 1963, 1965, 1966) and enjoyed his best performance in the 1965 World Series, including four hits in Game 6. Wills also compiled a .357 batting average in six All-Star games and was named MVP of the 1961 games. Wills later worked as a commentator for NBC-TV and cable television, managed winter league teams in Mexico, and served as an instructor for the Dodgers (1977). In 1976, he authored *How to Steal a Pennant*. Willis replaced Darrell Johnson as manager of the Seattle Mariners (AL) in August 1980, making him the third black major league manager following Frank Robinson* and Larry Doby.* The Mariners compiled a 20–38 record under Wills to finish in last place, 38 games behind the Kansas City Royals. As Mariners' manager, Wills was fined $500 and suspended for two games in April 1981 for ordering the batters' boxes lengthened illegally. Wills was fired on May 6, 1981 after the Mariners started the season with a 6–18 record.

In 1958, Spokane (PCL) manager Bobby Bragan encouraged Wills to become a switch-hitter. Dodgers manager Walter Alston* later considered him "an absolute marvel." Wills, the son of a minister, grew up in the slums of Washington, DC with his 12 siblings. His main hobbies are playing the banjo and training bird dogs. His son, Elliot "Bump," played second base for the Texas Rangers (AL, 1977–1981), Chicago Cubs (NL, 1982), and Hankyu, Japan Braves. Wills works in public relations for the Los Angeles Dodgers Community Service Department.

BIBLIOGRAPHY: Maury Wills file, National Baseball Library, Cooperstown, NY; Walter Alston with Si Burick, *Alston and the Dodgers* (Garden City, NY, 1966); John Benson et al., *Baseball Top 100* (Wilton, CT, 1997); *TSN Official World Series Records, 1982*; John Devaney, "Maury Wills: A Revealing Look at a Man on the Go," *Sport* 41 (May 1966), pp. 72–77; "Ex-Dodger Wills Talks about Life after Baseball, Drugs," *Jet* 77 (March 12, 1990), p. 49; *TSN Baseball Register, 1981*; Tot Holmes, ed., *Dodgers Blue Book* (Los Angeles, CA, 1983, 1985); William Leggett, "Stealing Onto the Air," *SI* 41 (August 19, 1974), p. 45; "Mariners Oust Wills," *NYT*, May 7, 1981, p. B15; Larry Moffi and Jonathan Kronstadt, *Crossing the Line* (Jefferson, NC, 1994); Thomas Aylesworth and Benton Minks, *The Encyclopedia of Baseball Managers* (New York, 1990); William F. McNeil, *The Dodgers Encyclopedia* (Champaign, IL, 1997); Walter Alston with Jack Tobin, *A Year at a Time* (Waco, TX, 1976); Stanley Cohen, *Dodgers! The First 100 Years* (New York, 1990); Tommy Holmes, *The Dodgers* (New York, 1975); Donald Honig, *Dodgers* (New York, 1986); Richard Wittingham, *An Illustrated History of the Los Angeles Dodgers* (New York, 1982); *The Baseball Encyclopedia*, 10th ed. (New York, 1996); Maury Wills, "The Great Stealer Tells Some Secrets," *Life* 53 (September 28, 1962), pp. 50–52; David Smith, "Maury Wills and the Stolen Base," *BRJ* 9 (1980), pp. 120–127; Richard L. Burtt, *The Pittsburgh Pirates: A Pictorial History* (Virginia Beach, VA, 1977); Bob Smizik, *The Pittsburgh Pirates: An*

Illustrated History (New York, 1990); Dan Turner, *The Expos Inside Out* (Toronto, Canada, 1983); Maury Wills and Don Freeman, *How to Steal a Pennant* (New York, 1976); Maury Wills and Mike Celizic, *On the Run* (New York, 1991).

Jack P. Lipton

WILSON, Arthur Lee "Artie" (b. October 28, 1920, Springville, AL), player, excelled as a defensive shortstop for the Birmingham, AL Black Barons (NAL) during the 1940s. A master of the double play, he also won batting titles in 1947 and 1948 with .370 and .402 averages. The ideal left-handed leadoff batter demonstrated speed on the bases and hit the ball to the opposite field, compiling a high batting average. He notched batting averages of .346 in 1944 and .374 in 1945, finishing second to Sam Jethroe* each time. The 5-foot 10-inch, 160-pound speedster also ranked among the NAL leaders in stolen bases each season.

In his five NAL seasons from 1944 to 1948, Wilson appeared in four East-West All-Star Games, missed only the 1945 classic, and helped the Birmingham Black Barons win NAL pennants in 1943, 1944, and 1948. Unfortunately, the Black Barons lost the World Series to the NNL's Homestead, PA Grays in each instance.

After the color line was eradicated, Wilson made the transition to the major leagues with the New York Giants (NL). Initially, he became the center of a controversy between the New York Yankees (AL) and the Cleveland Indians (AL), with both teams claiming him. Commissioner Happy Chandler* resolved the disagreement by ruling in favor of the New York Yankees. Wilson entered organized baseball in 1949 and enjoyed two PCL seasons with the Oakland, CA Oaks, batting .348 and .312 and earning a place on the New York Giants' (NL) roster in 1951. Opponents used a shift on him like he was a right-handed pull-hitter, but he just could not pull the ball to overcome the shift. Wilson was used sparingly, hitting .182 in only 22 major league at-bats. The Giants promoted Willie Mays* later in the season, farming out Wilson to Minneapolis, MN (AA) and Oakland, CA for the remainder of the season.

Wilson starred in the PCL, compiling batting averages of .316, .332, .336, .307, .293, and .263 from 1952 through 1957. He led the PCL in hits in 1952 and in triples in 1953 and 1954. His best seasons came with Seattle, WA, but he also played with Portland, OR, Oakland, CA, and Sacramento, CA. After four years away from baseball, he returned to Portland, OR in 1962. The layoff proved too much to overcome, as he finished the season with Kennewick, WA (NWL). Wilson retired with a .312 minor league batting average and opened a car dealership in Portland, OR.

BIBLIOGRAPHY: Artie Wilson file, National Baseball Library, Cooperstown, NY; *The Baseball Encyclopedia*, 10th ed. (New York, 1996); Chicago (IL) *Defender*, 1944–1948; Larry Moffi and Jonathan Kronstadt, *Crossing the Line* (Jefferson, NC, 1994); Noel Hynd, *The Giants of the Polo Grounds* (New York, 1988); Robert W. Peterson, *Only the Ball Was White* (Englewood Cliffs, NJ, 1970); James A. Riley, *The All-Time All-Stars of Black Baseball* (Cocoa, FL, 1983); James A. Riley, *The Biographical Encyclopedia of the Negro Baseball Leagues* (New York, 1994); James A. Riley, interviews with former Negro League players, James A. Riley Collection, Canton, GA; Mike Shatzkin, ed., *The Ballplayers* (New York, 1990).

James A. Riley

WILSON, Ernest Judson "Jud" (b. February 28, 1899, Remington, VA; d. June 26, 1963, Washington, DC), player, performed in the Negro League and Caribbean Winter League. The powerful, 5-foot 8-inch, 195-pound Wilson, who had an unusual build, had a Herculean torso tapering to a small waist and was slightly bowlegged and pidgeon-toed. The sincere, fearless Wilson exhibited a moody, ill-tempered nature. These traits resulted in frequent fights, sometimes involving the police and leading to occasional arrests. An unyielding desire to win earned him a reputation for being a mean, nasty, talented competitor. Wilson variously held contempt for umpires, opposing players, and teammates. Wilson's strength produced vicious line drives that jumped off his bat. The left-handed Wilson crowded the plate and regularly was hit by pitches. His limited defensive skills at third base caused numerous knots and bruises. He often smothered or blocked balls rather than catching them and used his strong arm to throw out runners.

After serving in the U.S. Army in 1918, Wilson played sandlot baseball in a Washington, DC ghetto and with the Baltimore Black Sox (ECL, ANL) from 1922 through 1930. The Black Sox won the 1929 ANL title and featured stars Wilson at first base, manager Frank Warfield* at second, Dick Lundy* at shortstop, and Oliver Marcelle* at third. Wilson in 1931 moved to the Homestead, PA Grays (EWL) and split the next season between Homestead and Pittsburgh Crawfords (NNL). From 1933 through 1939, he performed with the Philadelphia Stars (NNL). The 1934 Stars won the second half of a split season and claimed the NNL crown after a disputed series with the first half titlist Chicago American Giants. Wilson joined the Washington (Homestead) Grays (NNL) in 1940 and played there until retiring in 1945. Washington captured the NNL championship each year, winning the 1943 and 1944 Black World Series and dropping the 1942 and 1945 classics.

Wilson's awesome hitting skills included a .345 career Negro League batting average. His sparkling Winter League career averages included .372 in Cuba and .412 in Puerto Rico. During his prime, Wilson led or ranked near the top of his leagues in most offensive categories. He competed in three East-West (Negro League) All-Star Games, batting .435 and driving home the only run in the 1934 classic. In exhibition games against white major leaguers, he posted a .442 batting mark. Subsequently, he worked for several years for a road crew building Washington, DC's Whitehurst Freeway. Wilson, whose wife, Betty, came from rural Virginia, eventually suffered epileptic seizures and was institutionalized.

BIBLIOGRAPHY: John B. Holway, "Boojum, Jud Wilson," John Holway Collection, Springfield, VA; John B. Holway, *Blackball Stars* (Westport, CT, 1988); James A. Riley, *The Biographical Encyclopedia of the Negro Baseball Leagues* (New York, 1994); Robert W. Peterson, *Only the Ball Was White* (Englewood Cliffs, NJ, 1970); James A. Riley, *The All-Time All-Stars of Black Baseball* (Cocoa, FL, 1983).

                              Merl F. Kleinknecht and John B. Holway

WILSON, James "Jimmie" (b. July 23, 1900, Philadelphia, PA; d. May 31, 1947, Bradenton, FL), player, manager, and coach, was one of 10 children of Robert Wilson, a textile worker, and Agnes (McCauley) Wilson, who immigrated from Scotland to northeast Philadelphia in 1898. Wilson, who left school at age 14 to work full-time in a hosiery mill, played semiprofessional soccer and began semiprofessional baseball in 1919. Most notably, he joined the strong Bethlehem Steel Company Soccer Club. A righthanded batter and catcher in baseball, Wilson was signed in September 1920 by manager Chief Bender* of New Haven, CT (EL) upon Connie Mack's* recommendation. After Wilson spent three seasons there, New Haven sent him in February 1923 to the Philadelphia Phillies (NL) for pitcher Stan Baumgartner and catcher Jack Withrow.

Wilson caught regularly for the Philadelphia Phillies until traded in May 1928 to the St. Louis Cardinals (NL). He remained with the St. Louis Cardinals through 1933, appearing in the 1928, 1930, and 1931 World Series. Manager Frank Frisch* developed inexplicable hostility towards the popular Wilson and returned him to the Philadelphia Phillies, where the latter piloted the hapless Phillies five seasons. The Philadelphia Phillies finished seventh three times and last twice. President Gerry Nugent sold stars Chuck Klein,* Dolf Camilli,* and Bucky Walters* to avert the franchise's financial collapse. The patient, perceptive Wilson had converted Walters from a journeyman infielder to an ace pitcher. The friendly, durable Wilson ceased catching regularly in 1937 and resigned as manager in 1938.

Wilson coached for the Cincinnati Reds (NL) in 1939 and 1940. When the Cincinnati Reds suffered a dearth of catchers, the 40-year-old coach returned behind the plate in September 1940. He helped the Reds win the seven-game World Series against the Detroit Tigers, batting .353 and fielding flawlessly. An AP poll named his performance the top sports comeback of 1940. Wilson managed the Chicago Cubs (NL) from 1941 until May 1944 to second division finishes. In nine managerial seasons, he compiled a 493–735 win–loss mark.

Wilson again coached for the Cincinnati Reds in 1944 and 1945 and operated a citrus produce business in Bradenton until suffering a fatal heart attack. He married Serena Edwards in April 1921 and had two children, Robert, killed in action during World War II, and Jane Isabel.

The 6-foot 1½-inch, husky, intelligent receiver participated in 1,525 games during 18 major league seasons and batted .284, well above the average for catchers. He knocked in 621 runs and played in the 1933 and 1935 All-Star Games. He possessed excellent mechanical catching skills and consistently demonstrated uncanny ability in handling pitchers.

BIBLIOGRAPHY: James Wilson file, National Baseball Library, Cooperstown, NY; Stan Baumgartner, "Wilson, Former Catcher and Manager, Stricken in Florida Home at Age of 46," *TSN*, June 11, 1947; John Benson et al., *Baseball's Top 100* (Wilton, CT, 1997); C. William Duncan, "Jimmie Wilson, Scotch and Thrifty . . . ," *TSN*, February 8, 1934; Eddie Gold and Art Ahrens, *The New Era Cubs, 1941–1985* (Chicago, IL, 1985); Harold (Speed) Johnson, comp., *Who's Who in Major League Base Ball* (Chicago, IL, 1933); Frederick G. Lieb and Stan Baumgartner, *The Philadelphia Phillies* (New York, 1953); Gordon Mackey, "Jimmie Wilson, Pilot Who Rolls His Own . . . ," *TSN*, April 4, 1935; John Thorn et al., eds., *Total Baseball*, 5th ed. (New York, 1997); Thomas Aylesworth and Benton Minks, *The Encyclopedia of Baseball Managers* (New York, 1990); Allen Lewis, *The Philadelphia Phillies: A Pictorial History* (Virginia Beach, VA, 1981); Rich Westcott and Frank Bilovsky, *The New Phillies Encyclopedia* (Philadelphia, PA, 1993); Ritter Collett, *The Cincinnati Reds* (Virginia Beach, VA, 1977); Lee Allen, *The Cincinnati Reds* (New York, 1948); Frederick G. Lieb, *The St. Louis Cardinals* (New York, 1945); Bob Broeg, *Redbirds: A Century of Cardinals' Baseball* (St. Louis, MO, 1981); Bob Broeg and Jerry Vickery, *St. Louis Cardinals Encyclopedia* (Grand Rapids, MI, 1998); Rob Rains, *The St. Louis Cardinals* (New York, 1992); Robert Gregory, *Diz* (New York, 1992); Frank Frisch as told to J. Roy Stockton, *Frank Frisch: The Fordham Flash* (Garden City, NY, 1962).

Frank V. Phelps

WILSON, Lewis Robert "Hack" (b. April 26, 1900, Ellwood City, PA; d. November 23, 1948, Baltimore, MD), player, grew up in Chester, PA, quit school at an early age, and worked for a print shop, railroad company and shipyard. His professional baseball career began in 1921 with Martinsburg, WV (BRL). In 1923, he played for Portsmouth, VA (VL) and the New York Giants (NL). In 1925, he was assigned to Toledo, OH (AA) and was chosen by the Chicago Cubs (NL) in that year's post-season draft. The Cubs paid $5,000 for draft rights to Wilson, inspiring the phrase, "A Million Dollar Slugger from the Five and Ten Cent Store." Wilson played outfield for the Chicago Cubs from 1926 through 1931 and became one of the NL's top sluggers. Besides hitting a then NL record 56 HR in 1930, he paced the NL in HR from 1926 to 1928. He drove in 190 runs in 1930 (a major league record that still stands), led the NL in RBI with 159 in 1929, and remains the only NL player to have over 150 RBI two consecutive seasons. In 1930, Wilson recorded a phenomenal .723 slugging percentage. Wilson, whose career batting average was a respectable .307, hit a career-high .356 in 1930 and led the NL five times in strikeouts and twice in walks.

During a 12-year major league career, he compiled 1,461 hits, 266 doubles, 67 triples, 244 HR, 884 runs scored, 1,062 RBI, 713 strikeouts, and a .545 slugging average. Although a good defensive player, Wilson became the goat of the 1929 World Series by losing a fly ball in the sun. This miscue enabled the Philadelphia Athletics to rally from an 8–0 deficit in the seventh inning of the fourth game and win, 10–8. Philadelphia won the World Series, despite Wilson's .471 batting average. After his spectacular 1930 season, Wilson signed a record $40,000 contract for the next season. Rogers Hornsby* became Cubs manager and clashed with Wilson frequently, causing the outfielder's production to plunge. From 1932 to August 1934, he played for the Brooklyn Dodgers (NL). Wilson was traded in August 1934 to the Philadelphia Phillies (NL) and released the following the season.

After playing with Albany, NY (IL) in 1935 and Portland, OR (PCL) in 1936, Wilson left baseball. He was divorced, lived in Martinsburg, WV, and operated a saloon in Chicago, IL. Wilson finally settled in Baltimore, MD, where he worked in a defense plant during World War II and later as a groundskeeper and swimming pool manager for the city parks system. In 1948, he quit that job and died of internal hemorrhaging complicated by influenza.

Wilson, resembling a veritable fire hydrant, stood only 5 feet 6 inches, weighed about 190 pounds, and wore a size 18 collar and size 6 shoes. A notorious disciplinary problem off the field, he shortened both his baseball career and his life by excessive drinking. Nicknamed "Hack," he resembled Russian strongman and wrestler George Hackenschmidt, popular in Wilson's youth. Some compared Wilson to Hack Miller, a Cubs outfielder of the mid-1920s. After a long campaign by his supporters, Wilson was elected to the National Baseball Hall of Fame in 1979.

BIBLIOGRAPHY: Robert Boone and Gerald Grunska, *Hack* (Highland Park, IL, 1978); Hack Wilson file, National Baseball Library, Cooperstown, NY; Eddie Gold and Art Ahrens, *The Golden Era Cubs, 1876–1940* (Chicago, IL, 1985); Warren Brown, *The Chicago Cubs* (New York, 1946); Jim Enright, *Chicago Cubs* (New York, 1975); Frank Graham, *The Brooklyn Dodgers* (New York, 1945); Richard Goldstein, *Superstars and Screwballs* (New York, 1991); Charles C. Alexander, *Rogers Hornsby* (New York, 1995); Don Nelson, "A Tale of Two Sluggers: Roger Maris and Hack Wilson," *TNP* 1 (Fall 1982), pp. 32–33; Ralph Hickok, *Who Was Who in American Sport* (New York, 1971); Gene Karst and Martin J. Jones, Jr., *Who's Who in Professional Baseball* (New Rochelle, NY, 1973); Mark Kram, "Why Ain't I in the Hall?" *SI* 46 (April 11, 1977), pp. 88ff; *The Baseball Encyclopedia*, 10th ed. (New York, 1996); *NYT*, November 24, 1948, March 8, 11, 1979; Lowell Reidenbaugh, *Baseball's Hall of Fame-Cooperstown* (New York, 1993); Warren Wilbert and William Hageman, *Chicago Cubs: Seasons at the Summit* (Champaign, IL, 1997).

John E. Findling

WILSON, Willie James (b. July 9, 1955, Montgomery, AL), player, graduated from Summit, NJ High School in 1974 with 250 college football offers. When the Kansas City Royals (AL) baseball club offered him a reported $50,000 bonus and selected him in the first round of the draft, he signed a contract and actually received $90,000. Wilson played minor league baseball for Sarasota, FL (GCL) in 1974, Waterloo, IA (ML) in 1975, Jacksonville, FL (SL) in 1976, and Omaha, NE (AA) in 1977. In three of four minor league seasons he led his respective leagues in stolen bases.

The speedy 6-foot 3-inch, 190 pounder, who threw and batted right-handed, joined the Kansas City Royals full-time in 1978 and began switch-hitting upon the request of manager Whitey Herzog.* As a rookie, Wilson probably ranked as the fastest player in the major leagues. He sprinted from home plate to first base in 3.9 seconds, routinely took extra bases, and occasionally scored from second base on singles, but saw limited action. The regular left fielder in 1979, Wilson batted .315 and led the AL with 83 stolen bases. In 1980, he exploded with an all-time major league leading 705 official plate appearances and paced the AL with 133 runs and 230 hits. Wilson's 15 triples tied the AL season record, while his 32 consecutive stolen bases equalled the all-time AL mark. Besides hitting .326, he placed among the top ten in at least seven offensive categories and won the Gold Glove for defensive excellence.

In 1982, Wilson's .332 batting average and 15 triples comprised AL season bests. For the first time since he became a Royals starter, his batting average in 1983 fell below .300. At the season's end, he was indicted on a misdemeanor cocaine charge and suspended from baseball. After returning to the Royals in May 1984, Wilson became active in antidrug programs for youth and quickly regained his pre-1983 form. In 1985, he batted .278, made 168 hits, led the AL with an AL record 21 triples, and stole 43 bases to help the Royals win the AL pennant. Two years later, Wilson paced the AL again in triples with 15 and led AL outfielders with a .997 fielding percentage. He won his fifth AL triples crown with 11 in 1988 and remained with the Royals through 1990. In December 1990, the Oakland A's (AL) signed him as a free agent. His major league career ended with the Chicago Cubs (NL) in 1993 and 1994.

In 19 major league seasons, Wilson batted .285 with 1,169 runs scored, and 2,207 hits. His speed produced 668 stolen bases and the highest AL stolen base percentage (around .830). During his career, Wilson also compiled 281 doubles, 147 triples, 41 HR, and 585 RBI.

Wilson appeared in two All-Star Games, the 1981 Western Division Series, four AL Championship Series, and the 1980 and 1985 World Series. He hit only .154 and struck out a record 12 times in the 1980 World Series against the Philadelphia Phillies. In the 1985 World Series triumph over the St. Louis Cardinals, Wilson batted .367 and made 11 hits, three RBI, and three stolen bases. He also batted over .300 in the AL Championship Series against the New York Yankees in 1980 and Toronto Blue Jays in 1985 and in the 1981 Western Division Series. He seldom hit into double plays, setting an AL record by grounding into only one in 1979. Wilson lives with his wife, Kathy, and two children in Leawood, KS.

BIBLIOGRAPHY: Willie Wilson file, National Baseball Library, Cooperstown, NY; Sid Bordman, *Expansion to Excellence* (Marcelline, MS, 1981); Alan Eskow, *A Royal Finish* (Chicago, IL, 1985); John Garrity, *The George Brett Story* (New York, 1981); Joe Flaherty, "Wilson Making Every Hit Count," *NYT Biographical Service* (August 1982), pp. 1112–1114; Douglas S. Looney, "Fleetest of the Royal Fleet," *SI* 48 (April 24, 1978), pp. 54–56; Jim Kaplan, "K.C. Takes Off on Willie's Wings," *SI* 51 (September 10, 1979), pp. 26–27; Jim Kaplan, "Will He Be Willie Again?" *SI* 54 (February 9, 1981), pp. 78–79; *The Baseball Encyclopedia*, 10th ed. (New York, 1996); *TSN Official Baseball Register*, 1995; "Two Rookies with a Royal Look," *NYT Biographical Service* (May 1978), p. 602.

Gaymon L. Bennett

WILTSE, Dorothy. *See* Dorothy Wiltse Collins.

WILTSE, George LeRoy "Hooks" (b. September 7, 1880, Hamilton, NY; d. January 21, 1959, Long Beach, NY), player, coach, and manager, attended elementary school only and married Della S. Schaffer on November 23, 1904. After pitching minor league baseball for Scranton, PA (PSL) and Troy, NY (NYSL) in 1902 and 1903, the 6-foot, 185-pound left-hander reached the major leagues in 1904 and remained through 1914 with manager John McGraw's* New York Giants (NL). He divided the 1915 campaign between Jersey City, NJ (IL) and the Brooklyn Feds (FL). The following three campaigns were split among Albany, NY (NYSL), Reading, PA (NYSL) and Buffalo, NY (IL). Wiltse pitched with Buffalo until 1923 and reappeared briefly with Reading, PA (IL) in 1926. During these twilight minor league years, he sometimes played at first base. Managerial assignments included Jersey City in 1915, Albany in 1916, Reading in 1917, Buffalo from 1918 to 1924, and Reading in 1926. The New York Yankees (AL) hired him as a coach in 1925.

During his early seasons with the New York Giants, Wiltse reached stardom. After compiling the fourth highest NL winning percentage (.714) in 1905, he in 1908 won a career-high 23 games. On July 4, 1908, Wiltse pitched a 10-inning no-hitter against the Philadelphia Phillies and missed a perfect game only because he hit a batter with two outs in the ninth inning. He won 20 games in 1909, but saw his pitching skills dwindle rapidly thereafter. His career major league statistics, including his FL season, came to 139 wins, 90 losses, a strong .607 winning percentage, and a 2.47 ERA.

Wiltse's other claim to fame came as an emergency first baseman in the 1913 World Series against the Philadelphia Athletics. The second game had developed into a tense, scoreless pitching duel between Christy Mathewson* and Ed Plank.* In the last half of the ninth inning, the Athletics placed runners on second and third base with none out. Wiltse, playing first base with a finger glove, threw out successive runners at home plate after fielding grounders. One stop proved spectacular. The New York Giants won the game in the tenth inning, 3–0. Subsequently, Wiltse sold real estate.

BIBLIOGRAPHY: *The Baseball Encyclopedia*, 10th ed. (New York, 1996); J. C. Taylor Spink, comp., *TSN Daguerreotypes of Great Stars of Baseball* (St. Louis, MO, 1961); George Wiltse file, National Baseball Library, Cooperstown, NY; Frank Graham, *The New York Giants* (New York, 1952); Noel Hynd, *The Giants of the Polo Grounds* (New York, 1988); Charles C. Alexander, *John McGraw* (New York, 1988); Ray Robinson, *Matty: An American Hero* (New York, 1993); Frank Graham, *McGraw of the Giants* (New York, 1944); Fred Stein and Nick Peters, *Giants Diary* (Berkeley, CA, 1987); G. F. Fleming, *The Unforgettable Season* (New York, 1981).

Lowell L. Blaisdell

WINFIELD, David Mark "Dave" (b. October 3, 1951, St. Paul, MN), baseball player and all-around athlete, is the son of dining car waiter Frank Winfield and Arline (Allison) Winfield. After his father left the family in 1954, he grew up with his mother, a St. Paul school employee, and his grandmother. At St. Paul Central High School, he did not play baseball until his junior year and yet made the All-City and All-State teams as a senior. Although drafted by the Baltimore Orioles (AL) in 1969, Winfield instead attended the University of Minnesota and made the baseball team his sophomore year as a right-handed pitcher. An arm injury forced Winfield off the mound as a junior, but he pitched again his senior year with a 13–1 record, batted .385, and slugged nine HR. He was named MVP of the 1973 NCAA College World Series.

Drafted by four teams in three sports, the 6-foot 6-inch, 220 pounder signed with the San Diego Padres (NL) for a bonus estimated at between $50,000 and $100,000. The Padres wanted him as an everyday player and immediately inserted him as a starting outfielder. The right-handed batting Winfield hit a respectable .277 in 1973 and belted 20 HR in 1974. He raised his batting average to .308 in 1978 and 1979 and led the NL with 118 RBI, 333 total bases, and 24 intentional walks the latter season. Always among defensive leaders, he led the NL in assists with 15 in 1976 and received the NL Gold Glove Award in 1979 and 1980.

Frustrated by playing on a losing team, Winfield signed as a free agent with the New York Yankees (AL) in December 1980. His 10-year contract, then the most lucrative in sports, was estimated worth up to $25 million. In his first six seasons in New York, Winfield averaged 89 runs on 158 hits compared to 74 runs scored and 141 hits at San Diego. His average HR output rose from 19 to 25, while his RBI increased from 78 to 101. In 1984 Winfield battled teammate Don Mattingly* for the AL batting title to the last day of the season, finishing second with .340. The next year, he finished third in the AL in RBI (114) and second in game-winning hits (19). He led the AL with 17 assists in 1982 and made only two errors in 1984 for a .994 fielding average to earn his third AL Gold Glove. Winfield often saved extra base hits and runs with his bullet-like throws from the outfield. In 1985, he earned another Gold Glove.

On July 17, 1986, Winfield tripled for his 2,000th major league hit in a 14–3 victory over the Texas Rangers. He batted .322 in 1988 and spent 1989 on the disabled list. In May 1990, the New York Yankees traded Winfield to the California Angels (AL). He earned *TSN* Comeback Player of the Year award that year. During 1991, he clouted three HR on April 13 against the Minnesota Twins and hit for the cycle on June 24 against the Kansas City Royals. In December 1991, Winfield joined the Toronto Blue Jays (AL) as a free agent. He batted .290 with 26 HR and 108 RBI in 1992 and clouted two HR to help the Toronto Blue Jays capture the AL Championship Series against the Oakland A's. Although batting only .227 in the 1992 World Series against the Atlanta Braves, Winfield knocked in the winning run to clinch the final game. He spent 1993 and 1994 with the Minnesota Twins (AL). On September 16, 1993, Winfield became the 19th major league player to get 3,000 hits with a ninth-inning single off Dennis Eckersley* of the Oakland A's. His major league career ended with the Cleveland Indians (AL) in 1995.

In 22 major league seasons, Winfield batted .285 with 1,669 runs scored, 3,110 hits, and 223 stolen bases. His 1,093 extra base hits included 540 doubles, 88 triples, and 465 HR. He ranked among the top ten in career at-bats, games, and total bases and among the top 20 in career hits, HR, and RBI. He appeared in every All-Star game from 1977 to 1988, batting .361, and also played in the 1981 AL Division Series, AL Championship Series, and World Series.

A bachelor, the Ft. Meyers, FL resident still operates the Winfield Foundation with his brother, Steve. The foundation has sponsored several charities for underprivileged youth, including free seats for baseball games, All-Star Game children's parties, and yearly scholarships. Besides decorating homes, he designs his own clothes and enjoys photography.

BIBLIOGRAPHY: Phil Berger, "The Yankees' $20 Million Gamble," *NYT Magazine* (March 29, 1981), pp. 26–40; Ira Berkow, "Winfield Looks Back on Satisfying Season," *NYT Biographical Service* (November 1981), pp. 1,609–1,611; Barbara Carlisle Bigelow, ed., *Contemporary Black Biography*, vol. 5 (Detroit, MI, 1994), pp. 285–288; *CB* (1984), pp. 42–45; Joseph Durso, "All-round Athlete," *NYT Biographical Service* (December 1980), pp. 1,832–1,833; Ron Fimrite, "Good Hit, Better Man," *SI* 51 (July 9, 1979), pp. 32–34; Ron Fimrite, "Richest Kid on the Block," *SI* 54 (January 5, 1981), pp. 22–26; William Oscar Johnson, "Al Gave It His All," *SI* 54 (January 5, 1981), pp. 26–35; Robert E. Kelly, *Baseball's Best* (Jefferson, NC, 1988); W. Ladson, "The Sport Q & A: Dave Winfield," *Sport* 82 (August 1991), pp. 84–86; Tim Kurkjian, "Mr. Longevity," *SI* 79 (September 27, 1993), p. 55; David L. Porter, ed., *African-American Sports Greats* (Westport, CT, 1995); Rick Reilly, "I Feel a Whole Lot Better Now," *SI* 76 (June 29, 1992), pp. 56–60; *The Baseball Encyclopedia*, 10th ed. (New York, 1996); *TSN Official Baseball Register, 1996*; D. Whitford, "What Do You Think of Dave Winfield?" *Sport* 77 (October 1986), pp. 92–94; Dave Winfield with Tom Parker, *Winfield: A Player's Life* (New York, 1988); Dave Winfield file, National Baseball Library, Cooperstown, NY; Peter C. Bjarkman, ed., *Encyclopedia of Major League Baseball Team Histories National League* (Westport, CT, 1991); Mark Gallagher, *The Yankee Encyclopedia*, vol. 3 (Champaign, IL, 1997); Dick Lally, *Pinstriped Summers* (New York, 1985); *WWA*, 43rd ed. (1984–1985).

Gaymon L. Bennett

WINKLES, Bobby Brooks (b. March 11, 1930, Tuckerman, AR), player, coach, manager, and sportscaster, signed a professional baseball contract with the Chicago White Sox (AL) organization in 1951 while attending Illinois Wesleyan University. After completing his bachelor's degree in philosophy there in 1952, he served a stint in the U.S. Army Infantry and married Ellie Hoeman on February 28, 1953. Winkles earned his master's degree in physical education from the University of Colorado in 1956 while playing shortstop with Colorado Springs, CO (WL). His best seasons as a player came at Colorado Springs, where he batted between .286 and .298 over four seasons.

After his seven-year minor league career ended, Winkles inherited a nondescript baseball program at Arizona State University in 1959. His Arizona State Sun Devils won 524 games and lost only 173 contests for a .752 winning percentage over the next 13 seasons and captured NCAA Championships in 1965, 1967, and 1969. Arizona State players included Reggie Jackson,* Rick Monday,* and Sal Bando,* three sluggers with the outstanding Oakland A's in the 1970s. During Winkles' tenure, only the University of Southern California Trojans fielded a more successful collegiate baseball program.

The California Angels (AL) hired Winkles in December 1971 as their first base coach. Some regarded the Angels' move of enlisting a coach with a demonstrated ability to teach young players as a brilliant innovation, while others warned that Winkles would have trouble switching from the emotional college game to the more hardened environment of the professional game. After spending one season on the coaching lines, Winkles was appointed the California Angels manager in October 1972. The California Angels finished with a 79–83 win–loss mark under Winkles, placing fourth in the AL Western Division. After California struggled to a 30–44 start in 1974, Dick Williams* replaced Winkles as manager. Winkles coached for the Oakland Athletics for the remainder of 1974 and in 1975 before crossing the Bay to coach the San Francisco Giants (NL) for the 1976 and 1977 campaigns. In June 1977, he replaced Jack McKeon as Oakland A's manager and guided the Athletics to a 37–71 win–loss finish. Although Oakland started well (24–15) in 1978, owner Charlie Finley* then rehired McKeon as the Athletics manager. In four seasons as a major league pilot, Winkles compiled a 170–213 win–loss record. Winkles coached for the Chicago White Sox (AL) from 1979 to 1981 and for the Montreal Expos (NL) from

1986 through 1988. He announced for the Montreal Expos from 1992 through 1994.

BIBLIOGRAPHY: Bobby Winkles file, National Baseball Library, Cooperstown, NY; *Arizona State University Baseball Media Guide*, 1966–1971; *The Baseball Encyclopedia*, 10th ed. (New York, 1996); Los Angeles (CA) *Times*, 1971–1974; *TSN Baseball Register, 1978*; Thomas Aylesworth and Benton Minks, *The Encyclopedia of Baseball Managers* (New York, 1990); Ross Newhan, *The California Angels* (New York, 1982); Bruce Markusen, *Baseball's Last Dynasty* (New York, 1998); Jack McKeon with Tom Friend, *Jack of All Trades* (Chicago, IL, 1988).

Cappy Gagnon

WINSCH, Jean Faut. *See* Jean Faut Winsch Eastman.

WINTER, Joanne Emily (b. November 24, 1924, Chicago, IL; d. September 22, 1996, Scottsdale, AZ), player, was the daughter of George Winter, of German ancestry, and Edith (Watson) Winter, of Scottish ancestry, and attended Proviso Township High School. She participated in swimming, volleyball, basketball, soccer, track and field, tennis, and handball as a youth near Chicago. She literally lived in Johnny Conlon's gymnasium and dropped out of school at age 15. Winter joined the Oak Park Coeds softball team at age 11. Winter carned $15 a week playing softball for the Parichy Roofing Company team, better known as the "Bloomer Girls," and then joined the Admiral Music Maids. After four years of semiprofessional competition, she tried out for the AAGPBL. Her family had moved to Phoenix, AZ, where she had signed with the Phoenix, AZ Ramblers. She joined the Racine, WI Belles (AAGPBL) in 1943. The AAGPBL was portrayed in the film *A League of Their Own*, with Winter joining several former players as consultants. The 5-foot 8-inch, 138-pound right-handed Winter excelled as a pitcher for eight campaigns from 1943 to 1950 with the Racine Belles. Winter split 22 decisions in 1943, helping the Belles win the AAGPBL pennant and championship. After struggling with a 22–45 mark the next two seasons, she learned from a Mexican hurler how to throw a sling-shot delivery. The rising pitch baffled hitters and transformed her into one of the league's best pitchers. Her superb 1946 season included 33 wins, only nine losses, 17 shutouts, and a record 63 consecutive scoreless innings and six consecutive shutouts. She made the All-Star team for the first time, helping the Belles capture another pennant and championship. Racine defeated the Rockford, IL Peaches 1–0 for the title, as Winter stranded 19 runners on base. Winter's 33 victories tied her with Connie Wisniewski* for most triumphs in a season. After compiling a 22–13 slate in 1947, Winter finished 25–12 to make the All-Star team a second time and help Racine garner another pennant. Winter pitched overhand in 1948, sharing the AAGPBL leadership with 25 victories and amassing an AAGPBL-leading 256 strikeouts and 329 innings in what she termed the "third American Baseball

League." Leo Murphy, former Pittsburgh Pirates (NL) catcher, helped Winter convert to a three-quarters delivery following the 1948 season after the AAGPBL banned the underhand delivery. Winter developed back problems and suffered losing records the next two seasons. She and several other primarily underhand pitchers joined the Admirals of the ChNL for a higher salary. The Admirals paid her $150 a week and gave her a $400 bonus for winning 25 games. Winter's composite AAGPBL record included 133 victories and 115 losses with a 2.06 ERA. She struck out 770 batters and surrendered 1,470 hits in 2,159 innings. Her AAGPBL record included most losses in a season (23), second most career losses, innings pitched, and games pitched (287), and third best career victories.

Winter competed four more years in professional leagues in Chicago and moved to Phoenix, AZ in 1955 with her father. She hurled for the Phoenix A-1 Queens, winning 36 of 42 games and leading them to the 1958 State Women's championship. Winter, an accomplished athlete, taught tennis and won the Arizona State Women's Golf championship four times. She joined the LPGA in 1962, competing in 25 tournaments. Her LPGA career ended in 1965 due to a back injury caused by an auto accident. Winter's ability to compete in two professional sports marked a rarity for women in the 1960s.

Winter, one of 14 original Master Professionals in the LPGA Teaching and Club Professional Division, found her niche as a master teacher of golf for 30 years. She tutored many students from beginners to tour professionals, including Jerilyn Britz, Robin Walton, Alice Miller, Heather Farr, and Dina and Danielle Ammaccapane. Winter, founder of the Arizona Silver Belle Championship Golf tournament, coached women's golf at Scottsdale CC and Arizona State University.

Winter received many honors and awards, including LPGA Teacher of the Year in 1969 and the Ellen Griffin Rolex award in 1995. This award, named after one of the best known female teachers in American golf history, recognizes individuals who have demonstrated by their teaching skill the same spirit, love, and dedication possessed by Griffin. The unselfish Winter excelled in two sports and shared her expertise with thousands of students young and old.

BIBLIOGRAPHY: Gai Ingham Berlage, *Women in Baseball* (Westport, CT, 1994); Barbara Gregorich, *Women at Play* (San Diego, CA, 1993); Sharon Roepke, *Diamond Gals* (Flint, MI, 1988); Susan Johnson, *When Women Played Hardball* (Seattle, WA, 1994); Payson (AZ) *Roundup*, December 6, 1995; Arizona *Republic*, September 26, 1996; W. C. Madden, *The Women of the All-American Girls Professional Baseball League* (Jefferson, NC, 1997); James E. Odenkirk, personal interview with Joanne Winter, Scottsdale, AZ, April 15, 1996; *NYT*, September 26, 1996, p. D-23.

James E. Odenkirk

WINTERS, Jesse "Nip" (b. 1899, Washington, DC; d. December 1971, Hokessin, DE), player, pitched for 11 teams in a 14-year Negro League career.

The imposing 6-foot 5-inch, 225-pound left-hander commanded one of the Negro League's best curve balls and enjoyed an exceptional stint from 1924 through 1927 with the Philadelphia Hilldale Daisies (ECL). His effectiveness and capabilities, however, were hampered by excessive drinking.

In 1919, Winters began his diamond career with Chappie Johnson's* Norfolk, VA Stars. After moving in 1921 to the Atlantic City, NJ Bacharach Giants (ECL), he posted a three year 13–8 record. Upon joining the Philadelphia Hilldale Daisies in 1924, Winter established himself among the Negro League's premier hurlers. National Baseball Hall of Famers Judy Johnson* and "Pop" Lloyd* starred for the Hilldale Daisies. Winters won 69 games and lost only 28 from 1924 through 1927, leading the ECL with 19 triumphs in 1924 and 21 victories in 1925. He starred in the inaugural 1924 Negro League World Series, winning three of four decisions with a 1.16 ERA for the ECL titlists against the Kansas City Monarchs. The Kansas City Monarchs' ultimate World Series victory may have diminished Winters' heroics, but he gained some revenge with a complete game victory in 1925. The same teams repeated their league triumphs, but the Hilldale Daisies triumphed in the postseason series, five games to one. Winters, a skillful hitter, occasionally pinch hit or played first-base, batting .345 in 1925 and .314 in 1926. In exhibition games against the Babe Ruth* All-Stars, he split two mound decisions with Hall of Fame pitcher Lefty Grove.*

After posting a 15–5 record in 1926 and a 14–8 mark in 1927, Winters was suspended for lackadaisical play and probably for excessive drinking. The Hilldale Daisies in 1928 traded him to the New York Lincoln Giants, but he never again achieved notable success with eight clubs through 1933. With the Lincoln Giants and the Homestead Grays, Winters won 11 games and lost 12 in 1928 and 1929. In 1931 and 1932, his combined record fell to just two wins and six losses.

Although drinking habits plagued him, Winters worked sporadically as a handyman. A 1952 fan poll, conducted by the *Pittsburgh Courier*, listed him on the Negro Leagues Second Team All-Time All-Stars.

BIBLIOGRAPHY: *The Baseball Encyclopedia*, 10th ed. (New York, 1996); Dick Clark and Larry Lester, eds., *The Negro Leagues Book* (Cleveland, OH, 1994); John B. Holway, *Voices From the Great Black Baseball Leagues* (New York, 1975); Robert W. Peterson, *Only the Ball Was White* (Englewood Cliffs, NJ, 1970); James A. Riley, *The All-Time All-Stars of Black Baseball* (Cocoa, FL, 1983); James A. Riley, *The Biographical Encyclopedia of the Negro Baseball Leagues* (New York, 1994); Mike Shatzkin, ed., *The Ballplayers* (New York, 1990).

David Bernstein

WISE, Richard Charles "Rick" (b. September 13, 1945, Jackson, MI), player, is the son of Clifford C. Wise, a teacher, and Barbara J. (Putnam) Wise and graduated in 1963 from James Madison High School in Portland, OR, where he starred as a high school athlete. He married Susan Lakey on February

18, 1967 and has two children, Stacey and Richard, Jr. His brother, Tom, played infield in the Houston Astros (NL) organization from 1970 through 1974.

The Philadelphia Phillies (NL) signed the 6-foot 2-inch, 195-pound right-handed pitcher in 1963 and optioned him to Bakersfield, CA (CaL). Wise spent 1964 with the Philadelphia Phillies as an 18-year-old, finishing 5–3 with a 4.04 ERA. The Philadelphia Phillies appeared headed for the NL pennant, but collapsed in September. The hard-throwing Wise pitched in 1965 for Little Rock–based Arkansas (PCL) and part of 1966 for San Diego, CA (PCL) before rejoining Philadelphia. Wise remained with the Philadelphia Phillies through 1971, boasting a 15–13 mark and 3.23 ERA in 1969. In 1971, he compiled a 17–14 record and career best 2.88 ERA. His greatest thrill came against the Cincinnati Reds on June 23, 1971, when he set a major league record by hurling a 4–0 no-hit victory and hitting two HR. The two-time All-Star tied a major league mark for pitchers by hitting two HR twice that season.

In February 1972, the Philadelphia Phillies traded Wise to the St. Louis Cardinals (NL) for Steve Carlton.* Wise, who found Hank Aaron* the most difficult batter to face, finished 16–16 with a 3.11 ERA in 1972 and posted a 16–12 mark in 1973. He started the All-Star Game for the NL, hurling two innings for the victory. In October 1973, the St. Louis Cardinals sent Wise to the Boston Red Sox (AL) for Reggie Smith.* Wise led the Red Sox with a 19–12 mark and 3.95 ERA in 1975, compiling a 1–0 record and 2.45 ERA in the AL Championship Series against the Oakland A's. He won his only World Series appearance against the Cincinnati Reds, relieving in the dramatic sixth game. For the Boston Red Sox, he finished 14–11 in 1976 and 11–5 in 1977.

A March 1978 trade sent Wise to the Cleveland Indians (AL) for Dennis Eckersley.* Wise struggled with 19 losses in 28 decisions for the last place Cleveland Indians in 1978, but led their staff with a 15–10 record in 1979. In November 1979, the San Diego Padres (NL) acquired him as a free agent. He won 10 games the next two campaigns with the San Diego Padres before retiring as a player. In 506 major league games, Wise compiled a 188–181 win–loss record and 3.69 ERA with 1,647 strikeouts in 3,127 innings. He hurled four career one-hitters and batted .195 with 15 HR (including two grand slams) and 66 RBI.

The Beaverton, OR resident served as a pitching coach with Madison, WI (ML) in 1985 and 1986, Sarasota, FL (GCL) in 1987, Auburn, NY (NYPL) in 1988 and 1989, New Britain, CT (EL) in 1991 and 1992, and Pawtucket, RI (IL) from 1993 to 1995.

BIBLIOGRAPHY: Richard Wise file, National Baseball Library, Cooperstown, NY; William Leggett, "Enter an All-Around Wise Guy," *SI* 35 (July 5, 1971), p. 40; David L. Porter, telephone conversation with Richard Wise, March 8, 1996; *San Diego Padres Media Guide*, 1982; *TSN Official Baseball Register*, 1982; Richard Wise, letters to David L. Porter, March 9, 1996, April 3, 1996; Allen Lewis, *The Philadelphia Phillies: A Pictorial History* (Virginia Beach, VA, 1981); Frank Dolson, *The Philadelphia Story* (South Bend, IN, 1981); Allen Lewis and Larry Shenk, *This Date in Philadelphia Phillies History* (New York, 1979); Rich Westcott and Frank Bilovsky, *The New Phillies Encyclopedia* (Philadelphia, PA, 1993); Bob Broeg, *Redbirds! A Century of Cardinals' Baseball* (St. Louis, MO, 1981); Rob Rains, *The St. Louis Cardinals* (New York, 1992); Bob Broeg and Jerry Vickery, *St. Louis Cardinals Encyclopedia* (Grand Rapids, MI, 1998); Howard Liss, *The Boston Red Sox* (New York, 1982); Robert Redmount, *The Red Sox Encyclopedia* (Champaign, IL, 1998); Peter Golenbock, *Fenway* (New York, 1984); Peter Gammons, *Beyond the Sixth Game* (Boston, MA, 1985); Dan Shaugh- nessy, *The Curse of the Bambino* (New York, 1990); Jack Torry, *Endless Summers* (South Bend, IN, 1995); Terry Pluto, *The Curse of Rocky Colavito* (New York, 1994); Jack McKeon with Tom Friend, *Jack of All Trades* (Chicago, IL, 1988).

David L. Porter

WISE, Samuel Washington "Sam," "Modoc" (b. August 18, 1857, Akron, OH; d. January 22, 1910, Akron, OH), player, hit productively and fielded erratically through 11 major league seasons. The son of Pennsylvania-born Samuel Wise and Sarah (Weary) Wise, he began playing professionally with the independent Akron, OH club in 1880 and made two hits in his only major league game for the Detroit Wolverines (NL) in 1881. In 1882, he signed with both the Cincinnati Red Stockings in the newly formed AA and with the Boston Red Caps (NL), helping precipitate a contract war between the two leagues. The Cincinnati Red Stockings sued the Boston Red Caps unsuccessfully in what historian David Pietrusza terms "the first instance in which the courts became involved in baseball."

Wise played infield seven years for the Boston Red Caps and Boston Bean- eaters, performing chiefly at shortstop. In 1883, he led NL shortstops with 88 errors. But the Boston *Globe* squelched rumors that Wise was fixing games: "Considering the chances he tries for and accepts, it is wonderful that his record is as good as it is." He led NL shortstops in chances per game in 1885 and 1888.

In 1886, an injured arm forced Wise to play mostly at first base. The 5- foot 10½-inch, 170-pound Wise, who hit left-handed and threw right- handed, returned to shortstop in 1887 and enjoyed his finest offensive season. He recorded major league career highs in batting average (.334, fifth in the NL), slugging average (.522, fourth in the NL), and runs scored (103). After leaving the Boston Beaneaters for the Washington Statesmen (NL) in 1889, he played primarily at second base for the rest of his major league career.

Wise jumped to the Buffalo Bisons in the renegade PL for 1890, hitting .293 and achieving career highs in doubles (29) and RBI (102). With the demise of the PL, the Baltimore Orioles (AA) signed Wise for 1891. In 1892, he played in the minor leagues with Rochester, NY (EL) and Binghamton, NY (EL). Upon joining the Washington Senators (NL) for a final major league season in 1893, Wise played near his peak. He batted .311 with a career-high 162 hits and led NL second basemen in chances per game. In six subsequent minor league seasons, he hit over .300 five times.

Wise later umpired in the OPL and worked as a foreman for the Dia Rubber Company in Akron. He died of peritonitis and was survived by his wife. In 1,175 major league games, Wise batted .272 with 1,281 hits, 834 runs scored, and 672 RBI.

BIBLIOGRAPHY: Samuel Wise file, National Baseball Library, Cooperstown, NY; Daniel E. Ginsburg, *The Fix Is In* (Jefferson, NC, 1995); Frederick Ivor-Campbell et al., eds., *Baseball's First Stars* (Cleveland, OH, 1996); David Pietrusza, *Major Leagues* (Jefferson, NC, 1991); John Thorn et al., eds., *Total Baseball*, 5th ed. (New York, 1997); Harold Kaese, *The Boston Braves* (New York, 1948); Gary Caruso, *The Braves Encyclopedia* (Philadelphia, PA, 1995); Shirley Povich, *The Washington Senators* (New York, 1954); Morris Bealle, *The Washington Senators* (Washington, DC, 1947).

Frederick Ivor-Campbell

WISHAM, Mary Nesbitt "Wish" (b. February 1, 1925, Greenville, SC), player, is the daughter of Grady Nesbitt, a shipping foreman in a textile mill, and Lucille (Dubberly) Nesbitt and had two brothers. Her step-grandfather inspired her to play baseball and taught her to throw as hard as she could, using him as a target. Her parents divorced when she attended elementary school.

Wisham, whose baseball hero was Stan Musial,* carried a tote bag with a baseball bat, balls and gloves to school daily so that she and her friends could play ball at recess and during lunch breaks. She played in a fast-pitch softball league at age 12 and participated on some championship teams in Florida. She attended Ponce De Leon High School in Coral Gables, FL and transferred her senior year to Central High School in Chattanooga, TN, where she played basketball, tennis, and volleyball and enjoyed considerable success as a sprinter and long jumper in track and field. AAGPBL scout Jimmy Hamilton saw her play for a Chattanooga, TN men's team and invited her for a tryout.

The 5-foot 8-inch, 155-pound left-hander, who also performed under the name of Crews, pitched and played first base for the Racine, WI Belles (AAGPBL) from 1943 to 1945 and for the Peoria, IL Redwings (AAGPBL) in 1947, 1948 and 1950. In 1943, Wisham pitched for the All-Star team under the lights at Wrigley Field in Chicago, IL. She compiled an impressive 26–13 mark in 1943 and a 23–17 record in 1944 with her knuckleball. A broken collarbone caused her to have less effective control of her pitches and she became a first baseman.

Wisham helped pitch the Racine Belles to the 1943 AAGPBL Championship and ranked among the top 10 AAGPBL hitters for five out of her six seasons. She tied Helen Callaghan St. Aubin* for the batting crown in 1945, with a .319 average. She did not play in 1946, but returned to the

AAGPBL for the next four seasons. In 1948, she led Peoria in batting and paced the AAGPBL in extra base hits (39) and doubles (24). Her career-best .340 batting average came in her concluding season in 1950. "I really loved the game," she commented. "I ate, slept and talked baseball constantly. We were one big happy family and felt really close to our coaches." In six AAGPBL seasons, she batted .282 with 419 hits, 13 HR and 186 RBI, and compiled a 65–49 win–loss record with a 2.44 ERA in 935 innings.

In 1946, she married Vester Wisham. They had four children, David (deceased), Luree, Mary Elizabeth, and Todd. Wisham, who drove a school bus for 22 years until 1990, regards her Christian faith as being the cornerstone of her life. She has always enjoyed musicals and has often seen baseball movies. Wisham played softball until a hamstring injury at age 65 and umpires Little League games in her Holister, FL community.

Wisham's career highlight came at Peoria, IL, where she hit a game winning grand slam HR before over 10,000 spectators. Interlachen, FL honored her with the Mary Wisham Ballfield. She belongs to the AAGPBL Gallery at the National Baseball Hall of Fame.

BIBLIOGRAPHY: Scott A.G.M. Crawford, telephone interview with Mary N. Wisham, April 15, 1996; AAGPBL files, Northern Indiana Historical Society, South Bend, IN; Tim Wiles, National Baseball Hall of Fame, Cooperstown, NY, letter to Scott A.G.M. Crawford, December 14, 1995; W. C. Madden, *The Women of the All-American Girls Professional Baseball League* (Jefferson, NC, 1997); Scott A.G.M. Crawford, telephone conversations with Dottie Collins, AAGPBLPA, February 1996.

Scott A.G.M. Crawford

WISNIEWSKI, Connie "Iron Woman," "Polish Rifle" (b. February 18, 1922, Detroit, MI; d. May 4, 1995, FL), player, was one of six children born to Stanley Wisniewski and Frances Wisniewski and attended Detroit schools, graduating from the High School of Commerce. Wisniewski played softball on local sandlots and for Detroit's Hudson Motors team. She was nicknamed "Iron Woman" for hurling both games of a doubleheader and pitched Hudson Motors to the city championship. She joined the Milwaukee Chicks (AAGPBL) as a pitcher and outfielder in 1944 after a scout saw her playing softball. Her mother persuaded her playing baseball was better than serving in the U.S. Army for four years. Wisniewski competed in the AAGPBL for nine seasons from 1944 to 1952, compiling a .697 winning percentage in 1944 to lead Milwaukee to the pennant and playoffs. She was named the AAGPBL's first Player of the Year and an All-Star in 1945 with the Grand Rapids, MI Chicks. The Grand Rapids Chicks had moved from Milwaukee before the 1945 season. Wisniewski led the AAGPBL in games pitched (46) in 1945, hurling both games of a doubleheader once. She also paced the AAGPBL in ERA (0.81), victories (32), winning percentage (.744), and innings (391). In 1946, she again paced the AAGPBL hurlers in winning percentage (.786) and ERA (0.96) and tied Joanne Winter* for victories (33), repeating as an All-Star.

Wisniewski pitched her first five seasons, compiling an impressive 107–48 won–lost record, .690 winning percentage, and superb 1.48 ERA. When the AAGPBL switched from an underhand to an overhand pitching motion, she failed to make the adjustment to the changed pitching motion and moved to the outfield as a regular. She won only 16 of 30 decisions in 1947, but batted .291 as an outfielder. In 1948, Wisniewski ranked third in batting (.289) and led the AAGPBL with seven HR. After ranking second in batting in 1949, she bolted to the NGBL in 1950. Wisniewski returned to the AAGPBL in 1951 and batted for Grand Rapids. She also played in the All Star game as an outfielder in 1948, 1949, 1951, and 1952.

Her phenomenal pitching record earned her the sobriquet the "Christy Mathewson* of women's baseball." After retiring from baseball in 1953, Wisniewski worked for General Motors in Detroit, MI for 28 years. She played on the company softball team and joined its golfers league. Wisniewski also owned a restaurant, "The Chick's Dugout." She retired to Clearwater, FL, where the warmer weather allowed her to continue playing golf.

BIBLIOGRAPHY: Gai Berlage, *Women in Baseball* (Westport, CT, 1994); AAGPBL Statistics, 1944–1949; Lois Browne, *The Girls of Summer* (New York, 1992); W. C. Madden, *The Women of the All-American Girls Professional Baseball League* (Jefferson, NC, 1997); Barbara Gregorich, *Women at Play* (San Diego, CA, 1993).

Leslie Heaphy

WOLF, William Van Winkle "Chicken Wolf," "Jimmy" (b. May 12, 1862, Louisville, KY; d. May 16, 1903, Louisville, KY), player and manager, was nicknamed "Chicken Wolf" by Pete Browning* while with the Louisville Eclipse (AA). Wolf disobeyed his manager's orders not to eat too much stewed chicken before a game and then was charged with several errors during the game.

Wolf may be the only major leaguer to play in the AA from its inception in 1882 to its last year in 1891, setting AA career records for most games (1,195), hits (1,438), doubles (213), triples (109), and total bases (1,925). The Louisville Eclipse signed Wolf as a 19 year old to play right field in 1882 for $9 per week. *SL* called him the lowest paid professional baseball player in history. A fine fielder, he led AA outfielders in assists in 1882 and shared honors for most double plays (6) in 1883. The durable Wolf played in every Louisville game from 1883 to 1885 and in 1887 and 1890 and ran the bases well. Although clouting only 18 career HR, he belted two on August 22, 1886 against the Cincinnati Red Stockings.

Wolf received his only taste as a major league manager in 1889 when the Louisville Colonels (AA) finished with only 27 wins and 111 losses. Since the Louisville Colonels rotated managers at whim, Wolf took his turn and produced a woeful 14–51 record. The veteran ballplayer provided the Louisville Colonels with both leadership and support. His best major league season came in 1890, when the Colonels won the AA pennant. In 1890, Wolf paced the AA with a .363 batting average and 197 hits and batted .360 with eight RBI in the World Series against the Brooklyn Bridegrooms. When the AA folded after the 1891 season, he ended his professional baseball career with Syracuse, NY (EL) in 1892 and Buffalo, NY (EL) in 1893.

Wolf returned to Louisville and worked for the city fire department. In a freak accident, he was thrown from a horse-drawn vehicle while rushing to a fire and hit his head on a cobblestone street. The injury rendered him mentally unbalanced for the rest of his life. He died in the Lakeland Insane Asylum in Louisville.

BIBLIOGRAPHY: William Wolf file, National Baseball Library, Cooperstown, NY; Peter Filichia, *Professional Baseball Franchises* (New York, 1993); James K. Skipper, Jr., *Baseball Nicknames* (Jefferson, NC, 1992); David Nemec, *The Beer and Whisky League* (New York, 1994); Philip Von Borries, *Legends of Louisville* (West Bloomfield, MI, 1993); Philip Von Borries, *Louisville Diamonds* (Paducah, KY, 1997); David Nemec, *The Great Encyclopedia of 19th Century Major League Baseball* (New York, 1997); John Thorn et al., eds., *Total Baseball*, 5th ed. (New York, 1997); Robert L. Tiemann and Mark Rucker, eds., *Nineteenth Century Stars* (Kansas City, MO, 1989).

Scot E. Mondore

WOOD, Howard Ellsworth. *See* Joe "Smoky Joe" Wood.

WOOD, Joe "Smoky Joe" (b. Howard Ellsworth Wood, October 25, 1889, Kansas City, MO; d. July 27, 1985, West Haven, CT), player and coach, was the son of attorney John Wood and homemaker Rebecca (Stephens) Wood and grew up in Ouray, CO and Ness City, KS. He married Laura O'Shea on December 20, 1913 and had four children, Stephen, Robert K., Joseph P., and Virginia. In 1943, Joseph P. played 60 games with the Detroit Tigers (AL). A devoted family man, the modest, sincere, fair-minded, and friendly Wood signed a contract for $20 in 1906 to play baseball with the touring Kansas City Bloomer Girls. In 1907 he played briefly with Cedar Rapids, IA (3IL) and joined Hutchinson, KS (WA), where he struck out 224 batters in 196 innings. After being sold in 1908 to Kansas City, MO (AA), he was purchased that summer by the Boston Red Sox (AL) and signed for $2,600.

With the Boston Red Sox in 1911, he compiled a 23–17 mark, struck out a then club-record 231 batters, and on July 29 pitched a no-hitter against the St. Louis Browns. In 1912 the 5-foot 11-inch, 180-pound right-hander won 34 of 39 regular season decisions and three World Series contests to help Boston defeat the New York Giants, four games to three. During 1912, he tied the AL consecutive victory pitching record (16), struck out 258 batters, led the AL in shutouts (10), victories, winning percentage (.872), and complete games (35), and compiled a sparkling 1.91 ERA. In early 1913, Wood fell on slippery grass while fielding a bunt and broke his pitching-hand thumb. Although pitching occasionally in 1913 and 1914 and leading the AL in winning percentage (.750) in 1915 with a 15–5 mark and 1.49 ERA, Wood hurled in almost continuous pain and never recovered his fast-ball. Pitching phenom Walter Johnson* in 1912 had commented, "No man alive can throw a baseball harder than Joe Wood."

Wood sat out the 1916 season, unable to raise his right arm. Ranked first in Red Sox career winning percentage (.674) and ERA (1.98), Wood was recommended by Tris Speaker* as an outfielder to Cleveland Indians (AL) manager Lee Fohl. In February 1917, the Red Sox sold him to the Indians for $15,000. With Cleveland from 1917 through 1922, he batted .298 and proved that a forced retirement pitcher could stay in the major leagues as an outfielder. As a pitcher, he compiled 116 wins and 57 losses for a superb .671 record, 2.03 ERA, and 989 strikeouts in 1,434.1 innings. Wood completed 121 of 158 starts and hurled 28 career shutouts. A .283 lifetime batter, he compiled 553 hits, 118 doubles, 31 triples, 23 HR, 266 runs scored, and 325 RBI. He participated on world championship teams with the 1912 and 1915 Boston Red Sox and 1920 Cleveland Indians. From 1923 to 1942, Wood piloted Yale University to a composite 283–228–1 mark. In 1984, Yale awarded Wood an honorary Doctor of Humane Letters degree. Wood's main impact upon baseball was his courageous, successful decision to become an outfielder after an arm injury had ruined his brilliant pitching career.

BIBLIOGRAPHY: Mark Alvarez, "An Interview with Joe Wood," *BRJ* 16 (1987), pp. 53–56; John Benson, *Baseball's Top 100* (Wilton, CT, 1997); Joe Wood file, National Baseball Library, Cooperstown, NY; Frederick G. Lieb, *The Boston Red Sox* (New York, 1947); Howard Liss, *The Boston Red Sox* (New York, 1982); Robert Redmount, *The Red Sox Encyclopedia* (Champaign, IL, 1998); Dan Shaughnessy, *The Curse of the Bambino* (New York, 1990); Franklin Lewis, *The Cleveland Indians* (New York, 1949); *Boston Red Sox Media Guide, 1984*; Ellery H. Clark, Jr., *Boston Red Sox: 75th Anniversary History* (Hicksville, NY, 1975); Ellery H. Clark, Jr. (Red Sox Analytical Letter Collection), correspondence with Harry Hooper, "Duffy" Lewis, Joe Wood; Ellery H. Clark, Jr., *Red Sox Fever* (Hicksville, NY, 1979); Ellery H. Clark, Jr., *Red Sox Forever* (Hicksville, NY, 1977); Ellery H. Clark, Jr., interviews, Everett Scott, September 1924, Tris Speaker, June 1926, June 1927, Bill Carrigan, May 1928, Buck O'Brien, July 1950, Joe Wood, June 1974, July 1982, August 1983, Larry Gardner, July 1974, Robert K. Wood, July 1983; Jack Lautier, *Fenway Voices* (Camden, ME, 1990); Wil A. Linkugel and Edward J. Pappas, *They Tasted Glory* (Jefferson, NC, 1998); Lawrence Ritter, *The Glory of Their Times* (New York, 1966); Morris Eckhouse, *Day-by-Day in Cleveland Indians History* (New York, 1983); *The Baseball Encyclopedia*, 10th ed. (New York, 1996).

Ellery H. Clark, Jr.

WOOD, Wilbur Forrester, Jr. "Mr. Knuckles" (b. October 22, 1941, Cambridge, MA), player, is the son of Wilbur Wood, Sr. and was signed by the

Boston Red Sox (AL) to a $30,000 bonus in 1960. The 18-year-old southpaw split the 1960 season between Waterloo, IA (ML) and Raleigh, NC (CrL), winning four of nine decisions. After compiling an 8–5 win–loss record at Winston-Salem, NC (CrL) in 1961, Wood pitched six games for the Boston Red Sox and finished the campaign at Johnstown, PA (EL). In 1962 at York, PA (EL), Wood led the EL in games started and innings pitched, won 15 decisions, and boasted a 2.84 ERA. In September 1962, Boston Red Sox manager Pinky Higgins* gave him a single start. Wood shuttled between Seattle, WA (PCL) and the Boston Red Sox in 1963 and 1964, unable to translate his minor league success to the major league level. The Boston Red Sox sold the 6-foot, 190-pound left-hander to the Pittsburgh Pirates (NL) in time to lose two games in September 1964. Wood spent the entire 1965 season as a middle reliever in a Pittsburgh Pirates bullpen that featured Al McBean and Don Schwall. In 1966, Pirates reliever Elroy Face* regained health and Pete Mikkelson enjoyed the best season of his career. Pittsburgh dispatched Wood to Columbus, OH (IL), where he won 14 and led the IL and ERA and innings pitched.

The Chicago White Sox (AL) acquired Wood for pitcher Juan Pizarro* in October 1966. Wood joined Hoyt Wilhelm,* one of the premier relievers of all time, in the White Sox bullpen. Professionally, Wood had relied on a fastball and a curveball. Wilhelm worked with Wood on developing the knuckleball quickly. Wood recorded a 2.45 ERA in 51 appearances in 1967 and led the AL in games pitched over the next three campaigns with AL records of 88, 76, and 77, respectively. Between 1968 and 1970, Wood won 31 games in relief and saved 52 other contests.

Chicago White Sox manager Chuck Tanner* moved the durable Wood to the starting rotation in 1971. Wood responded with 22 wins, 22 complete games, and a sparkling 1.91 ERA. Fourteen of those victories came on only two days' rest. In 1972 Wood started an incredible 49 games and hurled 376.2 innings, the most frames pitched in a major league season since 1917. He won 24 of 41 decisions and led the AL in victories, but also set a major league record for pitchers by striking out 65 times at bat. *TSN* voted him AL Pitcher of the Year in 1972. The following year, Wood finished 24–20 to become the first pitcher to win and lose 20 contests in the same season since Walter Johnson* in 1916. He paced the AL in both wins and innings pitched. On July 20, 1973, he started and lost both games of a doubleheader against the New York Yankees. Wood compiled a 20–19 win–loss mark in 1974 and a 16–20 slate in 1975. From 1971 to 1975, he amassed nearly 1,700 innings as a starter. A line drive by Ron LeFlore* of the Detroit Tigers fractured Wood's kneecap on May 9, 1976 and cost him the rest of the season. Wood pitched again for the White Sox in 1977 and 1978, but did not regain his previous effectiveness. Wood, the only great left-handed knuckleball pitcher, retired with 651 appearances, 164 wins, 156 losses, 57 saves, 24 shutouts, 1,411 strikeouts, and 724 walks in 2,684 innings. Wood, who married Sandra Malcolm on November 6, 1963, owned and operated a fishing supply store in Boston, MA. He has worked since 1988 as a salesman for Geneva Pharmaceutical Company.

BIBLIOGRAPHY: Wilbur Wood file, National Baseball Library, Cooperstown, NY; Ross Forman, "Wilbur Wood," *SCD* 25 (May 29, 1998), pp. 170–171; Richard Lindberg, *Sox* (New York, 1984); Richard Lindberg, *Who's on Third?* (South Bend, IN, 1983); Bob Vanderberg, *Sox: From Lane and Fain to Zisk and Fisk* (Chicago, IL, 1982); Zander Hollander, ed., *The Complete Handbook of Baseball 1977* (New York, 1977); Rich Marazzi and Len Fiorito, *Aaron to Zuverink* (New York, 1982); Mike Shatzkin, ed., *The Ballplayers* (New York, 1990); John Thorn and John B. Holway, *The Pitcher* (New York, 1987).

Frank J. Olmsted

WOODLING, Eugene Richard "Gene," "Old Faithful" (b. August 16, 1922, Akron, OH), player, coach, and scout, is one of four sons of Harvey Woodling and Alvada Woodling and graduated in 1940 from Akron East High School, where he participated in swimming, baseball, basketball, and football. One of his brothers won a swimming championship at Ohio State University.

Woodling's professional baseball career began in 1940 when he was signed by Cleveland Indians (AL) scout Bill Bradley* and assigned to Mansfield, OH (OSL). He played with three other minor league teams before the Cleveland Indians brought him up in September 1943. He spent 1944–1945 in the military and returned to the Cleveland Indians for 61 games in 1946, batting an uninspiring .188. In December 1946, the Cleveland Indians traded him to the Pittsburgh Pirates (NL) for catcher Al Lopez.* His one season with the Pittsburgh Pirates saw him hit .266 in only 22 games. Woodling's next two years were spent in the minor leagues with Newark, NJ (IL) and San Francisco, CA (PCL). He feasted on PCL pitching with a .385 batting average in 1949 and joined the New York Yankees (AL) for the next five years. His best years in New York came when he hit .309 in 1952 and .306 in 1953, when he led the AL with a .429 on base percentage. When he left the New York Yankees for the Baltimore Orioles (AL) in a record 17-player trade in December 1954, his career batting averaged stood at .280. Upon retiring eight years later, his career batting average had improved to .284. The 5-foot 10-inch, 195-pound Woodling, who batted left-handed and threw right-handed, hit .300 or better in six of his 17 seasons. Woodling played from June 1955 until April 1958 with the Cleveland Indians and from April 1958 through 1961 with the Baltimore Orioles. His career-best .321 batting average with the Cleveland Indians in 1957 placed him third among AL hitters that year. From 1957 to 1960, Woodling frequently ranked among the top five hitters in production, total average, on-base percentage, and clutch-hitting index. His major league career ended in 1962, when he hit .274 for the expansion New York Mets (NL) and the Washington Senators (AL).

The outspoken Woodling appeared in five consecutive World Series from 1949 to 1953, compiling a .318 batting average for the triumphant New York Yankees. He scored 21 runs and walked 19 times in 26 World Series games. He is proudest of his hitting feats with the 1959 Baltimore Orioles, with his RBI winning several contests. In 1,796 major league games spanning 17 seasons, he made 1,585 hits with 257 doubles, 147 HR, 830 RBI, and 921 walks.

Woodling, who coached for the Baltimore Orioles from 1964 through 1967, worked for the Eaton Corporation, scouted part-time for the Cleveland Indians, raised horses and enjoys fishing and traveling. He was the beneficiary of oil wells on his Medina, OH property. He married Betty Nicely in October 1942, resides in Remsen Corners, OH, and has three children, Pamela, Gene, and Kimberly.

BIBLIOGRAPHY: Gene Woodling file, National Baseball Library, Cooperstown, NY; Dom Forker, *The Men of Autumn* (Dallas, TX, 1989); Rich Marazzi and Len Fiorito, *Aaron to Zuverink* (New York, 1982); Tom Meany, ed., *The Magnificent Yankees* (New York, 1952); Larry Moffi, *This Side of Cooperstown* (Iowa City, IA, 1996); Mike Shatzkin, ed., *The Ballplayers* (New York, 1990); John Thorn et al. eds., *Total Baseball*, 5th ed. (New York, 1997); Jack Torry, *Endless Summers* (South Bend, IN, 1995); John Phillips, *Winners* (Cabin John, MD, 1987); Morris Eckhouse, *Day-by-Day in Cleveland Indians History* (New York, 1983); *TSN Official Baseball Register*, 1962; Rich Westcott, *Diamond Greats* (Westport, CT, 1988); Gene Woodling, letter to Lee Scanlon, 1994; Dave Anderson et al., *The Yankees* (New York, 1979); Ted Patterson, *The Baltimore Orioles* (Dallas, TX, 1995); Peter Golenbock, *Dynasty* (New York, 1975); Robert W. Creamer, *Stengel: His Life and Times* (New York, 1984); Mark Gallagher, *The Yankee Encyclopedia*, vol. 3 (Champaign, IL, 1997).

Lee E. Scanlon

WOODS, Parnell L. (b. February 26, 1912, Birmingham, AL; d. July 22, 1977, Cleveland, OH), player and manager, was the son of Bernard Woods and Belzora (Bruton) Woods. He was survived by his wife, Rosa K. (McGiven) Woods, and six children.

Woods launched a 19-year professional baseball career with the Birmingham, AL Black Barons in 1933 and was still playing with the club in 1937, when it helped charter the NAL. After performing with the Birmingham Black Braves in 1938, he joined the Jacksonville, FL Red Caps (NAL). The Jacksonville Red Caps performed as the Cleveland Bears (NAL) in 1939 and 1940 and returned to Jacksonville in 1941.

Woods left the Red Caps in the spring of 1942 to manage the infant Cincinnati Buckeyes (NAL). The Negro League's youngest pilot guided the Cincinnati Buckeyes to the first half NAL title and moved with the Buckeyes to Cleveland in 1943. He managed the Buckeyes through 1944, relinquishing the reins to Quincy Trouppe* in 1945. After captaining the Cleveland Buckeyes in 1945, Woods played professional baseball the next three seasons in

Venezuela. He reappeared briefly with the transplanted Louisville, KY Buck-eyes (NAL) in 1949 and finished 1949 with Oakland, CA (PCL), batting .275 in 40 games for the Oaks. He returned to the NAL in 1950 with the Memphis, TN Red Sox and ended his baseball career in 1951 with the Chicago American Giants (NAL).

The 5-foot 9-inch 170-pound right-hander ranked among the best third basemen, appearing in five Negro League East-West All-Star Games. He initially performed in the 1939 contest and started at third base for the West in 1940, 1941, 1942 and 1951. Woods also was selected an All-Star in Venezuela, leading the 1947 VWL in batting average (.354), runs scored (28), doubles (13), and triples (3). He is credited with NAL batting averages of .343 in 1939, .318 in 1940, .343 in 1942, .329 in 1944, .335 in 1945, and .375 in 1951. He compiled a .316 NAL career batting average and .306 composite mark as a professional. He also played PRWL baseball in the 1939–1940 season and CUWL baseball in the 1947–1948 campaign.

Woods' offensive ability was complemented by his defensive talent. In 1944, he led NAL third basemen with a .948 fielding average. Woods helped the Cleveland Buckeyes capture the NAL pennant and sweep the Negro Leagues' World Series in 1945. The third baseman made the Negro Baseball Pictorial Year Book All-America baseball team for both the 1944 and 1945 seasons. He served as business manager of the world famous Harlem Globe-trotters basketball team for 27 years.

BIBLIOGRAPHY: Dick Clark and Larry Lester, *The Negro Leagues Book* (Cleveland, OH, 1994); *Cleveland Call & Post*, 1942–1946; *Cleveland Plain Dealer*, July 26, 1977; G. Becerra Mijares, *Beisbol Venezolano* (Venezuela, 1966); *Negro Baseball Pictorial Year-book* (Washington, DC, 1945, 1946); James A Riley, *The Biographical Encyclopedia of the Negro Baseball Leagues* (New York, 1994); James A. Riley, *The All-Time All-Stars of Black Baseball* (Cocoa, FL, 1983).

Merl F. Kleinknecht

WRIGHT, Burnis "Bill," "Wild Bill" (b. June 6, 1914, Milan, TN; d. August 3, 1996, Aguacalientes, Mexico), player and coach, excelled as a big, strong, swift outfielder with the Elite Giants' (NNL) franchises in Nashville, TN (1932–1934), Columbus, OH (1935), Washington, DC (1936–1937), and Baltimore, MD (1938–1939, 1942, 1945). One of the league's fastest players, he batted fourth and hit the long ball when needed. The switch-hitter per-formed best in the clutch, exhibiting a compact swing and making good contact. Wright hit better from the left side. He was selected seven times to the East-West All-Star squad, including five consecutive appearances from 1935 to 1939 and others in 1942 and 1945, and batted .318 in All-Star competition.

His nickname "Wild Bill" came when just a teenaged pitcher who lacked control for a local team, the Milan Buffalos, in 1931. The next year, owner Tom Wilson's Nashville Elite Giants gave him a tryout, but he hurt his arm by throwing too hard in the cold weather and was switched to the outfield. With Wilson's club for 12 seasons, he was credited with batting averages of .300, .244, .300, .244, .293, .410, and .316 for his first seven seasons from 1932 through 1938. The 1939 season marked the highlight for both the Baltimore Elite Giants and Wright. The Elite Giants defeated the Homestead, PA Grays (NNL) in a postseason playoff after Wright copped the NNL batting title with his extraordinary .488 average.

Wright succumbed to the lure of Mexico in 1940 and remained in the MEL for the balance of his career except for two seasons during World War II, when he returned to Baltimore due to his draft status. In these last two Negro League seasons, he batted .303 in 1942 and .371 in 1945 and registered a .517 slugging percentage the latter season. He finished with a lifetime .361 batting average in the Negro Leagues. In the MEL, he quickly became one of Mexico's most productive and most popular players, registering batting averages of .360, .390, .366, .355, .301, .305, .326, .282, .299, and .362 while playing primarily with the Mexico City, Mexico Reds. Wright led the MEL in several categories during his career there, tying for the lead in doubles while ranking fifth in batting average in 1940. In 1941, he led the MEL in both stolen bases and batting average. Wright's ultimate accomplishment came in 1943, when he won the triple crown and missed the stolen base crown by only a single theft. The 6-foot 4-inch 220-pounder circled the bases in 13.2 seconds and proved a skilled drag bunter, a combination enabling him to avoid a prolonged batting slump.

After a baseball career that spanned a quarter of a century as a player from 1931 to 1956 and an additional three seasons as a coach, he made Mexico his permanent home with his Hawaiian wife. The popular outfielder opened a restaurant, Bill Wright's Dugout, in Aguascalientes, Mexico. During his long career, he attained legendary status on the Mexican baseball diamonds and was elected to the Mexican Hall of Fame in 1982.

BIBLIOGRAPHY: *Afro-American*, 1935–1948; *The Baseball Encyclopedia*, 10th ed. (New York, 1996); Brent P. Kelley, " 'Wild Bill' Wright 'The Black Joe DiMaggio,' " *SCD* 23 (August 30, 1996), p. 140; Robert W. Peterson, *Only the Ball Was White* (Englewood Cliffs, NJ, 1970); James A. Riley, *The All-Time All-Stars of Black Baseball* (Cocoa, FL, 1983); James A. Riley, *The Biographical Encyclopedia of the Negro Baseball Leagues* (New York, 1994); James A. Riley, interviews with former Negro League players, James A. Riley Collection, Canton, GA; James A. Riley, "Wild Bill Wright: A Mexican League Legend Comes Home," *OTBN* (1991), p. 17; Mike Shatzkin, ed., *The Ballplayers* (New York, 1990).

James A. Riley

WRIGHT, Forest Glenn "Buckshot" (b. February 6, 1901, Archie, MO; d. April 6, 1984, Olathe, KS), player, manager, and coach, ranked among the finest shortstops of the 1920s and 1930s. He possessed great range and a rifle arm, earning him the nickname "Buckshot." Besides setting a still record 601 assists at shortstop in 1924, he executed an unassisted triple play on May 1, 1925. In 1925, he made both *TSN* and *BM* All-Star teams. Wright's parents, Robert Lee Wright and Alberta (Musick) Wright, operated a farm and hardware store. Wright wed Margaret Josephine Benn in 1929 and had one son and one daughter. Divorced in 1940, he later remarried. After completing high school in Archie, MO in 1919, he attended the University of Missouri for two years and played football and basketball there. An outstanding sandlot baseball player, he left Missouri in the spring of 1921 and signed as a shortstop with the Kansas City, MO Blues (AA). Wright played with Independence, MO (SWL) in 1921 and performed impressively in 1922 and 1923 with Kansas City.

The Pittsburgh Pirates (NL) purchased him before the 1924 season for $40,000. An instant star, the 5-foot 11-inch, 170-pound, right-handed Wright hit .287 and drove in 111 runs in 1924 and batted .308 with 121 RBI the following year. He and "Kiki" Cuyler* each slugged 18 HR in 1925, which remained the Pittsburgh record for a decade. Wright, an important cog in the Pirates lineup for five years, starred on the 1925 and 1927 NL pennant-winning teams. In December 1928, Pittsburgh needed left-handed pitching help and peddled him to the Brooklyn Dodgers (NL) for Jesse Petty. In a handball game that winter, he crushed his right shoulder, damaging his throwing arm, and consequently missed much of the 1929 season. Shoulder surgery in August enabled him to throw again, but his arm no longer possessed "buckshot" velocity. Nevertheless, Wright enjoyed his best offensive year in 1930 by hitting .321, driving in 126 runs, and belting 22 HR. His HR output remained the NL record for shortstops until 1953. Wright captained the Dodgers for several years, but his play declined and Brooklyn released him in 1933. Wright, who played with Kansas City, MO (AA) in 1934 and briefly with the Chicago White Sox (AL) in 1935, compiled an 11-year major league career .294 batting average. In 1,119 games, he made 1,219 hits, 203 doubles, 76 triples, 94 HR, 584 runs scored, 723 RBI, and 38 stolen bases. Wright managed Wenatchee, WA (WeIL) from 1937 to 1939 and later coached for Hollywood CA (PCL).

BIBLIOGRAPHY: Glenn Wright file, National Baseball Library, Cooperstown, NY; Frederick G. Lieb, *The Pittsburgh Pirates* (New York, 1948); Richard L. Burtt, *The Pittsburgh Pirates: A Pictorial History* (Virginia Beach, VA, 1977); Bob Smizik, *The Pittsburgh Pirates: An Illustrated History* (New York, 1990); Frank Graham, *The Brooklyn Dodgers* (New York, 1945); William F. McNeil, *The Dodgers Encyclopedia* (Champaign, IL, 1997); Richard Goldstein, *Superstars and Screwballs* (New York, 1991); Stanley Cohen, *Dodgers! The First 100 Years* (New York, 1990); Tommy Holmes, *The Dodgers* (New York, 1975); "Glenn Wright's Sensational Comeback," *BM* 46 (January 1931), pp. 351–352; Harold "Speed" Johnson, *Who's Who in Major League Baseball* (Chicago, IL, 1933); F. C. Lane, "The All-American Baseball Club of 1925," *BM* 36 (December 1925), pp. 305–308, 331–334; Walter Langford, "An Interview with Glenn Wright," *BRJ* 19 (1990), pp. 71–76; Eugene Murdock, "Glenn Wright,

Last of the 1925 All-Stars," *BRJ* 8 (1979), pp. 109–113; Eugene Murdock interview, Glenn Wright, June 23, 1978, Fresno, CA; *The Baseball Encyclopedia*, 10th ed. (New York, 1990); John J. Ward, "Has Pittsburgh Found a Worthy Successor to Hans Wagner?" *BM* 35 (November 1925), pp. 538, 568.

Eugene Murdock

WRIGHT, George (b. January 28, 1847, Yonkers; NY; d. August 21, 1937, Boston, MA), baseball and cricket player, golfer, and sporting goods entrepreneur, was the brother of **William Henry "Harry" Wright** (b. January 10, 1835, Sheffield, England; d. October 3, 1895, Atlantic City, NJ), baseball player and manager, cricket player, and bowler, who brought respectability to professional baseball and paved the way for the first pro league. In 1869, Harry transformed Cincinnati's Red Stockings into baseball's first openly pro team. With his younger brother, George, as their star player, the Red Stockings won 87 consecutive games over two seasons and showed that pro baseball could succeed.

Harry emigrated as an infant to New York with his parents, Samuel Wright, a professional cricket player, and Ann (Tone) Wright. After attending New York schools to age 14, he worked for a jewelry manufacturer. In 1857, he joined Staten Island's St. George Cricket Club as a pro bowler and assistant to his father, who coached the club. Harry and George saw their first baseball game that same year at Elysian Fields, Hoboken, NJ, where cricket and baseball clubs played on adjacent grounds. Both brothers liked the new game. Harry joined the New York Knickerbockers as an outfielder, while George played with the junior club of New York's Gothams. At age 15 George was elevated to the Gotham seniors, where he played various positions before settling at shortstop. During this time, he was also named assistant pro of the St. George Cricket Club. He spent 1865 as a pro with the Philadelphia Cricket Club and also played baseball with Philadelphia's Olympics. He returned to the Gotham Seniors the following year, but in July joined another New York club, the Unions of Morrisania. In 1867 20-year-old George captained and played shortstop for the Washington, DC Nationals, but returned to the Unions of Morrisania in 1868.

Harry, meanwhile, was hired by the Union Cricket Club of Cincinnati, OH in August 1865 as instructor and player. The following summer, he helped organize and captained the Cincinnati Base Ball Club (which became known as the Red Stockings after Harry added scarlet stockings to the uniform in 1867). When the Red Stockings in November 1867 offered him a salary equal to that paid him by the Union Cricket Club, Harry quit cricket to concentrate on baseball. With Harry and several other pros on the club, the Red Stockings in 1868 won the championship of the Midwest.

In 1869 Harry brought George to Cincinnati, where he assembled for the Red Stockings baseball's first fully professional team. George's skillful and innovative fielding (he was the first shortstop to position himself out beyond the baseline) and astonishing hitting (49 HR, .629 batting average) helped lead the team to an undefeated season in 57 games against challengers from Boston, MA to San Francisco, CA. Although the Red Stockings disbanded after a less successful 1870 season, their early success demolished long-held prejudices against pro baseball and led to the formation in 1871 of the NAPBL.

George Wright was the first player signed by the Boston Red Stockings (NA), while Harry was hired soon after as team manager and center fielder. The Boston Red Stockings finished third that year, but from 1872 through 1875 Harry piloted the club to four successive NA championships. In these five years, the Red Stockings compiled a 226–60 won–lost record for an impressive .790 winning percentage. George compiled a five-year .350 batting average, the NA's fourth highest. In hits (484) and runs scored (401) he ranked second only to teammate Ross Barnes.*

When the NA folded after the 1875 season, the Wright brothers joined the Boston Red Stockings of the new NL. Harry concentrated on managing, but George played regularly for four more years. Although his batting average fell to .274, George continued to field skillfully (except for 1877, when he played second base and led the NL in errors), leading NL shortstops twice in putouts and assists and once in fielding average. Stung by the defection to the Chicago White Stockings of their "big four" (Barnes, Cal McVey,* Al Spalding,* and Deacon White*), Boston placed only fourth in its initial NL season. But manager Harry lured Hartford Dark Blues pitcher Tommy Bond,* who twice led the NL in wins and paced Boston to NL pennants in 1877 and 1878.

George managed and played shortstop for the Providence Grays (NL) in 1879. In his only year as a manager, he in 1879 led the Grays to the NL pennant by five games over Harry's second place Red Stockings with a 59–25 mark. George founded a sporting goods firm when he first went to Boston in 1871. In 1879, Henry A. Ditson joined him to form Wright & Ditson. Although he played a few games for Harry's Red Stockings in 1880–1881 and half a season for Harry's Providence Grays in 1882, George concentrated on the sporting goods business. He supported the outlaw UA in its one year of existence (1884), investing in the Boston Reds and persuading the UA to use Wright & Ditson baseballs.

Harry managed the Providence Grays (NL) in 1882 and 1883 and Philadelphia Phillies (NL) from 1884 through 1893. Although he won no championship after 1878, Harry guided Providence in 1882 and Philadelphia in 1887 to close second place finishes. In 18 years of NL play, Harry's teams won 999 games and lost 825 contests for a .542 winning percentage. Harry's integrity, sense of fair play, and gentle firmness in managing ballplayers were widely admired qualities. In 1890, a severe eye disorder left him nearly blind. His return to Philadelphia after several months' absence brought an outpouring of affection from players and fans. When he retired from managing after the 1893 season, the NL created for him the largely honorary post Chief of Umpires. He died of pneumonia in 1895. Married three times, Harry first wed Mary Fraser of New York, then Carrie Mulford of Cincinnati, OH. His third wife, a sister of the first, survived him, as did seven of his eight children.

George lived to age 90, surviving his wife, Abbraria "Abbie" (Coleman) Wright. After retiring from baseball, he played cricket for many years and golf for over 40 years. He introduced golf to Boston, MA in 1890, importing equipment from England and setting up New England's first nine-hole golf course. He also figured prominently in introducing Canadian ice hockey to the United States and developing America's interest in tennis. His two sons, Beals (OS) and Irving, won national tennis championships. He died from myocarditis and pneumonia and was survived by his sons and two daughters.

George, through his sporting goods company and his promotion of sports other than baseball, probably had the greater impact on American sport in general, but Harry had a more profound influence on baseball. Although George surpassed Harry as a ballplayer, Harry gained acceptance for professional baseball and set the game on its present course. Harry's example of moral vigor in 26 years as manager helped establish the integrity and stability of the pro game. Both brothers are enshrined in the National Baseball Hall of Fame. George, elected in the year of his death, was among the earliest chosen. Harry, whose contribution to baseball was less visible, was elected belatedly in 1953.

BIBLIOGRAPHY: W. S. Barnes, Jr., "Grand Old Man of Baseball Set Notable Sports Record," Boston *Globe*, August 22, 1937; Boston *Globe*, August 23, 1937; Gerald Casway, "A Monument for Harry Wright," *TNP* 17 (1997), pp. 35–37; Henry Chadwick Scrapbooks, Albert Spalding Collection, New York Public Library, New York, NY; Sam Crane, "George Wright," New York *Journal*, November 23, 1911; Sam Crane, "Harry Wright," New York *Journal*, March 27, 1915; *DAB* 20 (1936), p. 554; *DAB* 22, Supp. 6 (1956–1960), p. 737; "George Wright Recalls Triumphs of 'Red Stockings,'" New York *Sun*, November 14, 1915; Ernie Harwell, "Brilliant Career of Harry Wright Shows Greatness of Pro Ball's Dad," *TSN*, November 18, 1953; Brad Herzog, *The Sports 100* (New York, 1995); Frederick Ivor-Campbell et al., eds., *Baseball's First Stars* (Cleveland, OH, 1996); William J. Ryczek, *Blackguards and Red Stockings* (Jefferson, NC, 1992); William J. Ryczek, *When Johnny Comes Sliding Home* (Jefferson, NC, 1998); Greg Rhodes and John Erardi, *The First Boys of Summer* (Cincinnati, OH, 1994); Gary Caruso, *The Braves Encyclopedia* (Philadelphia, PA, 1995); John Thorn et al., eds., *Total Braves* (New York, 1996); George Tuohey, comp., *A History of the Boston Base Ball Club* (Boston, MA, 1899); Thomas Aylesworth and Benton Minks, *The Encyclopedia of Baseball Managers* (New York, 1990); Frederick G. Lieb and Stan Baumgartner, *The Philadelphia Phillies* (New York, 1953); Harold Kaese, *The Boston Braves* (New York, 1948); Craig Carter, ed., *TSN Daguerreotypes*, 8th ed. (St. Louis, MO, 1990); Preston D. Orem, *Baseball 1845–1881* (Altadena, CA, 1961); *The Baseball Encyclopedia*, 10th ed. (New York, 1996); Harold Seymour, "Baseball's First Professional Manager," *OHQ* 64 (October 1955), pp. 406–423; Harry

Simmons, "100 Years Ago—Birth of First Baseball League," *TSN*, May 1, 1971; Albert G. Spalding, *America's National Game* (New York, 1911); Rich Westcott and Frank Bilovsky, *The New Phillies Encyclopedia* (Philadelphia, PA, 1993); George Wright file, National Baseball Library, Cooperstown, NY; Harry Wright correspondence, Albert Spalding Collection, New York Public Library, New York, NY; Harry Wright file, National Baseball Library, Cooperstown, NY.

                                                                                        Frederick Ivor-Campbell

WRIGHT, Taft Shedron (b. August 10, 1911, Tabor City, NC; d. October 22, 1981, Orlando, FL), player and manager, grew up near Lumberton, NC and graduated from Lumberton High School. Wright, who switched from pitcher to the outfield early in his minor league career, played in Charlotte, NC (PiL) in 1933, Atlanta, GA (SL) in 1934, Albany, NY (IL) in 1935, and Chattanooga, TN (SL) in 1936 and 1937.

Wright, who threw right-handed but batted from the left side, made the major leagues in 1938 with the Washington Senators (AL), batting .350 and leading the AL with 13 pinch-hits. After hitting .309 with the Washington Senators in 1939, he was traded that December to the Chicago White Sox (AL). Wright batted .337 in 1940, .322 in 1941, and .333 in 1942 and drove in at least one run in 13 consecutive games in 1941. He spent from 1943 to 1945 in military service and rejoined the Chicago White Sox in 1946. He rarely regained his pre-war form, although batting .324 in 1947. He completed his major league career in 1949 with the Philadelphia Athletics (AL). It was joked that the roly-poly 5-foot 10-inch, 180-pounder, who did not look like a baseball player, had his uniforms made by a tent-maker. The line-drive hitter compiled a .311 lifetime major league batting average and twice drove in more than 90 runs, clouting only 38 HR among his 1,115 hits.

Wright and his wife, Mary, had three children, Richard, Taft, Jr., and Sherry. He managed Ottawa, Canada (IL) in 1954, Amarillo, TX (WTNML) in 1955, and Orlando, FL (FSL) in 1956, batting .353 at age 45. Wright was inducted into the North Carolina Sports Hall of Fame in 1992.

BIBLIOGRAPHY: Clifford Bloodgood, "He Drives in Runs for Washington," *BD* 64 (January 1940), pp. 367–368; Taft Wright file, National Baseball Library, Cooperstown, NY; Shirley Povich, *The Washington Senators* (New York, 1954); Morris Bealle, *The Washington Senators* (Washington, DC, 1947); Warren Brown, *The Chicago White Sox* (New York, 1952); Richard Lindberg, *Sox* (New York, 1984); Jerome C. Romanowski, *The Mackmen* (Upper Darby, PA, 1978).

                                                                                                Jim L. Sumner

WRIGHT, William Henry "Harry." See George Wright.

WRIGLEY, Philip Knight "Phil" (b. December 5, 1894, Chicago, IL; d. April 12, 1977, Elkhart, WI), executive, was the longest active representative of a once flourishing but long anachronistic baseball practice, the family-owned team. He succeeded his father, William Wrigley, who founded a fortune on chewing gum and owned the Chicago Cubs (NL). Wrigley graduated from Phillips Academy in Andover, MA in 1914 and served at Great Lakes Naval Station in World War I. He married Helen Blanche Atwater on March 26, 1918 and had two daughters and one son, William, who succeeded Philip as Cubs owner on the latter's death. In 1981, William ended the 60-year Wrigley ownership by selling the Cubs to the Chicago Tribune Corporation.

Wrigley, who had varied interests and a complex personality, possessed remarkable mechanical aptitude. Innovative skill and business acumen enabled him to expand the chewing gum business into a worldwide enterprise. He served on or headed many boards, civic enterprises, and philanthropic organizations and as NL vice-president from 1947 to 1956. In contrast to his gregarious father, Wrigley preferred privacy, a trait that many interpreted as indifference to baseball.

Wrigley's lengthy supervision of the Chicago Cubs spanned from his father's death in 1932 until his own death. His Cubs won NL pennants in 1932, 1935, 1938, and 1945, but captured no World Series. During his last 32 years, the Cubs produced no NL pennant winners. In later life, Wrigley lost the deep commitment to the team's fortunes that success in sports requires. His propensity for innovation proved fitful, diffuse, and impractical when applied to baseball. He inappropriately used the notorious college of coaches to replace the time-proved manager and employed a retired naval athletic director without baseball experience as superintendent. And yet, decades after all other teams had converted to night games, his Cubs continued to play only day baseball. The latter quaint practice and other fan-oriented gestures helped create an amazingly loyal fandom in the face of adversity, but did nothing to make the Cubs a contender. With the advent of corporation ownership, huge television contracts, and player free agency, the Wrigley family ownership could not cope with the many special interests comprising billion dollar baseball. Regrettably, Wrigley left a team that had not won in 32 years.

BIBLIOGRAPHY: Phil Wrigley file, National Baseball Library, Cooperstown, NY; Warren Brown, *The Chicago Cubs* (New York, 1946); Jim Enright, *Chicago Cubs* (New York, 1975); Chicago *Sun-Times*, April 12, 1977; Edwin Darby, *The Fortune Builders* (New York, 1986); Leo Durocher, *Nice Guys Finish Last* (New York, 1975); Jim Langford, *The Game Is Never Over* (South Bend, IN, 1980); *TSN*, February 4, 1932, January 12, 1956, February 12, 1966, July 4, 1981; Bill Veeck with Ed Linn, *Veeck—As in Wreck* (New York, 1962); *WWWA*, 7 (1977–1981), p. 630.

Lowell L. Blaisdell

WYATT, John Whitlow "Whit" (b. September 27, 1907, Kensington, GA; d. July 16, 1998, Carrollton, GA), player, coach, and manager, was the son of James Colquit Wyatt, a railroad engineer, and Leila (Whitlow) Wyatt and was a right-handed pitcher known for his outstanding slider. His professional baseball career began in 1928 with Evansville, IN (3IL). After Wyatt compiled a 22–6 win–loss record there in 1929, the Detroit Tigers (AL) purchased him that September. He spent 1930 with the Detroit Tigers and was optioned to Beaumont, TX (TL) in 1931. After being recalled in 1932, he pitched for the Detroit Tigers until May 1933. The Detroit Tigers then traded Wyatt to the Chicago White Sox (AL). He remained with the Chicago White Sox until the spring of 1936, when he was acquired by Kansas City, MO (AA). The Cleveland Indians (AL) purchased Wyatt, but he enjoyed little success there in 1937 and was sent to Milwaukee, WI (AA) in 1938. Wyatt's 23–7 record in 1938 there prompted the Brooklyn Dodgers (NL) to purchase his contract. He became the mainstay of the Brooklyn pitching staff from 1939 until dropping to a 2–6 win–loss record in 1944. In March 1945, the Brooklyn Dodgers sold him to the Philadelphia Blue Jays (NL). After Wyatt's 0–7 record that year, Philadelphia unconditionally released him in February 1946.

In 16 major league seasons, Wyatt appeared in 360 games, won 106 and lost 95 with 872 strikeouts and 642 walks in 1,761 innings, and compiled a 3.79 ERA. His best year came in 1941, when he posted a 22–10 record to lead the NL in victories. He was selected to the NL All-Star teams from 1939 through 1942, but participated only in the 1940 and 1941 games. He pitched two innings in each, allowing only one hit. Wyatt started for Brooklyn against the New York Yankees in the 1941 World Series, compiling a 2.50 ERA, winning the second game, and losing the fifth contest. Wyatt encountered mediocre success as a pitcher until learning to control a sharp-breaking slider and to pitch inside and high to batters. His brushback pitches as a Brooklyn Dodger led to beanball battles with the Boston Braves and Chicago Cubs.

Wyatt remained out of organized baseball from 1946 until 1950, when the Atlanta, GA Crackers (SA) signed him as a coach. Wyatt remained there as a coach through 1953 and pitched in one game in 1951. Atlanta named him manager in 1954, when the Crackers won the SA pennant, SA playoff championship, and Dixie Series against the TL winner. Wyatt coached for the Philadelphia Phillies (NL) from 1955 through 1957 and Milwaukee Braves (NL) from 1958 to 1965. He remained with the Braves when they moved to Atlanta in 1966 and retired as a coach after the 1967 season.

Wyatt, who married Edna Carle White on February 4, 1933, had one son and one daughter. He lived on his farm in Buchanan, GA, and enjoyed hunting.

BIBLIOGRAPHY: Whitlow Wyatt file, National Baseball Library, Cooperstown, NY; Furman Bisher, *Miracle in Atlanta* (Cleveland, OH, 1966); Frank Graham, *The Brooklyn Dodgers* (New York, 1945); Paul Green, "An Interview with Whitlow Wyatt," *SCD* 13 (March 28, 1986), pp. 172–220; Thomas Liley, "Whit Wyatt—The Dodgers' 1941 Ace," *TNP* 11 (1992), pp. 46–47; Peter Golenbock, *Bums* (New York, 1984);

Robert L. Tiemann, *Dodger Classics* (St. Louis, MO, 1983); Fred Smith, *995 Tigers* (Detroit, MI, 1981); Warren Brown, *The Chicago White Sox* (New York, 1952); Richard Goldstein, *Superstars and Screwballs* (New York, 1991); William F. McNeil, *The Dodgers Encyclopedia* (Champaign, IL, 1997); Stanley Cohen, *Dodgers! The First 100 Years* (New York, 1990); Tommy Holmes, *The Dodgers* (New York, 1975); *TSN Official Baseball Register*, 1966.

Ralph S. Graber

WYNN, Early, Jr. "Gus" (b. January 6, 1920, Hartford, AL; d. April 9, 1999, Venice, FL), player, manager, coach, scout, and sportscaster, grew up in Hartford, AL and attended Geneva County High School, where he excelled in football and baseball. His father, Early, Sr., worked as an auto mechanic. At age 16, Wynn signed as a pitcher with the Washington Senators (AL). Although appearing in three games for the Washington Senators in 1939, Wynn spent from 1937 to 1941 hurling for Sanford, FL (FSL), Charlotte, NC (PiL), and Springfield, MA (EL). The 6-foot, 190-pound right-hander returned to Washington late in 1941 and pitched through 1948 for the Senators, except for spending 1945 in the U.S. Army.

After enjoying only average success with Washington, Wynn was traded to the Cleveland Indians (AL) in December 1948. Cleveland coach Mel Harder* taught him the finer points of pitching. Wynn became one of the game's toughest competitors. His brushback pitch was feared by everyone. He won at least 20 games four times for the Indians, leading Cleveland to the AL pennant in 1954. In December 1957, Wynn was traded to the Chicago White Sox (AL). At age 39, he won an AL-leading 22 games for the pennant-winning 1959 White Sox and captured the Cy Young Award. Wynn in 1962 triumphed in seven games, one victory short of the coveted 300 mark. Chicago released Wynn in November 1962. The Cleveland Indians signed him in June 1963. On July 13, 1963, he became the 14th pitcher in major league history to win 300 or more games in recording his last victory.

Wynn, one of a few players whose major league career spanned four decades, established the AL record for most years pitched (23). He led the AL in strikeouts twice (1957–1958), innings pitched three times (1951, 1954, 1959), victories twice (1954, 1959), shutouts once (1960), and ERA once (1950) and ranks high on the all-time major league lists in several departments. In 691 games, he started 612 contests (15th), completed 290, won 300 (19th), and lost 244 (13th). Wynn hurled 4,564 innings (19th), allowing 2,037 runs, 4,291 hits, and 1,775 bases on balls (4th). With a lifetime 3.54 ERA, he struck out 2,334 batters (31st), won at least 20 games five times, and pitched 49 shutouts (21st). In World Series competition, Wynn triumphed in one game and lost two. He pitched in seven All-Star games, earning the victory for the AL in 1958. As a batter, Wynn slugged 17 HR and made 365 career base hits.

Wynn served as a pitching coach for the Cleveland Indians from 1964 to

1966 and Minnesota Twins (AL) from 1967 to 1969. He managed Evansville, IN (AA) in 1970, Wisconsin Rapids, WI (ML) in 1971, and Orlando, FL (FSL) in 1972 and broadcast for the Toronto Blue Jays (AL) in 1977 and later for the Chicago White Sox. Wynn also co-owned a Florida construction company and restaurant–bowling alley. In 1939 he married Mabel Allman, who was killed two years later in an automobile accident. They had one son, Joe Early. Wynn married Lorraine Follin in September 1944 and has a daughter, Shirley. In 1972 he was elected to the National Baseball Hall of Fame.

BIBLIOGRAPHY: Early Wynn, Jr. file, National Baseball Library, Cooperstown, NY; Shirley Povich, *The Washington Senators* (New York, 1954); John Phillips, *Winners* (Cabin John, MD, 1987); Morris Eckhouse, *Day-by-Day in Cleveland Indians History* (New York, 1983); Bob Feller with Bill Gilbert, *Now Pitching Bob Feller* (New York, 1990); Bruce Dudley, *Bittersweet Season* (Annapolis, MD, 1995); John Thorn et al., *Total Indians* (New York, 1996); Craig Carter, ed., *TSN Daguerreotypes*, 8th ed. (St. Louis, MO, 1990); Lowell Reidenbaugh, *Baseball's Hall of Fame-Cooperstown* (New York, 1993); Richard Lindberg, *Who's on Third?* (South Bend, IN, 1983); Richard Lindberg, *Sox* (New York, 1984); David Condon, *The Go-Go Chicago White Sox* (New York, 1960); Bob Vanderberg, *Sox: From Lane and Fain to Zisk and Fisk* (Chicago, IL, 1982); *TSN*, July 25, 1981, pp. 30–31; *TSN Official Baseball Record Book, 1997*.

John L. Evers

WYNN, James Sherman "Jimmie," "The Toy Cannon" (b. March 12, 1942, Hamilton, OH), player, overcame his small 5-foot 9-inch, 160-pound frame to become a surprising right-handed power hitter. In his 15-year major league career, Wynn clouted 291 HR and hit a career high 37 HR for the Houston Astros (NL) in 1967. This remarkable feat followed the nadir of Wynn's career. On August 1, 1966, he had crashed into an outfield wall, smashing his left elbow and wrist. The Astros originally feared that the injury would end his career, but "The Toy Cannon" recovered impressively.

Wynn, best known as a member of the Houston Colt 45s and Houston Astros (NL) from 1963 to 1973, performed in the minor leagues at Tampa, FL (FSL) in 1962 and San Antonio, TX (TL) in the first half of 1963. Although playing some infield in the minor leagues and in his first major league season, Wynn soon established himself as the starting center fielder for the Houston Colt 45s.

After a poor season with the Houston Astros in 1973, Wynn was traded that December to the Los Angeles Dodgers (NL) for Claude Osteen* and Dave Culpepper. Wynn hit .271 with 32 HR, earning 1974 *TSN* NL Comeback Player of the Year honors. Wynn became a crowd favorite of the Los Angeles fans in the outfield pavilion at Dodger Stadium. In November 1975, the Dodgers traded the popular Wynn, Lee Lacy, Tom Paciorek, and Jerry Royster to the Atlanta Braves (NL) for Dusty Baker* and Ed Goodson. His last major league clubs included the Atlanta Braves in 1976, New York Yankees (AL) in 1977, and Milwaukee Brewers (AL) in 1977.

On June 15, 1967 and May 11, 1974, Wynn hit three HR in single games against the San Francisco Giants and San Diego Padres. A feared, patient hitter, Wynn tied the NL record for walks with 148 in 1969. Ironically, Wynn also led the NL in strikeouts with 137 in 1967. Wynn, an NL All-Star in 1967, 1974, and 1975, batted .500 in six at-bats and hit a HR in the 1975 classic. His only postseason play came with the 1974 Dodgers in the NL Championship Series and World Series.

Wynn attended Central State College in Wilberforce, OH and enjoys jazz music. Wynn, along with future major league stars Rusty Staub,* Joe Morgan,* and Jerry Grote, appeared in the all-rookie lineup that the Colt 45s fielded on September 27, 1963. Wynn, a complete ballplayer, demonstrated power, compiled a respectable .250 career batting average, stole 225 bases, and drove in 964 runs. Defensively, he led NL outfielders in putouts in 1965 and 1967, paced the NL in double plays in 1968, and shared the double-play lead in 1971. Wynn twice batted in more than 100 runs, recording 107 runs in 1967 and 108 in 1974. He married Ruth Mixon on December 20, 1963.

BIBLIOGRAPHY: James Wynn file, National Baseball Library, Cooperstown, NY; *The Baseball Encyclopedia*, 10th ed. (New York, 1996); Joe Hoppell and Craig Carter, eds., *TSN Baseball Trivia Book* (St. Louis, MO, 1976); *TSN Baseball Register, 1978*; Paul Burka, "Houston Astros," *TM* (December 1980), pp. 156–161, 264–271; Peter C. Bjarkman, ed., *Encyclopedia of Major League Baseball Team Histories: National League* (Westport, CT, 1991); William F. McNeil, *The Dodgers Encyclopedia* (Champaign, IL, 1997); Tommy Holmes, *The Dodgers* (New York, 1975); Donald Honig, *Dodgers* (New York, 1986); Richard Whittingham, *An Illustrated History of the Los Angeles Dodgers* (New York, 1982); "Wynn of the Losers," *Time* 90 (July 7, 1967), p. 64; "Yanks Buy Wynn, Right-Handed Slugger," *NYT*, December 1, 1975, pp. B9, B11.

Jack P. Lipton and Susan M. Lipton

Y

YASTRZEMSKI, Carl Michael "Yaz" (b. August 22, 1939, Southampton, NY), player and coach, was one of the dominant AL hitters from 1961 until retiring in 1983. He followed Ted Williams* as left fielder for the Boston Red Sox (AL) and amassed the sixth highest hit total (3,419) in major league history. The son of Carl Yastrzemski and Hattie Yastrzemski, he grew up in a farm environment and helped his father, a semiprofessional baseball player and youth athletic coach. A devout Roman Catholic, Yastrzemski served as an altar boy and as a student body leader (twice class president) at Bridgehampton, NY High School. An all-around athlete, he set a Long Island high school record in basketball by scoring 628 points in 1957. He caught, pitched, and played outfield in baseball and impressed major league scouts by batting .506 one season.

After his 1957 graduation from Bridgehampton High School, Yastrzemski attended the University of Notre Dame for one year on a baseball scholarship. He tried out with the New York Yankees (AL), but signed a contract with the Boston Red Sox for a $108,000 bonus. After batting .377 with Raleigh, NC (CrL) in 1959 and .339 for Minneapolis, MN (AA) in 1960, he joined the Red Sox when Ted Williams retired. Under pressure from the inevitable comparison with Williams (Williams was a natural pull hitter, while Yastrzemski batted to all fields), he started slowly with a .266 batting average, only 11 HR, and 80 RBI his rookie year. During the next five seasons, he led the AL in hitting once (.321 in 1963) and averaged .299 at the plate with 84 HR and 381 RBI for a regular second division finisher.

After Dick Williams* was named manager in 1967, Yastrzemski enjoyed an extraordinary season and led the Red Sox to the AL pennant. In 1967, he won the AL Triple Crown with a .326 batting average, 121 RBI, and 44 HR (tied with Harmon Killebrew*) and led the AL in hits (189), total bases (360), and runs scored (112). In the final two decisive regular season games against the Minnesota Twins, he made seven hits in eight at-bats. In the World Series against the St. Louis Cardinals, he batted .400 and fielded brilliantly in the Red Sox' seven-game losing effort. He was named the AL MVP, *SI*'s Sportsman of 1967, and AP Male Athlete of the Year. He repeated as batting leader in 1968 with a .301 mark, the lowest such figure in major league history. Yastrzemski achieved a career-high .329 batting average in 1970 and 40 HR in both 1969 and 1970. During his 23 major league seasons, Yastrzemski's production varied considerably, with six .300 or better seasons and nine seasons with .270 or less, HR totals ranging from 44 to 7, and RBI figures varying from 121 to 50.

In the Red Sox pennant year of 1975, Yastrzemski batted .455 in the team's stretch drive and compiled a .310 mark against the victorious Cincinnati Reds in the World Series. The seven-time Gold Glove winner played errorless outfield for 140 games in 1977. Defensively, he made 10,437 putouts, 775 assists, and 135 errors in 23 seasons. Yastrzemski batted .294 in 14 All-Star games (1963, 1967–1972, 1974–1977, 1979, 1982–1983). At 6 feet tall and 180 pounds, he ranked among the outstanding throwers and most feared DH in modern AL history. Yastrzemski led the AL five times in on-base percentage, three times in batting average, doubles, runs scored, and slugging percentage, twice in hits and walks, and once in HR and RBI. His overall production put him among the all-time leaders in several categories. Yastrzemski ranked second in games played (3,308), third in at-bats (11,988), fourth in walks (1,845), sixth in hits (3,419), seventh in doubles (646), and eleventh in RBI (1,844). The former Highland Beach, FL resident married Carol Ann Casper in January 1960, has two daughters, Mary and Ann, and one son, Mike, and graduated from Merrimack College in 1966. Mike was a DH in the Chicago White Sox (AL) farm system. Yastrzemski, who serves as a hitting instructor for the Boston Red Sox, was elected to the National Baseball Hall of Fame in 1989.

BIBLIOGRAPHY: David Falkner, "For Yastrzemski, the Fire Still Burns" *NYT Biographical Service* 17 (October 1986), pp. 1262–1263; John Benson et al., *Baseball's Top 100* (Wilton, CT, 1997); *CB* (1968), pp. 445–447; Peter Golenbock, *Fenway* (New York, 1992); Jack Lautier, *Fenway Voices* (Camden, ME, 1990); Bill McSweeney, *The Impossible Dream* (New York, 1968); Dan Shaughnessy, *The Curse of the Bambino* (New York, 1990); Carl Yastrzemski file, National Baseball Library, Cooperstown, NY; Robert Redmount, *The Red Sox Encyclopedia* (Champaign, IL, 1998); Ken Coleman and Dan Valenti, *The Impossible Dream Remembered* (Lexington, MA, 1987); Peter Gammons, *Beyond the Sixth Game* (Boston, MA, 1985); Howard Liss, *The Boston Red Sox* (New York, 1982); Carl Yastrzemski with Al Hirshberg, *Yaz* (New York, 1968); *The Lincoln Library of Sports Champions*, vol. 14 (Columbus, OH, 1978); *The Baseball Encyclopedia*, 10th ed. (New York, 1996); Carl Yastrzemski and Gerald Eskenazi, *Yaz, Baseball, the Wall, and Me* (New York, 1990).

Leonard H. Frey

YAWKEY, Thomas Austin "Tom" (b. Thomas Austin, February 21, 1903, Detroit, MI; d. July 9, 1976, Boston, MA), owner and sportsman, was the son of Thomas J. Austin and Augusta L. Austin and the adopted son of uncle William H. Yawkey, who owned the Detroit Tigers (AL) and was a millionaire from timber and mining investments. Yawkey, who was educated in private academies and at Yale University, inherited a vast family fortune as a teenager and built its value to approximately $200 million at his death. His first marriage to Elsie Sparrow, in which they adopted a daughter, Julie, ended in divorce. In December 1944, he married Jean Hollander.

Yawkey purchased the struggling Boston Red Sox (AL) in 1933 and for the next 44 years spent heavily to build winning teams. During the depressed 1930s, his wealth enabled the Red Sox to secure star players from poorer teams. Yawkey acquired Lefty Grove* and Jimmie Foxx* from the Philadelphia Athletics (AL) and shortstop Joe Cronin for $250,000 from the Washington Senators (AL). His large investments in the Boston farm system produced some exceptional players, including Ted Williams,* Carl Yastrzemski,* and Jim Rice.* Despite these efforts, Boston did not keep pace with the arch-rival New York Yankees. The Red Sox won only three AL pennants (1946, 1967, 1975) and lost each World Series in seven games. The popular owner revived fan interest in the Red Sox and increased attendance at Fenway Park, which he rebuilt in 1934.

Critics claimed that Yawkey overpaid and pampered his players, diminishing his team's desire to win. A paternalistic employer, he paid high salaries even to mediocre players and exhibited personal interest in their welfare. His generosity also extended to numerous charities. Soon after World War II, Yawkey cooperated with attempts to resist racial integration of the major leagues. Boston did not add a black player to its roster until 1959, being the last major league team to integrate.

An avid sportsman and conservationist, he established the Tom Yawkey Wildlife Center in coastal South Carolina to protect migrating birds. He saved his deepest affection for the Red Sox, which he owned a record 44 years and which remained one of the last individually owned major league franchises. Always protective of his privacy, Yawkey proved a strong voice in major league councils and served as AL vice-president from 1956 to 1973. He was elected to the National Baseball Hall of Fame in 1980.

BIBLIOGRAPHY: Peter Golenbock, *Fenway* (New York, 1992); David Halberstam, *Summer of '49* (New York, 1989); Al Hirshberg, *What's the Matter with the Red Sox?* (New York, 1973); Robert Redmount, *The Red Sox Encyclopedia* (Champaign, IL, 1998); Howard Liss, *The Boston Red Sox* (New York, 1982); Ken Coleman and Dan Valenti, *The Impossible Dream Remembered* (Lexington, MA, 1987); Bill McSweeney, *The Impossible Dream* (New York, 1968); Al Hirshberg, "The Sad Case of the Red Sox," *SEP* 232 (May 21, 1960), pp. 38–39, 87–88; James S. Kunen, "The Man with the Best Job in Boston," *BoM* (September 1975), pp. 60–63, 97–102; Frederick G.

Lieb, *The Boston Red Sox* (New York, 1947); *NYT*, July 10, 1976; *TSN*, July 24, 1976; Jules Tygiel, *Baseball's Great Experiment* (New York, 1983).

Joseph E. King

YOKELY, Laymon Samuel "Norman," "Cornerpocket," "Mysterious Shadow" (b. May 30, 1906, Winston-Salem, NC; d. January 1976, Baltimore, MD), player, began his professional baseball career with the Baltimore Black Sox (ECL) in 1926 after pitching for the Livingstone College baseball team in Salisbury, NC. Yokely continued his education during the off-season. The Baltimore Black Sox' pitching ace from 1926 to 1932 hurled six no-hitters. The fastballer's best season came in 1929, when his 17 victories sparked the Baltimore Black Sox to the ANL pennant.

Yokely's popularity made him a matinee idol, but a sore arm caused from overwork shortened his career. Rumors abounded that he was "washed up." Despite having lost his effectiveness, Yokely attempted a comeback. Manager Dick Lundy* recycled the right-hander in 1932. The Baltimore Black Sox led the EWL when it broke up in mid-season.

Yokely's modest comeback continued in a supportive role with the 1934 NNL champion Philadelphia Stars. He pitched with the Philadelphia Stars for the remainder of the decade except for a short stint with the Washington Black Senators (NNL) in 1938. In 1939, Yokely boasted 25 wins with the Stars and 15 triumphs with the semipro Philadelphia Bacharach Giants.

The 6-foot 2-inch, 210 pounder finished his baseball career with the Edgewater Giants from 1940 to 1943 and the World War II-depleted Baltimore Elite Giants (NNL) in 1944. He operated his own Baltimore team, Yokely's All-Stars, from 1945 to 1959, when he opened Yokely's Shine Parlor. National Baseball Hall-of-Famer Leon Day* idolized Yokely.

BIBLIOGRAPHY: *Afro-American*, 1926–1944; Chicago (IL) *Defender*, 1926–1944; Robert W. Peterson, *Only the Ball Was White* (Englewood Cliffs, NJ, 1970); Philadelphia (PA) *Tribune*, 1926–1944; Pittsburgh (PA) *Courier*, 1926–1944; James A. Riley, *The All-Time All-Stars of Black Baseball* (Cocoa, FL, 1983); James A. Riley, *The Biographical Encyclopedia of the Negro Baseball Leagues* (New York, 1994); James A. Riley, interviews with former Negro League players, James A. Riley Collection, Canton, GA.

James A. Riley

YORK, Preston Rudolph "Rudy," "Chief" (b. August 17, 1913, Ragland, AL; d. February 5, 1970, Rome, GA), player, coach, and manager, won acclaim for setting the one-month major league record of 18 HR in August 1937. York, who was one-eighth Cherokee Indian and part Irish, grew up in Carterville, GA, where he married Violet Dupree in June 1932 and lived until his death. He dropped out of school and began playing on semiprofessional and company baseball teams in Atco, GA. In 1933, the Detroit Tigers (AL) signed him. The muscular, 6-foot 1-inch, 210-pound right-hander quickly proved a dominant hitter. His outstanding minor league career from 1933 to 1936 included stops at Knoxville, TN (SA), Shreveport, LA (EDL), Beaumont, TX (TL), Ft. Worth, TX (TL), and Milwaukee, WI (AA). York received MVP awards in the TL in 1935 and AA in 1936.

Managers always experienced problems finding a position for York. Sportswriter Red Smith (OS) commented, "No matter where he was stationed in the field, Rudy York always played the same position. He played bat. He was slow, unskilled, awkward, sincere, tireless, and stronger than dirt." York started as a catcher in his rookie season with the Detroit Tigers (AL) in 1937, which was perhaps his best major league campaign. He drove in 93 runs with his first 90 hits, producing 103 RBI in 104 games. He clouted 18 HR in August 1937, the major league record for a single month until Sammy Sosa* belted 20 in June 1998. For the season, York homered a career-best 35 times.

York performed nine seasons with the Detroit Tigers from 1937 to 1945, averaging 27 HR and 104 RBI per campaign. Detroit attempted unsuccessfully to make him an outfielder and then shifted him to first base in 1940. The Tigers captured the AL pennant that season, as York contributed a personal high 134 RBI, batted .316, and hit 33 HR. With Detroit, he started in three All-Star games (1941–1943), appeared in two other All-Star games (1938, 1944), and participated in the World Series against the Cincinnati Reds in 1940 and the Chicago Cubs in 1945. In 1943, he led the AL with 34 HR and 118 RBI and was named All-AL first baseman. After being traded to the Boston Red Sox (AL) in January 1946, he contributed 119 RBI to help the club take its first pennant since 1918. Upon completing his major league career with the Chicago White Sox (AL) in 1947, he had compiled 277 career HR, 1,152 RBI, and a .275 batting average.

Despite York's hitting ability, problems plagued the big slugger. York's fielding difficulties caused disfavor with Detroit followers, who mercilessly booed him. He admitted to a drinking problem, but claimed that his reputation for imbibing was blown "all out of proportion." Despite his major league salary, he complained toward the end of his life that he "had nothing to show for it except a brick bungalow."

York returned to Carterville, GA and worked as a house painter and forest-fire fighter. York played briefly in the minor leagues with Griffin, GA (GFL), Union City, TN (KL), Youngstown, OH (MSL), Oil City, PA (MSL), and New Castle, PA (MSL) through 1951. He returned to organized baseball in 1957 as manager of North Platte, NE (NeSL), coached one year with Memphis, TN (SA), and coached for the Boston Red Sox (AL) from 1959 through 1962, managing one loss in 1959. Lung cancer caused his death.

BIBLIOGRAPHY: Robert Redmount, *The Red Sox Encyclopedia* (Champaign, IL, 1998); Dan Shaughnessy, *The Curse of the Bambino* (New York, 1990); Howard Liss, *The Boston Red Sox* (New York, 1982); Frederick G. Lieb, *The Boston Red Sox* (New York, 1947); Richard Bak, *A Place for Summer* (Detroit, MI, 1998); William M. Anderson,

The Detroit Tigers (South Bend, IN, 1996); Rudy York file, National Baseball Library, Cooperstown, NY; Frederick G. Lieb, *The Detroit Tigers* (New York, 1946); Joe Falls, *Detroit Tigers* (New York, 1975); Fred Smith, *995 Tigers* (Detroit, MI, 1981); Furman Bisher, "The Cherokee Has No Regrets," *BD* 13 (July 1954), pp. 47–51; Furman Bisher, "Rudy York's Letter to His Son," *BD* 29 (June 1970), pp. 75–79; Arthur Daley, "The Saga of First Sackers from Cap Anson to Rudy York," *BM* 73 (June 1944), pp. 237–239; Tom Hufford, "Rudy York, the Big Gun of August," *BRJ* 4 (1975), pp. 12–15; Ira L. Smith, *Baseball's Famous First Basemen* (New York, 1956); Lyall Smith, "How York Used Batting Science for Homer Mark," *BD* 21 (July 1962), pp. 75–77; George Sullivan and David Cataneo, *Detroit Tigers* (New York, 1985); John C. Hawkins, *This Date in Detroit Tigers History* (Briarcliff Manor, NY, 1981); Joe Falls, *The Detroit Tigers: An Illustrated History* (New York, 1989).

William E. Akin

YOST, Edward Fred Joseph "Eddie," "The Walking Man" (b. October 13, 1926, Brooklyn, NY), player and coach, is the son of Fred Yost and Mary Yost. Nicknamed "Eddie" and "The Walking Man," he earned bachelor's and master's degrees from New York University (NYU). In September 1944, Yost joined the Washington Senators (AL) before his 18th birthday. He had no minor league experience and had not played at NYU, but was spotted playing semiprofessional baseball in New Jersey by Washington Senators' scout Joe Cambria. After spending all of 1945 and most of 1946 in the U.S. Coast Guard, Yost joined the Washington Senators for eight games in September 1946.

Cecil Travis,* the Washington Senators' star third baseman, could not regain his former ability the next season because of ailing feet. Yost, therefore, was installed at third base and remained a fixture there through 1958, although occasionally playing other infield positions and the outfield. The Washington Senators traded Yost in December 1958 to the Detroit Tigers (AL), where he played in 1959 and 1960. In November 1960, the Los Angeles Angels (AL) selected him in the AL expansion draft. Yost completed his career as a player with the Los Angeles Angels in 1961 and 1962.

Known for drawing walks, Yost possessed the patience to look over pitches better than any other contemporary player. Yost ranks 8th on the major league career walk list with 1,614, a significant achievement because he did not possess hitting power or receive many intentional walks. He led the AL batters in walks six times and paced the AL with 36 doubles in 1951 and 115 runs scored in 1959. Although Yost's career batting average came to only .254, his on-base percentage reached .395. He led the AL in on-base percentage with .437 in 1959 and .416 in 1960. His 1,863 hits included 337 doubles, 56 triples, and 139 HR. Defensively, Yost ranks third in most putouts lifetime by a third baseman with 2,356 and started 345 double plays. The durable performer ranks 8th in games played at third base and formerly held the record for most years leading AL third basemen in putouts with eight. He also paced the AL in fielding percentage in 1958 and 1959. The intelligent player and strategist coached for the Washington Senators from 1963 to 1967, New York Mets (NL) from 1968 to 1976, and Boston Red Sox (AL) from 1977 to 1986.

BIBLIOGRAPHY: Gene Karst and Martin J. Jones, Jr., *Who's Who in Professional Baseball* (New Rochelle, NY, 1973); Brent Kelley, "An Interview with 'The Walking Man,'" *SCD* 16 (October 13, 1989), pp. 190–192; Brent P. Kelley, *Baseball Stars of the 1950s* (Jefferson, NC, 1993); Shirley Povich, *The Washington Senators* (New York, 1954); John Thorn et al., eds., *Total Baseball*, 5th ed. (New York, 1997); *TSN*, October 6, 1954; Eddie Yost file, National Baseball Library, Cooperstown, NY; Morris Bealle, *The Washington Senators* (Washington, DC, 1947); Joe Falls, *Detroit Tigers* (New York, 1975); Fred Smith, *995 Tigers* (Detroit, MI, 1981); William M. Anderson, *The Detroit Tigers* (South Bend, IN, 1996); George Sullivan and David Cataneo, *Detroit Tigers* (New York, 1985); Ross Newhan, *The California Angels* (New York, 1982).

Ralph S. Graber

YOUNG, Denton True "Cy" (b. March 29, 1867, Gilmore, OH; d. November 4, 1955, Newcomerstown, OH), player and manager, was the son of farmer McKenzie Young and Nancy Mot (Miller) Young. He grew up on a Gilmore, OH farm and married neighboring farm daughter Robba Miller in November 1892. They had no children. Young played third base in 1889 for the Tuscarawas County baseball team. In 1890, he began his professional baseball career with Canton, OH (TSL) and compiled a 15–15 win–loss mark as a pitcher. The same season, he signed with the Cleveland Spiders (NL) for $300 and became the squad's only winning hurler with a 9–7 mark. Cleveland raised his salary to $1,400 for the 1891 season. Young, who worked vigorously on the farm when not playing baseball, credited much of his athletic success to his excellent physical condition. He demonstrated remarkable concentration on hitters and was admired as a gentleman by teammates, opponents, umpires, and fans.

With the Cleveland Spiders from 1890 to 1898, Young compiled a 241–135 mark and hurled a September 18, 1897 no-hitter against the Cincinnati Reds. For the St. Louis Cardinals (NL) in 1899 and 1900, he finished with a 45–35 record and saw his annual salary increased to $2,400. After the 1900 season, president Ban Johnson* persuaded him to jump to the Boston Pilgrims of the new AL with a $3,000 salary. Young won 192 of 304 decisions for the Boston Pilgrims–Red Sox from 1901 to 1908 and pitched a perfect game on May 5, 1904 against the Philadelphia Athletics. At age 41, he hurled a no-hitter on June 30, 1908 against the New York Highlanders. A member of championship Boston Pilgrims squads in 1903 and 1904, he won two of three decisions in the first modern World Series (1903) to help the Boston Pilgrims defeat the Pittsburgh Pirates, five games to three. In early 1907, Young temporarily managed the Boston Red Sox to a 3–3 mark.

During his final season with the Red Sox, the AL players and Boston fans honored Young in August 1908 and presented him with a large silver cup, money, and other gifts. Young on September 15 gave his Boston teammates a complimentary dinner at Putnam's Hotel and had each course named for one of the athletes. Young already had won a record 19 games at the Huntington Avenue Grounds in 1901 and had pitched 45.2 consecutive scoreless innings in 1904. No other Red Sox pitcher has recorded more career total innings, games started, complete games, victories, strikeouts, and shutouts with the club. In February 1909, the Cleveland Naps (AL) purchased him for $12,500. After compiling a 29–29 record for Cleveland from 1909 to July 1911, Young finished his career in 1911 with a 4–5 mark for the Boston Rustlers (NL) and returned to his Peoli, OH farm.

With five clubs spanning 22 years, Young holds the major league records for most wins (511), complete games (749), and innings pitched (7,356); ranks 9th in games appeared in (906) and in shutouts (78); and registered a strikeout–walk ratio of .697 percent to .303 percent. The right-hander started 815 games, struck out 2,803 batters, lost 316 games, and compiled a 2.63 ERA. Young led the NL in fewest walks per nine-inning game in 1890 and from 1893 to 1900. He achieved the same honor seven times, including the 1903–1907 seasons in the AL. Young reached the 20-game victory plateau 15 seasons, 25 games 11 times, and 30 games five times (1892–1893, 1895, 1901–1902). Young paced his league in shutouts seven times; in most wins five times; in complete games three times; in win–loss percentage, ERA, innings pitched, and strikeouts twice; and in games, losses, games started, and hits surrendered once.

Until his final years, Young remained strong and active on his Peoli, OH farm. The much-honored hurler was elected to the National Baseball Hall of Fame in 1937. Since his death, the major leagues have given the Cy Young Award annually to the major league's top hurler. In 1982, Boston fans voted him to the first Red Sox "dream team" as right-handed pitcher. The 6-foot 2-inch, 210-pound Young relished facing Rube Waddell* and other outstanding contemporary pitchers and used four effective pitches. Abbott Thayer's painting at Cooperstown shows him in his 1908 Red Stocking blouse, delivering an overhand fastball. The first Boston and AL pitching folk hero, Young became the city's best-liked player since King Kelly,* helped popularize the new AL and became a gracious legend. He made Major League Baseball's All-Century Team.

BIBLIOGRAPHY: Cy Young file, National Baseball Library, Cooperstown, NY; John Benson et al., *Baseball's Top 100* (Wilton, CT, 1997); *Boston Red Sox Media Guide 1998*; Bob Broeg, "Durable Ace Cy Young—A 511 Game Winner," *TSN*, April 17, 1971; Ellery H. Clark, Jr., *Boston Red Sox: 75th Anniversary* (Hicksville, NY, 1975); Ellery H. Clark, Jr., correspondence with Norwood Gibson, Fred Parent, Cy Young, Boston Red Sox Analytical Letter Collection, Ellery H. Clark, Jr., Papers, Annapolis, MD; Ellery H. Clark, Jr. interviews, Lou Criger, June 1928, Cy Young, July 1928, October 1954, George La Chance, June 1929, Kip Selbach, January 1955, Norwood Gibson, June 1955, Fred Parent, July 1965; Ellery H. Clark, Jr., *Red Sox Fever* (Hicksville, NY, 1979); Ellery H. Clark, Jr., *Red Sox Forever* (Hicksville, NY, 1977); *The Baseball Encyclopedia*, 10th ed. (New York, 1996); Paul F. Doherty, "Cy Young's Final Fling," *BRJ* 8 (1979), pp. 6–8; Frederick Ivor-Campbell et al., eds., *Baseball's First Stars* (Cleveland, OH, 1996); Ronald A. Mayer, *Perfect!* (Jefferson, NC, 1991); Alvin Peterjohn, "Cy Young's First Year," *BRJ* 5 (1976), pp. 83–89; J. Thomas Hetrick, *The Misfits!* (Jefferson, NC, 1991); John Phillips, *The Spiders—Who Was Who* (Cabin John, MD, 1991); Frederick G. Lieb, *The St. Louis Cardinals* (New York, 1945); Franklin Lewis, *The Cleveland Indians* (New York, 1949); Bob Broeg, *Redbirds: A Century of Cardinals' Baseball* (St. Louis, MO, 1981); John Thorn et al., eds., *Total Indians* (New York, 1996); Rob Rains, *The St. Louis Cardinals* (New York, 1992); Bob Broeg and Jerry Vickery, *St. Louis Cardinals Encyclopedia* (Grand Rapids, MI, 1998); Frederick G Lieb, *The Boston Red Sox* (New York, 1947); Howard Liss, *The Boston Red Sox* (New York, 1982); Robert Redmount, *The Red Sox Encyclopedia* (Champaign, IL, 1998).

Ellery H. Clark, Jr.

YOUNG, Nicholas Emanuel (b. September 12, 1840, Amsterdam, NY; d. October 31, 1916, Washington, DC), cricket player and baseball executive, was born in Johnson Hall, the colonial estate of Sir William Johnson. He was the son of Almarian T. Young, a descendant of Dutch settlers and wealthy mill owner, and Mary (Miller) Young. After serving in the Union Army during the Civil War, Young became a clerk and auditor in the U.S. Treasury Department. An outstanding cricket player in his youth, he performed for the Olympic Club of Washington and acted as secretary and business manager of the professional National Club. Young married Mary E. Cross of Washington, DC in 1872 and had four children, Robert H., Ford E., Hulbert, and Lee. In March 1871, he organized a meeting of professional baseball clubs. This group formed the first professional league, the NAPBL, and selected Young as the NA secretary. When the NL was formed in 1876, Young became its secretary-treasurer.

In 1885, Young succeeded his friend and Washington colleague A. G. Mills as NL president. Young's selection resulted from a split between club owners and the NL president, who took a hard line in treating the rival UA. The owners, anxious for accommodation, chose Young because he offered no objection to their desires. Young seldom attempted to influence events during his tumultuous years as NL president. Baseball historian David Quentin Voigt characterized Young's tenure thus: "Having neither the authority nor the *charisma* to be a policy-shaper, Young was the perfect figurehead." Since his job depended on the owners, Young tried to avoid disputes. When the NL owners split into two factions after the 1901 season, reformers attempted to replace Young with Albert G. Spalding.* The owners eventually reached a compromise requiring both Spalding and Young to withdraw their candidacies. Young dutifully stepped down and returned to his government job. The well-liked Young, affectionately called "Uncle Nick" in his last years as NL president, served baseball for over 30 years, but provided ineffective leadership. He served on the Mills Commission in 1905 to review and determine the origins of baseball and later attended many Washington Senators (AL) games.

BIBLIOGRAPHY: Nicholas Young file, National Baseball Library, Cooperstown, NY; Lee Allen, *The National League Story* (New York, 1961); Arthur Bartlett, *Baseball and Mr. Spalding* (New York, 1951); Frederick Ivor-Campbell et al., eds., *Baseball's First Stars* (Cleveland, OH, 1996); William J. Ryczek, *Blackguards and Red Stockings* (Jefferson, NC, 1992); David Quentin Voigt, *The League That Failed* (Lanham, MD, 1998); David Pietrusza, *Major Leagues* (Jefferson, NC, 1991); Francis C. Richter, "Recalled by a Missive from 'Uncle Nick' Young," *SL* 13 (February 31, 1906); Harold Seymour, *Baseball: The Early Years* (New York, 1960); David Quentin Voigt, *American Baseball*, vol. 1 (Norman, OK, 1966).

William E. Akin

YOUNGS, Ross Middlebrook "Pep" (b. Royce Middlebrook Youngs, April 10, 1897, Shiner, TX; d. October 22, 1927, San Antonio, TX), player, grew up in the semi-arid plains. At West Texas Military Academy, he starred in football and track and played baseball. Youngs sparkled in the infield for Sherman, TX (WA) in 1916, leading the WA in batting average (.362), hits (195), runs scored (103), and at-bats (539). The New York Giants (NL) purchased him after that season. He played at Rochester, NY (IL) for most of the 1917 campaign learning the outfield, and batted .346 when brought up to the New York Giants at season's end. During eight full years with New York, Youngs invariably ranked among NL leaders in several offensive categories and led the NL in runs scored (121) in 1923 and in doubles (31) in 1919. The confident, husky, 5-foot 8-inch, 162-pound right-hander batted .322 lifetime and became the first player in World Series history to make two hits in a single inning, slashing a double and triple against the New York Yankees in the seventh inning of the third game in 1921. In four consecutive World Series from 1921 through 1924, Youngs appeared in all 26 games and batted .286. A superb throwing arm and above average speed helped offset his often overly enthusiastic style of defensive play. Youngs led the NL in assists three times and errors twice.

Youngs' batting average fell below .300 for the first time in 1925, when the Giants slipped to second place following four consecutive pennants. Called by Giants manager John McGraw* "my greatest outfielder," Youngs tragically was struck down in his prime by Bright's disease. After Youngs' ailment was discovered during spring training in 1926, the Giants hired a full-time nurse to travel with him. Using every physical and emotional resource, Youngs managed a .306 batting average in 95 games and also helped teach 17-year-old Mel Ott* the subtleties of covering the outfield. In 1927, Youngs was bedridden the entire season and saw the Giants fall to fifth place in the standings before succumbing. McGraw hung a picture of Youngs alongside a photograph of Christy Mathewson* behind his desk. In 1,211 career games, Youngs compiled 1,491 hits, 236 doubles, 93 triples, 812 runs, 592 RBI, 153 stolen bases, and a .441 slugging percentage. As baseball still trembled under the suspicions aired in the Chicago Black Sox scandal, claims were made in 1924 that Youngs was taking bribes from New York gambling concerns. His quick, direct denial of these charges, along with his well-respected abilities and overall character, led to his immediate exoneration. In 1972, he was inducted into the National Baseball Hall of Fame.

BIBLIOGRAPHY: Ross Youngs file, National Baseball Library, Cooperstown, NY; Noel Hynd, *The Giants of the Polo Grounds* (New York, 1988); Frank Graham, *The New York Giants* (New York, 1952); Frank Graham, *McGraw of the Giants* (New York, 1944); Charles C. Alexander, *John McGraw* (New York, 1988); Fred Stein and Nick Peters, *Giants Diary* (Berkeley, CA, 1987); Gene Karst and Martin J. Jones, Jr., *Who's Who in Professional Baseball* (New Rochelle, NY, 1973); Craig Carter, ed., *TSN Daguerreotypes*, 8th ed. (St. Louis, MO, 1990); *NYT*, October 23, 1927; *The Baseball Encyclopedia* 10th ed. (New York, 1996); Lowell Reidenbaugh, *Baseball's Hall of Fame-Cooperstown* (New York, 1993); James D. Smith III, "Bowing Out on Top," *TNP* 2 (Fall 1982), pp. 73–81; *TSN*, October 27, 1927.

Alan R. Asnen

YOUNT, Robin R. (b. September 16, 1955, Danville, IL), player, is the son of engineer Philip Yount and Marion Yount and moved when he was a year old to Woodland Hills, CA, where his father became an aerospace engineer with Rocketdyne. His older brother, Larry, pitched briefly with the Houston Astros (NL) in 1971. Yount graduated from Taft High School in Woodlawn, CA and played football and baseball there. After being named City Baseball Player of the Year in 1973, he was selected by the Milwaukee Brewers (AL) in the first round of the free agent draft. The 6-foot, 170-pound, right-handed Yount played one year (1973) in the minor leagues with Newark, NY (NYPL), where he was named All-Star shortstop. Upon joining the Brewers in 1974 at age 18, he became the youngest player in the major leagues and one of the youngest regulars in baseball history. The Brewers employed Yount as starting shortstop from 1974 to 1984, but an injured right shoulder forced him to play the outfield in 1985. Yount underwent surgery in September 1985 and made a fine comeback in 1986. He spent the remainder of his major league career through 1993 as an outfielder with Milwaukee.

In 1982, he was named Major League Player of the Year and AL MVP after leading the Brewers to the AL pennant. Besides batting .331, he paced the AL in hits (210), doubles (46), and slugging percentage (.578). Yount also scored 129 runs, drove in 114 tallies, and hit 29 HR. He batted .414 in the World Series and made 12 hits, 1 HR, and 6 RBI, as the Brewers lost in seven games to the St. Louis Cardinals. He established a World Series record with two four-hit games. Yount made the AL All-Star team in 1980, 1982, and 1983. His second AL MVP Award came in 1989, when he batted

.318 with 195 hits, 21 HR, and 103 RBI. On September 9, 1992, he singled in the bottom of the seventh inning to become the 17th major league player to reach 3,000 hits.

Consistency has characterized Yount's major league career. In 20 major league seasons, Yount batted .285 with 3,142 hits, 583 doubles, 126 triples, 251 HR, 1,632 runs scored, 1,406 RBI, and 271 stolen bases. Yount led AL batters in doubles (49) in 1980 and (46) in 1982, triples (10) in 1983 and (11) in 1988, and slugging average (.578) in 1982. He paced AL shortstops in putouts (290), total chances (831), and double plays (104) in 1976. Yount also led AL shortstops in fielding average (.985) in 1981 and AL outfielders with .997 in 1986 and in assists (489) in 1982. He was named shortstop on *TSN* AL All-Star teams in 1978, 1980, 1982, and 1989, named to *TSN* Silver Slugger team as the best hitting AL shortstop in 1980 and 1982, and AL outfielder in 1989 and chosen on the AL All-Star fielding team in 1982.

Yount signed a lucrative multi-year contract in 1978 after holding out and threatening to join the professional golf tour. He married high school sweetheart Michele Edelstein after the 1977 season and has three children, including daughters Melissa and Amy. He serves as vice president of the MLBPAA. In 1999, he was elected to the National Baseball Hall of Fame.

BIBLIOGRAPHY: *CB Yearbook* (1993), pp. 615–618; Peter Gammons, "Forever a Kid," *SI* 72 (April 30, 1990), pp. 76–80; Robert E. Kelly, *Baseball's Best* (Jefferson, NC, 1988); Robert Grayson, "The Class of '99," *SCD* 25 (December 25, 1998), pp. 80–81; *Milwaukee Brewers 1983 Official Yearbook*; *Milwaukee Brewers 1989 Official Yearbook*; Peter C. Bjarkman, ed., *Encyclopedia of Major League Baseball Team Histories American League* (Westport, CT, 1991); Robin Yount file, National Baseball Library, Cooperstown, NY; Jeff Everson, *This Date in Milwaukee Brewers History* (Appleton, WI, 1987); *Milwaukee Brewers Media Guide, 1975–1993*; *The Baseball Encyclopedia*, 10th ed. (New York, 1996); *TSN Official Baseball Record Book, 1998*; John Benson et al., *Baseball's Top 100* (Wilton, CT, 1997); *TSN Official Baseball's Register, 1994*.

Jack R. Stanton

Z

ZACHARY, Jonathan Thompson Walton "Tom," "Ol' Tom" (b. May 7, 1896, Graham, NC; d. January 24, 1969, Burlington, NC), player, was a left-handed pitcher perhaps best known for surrendering Babe Ruth's* 60th HR on September 30, 1927. The 6-foot 1-inch 187 pounder pitched 19 major league seasons, compiling a record of 186 wins, 191 losses, and a 3.73 ERA. He also won three World Series games without a loss, including a 2–0 mark for the victorious Washington Senators against the New York Giants in the 1924 fall classic.

Zachary attended Guilford College and spent the summer of 1918 in Philadelphia, PA awaiting an overseas assignment with a Red Cross unit. He approached manager Connie Mack* about playing for the Philadelphia Athletics (AL). Mack agreed, but insisted that Zachary should play as Zach Walton. Zachary won both decisions in 1918.

From 1919 to 1926, Zachary pitched for the Washington Senators (AL) under his real name. Later, he hurled for the St. Louis Browns (AL) from 1926 to July 1927, Washington Senators from July 1927 to August 1928, New York Yankees (AL) from August 1928 to May 1930, Boston Braves (NL) from May 1930 to May 1934, and Brooklyn Dodgers (NL) from June 1934 to April 1936 before finishing his major league career in 1936 with the Philadelphia Phillies (NL). Zachary later recalled, "I always said if I ever got stuck in that Baker Bowl it would be time to quit."

Ruth's renowned 60th HR of the 1927 season was hit off Zachary down the right field line. Zachary argued vehemently with umpire Bill Dinneen* to no avail that the ball was foul. When the two rivals met in Yankee Stadium at a 1947 Old-Timers gathering, Ruth remarked to Zachary, "You crooked-arm sonofabitch, are you still claiming that ball was foul?"

Zachary's most remarkable season came in 1929, when he won 12 games without a loss as both a starter and reliever, ironically, for the New York

Yankees. Zachary retired to Graham, NC, where he worked in real estate and land development. He and his wife, Etta, had two children, Sally and Tom, Jr.

BIBLIOGRAPHY: Frank Graham, *The Brooklyn Dodgers* (New York, 1945); Robert S. Fuchs and Wayne Soini, *Judge Fuchs and the Boston Braves, 1923–1935* (Jefferson, NC, 1998); Gary Caruso, *The Braves Encyclopedia* (Philadelphia, PA, 1995); Al Hirshberg, *The Braves, the Pick, and the Shovel* (Boston, MA, 1948); William F. McNeil, *The Dodgers Encyclopedia* (Champaign, IL, 1997); *The Baseball Encyclopedia*, 10th ed. (New York, 1996); Robert W. Creamer, *Babe: The Legend Comes to Life* (New York, 1974); Shirley Povich, *The Washington Senators* (New York, 1954); Morris Bealle, *The Washington Senators* (Washington, DC, 1947); Henry W. Thomas, *Walter Johnson* (Washington, DC, 1995); Bill Borst, ed., *Ables to Zoldak*, vol. 3 (St. Louis, MO, 1990); Bill Borst, *Still Last in the American League* (West Bloomfield, MI, 1992); Frederick G. Lieb, *The Baltimore Orioles* (New York, 1955); Frank Graham, *The New York Yankees* (New York, 1943); Mark Gallagher, *The Yankee Encyclopedia*, vol. 3 (New York, 1997); Harold Kaese, *The Boston Braves* (New York, 1948); Tom Zachary file, National Baseball Library, Cooperstown, NY.

David S. Matz

ZERNIAL, Gus Edward (b. June 27, 1923, Beaumont, TX), player, is the son of Gustavous Zernial, a carpenter, and Emma (Alexander) Zernial and ranked among the leading AL power hitters of the 1950s. Zernial initially played first base, a position for which his 6-foot 2½-inch, 210-pound frame was well suited. He shifted to the outfield, however, before entering professional baseball at Waycross, GA (GFL) in 1942. The Atlanta, GA Crackers (SA) acquired Zernial's contract, but he joined the U.S. Navy in 1943 for World War II service. Upon Zernial's return to baseball in 1946, the Cleveland Indians (AL) and Chicago White Sox (AL) successively drafted him. After spending two strong seasons with Hollywood, CA (PCL), he began the 1949 season with the Chicago White Sox. An excellent start was stalled when he broke his right collarbone while making a tumbling catch against the Cleveland Indians on May 28. The accident ostensibly demonstrated Zernial's shortcomings as an outfielder, but he returned to action on July 29 and finished the 1949 season with a .318 batting average. He batted .280 in 1950, setting the then Chicago White Sox HR record with 29, and drove in 93 runs.

Although Zernial seemed to be the power hitter to which the club had long aspired, the Chicago White Sox traded him in April 1951. Chicago acquired Orestes Minoso,* a fast line-drive hitter with skills more suitable to Comiskey Park. The three-way deal sent Zernial to the Philadelphia Athletics (AL), whose small Shibe Park helped his HR output. In 1951, he led the AL with 33 HR and 129 RBI. In the Athletics' last season in Philadelphia, he fell while chasing a fly ball against the Boston Red Sox on July 11, 1954 and broke his left collarbone. He accompanied the Athletics to Kansas

City in 1955 and played there through the 1957 season. The Kansas City Athletics traded Zernial in November 1957 to the Detroit Tigers (AL), where he finished his major league career in 1959. As an 11-year major leaguer, Zernial hit 237 HR, drove in 776 runs, batted .265, and compiled a .486 slugging average.

Zernial, who is of Dutch-German extraction, married Gladys Hale on April 30, 1946. After their divorce, he married Maria Sims in January 1961 and has four children, Susan, Gus, Jr., Jim, and Lisa. Zernial broadcast sports for a CBS Radio and Television affiliate in Fresno, CA from 1960 to 1976 and worked as a financial service officer for a bank. He helped purchase the Fresno, CA Grizzlies (PCL) franchise.

BIBLIOGRAPHY: Gus Zernial file, National Baseball Library, Cooperstown, NY; *The Baseball Encyclopedia*, 10th ed. (New York, 1996); Paul Green, " 'I Could Always Handle the Stick': SCD Talks to Gus Zernial," *SCD* 15 (December 30, 1988), pp. 136–138; Rich Marazzi, "Gus Zernial Smacked Seven Homers in Four Games," *SCD* 25 (October 9, 1998), pp. 80–81; Warren Brown, *The Chicago White Sox* (New York, 1952); Richard Lindberg, *Who's on Third?* (South Bend, IN, 1983); Richard Lindberg, *Sox* (New York, 1984); Ernest Mehl, *The Kansas City Athletics* (New York, 1956); Fred Smith, *995 Tigers* (Detroit, MI, 1981); Bob Vanderberg, *Sox: From Lain and Fain to Zisk and Fisk* (Chicago, IL, 1982); *WWIB, 1959*, 44th ed.

                                                                    George W. Hilton

ZIEGLER, Alma "Gabby," "Ziggy" (b. January 9, 1921, Chicago, IL), player, is the daughter of Frank Ziegler, a printer, and Mae (Connal) Ziegler and had one brother. She played baseball as a child in Chicago. In 1933, her family relocated from Chicago to Los Angeles, CA because of the economic Depression. Ziegler expressed disappointment over very little organized women's school sport, but recalled that various girls athletic associations in the Los Angeles area provided compensation. Her hectic later teenage years involved memberships on several softball, basketball, and speedball teams. She began playing organized softball in high school and tried out for the AAGPBL in Los Angeles.

The 5-foot 3-inch, 125-pound Ziegler, who batted and threw right-handed, played second base and shortstop and pitched. She began her AAGPBL career with the Milwaukee Chicks in 1944 and spent from 1945 to 1954 with the Grand Rapids Chicks (AAGPBL). Although originally nick-named "Gabby," she eventually was called "Ziggy" by the Grand Rapids home crowds. Grand Rapids fans honored her with "A Night for Ziggy." In 1944 she started at second base and helped the Milwaukee Chicks win an AAGPBL pennant and championship. The Grand Rapids Chicks captured the AAGPBL Championship in 1947, as Ziegler led second basemen in fielding percentage and the AAGPBL in walks (62). After compiling a 9–6 record as a pitcher to help Grand Rapids win an AAGPBL pennant in 1948, she led second basemen in fielding percentage in 1949. Besides being selected

MVP in 1950, Ziegler made the All-Star Team in 1950 and 1953 and led AAGPBL pitchers in 1951. She proved an excellent pitcher during the overhand era. Her pitching arm demonstrated both resiliency and accuracy. Ziegler returned to the mound in 1950, compiling a 19–7 record and leading the league with a .731 fielding percentage. She pitched 235 innings in 35 games with a 1.38 ERA in 1950 and 171 innings in 22 games with a 14–8 record and 1.26 ERA in 1951. She led the AAGPBL with 25 sacrifices in 1952 and second basemen with a .954 fielding percentage in 1953, when the Chicks won another championship. Ziegler managed one of the playoff games when the umpire ejected the team manager. In 11 AAGPBL seasons, Ziegler batted .173 with 628 hits and 383 stolen bases and compiled a 60–34 record and .638 pitching percentage with a 1.94 ERA. She also played the second most games (1,154) in league history.

Ziegler, who is single, worked as a court reporter for a superior court judge in Los Angeles. After completing a college stenography program, she moved to the San Luis Obispo, CA area and accepted another court reporter position. Ziegler retired in 1980 after more than 25 years as a courtroom fixture. She enjoys legal courtroom drama fiction, citing John Grisham as her favorite author. Since 1980, Ziegler has been an extremely active member of the Morro Bay Women's GC and participates in the "Meals on Wheels" outreach program in Los Osos, CA.

Ziegler's only regret came with the dissolution of the AAGPBL. "The only tragedy in my life was when the league [AAGPBL] disbanded," she lamented. "I was heartbroken and found the whole thing very difficult to accept." She speaks annually on the California Polytechnic University campus. "I talk to the students about a wonderful time in my life and about a great group of women—the All-American Girls Professional League."

BIBLIOGRAPHY: W. C. Madden, *The Women of the All-American Girls Professional Baseball League* (Jefferson, NC, 1997); Scott A.G.M. Crawford, telephone interview with Alma Ziegler, April 16, 1996; AAGPBL files, Northern Indiana Historical Society, South Bend, IN; Tim Wiles, National Baseball Hall of Fame, Cooperstown, NY, letter to Scott A.G.M. Crawford, December 14, 1995; Scott A.G.M. Crawford, telephone conversations with Dottie Collins, AAGPBLPA, February 1996.

Scott A.G.M. Crawford

ZIMMER, Charles Louis "Chief" (b. November 23, 1860, Marietta, OH; d. August 22, 1949, Cleveland, OH), player, manager, umpire, and executive, began his professional baseball career with Ironton, OH (OL) in 1884. As captain of the Poughkeepsie, NY Indians (HRL) in 1886, he batted .409 and acquired the nickname "Chief." Zimmer was given brief major league trials with the Detroit Wolverines (NL) in 1884 and New York Metropolitans (AA) in 1886. He played most of 1887 with Rochester, NY (IL) and joined the Cleveland Blues (AA), where he became one of the finest catchers of his era.

Authorities credit Zimmer with being the first catcher to position himself close behind the batter for every pitch. Catchers previously moved up only with men on base. The quiet, 6-foot, 190-pound right-hander shared catching duties with Charles "Pop" Snyder in 1888 and became Cleveland's principal catcher in 1889, when the club transferred from the AA to the NL as the Spiders. After the season, he signed with the Cleveland Infants in the short-lived PL. Unlike most of his teammates, who remained in the PL, Zimmer returned to the Cleveland Spiders (NL) before the 1890 season. He became rookie pitcher Cy Young's* battery mate, catching a career-high 125 games and 111 in a row, both major league records. Zimmer, a carpenter apprenticed with a cabinet maker, built the furniture and the house in which he, his wife, and three daughters lived in Cleveland, OH.

In 1898, Lou Criger replaced Zimmer as Young's primary catcher. When the next season opened, Zimmer was one of only two Cleveland players remaining from the 1898 Spiders roster. Most Spiders had been sent to strengthen the St. Louis Browns (NL). But Cleveland considered Zimmer too expensive for its failing club and released him in June. Zimmer signed with the Louisville Colonels (NL) for the rest of the 1899 season and joined the Pittsburgh Pirates (NL) with many teammates in 1900, when Louisville was dropped from the NL.

In June 1900, Zimmer was elected president of the newly formed PAPBP. He created a loophole through which NL players could jump to the renegade AL in 1901 without losing the PAPBP-negotiated rights. Zimmer remained in the NL until the Pittsburgh Pirates released him during the 1902 season. He signed with Tacoma, WA (PNL), but was released and returned to the Pittsburgh Pirates (NL) for the remainder of the season. He managed the Philadelphia Phillies (NL) to seventh place with a 49–86 win–loss record in 1903 while catching part-time. Zimmer umpired in the NL in 1904 and the EL in 1905. After serving as part owner–manager of Little Rock, AR (SA) in 1906 and an SA umpire in 1907, Zimmer retired from baseball.

Zimmer batted over .300 four times and compiled a .269 career batting average, with 1,224 hits in 1,280 games. Fielding, however, marked his forte. He led NL catchers several seasons in putouts, assists, double plays, and fielding average. His 1,580 career assists rank fifth all-time among major league catchers, as do his 105 fielding runs (a statistic devised by Pete Palmer to evaluate players' overall fielding effectiveness). In four World Series (1892, 1895, 1896, 1900), Zimmer batted .250 with 16 hits and seven RBI. Aficionados of baseball board games regard his colorful Zimmer's Base Ball Game (1893) as the most beautiful ever produced.

BIBLIOGRAPHY: J. Thomas Hetrick, *Misfits!* (Jefferson, NC, 1991); Thomas Aylesworth and Benton Minks, *The Encyclopedia of Baseball Managers* (New York, 1990); Franklin Lewis, *The Cleveland Indians* (New York, 1949); Frederick G. Lieb, *The Pittsburgh Pirates* (New York, 1948); John Phillips, *The Spiders: Who Was Who* (Cabin John, MD, 1991); Harold Seymour, *Baseball: The Early Years* (New York, rpt., 1989);

Mike Shatzkin, ed., *The Ballplayers* (New York, 1990); John Thorn, et al., eds., *Total Baseball*, 5th ed. (New York, 1997); Charles Zimmer file, National Baseball Library, Cooperstown, NY.

Frederick Ivor-Campbell

ZIMMER, Donald William "Don," "Popeye" (b. January 17, 1931, Cincinnati, OH), player, coach, and manager, is the son of Harold Zimmer, a produce wholesaler, and Lorraine (Ernst) Zimmer and starred in three sports at Western Hills High School in Cincinnati. He signed with the Brooklyn Dodgers (NL) after graduation in 1949 and married Jean Carole "Soot" Bauerle at home plate in Elmira, NY on August 16, 1951. The couple have two children, Thomas and Donna, and reside in Treasure Island, FL.

Zimmer epitomized a prototypical baseball man, being highly competitive, devoted to the game, and popular with his teammates. He joined the Brooklyn Dodgers in 1954 as a utility infielder. Although being on World Series winners with the Brooklyn Dodgers in 1955 and Los Angeles Dodgers (NL) in 1959, Zimmer suffered considerable frustration in baseball. In 1953, scouts considered him baseball's top minor league prospect. Zimmer possessed a superior throwing arm, soft hands, good foot speed, and outstanding power for his 5-foot 9-inch, 160-pound frame. Through early July 1953, Zimmer led the AA with 23 HR and 63 RBI. Near-fatal injuries and the depth of the Brooklyn Dodgers talent kept him from reaching his tremendous potential.

In July 1953, Zimmer was almost killed when Jim Kirk's pitch fractured his skull while with St. Paul, MN (AA). He lay unconscious for 13 days and was hospitalized for a month. He lost his speech for six weeks and lost 44 pounds. In 1956, a fast ball by Hal Jeffcoat of the Cincinnati Reds broke his cheek and almost blinded him. Although knowing that another beaning could cost his life, Zimmer persevered. He enjoyed his best season as a major league shortstop for the Los Angeles Dodgers in 1958, batting .262 with 17 HR and participating in 100 double plays.

In April 1960, the Los Angeles Dodgers traded Zimmer to the Chicago Cubs (NL). In his second year with the Chicago Cubs, he was appointed team captain and made the All-Star team. His last four major league seasons were spent with the New York Mets (NL) and Cincinnati Reds (NL) in 1962, Los Angeles Dodgers (NL) in 1963, and Washington Senators (AL) from 1963 to 1965. He concluded his 12-year major league career with a .235 batting average, 91 HR, and 352 RBI.

After playing one season in Japan, Zimmer began his managerial career in 1967. His first major league managerial assignment came in 1972 as pilot of the San Diego Padres (NL). He enjoyed success as Boston Red Sox (AL) manager from 1976 to 1980, but was disappointed when the 1978 team squandered a 13-game lead and lost to the New York Yankees in a playoff. Zimmer also piloted the Texas Rangers (AL) in 1981 and 1982 and Chicago

Cubs (NL) from 1988 through 1991. Chicago won an NL Eastern Division title in 1989, as Zimmer earned NL Manager of the Year honors. When Joe Torre* underwent prostate cancer surgery in 1999, Zimmer piloted the Yankees to a 21–15 record. His major league clubs compiled a 906–873 win-loss record. He coached with the Montreal Expos (NL) in 1971, Boston Red Sox from 1974 through 1976 and in 1992, New York Yankees (AL) in 1983, 1986, and since 1996, Chicago Cubs from 1984 to 1986, San Francisco Giants (NL) in 1987, and Colorado Rockies (NL) from 1993 to June 1995.

BIBLIOGRAPHY: T. Balf, "Baseball the Way It Used to Be," *Sport* 79 (April 1988), p. 55; Don Zimmer file, National Baseball Library, Cooperstown, NY; Eddie Gold and Art Ahrens, *The New Era Cubs, 1941–1985* (Chicago, IL, 1985); Ray Fitzgerald, " 'No Manager's Got a Better Job,' " *Boston Sunday Globe*, August 14, 1977, pp. 19ff; Ed Linn, "Don Zimmer and the Ballplayer's Code," *Sport* 40 (July 1965), pp. 47–49; Rich Marazzi, "1995: The 'Boys of Summer' Have Their October," *SCD* 22 (May 5, 1995), pp. 160–162; Rich Marazzi, "Don Zimmer: A Half Century as a Major Leaguer," *SCD* 25 (February 6, 1998), pp. 142–144; Rich Marazzi, "Manager of the Year Award in 1989 Was a Highlight for Zimmer," *SCD* 25 (February 13, 1998), pp. 80–81; Rich Marazzi, "Don Zimmer Remembers a Generation of Legendary Players," *SCD* 25 (February 20, 1998), pp. 70–71; Steve Wulf, "Meet the New Boss," *SI* 74 (June 3, 1991), pp. 66ff; James R. Hartley, *Washington's Expansion Senators (1961–71)* (Germantown, MD, 1998); Thomas Aylesworth and Beton Minks, *The Encyclopedia of Baseball Managers* (New York, 1990); Robert Redmount, *The Red Sox Encyclopedia* (Champaign, IL, 1998); William F. McNeil, *The Dodgers Encyclopedia* (Champaign, IL, 1997); Phil Rogers, *The Impossible Takes a Little Longer* (Dallas, TX, 1991); Peter Golenbock, *Bums* (New York, 1984); Leigh Montville, "The Face of Genius," *SI* 71 (September 25, 1989), pp. 58–64; Robert Obojski, " 'Popeye' Signs on as Yankees Coach for '96," *SCD* 22 (December 22, 1995), pp. 100–101.

Allen E. Hye

ZIMMERMAN, Henry "Heinie," "The Great Zim" (b. February 9, 1887, New York, NY; d. March 14, 1969, New York, NY), player, described himself as "The Great Zim" and might have stepped directly from the pages of Ring Lardner's *You Know Me Al*. He played sandlot baseball with the Bronx Giants and married Helene C. Chasar in 1912. After their divorce in March 1916, he married Bertha K. Noe on June 24, 1919. They had no children.

His professional baseball career began in 1906 with Wilkes-Barre, PA (NYSL). By late August 1907, he made the major leagues with the Chicago Cubs (NL). The Chicago Cubs in August 1916 traded Zimmerman to the New York Giants (NL) for Larry Doyle.* Although an outstanding third baseman, he began his major league career as a second baseman and also played at shortstop and first base.

An outstanding offensive player, the 5-foot 11-inch, 176-pound, right-handed Zimmerman enjoyed particularly productive seasons in 1912 and 1913. Zimmerman led the NL in batting (.372), hits (207), doubles (41), slugging percentage (.571), and HR (14) in 1912 and paced the NL in RBI with 83 in 1916 and a career-high 102 in 1917. Managers found Zimmerman "played episodically, showing bursts of brilliance followed by periods of lassitude." Zimmerman remains best known for his fielding play in the 1917 World Series against the Chicago White Sox. During a rundown between third base and home plate, Zimmerman chased base runner Eddie Collins* of the Chicago White Sox toward home. On discovering that the New York Giants catcher and pitcher had left the plate unguarded, Zimmerman attempted unsuccessfully to catch up with Collins. Collins scored what proved to be the winning run. When asked about the play after the game, Zimmerman retorted, "Who the hell was I going to throw the ball to? [Bill] Klem?"

The New York Giants released Zimmerman in September 1919. In 13 major league seasons, Zimmerman batted .295, made 1,566 hits, slugged 275 doubles and 105 triples, and knocked in 796 runs. During the early 1920s, he and Hal Chase* were implicated in various attempts to bribe other New York Giants players to lose games and were banned for life. Zimmerman, who continued to live in New York City, in 1920 organized and played semiprofessionally with the Bronx Giants. He supposedly worked as a steamfitter until his retirement, but also kept associations with the New York underworld. He allegedly co-owned a speakeasy with bootlegger Dutch Schultz in 1929 and 1930.

BIBLIOGRAPHY: Charles C. Alexander, *John McGraw* (New York, 1988); Warren Brown, *The Chicago Cubs* (New York, 1946); Eddie Gold and Art Ahrens, *The Golden Era Cubs, 1876–1940* (Chicago, IL, 1985); Jim Enright, *Chicago Cubs* (New York, 1975); Warren Wilbert and William Hagemen, *Chicago Cubs: Seasons at the Summit* (Champaign, IL, 1997); Frank Graham, *The New York Giants* (New York, 1952); Noel Hynd, *The Giants of the Polo Grounds* (New York, 1988); Fred Stein and Nick Peters, *Giants Diary* (Berkeley, CA, 1987); Joseph Durso, *The Days of Mr. McGraw* (Englewood Cliffs, NJ, 1969); Frank Graham, *McGraw of the Giants* (New York, 1944); Daniel E. Ginsburg, *The Fix Is In* (Jefferson, NC, 1995); Bill James, *The Historical Baseball Abstract* (New York, 1986); John Thorn and Pete Palmer, eds., *The Hidden Game of Baseball* (Garden City, NY, 1984); *TSN Baseball Register, 1955*; Henry Zimmerman file, National Baseball Library, Cooperstown, NY.

Leverett T. Smith, Jr.

ZISK, Richard Walter "Richie" (b. February 6, 1949, Brooklyn, NY), player and coach, is the older of two sons of Walter Zisk, a production supervisor at a chemical plant and semiprofessional baseball player, and Veronica (Murowski) Zisk, both of Polish descent. His family resided in Livingston, NJ until he was age 14 and then moved to Parsippany, NJ. Zisk graduated from Parsippany High School, where he played baseball and was named All-State twice, and attended Seton Hall University for two years. The Pittsburgh Pirates (NL) selected him in the third round in the June 1967 free agent draft. He hit .307 with Salem, VA (ApL) in 1967 and then played at Gastonia, NC (WCL) in 1968 and Salem, VA (CrL) in 1969. In 1970 at Waterbury, CT (EL), he led the EL with 34 HR. With Charleston, WV (IL), he paced the IL in RBI (109) in 1971 and HR (26) in 1972. He received brief trials with the Pittsburgh Pirates in 1971 and 1972 and then came up to stay in 1973. Over the next four years, he averaged .299, 17 HR, and 80 RBI per season. The Pittsburgh Pirates traded Zisk to the Chicago White Sox (AL) in December 1976. The Texas Rangers (AL) signed him as a free agent in November 1977. Recurring knee injuries increasingly limited his range in the outfield, making him spend more time as a DH. In December 1980, he was traded to the Seattle Mariners (AL). He hit .311 in 94 games in 1981, being named *TSN* Comeback Player of the Year and *TSN* and UPI DH of the Year. His knee problems became increasingly severe, however, and forced his retirement after the 1983 season.

A right-handed, line drive hitter, the 6-foot 1-inch, 200-pound Zisk sprayed the ball well to all fields. In 1,453 major league games, he hit .287 with 207 HR and 245 doubles. Defensively, he possessed a strong arm. Although lacking mobility, he made an All-Star fielding team at the Class AAA level.

Zisk married Barbara Louise Boice on May 27, 1969 and has three children. After retiring as a player, he completed a bachelor's degree in communications. From 1987 through 1999, he served as the minor league hitting instructor for the Chicago Cubs (NL). In December 1999, he became manager of Daytona, FL. He lives in Lighthouse Point, FL with his family.

BIBLIOGRAPHY: *The Baseball Encyclopedia*, 10th ed. (New York, 1996); Luther W. Spoehr, interview with Richie Zisk, February 9, 1994; Richie Zisk file, National Baseball Library, Cooperstown, NY; Richard L. Burtt, *The Pittsburgh Pirates: A Pictorial History* (Virginia Beach, VA, 1977); Bob Smizik, *The Pittsburgh Pirates: An Illustrated History* (New York, 1990); Bob Vanderberg, *Sox: From Lane and Fain to Zisk and Fisk* (Chicago, IL, 1982); Richard Lindberg, *Who's on Third?* (South Bend, IN, 1983); Phil Rogers, *The Impossible Takes a Little Longer* (Dallas, TX, 1991); Tracy Ringolsby, "Shipwrecked in Seattle," *Sport 75* (March 1984), pp. 61–71; Peter C. Bjarkman, ed., *Encyclopedia of Major League Baseball Team Histories American League* (Westport, CT, 1991).

Luther W. Spoehr

Appendix 1
Entries by Place of Birth

The following lists the entries alphabetically by their state, or, in selected instances, American territory or foreign nation of birth.

Alabama (44)

Aaron, Henry
Alexander, Doyle
Bankhead, Samuel
Brown, Larry "Iron Man"
Bruton, William
Carroll, Clay
Davis, Lorenzo "Piper"
Davis, Virgil "Spud"
Dismukes, William
Finley, Charles O.
Foster, George
Gamble, Oscar
Irvin, Monford
Key, James "Jimmy"
Lary, Frank
McCovey, Willie
McDuffie, Terris
Manush, Henry
May, Lee
Mays, Willie
Moore, Terry
Newsom, Louis "Bobo"
Otis, Amos
Paige, Leroy "Satchel"
Radcliffe, Alexander
Radcliffe, Theodore "Double Duty"
Scales, George
Sewell, James Luther "Luke"
Sewell, Joseph
Sewell, Truett "Rip"
Smith, Osborne "Ozzie"
Stephenson, Jackson Riggs
Street, Charles "Gabby"
Sutton, Donald
Tabor, James
Thornton, Andre
Trucks, Virgil "Fire"
Veale, Robert, Jr.
Williams, Billy
Wilson, Arthur
Wilson, Willie
Woods, Parnell
Wynn, Early
York, Preston Rudolph

Alaska (1)

Schilling, Curtis

Arizona (3)

Denny, John
Hemus, Solomon "Solly"
Keagle, Merle "Pat"

Arkansas (21)

Brock, Louis
Davis, Willie
Dean, Jay "Dizzy"
Douthit, Taylor
Gardner, Floyd "Jelly"
Jackson, Travis
Johnson, Alexander
Kell, George
Kessinger, Donald
Kinder, Ellis
Lollar, John Sherman
McReynolds, Walter Kevin
Mathis, Verdell "Lefty"
Monday, Robert "Rick"
Moon, Wallace
Moseby, Lloyd
Robinson, Brooks
Roe, Elwin "Preacher"
Sain, John
Vaughan, Joseph "Arky"
Warnecke, Lonnie

California (148)

Aguilera, Richard "Rick"
Appier, Robert Kevin
Arlett, Russell
Ashford, Emmett
Bailey, Robert
Baker, Johnnie, Jr., "Dusty"
Blackwell, Ewell
Bonds, Barry
Bonds, Bobby
Bonham, Ernest
Boone, Raymond
Boone, Robert
Bowa, Lawrence
Briles, Nelson
Brunansky, Thomas
Buckner, William
Burleson, Richard "Rick"
Burroughs, Jeffrey
Butler, Brett
Camilli, Adolph
Caminiti, Kenneth
Carr, George
Carter, Gary

Chance, Frank
Chase, Harold
Collins, Dorothy Wiltse "Dottie"
Cowens, Alfred
Crandall, Delmar
Cravath, Clifford "Gavvy"
Cronin, Joseph
Crosetti, Frank
Dancer, Faye
Danning, Harry
Davis, Eric
Davis, La Vonne Paire "Pepper"
DeCinces, Douglas
Demaree, Joseph Franklin "Frank"
Dierker, Lawrence "Larry"
DiMaggio, Domenic
DiMaggio, Joseph
Doerr, Robert
Downing, Brian
Doyle, Dorothy Harrell "Snookie"
Drysdale, Donald
Dykstra, Leonard
Eckersley, Dennis
Elliott, Robert
Evans, Darrell
Evans, Dwight
Fielder, Cecil
Fonseca, Lewis
Forsch, Robert
Fregosi, James
Freitas, Antonio, Jr.
French, Lawrence
Galan, August
Garcia, Edward Miguel "Mike"
Gentile, James
Goldsmith, Fred
Gomez, Vernon "Lefty"
Gordon, Joseph
Gwynn, Anthony
Hack, Stanley
Hafey, Charles "Chick"
Harvey, Harold Douglas
Heilmann, Harry
Held, Woodson "Woodie"
Henderson, David
Hendrick, George, Jr.
Hernandez, Keith
Hooper, Harry

Hrabosky, Alan
Jefferies, Gregory
Jensen, Jack
Johnson, Deron
Johnson, Randall "Randy"
Jones, Douglas
Jones, Randall "Randy"
Joost, Edwin "Eddie"
Kamm, William
Kelly, George
Koenig, Mark
Kremer, Remy "Ray"
Kress, Ralph "Red"
Lange, William
Langston, Mark
Lansford, Carney
Lary, Lynford "Lyn"
Lazzeri, Anthony
Lee, Thornton
Lee, William F. "Bill"
Lemon, Robert
Lewis, George "Duffy"
Lombardi, Ernest
Lonborg, James
McDougald, Gilbert
McDowell, Jack
McGee, Willie
McGraw, Frank, Jr., "Tug"
McGregor, Scott
McGwire, Mark
McNamara, John
Maloney, James
Martin, Alfred "Billy"
Matthews, Gary
Meusel, Emil
Meusel, Robert
Meyers, John "Chief"
Mitchell, Kevin
Murray, Eddie
Nettles, Graig
Nolan, Gary
O'Doul, Frank "Lefty"
Ojeda, Robert "Bob"
Overall, Orval
Pearson, Marcellus Montgomery
   "Monte"
Pendleton, Terry
Petry, Daniel

Pinelli, Ralph "Babe"
Priddy, Gerald
Quisenberry, Daniel
Righetti, David
Rigney, William
Rudi, Joseph
Ruether, Walter
Sax, Stephen
Scott, Michael
Seaver, George Thomas
Smalley, Roy, III
Smith, David S.
Snider, Edwin "Duke"
Speier, Christopher
Stewart, David
Stieb, David
Strawberry, Darryl
Stuart, Richard
Suhr, August "Gus"
Thompson, Jason
Trammell, Alan
Triandos, Gus
Ventura, Robin
Wallach, Timothy
Washington, Claudell
Watson, Robert
White, Roy
Williams, Matthew
Williams, Theodore
Yount, Robin

Colorado (1)

Gossage, Richard "Goose"

Connecticut (16)

Blass, Stephen
Bulkeley, Morgan
Connor, Roger
Corcoran, Thomas
Dropo, Walter
Hanlon, Edward "Ned"
Hutchinson, William
Lynch, Thomas
McAuliffe, Richard "Dick"
Murnane, Timothy
O'Rourke, James
Piersall, James

Topping, Daniel
Vaughn, Maurice "Mo"
Vincent, Francis, Jr.
Weiss, George

Delaware (7)

Carpenter, Robert, Jr.
Green, George Dallas
Lobert, John "Hans"
McDonald, Webster
McGowan, William
McMahon, John
Willis, Victor

District of Columbia (7)

Blue, Luzerne
Devlin, Arthur
Hines, Paul
Money, Donald
White, Guy
Wills, Maurice
Winters, Jesse "Nip"

Florida (32)

Bell, Jay
Bichette, Alphonse Dante
Billingham, John "Jack"
Carlton, Steven
Coleman, Vincent
Davis, Glenn
Dawson, Andre
Garvey, Steve
Gooden, Dwight
Grant, James "Mudcat"
Harris, E. Victor
Howser, Richard
Johnson, David
Johnson, Howard
LaRussa, Anthony, Jr.
Lloyd, John Henry
Lopez, Alfred
Lundy, Richard
McGriff, Frederick
McRae, Harold
Martinez, Constantino "Tino"
O'Neil, John, Jr., "Buck"
Parrish, Larry

Piniella, Louis
Powell, John Wesley
Raines, Timothy K.
Rhoden, Richard
Rivers, John Milton "Mickey"
Sheffield, Gary
Thigpen, Robert
Trent, Theodore
White, William K.

Georgia (27)

Bagby, James, Sr.
Brown, James Kevin
Butts, Thomas "Pee Wee"
Byrd, William
Casey, Hugh
Chandler, Spurgeon "Spud"
Cobb, Tyrus "Ty"
Cockrell, Phillip
Dixon, Herbert
Fairly, Ronald
Gibson, Joshua
Grissom, Marquis
Joyner, Wallace
Manning, Maxwell "Max"
Mize, John
Moore, Walter "Dobie"
Moses, Wallace
Redding, Richard
Robinson, Jack
Rucker, George Napoleon "Nap"
Stallings, George
Terry, William H.
Thomas, Frank E.
Travis, Cecil
Trouppe, Quincy
Walker, Fred
Wyatt, John Whitlow

Hawaii (2)

Darling, Ronald
Hough, Charles

Idaho (3)

Jackson, Lawrence
Killebrew, Harmon
Law, Vernon

Illinois (82)

Barfield, Jesse
Barlick, Albert
Bartell, Richard
Bauer, Henry
Berger, Walter
Bluege, Oswald
Bottomley, James
Boudreau, Louis
Campbell, Bruce
Cavarretta, Philip
Comiskey, Charles
Conlan, John "Jocko"
Cutshaw, George
Dalrymple, Abner
Donlin, Michael
Doyle, Lawrence
Dressen, Charles
Eckert, William
Evans, William
Fletcher, Arthur
Foss, Betty Weaver
Friend, Robert
Gaetti, Gary
Giles, Warren
Gura, Lawrence
Haller, Thomas
Harridge, William
Henderson, Rickey
Herzog, Dorrell "Whitey"
Jacobson, William
Jethroe, Samuel
Keating, Edythe Perlick
Kluszewski, Theodore
Kreevich, Michael
Leibrandt, Charles, Jr.
Leifield, Albert
Leonard, Emil "Dutch"
Lindstrom, Frederick
Long, Herman
Lundgren, Carl
Luzinski, Gregory
Lynn, Fredric
Lyons, James
McGinnis, George "Jumbo"
McGinnity, Joseph
McLain, Dennis

McManus, Martin
Mostil, John
Oberkfell, Kenneth
O'Day, Henry
O'Farrell, Robert
Patterson, Andrew "Pat"
Pfeffer, Edward "Jeff"
Pipp, Walter
Powell, John Joseph
Puckett, Kirby
Rader, Douglas
Reuschel, Ricky
Rice, Harry
Roberts, Robin
Ruffing, Charles "Red"
Saberhagen, Bret
Schalk, Raymond
Schoendienst, Albert "Red"
Schroeder, Dorothy "Dottie"
Seitzer, Kevin
Sheely, Earl
Sheridan, John
Shively, Twila
Skowron, William
Smith, Lonnie
Spalding, Albert
Stock, Milton
Sundberg, James
Turley, Robert
Veeck, William, Jr.
Wagner, Audrey
Weaver, Joanne
Winter, Joanne
Wrigley, Philip
Yount, Robin
Ziegler, Alma "Gabby"

Indiana (36)

Adams, Charles "Babe"
Brown, Mordecai "Three Finger"
Bush, Owen "Donie"
Carey, Max
Charleston, Oscar
Crandall, James "Doc"
Cuppy, George "Nig"
Dauss, George
Erskine, Carl
Fehr, Donald

Fitzsimmons, Frederick
Fox, Ervin "Pete"
Frick, Ford
Hargrave, Eugene "Bubbles"
Herman, William
Hodges, Gilbert
John, Thomas
Klein, Charles
Larsen, Don
Lofton, Kenneth
Mattingly, Donald
Meekin, Jouett
Nehf, Arthur
Ramsey, Thomas "Toad"
Reed, Ronald
Rice, Edgar
Roush, Edd
Rusie, Amos
Scott, Lewis Everett "Deacon"
Splittorff, Paul, Jr.
Stahl, Charles "Chick"
Strong, T. R. "Ted"
Thompson, Samuel
Trout, Paul "Dizzy"
Warfield, Francis "Frank"
Williams, Fred

Iowa (19)

Anson, Adrian "Cap"
Bancroft, David
Boddiker, Michael
Clarke, Fred
Coombs, John
Faber, Urban "Red"
Feller, Robert
Hoffer, William "Bill"
McVey, Calvin
Menke, Denis
Miller, Edmund "Bing"
Severeid, Henry "Hank"
Stone, George
Trosky, Harold
Vance, Arthur "Dazzy"
Voyce, Inez
Weimer, Jacob "Jake"
Whitehill, Earl
Wilkinson, James L.

Kansas (20)

Auker, Eldon
Brewer, Chester
Cabell, Enos, Jr.
Cheney, Laurance "Larry"
Cooley, Duff
Daulton, Darren
DeMoss, Elwood
Giles, George
Grantham, George
Grimsley, Ross, II
Hendrix, Claude
Horner, Robert
Houk, Ralph
Johnson, Oscar "Heavy"
Johnson, Walter
Mauch, Gene
Russell, William
Tinker, Joseph
Torrez, Michael
Wickware, Frank

Kentucky (26)

Beckwith, John
Bell, David "Gus"
Browning, Louis "Pete"
Buhner, Jay
Bunning, James
Camnitz, Samuel Howard
Chandler, Albert "Happy"
Chapman, Raymond
Combs, Earle
Derringer, Paul
Greenwell, Michael
Gullett, Donald
Hughes, Samuel
McGann, Dennis "Dan"
Mays, Carl
Page, Theodore "Ted"
Pfeffer, Nathaniel Frederick
Pulliam, Harry
Reese, Harold "Pee Wee"
Spence, Stanley
Stephens, Vernon
Tannehill, Jesse
Thomas, Clinton

Veach, Robert
Weyhing, August
Wolf, William "Chicken"

Louisiana (28)

Adcock, Joseph
Belle, Albert
Blue, Vida
Bonura, Henry "Zeke"
Bremer, Eugene, Sr.
Brown, Willard
Clark, William Nuschler, Jr.
Clark, William Watson "Watty"
Dedeaux, Raoul "Rod"
Dickey, William
Dyer, Edwin
Finley, Charles E. "Chuck"
Garr, Ralph
Guidry, Ronald
Hale, Arvel Odell "Sammy"
Harper, Tommy
Lee, William C.
Lyons, Theodore
Malarcher, David
Marcelle, Oliver
Ott, Melvin
Parnell, Melvin
Pollet, Howard
Richard, James Rodney
Smith, Carl Reginald
Smith, Lee, Jr.
Staub, Daniel
Suttles, George

Maine (4)

Carrigan, William
Gore, George
Sockalexis, Louis
Stanley, Robert

Maryland (21)

Anderson, Brady
Baines, Harold
Baker, John Franklin
Childs, Clarence
Foutz, David

Foxx, James
Grove, Robert "Lefty"
Herzog, Charles "Buck"
Johnson, William "Judy"
Jones, Stuart "Slim"
Kaline, Albert
Keller, Charles
Kuhn, Bowie
Mathews, Robert
Nicholson, William
Phelps, Ernest "Babe"
Ripken, Calvin, Jr.
Rommel, Edwin
Ruth, George Herman "Babe"
Wendelstedt, Harry, Jr.
Werber, William

Massachusetts (48)

Bagwell, Jeffrey
Bancroft, Francis
Bedrosian, Stephen
Belanger, Mark
Buffinton, Charles
Callahan, James "Nixey"
Chesbro, John
Clarkson, John
Cochrane, Gordon "Mickey"
Collins, John F. "Shano"
Conigliaro, Anthony "Tony"
Cummings, William "Candy"
Day, John B.
Donovan, Richard "Dick"
Donovan, William
Durocher, Leo
Dwyer, John Francis "Frank"
English, Madeline "Maddy"
Farrell, Charles "Duke"
Fletcher, Elburt "Elbie"
Giamatti, Angelo Bartlett
Glavine, Thomas
Grant, Frank
Hebner, Richard
Hegan, James
Keefe, Timothy
Kelley, Joseph
McCarthy, Thomas
McGunnigle, William

McInnis, John
Mack, Connie
Maranville, Walter "Rabbit"
Miller, Stuart
Moran, Patrick
Morrill, John
Mutrie, James
Raschi, Victor
Reardon, Jeffrey
Reardon, John "Beans"
Robinson, Wilbert
Ryan, James
Sanford, John "Jack"
Siebert, Richard
Soden, Arthur
Tenney, Fred
Terry, William Adonis
Traynor, Harold "Pie"
Wood, Wilbur, Jr.

Michigan (40)

Altobelli, Joseph
Ball, George Walter
Briggs, Walter
Buhl, Robert
Cicotte, Edward
Cuyler, Hazen "Kiki"
Fournier, John
Freehan, William
Gehringer, Charles
Gibson, Kirk
Grich, Robert
Haylett, Alice
Hentgen, Patrick
Kaat, James
Kurys, Sophie
Lau, Charles
McHale, John
MacPhail, Leland, Sr., "Larry"
Marshall, Michael
Mayberry, John
Myer, Charles
Navin, Frank
Newhouser, Harold
Northrup, James
Pappas, Milton
Pierce, Walter William
Radatz, Richard

Randall, Maxine Kline
Reulbach, Edward
Robinson, Cornelius "Neil"
Sanderson, Scott
Simmons, Ted
Smoltz, John
Tanana, Frank
Tresh, Thomas
Virdon, William
Welch, Robert
Wise, Richard "Rick"
Wisniewski, Connie
Yawkey, Thomas

Minnesota (15)

Bender, Charles "Chief"
Bush, Leslie "Bullet Joe"
DeMontreville, Eugene
Gandil, Arnold "Chick"
Gullickson, William
Harris, Anthony Spencer
Hrbek, Kent
Kelly, J. Thomas
Koosman, Jerry
Lane, Ferdinand C.
Maris, Roger
Molitor, Paul
Morris, John
Walberg, George "Rube"
Winfield, David

Mississippi (11)

Bell, James "Cool Papa"
Bush, Guy
Easterling, Howard
LeFlore, Ronald
Lemon, Chester
Melton, Edwin William "Bill"
Parker, David
Passeau, Claude
Scott, George, Jr.
Walker, Gerald
White, Frank, Jr.

Missouri (67)

Allison, William Robert
Beckley, Jacob

Berra, Lawrence "Yogi"
Boyer, Cletis
Boyer, Kenton
Breitenstein, Theodore "Ted"
Busch, August, Jr.
Cone, David
Cooper, Morton
Cooper, William Walker
Crutchfield, John
Currie, Reuben
Davis, Curtis
Dickson, Murry
Donaldson, John
Duncan, Frank, Jr.
Evers, Walter "Hoot"
Florreich, Kathleen Lois
Frey, Linus "Lonny"
Galvin, James "Pud"
Goodman, Ival
Griffith, Clark
Grimm, Charles
Henke, Thomas
Holliday, James "Bug"
Hollocher, Charles
Holtzman, Kenneth
Howard, Elston
Hubbell, Carl
Hunt, Ronald
Joyce, William
Keane, John
King, Charles "Silver"
Kling, John
Leach, Frederick
Lucas, Henry
McBride, Arnold "Bake"
Mueller, Donald
O'Connor, John "Jack"
Orth, Albert
Porter, Darrell
Reiser, Harold "Pete"
Reuss, Jerry
Rogers, Stephen
Ruel, Herold "Muddy"
Shellenback, Frank
Siebern, Norman "Norm"
Siebert, Wilfred, III, "Sonny"
Sievers, Roy
Smith, Alphonse "Al"

Smith, Edward Mayo
Steinfeldt, Harry
Stengel, Charles "Casey"
Stottlemyre, Melvin, Sr.
Sutcliffe, Richard
Tebeau, Oliver "Patsy"
Tesreau, Charles "Jeff"
Tobin, John
Van Haltren, George
Wagoner, Betty
Weaver, Earl
Werden, Percival "Perry"
Williams, Claude "Lefty"
Williams, James
Williams, Richard
Wood, Joseph
Wright, Forrest Glenn

Montana (1)

McNally, David

Nebraska (9)

Alexander, Grover Cleveland
Ashburn, Don Richie
Boggs, Wade
Budig, Gene
Crawford, Samuel
Gibson, Robert
Harder, Melvin
Hopp, John, Jr., "Hippity"
Southworth, William

New Hampshire (6)

Adams, Daniel
Flanagan, Michael
Latham, Walter Arlington
Rolfe, Robert "Red"
Selee, Frank
Tyler, George "Lefty"

New Jersey (20)

Case, George, Jr.
Cramer, Roger "Doc"
Feeney, Charles "Chub"
Fraser, Ronald
Gleason, William "Kid"
Goslin, Leon "Goose"

Hamilton, William
Hayes, Frank
Jamieson, Charles
Medwick, Joseph "Ducky"
Messersmith, John "Andy"
Newcombe, Donald
Perranoski, Ronald
Richardson, Abram "Hardy"
Shindle, William
Stoneham, Charles
Stoneham, Horace
Summers, William
Tiernan, Michael
Vander Meer, John

New Mexico (2)

Kiner, Ralph
Stephens, Vernon

New York (113)

Antonelli, John
Barnes, Roscoe
Biggio, Craig
Bonilla, Roberto "Bobby"
Breadon, Sam
Brouthers, Daniel
Brush, John, Jr.
Burns, George J.
Cammeyer, William
Candelaria, John
Cartwright, Alexander
Cash, David, Jr.
Chamberlain, Elton "Icebox"
Chapman, John "Jack"
Colavito, Rocco
Collins, Edward
Collins, James
Corcoran, Lawrence
Creighton, James
Cuccinello, Anthony
Dahlen, William
Davis, George
Davis, Herman Thomas
Dinneen, William
Dougherty, Patrick "Patsy"
Ebbets, Charles
Evers, John

Face, Elroy
Ferguson, Robert V.
Ford, Edward "Whitey"
Fowler, John
Franco, John
Freedman, Andrew
Frisch, Frank
Gehrig, Henry Louis "Lou"
Gordon, Sidney
Greenberg, Henry
Griffin, Michael
Groh, Henry
Harris, Stanley "Bucky"
Herman, Floyd "Babe"
Hershiser, Orel, IV
Heydler, John
Holmes, Thomas
Howell, Henry "Harry"
Hoyt, Waite
Hulbert, William
Judge, Joseph
Jurges, William
Keeler, William
Kelly, Michael
Klem, William
Konstanty, James
Koufax, Sanford "Sandy"
Leach, Thomas
Leonard, Dennis
Logan, John, Jr.
Lopat, Edmund
Luciano, Ronald
McCormick, Frank
McGraw, John
McMahon, Donald
McPhee, John "Bid"
Maglie, Salvatore
Malzone, Frank
Martinez, Edgar
Mele, Sabath "Sam"
Miller, Marvin
Mills, Abraham
Mogridge, George
Morris, Edward "Cannonball"
Murphy, John
O'Laughlin, Francis "Silk"
O'Malley, Walter
Orr, David

Ozark, Daniel
Palmer, James
Paul, Gabe
Pearce, Richard
Pepitone, Joseph
Petrocelli, Americo
Podres, John
Radbourne, Charles
Rizzuto, Philip
Rudolph, Richard
Ruppert, Jacob
Schang, Walter
Schulte, Frank
Schumacher, Harold
Score, Herbert
Seymour, James
Singleton, Kenneth
Spahn, Warren
Stark, Albert D.
Start, Joseph
Stirnweiss, George "Snuffy"
Sutton, Ezra
Torre, Joseph
Tudor, John
Van Slyke, Andrew
Viola, Frank, Jr.
Welch, Michael
Whitaker, Louis, Jr.
White, James
White, William
Whitney, James
Wiltse, George "Hooks"
Wright, George
Yastrzemski, Carl
Yost, Edward
Young, Nicholas
Zimmerman, Henry
Zisk, Richard

North Carolina (28)

Abernathy, Theodore "Ted"
Allen, John
Appling, Lucius
Barnhill, David
Burgess, Forrest "Smoky"
Craig, Roger L.
Crowder, Alvin "General"
Ferrell, Richard

Ferrell, Wesley
Goodman, William
Grace, Mark
Greenlee, William A.
Hart, James Ray
Hunter, James
Jones, Charles W.
Lanier, Hubert Max
Leonard, Walter "Buck"
Lewis, John, Jr., "Buddy"
Lockman, Carroll "Whitey"
Meadows, Henry Lee
Perry, Gaylord
Perry, James
Slaughter, Enos
Temple, John
Wilhelm, James Hoyt
Wright, Taft
Yokely, Laymon
Zachary, Jonathan Thompson

Ohio (104)

Allen, Ethan
Alston, Walter
Ames, Leon
Bando, Salvatore
Bradley, William
Bescher, Robert
Bresnahan, Roger
Brown, Raymond
Burns, George H.
Caylor, Oliver Perry
Chambliss, Carroll Christopher
Chance, Wilmer Dean
Clemens, William Roger
Crosley, Powel, Jr.
Delahanty, Edward
Delahanty, James
Elberfeld, Norman "Kid"
English, Elwood "Woody"
Ewing, William "Buck"
Fingers, Roland
Flick, Elmer
Fothergill, Robert
Frey, James
Galbreath, Daniel
Galbreath, John W.
Garver, Ned

Gowdy, Henry "Hank"
Haddix, Harvey
Haines, Jesse
Hartsel, Tully "Topsy"
Henrich, Thomas
Hisle, Larry
Howard, Frank
Hoy, William "Dummy"
Huggins, Miller
Jochum, Betsy
Johnson, Byron
Johnson, George "Chappie"
Johnson, Grant
Johnson, Kenneth Lance
Jones, Samuel Pond
Jones, Samuel "Toothpick"
Justice, David
Kamenshek, Dorothy "Dottie"
Kauff, Benjamin
Kennedy, William "Brickyard"
Kuhel, Joseph
Landis, Kenesaw Mountain
Lane, Frank
Larkin, Barry
Leever, Samuel
Leonard, Hubert "Dutch"
Leyland, James
Lyons, Dennis
McGuire, James "Deacon"
McKean, Edward
McNaughton, Alice Hohlmayer "Lefty"
Maddox, Garry
Marquard, Richard "Rube"
Montgomery, Jeffrey
Moore, Earl
Mullin, George
Munson, Thurman
Niekro, Joseph
Niekro, Philip
Nuxhall, Joseph
Oliver, Albert
O'Neill, Paul
Paskert, George "Dode"
Peckinpaugh, Roger
Pfiester, John "Jack"
Post, Walter "Wally"
Reilly, John
Richmond, J. Lee

Rickey, Wesley Branch
Rigler, Charles "Cy"
Root, Charles
Rose, Peter
Roseboro, John
Sallee, Harry "Slim"
Schmidt, Michael
Selbach, Albert "Kep"
Seybold, Ralph "Socks"
Shocker, Urban
Sisler, George
Somers, Charles
Steinbrenner, George, III
Stenzel, Jacob
Stone, Steven
Taylor, John W.
Tekulve, Kenton
Tettleton, Mickey
Trautman, George
Uhle, George
Vosmik, Joseph
Walker, Moses
Wheat, Zachariah
White, King Solomon
Wise, Samuel
Woodling, Eugene
Wynn, James
Young, Denton "Cy"
Zimmer, Charles "Chief"
Zimmer, Donald

Oklahoma (27)

Barnes, Jesse
Barr, George
Bench, Johnny
Blair, Paul
Brecheen, Harry
Callison, John
Carter, Joseph, Jr.
Clift, Harlond
Cox, Robert
Dark, Alvin
Dobson, Joseph
Hudlin, George Willis
Johnson, Robert
Johnson, Roy
McDaniel, Lyndall
Mantle, Mickey

Martin, Johnny "Pepper"
Mitchell, Loren Dale
Murcer, Bobby
Radcliff, Raymond "Rip"
Ray, Johnny
Reynolds, Allie
Rogan, Wilbur
Stargell, Wilver
Thompson, Henry "Hank"
Waner, Lloyd
Waner, Paul

Oregon (7)

Baker, Delmar
Jansen, Lawrence
Kingman, David
Lolich, Michael
Murphy, Dale
Pesky, John
Williams, Kenneth

Pennsylvania (119)

Adams, Earl "Sparky"
Allen, Richard "Dick"
Baldwin, Marcus
Beckert, Glenn
Bell, David
Bennett, Charles
Bierbauer, Louis
Bishop, Max
Burns, Thomas E.
Burns, Thomas P. "Oyster"
Campanella, Roy
Chylak, Nestor, Jr.
Clark, Jack
Clements, John "Jack"
Collins, James Anthony "Ripper"
Coveleski, Harry
Coveleski, Stanley
Crawford, Henry "Shag"
Daly, Thomas
Daubert, Jacob
Davis, Harry
Devlin, James
Doak, William
Dugan, Joseph
Dunlap, Frederick

Dunn, John
Dykes, James
Eastman, Jean Faut Winsch
Ennis, Delmer
Fox, Nelson
Francona, John "Tito"
Freeman, John "Buck"
Furillo, Carl
Garber, Henry Eugene
Griffey, George Kenneth, Jr., "Ken"
Griffey, George Kenneth, Sr.
Gumbert, Harry
Hallman, William
Harris, Joseph
Hecker, Guy
Hickman, Charles "Piano Legs"
Honochick, George James "Jim"
Jackson, Reginald
Jennings, Hugh
Jones, Fielder
Killen, Frank
Kilroy, Matthew
Kurowski, George "Whitey"
Larkin, Henry "Ted"
Lasorda, Thomas
Leonard, Jeffrey
Lowe, Robert
Lyle, Albert "Sparky"
McBride, James Dickson
McCarthy, Joseph
McDowell, Samuel
McKechnie, William
Magee, Sherwood
Malone, Perce "Pat"
Mathewson, Christopher
Matlack, Jonathan
Meyerle, Levi
Miller, Edward R.
Milligan, John "Jocko"
Murphy, Daniel
Murray, John "Red"
Murtaugh, Daniel
Musial, Stanley
Mussina, Michael
O'Neill, Stephen
Page, Joseph
Parrish, Lance
Pennock, Herbert

Peters, Guy
Piazza, Michael
Plank, Edward
Posey, Cumberland
Purkey, Robert
Quinn, John
Rhines, William
Richard, Ruth
Ritchey, Claude
Rowe, John "Jack"
Sauer, Henry
Shaffer, George "Orator"
Shantz, Robert
Shawkey, James Robert
Sheckard, Samuel James
Sherdel, William
Shibe, Benjamin
Shollenberger, Fern
Simmons, Curtis
Smiley, John
Smith, Elmer Ellsworth
Smith, Frank Elmer
Stanky, Edward
Stivetts, John
Stovey, George
Stovey, Harry
Strunk, Amos
Sutter, Howard Bruce
Tanner, Charles "Chuck"
Tenace, Fury Gene
Thomas, Frank J., Jr.
Thomas, Roy
Titus, John
Vernon, James "Mickey"
Vuckovich, Peter
Waddell, George "Rube"
Wagner, John "Honus"
Wallace, Roderick
Walsh, Edward
Walters, William "Bucky"
Ward, John Montgomery
Weaver, George "Buck"
Wertz, Victor
Williamson, Edward "Ned"
Wilson, James "Jimmie"
Wilson, Lewis "Hack"

Rhode Island (5)

Briggs, Wilma
Duffy, Hugh
Gromek, Steven
Hartnett, Charles "Gabby"
Lajoie, Napoleon

South Carolina (18)

Doby, Lawrence
Driessen, Daniel
Hoyt, Dewey LaMarr
Jackson, Joseph
Jones, Willie
Mahon, Elizabeth
Marion, Martin
Mungo, Van Lingle
Pratt, Derrill
Randolph, William, Jr.
Rice, James
Richardson, Robert, Jr.
Rosen, Albert
Smith, Charles
Taylor, Benjamin
Taylor, Charles I.
Thomas, James Gorman, III
Wisham, Mary Nesbitt

South Dakota (2)

Anderson, George "Sparky"
Scott, James

Tennessee (25)

Alexander, David Dale
Bailey, Lonas Edgar "Ed"
Bridges, Thomas
Caruthers, Robert
Chapman, William Benjamin
Cullenbine, Roy
Garner, Phillip
Gilliam, James
Hahn, Frank "Noodles"
Harvey, Bryan
Kimbro, Henry
Lucas, Charles "Red"
MacPhail, Leland, Jr.
Milan, Jesse Clyde

Osteen, Claude
Petway, Bruce
Pinson, Vada
Sams, Doris
Stearnes, Norman "Turkey"
Stone, John
Toney, Frederick
Turner, James
Wagner, Leon
Walker, Clarence "Tillie"
Wright, Burnis "Bill"

Texas (58)

Allen, Newton
Banks, Ernest
Baylor, Don
Boggess, Lynton "Dusty"
Brown, David
Buford, Donald
Cash, Norman
Collins, Harry "Rip"
Cooper, Cecil
Donohue, Peter
Drabek, Douglas
Fain, Ferris
Falk, Bibb
Flood, Curtis
Foster, Andrew "Rube"
Foster, Willie
Gant, Ronald
Gaston, Clarence "Cito"
Gustafson, Clifford
Hargrove, Dudley Michael
Higgins, Michael "Pinky"
Hooton, Burt
Horlen, Joel
Hornsby, Rogers
Hughson, Cecil "Tex"
Knoblauch, Edward Charles "Chuck"
McMillan, Roy
Mackey, Raleigh
Maddux, Gregory
Marberry, Fredrick
Mathews, Edwin, Jr.
Moore, Joseph "Jo Jo"
Moore, William Wilcy "Cy"
Moreland, Bobby Keith

Morgan, Joe
Mumphrey, Jerry
Philley, David
Reynolds, Carl
Richards, Paul
Robinson, Frank
Robinson, William Edward "Eddie"
Rowe, Lynwood "Schoolboy"
Runnels, James "Pete"
Ryan, Lynn Nolan
Santop, Louis
Serrell, William "Bonnie"
Smith, Hilton
Speaker, Tristram
Templeton, Garry
Vaughn, James
Walker, William Curtis "Curt"
Wells, Willie
West, Samuel
White, Chaney
Whitney, Arthur "Pinky"
Williams, Joe
Youngs, Ross
Zernial, Gus

Utah (2)

Franks, Herman
Hurst, Bruce

Vermont (3)

Fisk, Carlton
Gardner, William Lawrence
Tebbetts, George "Birdie"

Virginia (16)

Alley, Leonard Eugene "Gene"
Brodie, Walter "Steve"
Dandridge, Raymond
Davis, John Howard
Day, Leon
Ferguson, Charles J. "Charlie"
Hamner, Granville
Henderson, Arthur "Rats"
Horton, Willie
McQuinn, George
Nash, William

Phillippe, Charles
Poles, Spottswood
Rixey, Eppa
Sanders, Alexander Bennett "Ben"
Wilson, Ernest Judson

Washington (10)

Averill, Earl
Brown, Robert
Cey, Ronald
Hutchinson, Frederick
Kison, Bruce
Myers, Randall
Sandberg, Ryne
Santo, Ronald
Staley, Gerald
Torgeson, Clifford Earl

West Virginia (11)

Barnard, Ernest
Brett, George
Burdette, Selva Lewis
Burkett, Jesse
Cooper, Arley Wilbur
Glasscock, John
Harrah, Colbert "Toby"
Hoblitzell, Richard
Kruk, John
Mazeroski, William
Seminick, Andrew

Wisconsin (18)

Beaumont, Clarence
Cross, Lafayette
Felsch, Oscar "Happy"
Gantner, James
Grimes, Burleigh
Hauser, Joseph
Joss, Adrian
Keltner, Kenneth
Konetchy, Edward
Kuenn, Harvey
Luderus, Frederick
Merkle, Frederick
Nichols, Charles "Kid"
Pafko, Andrew
Rennert, Laurence "Dutch"

Rowland, Clarence "Pants"
Selig, Allan "Bud"
Simmons, Aloysius

Wyoming (1)

Browning, Thomas

AMERICAN TERRITORIES (15)

Puerto Rico (15)

Alomar, Roberto
Baerga, Carlos
Cepeda, Orlando
Clemente, Roberto
Cruz, Jose
Gonzalez, Juan
Hernandez, Guillermo "Willie"
Lezcano, Sixto
Montanez, Guillermo "Willie"
Pizarro, Juan
Power, Victor
Rodriguez, Ivan
Santiago, Benito
Sierra, Ruben
Tartabull, Danilo "Danny"

FOREIGN NATIONS (76)

Alou, Felipe—Dominican Republic
Alou, Mateo—Dominican Republic
Anderson, John—Norway
Aparicio, Luis, Jr.—Venezuela
Armas, Antonio "Tony"—Venezuela
Avila, Roberto—Mexico
Bell, George—Dominican Republic
Blyleven, Rik Aalbert—Denmark
Bond, Thomas—Ireland
Brown, Thomas T.—England
Campaneris, Dagoberto "Bert"—Cuba
Canseco, Jose, Jr.—Cuba
Cardenal, Jose—Cuba
Cardenas, Lenardo "Leo"—Cuba
Carew, Rodney—Panama
Carty, Ricardo—Dominican Republic
Cedeno, Cesar—Dominican Republic
Chadwick, Henry—England
Concepcion, David—Venezuela
Connolly, Thomas—England
Cuellar, Miguel "Mike"—Cuba

Davis, Charles "Chili"—Jamaica
Dihigo, Martin—Cuba
Donovan, Patrick—Ireland
Doyle, John—Ireland
Dreyfuss, Barney—Germany
Fernandez, Octavio Antonio "Tony"—
  Dominican Republic
Ford, Russell—Canada
Fox, Helen Nicol "Nickie"—Canada
Franco, Julio—Dominican Republic
Galarraga, Andres—Venezuela
Gibson, George—Canada
Griffith, Calvin—Canada
Guerrero, Pedro—Dominican Republic
Hall, George—England
Heath, John Geoffrey "Jeff"—Canada
Higham, Richard—England
Hiller, John—Canada
Jenkins, Ferguson—Canada
Luque, Adolfo—Cuba
McCormick, James—Scotland
Marichal, Juan—Dominican Republic
Martinez, Jose Dennis—Nicaragua
Martinez, Pedro—Dominican Republic
Martinez, Ramon—Dominican
  Republic
Mendez, Jose—Cuba
Minoso, Saturnino Orestes—Cuba
Mullane, Anthony—Ireland
Oglivie, Benjamin—Panama
Oliva, Pedro "Tony"—Cuba
O'Neill, James "Tip"—Canada

Orta, Jorge—Mexico
Palmeiro, Rafael—Cuba
Pascual, Camilo—Cuba
Pena, Antonio—Dominican Republic
Perez, Anatasio "Tony"—Cuba
Puhl, Terry—Canada
Reach, Alfred—England
Rijo, Jose—Dominican Republic
St. Aubin, Helen Callaghan Candaele—
  Canada
Samuel, Juan—Dominican Republic
Sanguillen, Manuel "Manny"—Panama
Selkirk, George "Twinkletoes"—
  Canada
Sosa, Samuel—Dominican Republic
Taylor, Antonio "Tony"—Cuba
Tener, John—Ireland
Thomson, Robert—Scotland
Tiant, Luis, Jr.—Cuba
Torriente, Christobal—Cuba
Trillo, Jose Manuel "Manny"—
  Venezuela
Valenzuela, Fernando—Mexico
Valo, Elmer—Czechoslovakia
Von der Ahe, Christian—Germany
Walker, Larry, Jr.—Canada
White, Devon—Jamaica
Wright, Harry—England

Unknown (3)

Hill, J. Preston
McClellan, Dan
Monroe, William

Entries by Main Position Played

The following lists the entries alphabetically by the main position played. Outfielders are listed as a group rather than as left, center, and right fielders. Entries are listed at the position played most often in the major, minor, Negro, or All-American Girls Professional Baseball leagues.

First Basemen (132)

Adcock, Joseph
Alexander, David
Allen, Richard "Dick"
Altobelli, Joseph
Anson, Adrian "Cap"
Bagwell, Jeffrey
Beckley, Jacob
Blue, Luzerne
Bonura, Henry "Zeke"
Bottomley, James
Brouthers, Dennis
Buckner, William
Burns, George H.
Camilli, Adolph
Carew, Rodney
Carr, George
Cash, Norman
Cavarretta, Philip
Cepeda, Orlando
Chambliss, Carroll Christopher
   "Chris"
Chance, Frank
Chase, Harold

Clark, Jack
Clark, William, Jr.
Collins, James "Ripper"
Comiskey, Charles
Connor, Roger
Cooper, Cecil
Daubert, Jacob
Davis, Glenn
Davis, Harry "Jasper"
Davis, Lorenzo "Piper"
Doyle, John
Driessen, Daniel
Dropo, Walter
Fain, Ferris
Fairly, Ronald
Fielder, Cecil
Fletcher, Elburt "Elbie"
Fonseca, Lewis
Foss, Betty Weaver
Fournier, John
Foxx, James
Galarraga, Andres
Gandil, Arnold "Chick"
Garvey, Steve

Gehrig, Henry Louis
Gentile, James
Giles, George
Grace, Mark
Greenberg, Henry
Grimm, Charles
Hargrove, Dudley Michael
Harris, Joseph
Hernandez, Keith
Hickman, Charles "Piano Legs"
Hoblitzell, Richard
Hodges, Gilbert
Hrbek, Kent
Johnson, Deron
Joyner, Wallace
Judge, Joseph
Kamenshek, Dorothy "Dottie"
Kelly, George
Killebrew, Harmon
Kluszewski, Theodore
Konetchy, Edward
Kruk, John
Kuhel, Joseph
Larkin, Henry "Ted"
Leonard, Walter "Buck"
Lockman, Carroll "Whitey"
Luderus, Frederick
McCormick, Frank
McCovey, Willie
McGann, Dennis "Dan"
McGriff, Frederick
McGwire, Mark
McHale, John
McInnis, John
McQuinn, George
McVey, Calvin
Martinez, Constantino "Tino"
Mattingly, Donald
May, Lee
Mayberry, John
Merkle, Frederick
Mize, John
Montanez, Guillermo "Willie"
Morrill, John
Murnane, Timothy
Murray, Eddie
O'Neil, John, Jr., "Buck"
Orr, David

Ozark, Daniel
Pepitone, Joseph
Perez, Anatasio "Tony"
Pipp, Walter
Powell, John Wesley "Boog"
Power, Victor
Reilly, John
Robinson, William Edward "Eddie"
Runnels, James "Pete"
Scott, George, Jr.
Sheely, Earl
Shively, Twila
Siebern, Norman "Norm"
Siebert, Richard
Sievers, Roy
Sisler, George
Skowron, William
Start, Joseph
Stuart, Richard
Suhr, August "Gus"
Suttles, George
Taylor, Benjamin
Tebeau, Oliver "Patsy"
Tenney, Fred
Terry, William
Thomas, Frank E.
Thompson, Jason
Thornton, Andre
Torgeson, Clifford Earl
Trosky, Harold
Tucker, Thomas
Vaughn, Maurice "Mo"
Vernon, James "Mickey"
Voyce, Inez
Watson, Robert
White, William
Wisham, Mary Nesbitt
York, Preston Rudolph

Second Basemen (89)

Adams, Earl "Sparky"
Allen, Newton
Alomar, Roberto
Anderson, George "Sparky"
Avila, Roberto
Baerga, Carlos
Barnes, Roscoe
Beckert, Glenn

Bierbauer, Louis
Biggio, Craig
Bishop, Max
Cash, David, Jr.
Childs, Clarence
Collins, Edward
Cutshaw, George
Daly, Thomas
Delahanty, James
DeMontreville, Eugene
DeMoss, Elwood
Doerr, Robert
Doyle, Lawrence
Dunlap, Frederick
Evers, John
Fowler, John
Fox, Nelson
Frey, Linus
Frisch, Frank
Gantner, James
Garner, Philip
Gehringer, Charles
Gilliam, James "Junior"
Gleason, William "Kid"
Gordon, Joseph
Grant, Frank
Grantham, George
Grich, Robert
Hale, Arvel Odell "Sammy"
Hallman, William
Harris, Stanley "Bucky"
Herman, William
Herzog, Charles "Buck"
Hornsby, Rogers
Huggins, Miller
Hughes, Samuel
Hunt, Ronald
Johnson, David
Knoblauch, Edward Charles "Chuck"
Kurys, Sophie
Lajoie, Napoleon
Lazzeri, Anthony
Lopes, David
Lowe, Robert
McAuliffe, Richard "Dick"
McManus, Martin
McPhee, John "Bid"
Martin, Alfred "Billy"

Mazeroski, William
Monroe, William
Morgan, Joe
Murphy, Daniel
Murtaugh, Daniel
Myer, Charles "Buddy"
Orta, Jorge
Pfeffer, Nathaniel Frederick
Priddy, Gerald
Randolph, William
Ray, Johnny
Reach, Alfred
Richardson, Abram Harding
Richardson, Robert, Jr.
Rigney, William
Ritchey, Claude
Robinson, Jack
Samuel, Juan
Sandberg, Ryne
Sax, Stephen
Schoendienst, Alfred "Red"
Serrell, William "Bonnie"
Stanky, Edward
Stirnweiss, George "Snuffy"
Taylor, Antonio "Tony"
Temple, John
Trillo, Jesus Manuel "Manny"
Warfield, Francis "Frank"
Whitaker, Louis, Jr.
White, Frank, Jr.
White, King Solomon
Williams, James
Ziegler, Alma "Gabby"

Third Basemen (99)

Bailey, Robert
Baker, John Franklin
Bando, Salvatore
Bell, David "Buddy"
Bluege, Oswald
Boggs, Wade
Bonilla, Roberto, Jr.
Boone, Raymond
Boyer, Cletis
Boyer, Kenton
Bradley, William
Brett, George
Brown, Robert

Burns, Thomas E.
Cabell, Enos, Jr.
Caminiti, Kenneth
Cey, Ronald
Clift, Harlond
Collins, James
Cross, Lafayette
Dandridge, Raymond
DeCinces, Douglas
Devlin, Arthur
Dressen, Charles
Dugan, Joseph
Dunn, John
Dykes, James
Easterly, Howard
Elliott, Robert
English, Madeline "Maddy"
Evans, Darrell
Gaetti, Gary
Gardner, William Lawrence
Groh, Henry
Hack, Stanley
Hart, James Ray
Hebner, Richard
Higgins, Michael "Pinky"
Horner, Robert
Johnson, Howard
Johnson, William "Judy"
Jones, Willie
Joyce, William
Kamm, William
Kell, George
Keltner, Kenneth
Kurowski, George "Whitey"
Lansford, Carney
Latham, Walter Arlington
Lewis, John, Jr., "Buddy"
Lindstrom, Frederick
Lobert, John "Hans"
Lyons, Dennis
McGraw, John
McKechnie, William
Madlock, Bill, Jr.
Malarcher, David
Malzone, Frank
Marcelle, Oliver
Martinez, Edgar
Mathews, Edwin, Jr.

Melton, Edwin William "Bill"
Meyerle, Levi
Molitor, Paul
Money, Donald
Nash, William
Nettles, Graig
Oberkfell, Kenneth
Parrish, Larry
Patterson, Andrew "Pat"
Pendleton, Terry
Pinelli, Ralph "Babe"
Radcliffe, Alexander
Rader, Douglas
Robinson, Brooks
Rolfe, Robert "Red"
Rosen, Albert
Santo, Ronald
Schmidt, Michael
Seitzer, Kevin
Shindle, William
Shollenberger, Fern
Steinfeldt, Harry
Stock, Milton
Sutton, Ezra
Tabor, James
Thompson, Henry "Hank"
Traynor, Harold
Ventura, Robin
Wallach, Timothy
Werber, William
White, James
Whitney, Arthur "Pinky"
Williams, Matthew
Wilson, Ernest Judson
Woods, Parnell
Yost, Edward
Zimmer, Donald
Zimmerman, Henry

Shortstops (93)

Adams, Daniel
Alley, Leon Eugene "Gene"
Aparicio, Luis, Jr.
Appling, Lucius
Bancroft, David
Banks, Ernest
Bartell, Richard
Beckwith, John

Belanger, Mark
Bell, Jay
Boudreau, Louis
Bowa, Lawrence
Burleson, Richard "Rick"
Bush, Owen "Donie"
Butts, Thomas "Pee Wee"
Campaneris, Dagoberto "Campy"
Cardenas, Leonardo "Leo"
Chapman, Raymond
Concepcion, David
Corcoran, Thomas
Cronin, Joseph
Crosetti, Frank
Dahlen, William
Dark, Alvin
Davis, George
Doyle, Dorothy Harrell "Snooky"
Durocher, Leo
Elberfeld, Norman "Kid"
English, Elwood "Woody"
Fernandez, Octavio Antonio "Tony"
Fletcher, Arthur
Fregosi, James
Glasscock, John
Hamner, Granville
Harrah, Colbert "Toby"
Held, Woodson "Woody"
Hemus, Solomon "Solly"
Hollocher, Charles
Howser, Richard
Jackson, Travis
Jennings, Hugh
Johnson, Grant
Joost, Edwin
Jurges, William
Keane, John
Kessinger, Donald
Koenig, Mark
Kress, Ralph "Red"
Kuenn, Harvey
Larkin, Barry
Lary, Lynford "Lyn"
Lloyd, John
Logan, John, Jr.
Long, Herman
Lundy, Richard
McKean, Edward

McMillan, Roy
Maranville, Walter "Rabbit"
Marion, Martin
Menke, Denis
Miller, Edward R.
Moore, Walter "Dobie"
Pearce, Richard
Peckinpaugh, Roger
Petrocelli, Americo
Reese, Harold "Pee Wee"
Ripken, Calvin, Jr.
Rizzuto, Philip
Rowe, John "Jack"
Russell, William
Schroeder, Dorothy "Dottie"
Scott, Lewis Everett "Deacon"
Sewell, Joseph
Smalley, Roy, III
Smith, Osborne "Ozzie"
Speier, Chris
Stephens, Vernon
Templeton, Garry
Tinker, Joseph
Trammell, Alan
Travis, Cecil
Vaughan, Joseph "Arky"
Wagner, John "Honus"
Wallace, Roderick
Ward, John Montgomery
Weaver, George "Buck"
Wells, Willie
Wills, Maurice
Wilson, Arthur
Wise, Samuel
Wright, Forrest Glenn
Wright, George
Yount, Robin

Outfielders (366)

Aaron, Henry "Hank"
Allen, Ethan
Allison, William Robert
Alou, Felipe
Alou, Mateo
Anderson, Brady
Anderson, John
Arlett, Russell
Armas, Antonio "Tony"

Ashburn, Don Richie
Averill, Earl
Baines, Harold
Baker, Johnnie "Dusty"
Barfield, Jesse
Bauer, Henry
Baylor, Don
Beaumont, Clarence "Ginger"
Bell, David "Gus"
Bell, George
Bell, James
Belle, Albert
Berger, Walter
Bescher, Robert
Bichette, Alphonse Dante
Blair, Paul
Bonds, Barry
Bonds, Bobby
Briggs, Wilma
Brock, Louis
Brodie, Walter "Steve"
Brown, Thomas T.
Brown, Willard
Browning, Louis "Pete"
Brunansky, Thomas
Bruton, William
Buford, Donald
Buhner, Jay
Burkett, Jesse
Burns, George J.
Burns, Thomas P. "Oyster"
Burroughs, Jeffrey
Butler, Brett
Callison, John
Campbell, Bruce
Canseco, Jose, Jr.
Cardenal, Jose
Carey, Max
Carter, Joseph, Jr.
Carty, Ricardo
Case, George, Jr.
Cedeno, Cesar
Chapman, John "Jack"
Chapman, William Benjamin
Charleston, Oscar
Clarke, Fred
Clemente, Roberto
Cobb, Tyrus

Colavito, Rocco
Coleman, Vincent
Collins, John F. "Shano"
Combs, Earle
Conigliaro, Anthony "Tony"
Conlan, John "Jocko"
Cooley, Duff
Cowens, Alfred "Al"
Cramer, Roger "Doc"
Cravath, Clifford
Crawford, Samuel
Crutchfield, John
Cruz, Jose
Cuyler, Hazen "Kiki"
Dalrymple, Abner
Dancer, Faye
Davis, Charles "Chili"
Davis, Eric
Davis, Herman Thomas
Davis, John Howard
Davis, Willie
Dawson, Andre
Delahanty, Edward
Demaree, Joseph Franklin "Frank"
DiMaggio, Domenic
DiMaggio, Joseph
Dixon, Herbert
Doby, Lawrence
Donlin, Michael
Donovan, Patrick
Dougherty, Patrick "Patsy"
Douthit, Taylor
Duffy, Hugh
Dykstra, Leonard
Ennis, Delmer
Evans, Dwight
Evers, Walter "Hoot"
Falk, Bibb
Felsch, Oscar "Happy"
Flick, Elmer
Flood, Curtis
Foster, George
Fothergill, Robert
Fox, Ervin "Pete"
Francona, John "Tito"
Freeman, John "Buck"
Frey, James
Furillo, Carl

Galan, August
Gamble, Oscar
Gant, Ronald
Gardner, Floyd "Jelly"
Garr, Ralph
Gaston, Clarence "Cito"
Gibson, Kirk
Gonzalez, Juan
Goodman, Ival
Gordon, Sidney
Gore, George "Piano Legs"
Goslin, Leon
Greenwell, Michael
Griffey, George Kenneth, Jr., "Ken"
Griffey, George Kenneth, Sr.
Griffin, Michael
Grissom, Marquis
Guerrero, Pedro
Gwynn, Anthony
Hafey, Charles
Hall, George
Hamilton, William
Hanlon, Edward "Ned"
Harper, Tommy
Harris, Anthony Spencer
Harris, E. Victor
Hartsel, Tully "Topsy"
Hauser, Joseph
Heath, John Geoffrey
Heilmann, Harry
Henderson, David
Henderson, Rickey
Hendrick, George, Jr.
Henrich, Thomas
Herman, Floyd
Herzog, Dorrell "Whitey"
Higham, Richard
Hill, J. Preston
Hines, Paul
Hisle, Larry
Holliday, James "Bug"
Holmes, Thomas
Honochick, George James "Jim"
Hooper, Harry
Hopp, John, Jr., "Hippity"
Horton, Willie
Howard, Frank
Hoy, William "Dummy"

Irvin, Monford
Jackson, Joseph
Jackson, Reginald
Jacobson, William
Jamieson, Charles
Jefferies, Gregory
Jensen, Jack
Jethroe, Samuel
Jochum, Betsy
Johnson, Alexander
Johnson, Kenneth Lance
Johnson, Oscar "Heavy"
Johnson, Robert
Johnson, Roy
Jones, Charles
Jones, Fielder
Justice, David
Kaline, Albert
Kauff, Benjamin
Keagle, Merle "Pat"
Keating, Edythe Perlick
Keeler, William
Keller, Charles
Kelley, Joseph
Kelly, Michael
Kimbro, Henry
Kiner, Ralph
Kingman, David
Klein, Charles
Kreevich, Michael
Lange, William
Leach, Frederick
Leach, Thomas
LeFlore, Ronald
Lemon, Chester
Leonard, Jeffrey
Lewis, George "Duffy"
Lezcano, Sixto
Lofton, Kenneth
Luzinski, Gregory
Lynn, Fredric
Lyons, James
McBride, Arnold "Bake"
McCarthy, Thomas
McGee, Willie
McGunnigle, William
McRae, Harold
McReynolds, Walter Kevin

Maddox, Garry
Magee, Sherwood
Mahon, Elizabeth
Mantle, Mickey
Manush, Henry
Maris, Roger
Martin, Johnny "Pepper"
Matthews, Gary
Mays, Willie
Medwick, Joseph
Mele, Sabath "Sam"
Meusel, Emil
Meusel, Robert
Milan, Jesse Clyde
Miller, Edmund
Minoso, Saturnino "Minnie"
Mitchell, Kevin
Mitchell, Loren Dale
Monday, Robert "Rick"
Moon, Wallace
Moore, Joseph "Jo Jo"
Moore, Terry
Moreland, Bobby Keith
Moseby, Lloyd
Moses, Wallace
Mostil, John
Mueller, Donald
Mumphrey, Jerry
Murcer, Bobby
Murphy, Dale
Murray, John "Red"
Musial, Stan
Nicholson, William
Northrup, James
Oglivie, Benjamin
Oliva, Pedro "Tony"
Oliver, Albert
O'Neill, James "Tip"
O'Neill, Paul
O'Rourke, James
Otis, Amos
Ott, Melvin
Pafko, Andrew
Page, Theodore "Ted"
Palmeiro, Rafael
Parker, David
Paskert, George "Dode"
Philley, David

Piersall, James
Piniella, Louis
Pinson, Vida
Poles, Spottswood
Posey, Cumberland
Post, Walter "Wally"
Pratt, Derrill
Puckett, Kirby
Puhl, Terry
Radcliff, Raymond "Rip"
Raines, Timothy
Reiser, Harold "Pete"
Reynolds, Carl
Rice, Edgar
Rice, Harry
Rice, James
Rivers, John Milton "Mickey"
Robinson, Cornelius "Neil"
Robinson, Frank
Rose, Peter
Roush, Edd
Rudi, Joseph
Ruth, George Herman "Babe"
Ryan, James
St. Aubin, Helen Callaghan Candaele
Sauer, Henry, Jr.
Schulte, Fred "Wildfire"
Selbach, Albert "Kep"
Selkirk, George "Twinkletoes"
Seybold, Ralph "Socks"
Seymour, James
Shaffer, George "Orator"
Sheckard, Samuel James
Sheffield, Garry
Sierra, Ruben
Simmons, Aloysius
Singleton, Kenneth
Slaughter, Enos
Smith, Alphonse "Al"
Smith, Carl Reginald
Smith, Charles
Smith, Edward Mayo
Smith, Elmer Ellsworth
Smith, Lonnie
Snider, Edwin
Sockalexis, Louis
Sosa, Samuel
Southworth, William

Speaker, Tristram
Spence, Stanley
Stahl, Charles "Chick"
Stargell, Wilver
Staub, Daniel "Rusty"
Stearnes, Norman "Turkey"
Stengel, Charles "Casey"
Stenzel, Jacob
Stephenson, Jackson Riggs
Stone, George
Stone, John
Stovey, Harry
Strawberry, Darryl
Strunk, Amos
Tanner, Charles
Tartabull, Danilo "Danny"
Thomas, Clinton
Thomas, Frank Joseph, Jr.
Thomas, James Gorman, III
Thomas, Roy
Thompson, Samuel
Thomson, Robert
Tiernan, Michael
Titus, John
Tobin, John
Torriente, Christobal
Tresh, Thomas
Valo, Elmer
Van Haltren, George
Van Slyke, Andrew
Veach, Robert
Virdon, William
Vosmik, Joseph
Wagner, Audrey
Wagner, Leon
Wagoner, Betty
Walker, Clarence "Tillie"
Walker, Fred "Dixie"
Walker, Gerald
Walker, Larry, Jr.
Walker, William Curtis "Curt"
Waner, Lloyd
Waner, Paul
Washington, Claudell
Weaver, Joanne
West, Samuel
Wheat, Zachariah
White, Chaney

White, Devon
White, Roy
Williams, Billy
Williams, Fred
Williams, Kenneth
Williams, Richard
Williams, Theodore
Williamson, Edward "Ned"
Wilson, Lewis "Hack"
Wilson, Willie
Winfield, David
Wolf, William "Chicken"
Woodling, Eugene
Wright, Burnis
Wright, Harry
Wright, Taft
Wynn, James
Yastrzemski, Carl
Youngs, Ross
Zernial, Gus
Zisk, Richard

Catchers (89)

Bailey, Lonas Edgar "Ed"
Baker, Delmar
Bench, John
Bennett, Charles
Berra, Lawrence "Yogi"
Boone, Robert
Bresnahan, Roger
Brown, Larry "Iron Man"
Burgess, Forrest "Smoky"
Campanella, Roy
Carrigan, William
Carter, Gary
Clements, John "Jack"
Cochrane, Gordon "Mickey"
Cooper, William Walker
Crandall, Delmar
Crawford, Henry "Shag"
Danning, Harry
Daulton, Darren
Davis, LaVonne Paire "Pepper"
Davis, Virgil "Spud"
Dickey, William
Duncan, Frank, Jr.
Ewing, William "Buck"
Farrell, Charles

Ferrell, Richard
Fisk, Carlton
Franks, Herman
Freehan, William
Gibson, George
Gibson, Joshua
Gowdy, Henry "Hank"
Haller, Thomas
Hargrave, Eugene "Bubbles"
Hartnett, Charles "Gabby"
Hayes, Frank
Hegan, James
Houk, Ralph
Howard, Elston
Johnson, George "Chappie"
Kling, John
Lau, Charles
Lollar, John Sherman
Lombardi, Ernest
Lopez, Alfonso
McGuire, James "Deacon"
Mack, Connie
Mackey, Raleigh
McNamara, John
Meyers, John "Chief"
Milligan, John "Jocko"
Moran, Patrick
Munson, Thurman
O'Connor, John "Jack"
O'Farrell, Robert
O'Neill, Stephen
Parrish, Lance
Pena, Antonio
Petway, Bruce
Phelps, Ernest "Babe"
Piazza, Michael
Porter, Darrell
Richard, Ruth
Rickey, Wesley Branch
Robinson, Wilbert
Rodriguez, Ivan
Roseboro, John
Ruel, Herold "Muddy"
Sanguillen, Manuel "Manny"
Santiago, Benito
Santop, Louis
Schalk, Raymond
Schang, Walter

Seminick, Andrew
Severeid, Henry "Hank"
Sewell, James Luther "Luke"
Simmons, Ted
Stallings, George
Street, Charles "Gabby"
Sundberg, James
Tebbetts, George "Birdie"
Tenace, Fury Gene
Tettleton, Mickey
Torre, Joseph
Triandos, Gus
Trouppe, Quincy
Walker, Moses
Wilson, James "Jimmie"
Zimmer, Charles "Chief"

Pitchers (444)

Abernathy, Theodore "Ted"
Adams, Charles "Babe"
Aguilera, Richard "Rick"
Alexander, Doyle
Alexander, Grover Cleveland
Allen, John
Ames, Leon
Antonelli, John
Appier, Robert Kevin
Auker, Eldon
Bagby, James, Sr.
Baldwin, Marcus
Ball, George Walter
Bankhead, Sam
Barnes, Jesse
Barnhill, David
Bedrosian, Stephen
Bender, Charles "Chief"
Billingham, John "Jack"
Blackwell, Ewell
Blass, Stephen
Blue, Vida
Blyleven, Rik Aalbert
Boddiker, Michael
Boggess, Lynton "Dusty"
Bond, Thomas
Bonham, Ernest
Brecheen, Harry
Breitenstein, Theodore "Ted"
Bremer, Eugene, Sr.

Brewer, Chester
Bridges, Thomas
Briles, Nelson
Brown, David
Brown, James Kevin
Brown, Mordecai "Three Finger"
Brown, Raymond
Browning, Thomas
Buffinton, Charles
Buhl, Robert
Bunning, James
Burdette, Selva Lewis
Bush, Guy
Bush, Leslie "Bullet Joe"
Byrd, William
Callahan, James "Nixey"
Camnitz, Samuel "Howie"
Candelaria, John
Carlton, Steven
Carroll, Clay
Caruthers, Robert
Casey, Hugh
Chamberlain, Elton "Icebox"
Chance, Wilmer
Chandler, Spurgeon "Spud"
Cheney, Laurance "Larry"
Chesbro, John
Cicotte, Edward
Clark, William Watson "Watty"
Clarkson, John
Clemens, William Roger
Cockrell, Phillip
Collins, Dorothy Wiltse "Dottie"
Collins, Harry "Rip"
Cone, David
Coombs, John
Cooper, Arley Wilbur
Cooper, Morton
Corcoran, Lawrence
Coveleski, Harry
Coveleski, Stanley
Craig, Roger
Crandall, Otis "Doc"
Creighton, James
Crowder, Alvin "General"
Cuellar, Miguel "Mike"
Cummings, William "Candy"
Cuppy, George "Nig"

Currie, Reuben
Darling, Ronald
Dauss, George
Davis, Curtis
Day, Leon
Dean, Jay "Dizzy"
Denny, John
Derringer, Paul
Devlin, James
Dickson, Murry
Dierker, Lawrence "Larry"
Dihigo, Martin
Dinneen, William
Dismukes, William
Doak, William
Dobson, Joseph
Donaldson, John
Donohue, Peter
Donovan, Richard "Dick"
Donovan, William
Drabek, Douglas
Drysdale, Donald
Dwyer, John Francis "Frank"
Eastman, Jean Faut Winsch
Eckersley, Dennis
Erskine, Carl
Faber, Urban "Red"
Face, Elroy
Feller, Robert
Ferguson, Charles J. "Charlie"
Ferrell, Wesley
Fingers, Roland
Finley, Charles "Chuck"
Fitzsimmons, Frederick
Flanagan, Michael
Florreich, Kathleen Lois
Ford, Edward "Whitey"
Ford, Russell
Forsch, Robert
Foster, Andrew "Rube"
Foster, Willie
Foutz, David
Fox, Helen Nicol "Nicky"
Franco, John
Freitas, Antonio, Jr.
French, Lawrence
Friend, Robert
Galvin, James "Pud"

Garber, Henry Eugene
Garcia, Edward Miguel "Mike"
Gibson, Robert
Glavine, Thomas
Goldsmith, Fred
Gomez, Vernon
Gooden, Dwight
Gossage, Richard "Goose"
Grant, James "Mudcat"
Green, George Dallas
Griffith, Clark
Grimes, Burleigh
Grimsley, Ross, II
Gromek, Stephen
Grove, Robert "Lefty"
Guidry, Ronald
Gullet, Donald
Gullickson, William
Gumbert, Harry
Gura, Lawrence
Haddix, Harvey
Hahn, Frank "Noodles"
Haines, Jesse
Harder, Melvin
Harvey, Bryan
Haylett, Alice
Hecker, Guy
Henderson, Arthur "Rats"
Hendrix, Claude
Henke, Thomas
Hentgen, Patrick
Hernandez, Guillermo "Willie"
Hershiser, Orel, IV
Hiller, John
Hoffer, William "Bill"
Holtzman, Kenneth
Hooton, Burt
Horlen, Joel
Hough, Charles
Howell, Henry "Harry"
Hoyt, Dewey LaMarr
Hoyt, Waite
Hrabosky, Alan
Hubbell, Carl
Hudlin, George Willis
Hughson, Cecil "Tex"
Hunter, James
Hurst, Bruce

Hutchinson, Frederick
Hutchinson, William
Jackson, Lawrence
Jansen, Lawrence
Jenkins, Ferguson
John, Thomas
Johnson, Randall "Randy"
Johnson, Walter
Jones, Douglas
Jones, Randall "Randy"
Jones, Samuel Pond
Jones, Samuel "Toothpick"
Jones, Stuart "Slim"
Joss, Adrian
Kaat, James
Keefe, Timothy
Kennedy, William "Brickyard"
Key, James "Jimmy"
Killen, Frank
Kilroy, Matthew
Kinder, Ellis
King, Charles "Silver"
Kison, Bruce
Konstanty, James
Koosman, Jerry
Koufax, Sanford
Kremer, Remy
Langston, Mark
Lanier, Hubert Max
Larsen, Don
Lary, Frank
Law, Vernon
Lee, Thornton
Lee, William C.
Lee, William F. "Bill"
Leever, Samuel
Leibrandt, Charles, Jr.
Leifield, Albert
Lemon, Robert
Leonard, Dennis
Leonard, Emil "Dutch"
Leonard, Hubert "Dutch"
Lolich, Michael
Lonborg, James
Lopat, Edmund
Lucas, Charles "Red"
Lundgren, Carl
Luque, Adolfo

Lyle, Albert "Sparky"
Lyons, Theodore
McBride, James Dickson
McClellan, Dan
McCormick, James
McDaniel, Lyndall
McDonald, Webster
McDowell, Jack
McDowell, Samuel
McDuffie, Terris
McGinnis, George "Jumbo"
McGinnity, Joseph
McGraw, Frank, Jr., "Tug"
McGregor, Scott
McLain, Dennis
McMahon, Donald
McMahon, John J.
McNally, David
McNaughton, Alice Hohlmayer
Maddux, Gregory
Maglie, Salvatore
Malone, Perce "Pat"
Maloney, James
Manning, Maxwell "Max"
Marberry, Fredrick
Marichal, Juan
Marquard, Richard "Rube"
Marshall, Michael
Martinez, Jose Dennis
Martinez, Pedro
Martinez, Ramon
Mathews, Robert
Mathewson, Christopher
Mathis, Verdell "Lefty"
Matlack, Jonathan
Mays, Carl
Meadows, Henry Lee
Meekin, Jouett
Mendez, Jose
Messersmith, John "Andy"
Miller, Stuart
Mogridge, George
Montgomery, Jeffrey
Moore, Earl
Moore, William Wilcy "Cy"
Morris, Edward "Cannonball"
Morris, John "Jack"
Mullane, Anthony

Mullin, George
Mungo, Van Lingle
Murphy, John
Mussina, Michael
Myers, Randall
Nehf, Arthur
Newcombe, Donald
Newhouser, Harold
Newsom, Louis "Bobo"
Nichols, Charles "Kid"
Niekro, Joseph
Niekro, Philip
Nolan, Gary
Nuxhall, Joseph
Ojeda, Robert "Bob"
Orth, Albert
Osteen, Claude
Overall, Orval
Page, Joseph
Paige, Leroy "Satchel"
Palmer, James
Pappas, Milton
Parnell, Melvin
Pascual, Camilo
Passeau, Claude
Pearson, Marcellus Montgomery
    "Monte"
Pennock, Herbert
Perranoski, Ronald
Perry, Gaylord
Perry, James
Peters, Gary
Petry, Daniel
Pfeffer, Edward "Jeff"
Pfiester, John "Jack"
Phillippe, Charles
Pierce, Walter William
Pizarro, Juan
Plank, Edward
Podres, John
Pollet, Howard
Powell, John Joseph
Purkey, Robert
Quinn, John
Quisenberry, Daniel
Radatz, Richard
Radbourne, Charles
Radcliffe, Theodore

Ramsey, Thomas "Toad"
Randall, Maxine Kline
Raschi, Victor
Reardon, Jeffrey
Redding, Richard
Reed, Ronald
Reulbach, Edward
Reuschel, Ricky
Reuss, Jerry
Reynolds, Allie
Rhines, William
Rhoden, Richard
Richard, James Rodney, Jr.
Richmond, J. Lee
Righetti, David
Rijo, Jose
Rixey, Eppa
Roberts, Robin
Roe, Elwin "Preacher"
Rogan, Wilbur
Rogers, Stephen
Rommel, Edwin
Root, Charles
Rowe, Lynwood "Schoolboy"
Rucker, George Napoleon
Rudolph, Richard
Ruether, Walter "Dutch"
Ruffing, Charles "Red"
Rusie, Amos
Ryan, Lynn Nolan
Saberhagen, Bret
Sain, John
Sallee, Harry "Slim"
Sams, Doris
Sanders, Alexander Bennett "Ben"
Sanderson, Scott
Sanford, John "Jack"
Schilling, Curtis
Schumacher, Harold
Score, Herbert
Scott, James
Scott, Michael
Seaver, George Thomas
Sewell, Truett "Rip"
Shantz, Robert
Shawkey, James Robert
Shellenback, Frank
Sherdel, William

Shocker, Urban
Siebert, Wilford, III, "Sonny"
Simmons, Curtis
Smiley, John
Smith, David S.
Smith, Frank Elmer
Smith, Hilton
Smith, Lee, Jr.
Smoltz, John
Spahn, Warren
Spalding, Albert
Splittorff, Paul, Jr.
Staley, Gerald
Stanley, Robert
Stewart, David
Stieb, David
Stivetts, John
Stone, Steven
Stottlemyre, Melvin, Sr.
Stovey, George
Sutcliffe, Richard
Sutter, Howard Bruce
Sutton, Donald
Tanana, Frank
Tannehill, Jesse
Taylor, John "Jack"
Tekulve, Kenton
Tener, John
Terry, William Adonis
Tesreau, Charles "Jeff"
Thigpen, Robert
Tiant, Luis, Jr.
Toney, Frederick
Torrez, Michael
Trent, Theodore "Ted"
Trout, Paul "Dizzy"
Trucks, Virgil
Tudor, John
Turley, Robert
Turner, James
Tyler, George "Lefty"
Uhle, George
Valenzuela, Fernando
Vance, Arthur "Dazzy"
Vander Meer, John
Vaughn, James "Hippo"
Veale, Robert, Jr.
Viola, Frank, Jr.

Appendix 3
Major League Managers

The following entries, listed alphabetically, managed at least one major league game.

Adcock, Joseph
Alou, Felipe
Alston, Walter
Altobelli, Joseph
Anderson, George "Sparky"
Anson, Adrian "Cap"
Appling, Lucius "Luke"
Baker, Delmer
Baker, Johnnie "Dusty"
Bancroft, David
Bancroft, Frank
Barrow, Edward
Bauer, Henry
Baylor, Donald
Bell, David "Gus"
Berra, Lawrence "Yogi"
Bluege, Oswald
Bond, Thomas
Boone, Robert
Bottomley, James
Boudreau, Louis
Bowa, Lawrence
Boyer, Kenton
Bradley, William
Bresnahan, Roger
Brown, Mordecai "Three Finger"
Brown, Thomas T.

Buffinton, Charles
Burns, Thomas E.
Bush, Owen
Carey, Max
Carrigan, William
Caruthers, Robert
Cavarretta, Philip
Caylor, Oliver P.
Chance, Frank
Chapman, John
Chapman, William Benjamin
Clarke, Fred
Clements, John
Cobb, Tyrus
Cochrane, Gordon "Mickey"
Collins, Edward, Sr.
Collins, James
Collins, John "Shano"
Comiskey, Charles
Connor, Roger
Coombs, John
Cox, Robert
Craig, Roger
Crandall, Delmar
Cravath, Clifford
Cronin, Joseph
Cross, Lafayette

Dahlen, William
Dark, Alvin
Davis, George
Davis, Harry "Jasper"
Davis, Virgil "Spud"
Day, John
Dickey, William
Doby, Lawrence
Donovan, Patrick
Donovan, William
Doyle, John
Dressen, Charles
Duffy, Hugh
Durocher, Leo
Dwyer, John
Dyer, Edwin
Dykes, James
Ebbets, Charles
Elberfeld, Norman "Kid"
Elliott, Robert
Evers, John
Ewing, William "Buck"
Falk, Bibb
Ferguson, Robert V.
Fitzsimmons, Frederick
Fletcher, Arthur
Fonseca, Lewis
Foutz, David
Franks, Herman
Fregosi, James
Frey, James
Frisch, Frank
Galvin, James
Garner, Philip
Gaston, Clarence "Cito"
Gibson, George
Glasscock, John
Gleason, William "Kid"
Gordon, Joseph
Gore, George
Gowdy, Henry
Green, George Dallas
Griffin, Michael
Griffith, Clark
Grimes, Burleigh
Grimm, Charles
Groh, Henry
Hack, Stanley

Hallman, William
Hanlon, Edward "Ned"
Harder, Melvin
Hargrove, Dudley Michael
Harrah, Colbert "Toby"
Harris, Stanley "Bucky"
Hartnett, Charles "Gabby"
Hecker, Guy
Hemus, Solomon "Solly"
Herman, William
Herzog, Charles "Buck"
Herzog, Dorrell "Whitey"
Higgins, Michael "Pinky"
Higham, Richard
Hodges, Gilbert
Holmes, Thomas
Hornsby, Rogers
Houk, Ralph
Howard, Frank
Howser, Richard
Huggins, Miller
Hutchinson, Frederick
Jennings, Hugh
Johnson, David
Johnson, Roy
Johnson, Walter
Jones, Fielder
Joost, Edwin
Joyce, William
Jurges, William
Keane, John
Kelley, Joseph
Kelly, Jay Thomas
Kelly, Michael
Kessinger, Donald
Kling, John
Kuenn, Harvey
Kuhel, Joseph
Lajoie, Napoleon
Larkin, Henry "Ted"
LaRussa, Anthony
Lasorda, Thomas
Latham, Walter Arlington
Lemon, Robert
Leyland, James
Lobert, John "Hans"
Lockman, Carroll "Whitey"
Lopat, Edmund

Lopez, Alfonso
Lowe, Robert
Lyons, Theodore
McBride, James Dickson
McCarthy, Joseph
McCarthy, Thomas
McCormick, James
McGraw, John
McGunnigle, William
McInnis, John "Snuffy"
Mack, Connie
McKechnie, William
McManus, Martin
McMillan, Roy
McNamara, John
McPhee, John "Bid"
McRae, Harold
McVey, Calvin
Maranville, Walter "Rabbit"
Marion, Martin
Martin, Alfred "Billy"
Mathews, Edwin, Jr.
Mathewson, Christopher
Mauch, Gene
Mele, Sabath "Sam"
Milan, Jesse Clyde
Moore, Terry
Moran, Patrick
Morrill, John
Murnane, Timothy
Murtaugh, Daniel
Mutrie, James
Nash, William
Nichols, Charles "Kid"
O'Connor, John
O'Day, Henry
O'Farrell, Robert
O'Neill, Stephen
O'Rourke, James
Orr, David
Ott, Melvin
Ozark, Daniel
Pearce, Richard
Peckinpaugh, Roger
Perez, Anatasio "Tony"
Pesky, John
Pfeffer, Nathaniel Frederick
Piniella, Louis

Rader, Douglas
Reach, Alfred
Richards, Paul
Rickey, Wesley Branch
Rigney, William
Robinson, Frank
Robinson, Wilbert
Rolfe, Robert "Red"
Rose, Peter
Rowe, John
Rowland, Clarence "Pants"
Ruel, Herold "Muddy"
Runnels, James "Pete"
Russell, William
Schalk, Raymond
Schoendienst, Albert "Red"
Selee, Frank
Sewell, James Luther
Shawkey, James Robert
Sisler, George
Smith, Edward Mayo
Southworth, William
Spalding, Albert
Speaker, Tristram
Stahl, Charles "Chick"
Stallings, George
Stanky, Edward
Start, Joseph
Stengel, Charles "Casey"
Stovey, Harry
Street, Charles "Gabby"
Tanner, Charles
Tebbetts, George "Birdie"
Tebeau, Oliver "Patsy"
Tenace, Fury Gene
Tenney, Frederick
Terry, William H.
Tinker, Joseph
Torre, Joseph
Traynor, Harold "Pie"
Van Haltren, George
Vernon, James "Mickey"
Virdon, William
Von der Ahe, Christian
Wagner, John "Honus"
Wallace, Roderick
Walsh, Edward
Walters, William "Bucky"

Ward, John Montgomery
Weaver, Earl
White, James "Deacon"
White, William H.
Williams, Richard
Williams, Theodore
Wills, Maurice
Wilson, James
Winkles, Bobby

Wolf, William "Chicken"
Wright, George
Wright, William Henry "Harry"
York, Preston Rudolph
Yost, Edward
Young, Denton "Cy"
Young, Nicholas
Zimmer, Charles "Chief"
Zimmer, Donald

Appendix 4
Major League Executives

The following entries, listed alphabetically, served as major or Negro league executives.

Aaron, Henry "Hank"
Adams, Daniel
Bancroft, Francis
Bando, Salvatore
Barnard, Ernest
Barrow, Edward
Bell, David "Buddy"
Bluege, Oswald
Boone, Robert
Brett, George
Briggs, Walter
Brown, Robert
Brush, John, Jr.
Budig, Gene
Bulkeley, Morgan
Busch, August, Jr.
Cammeyer, William
Carpenter, Robert, Jr.
Cartwright, Alexander
Caylor, Oliver Perry
Chadwick, Henry
Chandler, Albert "Happy"
Clarke, Fred
Cochrane, Gordon "Mickey"
Collins, Edward, Sr.
Comiskey, Charles
Crosley, Powel, Jr.

Day, John
*Dismukes, William
Doby, Lawrence
Dreyfuss, Barney
Ebbets, Charles
Eckert, William
Evans, William
Evers, Walter "Hoot"
Feeney, Charles "Chub"
Fehr, Donald
Ferrell, Richard
Finley, Charles O.
*Foster, Andrew "Rube"
Freedman, Andrew
Frick, Ford
Galbreath, Daniel
Galbreath, John W.
Gehringer, Charles
Giamatti, Angelo Bartlett
Gibson, Robert
Giles, Warren
Green, George Dallas, Jr.
Greenberg, Henry
*Greenlee, William
Griffith, Calvin
Griffith, Clark

Haller, Thomas
Harper, Tommy
Harridge, William
Herzog, Dorrell "Whitey"
Higgins, Michael
Houk, Ralph
Hubbell, Carl
Hulbert, William
Irvin, Monford
Johnson, Byron
Kuhn, Bowie
Landis, Kenesaw Mountain
Lane, Ferdinand C.
Lane, Frank
Lasorda, Thomas
Lockman, Carroll "Whitey"
Lucas, Henry
Lynch, Thomas
McCovey, Willie
McHale, John
Mack, Connie
MacPhail, Leland, Sr., "Larry"
MacPhail, Leland, Jr., "Lee"
Mathewson, Christopher
Miller, Marvin
Mills, Abraham
Morrill, John
Murphy, John
Musial, Stanley
Navin, Frank
O'Malley, Walter
Paul, Gabriel
Peckinpaugh, Roger
Piniella, Louis
*Posey, Cumberland, Jr.
Pulliam, Harry
Randolph, William, Jr.
Reach, Alfred
Richards, Paul
Rickey, Wesley Branch

Rigney, William
Robinson, Frank
Robinson, Wilbert
Robinson, William Edward
Rosen, Albert
Ruel, Herold "Muddy"
Ruppert, Jacob, Jr.
Rowland, Clarence "Pants"
Selig, Allan H. "Bud"
Selkirk, George
Shibe, Benjamin
Soden, Arthur
Somers, Charles
Spalding, Albert
Stargell, Wilver
Steinbrenner, George, III
Stewart, David
Stoneham, Charles
Stoneham, Horace
*Taylor, Charles I.
Tebbetts, George "Birdie"
Tener, John
Topping, Daniel
Trautman, George
Veeck, William, Jr.
Vincent, Frances, Jr., "Fay"
Von der Ahe, Christian
Ward, John Montgomery
*Warfield, Francis
Weiss, George
White, James
White, William D.
*Wilkerson, James
Wright, George
Wright, William Henry "Harry"
Wrigley, Philip
Yawkey, Thomas
Young, Nicholas

*Negro Leagues

Appendix 5
Major League Umpires

The following entries, listed alphabetically, umpired at least one major league game.

Ashford, Emmett
Barlick, Albert
Barr, George
Beckley, Jacob
Boggess, Lynton "Dusty"
Chylak, Nestor, Jr.
Clements, John J.
Conlan, John "Jocko"
Connolly, Thomas, Sr.
Corcoran, Thomas
Crawford, Henry "Shag"
Dinneen, William
Donatelli, August
Doyle, John
Dwyer, John
Evans, William
Ferguson, Robert V.
Galvin, James "Pud"
Goldsmith, Fred
Harvey, Harold Douglas
Hecker, Guy
Heydler, John
Higham, Richard
Honochick, George James
Jones, Charles Wesley
Keefe, Timothy

Klem, William
Latham, Walter Arlington
Luciano, Ronald
Lynch, Thomas
McGowan, William
McInnis, George "Jumbo"
Magee, Sherwood
Marberry, Fredrick
Morrill, John
O'Day, Henry
O'Loughlin, Francis "Silk"
Orth, Albert
Palermo, Stephen
Pinelli, Ralph "Babe"
Reardon, John "Beans"
Rennert, Laurence "Dutch"
Rommel, Edwin
Rowland, Clarence "Pants"
Scott, James
Sheridan, John F.
Stark, Albert "Dolly"
Summers, William
Wallace, Roderick
Walsh, Edward
Warneke, Lonnie
Wendelstedt, Harry, Jr.

Appendix 6

National Baseball Hall of Fame Members

The following entries, listed alphabetically, are members of the National Baseball Hall of Fame in Cooperstown, New York.

Aaron, Henry
Alexander, Grover Cleveland
Alston, Walter
Anson, Adrian "Cap"
Aparicio, Luis, Jr.
Appling, Lucius "Luke"
Ashburn, Don Richie
Averill, Howard Earl
Baker, John Franklin "Home Run"
Bancroft, David
Banks, Ernest
Barlick, Albert
Barrow, Edward
Beckley, Jacob
Bell, James "Cool Papa"
Bench, Johnny
Bender, Charles "Chief"
Berra, Lawrence "Yogi"
Bottomley, James
Boudreau, Louis
Bresnahan, Roger
Brett, George
Brock, Louis
Brouthers, Dennis "Dan"
Brown, Mordecai "Three Finger"
Bulkeley, Morgan
Bunning, James

Burkett, Jesse
Campanella, Roy
Carew, Rodney
Carey, Max
Carlton, Steven
Cartwright, Alexander
Cepeda, Orlando
Chadwick, Henry
Chance, Frank
Chandler, Albert "Happy"
Charleston, Oscar
Chesbro, John
Chylak, Nestor, Jr.
Clarke, Fred
Clarkson, John
Clemente, Roberto
Cobb, Tyrus
Cochrane, Gordon "Mickey"
Collins, Edward
Collins, James
Combs, Earle
Comiskey, Charles
Conlan, John "Jocko"
Connolly, Thomas
Connor, Roger
Coveleski, Stanley
Crawford, Samuel

Cronin, Joseph
Cummings, William "Candy"
Cuyler, Hazen "Kiki"
Dandrige, Raymond
Davis, George
Day, Leon
Dean, Jay "Dizzy"
Delahanty, Edward
Dickey, William
Dihigo, Martin
DiMaggio, Joseph
Doby, Lawrence
Doerr, Robert
Drysdale, Donald
Duffy, Hugh
Durocher, Leo
Evans, William
Evers, John
Ewing, William "Buck"
Faber, Urban "Red"
Feller, Robert
Ferrell, Richard
Fingers, Roland
Fisk, Carlton
Flick, Elmer
Ford, Edward "Whitey"
Foster, Andrew "Rube"
Foster, Willie
Fox, Nelson
Foxx, James
Frick, Ford
Frisch, Frank
Galvin, James "Pud"
Gehrig, Henry Louis
Gehringer, Charles
Gibson, Joshua
Gibson, Robert
Giles, Warren
Gomez, Vernon "Lefty"
Goslin, Leon "Goose"
Greenberg, Henry
Griffith, Clark
Grimes, Burleigh
Grove, Robert "Lefty"
Hafey, Charles "Chick"
Haines, Jesse
Hamilton, William
Hanlon, Edward "Ned"
Harridge, William

Harris, Stanley "Bucky"
Hartnett, Charles "Gabby"
Heilmann, Harry
Herman, William
Hooper, Harry
Hornsby, Rogers
Hoyt, Waite
Hubbell, Carl
Huggins, Miller
Hulbert, William
Hunter, James "Catfish"
Irvin, Monford
Jackson, Reginald
Jackson, Travis
Jenkins, Ferguson
Jennings, Hugh
Johnson, Byron
Johnson, Walter
Johnson, William "Judy"
Joss, Adrian "Addie"
Kaline, Albert
Keefe, Timothy
Keeler, William "Wee Willie"
Kell, George
Kelley, Joseph
Kelly, George
Kelly, Michael
Killebrew, Harmon
Kiner, Ralph
Klein, Charles
Klem, William
Koufax, Sanford
Lajoie, Napoleon
Landis, Kenesaw Mountain
Lasorda, Thomas
Lazzeri, Anthony
Lemon, Robert
Leonard, Walter "Buck"
Lindstrom, Frederick
Lloyd, John Henry
Lombardi, Ernest
Lopez, Alfonso
Lyons, Theodore
McCarthy, Joseph
McCarthy, Thomas
McCovey, Willie
McGinnity, Joseph
McGowan, William

McGraw, John
Mack, Connie
MacPhail, Leland, Jr., "Lee"
MacPhail, Leland, Sr., "Larry"
Mantle, Mickey
Manush, Henry
Maranville, Walter "Rabbit"
Marichal, Juan
Marquard, Richard "Rube"
Mathews, Edwin, Jr.
Mathewson, Christopher
Mays, Willie
Medwick, Joseph "Ducky"
Mize, John
Morgan, Joe
Musial, Stanley
Newhouser, Harold
Nichols, Charles "Kid"
Niekro, Philip
O'Rourke, James
Ott, Melvin
Paige, Leroy "Satchel"
Palmer, James
Pennock, Herbert
Perez, Atanasio
Perry, Gaylord
Plank, Edward
Radbourn, Charles "Hoss"
Reese, Harold "Pee Wee"
Rice, Edgar
Rickey, Wesley Branch
Rixey, Eppa
Rizzuto, Philip
Roberts, Robin
Robinson, Brooks
Robinson, Frank
Robinson, Jack
Robinson, Wilbert
Rogan, Wilbur
Roush, Edd
Ruffing, Charles "Red"
Rusie, Amos
Ruth, George Herman "Babe"
Ryan, Lynn Nolan
Schalk, Raymond
Schmidt, Michael
Schoendienst, Albert "Red"

Seaver, George Thomas
Selee, Frank
Sewell, Joseph
Simmons, Aloysius
Sisler, George
Slaughter, Enos
Snider, Edwin "Duke"
Spahn, Warren
Spalding, Albert
Speaker, Tristram
Stargell, Wilver
Stengel, Charles "Casey"
Sutton, Donald
Terry, William
Thompson, Samuel
Tinker, Joseph
Traynor, Harold "Pie"
Vance, Arthur "Dazzy"
Vaughan, Joseph "Arky"
Veeck, William, Jr.
Waddell, George "Rube"
Wagner, John "Honus"
Wallace, Roderick
Walsh, Edward
Waner, Lloyd
Waner, Paul
Ward, John Montgomery
Weaver, Earl
Weiss, George
Welch, Michael
Wells, Willie
Wheat, Zachariah
Wilhelm, James Hoyt
Williams, Billy
Williams, Joe
Williams, Theodore
Willis, Victor
Wilson, Lewis "Hack"
Wright, George
Wright, William Henry "Harry"
Wynn, Early
Yastrzemski, Carl
Yawkey, Thomas
Young, Denton "Cy"
Youngs, Ross
Yount, Robin

Appendix 7
Negro League Entries

The following is a list of the baseball figures profiled who spent all or most of their professional baseball careers in the Negro Leagues.

Allen, Newton
Ball, George Walter
*Bankhead, Samuel
Barnhill, David
*Beckwith, John
*Bell, James "Cool Papa"
Bremer, Eugene, Sr.
*Brewer, Chester
Brown, David
*Brown, Larry "Iron Man"
Brown, Raymond
****Brown, Willard
Butts, Thomas "Pee Wee"
Byrd, William
Carr, George
*Charleston, Oscar
*Cockrell, Phillip
Crutchfield, John
Currie, Reuben
*Dandridge, Raymond
Davis, John Howard
*Davis, Lorenzo "Piper"
Day, Leon
*DeMoss, Elwood
*Dihigo, Martin
**Dismukes, William
Dixon, Herbert

Donaldson, John
*Duncan, Frank, Jr.
Easterling, Howard
**Foster, Andrew "Rube"
*Foster, Willie
Fowler, John
Gardner, Floyd "Jelly"
Gibson, Joshua
*Giles, George
Grant, Frank
***Greenlee, William A.
*Harris, E. Victor
Henderson, Arthur "Rats"
*Hill, J. Preston
Hughes, Sammy
*Johnson, George "Chappie"
*Johnson, Grant
Johnson, Oscar "Heavy"
*Johnson, William "Judy"
Jones, Stuart "Slim"
Kimbro, Henry
Leonard, Walter "Buck"
*Lloyd, John Henry
*Lundy, Richard
*Lyons, James
*McClellan, Dan
*McDonald, Webster

McDuffie, Terris
*Mackey, Raleigh
*Malarcher, David
Manning, Maxwell "Max"
Marcelle, Oliver
Mathis, Verdell "Lefty"
*Mendez, Jose
Monroe, William
Moore, Walter "Dobie"
*O'Neil, John, Jr., "Buck"
Page, Theodore "Ted"
****Paige, Leroy "Satchel"
Patterson, Andrew "Pat"
*Petway, Bruce
Poles, Spottswood
**Posey, Cumberland
Radcliffe, Alexander
*Radcliffe, Theodore "Double Duty"
*Redding, Richard
Robinson, Cornelius "Neil"
*Rogan, Wilbur
Santop, Louis
*Scales, George
Serrell, William "Bonnie"
Smith, Charles

Smith, Hilton
Stearnes, Norman "Turkey"
Stovey, George
Strong, T. R. "Ted"
*Suttles, George
*Taylor, Benjamin
**Taylor, Charles I.
Thomas, Clinton
****Thompson, Henry "Hank"
Torriente, Christobal
Trent, Theodore
*Trouppe, Quincy
**Warfield, Francis "Frank"
*Wells, Willie
White, Chaney
**White, King Solomon
Wickware, Frank
***Wilkinson, James L.
Williams, Joe
****Wilson, Arthur
Wilson, Ernest Judson
Winters, Jesse "Nip"
*Woods, Parnell
Wright, Burnis
Yokely, Laymon

*Players and managers
**Players, managers, and executives
***Executives
****Also played major league baseball

Appendix 8

All-American Girls Professional Baseball League Entries

The following entries, listed alphabetically, played in the All-American Girls Professional Baseball League.

Briggs, Wilma
Collins, Dorothy Wiltse* "Dottie"
Dancer, Faye
Davis, LaVonne Paire* "Pepper"
Doyle, Dorothy Harrell* "Snooky"
Eastman, Jean Faut* Winsch**
English, Madeline "Maddy"
Florreich, Kathleen Lois
Foss, Betty Weaver*
Fox, Helen Nicol* "Nicky"
Haylett, Alice
Jochum, Betsy
Kamenshek, Dorothy "Dottie"
Keagle, Merle "Pat"
Keating, Edythe Perlick*
Kurys, Sophie
McNaughton, Alice Hohlmayer*
    "Lefty"

Mahon, Elizabeth
Randall, Maxine Kline*
Richard, Ruth
St. Aubin, Helen Callaghan* Candaele**
Sams, Doris
Schroeder, Dorothy
Shively, Twila
Shollenberger, Fern
Voyce, Inez
Wagner, Audrey
Wagoner, Betty
Weaver, Joanne
Winter, Joanne
Wisham, Mary Nesbitt*
Wisniewski, Connie
Ziegler, Alma "Gabby"

*Maiden name, if married
**First married name, if married twice

Index

Page numbers in **bold** refer to main entries.

Contributors

The following people contributed baseball entries to one or more volumes. They are listed alphabetically with their official position at the time of their last contribution.

William E. Akin, Academic Vice President, Ursinus College, Collegeville, PA.

Charles C. Alexander, Distinguished Professor of History, Ohio University, Athens, OH.

Louis J. Andolino, Associate Professor of Political Science, Rochester Institute of Technology, Rochester, NY.

Sheldon L. Appleton, Professor of Political Science, Oakland University, Rochester, MI.

Alan R. Asnen, freelance writer, Columbia, SC.

C. Robert Barnett, Professor of Physical Education, Marshall University, Huntington, WV.

Thomas H. Barthel, Professor, Herkimer County Community College, Herkimer, NY.

Terry A. Baxter, consultant, Cedar Rapids, IA.

Gaymon L. Bennett, Professor of English and Chairman, Department of English, Northwest Nazarene College, Nampa, ID.

David Bernstein, Professor of History, California State University, Long Beach, CA.

Peter C. Bjarkman, freelance writer, Lafayette, IN.

Lowell L. Blaisdell,** Professor of History, Texas Tech University, Lubbock, TX, resides in Denton, TX.

Stephen D. Bodayla,* Chairman of the Department of History, Marycrest College, Davenport, IA.

William A. Borst, freelance writer, radio host, and Adjunct Professor, Webster University, St. Louis, MO.

Robert T. Bowen, Jr.,** Professor of Physical Education, University of Georgia, Athens, GA.

Frank P. Bowles,** Associate Professor of English, University of Northern Colorado, Greeley, CO.

Jack C. Braun, Associate Professor History, Edinboro University, Edinboro, PA.

Gerald E. Brennan, bookstore manager, Chicago, IL.

Robert J. Brown, Associate Professor of History and Political Science, Rochester Institute of Technology, Rochester, NY.

Robert S. Butcher, Director of Media Operations, Columbus Clippers Baseball Club, Columbus, OH.

Stan W. Carlson,* freelance writer, editor, and publisher, Minneapolis, MN.

Peter J. Cava, Press Information Director, USA Track & Field, Indianapolis, IN.

Dennis T. "Tom" Chase, librarian, Berea, KY.

Dennis S. Clark, Instructor, Alternative Secondary Program, Lane Community College, Eugene, OR and Ph.D. candidate, Education Policy and Management, University of Oregon, Eugene, OR.

Ellery H. Clark, Jr.,* Professor of Naval History, U.S. Naval Academy, Annapolis, MD.

Scott A.G.M. Crawford, Professor of Physical Education and Graduate Coordinator, Eastern Illinois University, Charleston, IL.

L. Robert Davids,** Federal Government public affairs officer and founder, Society for American Baseball Research, Washington, DC.

John E. DiMeglio,** Professor of History, Mankato State University, Mankato, MN.

Leslie Eldridge, librarian, Boise Public Library, Boise, ID.

John T. English, Professor, School of Education, The University of Puget Sound, Tacoma, WA.

Bruce Erricson, county employee and actor, San Diego, CA.

Phillip P. Erwin, editor-publisher, *Baseball Insight*, Portland, OR.

John L. Evers,** high school teacher and administrator, Carmi, IL.

Albert J. Figone, Professor and Graduate Coordinator, Department of Physical Education, Humboldt State University, Arcata, CA.

John E. Findling, Professor of History, Indiana University Southeast, New Albany, IN.

David Fitzsimmons,** Professor, Wright State University, Dayton, OH.

Joel S. Franks, Lecturer, Department of Social Science, San Jose State University, San Jose, CA.

Leonard H. Frey,** Professor, Department of Linguistics, San Diego State University, San Diego, CA.

Ronald L. Gabriel, consultant, publisher, Chevy Chase, MD.

Cappy Gagnon, Director of Volunteer Programs, Legal Services Program of Northern Indiana, South Bend, IN.

Richard H. Gentile, freelance writer and editor, South Easton, MA, and Ph.D. candidate, History, Boston College, Boston, MA.

Larry R. Gerlach, Professor of History, University of Utah, Salt Lake City, UT.

James N. Giglio, Professor of History, Southwest Missouri State University, Springfield, MO.

Horace R. Givens,** Professor of Accounting, University of Maine, Orono, ME.

Roger A. Godin, former Curator, U.S. Army Ordnance Museum, Aberdeen Proving Ground, resides in St. Paul, MN.

David A. Goss, Professor of Optometry, Indiana University, Bloomington, IN.

Ralph S. Graber,** Professor of English, Muhlenberg College, Allentown, PA.

Lloyd J. Graybar,** Professor of History, Eastern Kentucky University, Richmond, KY.

John Hanners, Professor, Chair, Department of Communication and Theatre, East Texas State University, Commerce, TX.

James W. Harper, Associate Professor of History, Texas Tech University, Lubbock, TX.

John David Healy, lawyer, Little Falls, NJ.

Leslie Heaphy, Assistant Professor of History, Kent State University, Stark Campus, Canton, OH.

John Hillman, certified public accountant, Waco, TX, and lecturer, Department of Accounting, Southwest Texas State University.

George W. Hilton,** Professor of Economics, University of California, Los Angeles, resides in Columbia, MD.

John B. Holway, writer and baseball author, Springfield, VA.

Louis E. Hunsinger, Jr., freelance writer, Williamsport, PA.

John R. Husman, human resources manager, lives in Sylvania, OH.

Allen E. Hye, Associate Professor of German, Wright State University, Dayton, OH.

Chad Israelson, graduate student, Department of History, University of Nebraska, Lincoln, NE.

Frederick Ivor-Campbell, freelance writer and historian, Warren, RI.

William Ivory, writer and baseball coach, St. Albans, Washington, DC.

Harry A. Jebsen, Jr., Professor of History, Capital University, Columbus, OH.

Robert E. Jones, research analyst, Aumsville, OR.

Thomas D. Jozwik, insurance inspector, Milwaukee, WI.

Thomas L. Karnes,** Professor of History, Arizona State University, Tempe, AZ, resides in Round Rock, TX.

Gene Karst,** baseball publicity director and freelance writer, Branson, MO.

Brian R. Kelleher, press relations publicist, Saratoga, NY.

Joseph E. King, Professor of History, Center for History of Engineering and Technology, Texas Tech University, Lubbock, TX.

Merl F. Kleinknecht, U.S. Postal Service employee, Galion, OH.

Kent M. Krause, Instructor, Department of History, University of Nebraska, Lincoln, NE.

Dan E. Krueckeberg, writer and consultant, Webster Groves, MO.

Raymond D. Kush, senior editor, Minneapolis, MN.

Tony Ladd, Professor and Chair, Kinesiology and Athletics, Wheaton College, Wheaton, IL.

Jay Langhammer, Sales Manager, Freeman Exhibit Company, freelance writer, and sports editor of fraternity magazines, Fort Worth, TX.

Brian L. Laughlin, student, Creighton University Law School, Omaha, NE.

Joseph Lawler (Nicoteri), Librarian, University of Rhode Island, Kingston, RI.

Mary Lou LeCompte, Assistant Professor, Physical and Health Education, University of Texas, Austin, TX.

Larry Lester, software developer and freelance writer, Kansas City, MO.

Robert D. Linder, Professor of History, Kansas State University, Manhattan, KS.

B. Randolph Linthurst,** Public Information Director, State of New Jersey, Trenton, NJ, resides in Sun City Center, FL.

Jack P. Lipton, attorney at law and psychologist, Venice, CA.

Susan M. Lipton, researcher, Venice, CA.

Carl Lundquist,** author and sportswriter, Port Orange, FL.

Michael J. McBride, Professor and Chairman, Department of Political Science and Dean of Foreign Studies, Whittier College, Whittier, CA.

Arthur F. McClure,* Professor and Chairman, Department of History and Anthropology, Central Missouri State University, Warrensburg, MO.

Norman L. Macht, freelance writer, Easton, MD.

Gordon B. McKinney, Professor of History, Western Carolina University, Cullowhee, NC.

William E. McMahon, Professor of Philosophy, University of Akron, Akron, OH.

Douglas D. Martin, Professor of History, Towson State University, Towson, MD.

David S. Matz, Associate Professor of Humanities, University of Pittsburgh at Bradford, Bradford, PA.

David B. Merrell, Dean, College of Liberal and Fine Arts, and Chairman, Department of English, Abilene Christian University, Abilene, TX.

Charles R. Middleton, Associate Dean, College of Arts and Sciences, University of Colorado, Boulder, CO.

Richard D. Miller,** Air Force chaplain and freelance writer, Fort Thomas, KY.

William J. Miller,** Associate Professor of History, St. Louis University, St. Louis, MO, resides in Mansfield, MO.

Scot E. Mondore, Senior Researcher, National Baseball Library, Cooperstown, NY.

Eugene Murdock,* Professor of History, Marietta College, Marietta, OH.

Clark Nardinelli, Assistant Professor of Economics, Clemson University, Clemson, SC.

John E. Neville, Assistant Professor, Health and Physical Education Department, Youngstown State University, Youngstown, OH.

Douglas A. Noverr, Professor of American Thought and Language, Michigan State University, East Lansing, MI.

James E. Odenkirk,** Professor, Department of Exercise Science and Physical Education, Arizona State University, Tempe, AZ, resides in Boise, ID.

Frank J. Olmsted, Theology teacher, De Smet Jesuit High School, St. Louis, MO.

Joseph M. Overfield,** Vice-President, Monroe Abstract & Title, Tonawanda, NY.

Anthony J. Papalas, Professor of History, East Carolina University, Greenville, NC.

Edward J. Pavlick, freelance writer, Milwaukee, WI.

Robert W. Peterson, freelance writer, Ramsey, NJ.

Frank V. Phelps,** freelance writer, King of Prussia, PA.

David L. Porter, Shangle Professor of History, William Penn University, Oskaloosa, IA, and freelance writer.

Kevin R. Porter, office manager, solar ovens distributor, Sacramento, CA.

Donald J. Proctor, Professor, University of Michigan-Dearborn, Dearborn, MI.

Samuel O. Regalado, Associate Professor of History, California State University, Stanislaus, Turlock, CA.

Steven A. Riess, Associate Professor of History, Northeastern Illinois University, Chicago, IL.

James A. Riley, freelance writer, editor, and publisher, Canton, GA.

John G. Robertson, freelance writer, Cambridge, Canada.

Victor Rosenberg, student, John Marshall Law School, Cleveland, OH, and freelance writer, Mayfield Heights, OH.

John P. Rossi, Professor of History, LaSalle University, Philadelphia, PA.

Emil H. Rothe,* high school teacher and administrator, Chicago, IL.

Robert L. Ruck, Assistant Professor of History, Chatham College, Pittsburgh, PA.

Mark D. Rucker, President, Transcendental Graphics, Boulder, CO.

Steven P. Savage, Professor, Department of Anthropology, Sociology, and Social Work, Eastern Kentucky University, Richmond, KY.

Lee E. Scanlon, Associate Professor, Department of Communicative Arts and Sciences, Eastern New Mexico University, Portales, NM and sports announcer.

Eric C. Schneider, Program Associate, Delaware Humanities Forum, Wilmington, DE.

William J. Serow, Professor, Department of Economics, Florida State University, Tallahassee, FL.

Fred M. Shelley, Assistant Professor of Geography, University of Southern California, Los Angeles, CA.

William M. Simons, Professor of History, State University College, Oneonta, NY.

Douglas G. Simpson, high school English and Journalism teacher, Issaquah, WA.

James K. Skipper, Jr.,* Professor of Sociology, University of North Carolina at Greensboro, Greensboro, NC.

Duane A. Smith, Professor of History/Southwestern Studies, Fort Lewis College, Durango, CO.

James D. Smith III, Pastor, Claremont Emanuel Baptist Church, San Diego, CA and Adjunct Professor, Bethel Seminary West, San Diego, CA.

Leverett T. Smith, Jr., Jefferson-Pilot Professor of English, North Carolina Wesleyan College, Rocky Mount, NC.

Lowell D. Smith, Ph.D. candidate, Department of History, University of Nebraska, Lincoln, NC.

Eric Solomon, Professor, San Francisco State University, San Francisco, CA.

Lyle Spatz, freelance writer, Edgewater, MD.

Luther W. Spoehr, Professor, Education Department, Brown University, Providence, RI.

Jack R. Stanton, Senior Vice-President, Advertising and Public Relations Agency, Minneapolis, MN.

Fred Stein,** environmental consultant, resides in West Palm Beach, FL.

A. D. Suehsdorf,** editor, Ridge Press, Sonoma, CA.

Jim L. Sumner, Historian, North Carolina State Historical Preservation Office, Raleigh, NC.

William A. Sutton, Professor of Sports Management, Ohio State University, Columbus, OH.

Edward J. Tassinari, Adjunct Professor, Humanities Department, New York State Maritime College and freelance writer, Scarsdale, NY.

Frank W. Thackeray, Professor of History, Indiana University Southeast, New Albany, IN.

Sarah L. Ulerick, Professor, Geology Department, Lane Community College, Eugene, OR.

Robert B. Van Atta,** freelance writer and history editor, Greensburg *Tribune*, Greensburg, PA.

David Q. Voigt,** freelance writer and Professor of Sociology and Anthropology, Albright College, Reading, PA.

Edward J. Walsh, Professor of English, Slippery Rock University, Slippery Rock, PA.

Robert G. Weaver,** Professor of English, Pennsylvania State University, University Park, PA, resides in Petersburg, PA.

Robert E. Weir, Associate Professor of Liberal Arts, Bay Path College, Longmeadow, MA.

James E. Welch, Professor of Business Administration, Human Resource Management, and Industrial Relations, Kentucky Wesleyan College, Owensboro, KY.

Jerry J. Wright, Professor of Kinesiology, Pennsylvania State University, Altoona Campus, Altoona, PA.

David W. Zang, Assistant Professor, Department of Physical Education, Towson State University, Towson, MD.

Darryl R. Zengler, historian and Ibar Settlement Company employee, Pasadena, CA.

John H. Ziegler, Professor of English, Film, and Humanities, Cochise College, Sierra Vista, AZ.

Lawrence E. Ziewacz, Assistant Professor, Department of American Thought and Language, Michigan State University, East Lansing, MI.

*deceased

**retired